Gift from Chuck Krauskopf

Functional Psychological Testing

Principles and Instruments

Functional Psychological Testing

Principles and Instruments

Edited by

Raymond B. Cattell

and

Ronald C. Johnson

BRUNNER/MAZEL, *Publishers* • New York

Library of Congress Cataloging in Publication Data
Main entry under title:

Functional psychological testing.

   Bibliography: p. 545
   Includes index.
   1. Psychological tests. I. Cattell, Raymond B.
(Raymond Bernard) 1905-   . II. Johnson, Ronald C.
(Ronald Charles) [DNLM: 1. Psychological Tests.
BF 176 F979]
BF176.F86 1985   150′.28′7   85-443
ISBN 0-87630-363-7

Published by
Brunner/Mazel, Inc.
19 Union Square West
New York, New York 10003

Contents

Preface *by Raymond B. Cattell*   ix
Preface *by Ronald C. Johnson*   xv
Contributors   xvii

PART I: *Psychometric Principles in Testing*

1. Structured Tests and Functional Diagnoses   3
   Raymond B. Cattell

2. General Principles Across the Media of Assessment   15
   Raymond B. Cattell

3. The Actual Trait, State, and Situation Structures
   Important in Functional Testing   33
   Raymond B. Cattell

4. The Psychometric Properties of Tests: Consistency,
   Validity, and Efficiency   54
   Raymond B. Cattell

5. Scales and the Meaning of Standardized Scores   79
   Raymond B. Cattell

6. Selecting, Administering, Scoring, Recording, and Using
   Tests in Assessment   105
   Raymond B. Cattell

7. Solid State Psychology: The Role of the Computer in
   Human Assessment   127
   Samuel E. Krug

8. The Wider Scientific and Social Aspects of Psychological
   Testing   142
   Ronald C. Johnson, Barbara D. Porteus, and
   Raymond B. Cattell

PART II: *Available Structured Tests for Functional Psychometry*

9. Intelligence and Primary Aptitudes: Test Design and
   Tests Available   166
   Robert E. Woliver and *Stephen D. Saeks*

10. Achievement and Proficiency Measures   189
    Daniel D. Blaine and *Philip Merrifield*

11. Personality Assessment by Observers in Normal and
    Psychiatric Data   208
    Ronald C. Johnson

12. Personality Assessment by Questionnaire   237
    Keith Barton

13. Personality Assessment by Objective Tests   260
    James M. Schuerger

14. Evaluating Motivation Structure, Conflict, and
    Adjustment   288
    Arthur B. Sweney, Michael T. Anton, and *Raymond
    B. Cattell*

15. Measuring Attitudes, Interests, Sentiments, and Values   316
    Richard L. Gorsuch

16. Measuring Emotional States and Temporary Role
    Adoptions   334
    Keith Barton

PART III: *The Art of Testing in Psychological Practice*

17. Clinical Diagnosis and Psychotherapeutic Monitoring   348
    Brian F. Bolton

18. The Art of Clinical Assessment by the 16P.F., CAQ,
    and MAT   377
    Heather B. Cattell

19. Industrial and Vocational Selection   425
    Charles Noty

20. Classroom Achievement and Creativity   447
    John S. Gillis

21. Psychological Characteristics of Groups   466
     John S. Gillis

22. Legal Considerations for the Psychologist and Some
    Practical Suggestions   486
     Paul M. Ganley

23. Dodging the Third Error Source: Psychological
    Interpretation and Use of Given Scores   496
     Raymond B. Cattell

References   545
Author Index   573
Subject Index   578

Preface

Raymond B. Cattell

The last 20 years of this century are likely to be known as the point at which psychological testing and diagnosis "turned a corner." The turn, already beginning, is from relatively blind, rule-of-thumb, cookbook tests and procedures to what this book defines as *functional psychological testing* based on quantitative personality theory and susceptible to powerful aid from computer use. No longer is it sensible for each of fifty thousand psychologists to make up on the weekend a test for some pet trait term that has been the whim of the week. The technology of sound test construction has become formidable, and tests now have to be based on a full understanding of factorial personality structure and the dynamic calculus. The sources of development of ability, personality, and dynamic structure have now emerged from the mists of speculation, revealing clear-cut structural concepts demanding tests that validly represent the meaning of each.

Since the term "structural testing" has here and elsewhere sometimes been used alternatively, to make this approach distinctive, let us explain why we have finally given the name *functional* testing to the movement spearheaded by this book. The vital reason is that addressing tests to real trait structures and dimensions of state change opens up a fascinating prospect of use of the now rapidly developing science of personality itself, based increasingly on quantitative laws and significant prediction. Naturally, it requires of the practitioner a scientific understanding of personality founded on quantitative data and mathematical models, for, since the middle of the century, testable psychological theory, founded on bivariate and multivariate experiment, e.g., in the clinical field, has begun to crystallize in predictive laws and definite concepts. Thus, testing, of the kind here described, can begin to be functional in the greater sense of, for example, knowing the age curves of development of diverse traits, recognizing the degree of heritability as it affects psychotherapy and maturation predictions, relating source trait scores to a wider span of life criteria, introducing quantities (vectors) for the principal cultural situations, expressing the clinical roots of internal conflict in checkable quantitative analyses, and so on.

As if by an act of a beneficent providence, the physicists gave birth to the computer just when leading psychologists were striving to show that psychology could penetrate its major problems only by sophisticated multivariate methods and models. The new practice has not yet penetrated very far, for though the harvest is generous the laborers are few. Much of the research basic to the present test application is the work of a band of perhaps no more than a couple of hundred psychologists here and abroad. The expansion of its utility, moreover, depends largely now on practitioners themselves, who are seemingly always too busy applying old methods to contribute to new methods. This is evident especially in the clinical field, as a comparison of the slimness of *Multivariate Experimental Clinical Psychology* with the diffuse verbal output of most other clinical and psychiatric journals will at once show. Consequently, we do not at this moment have at hand for this book more than a fraction of the clinical profiles, the behavioral equations for success by different therapies, the necessary constants and indices, the magnitudes of weights for predicting real life criteria, the learning constants for various life experiences (in path learning analysis), and so on that should be the consulting room equipment of practitioners who take the demonstrable effectiveness of their services seriously.

This assessment of the direction that psychological testing will take pitchforks us into the old cauldron of what is, intellectually, a stale debate about intuitive versus psychometric practice. From Meehl (1954) and countless conclusive experiments since, we know that as far as any assessable criterion is concerned practitioners who rest their case on measurement come out significantly more effective than those who stare complacently into the crystal ball of their "experience" and intuitive powers. No wonder that after

watching 20 years of further "slovenly intellectual tradition in clinical psychology and psychiatry," as Meehl (1973) forcefully calls it (in a passage of fine analytical quality), this outstanding leader in clinical psychology feels compelled to add, "professionals in these fields are so habituated to superficiality of thought. . . , that trying to explain anything that involves the making of complex or subtle distinctions . . . is usually a waste of time." He further points out that accepting the clinician's recognition that "the mind is terribly complicated" is no excuse for evasion and rejection of mathematical and statistical aids.

Unquestionably, in our opinion, the psychological practice of the next two or three decades will show an increasing use of source trait concepts and knowledge of their natural history, as well as of the dynamic calculus and its measurement concepts, greatly aided by computer predictions and analyses. Indeed, both psychology and medicine are likely, in the next 20 years, to discover an array of insightful laws, especially in the realm of systems theory, that, by their complexity, will require substantial computer program aids for their application. This will inevitably lead to altogether more effective diagnosis and treatment. However, this will by no means rule out experienced intuition. Intelligent synthesis of these quantitative contributions and complexities requires the human mind. Moreover, any use of computer calculation requires wary recognition that all mathematical model predictions operate in a world of statistical error—and also of influences still outside present organized knowledge. The difference is that intuition should be used at a higher level in the pyramid of observations. It will be at its finest application not in immediate consulting room notes and physical observations, but in integrating the second and third derivatives (to borrow a mathematical metaphor) from the estimates and predictions which the computer sends back from the consulting room test results, observational notes, and biographical data.

I think we can confidently expect that the reader will come to feel the full meaning of this in what our present contributors illustrate in their various fields. However, let us also not forget, regarding the present wave of enthusiasm for computers: 1) that they are only as good as the programs put into them, i.e., as the kinds of measurement and psychological law models that research on personality has reached, and 2) that the human mind can perform many things that the computer cannot. Each has its area of special advantage, and clinical intuition in the best sense, employed at the apex of the process of synthesis of measures, calculations and observations, remains indispensable.

If the science and technology of psychology advance as anticipated above, we face something of the magnitude of a revolution in both the education of the practitioner and the organization of psychological services. The initial obvious difficulty, which will occur as soon as books such as *Functional Psychological Testing* get into circulation, will be a generation gap in test usage between the new practitioners and those trained in the fifties, sixties, and seventies—unless the latter get time to read. One can also surely foresee that part of that revolution will occur in *organization* of personnel and services. In the world of practice one constantly comes up against the fact that the community demand for psychological services is so extensive and expensive that much testing must be administered—and, indeed, interpreted—by teachers, social workers, employment officers, nurses, and school counselors, whose training is far short of allowing them to read easily, for example, the present book. Even in the old and widely established field of achievement testing, the technological expertise of the nationwide Educational Testing Service is with difficulty rendered clear to teachers and amateur critics on school boards. Most test publishers now say that, in accordance with the realities discussed in APA test committees, they are bound to issue test information at two levels: first as a *manual* which the above type of less instructed test user can follow in test administration, and secondly as a *handbook* which does not hesitate to give the full technical complexities of information that an adequately trained psychologist needs for expert work.

There is not appropriate space here to explore the possibilities of what the revolution may produce in the structure of services, but I see little alternative to a hierarchy, such as is developing in rough outline already in medicine in several countries in the form of "medics and paramedics." Therein the reality will be accepted that, as recognized in Meehl's phrase above, the human mind is exceedingly complex and we have somehow to make maximum use of a complex science by a pyramidal organization spreading the expertise of the most highly trained. In fact, the future may show that relatively few can be educated to make decisions from the intricate multivariate models and computerized use of functional testing based on new scientific vistas in psychology. However, we can hope that, as in most areas of new technology, this revolution will essentially settle down to employing the same fraction of the population, for the volume of services needed interdicts the possibility of "technological unemployment." Nevertheless, new styles of education and organization will certainly be called for. Meanwhile we are presenting here what we believe to be the most up-to-date findings and principles in the underlying technical testing practice needed for such organization. Having done this, we must leave it to new service organizations and suitable professionally approved standards of qualification to make the best use of these advances.

If we adhere to the standards of functional testing and a clear orientation to the direction where new test construction must now appear, it follows that we *cannot* honestly give prominence here to what can be broadly and briefly indicated as "cookbook tests." We have limited space, and we do not claim to be setting out a catalogue of produced tests (as Buros thoroughly does). Such catalogues (as Oscar Wilde said of history) often constitute "an account of things that should never have happened." Instead, our space is used to give the fullest account of the psychometric properties, availabilities, and best utilizations of tests aimed at and based on carefully investigated unitary structures, unitary processes, taxonomically established types, and state dimensions. Immediately, in discussions of this plan with certain practitioners, we have been confronted with astonished remarks that "X is a very widely used, popular test and is taught in most courses, yet you mention it only briefly. You rather tactlessly expose its scientific shortcoming by the rigorous new standards you apply to all tests, and pass on without putting the student through the time-hallowed, detailed rituals normally taught. This will not make your book popular in existing testing courses."

We must reply in the field of science as well-known leaders have replied in religion: "I can, in honesty, do no other." Several of the tests to which we have given the short shrift they really deserve are actually sustained in the field of testing by a combination of commercial enterprise and teacher laziness. Others remain socially prominent, though scientifically in hiding, by sheer academic momentum i.e., by teachers teaching what they were taught by a previous generation of teachers, in a Mandarin culture that could go on for generations. To seize one particular bull by the horns, let us face the fact that the Rorschach test is taught everywhere and is on the "demanded" list of various psychiatric and other institutions. It *does* have some predictive value, if by prediction we mean some modest power in assignment to DSM pigeonholes, but it

relates to no demonstrated personality and dynamic unitary traits (unless we consider schizophrenic thought process, which appears as a unitary factor in the CAQ) and the thousands of articles about it are mainly a monument to what can be done by sedulous, detailed, blind, empirical data-gathering by overwhelming numbers of devotees. And if the psychometric evaluations of Rorschach and the like by good psychometrists such as Thurstone and Cronbach are heeded, the victory is one of achieving a few barely statistically significant relations accompanied by no insight.

The Rorschach is far from being the poorest example of the cookbook approach, and is cited mainly because it is so excessively used. Nor do we overlook the possibility that responses in many such inherently not very potent tests can become useful as the beginnings of free associations, as in the TAT, and lead to valuable intuitions about specific emotional ties. However, one could add that tea leaves in the bottom of a cup, or perusal of palmar lines, might be an almost equally effective beginning for associations and ways of thinking. Moreover, the meaningful trait scores on, for example, the MAT, the Eysenck Scales or the 16 P.F. primaries can be an equally good starting point for associating to biographical insights, while economically providing at the same time such objective measurement of defined dynamic and personality traits as the TAT and Rorschach cannot provide. Indeed, one can resort to associations to the client's particular item responses in these tests with more associational richness than is possible with older tests (see Chapters 14, 17, and 18).

There is an unmistakable current movement in applied psychology to step outside the personality of the client to make strong allowance for family and community psychology. This, if not excessive, is a long-needed balance. Unfortunately, it is in part motivated by disillusionment with the practical efficacy of consulting room methods, which has been due to poor quantitative measurement and models to apply thereto. To turn the same poor conceptual and psychometric methods on community psychology, with its greater complexity, is to go from disillusionment to despair. The escape from failure is to turn to better quantitative, scientific, mathematical methods in both. All chapters here give due regard to the recent models for handling situational, social factors, but Chapters 14, 15, 17, 18, 19, and especially 21, with its quantification of group syntality and synergy, as well as ethnic and social class patterns, introduce a positive handling of community measurement.

From stating the main scientific position, let us turn next to the details of structure of the book and how to get the best from it. First let us point out that it has three clearly separable parts, which could be separate volumes, as follows:

Part I (Chapters 1 to 8) deals with general psychometric principles in testing and, since these refer especially to functional testing, it begins with a brief systematic statement of what structures are presently known in traits, states, and situations. It proceeds in Chapters 3, 4, and 5 to a brief, self-contained, but comprehensive treatment of psychometric concepts and formulae, and so to test selection and predictive aid to be obtained from the computer, with actual illustrations of the use of linear relations in the behavioral equation and of type assignment calculations, etc. This first "general purpose" psychometric-statistical part concludes with a chapter supplementing the technical overview with a view, of equal generality, of the social and professional aspects of all testing.

Part II (Chapters 9 to 16) gives an account of particular tests and assessment methods for each of the main trait areas—abilities (Chapters 9 and 10), personality (Chapters 11, 12, and 13), and dynamic modalities (Chapters 14, 15, and

16). These chapters on actual tests proceed from the best established available devices in abilities and achievement, to those in personality ratings, questionnaires, objective personality tests, dynamic measures of motivation and attitude, and so on to psychological states and the adoptable roles that interact with personality. This part aims to deal with the most effective tests and their properties, bringing to bear more concern for technical foundations than has been possible in the older "catalogue" literature. This concentration has been possible only by reduction of the number of tests seriously considered, as selected by the professional experience and psychometric wisdom of the many distinguished contributors to this book. Basic psychometric principles of dependability, practicality, and potency have been faithfully and critically applied, along with the background of structural knowledge available today, to offer the professional psychologist a dependable and adequate core of tests for all purposes.

Part III (Chapters 17 to 23) deals with the art of "testing practice" itself, in all its fields—essentially clinical, industrial, educational, and social. The social Chapter 22 deals explicitly with those legal and community relationships that concern the practitioner. Finally, since part of the art of intelligent testing is to take realistic account of sources of error, a comprehensive treatment is given in Chapter 23 of the nature, magnitude, and treatment of diverse error sources.

While these three parts are quite distinct in their aims and coverage, so that each could be used—in teaching for example—as a volume on its own, they share throughout a consistency in their orientation to functional principles in testing. Similarly, although each chapter expresses the individuality of an expert in a particular area, the reader will find few inconsistencies of scientific standards and generally good cross-referring and integration. In fact, there are sufficient chapter cross-references to enable the reader to transcend frontiers and perceive integrations and extensions. It has seemed better to avoid gaps than overlaps, so the reader must expect a few repetitions—these will aid learning. A common bibliography, necessarily extending more into deeper research foundations than is usual in a practical handbook, concludes the text.

Although teaching and special practitioners' areas might have been convenienced by division into three volumes, the reading of all three parts is desirable to get a really thorough understanding of each. Nevertheless, both in teaching courses and when the practitioner draws a volume from the shelf for immediate consultation, there is convenience in the separation. For example, a mature prac-

titioner, fully qualified in matters of statistics and in the problems of his or her own field, might want to more frequently consult Part II, setting out the validities, reliabilities, standardization, etc. of the principal tests. On the other hand, the teacher of a first basic course in psychometrics might want to take Part I as the main text (supplemented perhaps by a standard statistics textbook), with brief dips into the other parts. Lastly, a teacher giving workshops to psychologists already having a background in both psychometrics and the world of available tests will find the experiences of the various writers on the art of testing in diverse fields, described in Part III, a meaty adjunct to the workshop discussions.

Preface

Ronald C. Johnson

The seven deadly sins are pride, wrath, envy, lust, gluttony, avarice, and sloth. I have seen comparatively few evidences of gluttony among my psychological colleagues; the rest of the sins seem to be observably present. It is the sin of sloth that I wish to address.

First, I must confess my own sloth. Having undergone the obligatory exposure to Cattell in graduate school, I retained a vast respect for him and for his work but read very little of it for almost 20 years. It was *hard*; lots of formulae, many invented words without any easy associations, a pretty difficult writing style in terms of Flesch count. Not the sort of thing to scan while undergoing the preliminary rituals of a department meeting. I became interested in Cattell's work after he joined us here at the University of Hawaii. He is lively and stimulating. Graduate students got a lot out of what he had to say. Thinking that if they could master Cattell's message, then so could I, I began to overcome my sloth and read what he had written. This was fortunate, because soon after I began to read Cattell I was asked to review one of his books for *Contempo-*

rary Psychology. This required me not only to read Cattell, but to read him well. I was most impressed. If we are in the business of defining and measuring personality, then we'd best be serious about it. Cattell was and is. Words that I had dismissed as neologisms clearly were necessary new words; already existing words don't convey the exact intended meaning and have associations that are not appropriate. His major concepts are not difficult to grasp once one is immersed in his approach to personality for some time—a couple of books worth of time.

I was again impressed by Cattell's work on psychological measurement when we began to analyze personality data from the Hawaii Family Study of Cognition. I always was impressed by the range of his work; I became impressed by the depth. For example, the meaning that a given personality scale score has, in describing an individual, clearly is influenced by the age of the individual. Being highly rebellious at age 18 has different psychological meaning than it does at age 48. We found that psychological test constructors and users generally show little concern for age effects. Cattell, to the contrary, provided excellent age norms for his measures. I lost a fair amount through the sin of sloth; I would have done better research had I been aware of Cattell's research. Beware of the sin of sloth. A book by Cattell is a book about Cattell's ideas. A book on psychological testing by Cattell is a book devoted chiefly to functional psychological testing; to the kind of testing and use of tests common to Cattell and his many students. His approach is sufficiently different from that of the majority of personality psychologists and psychological testers that this is a natural consequence, not the result of self-pride.

I have come to the conclusion, across some years of contact, a fair amount of reading, and my involvement with the present book, that Cattell is right: His approach is the most likely to lead to an understanding of both stable and dynamic aspects of personality both within the areas of "pure" sciences and in applied fields. It will be hard going for the reader *unless* the reader is willing to work at it. If the reader is willing, then I believe that reading this book will be most worthwhile. While it is improbable that the positions represented herein all will be proved correct in every particular, I believe that they always are testable and usually will be verified. One thing is certain, functional psychological testing leads the researcher and also the clinician onward—puts the ideas to the test, refines them, repeats it—and this is the essence of science.

I urge the potential reader to avoid the sin of sloth and to make the effort to read, think about, and understand *Functional Psychological Testing*.

Contributors

Michael T. Anton, M.A.
Graduate Student
School of Professional Psychology
Dayton, Ohio

Keith Barton, Ph.D.
Professor, Human Development *and*
Co-hairperson, Department of Applied
    Behavioral Sciences
University of California
Davis, California

Daniel D. Blaine, Ph.D.
Acting Dean and Professor
Educational Psychology
College of Education
University of Hawaii at Manoa
Honolulu, Hawaii

Brian F. Bolton, Ph.D.
Professor
Arkansas Rehabilitation Research and
    Training Center
University of Arkansas
Fayetteville, Arkansas

Heather B. Cattell, Ph.D.
Clinical Psychologist in Private Practice
Honolulu, Hawaii

Raymond B. Cattell, Ph.D.
Professor Emeritus
University of Illinois *and* Director,
    Cattell Institute
Honolulu, Hawaii

Paul M. Ganley, J.D.
Attorney at Law
Carlsmith, Wichman, Case, Mukai and
    Ichiki *and*
Trustee, Estate of S.M. Damon
Honolulu, Hawaii

John S. Gillis, Ph.D.
Professor
Department of Psychology
St. Thomas University
Fredericton, New Brunswick
Canada

Richard L. Gorsuch, Ph.D.
Professor of Psychology *and* Director of
    Research
Fuller Theological Seminary
Graduate School of Psychology
Pasadena, California

Ronald C. Johnson, Ph.D.
Professor, Department of Psychology
    and
Director, Behavioral Biology Laboratory
University of Hawaii at Manoa
Honolulu, Hawaii

Samuel E. Krug, Ph.D.
President
MetriTech, Inc.
Champaign, Illinois

Philip Merrifield, Ph.D.
Professor, Department of Educational
  Psychology
New York University
New York City, New York

Charles Noty, Ph.D.
Professor
Management and Personnel
  Administration
Heller College of Business
Roosevelt University
Chicago, Illinois

Barbara D. Porteus, Ph.D.
Clinical Psychologist, State Department
  of Mental Health
and
Clinical Professor, Psychology
  Department
University of Hawaii at Manoa
Honolulu, Hawaii

Stephen D. Saeks, M.A.
Director, Program Development and
  Training
Cattell Research Institute *and*
Doctoral Student in Clinical Psychology
University of Hawaii at Manoa
Honolulu, Hawaii

James M. Schuerger, Ph.D
Professor of Psychology
Cleveland State University
Cleveland, Ohio

Arthur B. Sweney, Ph.D.
Professor
Wichita State University
Wichita, Kansas

Robert E. Woliver, Ph.D.
President
Hawaii School of Professional
  Psychology
Honolulu, Hawaii

PART I

Psychometric Principles in Testing

CHAPTER 1

Structured Tests and Functional Diagnoses

Raymond B. Cattell

TEST-CENTERED AND CONCEPT-CENTERED PSYCHOMETRY

Anyone versed in the history of science recognizes that the introduction of *measurement* has marked the true birth of each science—as of astronomy out of astrology and chemistry out of alchemy. Similarly, in the applied sciences, e.g., in medicine, accurate and meaningful *diagnosis* has inaugurated effective treatment. Therefore, the movement of psychology during this last generation from personality theories without calculations and reflexological ("behaviorist") treatment without diagnostic testing marks a hopeful advance toward some maturity in our science.

We shall treat testing here both as an expression of growth in theory and as a means to improve practice and research. With this new perspective, the present book should function both as a data basis for courses in personality and ability theory and as a faithful handbook on the shelf of the new-style practitioner who bases his

or her diagnoses and monitoring on basic personality theory.

The meaning of *functional* and *structured* in regard to this newer testing approach needs to be explained. Even when testing has, in the past, been well incorporated as a central course for psychologists, it has tended to be a *test-centered* rather than a *theoretical-concept-centered* presentation. It seems that test construction has been so widespread a hobby among psychologists that thousands of psychologists have constructed tens of thousands of *ad hoc* tests; Buros (1972), incidentally, gives us a bewildering glimpse of this jungle. Many of these—indeed most—have a "theoretical" basis that is subjective, parochial in area, and unproven; also, although tests like the Rorschach, the Bender, the TAT, and, one may even add, the WAIS stand out among them as so socially well rooted that few users question them, the fact is that most have acquired what validity they have by diligent search for criterion associations and structure *after* their construction, rather than from good initial theoretical construction. It is tests like the above which led, in the intelligence field for example, to the theoretical cul-de-sac that "intelligence is defined as what intelligence tests measure." We shall show, in surveying the relevant fields, that tests of this kind are not such as would satisfy a psychologist growing up in the standards of a scientific psychology.

Concept-centered development, on the other hand, has first examined personality structure (not necessarily rejecting psychoanalytic, Jungian or other pre-quantitative, pre-experimental sketches of structure) by factor analytic and other multivariate experimental methods. It has then begun to shape tests psychometrically valid against the discovered structural maps of human behavior. This is what is meant by *structural psychometrics*, which leads to *functional testing*. Testing deserves to be called functional when it uses growing psychological knowledge of the genetic and learning roots of traits and their modes of action in life, which permits prediction, as well as clinical understanding, to go beyond any blindly statistical use of scores, such as might be done with Rorschach-like or MMPI scores or numerous *ad hoc* scale scores that have been related to behavior statistically but not to personality structure. (When we say "beyond" we do not mean that mathematical-statistical procedures are neglected, but that they are applied to a world of *psychological* laws, not merely statistical ones.)

By contrast, to, say, the Rorschach cookbook, when one has scores for the trait of, say, *surgency*, one knows that it is more genetically than environmentally determined (H = .70), that it shows a life course of rise to the early twenties and a steady fall thereafter, that it is reduced in marriage, that it predicts success as a leader in small groups, and so on. Or if one has separate scores for *fluid*, g_f, and *crystallized* intelligence, g_c, one knows they will have different life courses, susceptibility

to brain damage, response to learning, etc., permitting functional understanding in a way never possible with a conglomerate score as in the WAIS and many older tests.

More modern analytic methods, it is true, have been brought to bear on older tests (both the WAIS and the MMPI have been postnatally factored, showing a different structure from that intended on the scale names). Since the subsequent scientific use of such tests is as awkward as a stage coach with a gasoline engine tied to the shafts, postnatal reconstructions are apt to become postmortem. The history of psychometric activities of this kind brings us to recognize an important duality within the stream of psychometrics itself. In its earlier phases, mainly before World War II, the emphasis was on what may, for distinction, be called *itemetrics*. After that came what we may call a development of *structured psychometrics* —and perhaps today we are on the verge of what may be called *structured systems* theory in psychometrics.

Itemetrics was principally concerned with the *statistical properties of different item forms in different scale forms*. Among less sophisticated practitioners it led to the apotheosis of homogeneity (often miscalled reliability and commonly measured as agreement of items with the pool) as the chief virtue of a scale. If the scale happened to be well conceived in relation to structure, this could (but need not) result in all items being good; but more often, because the original conception, subjectively chosen and arbitrary, the procedure made the worst of a bad job. Let us recognize that by developing certain valuable precisions of psychometric thinking the itemetric phase nevertheless did much for psychology. It produced such formulae as the Spearman-Brown, the Kuder-Richardson, Cronbach's alpha, various scaling principles, regard for the normal curve, tests of significance, use of multiple and other criterion correlations, various treatments of error, as in the attenuation formula, and so on. But, as far as personality theory was concerned, it lived in a world of "items" and subjective guesses about what such things as extraversion, super-ego, intelligence, persistence, etc., might be. It also kept test construction in a groove of questionnaire-like, verbal items, atomistic thinking, and a technical vocabulary inapt to further advance. Had other psychologists not taken off these blinders the whole domain of objective (performance) personality tests, of objective dynamic drive measures, and of linkage with laboratory measures (such as the GSR, acidity of saliva, frequency of reaction time errors, etc., for measuring anxiety, for example) would never have developed (see Chapter 13). Nor would concepts of developmental psychology, the behavior genetics of traits and modulation theory of psychological states, etc., have found a home in psychometric practice.

WHAT STRUCTURAL PSYCHOMETRICS IMPLIES

By contrast to the above, *structural psychometrics*, as the name indicates, was concerned from the beginning with the use of new statistical-experimental tools, such as factor analysis in its R-, dR-, and P-technique forms, in order to find the *natural structure*, within our culture and genetic pool, of abilities, personality-temperament traits, dynamic drives, and dimensions of state change. Its first aim was in fact not testing at all, but the shifting of earlier clinical and Jamesian-like concepts of personality on to a new foundation of quantitative multivariate experimental research on traits, states and their interactions. It succeeded, through the work of Spearman, Thurstone, Horn, Hakstian, Krug, Guilford, Eysenck, Pawlik, Hundleby, Sweney, some 50 colleagues of the present writer, and many independent laboratories here and abroad, in recognizing a rich and firm basis of unitary structures and processes. Thence began an understanding of development and inter-

action with situations which moved personality theory to an entirely new basis, clear of the previous quagmire of verbal speculation.

The construction of truly structured tests followed only after this work was completed, at least to a first approximation. And as an incidental result of the delay and deliberateness of the scientific approach, the structural tests found themselves entering a field already extensively occupied by the aboriginal prestructural scales and tests. They sometimes found themselves unwelcomed. Indeed, a student of sociology of science would realistically recognize even today that psychometric courses are often a strange mixture of the new and the obsolete. Progressive graduate students are still battling with the vested habits of a generation of teachers whose training preceded factor analytic and other quantitative bases for modern ability, personality, and dynamic concepts, and who aim to keep safely to the popular traditions.

In Chapter 2 we will proceed, because of these gaps in some current texts, briefly to present the evidence for the structures of traits and states on which subsequent understanding of tests will stand. At this point it is enough to present the historical situation and to make clear that popularity or antiquity of practice will not be entertained as a basis for psychometric judgments on tests and procedures presented here.

The multivariate experimental methods by which research on trait and state structure—and their interactions in the total personality—has been advanced are somewhat complex. Both the social worker and the psychiatrist are likely to have some problems in communicating with the psychologist on newer psychometric concepts and the use of formulae in computer diagnosis or job performance prediction. Unfortunately, the concepts that an advancing psychology has to deal with have often been presented in such forbiddingly mathematical terms and purely statistical, unpsychological settings that cautious teachers have considered such matters as the *behavioral equation* unteachable to undergraduates. This means that graduate students start out imprinted in a merely qualitative, verbal evaluation of theory, which they seldom outgrow. Actually, if psychology undergraduates are no different in quality from those in physics, chemistry, or engineering, they could well absorb the idea, for example, of the simple linear behavior specification equation and satisfactory concepts of test validity and consistency in terms of checks on the unitary structure and growth of alleged traits.

After this comment the writer is reluctant to seem to back down from the ideal of a firm foundation, by saying that this book itself can have no space for a full account of factor analysis, discriminant functions, higher order factor analysis, the differences among R-, dR-, and P-techniques, etc., on which the research concepts of personality in the next chapter rest. However, by a combination of some simplified presentation here and reference to quite readily available background reading, the needs of the advanced research reader for precision and of the immediate practical user for research background may be tolerably met.

To turn now to the concept to which we have been alluding, let us recognize that the concept of a *unitary common trait* in structural psychometrics is based on

1) Evidence from correlation of many behavioral variables measured across many people that they "go together"—in individual differences—in a number of "clusters." (A factor is not just a cluster, but an underlying common source of variance that enters a cluster.) Such individual difference factoring is called *R-technique* and the resulting factors—such as verbal ability, V, fluid intelligence, g_f, ego strength, C, as described in the next chapter—are called

source traits, because a single underlying source, determiner, or influence can be inferred and sometimes observed to account for the experimentally obtained positive correlations.

2) If the unitariness is fully functional, it must also be demonstrated by correlations in the day-to-day *fluctuations* (change measures) of a source trait. Thus, if people are measured on some dozens of variables on Monday and again on Friday, the correlations of their shifts in performance should also be resolvable into the same factors. This factoring of difference scores is called *dR-technique* and it shows that many or most source traits, such as intelligence, ego strength, superego strength, extraversion, and the various ergic tensions (sex, hunger, curiosity, self-assertion) originally located by R-technique also show a unitariness of daily change by dR- technique.

3) Observations on long-term development also show that the parts of source traits grow and decline together. For example, Horn, Baltes, and others have shown that the expressions of fluid intelligence, $3g_f$, on the one hand, and crystallized intelligence, g_c, on the other, change through life (within each set) together, but on quite different curves for the two source traits *per se*.

4) It will be noted that so far we have talked of *common traits*, since the analytical procedures above deal with common variation within a population of people. Now the psychologist, especially if he or she is a clinician, is much concerned with doing justice in testing to the *uniqueness* of the individual and his or her problems. The uniqueness of the individual can be caught in two ways. First it can, in part, be described as a *unique combination of common factor scores*, such as stands out when we draw a profile on, say, Thurstone's primary mental abilities test or the 16 P.F. Predictions from such unique profiles

will, in fact, come fairly close to estimating much of the individual's behavior.

There is a second aspect of uniqueness not caught by this. Fortunately, we have available a factor analytic device for getting the unique trait *structures* of the single *person*—hence called *P-technique*. Here the person is measured on, say, 50 behavior variables every day for perhaps 100 days and the correlations over time are factored. Experiment soon found that in most such studies recognizably the same factors—as unique factors—emerged as had been found in the common factors of R- and dR-techniques. That is to say, the loading pattern of anxiety or surgency or verbal ability was easily recognizable as that in the common factor, but with some individual special emphases.

This should not surprise us, for the medical doctor, for example, depends on the same assumption of identity, namely, that though every individual's anatomy and physiology are in fact unique, the surgeon can depend on a heart, a liver, a facial nerve structure, etc., being in much the same place and similar in functioning. Here, too, as in our first form of individual uniqueness, the individuality is partly in the particular combination of sizes and strengths of the organs. However, psychology is more culturally involved than medicine, and traits are more subject to experience. So, although admittedly personal history counts in both, it counts decidedly more where we come to an individual's particular interests, attachments, values, phobias, and conflicts than in physiology.

Regarding patterns, factor analytic findings suggest that different kinds of traits differ in susceptibility to uniqueness of form. Primary abilities and temperament traits, like exvia, surgency, and premsia, seem to have much the same expression (loading pattern) in most people in a given culture. It is in dynamic

interest traits that uniqueness, as revealed by comparison of R- and P-technique results, becomes prominent and inescapable. True, both R- and P- show in that realm a) the same principal ergs (drives), such as fear, sex, assertion, parental protectiveness, etc., and b) the same principal sentiment ("sem") structures, to home, job, religion, hobby, etc., acquired to different degrees. But in the latter realm an appreciable degree of uniqueness of attachments is evident; when we come to the dynamic structures that have been called "complexes," this attention to the unique is especially demanded.

The actual magnitude and attainable degree of accuracy of behavior predictions that can be made from *common* trait measures have been a matter of sharp debate, especially by reflexologists whose atomistic views of behavior predispose them to doubt even the existence of such unitary structures! However, no matter what theoretical predilections one has, the experimental fact is that major functions of the variance of measured criteria in everyday life can be predicted from common trait batteries. For example, Cattell and Butcher (1968) showed that almost 70% of school performance could be predicted from a combination of scores on common factor patterns of ability, personality, and dynamic source traits. Even apart from any subsequent factoring of the matrix of correlations among natural or laboratory or test performances, the sheer magnitude of correlations visible makes an atomistic view of the structure of human nature quite untenable. In everyday life variables, the correlations are far beyond what one would expect from random (atomistic) numbers.

The arguments in this area could advantageously move on nowadays from "Is there structure?" to asking how these structures arise. The rapid advance of behavior genetics in the last decade shows that a number of source traits, such as fluid intelligence, g_f, spatial ability, S, surgency, F, and premsia, I, have such high heritability that their unities must arise to a large extent from coordinated inner maturation and perhaps from dependence on physiological roots, such as cortical size for g_f or some chemical pacemaker for F. Other source traits, however, such as superego strength, G, guilt proneness vs. self-esteem, O, radicalism-conservatism, Q_1, and ergic tension, Q_4, which have relatively trivial heritability, must arise from learning exposure to unitary institutions, e.g., in home training, etc., simultaneously building up a whole ring of specific behaviors together.

Developmental study of source traits is in its infancy, because developmental psychologists have had measures of well-replicated traits available only for 10 to 20 years. But it is evident already that, although we talk of "fixed" traits and find they can be separated from *psychological state* measures, few traits can be regarded as "measured once and for all" for the given person. Stature and strength of grip are physical measures that increase markedly through childhood and are expected to be relatively fixed through mature years, but even stature changes a little when a person stands up all day. Psychological unitary factors that we consider traits, not states, nevertheless have varying *stability* coefficients (Chapter 4). Intelligence, for example, is high and ergic tension is low—but all can change. However, it seems a statistical fact that under ordinary everyday life conditions individual trait level ranks do not change much past 30 years of age, and even before then it is in practice worth maintaining score profiles in, say, clinical records for use over a few years, until the next checkup.

THE USE OF SOURCE TRAITS IN THE BEHAVIORAL EQUATION AND IN TYPE FITTING

The psychologist using source traits as just defined in research terms does not need to immerse himself in factor analytic technicalities, any more than the user of a good camera needs to know the expertise of grinding lenses. The personality student does, however, need to have a *logical*, conceptual understanding and to know where to turn for factor analytic expertise when in danger of having some shoddy concept and scale foisted upon him. Granted that he understands conceptually how source traits have been established and what their natures and properties are, he can, without highly specialized statistics, use them to get better insights and results than are possible without them. Just so a doctor who does not know how to synthesize thyroxin or what the physics underlying improvements in X-ray machines may be, can nevertheless use both these agents effectively in his practice.

A criticism sometimes voiced of factor analytic breakdown into traits—which, incidentally, could be applied with equal obtuseness to other scientific analysis, such as of rocks into chemical elements—is that the analysis loses the whole person. The argument confuses analysis with destruction, and claims that "all the king's men could not put Humpty Dumpty together again!" But all meaningful synthesis begins with the illumination of an analysis.

The casual critic may say he cannot conceive how this synthesis from traits can be brought about, but the expert can demonstrate with practical results that analysis and synthesis will generally do better than the "wholistic" intuitions of the clinician or vocational counselor.

The style of the combination of functional measurement and psychological knowledge that will be developed in this book (with the next steps in Chapter 4, and Parts III and IV) can be illustrated in an introductory way by the *behavioral equation*. This—in factor terms sometimes called the "specification equation"—is the backbone of all further mathematical models and computer calculations in analysis and predictive syntheses. It states that a given behavior, act, or performance, which we may designate a_{hij} can be estimated through *adding* the factor scores of the individual i, each first weighted by a loading, b (for behavioral index), which is peculiar to that act. That is to say, it is special to the stimulus situation which we will designate as k and the mode of response, which we shall regularly call j. a is then a numerical value—usually a standard score—for the amount of j behavior.

The behavioral equation then takes the form:

$$a_{hij} = b_{hj1}T_{1i} + b_{hj2}T_{2i} + \ldots + b_{hjn}T_{ni} \quad (1\text{-}1)$$

where the T's with their subscripts are n source traits (ability, temperamental, and dynamic) scored for person i. Note that the b's are each peculiar to the behavior j and each given trait. They describe that trait's involvement in that behavior.

A thoughtful psychologist, while recognizing that this has the virtue of allowing that any act is a function of *all* traits, i.e., is an expression of the *total personality*, may yet object that it employs a *simple addition* of the trait contributions, rather than the more complex relations that can be imagined. The answer to this reasonable doubt is that very few indeed of the empirical predictive results yet examined have been improvable by shifting to nonlinear relations, and that, though one or two interesting curvilinear relations *have* been found, we must in the general case "learn to walk before we run" and resort to products, etc., only when forced to such complications.

A concrete illustration of the behavioral equation, taken from the 16 P.F. Handbook, is as shown in (1-2).

$$a_{hij} = .44A_i - .11B_i + .11C_i - .22E_i + .11F_i$$
$$- .11G_i + .22H_i - .33L_i - .11M_i + .11N_i +$$
$$.11O_i + .44Q_{2i} + .22Q_{3i} - .22Q_{4i} + 1.87$$
$$(1\text{-}2)$$

Here h is the situation of being a retail salesman, j is the typical performance of a salesman, scored, as a, as *mean weekly sales*. Other concrete examples will be given in appropriate areas. The trait scores (T's in 1-2) are here, in A, B, etc., the individual's sten scores on 16 P.F. factors, as alphabetically indexed. The 1.87 is a constant that has to do with a mere numerical contribution in factor equations because common factors do not account for the full unit variance of a_{hj}, and we wish to get a in standard scores from entering the T's in standard scores. (The coincidence of the values being .11, .22, .33, etc. instead of .1, .2, .3, etc. is also an artifact of correction to unit variance.)

Since the weights—the b's, called behavioral indices—are found by correlating the source trait scores with the criterion and then transforming from correlations to weights (calculation allowing for the correlations among the source traits), it will be seen that the behavioral equation can be regarded statistically as a typical instance of a *multiple regression equation*. However, the behavioral equation differs from any general multiple regression in that it does not start with the miscellaneous collection of variables that can be put into any regression equation, but strictly refers to *source traits*. That is to say, it economically and meaningfully represents the dimensionality of personality by only as many (oblique) common factors as are necessary.

A basic division in the predictive use of a profile of source trait scores that we shall encounter again and again in succeeding chapters is that between the above linear behavioral equation and the use of a *species type* calculation. In the latter, if we have, say, the test profile of the best type of policeman, we hold the candidate's profile against it and see how much it resembles it. There are calculations for expressing this as a profile similarity coefficient, and a vocational counselor might find Bill Smith's profile resembling a policeman's .7, a plumber's $-.2$, and a mailman's .3. This has long been done in psychiatric diagnosis, and the Clinical Analysis Questionnaire (CAQ), for example, now gives a 24-element profile defining each of the main DSM syndromes, so that a psychometric approach becomes possible. That for narcotic addicts, for example, is given in Figure 1.1.

A clinician may be content to judge by eye the similarity of the profile of a given client to say, a central schizophrenic profile, but a more precise approach is possible, with a little computer aid, by using the above *pattern similarity coefficient, r_p*. An evaluation of profile similarity can be used also in industrial psychology when one knows the profile of the type of person who stays steadily and successfully in a given job. More detailed treatment and illustration both of the "competence" method of estimation by the behavioral equation and the "adjustment" method by pattern similarity to a type, will be given later (Chapter 23), but it will be recognized that the type method implies a nonlinear relation (a person could, for example, overshoot the ideal type level for a given adjustment, which requires a switch from a positive to a negative *b* in the behavioral equation. However, the behavioral equation, especially with some nonlinear terms, is generally better when we are out to estimate a specific performance.

THE INSIGHTFUL USE OF FUNCTIONAL TESTING PRINCIPLES

A psychological test can be only as good as the ideas of the psychologist who constructed it and the practitioner who interprets it. His or her competence needs to extend to correct and more refined statistical use (as in Chapters 4, 5, 7, and 23), on the one hand, and to sound knowledge of personality structure and psychological theory on the other (as in Parts II and III here). The good knowledge of personality theory can come into its own only with the employment of *structured* tests representing the concepts with which personality theory deals.

The supposed antithesis of statistical and psychological understanding, as sometimes debated, may have been true of itemetrics, but there is really no such conflict existing in the realm of functional psychometrics. The application of psychological laws to structured assessments from functional test measurement implies a clear logical-mathematical model. However, one may reason from the test results "in one's head" or by expressing the model with computer and mathematical aids. Some clinicians who would make a contrast between the computer treatment of test results and the "artistic" treatment which they claim to have acquired and which they claim to be superior may be on unsafe ground. Some members of an older generation of clinicians are apparently simply avoiding having to learn what the mathematical models are, underlying their reasoning, and are losing what statistics could tell them. In the cases where claims to a mystique of clinical insight have been brought to compete with formulae, as in Meehl's classical attack (1954), the claims to the former have generally proved hollow. It is not unusual for a clinician or industrial psychologist or psychiatrist to voice enormous conviction "from experience" in the power of whatever test or method he or she uses. A similar occupational disease pervaded medieval textbooks of medicine; even in medicine today some would give more importance to "clinical insight" and the right bedside manner than to efficient modern quantitative diagnostic procedures. Admittedly, having the results of good instrumentation avails not at all if the clinician lacks the insight to put them together. But we are speaking here of the first phase—that concerning the accuracy of the observations themselves. A perhaps classic examination of this, in addition to Meehl's, is that of Cattell and Scheier (1961) who obtained the services of the two psychiatrists in a certain city with the greatest professional reputation as diagnosticians and had them rate anxiety

NARCOTIC ADDICTS

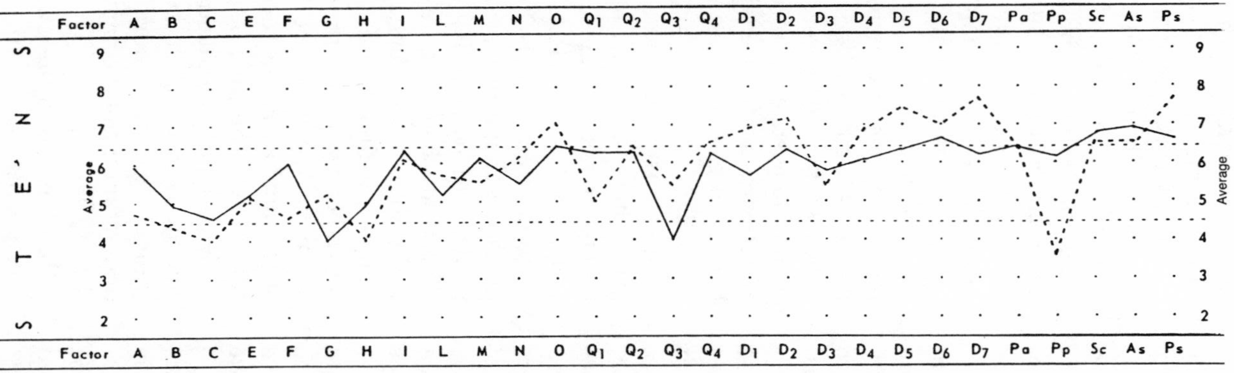

Factor	A	B	C	E	F	G	H	I	L	M	N	O	Q1	Q2	Q3	Q4	D1	D2	D3	D4	D5	D6	D7	Pa	Pp	Sc	As	Ps

GROUP	SEX	N	A	B	C	E	F	G	H	I	L	M	N	O	Q1	Q2	Q3	Q4	D1	D2	D3	D4	D5	D6	D7	Pa	Pp	Sc	As	Ps
Narcotic Addicts	m	64	M	5.9	4.9	4.6	5.2	6.0	4.0	4.9	6.4	5.2	6.1	5.4	6.5	6.3	6.3	4.0	6.3	5.7	6.4	5.8	6.1	6.4	6.7	6.3	6.5	6.2	6.8	6.9	6.7
			σ	1.8	1.7	2.1	1.9	1.7	1.8	1.9	1.8	2.0	1.6	2.5	2.1	1.8	1.8	1.8	1.9	2.0	2.0	2.2	1.7	1.7	2.1	1.8	2.0	2.0	1.9	1.5	1.8
Narcotic Addicts	f	11	M	4.7	4.4	4.0	5.1	4.6	4.0	6.1	5.7	5.5	6.1	7.1	5.0	6.5	5.4	6.6	6.9	7.2	5.4	6.9	7.4	7.0	7.7	6.4	3.6	6.6	6.6	6.6	7.7
			σ	2.1	1.7	2.3	1.8	1.3	2.1	2.2	1.9	2.1	2.5	1.8	2.7	1.3	1.7	2.5	3.0	1.7	1.4	2.0	2.1	1.9	2.3	2.4	2.3	2.8	1.9		1.3

Narcotic Addicts ——— (solid line, male)

Narcotic Addicts - - - - - (dashed line, female)

Note: The meaning of the factors is most fully discussed in Chapter 12: The male group alone is large enough for a dependable mean profile.

Figure 1.1. Example of a 24 source trait personality profile

level in some 80 clients. Their mutual agreement was revealed to be very low, as shown by a correlation of +0.3. But, what is perhaps most interesting, the agreement of *each* with a factored *measure* of anxiety was greater than their mutual agreement.

When matters reach the complexity of making a psychological diagnosis, or anticipating what comes next on the stock exchange, or directing a rocket to photograph Saturn, the number of elements involved, their magnitudes, and the equations of their interactions generally become too much for the human mind to handle unaided. We know from experiment that there are certain limits to immediate memory and the capacity to perceive relations. If, say, 20 influences enter into predicting a certain result, it can be shown that the human mind ceases to benefit from information supplied after about the first six, whereas the computer will go on to use all 20 in a steadily improving prediction. (Some stockbrokers and economists want to think in terms of only three or four!)

A simple example is the prediction of a child's school grades, where we know (see Cattell and Butcher, 1968, and Chapter 19 here) that at least a dozen ability and personality factors enter significantly into the prediction (or see equation 1-2 above where there are 14 loadings). But if we had to deal only with the child's intelligence score, his superego score, and an objective test of his interest in school, the best intuitive psychologist could not estimate the grade in his head—by artistic judgment—as well as the behavioral equation and a computer could do.

However, it is an unfortunate consequence of the neglect of scientific personality research with structural measures that we do not possess today more than a few of the necessary dependable behavioral equations and psychiatric profiles on the main ability and personality source traits. Nor do we have as much as research by now should have provided in terms of

evidence on genetic determinations, on developmental learning curves in relation to environments, on therapies, etc., necessary to a truly dependable practice. The fact is that all the structured tests and situational indices that expert psychological calculation and judgment need are *beginning* to be established by research but that currently the psychologist in much of his work still has to combine "in his head" the personality and dynamic measures, the personal history, the physical health, the personal appearance, the family and job situation, the client's aspirations, and countless other things. It behooves him, however, to know where better knowledge for statistical treatment of measurements is available and, it is hoped, to contribute to such knowledge himself.

One must point out, moreover, that even where the empirical weights for formulae are not available, the psychologist who uses structured tests can reason with extra accuracy because he is dealing with measures that directly represent concepts in general personality and motivation theory. Much of the growth of personality and ability theory around measurable and uniquely definable traits, states, and processes belongs to only the last two decades, and not all psychologists have experience of the application of theory or the measurements. The kind of application here anticipated can be illustrated for all psychologists, however, by reference to intelligence testing, where the associated understanding of the implications has had time to develop.

Here he knows the I.Q. values tend to be constant; that growth will cease around 16; that abilities like verbal skill in synonyms and mathematics will determine much of I.Q., whereas drawing, music, spelling, etc. will have little association; that brain injury will reduce I.Q.; that offspring will perhaps inherit it, and so on. If he is in touch with recent developments, he will know (Horn & McArdle, 1980) further how to calculate age progressions separately for fluid and crystallized intelligence and so on.

While most practitioners have been reasonably sure of such psychological projections only with intelligence scores, research has entered a new domain and been building up equally effective knowledge about general personality factors, such as affectia, A, ego strength, C, dominance, E, surgency, F, exvia-invia, QI, anxiety, QII, and so on. For example, we know that the most universal feature in all pathological profiles is low C (ego strength); that C has only moderate heritability; that it is lowered by chronic physical illnesses and raised by psychotherapy and some kinds of chemotherapy; that it is a key determiner of anxiety, and so on. In brief, we can hope that the future will shortly be as filled with exact and useful knowledge embedded in psychological laws about a dozen or more personality factor and state measurements as the past has been with firm practical knowledge about the technology of intelligence testing.

As this derivation from use of structured tests grows, practicing psychometrists will find themselves dealing with the identical qualities of human character that have long fascinated novelists, biographers, dramatists, historians, politicians, and all who have aimed at some sort of science of personality. But they will occupy this fascinating area with greater conceptual precision and power of prediction, for research is yearly putting into the hands of psychologists tools of such penetration and formulae of such precision as should enable them far to outdistance these able amateurs. This consummation, however, depends on two contingencies: 1) progress in applied research with the new instruments, and 2) acquisition of more mathematical and psychological discipline and finesse than was possessed by the practitioner trained only in the relatively "cookbook" methods of the last generation. As Chapter 7 stresses, increased potency brings increased responsibility. A third aspect of

this growth is an ethical sensitivity that will ensure these new and powerful scientific tools being of benefit to society.

SUMMARY

Science, in basic research and in effective technological applications, begins with *measurement*. In psychology a fundamental distinction must be drawn between measures that are merely *test-centered*, as is still the case in literally thousands of arbitrarily constructed tests on subjective notions, and those that are based on what can properly be called *structured tests*. The latter arise from multivariate experimental research and are *theoretical-concept-centered*. That is to say, they have awaited the results of replicated research on ability and personality structure before beginning test development. Structural psychometrics, using unitary trait and state measures, leads to *functional testing* because measures can be related to known trait criterion expressions, process changes, and personality laws in mathematical functions.

An intelligent use of structural psychometrics requires that psychologists have a logical, if not detailed, statistical understanding of the methods, phenomena, and concepts involved in studying the architecture of unitary traits and states. They should know that *common* trait structures are found by uniquely resolved R-technique factor solutions, whereas *unique* personal traits are revealed by P-technique factoring. Part of the unitary trait proof is that the correlations appear not only in individual differences, but in *common change* of the behavioral parts with situations and age development, as revealed by dR-technique.

Historically, structured tests, aimed at these unitary targets, have come relatively recently into a field of psychometric practice already occupied by subjectively concocted but now traditionally widely used tests. Yet the former are able to perform, by a few dozen meaningful source trait constructs, what was attempted by a thousand or so *ad hoc* tests. This simplification and linking up with theory have become accepted only slowly and belatedly, because of the usual lag between research and practice and the conservatism of earlier trainees.

It is a conceptual mistake to use the label "a trait theory of personality" because *any* taxonomy in *any* science starts analytically with characteristics and properties, i.e., traits. The mistake, tending to be supported by orthogonal factoring, lies in assuming that this basic research on the architecture of personality deals with isolated and fixed traits and takes no account of the *growth* and the *interaction* of the traits in total, integrated personality behavior. The *behavioral equation* understands and quantitatively estimates any performance response of the total personality as the summation of numerous trait endowments, each weighted by the given trait's characteristic involvement in that situation.

This model is mathematically the simplest possible and will doubtless need fitting better to nature here and there by product instead of simple summation relations, as well as by some nonlinear relations. However, it already gives the practicing psychologists, where the weights have been researched, a far better diagnosis or prediction of, say, school achievement, recovery from delinquency, probability of marital success, executive performance in business, etc., than has been possible by unaided clinical interview, etc.

One can derive a second contribution to practical utility from an individual profile of unitary source trait scores. Instead of estimating a performance by the behavioral equation, one proceeds here by the pattern similarity coefficient, to find the degree of belongingness of that individual to various psychological *types*, e.g., those used in psychiatry as syndrome concepts. Although little research has yet been done

to use the objective *Taxonome* program to find what types truly exist, when this is accomplished the diagnostic assignment process is likely to reach new levels of reliability. Although the expression of an individual's resemblance to a number of reference types respects some curvilinear relations overlooked by the ordinary linear behavioral equation, the latter is more appropriate for a majority of applied "estimates."

Nothing in the above call for more precise, meaningful, and mathematically implemented testing should be considered to detract from the importance in practice of a) intuitive, artistically experienced judgments *when made on the basis of theoretically meaningful measurements*, or b) a personal, sympathetic, and humanitarian bond to the client (any more than a surgeon's precision in anatomy detracts from such relationship).

Functional testing means transcending simple, immediate, statistical behavioral equation usage by invoking psychological laws about the traits, processes, and states which psychologists can bring to bear conceptually as soon as they deal with structurally based measurements. These laws encompass such regularities as in empirical age curves found for unitary traits (such as revealed the notion of constancy of I.Q.), in growing knowledge of the differing heritabilities of traits, in information about characteristic trait learning changes in various life situations, in the modulation equation for psychological states, in psychophysiological relations, and in such generalizations as are beginning to emerge concerning psychotherapeutic effects from monitoring by temperament and dynamic trait measurements. Functional testing use is thus possible and effective only for the psychologist trained in modern personality theory which, as Cattell and Dreger's (1977) contributors have tried to show, can now be rooted in experiment and measurement.

CHAPTER 2

General Principles Across the Media of Assessment

Raymond B. Cattell

THE MEANING OF THE BASIC BEHAVIORAL EQUATION: COMBINING PROFILES OF PERSONS AND SITUATIONS

Progress in linking personality theory to appropriate measurement procedures has been so great in the last decade that to know only the principles in use in say, 1960, is to be obsolete as far as present possibilities are concerned. Exhaustive lists of thousands of published tests were published by Buros (1972) and others, but requiring students to be familiar with them is not the way to qualify them as practicing psychologists. In T. S. Eliot's aphorism, "Wisdom is more than knowledge and knowledge is something more than information."

As to the choice of tests, it is unfortunately not unusual to find, both in regular test administrations, as in a school system or VA or state hospital, and in the domain of research, that the psychologist, nervously concerned to cover all that may be relevant, has used an unduly lengthy and redundant battery. When such batteries are examined with present knowledge about structures, many traditional tests are found to be mixed in factor structure individually and unnecessarily overlapping in combination in some traditional "battery." Uncertain in their grasp of test evaluation, some psychologists have thrown in "everything but the kitchen sink." It has also not been unusual for statisticians rather than psychologists to be called in to remedy this by finding a *statistical* reduction. Unfortunately, the statistician is likely to proceed to reduction and economy by what is known as principal components analysis and discriminant functions. However, it is important not only to cover the domain with a minimum, manageable number of test measures but also to make sure that the reduction is one supplying knowledge of structurally unitary and functionally meaningful trait and state dimensions.

In Chapter 3 we shall concentrate on examining present knowledge of just what the necessary unitary source traits and psychological state dimensions are. That is to say, we shall deal in a condensed way with the psychology of personality taxonomy itself and with the architecture of temperament, ability, and dynamic structure. However, there are some general issues logically prior to considering such lists. Traits and states are identified by analysis of data and we must ask what is the full range and nature of observable data on personality. Equally basic, though more theoretical in nature, is the question of the basic model in terms of which we see traits and situations interacting in the total setting.

Beginning with general principles, we have to take note that some students seem to have been taught in the sixties and seventies that a "trait theory of personality" ignores "the situation." In the first place, a trait theory is not a special approach describing characteristics and properties of certain entities. Sciences *begin* taxonomically by describing the "traits" of sodium, of the amoeba, of the proton, and so on because fixing characteristics is part of scientific definition. Secondly, it is not the personality psychologist (at least not the leading researchers) who have neglected the situation, but, on the contrary, the reflexologists (Watsonian "behaviorists") who have neglected the person. The atomistic, reflexological basic equation is:

$$R = (f)S \qquad (2\text{-}1)$$

where R is response, (f) some function, and S the stimulus. The personality theorist's basic formula by contrast is:

$$R = (f)P.S \qquad (2\text{-}2)$$

where P is the characteristics of the person (to many Skinnerian reflexologists merely a "black box")—in short his or her "traits." Since S is also in the equation, the personality theorist has never denied the importance of the situation.

Let us recognize now that what we introduced in the last chapter as the behavioral equation expressed the highly generalized "philosophy" of person and situation in equation 2-2 in a scientifically more committed and testable form. The "environment"—the total situation—is actually present in the b values, which describe the stimulus and mode of response in the situation in terms of what we shall come to see is a very useful "vector" or profile. However, as we pursue this representation more thoroughly we shall see that the b's can be split up further, in response to finer concepts about the environment. This refinement begins with the recognition that the environment with which the person deals has two parts: a *focal stimulus* which we have represented in all writings on this subject by h; and an *ambient situation*, which we shall now represent by k. For example, a man crossing a field may encounter a bull who is the *focal stimulus, h*, but his behavior will depend not only on the stimulus but on the *ambient situation, k*, which might be that a) there are or are not also cows in the field; b) he is only a short distance from the gate; and c) his fiancée is watching him from the gate. The focal stimulus plus the ambient situation constitute the *total situation* (S in 2-2). Both the stimulus and the ambient situation can be broken down into dimensions by which they can be defined. There are other developments that the personality theorist will enjoy (Cattell, 1979c, 1980a), but at present we will not pause to describe them because they are not immediately necessary to the practitioner.

Behavioral response, R, can be anything from an act of a few moments—defined as to pattern, in the above case, say, by "running to the gate," and measured by speed—to a performance over years, as when we take the college grade performance of a young man who is in the ambient situation of wanting to earn enough, say, to get married. In either case, we represent the actual response score in certain suitable behavioral units. To look next at this performance or response act, which we shall call a (no longer broadly by R), more closely we must assign to it four identifying subscripts (in equation 2-3), namely, h, i, j, and k, instead of the three by which we first illustrated it.

$$a_{hijk} = b_{hjk}T_{1i} + b_{hjk2}T_{2i} + \dots + b_{hjkp}T_{pi} \qquad (2\text{-}3)$$

The $hijk$ at the foot of a may be said to be the full "signature" of a. It simply says that it is a response to a particular focal stimulus h by individual i, the response taking the behavioral form j, and the whole occurring in the ambient situation k. Next, let us note that each behavior index, b, is also peculiar to a particular T and therefore it has a 1, 2, subscript, etc., up to p (assuming a total of p traits) tacked on to it. The traits are *common* ones but of a magnitude peculiar to the individual i; therefore all have i as a subscript. But, as recognized in the b's, they also have numbers 1, 2 up to p attaching their values specifically to the operative traits. The personality factors, abilities, and dynamic traits that enter into that behavior (the statistician will note that we don't wish

to complicate by adding *unique* factors, absolutely specific to behavior a_{hjk}, at this point) will all have some weight, positive or negative.

Now the reader will readily recognize that the spectrum or vector of ordered numbers for (T_{1i}, T_{2i}, $T_{3i} \dots T_{pi}$) consists of the scores defining the uniqueness of the individual as a peculiar, *unique* pattern—a profile—in terms of *common* source trait scores. A geometer might like to represent the trait dimensions as a set of coordinates so that any person, by his or her scores on these dimensions, would then be represented by a uniquely positioned point in the multidimensional space of the coordinates. More commonly, we are used to setting out the uniqueness of this personality as a *profile* of scores, as illustrated in Figure 2.1, which is given for clinical interest as that for the typical psychopathic individual.

As mentioned above, what is not so often realized is that the b's—the *behavioral indices* as we have called them—also constitute a unique profile, but in this case

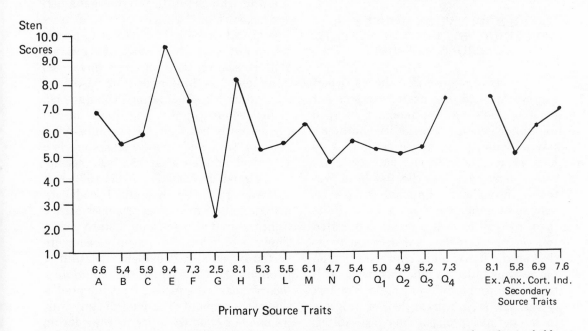

This is the typical, mean profile from 15 individuals diagnosed by psychiatrists as psychopaths (probably "anti-social personalities" in the DSM-III). From Cattell, Eber, and Tatsuoka (1970), p. 279.

Figure 2.1. An individual personality as a unique profile in common trait scores

representing that particular total *environmental situation*. Each *b* says how much a particular trait is involved in the reaction in that situation. If, for example, the b_x value for the T_x, which represents the strength of the sex erg, *x*, is large, we would call it an amorous situation, whereas if the biggest *b* value were on the fear erg it would be a fearful, avoidance-causing, security-seeking situation and response. And if *b* were large for the intelligence score, we would recognize it as a complex, puzzling situation. The *vector* (as named by the mathematician) or the *spectrum* or *profile*, as we may call it in more common terms, presented by these behavioral indices is thus as complete a statement about the *psychological meaning of the situation* (to people generally) as the *T*'s are a statement about the *personality of the individual*. Later we can apportion part of the *b* to the situation *per se* and part to the type of response that is typically made as part of the situation, i.e., to *k* and *j* respectively.

THE MODULATION MODEL FOR INCLUDING PSYCHOLOGICAL STATE AND ROLE MEASURES

Everyone recognizes that the way a person acts depends as much on his or her emotional state at the moment as upon his or her general personality characteristics. Some great historical moments have been said to depend on states. Napoleon may have lost the Battle of Waterloo through the unusual fatigue he showed on that day. Criminal law, in its turn, recognizes that a crime committed in a certain state does not necessarily reflect on the individual's character and on his responsibility as much as it would if he had been in a different state. The last decade has seen a great deal of progress in the definition of psychological states, basically through research by dR-technique and P-technique (Cattell, 1973a).

Although relatively good measurements of emotional and dynamic states have recently been provided in questionnaires by Curran and others and in objective tests by Nesselroade and by Scheier (see Chapter 15), practicing psychologists seem to have been in some doubt as to how to apply them. Obviously, states cannot be used in quite the same predictive way as traits. When traits are measured we can put the individual's profile *on file* and bring it out to apply to this or that situation as required, reasonably assuming that the trait scores will remain the same for months and in many cases for years. Obviously, this cannot be done with states.

If one could get knowledge about the individual's state level by measuring it *at the moment he or she begins a given performance*, then obviously one would not be predicting in the sense of *foretelling*, since one has to be there at the moment. However, one can, even then, make some use of such measures; e.g., if we know a person's anxiety level in an achievement exam, and how much anxiety reduces recall, we can make a definite quantitative allowance for the state and thus get a better measure of the person's real, characteristic attainment level. As it happens, the recent research on states has revealed that several unitary scores we have been accustomed to think of as *traits* also have *some* state-like fluctuation. The question of just where the dividing line is drawn conceptually between, for example, anxiety as a trait and anxiety as a state is a technical problem that has been considered elsewhere (Cattell, 1973a, 1979c).

However, a new theoretical model for utilizing state measures promises escape from the inability to foretell state levels. This model, which has recently been supported by empirical evidence (Cattell & Brennan, 1985), is called the *modulation theory* model. It supposes that the prediction of the amount of action from any trait (remember that we are now considering traits as slightly modulable) involves considering that the total situation $(h + k)$ a) *modulates (i.e., changes predictably) the level of the trait before the trait or state begins to act on the behavior,* and b) is then involved to the degree characteristic of the trait in determining the response, as previously represented by *b*.

Thus, in the case of our friend looking at the bull, the ambient situation would first raise the level of the fear state to a degree predictable from his timidity; the level of the fear state would then determine the rate at which he runs. This means that any *b* term obtained in the behavioral equation really has two parts hidden within it: 1) a modulator index which we will write s_{hk} and which tells *how much the stimulus,* h, *for the particular situation,* k, *typically raises the level of* T; and 2) a term *v* such that *v* describes the extent to which the state, at whatever level it reaches, is involved in the behavior per unit of its level, i.e., it is what we first took the *b* term to be. Thus *v*, in statistical terms, would be an ordinary regression coefficient, which tells the rate of change of speed of running with increase in the fear erg just as the *v* for intelligence in learning mathematics would say what movement in the latter arises from a unit increment in the former. The value *s* for the increase in the fear erg would be specific to the situation *hk*—a value characteristic of people in general. Finding the numerical values for the two terms v_{hj} and s_{hk} can be accomplished by experimental-statistical means described elsewhere (Cattell, 1971a, 1973a; Cattell & Brennan, 1983 and Chapter 16). In terms of a formula, the above statements condense to:

$$b_{hjk} = v_{hj} \times s_{hk} \qquad (2\text{-}4)$$

The symbol *v* is appropriate because we may call it the *involvement index* telling how much the given trait is involved in determining the response *j* to the focal stimulus *h*. The modulator index s_k is best understood by thinking of states, such as anxiety, amorousness, and anger, though it applies in smaller magnitudes also to

traits. Horn (1972), for example, has shown that even intelligence modulates somewhat from day to day. The value *s* is something that defines how much the *average person* experiences modulation in the given situation.

In full treatment of this problem, such as will be developed in Chapter 15 on states, it is necessary to develop and define the concept of a trait or state liability L_i. This scores the individual's liability to experience the given emotion, under unit provocation. In that case we have as an equation 2-5, which expresses the contribution to the act *a* of a given liability, a given modulating situation, and a known involvement of the state in the action.

$$a_{hijk} = v_{hjx}s_{hkx}L_{xi} \qquad (2\text{-}5)$$

(In this, incidentally, until future research clarifies, we assume *s* depends on the focal as well as the ambient situation.)

Although we began by considering *b* to represent the situation and its appropriate kind of response, we now recognize that the description of a *situation as such* depends much more on the *s* than on the *v* part of *b*. The *s*'s say what the situation means in terms of its emotion-provoking pattern, whereas the *v*'s strictly tell us only about the reaction or performance *j* in that particular situation. However, we cannot leave *v* out because the description of what the performance is in a situation is part of the subject's total understanding and perception of the situation. The situation of a red light contains the idea that you put a foot on the brake. But as far as the *cognitive and emotional meaning*, i.e., not the action, is concerned the *s*'s tell the story.

The psychological measurement of situations is new. It was confined initially simply to determining the relative variance of trait and situation in determining variance of behavior (Endler & Hunt, 1969; Endler & Magnusson, 1976). This approach, developed further, leads to comparing persons' *perceptions* of situations with the *realities* of situations, and explaining the deviations, as in attribution and *spectrad* theory, more fully discussed in Chapter 23.

States and roles are considered together in the modulation model because they behave in the same way. That is why Barton, in the fuller treatment of states in Chapter 16, also includes the psychology of role measurement. Typically, a role is something a person takes on temporarily, in relation to a situation, as when a policeman puts on his uniform or a teacher enters a classroom. As Shakespeare insisted (*As You Like It*), "One man in his time plays many parts." He or she then acts, while in the role-evoking situation, in a way that could not be fully predicted from what one commonly calls personality traits. The brief presentation of state modulation here cannot make the issues fully clear to the reader (see Chapter 15 for expansion and illustration), but we should be guilty of helping perpetuate a limited perspective if our introduction of the behavioral equation did not recognize this real and important aspect of it. In short, a realistic behavioral equation must contain, over and above the T terms that cover the totality of the personality, further terms in the form both of L's—liabilities to states—and of R's—acquired "liabilities" or readinesses to take on particular roles. They are formally alike in modulating their expressions strongly with ambient situations, k's.

Unfortunately, research and theory in this area are not yet backed enough by provision of equipment for practice. Not only do we lack s values for important state and role situations, but even the coarser b values, more grossly defining situations than v and s, have rarely been provided for the salient situations met in applied research. The only testing handbooks, as far as the present authors know that have presented vectors of k's for situations are the 16 P.F., the MAT, and the O-A Kit handbooks, though scattered re-

search articles can be found with relevant values.

As we turn now to focus on the next issue in this chapter—the principles and methodology in getting the basic data for traits—it should be kept firmly in mind that the situations are never omitted. Moreover, as we shall see, it is through the firmer definition and measurement of traits themselves that it has now become possible and appropriate for practitioners to begin accumulating situation profiles important in their work.

A SYSTEMATIC OVERVIEW OF THE MODALITIES OF BEHAVIOR AND THE POSSIBLE MEDIA FOR ASSESSING THEM

In almost all situations of practical testing, time is a tyrant. Consequently, efficient testing requires not only that the psychologist have sufficient knowledge of the nature of personality, ability, and dynamic structure to avoid wasteful duplications, but also that this same perspective on the architecture of human nature shall help him to know when his purposes permit certain areas to be dropped out. However, in principle, and especially in an exploratory study, if good psychometrists are asked what aspects of personality they are concerned with measuring, the reply will be in line with the principle that the total personality enters into each performance, "all of them." Only in well-understood domains, e.g., school achievement prediction, are they likely to know that some aspects are so little involved that they can get adequate prediction from measuring a limited spectrum. (However, they should know better than to use an intelligence test alone when asked to give the best prediction of school achievement!)

In considering dimensions and modalities to be measured, let us, incidentally, not forget that a psychologist may also be called at times to measure the performances and natures of *groups* as persistent organisms. A group's "personality" has been described as its *syntality* (Cattell, 1972a; Cattell & Woliver, 1980). The dimensions of syntality can be analyzed into meaningful "source traits," just as for personality, namely into abilities, and the equivalents of personality (types of excitability, morale, cohesiveness, etc.) and dynamic needs (group interests and concerns). The main syntality dimensions for measuring national cultures and the batteries that can be applied to the performances of small groups will be discussed in Chapter 19.

As far as the basis of observation and measurement of traits and states is concerned, it can be recognized at once that there are three, and only three, *media*, as we shall call them, namely:

1) Behavior in the everyday life situation recorded or rated by observers (*L-data* below). This is what Lorenz would call *ethological* data, carried from the animal to the human world.
2) Reports from mental interiors, by questionnaire or consulting room answers, also dealing with everyday behavior and introspection (*Q-data* below).
3) Responses to defined, laboratory-like experimental test situations (not questionnaires) objectively measured (*T-data* below).

The properties of and possible inferences from these three media of observation are so distinctive that it is important to understand them before examining trait abstractions as such in the next chapter.

A word must also be said at this point about trait *modalities*, if only to avert what seems a common confusion of *media* and *modality*, for it happens that there are also three modalities of measurement yielding three modalities of traits based thereon. These are the divisions familiar to all psychologists as 1) abilities, 2) temperament (general personality traits), and

3) dynamic traits (interests, drives, role traits, sentiments, values, and attitudes). The arguments for considering three main divisions convenient and apt are for most psychologists based on common sense and intuition, but when borderline instances occur (like odd legal cases that "make bad law") we are driven to find the more basic operational separation. This operation basis in the form of measurement is set out in Cattell and Warburton (1967, p. 73).

Table 2.1 sets out the cross-classification of modalities and media. It has the immediate utility of allowing us to see comprehensively what a psychologist can do about measurement, particularly in warning us of restrictions in the cases when the *validity of a medium becomes questionable for a particular modality*.

For example, common sense alone tells us that we do not measure abilities very validly by self-estimates, in Q-data, by items such as "Are you highly intelligent?" We must also take the position, though it is not shared by psychologists who have, for instance, used questionnaires to assess strengths on Murray's list of "needs," that the measurement of the real strength of interests and motives by conscious questionnaire responses is of doubtful validity. Anyone familiar, on the one hand, with the findings of psychoanalysis or, on the other, with diplomacy, would surely expect that this would be a poor medium for that modality; this issue will be examined more closely in Chapter 12.

Table 2.1 gives us a broad overview, placing, for example, an interview, in which S's total behavior, expressions, delays in answer, etc., are included, as L-data, but recognizing that consulting room evaluations, in which emphasis is on the nature of the patient's *introspections*, and ordinary questionnaire data are largely Q-data. However, the sources of evidence in psychological evaluation and diagnosis have more subtle subdifferentiating characteristics than those broadly given in the top row of Table 2.1, and if psychologists are to be sensitive to the quality of data they must have a more sophisticated analysis and clear frame of reference, as developed in Table 2.2.

On Table 2.2 we note first that each of the three media can be split into two forms. Thus, in the Q medium the responses (not the stimuli and mode of presentation) made and scored can be treated in two different interpretive frameworks. When a person says "No" to a Q item "Do you feel faint at the sight of blood?" or "Yes" to "Will you vote for X at the next election?" we can take this at its face value in describing behavior, as, alas, most questionnaires, biographical inventories, and surveys commonly do. Alternatively, we can, in what we define above as the Q' use of questionnaire evidence say, "No, this is not evidence of what he actually does or will do in everyday life, but only evidence of what he does *in this test situation*, namely making a mark by this item." For the psychometrist fully to realize what he is inferring in the Q' usage, he should think of the situation where he gives a questionnaire in a language which he himself does not understand. He would then have to find the predictive meaning of checking response "No" to question number 23 (which he himself cannot read) by correlating that test behavior (making a check mark) with personality factors *in behavior* (L- or T-data) or some specific life criteria. The psychologist might then find (if he now proceeds with scientific consistency to ignore the fact that he knows the questionnaire language) that in the above question on fainting, the subject checking yes is not actually unusually sensitive about the

TABLE 2.1

What Is Measured and How:

Media of Observation and Measurement

II PSYCHOLOGICAL MODALITY	T-DATA OBJECTIVE TESTS	Q-DATA QUESTIONNAIRES	L-DATA OBSERVATIONS IN LIFE BY
of Trait, State, or Specific Behavior[a] Measured	Behavioral Performances in which S does not really know on what aspects of his response he is being evaluated	Includes consulting room responses, questionnaires and self-ratings. Is based on introspection and self-evaluation	(a) Ratings (L) or (b) Recorded Events (L) (b) can be truly objective (a) is filtered through mind of the observer, as in an interview
Abilities	Valid	Non-valid	Valid
Temperament or general personality traits	Valid	Valid	Valid
Dynamic traits and interests	Valid	Questionably valid	Valid

[a]A specific piece of behavior by T-, Q-, or L-data would not necessarily classify as an instance of purely one modality.

TABLE 2.2
Differentiating Dimensions of the Properties of the Three Media of Observation and
Their Subforms

		Full cooperation required	Life situation stimuli and re-sponses	Observed over 24 hrs.	Subjective "floating" norms	Fixed situation and response modes, i.e., tests vs. other modes of assessment	Calculable homoge-neity of observers
		(1)	(2)	(3)	(4)	(5)	(6)
L-data	L(R) Observer Rating	no	yes	no	yes	no	yes
	L(B) Biographical Time Sampling	no	yes	no	no	no	yes
Q-data	Regular Q Description accepted	yes	yes	yes	yes	yes	no
	Q¹ Only checking behavior used	yes	yes	no	no	yes	no
T-data	TQ¹ Only checking behavior used	yes	no*				
	Regular T Objective Laboratory Type of Measurement	yes	no	no	no	yes	yes

*The items refer to life; the responses to them here are "laboratory" data

sight of blood, but is merely more truthful about confessing to this weakness. In fact, a "Yes" response on this item has been shown by experiment to have its significant positive loading on the superego (conscientiousness) factor!

THE ADVANTAGES AND LIMITATIONS OF THE MEASUREMENT MEDIA FOR VARIOUS MODALITIES

It behooves the psychometrist, therefore, to reach explicit conclusions about the better media for certain modalities. Even the man in the street recognizes that if we treat a questionnaire as Q-data, i.e., believe what the person says in his or her answers, we are liable to be misled (especially among, say, prisoners seeking parole) by conscious faking or unconscious motivational distortion. This is not peculiar to Q-data, for ratings (L(R)-data) are often so biased by the role or the personality of the rater as to be virtually useless, e.g., in testimonials. Such distortions and the ways of correcting for them by trait

view theory, MD scales, spectrad theory, etc., are more intensively pursued in Chapter 23.

Another weakness of both L(R)- and Q-data, but especially the former, is the "floating standardization." When a rater is asked, "How sociable is John?" or a questionnaire respondent, "How sociable am I?" it is obvious, and demonstrable, that one rater has a different idea of the mean (that is, of the real mean that holds across all subjects observed) from another. Or the rater may take as his mean not what he believes the real mean to be but what he thinks other persons answering the questionnaire will consider the mean to be. (For example, what is average sociability?) Again, in L-data, quite marked differences sometimes occur in rating the same child by a parent and a teacher, and this is not entirely due to seeing the child in different situations and roles, but to the parent's idea of the "average" being formed largely by experience of the different sibs in that family and the teacher's largely by the given class. Developmental studies based on ratings are particularly poor because the same child is almost always rated, say, at 6 and at 16 by different raters (and also in different situations). The questionnaire at least has virtually the same observer person on two occasions and the T-data response measure has laboratory constancy.

To evaluate media of measurement more closely, let us consider their parameters more analytically, under some six dimensions, as set out in Table 2.2. Parenthetically, we do not here consider "group or individual" administration and other more superficial (but sometimes practical) considerations that will be taken up in Chapter 6.

1) Cooperation Required in Subjects

Tests (which are either T or Q) require the cooperation of the subject, whereas L-data do not. In much of the carping public criticism of testing a decade or so ago it seemed quite overlooked that avoiding tests would not actually avoid valuation of abilities in one's job or of one's personality. This goes on inevitably in gossip of one's peers and assessment by one's boss—as inevitably as death and taxes. When a child is chosen for a scholarship by the head teacher instead of by objective tests, what one sidesteps is mainly reliability and validity! Against this disadvantage of comparative bias and unreliability in L-data, one balances the disadvantage that with tests (Q and T) uncooperative subjects can either fake or completely sabotage results. A characteristic of L-data (and some T-data in some situations —Cattell, Korth, and Bolz (1973) on dogs; Carpenter (1934), Lorenz (1971) and Tinbergen (1951) on ethology of wild animals; Skinner and countless others on rats and pigeons) is that it is obtainable not only without the subject's cooperation, but also without the subject's knowledge or consent, which involves some ethical nuances concerning use.

2) Occurring in the Life Situation or in an Artificial Laboratory Setting

Q- and L-data are basically contrasted with most T-data in that they deal with behavior in the life situation, not in the laboratory or in life-abstracted group test performances. As far as testing is concerned, this dimension is an important difference but not a pure advantage in either direction. However, as Pawlik (Hundleby, Pawlik & Cattell, 1965) points out, there is an advantage to L- and Q-data in research, in leading more easily to an initial theoretical *interpretation* of the source trait patterns found, for the meaning of factors is visible in the everyday life performances of the loaded constituent items, giving a "built in" theory. Certainly it has been possible to define the traits involved in L and Q measures more readily than in factors from complex, life-remote, laboratory behavior. It is also easier to be sure that one is covering the "personality sphere" of total life behavior in Q- and L-data (by the dictionary). Thus, we are assured in these media that our factoring is covering the full spectrum of traits.

3) Fraction of Daily Behavior Sampled

However, one should next not overlook a fairly important difference between these L and Q media themselves, namely, that ratings by observers are commonly confined to a few particular hours of the day and relatively narrow situations, e.g., school, job, whereas in Q-data the subject observes himself for 24 hours, including his dreams.

4) Floating Standard of Norms

As discussed above, a drawback of Q and L is that what is considered the mean is peculiar to the observer.

5) Standard, Definable Situation, and Response

A parameter which groups the media differently once again (namely with Q and T on one side and L on the other) is the ability to use a standard test situation in the two first. They have definite instructions and defined modes of response. Some L observations can in this respect, however, count as halfway hybrids, as in time sampling and a standard interview. Essentially, however, this dimension distinguishes what we call tests from other media.

6) Calculable Homogeneity Between Observers

The scores assigned by one outside observer can be compared with those of another in L- and T-data but not in Q or Q′, for in these latter there is only one observer—the subject introspecting on his or her own behavior. One can, of course, get a dependability reliability in Q-data. The coefficient, which is unlikely to be high in L(R)-data but could be high in L(B)- and very high in T-data, is one that might carelessly be called a "reliability" coefficient but is actually a homogeneity coefficient (see Chapter 4). That is to say, it is the agreement of two parts or aspects *simultaneously* recorded, not a repeat reliability. The homogeneity coefficient that one can get in a questionnaire is not the homogeneity of observers as one can call them, but a very different thing—the homogeneity among items in the scale. Incidentally, the media differences present good illustrations of the differences of the four forms of test consistency coefficients: dependability, homogeneity, administrative reliability, and transferability (see Chapter 4).

Little, surely, needs further to be said about the advantages and disadvantages of the poles of the six dimensions set out in Table 2.2. Many depend on the assessment situation in which the psychologist is placed. L-data are often used as the concrete *criterion* (*not* the *concept* [or construct] criterion; see Table 2.2) against which T- and Q-data are validated. That is sound if it is L(B), i.e., records, but otherwise L(R) is weak as either a criterion or predictor because ratings are so contaminated with the personality of the observer, even when otherwise well-founded on long, intimate observation. In demonstrating the statistical poorness of that variety of L(R)-data we call the interview, Eysenck scarcely exaggerates when he says it tells more of the personality of the interviewer than the interviewee.

Not all the properties of methods of assessment that a psychologist needs to consider have been covered in Table 2.2. One that unfortunately enters—psychologists being human—is that it takes more effort, training, and precision to give an objective test than to hand out a questionnaire. Another is that to get ratings that mean anything one needs fortunate circumstances in having, for example, some six or more raters per person (see Chapter 9), diverse behavioral situations under observation, and other conditions.

TEN MAIN DIMENSIONS FOR CLASSIFYING TESTS

The further differentiating dimensions we need to study apply not to the whole field of media assessment but to sections. Since this book is primarily concerned with tests, we turn in Table 2.3 to focus on the dimensions specifically of tests as such.

The *group vs. individual* dimension has in many test evaluations been given more importance as a dichotomy than it deserves. All group tests are also practicable individual tests, with a "group" of one. And, many tests starting as individual

TABLE 2.3
Classifying Dimensions for Tests Per Se: Q- and T-data

1. Group vs. Individual Administration
2. Conspective (Key-scored) vs. Subjective Evaluation
3. Items vs. Subtests (Global, Patterned Performance)
4. Timed vs. Untimed
5. Open-ended, Inventive vs. Selective, Multiple Choice
6. (a) Machine Scorable and (b) Machine Interpretable vs. Requiring Psychologist's Scoring
7. Normative vs. Ipsative Scoring
8. Overt Behavior vs. Physiological Response
9. Cross-cultural vs. Culture-bound
10. Criterion Validity Testable vs. Face Valid

tests conversely (as achieved in, for example, the latest Objective-Analytic (O-A) Kit (Cattell & Schuerger, 1978) can, with sufficient ingenuity, be transformed from "laboratory" to group administrable forms. The myth that all advantages lie with individual forms has been too long unquestioned. In the first place, the conditions of individual testing are, in real life, less standard, for few administrators can refrain from adapting to the given individual (in difficulties!)—and a natural, compulsive *teacher* is hidden in many psychologists! Even when the verbal presentation is kept standard, cues are given in individual contact by expressions, gestures, or tones of voice that cannot be standardized. (This is why the Pre-School Questionnaire by Dreger and Cattell has been set up by a standard, female voice *on a tape*.) The real virtue of the individual test is certainly not its "standardization" of conditions, but simply that it guarantees attention to the test in the psychotic, the young child, and other cases not very commonly met in general educational and industrial testing. Much testing is individual simply because clients come one at a time.

The defect of group administration is the difficulty, in a whole classroom, of obviating individual failure to follow instructions, detecting cheating on time limits, etc., but using proctors in a large group or restricting groups to four to six removes this danger. The cost of the school psychologist's time is also a saving in group testing, and even in clinics tests can often be arranged for four or so clients together, with a corresponding saving. An interesting innovation by Eber (see Krug, Chapter 7) is a set-up of a half dozen phone-box-like testing booths giving the privacy of individual testing with automated instructions or central phone communication and timing by the psychologist. Psychologists of the last generation made a fetish of the superiority of individual testing, which is not supported by actual experience. This fetish long held up adaptive advances to group administration and the use of group tests as individual tests. Meanwhile, today we are seeing a rapid development not just of machine scoring, but of machine testing by tests on TV screens with push-button responses, and so on.

The term *conspective* comes from *con* and *spectare*—to look at together. It concerns how far two psychologists looking at the *same* test performance will agree on the assigned score. Among different tests there can be inherent differences in such reliability of agreement and the *conspection coefficient* has therefore been introduced as a correlation to assess this. (We have already noted that what we might like to have as an *inner* conspection coefficient cannot be worked out for Q-data, because only one person can look at his or her own memories and introspections.) However, with the key-scored test design perfect conspection between scorers can be reached for Q- and T-data. Let us note that though 2) *conspectiveness* (in Table 2.3) relates to 5) *open-ended versus multiple-choice*, it is not identical. (Most of the nine dimensions in Table 2.3 have this cross-permissive independence.) It is *possible* to have a key for *inventive* (open-ended) answers, e.g., in some tests in the O-A Kit where only certain produced words are accepted, and in that case there is still a conspection correlation of 1.0.

The other end of this dimension—purely subjective evaluation—is strictly not to be tolerated in tests *per se*. A test with this form of scoring is strictly a rating (L(R)-data) and has the properties we have seen in ratings. An attempt to make this approach more objective was made years ago by Sir Cyril Burt with children's drawings and essays by the use of standard graded products to be matched (examples in Cattell, 1936) as nearly as possible by a given product. However, Burt himself confessed that, when he was scoring essays with another examiner, the model he had written out for the ideal 10-point essay score was accidentally included with the batch sent to the other examiner and was failed by the latter! The poor conspect reliability of experts' evaluations of much modern artwork illustrates in a wider context the unsolved difficulties of using open-ended scoring, as well as open-ended response, in psychological tests. One must realistically recognize that it sadly reduces the value of such tests as the TAT, Rorschach, and Draw-A-Man (as a personality test, not as the Goodenough ability test).

The psychologist should be wary of the misuses of the word "objective" in regard to tests. As Tables 2.1 and 2.2 have made clear, *objective means T-data*, defined as a test in which the subject is not giving his own estimate of himself, as in Q-data, but simply *performing* (as in an intelligence test or the O-A Personality Battery) and is being scored on aspects of his behavior of which he is not aware. Confusion has arisen from using "objective" for tests that are merely objectively *scorable*, i.e., completely *conspective* questionnaires. The correct terms for distinguishing these two properties are *objective* and *conspective*, and each can exist without the other.

The third dimension in Table 2.3—*patterned vs. item scoring*—is one unknown to the itemetric psychometry that originally grew up around questionnaires and item-izable tests. Especially in laboratory psychology, e.g., in a track-tracer performance, or in physiological approaches, e.g., the change in skin resistance or acidity of saliva in a stress interview, or in the O-A Battery where one uses a *ratio* of emotional to unemotional words recalled, and other ratio, difference, etc. scores, the total test score cannot be broken down into items. Most of these non-item tests essentially present a *global* situation and deal with a *pattern* of response.

A score on a factorial source trait in an ability test or the O-A Personality Kit will typically consist of a weighted sum of scores on perhaps six to eight subtests of that type. It is true that in an intelligence test some of these subtests, but not all, *may* break down themselves into items (analogies, synonyms), but the subtests in objective personality measures are, as stated, often wholistic ratios, etc., which demand different psychometric principles and calculation formulae from those used so long in itemetrics (see Chapter 23). In passing we may note that the laws of distribution, reliability, etc., of such *structured test* scores have been neglected relative to the simpler itemetric generalizations. A collection of subtests can in some respects only be treated like a series of items (but in larger units) because itemetrics requires an atomistic similarity in form that is not present in the diverse subtests that go into a factor battery. This difference affects test consistency and validity concepts and calculations with new tests, as studied in more detail in Chapter 23.

The dichotomous dimension of *timed vs. untimed* tests is important not only in practice but in theory. In practice, the only difference is that in the one case one needs one bit of apparatus—a stopwatch, or, better, a preset alarm timer—and a sharp eye for cheating on time. Except for this the timed test is certainly more convenient. In questionnaires, for instance, typically untimed, one may be very late for dinner waiting for the slowest of 200 subjects to finish!

In the theoretical domain, however, the timed test may have problems. Is one testing the same thing when the subject does or does not have to hurry? Thorndike, for example, thought not, and his followers learned to distinguish in intelligence between "power" (untimed) and "speed" measures. Spearman, on the other hand, showed that one gets virtually the same rank order of subjects when they take as long as they like and when they work fast to a time limit. His result, however, was achieved with subjects all of the same age. The question of whether one is testing the same trait with timed and untimed tests with a mixed age group is generally answered in the negative, along with warnings about complexities.

At a purely test mechanics level, a timed test means that the faster individuals move on to a set of items that is not touched by the slower, and later items may have, either unavoidably or by design, a somewhat different constitution or difficulty. (In a properly constructed intelligence test the latter items are, for example, ranked in increasing difficulty, and this rule has been followed in most tests from the Binet to the Culture-Fair.) The same tests given timed and untimed consequently require some differences in calculations of effects of length, etc., upon consistency and validity coefficients, from those itemetric formulae dealt with in

Chapters 4 and 23.

In general, a speed condition introduces a new pattern to the test's validities. Indeed, the personality factor *exuberance*, U.I.21, in the O-A Battery is measured largely by speed, without regard to content.

An important dichotomy of tests, as the fifth category in Table 2.3 reminds us, is that between *inventive* answers, e.g., where the subject must produce some word not there, or *selective* responses where the subject selects, usually from a multiple choice, the given response that he thinks best. The former is commonly called "open-ended" and although it *can* be key-scored, by checking S's output against the psychologist's key list of acceptable answers, it is often vitiated as a satisfactory test device by subjective scoring. A conspective use of inventive answers *without* a key occurs in many objective tests, e.g., of fluency on a topic when the score is simply the number of words produced in a given time.

Multiple choice is by far the most satisfactory item test form where machine key scoring is employed. It does have the disadvantage that with n alternatives there is a $1/n$ chance of being right by luck. If n is 2 this is serious; however, if to escape it one makes n large (say 6 or 7), it slows reading so that fewer items can be covered in a given time. In any case, an approximate correction for number right by luck can be made by subtracting $1/n$ from the number right. This is not as good an answer to the problem as it may at first seem, because in an intelligence test with ranked difficulty of items there is little guessing in the earlier items and $1/n$ should apply only to the later items done. In a timed test, with S's reaching different numbers done, it is nevertheless better than no correction at all. The itemetric literature of the 1930s through 1950s teems with ingenious schemes for improving multiple choice tests, e.g., making wrong responses spuriously attractive to those who do not know the right answer, thus reducing their "luck." But in a brief overview we cannot stray into these refinements.

The sixth dichotomy is of a somewhat different class from the others and needs discussion in contiguity with inventive vs. selective design and other alternatives. On the mechanical scoring end we have made a distinction between a) machine scoring and b) obtaining useful derivatives and interpretations of the scores by machine. Although procedure b) is naturally often connected with a), since entering the computer with a) makes it easy to follow on with b), yet b) is naturally independent and applicable to almost any test form and mode of initial scoring.

Machine scoring in the past has meant responding to the test on an *answer sheet* first. This has been so convenient to the psychologist that one suspects its weaknesses have never been intensively explored. In a personality test individual differences in whatever instrument factor (Chapter 23) is involved in transmitting answers from test to sheet may not be important—except as it increases random error. But in ability tests short distance memory, g_{ml} (Horn's SAR) could become, with speeded tests on answer sheets, a real intrusion into whatever special ability is being measured, e.g., in the CAB (Chapter 8). However, as psychologists settle on the most worthwhile tests for their domain of practice, it becomes practicable to invest in more apparatus. In the last five years or so a number of tests, e.g., the 16 P.F. and CAQ, have been put on a screen presentation, by cassette, such that subjects can respond by a button, and the scores on the various scales can be made available as soon as the test is completed (see Chapter 7). This eliminates the objection to the answer sheet, though that device is likely always to be with us for group testing.

The second use of the computer—b) above—is of much broader importance

and is fully discussed in Chapter 7. It involves operating upon the scores as soon as they are recorded to yield predictions by the behavioral equation of various criteria, use of the pattern similarity coefficient to test the individual's fit to job profiles or psychiatric syndrome patterns, and a verbal "narrative output" description of the client in terms suitable for communication to agencies. The Institute for Personality and Ability Testing, Dr. Herbert Eber, Dr. Samuel Krug, and many others have now developed programs with such art that it is mostly impossible to distinguish the computer's "narrative description" (as it is commonly called) from a clinician's ordinary written report of the case. (It is distinguished, if anything, by nicer use of correct terms and accuracy of probabilities than in the average noncomputer case writeup!)

The *normative vs. ipsative* scoring dimension will be studied in all implications in Chapters 4 and 23, as it involves several aspects of standardization. What we can point out here is that the choice between an ipsative and a normative translation of the raw scan can sometimes be made *after* the test is scored. But more often it is unavoidably and irrevocably built into the test's construction and its scoring. In general, we compare a given score with the distribution over a population of *persons*, as in an I.Q. Such a basis of comparison is called *normative* standardization. But sometimes we compare with the distribution of other traits within one person. This occurs in Q-sort, but also in an area of wider importance, that of interest and motivation scores (Chapter 13). When we conclude, for example, that Smith's interest in athletics can be considered one-quarter of his total interests, that interest may not, normatively, be as great as Jones's, which is a sixth of *his* total interest. But in ipsative scoring we are only comparing interests *within* each person.

It escaped notice for some time that certain interest tests, like the Kuder and Strong, by using a forced choice between each of a set of interests paired in some or all possible ways, compelled the *total* interest to be the same for everyone, and thus forced a negative correlation among the constituent interests, which become automatically ipsatively scored. (The consequences of this for factor analytic structure have been explored by Jackson [1971] and Cattell and Brennan [1983].) Where possible it is undoubtedly best to use tests that can lead to normative scores. Only rarely will one wish to derive ipsative scoring when not actually forced by the inherent nature of the test design. In any case, *either* mode of scoring implies reaching a standardization. Incidentally, we have *not* thought it necessary to use a dimension here of standardized vs. unstandardized, since without a standardization to interpret scores we scarcely have what can be called a test.

The dimension in Table 2.3 of *overt behavior vs. physiological response* is not identical with Q vs. T media. Objective tests use both overt behavior and physiological response. For example, U.I.24, Anxiety, in the O-A Kit (Cattell & Schuerger, 1978, and Chapter 12) uses, on the one hand, such behavior as is expressed in "degree of emotionality of comment" and, on the other, shorter lag in pulse response to the cold pressor, and greater trapezius muscle tension on the myograph. For the personality factors and states that turn out to be temperamental (in the sense of constitutional), more physiological subtests will undoubtedly be found in the present O-A Battery and incorporated in extended batteries in the future. Even intelligence, g_p as Ertl (1966) has shown, can have its factor validity increased by electroencephalographic analysis.

The ninth dimension in Table 2.3, *cross-cultural fitness*, must be recognized as actually referring as much to a trait as to a test. There can be no cross-cultural quality to a test aiming at a trait completely

peculiar in form to one culture! Strength of attachment to a Japanese tea ceremony or level of skill in wind-surfing can scarcely be tested in, say, the population of Niger. However, it turns out that the major primary and secondary personality and ability factors, e.g., in the 16 P.F. and the Culture-Fair Intelligence Test, have appeared wherever factoring has been done, and, as far as research has gone, can be said to represent traits of basic human nature everywhere.

Even so, there are differences in the loadings of items within what is recognizably the same pattern, and one must distinguish between a test which is a) translatable and scorable for an agreed trait, as in the dozen translations of the 16 P.F. or in the crystallized intelligence factor represented by the WAIS, and b) usable across cultures *as it stands*, as when literally the same test form of the Culture-Fair Intelligence Test is used in the U.S., Germany, Taiwan, and Japan, or when physiological tests are used to measure U.I.24, Anxiety, or hand tremor and acceleration of metabolic rate in U.I.21, Exuberance (Cattell & Schuerger, 1978). Strictly cross-cultural tests in the b) sense are rare, the Culture-Fair Test of g_f and the measures of anxiety, U.I.24, being almost unique; but in the first sense there are now several important tests, e.g., the O-A, the WAIS, MMPI, EPI, and 16 P.F., on which psychologists can get results with hope of comparing their findings with those in a number of other cultures.

The tenth and last test dimension to be discussed is one which carries us over into the expanded discussions of Chapter 4. Is the test one whose validity can be precisely evaluated or is this inherently impossible? (We center the dimension on validity here, but in fact we deal with a test property that involves all the psychometric properties—reliability, homogeneity, efficiency—that surround validity.)

Just as we have said that a test that is

unstandardized is scarcely a test, and we have consequently entered no such dimension, so one should perhaps pay little attention to a validity-nonvalidity dimension, in that a test without some validity is pointless. However, there is, or at least has been, among psychologists a concept of validity that is nonpsychometric and is most often given the name of "face validity." There is one legitimate sense of face validity, namely, that in achievement tests one on geography should obviously deal with geography and one on chemistry with chemistry. But where personality and even much of ability testing is concerned, no one can accurately tell from a *look* at the content items with what validity a particular personality or ability factor is being measured.

One is free, of course, within limits (Chapter 3) to *call* a factor what he or she thinks its meaning is. The criterion relations will eventually decide whether the name is apt, and we are then dealing only with a matter of semantics. The real trouble with face validity is that naive individuals trust their "insights," believing they can decide by inspection whether an item or subtest measures whatever factor is claimed to underlie the test. For example, both teachers and business executives, who rightly emphasize ability to write intelligently, are apt to reject the Culture-Fair Intelligence Test on "face validity" because they see no words in it! But actually, since fluid intelligence *is* involved in writing intelligently (and especially in *learning* such performance), having a correlation of about + .4 with English grades in the U.S.A. and the same with Chinese language grades in China, one would expect it to predict learning in words as readily as a traditional verbal intelligence test.

The erroneousness of face validity, however, arises more frequently in *over-* than *under*estimation of validity of a test. Such overestimation often comes from ego involvement of practitioners in the tests they were taught to administer in their training years and on which they have never examined the research evidence since—and sometimes not before! Such valuation from authority, or from personal experience constantly biased in recall, is as remote from true psychometric evidence of validity as is face validity. I have ventured, in earlier writings, to suggest its cognate status by calling it "faith" validity! Much use of "crystal ball" tests lingering on today has only this kind of validity—by anecdote, personal involvement, self-deception through selective memory, and so forth.

Numerical levels on validity and consistency are not discussed in Table 2.3, being left for Chapter 4. These are broader dimensions, and the tenth is not level of validity, but whether the test has the property of being psychometrically evaluated on validity. Some more esoteric dimensions that can be applied to tests are set out in Cattell and Warburton (1967, Chapter 6).

SUMMARY

This chapter examines two basic preliminary issues in psychological testing:

1) How are measures on individual people's *traits* (or other organisms) to be combined with quantifications of *situations* in predicting behavior or diagnosing causes of behavior. A basic answer is given through the behavioral equation, leaving more extensive discussion to Chapters 3 and 23.
2) What are the characteristics, limitations and advantages of the available varieties of observational evidence on traits, processes, and states in individuals?

As to the first issue, the behavioral equation is shown to combine the profile of the individual and the profile of the stimulus situation (representing each uniquely) in a simple linear and additive model which has been shown to fit well up to the limits of most recent experiments.

Modern testing, especially in a clinic, but also in allowing for changing estimations in school or industry, requires that the behavioral equation include, beside trait scores, psychological *state* and *role adoption* measures. This becomes practicable through *modulation theory*, the model of which uses a) measures of a trait of personal *liability (proneness) to a particular* state or acquired readiness to adopt a role, and b) knowledge of the population vector of modulation indices for common life situations capable of provoking emotional states.

As to the bases of perceived data for trait, state, and situation assessment, there are just three *media of observation*:

1) *L-data*: behavior in everyday life. This can be either rated by observers (L(R)) or recorded by time sampling of events (L(B)), as in biographical material.
2) *Q-data*: behavior self-rated from introspection, as in questionnaire or consulting room. (This is called Q'-data when not taken at face value but as behavior on a test.)
3) *T-data*: objective performance tests (essentially as in a laboratory). Logically, Q'-data falls with objective performance, T-data, but by usage is classed with Q-data.

The manner of collecting and scoring data also leads to a second tripartite division, namely in the naming of the emergent traits as ability (or cognitive), temperament (or *general* personality), and dynamic (interest and motivation). Psychologists have been so confident of their "commonsense" ability to allocate any trait to one of these categories that no operational separation was proposed before that of Cattell and Warburton (1967). The operational distinction, needed in borderline cases, is associated with further properties that make this tripartite categorization by *modalities* a useful one.

From a test design viewpoint it is useful to look at the three-media by three-modality table, since not all of the three media of observation are equally effective and valid for the various modalities of traits and states. For example, the L- and T-media bases are better (less open to bias) than Q-data where the assessment of abilities or the strengths of interests and motives is concerned, as clinical analysis shows. However, L-data also have observer bias. Q- and L-data have certain advantages in trait-state coverage from dealing with everyday life behavior. T-data are unique in being essentially free of the motivational and observer-personality distortions in L- and Q-data through the latter's quantities being filtered through the human mind and otherwise injected with bias.

True tests—possible only in Q- and T-data—can be defined, individually, with respect to position on ten main dimensions, as well as some less essential ones. Probably the most important (see Table 2.3) are:

• Timed vs. untimed
• Key-scored (conspective) vs. subjectively evaluated
• Inventive (open-ended) vs. selective (multiple choice)
• Itemized, atomistic vs. pattern-scored
• Normatively vs. ipsatively standardized

CHAPTER 3

The Actual Trait, State, and Situation Structures Important in Functional Testing

Raymond B. Cattell

TRAITS TRANSCEND MEDIA OF MEASUREMENT

The points made in Chapter 2 concerning "angles of observation" for personality plainly imply that there exists a structure of personality in and of itself, of which we may get views of varying accuracy according to the medium of measurement. Meanwhile we have made it clear that, although initial research on structure must grope with all kinds of measurement, as soon as a scientific taxonomy of personality structure in a given culture emerges, the practicing psychologists are wise to aim their tests at the meaningful unitary structures that emerge. This is what we mean by functional testing.

Although the unitary structures, state dimensions, and typical processes in personality are by no means fully mapped, some 50 years of intensive programmatic work with increasingly sophisticated fac-

tor analytic and other multivariate experimental methods have yielded no small harvest of structural knowledge. What is perhaps three-quarters of the domain of abilities have been reliably mapped; over 40 personality factors (including primary and secondary structures) have been rendered measurable, and the complex world of motivation has yielded up knowledge of innate human drive structures (ergs) and culturally acquired sentiments (sems). The research particulars of these findings and the scientific formulation of the concepts are available in a voluminous literature of personality theory (for example, in Cartwright, 1974, 1979; Lindzey & Hall, 1975; Smith & Vetter, 1982; Eysenck, 1960, 1970; Cattell, 1979c, 1980a; Pervin, 1975; Pawlik, 1968; and Wiggins, 1973), so that here we can appropriately confine ourselves to the structures as objects of measurement.

At first delving into research it may not

be obvious that the factorings in L-, Q- and T-data are approaching the same structures. The principle which we have expressed above—of a structure existing apart from viewpoint—has been technically expressed in the *principle of indifference of indicator*. In the more operational setting of factor analytic experiment, this is attested by the existence of *instrument-transcending trait factors*. The latter shows by a factor X being found loaded by measures of X by variables in medium or instrumentality A *and* in medium B. However, two extra, smaller, "instrument" factors may appear from factoring the joint set of media variables, one loading instrumentality A variables and one the tests that have in common instrumentality B. This is illustrated in Table 3.1. Further discussion and practical illustration of instrument factors will be found in Cattell (1961a, 1973a), Cattell and Digman (1964), and Campbell and Fiske (1959). They are most prominent in objective dynamic trait measures, and so more deliberate attention will be given them in Chapters 13, 14, and 23.

The principle of indifference of indicator

has not been given nearly as much research attention as it deserves, but where experiments are done they support it. The source traits indexed as A, B, C, D, etc., in Q-data, e.g., in the 16 P.F. and HSPQ, are obviously aligned in meaning, one to one, with the dozen or more factors in experimentally well-designed rating, L-data studies. Consequently, most psychologists have accepted the common indexing, e.g., A, affectia; C, ego strength; F, surgency, etc., as contingently applying to the same source traits in Q and L factorings. However, direct investigation factoring L and Q together (Cattell, Pierson, & Finkbeiner, 1976) recently showed a beautiful alignment in virtually all cases. It is interesting, however, that some *apparent* differences of behavioral descriptions (not of common loading) exist between the "mental interiors" of the introspective Q and the outwardly seen "behavioral exterior" of L-data. For example, the shyness reported in questionnaire H(-) gets some ratings of "pride" from observers, and the high F-factor people think themselves very sociable, while observers think they are more attention-getting. These

TABLE 3.1

Instrument-transcending and Instrument Factors in Common Factoring of Two Media or Instrumentalities

Variable and Mode at Measurement						Source Trait X	Source Trait Y	Instrumentality or Medium		
								A	B	C
1	Source	Trait	X,	Medium	A	x		x		
2	"	"	"	"	A	x		x		
3	"	"	"	"	B	x			x	
4	"	"	"	"	B	x			x	
5	"	"	"	"	C	x				x
6	"	"	"	"	C	x				x
7	"	"	Y	"	B		x		x	
8	"	"	"	"	B		x		x	
9	"	"	"	"	A		x	x		
10	"	"	"	"	A		x	x		

x = significant loading. Although instrument transcending psychological source trait patterns on the one hand and instrument factors on the other can be recognized as distinct, the estimation of, say, source trait A will always be contaminated with some instrument factor and the best we can do is reduce bias from any one by using varied instruments, e.g., adding scores on variables 1, 3 and 5 to get source trait X score.

are interesting small departures not affecting the main alignment.

However, one must recognize that at the present moderate levels of validity reached by actual source trait questionnaire scales, the direct correlations between the Q scale and the observer L rating for a given factor by a typical observer are not really high. This is because, in addition to sharing the common personality factor, each has a different instrument factor pushing variance into it. The fact that these Q and L "markers" when factored together have their highest loadings on the same factor tells the essential story. However, in statistical terms, if the L and the Q marker each have, say, a .7 validity on this instrument-transcending source trait factor, their mutual correlation is going to be only 0.5. Thus, the self-sentiment and the superego as measured by objective dynamic devices *in the MAT* (Motivational Analysis Test) have so far not exceeded this level in correlations with, respectively, measures of Q_3 (self-sentiment) and G (superego) in the questionnaire medium. Further *progressive rectification* (see Chapter 23) of the scales may raise these r's somewhat, but in any case there is some possibly useful information in the instrument differences. For example, the MAT Q_3 might give mostly the actual investment strength, but the questionnaire Q_3 might give more the degree of cognitive awareness of that strength. In any case, this phenomenon forces us to conclude that we should ideally reach the best possible estimate of any required instrument-transcending trait by not depending on a test in one medium. This is an onerous ideal but the implication is that we reduce the contamination of one medium by adding across several media or devices. It can be shown mathematically (Ch. 4) that in such additions the variance contribution of the common, desired element piles up faster than that of the contaminants.

The principle requiring the same factors to appear—though in different dress —in different media received for years support in the L and Q media, but researchers were baffled by a complete inability to show order between the well-aligned L-Q source traits, on the one hand, and the T-data factors indexed as U.I.16, U.I.17, U.I.18, etc., on the other. At last a partial breakthrough appeared when certain *second-order* factors in L-Q proved to be *first-order* factors in T-data. Second-order (stratum) factors are factors among L and Q primary factors. Anxiety and ex-via-invia are well-known instances. The second-order anxiety factor (QII, covering primaries C-, H-, O, Q_5- and Q_4) aligned with U.I.24, the anxiety factor among objective tests, while other alignments studied have been QII = U.I.32, extraversion, QVIII = U.I.17, inhibitory control, some standing firmly to replication, others less steady over populations.

It is hoped that other identities will soon be found, but at present we must also entertain the possibility that the nature of one medium is so much more sensitive than another in a certain area that certain traits will have substantial variance in it but be too small in variance to be clearly recognized in another. Thus, in T-data some temperament traits with largely physiological, unconscious expression might not enter the person's self-concept, which is what we really have in Q-data. The ratio of 35 presently known primary Q traits to 20 T-data might favor the theory just broached that the latter arise as second stratum patterns from the naturally more numerous first stratum Q-L factors. But the slowness with which further examples are presently being located suggests also that there may be some areas of behavior in which they do not overlap. Yet, the size of behavioral areas covered cannot be very different because so far, the *criterion predictions* from T-data have easily rivaled those from Q measures at the same stage of research, despite the relative present obscurity of some of the T-data pattern meanings.

AN OVERVIEW OF ABILITY STRUCTURES

To give an adequate account of the number, nature, and developmental courses of the principal personality and ability traits is obviously a task to be accomplished only by some major textbooks in core courses in psychology and psychiatry. Certainly, to handle the usual legitimate doubts, criticisms, and debates that naturally arise would also require a volume on methodology and the history of research. At present, the comparative simplicity of the findings and methods in primary and secondary ability structures makes that area better known to psychologists. Consequently, we shall begin the substance of this chapter with description of the important *ability traits* and then move on to the methodologically more complex proofs of *temperament* and *dynamic* trait structures and a few touches of illustration of properties. Fortunately, there are textbooks in each subarea (and many hundreds of research articles) that can be referred to as explaining what we must briefly, and sometimes therefore with seeming dogmatism, state as a position here. It is, at any rate, a position reached in all cases by many years of experience, experiment, and careful psychological reasoning.

The number of primary abilities first located and defined by Thurstone as about half a dozen has now reached (and perhaps in the interim passed) the list of 20 in Table 3.2.

Of course, one can always break skills down into much smaller performances than these, but they would be very narrow specifics. For example, a capacity like numerical ability shows some "specifics" (narrow common factors) separately for addition, subtraction, multiplication, and division. Persons constantly adding, as in a store, could be "disproportionately" good in that specific sense.

In books about testing in this area the terms "ability" and "aptitude" have been bandied about with good intent to distinguish them but with much inconsistency of use from writer to writer. Possibly the commonest use is to employ ability for a capacity *in being*, and aptitude for some natural, more constitutional, or genetic predisposition. Actually, the size of the genetic components in the most important of the above *agencies* (as we call them in Chapter 8) has been assessed by at least a dozen careful investigators, and the general conclusion (see recent integration of studies in Cattell, 1982) is that *all* have some genetic component, but that it is highest (heritability around 58%) in *spatial ability, fluency*, and *verbal ability*, and lowest in numerical ability, reasoning, retrieval memory and several others. The high value in verbal ability may actually be due to its high loading in fluid intelligence, which is appreciably heritable. "Aptitude" may perhaps therefore best be used for the genetic part of a primary ability.

Second-stratum—henceforth *secondary*—factors are, as stated above, located as factors among factors. There may also be *tertiaries* and still higher orders developed from these. Often by the second order the factors, though broad in influence, are "shallow," i.e., contributing only moderately to the original, directly measured test variables. Their nature *may* not even be strictly psychological, but could be causes residing in broad social influences, on the one hand, e.g., social status structure producing correlation of intelligence and emotional control, or in broad physiological influences, on the other, e.g., several primary abilities deriving from total cortical undamaged cell count.

It is usual to speak of intelligence, fluency, speed, memory, etc., as second-order factors among primaries, and such in fact they are in factorial operations as recorded by their loadings on primaries in Table 3.2. But the *triadic theory* of ability structure (Cattell, 1971a) ultimately sees evidence for *three* tiers:

TABLE 3.2
Twenty Primary Abilities Examined for Higher Stratum Factors
Oblique Primary-Factor Pattern Matrix at Optimal Position of Simple Structure

Alternative Universal Index Number	Primary ability	U.I.I g_c	U.I.II g_f	U.I.III g_v	U.I.IV g_{ps}	U.I.V g_m	U.I.VI g_r	h^2
U.I. 1	Verbal Ability (V)	**59**	− 02	− 06	18	05	06	52
2	Numerical Ability (N)	− 05	**45**	01	29	**32**	− 02	60
3	Spatial Ability (S)	07	**68**	**37**	03	02	04	54
4	Speed of Closure (Cs)	02	02	**28**	**89**	−**33**	− 04	63
5	Perceptual Speed and Accuracy (P)	− 25	**40**	**27**	**37**	− 01	00	40
6	Inductive Reasoning (I)	00	**42**	22	23	13	02	40
7	Flexibility of Closure (Cf)	02	23	**27**	26	00	11	24
8	Associative Memory (Ma)	03	06	− 02	00	**66**	− 03	46
9	Mechanical Ability (Mk)	**57**	17	**37**	− 03	− 02	− 09	40
10	Span Memory (Ms)	− 13	05	00	**31**	11	22	22
11	Meaningful Memory (Mm)	12	03	01	06	**38**	06	25
12	Spelling (Sp)	10	− 13	03	**63**	05	− 04	42
13	Auditory Ability (AA)	17	00	24	23	− 03	11	18
14	Esthetic Judgment (E)	09	01	06	− 08	04	**32**	13
15	Spontaneous Flexibility (Fs)	13	24	23	09	07	**27**	29
38	Ideational Fluency (Fi)	01	28	01	04	00	**78**	70
39	Word Fluency (W)	07	09	02	**53**	02	06	40
40	Originality (O)	19	02	15	− 01	− 16	**41**	23
41	Aiming (A)	00	− 06	**44**	02	17	− 01	26
42	Representational Drawing (RD)	− 04	− 07	**42**	07	17	03	27

Note: Decimal points have been omitted. Salient factor pattern coefficients, or loadings used to interpret particular factor, appear in boldface. g_c = Crystallized Intelligence, g_f = Fluid Intelligence, g_v = Visualization Capacity, g_{ps} = General Perceptual Speed, g_m = General Memory Capacity, and g_r = General Retrieval Capacity.
  Since there has been some tendency to equate crystallized intelligence, g_c, with "verbal or scholastic intelligence" (Vernon, 1969a), it should be pointed out that crystallized intelligence arises from investing g_f in *any* complex cultural area. This is well-illustrated here by mechanical ability being just as much such an acquired intelligence as verbal ability.
(From "Higher Stratum Ability Structures" by Hakstian, A. R., & Cattell, R. B., vol. 70, in the *Journal of Educational Psychology* (1978))

1) *primary agencies, a's*, like verbal, numerical, spatial and other well-known narrower abilities;
2) *provincial powers, p's*, where neural evidence suggests special associations built around *sensory input and motor* brain area centers, where local analysis goes on; and
3) *general capacities, c's, or g's*, which contribute widely to virtually all performances.

Some six or seven of the last general capacities arise from factoring a really broad array of primaries (one less confirmed general capacity—long distance meaningful memory [Kelley, 1964]—has been omitted from Table 3.2). Much is known about the capacities (*g's*), especially fluid and crystallized intelligence (see Chapter 8). But the provincial sensory motor powers, *p's*, have been less explored and, although Seashore, Lansome and others long ago explored auditory-musical capacity, it is only recently that an auditory ability factor (Horn & Stankow, 1979)—a *power* centered on discrimination and association around the auditory input—has been shown as a factor spreading over agencies and below the level of general capacities. The triadic theory in Table 3.3, like the chemist's periodic table in 1840, therefore, must be assumed still to have gaps in it. Moreover, although the

p's will tend to appear in factoring along with the g's, as second-order factors, the triadic theory supposes that when we are able to resolve correlations into path coefficients, the causal chains would probably show them in an intermediate position, as in Table 3.3, complexly interacting with g's to contribute to the level of development of the narrower agencies that people actually use in immediate test performances. For example, spatial ability might develop out of interaction of visual and kinesthetic p's, in which the higher relation-perceiving capacities of fluid intelligence, g_f, have additionally been invested. Further discussion of the nature of the structures is deferred to Chapter 8.

AN OVERVIEW OF PERSONALITY STRUCTURES FOUND IN L-Q MEDIA

Although the total personality sphere of behaviors is believed to be covered by our dictionary derived from gossip down the ages, there turned out to be a few instances of factors being found in Q-data before being recorded in L-data. For that reason the letters of the alphabet through P were assigned to the L-data-matched factors, roughly in declining order of variance. But on reaching Q, since it so happened that some new factors were found only in questionnaires, these were contingently given labels Q_1, Q_2, Q_3, etc. Twenty-three primaries—three put at the end of the Q's as insufficiently confirmed—have thus ultimately been found in items covering normal behavior, as listed in Table 3.4A.

On factoring *abnormal* behavior items in questionnaires, as in the MMPI, extended by certain well-known depression and psychopathic scales, 12 factors were located not found in the normal personality sphere (see Table 3.4B.). They are tentatively considered the patterns of certain "disease process" syndromes. A fresh symbol system was started for the 12 "abnormal" factors, beginning with D1 through D7 for the seven dimensions of depression and proceeding for the convenience of psychiatry with mnemonic sym-

TABLE 3.3
The Triadic Theory of Ability Structure
A. Examples of Agencies, Provincial Powers, and General Capacities

Primary Abilities or Agencies a's		Provincial Powers p's	General Capacities c's	
Verbal ability	a_v	Visualization association area, p_v	Fluid intelligence	g_f
Numerical ability	a_n	Auditory association area, p_a	Crystallized intelligence	g_c
Spatial ability	a_s	Kinesthetic motor control association area, p_k	Cognitive speed	g_s
Mechanical	a_m		Short-term memory	g_m
Esthetic judgment	a_e		Retrieval capacity (fluency)	g_r
Aiming	a_a			
Word fluency	a_w			
Drawing	a_d			
Perceptual speed	a_p			

Note that *only an illustrative set* of primary abilities—agencies, a's—from Table 3.2 is used here. The provincial (sensory-motor) *powers* would be expected by the triadic theory eventually to include a demonstrated olfactory skill and taste association and perhaps a tactile power distinct from the kinesthetic cerebellar power.

TABLE 3.3

B. Interaction of Capacities, Provincials and Agencies with Other Modalities in Determining Score on a Variable

| | *Abilities* | | |
| Powers | | Agencies | |
1 CAPACITIES	2 PROVINCIALS	3 AGENCIES	CONTRIBUTORS BEYOND ABILITIES
[Unity of Action over the Whole Cognitive Field]	[Unity of Organization of Neural Sensory or Motor Zone in Brain]	Aids [Unity of Learned Transfer]	Effector Proficiencies [Unity of Dynamic Learning]	Dynamic and Personality Noncognitive Contributors Outside Triadic Components
Examples: g_f, g_s, g_r, etc. g_x,	Examples: p_v, p_a, p_m, etc.	Examples: a_g, a_n, a_v, a_m, etc.	

Variables: Actual Performances
$v_1, v_2, v_3, v_4, v_5, v_6, v_7, v_8, \ldots v_n$

bols, e.g., Pa for paranoid, Pp for psychopathic, etc., as in the MMPI.

Although the 28 normal and abnormal primaries are firmly supported by factoring not only in the U.S. but also in several foreign countries, the 15 secondaries have been somewhat poor in replication on patterns QV, QVI, QIX, QX, QXL, QXII and QXIV. But QI, QII, QIII, QIV, QVII, QVIII, QXIII and QXV (roman numerals are now used for secondaries) are well replicated, meaningful, and useful for practical measurement. The rest call for more research. QVII loads little more than B, crystallized intelligence, among the primaries, and since fluid intelligence, g_f, is invested in g_c, which in the 16 P.F. is labeled B, the secondary QVII is probably to be equated with fluid intelligence.

QI uniquely defines exvia-invia (extraversion) and QII anxiety—uniquely because *unless* these secondaries are approached through factoring and rotation of the primaries, their scale positions are arbitrary, having no hyperplane, as in the EPI. It shows a poor grasp of research in this area that a) many psychologists have

been content to handle personality assessment and prediction through just two or three secondary scales, e.g., exvia and anxiety (neuroticism) in Eysenck's EPI, or even extraversion-introversion only in the Myers-Briggs—sophisticated factor analytic methods show, as common sense and literature would expect, that human nature is far more complex than two or three dimensions, and altogether too much is left out by such "conveniences"; and b) if one wishes to use secondaries, they can be more accurately and uniquely scored by the weighted combinations of the primary scores given in the handbooks of the 16 P.F., HSPQ, CAQ, etc. Comrey's scale (1970) and the Guilford-Zimmerman (1949), though they do not yield scores on secondaries (being orthogonally rotated in the latter's primaries), at least respect the real multiplicity of human personality dimensions.

It is not our purpose here to examine questionnaire or other scales as such —which is done in Chapters 11 and 12— but inasmuch as they are related variously to the basic structured concepts we are viewing here, it is relevant to mention them.

There are two theories about the nature of second-order factors: 1) that they are "emergents" from the interaction of primaries in the life situation; and 2) that they are broad underlying influences—as intelligence is to primary abilities—which contribute to begetting the primary growths. In any case, *depth psychometry* (Cattell, 1973) argues that we should get both primary and secondary scores for a given individual. It is a mistake to assume that, because Jung's exvia and Freud's anxiety are the two largest secondaries, they suffice. Statistically, as much variance predictions come from the next five secondaries QIII, QIV, QV, etc., and they should be given due notice.

In each case the psychologist would do well to understand and have in mind the primaries that are served by the given secondary. To make this clear the constitution of secondaries is illustrated in Ta-

TABLE 3.4

The Structure of Primary and Secondary Q-L Personality Factors

A. In Normal Behavior Range

Primary Index Number	Primaries (1st Order) Polar Label	Primary Index Symbol	Secondary Index Number	Secondaries (2nd Order) Polar Label
Q_1	Sizia vs. Affectia	A	QI	Exvia vs. Invia
Q_2	Crystallized Intelligence	B	QII	Anxiety
Q_3	Ego strength	C	QIII	Cortertia
Q_4	Phlegm vs. Excitability	D	QIV	Independence
Q_5	Submissiveness vs. Dominance	E	QV	Discreetness
Q_6	Desurgency vs. Surgency	F	QVI	Prodigal subjectivity
Q_7	Superego strength	G	QVII	Fluid intelligence
Q_8	Threctia vs. Parmia	H	QVIII	Inhibitory Social Control
Q_9	Harria vs. Premsia	I	QIX	Social Dedication
Q_{10}	Zeppia vs. Coasthenia	J	QX	Phlegmatic Self-Assurance
Q_{11}	Boorishness vs. Mature Socialization	K		Overactiveness
Q_{12}		L	QXI	Pessimism
Q_{13}		M	QXII	
Q_{14}	Artlessness vs. Shrewdness	N		
Q_{15}	Untroubled adequacy vs. Guilt proneness	O		
Q_{16}	Sanguine Casualness	P		
Q_{17}	Conservatism vs. Radicalism	Q_1		
Q_{18}	Group adherence vs. Self-sufficiency	Q_2		
Q_{19}	Self-sentiment (Esteem)	Q_3		
Q_{20}	Ergic Tension	Q_4		
Q_{21}	Group Dedication	Q_5		
Q_{22}	Social Panache	Q_6		
Q_{23}	Explicit Self-expression	Q_7		

Note:
Connections of secondaries illustrated for two cases (QI and QVIII).

TABLE 3.4 *(cont'd)*
The Structure of Primary and Secondary Q-L Personality Factors
B. In Abnormal Behavior Data

Primary Index Number	Primaries	Primary Index Symbol	Second Orders
Q_{24}	Hypochondriasis	D1	Essentially
Q_{25}	Suicidal Disgust	D2	a Class of
Q_{26}	Brooding Discontent	D3	Depressions
Q_{27}	Anxious Depression	D4	QXIII
Q_{28}	Low Energy Depression	D5	General Depressions
Q_{29}	Guilt with Resentment	D6	
Q_{30}	Bored Withdrawal	D7	QXIV
Q_{31}	Paranoia	Pa	Psychosis (Total)
Q_{32}	Psychopathic Deviation	Pp	
Q_{33}	Schizophrenia	Sc	QXV
Q_{34}	Psychasthenia	As	Pathological
Q_{35}	General Psychosis	Ps	Depression

The end scored positive, in factors with bipolar loadings, is given at the right. Apart from alphabetic indexing, the primaries, here and elsewhere, e.g., Cattell, 1973a, are in arabic and the secondaries in roman.

The full description of the nature, age curves, genetic ingredient, life criterion prediction power, sex and national culture differences, etc. on these factors must be left to textbooks, e.g., Cartwright, Cattell, Lindzey & Loehlin, Pervin, and others, as part of general personality theory. Some, like ego strength, C, superego strength, G, exvia-invia, QI, confirm, to precision, structures already clinically recognized by Freud, Jung, and others. Others are new and consequently have new names.

It is interesting in this connection to note that the largest temperamental dimension noted clinically—cyclothyme vs. schizothyme—by Kraepelin and Bleuler, and elaborated by Kretschmer, turned out also to be the largest variance factor here, therefore indexed A and labeled Sizia vs. Affectia, Cyclo-Schizo has a pathological suggestion awkward in describing normals. Affectia connotes the expressive and changeable affect of the cyclic pole and sizia (from Latin for flat) the flatness of affect in A –. Thus we find in ratings that A + people are warm-hearted, easygoing, emotionally expressive, while A – are detached, cool, and stiff. Descriptions for the other source trait factors in Table 3.4 are given in the textbooks and handbooks cited.

ble 3.4 by lines joining them to the constituent primaries, but this is done only in the case of extraversion (exvia), to avoid visual tangles. As is well known, Anxiety, QII, shows itself very clearly by loadings on C(-), ego weakness; H(-), parmia (parasympathetic predominance); O, guilt proneness; $Q_3(-)$, low self-sentiment (esteem); and Q_4, high ergic tension, by frustration.

WHAT ARE THE STRUCTURES FOUND IN T-DATA?

It has already been mentioned that interpreting the nature of the structures found in objective tests has been more of a challenge to personality theory than interpreting those clothed in the everyday life reference data of L and Q factor patterns. The dawn of evidence of secondaries in L-Q being sometimes primaries in T has, as stated, greatly helped in some interpretations. The fact that there are some 15 secondaries in Q and some 20 T-data personality traits (but probably only a dozen sufficiently replicated at the time of writing) itself confronts us with no insuperable discrepancy for matching, because T-data, being more recent in investigation, probably still has to yield a few more discoveries. However, as noted, the solution to matching is unlikely to be a one-to-one alignment of primaries in each, i.e., in T and in L-Q factors.

The known T-data source traits are listed in Table 3.5, with their Q matches, where these latter are already apparent. As Hundleby, Pawlik, and Cattell (1965) show, they have each been replicated, on average, in about ten researches.

As regards naming and indexing a T-data series of source traits, it will be rec-

TABLE 3.5

The Main Unitary Personality Dimensions Replicated in Objective (T-Data) Measures
(with Q-Data Matches)

1. U.I.16: Ego Standards (or Competitiveness)

Some associations would suggest this is ego strength in the classical psychoanalytic sense, and also in the sense of Factor C+ as ego strength in questionnaires. However, the title "hedges" on this identification deliberately because U.I.16 has a stronger emphasis on self-assertion and achievement than is usual in ego strength.

The subtests show boldness, competitive assertiveness, speed of action and decision, some rejection of authority, and breadth (an "up-to-dateness") of interests and attitudes. It is lower than normal in psychotics, neurotics, delinquent gangs, in lower social status, in persons of small physique, and those showing poorer school performance.

2. U.I.17: Control

A factor of good upbringing, corresponding to second-order QVIII.

3. U.I.19: Independence vs. Subduedness

This is a factor determining in its subtests independence, criticalness, accuracy, capacity for intensive concentration and perceptual "field independence" as studied by Witkin (1962) and others. It is a positive predictor of success in school and in some military (submarine) and scientific performances. There is quite a high hereditary component.

Psychotics and neurotics are significantly lower than normals, and males significantly higher than females.

4. U.I.20: Evasiveness

This quite subtle trait has been the hardest to name, at least in any well-known single term. Descriptively close labels have been offered in "social, emotional evasiveness" (Hundleby, Pawlik, & Cattell, 1965), "dependent instability," and "posturing acceptance of social values," while interpretive labels have been given by psychiatrists as "bound anxiety" or "characterological anxiety" and "compensation for insecurity." The individual is superficially culturally conforming, but suggestible also to inconsistent (delinquent) values. He shows emotional instability (but not of the deep, C—, ego weakness form) and neurotic lack of objectivity, with some hostility and guilt proneness; but is sociable and dependent. Adult delinquents score high on the factor, but so, also, do involutional depressives.

5. U.I.21: Exuberance

Because this loads on some tests in the ability field it has sometimes been confounded with "ideational fluency" or "divergent thinking," but it is much broader than a purely cognitive pattern.

All manifestations are clearly those of high spontaneity, fluency, imaginativeness, speed of social and perceptual judgment, fast natural tempo, and sacrifice of accuracy to speed.

A significantly subnormal score is found on this factor for both neurotic and psychotic patients, and particularly for all depressives.

6. U.I.23: Capacity to Mobilize vs. Regression

Also called Mobilization vs. Neurotic Regressive Debility and Neuroticism.

The measures are of flexibility, general competence (simulating intelligence at times), emotional balance (especially absence of depression), and endurance of stress. It appears to be about 50/50 hereditary and environmental. At the negative pole it is associated with neuroticism, and at an early stage was called Neuroticism by Eysenck (1947), though it is only one of a half dozen source traits equally or more strongly associated with neuroticism and is better called regression. This negative pole has some qualities of the psychoanalytic concept of regression, in showing a falling off of interest and vigor along with decline in capacity to organize one's thoughts. The fact that U.I.23 is low in schizophrenics, depressives, and manics points to its association with disorganization as such. Competence in school, in stressful jobs, etc., is significantly related to the positive pole, as is freedom from "passing out" under stress.

7. U.I.24: Anxiety

This well-defined factor, aligning also well with QII, the second-order anxiety factor in questionnaires (C−, H−, L+, O+, Q_3−, Q_4+), has in some writings been called "emotionality." But it is *anxiety*, by every criterion—clinical, behavioral, situational, and physiological—that has ever been applied (Cattell & Scheier, 1961; Cattell, Schmidt, & Bjerstedt, 1972; Spielberger, 1966, 1972). It is high in neurotics and highest in anxiety neurotics, but not different from normals in schizophrenics (hence a diagnostic discriminator). However, high scores are not *invariably* pathological since "healthy" anxiety can be high situationally.

8. U.I.25: Realism vs. Tensidia

Also called Normality vs. Psychoticism by Eysenck and, more descriptively, Less-Imaginative, Task-Oriented Realism vs. Tense, Inflexible Dissociation from Reality.

It loads accuracy, speed, rejection of disturbing, imaginative intrusions, and a realistic orientation to tasks. At the negative pole, which has been rated by some psychiatrists as a form of anxiety and correlates with O+, guilt proneness, and Q_4+, tension, it shows emotional tension and a rigid, subjective inflexibility to reality indications. Tensidia is an acronym term attempting to capture this tense, inflexible, insensitiveness to reality. It has, by Eysenck's data and our own (1981), a fairly strong hereditary determination. At the tensidia pole it correlates significantly with *both* psychosis and neurosis and is particularly low in depressives. Realism (positive U.I.25) is higher in normals relative to all pathological syndromes.

9. U.I.28: Asthenia vs. Self-Assurance

Sometimes called Dependent, Negativistic Asthenia vs. Undisciplined Self-Assurance.

This is a complex pattern believed to express ambivalence from a conflict between severe, demanding parental upbringing in socialization and the growing individual's own need for self-realization (Cattell, 1964a). There is conformity, but with resentment and a continual asthenia born of unresolved conflict. Neurotics are above average, while delinquents, drug addicts, and some kinds of alcoholics are actually *below* normal, i.e., more self-assured and undisciplined.

10. U.I.32: Exvia vs. Invia

The questionnaire correlations repeatedly found with QI (A+, E+, F+, H+, Q_2−) demonstrate this to be the exvia-invia core of the popular "extraversion-introversion" notion. Schizophrenics, but also manics and depressives, are significantly below normal, i.e., more inviant, as are neurotics. It has no relation, or only a slightly negative relation (as found also in questionnaire, QI, exvia measures), to school grades. EEG activation measures, when subjects are active (calculating) are greater for exviants than inviants. Contingently, one can assume most proven extraversion-introversion criteria, e.g., in Eysenck (1947), to be related to this factor.

11. U.I.33: Discouragement vs. Sanguineness

This is clearly, from its content and associations, a factor of pessimism and discouragement of a lasting nature. Higher score is associated with lower socioeconomic status, poorer physique, lower self-ratings on confidence, cooperativeness, and calm objectivity. Schizophrenics tend to be above average and delinquents below average (both very significantly) on U.I.33, discouragement.

The less used T-data source traits U.I. 18, 22, 26, 27, 29, 30, and 31, not described here may be seen in Cattell and Schuerger (1978).

ognized that abilities are also T-data, and that psychologists have in several instances wondered whether certain T-data patterns are really abilities or temperament traits. Consequently, it has seemed reasonable to index these two modalities in the same T series and the L-Q media in a separate series until evidence shall join them. The ability and temperament T factors have been given *universal index, U.I., numbers* whereas the L-Q have been given *alphabetic identities* (or Q numbers also in Table 3.4). Because French (1951) had identified 15 ability factors by 1951, running from U.I.1 to U.I.15, when the first collation of checked T-data personality factors became published the personality series, therefore, began at U.I.16 and ran to U.I.36. However, three or four among these 21 patterns, mainly the last, needed either more replication or more high loaded tests to give a decent measurement validity. Incidentally, just as the A, B, C, etc., order given L-Q source traits expresses their declining order of contribution to the personality sphere, so the U.I.16-U.I.36 sequence does for T-data, though in a less certain sampling of the personality sphere.

As to naming, we encounter a difficult problem, the nature and importance of which seem not to have been understood by psychologists with limited perspective on the history of science. These latter object to new names, perhaps partly because, as William James and others have pointed out, psychologists have been fooled—and continue to be fooled—by the pedantry and pomp of calling old things by new names. A junk heap of new terms in personality and other areas of psychology —especially with "theory" attached—that have proved to add nothing firm to our science, would indeed be a mountainous garbage heap and one that some satirist should describe.

Whenever, however, something genuinely new appears in science—and this would be as true of replicated factor mea-

sures as of protons, quanta, or new chemical elements in the physical sciences—it is vital to have a new name.* In psychology, and to some extent in medicine, the temptation is to stay with a popular name, because the professional practitioner has to talk with his clients. Thus, the psychologist who clearly recognizes the properties of *exvia* as a second-order factor, QI, and as U.I.32 in the O-A Battery, is forced to speak of exvia as "sociability," while the doctor may refer to osteo-arthritis as rheumatism. But the truth is that there are at least four primaries that could be called "sociability," each with different properties and predictions, and similarly several very distinct medical diseases that the man in the street is content to call rheumatism.

In a few source traits the factor pattern is so clearly already popularly but vaguely recognized that one is tempted to use the popular term. Extraversion, it is true, once had a special definition by Jung (though now recognized as corresponding to no replicable reality). What we see factorially today is an instrument-transcending source trait QI or U.I.32 which, because it can now be tied down and measured with dependable validities, is named *exvia-invia* (since extraversion-introversion has long become a vague and shifting journalists' expression, used differently by different writers). That is to say, the U.I.32 or QI patterns have been uniquely replicated in a factor pattern on items and per-

---

*As indicated above, it is easy to assume, since psychology especially has been charged with verbal pomp, as by William James and others, that what is genuine concentration on new technical names and notations is mere academic pedantry. The problem of precise technical names in their various taxonomies has been substantially solved in other biological and physical sciences, but sometimes only after neglect of terms and indices has caused headaches. The problem is rampant in other newer sciences besides psychology. Thus, the paleontologist Howells deplores that "the multiplicity of names [assigned to the same sets of subspecies fossils] has interfered with an understanding of the evolutionary significance of the fossils that bear them."

formance tests which different psychologists can objectively reach.

The problem is that even with initially precisely attached technical terms certain further discoveries sometimes demand sufficient reinterpretation to call for a new term—as when "dephlogisticated air" became oxygen. (Lavoisier's new name for that element in the end proved to be wrong, as acids were found that lacked it. Nevertheless, one must stop *somewhere* in continued refinements—and oxygen is now a sound technical term.) Now, in replicated personality factors about half of the known personality patterns have had to live for about 20 years in a limbo of *describable* but *uninterpretable* loading patterns. It happened that L-Q factors A, B, C, and D were at once recognizable, but further along came I, L, M and N, for example, which were intriguingly new. It is in such cases that it is important to hold the pattern identity as a firm reference in the literature by a *symbol* notation, and an admittedly contingent new term, while the pack of researchers hunts down the essential nature and origins, before assigning an interpretive final name. Meanwhile, it would be best to use a label as *descriptively* exact as possible, but *new*. This is what has been attempted in such acronym-like terms as *inconautia* (incontinent autism) for U.I.34 and *stolpar-somnia* (stolid, parasympathetic-system-dominated, somnolent temperament) for U.I.35, which hopefully will soon be replaced. In other cases a partial attempt at interpretation has been made, as in *surgency* (from Latin *surgere*, to rise up), since F shows centrally a rapid rising up of ideas and impulses, or in *cortertia*, for U.I.22 (QIII) since a high *cort*ical al*ert*ness level (activation) characterizes the behavior.

The source traits in Table 3.5 are so new (for example, so far as several personality textbooks are concerned) that more discussion and interpretation will be necessary here than in regard to the other

media.* This fuller discussion is undertaken in Chapter 12.

AN OVERVIEW OF DYNAMIC TRAIT STRUCTURES

To clinicians like Freud, Jung, Adler, and their intellectual descendants, to personality psychologists like McDougall, Murray, and William James, and to the world's novelists (especially when of the caliber of Henry James), the dynamic modality structure into which we now look has been the heart and soul of psychology. Experimental psychologists—including rat-runners—have not neglected the challenge of this domain, especially in the last half century. However, the classical *bivariate* experiment, seeking strict controls, naturally proved inadequate (except in animal research), and it remained for *multivariate* experiment to shape into testable scientific models the teeming and tangled complexities of human motivation that had hitherto been left to the clinician and the dramatist.

The elemental variables upon which factor analysis has been brought to bear have mainly been attitudes, either self-evaluated (Q-data), or, better, objectively measured (T-data). The underlying structures connecting the observed specific interests and behaviors need not, of course, be *conscious*, for correlation will reveal them even if they are not. Incidentally, in these experiments, the attitudes measured are not a pencil and paper checking of "for or against" as in sociology and polling, but are set in the experimental *stimulus-response* paradigm, "In this (life) situation I want so much to do this with

---

*In regard to the T-data source trait list in Table 3.5, the reader is reminded that in a sense it is incomplete because the T-data ability factors U.I.1 through U.I.15 are omitted. Also, it will be noted (Table 3.2) that the primary abilities alone are now 20, and that with new secondaries French's original indexing to 15 will have to be carried beyond personality U.I.36 into the U.I.40 regions.

that." As Chapter 13 will clarify, the response is a measurable performance or course of action, as symbolized by A_j in equation 3-1, where D is dynamic structure and S is situation.

$$A_j = (f)D.S \qquad (3\text{-}1)$$

By measuring a wide array of attitude-interests in a large sample of people, using objective motivation measurement devices (GSR, perception, fluency, word association, reaction time), the multivariate experimenter has succeeded in factoring out the innate drives (ergs) and acquired sentiment structures (sems) that underlie the visible specific interests. The methods of measurement will be seen in more detail in Chapter 13, but meanwhile we shall look at the harvest of structural findings in Table 3.6.

In spite of the forebodings of many psychometrists that factor analysis would be less able to track down the main structures in the subtle world of interests than in abilities and temperament traits, the results have been very clear. The structures discovered consist first of the main mammalian drives (on *this* operational basis, as found, in man, called *ergs*) as listed in Table 3.6.

Although these factor patterns, recognized as loading in, say, the fear drive all used attitudes involving the seeking of security, and in the sex erg all attitudes involving sex interest, are clear, they do not yet include *all* the ergs that have been hypothesized on ethological and other grounds, as, e.g., in McDougall's or Murray's lists, or Lorenz's observations on primates. This may be because such lists as Murray's, Maslow's, and Dreger's were the product of armchair analysis or because factor analytic work with objective tests has not been extended as quickly and as widely as a scientist might hope. Much research is still needed to expand the hypothesized and unreplicated patterns, and to search out the full domain of expression of each erg.

TABLE 3.6

The Chief Replicated and Adumbrated Ergic Patterns Appearing as Dynamic Structure Factors in Humans

Goal title	Emotion	Status of evidence
Food-seeking	Hunger	Replicated factor; measurement battery exists
Mating	Sex	Replicated factor; measurement battery exists
Gregariousness	Loneliness	Replicated factor; measurement battery exists
Parental	Pity	Replicated factor; measurement battery exists
Exploration	Curiosity	Replicated factor; measurement battery exists
Escape to security	Fear	Replicated factor; measurement battery exists
Self-assertion	Pride	Replicated factor; measurement battery exists
Narcissistic sex	Sensuousness	Replicated factor; measurement battery exists
Pugnacity	Anger	Replicated factor; measurement battery exists
Acquisitiveness	Greed	Replicated factor; measurement battery exists
Appeal	Despair	Factor, but of uncertain independence
Rest-seeking	Sleepiness	Factor, but of uncertain independence
Constructiveness	Creativity	Factor, but of uncertain independence
Self-abasement	Humility	Factor, but of uncertain independence
Disgust	Disgust	Factor absent for lack of markers
Laughter	Amusement	Factor absent for lack of markers

From Cattell, R. B. & Child, D., *Motivation and Dynamic Structure*, 1975.

A totally different kind of pattern from that of ergs was apparent from the beginning among the factors emerging from the totality of attitudes. It loaded attitudes with obviously *varied* ergic origins but a *common* social institutional goal. These obviously acquired dynamic structures, responsive to institutional teaching by the family, the church, etc., have been called *sentiments* (or *sems* for short) as listed in Table 3.7.

In this case the factors are supported also by findings with nonobjective mea-

surement (checklist), questionnaire devices, as shown by the researches listed. It is obvious from their form that they are each the result of a set of rewarded attitude learnings about a particular sentiment object. A score on such a factor would represent the length of common learning on the given attitude set and the amount of satisfaction the individual habitually gets from that attachment to the given object (concrete or conceptual).

The MAT, SMAT, TAT, VIM, etc., objective dynamic structure tests available

TABLE 3.7

The Main Sentiment Traits Obtained as Dynamic Structure Factors Among Attitudes, by Objective and by Questionnaire Experiments*

S_1	*Profession* (1)	S_{15}	*Theoretical-logical.* Thinking, precision (2) (8) (10)
S_2	*Parental family, home* (1)		
S_3	*Wife, sweetheart* (1)	S_{16}	*Philosophical-historical.* Language, civics, social-cultural, esthetic rather than economic (2) (3) (6) (7)
S_4	*The self-sentiment* (1). Physical and psychological self		
S_5	*Superego* (1)		
S_6	*Religion.* This has emphasis on doctrine and practice, on high social and low esthetic values (1) (4) (7) (8)	S_{17}	*Patriotic-political* (1) (7)
		S_{18}	*Sedentary-social games.* Diversion, play club and pub sociability; cards (2) (10)
S_7	*Sports and fitness.* Games, physical activity, hunting, military activity (1) (2) (3)	S_{19}	*Travel-geography.* Possibly Guilford's autism here
		S_{20}	*Education-school attachment*
S_8	*Mechanical interests* (1) (2) (5)	S_{21}	*Physical-home-decoration-furnishing*
S_9	*Scientific interests.* High theoretical, low political; math. (2) (3) (4) (5) (6) (7) (9)	S_{22}	*Household-cooking*
		S_{23}	*News-communication.* Newspaper, radio, TV
S_{10}	*Business-economic.* Money administrative (2) (3) (4) (5)	S_{24}	*Clothes, self-adornment*
S_{11}	*Clerical interests* (2) (4)	S_{25}	*Animal pets*
S_{12}	*Esthetic expressions* (2) (10)	S_{26}	*Alcohol*
S_{13}	*Esthetic-literary appreciation.* Drama	S_{27}	*Hobbies not already specified*
S_{14}	*Outdoor-manual.* Rural, nature-loving, gardening, averse to business and "cerebration" (2) (5) (6)		

*References:
(1) Cattell (1973)
(2) Guilford et al. (1954)
(3) Thurstone (1931)
(4) Gundlach and Gerum (1931)
(5) Torr (1953)
(6) Carter, Pyles, Bretnall (1935)
(7) Ferguson, Humphreys, Strong (1941)
(8) Lurie (1937)

(9) Strong (1949)
(10) Thorndike (1935)
See also
(11) Cottle (1950)
(12) Hammond (1945)
(13) Crissy and Daniel (1939)
(14) Vernon (1949)
(15) Miller (1968)

From Cattell, R. B. & Child, D., *Motivation and Dynamic Structure*, 1975.

(see Chapter 13) at present contain dynamic source traits (ergs and sems) based on only the most replicated factors from the researches above. The factors chosen, such as sex, fear, and assertiveness among ergs, and home, career, and superego among sentiments have, more frequently than in the case of abilities and temperament traits, also had their outlines *substantiated by dR- and P-techniques*. That is to say (as seen in the next section), they manifest their functional unitariness also in the common oscillation of the levels of their attitude elements with changing inner and outer circumstances. In fact, the role of the situation in measurement becomes particularly evident in the dynamic field. We can properly speak of dynamic trait structures, but what we actually measure in an erg of, say, hunger or sex, is an *ergic tension* level which is partly a function of the person's trait (the *liability*, L, as we called it in discussing states) and partly of the inner or outer temporary situation—the modulating influence, s_k, as we defined it for states.

The more detailed bases for understanding these dynamic structures are collected in books (Cattell, 1985c; Cattell & Child, 1975), where the *dynamic calculus* principles are set out illustrating that the measurement analysis here in fact constitutes a quantitative development of psychoanalysis. The practicing analyst will indeed recognize that the trait concepts and tests here are giving him a surer "quantitative psychoanalysis."

STATES AND SITUATIONS

The architecture of personality, as established above, by more objective multivariate experimental methods than clinical observation could attain, has to cover not only unitary *traits* in the three modalities, but also the machinery of *states* and *processes*. Already we have met the notion that underlying the level of each state, on a given occasion, there is

a) a characteristic proneness or *liability* to that particular trait for the particular person, L_{xi}, and b) a characteristic average human reaction to the given situational occasion, k, as s_{kx}. This has been described under *modulation* theory above.

The separation of state dimensions from trait dimensions requires the use of dR- and P-technique factoring, in contrast with R-technique results, as explained in more technical detail elsewhere (Cattell, 1973a, Chapter 6). Although there has been sufficient success in the pioneer work, both in the Q and T media to reveal the rich possibilities, research reinforcements are much needed to clear up certain questions that have arisen. One provocative finding is that state factors, though quite distinct by simple structure, nevertheless have higher correlations (over time) than have been met in the correlations among traits. For example, depression-elation correlates negatively with arousal-torpor and anxiety correlates both with depression and with invia as a state. Secondly, there is a difficulty, within one state, in separating the state from the residual trait *as a measurement* (not as a distinct factor pattern), because of overlapping loaded items. This is particularly evident in anxiety (characterological and state) and exvia-invia (characterological and state). It is not a problem of recognizing separate identities but of getting properly separated scores. Mutual partialling, as in Figure 3.1, should eventually overcome this. Parenthetically, it was not realized until these dR and P studies were done that exvia-invia, regarded since Jung as a temperament *trait*, is actually also a state along the dimension of which people vary appreciably from day to day.

States as commonly spoken of by the layman and professional alike, e.g., anxiety, depression, arousal, are at the *second-order* (stratum) level relative to the primary factors in the 16 P.F., HSPQ, etc. This conclusion is supported by the discovery of states, e.g., in the U.I.24 anxiety objective subtests by Scheier and by Nes-

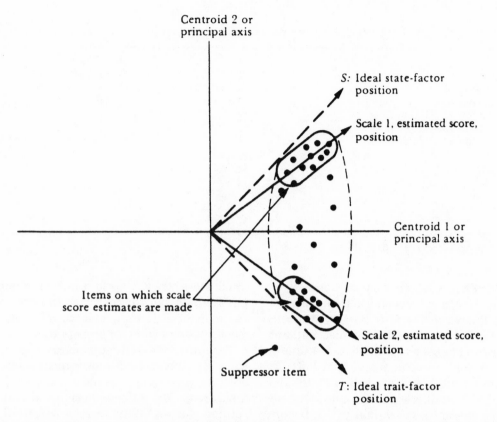

Mutual partialling to produce independence of estimated scale scores otherwise correlated. The correlation of estimates is due to the available items for the state having some loading on the trait and vice versa. The correction is shown here grossly for the scales, but it could be applied to each item.

Figure 3.1. Scheme for separation of incompletely separable state and trait measurement scales by mutual partialling

selroade, since T-data would be expected to be at the second order relative to Q-L. There *is* evidence, however, of states corresponding to the patterns of Q *primaries*, but they seem to have been too refined in form to have caught the observation of, and been named by, the man-in-the-street and the clinician. Table 3.8 lists the state dimension factors recognized so far on second-order Q- and first-order T-data.

A word is needed about depression, because psychiatric scales for various ideas of what depression is have proliferated on a nonexperimental basis, mixing and confusing the concepts of some eight distinct depressions which factor analysis has discovered. There seem to be definitely *eight* depression factors at the primary level (Kameoka, 1979; Cattell & Bjerstedt, 1967) and three at the second order. Among the latter, Depression I is by far the largest and it is this that is incorporated in the Curran-Cattell Eight State (1976) and in the IPAT Depression Scale. The use of these is so recent that neither the precise natures of the eight primaries nor of the second and third of the secondary factors have received sufficient research examination. Being clearly factor analytically identifiable, they must have helpful diagnostic and prognostic meanings, e.g., in regard to the type of diagnosis that will be most apt for a given case and the most effective clinical drug treatment.

TABLE 3.8

The Principal General State Dimensions Discovered by dR- and P-Techniques

Exvia-Invia	Q.S.I	U.I.S.32
Anxiety	Q.S.II	U.I.S.24
Cortertia	Q.S.III	U.I.S.22
Independence	Q.S.IV	U.I.S.19
Depression vs. Elation I	Q.S.V	
Depression vs. Energy II	Q.S.VI	
Depression vs. Calmness III	Q.S.VII	
Stress	Q.S.IX	
Fatigue	Q.S.X	
Arousal	Q.S.XI	
Regression	Q.S.XII	U.I.S.23
Guilt Superego	Q.S.VIII	
Psychoticism (Contact loss)	Q.S.XIII	

For research survey see Cattell, 1973a, Chapter 6.

The factors which separate depressives under treatment from normal controls are also known in the O-A Battery (Cattell, Price, & Patrick, 1981). A discriminant function has been presented for maximum separation (see Chapter 16 and Patrick, Cattell, Price, & Campbell, 1981b). Actually, Cattell, Schmidt, and Bjerstedt (1972) found these originally. U.I. factors 16, 19, 20, 21, 22, 23, 24, 25, 28, 29, 30, and 33 are all significantly related to the depressive-nondepressive distinction, but which operate as traits and which represent states is not yet known.

A valuable result of dR- and P-technique in the state area is the separation of anxiety and stress (for physiological associations see Cattell & Scheier, 1961). Stress might more fully be designated "effort stress" since it appears with hard mental or physical work in the complete absence of anxiety or emotional upset. Both IPAT researchers (Cattell & Scheier, 1961; Krug, 1977b; Kameoka, 1979) and Spielberger and students (Spielberger, Gorsuch, & Lushene, 1970) have pioneered the separation of anxiety as a state and anxiety as a trait. It unfortunately appears by dR analysis (Cattell, 1973a, Research Table 38) that Spielberger's anxiety *state* contains much depression, while the trait in that scale contains

much state stress. Careful rotation might purify these, but the confusion illustrates the danger of deciding subjectively what is a stress and what an anxiety item.

Technical research demands are high in solving problems in this area and the substantial correlations found among state measures, even in the extensive and well-rotated Curran (1968; Curran & Cattell, 1976) research, have caused some difficulties of interpretation for psychologists entering state measurement, e.g., with drug research and relaxation therapies. Of course, it is easy if one is prepared to ascribe the correlation to higher order factors not previously conceived by psychologists to determine (and switch measurement to) third-stratum factors, as in Table 3.9, which suggest broader mood states, one broad mood covering anxiety, an inviant outlook and general fatigue, and another stress with tendency to regress, and so on, but most conceptual and practical research will surely do best to keep to the second-stratum level using anxiety, stress, exvia, fatigue, etc., as distinct factors, though correlated.

The above are what have been called *general* psychological states, but the studies of change with time and situation in what we have listed as the dynamic traits (Tables 3.5 and 3.6) clearly show that

TABLE 3.9
Broader Mood Change Factors
Found Among (Second-Order) Psychological States

	Variables	Curran dR-Technique				Variables	Barton P-Technique			
		α	β	γ	δ		α	β	γ	δ
I	Exvia	−66	−04	−12	47I	Exvia	−41	−03	−61	48
II	Anxiety	87	−02	−03	07II	Anxiety	79	02	04	03
III	Depression	09	−82	26	−13III	Depression	−04	−75	−10	02
IV	Arousal	−10	35	08	84XI	Arousal	−08	53	−07	06
V	Fatigue	42	54	11	−08X	Fatigue	04	35	01	−95
VI	Stress	06	12	73	−07IX	Stress	03	08	69	−01
VII	Regression	−05	−04	46	−56XII	Regression	−02	−02	42	26
VIII	Guilt	−08	−47	−19	−15VIII	Random	36	−01	41	−55

Note: Decimal points omitted as in all factor-loading tables.
From Cattell, R. B., *Personality and Mood by Questionnaire*, 1973.

these also underlie states.* Thus, in the state domain of dynamics we actually concern ourselves with an ergic (rhymes with allergic) tension level of *arousal* for each erg (hard g) and with an excitation (*activation*) level for each sentiment. The relation of trait to state strength in these dynamic structures is fully discussed in a model elsewhere (Cattell, 1980a); but it is essentially the same as for general states in that each person has a given *liability trait* score, which gets modulated in a situation to a state, as $S_{xi} = s_k L_{xi}$ as given above.

The relation of general states (depression, stress, invia) to dynamic states is still experimentally uninvestigated, but

the theory is that the former derive in part from the average fate of the dynamic traits, resulting from experiences in the Adjustment Process Analysis chart (Cattell, 1980a, p. 307) and partly from physiological conditions. The measurement of states is important in much basic dynamic and cognitive process research and, in the applied field of practice, in monitoring the effectiveness of therapeutic steps and the aptness of given therapeutic methods.

This section heading has included the term *situations*, because it is in connection with states that they are most studied. But, to keep in focus the general behavioral equation model given at the beginning, let us repeat that the situation in the behavioral equation, for a given performance, is represented in the vector of *b* values. However, we have also pointed out that each behavioral index, *b*, can, with sufficient experiment, be broken down into a *v* and an *s*, the latter being the modulator peculiar to the situation. It is this *s* that fixes a state level (along with the person's L, see Chapter 16), while *v* describes the involvement of the state as such in producing action.

Usage of modulator values can probably be neglected as trivial, as long as we deal only with traits. But, as Chapter 15 indicates, the future holds promise of more

---

*These are "ergic tension" levels. The theoretical question arises: Can these be equated with what have been called primary emotions? As McDougall (1908) clearly brought out, there goes along with each "instinct" (translate "erg") the corresponding emotion (fear, curiosity, lust, pity). In 1929 I found from extensive introspective protocols that the GSR is not a measure of reported emotion but of reported conation (drive tension). The distinction between *affect* and *conation*, known to Plato, Aristotle, and the Scholastics was lost in much psychological writing in this century. The distinction is operationally real, however, as such studies as the above (Cattell, 1929) show. To the above question, therefore, the best answer at present is that what we measure by objective tests as *ergic tension states* is the *conative* component to which the attached emotion is a secondary memory-aiding epiphenomenon.

comprehensive and accurate psychological prediction and evaluation when vectors of modulators for situations have been worked out. Incidentally, the reader will recognize that the correction of a real performance for *state* action by a vector of modulators is not to be confused with the correction of a rating by a vector of weights through trait view effects. This deserves mention because the formal processes are rather similar.

SUMMARY

The basic principle of functional measurement is that the mapping of trait and state structure must precede the work on tests, which need to be well directed to what functional unities in behavior exist. Hence, the present chapter is a thumbnail sketch of the outcome of all that has been done to create a taxonomy of human traits and states.

According to the *theory of indifference of indicator*, the same source trait structures in personality will be factorially revealed despite differences in the media of measurement. Provided the same behavioral variable domains are covered, the L, Q, and T media will pick up the same patterns though in "different dress." Factors from the three media can, at least in some cases, be put together and appear in a single "instrument transcending" factor. This holds from L to Q directly and from L-Q to T in that a number of secondaries in L-Q match primaries in T.

Source traits in the ability field have been the longest studied and replicated in pattern. The triadic theory of ability structure recognizes 1) *a*'s, *agencies*, which are primary ability factors presumably acquired as skills from investment of underlying broader capacities in particular areas of required acquisitions—hence they are agencies (in Piaget's sense) for various cognitive developments such as numerical ability, grammatical sense, perceptual skill. About 20 are currently known and measurable. Next, the triadic theory recognizes, 2) *p*'s, *provincial powers*, which are associations specific to interpretation of input in each of the sensorimotor neural areas, and 3) *g*'s, *general capacities*, in the highest order of factoring yet experimentally defined, of which there are about six or seven, such as fluid and crystallized intelligences, fluency (retrieval capacity), short distance memory, speed, etc.

In personality, by L- and Q-data research, some 35 source trait factors have been replicated, of which 12 fall in abnormal behavior. Some 14 second orders are found among them, which secondaries, e.g., exvia-invia, anxiety, cortertia, are broader in behavioral area and shallower in variance contribution than the primaries. A development of psychological practice called *depth psychometry* aims (as provided for in the 16 P.F.) to get scores *simultaneously on primaries and secondaries*. The particular balance of primaries that make up the secondary score from primary scores in a particular individual tells us more than from knowing scores of primaries or secondaries alone. The "hardiest" of scores, however, are those of primaries, since research has established the continuity of the source trait patterns across the life span development, and their similarity in number and nature across different national cultures in the modern world.

Some 20 source traits have been found in objective, performance test indicators of personality, some of which line up with L-Q secondaries and all of which have been found to have substantial predictive or diagnostic value in clinical and other applied areas despite debate about their interpretation. Theories about their nature have been developed in only about half of them. But, as indubitable behavior *structures*, they generally hold across ages and cultures, and are therefore identified by universal index numbers to hold identities while research proceeds.

Among students of human behavior, from clinicians to dramatists, the most important characteristics of personality architecture have been considered to reside in the *dynamic structure* modality. Factorially, the chief unitary structures found there turn out to be either ergs (equivalent to mammalian drives) or sems (sentiments) which are cognitively bound aggregates of attitudes acquired around the conditionings by cultural institutions. Objective test devices have now been set up at the adult and child levels (the MAT and SMAT, Chapter 13) for some 10 dynamic traits, but more than a dozen drives (ergs) and perhaps two dozen semic structures are indicated by research so far and may in time be brought into the orbit of practical motivational testing.

Psychological state dimensions have been located, defined as patterns, and rendered measurable by dR- and P-technique factoring. They fall into two classes: 1) *general* "mood" states, and 2) specific *ergic* tension level dimensions. The former are, as so far found, about 8-10 in number, and are at the second order as far as L-Q traits are concerned. The latter correspond in nature and number to the list of dynamic structures, from which they derive by modulation.

Ultimately, the psychologist in practice will need to have a taxonomy of situations and to be able to handle the average effects of standard, frequently encountered, everyday life situations. An effective theoretical model is available, as yet with few established situation values, assessing the situation as a profile of loadings in the behavioral equation. With due refinement the vector is not the numerical value of the b's, but of the modulators, s's, to be

extracted from the b's—the vector (profile) of behavioral indices. Thus the description of the situation is, more specifically, the vector of modulator indices—values for trait change response in the given situation. Psychological measurement tables should ideally contain as much information on situations as on traits, but at present few profiles are available. One of the practically important uses of situational vectors is in correcting distortion in test results according to the situation of testing.

The uniqueness of the individual—and a substantial prediction of his or her performances—can be obtained from the unique combination of his or her scores on common traits, though the unique form of biographical interest investments and motivations can probably be better expressed by P-technique traits.

Knowledge of the well-replicated factorial source traits, and of their properties—heritability, life curves, response to experience, criterion predictions*—must include an overview of all, for *all* are likely to be involved in any diagnosis or prediction.

---

*In prediction of criteria we include also prediction of all kinds of existing special test scales, some having importance, by reason of inadequate definition, only as contemporary fashions, e.g., "authoritarian" scales, sensitivity, emotional empathy, inner vs. outer control, "higher level motivation." Most of these can be estimated from the combinations of basic personality and motivation traits that go into them, the combination depending on the subjective definition entering scale construction. The translations of simple structure source traits to the orthogonal Guilford-Zimmerman factors are given in Cattell and Gibbons (1967).

CHAPTER 4

The Psychometric Properties of Tests:
Consistency, Validity, and Efficiency

Raymond B. Cattell

A DEFINITION OF TESTS AND THEIR VARIETIES

Since tests are used to evaluate people and sometimes affect their lives in serious ways, a social conscience, if not a scientific ideal, should cause us to do our utmost to make them valid and reliable. We therefore turn now from examining the genuineness of traits to examining the genuineness of tests. First, the way in which choice of media of measurement affects measurement properties has been set out in Chapter 2. Second, we have seen in Table 2.3 ten comprehensive dimensions in terms of which any variety of test can be "placed." If we narrow discussion to the most reliably acceptable among these, we come in Table 4.1 to the framework most suitable for discussion of test properties

in this chapter. As far as questionnaires are concerned, we are in a definitive corner of this table—the reactive, restricted, selective, single-response, ordered, and homogeneous test. But objective (T-data) subtests range over the whole dimensionality.

In separately considering tests, apart from the other forms of assessment (L(B)-data), a test should be defined. Probably the most comprehensive definition is *a standard, portable stimulus situation, containing a defined instruction and mode of response, in which a consenting subject is measured on the response in a predefined way, the measure being designed and used to predict other behavior, elsewhere.*

It will be noted that Tables 2.3 and 4.1 supplement each other in that Table 4.1 turns to the internal construction of tests, whereas Table 2.3 is concerned with utilization, e.g., as group or individual, conspective or nonconspective scorableness, orientation to concrete or conceptual validity, and so forth.

Looking for a moment at the intrinsic properties of Table 4.1, let us note first that the dichotomies are relatively independent, so that one could approach therewith 2^8 types of tests, were it not that some dimensions are mutually tied. For example, the last seven dichotomies can apply only to the first category of number one. The dimensions are not claimed to be completely exhaustive, but they *do* have the status of operational, nonsubjective bases of test classification for the great majority of tests. They provide at least a beginning for a rational, descriptive test taxonomy.

Less fundamental dichotomies *can* be added to the basic 8, such as 9 and 10. Those dichotomize with respect to: 9) *Immediate Meaning vs. Referent Meaning* (how much symbolism is involved in the test stimulus material), and 10) *Itemized vs. Global Structure in Presentation and Scoring.* This is important in connection with what the previous chapter has said about *itemetrics* being only a part of *psychometrics.* Here, accordingly, is the distinction between a test that will atomize into items and one which will not, e.g., a physiological measure, or a measure which is a complex derivative, e.g., an acceleration, or a ratio of items or item groupings. (This is somewhat similar to the difference between a digital and an analogue computer.)

TABLE 4.1
A Descriptive-Operational Taxonomy of Tests by Internal Construction

1. *Reactive or Nonreactive.* Is the person to react to a stimulus, or to try not to react (as in some self-control tests)?

2. *Restricted or Free Response.* Is the mode of response highly prescribed, e.g., to react with any single word, or left free, e.g., to react with word, sentences, actions as one feels inclined?

3. *Inventive or Selective* (sometimes called "open-ended" or "closed"). Does S respond with anything from his or her repertoire that fits the given restricted instruction, or are his or her choices also restricted to a set of responses provided by the experimenter? Notice the difference from 2 above.

4. *Single or Extended, Repetitive Response.* Does S give a single response, or is he or she asked to "perform" by giving as many responses as possible to the single stimulus, as, for example, in a fluency test or a continuing cancellation or computation performance?

5. *Ordered or Unordered Sequence.* Does the instruction task include reacting in a certain order, as when S is told attempt items in this order given, or is he or she allowed to tackle the whole, beginning and proceeding where he or she likes?

6. *Homogeneous or Patterned.* Does one make the same kind of response from beginning to end, e.g., as in an intelligence test, or is there a developing pattern, e.g., in constructing a model?

7. *Natural Manner of Response or Pursuit of a Limit.* The most common case of this is "answer at your own rate" versus "answer as fast as possible," but it can also apply to, for example, "answer as you first feel" versus "answer with the utmost honesty."

8. *Making a Concluding Reaction or Reacting to One's Own Reactions.* In some test situations the reaction terminates the subject's task. In others—and this is increasingly true of new objective personality tests—the test may require him or her to evaluate it, associate to it, or memorize it. The psychoanalytic free association "test" is a "reacting to reaction" test, in which, typically of such tests, the original stimulus (excepting the instruction) is relatively unimportant.

From the *Compendium of Objective Personality Tests*, Cattell and Warburton (1967) who have suggested that a taxonomy of tests at a descriptive level can most fundamentally be drawn up on the above characters.

The "other behavior elsewhere" in the above test definition is commonly "the criterion," and, as we shall see in discussing validity, criteria also need to be classified by their characters.

THE VARIETIES OF TEST CONSISTENCY: THE DEPENDABILITY AND USAGE COEFFICIENTS

The first property commonly demanded of a test is consistency. There is a feeling that, of tests as of men, Polonius's dictum is correct: "To thine own self be true . . . thou canst not then be false to any man." And indeed it is true—but only provided consistency concepts are correct—that a test which is not consistent with itself can scarcely hope to predict anything else. A first common source of confusion here is the elementary habit of thinking consistency is covered by "test reliability," whereas in fact it has four major distinct aspects, and more than four coefficients to evaluate it.

The four aspects could be logically deduced from the Basic Data Relation Matrix or Data Box (Cattell, 1946, 1966b), which has Cartesian coordinates of individual 1) people, 2) stimuli, 3) response forms, 4) occasions (ambient situations), and 5) observers. These five signatures are required uniquely to fix any psychological event. They also indicate the diverse series of "ids" over which a test can be examined for consistency. However, since a test locks, in a fixed unity, *a given stimulus to a given response form*, there are actually four remaining coordinates over which consistency can show itself, namely:

1) Is the test (stimulus-response form) consistent across occasions? This is often popularly called a "test-retest reliability," best shortened to *dependability coefficient, r_d.*
2) Is it consistent across observers? This covers both administration and scoring

which we refer to respectively as *administrative* and *scoring conspect reliability coefficients, r_a and r_{sp}.*
3) Is it consistent across the various stimulus-response elements into which the test might be broken down? This gives the *homogeneity coefficient, r_h.*
4) Is it consistent in what it is supposed to measure across different kinds (populations) of people? This concerns the *transferability reliability, r_t.*

These fundamental and comprehensive divisions of test consistency are summarized in Table 4.2 and will be discussed in sequence.

Although these four are logically and analytically on a par, by virtue of derivation from the Data Box, they are not operationally so, their coefficients standing at various degrees of derivation from direct experimental data, as will be seen.

The Dependability Coefficient, r_d, as just indicated, is often called the test-retest reliability coefficient, though due to the ambiguity of "reliability" in common use we have for some years practiced calling it instead the *dependability* of a test. The correlation used is that between a first and second administration of the test, on a typical population sample, *at an interval so short that the trait or state itself will not have altered.* And it must be by the same examiner so that it does not suffer from variance due to source 2—usage by different administrators.

In the formulae which follow we are going to deal with sources of variance in a test score defined as follows:

$\sigma_t^2 =$ variance of true score

$\sigma_f^2 =$ variance of the trait itself, i.e., *functional fluctuation* of true score over a standard mean change of time and situation

$\sigma_e^2 =$ error of measurement due to the retest as such, and arising from properties, e.g., ambiguities, in the test itself.

TABLE 4.2
Divisions of Test Consistency

	Consistency		
Across Occasions	Across Administrators	Across Test Parts	Across Populations (Different Groups)
r_d	r_a	r_h	r_t
Dependability Coefficient (r_s, the stability coefficient is not wholly a test property)	Reliability Coefficient (r_{sp} is the conspect reliability for administrator's *scoring* only)	Homogeneity Coefficient	Transferability Coefficient

The size of the dependability coefficient will then be:

$$r_d = \frac{\sigma_t^2 + \sigma_f^2}{\sigma_t^2 + \sigma_f^2 + \sigma_e^2} \qquad (4\text{-}1)$$

(Note that in correlations of completely symmetrical tests it is r and not r^2 that defines the percent of total variance of one test common to the other test.) The dependability coefficient has to be operationally so defined because the trait fluctuation is caught at the same level in the immediate retest: Hence σ_f^2 appears in both numerator and denominator. The denominator is the total observed variance.

But one must include in "over occasions" consistencies also the case where perhaps a month or more separates test and retest, permitting trait fluctuation. This is a different coefficient from r_d and we call it the *coefficient of stability, r_s*. It is defined by

$$r_s = \frac{\sigma_t^2}{\sigma_t^2 + \sigma_f^2 + \sigma_e^2} \qquad (4\text{-}2)$$

It is vital to note that the stability coefficient *is not a true property of the test alone*, but is substantially determined also by the property of the *trait* (or mixture of traits). For the personality theorist the differences of traits in their degree of fluctuation is important information, and, for a moment, we will digress to show what the *coefficient of trait constancy* is. It has nothing to do with error of test measurement but is simply true of a trait:

$$r_{tc} = \frac{\sigma_t^2}{\sigma_t^2 + \sigma_f^2} \qquad (4\text{-}3)$$

It can easily be shown that this is derivable from the observed r_d and r_s, as can be seen algebraically from their formulae, thus

$$r_{tc} = \frac{r_s}{r_d} \qquad (4\text{-}4)$$

It is virtually *always* a virtue of a test to have a high *dependability* coefficient, but not necessarily to have a high *stability* coefficient. There have been a few judgments, e.g., in Buros's *Mental Measurements Yearbook* where what is really a state test is criticized for low "reliability." Actually, a stability coefficient greater than zero (across several occasions) for a scale claiming to be a state scale would show that the state test is worthless! It would then be confounding some trait measurement with the state measurement. Nevertheless, a psychological scale even for a state should have a high *dependability* coefficient.*

The second coefficient in Table 4.2—that between retests when different investigators use the test—may seem to be more a property of the investigators than the tests. The data *can* in fact be used to evaluate the reliability of different investigators. But that is not the object here, where we assume the testers are just a random sample of all investigators and that when we compare dependability coefficients of one test with another we are out to compare some property in test A that makes it more or less reliable than test B in the hands of the *typical* examiner using it. If σ_e^2 in equations above is defined as the error variance on readministering the test by the *same* examiner, we must now introduce a source of error (a third source of non-true score) due to having a different examiner; a_2 rather than a_1. The correlation between scores given by two administrators when the retest is immediate will be:

$$r_{da} = \frac{\sigma_t^2 + \sigma_f^2}{\sigma_t^2 + \sigma_f^2 + \sigma_e^2 + \sigma_a^2} \qquad (4\text{-}5)$$

where σ_a^2 is the administrative variance in shifting from a_1 to a_2 or any other pairs of administrators. If now we want an expression strictly to evaluate the *reliability of administrative usage* as such, we must rule out the error, σ_e^2, due to the test defect that occurs even when the same examiner repeats, and thus write:

$$r_a = \frac{\sigma_t^2 + \sigma_f^2}{\sigma_t^2 + \sigma_f^2 + \sigma_a^2} \qquad (4\text{-}6)$$

This can be derived from r_{da} and the ordinary dependability coefficient thus:

$$r_a = \frac{r_{da} r_d}{r_d - r_{da}(1 - r_d)} \qquad (4\text{-}7)$$

This *administrative usage coefficient, r_a,* cancels out the error due simply to readministration *per se* and tells us how much the nature of the test in the hands of different users contains a source of unreliability. (This is a property of the test rather than the administrators if we average over several of the latter. A low value might reflect, for example, an ambiguity of instructions.) Actually, if one wishes to examine the properties of tests more intensively, inconsistency here can be broken down further into contributions from properties of a) instructions, b) test form and timing requirements, and c) scoring interaction with the personalities of psychologists.

The scoring as such, though involved in r_a, is so important that we have formulated it separately in the *conspect reliability* or *conspection* coefficient, which is simply the degree of agreement of two examiners when they have *results* from the same administration, i.e., *have to evaluate the same response outputs by the same list of subjects put before them* and have only to interpret the given results. As pointed out, the conspect reliability of a keyed multiple choice test, such as an intelli-

---

*These theoretical concepts are beautifully illustrated in an experiment with anxiety scales by Nesselroade, Jacobs, & Preshnow (in press). They analyze the correlation matrix for two immediate anxiety measures on each of three fairly remote occasions, showing by the maximum likelihood "checking factor analysis" that the fit to the state model is decidedly superior to the trait model.

gence test or the Motivation Analysis Test (MAT), should be perfect, at 1.0, whereas that for, say, the TAT, or the Rorschach, or an essay output, or an interview, may typically be as low as 0.3 to 0.4.

Thus, to this point we have seen that consistency over the occasion (time situation) and the observer coordinates of the Data Box needs no fewer than three coefficients clearly to analyze its parts, namely the

dependability coefficient, r_d

administrative usage coefficient, r_a

conspect coefficient, r_{sp}

besides the

stability coefficient, r_s

(and the trait constancy coefficient, r_{tc}, which derives from it). The last, r_s, is a mixed coefficient that involves the properties of the trait measured, *as well as* those of the test.

It will be noted both here and in the remaining consistency coefficients that we are examining the two measures concerning how far they put the subjects in the same rank order. Two administrations could, however, differ also in mean, in raw score, or in standard scores from a combined first and second administration. This difference of mean, divided by the sigma of the two and inverted to be large when "good," we shall call the corresponding *index*. Thus the *dependability index* would be

$$I_d = \frac{\sigma^2_{1+2}}{(M_2 - M_1)^2} \qquad (4\text{-}8)$$

where 1 + 2 means the combined distribution. Since the mean typically shifts between the first and second administration of an intelligence test, but not of a questionnaire personality test, one would expect a better (larger) I_d for the questionnaire than for an intelligence test, though the r_d's might be in the reverse order. For each of the four *coefficients* above there is a corresponding *index* that

would be of interest for some test uses and should not be forgotten.

THE VARIETIES OF TEST CONSISTENCY: THE HOMOGENEITY AND TRANSFERABILITY COEFFICIENTS

Homogeneity, as the term indicates, is the uniformity among parts of a test: It has several forms and the most obvious division of these is that between the magnitude of *intercorrelation of items, or subtest parts*, on the one hand, and that between *two supposed equivalent forms* on the other. The latter we may call the *equivalence homogeneity* measured by the *equivalence coefficient* calculated between the two forms.

Attention to test homogeneity came early in psychometrics—in the itemetric phase—and was then calculated as the "split-half reliability" and later by various statistical improvements that followed on it such as the Kuder-Richardson and Cronbach's alpha. In the simplest form one merely took a random split of the items, often as the odd-numbered items against the even, and correlated the two pools. Naturally, that coefficient varied by chance, for a given test, according to the accident of sampling of items. The Kuder-Richardson improved on this by virtually taking the mean r for many or all possible splits, thus:

$$r_h = r_{xx} = \frac{n}{n-1} \cdot \frac{s_x^2 - \sum_{i=1}^{n} p_i q_i}{s_x^2} \qquad (4\text{-}9)$$

when n = number of items, $s2$ = observed variance of scores on test, $p_i q_i$ = product of proportion of passes and fails for any item i.

Cronbach's alpha coefficient of homogeneity got at the ideal in a different way:

$$r_h = \alpha = \frac{MS_p - MS_r}{MS_p + \frac{n_i - n_i^1}{n_i^1} MS_r} \qquad (4\text{-}10)$$

where MS is "mean square," MS_r is the residual mean square when MS_p, the mean square over all persons, has had subtracted from it the variance between items, and n_i^1 and n_i are the numbers of conditions of a facet. This is also formally the same as an *intraclass* correlation coefficient (Haggard, 1958). An intensive study of homogeneity and reliability statistics is available in Cronbach, Gleser, Nanda, and Rajaratnam (1972) and a good up-to-date review with illustrations in Scott (1963).

As occurs at several points in psychometrics, *structured psychometry*, dealing with factor (unitary trait) concepts, eventually requires some additional or modified formulations from those in the itemetric heritage. Cattell (1957c) in *"Formulae and Table for Obtaining Validities and Reliabilities of Extended Factor Scales"* and Cattell and Radcliffe (1962) in *"Reliabilities and Validities of Simple and Extended Weighted and Buffered Unifactor Scales"* extend consideration of the above to structured tests. However, it has seemed best to defer the specializations in the latter to the statistical Chapter 23.

With dependability consistency and homogeneity consistency now distinguished, we shall need to enter on some of their derivatives, mutually, and in respect to the validity coefficients still to be defined. Relatives have to be considered also to 1) style of items, notably the changing proportion of yes and no answers in dichotomous items, 2) the relation of homogeneity to validity with changing mean r's of items with the factor, and 3) the changing correlation between parallel forms (*equivalence homogeneity*) with increasing length. The other auxiliary derivatives will be treated elsewhere.

The third of those just mentioned has long been familiar in the field as the Spearman-Brown Prophecy Formula, thus

$$r_{nn} = \frac{nr_d}{1 + (n - 1)r_d} \qquad (4\text{-}11)$$

where r_{nn} is the consistency of the test increased in length by a multiple, of value n and r_d is the *present* (short) dependability or homogeneity coefficient. It should be noted that this can be applied equally to the homogeneity as an *equivalence r_e* between two forms or to the dependability coefficient as an immediate test retest. In fact, it can also be considered in relation to the time length of a test, for, when items are similar in size, to double the number of items is to double the testing time required.

As stated above, some three formulae, increasing in sophistication from the first onward (the odd-even split half) have been in use to measure homogeneity and the standard errors of these can be examined in Cronbach et al. (1972). Homogeneity is also often approached as the mean mutual correlation of all items or the mean correlation of all items with the pool of items. To examine the question of whether high homogeneity is actually desirable one has to ask, logically, what the "pool" means. It is, factorially, the sum of whatever common factors the items share, plus all their specifics.

The center of gravity of the pool moves around with each new item that is added. Consequently, the custom in the past—in the itemetric age—of evaluating not just the homogeneity contribution but the very "validity" of an item by its correlation with the "face valid" pool involves a thoroughly bad principle. A scale for this or that so made has no fixed meaning and chases its own tail. Even if it began as largely some desired factor X, it would shift from its centroid according to "which side" the items of high homogeneity happened to get added. Nothing prevents such a scale from wandering far from the original factor. Not only is homogeneity beyond a certain level undesirable (see below), but seeking to maximize it is also a potent source of distortion from the factor true position. (See "test homogeneous-factor heterogeneous in Figure 4-5.) A special problem in determining the correlation of an item with the pool is that if the item is already in the pool score its correlation will be raised by the artefact that its *specific* (beyond the common factors) is already in the pool score. Guilford (1965) has given us a means of correcting for this but it gets tediously impracticable with a lot of items.

Before leaving homogeneity, it is necessary to recognize that most discussions of homogeneity are confined to *test homogeneity* (see Figure 4.5). An important alternative is *factor homogeneity*, the extent to which the given set of items measures only one factor. A typical item will have a common factor composition, by variance, in the orthogonal case of:

$$Ta = b^2_1 + b^2_2 + \ldots b^2_p \qquad (4\text{-}12)$$

where the specific is omitted. An expression for the *factor* homogeneity (the mean intercorrelation of items due to a desired factor) of a test for a given factor x would be

$$r_{hfx} = \frac{\overset{p = n \quad q = n - 1}{\Sigma \quad \Sigma} b_p b_q}{n_{c2}} \qquad (4\text{-}13)$$

n being the number of items, b_p and b_q being any two items, and c the number of combinations. A simpler approximation to this would be

$$r_{hx} = \frac{\overset{p = n}{\Sigma} b^2_{px}}{n} \qquad (4\text{-}13a)$$

Finally, in considering test consistency with regard to those coordinates of the Data Box that are most relevant, we come to a fourth and much neglected coefficient—the *coefficient of transferability* (see Table 4.2). After consistency over occasions, over administrations, and over test parts comes consistency over people. That is to say, does the test go on consistently measuring what it is supposed to measure when it is shifted to other groups? (These group samples, of course, must, for fairness, be within the population the test designer *said* could be tested.) A topical instance is whether an intelligence test for the majority goes on measuring the same thing when applied to a minority group. The intention of a test, as to the conceptual validity it aims at, is defined by the factors it measures. Some tests may be deliberately factorially quite mixed and even those aimed at a particular pure factor will in fact have some contaminating loadings on others. We are not concerned here with what the particular composition may be but only with the consistency with which that composition is maintained across groups. If we like to keep to a correlation for expressing consistency, then the *transferability coefficient* between two groups 1 and 2 would be

$$r_t = \frac{\overset{k}{\Sigma} (b_1 b_2)}{\sqrt{\overset{k}{\Sigma} b^2_1 \overset{k}{\Sigma} b^2_2}} \qquad (4\text{-}14)$$

the b's being behavioral indices in standard scores, from factoring the test in the two groups, 1 and 2. However, we know that in comparing factor loading patterns the congruence coefficient r_c is better than the ordinary correlation, r, so in the case of the transferability consistency coefficient it would be better to shift to congruence. This we reach simply by using for the b's in equation 4-14 *the literal values for the b's*, not the b's changed to standard scores, as in getting r, and we can then denote the coefficient as r_{ct} (not to be confused with r_{tc}, the trait constancy coefficient).

In evaluating tests as to transferability consistency, it would be highly desirable to have a *standard array of subgroups* or populations across which it is agreed to compare them. For example, the Culture-Fair Intelligence Tests, the WAIS, the Humor Test of Intelligence, and Draw-A-Man (Goodenough intelligence test version) might be compared as to factor patterns (and validity therefore on g_f and g_c) across defined social class and ethnic groups in the U.S.A. Compared across countries, in literally the same (untranslated) form, it is evident that the first and last would score much higher transferability consistency than the other two.

Although, as Table 4.2 sets out, there are basically only four general kinds of consistency coefficients, yet there are subforms that need setting out in a final overview as follows:

Varieties of Test Consistency Coefficients

1) *Dependability* (across time)
   r_d,   immediate test-retest, *dependability* coefficient
   r_s,   longer term retest, *stability* coefficient (not wholly a test property)
   (r_{tc} derived from r_s/r_d, a trait, *not a test parameter*, but the *trait constancy* coefficient)
2) *Administrative Usage Consistency* (across administrators, observers, examiners)
   r_a,   derived from r_d and r_{a1a2}, *administrative reliability* coefficient
   r_{sp},   *conspect reliability*, evaluates an aspect of r_a—the scoring consistency (Note distinction of symbol from r_s above, and from r_p, the pattern similarity coefficient.)
3) *Homogeneity* (across test parts)

   r_h,   scale item homogeneity coefficient
   r_e,   *equivalence*, homogeneity of two forms
   r_{hf},   *factor homogeneity* coefficient
4) *Transferability* (across populations)
   r_t,   the factor trueness *transferability coefficient* with the sophistication index as a subtype thereof on its own
   r_{ct},   calculated as a congruence coefficient.

It will be noted that these four parameters of consistency, corresponding logically to the four degrees of freedom in the Data Box, could be either for a particular test, or, by averaging across a class of tests, could yield information on properties of particular *forms* and *modes* of test construction.

THE VARIETIES OF VALIDITY

The validity of a test is, of course, its ability to measure what the psychologist sets it up to measure. Generically it can be defined as the ability to predict a desired "criterion" behavior that is outside itself. Good validity is the test virtue without which all other virtues—dependability, transferability, and usage reliability in administration and scoring—are useless. On the other hand, good validity can nevertheless be rendered null and void by poor dependability, etc.

There are three meaningful categorical dichotomies with respect to which the concepts of validity can be classified, and hence $2^3 = 8$ "types" (combined properties) of validity.

The three dimensions themselves, set out in Figure 4.1, will first be considered as to psychological meaning, before considering any formulae.

1) *Concrete to conceptual.* A concrete validity involves relating the test to a

quite specific behavior, e.g., performance in operating a cash register, or typing, or flying an airplane. Since a concrete life performance is rarely restricted to the action of a pure factor source trait, this kind of validity is generally called for in relation to *special-purpose tests*, specifically made up to select people in relation to a concrete performance. A whole battery of *general*-purpose (basic source trait) tests can, however, by a multiple R, estimate a special criterion and have a concrete validity. On the opposite side of this dichotomy is *conceptual validity*. In the case of a conceptual test, e.g., for the concepts of intelligence, exvia, depression, there is no corresponding "concrete validity coefficient," for the simple reason that no single piece of behavior in daily behavior wholly represents that concept. For example, one cannot obtain a conceptual validity of an intelligence or anxiety test against some specific real life behavior because no piece of complex, concrete life behavior can be pointed to as being pure intelligence or pure anxiety uncompli-

cated by other trait expressions. When a psychologist says, "This intelligence test has a validity against school achievement of 0.6," he is confused and should more logically say "It has a *relevance* to school achievement of 0.6." For school achievement involves much more than intelligence.

Concept validity is sometimes also called, in fact has often been called—again with potential for confusion—"construct validity." In science a construct is an abstraction deriving immediately from data, usually by inductive reasoning, whereas a concept is a higher level abstraction, resting on several feet in different areas of inductive observation and inference (Cattell, 1966b). The notion of a cat chasing a mouse is a construct, the concept of one animal being a prey to another in a regular ecological food chain is a concept. Thus, intelligence, anxiety, sexual ergic tension, and most of the important things psychological theory needs to measure are *concepts*, because they are rooted in a wide array of observations, spanning diverse

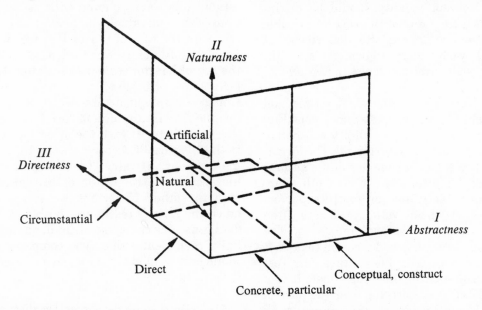

These are dichotomous "dimensions," i.e., a form of validation is either at one pole or the other. As the text explains, this would yield $2^3 = 8$ "types" of validity, but some have not yet been used in practice.

Figure 4.1. The three categorization dichotomies of validity

inductive areas. However, traits and states have usually been tied down as concepts, for test reference, as instrument transcending *factor* patterns with associated broad properties and relations. A one-shot research factor pattern may be, immediately, a construct, but replicated in diverse ways, it is so unique and firm an entity that a wide array of experimentally demonstrable associations are reliably built around it as a concept, in a theoretical frame. For example, the anxiety factor is shown to be systematically higher in neurotics, to fall under tranquilizers, to interfere with memory, to bring on higher ketosteroid excretion, and so on. Furthermore, the original pattern is shown to repeat itself in dR- and P-technique experiment, and evidence is usually present in its capacity to distinguish previously recognized clinical types, and to correspond to certain developmental concepts.

Consequently, when we correlate a test score with factor score estimate we are obtaining a *concept-validity* not a *construct* validity of only temporary interest. This concept validity should be distinguished from any of the several possible *concrete validities* as often described, but which would more accurately, scientifically be described as concrete *relevances*.

2) *Natural to artificial.* A second and probably less important dimension (Figure 4-1) along which validity can be polarized is *natural vs. artificial.* The former is a check against behavior in the natural world; the latter against some other laboratory, factitious, or testlike performance. Artificial validity, though often cited, is a poor, secondhand thing. The present writer has had occasion to protest against evaluating his Culture-Fair Test by correlation against the Binet! It is a protest against carrying over the form of "truth" involved in apostolic succession in theology to the procedures in the world of science. In science no one would think of testing the correctness of a caesium time

watch against Captain Cook's chronometer, or the latter against the 12th century clock in Wells' cathedral. A correlation for "artificial" validity is an interesting but not a required test property.

3) *Direct to indirect* (circumstantial). The third dimension seems to have been almost completely neglected by psychometrists. Yet, although direct validity against a factor is indispensable, indirect validity is a valuable supplement. In indirect validity we correlate the test for X not with X but with A, B, C, D, etc. and see if the test's correlations with A, B, C, D, etc. are the same as those found for X. In a twilight I vaguely see a bird that flies like a duck, swims like a duck, walks like a duck, but perhaps does not seem to quack like a duck. The validity of the judgment that it is a duck is positive but imperfect. The courtroom also uses circumstantial validity. This man in custody has a top hat, was seen by Sherlock Holmes on Baker Street at 11 P.M. on the 14th, etc., and has other properties Holmes can establish as corresponding with associations of the individual who committed the crime. In the case of the 16 P.F. test we have a profile of 15 correlations of, say, the actual L factor scale with the other 15 factors. We also have, in rotation of exemplary simple structure, which identifies the *true* L, a profile of correlation of this pure factor L with the other factors in the 16 space. If we compare the 15 cosine (correlation) values for the two profiles, scale and true factor, of correlation with the other 15 factors, we see how much the *L scale* resembles the *L factor*, giving us a circumstantial (indirect) validity coefficient value. The comparison would best be made by a congruence coefficient.

All validities in psychometric discussion can be resolved into positions on the above dichotomies (Figure 4.1) except, as we have said, *content* validity, and face or faith validity. A popular notion that is superfluous—and also intrinsically *misleading*—is "concurrent vs. predictive" validity. In the first place this asks for trouble verbally by using predictive when it means foretelling. (It is true that outside psychological statistics predictive in the dictionary does include foretelling, but in psychometry, we need to distinguish *prediction*, always used in a *statistical* timeless sense, having nothing to do with projection into the future, from *foretelling*, involving a forward time projection. But the main falsity of this concurrent vs. predictive term is that it purports to deal with a property (validity) of the test but actually concerns a property of the trait! If I cannot tell from an anxiety test score on Monday how anxious the patient will be on Saturday *that "predictive validity" is no reflection on the validity of the test*, and indeed, has nothing to do with the test. It involves the same pitfall as failing to distinguish I_d and I_{fe}, in the realm of consistency.

The legitimate thing to examine in a test is its concurrent validity, which needs no adjective because there is no other! So-called predictive validity is something for the psychologist to work out from his knowledge of the test validity and the trait constancy (s_k values, Chapter 15) in the forthcoming situations. In short, since all test validity is "concurrent" the term is superfluous, and a source of confusion, because a good depression state scale, for example, is actually a *more* valid test if its so-called predictive validity is lower. The sooner textbook writers cease repeating this concurrent predictive fable, the lighter will be the students' burden! Although 8 "types" of validity are possible from Figure 4-1, no others than those we have discussed bear much importance. It turns out that psychology is most concerned with the *direct-conceptual*, and secondarily with *direct concrete* (in special-purpose tests) combinations. However, although *circumstantial-conceptual* validity

is rarely calculated it is a valuable third form, and it would often raise confidence to have a direct validation checked by an indirect validation.

Let us next look more closely at the calculation of the *concept validity* either of a set of items in a scale or a batch of factor subtests (as in an intelligence test or the O-A Kit). Into this calculation there enters, as in getting any multiple correlation, a) the correlations of the items or subtests among themselves, and b) the correlation of each with the factor. The latter can be obtained from either i) correlating each test score with an estimate of factor score from all the other tests with reasonably good correlation with the factor, or ii) "factoring in" the given scale with variables in the general factor analysis of that and other factors, and determining the correlation in the simple structure factor space. The latter, which is the better method if one has time to factor and to get a really refined simple structure on sufficient variables can be read in a book on factor analysis, e.g., Cattell (1978); Gorsuch (1970); Harman (1976).

The first method underestimates validity to the extent that the factor score is not estimated with full variance. However, the test constructor is probably more likely to use it, for convenience, so it will be set out here. The researcher unfamiliar with matrix algebra can refer to the books just mentioned, since the following is most economically expressed in matrices.

Here R is the $n \times n$ correlation matrix among the items or subtests and V_{fs} is the factor structure matrix giving the correlations of these elements with the factors. With a single factor, V_{fs}, is a single column vector. Then the weights to be given the elements in putting their scores together to get the best factor score are in the column V_{fe} (*fe* = factor estimate).

$$V_{fe} = R^{-1}V_{fs} \qquad (4\text{-}15)$$

The concept validity of the scale or battery, obtained as a multiple correlation R_{fv} is then

$$R_{fv} = (V^1_{fe} V_{fs})^{1/2} \qquad (4\text{-}16)$$

(In non-matrix terms this may look more familiar as $R^2_{fv} = w_1 r_1 + w_2 r_2 + \ldots + w_n r_n$, where there are n elements.) As Horn (1965) and others have pointed out, the average validity across samples falls relatively little from using equal weight for items rather than exact weights.*

Finally, a word must be said about the difference between factor validity and factor trueness, one hopes sufficiently explained by Figure 4.2.

---

*We would also point out to psychometrists as such that Kaiser and others have shown that the correlation of estimated factor scores with other factors and variables becomes very variable about the true expected value as the validity of estimate falls. (If r_{fa} is the r of the factor with criterion or subtest a and r_v is the validity of estimate the expected correlation of the estimate with a would be $r_d r_{fa}$.)

SOME CONDITIONS AFFECTING CONCEPT AND CONCRETE VALIDITY EVALUATIONS

It is sometimes assumed that the criterion is entirely reliable but that the test is not. If the criterion happened to be, say, the dollars earned per year by each of 200 carpet salesmen in New York City, and the records are sound, then the values *are* the amount earned that year and no uncertainty arises. But, conceptually, this figure is one from several possible years and several possible groups of salesmen and in any real generalization it is this average that we have in mind. One is prone to forget that very rarely indeed is the criterion to be considered free from sampling error and measurement error. Therefore, if we want to know the most *likely* value for the true validity of a test we should correct the obtained coefficient for both the unreliability of the test and of the criterion, as follows:

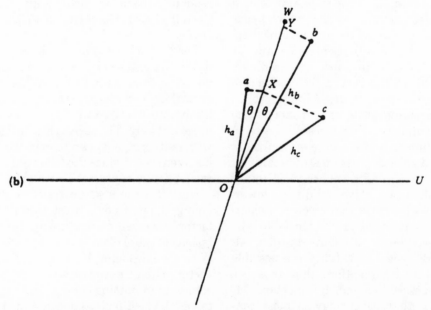

On the (oblique) wanted factor, W, tests a and b have an equal degree of trueness, c being lower in trueness (contaminated by more of the unwanted factor, U). Tests a and c have equal validity, but different trueness and are exceeded in validity by b.

Figure 4.2. Distinction of factor trueness and factor validity

$$r_v' = \sqrt{\frac{r_v}{r_{d/t} \; r_{d/c}}} \qquad (4\text{-}17)$$

where r^1_v is the improved estimate and the denominator contains the two dependability coefficients. On the other hand, if we wish to correct for unreliability only in the test itself we have

$$r_v'' = \sqrt{\frac{r_v}{r_{d(t)}}} \qquad (4\text{-}18)$$

where r_v'' is the estimated true value, r_v the observed, $r_{d(t)}$ the test reliability, and $r_{d(c)}$ the criterion reliability.

There is a sense in which a criterion can itself suffer from *invalidity* as well as unreliability. We have already seen such a case in conceptual validity where a factor can be estimated, as the criterion, either 1) where the test has been "factored in" with many variables marking the factor, the carefully rotated factor is the *true* criterion. It is so to the extent that the sampling of variables and people, and the factoring, are correct. The test-factor correlation is then with a true criterion or 2) when the test is correlated with an *estimate of the factor score* from a battery, it will have generally a lower value, because the estimate is imperfect (as Kaiser and Guttman emphasize). Equations 4-17 and 4-18 are correct only for unreliability (strictly *undependability* in our classification of consistency coefficients above). If our factor criterion is by *estimation* (2 above) then we need to correct also for invalidity of that estimate, then equation 4-17 becomes:

$$r_v = \frac{r_v' r_e}{\sqrt{r_{d(t)} r_{d(c)}}} \qquad (4\text{-}19a)$$

where r_v as before is the correlation of the battery with the weighted estimated factor score, $r_{d(t)}$ is the test dependability, $r_{d(c)}$ is the dependability of the battery estimate of the factor, r_e is the correlation of

the estimated factor score with the true factor (the multiple R from all tests used in the estimation (equation 4-16) and r'''_v is the validity of the test against the pure factor if there were no invalidity in its estimate as the criterion and no occasion to expect undependability. This is a value worth knowing for theoretical purposes when we wish to argue from test correlations to possible true factor correlations. The same relation would be true of a *concrete* criterion if we knew it had for some reason a validity less than 1.0 in what it purports to represent.

As expanded upon in the next section, the practicing psychologist looking at a test critic's shop window in a book like Buros's (1978) or in test catalogues recording alleged reliabilities and validities often comes away with about the same correctness of evaluation as in considering a list of promising Wall Street stock prospectuses. He finds it difficult—for lack of qualifying data—to allow for the several necessary corrections indicated above and that he knows should be applied to the given figures on validity and reliability. He is, in fact, a victim of oversimplified reporting. A simple case of such reporting is comparing dependabilities of tests without recording how long each test takes. Another is reporting what are actually homogeneities as dependabilities (reliabilities). Another is reporting in a test aimed at a *concept* (anxiety, intelligence) only *artificial* validities, e.g., against older intelligence tests, instead of factorial or other concept validities.

Test length is always important to the practicing psychologist because of time, and it must be admitted that in common practice two systematic errors are prevalent: 1) cutting down below a length for decent validity, and 2) representing some factors twice or more in overlapping tests while omitting others. For example, in doing school achievement estimates, to spend 90 minutes on two intelligence tests for g_c and then 35 minutes on 16 personality factors in the 16 P.F. (instead of doubling the latter by A and B forms and cutting down on the former) is poor planning.

Let us examine what precisely increased length does for validity. The appropriate formula is

$$r_{v(n)} = \frac{r_v'}{\sqrt{\dfrac{1 - r_d}{n} + r_d}}$$ (4-19b)

where n is the number of times the test length is increased and r_d is the reliability before extension. It will be noted that validity does not increase with length as rapidly as reliability, and no amount of extension of length will make a low validity test really substantially valid. (With an $r_d = .8$ and $r_v' = .7$, an n of 2 and of 3 raise reliability-dependability by a multiple of 1.11 and 1.15 (equation 4-11) respectively, and validity by one of 1.03 and 1.05.)

The next question concerns the relation of validity to homogeneity. A shortcut the reader will sometimes see taken to determine the validity of a scale is to take the square root of the equivalence coefficient obtained between *two* such equivalent scales. In the case of the concept validity of a test a that has *only error and specific factor* in its measurement besides the wanted factor f, the proposition holds that

$$r_{a_1 a_2} = r_{a_1 f} \cdot r_{a_2 f}$$ (4-20)

where a_1 and a_2 are the equivalent scales and r_{a1f} is validity of a_1. Thus, if symmetry holds and the two specifics are different, as just supposed, then the validity of the a scale is:

$$r_{af} = \sqrt{r_{a_1 a_2}}$$ (4-21a)

By the same formal model validity can be related to dependability. If there are no specifics and only error in the scale, then validity is simply

$$r_{af} = \sqrt{2r_{da}}$$ (4-21b)

But this is in almost all tests an unrealized ideal—a limit—useable only as a rough guide properly recognized as an upper limit. Similarly, equation 4-21a is systematically in error by assuming the scales a_1 and a_2 have only the required factor (or criterion) in common and nothing else. Whereas usually the same intruding broad factors are in common —unless suppression action is perfect.

It helps in all these analyses of relations of coefficients to remember that the variance of any test can be broken down, realistically, into as many components as shown here:

$$\sigma_t^2 = \sigma_w^2 + \sigma_{wf}^2 + \sigma_u^2 + \sigma_{uf}^2 + \sigma_s^2 + \sigma_{sf}^2 + \sigma_e^2$$ (4-22)

Let us now break down the variance of a test, as shown in equation 4-22. Here σ_w^2 is the wanted broad (common) factor we aim to measure, σ_u^2 is the *unwanted* common factor, (*not* the *unique, u,* factor often used in some factor formulae). σ_s^2 is the specific factor to that test, and σ_e^2 is the error of measurement peculiar to each occasion. The subscript f is the trait *fluctuation* part, from occasion to occasion. While equation 4-22 reminds us, comprehensively, that oscillation is *always* there, several of the broad principles we now need to discuss *can* be handled without involving it.

First, to link up with, and illuminate further, what was said about *consistency* coefficients, we can note how those listed earlier form a series as follows. With unit total test variance, as in a standard test score, the variances, as fractions, in calculating the dependability coefficient, are seen as follows on p. 69.

Note the denominator in all expresses full (unit) observed variance. (*$r_{h(e)}$ is homogeneity judged in the form of the equivalence of two parts.)

In the consistency breakdown the σ_e^2

$$r_d = \frac{\sigma_w^2 + \sigma_{wf}^2 + \sigma_u^2 + \sigma_{uf}^2 + \sigma_s^2 + \sigma_{sf}^2}{(\sigma_w^2 + \sigma_{wf}^2 + \sigma_u^2 + \sigma_{uf}^2 + \sigma_s^2 + \sigma_{sf}^2 + \sigma_e^2)} \tag{4-23}$$

Homogeneity as equivalence is:

$$*r_{h(e)} = \frac{\sigma_w^2 + \sigma_{wf}^2 + \sigma_u^2 + \sigma_{uf}^2}{(\sigma_w^2 + \sigma_{wf}^2 + \sigma_u^2 + \sigma_{uf}^2 + \sigma_s^2 + \sigma_{sf}^2 + \sigma_e^2)} \tag{4-24}$$

The stability coefficient is:

$$r_s = \frac{\sigma_w^2 + \sigma_u^2 + \sigma_s^2}{(\sigma_w^2 + \sigma_{wf}^2 + \sigma_u^2 + \sigma_{uf}^2 + \sigma_s^2 + \sigma_{sf}^2 + \sigma_e^2)} \tag{4-25}$$

The validity coefficient is:

$$r_v = \sqrt{\frac{\sigma_w^2 + \sigma_{wf}^2}{(\sigma_w^2 + \sigma_{wf}^2 + \sigma_u^2 + \sigma_{uf}^2 + \sigma_s^2 + \sigma_{sf}^2 + \sigma_e^2)}} \tag{4-26}$$

term is the key to the breakdown into further coefficients (as in Table 4.2). Different coefficients appear, e.g., r_{sp}, $r_{sp(a)}$, etc., through distinguishing interexaminer, scoring, and test construction sources of error.

Although invalidity is often treated as if it were due to intrusion of specific factors, the fact is that in any test yet constructed the invalidity is due not only to the unwanted specific factor, but also to unwanted *broad* (common) factors. Thus, intelligence test performances may sometimes contain some personality factors, such as superego strength. Good design calls for attempts at what is here discussed as "suppressor action," to reduce variance due to these unwanted common factors. Thus, if one item loads .4 on the wanted factor F_w, but also, inevitably, .3 on some unwanted broad factor, F_u, then the designer must find another item that

loads positive on F_w but $-.3$ on F_u. Such suppression is illustrated most simply in Figure 4.3 where only one unwanted factor is concerned. The principle is the same with several unwanted broad factors.

It is sometimes a nice question whether a more valid but less true (Figure 4.2) or a more true but less valid test is to be preferred. The answer for most work is the former, for if a test is less valid the finding that it is nevertheless quite true means only that it is not contaminated with factors that *we know* or has a huge specific. Since its communality is small in the domain we are factoring, there *must* be other unknown factors, beyond the one we want, that take up much of the variance of the test. For research or applied work in which we know we are not going to be concerned with other, outside, factors, however, trueness can be a useful virtue.

In discussing consistency we have already referred to the persistence of the widespread view that high homogeneity is in itself a virtue. Figure 4.3 illustrates the falsity of this clearly. Because a diagram is confined to two dimensions, we are admittedly using an extreme case—where two items can together give (summed) perfect validity (granted no specifics or experimental error) even with a correlation of zero between them! The principle holds in more dimensions, but with limiting "side-conditions." Where, as is inevitable, items bring in many contaminating unwanted broad factors, a high validity can no longer be achieved without allowing the homogeneity to rise above zero. As Cattell and Tsujioka (1964) showed, there is then a fixed relationship between the number of items, the number of unwanted dimensions, the mean r of items with the factor and the highest

mean r they will reach among themselves, i.e., the homogeneity. The detailed formulae can be seen elsewhere (Cattell, 1973a), but the upshot is shown in Figure 4.4.

Each of the four curves handles a particular combination of item homogeneity and item validity, and shows how the validity of the resulting scale then increases with number of items. It will be seen that throughout the range taken from A to D, an increase in scale validity is possible with an increase of the items loading on the factor combined with a *decrease* in the homogeneity.

It might seem that in test construction it would be ideal to use items that are as nearly as possible pure measures of the factor and that would therefore involve us in no search for suppressor action. In that case they would cluster with very high

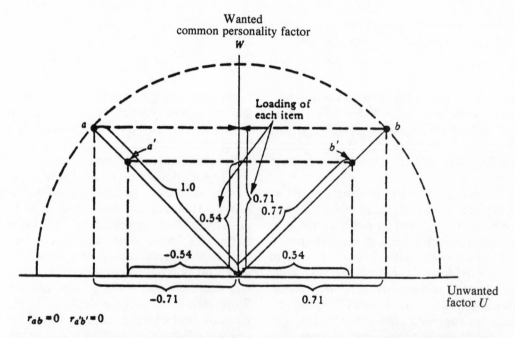

a and b are two tests fully accounted for by variance on the common factors W (on which validity is wanted) and U on which suppressor action reduces their loading to zero (being equal and opposite).

a' and b' illustrate the much more common condition in which there is specific factor variance in the two subtests or items. They still remain uncorrelated and exercise full suppression of U, but no longer give full validity as a scale for W.

Figure 4.3. The nature of suppressor action in achieving conceptual validity

homogeneity close about the vertical axis in Figure 4.3. Except for undependability the test scale would then theoretically need only *one* item (question) instead of the many needed in suppressor action!

Actually, this does not satisfy the requirements even of theory when all is considered, for there are other properties of an item than its immediate concept validity. There are its dependability, in the various

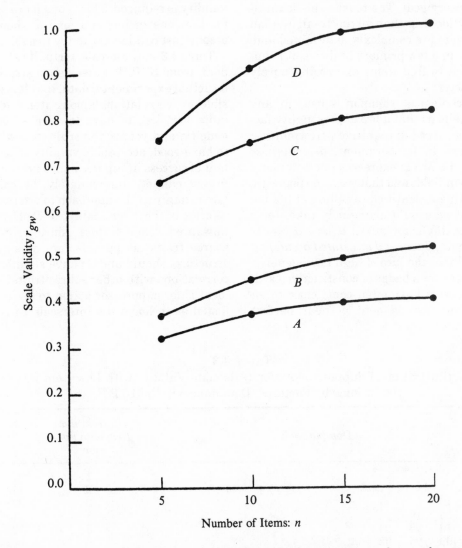

Relations of item and scale parameters: in a plot of relations of r_{jw}, r_{jm} and n under stated assumptions. Curve A: $r_{jw} = 0.2$, $r_{jm} = 0.2$. Curve B: $r_{jw} = 0.2$, $r_{jm} = 0.1$. Curve C: $r_{jw} = 0.4$, $r_{jm} = 0.2$. Curve D: $r_{jw} = 0.4$, $r_{jm} = 0.1$.

r_j is the correlation of items (mean or on each) with the required criterion factor, W. r_{jm} is the correlation (mean) of items with one another, i.e., the homogeneity. r_{jw} is the correlation of the whole scale with the wanted factor, i.e., it is the scale validity. An increase of r_{jw} without some increase in r_{jm} implies that items are being taken in a broader domain, embracing more "unwanted" common factors in suppressor action. The highest scale validity is obtained by a combination of high r_{jw} with low homogeneity, r_{jm}, as shown in Scale D.

Figure 4.4. The relation of homogeneity to validity of scale and items

above senses, and its distribution of alternative responses defining the fitness of its degree of "difficulty." In any case, the notion that good construction means one item, or even a whole scale of items, high loaded on the factor—and nothing else—is an illusory goal. The reason this is an illusory ideal is that virtually all human behaviors are complexly determined and, except in a few primary abilities, it is impossible to find items expressing purely one factor.

Psychological common sense, in any case, tells us that a broad personality factor, e.g., *speed* in cognitive performances, *surgency* in temperament, *assertiveness* (as in the MAT) expresses itself in many different fields and that from the principle of getting a stratified sampling of life behavior we should necessarily take items having the factor *mixed with a diversity of specific factors and unwanted broad factors*. Under the lure of high homogeneity, mistaken for a badge of constructive skill, test makers have often come close to an apparent achievement of near perfect

homogeneity (as in, for example, a Guttman scale) but on factoring it turns out that they have achieved homogeneity by arranging for items all to share in what is really a narrow specific factor, added to the common variance of the factor whose validity is required. This is one more peril for the constructor, and for the shopper among test catalogues, to try to avoid.

Table 4.3 shows a scale, virtually at random, from 16 P.F. scales demonstrating, on actual experimental data, that it is possible for correlations among items to be quite low, i.e., to have low scale homogeneity, and yet for the scale as a whole to have good, acceptable validity. The extent of success in suppression of unwanted factors cannot, unfortunately, be calculated simply as the approach to a zero correlation of the given scale as a whole with unwanted other factors, since primary source traits, as pure factors at simple structure, should and *do* have significant correlations with other source traits. The ideal is for suppressor action to be so adjusted as to leave the interscale correla-

TABLE 4.3

Typical Illustration of Suppressor Action (Adequate Validity with Low Item Inter-correlations) by Factor E (Dominance) in the 16 P.F.

Dominance E												Item	Correlation Item with Factor
												1	37
17												2	41
08	10											3	33
15	05	16										4	21
05	16	03	04									5	13
06	09	05	02	-02								6	04
14	14	09	15	02	03							7	22
13	06	05	04	13	20	08						8	53
09	08	-00	-00	07	-03	02	-00					9	11
-00	06	-03	00	-02	18	02	13	06				10	31
-00	06	-03	02	24	-03	-01	14	13	06			11	08
02	01	01	10	13	10	00	16	07	31	15		12	32
09	10	05	11	07	05	14	19	00	10	09	13	13	31

R scale validity by weighting = 0.84. Mean item validity = 0.26. r_{sw} scale validity by Formula (9-11) = 0.67.
    The table shows the intercorrelations of the 13 items in the given scale and their correlations with the factor in a factor analysis.

tions corresponding to the real interfactor correlations. A solution exists for this construction problem, with the associated calculations, but it must be left to separate advanced reading. It involves some assumptions linking item validity, r_{jw}, with the correlation of items with one another, r_{jm}, with the size of factor space, k, with the communality, h^2, and with the number of items, n (Cattell, 1973a; Cattell & Tsujioka, 1964; Gulliksen, 1930; Hunter, 1972). We have left such questions, along with a more intensive examination of the Cattell-Radcliffe translations of some classical itemetric formulae into the formulae that operate from the point of view of structured test concepts, to Chapter 23. Meanwhile, it can be said that in several factored tests the ideal of having the source trait scales intercorrelate in much the same way as the source traits themselves is tolerably realized. (See Tables 10.1 and 10.2, pp. 113 and 114, of Cattell, Eber, & Tatsuoka, 1970, on the 16 P.F. primaries.)

SOME BROADER PERSPECTIVES: UTILITY, EFFICIENCY, AND STANDARDIZED COEFFICIENTS

To get perspective at a glance on concepts we have so far reached, one may look at a graphic representation in Figure 4.5. It shows (by the convention of correlations as cosines in factor space) the way to avoid confusions in discussion between *test homogeneity* and *factor homogeneity*, and other concepts that get mixed in the transition from itemetric to structured psychometry.

It shows us, in the close-packed set of items in d, for example, that items can be highly test-homogeneous, but factorially heterogeneous; that items can be test-heterogeneous but yield a scale that (by suppressor action) is factor-true; and again, that factor validity and factor trueness are different.

Here we shall proceed to some final comments on the relations of test evaluation coefficients, and then to some newer coef-

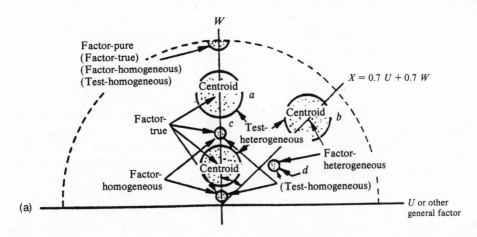

This figure also illustrates first the difference between what has been called (by Guilford and others) a *univocal* and what may be called a *unitractic* scale measure. The former, as X above, is factor analytically a measure of a single factor (except for suppressor intrusions), since if b is a small circle it would measure essentially only X. But though statistically one factor, e.g., by principal components scree test or Spearman's tetrad difference, it is not a single source trait (like the vertical and horizontal factor traits positioned by simple structure), but a mixture of two trait factors W and U. As shown, it constitutes a vector between these traits, mixing them about equally.

Figure 4.5. Concepts of (a) types of homogeneity, (b) unitractic and univocal scales, and (c) trueness and validity, illustrated in two dimensions

ficients corresponding to concepts the practitioner nevertheless needs. As to the former, a practical problem that often arises in calculating test validity with a *concrete* criterion concerns the calculation of the criterion score itself. As we have said, a single concrete criterion can seldom be considered completely valid for representing the criterion concept. However, the extent and nature of the invalidity, even when we are not out after a concept, but simply a specific life performance, often become debatable.

Any long-term life performance score is a composite of more specific performances and different psychologists may favor different weights for the parts. Success as a bus driver, for example, might combine freedom from accidents, punctuality at bus stops, sense of comfort in the passengers, and so on. Horst (1962) and others, in articles on "the most predictable criterion," have pointed to calculations wherein, by weighting components of the criterion and of the test battery, weights for tests and criterion elements can be found that give the best prediction of that criterion from that set of tests. They are thus objectively determined. This is "objective," but not necessarily right, for the criterion has now become the plaything of the test, shaping itself to be best predicted. Some agreed social or other real contribution of the criterion behavior should be the basis of giving weights to its parts rather than augmentation of its agreement with a particular set of tests. This is perhaps an example of how psychometrists are sometimes led by admiration for a statistical *tour de force* to neglect psychological good sense—but there are worse examples in terms of trying to squeeze the utmost out of an originally poor choice of tests, and in some uses of discriminant functions and canonical correlations, etc.

Probably the two commonest failures to make good use of information about test validities and consistencies come from 1)

neglecting to look at test length and 2) forgetting relative scoring objectivity (as revealed in *conspection* coefficients). Time is always precious to psychologists and generally also to the client. As pointed out in Chapter 2, the first economy the well-informed psychologist can make is to avoid duplication and overlap of tests in getting at the array of source traits he actually needs as relevant. Such duplication happens especially in unfactored tests. The second economy comes in choosing tests by looking past the validities listed in the handbooks to the concept of *validity per minute*. After all, since validity and reliability change with length —and, therefore, time allowed— judgments of the relative power of tests must be made on coefficients standardized to time. Instead of an artificial reduction to "per minute," per 15 minutes or half hour might be more convenient. In fact we would propose to call the validity of tests standardized by equation 4-19 to 15 minutes their *coefficient of efficiency, r_q*.

Psychologists comparing the validities of factors in, say, the 16 P.F. with those of intelligence tests, are apt to overlook that each scale in the former (with 40 minutes for the whole test) takes approximately 2½ minutes, against perhaps a half hour for the latter. Of course, test constructors should provide greater available length for psychologists—especially researchers—than 2½ minutes, as Cronbach suggests. But the 16 P.F., in fact, meets Cronbach's need by having equivalent A, B, C, D, and E forms by which the psychologist who wishes a good minimum time per factor—say, about 12 minutes —more akin to the intelligence factor as usually tested, can get it by using more of the equivalent forms.

A second derivative coefficient that is important for perspective is the *utility coefficient*. It has been pointed out that structured testing deals with defined source traits and states, and since the educated psychologist knows many functional facts and laws about these source traits, the use of a structured test gives him far more power than with *ad hoc* (criterion-specific) or subjectively defined and constructed scales. Of two tests with equal reliability and validity, against some given concrete criterion one may have much fuller predictive power because its source trait identity is known and it thus has also concept validity. The *utility* of a test may be defined in general scientific terms as a function of the amount of scientific information, in files and textbooks, accumulated and available on the *trait* involved. To make this utility concept more empirical and operational we could measure it for any given test as *the average validity over a standard set of situations agreed upon by psychometrists as representative of predictive needs and involving diverse remotenesses and transformations from the immediate testing situation*. This distinction might seem to be confused with the abandoned labels of concurrent versus predictive validity, but the greater *utility* of a test, through greater psychological knowledge about the trait or state it measures, applies alike to immediate and future prediction, the latter resting on psychological knowledge of the properties of the trait. Despite their value in test selection at present no psychometric research exists attempting to take our current armamentarium of tests and evaluate them individually in terms of their utility coefficients.

The third derivative parameter of wide scope—like r_e and r_u going beyond consistency and validity—is the *universality index, I_e*. The intention here is to generalize the transferability coefficient, r_t, which applied strictly to consistency of validity *across populations*, to an index of consistency of *all* parameters of a test, across all situations, e.g., of validity, dependability, homogeneity, across cultures, ages and administrators. It could be expressed as a mean absolute correlation, r_e or as an index I_e, investing the standard

deviation of the r_v, r_d, etc. coefficients across the standard selection of subcultures and administrative conditioning. This would quantify what we would think of—and much desire—as the general "hardiness" of a test. Like the utility coefficient the universality index is something that test users may hope to see in tables only in the future.

For the designer of a test installation, i.e., a regularly used battery for particular schools, military, or business institutions, one more index is important—*the economic cost per person (client) per unit amount of predictive information obtained*. It needs no argument surely to convince psychologists that the knowledge/cost ratio is important, since its alleged level is often basically the reason for a decision to employ or not to employ a psychologist. A single index to evaluate this has to be derived from several of the coefficients above, notably from the utility coefficient, from the conspection coefficient telling how objective the scoring is, and from such practical considerations as the degree of group rather than individual administration possible, and the possibilities of computer use for scoring and for deriving a variety of predictions. The improvements by Gillis and Krug at IPAT (see Chapter 7), Eber, Ford, Brennan, Fuller, Schmidt, and Häcker (in Germany) and others in advancing clinical diagnostic procedures and industrial testing over the last two decades in this area have been remarkable (see also Timm, 1968), and we can be sure that, however the knowledge/cost ratio is finally calculated, the up-to-date practitioner today can improve substantially on values from the practices of a decade ago.

Finally, among test parameters we should consider *vulnerability* to cheating, to unconscious motivational distortion, and to undetected sabotage. This requires so much discussion of new concepts and calculations that it has been deferred to the general treatment of error in Chapter

23. But r_e as we may call the coefficient of vulnerability (Chapter 23) is in practice as important as all the others.

With the parameters of the available tests—duly standardized—before him or her, the psychologist deciding on a battery for a given client or the test installation for a given service still has some "artistic" decisions to make. That he or she will avoid a) unfactored tests, except in a few special-purpose tests goes without saying, as also does b) his or her avoidance of the redundancy and overlap currently often seen. In the interests of social cooperation he or she may also recognize, more than it is the present habit to do, that it is the same person (client) that goes into school, into a job, and perhaps into a clinic. Consequently, professional cooperation requires that files centered as far as possible on the *same* basic personality-ability dimension (rather than the local coinage of a parochial area of practice) be considered in setting up a test installation.

The most general principle that enters into this final choice, for almost any use, predictive or diagnostic, is to be sure to get *as many factor source traits as are relevant*, in the given time, rather than give all available time to more valid and reliable measures on one or two—as would be possible for each with greater time. The tendency has already been mentioned above for school psychologists to give disproportionately large amounts of time to intelligence tests, at the expense of personality and motivation. On the A form of the 16 P.F. alone, intelligence and 15 other factors are measured in 40 minutes, equally at 2½ minutes each. This will, despite lower individual reliabilities, for almost all purposes give greater criterion prediction than, say, 40 minutes on an intelligence test alone or on, say, just two or three secondary factors like extraversion, anxiety, etc., each 40 items long.

Naturally one regrets being forced by some absolute available time to accept lower reliabilities. The model here is, of course, that of the multiple correlation, R. If the several tests are of factorial source traits (rather than a miscellaneous set of unfactored special-purpose tests) and therefore largely uncorrelated, *several* such tests of low dependability coefficient level will give (relevances being about equal) a decidedly higher prediction than from one of them measured with impeccable reliability by taking up the whole testing time. For example, a single predictor test of reliability 0.8 whose validity has been increased from, say, .50 to .53 by increasing its length six times (to fill the time available) is going to give a poorer prediction than six tests of the same inherent validity but kept at one-sixth of that length and therefore lower actual validity (equation 4-19). The same principle occurs in information theory, where it is recognized that there is a greater gain from several "bits" of information of moderate positive reliability than from one bit that is perfectly reliable. A somewhat similar argument for multiple measures occurs also in the strategy of basic exploratory research. An investigator may be preoccupied with a speculative hypothesis that factor X is connected with phenomenon Y. Knowledge would advance faster in the domain of Y if he entered with scales for X *and several other factors*, for he is likely to find to his surprise some quite significant connection of Y with the others, and the somewhat greater reliability that he would have given X by excluding the others from sharing the time has little relevance to establishing *some* significant relation of X to Y.

SUMMARY

Tests, a subvariety within general psychological assessments studied in Chapter 3, have several descriptive parameters, and some eight characters in their construction which fix the nature of any particular test in ways to be kept in mind in test choice.

The *consistency* of a test—its agreement with itself—can be seen in its fundamental characters most clearly by reference to the Basic Data Relation Matrix that applies to all psychological experiments. This tells us that there can be consistency 1) across *occasions*—the *dependability coefficient*, r_d, 2) across *test parts*—the *homogeneity coefficient*, r_h (with *equivalence* of forms, $r_{h(e)}$ as a special case), 3) across *observers*—test administrators — giving the *administrative consistency coefficient*, r_a (when applied to *scoring only* across observers consistency is called the *conspect coefficient*, r_{sp}), 4) across *populations*, yielding a *transferability coefficient*, r_t.

Formulae are given for each of the above, showing how the common variance which defines the correlation, undergoes successive systematic reductions by exclusion of error of measurement, trait fluctuation, specific factor variance, etc. It is pointed out that the long-term retest *stability coefficient*, r_s, is *not* a pure test consistency coefficient and that, when test consistency is taken out, it gives a measure of *trait* constancy, r_{tc}.

Test validity has varieties of meaning varying with respect to three dichotomies: 1) *conceptual* (abstract) to *concrete*, 2) *natural* to *artificial*, and 3) *direct* to *indirect*. *Conceptual* (sometimes rather doubtfully called "construct") validity is the correlation with the concept (intelligence, anxiety, etc.). The concept is defined in an immediate sense most frequently by a simple structure (R- and dR-replicated) factor pattern, but also by supplementary properties shown to be associated with the factor. *Concrete* validity, usually referring to a special purpose, *ad hoc* test, is the test correlation with a concrete, particular behavior. Most *factor* (source trait) tests have concrete *relevances* rather than validities, since a real-life performance can virtually never be found representing a single pure source trait. Thus, a relevance coefficient cannot be an exact test of the factor test's validity. Face validity and concurrent vs. predictive validity concepts are rejected as false and obsolete terms.

Test validities, as initially recorded, e.g., in test catalogues and reviews, need adjusting, for any dependable comparison by reference to a variety of circumstances, such as criterion validity, population range, and, especially, test length and reliability. Since most test construction, alike in Q- and T-data, requires "suppressor action" to reduce unwanted common (broad) factors, and is needed also on psychological principles for due breadth of behavior sampling, high homogeneity is usually neither attainable nor desirable. Formulae are available for the best validity obtainable in relation to homogeneity, number of items, and correlations of items with the criterion factor.

Operational definitions are given for *factor trueness, factor validity, factor homogeneity, test homogeneity, univocal scales*, and *unitractic scales*.

Psychologists need to use quantifiable test parameters beyond those covered by consistency and validity, namely, the coefficients of *efficiency, utility*, and *universality*, and an *economic index* (knowledge/cost ratio). The latter is the ultimate arbiter where psychological services are to be provided from a limited budget. It has to take into account the time demands on personnel at different salary levels, in relation to number of clients and the efficiency of the test diagnostic procedures.

In most testing, dividing available time across a fairly extensive array of factored tests, even at the cost of the reliability reduction that comes with shortened tests, will give higher predictions than spending time on one or two tests to get high reliabilities.

The test parameter of *vulnerability* and the special Cattell-Radcliffe transformations of formulae from itemetric to certain structural testing uses are deferred for specialized discussion in Chapter 23.

The number of coefficients required

fully to evaluate the psychometric properties of a test is around a dozen. As yet insufficient cooperation has been attained among applied psychologists to put together the data basis for these with respect to a reasonable choice of core tests, but eventually we may expect such "desk information."

CHAPTER 5

Scales and the Meaning of Standardized Scores

Raymond B. Cattell

BASES OF STANDARDIZATION: SETS IN THE BASIC DATA RELATION MATRIX (BDRM)

From the preceding chapters we can assume that the practicing psychologist has availed him- or herself of a test oriented to a meaningful personality, ability, or motivation structure, and of known validity and self-consistency. To use this instrument efficiently he or she now needs to have clear principles for scoring it.

Since the scales in a questionnaire or the subtests in an intelligence test or objective personality battery differ in level of difficulty, in number of items, and in other ways, a person's *raw score* giving the number responded to in a given "correct" way means little or nothing in itself. Using a standardized test means giving the raw score meaning by comparison to certain reference values among raw scores found in certain populations. Referring to reference points brings us not only into test standardization, but also into the meaning of scaling, involving problems in

possible arithmetical uses of scores. Both of these matters will be dealt with in the same chapter.

The concept of standardization has been treated in many texts narrowly as a problem of standardizing over *people*. With the broader vision of psychological measurement as applying not only to traits but to states, situations, interactions, groups, change scores, etc., a more comprehensive framework is needed. This is provided here, using the concept of the *Basic Data Relation Matrix* (BDRM) or *Data Box* (Cattell, 1946, 1966b).

The Basic Data Relation Matrix (Data Box) tells us how far we can go in extending a measurement concept, and keeps us clear on what we are leaving out if we wish to. Let us repeat that it recognizes that every measurement of behavior has five signatures which uniquely define it: 1) a *person* (or other reacting organism), i; 2) a *stimulus, h*; 3) an *occasion* (defining time and place and being synonymous with a *situation*), k; 4) a *form of response* to be measured, j; and 5) an *observer, o*,

79

and his instrument, through which experimental error enters the measurement. Throughout this book and other writings, these have consistently been symbolized as above by h for stimulus, i for individual, k for ambient situation, j for type of response, and o for observer, so that any numerical score a is written a_{hijko}.

The full *five*-dimensional Data Box cannot be visually represented, so in Figure 5.1 only three coordinates are given in ordinary spatial perspective and the other two are "tacked on" to remind us that further space exists. The Data Box suffices to remind us that the sources of variation

in a test score—which is a k-j combination —come from variations of people, of situations, and of observers (also of stimuli and response forms), and that consequently we can talk of standardizations across people, across situations, and across observers.

Although we stated in Chapter 4 that the dimensions of consistency—dependability, homogeneity and transferability—derived logically from the dimensions of the Data Box, namely into "over occasions," "over administrators" (observers), and "over test parts" (stimulus-response units), as in Table 4.2, we did not

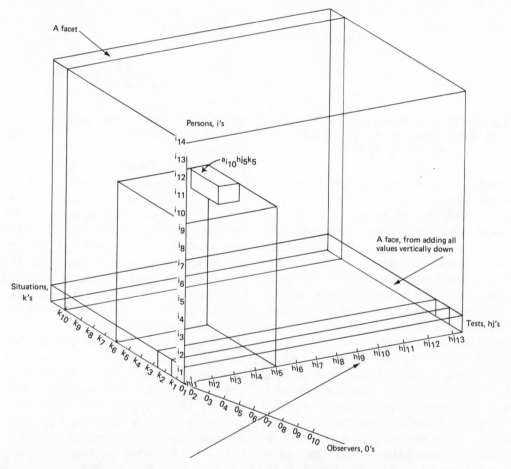

Two sets—h's, stimuli, ij's response forms—are here collapsed in a single *Test* coordinate set.

*Id is a needed generic term to refer to individual "patterns" of all kinds—people, stimuli, situations, response forms, observers.

Figure 5.1. Sources of variation (sets of ids*) within the data box

need to go into the Data Box properties as thoroughly as we now need to with regard to variance breakdowns in standardization.

For clarity of discussion it is good to have terms for the most commonly used settings for standardization. If, as most commonly occurs—and as occurs systematically here—we are talking of tests, we note first that a test fuses two of the coordinates of the Data Box into one. For, by the instruction, a test ties a particular form of response to a particular stimulus and we have a single series of hj's. A test score, therefore, is free to vary across the three remaining series—people, situations, and observers. The first setting used for standardization—across people—has by tradition become named "normative." *Normative* standardized scores, therefore, tell you where the given person stands relative to other people. (Incidentally, do not confuse *normatization* with *normalization*, discussed below.)

The first alternative standardization to the ordinary normative standardization that we shall deal with is *ipsative* standardization. This we have already run into above, in another connection, but we shall deal with it exhaustively here before proceeding to yet further, though less important, varieties of standardization. Normative standardization is of a test across people, but according to the Data Box we could also go across occasions and across observers, the score being that of a single person. The across occasions would be appropriate for converting a *state* raw score to standardized form.

As mainly used, ipsative standardization is standardization *within an individual*, and normative within a population. But the chances of confusion in using these terms are considerable because actually there are decidedly more forms than are revealed by the Data Box. If we stick to tests, i.e., hj as a unitary entity, then an individual can have performance distributions over occasions and observers, as noted. But if we shift from people

as the referent, a situation can be standardized over people and observers, and an observer over people and situations. Further, if we care to split the test and refer to a common performance over many different stimuli, i.e., if we let four of the five dimensions vary separately, then an ipsative score, i.e., one having to do with variation in a single individual, can have three forms: over occasions and observers as before, and now also over the range of stimuli.* A similar increase then happens for the score ranges associated with a situation (over people, observers, and stimuli) and an observer. Although these are not just "academic" analyses, since they have central relevance, for example, to social psychology, attribution theory and perception, the reader must be referred for the development of nomenclature and conceptions to the *Handbook of Multivariate Experimental Psychology* (Cattell, 1966b; Nesselroade & Cattell, 1985). Here we shall use *normative* in the usual way for tests over people and *ipsative* for test score ranges and standardization within one person, as in giving a person a standardized score, on a state, across occasions.

Even so, we have to recognize within ipsatization a further distinction between what we can best call *distributive ipsative* and *fractional ipsative*. *Fractional ipsative* (sometimes called performative) can be used on data where a figure can be obtained as a sum of the *total* performance of the individual over an agreed total of occasions or directions of interest. For ex-

---

*Implicit in the discussion here is the difference known to the student of statistics between *nominal* weight and *real* weight. If all subtests are put in standard scores, they are of equal nominal weight. Because they typically have appreciable a) mutual correlation and b) differing correlations with the factor that gives concept validity to them, one would have to calculate their multiple regression weights (b's, on the factor) to get the best true weights. If one wants to give them equal real weight, the raw score deviations would be multiplied by the inverse of these; but actually the best estimate of the factor would require them to be given b weights, not equal real weights. See Chapter 9 in Cattell (1973a) for further discussion and illustration.

ample, each of dozens of activities (performances) could be scored for a given individual according to the fraction of the 24-hour day he or she spends on them. (These fractions could, of course, *secondarily* be put into deciles or standard scores.) Actually, quite a lot of psychological measures are really *fractional ipsative* and this has not always been recognized in manipulating the results, i.e., in subsequent statistical treatment of the scores. One odd character they will have is that the correlations among the part scores, when carried out over a sample of people, must average to a negative value. Whenever a fixed total time or energy value score exists, fractional ipsative scores, correlated over people, will give odd results in factor analyses, etc. The widely used preference tests of interest, e.g., in the Strong or Kuder, have this character, for if, say, 12 words, each a special fractional interest, are paired in all possible ways (66), a higher score on one interest response means a lower score on others.

In a *distributive ipsative* standardization (as in scoring Mr. Smith on an anxiety scale over 100 days) this problem does not directly arise, and sigma and mean are used as in normative standardization. However, within distributive ipsative standardization we again run into a twofold division in current practices. The standardization can be full ipsative, i.e., with a sigma of 1.0, or only semi-ipsative, where different persons would have the same mean (0.0) for their many scores but differing standard deviations. As will be considered later, the choice of any raw score transformation must be consistent with psychological assumptions. For example, are we prepared "democratically" to assume that one person's total interest is as good as another's (thus using fractional ipsative scoring)? Or do we think we have measurement operations which permit using a concept that people have different total interest scores (thus using normative scores)?

While looking around at aspects of standardization that psychometric texts do not often handle, we may note also the several possible *set-combined standardizations*. For example, a psychologist might give an anxiety *state* scale to a thousand persons. It does not much matter whether all scores are on the same day (unless there was an earthquake), for each subject's day has his or her own incidence of anxiety provokers. The important point is that this basis of normative standardization is actually *simultaneously a standardization across individual differences and occasion differences*. It covers the scores in the cells of facet X in the Data Box in Figure 5.1. As an accommodation to practical difficulties, we might accept this temporarily as a standardization of the state scale concerned. But actually the variance in the standardization is the *sum* of two variances, namely intraindividual (state) and interindividual (trait) anxiety variance. We would like to rest only on the former, but without multiple occasion data we have to be content with the sum.

The number of combined-variance standardizations possible is large: ten kinds of two-sets, ten three-sets, five four-sets, and one five-set. (Further, each two-set can be either a face or as many facets as there are ids elsewhere, e.g., one could get a person-situation distribution for each of n observers.) The only one of these that is likely to have much practical importance and use is the five-set. Social psychology, particularly, may find it appropriate to deal with the total human variation in score over people, stimuli, situations, response forms, and observers recordings, for that is life as it occurs. But in other calculations we may want to hold some of the five sources of variance constant. What this section essentially teaches is that we should be *aware* of what sources are implied in the standardizations we use.

Thus, with the reminder in this section of the wider possible meanings of "reference population" and the description of systematic ways and terms for handling reference populations, we shall turn to the statistical standardization procedures that apply to all.

STANDARDIZATION TRANSFORMATIONS: CENTILE RANKS, Z SCORES, STENS, AND STAVES

Every well-appointed test one meets provides rules to go from a raw score to some kind of standardization value. One needs to be alert to the properties of the latter, in terms of what calculations can be done with it.

Although the question of scaling of tests is more fully dealt with below, the simple classical possibilities must be recognized here at the outset. They are:

1) Merely *categorical*, placing the given case as "blue" or "monocotyledonous," or in psychology, as schizophrenic, hysteric, carpenter, republican, etc.
2) *Rank order*, recognizing that a continuum exists on the given trait, etc., but refraining from any ascription of quantitative values thereon.
3) *Equal interval*, claiming that the units of the scale are equal, at different levels, but accepting inability to designate an absolute zero.
4) *Ratio*, claiming that a true zero can be located, so that the ratio of one score to another can be calculated, over and above a mere difference in units, as in 3. Occasionally equal intervals are not implied when an absolute zero is.

The firm and early progress of the physical sciences has been partly due to their being able to use ratio scales practically everywhere. The biological sciences, from statures to red cell counts have done much the same. The social sciences can get a zero for election results, crimes per year, and so on. But what is the absolute zero of exvia, or intelligence, or anxiety? And are we safe in counting equal numerical *raw* score intervals on, say, the item scores in a depression scale as *truly* equal steps?

Psychology has fallen back sometimes on categorical/qualitative designations, but most often on rank order properties. However, as we shall argue later, with some more extensive research guided by such principles as the *relational simplex* and *pan-normalization*, it could advance to meaningful equal intervals and even to essential zero values (absolute scores) in some cases. Meanwhile, let us recognize that virtually all existing psychological measurement is really rank order. We do not know, for example, that an increment from 110 to 111 on an ordinary intelligence test, e.g., the WAIS, is equal to one from 109 to 110: We only know that 109, 110, and 111 are in that rank order. But, as in the fairy tale about the Emperor's clothes, we constantly live in the illusion that our measures are "clothes" at least hiding our bareness in equal interval properties. However, if a concerted effort were made by psychologists along the lines of pan-normalization, the relational simplex, and modulation theory (below), it is probable that we could transcend this disabling limitation for measures of the most important ability and personality factors. As we now talk about standardization, we must at any rate follow the fashion of assuming that we have equal unit intervals in the members we add. The concepts can be shifted, when needed, to the lesser assumption of rank order or the further assumption of a normal distribution on a continuum.

The two common alternatives in going from a "meaningless" raw score to a standardized, meaningful equivalent are:

1) To go to a statement of rank, with or without assumption of a normal distribution. Percentiles (better "centiles") are expressions of rank. They are inverted from rank, however, so that a

large number means a high score, i.e., the person third from the top in 100 is at the 98th centile. With a normal distribution the difference in raw score between the 55 and 65 centile is much less than between 85 and 95, which makes it logically impossible to add and average centile scores.

2) To go from raw scores to scale unit intervals of a more common kind, e.g., such that something like 10 or 100 units span the population (rather than, say, some inconvenient raw score range from 375.15 to 519.36). Again this can be with or without the requirement that the population be normally distributed on the new units. If the raw score unit range is small—say 20 to 55—one obviously cannot transform to a 100-unit scale range. There must be a reduction, say, to a 10-point range, as in stens, or even a five-point, as in staves, according to the raw score range. But usually, with a decent raw score range, one would not go to such gross units as staves because a) one loses some precision present in one's information, and b) as a result of the coarseness various derivates are distorted. For example, in getting correlations a grouping to fewer than about 12 points lowers the true correlation of the finer scaling and calls for Sheppard's correction.

The beginning of calculation of transformations to stens or any other standardized score is the calculation of a standard score *per se*, which, as every student knows, comes from:

$$\sigma = \sqrt{\frac{\Sigma d^2}{N}} = \sqrt{\frac{\Sigma(X - M)^2}{N}} \qquad (5\text{-}1)$$

where σ (sigma) is the standard deviation, M is the mean of all scores, X is any raw score, d is $(X - M)$, and N is the number of cases.

The standard score, z of any individual i is then

$$z_i = \frac{X_i - M}{\sigma} \qquad (5\text{-}2)$$

So far the standard scores reached would have whatever irregular distribution the original raw scores had. But if we care to assume the distribution should really be normal, then we can, by using the information in Figure 5.2, get *normalized standard scores*. In these scores very few people indeed will have standard scores outside $+2$ and -2, and the mean standard score will be 0.

If we agree to let a *sten* be equal to half a standard deviation, then 10 equal intervals, as Figure 5.2 shows, will include all but 1% of the population and those few extremes we can reasonably include in sten 1 and sten 10. The normal curve has a fixed relationship between any given standard score and the percent of the population it "ropes in" between itself and the mean, which is in the true normal curve exactly at the 50% percentile. Thus, if the raw scores are collected according to rank, in the percentages required by the normal curve we know that the cutting score between these fractions represents a given standard score and given sten score. Figure 5.3 shows the usual "ogive" curve relation between centiles and raw scores, when the latter are essentially at equal intervals. The cuts we have just described can be made on this curve. At the same time a glance at this curve suffices to make clear why centiles are set aside from future scale calculations in this chapter, leaving them as suitable only for a descriptive, perspective-giving number.

Stens are used in, for example, the 16 P.F. and HSPQ, in both ordinary, direct stens, labeled *d-stens*, and normalized stens, labeled *n-stens*. The former, based on use only of the mean and sigma of the raw scores, will usually not distribute normally. Thus *d*-stens may be skewed, and

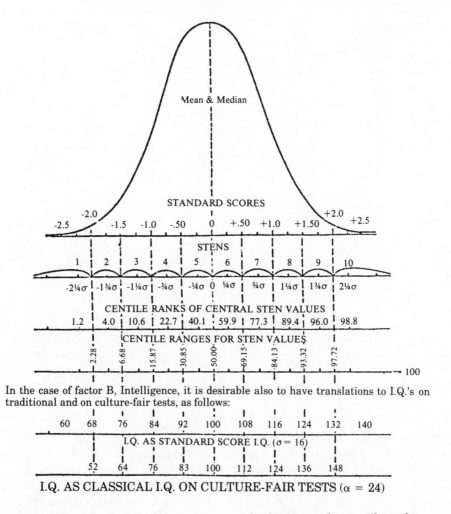

In the case of factor B, Intelligence, it is desirable also to have translations to I.Q.'s on traditional and on culture-fair tests, as follows:

I.Q. AS CLASSICAL I.Q. ON CULTURE-FAIR TESTS ($\alpha = 24$)

Figure 5.2. Translations from stens to standard scores and to centile ranks

may have extreme cases that could receive a sten score above 10. They will also not have a mean precisely at 5.5 as n-stens do. If Burt and Howard's (1956) distribution data are correct, the I.Q. does not distribute itself quite normally in Britain but skews upward. Minor deviations of this kind from normality, and common variations in sigma in various subpopulations have induced some psychometrists to use a normalized "standard score I.Q.," usually with an artificial sigma of 16 and a mean exactly at 100. The same resort to a normal curve is likely to be popular in other psychological measures.

Whatever transformations one makes, z is the essential beginning and basis of the new units. As mentioned above, when raw scores are in whole units, *any* transformation is likely to lose information since an exact equivalent to, say, a centile may call for splitting a whole unit that in some scales just cannot be split. This is evident in the kind of case mentioned above where one is driven, say, to attempt to expand a 7-point raw score range into a 10-point sten range. On the other hand, if one has, say, a 254 raw score range it may still be better to use stens than a 100-point unit transformation. For it is appro-

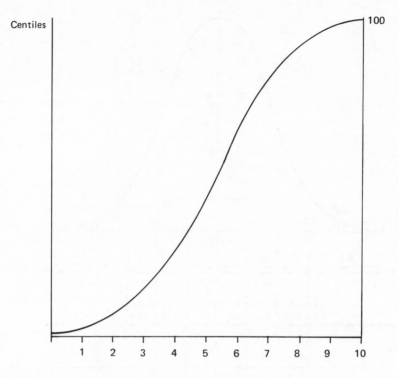

Figure 5.3. Curve (ogive) of relation of centiles to equal interval point raw scores

priate to consider the reliability of the raw score value, and if a raw score value has, say, a standard error of measurement of ±5.0 (see Chapter 23) in a 254 range, a sten is more reasonable than the use of 100 units. A decision hinges on the purely practical point that we do not want to bother our minds or deceive our clients by using a much finer scale than the real reliability, discriminating power, and validity of the data warrant.

A last point concerns the soundness of the rationale for depending on the normal curve of distribution. The formula for the height of the curve, Y, at any distance along the base, X, is:

$$Y = \frac{N}{\sigma\sqrt{2\pi}} \; e - (X - u)^2/2\sigma^2 \qquad (5\text{-}3)$$

where u is the mean score, X the standard deviation, e is exponential e, and N the number of cases. This is mathematically precise enough, but what is the naturalistic argument for respecting it?

In nature the normal curve tends to be found in populations of one species where the measurement of each individual is due to *many* influences, all of which act to different degrees on all individuals. According to the constants, the curve can be relatively pointed (leptokurtic) or relatively flattened (platykurtic). It is probable that convenience (as in Figure 5.2), rather than firm evidence of aptness to the given population, more frequently dictates its use. In some research fields social discoveries might be lost by using n-stens instead of d-stens, or normalized z rather than direct z. The basis of decision might then be, "Is the skewness of the raw score data significant in relation to the size of sample?" On the other hand, as indicated above in this section, if we have severe doubts about the raw score units being equal at different points in the scale, and suspect the skewing is not real, but due to "ceiling" or "floor" effects (cramping of units at scale ends), it may well be safer to turn to the assumptions of pan-normalization and admit we have no evidence justifying *d*-stens.

When there is no suggestion or evidence of raw score units being unequal in scale terms, it is generally wiser *in research*, where one has experimental or control groups or is dealing with correlation, to forget about applying any standardization transformations and use raw scores, thereby losing no information. Only in practice and applied psychology is it usually essential to know the "population meaningful" standardized values.

SOME REFINEMENTS OF CENTILE-STEN SCORING

Following from the above is a minor but sometimes confusing matter of whether to deal with fractional stens when greater accuracy is justified, by a wide numerical raw score range, than the coarse ten-interval units. When we thus use whole numbers (integers) for stens and refrain from decimal points, then a fair range of raw scores will correspond to, and be included in, one sten value. For example, a sten of 7 extends (see Figure 5.2) from half a sigma (half a standard deviation) above the mean (which is a sten of 6.5) to one sigma above the mean (sten of 7.5). In percentiles these boundaries are 69.15 to 84.13 so that any raw score between these percentiles is called a 7 sten.

However, a distortion arises here because the cases within the boundaries of the seventh sten are substantially skewed, as Figure 5.2 reminds us. The mean score of all people between those boundaries will not be at the center of the sten, namely at 7.0, but to one side—the lower side. (This distortion can also be seen in the ogive curve in Figure 5.3.)

If we wish this interval to yield a mean which is *exactly* at a 7.0 sten, i.e., $\frac{3}{4}\sigma$ above the group mean, we should shift our boundaries outward from the mean, by a small quantity which can be calculated, to give percentiles for these boundaries (and corresponding raw scores) a little different from those ordinarily used.

But there are tolerably good reasons for sticking to the simpler procedure and letting the slight distortion we are discussing be taken care of by Sheppard's and other corrections when we wish to derive more accurate estimates of sigmas, correlations, etc., from raw score groupings into sten scores. One reason is that we may wish (see below) to translate raw scores into the kind of stens that are *not* left as integers, but which proceed to as many decimal points as we wish. In that case the bounding values to the sten interval, say, 6.50 and 7.50 in this case, should fall exactly as we now have them —at the raw scores corresponding to percentiles of 69.15 to 84.13. However, in that case the exact 7.00 sten will correspond to the raw score for percentile 77.3, which is different from the middle of the 6.50 to 7.50 interval, as well as from the average of all scores (raw or normalized) in the interval.

There is a "fussiness" about these problems of converting from raw to standard scores with a normal distribution that the reader would probably like to avoid! But especially if we refine sten scores to have decimal points, e.g., 7.3, 7.4, 7.5, the conversion *has* to take account of the skewing, if we are to be fully accurate. At any rate, in calculating means and standard deviations from coarsely grouped data —and ten (sten) groups come just within that definition as far as effects are concerned—it is useful to know by a histogram what distribution one has, and to use Sheppard's correction (see Dunlap & Kurtz, 1932, p. 111) when it is applicable.

As indicated above, an equally serious but different source of inaccuracy arises when the range in the raw scores themselves is a little larger (or even smaller) than the number of stens (10) or stanines (9) or other grouped standard score one may be using. In multifactor (omnibus) questionnaires, when perhaps nearly 20 factors have to be measured in an hour, it is unavoidable that each factor will have perhaps only a dozen items to represent it, and the range of *raw* scores may then be only 10. (Note that a reduced range of score say to eight when there are 12 items does *not* imply that some of the dozen items are unnecessary.) If the scale range be as few as eight, then one raw score would have to be equated to two normalized stens; in fact, this would happen twice.*

Despite these boundary problems, standard scores, e.g., as sten scores, are in most applied psychology indispensable. For example, various attempts to design tests to make the *raw* scores on equivalent A and B forms exactly equal, or to make a raw score directly equal to some final standardized value, of the type of the I.Q., are *tours de force* rarely successful to any acceptable degree of accuracy. All individual work and much group (classroom) averaging must be referred to norms.

To provide researchers with reference points which they will need, most tests, including such tests as the 16 P.F., set out not only the desired norms but also the basic information on the *mean* and *standard deviation* of the raw scores. The observant student will notice, however, that

this raw mean is not the same (quite) as the mean deriving from looking at the table for the normalized stens, because a sten of 5.5 (the mean of all ten stens) is fixed by the median raw score, not the mean. And insofar as there is some asymmetry in the raw score distribution, the raw scores corresponding to two *n*-stens above and below the mean will in one case slightly exceed and in the other slightly undercut the value given by the raw sigma in the tables.

THE REFERENCE POPULATIONS IN STANDARDIZATION, BY AGE, SEX, ETHNIC GROUP, ETC.

In the first part of this chapter we pointed out that the reference groups in a standardization need not be only people, but can also be occasions, observers, etc., to the limits of the BDRM (Data Box). Here we shall deal largely with people and occasions, for the others are at present esoteric. Incidentally, people and occasions also present us with the most important occasion for *combined distributions*. For strictly, since traits fluctuate, the standardization of *traits* should be based on a score for each person that is actually his or her *mean score over many occasions* of measurement. At present it would be hard indeed to find any test for which this has been done and all the presented standard deviations—even for I.Q.—contain a modicum of state variance. The state variance, given the distribution of psychological state measures, e.g., anxiety, depression, ergic tensions, for the average person, would then be the remaining variance when this true, stable trait (or central personal state level) variance is subtracted from the combined variance.

Standardization always refers to a *real* population, which one must be careful not to equate in properties with the statistician's abstract population one has seen defined in statistics classes. The real population is often a Christmas pudding of

---

*Scores for a single person can distribute themselves across the four remaining Data Box sets—stimuli, situations, response forms and observers—or three remaining if we run stimulus-response forms together in pairs as "tests." But there is no need for special terms, other than "observer distributed ipsative" or "occasion distributed ipsative." However, some four other forms of ipsative scoring exist that are scarcely ever mentioned—those hinging on an individual situation, observer, stimulus, etc., instead of an individual person. When used they have the usual *distributive* or *fractional* ipsative standardization properties.

distinct types of constituents, imperfectly mixed. If a standardization for the U.S. population is to be sound, it is necessary—since all 220 million cannot be tested—to sample from different ethnic and status groups with proportions equal to—or weighted to be equal to—the proportions of the subgroups in the whole population. This we call a *stratified sample* standardization.

However, sometimes psychologists may want what we may call a special reference group—men alone, women alone, Mexican-Americans, blacks, college students, etc.—when they know that their purpose is going to be to score relative to that subpopulation. Distinct ethnic and social class standardizations are not often appropriate—like job quotas they may imply racism—but grouping by sex and by age frequently is. Decades of common education seem not to have altered the higher scores in primary abilities of women on verbal and men on spatial. If psychologists were selecting for women's positions on the ordinary norms for spatial ability, they might get the impression that they had a poor sample of candidates. If one wishes to refer to separate sex or age populations, the alternatives are to compound separate norms or use common norms and add a suitable constant. The 16 P.F. Handbook and Manual, for example, do the latter, because finding one's way through many different standardization tables (10 age groups $\times$ 2 sexes $=$ 20) increases work, time, and errors.

Some comments in Buros (1965) and other writings on tests suggest that a sense of proportion is needed in evaluating the adequacy of test standardizations. Often some critics bemoan a basis of 2,000 or 3,000 cases as too little, while other users employ tests central in their work with only 500 cases. (At last count of two common tests, the MMPI was 900 and the 16 P.F. over five thousand.)

Certainly there are more important features in evaluating a test than its resting on a gigantic standardization—though the latter is often unreasoningly worshipped. Validity is surely more basic, and in standardization taking the trouble to get a well-stratified sample is more important than great size. For most practical purposes a standardization in the neighborhood of 2,000 cases, or, with good fortune, up to 5,000, is entirely adequate. The demands of some test reviewers for a minimum of 20,000 or 30,000 are misguided from two standpoints. First, if we consider the standard error of a mean—$\frac{\sigma}{\sqrt{N}}$—and the population sigma as being (for an average length of test) in the region of 20 raw score points (or 15 in the case of I.Q.), then, with even just a thousand cases there is about a 50/50 chance of the true standard score being within approximately ½ point of the obtained value for an individual on the given standardization, and one chance in 20 of its being one unit different from that obtained if the standardization were on an infinite population. Using 10,000 cases will only reduce the standard deviation of the mean (and any sten cutting point) to ⅙ of an I.Q. point. For comparisons of groups, i.e., seeking and evaluating differences of group means, larger numbers have advantages; but for doing all that can be done with the individual case, and with a sense of proportion regarding other sources of error, a 2,000 to 4,000 standardization N is entirely satisfactory. (Even with this more down-to-earth perspective, however, the basis of only 900 in the MMPI standardization is a weakness in its diagnostic use.)

A second practical consideration is that the heavy cost of standardizations reaching the 10,000 level, or more, means that test corporations will be indisposed to restandardize as often as the secular trend in many psychology scores requires. It is often overlooked that standardizations are local in time as well as place. The surveys of Tuddenham (1948), Finch (1946), Vernon (1969a), and others show that crystallized intelligence test scores, probably because of improvement in school educational levels (contaminating tests like the WAIS, WISC, etc.) rose by nearly half a standard deviation between World Wars I and II. The costly standardization of, say, the Stanford Binet, on over 50,000 cases, is thus out of date before it is even calculated, and a few years can make it more erroneous for the user than it would be if it were calculated afresh each year on as few as a thousand cases.

Incidentally, the present writer's (1953) retest of the 10-year-olds in a large city after 13 years, with Culture-Fair I.Q. measures, shows that, as theory would expect, no such significant change occurred. As might be expected, innate intelligence scarcely altered, but school performances increased markedly. On the other hand, there is evidence (which must presently be considered only an indication, because not on a large sample and published) that mean scores on extraversion—as defined in second orders in the 16 P.F. and Eysenck's EPI—crept upward between 1950 and 1970, and that scores on superego, g, may have fallen somewhat. The refinement of tracking epogenic curves (curves peculiar to an epoch: Cattell, 1970c; see Table 7-3 in 1971a) has yet scarcely been contemplated in psychological research, but an intelligent treatment of standardization requires that such trends be assessed and ultimately we may expect corrections for standardizations per calendar year to be published. Well-stratified samples of 5,000 would probably suffice for this.

As tests with good transferability, r_t, coefficients, i.e., usable with equal validity on different subcultures and even different nations, become more common, regard for standardization differences like those of age groups and of the sexes will need to be more exactly focused. The evidence is irrefutable that, for whatever reasons, significant differences of minority ethnic groups exist on intelligence tests and on personality measures (Jensen,

1973; Knapp, 1963; Lynn, 1971, 1977; Cattell, Eber & Tatsuoka, 1970). They exist even between two countries as similar as the U.K. and the U.S.A. (Saville, 1972), between areas of Britain (Lynn, 1977) and between some large U.S. cities (Thorndike & Woodyard, 1942). Whether there is some genetic component or whether these differences are wholly cultural is unknown, but Buj (1981) has shown that even with culture-fair scales significant mean intelligence differences exist among some 12 or more European countries. If one is selecting or predicting within a larger, embracing population and culture the inclusive composite norms are needed but, as we are normally concerned with predictions *within* a subgroup, the norms for that subgroup as such need to be known.

No sex differences of mean have been found on intelligence, but significant differences are found on primary abilities, notably on spatial and verbal abilities. And on primary and secondary personality factors in the 16 P.F. significant sex differences on the *same* personality factors have been found in the U.K. and U.S.A. (and possibly elsewhere) in the same directions.

The main dimension that definitely calls for specific subgroup norms is age. For every ability or personality trait yet researched significant "ecogenic" (Cattell, 1973a) age changes have been found to exist across the life span. Psychologists have long been accustomed to comparing the brightness of two individuals by correcting to mental age scores their actual scores. In that case, as Stern found, nature had conveniently arranged that the quotient—the I.Q.—should stay essentially constant over the growth period. But what we find in the personality factors is something more varied and complex. Figures 5.4 and 5.5 illustrate the need to watch age in personality standardizations, and numerous other plots can be found elsewhere (Cattell, 1973a; Cattell & Schuerger, 1978).

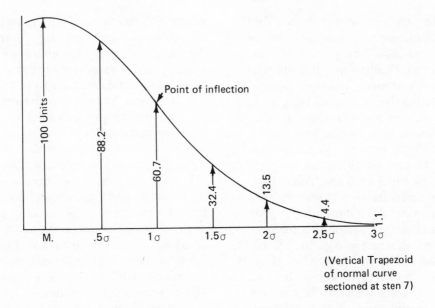

Figure 5.4. Problems in interpolating N. Extrapolating in centile-sten relations

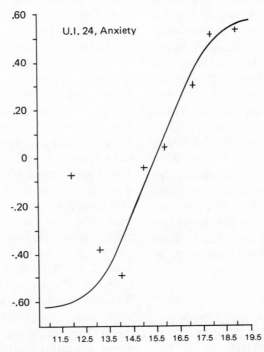

(a) Surgency (Factor F in 16 P.F.) Raw Score
 Variance Across Population = 81 stens squared
 Variance Across Age = 4 stens squared

(b) Anxiety (U.I.24 in O-A Battery)
 Variance Across Population = .90 stens squared
 Variance Across Age = .25 stens squared

Note: These are cross-sectional not cursive curves.

Figure 5.5. Illustration of norm corrections indicated by two age curves

Thus the psychologist can already find tables (sometimes reducible to formulae) to predict the most likely score of Jane on surgency at 25 when her present score at 15 is such and such. However, as the studies of Baltes (1968), Cattell (1971a), Horn (1970), Schaie and Strother (1968), and others show, even intelligence requires a more difficult type of age allowance between 20 and 80 than the simple I.Q. gives. (See Figure 5.6 and Table 9.2.)

Age standardization allowances are actually now available for both the primary *and* the secondary personality factors, and both in questionnaires, e.g., 16 P.F., HSPQ, etc., and objective tests (O-A Battery). However, one has to get along *outside* structured tests with the fact that a regrettable proportion of tests still in popular use lack them.

References have been made above to the complication of age allowance occasioned by the different life courses of several source traits—particularly in personality—and by the different possible analyses of life span curves by *cross-sectional* (same calendar date, different age groups), *cursive* (same cohort through different ages), *fixed epoch*, etc. calculations. These have been sufficiently discussed by Baltes (1968), Cattell (1969a, 1970a, 1970b), Horn (1970), Nesselroade and Reese (1973), and others elsewhere. Here we shall refer the reader to the adequate but condensed presentation in Figure 5.5. That presentation indicates that there are at least a half dozen different referent standardizations that could, in refined treatment, be used for "age correction" tables.

STANDARDIZATION IN RELATION TO TEST SCALE OR BATTERY CONSTRUCTION

It is appropriate at this point, given the above attention to basics in varieties of standardization, to turn to some more refined issues in scaling and their interactions with standardization. We shall not begin with the theoretically more difficult questions of equal unit and absolute zero (ratio) scaling values, which are deferred to this chapter's last section, but shall look at more practical matters in existing test constructions. Even these can be recondite and practicing psychologists may even want to restrict their reading on standardization by ending with the above section and jumping to the chapter summary.

It was the general assumption in the early pencil-and-paper age of testing (before multivariate experimental psychology introduced source trait factors and, by creating objective tests too, fused the scope of individual difference study with the realm of laboratory experiment) that all tests were made of "items." This is no longer true of many objective tests of personality factors and of most objective motivation tests, though in the interests of group administration these new test forms are often eventually brought into pencil and paper form, which is not the same as "itemetric." Besides, when the group forms are also supplemented, when possible, as provided in the handbooks, by such laboratory tests as the GSR, tachistoscopic exposures, varied reaction times, and auditory patterns of stimuli on tape, their difference from the itemetric framework is even more emphatic. The model of "atomicity" was acceptable with the item form and encouraged a superstructure of testing theory which the present writer has here and elsewhere designated "itemetrics." A number of outstandingly competent psychometrists, who can be illustrated by Brown, Coombs, Cronbach, Cureton, Flanagan, Gulliksen, Guttman, Kruskal, Lindquist, Lord, McNemar, Messick, Ross, Spearman, Tatsuoka, Thurstone, Torgerson, and others, worked out some essential and beautiful formulae and equations for scales on this basis. These pioneers, in fact, brought about a three- or four-decade "golden age" in the development of this domain of psychology as a mathematically based science. That did more, perhaps, even than reflexolog-

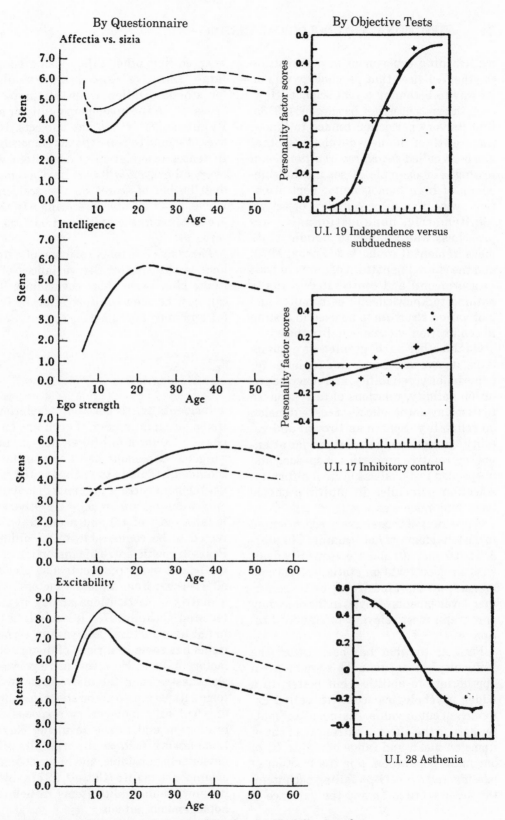

By Questionnaire

Affectia vs. sizia

Intelligence

Ego strength

Excitability

By Objective Tests

U.I. 19 Independence versus subduedness

U.I. 17 Inhibitory control

U.I. 28 Asthenia

Age trends for primaries *A, B, C,* and *D*. Thin line is females; thick line is males

Figure 5.6. Normal age changes in personality source traits, by questionnaire and objective test measurement

ical learning experiment to demonstrate to other sciences that psychology was on its way to becoming a real science. However, the present writer has argued (1973a) that its very perfection tended to hinder the growth of the new development that has been called *structured and functional* testing. For example, it set up the shibboleth of high homogeneity; kept attention away from more complex, objective, nonitemetric, nonquestionnaire approaches; was unable to handle state measurement (Cronbach & Furby, 1970) and the changing pattern of a source trait measurement; and contributed virtually nothing to knowledge of personality and motivation *structure* to be used in testing in conjunction with personality theory.

On the other hand, granted its assumptions, it gave us concepts and formulae for homogeneity, reliability, and concrete criterion validity, relations of test variance to item variances, effects of test extension on reliability (Spearman-Brown) and validity, correction of correlations for attenuation, relative properties of speeded and unspeeded tests, effects of item difficulty, selection principles in multiple choice tests, and much else.

Since most of these have been presented in various chapters here (mainly Chapters 3, 11, 14, and 20) and are very fully dealt with in good texts on statistical psychometrics, we shall touch only on those further developments of topics in the preceding paragraph most relevant to standardization.

First as to what has been called the "difficulty" of an item: This was a term appropriate to abilities, but better, in a wider psychological context, called *extremity* of cut or value. An important matter here is the effect of extremity of cut of items on mean and range of scales. If, in our main population, p is the fraction of passing and q, i.e. $(1-p)$, failing each item, the mean score is $\frac{\Sigma p}{N}$ and the variance is pq, giving σ (sigma) $= \sqrt{pq}$. It will be noted that this sigma is greatest when p

$= q$, so that other things being equal a large, "sensitive" range is made available for standardization when all items are "passed" (in the given personality or ability direction) by *half* the subjects. However, it should be noted that as homogeneity increases (correlation of each item with every other), one will then have a bimodal distribution of scores on the scale as a whole, half the subjects scoring n (if there are n items in the scale) and half scoring zero.

The range (variance) of a test of n items long is the sum of the variances of all items plus twice their covariance. This can best be seen in illustration in Table 5.1 and in equation 5-4.

$$\sigma_n^2 = \begin{array}{cc} x = n_2 \\ \Sigma \sigma_x \end{array} + \begin{array}{cc} xy = n(n=1) \\ \Sigma r_{xy}\sigma_x\sigma_y \end{array} \tag{5-4}$$

Incidentally, to get the correlation of items for equation 5-4, if each has only a pass ($+1.0$) or a fail (0) value, i.e., not a range of scores, one needs to use the *phi* coefficient. This is the same as the product-moment correlation in its distribution only when $p_x = q_x = p_y = q_y$. Otherwise, it falls short of 1.0 and needs to be corrected to be comparable to an ordinary Pearson coefficient. This distortion of the coefficient by extreme cuts also produces effects regarding "difficulty factors" when a matrix of correlations among items is factored (Cattell, 1978). It reminds us that handling structural analyses in terms of items has some real risks of distortion in factor analysis. However, more pervasive weaknesses than the above arise in factoring items due to a) the sheer instability of a subject's momentary response to a brief item and to the resulting correlations among such small, brief bits of behavior being unstable, and b) the obscuring of simple structure (Cattell, 1973a) by using low communality items rather than homogeneous parcels.

The parcel factoring techniques can be read elsewhere (Cattell & Burdsal, 1975;

Cattell, 1974b), but now we turn to a different problem in item test construction, in that with just two alternatives the subject has a 50/50 chance of being "right" when he or she knows nothing. As stated earlier, increasing the number of alternatives in a multiple choice reduces this error but, if the number is raised to, say, five or six, it slows down decision speed to where one has to test with significantly fewer items in the available time. Since, ordinarily, the bolder subjects will guess more and others less, it is desirable to demand in the instructions that *all* subjects make guesses on *all* items and then correct for guessing by:

$$S = R - W/(k\text{-}1) \qquad (5\text{-}5)$$

where S is corrected score, R the number right, W the number wrong and k the number of alternatives in the multiple choice. As pointed out earlier, this goes somewhat astray in an intelligence test where items are graded in difficulty, so that guessing only begins at a certain point.

Most item construction calls for skills, e.g., avoiding designs vulnerable to response sets, and using, for example, the principle (Cattell, 1973a) of giving meretricious attraction (for persons who cannot solve the item) to the wrong alternative. There are various other test construction skills, such as adjusting to vocabulary, etc., that are only tangentially relevant to variance and standardization. Except when *concept* (factor) validity of items with *suppressor* action is used, the selection of items in an itemetric methodology

TABLE 5.1

The Variance of a Test Scale Consisting of n Items

	1	2	3	4		n
1	s^2_1	$r_{12}s_1s_2$	$r_{13}s_1s_3$	$r_{14}s_1s_4$		$r_{1n}s_1s_n$
2	$r_{12}s_1s_2$	s^2_2	$r_{23}s_2s_3$	$r_{24}s_2s_4$		$r_{2n}s_2s_n$
3	$r_{13}s_1s_3$	$r_{23}s_2s_3$	s^2_3	$r_{34}s_3s_4$		$r_{3n}s_3s_n$
4	$r_{14}s_1s_4$	$r_{24}s_2s_4$	$r_{34}s_3s_4$	s^2_4		$r_{4n}s_4s_n$
n	$r_{1n}s_1s_n$	$r_{2n}s_2s_n$	$r_{3n}s_3s_n$	$r_{4n}s_4s_n$		s^2_n

has usually aimed to get validity against an *external concrete* criterion, and simultaneously to aim at homogeneity by trying to approach $p = q$ and, especially, raising r_{xy}. Both of these "itemetric" procedures raise homogeneity, often beyond the optimum value for an important broad personality factor. However, from a standardization point of view the raised extremity homogeneity will give, for a given number of items, a wider raw score range and therefore (with few items, say, 12) less awkwardness in going to stens and integral decile or centile cuts.

Secondary goals in item selection are to avoid skewed raw score distribution and to bring parallel A and B forms of a test reasonably close in their *raw* score means and sigmas. However, one must suspect any claim that raw score equality of mean and sigma has been so perfectly attained that it is unnecessary to convert to standard scores, e.g., before adding. In timed ability tests it goes without saying that preparatory research must aim to get the order of difficulty of items reliably increasing from the beginning to the end, so that the less able is not held up on a too difficult item while easier items are still ahead.

Moving on now from construction and other influences on the norms of *itemetric* type tests, we come to the further technicalities belonging to *structured* tests, scored for factors. In functional testing with such batteries or scales, a whole lot of new principles enter, affecting scoring and standardization, dealt with in Chapter 23. Further, since certain matters of scoring, for both itemetric and structured constructions, are dealt with essentially from the standpoint of efficient test installation choices in Chapter 6, only the more directly standardization-relevant matters will be handled here. And the question of separation of error as such, from response sets, from faking for social desirabilities, etc., is also handled elsewhere, under analysis of general error effects in Chapter 23.

In functional testing, dealing with true source trait or state factors, one usually has in T-data, objective tests some four to eight distinct subtests whose scores are to be added to give the total final estimate of the factor source trait. This compositeness of the final "scale" score from the battery is not the only difference from itemetric form or the questionnaire medium that characterizes objective tests and their scores. In *objective* tests of personality and motivation, as in ability tests like the Binet (which is also objective, T-data), the score is often a *pattern* score.

In the simplest pattern we may have nothing more complex than a *ratio* of reactions under two different conditions, or a measure of acceleration in "warming up," or a ratio of two ratios (see Chapter 12, and the roughly 500 objective tests in Cattell & Warburton, 1967). The distribution of ratio scores is a tricky calculation (see Cattell, 1982a, p. 294) from the contributory scores, but fortunately, to get that distribution we have only to plot the empirical outcomes, not go back to a calculation from item properties. This is because the factor sum of, say, ten subtest scores, is usually close to normal despite oddities in one or two of the subtests. Incidentally, one must distinguish between pattern *scoring*, to get a single score, and *predicting* from patterns. The latter is done in the 16 P.F., where the scales themselves are itemetric, but prediction from them may be most effective from a *profile pattern*, as described in Chapter 21. Direct introduction of pattern qualities into scales was undertaken by Walker (1940) and by Guttman (1959). A Walker-Guttman scale is one in which all possible extremity (difficulty) comparisons are made among proposed items and only those items retained which fall, consistently in all paired comparisons, into a single hierarchy. In practice it has turned out that only factorially very narrow scales, e.g., verbal attitude scales for favorability to a particular object, can meet these conditions. The Guttman technique is, therefore, unsuitable for the low homogeneity-construction necessary for broad, psychologically important personality and ability factors.

The question that arises in getting a "factor scale" from adding the subtests in a factor battery, e.g., in the O-A or the Culture-Fair Intelligence Test, is to fit them together with appropriate weights for the best estimate of the factor. Such tests as the WAIS or WISC, having (prior to such analyses as those of Cohen, Saunders, and Horn—and perhaps since) no exact definition of concept validity against a single demonstrated and targeted factor, cannot aspire to this. Many intelligence and other tests simply throw the unweighted raw scores together, and some even naively assume that this is an "equal weight" procedure. If equal weight is the aim, then the subtest scores should strictly be transformed from raw into standard scores, as is done for example in the four subtests of the Motivation Analysis Test (MAT). Actually, though an improvement, this still gives only equal *nominal* weight to the subtests. As a multiple R will tell us, the subtest intercorrelations make the true weights actually different from the nominal equal weights. In the best scoring we *want* them to be unequal, but in the special way required to maximize the factor estimate. For this purpose we need to calculate the factor estimation matrix, V_{fe}, which is a special case in factor terms of the general weighting calculation shown in equation 5-6.

The handbooks and tables for very few tests give the required weights, as do those for the MAT, the O-A Kit Batteries, and a few others. It may be that publishers can defend this omission on the grounds that few psychologists in the past have been able or willing to handle such paradoxes. A seeming reason for avoiding them is that, as Horn (1970) and others have shown, there is often insufficient "hardiness" of weights, across different samples, to give a significant advantage to such careful score estimation over estimation with merely *equal* weights. The

rougher procedure even of adding *raw* scores (when they are nearly equal in sigma) is defensible when all the subtests are of high loading. But when, as in estimating broad secondaries from primary scale scores on tests like the 16 P.F., CAQ, etc., the loadings are necessarily very varied, then the better procedure is called for. The progressive psychologist will realize that circumstances have altered in the last decade and that anyone with access to a computer, or a scoring service within easy phoning (see Chapter 7), nowadays meets no labor in getting the more accurate factor score. As far as programming is concerned, the setup, in terms of matrix operations, is very simple. The formulation is:

$$W = R^{-1} V_{fs} \qquad (5\text{-}6)$$

where V_{fs} is the column of subtest correlations with the factor, R is the square matrix of correlations among the subtests, and W is the desired column of weights for the subtests.

As the highest ideal of procedure one would have to recognize that since R and V_{fs} alter with the population—notably, for example, with different age groups and the same types of subtest—the matrices should be adjusted to new populations. Incidentally, weighting *could* advantageously be used with single items too, but itemetric practice has rarely done this. Table 4.3, showing the correlations R among items on the Dominance, E, scale and the V_{fs} values and the increase in validity gained from using the ensuing weights, presents an empirical argument for using this weighting procedure (not forgetting though our counterargument from instability of items). Incidentally, it should be noted that when we have standard scores in the subtests to be added, and add them with the weights in W, this does not *immediately* give standardized scores for the factor, though it does retain the mean of zero. The reason is simply that no multiple regression equation gives *complete* estimation. Thus,

$$R^2 = r_{ca}\, w_{ca} + r_{cb}\, w_{cb} + \ldots + r_{cn}\, w_{cn} \qquad (5\text{-}7)$$

falls short of unity, and if we want to convert to standard scores we must divide by the sigma thus derived.

There remains to be considered, in continuous scales, the effect on the true standardized score of contamination of the would-be factor-concept-valid scale by intrusions of unwanted factors. For example, Fulker argues that differences of *motivation* in intelligence test-taking may account for an appreciable fraction of the score. Generally, this intrusion is best handled at a later stage in the calculation processes beyond scoring and scaling units, and is so handled in Chapter 23 by taking motivation strength scores along with the intelligence test scores and using "computer synthesis." But occasionally one needs to be aware of effects directly in the scaling itself. It happens that the common practice of intelligence testing can provide an example of this and its handling, as follows.

The practice (since Stern) of dividing a mental age—derived from the performance curve of the average person—by the actual age is peculiar to the intelligence trait. It happens to be useful in intelligence (though only up to 15) because of the unusual property that the ratio—over that brief fraction of life—tends to be constant for individuals. Incidentally, Thurstone (1928a) brought evidence that it would be more constant if divided by age since conception (age +9 months). Now the recent research developments which have split the concept of intelligence into fluid and crystallized intelligence (Chapter 8) have shown such a major difference in the size of sigmas of I.Q.—from 15 or 16 in traditional, crystallized intelligence test measures to 24 or 25 in fluid, culture-fair test measures—that we are faced with a basic question on the meaning of standardization, appropriate for discussion here. As far as the solution for intelligence itself

is concerned, we have touched on it in Chapter 9, and can expand in a footnote here.* It is to take leave of the actual I.Q. ratio distributions and set up a convenient standard score I.Q.

---

*The sigma of the I.Q. is the function of the variance of *individuals* in their scores at a given year to the variance of the *means* of children's scores across a given number of years. If the former performances become more varied they give a greater variation in mental ages, since the latter are based on years defined by mean performances. If this is at a certain value, σ_{gf}, for fluid intelligence, then when each individual's performance becomes in traditional test, a sum of $g_f + s = g_c$, where s is schooling, the new sigma is the root of the new variance: $\sigma_{g_c}^2 = \sigma_{gf}^2 + \sigma_s^2 + 2r_{gfs}\,\sigma_{gf}\,\sigma_s$. The same variance-covariance relation holds for the sigma of child *means* taken over a number of years. But whereas for the *means* r_{gs} is close to $+1.0$, i.e., each year's increase in g_c is closely matched by increase in total schooling, this is not true for individuals, in the first equation. Indeed, the behavior genetics findings (Cattell, 1982a) are that r_{gfs} *is zero or negative. The hypothesis is that classroom education and the teacher's need to keep bright and dull in step, as well as other causes, produce this poor or even negative correlation of genetic and environmental contributions. Whatever the cause may be, the expected statistical consequence of this difference of r's for individuals and for year means* would be that I.Q. variance on traditional, g_c, tests would be *smaller* than for culture-fair, g_f, tests. This proves to be the case, for when I.Q. is correlated in the classical manner, the standard deviation is about 24 for culture-fair tests and 16 for traditional tests.

In face of this, as well as the variations of variance among traditional intelligence tests (due to their differing contamination with school achievement contest), Johnson (1948) and others suggest a "standard score I.Q." This could be literally a standard score, ranging from -3 through 0 (I.Q. 100) to $+3$, but most psychologists seem to have voted for retaining the I.Q. units and simply bringing all tests to one and the same numerical value for the sigma. The question is what value, and though a good argument can be made for the culture-fair value of $\sigma = 24$ points of I.Q. being more correct, it would perhaps be more gracious for the new to accept the fact that the old is embedded now in more psychologists' minds, and to agree to the traditional standard deviation of 16. At any rate, the culture-fair tests publish both the norms by the classical I.Q., i.e., as reached by mental ages over actual ages, the sigma of which works out at 24, and the standard score I.Q., which accepts 16. The difference is, of course, that by the latter 15.9% of people will be above an I.Q. of 116 and by the former the same percentage will be found above 124. It is a matter either of adjusting our thinking to the culture-fair notion that I.Q.'s above, say, 120, are not quite as rare as we have thought, or of bringing all tests to a standard score I.Q. with a sigma deviation falling at 116 and 84.

The point is that in general a standardization has what values we like to give it. We can divide the raw range between freezing and boiling into 180 units as in Fahrenheit or 100 as in Celsius. Nevertheless, there are two ways in which one standardization may be better than another: It may have some relation to important external events, as in placing the freezing of water at 0°; and it may have more convenient calculating properties, as the decimal system does relative to the duodecimal. In psychology we have scarcely reached the stage where much guidance can be gathered from either. We may use stens rather than stanines because the former fits our decimal thinking, and we may fix the average I.Q. at 100, but there are few other signs of such guidance.

There is one area, however, where we see promise of getting a true zero, as mentioned above under scaling, and that is in measuring states and situations. If the modulation model, $S = sL$, holds, as the recent work of Cattell and Brennan (1983) suggests it does, at least for anxiety and depression, then we have not only a true zero to be fixed on a state scale, but also a zero to be fixed in the continuum of provocative situations for the given psychological state (see Chapter 15). This is a zero s_k (modulator value), and since from a good sample of life situation s_k's we can find a nonstimulating situation, this may also suggest a numerical unit for standardization.

The particular standardization concept with which we shall close, however, is that indicated in the footnote on page 98, by the contamination of fluid intelligence in a crystallized intelligence measure. Logically we are dealing with the reciprocal situation to that of weighting subtests to get a pure factor score. There we used the multiple R to combine; in the case of a measure that is contaminated by something we do not want we are using a partial correlation to get rid of the contaminator. What does that do in terms of going from the combined raw score to a standard score on the element we want? Obviously, since partialling out will reduce the variance, according to the variance in the parceled variable (say, motivation in the case of intelligence), the standardization table will be shifted to a new base. As a practical matter it may be true, as Spearman claimed to show, that *capacity to perceive relations* is little affected by motivational effort over a reasonable range of motivation, while other abilities, such as fluency, speed, and perhaps visualization, *are* affected by motivation level. Accordingly, we should ideally parcel out and get rid of motivation contamination from ability, just as reciprocally we aim in the MAT to get rid of ability contamination in motivation.

The procedures for partialling out ability from motivation scores are more adequately discussed under Motivation Measurement in Chapter 13. The converse is practically never done, but as a general problem, and in relation to standardization purposes, we may note that two ways of correcting have been tried: 1) parceling out ability from motivation by getting a separate score for each person for ability in the way just discussed; and 2) ipsatizing scores over all interests measured through any one vehicle. The first requires that an estimate be obtained of the person's ability, e.g., memory, and of its correlation with each interest measure, and that we partial it out (which can be done by a table from the memory score). Then, with this "decontaminated" score we would look in a sten or other standardization table made up for decontaminated scores. The second requires that we bring each person, over *all* his or her interests measured by memory (or other vehicle), to the same mean (semi-ipsatization) or to both the same mean and sigma (full ipsatization) as anyone else. Let us note that though the problem has been ignored, any one of the numerous paired-preference design tests now in use actually inevitably yields an ipsatized score. Thus, in the simplest case, if all items represent just *two* major interests, it is easy to see that the score on one, A, is the complement to the score on the other, B, because the total (A + B) must remain constant. Thus A and B will correlate −1.0.

There are psychological as well as statistical truths to be discussed, in Chapter 13, regarding this form of scoring as it concerns motivation. But from the point of view of standardization it suffices if we note that we typically follow in practice a *double* standardization with such tests. First, we enter an ipsatizing table with the person's total score for all tests with the device, e.g., memory, autism, GSR, and read off his or her percentages in each field of interest. Second, we take this figure for the given interest and look up his or her score in a normatizing table (standardizing across people). (Note that with regard to using vehicle devices, such as memory, we must go out *deliberately* to ipsatize, by use of the ipsatizing table procedure above. But with *preference* tests the ipsatization is already done by the time we get the score, with which we enter the normatization table.) The standard score so obtained will naturally have some peculiar properties compared to the ordinary normatized score. First, the sum of all interests of one person will be the same as another's, i.e., it will be no use looking experimentally for differences in total interests. Second, the correlations of one interest with another, carried across all interests, will average significantly negative (actually l/n-l where there are n interests paired in all possible ways). This is perhaps the most striking, though by no means the only, instance of the particular form of a standardization procedure affecting the kind of results one can get by subsequent analyzing of data.

Our concern so far has been with continuous scales, produced for example by items that overlap, or by weighted subtests, etc., but there are also categorical, classifying scales, which are often not even ordinal or are nonparametric in that

no distribution is known or assumed among them. Such procedures are, in simple form, as old as history (the Old Testament records classification by a "shibboleth") and in nonordinal form are used by the diagnosing psychiatrist. The ordinal use was perhaps first shaped for psychologists by Burt (1917) whose Draw-a-Man test was incorporated by Cattell (1936, p. 128) using the notion of a median specimen product for each year of age. This was handled in a somewhat less "wholistic" way in Goodenough's use of Draw-a-Man not as a drawing test but as an intelligence test (Chapter 8). The principle in a wholistic standardization can only be that of empirically producing representative patterns and leaving to human judges the judgment of resemblance of a given case to the standardized case. Where something like age is not available (as in Burt's drawing test for fixing the originals), one must fall back on judges for the point scale itself, as Thurstone did with attitude statements and Flanagan and other military psychologists in ranking "critical incidents" for criterion performance. This "wholistic scaling" is little different from the "wholistic categorizing" in the psychiatrist's pigeonholing of diagnostic cases.

These procedures have in general not had very good psychometric properties, in validity and dependability, on either the pattern scale production or its use. Judgments of paintings, essays, and musical productions and performances can be aided by median representatives and practiced judges, but remain poor. One wonders if a computer weighting of pattern elements and their interactions may not be the answer. Indeed, some heroic attempts *have* been made in ordinal scaling to use mathematical functions of elements in the patterns, a notable case being Ellis Page's tolerably successful experiment in scoring essays by computer and Art McKenna's scoring of drawings.

Incidentally, throughout this section, by reason of scaling and scoring being interwoven problems, we have necessarily trespassed somewhat on Chapter 6's scoring discussions, but in Chapter 6 the emphasis is more on practical procedures in scoring.

ATTEMPTS, IN THE SIMPLEX AND PAN-NORMALIZATION PRINCIPLES, AT SCALES ADEQUATE FOR FURTHER CALCULATION

The primary concern of this chapter is really standardizations and norms, but, obviously, *unless* we get equal interval scales standardizations will be distorted. And without the further property of ratio scales (absolute zero), certain ratio comparisons of standardized scores across tests and situations cannot be made. In the presence of other scientists psychologists must blush at continuing with the fantasy of making calculations with scales which still lack the properties necessary for such calculations. Meanwhile, there have been available for nearly 20 years two models by which, with some work to refine and apply them, the psychologist might move on from this embarrassing situation.

The first—pan-normalization—begins with the general proposition already stated above: that multiply determined dimensions, i.e., those into which many independent contributors enter, are likely to be normal, in an integrated, single species population. Most psychologists accept this, finding pragmatically that the assumption of normality very rarely gets contradicted by untoward outcomes. Pan-normalization, however, proceeds further than transforming raw scores to normalized scores in a single group. It requires transformations that maximize the approach to normalization *simultaneously over a universe of samples and populations* (hence "pan-"). That is to say, the rescaling which gives a normal distribution in the upper half of, say, a group of children all exactly 10 years old should be the same

as that which gives a normal distribution in the lower half of, say, a sample all exactly at 12 years of age. In other words, where the raw score ranges overlap, the scale transformation chosen should maximize the degree of it to a normal curve in both groups. An initially imperfect computer program has been worked out by Brennan (see Cattell & Brennan, 1985), which begins with two or more sets of data using a particular raw score scale, each set being from an integrated population and overlapping in some degree in raw score levels with the other(s). It then aims to bring about a transformation of raw scores that will maximize the normality of distribution, simultaneously evaluated over each of the different sets of data. It is promising but requires further research.

The second insufficiently tried approach to equal interval scales is that based on the *relational simplex* theory. This theory is based on the postulate that more relations in nature are linear than otherwise. Since a correlation between two variables that are truly linear in relation is reduced if one of them is transformed to a nonlinear form, the mean correlation of one variable with many will tend to be reduced if it is rescaled to give more nonlinear relations. A variable is most probably at its correct scaling, therefore, when the particular way in which it has become scaled gives the *highest* mean correlation with variables with which it has any significant correlation at all. This can be seen from another angle in terms of the improvement of magnitude that occurs in correction of correlations for attenuation, since "error" distortion of the true scores can be seen as departure from correct scaling.

The best equal interval scaling for a variable can be found by this examination of correlations, however, only by trial and error, stretching it here and contracting it there, in transformations from the raw score to trial scale units. There is no way of finding a maximum, for example, by differential calculus. One has to proceed empirically with sequential transformations until the highest mean r with a stratified sample of the universe of related variables is found. Fortunately, computer programs are possible for going systematically through possible transformation "distortions," as Lingoes (1966) has shown. To avoid specific biases in small samples, a moderately large number of variables is needed and the scale transformations would be continued to the finding of a maximum mean correlation of each variable in turn with all the others. That is to say, one would go through an iterative process with the mean r in the triangular matrix being the criterion at each step. With too small a sample of variables there might be a risk of maximizing through all scales *agreeing* on some distortion of units at the same level, but this becomes increasingly improbable with a widely chosen sample. The approach would be impracticable without high speed computers, and there are further technical aspects that must be left for discussion elsewhere (Cattell, 1963a, 1973a). But the above may clarify the central principle of the *relational simplex theory*, which is that true units are reached when the relationships become clearest (a simplex), since in general faulty units will tend to obscure any systematic relation.

Initially, the relational simplex principle is one for transforming raw score units into equal interval units, across the given range of raw scores. But it also has possibilities for the second problem: that of detecting absolute zeros on various scales. Imagine that one correlated air pressure with temperature, in a closed mechanical system that would freely admit air if the pressure should fall below a certain point (creating a true zero to the pressure range). Then (by the joint action of Boyle's and Charles's laws), the r would be very high over all ranges until the temperature fell beyond the regression value corresponding to that zero. The moment the correlated range fell below that value, the onset of decline in r would thus signal the appearance of an absolute zero in the one variable. (It will be realized that our raw score scale for pressure would have values ranging below that point.)

However, there are other approaches to be considered to the detection of an absolute zero in a psychological scale, where the raw score scale one has made up is liable either to register zero *before* true zero is reached for the state or trait or to register some positive value at a point where true zero *has* already been passed. (This apart from the special case which Nesselroade and Reese (1973) points out: that all *change* scores necessarily have a true zero.) Thurstone (1928) pointed out one approach in his article, "The Absolute Zero in Intelligence Measurement." Three principles for finding an absolute zero have been suggested by Cattell (1972b). They may be designated: 1) repeated measurement steps; 2) inherent properties; 3) a secondary use of the relational simplex principle. The first is not too promising and is left for study in the place indicated. The last has been discussed above. The second branches into four forms: 1) that the amount of fluctuation of a given trait will be proportional to its absolute score; 2) that the magnitude of dispersion (sigma) of a trait in various populations will (in part) be proportional to the absolute (mean) level; 3) that rate of change, e.g., growth, or learning modification, of a trait will (in part) be a function (perhaps nonlinear) of its absolute level; and 4) that in some cases the magnitude of the inherent property is a simple function of time or age. If sediment deposits in a lake at one inch per year, and we know the stream depositing has run in for only 10 years, the true zero for that kind of deposit, in a boring core with obscure visual boundaries, is actually 10 inches down. Psychological examples of this last method might occur in organic disease processes, where the score on "impairment" needs fixing on an absolute scale.

Most attention has been given to principle 2, specifically in regard to the modulation effect of situations on states. When we make up, for example, an anxiety scale, it will be uncertain, in, say, a 100 raw score scale, whether a true zero on anxiety is perhaps, at a raw score of, say, 8, or whether a zero on the scale still represents an appreciable amount of anxiety. The essence of the modulation theory approach has been sketched above, but there are assumptions (Cattell, 1963, 1972, 1973) too complex to make explicit at the tail end of this section, and which will be handled in Chapter 15 on state measurement. Practicing psychologists may perhaps feel that the amount of concern we have shown for getting assurance of equal interval and even absolute scales has led us excessively into "academic" issues. It is not so if psychology is to make progress as a science, for unless the necessary serious research is done soon on equal interval and ratio scale design, practitioners will remain deprived of diagnostic and predictive laws that could lift them to a higher level of professional potency.

SUMMARY

"Standardization" has too long been considered and developed only "over people." Nowadays, with more regard for states and for situations, a comprehensive model is necessary applicable to all dimensions. Indeed, even the standardization over people cannot be properly understood without considering variance also from the other sources of "ids." The Basic Data Relation Matrix, or Data Box, recognizes five sets of ids—people, situations, observers, etc.—any psychological event being a combination formed by one from each series. From the Data Box one sees that standardizations can be made

from measures over single sets or over the variance of combined sets, thus offering "higher and lower degree" standardizations.

In standardization using scales referring to a continuous dimension, raw scores are given standardizations either in ranks, e.g., centiles, or in standard score intervals; z scores, T scores, stens, staves, etc. The relations of these two *may* assume normal distribution, with z scores and centiles in a fixed relation, as in *n-stens*, or be free to depart from that assumption, as in *d-stens*.

The calculations of norms have certain detailed intricacies, e.g., in intrapolation and extrapolation, fixing the central value of a slice in the normal curve, handling tied ranks, handling empty intervals in skewed distributions, recognizing lepto- and platykurtic distributions, etc., that a psychometrist ultimately needs to be familiar with.

It is important to be clear as to what the reference population is on which any standardization sample is based. Also, to get the improvement of a stratified sample, as distinct from a random sample, one must know the proportion of subgroups in the reference population. Care in stratification is more important than magnifying sheer sample size—at least, once a tolerable number (2,000-10,000 in most kinds of test) is reached. Although substandardizations for men and women, minorities, classes, undergrads, etc., are useful adjuncts needed for special purposes, most uses of tests in estimating relative real life performances call for ruling out "race, creed and color." Two classes, however, need special bases—age, and, sometimes, sex—and this means either separate norm tables or "allowance" tables.

Under age one can have either cross-sectional or cursive norms. From these one can make further age standardizations in terms of ecogenic and epogenic curves. The latter heed the character of a particular historical epoch. Incidentally, the fact that most norms change with epoch makes a standardization on, say, 5,000, made every 10 years, more satisfactory than one on, say, 50,000 made only every 40 years. Traditional intelligence tests (Binet, Simplex, WAIS, etc.) in any case have "creeping norms" due to changing educational effects on crystallized intelligence, but culture fair norms have shown higher and virtually complete constancy over decades.

The study of scaling in test construction is best made in conjunction with standardization, since test construction affects the latter. Scaling and the test properties related to it have been excellently worked out by a generation of psychometrists on the *itemetric model*. A very thorough treatment of the itemetric equations and the principles of test construction in the domain is available in the classical surveys by Lindquist (1961) and Torgerson (1958) and texts by Coombs, Cronbach, Ferguson, Frederiksen, Guilford, Gulliksen, Luce, Nunnally, Suppes and others, whence a perspective only on essentials is given here.

Functional testing is different from itemetric testing in resting on structural concepts in the person, as well as in the test. The main concepts in structured testing scaling are those associated with factor score estimation from variously weighted subtests and the partialling out of unwanted factors from distributions.

In addition to scales based on the assumption of continuous dimensions, there are categorical and nonparametric scalings without assumptions of continuity, ranking, or distribution properties. These (and *some* continuous scales) may be handled by reference to "representative types," as in psychiatric diagnosis or evaluating drawings, musical compositions, essays, etc., in which the significance of a total *pattern* is implicit. However, the alternatives of scoring by continuous dimensions or by types is probably better handled at a later stage of operations than the test construction and standardization by critical samples—in fact, by principles set out in Chapters 2 and 23.

The advance of psychology as a true science, as well as more sophisticated practice, has been brought to a standstill by failure of measurement to progress beyond categorical and ordinal to equal interval and absolute scales. Two principles —*pan-normalization* and the *relational simplex*—have been proposed for progress to equal intervals and three (plus the relational simplex again) for reaching absolute zeros. One of the latter—the modulation principle—has been shown to be practicable for absolute scaling of psychological *state* scales. Extensive and programmatic research is needed before these can actually provide better scales for most tests with which practice is concerned.

Some further practical aspects of scoring in relation to scaling are taken up more suitably in the next chapter, as well as in the chapters on special testing areas, and finally in some more advanced discussions in Chapters 7 and 23.

CHAPTER 6

Selecting, Administering, Scoring, Recording, and Using Tests in Assessment

Raymond B. Cattell

ALL-ROUND PROPERTIES OF TESTS TO BE CONSIDERED IN SELECTION

Psychologists who put first things first, as we have aimed to do in this book, will understand validity, reliability and standardization and, hopefully, put them before convenience, brevity, and machine aid in scoring, valuable though these latter are. However, one must point out that it has unfortunately been true that better diagnostic methods are sometimes not used, e.g., objective tests in place of questionnaires, because they are harder to give or score. One can expect, fortunately, that if a test is more potent it will in due course get such attention to improving scoring methods, etc., as will bring it, as far as possible, into routine use.

The number of psychological tests available today is fabulous, as a perusal of Buros's *Mental Measurements Yearbook* and many test catalogues will show. A prelim-

inary condensation is therefore needed, by clear principles, in each area, and thus has been attempted by the authors in Part II of this book, area by area. There they apply the special standards needed in each. However, there remain some general principles of selection, scoring, etc., deriving from the theoretical bases in the preceding chapters, that are universal and can best be discussed here. In particular, we can discuss the balancing of the virtues of validity, reliability, standardization, administration time, convenience, scoring, recording, and the provision of criterion and supportive information for sound interpretation, covered in the preceding chapters.

First let us look in Table 6.1 at the comprehensive classification of tests. It is interesting to compare it with the classification of traits, states, and situations in the tables in Chapter 3 and with the analysis of test dimensions in Cattell and Warburton (1967, p. 76) summarized in Table 6.1 here, whereby the reader will acquire a truly comprehensive view of the taxonomy of psychological tests.

Table 6.1 is self-explanatory, though we may point to the need for keeping in mind the clear distinction between structured *unitary trait* tests, e.g., for fluid intelligence, surgency, superego, and *special purpose* tests (IIb and IIIb in Table 6.1), which already provide in a single instrument the prescribed mixture for a particular selection purpose, e.g., for selecting machine operators, guards, suicidal depressives. We would argue that the justifications for special-purpose tests, concretely validated against criterion group differences by a discriminant function weighting, or weights from a specification of performance, are fewer than some prac-

TABLE 6.1

Classification of Available Tests by Trait Structure and Modality

A. TRAITS

I. Cognitive Modality

1) Abilities and Aptitudes
   Intelligence Tests, Culture-Fair and Traditional,
   Specific Aptitude (Primary Ability) Tests
2) Achievement and Proficiency
   Scholastic Achievement, General and Specific
   Proficiencies in Specific Occupations
   Proficiencies in Specific Hobbies, etc., e.g., Athletics

II. Temperament Modality

General Personality Dimensions
   (a) Oriented to Unitary Traits
      Questionnaire Scales. Multifactor
      Objective Test Batteries. Multifactor
      Questionnaire Scales. Single Factor, e.g., Anxiety
      Objective Test Batteries. Single Factor
   (b) Oriented to Special Purposes (Composites)
      Questionnaires, e.g., Neuroticism Scale
      Objective Tests, e.g., Battery for Officer Selection

III. Dynamic, Interest Modality

Dynamic Structures, Conflict
   (a) Oriented to Unitary Traits
      Questionnaire, Preference Statement Tests
      Objective Motivation Measurement Tests, e.g., MAT, SMAT
      Measures of Conflict Adjustment
   (b) Oriented to Special Purpose Areas
      Questionnaire, Check List, e.g., Strong and Kuder Tests

B. STATES

   Questionnaires, e.g., on Anxiety, Clyde Mood Scale and Curran's 8-State Battery
   Objective Tests, e.g., Scheier's 8 Parallel Form Anxiety Battery

C. SITUATIONS

   Family Atmosphere Dimension Measures
   Intrafamilial Attitudes
   Child Upbringing Practices
   Social Worker Scales for Evaluating Homes

titioners assume. Their advantages are that they can be relatively short, require no further computation from parts, and can often be administered even by a foreman or a clerical worker. Their disadvantages are, first, that they are "blind," i.e., unable to tell the psychologist on which trait the candidate is particularly succeeding or failing. This lack restricts the knowledgeable psychologist's capacity to extrapolate by personality laws into future outcomes. Second, the weights of the needed components for the best criterion prediction may change with sample or epoch without one being aware of it or able to adjust for it. Third, the results can be used for no other purpose, whereas a profile on basic personality traits and primary abilities can be taken from the file for several uses. Nevertheless, up to the recently increased understanding of functional testing, the appeal of immediate convenience has kept special-purpose tests fashionable somewhat beyond their real aptness.

In Table 6.2 are summarized the main points one needs to keep in mind in choosing a test. (As stated, these are general; Chapters 8 through 21 below give the further experience valuable in specific areas.) The chooser of tests today needs to have his points as complete and clearly in focus as a buyer does the points of a horse when dealing with a horse trader. The points specifically concerned in *administration* are given separately later in Table 6.3.

In regard to the ten points in Table 6.2, some interactions are to be considered. An instance would be balancing 2—a high level of reliability-validity, proportional of course to testing time—in its interaction with 6 and 9—getting maximum prediction from a limited available time. As discussed elsewhere, more information and prediction are gained from an hour given to measuring, say, 12 independent personality and ability factors with the lower reliability of 5 minutes each than by giving the whole hour to one factor and thereby getting very high reliability.

One may note also that older tests will tend to have more concrete criterion relevances, but, being older, they are more likely to be prestructural tests, using rule-of-thumb relevances, as in Rorschach, that cannot be brought into relation with personality structure and theory based on multivariate experimental research. As for point 10, it is to be expected in all such arts and sciences as medicine, engineering, and psychology, that a test will be considered "difficult to use" by those who graduated before it came into use. Experience suggests that few psychologists pick up new techniques *from reading as individuals*, and that workshops are for most the necessary solution.

Current traditional training programs in the skills of test administration are not always geared to test progress and must be regarded as in transition. For example, only the most up-to-date courses prepare the student for the growing use of automation. Again, few get adequate training in the *objective* personality test batteries, such as the O-A Battery (even on one or two "token" factors in the Kit, of outstanding practical importance, such as U.I.24, anxiety, U.I.32, exvia-invia). There has been neglect also of the clinical need for continuous monitoring, and the tests adapted thereto, such as the 8 Parallel Form Anxiety Battery, the Neurotic Regression (U.I.23) battery and so on (see, however, Karoly & Steffens, 1980). The disproportion between demanding of a student almost a semester's training in giving the Binet or its derivates as individual tests for just one factor, g_c, while allowing the researcher to pick up the Nesselroade repeat anxiety state test or the O-A Handbook and march straight in to give a test of 8 to 10 different personality factors with scarcely any practice surely indicates an astigmatism that some college test and measurement courses still need to rectify.

In a rapidly changing technology some lag is inevitable, but surveys suggest that the most general and pervasive emphasis

TABLE 6.2

Points in Selecting a Test

1) Does it have demonstrated *concept validity* (Chapter 4), so that it is functional for application of psychological laws regarding personality and ability structure?

2) Are its psychometric properties of *consistency* (reliability, homogeneity, efficiency, etc. [Chapter 4]) given for adequate samples?

3) Is its basic *standardization* adequate, and does it have substandardizations (or corrective tables) for age and sex?

4) Is there a firm basis for standardization in the nature of the *scoring*? Multiple choice tests have a conspection coefficient of 1.0, but *open-ended* tests, e.g., the TAT, have low values of r_c (Chapter 4), as also do the assessments of psychiatrists using classification systems like the DSM. Open-ended test scoring is, however, not absolutely synonymous with poor conspection, since lists of meaning of most possible responses can be provided, e.g., in the Holtzman form of the Rorschach. Included in this area of evaluation is also "In a speed test are the items reliably placed in order of difficulty?," "Is the vocabulary 'safe' and the behavioral realm appropriate for the age or minority group?"

5) Does the test have a sufficiency of parallel forms—A, B, C, etc.—including adaptations to low literate subcultures, e.g., like E and F in the 16 P.F.? Parallel forms, though costly to construct, are valuable a) to the researcher (experiment-control groups, immediate repeat measures) and b) to the practitioner, in monitoring therapy, in giving shorter or longer tests.

6) Is the length of the test appropriate? Naturally, there is a great temptation in practice to use short tests. Relative reliability and validity are a direct function of length (Chapter 4). It is a fact that Form A of the 16 P.F. is used each year about 10 times as frequently as B, C, and D together. This means that most practitioners feel they can give only 2-3 minutes to each primary personality factor (average total time 38 minutes)! In cases on which much hinges it would be more professionally satisfactory to reach the reliability at least of giving A + B (for which norms are given). The character in a test which we might call "extensibility" (several equivalent forms) is to be prized because it allows the user to reach the maximum reliability and validity when his time allowance permits extension.

7) Is the test well supplied with tables of *relevances*? As we have seen (Chapter 4), the expression "concrete validity" is really meaningless except for special-purpose tests, and "relevance" is more apt. To say that an intelligence test has concrete validity because it correlates .5 with ability to learn Greek involves the gratuitous assumption that we *know* that this ability is so much involved in Greek. Possibly it is memory that is principally involved and criterion *r* as high as .5 actually means that the supposed intelligence test is subtantially contaminated with ability to memorize.

When tests are well founded on (concept) validity against a unitary trait, it is more correct to speak of their *relevance* to this, that or the other concrete criterion. In Chapter 4 the *utility coefficient* has been defined as a measure of the general degree of relevance of a particular factor, and other things being equal it will pay to concentrate on tests of high (but independent) relevance in life. The forms in which knowledge of relevance are made available are mainly a) specification equations, and b) profiles for occupational groups, clinical categories, etc., but also c) age trends, d) prognoses in treatment, e) degrees of inheritance, f) importance in marriage, and countless other life relations.

It is an astonishing commentary on the organization of psychology that with some 30,000 practitioners in the U.S.A., the effort to obtain these valuable quantitative probabilities, profiles, specification equations for structured tests in common use has yet scarcely been made. The 16 P.F. and its associated trait measures in the CAQ, HSPQ, etc. have barely achieved more than a dozen reliable specification *equations*, though they and the MAT have reached a considerable number of occupational and clinical *profiles*. The MMPI has accumulated many profiles for clinical types. The Rorschach, though possessing no specification equations, has a heap of associations of specific signs to specific diagnoses. Intelligence tests have correlations abundantly and redundantly worked out to concrete relevances. But beyond the above tests the writers of this book have been unable to find more than half a dozen tests concerning which predictions on more than three or four criteria (at most) have been precisioned. Among these practical *relevance values*, as we may comprehensively call them, should be counted also the readiness of the test to be scored for higher order factors, from the initial primaries. This secondary calculation makes it unnecessary to use additional tests. For example, a crystallized intelligence score can be obtained from the primary abilities in Hakstian's CAB, making a WAIS unnecessary, and extraversion, anxiety (neuroticism), psychoticism, and other secondaries can be obtained from the CAQ. The combination of primaries and secondaries by the same test makes *depth psychometry* (Cattell, 1973) possible.

8) Does the test have defenses against faking, accumulation of response sets, e.g., position and acquiescence effects (see Scott, 1963, 1965), motivational distortion by diverse social and other desirability situations, mutual factor contamination, etc. available? A motivational distortion scale, as in the 16 P.F., MMPI, etc. is a first crude beginning, but more sophisticated methods, applicable to all factored scales, are discussed in Chapter 23. It is, unfortunately, an understatement to say that nine-tenths of all tests in Buros' compendium lack such aids.

9) Do the tests provide data that, when needed, can be used in other fields? This includes the notion of whether it can be clearly used with other tests, without overlap, to give maximum prediction. It was a feature of the early, theory-less, "muddling through" (or *not* through) stage in test construction that clinicians, educators, and industrial, occupational psychologists developed tests useful and meaningful *only* in their own areas, e.g., the Strong Interest Blank in the occupational interest field. The modern critical and constructive approach to this past tradition has been (Jensen, 1981; Cattell, 1936, 1946, 1973a) to emphasize that the same "client" steps into all three areas of consultation and that, by using specification equations from the same central personality and ability measures applied to the different situations, both insight and economy would be assisted. In the widest sense this even requires that some universality be demonstrated across nations and cultural subgroups for the major source traits, but that is, perhaps, more of an aid to the universality of science than to practice within one country.

10) Are the administration and scoring susceptible to technical aids? If a test is excellent on the preceding nine points, no good professional psychologist would reject it because it puts demands on his skill in administration and his understanding of complex scoring—any more than a good surgeon would reject an operation of known high promise because of its technical demands upon him. Indeed, many simple questionnaires and tests, e.g., Draw-a-Man, are such as any layman could "administer" and any high school child (or tea-cup reader) score. The psychologist really vindicates his or her training when meeting the challenge of a truly technically demanding test. However, there remain the problems of consumption of time, of avoiding human inaccuracies and the need, perhaps, to get out a result before the client leaves. Most of the more advanced tests have well-constructed keys, avoiding human inaccuracies, or use a tape for instruction and timing, as in the O-A Battery, and have installations at computing centers for instant calculation of relevances, or for "narrative reports."

---

in training courses is on cognitive tests, with comparative neglect of the newer developments in the other two modalities—personality and motivation measures. Fortunately, various institutions now give summer refresher courses and short workshops which, for psychologists already possessing some experience in applied psychology, seem to function well.

As for use of tests in published research, as distinct from practice, some instances of indefinite results suggest that researchers as much as practitioners need attention to test administration. However natural it may seem to them to go straight into the use of a familiar laboratory test, they need to recognize that they cannot hope reliably to give certain group psychometric tests without the practice provided by two or three rehearsals. The word rehearsal is advisedly used because the role of tester is more than that of "experimenter" and involves the practice appropriate to a part in a play. While the practice that is still occasionally found of giving a whole semester of instruction for one or two tests is absurd—if only because of the half dozen distinct *areas* (modality divisions) of testing (Table 6.1 on p. 106) for which practice is equally needed—and probably excessive, practice in the art *is* necessary. For example, four or five "runs," in an internship-like situation, would not be excessive for tests like the GATB, the O-A Battery, the Rorschach, the MAT, the TAT, etc.

TESTS FROM AN ADMINISTRATION VIEWPOINT: ISSUES OF GROUP VS. INDIVIDUAL TESTING, TIME DEMAND, SUPERVISION, SKILLS, AND APPARATUS USE

It perhaps goes without saying that the first consideration in administration is getting the cooperation of the subject or client. Cooperation must not be taken for granted, and the establishment of rapport deserves some preliminary effort. The subject may come with unhappy recollections of school examinations, or a carryover of attitudes to the indignities of medical examination. His or her status as an equal collaborator with the psychologist in a useful inquiry should be agreeably discussed. Even so, the attitudes systematically differ in a clinic, in school, in industry and in, say, a prison population. Incidentally, allowances for unavoidable distortions of scores from these situations are discussed under trait view theory, Chapter 23.

The importance of motivation in getting accurate test results has, in one sense, been exaggerated, notably in declaring that higher results in some groups on *intelligence* tests are the consequence of greater competitive interest and motivation. The early work of Spearman showed that capacity to perceive relations—as distinct from several other cognitive performances such as fluency, cancellation, etc.—cannot be much improved by effort. The results of others also showed that children retain very much their same rank order despite increased monetary rewards for higher performance. On the other hand, the results of Blackburn and Cattell and others giving Benzedrine to depressives showed that unstimulated depressives score well below their true intelligence levels and that their scores rise significantly with medication. Administrative awareness of mood and motivation effects, and skill or special measures in minimizing distortion of results from them therefore remains impor-

tant. A counsel of perfection would be to give a psychological-state test, e.g., the Curran or the Barton (see Chapter 15), and the Motivational Analysis Test along with the intelligence test and partial out the effects of the former from the "intelligence score" according to a behavioral equation for the given type of test situation.

The very young and the middle-aged or elderly seem to offer the greatest difficulty in test administration, the first for obvious reasons, the second usually for reasons of status. Psychologists dealing with important business executives have experienced difficulty in getting them to do intelligence tests, and I understand from some psychologists who have tried that politicians are still more wary. Incidentally, this was one reason for developing an intelligence scale within the Humor Test of Personality (see Chapters 8 and 12), since these same executives will good-naturedly offer to express their tastes in humor. (Actually, perhaps because it is embedded in other scales in an omnibus test, psychologists seem to have done remarkably little to develop its use as a more acceptable intelligence test.)

The chief characteristics of tests themselves affecting their choice from an administration standpoint are listed in Table 6.3, which requires little explanation.

Regarding the first dimension—group or individual—I have pointed out that it has been a bit of prejudice that individual administration is always better than group (well proctored), although the reverse is often true. Indeed, in the development of test construction—since a group test can be given individually but not vice versa—the trend has been to make as many tests as possible group administrable. The historical development has been—particularly in objective personality tests (T-data, as in the O-A Kit)—that the validity of a new test has often been demonstrated first with individual administration and elaborate laboratory re-

TABLE 6.3
Considerations of Test Administration *per se* Involved in Evaluating or Preparing for a Test

1. Suitability for group and individual administration
2. Length, in items and time; distribution in parts of a battery
3. Required administrative skills, notably timing or absence of timing
4. Amount of apparatus required
5. Adaptation to subjects' reading and other skills; likelihood of test sophistication effects
6. Anticipating retesting, the availability of alternative, equivalent forms

search gear and the drive of progress has been—in these objective, trait and state measures—to create adaptations that are group administrable. The handbooks, both for the O-A Battery Kit in personality and the MAT in motivation measurement, record tests that had to be ingeniously (and also, sometimes with rather lowered validity) recast from the individual test form employed in research into the group administrable form that practice finds vastly more convenient. The same has occurred with the Rorschach and, of course, intelligence testing, where various Binet items, performance form boards, and forms originally made for individual testing with young children have had to be modified to group administrable forms. The handbooks, in the case of the group O-A and the MAT batteries, specifically set out, however, certain subtests that cannot be adapted to group administration but are available as supplements to validity when the psychologist is able to do individual testing.

Individual testing is essential with defectives and most psychotics where, without it, gross misunderstandings of instructions would occur and proper attention would not be assured. Moreover, the test situation is then an "interview" in which extratest observations during the procedure can be made. On the other hand, as mentioned above, the tester can in the individual situation be biased by the look of the subject, and his stopwatch timing, or even patience, can vary from case to case, whereas the group situation at least makes the same allowances for all. Per-

haps a much more serious bias is that the teacher in every psychologist makes it difficult for him or her to refrain from helping lame dogs over stiles, and thus helping, by gesture, extra time, and subtle signals, certain intelligent-looking individuals "overachieve" relative to their real level.

The line between group and individual administration, as far as control is concerned, is in any case becoming less sharp because of increased resources in mechanical aids. The O-A Battery, for example, has instructions and timing on tape, plus group-adapted screen projections of stimuli, etc. Dreger's Pre-School Personality Questionnaire likewise presents a taped voice with standard intonations that permits it to be given at any rate to two or three youngsters at a time. Since experience shows that testing, even in mental hospitals, can be done, with certain aids, likewise in groups of two or three, such a doubling or trebling of psychological service efficiency is not to be despised. In this connection Eber's innovation of putting several subjects in the privacy of small "telephone booths," and communicating by visual screens and headphones has been a successful demonstration of what enterprise can do to reduce the community costs of mental health service. Krug's Chapter 7 has much to offer in this area. Regardless of this particular "booth" design or its success, there are many aids to efficiency of test administration that some psychologists have been slow to adopt, despite possible economies that would help to keep diagnostic and therapeutic service at a bearable, public-acceptable cost level. Here the percipient person will see the implications of the choice of tests according to the coefficients of *efficiency, utility,* and *universality* as proposed in the psychometric evaluations of Chapter 4.

The above discussion has essentially handled issues 3, 4 and 5 in Table 6.3, except that one might add that the amount of apparatus—audiovisual aids, and even electronic recording of response from each chair, in order to give also *immediate scoring*—is surely likely to increase in group testing in the near future. Ertl's use of a brain wave analyzer to produce an intelligence score is an enterprising example, except that, as Horn (1970) has shown, a sufficient demonstration that his index is one purely of g_f and g_c has not yet been given (see Chapter 8). However, it is evident that the present move toward instrumentation for more mechanized test administration and scoring will lead to more supplementation of behavioral measures by physiological measures, which have been shown (Cattell & Scheier, 1961; Cattell & Bartlett, 1971) to load state factors of anxiety, stress, etc., in a way adding appreciably to validity.

The second issue—the consideration of length and testing time in administration—has also been essentially handled earlier, and will come up again under "installations." Three of the earlier points could probably well be reiterated here: First, many testing practices and installations make a poor use of time by falling into a highly uneven distribution of time among the factors they wish to measure. For example, in predicting school performance it is known that the three-quarters of the total variance that *can* be predicted is about equally divided as one-quarter from intelligence, one-quarter from personality, and nearly one-quarter from dynamic traits (motivation) (Cattell & Butcher, 1968) (see Chapter 17). Yet, in attempting such predictions or analyzing causes of underachievement, it is not unusual for school psychologists still to use up the available hour or so with an intelligence test only.

Second, from omissions we must next turn to redundancies. For example, it is not necessary to give a crystallized intelligence test along with a measure of primary abilities like the CAB, since the former can be very accurately reached as a weighted sum of primaries (as in Dixon & Johnson, 1980, p. 93). And it is not necessary to give extraversion and neuroticism or anxiety scales along with the 16 P.F., since they are well covered in the latter as easily derived secondaries. There are also mutual weightings for going to and fro from the Guilford-Zimmerman to the 16 P.F. (Cattell & Gibbons, 1967), which makes it superfluous to give both tests. And since the CAQ comes from factoring MMPI-like items (along with other pathological items), practically all of the latter scores can be derived from the former and a large fraction of the former from the latter by mutual multiple regression tables (Cattell & Bolton, 1969).

The reality of instrument factors may sometimes definitely call for "apparent" redundancy. For example, a score on exvia-invia can be reached alternatively by questionnaires (16 P.F. or EPI or Barton's CTS) by the O-A Battery, and by the Humor Test, but each carries into the score some instrument factors of the given medium. Consequently, a researcher intent on the most valid possible measure of exvia-invia might well seek the central validity that comes from summing all three. Or again, superego strength, G, and self-sentiment development, Q_3, are measurable both by questionnaire, e.g., the HSPQ, and by objective motivation measures, in MAT and SMAT. In practice, with severe time demands, one might want to keep to one of the alternative instruments, but in research, to reduce instrument factor distortion, two or three media could well be used, without being guilty of redundancy in the sense used above.

The third and last point to make regarding testing time is that the institutional dispensers of requests for diagnoses are often quite unrealistic in how much expense of time they allow as appropriate. At the present stage of psychology it is a sheer daydream to imagine one can get a reasonably sure diagnosis of an individual's personality and motivation in an hour or even two. Indeed, a psychologist using older instruments cannot get comprehensiveness and good validity even in the four hours which insurance companies commonly allow the practitioner. It becomes just possible, however, for one well versed in principles of test selection. Incidentally, the provision of "list of acceptable tests" that certain authorities, e.g., HMSA and the V.A., issue is desirable and necessary, to avoid charlatanism from astrology, phrenology, and various crystal ball fads. But such lists obviously need to be kept up-to-date by consultants well immersed in research. One must sadly comment that, as far as the newer standards of functional testing here described are concerned, some of those lists are definitely dated.

TESTS FROM AN ADMINISTRATION VIEWPOINT: ISSUES OF LANGUAGE SKILLS, TEST SOPHISTICATION, REPEATED TESTING

Complete change of language, using the technique of "back translation" (Sakai translates Jones' test into Japanese; Robinson translates back into English)—a technique which can reveal possible falsities—has presented no problem in personality factor questionnaires. When the data are thus firm, their *structure*, as revealed by independent factoring (Cattell, Pichot, & Rennes, 1961; Cattell, Schroeder, & Wagner, 1969; Cattell, Seitz, & Rausche, 1971), stays very much the same. But factor *levels* may be (culturally or genetically) significantly different across peoples. With *traditional* intelligence tests,

however, the procedure of translation to compare I.Q. scores is quite unsafe, because of dependence of several subtests, e.g., synonyms and analogies, simultaneously on the relative meaning of *several* words, each shifting a little from any possible exact equivalence in translation.

In practice, rather than in research, it is *within* countries, with different subcultural and ethnic groups, that problems really arise. The item (for F factor) "Have you a debonair and gay disposition?" was answered by an 18-year-old black student in a New York school with a very indignant "No!" Interest tests, of course, change from other than vocabulary differences, namely, from greater epochal changes in the objects of interest than occurs in the substance of ability and temperament (general personality) measures. One would ideally like to see every test of importance issued in separate language editions suitable for the chief cultural subgroups. In this domain, Heather Cattell, Raymond, Danko, Campbell, and others in Hawaii, have experimented with a Hawaiian Creole (pidgin English of the Pacific) form of the High School Personality Questionnaire which is not in the ordinary sense a translation but a subgroup adaptation. As in the cross-national translations (e.g., Cattell, 1970a; Schumacher & Cattell, 1974), the same 14 factors were found, though with different emphases on variance on C, O, and Q_3. In this and other factored personality questionnaires language differences have affected structure only trivially, though life situation aspects are sometimes redesigned to the culture.

Although culture-fair intelligence scales do not require language, it is usual to give the *instructions* in the language of the group. However, especially with experienced anthropologists, it has proved readily possible to proceed wordlessly, by pantomime, as in a teaching game, though more examples may then be necessary.

A problem in the ordinary use of test

standardizations is that some members of, say, a class, have previous experience of a test while others have not. There is no evidence in personality and motivation (as contrasted with ability: see Chapter 8) tests that this affects scores, but it does seem to affect the time required (in an untimed test). More striking than the effect on the subjects is the effect of repetition on the administrator! It is noticeable that when psychologists repeatedly administer an objective test like the Binet or the O-A Personality Battery, the time they require shrinks significantly over the first three or four administrations, although the stopwatch time fixed for *elements* of subtests as given to subjects remains standard. Skill in presentation of objective tests evidently is susceptible to training.

This suggests we should not forget that, with regard to required skills in the test administrator, there is a very great difference between the questionnaire, on the one hand (untimed and having its instructions written on it for the subject), and the objective personality test, with apparatus and nicely timed sequences, on the other.* Most intelligence tests have an administrative complexity somewhere between the questionnaire and the objective personality test. But regardless of these differences in procedure there is one skill, as mentioned above, that is required in all administration: the ability to establish

rapport with subjects, in individual or group situations, and to generate the appropriate motivation. Sometimes the test instructions themselves contain remarks to remove obstacles; sometimes the handbook gives the testee additional suggestions. However, in the last resort it is up to the psychologist to see by proper greeting, a pleasant, well-lit examination room, and an "exhortation" adapted to the interests of the particular group of clients that he or she achieves good rapport.

Returning to the practice effects on *subjects*, we have noted that—in ability tests particularly—those can be considerable. Typically, improvement of average score continues with lessening increment up to the fifth or sixth readministration. Two forms, A and B, of an ability test, made as equivalent as possible, show higher numerical raw scores in the norms for whichever is given second (hence A to B order must be retained). This practice effect is no real improvement of intelligence but merely what Vernon has called *test sophistication* and others, e.g., Donaldson, "*testmanship.*" It comes through increased familiarity with layout, instructions, time allowance, etc. What one does about this depends on finding out something about the experiences of the particular subjects. With complete novices it may be desirable to give A and B and throw A away, as just a practice run. The culture-fair tests are as liable to test sophistication as culture-

---

*In the practice of timing tests, experience unfortunately shows that there are very few testers who can time a series of subtests, etc., without occasional disturbing errors and lapses of attention, using an ordinary stopwatch. A device which can be set at the prescribed time as the test starts, and which will make a sharp sound or flash as the period ends, is far better, since the administrator already needs both eyes and ears to take in all that is going on, as a monitor, in a typical group test situation. Incidentally, one must distinguish, in thinking of time and tests, between exactly timed tests, as such, and the introduction of some "time pressure" into those kinds of untimed tests in which a classroom period makes pressure to finish a desirable and permissible practical atmosphere. In questionnaires, for example, it is good to prevent too much straggling by having a

norm in mind and saying at intervals, "You should be at about Number X now." This is an unavoidable necessity if everyone is to move to the next class or get home, for if people are left absolutely to "take their time" a skewed distribution results in which some finish a 20-minute test in two hours!

In the last few years there has been a rapid growth of use of "instructions on tape," since this has the advantage of building the test timing into the total machinery of administration, while also delivering instruction in standard tones (but check, first, that your machine is running at standard rate!). It is important that this constancy of instruction be extended also to the voice quality of the items themselves, especially when they have to be given young children, as in the Pre-School Personality Questionnaire.

embedded ones. But they have now been more generously provided with pretest practice illustrations than formerly, to reduce this involvement.

The "telescopic" or extension principle of test construction that we have mentioned, i.e., making as many as A, B, C, D, and E equivalent forms (as in the 16 P.F.) has value in other conditions than those initially mentioned. The *dependability* coefficient, r_d, it will be remembered, concerns an immediate retest; the *stability* coefficient, r_s, a retest after a week or two (Chapter 4). Since studies separating states from traits began (Cattell, 1973a; Nesselroade & Reese, 1973; Barton, 1976; Spielberger, 1972), it has been realized that even true traits oscillate somewhat and, indeed, stability coefficients for a typical intelligence test over a few weeks may be no higher than .8. According to equation 4-4, if the immediate dependability is itself 0.9, this gives the intelligence trait itself a constancy, r_c, also of 0.9. Accepting an r_d of 0.9 and a standard deviation of 16 points of I.Q. the usual calculation for the probable error (P.E. $= .67456\sigma$) shows that there will be a 50/50 chance that a subject's score on retest will be within 5 points (plus or minus) of his first I.Q. determination.

This points to the need, for serious prediction, e.g., scholarship selection, of two or three time-spaced measures duly averaged. And in psychotherapy when health insurance regulations allow only 10 hours for both the diagnosis and the treatment and put financial pressure on shortening the diagnosis to give more time for therapy, we face an unrealism in the situation, for effective therapy depends on diagnosis. Almost all testing practice is presently undercutting the optimum fraction of total time that needs to be spent for accurate evaluation.

Most tests—except ability tests—are such that they can be safely readministered as *the same form* when more than a week or two separates the testings, with

no demonstrable effect from repetition *per se*. If this finding is sustained in the case of the psychologist's preferred personality or state test then parallel forms are scarcely needed. But there is another reason for parallel forms than this or the need for a larger test, namely, that tests need to fit conveniently into "administration units." There are tests that, for psychological reasons, need to exceed in length the 40-45 minutes of a classroom or consultation period, and whose design should therefore break them into suitable administrative lengths. Along with this goes the need to avoid fatigue and resulting deterioration of attention in young children, depressive patients, etc. This explains why the ESPQ—the Early School Personality Questionnaire—and the Scale 1 Culture-Fair are broken into *parts* smaller than the *forms* on which standardization is made. That is to say, there is recognition in design that administration and scoring packets are different. Of course, any test which can be broken into subtests can be given in bits, but *parts* are aimed at an externally demanded useful length. For example, they may be designed to be ten minutes short of the class period (that period itself being taken as the shortest in various school systems). Where this breaking down of *forms* further into *parts* has been done, it is usually for the attention span of younger or clinical subjects, and in recognition that forms in use today allow little time for mishaps in handing out forms, explaining to individuals who have difficulties, collecting answer sheets, etc.

SCORING IN RELATION TO TEST DESIGN AND STANDARDIZATION: FURTHER SOCIAL AND TECHNICAL CONSIDERATIONS

Scoring has been considered in relation to scaling and standardization. It is now necessary to look at it from some further viewpoints concerned with practice. (In doing so we shall necessarily overlap to some extent with Chapter 5.)

A question that arises in scoring and standardization of tests in research is "Do I need (in a 'one-testing comparison design') a control group, when I have available the mean and sigma of the whole stratified sample that went into the standardization?" For example, if one wished to find on what personality factors women drug addicts differ from "normals," would it not suffice to make comparisons with, say, Cattell and Green's (1961) thoroughly stratified sample of the nation's adult women?

It is probable that research results would be more dependable and less often contradictory if what we might call "double control" (or even "multiple control") were used. That is to say, one needs to use, on the one hand, the national, stratified sample and, on the other, a group that is "control" in not possessing the particular symptom of the "experimental" group but *matched with it in every other assessable parameter*. Thus, in investigating the differences of psychotics from normals, Cattell and Tatro's (1966) data on the O-A show state hospital psychotics to have highly significant differences from national norm "normals," but that significances are much reduced when the comparison is made with a control group taken from the locality and socioeconomic level from which these state hospital cases were recruited. It is a nice question whether one should rest conclusions on the second of these comparisons, thus "partialling out" poor economic conditions, or consider that borderline psychotic conditions are an inherent associate of poverty.

One might say that the second approach merely illustrates the traditional practice of selectively matching experimental and control groups on all but the independent variable (which is the same as using covariance analysis to allow for known, observed, ulterior differences). There is, however, a real difference between taking controls in the population from which the experimental group came and matching for all parameters one happens to think of, which often fall short of the totality of those operative. If one seeks *personality* causes of, say, school backwardness by matching the controls for intelligence, socioeconomic status, amount of absenteeism, etc., much of the real cause in personality gets lost, because the two last variables are much involved with personality. The root principle we need in the matching and parceling out procedures is that knowledge of *causal chains* must be established before parceling out this or that. To reach sound conclusions, we would argue that double control groups are always necessary, which amounts to having the local matched control (the correct subgroup reference standardization) and at the same time the standardization for the larger group to which the individuals belong—usually the national norms.

It has been pointed out (Chapter 5) that the inventive, open-ended test has increasingly given way to multiple choice, though many educators have bitterly protested that something is lost when a patterned product, say the essay, is dropped from scoring on grounds simply of greater conspection reliability in the multiple choice. Decisions on that issue must be left to educators, but in personality research it is certain that whole factors would be lost if inventive tests were not used. This may well be why the O-A Battery has some substantial factors for which no matches can be found in multiple choice questionnaire tests. Actually, inventive test answers can be made more conspectively reliable. It has been pointed out that when a list of "approved responses" has been supplied to psychologists, based on an exhaustive survey of answers spontaneously given by a large sample, the conspection coefficient of scoring agreement for "creative response" tests can be virtually as high as in multiple choice. But to make such scoring as quick and convenient as the machine scoring of multiple choice is quite another matter. Conceivably a computer *could* be programmed to run off a comparison of the inventive, open-ended answers with a coded list of "acceptables," but at present no one has found a way—other than by human inspection—to recognize and code for machine scoring the words or drawings spontaneously given.

A problem within multiple choice scoring concerns the relative desirability, in personality and similar scales, where alternatives are on a continuum—very much, moderately, little, not at all—of wider and narrower ranges and gradations, i.e., more or fewer choices. In the fifties the "forced choice," involving always just two alternatives, became fashionable. Many itemetric studies—reliable but often not taking in all the conditions—were made on this and on such matters as the effect of speeded and unspeeded presentation; of instructions to guess when uncertain versus not to guess; of forced choice with construction to get equally aversive items; of shorter, vaguer versus longer more precise definition of behavioral situations; of the form "I do so-and-so . . ." versus "Do you do so-and-so?"; of answering directly on the form versus on an answer sheet, etc. Regarding the last, one might venture to say that machine scoring from a subject-marked answer sheet has inevitably become so popular that, as we have said, psychologists tacitly accept a conspiracy of silence on its possible drawbacks. For less bright adults or younger children the immediate transference of responses to numbered spaces on an answer sheet is possibly as difficult a process as for the average person to fill in an income tax form! There are no really extensive studies on how much is lost at different ages, etc. of subjects through unreliability from this source. The general opinion is that it is very little, but there is room for more ingenuity in making answer sheets foolproof or slipproof. Meanwhile, when in doubt the psychologist does well to revert to having answers made on the test form itself and getting clerical help to transfer to answer sheets. In any case one should make an answer sheet spot check, in the case of borderline competent groups.

In regard to forced choice, the argument is that less time is taken per item with two alternatives than with three or four alternative responses, which are commonly supposed to be, but may not be, on a continuum. The work of Travers (1951) and others some years ago seemed at times to favor forced choice, but it overlooked and failed to investigate the buildup of "resentment" which seems to occur from the forcing and leads to carelessness, when people are repeatedly required to make coarser judgments than their feelings warrant.

Questions of speeded versus unspeeded administration go deeper than administration conditions. As pointed out earlier, they get into issues of what factors one is really out to measure. As mentioned, during Spearman's basic inquiries on the nature of intelligence, he responded to criticisms of timed (speeded) tests by showing that when all subjects were given time to complete the test the rank order of subjects was, within error limits, just the same as when they were speeded. However, these subjects were all of the same age, and the performance was a complex one. In other conditions (*vide* the Baltes-Horn debates on fluid and crystallized intelligence), a distinct general speed factor in the ability realm gets mixed into the measure—a factor important in simple cognitive procedures and tied to age.

Some of the intrusions of speed when one does not want to include it can be kept out by good grading of ability items in order of difficulty. Indeed, in ability tests, from the time of the age-calibrated Binet test onward, it has been considered good design to arrange items in order of difficulty, because it ensures that test time is not wasted wrestling with a difficult item while easier ones later are untouched. In the culture-fair tests, further, the timing is planned to be such (since brighter persons work faster in the same age group) that most people meet the items unsolvable by them just as they run out of time. In this design, the scorer has no need to defend the approximation of taking the right fraction of the number wrong from the number right (equation 5-5). Parenthetically, the Culture-Fair also reduces the effect of chance error by having (in Classifications at least) *two* out of five right instead of one. The likelihood of hitting the correct *two* out of five by chance is one in ten, as against one in five for the single choice item. Even this degree of intrusion of luck can be further reduced by the "principle of specious or meretricious appeal," as it may be called, which makes the wrong answer speciously more attractive on superficial grounds in a way that the confident insight of the more intelligent person discounts.

When it is absolutely necessary for everyone to complete all items, as in most personality and motivation tests, an untimed test is unavoidable, if only to accommodate to differences of reading speed. A bunch of subjects left to finish in their own time produce a time distribution badly skewed to the long end. For this reason the administration instructions in some tests, e.g., the 16 P.F., advocate that the administrator should call out the item number at which most subjects should be operating at a few given points in the time lapse.

Just as order of difficulty needs attention in ability test design, so in some *objective* personality tests that are timed it becomes necessary to check that, say, the first ten items are a proper "even" sample from, say, the full twenty. For example, the test may measure "the fraction of approved statements recalled relative to those not approved." In this case the recall has to be tested on the fraction which each individual has covered in part one (approval checking). It then becomes important to design the items in the first part so that the earlier and later are as far as possible psychologically equivalent. This is a special case within the general issue of the reliability of speeded tests.

It is inevitable in testing that some subjects will have missing answers on some items. Of course, this is not a problem in speeded tests, where the blanks are part of the unachieved score. In unspeeded tests, however, there is nothing to do but fill these in which chance probabilities, e.g., half of the blanks "right," or the group's average fraction right on that item, in a forced choice, or one-quarter or a group average where there are four answers. In research, where the effect on *correlations* is concerned, there are well-known alternatives: 1) the missing items correlation program; 2) estimating the probable score on the item or subtest from its regression on the rest of the items or tests; and 3) entering simply the probable, average score of all subjects as score of the individual who has omitted response.

RECORDING THE OPERATING WITHIN THE THREE FILE SYSTEM

The question of the best use of recorded, standardized score results can be pursued most comprehensively only with regard to each of the special areas of application. Chapters 16, 17, 18, 19, and 20 in particular are concerned with that. However, there are important *general* principles and practices, which can here be built directly on the above foundations of test psychometry in Chapters 4 and 5. Here we shall develop them in an introductory way, leaving to Chapters 7 and 23 that more precise and detailed statistical handling of test results and records by computers and relatively complex formulae which some psychologists will wish to master.

In proper perspective, the handling of test records and their interpretation is not just a statistical matter, but requires re-sort to all that psychology—particularly personality and motivation theory—can bring to bear. In interpretation and com-munication of records, a problem arises that we have already briefly met, namely, the need for two languages and proce-dures, in communicating with other psy-chologists on the one hand and the general public and the subject on the other.

The situation is no different from that in medicine, but whereas a higher level of popular education in medicine has brought the patient and his or her rela-tives to where a doctor can communicate even with technical terms, tolerably understood, the popularization of psy-chology has been accompanied by so many fads and fictions that a more untidy lan-guage exists. There are some respects —especially in explaining to the layman the meaning of statistics and probability, where the subject matter is at least as technical and complex as that of medicine. It is a serious charge against current prac-titioners that, in seeking to speak to the public (also in paperbacks!) in vague and fanciful terms, they have come to speak to one another in nothing more precise. Like the elocutionist hired to teach the Cockney millionaire a better class of Eng-lish, they have themselves ended up with the coarser dialect.

To illustrate the problem, let us con-sider a profile on the 16 P.F. and its bear-ing on, say, vocational guidance, being discussed with an adolescent and his par-ents. Each factor is set out on a profile sheet with its technical title, e.g., ego strength, surgency, premsia, ergic ten-sion, which convey a number of precise technical implications to the psychologist. Alongside are the popular labels (in this case, respectively, "emotionally stable," "happy-go-lucky," "tenderminded," and "tense"), which unfortunately mean mainly what each person likes to think they mean. To explain further how the blend-ing of scores on these source traits in the behavioral equation allow the psycholo-gist to give certain *probabilities* of, say, success in this or that occupation, is yet another difficulty.

The popular equivalent of a technical statement, if it is to be the best possible, is almost always decidedly more volumi-nous than the technical statement. Dr. X may tell Dr. Y that Johnny is a case of phenylketonuria, but in explaining to the parent, one word has to become perhaps a thousand. A development (see Krug, Chapter 7) that helps the practitioner con-siderably here is what has tentatively been called a case "narrative output." In its new form this is a computer program but it is virtually a "verbal case report" when composed by the psychologist. As pointed out elsewhere, it is a mistake to think that the narrative printout will be stilted or repetitive in style, for when the program has been created by a first-rate author it is difficult to make a confident distinction between the computer and the "freehand" case report; if anything, the former makes fewer slips in verbal em-phasis, etc. And the well-designed nar-rative output escapes the moments when the psychologist nods in writing the tenth report for the day.

Incidentally, a common cause of dismay in traditional case reporting is the sheer bulk and repetitiousness of what is said about a client (from sources of differing reliability). The thickening bundle of pa-pers is an appreciable obstruction to re-ferring to the essentials of the case itself and an almost total obstruction to re-search across cases. The argument for re-ports based on structured testing is that they lead to a compactness of core mea-sures and to formulation of personality dynamics (and, incidentally [see Chapter 3], of descriptions of situations). Any case history could be written to read as a full-length novel, but psychologists are in practice for action, not esthetic contem-plation.

The report of case results, by either personal or computer writeup, should be furnished with an enrichment of psychometric behavioral *inferences* from the profile itself. In fact, the full report must contain a) succinct profiles of standard scores of states, traits, etc.; b) biographical and life situation particulars; c) changes of scores under time, therapy, and situational change; and d) changing life behavior. In vocational selection, for example, these would be the estimates, from specification (behavioral) equations, of relative fitness for a spectrum of jobs; in clinical assessment there would be pattern similarities to a variety of DSM psychiatric diagnostic types; in prison cases quantitatively stated prognoses of success for parole; and in therapy evaluations of the best points of manipulation in personality and environment. These are discussed in various chapters and quantitatively in Chapter 2.

For final recording and operating, the psychologist needs what was called a two-file system, but would perhaps more comprehensively now be called a *three-file system*. In the first he needs a comprehensive, well labeled, easily accessible file or shelf of the tests he has selected and settled upon for general use. Within that there can be what might be called different *test installations*, i.e., groups of tests carefully planned to give maximum information in a practicable testing time for a certain subarea of practice, e.g., court cases, suspected schizophrenics, school performance, business executive selection, etc. The value of designing and keeping to such a package or *installation* is that experience in administering, scoring, and interpreting a particular set accumulates valuable skills and an appropriate sense of confidence in interpreting varieties of results.

Some difference of emphasis regarding the subsets of tests in these installations will arise according to the psychologist's situational opportunities and philosophy of action. Many practitioners are in an institutional system where they are *not*

asked, "Find out as much as possible about this personality." Instead, the request is for a present specific judgment, e.g., "Tell us if this court referral is or is not a schizophrenic," or "Would Jones this year make good use of a scholarship at the university?" The implication of the first of the latter questions might be, "I want only to know of three signs on the Rorschach believed to be schizophrenia indicators that have been made by this client," or "I want to know if the pattern similarity of the source trait profile to that of escapees tells us if this adolescent will break out of his reformatory school," and so on.

Such restricted orders and prescriptions are seen, in the light of functional testing, often to lead to too narrow a test practice. There is scarcely any behavior that is not a function of the total personality (and the total situation), as the figures in the behavioral equations in this book clearly show. Nevertheless, the ill-conceived demands on the practitioner made by the general public, hospitals, courts, etc., cannot be brushed aside, and some restriction implied in the concept of test installations (functional test combination packages) is a practicable compromise with goals of high comprehensiveness, validity, reliability, and universality of reference. Thus, we have to concede that what might be called *narrow purpose installations*, perhaps even composed only of a few special-purpose, nonanalytical tests to give some immediate but insightless answer, are often needed, though their results are largely blind to the future and to wider possibilities in the client. In any case, the arrangement of tests in file 1 in convenient subset installations, or on a shelf by age levels, minority use, clinical, industrial and educational applications, etc., will help keep the psychologist aware of his full resources and give quick and convenient access to them.

The *second file* is, of course, simply the usual file of *client cases*, in most of which the same common *core* (at least) of personality, ability, and motivation profiles will be found. By their central reference to the main traits and states, these records will be useful *not only for the immediate cause of referral, but for other predictions, use by other psychologists, checks on later development and, of course, research.** If such comparable records were kept by enough practitioners, research would find a harvest of analyzable material sufficient for discoveries valuable not only to general practice but also to study of the rarer, more unusual patterns of behavior. Indeed, when one considers how much the practitioner is today in need of firm predictive evidence on all types of problems and all types of treatment, it comes near to being a professional scandal that the great majority of individuals involved in this profession contribute negligibly to research findings advancing their profession beyond the present science-poor methods. Doubtless, in a small proportion of dismal cases this is due to lack of any conscientious sense of obligation to advance the profession scientifically (rather than politically and economically). But in most, who are striving to raise the level of practice, it is simply the hopelessness of expecting, as an individual, to accumulate enough cases of, say, obsessional hand-washing, or suicide, or incest, to draw some firm statistical conclusions. (The single case theoretical "explanation" being justifiably unimpressive.) Attention in this second file to record keeping, centered on common measures as used by several practitioners, would thus, secondarily, have great value for research, once machinery is properly organized within the profession.

---

*This emphasis on a stable common technical language is surely not misplaced. In an area similarly beset by taxonomic confusion, the successful pioneer Broca (of the speech area location) pleaded for "a name for everything, one name only, and one that stands for nothing else."

The *third file* is one of behavioral specification equations, type profiles (as implied in DSM), age curves and other bases of practical prediction and diagnosis emanating from research. In principle, the chief source of well informed, wise, and effective action for the practitioner comes from simply putting together the information from file two and file three. That is to say, he or she has to bring together the data on the individual case with the psychological laws made precise in the equations and constants of the third file.

THE INTEGRATION OF INDICATIONS FROM TESTS AND INTERVIEW ASSESSMENTS OF SITUATION AND BIOGRAPHICAL BACKGROUND

The final use of the measures as conceived, made and groomed into precise meaning as measures, according to the techniques of the past five chapters, is variously divided into *assessment, diagnosis, prognosis, monitoring*, and *prediction*. The description and classification involved in the two first are rarely an end in themselves, and it is with their integration with the last three that we are here mainly to be concerned. To the scientist *per se* prognosis and guiding therapy rest on statistical prediction — prediction 1) of immediate behavior; 2) of what will ensue if the anticipated life situations take their course; and 3) (in monitoring) of what various tactical moves in treatment will do to modify the traits, states, symptoms, etc. recorded.

In Chapter 1 the reader has already met the basic principle of the behavioral equation. In principle, it can be properly applied either to a single response act or to the prediction of cumulative effects of a substantial period of life acts in a summary score of, say, school achievement at the end of a year, success in marriage after five years, or the cure of a psychiatric symptom after a normal period of treatment. For example, the 16 P.F. Handbook gives (p. 230) for college achievement of undergraduates (data from Graffam, 1967):

$$\text{Ach} = .05A + .23B - .10C - .27E + .05F + .31G - .02H + .23I - .05L - .02M - .03N - .11O + 12Q1 + .11Q2 - .18Q3 - .14Q4 \qquad (6-5)$$

In this prediction of cognitive achievement at least six personality factors are *not* significantly involved, but intelligence, B, and the remaining nine personality traits yield a multiple R of .63 with the criterion. Cattell and Butcher found with high school subjects a slightly different emphasis, as would be expected. At that age the same factors in the HSPQ gave loadings as follows:

$$\text{Ach (Stanford Test)} = .17A + .62B + .02C - .09D - .22E + .02F + .34G - .01H + .08I + .06J - .04O + .35Q2 + .18Q3 - .02Q4 \qquad (6-6)$$

In general, other school achievement specifications agree with these, in showing the main action from intelligence, B, submissiveness, E(−), strong superego, G, and self-sufficiency, Q_2, and, sometimes Q_3, self-sentiment, as the main predictors.

Unfortunately, the number of behavioral specification equations made available for primary personality, ability, and motivation factors is still woefully few. As Chapter 7 (Krug) shows, there are some for salesmen's earning levels, teaching success, air piloting, chances of "remission" in young delinquents, in which practitioners have gone to the trouble of getting real criterion data, but mostly practitioners seem unorganized or prepared to guess rather than establish these firm bases.

Average profiles, e.g., of people in many occupations are, on the other hand, much easier to get, though, as Chapters 19 and 23 point out, we cannot be sure that people in an occupation are those who *should* be! With some acceptable assumptions, as Tatsuoka and Cattell (1970) have shown

(see Chapter 23), a behavioral equation *can* be derived just from such more easily obtained average profiles, thus permitting a criterion estimate of probability of success in that occupation from any client's personality score profile.

Fortunately (in view of this shortage of specification equations), one can proceed in clinical diagnosis, and also in some counseling and guidance, without the prediction of an actual performance level. Using the alternate "adjustment calculation" method, it suffices to use the pattern similarity coefficient to express the similarity of the given CAQ, MMPI, etc., profile to the control pattern for, say, an accountant, a pilot, an anxiety neurotic, a process schizophrenic, or a manic-depressive (see Chapters 16, 17, and 23).

What the practitioner has to realize is that the behavioral equation and the pattern similarity ("adjustment") methods, with some derivatives, e.g., nonlinear specification (Chapter 23), are paradigms that really underlie all evaluation and decision processes in this domain. Since those processes occur "intuitively" in the mind of nonmathematical psychologists, they might be surprised to be told that they are, nevertheless, employing them. However, neither the intuitive nor the calculating type of practitioner should be content with what the tests *immediately* tell about the client at the given moment. As stressed in all functional testing, *psychological laws* must be and can be invoked to permit prognosis and treatments (educational or therapeutic) beyond what the test scores at that moment are capable of telling us in purely *statistical* laws.

Here the great claim of functional testing, based on verified structures, about which personality theory has developed, is that, in contrast to prestructural tests, they permit one to proceed beyond the immediately statistical values, so as to extend meaning and prediction by applying general psychological theory. The "intuitive" operator, we have recognized, will still do this by half-conscious or purely verbal processes, but the scientific user of mathematical models can, with the advance of multivariate experimental psychology, increasingly do so with altogether greater precision, using available *quantitative* psychological laws. Although this statement to some extent draws bank checks on the future, that future is already close in the current writing of progressive multivariate experimental psychologists, which we can illustrate in, for example, the syntheses of Buss and Poley (1976), Cartwright (1979), Cattell (1979a, 1980a), H. Cattell (this volume), Delhees (1975), Dreger (1972), Eysenck (1952, 1960), Fiske and Maddi (1961), Guilford (1959), Hundleby, Pawlik, and Cattell (1965), Karson and O'Dell (1976), Lawlis and Chatfield (1974), Lindzey and Loehlin (1979), Lynn (1971), Madsen (1977), Nesselroade and Reese (1973), Pawlik (1968), Pervin (1975), Royce (1973), Sahakian (1965); in Germany—Schmidt and Häcker (1975), and Schneewind (1977); Wessman and Ricks (1966), Witkin (1962). In these developments of the theoretical background the reader will meet findings that greatly extend the power of prediction from structured measurement.

Results from a prefunctional test such as the Rorschach rely at best on specific empirical relations of unknown causal origin. By contrast, a score on a source trait, for a person at a given age and in a given situation, opens up prediction beyond immediate empirical statistical equations, for it connotes knowledge of what the age change will be in the next few years; to what extent the trait is genetic; and, if we have adjustment process analysis vectors (Cattell, 1979c) for various life paths, what learning change may be expected from exposure to the life situations or therapies studied.

The behavioral equation, as made clear at the outset, gives equal weight to personality traits and to situations. In Chapters 2 and 3 we have shown how situations can be precisely psychologically described by vectors. But psychologists have at present worked out and made available virtually no such meaningful vectors. There are, in fact, in broad perspective, two things that the ordinary testing of common traits by tests as described omits up to this point, actually: 1) the integration with test results of the subject's present situation, and his or her biographical history leading to it; and 2) the specific, narrow personal investment of interests. (The broad ergic tension levels and major sentiments —career, home, religion, sport, etc.—*are* covered in measures by the MAT, etc.)

Obviously, these two further sources of information have to be handled in the interview and, if possible, along with whatever discussion of test results with the client is appropriate. Certain open-ended "projection"* tests like the TAT, or the analysis of dreams, or free association, or anything that is a suitable start for free

---

*Many practitioners need to grow beyond a use of the term "projective tests"—a term that was a misnomer from the beginning, and the careless use of which for a very vague collection of tests promotes conceptual confusion. The experimental and factor analytic evidence is (Cattell & Wenig, 1952) that there are two kinds (unitary tendencies in people) of projection: psychoanalytic dynamic and naive. The former is a dynamic defense mechanism in which the person attributes to others motives (usually undesirable) existing excessively in his or her own unconscious. The latter—naive projection—deals with consciously available knowledge whereby persons naively (or thoughtlessly) assume the mental processes of others are like their own, e.g., a child assumes his uncle is as fond of candy as he himself is.

Though the TAT, the Rorschach, the Draw-a-Man Test, etc. may involve true projection, they also involve several other defense mechanisms and processes. Inferences cannot be drawn on motivation from perceptual distortions on these tests, as the correlations show they can specifically from, say, Subtest 2 of the MAT. In fact, "projective" in some writings appears to mean nothing more than "not a questionnaire," i.e., it means for these writers what a more logical use of language would call *objective tests*. Clarity is served if within the objective tests we recognize subtests (as in the O-A, the TAT, the MAT, etc.) that happen to be truly projective, and others that involve a diversity of quite different principles (Cattell & Warburton, 1967).

association, brings the needed supplementation of common trait scores with specific attachments and biographical events.

Here we come to the clinical *art*—or "technique" if one wishes—of attaching the vaguely heard tune of the subject's own conception of his or her troubles to the firm and clear libretto of functional test results. In the motivation field, which is generally the most vital modality in clinical work, the source trait tests, such as the MAT and SMAT, give the most reliable information on the major drive levels and "institutional" attachment strengths, but claim no designation of the roots of these in personal experience or of the quirks of drive attachments outside common trait structures. Consequently, after the objective testing the psychologist is thrown back on the TAT, free association, etc., for the unique "finishing touches"! Actually, the psychologist who looks to tomorrow should not forget that there *does* exist a more objective technique even for unique dynamic traits, to trace the lattice of dynamic connections to the unique symptom and situation structure of the client, namely, P-technique. This has been amply clinically illustrated by Birkett and Cattell (1978), Cattell and Cross (1952) and others, and designs have been suggested for reducing its excessive time demand. But, as Chapter 13 will point out in more detail, this is "deluxe" diagnostic procedure presently beyond the reach of most practitioners, as well as their clients' pocketbooks.

It is here that clinical use of tests departs most from industrial and educational practice, for there the most that is called for in analysis and prediction of the individual case can be handled as the outcome of a unique combination of common trait scores. The final use of test results in the clinical area, by contrast, requires their integration with interests, symptoms, and environmental situations that are unique in pattern to the individual and obtained through biographical inquiry and consulting-room expertise.

SUMMARY

Ten major properties of tests have been studied in relation to the psychologist's appropriate *selection* of tests.

Considering test administration *per se,* issues of length and time distribution, required administrative skills, and need for apparatus aids have first been evaluated. Convenience in administration and scoring are important, but are placed after validity and reliability in this book, in the belief that testing practice should put effectiveness of service before other considerations. There is no question that in fact clients are being "short-changed" today because some psychologists wish to avoid mastering the complexities and difficulties of newer methods. For example, there has been a lag in substituting objective tests for questionnaires, in using culture-fair intelligence tests, in monitoring with state measurements, and in using objective measures of motivation structure, when these would be appropriate. (Their reasoning is on the same plane as that of the man who lost his key in the garage but looked for it in the living room because it seemed easier to see there!)

Other issues in administration and test choice concern the breadth of relevance of the test, r_e; its language fitness; its cycling of items and avoidance of position and acquiescence (by reversal) effects; its susceptibility to and provision of correction for faking; its scoring facility; its constructed freedom from acquiescence sets; its provision of equivalent forms to handle test sophistication effects; its meeting the requirement of being short yet expandable to adequate length in special circumstances; and its meeting the need for immediate retests.

Open-ended, inventive answer administration does not necessarily connote low *conspection reliability* among scorers, but it commonly does. At the least it has the drawback, e.g., in the TAT, Rorschach, etc., that no objective computer scoring for this design has been attainable. Forced choice (two answers) multiple choice is probably not as good as three or four alternatives. One should be wary in multiple choice of answer sheet use with persons of borderline capability. Speeded tests (not completed by all) call for care in equating early and late samples of items in personality tests, and for ranking in difficulty in ability tests. The difference of speeded and unspeeded scores is often not just a matter of effect on standardization, but alters the nature of the trait being measured. Corrections for guessing and for missed items (especially in untimed tests) are desirable.

The principles and varieties of standardization have been discussed in the preceding chapter. The *choice* of a standardization table, however, is often a further problem for the practicing psychologist. We have pointed out earlier that in research it is often preferable to work in raw scores rather than lose some precision in translating to standard scores. However, the use of a control group matched on associated variables is conceptually equivalent to parceling out some causes or consequences of the main trait under inspection. A *double control* design is here advocated in which the "oddity" of the experimental group is compared both with a matched control and with the standardization values for the general population.

In recording the test results there is one level purely of description and another of interpretive use in working with prediction treatment and criterion relations. In both, the psychologist has to master two levels of communication: 1) to the layman, and 2) to the psychologist or psychiatrist. The latter finds technical terms and formulae indispensable for conciseness and precision. The former need not be unstandardized even though in popular language. An initial case report on test results in general language can nowadays be well handled by computer "narrative output." This begins with description but usually proceeds beyond to criterion predictions by the behavioral equation and

pattern similarity resemblances to type profiles, thus enriching interpretation and prediction with concrete anticipations.

Although special conditions come into clinical, educational, and industrial test use, a broad principle applying to practice in all fields is the *three-file system*, calling for 1) a file of tests, organized in "installations" for a variety of specialized purposes; 2) a file of the individual case records, succinctly represented by profiles and narrative outputs, and biographical, situational notes; and 3) a file of referent weights for as many criterion specification equations as possible, and as many diagnostic mean profiles as can be accumulated for the main occupations, clinical syndromes, etc. The crux of good interpretive practice is in bringing 2) and 3) together for the most precise obtainable diagnosis and predictive estimates. Attention to a good three-file system will initially uncover the enormous gaps presently in the third file, and at the same time encourage keeping records that could be integrated across numerous isolated practitioners to remove those gaps.

The complete process of assessment, prediction (school and industry), classification, diagnosis, prognosis, monitoring, and tactically adjusting therapy goes beyond test results to their integration with knowledge of situational and biographical information. In this process the psychologist's experience and intuition—his or her "art"—come into their own. Nevertheless, the underlying logical framework lies in the model of type profiles and the linear or curvilinear behavioral equation.

Herbert Spencer has passed down to us the comment that "the more information a man has the more he is likely to be confused, unless he has clear principles." This is an apt warning in the practice of psychology today, which is liable to be overwhelmed by innumerable special-purpose tests and transient special emphases on treatment methods. Keeping in mind the multiple causation of behavior (again, the behavioral equation), and educated in the particulars of source trait and state structure, in ability, temperament and dynamic modalities, the psychologist can bring to bear all that experimentally based personality theory knows, e.g., concerning the normal age course of a given trait, its heritability index, or ratio, its susceptibility to situational learning (Path Learning Analysis, Cattell, 1980a) and therapeutic influences the modulation indices of life situations, its physiological associations, and similar research insights from many fields. However, scientific precision is as yet available to us only in patches. Thus, especially in clinical practice, the experienced art of integrating the firm test information with less condensable and validatable input on the biographical past and the present situation remains vital.

CHAPTER 7

Solid State Psychology: The Role of the Computer in Human Assessment

Samuel E. Krug

Although technology is not science, the existence of a flourishing technology often indicates the existence of a highly developed basic science.

Raymond B. Cattell (1957c)

THE CONTRIBUTION OF THE COMPUTER TO THE NEW MULTIVARIATE EXPERIMENTAL PHASE OF PSYCHOLOGICAL RESEARCH AND PRACTICE

Most of the empirical sciences tend to identify, at one time or another, with a relatively unique technology. For example, when we think of astronomy, the telescope comes almost automatically to mind. Mention a microscope and most people think of biology. As Cattell noted in the opening sentences of Chapter 1, it was the replacement of conjecture and speculation with objective measurement that marked the real beginning of each science. In most cases, the introduction of measurement

and the development of technology were concurrent events, since the technological devices represented media by which empirical observations were made and quantified.

For many years, psychology identified itself with the technology of the animal and physics laboratories—the cages, mazes, and mechanisms through which we sought general laws of behavior by carefully measuring response events under environmentally controlled conditions. This is not at all surprising when one considers that scientific psychology evolved from the late 19th century physics laboratories. But, during the course of the last century of progress we have noticed a gradual shift in technology, and "Apples" are now nearly as common as activity cages. This development reflects an increased willingness of modern psychology to analyze the roots of more complex behavioral phenomena. Just as physics required sophisticated particle accelerators to unlock the secrets of matter, so modern psychology required the computer to interrelate many diverse behavioral responses in order to identify their underlying causes.

In perhaps no area of psychological study has the presence of computers been more evident than that of personality assessment. For decades now, construction of personality inventories has relied extensively on high speed computers. Validity research on the basic personality model underlying the 16 P.F., for example, would have been virtually impossible were it not for the advanced machines available to Cattell at Illinois in the 1940s. It is difficult to conceive of Jackson's painstaking analyses of the 3000-item source pool for the PRF being completed within a lifetime, without computer assistance. With only a desk calculator available, it is unlikely that Comrey's factorings of individual MMPI scales would have progressed much beyond D or Hy. FHIDs would still be on the horizon and the *Comrey Personality Inventory* decades from reality.

Because the computer has played such a significant role in the development of so many structured inventories, it should not seem surprising to find it ever more frequently used in the application of these instruments.

THE ELECTRONIC ASSISTANT

There is a tendency on the part of many to view this outpouring of output as simply representing convenience, economy, or speed. Like Sherlock Holmes's Watson, the computer is viewed as a patient, perhaps naive, but always loyal second to the more perceptive, penetrating clinician. Even if this were all the computer offered,

there would still be many significant advantages that accrue to the test user.

For example, in the case of a structured technique—one which has conspective scoring, to use Cattell's terminology (see Chapter 4)—we normally assume the scoring process itself is a straightforward, unchallenging task. But, consider for a moment Cattell and Schuerger's *Objective-Analytic Test Battery* (Chapter 13). Although the scoring is certainly conspective in the sense that no judgment is required on the part of test administrators, the scoring calculations are necessarily so complex that unassisted (i.e., noncomputerized) use of the battery is generally impractical. In the case of the *Executive Profile Survey* (EPS), Lang and Krug (1978) adopted the variance reallocation procedure (Eber, Cattell, & Delhees, 1976) as the basic model to be used for combining items into scales. In this procedure every item is given some fractional weight in estimating each scale. As a practical matter, this means that for each examinee who has completed the EPS, the test administrator must multiply a 94-item response vector by a 94 × 11 matrix, a feat that could easily tax the patience (if not the calculation limits) of the most enthusiastic examiner. The same is true of the use of trait view theory.

In both instances, computers allow test users to include such sophisticated instruments in their assessment work and benefit from the resulting increases in reliability and validity, by faithfully carrying out the tedious, but necessary, calculations.

But, after the test is scored, is it time to unplug our electronic Watson and turn to the real task of assessment? Not really. In the case of certain well-established and well-researched inventories like the 16 P.F., the computer can provide a great deal of assistance in carrying out one or more of the various types of corrections that might apply.

For example, age trends have been very

carefully mapped for each of the primary scales of the 16 P.F. Across a wide age range from 16 to 70 years, the verdict seems to be that a quadratic function best fits data obtained with the longer and more reliable forms (A and B) of the test (IPAT, 1971). In certain cases, typically a research setting, when the experimenter wishes to control or partial out age effects, the computer literally performs in microseconds tasks that would otherwise stop the unassisted researcher cold.

In Chapter 23 Cattell discusses trait-view theory and its implications for improved validity in personality measurement. Its basic hypothesis is that there is no sharp distinction between substantive and stylistic sources of variance in personality measurement. In fact, Cattell's theory subsumes "style" as a redundant concept, under temperament factors. An individual's score on a personality scale, like any behavior, is a complex sum of many underlying personality and dynamic role factors. Trait-view theory further hypothesizes that the influence each factor exerts differs from situation to situation. Consequently, correction equations are uniquely defined for each test scale in each test-taking situation: the job-seeking situation, the anonymous research situation, the clinic intake situation, etc.

Empirical research has demonstrated the accuracy of the basic model. But this research (Krug & Cattell, 1971) also shows that trait-view corrections are so complex as to require the use of the computer if the method is to be practically implemented. Even the simpler approach by using distortion or "faking" scales (Cattell, Eber, & Tatsuoka, 1970; Krug, 1978a; Winder, O'Dell, & Karson, 1975) becomes unruly when many protocols are to be scored.

It should already be clear that current applications of computers in human assessment have gone far beyond simple convenience. To view the computer as nothing more than an assistant probably says more about our own insecurity than about reality.

The tests currently available to us increasingly represent sophisticated products of electronic technology. They are complex analog-to-digital converters —instruments that take living, breathing creatures and transform them in a twinkling from a few items into a vector of numbers. They require correspondingly sophisticated technologies to handle the D-A conversion: that is, the inverse process that transforms a vector of numbers (i.e., the test profile) into useful verbal hypotheses for consideration by a clinician, personnel officer, or counselor, via the laws of personality growth and motivational dynamics that these measurements have permitted to emerge in psychological theory.

THE USE OF BEHAVIORAL EQUATIONS AND PATTERN SIMILARITY COEFFICIENTS

In order fully to appreciate the computer's labor-saving contributions to applied measurement, let us diverge for a moment and consider in somewhat greater detail the complex calculations involved in the use of certain statistical prediction models.

Elsewhere, Cattell, Eber, & Tatsuoka (1970, p. 133) have suggested that behavioral predictions can be broadly classified as one of two types—effectiveness models or adjustment models—on the basis of the underlying statistical techniques used to make the prediction. The former assume that some independent measure of the behavior to be predicted is available for analysis. The latter assume that the average profile (i.e., the typical response pattern) of a representative sampling of individuals in a diagnostic class or occupational group can itself serve as a criterion against which to evaluate individuals. This distinction between methods corresponds approximately to what others (e.g., Wiggins, 1973) have considered linear versus configural prediction models.

In Cattell's system, the effectiveness method is represented by what he terms the *behavioral specification equation*, or simply the *behavioral equation*. At the level of operations this corresponds to a linear multiple regression equation in which scores on factorially identified source traits are used as the predictor variables. Under these circumstances Cattell feels that "the method lends itself much more to the application of psychological insight and laws than in the usual multiple regression equation where ad hoc variables (rather than unitary traits) form the predictors" (Cattell, Eber, & Tatsuoka, 1970, p. 147). This is because we can hang additional prediction on source traits, knowing what they are, how they change with experience, etc.

For example, Drevdahl and Cattell (1958; Cattell & Drevdahl, 1955) derived a specification equation for predicting creativity from empirical studies of adults in three major creative professions, including science, writing, and art. Their equation is:

$$\text{Creativity} = .99 - .33A + .33B + .17E - .33F + .16H + .33I + .16M - .16N + .16Q_1 + .33Q_2$$

The letters represent any individual's scores on the corresponding 16 P.F. scales and the decimal weights are those which were found to represent each factor's optimum contribution to the prediction of creativity. The constant, .99, is included for scaling purposes: When these weights are applied to sten scores on the 16 P.F. scales (standard scores with a mean in the reference population of 5.5, a standard deviation of 2.0, and a range of 1-10) and the constant is added, the predicted creativity score will also follow a sten distribution. In this particular example, Drevdahl and Cattell found that the predictive contributions of the remaining 16

P.F. factors (C, G, L, O, Q3, and Q4) were negligible (or redundant) when these 10 source traits were included in the equation.

As a numerical example, let us replace the letters in the equation with an actual person's sten scores as follows:

$$\text{Creativity} = .99 - .33 \times 2 + .33 \times 8 + 17 \times 6 - .33 \times 2 + .16 \times 6 + .33 \times 5 + .16 \times 8 - .16 \times 7 + .16 \times 10 + .33 \times 5 = .99 - .66 + 2.64 + 1.02 - .66 + .96 + 1.65 + 1.28 - 1.12 + 1.60 + 1.65 = 9.4$$

For an individual with this set of scores, creativity is predicted to be quite high, higher, in fact, than all but about 2% of people in the same population (e.g., adults, college students, or high school students, depending on which 16 P.F. norm table was used to convert this individual's raw scores).

It has been recognized in Cattell's theory that the linear model may fail to take into account the complex nature of the relationship between human characteristics and behavior and that nonlinear behavioral equations should be sought where necessary. He is dubious, however, about the criticism that the compensatory nature of the model could lead to predictions that run counter to logic. For example, the creativity equation presented above assigns a negative weight to factor F (impulsivity or surgency), which means that lower scores on factor F are predictive of higher creativity. But critics of the linear model might argue that the relationship holds only up to a point: Beyond some minimum level on factor F the individual may be too withdrawn, gloomy, or depressed to be creative. Cattell points out that this is no error of logic: The situation simply calls for the nonlinear form of the behavioral equation. The question, unfortunately, has generated much verbal activity and an extensive literature without any corresponding pursuit of experiment with known source traits. However, the general conclusion to be drawn from research by Ward (1954) and others is that the linear model seems to be more robust in actual cases, and more reliable as a prediction tool than many more complex prediction functions yet applied.

Regarding the compensatory nature of the behavioral equation, critics point out that it would be possible, for example, for an individual with a sten score of 1 on factor B (which suggests extremely limited intellectual resources) nevertheless to obtain a predicted creativity score of 10. How reasonable, they ask, is it to expect creativity in someone with an I.Q. below 70? One might answer that the combination of scores on the remaining factors necessary to produce this result is extremely improbable, or one could point to the occasional "idiot savant." The linear equation, then, remains an approximation to the nonlinear equations that have not yet been found, but it is remarkably effective over most ranges.

By its very nature the second general approach to prediction, the adjustment or "type placement" approach, is less sensitive to this kind of objection. As stated earlier, the central assumption is that the average profile of a reasonably homogeneous group proven adjusted over years to the occupation or representative of a diagnostic classification represents an optimum level of adjustment. E. K. Strong relied implicitly on this approach in his development of interest scales, although he relied on similarity at the level of individual item responses rather than at the level of factorially pure source traits.

Cattell has usually identified the adjustment approach with the use of the pattern similarity coefficient, r_p, a measure of the "distance" between two profiles scaled such that an r_p of 1.00 indicates no distance between the profiles, i.e., perfect similarity. An r_p of 0.0 corresponds to a distance between profiles that would be expected if the two were randomly drawn from some universe, or a chance level of

similarity. Negative r_p's indicate increasingly greater distances between profiles and less similarity.

The general formula for r_p is

$$r_p = \frac{E[\sum_i^k (x_{1i} - x_{2i})^2] - \sum_i^k (x_{1i} - x_{2i})^2}{E[\sum_i^k (x_{1i} - x_{2i})^2] + \sum_i^k (x_{1i} - x_{2i})^2} \quad (7\text{-}1)$$

where x_{1i} represents the score on the ith element of profile 1, x_{2i} the score on the ith element of profile 2, and $E[\sum_i^k (x_{2i} - x_{2i})^2]$ the expected value of the sum of squared differences between profiles with k profile elements. The numeric value of this quantity depends principally on the variance of the difference scores. When the profiles are expressed as z-scores, then the value is $2\varkappa^2_k$ where $\varkappa^2_k$ is the median (i.e., p = .50) chi-square value for k profile elements. When two individual 16 P.F. profiles are compared, then the numeric value is $8\varkappa^2_{16}$ or 122.7.

More often than not, the examiner will be interested in comparing an individual 16 P.F. profile to one of the more than 100 reference profiles for occupational or diagnostic groups reported in the handbook. For that common application the test authors have developed a refined formula that takes into account the extent to which the reference profile deviates from the general population, as well as the individual's deviation from the reference profile. The interested reader will wish to consult the original source (Cattell, Eber, & Tatsuoka, 1970, pp. 141-142) for details.

From the formula for the pattern similarity coefficient, the reader can quickly see that deviations from the "normative" profile in either direction subtract equally from the overall degree of similarity between the two profiles. When comparisons are made to an occupation like that of airline pilot which requires relatively high levels of emotional stability (the average sten score on factor C = 7.8 of 360 successful pilots), individuals whose factor C sten scores fall at 5 or at 10 are each "penalized" about equally for missing the mark. Psychologically, one might argue that the first person simply doesn't have sufficient emotional resources to deal with the demands of the cockpit, while the second person is perhaps too detached and insensitive to the human relations side of piloting.

THE GROWTH AND MANAGEMENT OF DATA BASES

It should be clear at this point that computers can offer considerable assistance in the interpretation of individual test results. But I do not mean to suggest that it is only the instruments and the statistical techniques for interpreting them that have become complex. The data bases that have developed in connection with these tests have grown at a rate outstripped only by Jack's beanstalk. Literally thousands of research articles lie in wait to help the knowledgeable and to trap the unwary test user. The various *Mental Measurements Yearbooks* issued between 1938 and 1978 catalogue some 57,846 research references involving more than 1000 different tests (Buros, 1978). Add to these individual studies the voluminous, otherwise unpublished, interpretive information frequently contained in test handbooks and manuals. Very soon, the test user is led to despair of ever being able to master a single instrument, let alone the entire field of personality assessment.

For example, in the case of the 16 P.F., several thousand researches now exist that empirically link the underlying characteristics it measures to significant outcomes in clinical, organizational, vocational, correctional, and educational settings. It is difficult, if not impossible, for the individual test user to index, store, and reliably retrieve this information.

Take as a single example the fairly well-defined area of vocational counseling and the implications the 16 P.F. holds for it.

Data reported in the 16 P.F. Handbook (Cattell, Eber, & Tatsuoka, 1970), supplemented by independent research in the professional literature, have permitted the accumulation of more than 100 occupational profiles based on over 25,000 cases. In many instances, separate profiles have been constructed for men and women. The counselor would undoubtedly find the similarities between an individual profile and this set of reference profiles a useful point of departure in the counseling activity. As noted in the previous section, a high degree of resemblance to the average profile for a number of engineers who have successfully pursued careers for some years could reasonably be interpreted to mean that the individual has the kind of qualities that will allow him or her to adjust to the unique personality demands of the engineering profession. But, as a practical matter, the calculation of even a few profile similarity coefficients, let alone 100, is beyond the time available to an unassisted clinician.

In addition to the large number of occupational reference profiles, the vocational counselor needs also to consider the various behavioral specification equations that have been worked out between the 16 P.F. scales and relevant performance criteria. In the occupational area, the counselor would presumably be interested in leadership equations (Cattell & Stice, 1954), creativity equations (Cattell & Drevdahl, 1955), and occupational theme equations (Walter, 1978), as well as the equations available for accident proneness, achievement potential, sales potential, and other criteria, as reported in the handbooks for the primary personality scales (16 P.F., HSPQ, ESPQ, CAQ, etc.).

Over and above the profiles and equations, there is still a massive amount of data in the vocational area which is relevant to the issue but which taxes the limits of most human memory banks and retrieval systems. For that reason Walter (1978), working in close association with IPAT psychologists, designed the *Per-*

sonal-Career Development Profile, a paragraph-style analysis of the 16 P.F. focused on self-directed career exploration and personal growth through self-insight. A sample is shown in Table 7.1.

This report systematically integrates the occupational data base with the set of scores at hand. Various occupational choices are suggested for consideration by the examinee and counselor and a comprehensive report on personality characteristics that have implications for vocational choice is provided.

Table 7.1
Sample 16 P.F. Personal-Career Development Profile*

JOHN SAMPLE	ID NUMBER 9894-61-423
SEX M	12/02/1982

AGE 32

Orientation to the 16 P.F. Questionnaire

Mr. Sample appears to have answered most of the questions in the 16 P.F. inventory sincerely and spontaneously. He seems to have been motivated to present as accurate a self-portrayal as possible. Even so, the information that follows in this report should be read and interpreted in the light of what is actually known about his personal life-style patterns.

General Overview Patterns

Mr. Sample's life-style is typical of people who value self-directedness and independence. He generally strives to achieve control of and freedom of choice in his personal life and work-related situations. He tends to derive his major gratifications in life from opportunities for personal achievement in the face of competition. He usually likes being influential over other people in his efforts to meet difficult challenges. He is likely to feel most comfortable on assignments which involve working conditions that are flexible, varied, and unstructured. If structure is required, he prefers to provide it, rather than to have it imposed on him. Mr. Sample is likely to accept a role of authority and leadership with a group of friends or co-workers if provided the opportunity. He is also likely to exercise his role in ways which most group members accept and understand.

Problem-Solving Patterns

Mr. Sample functions quite comfortably with problems and situations which involve abstract reasoning and conceptual thinking. He is usually able to integrate detail into meaningful, logical wholes. He is very mentally alert. He is likely to be quick to grasp ideas and to be a fast learner. Mr. Sample's approach to tasks and situations usually reflects a balance between getting things done and being aware of the subtle steps and consequences involved in the process of getting them done. He is essentially conventional and practical in his approach to life and its problems. He is usually attentive to the everyday requirements of situations.

Patterns for Coping with Stressful Conditions

On the whole, Mr. Sample appears to be well-adjusted. He seldom shows evidence of tension or anxiety, even under conditions of pressure and stress. He generally tries to approach situations calmly and even-temperedly. He seldom allows his emotional needs to interfere with or obstruct

---

*Copyright © 1977 by Verne Walter, Ph.D., Santa Monica, CA., and the Institute for Personality and Ability Testing, Champaign, IL. Reproduced by permission.

TABLE 7.1 *(cont'd)*

what he does or attempts to do in most situations and relationships. He is basically quite adaptable and flexible. He does not usually feel compelled to rigidly follow rules and established practices. He tends to be somewhat casual in his behavior. He usually follows his own impulses, intuitions, and urges as opposed to exercising conscious self-discipline over his feelings and behavior. Generally, when Mr. Sample is faced with conflict or opposition from others, he likes to challenge those who oppose him and to assert his views on the issues involved. However, if pressed far enough, he is likely to either give in or break off the relationship, whichever he considers to be more advantageous for the moment.

Patterns of Interpersonal Interaction

On the whole, Mr. Sample tends to direct his attention to people around him and to their concerns, rather than focusing unduly on himself and his own concerns. He usually strives to project personal warmth toward others. He is generally good-natured and likes group activities. Mr. Sample generally has a keen sense about his social obligations, and he is usually alert to what is appropriate in his social interactions with others. He tends to be assertive and competitive. He values his freedom from the influence of others. Although Mr. Sample generally prefers to be free from the influence of others, he is adaptable in relations with others. He normally identifies well with people who are competitive and who understand the importance of exercising control over what they do in efforts to be productive and attain desired results. Sometimes Mr. Sample may be in such a hurry to get things done that he tends to disregard how others who may be affected by his actions feel about issues or matters of importance to them. For the most part, he strives to be friendly and helpful to people, since he tends to be trusting and accepting of himself and the situations in which he finds himself. He is generally quite bold, spontaneous, and uninhibited when relating with others. He relates to most people with ease and personal comfort. If he were to assume a leadership role with others, his most typical approach for influencing others would likely be to get things accomplished through direction, persuasion, and a variety of means for challenging others.

Patterns for Career, Occupational, and Avocational Interests

Mr. Sample's profile suggests that he is likely to enjoy career-oriented and/or avocational activities which entail working out ways for accomplishing and doing things by convincing, directing, or persuading others toward attainment of organizational goals and/or economic gain, being near or at the center of group endeavors and solving problems through discussions with others, or by arranging relationships between people so as to enlighten, serve, or train them, and use of data-processing, office practice, verbal and numerical skills to organize information and tasks according to prescribed plans and well-established procedures and systems. Therefore, his profile appears to be similar to persons who express rather marked interests for one or more of the administrative, business management, consulting, legal/political, merchandising, or sales, educational, health care, religious, or social service, business-data processing system, financial, clerking, or office practice fields of endeavor.

Related Occupations of Interest

Mr. Sample's strongest interest themes are similar to those of people employed in some of the following occupations. In reviewing this list, he may find support for past or present career choices. Alternatively, he may find it helpful to review his interests, skills and experience with respect to occupations he may not have considered. There are indications he may find it relatively easy to identify with and relate to people who are successfully pursuing careers in some of these occupations: administrative services director, chamber of commerce executive, community service director, compensation-benefits director, consultant, customer service manager, food service manager, public relations director, retail store manager. Additional occupations Mr. Sample may wish to consider include: administrative manager, claim manager, credit manager, industrial relations manager, insurance manager, wholesaler, and advertising account manager, art center director, attorney, journalist-reporter.

TABLE 7.1 *(cont'd)*

The occupational information reported here is based on career preferences suggested by Mr. Sample's general personality orientation. The occupational listings should not be treated as specific job suggestions. Some may not appeal to him. Others may not relate well to his training and experience. However, each represents an option open to Mr. Sample in his personal growth and career planning at this point in time. A careful review may bring to mind other alternatives that represent even more appealing career paths.

Personal-Career Development Considerations

Mr. Sample shows a marked preference for activities and work which involve meeting and interacting with people. He generally experiences most satisfaction when he is in a position of leadership, and is able to direct the actions of others. Mr. Sample enjoys being in charge of endeavors, responding to challenges for accomplishment, and functioning in a business-like manner. He should perform well on trouble-shooting assignments in which he is given opportunities to tackle and solve complex problems. Mr. Sample is apt to feel most comfortable and experience most personal gratification if he is assigned work-related responsibilities in a controlled and structured environment. Provided that Mr. Sample is motivated to do so, Mr. Sample shows moderate interest for the kinds of disciplined activities required by formal academic training situations. He can be expected to function adequately when assigned to activities or work which do not demand many sudden adjustments on his part, but he should avoid taking on tasks and assignments which are stressful in nature. Mr. Sample's profile patterns suggest the presence of sufficient personal concerns that he may profit from supportive counsel as a means for acquiring the skills to cope effectively with the concerns and stresses he appears to be experiencing presently. Because of his personal concerns at this time, Mr. Sample should be cautious about his considerations of any decisions with respect to the career interest information in this report.

In terms of Mr. Sample's needs for self-growth and performance improvement, he could be encouraged to guard against: (*) his tendency at times to act with such enthusiasm that he may overlook important details or the need to prepare himself sufficiently for what he undertakes; (*) taking on assignments and tasks which may be too emotionally and physically demanding of him; (*) excessive demonstration or display of his emotions and feelings in stressful circumstances or situations; (*) any tendency to feel superior to others as well as efforts to force his ideas on them; (*) being in such a hurry to get things done that he disregards how others may feel about matters of importance to them; (*) tendencies to be somewhat less considerate of others and less sensitive about their needs than he could be at times; and (*) taking on activities or assignments which involve mundane, routine tasks with limited opportunity to think and reason conceptually or which may not fully challenge Mr. Sample's intellectual curiosity.

In conclusion, Mr. Sample desires to make a sincere impression when presenting himself to others.

Scores reported on this page have been computed by comparing 16 P.F. scores with profiles from the occupations listed below. Any review and consideration of them for career planning should be regarded as tentative rather than conclusive. These scores must be considered along with other relevant information about abilities, skills, interests, educational preparation, and work experiences.

OCCUPATIONAL TITLE	SCORE*	OCCUPATIONAL TITLE	SCORE*
Venturous-Influential (V)		Creative-Self Expressive (C)	
Occupations	9.4	Occupations	6.8
Administrators: Mid-Level	8.6	Artists	5.4
Airline Pilots	8.5	High School Teachers	3.1
Business Executives	4.7	University Administrators	7.5
Real Estate Agents	9.4	Writers	7.2
Sales: Wholesale	7.5		

*Scores range from 1 through 10. Scores of 1-3 are considered very low. Scores of 8-10 are considered very high. Scores of 4-7 are average.

TABLE 7.1 *(cont'd)*

OCCUPATIONAL TITLE	SCORE*	OCCUPATIONAL TITLE	SCORE*
Analytic-Scientific (A) Occupations	5.8	Procedural-Systematic(P) Occupations	7.0
Biologists	6.4	Accountants	6.7
Chemists	7.1	Bank Managers	9.2
Computer Programmers	10.0	Credit Union Managers	9.0
Engineers	3.4	Dept. Store Managers	2.5
Geologists	6.4	Personnel Managers	10.0
Physicians	2.6	Sales Managers/Supervisors	8.6
Physicists	6.2		
University Professors	1.9	Mechanical-Operative (M) Occupations	5.3
Nurturing-Altruistic (N) Occupations	7.1	Firefighters	10.0
		Plant Forepersons	8.1
Priests (R.C.)	2.8	Production Managers	9.8
Psychologists	8.1	Service Station Dealers	4.8
School Superintendents	7.0	Urban Police Officers	10.0
Teaching-General	5.9		

This page of 16 P.F. scores is intended for use by properly qualified professionals only. Scores should be treated confidentially, and the results embodied herein should not be substituted for other valid information about this person.

16 P.F. PROFILE

	LOW MEANING	1 2 3 4 5 6 7 8 9 10	HIGH MEANING
A 8	Autonomous-Reserved	*	Participating-Warm
B 9	Concrete Thinking	*	Conceptual Thinking
C 8	Affected by Feelings	*	Calm-Unruffled
E10	Considerate-Humble	*	Assertive-Competitive
F 7	Reflective-Serious	*	Talkative-Impulsive
G 4	Changeable-Expedient	*	Persistent-Conforming
H 8	Cautious-Shy	*	Socially Bold
I 5	Tough-Minded	*	Tender-Minded-Sensitive
L 3	Accepting-Trusting	*	Mistrusting-Oppositional
M 6	Conventional-Practical	*	Imaginative
N 8	Forthright-Unpretentious	*	Sophisticated-Shrewd
O 4	Confident-Self-Assured	*	Apprehensive-Concerned
Q1 5	Conservative-Traditional	*	Experimenting-Liberal
Q2 6	Group-Oriented	*	Self-Sufficient
Q3 3	Lax-Uncontrolled	*	Disciplined-Compulsive
Q4 4	Composed-Relaxed	*	Tense-Driven

BROAD PATTERNS

Extraversion is high (7.7).
Tough poise is above average (6.7).
Independence is high (7.6).
Preference for structured situations is extremely low (1.0).
Accident-error proneness is predicted to be average (6.0).
Potential to learn from on-the-job experience is average (4.8).
Potential to profit from formal academic training is above average (6.6).
Creativity and inventiveness are estimated to be average (6.1).
Preference for attaining a leadership role is above average (7.1).
Tendency to fake good (motivational distortion) is average (6.0).

---

*Scores range from 1 through 10. Scores of 1-3 are considered very low. Scores of 8-10 are considered very high. Scores of 4-7 are average.

COUNSELING CONSIDERATIONS

Adequacy of adjustment is high (8.4).
Level of anxiety is low (3.4).
Effectiveness of behavior controls is average (4.7).
Acting-out behavior tendencies are high (8.1).

THE ELECTRONIC CLINICIAN

From the previous example, it should be clear that it is not simply the fact that the computer is a more efficient information storage and retrieval unit than the clinician that makes it a valuable tool in psychology. Since Meehl's (1954) provocative essay on the topic, evidence pointing to the superiority of statistical (i.e., computer-like) predictions over clinical predictions continues to accumulate. After considerable debate and an outpouring of "horse-race" type research, the final verdict seems to be that computers are simply far more consistent than their human rivals in following well-established decision rules. On the other hand, it appears that computers have not learned to identify and isolate the variables that are relevant to a particular situation. Research now suggests that in many cases the best predictions are likely to be made by teaming the clinician with an electronic counterpart (Dawes, 1979).

To illustrate this point, consider Kleinmuntz's (1963) innovative analysis of the relative effectiveness of human and electronic diagnoses. Test protocols of 126 students exhibiting various degrees of adjustment were presented to 10 experienced clinicians who were asked to classify the individuals on a continuum ranging from well-adjusted (i.e., nominated by peers as especially well-adjusted) through a normal control sample to poorly adjusted (i.e., either in counseling for personal problems or else nominated by peers as poorly adjusted). From among the ten, the best clinician (that is, the one who had the highest rate of correct categorizations)

was given a small sample of the 126 profiles and asked to verbalize his thoughts as he went through the classification process. Kleinmuntz next edited, analyzed, and formalized the classification rules, as would be necessary for programming a computer. The resulting program was then used to classify all 126 protocols.

The interesting sequel was that the program, developed from the verbalization of the best clinician was superior not only to the other nine clinicians but even outperformed that tenth clinician on whom the program was modeled. Goldberg (1970) has conducted similar research to demonstrate that the computer or statistical model of the clinician generally outperforms the clinician.

The conclusion to be drawn is, of course, not that the computer is more perceptive, more innovative, or more penetrating in its analyses, but only that it is more consistent in its applications of principles, once those principles are defined. However, in the case of the linear equation, the computer can *find* the weights—expressing the "principles" governing the particular psychological action—which the clinician can do only very approximately.

COMPUTER-BASED TEST INTERPRETATION

Considering the usefulness of the computer in managing extensive data bases, it is not surprising that among the earliest computerizations were those for the MMPI and the 16 P.F., the two most widely researched personality questionnaires in the world. The former was developed without explicit reference to theory and as such, lies at the fringes of a book such as this on functional testing based on structural research and associated personality theory. However, the extent to which it is used makes it impossible to ignore it in any treatment or computer resources for personality assessment.

The earliest attempts to generate electronic MMPI reports were those carried out by Swenson and Pearson (1964) at the Mayo Clinic. This first approximation may be viewed as a relatively "bare bones" effort: Most of the interpretive statements were generated on the basis of single-scale elevations and very little attention was given to combinations of scores or configural patterns. Subsequent efforts to automate MMPI interpretation by Finney (1966), Fowler (1969), Lachar (1976) and Butcher (1982) generally operated at a much greater level of sophistication, and based interpretation on empirically validated two-point codes, special scales beyond the basic profile, and application of better researched rules for configural analysis. In terms of the depth of the underlying data base or statement library, few of the MMPI systems match that achieved by Caldwell (1979). His report selects from among 12,000 sentences and integrates those statements into a meaningful, paragraph-style report virtually indistinguishable from one that might have been written by an experienced clinician (Kleinmuntz, 1982).

Despite the diversity of system authors, most of these reports share a common point of view: Because MMPI-scale construction was oriented principally toward pathology, each report tends to focus almost exclusively on pathology.

In the case of the 16 P.F., which was instead more broadly anchored within the concept of the total personality sphere, the situation has been different. The earliest attempts to computerize the 16 P.F. were undertaken by Eber (1964). These first efforts resulted in a generic, global appraisal of the individual's total personality. They at the same time programmed and incorporated segments of output directed to diagnostic inferences, occupational patterns, and various other hypotheses that could reasonably be drawn from the basic profile.

But as new research constantly expanded the borders of 16 P.F. knowledge and produced extensive data bases in widely diverse areas, a different pattern with respect to program development began to emerge. Now the computer took on an additional role in test interpretation: the organization and selective access of an extensive data base. Computer-generated 16 P.F. reports since the early 1970s have generally been tailored to emphasize only those aspects of the total data base that are relevant to specific applications and deemphasize those aspects of the profile that are of relatively less concern to a particular user in a particular setting.

For example, Karson (1979) has generated an approach that takes an intensely clinical focus and attempts to identify the maximum amount of pathology evident in a single profile. In this instance, the computer logic is modeled on the report-writing activities of a single, skilled 16 P.F. analyst (Karson & O'Dell, 1975).

Walter's (1978) *Manual for the Personal-Career Development Profile*, discussed earlier, is an example in a different domain almost entirely oriented to the world of work, to *career* implications of the 16 P.F. profile, while it virtually ignores the *clinical* data base.

As its name implies, the *Marriage Counseling Report* (Krug, 1977a) was designed primarily to assist professionals working with troubled relationships. It has its theoretical roots in Cattell's principles of likeness or *congeniality* ("birds of a feather flock together") and *complementariness* or supplementation (a deficiency in the performance of one spouse may be covered up by a talent in the other). These refer respectively to the operative personality dynamics in marital *satisfaction* and the effectiveness of performance or team functioning. Building on empirical testing of these two principles (Barton, 1976; Barton & Cattell, 1973; Cattell & Nesselroade, 1967), this report systematically analyzes (verbally and numerically) the similarities and differences in personality structure of two 16 P.F. profiles.

More recent applications are found in the area of law enforcement (Dee-Burnett, Johns, & Krug, 1981), security screening (Krug, 1981), medical evaluation (Eber, 1977), stress management (Kulhavy & Krug, 1982), and time management (Kozoll & Behrens, 1982).

Although the 16 P.F. and the MMPI are probably the most extensively computerized tests, they are not alone. Kleinmuntz did some early experimenting with the Wechsler scales but apparently abandoned those efforts before 1970. Attempts have even been made to extend rigid computer interpretive techniques to unstructured responses obtained from the Rorschach (Piotrowski, 1964).

Computer-based interpretive reports have been developed for many other functionally based tests such as the *High School Personality Questionnaire* (Cattell & Cattell, 1969b), the *Children's Personality Questionnaire* (Porter & Cattell, 1975), the *Early School Personality Questionnaire* (Cattell & Coan, 1976), the *Motivation Analysis Test* (Cattell, Horn, Sweney, & Radcliffe, 1964b) and the *Clinical Analysis Questionnaire* (Krug, 1980). The *Executive Profile Survey* mentioned earlier (Lang & Krug, 1978), because of its complex scoring, remains exclusively computer-based. Parenthetically, there seems to be a trend in recent years to lock up the scoring and interpretation of some tests from the psychologist, by a "secret code" in the computer. That is true, for example, of the *Strong-Campbell Interest Inventory* (Campbell & Hansen, 1981), for which the scoring keys have never been made public, and the *Millon Clinical Multiaxial Inventory* (Millon, 1982) for which no hand-scoring key is available.

A recent development of considerable importance arises naturally from structural concepts. Basic research has demonstrated that structures found in the three main modalities—abilities, temperament and dynamic traits—are very largely independent (Cattell, 1971a, 1979b; Cattell & Butcher, 1968). Consequently, the multiple correlation predicting a criterion almost invariably benefits from using tests *covering all three modalities*, and the same can be said of clinical insights. The first developments in combining results from different tests have, as a computer service, scarcely yet spanned all modalities, but temperament and dynamic modalities have aptly been covered in the pioneer work of Eber who, in the early 1970s switched his emphasis from "interpreting a test" to the more interesting possibility of "answering questions about the test taker." In his description of a report oriented toward health maintenance, Eber (1977) notes that the program simultaneously evaluates: a) 16 P.F. personality variables to describe lifestyle; b) pathological factors measured by the *Clinical Analysis Questionnaire* to describe present psychiatric status; c) factors of the *Motivation Analysis Test* (Cattell et al., 1964b) to describe dynamic influences; and d) scales of Sweney's (1980) *Vocational Interest Measure* to provide perspective on the patient's occupational profile. Undoubtedly, this trend away from single test interpretation to solution-oriented reports will increase as authors continue to explore the integrative power of the computer.

Over the course of the last several years, there has been a notable increase in the range and diversity of computer-based assessment resources available. Within the size limitations of a single chapter it is not possible to include them all. For a complete resource guide to available computer-based products, the interested reader is referred to Krug (1984).

FURTHER HORIZONS FOR THE COMPUTER

During the last decade, examiners have been increasingly drawn to the test administration potential of the computer (Johnson & Johnson, 1981). The principal benefits of on-line testing include greater control of reaction time and immediate availability of scored output. Important as these may be, they may be frequently offset by the increased cost of on-line assessment. In many of these instances the computer simply presents an item on the screen and allows the examinee to select from among a set of acceptable responses.

However, in the case of "computer adaptive testing," the computer is used to analyze responses immediately and alter the presentation sequence of successive items based on its analysis. In the case of an ability test, for example, every examinee is presented with a different set of items from a source pool, each of which has been previously calibrated with regard to certain parameters or item characteristics (i.e., endorsement frequency, difficulty level, etc.). In the simplest case, two individuals at markedly different levels of the underlying trait will be given only those items that are most appropriate for them. When verbal ability is being measured, for example, the high-level examinee will be presented with proportionately more difficult items than a lower-level examinee. In short, examinees are presented with the least redundant set of items so that testing efficiency in terms of time is maximized. In most ability tests items are in order of difficulty so this means chopping off the lower and upper range, according to the first indications of performance. However, although testing time is shortened and the r_c coefficient is higher, the actual validity and dependability coefficients would drop, according

to classical test theory which inevitably associates greater measurement consistency and validity with a larger number of items.

As item response theory becomes more fully articulated and computer hardware becomes less expensive and more generally available, it seems quite likely that interest in automated test administration and computer adaptive testing will increase.

A review of all the ways in which the computer contributes to human assessment—scoring, analysis, interpretation, and even testing—is informative and impressive. New applications are constantly being discovered as the computer, and those who explore its capabilities, develop and mature. Wagman's (1980, 1982) work is especially interesting in this regard. Harnessing the "user-friendly" capabilities of the University of Illinois's PLATO system (a powerful, computer-based educational system), he designed a program to provide counseling services to students. The system teaches the client a general approach to problem solving, much as a human counselor might provide general suggestions for changing frustrating situations. Research suggests that computer counseling results in about the same degree of improvement as has been found for more traditional therapeutic approaches.

A quite special diagnostic use of the computer is likely to occur if the proposal (Chapter 16) for a condensed P-technique proves practicable. Therein a carefully designed set of emotion-provoking stimuli is presented and the magnitudes of GSR and other responses recorded. That would require a special stimulus-response video apparatus, but the response record could be immediately factor-analyzed by an on-line computer yielding the evidence on dynamic structure directly at the end of the session.

With respect to computer architecture, we are currently seeing the third or fourth generation of a technology that did not exist 40 years ago. In terms of computer application in the area of personality assessment, we stand perhaps at only the dawn of the second generation. Considering the contributions that have been made so far, the advances of the next several years will no doubt be dramatic and exciting.

SUMMARY

Technology is a child of science. The science of psychology, in terms of objective measurement of personality and ability structure, and of dynamic theory based on psychometrics, has come of age. This opens up the possibility of vast strides in the technology of psychological practice.

More sophisticated tests require more sophisticated scoring—for example, in the combining of subtests, as in the O-A Battery Kit, the correcting for age trends, the reference to specialized norms for subpopulations, etc. These tax the time of the practicing psychologist unless he or she brings in computer aids.

The two main forms of proceeding from test profiles to psychological conclusions on an individual are 1) the behavioral equation—at present linear but potentially nonlinear—predicting *performance*, and 2) the determination of fit to a type, predicting *adjustment* or fit. Numerical examples are worked out and cautions in the use of each discussed.

In Chapter 4 (and in more detail in Cattell, 1973a), the *utility coefficient, r_u,* of a test has been defined as the number of domains of prediction to which it has relevance. This coefficient derives both from the nature of the test and the data bases built up for it by life research. Tests centered on true broad unitary source traits will tend to have greater utility. Tests whose designers and users have covered broader data bases of evidence in clinical, educational and industrial fields will also have greater utility. Examples are given of systematic data base banks.

Once the psychological laws operating in a given field, as well as the principles defining the roles of each kind of source trait, begin to be established, practitioners are likely to have difficulty in making estimates in proportion to the complexities, even though they understand them, unless they use computer assistance. It has been shown, by Meehl and others, that the computer can handle diagnosis and prediction with greater accuracy than, say, an experienced clinician, once the number of facts to be taken into account exceeds a relatively small number. An example of computer handling is presented and discussed.

Computer-based interpretive reports are already available for the 16 P.F. and the MMPI, the HSPQ, the MAT and the CAQ. Those of the adult tests are also incorporated in reports addressed in detail to specific problems—the *Personal-Career Development Profile,* the *Marriage Counseling Report,* the *Executive Profile Survey,* the *Individualized Stress Management Plan,* the screening reports for law enforcement candidates, etc.

Further horizons for the computer appear in 1) on-line "immediate" testing-scoring, though this may remain too expensive if it ties up the computer; 2) computer adaptive testing, which aims to shorten testing time by confining to a crucial "difficulty" range which preliminary items results show to be appropriate for a given subject; 3) the rapid analysis of longitudinal test responses to changing stimuli in P-technique; and 4) the combination of testing with teaching as is already done in the cognitive area of teaching. Potentially this last could lead to "custom-tailored" therapy, combining general test results, including especially the *Motivation Analysis Test* results, with instruction fitted to the situation of the client. In approaching these horizons the computer is developing what might be thought of as the third generation of a technology that did not exist at all until about 1950.

CHAPTER 8

The Wider Scientific and Social Aspects of Psychological Testing

Ronald C. Johnson, Barbara D. Porteus, and Raymond B. Cattell

QUANTIFICATION: A NECESSITY

An art or craft may be well-developed without much in the line of quantitative information. Our ancestors first learned to smelt copper, lead, tin and, eventually, iron, without theory—though almost certainly with incantations—and without the aid of numbers. Qualitative information was needed—it had to be learned early that casting different metals required different temperatures, as well as other differences in treatment, and the experienced smith probably guessed correctly most of the time. However, the first step in the development of any science is to develop means by which the phenomena that form the subject matter of that science can be dealt with by means of numbers. The science of metallurgy emerged from a combination of craft knowledge and alchemy and was developed by employees of the Fugger mining dynasty in Germany in the 1500s. It was based on the use of numbers. It moved metallurgy from an art—dependent on the qualitative judgments of a master—into a science, producing replicable results through the use of quantitative methods.

Psychological assessment almost certainly was going on at the same time that our first efforts at smelting were occurring. The same residents of the Anatolian plateau who first learned to smelt iron almost certainly could and did at least roughly *rank order* their neighbors on their aptness at learning new skills and remembering that which was learned, on their degree of adherence to cultural values, on their degree of aggressiveness, and on many other personalogical attributes as well. They probably did as well in their rank ordering as do contemporary persons using a basically number-free qualitative approach to assessment.

There are master artists—master

craftsmen in psychology. Max Hutt often made remarkably accurate diagnostic statements on the basis of Bender-Gestalt scores; Theodore Reik, in *Listening with the Third Ear* (1949), recounts some of his most crucial insights regarding patients' psychodynamics derived from free associative techniques. Most psychologists or psychiatrists are not such masters, and those masters who do exist typically cannot transmit their intuitive knowledge to others, even when they serve long and close apprenticeships.

In order to begin to make the jump from art or craft to science, it is necessary to reduce the dimensions of concern to a manageable number of the most relevant ones, adequately sample each of these relevant domains, provide numerical values for the individual object of measurement telling us something of an individual's manifestation of these attributes relative to others in the same category and relating these domains to one another. A quantitative approach is necessary.

A quantitative approach necessarily loses some of the richness of human variability. Current personality questionnaires provide information regarding three to 28 bipolar personality dimensions, and undoubtedly lose some of the richness of individual variations on the thousands of personality traits described by Allport and Odbert (1936). This is the basis of complaint of the more humanistic psychologist against the psychometrist. But the humanist, concerned with uniqueness, is not in a position to develop an understanding of the commonality of factors underlying uniqueness and, in fact, having made the statement that personality is unique, can go no further; he or she cannot engage in the usual business of science or make generalizations or predictions. It is from numbers that statistical predictions can be made. These predictions permit the development of scientific laws which, once derived, augment the power of statistical predictions.

WHY TEST? ALTERNATIVES TO TESTING

One of the authors of this chapter (Johnson) recalls chiding—while a graduate student—his mentor, the late John E. Anderson, with regard to Anderson's very high regard for intelligence tests. This took a bit of daring—Anderson was more than a bit austere, and was not a believer in the notion that collegiality extended to graduate students. However, after listening to some fairly standard complaints about intelligence tests, such as possible social class bias, the probability that the most commonly used tests were constructed by psychologists to tap the domains on which they perform well (such as verbal fluency) at the expense of other domains (such as spatial ability) at which they do poorly, etc., Anderson responded with an anecdote about what the world was like back around the turn of the century, well before psychological tests came into much use.

He grew up on a ranch outside of Lander, Wyoming, and when he got old enough, was enrolled in the first grade of a one-room rural school. The youngest student was six-year-old Anderson; the oldest students were teenaged boys who already were top hands on the surrounding ranches but who were forced to go to school as well. As in Eggleston's *The Hoosier Schoolmaster* (1899), which had to do with the decades in which Indiana was the frontier on our westward trek, the schoolmaster had to establish authority by beating each of these aspiring cowhands in a rough-and-tumble fight. Having done so, the schoolmaster could begin to practice his art of teaching. It was a brutal time, and a time in which there was no recognition of individual differences in learning capability (unless one's brains had been jangled by being kicked in the head by a horse). Anderson, apparently a sensitive youngster, at least for Lander, Wyoming, at the turn of the century, had been somewhat dismayed by the fights between the schoolmaster and his students. He became even more dismayed to learn that the teacher used a whip. As Anderson pointed out, if one believes that each person is equally capable of learning, yet some do not learn, then this lack of learning results from a moral flaw. The nonlearner *chooses* not to learn. The whip will change this choice. Anderson was a good boy and a quick learner. He did not get whipped. But his memories stayed with him.

He responded further by saying that intelligence tests aren't perfect, by any means. *But* the mere existence of measures of individual differences is indicative of a belief in individual differences in capability and in the need for judging performance on relative rather than absolute grounds. He argued that despite possible misdiagnoses and despite problems regarding test validity, the testing movement *per se* was a remarkably important element in changing our views regarding the basis of individual differences, and in making us more accepting of and humane toward human variability.

Anderson enlarged on his theme. Tests *may* be constructed on such a fashion that a given test is biased in terms of social class or race ethnicity. However, the very introduction of testing on a broad scale ultimately forced those persons involved in testing, no matter what their preconceptions, to the realization that despite differences in mean scores (the bases of which still are a matter of hot debate), tremendous overlaps existed across groups. It may be that the contents or the proper responses to items in ability tests are class- or race-biased, although claims that such is the case are unconvincing. Even if such claims were true, they ignore the very important point that as soon as adequate psychometric tests were developed it became clear that so much overlap existed between groups that each individual had to be considered in his or her own right—*not* as a member of a group be-

lieved to be superior or inferior to other groups. This was a more major advance toward true equality than has yet come from the antitesting movements.

Eysenck may have been both too kind (regarding status) and too cruel (regarding personal comparisons) when he noted that Judge Peckham (Eysenck & Kamin, 1981, p. 88) shares a distinction with both Hitler and Stalin, when Judge Peckham, in the "Larry P. case" banned the use of psychometric tests in California, as did both Hitler and Stalin in their respective domains. Psychometric tests are by no means perfect, but they do allow a comparison of a given person with that person's presumed peers on a quantitative basis without regard to such other personal attributes as race, sex, or family status. Psychometric tests may be imperfect but they do lead to an understanding that deficiencies or deviations in behavior are a result of wide individual differences in capability and in mode of response to environmental stimuli, rather than solely a consequence of perversity, lack of motivation, or inclination toward evil ways on the part of individuals who do not meet society's expectations.

The Economic Value of Tests

One major area of psychological testing is in personnel selection in industry. So long as there are more job applicants than there are jobs, the employer can select—by means of psychological tests—those applicants most likely to be effective employees. To what extent does the use of tests actually lead to the hiring of more efficient employees? How much gain in economic efficiency results from selection on the basis of test scores? This section deals with these questions, and is based on a recent, very thorough review of the literature by Jensen (1981, 1984) who, in turn, based a sizeable portion of his presentation on the research of Hunter and Schmidt.

Jensen tabulated 537 future performance and concurrent validity coefficients of the General Aptitude Test Battery with job performance in 446 different occupations. The median predictive validity for g, general intelligence, was $+.27$; for g plus specific factors, $+.36$. Clearly, most of the predictive power comes from g. Most of the variance in performance is unaccounted for by g—or by g plus other scores. However, as will be discussed below, even this modest validity is of substantial economic importance. Selection tests are valuable in situations in which one has a substantial number of job applicants for a comparatively few jobs—one establishes a high cutting point for employment and even a validity of .25 or .30 is important.

Hunter, Schmidt, and co-workers analyzed the results of hundreds of different studies, based on data from hundreds of thousands of subjects. They concluded that the predictive validity of individuals' scores on tests of general ability are not situational-specific or job-specific. The predictive importance of g goes up as the level of employment goes up (Schmidt & Hunter, 1978; Schmidt, Hunter, Pearlman, & Shane, 1979; Hunter, 1980), but differences in test validity are small, even across quite different jobs. Tests that are valid predictors of success in training also are valid predictors of job performance (Pearlman, Schmidt, & Hunter, 1980).

Hunter and Schmidt (1982) have provided data regarding the economic effects of the use of tests in employee selection. Jensen summarized these data as presented below:

Here are some examples of Hunter and Schmidt's estimates.

In a study of budget analysts, Schmidt and Hunter (1981) estimated that the dollar value productivity of superior performers (top 15%) was $23,000 per year greater than that of low performers (bottom 15%). Computer programmers showed a comparable difference. Hunter and Schmidt point out that when these dollar losses are multiplied by the number of employees in an organization and by the number of years they are employed, the losses quickly mount into millions of dollars.

In a study of the Philadelphia Police Department, with 5000 employees, Hunter (1979) estimated that abandonment of a general ability test for the selection of police officers would cost a total of 180 million dollars over a ten-year period.

The estimated gain in productivity resulting from one year's use of a more valid selection procedure for computer programmers in the Federal government range from $5.6 to $92.2 million for different sets of estimation parameters (Hunter & Schmidt, 1982). For the whole Federal government, with 4 million employees, Hunter and Schmidt conservatively estimate that optimal selection procedures would save $16 billion per year.

Hunter and Schmidt (1982) have also estimated the cost-effectiveness of using tests for job selection on a national scale. They estimate, for example, that the difference in yearly productivity between random assignment of the work force to jobs and assignment based on a test with an average validity of only .45, applied in a working population of 90 million, would be about $169 billion. If general ability tests, to the extent that they are currently used in selection, were to be abandoned, the estimated loss in national productivity would be about $80 billion per year. If current selection standards were relaxed overall to amount to a selection cut-off at the 33rd percentile of the distribution of test scores, with the top two-thirds of the total distribution being selected, there would be an estimated productivity loss of $54 to $60 billion. On the other hand, if more optimal test selection procedures were practiced throughout the entire economy, Hunter and Schmidt estimate that the GNP would be increased by $80 to $100 billion per year. Even conceding possibly a fairly wide margin of error in these estimates, it is apparent that the economic consequences of using selection tests is far from trivial. (Jensen, 1981, pp. 37-38)

Several newspaper and magazine articles appeared at the time this chapter was being written, lamenting the decrease in productivity per worker during the previous year. Some of this decrease almost certainly can be attributed to the decreased use of psychologically sound tests in employee selection and placement. We blame OPEC for our economic woes. If Hunter and Schmidt are correct (and their estimates almost certainly are most conservative), the renewed and expanded use of tests by industry would result in a sufficient increase in production to pay a good portion of our fuel bill and to get our economy moving again.

Testing and the Clinician

An important responsibility of the clinician who has been asked to do a psychological evaluation is to clarify the purpose of the evaluation. Notwithstanding careful and due regard for professional and ethical considerations, qualified clinicians may assume that their assessment methods and techniques will assist in garnering valuable, insightful, and essential information for an analysis of the person they are to evaluate; their expertise and training and the research may bolster their confidence in making such an assumption. An issue, though seemingly obvious, however, is understanding the assumptions underlying the request for the evaluation, whether this comes from the person himself, his family, a social institution or system.

Often a referring agent does not want to spend—or does not have—a great deal of time or energy, or there may be other resistances to answering questions or clarifying the problems. This issue may be related to much larger ones—such as validity and test bias—but in practice may be related more on an individual level to elucidating what questions are being asked and who is asking the questions for what purposes. Raising this issue is not meant to imply that the person making the request has questions which are wrong or is intending something socially unacceptable. Rather, there are often unclear or nonspecific requests for evaluations which assume that the psychological

clinician can take care of the problem, will define the issues, and ultimately delineate a solution.

Psychologists sometimes are expected to know more than they do. Role expectations and demands by others can be substantial and should not be underestimated. The psychologist must be careful to clarify what he will and/or will not do, to be clear about his role. He may very well be able to give meaning to an unclear situation or problem; however, whether doing so is useful or relevant will depend on the reasons for the request for the evaluation. Sometimes questions are asked when no evaluation is necessary; the referring person may have general questions which do not require an evaluation of an individual and could be attenuated by consultation. Sometimes questions are asked for which the answers are not wanted and in fact could be unacceptable and countertherapeutic. The important point is that the clinical psychologist needs to evaluate the purpose for the request for the evaluation as carefully as he needs to evaluate the referred patient.

Other reasons for understanding the purpose for the request is that there is a wide variety of tests and techniques from which some need to be selected for measuring the relevant aspects of behavior and there is often a wealth of information available from a psychological evaluation from which the clinician must select relevant aspects in making his report. For example, an emotionally passive-aggressive, retarded child may be found to have problems because of these characteristics and could benefit from therapy and specialized education directed at remediating these problems, but the primary problem in the child's life may be parental rejection and a lack of a position of relative importance or status within the family. The intrafamilial factor may be what exacerbates the symptoms which led to the referral. If the referring agent and the psychologist have not clarified the purpose of the referral in depth, it is very possible the intrafamilial dynamics would not be delineated. Also, the psychological evaluation report needs to be made with considerable judgment, weighing all the findings and the individual's social context, which includes the purpose of the referral.

Often, when motivation, environmental factors, developmental factors or other adjustment criteria are aberrant, precarious, or at issue, there is a request for a psychological evaluation. For example, the client may be placed in an institution, such as an adolescent in a detention facility; there may be a family crisis; a child may be starting school, entering puberty, or not reading or talking or walking. This is often the time when the psychological evaluation is conducted. Test results must be questioned and interpreted carefully, as there are complex relationships between emotionality and intelligence. These are crucial times for the psychologist to be aware of the purpose of the referral for testing and to make careful judgments about the reliability of the findings and what is to be included in the evaluation report. It is important to remember that the psychologist is often seen as the expert and any negative generalizations about the client/testee may have long-lasting reactive effects, which were never intended by the psychologist. That is, those receiving the results may react negatively to the client/testee on the basis of the interpretation partly because the psychological report was negative (i.e., the psychological report may be accepted as an unchanging fact or "truth"), especially if the interpretation does not address the nature of the findings and the factors which may impinge on their reliability.

Other factors which impinge on the testing purposes include whether the information is going to be useful for remedial work and treatment and whether appropriate treatment is available. One may question if a recommendation for a certain kind of remedial work would be useful if it is not available, e.g., tutoring in reading or long-term group or individual therapy. If it is not available, one may wonder if making the recommendation may be setting the client up to feel disheartened or disillusioned with the "system" or, on the other hand, providing the basis for identifying a need for a service which must be identified before it can be provided for, improved, or changed in the future.

Clinical psychological evaluations can be used in a wide social context for a variety of reasons and provide one of the bases for decisions having legal and social consequences. An evaluation may be used in educational classification (e.g., learning-disabled, severely emotionally disturbed), in determining the necessity for services (e.g., diagnostic labeling for the provision for services by third-party payers), for making decisions concerning rights and responsibilities (e.g., in cases of mental incompetence, child or parent abuse and neglect, parole), and in personnel selection.

As mentioned earlier, test results can be used for describing, understanding and measuring changes in behavior. When directed at clinically prescribing change, as for specifying the need for therapy or a particular mode of therapy, the use of the psychological evaluation becomes somewhat more complex. Whether the diagnostician/evaluator becomes the therapist may be an issue. One of the advantages of the therapist and diagnostician being identical is that the therapist understands the evaluation, the relevance of the findings and the recommendations; the theoretical frames of reference are the same and there should be no difficulty with follow-up, assuming the client is willing. If the therapist is the same as the diagnostician who has identified needed areas for change and the diagnostician has had to make a report to another authority, such as a court, even though the diagnostician had the full consent of the client, the client may not be able to develop trust with the psychotherapist for a therapeutic relationship. If, on the other hand, the therapist is not the same psychologist as the diagnostician, the therapist may not accept the diagnostician's findings or their relevance, proceed with his own evaluation, and provide the kind of therapy directed by his own assessment and consistent with his theoretical framework. If this is the situation, the evaluation by the original diagnostician turns out to have been more for persuasive than therapeutic uses. A different kind of evaluation report, one which did not delineate the recommended therapeutic mode, might have been equally useful.

THE AUGMENTATION OF STATISTICAL PREDICTIONS BY SCIENTIFIC LAWS

It is easy for a psychologist who produces a reasonably comprehensive and thorough profile regarding his client to slip into the assumption that the values in his file *are* that person. There are four good reasons why they are not:

1) Even with, say, 15 ability factors, 28 personality traits, and a dozen motivation measures—which is more than one would achieve for the average client—there are regions, accounting for perhaps 25% of the behavioral sphere, for which the psychologist has no predictors.
2) The person is subject to change from the moment of testing.
3) Even apart from change, the psychometric reliabilities and validities of instruments are imperfect.
4) In the equations combining situation and personality, the psychologist at present has only a trivial list of well-determined situational behavioral indices (b's in the specification equation for various performances and situations).

The nature of the first of these sources of error and uncertainty is obvious. Though theoretically we handle the virtually infinite variety of human behavior by "specific abilities" and other traits (T_j's in the specification equation) there is in fact no hope of covering them. But the structured-learning theorist "takes arms against the sea of troubles" in which the reflexologist drowns, by recognizing broad and specific unitary structures, the discovered list of which already predicts the larger part of behavior. In test terms this means using a few omnibus measures such as the Thurstone primaries, the 16 P.F. and the MAT instead of cluttering the test kit with a host of special-purpose tests for hundreds of special purposes and criteria.

As for the second reason, the habit of thinking that our test measures represent fixed characteristics of the individual has probably been fostered by the accident that psychological testing began with intelligence tests, which deal with a characteristic of high constitutional determination and stability. From the now available pioneer nature-nurture researches (Cattell, 1982; Dixon & Johnson, 1980; Loehlin & Nichols, 1976) investigating heredity and *personality* factors, we can conclude that it is true that three or four of them (in the O-A Kit and 16 P.F.) have the constitutional firmness of intelligence (notably the temperament traits U.I.16, 19, 20, and 24) (see Chapter 12) (and Q data factors, F, H, and I) (see Chapter 11), but most have substantial environmental determination that could change them appreciably over the years. It is probable that a susceptibility to change with changing life situation is even more characteristic of dynamic traits and interests, as in the Kuder, Strong, and MAT data.

Consequently, when we think of our central predictive model, the behavioral specification equation as set out in Chapter 1, thus

$$a_{ij} = b_{jl}T_{lt} + \ldots + b_{jk}T_{ki} + b_j T_{ji} \qquad (8\text{-}1)$$

(where a is the action or performance, the b's are the weights on that performance for test j, and the T's are the trait strengths in the individual), we must never forget that these T values *can* change for the subject i. Whenever we make a prediction from an individual profile of T's, described in the two-file record system in the last chapter, by bringing it into conjunction with a profile of b's from the prediction file, we must ask *how long* it has been since the T profile was obtained.

Our task will then be to ask either, "What would be the typical amount of systematic error of estimate introduced by this much time lapse since the measures were obtained?" or "What do I know from the general laws of psychology that would permit me to reduce this error by anticipating the changes?" As to the first, a purely statistical answer is possible simply from the stability coefficients of the trait measurements psychometrically obtained for *given* intervals. This is a purely actuarial statement, which can be put in the form that "after two years a measure of surgency (F factor) has a 50/50 chance of being out by 1.3 stens" or "from the ages of 18 to 21 the typical member of our culture has an even chance of deviating from his original score on dominance (E factor) by more or less than 0.8 stens."

Actually, as the work of E. Lowell Kelly (1955), Nesselroade and Reese (1973), Schaie and Strother (1968), and others have shown, people do not usually change much in their personality and abilities (in rank relative to other people) after they reach 30 years of age. And even before that, though many traits have only a small hereditary determination, the inertia of functional autonomy or trait rigidity makes it possible to project with considerable confidence from a present trait score to a score a few years hence. Thus, even *without* scientific understanding of how and why changes occur, we can set up actuarial expectancies, on *purely statistical grounds*, as to how much "wobble" there is likely to be in our predictive

use of test measures over various time intervals. However, since part of the stability of traits is undoubtedly tied up with stability of situation, e.g., of the job and people with whom one associates, and since cultural change may alter the average stability of life situations, we should exercise due caution in carrying over the stability coefficients found at one place and time to another.

Obviously the second, not merely actuarial approach, in which one asks, rather, what scientific psychological laws will permit one to estimate the specific nature of the change, is a superior one. Already we have tolerably accurate laws about the life course of intelligence (Chapter 9), of surgency, of anxiety and many other 16 P.F. and O-A Battery personality factors (Chapters 12 and 13). With these we can extrapolate for an individual's score some years into the future in regard to the *average* age trend. This is discussed under particular trait measurements in Part II, but there is now an extensive literature, beginning in modern form with the analytical approach of Baltes (1968) and Cattell (1969a, 1970b, 1973c), followed by Horn (1970), Schaie (1973) and others. This distinguishes the typical ontogenetic, epoch-free age change from results due to changing culture with historical events. It aims to break down again into the endogenous (genetically determined) and the exogenous (environmentally determined, threptic) part. These analyses require particular operations, comparing *cursive* with *cross-sectional* series. The nature of these concepts and operations is most compactly indicated by the diagnosis in Table 8.1.

Among the major advantages of working with structured psychometric principles and tests, i.e., with tests targeted at known structures, are not only a) ready recourse to age trend curves, with the meaningfulness of the above epo- and ecogenic analysis, but also b) the utilization of knowledge, as it steadily accumulates from basic personality research, on how various life and learning experiences contribute to changes in the primary personality source traits.

Information on the first of these is substantial, covering by now most abilities (Horn & Cattell, 1966; Cattell, 1971a) and most primary personality traits (Cattell, 1973a; Cattell & Schuerger, 1978), as illustrated in Figure 5.6 (p. 93).

As to specific life effects, we have the five-year New Zealand study of Barton, Cattell, and Vaughan (1973), certain college studies (Graffam, 1967; Izard, 1962), and the clinical studies of Hunt et al. (1959) and Rickels et al. (1966) showing such effects as an increase in personality factors, E, F, and especially C (ego strength)

with therapy; the increase of C with belonging to a church (or equivalent); the increase of C with successful marriage; the increase of G (superego) with added responsibilities; the decline of E, dominance, with chronic illness, and its rise with leaving home, occupational promotion, and wider social contacts; the reduction of surgency, E, with marriage; the rise in I, premsia, in those who go to college compared to those who do not, and so on.

Although structural testing is new, the number of valuable diagnostic and prognostic insights that are rendered possible by its association with basic personality and ability research is already consider-

TABLE 8.1

Analysis of Life-Span Development Curves

(A) POSSIBLE COMBINATIONS OF OBSERVATIONS

	Same Age at Testing		Different Age at Testing	
	Same Birthday	Different Birthday	Same Birthday	Different Birthday
Same Year of Testing	No Series	Impossible	Impossible	SC
Different Year of Testing	Impossible	FCE	SL and CL	EE

Note: Only one category permits a further subdivision into same subjects or different subjects (from the same age group), namely, SL and CL.

(B) RESULTING SERIES

Calendar Year of Birth	Different Persons Tested Age at Testing						
	10	20	30	40	50	60	
1910	1920	1930	1940	1950	1960	1970	SL
1900	1910	1920	1930	1940	1950	1960	
1890	1900	1910	1920	1930	1940	1950	
1880	1890	1900	1910	1920	1930	1940	FE
1870	1880	1890	1900	1910	1920	1930	SC
1860	1870	1880	1890	1900	1910	1920	
1850	1860	1870	1880	1890	1900	1910	
	FCE						

Calendar Year of Birth	Same Persons Tested Age at Testing						
	10	20	30	40	50	60	
1910	1920	1930	1940	1950	1960	1970	CL$_1$
1900	1910	1920	1930	1940	1950	1960	
1890	1900	1910	1920	1930	1940	1950	CL$_2$

able, and highlights the comparative priority of working with "special-purpose" tests unrelated to structure. However, this is not the place to enter on basic personality theory itself, and for treatments related to measurements as here surveyed the reader must be referred to Cattell and Kline (1977), Cattell, *Personality and Learning Theory* (1979c, 1980a), Pervin (1975) or Wiggins (1973).

WHO SHOULD TEST? THE TRAINING REQUIREMENTS FOR THE PSYCHOLOGIST

The importance of theory for a practitioner is only equaled by the importance of the practitioner to theory. The history of medicine, for example, scintillates with basic contributions made by alert practitioners from daily experience, and in psychology, of course, we have Freud and Jung, whose theories came from good empirical observation.

What this professional training should be depends on what role the profession is to perform. In the early stage of psychological practice Cattell protested (in "Psychologist or Medical Man," 1932a) that the cramping effect of making the psychologist a mere handmaiden (appropriate when much testing was done by women B.A.'s) to the psychiatrist would prevent the rise of the fully qualified professional psychologist. In the next decade that danger passed, except in some countries of Mediterranean culture where the new profession of psychologist fought entrenched medical and religious conservatism. However, even with the rise of the licensed Ph.D. psychologist, presumably able to link psychometric diagnosis with therapy, the question of status training is still not clearly answered. One problem is that practice has splintered into clinical, educational, and industrial psychologists, into marriage counselors, child and family counselors, alcohol and drug specialists, etc.

If one looks over existing texts on psy-

chometry, one wonders for which of these they are written. Several talk mainly of educational psychometry or industrial selection tools and do not seem written for a psychologist in the fullest sense of the word. They belong with several others that are mere catalogues, avoiding the deeper psychological and structural questions.

As a rationale for this light skimming over basic psychology in the training of school counselors, child psychologists, and those in refresher courses, we are sometimes told a) that the individuals involved do not have enough general psychological and statistical background to go deeper, and b) that the job opportunities are so distributed that only a small fraction of those engaged in psychological testing can be induced to become fully qualified psychologists. As to b), it is undoubtedly true that perhaps 5,000 psychologists in the American Psychological Association are qualified, in university degree terms, to give and interpret tests, whereas perhaps 50,000 people around the country are engaged in some form of psychological test administration and interpretation.

Perhaps this discrepancy in the relation of skill to decisions required is not so serious as it would be in, say, the field of surgery or of commercial airline pilot flying qualifications. Yet some very disturbing things can happen, for example, to school children and clinical patients, as a result of misguided use of test results. The element of justice in the public outcry over psychological testing in schools a few years ago resided not so much in some of the arguments used against testing as such, as in the assertion that many people using tests did not know what they were doing.

Let us fairly recognize that a gross discrepancy exists today between the number of people engaged in testing and the number really qualified to offer a skilled, safe, and effective application of the results. Efforts to reduce this gap are being made from several directions, notably:

1) the setting up of state licensing laws for controlling the qualification of psychologists along the same professional lines as medical men;

2) the ethical practice of test publishers of supplying tests only to qualified users;

3) the encouragement by universities of those who wish to go into practice to proceed to adequate postgraduate work, either at the M.A. or the Ph.D. level—indeed, already in the last decade, the collaboration of universities and state licensing boards has resulted in a Ph.D. with internship being required for most work;

4) the planning of organizational hierarchies in practicing institutions as discussed here and later in this chapter, better to utilize available skills and sources of information.

To say "amen" to these propositions is not, however, to argue that all people doing testing need equal qualifications, or that all is well with the above plans. The institution, for example, of a *doctorate of psychology*, supposedly analogous to a doctor of medicine, and lacking the research training of the Ph.D., is not truly as adequate as the medical degree, because medicine has reached a substantial level of effectiveness, whereas psychology is where medicine was two centuries ago and may change in ways which only a researcher can follow. Twenty years after the doctorate it is pretty safe to say the Psy.D. will still be making use of the accepted knowledge of his or her graduation decade, whereas there is hope that the Ph.D. will have participated in and kept up with intervening research. However, some schools of professional psychology giving the Psy.D. *do* include emphasis on research training.

Thus, a doctorate may not always be a guarantee of understanding the latest psychometrics, and to this we would add that the absence of a doctorate should not prevent personnel from actually *giving* psychological tests. The meaning of the "hierarchy" concept above is that, in the name of good organization and of the best service to the public for money available, qualified technicians may well *give tests*, even though they may not be competent to interpret them. Administration and scoring are quite different, and the authors in practice have known a young clerical assistant to do a better job of administering tests to young children than some Ph.D.'s. There is thus no reason why, with certain tests, the actual administration of tests should not be delegated to a clerical assistant, teacher, or social worker properly trained by the supervising psychologist for that particular test situation. Researching with psychiatrists in private practice, Cattell and Rickels were unable to detect any difference between the test-retest score reliabilities of anxiety scales and regression batteries given by qualified persons and those given by alert clerical and nursing help. *It is in the conversion to standard scores, the interpretation, the diagnosis, and the computing of future predictions that the fully qualified psychologist is needed.* And even here, many analyses and predictions could be handled by technicians working in a central computer service.

However, centrally in any such school or clinical organization, and, it is hoped, in increasing numbers, one must have professional psychologists at least qualified to the M.A. and, as a general rule, to the Ph.D. level. In the training of such a psychologist it is essential that both statistical and clinical-personality experience be included. The presently much-debated issue of whether the clinical practitioner should also feel at home with scientific research methods is one not so easily answered. The prejudice of the writers is that as high a proportion as possible of practitioners should be research-trained, even if this means skimping somewhat on the training in "bedside manner." This argument is based, as stated above, on the probability that great strides will be made in practical techniques and tests during the next two decades, and that a purely "cookbook" practitioner will be unable to keep up with advances.

It is in the framework of social and scientific needs just stated that the present book moves away somewhat from the usual testing or psychometric test of the last decade. We have aimed at the education necessary for the Ph.D. psychologist in practice on his or her own or directing a clinic or industrial unit. The training for those who help in administration and scoring is something that he can give. He himself, or she herself, if in clinical psychology, does not have to be immediately familiar with such recondite statistical procedures as in factor analysis, multiple discriminant functions, and so on, but only what a factor is, conceptually, and how and why source trait and state scores are strung along in the specification equation. Beyond statistics he must surely understand the nature of various personality and ability traits and their natural history, nature-nurture ratios, age curves, responsiveness to learning, etc.—and, of course, their relations to the practically important criteria in his or her own field.

PUBLIC RELATIONS IN PSYCHOLOGICAL TESTING

It may be a truism to say that the public relations of a profession can be as good as and no better than the ethical and scientific standards to which it shows habitual commitment. All else is a matter of local and temporary ups and downs. Psychological associations, national and local, have done much in recent years to ensure good ethical standards of practice and, within the English-speaking countries particularly, the status of the psychologist seems now as well-assured, professionally, from the standpoint of the practitioner, and

ethically, from the standpoint of the public, as that of a member of the medical profession.

Our concern so far has been with the scientific standards. To be objective—and as candid as truth demands—there is a large variation in the thoroughness and up-to-dateness of technical psychological education, and many practitioners are undoubtedly falling far short of the best diagnostic and predictive service that could be given today. This book is concerned with tools and methods of diagnostic and predictive work rather than of therapy —except insofar as intercurrent testing should be an essential part of evaluating and redirecting therapy. The chief criticism from the public does not concern the psychologists' and psychiatrists' ethics but the poor level of effectiveness of therapy with psychotics, neurotics, addicts, and criminals. Certain notorious court cases, in which unreliability of diagnosis by psychiatrists and psychologists has been highlighted, have evoked real public distrust. This is not a charge of incompetence against the practitioners but against their specialty itself, as a presumed science. (It casts guilt only on those prosperous practitioners who do no research themselves, who refuse to inconvenience themselves for research by others, and who cover up ignorance with complacency.) When Eysenck (1952, 1961) pointedly and courageously presented evidence that neurotics psychiatrically treated by psychoanalysis and related methods improved no faster than those left to nature, or when Cureton (1947) showed that physical training reduced anxiety as much as the same time in therapy, their researches quickly brought violent attacks on their supposed weaknesses. The weaknesses were trivial and shared by the bulk of research in the clinical penumbra. The fact remains that therapy has much research to do before its methods become even tolerably effective.

By contrast, psychometry stands on a

very adequate theoretical basis and it is one of the few public applications of psychology that has introduced new levels of effectiveness, emerging in a pragmatically confirmed technology in school, industry, and clinic. (Learning theory also works, but reinforcement was known to Aristotle and every school teacher since, anyway.) But although the psychometrist is in good standing scientifically, he has had in the last 15 years a disaster—an unnecessary disaster—in public relations.

Endless social philosophy about rights to privacy, fears of slurs against minority groups, instances of misclassification in school, and the like has been poured out in the last decade, but the real motive behind much of this is simply that people in general dislike being tested. (Except the few who take the ancient word of wisdom "know thyself" seriously.) People dislike a checkup at doctor or dentist and the notion of a Day of Judgment long ago impaired enthusiasm for religion. Practically, a test may mean being denied a job or refused entry to a university, and it always contains implicitly the affront to narcissism that someone is better than oneself in some direction.

Every individual has a right to be tested or not to be tested, according to his choice, but he does not have the right to practice surgery, or risk the lives of 600 human beings as he flies a plane, without stringent tests. And though these are salient examples of the principle of *responsibility through examination*, it really permeates all society, and the person who declines to demonstrate his or her capacities while demanding a job is grossly unfair to his or her fellow citizens.

Although the psychometrist, standing on a fine scientifically checked technique, has nothing to fear ethically or scientifically, he nevertheless has suffered from the political rabble-rousers and the hair-splitting and Protean rationalization of test-allergy in the last decade. Some origins of this pungent intellectual smog were the

irateness of some minority groups performing poorly on tests, the hippie movement with its demand for removal of school and college examinations and, in Britain, the labor government's abolition of selection by intelligence test for more advanced secondary school education. The regression from reliability and justice of individual promotion or selection which followed was frightful. In Britain, evaluation by a teacher—ultimately a headmaster who could not know all his students—was substituted in many cases, with all its possibilities of personal bias, for the much-criticized intelligence test. In industrial situations "clinical evaluation," i.e., an interview, often replaced a test battery that had shown substantial criterion prediction.

Despite 40 years of statistical demonstration that the interview is significantly less reliable than the test battery, the unpopular tests were often dropped. "Popular" rather than "sound and serious" is the key word in this evaluation of testing, and journalists rather than professional psychologists have been allowed to shape public opinion. As late as December 1977, apparently unaware that the smog was beginning to disperse, a journalist in *Time* claimed that I.Q. scores "fluctuate widely," that "the more tests that are devised, the more educators seem to doubt their validity" and that "I.Q. tests ... which are biased in favor of middle-class children ... are being abandoned in favor of tests [of academic performance]." There is a mixture of fact, of values, and of going with the direction assumed desired by most readers in these journalistic forays. The fact, in this case, is that the traditional intelligence test *is* biased to academic performance (not, however, a prerogative of the middle class), which is why here and elsewhere Cattell (1940, 1979b) has urged psychologists to study culture-fair tests and the findings about fluid intelligence.

Undoubtedly, psychologists owe it to

the public to ascertain carefully if there are any elements of technical truth in the criticisms and they owe it to their profession to take all possible steps to ensure better public acceptance and understanding of testing. The technical criticisms refer to issues already well understood: that intelligence is not the only predictor of scholastic success; that a test taken on only one occasion lacks perfect reliability; that some logical argument can be given for other alternatives in a multiple-choice test, and so on. The sad situation is, as stated in our opening comments, that one has to go beyond the honest scientific issues and to deal, almost therapeutically, with personal and political misunderstandings of an emotional kind. If one listens with the ear of a clinician, as free association proceeds in the rambling argument, he will soon perceive that the criticism is not so much of *psychological* tests as of *any* testing and evaluation. It is the pleasure principle speaking out against competition and the tough realities of meeting real demands for efficiency.

An objection that refers specifically to personality and motivation tests is that they are an invasion of privacy. It cannot be denied that personality and motivation cannot at present be investigated deeply without confronting the client with some disturbing questions or applying some slightly stressful objective tests. However, as the French proverb has it, one cannot make an omelette without breaking some eggs. But some of the school questionnaires which have been under fire *have* asked unnecessarily lewd or psychopathic questions. It is generally possible, as has been carefully done in such school questionnaires as the HSPQ and CPQ, to find substitute items which prove to be equally well-loaded on a factor, but which provoke less disturbance or invite less faking.

On the other hand, a psychological examination will always involve intrusion into some private realms and, just as some children decline to take a shirt off for a medical examination, and some adults resent a blood sample being taken, so there will be a minority unhappy about any psychological examination. For that matter, vaccination has its opponents too, as does even the germ theory of disease. The question is whether the results of psychological and medical examinations can be shown to yield such benefits and avoid such greater evils that it is reasonable for the public to put up with them. It has already been admitted above that some users of mental tests and, for that matter, some psychologists qualified before modern advances occurred, will not make the wisest—or even safe—use of test results. It is here that the public criticism deserves to be taken very seriously indeed. We must henceforth make sure that test results do not fall into incompetent hands, that privacy is not violated by the sense of leaking information that is privileged, and that the action taken on test results is scientifically justified and as tentative as the present state of our knowledge requires.

It remains to be seen how far psychologists may become subject to the same epidemic of malpractice suits as has swept into medicine over the last few years. Presumably the law will settle down to defenses against predatory suits, but since the very object of psychological testing is clinical, job, and educational decisions, the better the technical validity, the less the risk. The bill of a few years back that employers must prove some significant validity for employment tests disposed of a lot of face (faith) valid, useless tests that trained psychometrists had previously criticized in vain. But it also demanded such expensive research demonstration that much sound testing was discontinued at the same time.

Another major problem in public relations concerns correctly communicating results to laymen. The term includes the child and his parents and, if we are talking of really adequate psychometric understanding, teachers and social workers as well. While one can get guidance from what medicine has learned over centuries, there are some novel features special to psychological diagnosis. A physical illness carries only a limited stigma (though it has taken 50 years for cancer to become discussable), but insanity, addiction, mental defect, and the like strike at the heart of the individual's self-regard and social reputation and that of his or her near kin. New heights of tactfulness, regard for privacy, and care in explanation are demanded; yet, one must question the correctness of a rigid rule that an educational psychologist should not disclose an I.Q. In the basic sense of helping adjustments and avoiding unreal ambitions, it is more dangerous and culpable not to disclose it.

The danger in disclosing results of any psychological test is largely that its meaning will not be understood. Eysenck's writing in *Uses & Abuses of Psychology* (1953) and *Sense & Nonsense in Psychology* (1968) help clarify some of these issues. The fact is that *in proportion to psychology's becoming a science, its more technical conclusions will become incomprehensible to the layman.* To accept an obligation to explain to the subject, as when a doctor explains the implications of erythropoietic porphyria, should not mean abandoning the precision of scientific findings in the interest of a sympathetic understanding with the client. Surely one must question the dogmatic or fanciful statement by some quite eminent leaders in the guidance field that one should never *use* concepts which cannot be understood by parents or others who have to be taken into the counseling discussion. Medicine would go back 200 years if doctors could use only methods and concepts which laymen could understand. In the 16 P.F. profile sheets, which are often used in discussions with clients, parents, etc., popular expressions are used, alongside the

technical expressions, but to the psychologist the latter carry much fuller information. In the final analysis it is the technical expression which is correct. Moreover, there are even advantages in the cryptic symbol (as in a prescription), for part of the trouble with explaining in popular terms to the client is that popular terms are loose and can easily permit the individual to make disturbing conclusions, whereas the technical term permits the psychologist to give explanations adapted to the given client.

THE RESPONSIBILITIES OF REVEALING AND DISCUSSING TEST RESULTS

What has just been introduced as a part of public relations deserves fuller discussion as a technique. The psychologist more than the doctor needs such techniques because they merge into therapy itself. For example, the psychologist in a school system has relationships with teachers, parents, children, P.T.A. committees, special schools, children's courts, mental hospitals, etc.; in relation to all of these groups, some explanation of what the testing installation is meant to do is necessary. We have argued for the installation in any institution, such as a school, a company or a clinic, of comprehensive and routine testing in intelligence, personality motivation tests, and of achievement areas, in order that information may be available simultaneously to several services. Obviously, the usefulness of a design of this complexity needs to be explained to all concerned by some formal lecture or conference sessions, repeated perhaps once or twice each year, to keep newcomers up-to-date and all in a state of good coordination.

The problems of communication and public relations become more specific to each field and situation from this point on, but some illustrations can be given. For example, the industrial psychologist has the special problem of satisfying his employer, the management, while keeping in mind that his task is to benefit both the employee and production. He will meet plenty of irrational criticisms from both sides. After a psychologist has been at great pains to eliminate face validity from his tests, and thus reduce the opportunity to fake, a company director may tell him that this test obviously is not measuring what it is supposed to measure. Foremen will criticize his promotion of a man other than the one who has made himself most popular to them, and workmen will pester their union leader if the psychologist seems too busy timing workers with a stopwatch or introduces some fatigue-reducing innovation which conflicts with tradition.

Any plan to organize the choice of tests and the methods of recording as advocated here (simultaneously for scholastic, clinical and vocational selection ends) will raise in clear form the often veiled question, "To whom do these results belong?" It is well to have a civilized and explicit exchange and responsibility worked out among administrative powers!

The public relations and communications of the practicing psychometrist have other important aspects than those with the general public and his clients. They include relations with research centers, as in universities, with institutions such as schools and law courts, and with the military. As to the first, the *average* applied psychologist forgets all too readily his debt to the researcher (who often pursues his work scarcely paid), without whom his practice would show no improvement, initial validity even, and ultimately no salary! The machinery for directing an optimum fraction of the rewards of practice to the research that makes its efficacy possible is still quite inadequate in most communities. The least the practitioner can do is to *open his cases to researchers and, especially, keep those long-term records through which practice can contribute*

to research what no short-term Ph.D. research can do. The setting up of test installations needs direction not only from keen thoughts about validity, reliability, and comprehensiveness, but also from the needs of research analysis of developmental laws and comparisons of therapeutic methods. Until recent laws were passed, one had the impression that, whoever might have the right to the test results (among the maneuvering of rival little empires), the one person who did *not* was the client himself! This, in the case of I.Q. results, has often been extended to denying parents access to records of the I.Q.'s of their children. This practice directly contradicts the wisdom of the philosopher's injunction to "know thyself." Further, it finds one end of the professional spectrum—the school psychologist—acting in exactly the opposite way to the other, the therapist, whose task in a "deep analysis" is maximally to confront the patient with the realities of his or her own personality. Of course, there is some common sense in both views. Ignorant or unstable people have been known to do foolish things on being told the truth of psychological and medical examinations. And social envy can make much friction out of publicly discussed alleged differences in I.Q.'s.

If the meanings of psychological measures and of statistics were properly understood and care was used with ignorant or unstable clients, the dangers of giving information would be greatly reduced. Socially it is already evident that in societies such as America, most British Commonwealth countries, and Scandinavian countries, where much education regarding psychology has gone on, difficulties over psychological testing have been reduced to much smaller proportions. But the key words are "ignorant" and "unstable," and over instability there is no control other than the intensive, hand-in-hand facing of facts which the therapist can maintain but the school psychologist, for example, has no time to concentrate on.

We leave this communication problem somewhat in a realm of "if's" and "but's" because there is an astonishing dearth of research on the effects of making ability and personality measurement results available to the subjects concerned. In the writers' experience, the discussion with a subject of some ability, such as I.Q. score, which is believed to be comparatively fixed, has been beneficial to the individual in removing some doubts and helping him or her more realistically to shape life goals. In principle such information is no different from that which a boy gets when he realizes his stature is not going to place him as tallest in class, or when a girl first sees her averagely attractive profile in a wardrobe mirror. If individuals can be wisely helped in integrating such facts and their aspirations into a well-integrated self-sentiment, so much the better. In some cases known to the writers, the discussion of a personality profile has led to decided steps toward self-improvement or to better control and expression of more fixed temperamental qualities. Conceivably, over time and in subtle ways, substantial changes will be found to occur in groups regularly informed of psychological test results compared with those who have no such service, illustrating the German adage "Selbst erkenntnis ist die erste Schritt zur Besserung" (Self-knowledge is the first step toward improvement.).

Meanwhile, the psychologist should make sure that in situations where test results *are* made known to the subject:

a) the subject is given an adequate understanding of what the traits are and our limits of understanding them;

b) an explanation is given (i) of the magnitude of errors of measurement, i.e., that every test score is an *estimate* with a *probability* of truth only, and (ii) of the fact that very few traits need stay fixed;

c) a skilled psychological decision is made, relative to the subject's maturity and stability, of how and how much information can be imparted.

But when all is said, assisting a subject to self-insight and improvement is one of the most onerous and most valuable duties of the psychologist. And perhaps the time will come when it will be economically feasible for the community to permit the psychologist not only to spend time with the deviants but also to give the time that may be necessary to discuss results constructively with every individual normal school child.

THE DESIRABLE QUALIFICATIONS OF TEST DESIGNERS AND PUBLISHERS

Having asked who should have access to tests, it is natural that we should ask also about the qualifications of those who design them. Here, as often, history and the ideal are not the same thing, and we should first realistically glance at history.

Every school teacher has been a maker of tests from time immemorial. We know now that much of this assessment of pupils has been of low validity and reliability—as witness, for example, the blindness of teachers to the talents of many individuals, regarded with scorn at school, who made remarkable contributions in later years. Such individuals might nowadays still make poor school performance, but their intelligence, personality, and motivation test results would open our eyes to the talent present and permit us to recognize what lies behind the mediocre classroom performance.

However, we are not so much concerned with dependence on school achievement tests at the cost of analysis of intelligence and personality (such as existed for centuries and exists in Russia and in American opponents of intelligence testing) as in the test-construction skills themselves.

As any comparison of, say, ETS products in attainment tests with most classroom products will show, there is now a body of advanced professional technique in evaluating progress in various fields for which the average teacher lacks the necessary statistical and computational resources. Such examinations, moreover, have three purposes (Cattell, 1937b): to assess the student's progress; to apply motivational pressure to study; and to assess the goodness of teaching. These purposes require subtle differences in construction.

The central conclusion is that, as in most cultural advances, a new specialization has appeared, and though it must be kept in a wholistic vision, test construction now calls for the hand of the psychometric specialist. Enough has been demonstrated about the enormous unreliability and vulnerability to bias of the essay type of examination, the superficiality of the interview, and the subjectivity of clinical diagnosis,* to justify placing the design of diagnostic tools in the hands of psychometrically critical and capable psychological specialists. These test specialists must keep close contact with the needs and insights of those in the field—the teachers, social workers, industrial psychologists, and psychiatrists. But test construction can no longer be safely left to the latter.

As a glance at our journals or at Buros's *Mental Measurements Yearbook* will show, published tests are today actually constructed by individual academic and professional psychologists, by private enterprise and so-called nonprofit test publishers, and by government and state organizations such as the public school systems, the military, and the civil service. Incidentally, some of the most extensive (but also, unfortunately, some of the most hurried and immediate-purpose) construction of tests ever undertaken was done by the military in World War II.

Because almost all institutions get hidebound, while some individuals do not, it would be fatal for basic progress in test design if a situation developed in which individuals could not construct tests and get them published. Committees can be depended upon to work meticulously and with common sense upon the last generation's ideas. Unfortunately, the optimistic individual creator will quickly discover that more resources are needed to produce a finished test than the average psychologist ever imagines.

Over and above the basic research on the structures to be measured, there is the long process of inventing many items, the rejection of a large proportion of them by validity tests at item analysis, as well as for inappropriate difficulty, for unexpected associations and responses found on trial, and for many other causes. Then there is the balancing of items for yes and no answers, and for suppression effects on unwanted factors or, in ability tests, their ranking in exact difficulty order. Next there is exploration of test formats and outlays, for visibility, clarity to the subject, and reduction of paper and printing costs. At that time the designer also will have to work out an answer sheet and a score key plan which gives maximum convenience to the scorer, at once for hand and machine scoring. This must be systematic yet not reveal patterns to the subject or result in undesirable practice and other sequence effects. The final instructions must be examined for clarity to different social subcultures or, if used internationally, across cultures. Finally there is the task of standardization, the obtaining of stratified samples, and the lengthy scoring and many-faceted analysis, e.g., of reliability, equivalence and stability coefficients, percentile, T-score, sten, etc. The user, moreover, will typically demand a standardization break-

---

*An experimentally checked instance is Cattell & Scheier's finding (1961) of a correlation of only 0.3 between two top psychiatric diagnosticians in assessing anxiety levels over some 80 patients.

down in multitables for men and women, for A, B, and (A + B) forms, separately, for students, for general population, and so on.

The inventive individual, creative within the science of psychometry, will also find himself up against vested interests, just as in other fields of science. And though no instance can be cited of a large concern buying up an invention in order to suppress it—as has occurred in applied physics and chemistry—vested interests have worked in other ways to preserve the status quo. Much of this large, test-using vested interest action is innocent. Psychologists keep most of their lives to the concepts and tests in which they were trained at graduation; comparisons of institutions and epochs require maintenance of the same tests; developmental diagnosis of individuals requires continuation of the same tests, and so on.*

If adequate innovation and experimental advance are to be maintained, the avoidance of a monopoly in test publishing is vital. This requires either private enterprise or checks and balances and freedom among government departments. The latter seems never to have worked as well as the former, and those who wish to check this might compare psychometric output in the U.S., Britain, West Germany, etc.,

with that in Communist countries. On the other hand, an enterprisingly run government department, because it does not have to depend on short-term commercial success, might introduce methods somewhat ahead of common demand of psychologists at the time. At least during the loosening up of customs which the two world wars produced, military psychometrics made great strides (see Vernon & Parry, 1949). As professors who have watched where their students go will probably testify, industry and university research tend to take the more enterprising individuals, and the civil service, the more safety-seeking. A social psychologist could probably document the long history of valuable inventions, etc. turned down by civil servants with little to gain and with tranquility and reputation to lose by taking anything but a safe conservative stand. And one may guess that the most effective system for psychological test advance and supply will turn out, as in the analogous situation of drug experiment and pharmaceutical supply, from private enterprise, to a suitable degree evaluated and controlled by government organizations which are not themselves involved or required to produce.

It goes without saying that there should be no monopolies in the commercial test publication field either. For it could be pointed out that there, also, some of the largest and best established firms have been among the most resistant to new ideas. It has been to their own cost, eventually, but that is not always perceived. At the present time there are, fortunately, more than a half dozen entirely independent test organizations in the U.S. alone, ranging from large concerns like the Educational Testing Service, the Psychological Corporation and the Institute for Personality and Ability Testing to the Sheridan Company (publishing Guilford's tests), Editest, the test publishing sections of Bobbs-Merrill and World Book. Abroad one might mention the Centre de Psy-

---

*An instance in point is the failure of college testing installations to make use of the Culture-Fair Scale 3—a test for high level adults—in their installations for evaluating entrants to graduate school. A suitable *achievement* test is available (and widely used) in the ETS Graduate Record Exam. But as an intelligence test the Miller Analogies came in years ago and has not been reevaluated. With its dependence on a single type of subtest, its heavy involvement of a primary—V factor—by its esoteric vocabulary it is almost certainly inferior in g_f saturation to the Culture-Fair Scale 3. Indeed, it has been shown to lower systematically the scores of physics, engineering, and medical students relative to those in English and liberal arts. A check by testing graduate students for some years jointly on the MA test and the CF Scale 3 could almost certainly show the latter to be a more fair and predictive test of general fluid mental capacity, g_f, and therefore of future performance.

chologie Appliquée in France, the University of London Press in England, the Organizatione Specciale in Italy and the Hogrefe & Berne agency in German-speaking countries. The National Council for Educational Research in Britain, the ACER in Australia, and the NZCER in New Zealand, as well as the Psychometric Institute in Johannesburg, though national in label are largely as private as commercial publishers. They confine themselves largely to test distribution and to research on the effectiveness of tests in applied situations of education and personal selection. Some of these organizations, like ETS (by the terms of its foundation by the colleges aiming at common entrance standards), concentrate largely on educational achievement, others, like IPAT, on personality and motivation (including clinical and medical realms), and still others, like Houghton Mifflin and the California Test Bureau (recently defunct), on particular intelligence tests of wide distribution.

Producing the best tests and maintaining them in available published form are a far more precarious enterprise than most psychologists realize. Publication of psychological books has clearly shifted to a more commercial emphasis in the last decade. Why should publishers put effort and money into producing a scientifically important book with a 5,000 upper limit of sales when they could sell 100,000 copies of a picture book in general psychology for undergraduates? Moreover, in the test field, important psychological research and reliable practice demand such things as tests designed long enough (an hour or two) to give high reliabilities, special tape and apparatus, supplements, as many as four equivalent forms of a given test, intelligence tests for unusual (non-school) age ranges, really adequate standardizations, and so on. Tests on such thorough research and production bases as here indicated may receive such small demand that they are published at a loss. Though

IPAT, NZCER, and ACER, for example, have had the public conscience to do this to a necessary extent, they obviously would vanish if they proceeded further in this direction.

The maintenance of a good test service in these rather precarious conditions has not been helped by the "piracy" and illegal reproduction, on Xerox copiers, etc., that certain individuals have practiced. Among students some of this robbery may be due to lack of informed appreciation of the costs that go into the production, validation, standardization, etc. of these "bits of paper." In other instances piracy *is* the correct term and both the Psychological Corporation and IPAT, to name but two, have done well for the profession to exact salutary damages in prosecutions of flagrant instances. And incidentally, the cost of a printed page of a test is, production-wise, far greater than that in plagiarising a page of a novel or textbook.

With increasing recognition of the logistics and costs of test production, and of the resemblances of the originality of the test constructor to those of the chemical inventor, the novelist, and the artist, it is not surprising that increasing emphasis has been placed, in the APA Test Committee and elsewhere, on exact regard for test copyright. When one considers also the heavy developmental expenditures which have gone into a test (word for word, as just indicated, a far more expensive project for the publisher than any novel), a certain jealousy of copyright, which should properly extend to single items, is understandable. Whereas quotation of a long paragraph of an author's views without permission can be illegal (perhaps unnecessarily so, since he has issued them for public), the "lifting" of an item or the mimeographing of a test for research was, until a few years ago, an almost accepted feature of the pioneer "frontier" days of test psychology. Any test user should be extremely careful about such special uses, as also about leaving tests around in lay circles in such a way that the standardization could become affected by the items becoming popular knowledge.

THE VALUE OF UNIVERSALLY AVAILABLE TESTS AND ORGANIZED SERVICES AROUND THEM

A fairly voluminous set of recommendations and requirements for satisfactory tests was published in 1954 by the APA Committee on Test Standards and has been revised and reissued in recent years (1974). At various points in chapters in this book reference has been made to particular issues therein, e.g., on validity, consistency, standardization, and criterion requirements.

Criticisms have greatly been made of the early conceptual frameworks promulgated by these committees. For example, there was overemphasis on concrete relative to concept (constant) validity, and no clear perception that the former should strictly be concerned as concrete *relevance*. The concept validity of an anxiety scale is the correlation of that text with the *anxiety factor*, and all we have to make sure of is that the factor is extracted from the domain of behavior semantically, traditionally referred to as anxiety.* The extent to which this scale should correlate with, say, neuroticism, ketosteroid excretion, impairment of immediate memory, and other assumed signs of anxiety is something to be discovered, as a *relevance* of anxiety—not set up *a priori* as a criterion of anxiety. For example, some psychiatrist might argue that the test should

show schizophrenics to be high on anxiety if it is a test of anxiety. Actually, this would be misleading, since schizophrenics have been shown not to differ significantly from normals when a battery is well-defined by the factor.

Other recommendations of that committee that are truly doubtful include the emphases on excessively large standardizations, which as we have seen, can arrest progress in test development and use. Tests should not have their value and validity judged by mere size of standardization. Another misvaluation springs from the confusion of dependability with homogeneity as desiderata in test consistency (see Chapters 4 and 23). In that connection the consistencies (reliabilities) requested to be reported in test handbooks by the APA are often meaningless, being artificially high through absence of a standard variance of the general population to which, in fairness, they should all be referred. And the committee made no recommendation at all that such indices should be calculated to a standard time length for all tests. Generally, as far as reliability is concerned, a well-designed test, providing A, B, C, etc. equivalent forms, will permit the psychologist what reliability he or she wishes to give the time for. As pointed out earlier, yet another weakness of psychometric conception was the naming of "concurrent" and "predictive" validities, when only the first is a property of the test, the second being the property of a trait or state. It would thus be a virtue for the "predictive validity" of a good state test to be zero (see Chapters 4, 5, and 23).

Although there is need for centralization and agreement in regard to test standards, it is probably better—at least until the science of psychometry is more mature—to leave the definition of standards to the interaction of the writings of the leading researchers in the field. A formal house of cardinals fits religion better than a progressing science. Yet there are considerable advantages both to research and to precise and informed practice to

---

*Even that semantic anchoring may not be necessary. If Spearman wanted to call his general factor "intelligence" it was appropriate that the hundreds of mental processes he included be designated popularly as "intelligent." Actually, he avoided entanglement with competing subjective, philosophical, and semantic interpretations of intelligence by calling his finally *g*-selected battery a "Test of *g*," leaving posterity to apply to *g* whatever term further research on its properties may require.

having a number of tests recognized as standard for certain purposes—until research indicates it is time to move on to others. As argued above, one must avoid monopoly, and perhaps a rule of thumb would be to have at least three acceptable parallel test systems (alternative sets of tests) available in the domains of ability, personality, achievement, motivation, and so on. The equivalences of meaning among them would soon become known and the psychologist's capacity for generalization from experience and experiment would be increased.

It has been argued above that, apart from achievement test construction for specific industrial and civil service proficiencies, the practice of "local" test construction can seriously be questioned. Nearly always a better product, founded on much more extensive research than the particular psychologist or small organization can muster, is already on the market. It is an illusion, as we have evidenced, for a psychologist to believe that he can concoct in a few evenings work and a few visits to the computer, an anxiety scale, or a creativity test, or a mathematics attainment test which can compare in validity, etc., with those on which test construction teams have lavished years of research.

There was a phase in medicine when the country doctor shook up his own prescriptions in the kitchen, but the modern doctor has to depend much more on vaccines, hormones, and new pharmaceuticals made with full technical resources by well-known drug houses, and the professional psychologist is increasingly in an analogous position. Probably most educational departments, clinics, and industries would do better to use their psychologists' services in actual service, or at most in evaluating what regular test constructors have made available, rather than in handicapped attempts at constructing tests which the organization can have the doubtful satisfaction of calling its "very own." There are in fact many advantages to a more universal test. In the first place, it is more likely to be based on well-investigated natural ability and personality structures, published in scientific journals and, in the second, it will give results admitting of wider comparison and generalization. In regard to the primary personality factors covered by the HSPQ, or a culture-fair intelligence test targeted on the fluid general intelligence factor, g_f, for example, these comparisons even extend to research results accumulating abroad, thus widening the possible scientific conclusions.

One of the few arguments in favor of the "homegrown" product, at least in schools and industries, is that steps can easily be taken to ensure that the answers to the tests do not get around, that coaching is minimal, etc. However, many test publishers keep equivalent forms of certain tests in reserve and unpublished, in the ordinary sense, for just such occasions. For example, a form of the Culture-Fair Intelligence Scale II is kept for a few concerns which guarantee to use it in circumstances where no copy can become public and which keep it under lock and key. In any case, the particular predictive formulae for assessing their special criteria from the best general ability and personality dimension measures remain the property of the firm or organization concerned.

Another major advantage of sets of tests in each domain that are of relatively universal status concerns the possibility, already considered, of computer scoring, criterion prediction, and narrative case report aids. Actually, this is best envisaged as part of a social organization of test data services and exchanges which is likely to develop considerably in the next decade. The obtaining of raw scores by electronic sight scanning of answer sheets, as well as the computer translations at the same time to standard scores and various derivatives therefrom, almost instantaneously, is an obvious development, already available by N.C.S., IPAT, I.B.M., and other computer organizations. So also are the weighting of these scores to give a variety of second-order scores; specification equation predictions of criteria, of diagnostic profile matchings, etc.; and provision of "writeups" in verbal descriptive narrative reports. They can be obtained rapidly, mostly by return mail; alternatively, the individual, linking his own computer by phone as a "satellite" console, can get them almost instantaneously.

What is still not an actuality, unless it be to a few pioneers, is a recording and analyzing service which will give instant aid to clinical and other decisions by applying relatively complex calculations based on psychological as well as statistical laws and including biographical data with test data. If this could be organized to be rapid enough in response, it could direct phases of the psychological examination or therapy even while they are being done. Perhaps psychologists should not feel too remiss about their present failure to develop these opportunities, since medicine, with its more established physiological laws, is only just beginning to contemplate such aids from multivariate calculations and monitorings. But the theoretical possibilities are fascinating and will improve with every advance in understanding the natural history and development of several trait factors in personality and ability, and in the scope of the dynamic calculus. Many therapeutic procedures have the form of games theory—there is a best possible next step to be decided in the light of original information and client change scores up to that point—and as psychology progresses it will be able to program for such moves. A second development in this area is an immediate analysis of dynamic structure by P-technique (see Chapters 17 and 18). The time may well come when the practitioner even in the smallest town will be able to "hitch his wagon to a star"—a Telstar—and immediately obtain the bearing upon his test results of a large library of information and formulae.

Probably such developments will be less delayed through any difficulties from the electronic physicist than through those inherent in organizing psychologists and their information needed in their technology. At present what we have called "the second file" in the *two-file system*, i.e., the research-accumulated specification equations, occupational and diagnostic profiles, norms, age, and situation trends, etc., on basic personality and ability structures, is very tenuous and spotty. Professional psychologists could do a great deal to get the second file organized by more systematic feedback to a few organizing centers of their case experiences with associated standard source trait measures. It would advance also by the usual growth of research publications cross-referencing to the work of others, providing they are using the same source traits and state measures, for, as pointed out in Chapter 1, it is one of the central advantages of structural tests that the information accumulated about them belongs not merely to the test but to the recognized trait or state. Appropriate statistical adjustments can generally make the criterion information which research has found for Test X concerning Trait A useful to the necessary degree of accuracy with, say, an improved successor to Test X, namely Test Y, for the same Trait A.

One can already see services developing to make predictive information available to practitioners within minimum delay. But it will grow only if they help in providing it. It is heartening to see that such supportive information is already compiled around a few important tests, as, for example, in the Hathaway and Meehl atlas to the MMPI (1951), in Rorschach handbooks, and in Karson and O'Dell (1976), Scheier's, Pierson's, Sweney's, Watson's and others' information bulletins on the 16 P.F., HSPQ, Anxiety Scales, the MAT, etc. (1975-1985). There is Smith's

Survey of WAIS Predictions, and Rodd's, Horn's and others' data on the culture-fair intelligence tests in crucial fields (see Cattell, 1971c). These foreshadow something of the rich store of information which the second file will surely hold for users of structured tests in the future.

SUMMARY

Quantitative data are necessary for the development of any science. Despite problems associated with the use of psychological tests, tests do today provide broadly a quantitative basis for the assessment of individual differences. The use of psychological tests has made us more aware of individual differences and has led to an understanding that there is wide variability in response tendencies within any given group and substantial overlap across all groups. The use of psychological tests in avoiding the square peg in the round hole employment and in aiding fair promotion demonstrably increases economic productivity. The benefits of psychological testing are substantial for the individual—especially the individual seeking psychological help—as well as for the society at large and for the economy. An understanding of the predictable associations between different test scores and of the theoretical bases for the existence of these associations further increases the utility of psychological tests.

We suggest that clerical assistants might well administer and mechanically score tests, but that the selection of what tests are administered and the interpretation of results require the use of professionals, and that these professionals should be better trained than is presently the norm. The adverse public image of psychological testing which appeared in the sixties and seventies is not to any extent a result of the nature of tests. In part it is a consequence of a general tendency—always present but now provided with trappings of legitimacy—of persons to seek to avoid evaluation. In part it is a result of the less than optimal competence of persons involved in testing. The tester must be aware of his or her obligations to each of a number of constituencies. The use of standardized tests of known validity and reliability is a necessity if tests are to be used effectively in benefiting the individual testee and society.

PART II

Available Structured Tests

for Functional Psychometry

CHAPTER 9

Intelligence and Primary Aptitudes: Test Design and Tests Available

Robert E. Woliver and Stephen D. Saeks

THE CLASSIFICATION OF ABILITIES

From this point, beginning Part II of this book, we turn from general psychometric principles to particular areas and the actual tests available in those areas. In each area it will be our aim to ask what is known about structure and to proceed to describe the tests available, their design, length, validity, and standardization, and clinical, educational, industrial or other fields of usefulness. The approach taken in this text is different from that taken in previously published texts on testing. In this volume, tests will be pre-

The authors wish to express their gratitude to: Jack McArdle for his support and assistance in obtaining valuable research data; John Horn for his permission to reprint his table (9.3) in this chapter; and the Institute for Personality and Ability Testing for background information on the CAB. The assistance we obtained from these people made this chapter easier to write and more informative than it would have been without them.

sented and examined on the basis of their merit and "statistically sound" design and construction, rather than on their previous degree of popularity. This volume seeks to direct practicing psychologists, on the basis of a fresh and basic look at research evidence, to those tests with which they might well seriously concern themselves.

Ability measurement can nowadays be seen in perspective as a confluence of two distinct streams, which, like the Blue and White Nile, mix rather poorly. One, which we may call the *intuitive* and immediately practical, begins with Binet (1905). The other, which we may call the *structure-directed*, begins in the same year and includes Spearman's g, along with its later division into g_f and g_c, the Thurstone and Hakstian primary abilities tests, and other factored measures.

Goodness of standardization, reliability, scoring convenience, etc., needs to be examined for the chief examples of both types, as these parameters are independent of the differences of the theoretical basis of validity. However, that difference of basis—and especially the sociocommercial situation that surrounds it—cannot be overlooked by any conscientious scientist. The importance and correctness of Spearman's and Thurstone's (and, later, Cattell's, Horn's, Guilford's and Hakstian's) factor analytic determination of ability structure, like many complex but fundamental innovations in science, took a surprisingly long time to become popularly accepted. Indeed, for most of 50 years many applied psychologists got increasingly entangled in a jungle growth of theoryless, subjective, unresearched, and arbitrarily developed scales.

The structured measures, on the other hand, came to fruition in practice later, because they are designed to be targeted on the findings of basic research regarding structure, which took nearly half a century to be completed to its present level. Thus, Spearman's criterion of validity by g-saturation, fluid and crystallized intelligence (1929, 1930), and Thurstone's primaries (1938), were for many years not well-understood in their implications. As factor analysis became more widely recognized and practiced, tests on a popular basis of subjective definitions, like the WAIS-R and WISC-R, were eventually factored. This "factoring after the event" actually led to the realization that the mélange involved several factors and required complicated ways of adding existing parts to scores to get intelligible concepts. Such derivations are considerably less desirable than measures based on structurally clean design in the first place.

Although the "cookbook" approach to test design and scoring affronted good theory, the structured approach, like a cultivated plant growing belatedly among rank weeds, was late in coming to view and only belatedly incorporated into test practices. This was due in part to the difficulty experienced by highly trained and practicing professionals in relinquishing their hold on the deeply ingrained procedures and theories of testing that they had been exposed to throughout their professional training and careers. The defense of the prestructural tests is that they involved concepts of intelligence which, though often different in different tests, fitted popular stereotypes and required no accommodation to entirely new ideas. The final defense of such arbitrary test construction has tended to be that tests so founded have been *validated against life criteria*.

Essentially, this argument raises the important issue of the difference between validity and relevance. Since no one knows the relative amounts of intelligence needed in various life performances (e.g., getting good grades in geography courses, succeeding as an actress, making money on the stock exchange), the life criterion argument and calculation are of limited value, at best. Spearman showed that a uniquely determinable general factor runs through all cognitive performances and loads most highly on those that are recognizably more complex. The older approach put the cart before the horse; the newer approach, having uniquely located the concept of relation-perception and measured it, can turn to find which everyday life performances demand more or less intelligence. It is important to note that these correlations may be said to indicate the *relevance* of intelligence to various occupations or performances, but they do not *validate* intelligence. It is already validated, in any given test, against the general factor. When Thurstone showed that factor analysis yields also primary abilities—like verbal, numerical, spatial, etc.—some psychologists at first concluded that this destroyed the theory of a broad g factor. But g was actually better defined than before, as a *second-order* factor (a "secondary") back of the primaries. All this history and its latest developments may be read in books and articles like those of Butcher (1968), Cattell (1971c),

Eysenck (1978a), Guilford (1972), Horn (1968), and others. Here we shall return to practical aspects, after summarizing the main structural conclusions in Figure 9.1.

As the work of Kaufman (1979) and others show, the WAIS, WISC, the Binet, and other such tests typically mix three or four of these factors. But since the traits concerned have different properties, age curves, predictions of criteria, and so on, the aim of a well-trained practitioner is to get measures as pure as possible of each, e.g., for analyzing the different reasons for classroom backwardness in different children. This is now possible because in the last two decades there has been production of relatively factor-pure tests. This is true of the primaries and of fluid intelligence, g_f, but unfortunately we still do not have well-standardized, handy measures for several of the big secondaries, like fluency, speed, memory 1, and memory 2. At least, however, out of the broad sweep of the field of cognitive processes from which these primaries and secondaries have been factorially isolated, the factors of fluid (g_f) and crystallized (g_c)

intelligence have shown themselves clearly and good tests exist for them, though crystallized intelligence has to be defined afresh for each culture. Some excellent batteries, like Thurstone's and the CAB, also exist for most of the primaries.

THE BROAD UPPER STRATUM CAPACITIES OF FLUID AND CRYSTALLIZED INTELLIGENCE, RETRIEVAL CAPACITY, VISUALIZATION, SPEED, AND MEMORY

Some idea has already been given in Chapter 3 of the structure of abilities as such. The picture that emerges—and which we must discuss further before going to actual tests—is that of 20 or so primary abilities, of the kind first discovered by Thurstone (1938) and extended by Hakstian and Cattell (1974, 1977), upon which, acting at the second stratum, we find six to eight broad secondaries: fluid intelligence, crystallized intelligence, fluency (retrieval capacity), speed, visualization, etc., as shown in Figure 9.1.

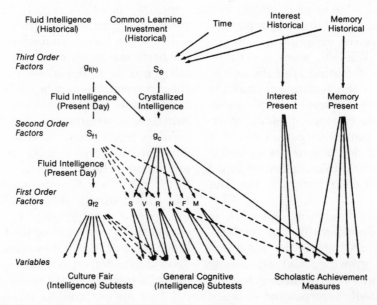

Figure 9.1. Relation of some higher ability source traits to primary abilities and cognitive test performances

At a still insufficiently investigated level, Cattell (1971a) has proposed the *triadic* theory of abilities, which supposes that what we now throw together as secondaries are actually at two levels, which he calls *general capacities—g's—*(fluid and crystallized intelligence, speed, retrieval) and *provincial powers—p's—*which correspond to the main sensory integration areas of the brain: visualization, auditory ability, tactile and kinesthetic capacity, and so on. Below these are the primary abilities or agents—*a's*—which are unitary developments out of the more constitutional dispositions above, produced as agencies for particular cultural fields by training developments in various situations.

The provincials, *p's*, are virtually never measured and, as far as the writers know, one would have to go to research articles at present, even for a test of *V*s, visualization. The general capacities, *c's* or *g's*, except for the intelligences, g_f and g_c, and some published measures of fluency (Cattell, 1937b) are also not available in ready-to-use standardized forms. It is thus to g_f, g_c, and the primary abilities that the psychometrist can confidently turn for well investigated and standardized tests.

The history of intelligence test construction is a curious story of compartmentalized advances. Among theoretically interested psychologists the discovery of a general intelligence factor by Spearman in 1905 and the extension to primaries by Thurstone led to important conceptual developments, particularly in Europe. But in America, the bulk of this activity followed Binet's product, leading to further devices and subtests that fitted school procedures and seemed, on "common sense" grounds, to be measures of intelligence. This rather grossly empirical, but widely understandable approach led to the Stanford Binet and such tests as the WISC-R and the WAIS-R. As stated, these have been competently factored, *after* their construction, but that does not alter the fact that their design lacked clear theory and

proceeded by patchwork additions. It is now clear that factor analytically they are a mixture of fluid and crystallized intelligence, with uneven weights for primary abilities. A division into verbal and numerical, for example, leaves a dozen other primaries unrepresented.

Meanwhile, after 50 years of near-stagnation, theory began moving again with the work of Guilford, on convergence and divergence, and Cattell and, later, Horn and his associates, on fluid and crystallized intelligence. The theory of fluid and crystallized intelligence rests on the discovery of two major general ability factors, positively correlated (oblique), which are briefly described below.

1) *Fluid general intelligence* shows itself in the general capacity to perceive relations, as well as relations among relations, in any area. It has a high degree of inheritance, is closely related to physiological capacity of the brain and as such (Hebb, 1949), ceases growth around 15 or so years, and declines with physiological decline (Horn, 1976) after about 25. It is particularly predictive of success in areas either to which all subjects are quite new, or in which all are equally overlearnt, as in spatial perceptions.

2) *Crystallized intelligence* shows itself in capacities in handling complex relations in fields in which the subjects have been taught, e.g., in the subjects of school learning and cultural-social learning generally. Its testing rests, however, on the narrower "scholastic" field in which most children have received common exposure. It represents the extent to which the individual has invested (used) his or her fluid intelligence in acquiring discriminatory habits in naturally complex cultural areas, e.g., verbal, mathematical, and other concepts. In those who continue education, it continues to grow beyond 15 or 16 in those areas and in those who

merely meet social problems it continues as social intelligence. In a balance
of learning and forgetting it maintains
its level throughout life.

With the factor-analytically discovered
differentiation of fluid (g_f) and crystallized
(g_c) general abilities, there are associated
a number of other properties, as follows:

1) A difference of age growth and de-

cline. Fluid abilities uniformly reach full
development around the age of 21 to 22
and then a steady decline begins. Crystallized abilities improve up to the age of
30-39. g_c declines slowly when compared
to g_f and this difference becomes greater
after 16 years of age.

2) A difference in the standard deviation of the I.Q. Since the individual differences are large relative to the age
increments, the I.Q.'s in culture-fair, fluid

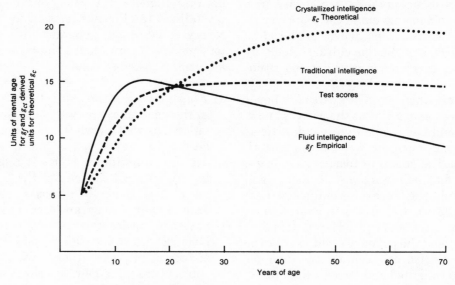

Age Changes Expressed as Correlations

	With Age Correlation
Crystallized Intelligence	
General Information	.44
General Comprehension	.42
Arithmetic Reason	.10
Vocabulary (Ad hoc)	.41
Vocabulary (PMA)	.43
Subtraction and Multiplication	.33
Fluid Intelligence	
Block Design	−.26
Picture Arrangement	−.27
Sheppard-Metzler Mental Rotations	−.37
PMA Pedigrees (Abstract Reasoning)	−.18
Immediate Memory	−.18
ETS Card Rotations	−.34

Data from Caucasian, Japanese and Chinese, samples totalling 453, in Johnson, R. C., and Ahern, F. M.
Correlations of Measures of Cognition and Personality with Age. (in press)

Figure 9.2. Age change life-span curves for fluid and crystallized intelligence

ability tests have a sigma of 24 points of I.Q., being thus almost exactly 50% larger than for traditional crystallized ability tests, where sigma stands roughly at 16 points. The formula (Cattell, 1963b) for this relation is:

$$\sigma_{I.Q.(f)} = k \sqrt{\frac{\sigma_{p(f)}^2}{\sigma_{a(f)}^2}}$$

$$\sigma_{I.Q.(c)} = k \sqrt{\frac{\sigma_{p(f)}^2 + \sigma_{p(c)}^2 + 2r_{p(f)p(c)}\,\sigma_{p(f)}\,\sigma_{p(c)}}{\sigma_{a(f)}^2 + \sigma_{a(c)}^2 + 2r_{a.f.ac}\,\sigma_{a(f)}\,\sigma_{a(c)}}}$$

where σp is sigma of true score across people at one age and σa is sigma of true means across the range of *ages*. The K value will simply depend on the number of years covered by the age means. Since $r_{af.ac}$ will be unity, and r_{fc} will be something between 0 and .5, it is clear that $\sigma_{I.Q.(c)}$ will normally be less than $\sigma_{I.Q.(f)}$. If all σs are approximately equal, and $r_{p(f)p(c)}$ is taken as zero we should get a culture-fair σ of approximately 25, as found, corresponding to a traditional test I.Q. sigma of 16. This formula has important consequences in comparing the I.Q.'s of individuals across different tests.

3) It follows, though it has not been fully checked, that the I.Q. (presumably from the "conception" zero age) of culture-fair fluid ability tests will be more constant than that of traditional tests, because the denominator in the latter, with children beyond 14 years, should vary from individual to individual depending on the age of cessation of his schooling. Even before that age, as the team at the London School of Economics (Cattell, 1984) has shown, the crystallized ability I.Q. is constant with cultural differences and with changes in the home background.

4) Brain injury may cause a local lack of ability in a crystallized ability measure, e.g., a verbal aphasia, but a general reduction of relation-educing capacity in fluid ability.

5) There is evidence that the nature-nurture ratio is higher in fluid ability than in crystallized. Twenty to 25% of variance in the latter is connected with the differences of environmental experience but, except for physical environmental injuries, the fluid ability level would be expected to be fixed constitutionally. Much of the debate about inheritance of "intelligence" arises from confusion of the two concepts.

Finally, in comparing the fluid and crystallized intelligence concept from a practical point of view one should remember that crystallized intelligence is not a stable entity. It changes its pattern with age, sex, social class, and obviously with national affiliation. It will thus not give a safe basis of comparison for persons of different social background, or for, say, 20- and 50-year-olds. Probably in the U.S., the best constancy of definition and measurement of crystallized intelligence results from using subtests covering crystallized investments in the last two years of high school. At the school age g_c and g_f have the correlations shown in Table 9.1.

A 50-year-old engineer and 60-year-old woman nurse might be tolerably compared on the basis of that common experiential period, though one's crystallized intelligence has since been defined in engineering technicalities and the other's in nursing skills. Fluid intelligence tests, on the other hand, have shown great constancy of factor loading pattern of subtests across cultures as diverse as the U.S., Germany, and Japan. Also, they have proved useful in cross-cultural comparisons. For example, virtually identical levels on literally the same culture-fair test form have been found for children of the same age in the U.S., Taiwan, Germany, etc. In Hawaii, use of the culture-fair tests showed that a substantial proportion of native Hawaiians sent to special classes as backward, based on their performance in traditional tests, were not, in fact, below average in intelligence. Incidentally, the fact that culture-fair subtests contain no

TABLE 9.1
The Correlation of Measures of Fluid and Crystallized General Intelligence

	g_f	g_c	Exvia	Anxiety
Fluid Intelligence g_f	1.00			
Crystallized Intelligence g_c	.47	1.00		
Exvia	.29	.17	1.00	
Anxiety	.35	.15	.17	1.00

From 277 13-14-year-olds (Cattell, 1963)
A special value of this study is that two major personality factors are included to help broaden the bases of accurate rotation. The value of +.47 is fairly typical over the school range, but in adult life we as yet have no agreement.

verbal material has caused some teachers and business personnel offices to conclude that they will not predict verbal ability. But since intelligence is substantially involved in verbal learning and the tests measure intelligence, it is not surprising that the culture-fair test score is significantly correlated with English language learning in the U.S. and the level of Chinese language learning in Hong Kong.

IMPLICATIONS OF STRUCTURAL THEORY FOR USE OF INTELLIGENCE TESTS IN PREDICTIONS AND ANALYSIS

Intelligence tests are used for scholarship selection (or selecting children for special educational streams), vocational guidance, and clinical diagnosis, notably on causes of backwardness and maladjustment. The type of test needed and the manner of its use will vary with these purposes.

In scholarship selection and prediction of future school performance generally, the aim is to get the best possible prediction, i.e., correlation between future achievement and the present battery score. As various research studies show, the correlation with achievement scores (provided we are speaking of children and of this year or next) is better for traditional than culture-fair tests. This should not

surprise us, for:

a) The g_c test is already contaminated with much achievement, i.e., it already has the criterion inside it.

b) Over and above this gain due merely to an artifact—the inclusion of the criterion in the predictor—there is a real psychological gain in that the learning rate in the near future is a function not only of intelligence but of special skills and concepts in the area concerned. These are called "aids" (Cattell, 1963b) and have been talked about a good deal by Piaget (1960). They might be illustrated in schoolwork by someone grasping the idea of an equation, or of coordinates, or the syntax of a sentence, and they act as aids to further "perceiving of relations" *in that area.* Research on transfer of training, however, shows that they have no wider transfer. They improve a local front on g_c but do 112 affect g_f. But we must remember that rate of learning will depend on g_c as well as g_f (in a g_c area) and that the g_c correlation with next year's achievement is not *only* because nine-tenths of the scholarship in next year's attainment is already contained in this year's crystallized intelligence test.

The casual conclusion of many teachers that because a traditional intelligence test correlates better than a g_f (culture-fair), as a rule, with next semester's attainment score, it is therefore a better intelligence test, misses the whole point of intelligence testing. Even in the school situation (and still more in the child guidance clinic), the purpose of intelligence testing is diagnostic. We want to know how much the backwardness is due to low intelligence and how much to lack of schooling, concentration, etc., and this places a burden on any single test of intelligence. If our objective, as in the non-individual general grade prediction or scholarship selection situation, is maximally to predict next year's attainment, then this can be better done, as Cattell and Butcher (1968) have shown, by combining personality and motivation measures with a culture-fair intelligence test, each one contributing approximately 25% of the variable.

And when we come to the larger world of adult performance, the g_c score on a regular, traditional intelligence test becomes increasingly beside the point. It is a historical relic of school achievement, reflecting tolerably the young person's intelligence at the time, but not his general relation-eduction capacity in present new fields. In adult life we have several g_c's instead of one: that of the farmer, with his rich crystallized skills in judging farm stock, land, and weather; that of the banker, with his subtle judgments in a world of figures; that of the air pilot, the doctor, and many others. It might be useful to develop g_c measures suitable for each. The diminishing correlation and common factor in adults show one can no longer depend on a single crystallized intelligence measure for really effective prediction. On the other hand, the g_f common factor retains its form and predictive capacity with adults.

In the following sections we shall describe the tests available first for fluid intelligence, g_f, and second for g_c, connecting the latter with the ensuing deviation of g_c from a primary-ability battery.

TESTS AVAILABLE FOR MEASURING FLUID GENERAL INTELLIGENCE, g_f

For measuring fluid general intelligence one thinks both of culture-fair tests and performance tests, but both have features and involve considerations beyond the fluid ability concept just discussed. Insofar as the fluid general ability test avoids crystallized acquired skills it must be culture-fair. But there is the possibility that it is involving—not at the critical success-failure level but as a necessary substrate—certain skills which are so overlearnt by everyone that, although acquired, they do not differentiate cultures. For example, spatial ability at a lowly level is involved in most perceptual tests, but people have to come to terms with space all the world over, and after three or four years of age they do not step over precipices or walk through closed doors.

However, when it comes to the purposes of the anthropologist, for example, working with remote and preliterate cultures, trivial features of g_f tests, unimportant within a broad culture, e.g., the culture of America, Europe and Russia, could become important. That is why the expression "culture-fair," expressing an equality within a fair range of cultures were substituted for "culture-free" suggesting that no acquired skills whatsoever might be involved. Sources of doubt about fairness over extreme cultural ranges concern working with pencil and paper, to a time limit, and without the usual school interest in competition. The tests have norms for untimed administration as well as timed, and the time limit has been shown (Cattell, 1949a, 1957b) not to be an essential part of g_f factor measurement. Having a known time limit for the tests is simply a convenience for schools and planning. Within fairly wide limits, and with untimed tests, differences of strength of motivation and interest have been shown to have surprisingly little influence on intelligence test scores (Spearman, 1929,

1930). The generation of sufficient interest in preliterates is a task which the anthropologist should be able to solve by his or her knowledge of the particular cultural reward systems.

As to performance tests of intelligence, it has been shown that: 1) except for quite low mental ages, they are decidedly poorer in saturation with the general intelligence factor than are either traditional (verbal-numerical) or culture-fair tests; and 2) they are reasonably culture-fair, as far as school training and language are concerned, but most dexterities are rapidly subject to learning and most performance tests involve both these and spatial abilities. Consequently, few current performance tests, be they of drawing or of object manipulation type, can be recommended as valid, dependable intelligence tests. On the other hand, the interest provoked by performance activity is valuable both for anthropological investigations of preliterates and for young children. A need at the present test design juncture is to produce forms of the culture-fair tests which adapt to primitives and young children by invoking "performance" activity with wooden models, etc., requiring the procedures in the present culture-fair tests.

Among the subtest designs which have proved well-saturated in g_f at most age levels are: series classifications, analogies, matrices, topology (Cattell), "dominoes" (Vidal), and the recent tests validated by Horn (1981). They have been brought together most systematically in the following tests:

1) The Cattell Culture-Fair Scales 1, 2 and 3 (in the U.S., Europe, Japan, and India)
2) The Raven Matrices (in England)
3) The Vidal Dominoes (in France)
4) The Australian Council of Educational Research (C. of Ed. Res.) Tests

A major drawback to the Raven Matrices—or any Matrices test alone—is that it "puts all its eggs in one basket," i.e., that unlike any good factor battery which "cancels out" specifics by having at least four or five distinct subtests, it compounds the general factor with whatever must be specific to one test device. A similar difficulty arises when using the Dominoes test. The Culture-Fair Tests, on the other hand, have four subtests which are alike in both forms A and B, and four others in the C and D forms. There are three scales to the Culture-Fair Test:

Scale 1   Ages 4-8 years
Scale 2   Ages 8-14 years
Scale 3   For superior adults

Thereby, it is possible in developmental and comparative studies to measure the fluid general ability factor consistently at different age levels by the same kind of test. Scale 2 is of a suitable difficulty for most adults, but has its maximum discrimination in occupations below the managerial and professional level. It is Scale 3 which is designed for university students, with a ceiling high enough to make it an excellent discriminator among superior adults. Among graduate students it would have the advantage over tests of the Miller Analogies type in that it does not overweight verbal ability, and thus deals fairly by the engineering, mathematics, and physics students relative to English and arts students. (At the same time, by the nature of g_f, although it does not involve a single language subtest, it predicts ability to learn in the language field as well as a traditional intelligence test.)

Scale 1 of the Culture-Fair series, in adapting to the special problems at the four-to-eight-year level, has to use more subtests than Scales 2 and 3. Some of the eight subtests are not fully culture-fair and some are not group administrable. It is, indeed, a test which is designed to meet several needs at once, namely:

1) A full eight-subtest, group administra-

ble test where the children are not of such different cultures that some verbal involvement is undesirable.

2) A six-subtest "shorter selection" where one must be culture-fair (and still group administrable).

3) A different six-subtest selection for the four- and five-year-olds, or others for whom individual administration is unavoidable.

Actually most of the Culture-Fair Scale 1 can be given to four- and five-year-olds in small groups (four to six at a time) and a minority of subtests can then be completed individually, allowing great saving of time.

The times required, reliabilities, standardizations, and other properties of the Culture-Fair Scales and Raven Matrices are set out in Table 9.2.

In Table 9.3 we have also shown, for comparison, a study by McArthur and Elley showing the saturation of the Culture-Fair if one takes out a general factor common to all intelligence tests.

One last comment regarding culture-fair tests, which needs to be made before leaving this section, is in the area of cross-cultural transferability of test scores. The problem of comparing scores of individuals in different minorities is most completely answered by the culture-fair tests, which contain scales for ages from four to "old age." However, in the case of primary abilities or of attainment tests, such as

TABLE 9.2
Culture-Fair Intelligence Test

Publisher:	Institute for Personality and Ability Testing
Forms:	3 scales for different populations and purposes.
	Scales 2 and 3 have A and B forms.
Age Ranges:	Scale 1. 4-8 years old and mentally retarded adults
	Scale 2. 8-14 years old and adults in the average range of intelligence
	Scale 3. grades 9-college and superior adults
Times:	Scale 1. 22-60 minutes
	Scale 2. 12.5 (30) minutes
	Scale 3. 12.5 (30) minutes
Norms:	Percentile
Reliability:	Correlates with WISC Verbal I.Q.: .62
	Correlates with WISC Full Scale I.Q.: .72
	Correlates with WAIS Full Scale I.Q.: .74

	RAVEN'S PROGRESSIVE MATRICES TEST
Publisher:	Psychological Corporation
Forms:	Three
	1. Standard Progressive Matrices
	2. Colored Progressive Matrices
	3. Advanced Progressive Matrices
Age Ranges:	Form 1. 6 years and older
	Form 2. 5-11 years; and mental patients and senescents
	Form 3. 11 years and older; of above average intellectual ability
Times:	Form 1. 45 minutes
	Form 2. 15-30 minutes
	Form 3. 40 (45) or 60 minutes
Norms:	Percentile
	8-14 years: norms for each half year
	20-65 years: norms for each five years
Reliability:	Correlation with Verbal and Performance tests of intelligence: .40-.75
	Test-Retest: .70-.90

TABLE 9.3

Factor Loadings (Test Validities) of Some Well-Known Intelligence and Achievement Tests

Test	Presumed[1] g_f	Presumed Cryst. Intell. or Educ. Factor
IPAT Culture-Fair (Scale 2A)	.75	
Rav. Progressive Matrices	.71	
Lorge-Thorndike Fig. Class.	.58	
Lorge-Thorndike No. Series	.55	
Lorge-Thorndike Fig. Anal.	.74	
Holz-Crowder Fig. Ch.	.50	
Holz-Crowder Series	.46	.21
Holz-Crowder Spatial	.40	
Occupat. Status Parent	.25	
Home Index	.25	.21
Reading Vocabulary	.34	.74
Reading Comprehension	.50	.62
Arith. Reasoning	.46	.34
Arith. Fundamentals	.45	.44
Language	.42	.59
Spelling	.20	.62
Laycock	.68	.51
Cal. Test Ment. Matur. Spatial	.61	
Cal. Test Ment. Matur. Logical	.66	
Cal. Test Ment. Matur. Number	.64	.20
Cal. Test Ment. Matur. Verbal	.46	.66

[1]On 271 Canadian Grade 7 boys and girls. Rotation, not fully for simple structure, by R. T. McArthur and W. B. Elley. The reduction of socioeconomic bias in intelligence testing. *British Journal of Educational Psychology*, 1963, *33*, 107-119. Correlations below .20 omitted.

those of ETS, there is no easy solution. However, Stricker (1982b), analyzing data on the GRE by race and sex, puts forward a new calculation (involving partial correlations) for identifying items that perform differentially (and therefore, need correction) in population subgroups. It may be that this approach will make it possible to use those tests which have not been so designed, to help provide items which will prove to have strength in measuring cross-culturally.

TESTS AVAILABLE FOR MEASURING CRYSTALLIZED GENERAL INTELLIGENCE

One of, if not the major, problem with using intelligence tests that are already on the market for measuring crystallized general intelligence (g_c) is that most of these tests are not specifically designed to measure g_c. This, however, is not an insurmountable problem, as the nature of g_c makes its measurement possible by the currently available tests.

As was previously stated, g_c is a reflection of an individual's "learned" intelligence. In other words, g_c is what an individual has learned both culturally and scholastically, and therefore it is measurable by tests of: verbal ability (skills); mathematical ability (skills); general information; and other similar areas of knowledge and/or skill.

At present, there are two major tests or sets of tests of intelligence which measure crystallized general intelligence: the Wechsler Scales (Wechsler Adult Intelligence Scale-Revised or WAIS-R; Wechsler Intelligence Scale-Revised or WISC-R; the Wechsler Preschool and Primary Scale of

Intelligence or WPPSI; and the Stanford-Binet Intelligence Scale. We will examine the latter of these first.

The Binet test began as a test of children's intelligence (in the broad sense of the term); however, it was later revised and extended so that an older population could be assessed. The test is designed to measure an individual's current degree of skill in various areas and then this measurement is compared to what has been established as "normal" for a given age. The Binet emphasizes verbal skills (Golden, 1979) and is thus very well suited for measuring crystallized intelligence.

Reliability studies have been performed on the Binet with encouraging results. A summary of some of these results can be seen in Table 9.4. McNemar (1942) performed some correlational studies, which examined the relationship between verbal ability and the overall mental age obtained on the test. McNemar's findings, which obtained correlations of .71-.86 between the vocabulary test and the mental ages on the entire test, support the contention that the Binet test is heavily weighted with verbal and thus crystallized intelligence. Additionally, the Binet has a median correlation with the WAIS of .78, suggesting a large degree of relationship between these two tests.

The Wechsler Scales (see Table 9.5), unlike the Binet, are broken down into subtests which are designed for a pattern or scatter analysis. The subtests of the Wechsler Scales are grouped into two broad categories: verbal and performance. The verbal scale corresponds with crystallized general intelligence (Kaufman, 1979) and will be examined here.

The verbal subtests of the WAIS-R are: information, digit span, vocabulary, arithmetic, comprehension, and similarities. These subtests, with the possible exception of the digit span subtest, measure areas of learned or acquired knowledge and skills.

The raw scores obtained on the Wechsler Scales are transformed into scaled scores, and then these scaled scores are added together and transformed into an I.Q. score.

Reliability studies on the Wechsler Scales have been performed in a number of areas. Stability coefficients have been obtained, for example, for the WAIS-R, and they show an overall correlation of .94 for the verbal subtests between two separate administrations of the test. Stability coefficients for the individual verbal subtests range from .79 for comprehension to .93 for vocabulary. Comparison of the verbal score on the WAIS-R with the individual scores on the verbal subtests range from .57 on the digit span to .85 on the vocabulary subtest. The average reliability of the verbal I.Q. by age was .97,

TABLE 9.4
Stanford-Binet

Publisher:	Houghton Mifflin Company
Forms:	2-M; third revision, 1960 (1972)
Age Range:	2-18
Time:	younger children—30-45 minutes
	older children—60-90 minutes
Norms:	3184 subjects (native-born whites)
	100 s_s at each ½-year interval from 1.5-5.5 years
	standardization sample
	200 S_s at each age from 6-14
	100 S_r at each age from 15-18
Reliability:	Age 2.5-5.5 yrs .83 (140-149 I.Q.) to .91 (60-69 I.Q.)
	Age 6-13 yrs .91 (140-149 I.Q.) to .97 (60-69 I.Q.)
	Age 14-18 yrs .95 (140-149 I.Q.) to .98 (60-69 I.Q.)

TABLE 9.5
Wechsler Intelligence Scales (WAIS-R, WISC-R, WPPSI)

Publisher:	Psychological Corporation
Forms:	WAIS-R
	WISC-R
	WPPSI
Age Ranges:	WAIS-R—16 and older
	WISC-R—6-17 years
	WPPSI—4-65 years
Times:	WAIS-R—60-90 minutes (approximately)
	WISC-R—50-75 minutes (approximately)
	WPPSI—50-75 minutes (approximately)
Norms:	WAIS-R—16 years-74 years 11 months
	WISC-R—6-16 years 6 months
	WPPSI—4 years-6 years 6 months
Reliability:	WAIS-R: overall full scale I.Q. − r = .97
	verbal scale I.Q. − r = .97
	performance scale I.Q. − 4 = .93
	WISC-R: overall full scale I.Q. − r = .96
	verbal scale I.Q. − r = .94
	performance scale I.Q. − r = .90

with a range of .83 on the digit span to .96 on the vocabulary subtest.

Recent research by Horn (1981) on the application of g_f - g_c theory to WAIS has: 1) given strong support for the multiple factor theory; and 2) clarified and expanded the existing body of knowledge in this area (see Table 9.6). The single most important point which has been stressed in the research of McArdle and Horn is that the WAIS is not unifactorial. Horn (1981) suggests that ". . . scoring based on the results of Table 9.6, for example, will provide measures that more nearly represent current theory about intellectual functioning than do the verbal-IQ, performance-IQ and total-IQ of the WAIS" (p. 56). At present, more research is needed to yield the necessary information to enable clinicians and researchers to utilize what Horn has suggested.* Therefore, the state of the art, in multifactorial assessment of intelligence, remains as has been described in this chapter.

As can be seen, the verbal components of both the Binet and Wechsler scales have high consistency, i.e., homogeneity between the scales and within the subtests, and high dependability coefficients for the tests over time. These tests also can be said, based on the aforementioned reliability information, to accurately measure g_c, because of the nature of what the tests are designed to measure and the nature of g_c.

A set of scales designed for testing crystallized intelligence, but on different principles from the WAIS, WISC, and Binet, is available in the Cattell Intelligence Scales (not to be confused with the IPAT Culture-Fair Scales above, also designed by Cattell). Instead of being factored *after* construction, as had to be done with the WAIS, WISC, and Binet, these scales were from the beginning built of the six subtest forms which Spearman had shown to have the highest g-saturation. The higher forms consist of some 20 items, carefully graded in increasing difficulty, for each of the subtests Synonyms, Classification, Opposites, Analogies, Completion, and Inferences. The first four have a balance of

---

*At the same time this chapter was written, a personal communication with J. McArdle revealed that this research is presently being conducted and the first results will be published later this year in the article "g_f-g_c Theory Applied to the WAIS," by McArdle and Horn (SDS).

TABLE 9.6

Structure of the Wechsler Adult Intelligence Scale (WAIS) Examined by Maximum Likelihood Fits for Different Hypotheses*

Subscale	Symbol	Reliability r_2	General-Factor Hypothesis g r_{cf}	h^2	Verbal-IQ Performance-IQ Hypothesis V	P	$r^2_{xt} h^2$	Three-factor g/g_c Hypothesis g_c	g_f	SAR	$r^2_{xt} \cdot h^2$	Four-factor g/g_c Solution Being Explored g_c	g_f	SAR	g_v
Information	IN	.91	.85	.19	.88		.14	.89			.12	.9			
Comprehension	CO	.78	.77	.19	.78		.17	.78			.17	.8			
Arithmetic	AR	.81	.69	.33	.69		.33	.40		.40	.28	.2	.3	.4	
Similarities	SI	.85	.77	.26	.76		.27	.60		.22	.26	.8	.2		
Memory Span	MS	.66	.57	.34	.55		.36			.76	.09			.7	
Vocabulary	VO	.95	.85	.23	.89		.16	.91			.13	.9			
Digit Symbol	DS	.92	.62	.54		.67	.47		.47	.28	.45		.3		.5
Picture Completion	PC	.85	.74	.30		.80	.21		.27	.59	.24		.3		.5
Block Design	BD	.83	.66	.39		.76	.25		.80		.19				.8
Picture Arrangement	PA	.66	.67	.21		.74	.11		.20	.57	.14		.3		.7
Object Assembly	OA	.69	.56	.37		.66	.25		.70		.21		.3		.7
Average Reliable Unique				.30			.25								
Chi-square for Fit			691		295			115							
Degrees of Freedom (df)			44		43			36							

*Based on McArdle and Horn, 1980, unpublished manuscript.

Note: $r^2_{xt} h^2$ represents the difference between the reliability, representing a variable's squared correlation with its own true score component, and the communality, representing a variable's squared multiple correlation with the common factor components of the other variables of the set. Thus $r^2_{xt} h^2$ is the true score variance not accounted for by common factors. The chi-square difference with one degree of freedom represents a nested-set. The difference indicates that the two-factor solution provides a better fit than the one-factor solution. The three-factor solution is similarly better than the two-factor solution but it need not be the only way to improve on the particular V-IQ and P-IQ two-factor solution and may not improve as much on other two-factor solutions as it improves on this one. This is because the two-factor solution is not a one-df nested-set of the three-factor solution and because there are three-factor and two-factor solutions for which the difference of chi-square may be as small as for the present solutions, and with the same degree of freedom.

verbal and nonverbal (culture-fair) examples, and in all cases increased difficulty is brought about not by using an
esoteric vocabulary, as in the Miller Analogies, but by requiring increasing nice
distinctions among common short words.

Discriminatory power is assisted by
having each scale for a relatively short
age range: Scale I, 8-11 years; Scale II, 11-
15; and Scale III for "Superior Adults."
Each scale has equivalent A and B forms.
The scales are long enough to give high
reliabilities and concept validities, as
checked by factor analysis, and require a
total of 66 minutes, timed, for the six subtests.

The tests are published in England (G.
G. Harrap and Co., 182 High Holborn,
London, WC 1) and have so far been standardized on an English population (2,000
to 3,000 on each). But Harrap and Co. also
publish from Toronto and Scale III is used
by the American Mensa Society (also the
British Mensa) for selection of exception-
ally high intelligence, and since it has
40,000 members it is proceeding to sophisticated standardization and scoring
for upper ranges in the U.S.

In England the test has been used to
ascertain the mean (and sigma) of intelligence for a representative range of common occupations, and also for a range of
types of school, including universities.

These are indications, notably in the
standard deviation of I.Q. (classically calculated) being higher than 16, that the
use of an infusion of culture-fair items,
and the employment of an ordinary "newspaper" size vocabulary has reduced the
usual overemphasis on the verbal factor
and resulted in a larger role of g_f relative
to g_c than in the WAIS, WISC, Miller, and
other tests that largely measure crystallized intelligence.

TESTS OF PRIMARY ABILITIES: THURSTONE'S PMA AND THE CAB

The reader should perhaps be reminded
of our earlier statement that under apti-

tudes we commonly understand the more
natural, constitutional ability structures,
more restricted in scope than general intelligence. There are, of course, many specific capabilities, such as clerical aptitude,
knowledge of tools, and skill in driving
buses, which seem to be largely acquired
and which are therefore considered in the
next chapter on attainments, informa-
tions, and skills.

However, it must be admitted that even
today the separation of the aptitudes from
the capabilities, and even of the personality factors from the aptitudes is not as
well-established as one would wish. If we
accept the very careful evaluation of the
literature by French (1953), and bring it
up to date by a survey of Guilford (1975)
and especially the recent literature of extensive and factor analytically precise
studies by Hakstian and Bennet (1977)
and Horn (1968, 1970), we reach a list of
reasonably well-established primary aptitudes, as in Table 9.7. However, it must
be pointed out that the personality factor
of exuberance, which accounts for so much
of the variance in fluency, *could* really be
the broader entity perceived as an "aptitude" in narrow experiments in the ability
field, and that Thurstone's "perceptual
ability" factor of speed of closure could
also be the outcropping in the ability field
of a more general personality factor.

"Abilities," as Cattell (1971a) states,
"can, in principle, always be measured by
speed, or the fewness of errors, in attaining an agreed result despite complexities"
(p. 25). Another important point when
looking at the concept of abilities is to differentiate it from the concept of aptitude.
Ability has the implication that a given
task can be performed at the present time,
whereas aptitude implies that the person
can be taught or trained to perform a specific task at some future time. Primary
abilities are factors which are highly intercorrelated and appear to be present,
innately, in some varying combination or
degree in everyone. The presence and
characteristics of these abilities have been

TABLE 9.7
Thurstone Test of Primary Mental Abilities

Publisher:	Science Research Associates, Inc.
Age Range:	Kindergarten-12th grades
Time Required:	Kindergarten-1st grade: 65-75 minutes in 2 sessions
	2nd-4th grades: same
	4th-6th grades: 52 minutes (107)
	6th-9th grades: 35 minutes (75)
	9th-12th grades: 74 minutes
Abilities Covered:	Kindergarten-6th grades
	1. verbal meaning
	2. perceptual speed
	3. number facility
	4. spatial relations
	6th-12th grades
	1. verbal meaning
	2. number facility
	3. reasoning
	4. spatial relations

demonstrated, since Thurstone (1938) first brought attention to them, through extensive factor-analytic studies.* One important outgrowth of these seminal works was the development of scales which could accurately measure an individual's mental ability by assessing primary ability levels. At present, there are two major batteries which are designed to comprehensively assess an individual's "intelligence" or mental ability by assessing the primary ability constructs: the Comprehensive Ability Battery (CAB), and Thurstone's Test of Primary Mental Abilities (PMA) (see Table 9.7).

Thurstone's PMA test (1938) was the first test which was designed to measure these primary ability constructs and is based on Thurstone's original factors and the five primary abilities which are measured by the PMA test: 1) verbal meaning; 2) perceptual speed; 3) number facility; 4) spatial relations; 5) reasoning. Thurstone's test does a more than adequate job of assessing these factors, but it does not include factors which have, in recent

years, been included as primary abilities.

The CAB, which is a more recent test, is able to assess what at present are considered to be the 20 primary abilities comprising human intelligence or mental ability. The 20 abilities which are assessed by the CAB are:

1) *Verbal,* the comprehension of words and ideas;

2) *Numerical,* an individual's facility in manipulating numbers quickly and accurately;

3) *Spatial,* the accurate perception of spatial figures and the ability to follow the orientation of figures when their position in a plane is rotated;

4) *Speed of closure,* the ability to quickly "perceive" a whole stimulus, when parts are missing;

5) *Perceptual speed and accuracy,* the ability to make rapid evaluations of features of visual stimuli;

6) *Inductive reasoning,* the ability to apply the process of induction to a general principle;

7) *Flexibility of closure,* the ability to disregard irrelevant stimulus material in a perceptual field and then to find key stimulus figures;

---

*For a detailed examination of the area of primary abilities, see Cattell (1971) *Abilities: Their Structure, Growth and Action.*

8) *Associative (or rote) memory,* the ability to recall material learned in a rote or nonmeaningful manner;

9) *Mechanical,* which requires more acquired knowledge or skill in the area of basic mechanical principles;

10) *Memory span,* or short-term memory;

11) *Meaningful memory,* the ability to recall meaningfully linked information;

12) *Spelling,* the ability to recognize misspelled words;

13) *Auditory ability,* divided into two parts. The first involves the ability to differentiate between tones which vary in pitch and the second which involves the ability to remember a sequence of tones;

14) *Esthetic judgment,* the ability to detect adherence to basic principles of good design or art;

15) *Spontaneous flexibility,* the ability to break traditional sets and use ideational flexibility to generate a large number of possible organizations of semantic material;

16) *Ideational fluency,* concerned with producing ideas about a given topic rapidly and with an abundance of concern over quality;

17) *Word fluency,* the ability to rapidly produce words, generally conforming to certain letter requirements, without a conceptual or meaning component's becoming a part of the task;

18) *Originality,* tasks of the "object synthesis" type;

19) *Aiming,* which relates to eye-hand coordination and abilities; and

20) *Representational drawing,* the ability to accurately reproduce given stimulus figures. (See summary in Table 9.8.)

It is evident, from the comprehensive nature of the above listed abilities, that the CAB is able to more efficiently differentiate and assess the specific abilities an individual may possess. Another strong point in favor of the CAB as a test of abilities is its usage of short tests for each of the 20 abilities rather than lengthier tests which have items that measure a number of variables. The attention that this test pays to the statistical concerns of test design further strengthens the power of this instrument.

THE ASSESSMENT OF ABILITY DEFICIT IN BRAIN DAMAGE

A special problem of testing encountered by the practitioner which should not be overlooked in this chapter is that concerned with testing relative to physiological diagnosis, particularly the neurological symptoms of brain damage.

It is well known, through the last decade of research by Horn and McArdle, Cattell, Nesselroade, Baltes and Schaie, and others, that fluid intelligence shows an age decline, on the average population, from about 22 onwards. This can be related to similar curves for several physiological variables and may be "normal." On the other hand, it can be considered along with the brain damage problem because it is possible that much of the decline is due to "neural insults" from intoxication, smoking, fevers, head injuries and other ills to which the flesh is heir. It is still possible that much of the aging effect is "normal," due to reduction of endocrines, etc., rather than to brain cell damage as such from accidents, drugs, strokes, and so forth. In any case assessment of brain damage from behavior calls upon use of measures of g's and a's (primaries) for its diagnosis. Thus, what we have symbolized as $g_m(i)$ —immediate memory, Horn's SAR—is a substantial indicator, by a declining score, of Korsakow's syndrome, and possibly g_r (retrieval) and g_s (general speed) are also indicators of brain physiological changes not yet precisely linked to them.

For many years several tests of general brain damage have been used which we now see amount to a comparison of g_f and g_c level, and could be expressed by comparison of the Culture-Fair Test score (or, with time short, with one subtest) and the g_c score from the WAIS (or with time

TABLE 9.8
The Comprehensive Abilities Battery (CAB)

Publisher:	Institute for Personality and Abilities Testing
Age Range:	15 years and older
Forms:	CAB 1 = 4 scores
	CAB 2 = 5 scores
	CAB 3/4 = 5 scores
	CAB 5 = 6 scores

Time Required: CAB 1: 21.75 (30 minutes)
CAB 2: 28 (35) minutes
CAB 3/4: 25-30 minutes
CAB 5: 32 (40) minutes

Abilities Covered: CAB 1:
1. verbal
2. numerical
3. spatial
4. speed of closure
CAB 2:
1. perceptual speed and accuracy
2. inductive reasoning
3. flexibility of closure
4. rote memory
5. mechanical
CAB 3/4:
1. memory span
2. meaningful memory
3. spelling
4. auditory
5. esthetic judgment
CAB 5:
1. spontaneous flexibility
2. ideational fluency
3. word fluency
4. originality
5. aiming and representational drawing

Reliability: 14 CAB scores and WAIS F.S.: r = .80 .92
14 CAB scores and WAIS Verbal: r = .69 .86
14 CAB scores and WAIS Performance: r = .70 .87
(corrected for restricted range)

short, simply the verbal vocabulary or synonym measure). With the average person, as Figure 9.2 shows, there is a steady fall in g_f, while the original level of g_f is measured by the high school markers in g_c. An unusually deviant difference of these two, as evaluated by age norm, should therefore operate as an indicator of brain damage. It is conceivable that Ertl's analysis of the electroencephalographic response to stimuli could also be so used. Ertl offers it as a measure of in-

telligence as such; however, although Horn's experimental check shows a quite significant correlation with mental age on intelligence tests, it is too low to permit substitution of EEG analysis for an intelligence test. Nevertheless, it may have a future in regard to brain damage.

Halstead's (1947) factor analysis of performances, including alleged clinical signs, led in due course to the extensive research and instrumentation (rather complex and expensive) which Reitan and his associates have greatly advanced regarding location of the area and extent of brain damage. As far as these test procedures can be described in a few paragraphs, the following means of assessment are available.

It is clear that anything which creates changes and/or "abnormalities" of the brain may well have an effect on the measurement of an individual's abilities. Therefore, it is important to have available tests which can detect and assess any "abnormalities" in the brain. At present, there are two basic approaches to neuropsychological assessment: 1) the single-test approach; and 2) the test-battery approach. The single-test approach is less frequently used in the assessment of brain damage; rather, such tests as the Bender-Gestalt Test (Bender, 1938), the Wechsler Memory Test (Wechsler, 1945), the Graham-Kendall Memory for Designs Test (Graham & Kendall, 1960) and other quick tests are used only to determine the presence and general location of brain damage; the assessment of specific location and extent of the damage is done using neuropsychological test batteries. There are two major neuropsychological test batteries currently in use at this time: the Halstead-Reitan Neuropsychological Battery and the Luria-Nebraska Neuropsychological Battery.

There are essentially 11 subtests to the Halstead-Reitan Battery. These consist of:

1) Minnesota Multiphasic Personality Inventory (MMPI);
2) Seashore Rhythm Test;
3) Wechsler Adult Intelligence Scale (WAIS);
4) Reitan-Klove Sensory-Perceptual Examination;
5) Halstead Finger Tapping Test;
6) Halstead Category Test;
7) Speech-Sounds Perception Test;
8) Trail Making Test;
9) Reitan-Indiana Aphasia Examination;
10) Tactual Performance Test; and
11) Lateral Dominance Examination.

The usage of these diverse tests as part of an overall battery allows the examiner to determine a number of important factors, such as: presence of impairment; degree of impairment; lateralization, which refers to which hemisphere the damage is in; and localization, which indicates where specifically within that hemisphere the damage is located.

The Halstead-Reitan Battery takes approximately six hours to administer and gives a varied and accurate measurement of an individual's neuropsychological functioning. This is the "older" of the two neuropsychological batteries and therefore has been more widely used. In recent years, however, a newer battery has come onto the scene, the Luria-Nebraska Battery. This test is an outgrowth of the work of the Russian neuropsychologist, A. R. Luria.

This test consists of 269 standardized items, each of which is administered separately. When all of the items in this battery are administered and scored, they yield "scores" in 11 areas:

1) Motor Functions;
2) Rhythm;
3) Tactile Functions;
4) Visual Functions;
5) Receptive Speech;
6) Expressive Speech;
7) Writing;
8) Reading;
9) Arithmetic;
10) Memory; and
11) Intellectual Processes.

In addition, there are scales which are based on items from other scales, which yield specific information. These scales are: the Pathognomonic Scale, which brings together items which are "... highly indicative of brain damage and are rarely missed by patients with thought disorder or by patients with peripheral neurological involvement" (Golden, Hammeke, & Purisch, 1980); and the Right and Left Hemisphere Scales, which give "initial measures of lateralization." When all of the items have been scored, the individual's scores can be plotted on a standardized form, which will yield a profile which depicts the individual's neuropsychological functioning.

Golden (1979) points out the various strengths and weaknesses of these two batteries. He states that one of the biggest advantages of the Luria over the Halstead is that the Luria takes only two and one half hours to administer as compared with six for the Halstead. Additionally, he points out that since the Luria breaks general functions into specific skills and deficits and since the items on this test are of a qualitative nature, the user is enabled to more easily and perhaps more accurately interpret the results. The Halstead, he says, has the major advantage of having been in use longer, and therefore, it has a more extensive background than the Luria.

Smith (1975) came up with what he considers the four essential goals of a neuropsychological battery. These goals are:

1) neurodiagnosis;
2) establishing baselines of the individual's functioning;
3) aiding in the prognostic assessment of the individual; and
4) aiding in treatment/rehabilitation planning for the individual.

Both of these batteries are quite effective in each of these areas, and their effectiveness and accuracy make them invaluable in general, but especially in interpreting the results of abilities tests with individuals with brain damage.

THE ASSESSMENT OF INTELLIGENCE AND PRIMARY ABILITIES IN YOUNG CHILDREN

While it is not the aim of this chapter to give a detailed presentation on the assessment of intelligence and primary abilities in children, the authors do wish to present briefly some of the tests which are currently available in this area. Tests such as the Stanford-Binet, the Wechsler Scales, the Culture-Fair Test, the Thurstone Primary Abilities Test and the CAB, which sometimes extend into the one-to-eight-year range that we are talking about here, have been described above. In the present range we deal with some tests intended to be true intelligence tests and others that observe developmental steps in behavior, sometimes in "experimental situations" like the Gesell and Ilg tests. Among those most requiring consideration are: 1) the Bayley Scales of Infant Development, 2) the Gesell Developmental Scales, 3) the Kaufman K-ABC Test, 4) the Merrill-Palmer, 5) the Psyche Cattell test, 6) the McCarthy scales for two- to eight-year-olds, and 7) the IPAT Culture-Fair Scale 1, for four- to eight-year-olds.

The Bayley Scales are used with children from the ages of 2-30 months. These scales yield two scores: 1) motor and 2) mental. In addition, 30 behavior ratings are obtained with this test. The strength of this test, in addition to its applicability to a very young population, is its careful standardization and the fact that it is a comprehensive measure.

The Gesell Scales are designed for use with children from the ages of four weeks to six years. These scales yield measures in four areas of behavior: 1) language; 2) adaptive; 3) personal-social; and 4) motor. The Gesell Scales, however, are not as well-standardized as the Bayley Scales. The increased research with and development of the Wechsler Scales for younger children has resulted in a loss of popularity of these tests, so that they are less frequently used today, though the Gesell Scales are valuable in a broad assessment of developmental level.

Regarding the measurement of primary abilities in children, a further test to be presented is the McCarthy Scales of Children's Abilities. This test is for use with children between the ages of 2.5 and 8.5 years. It yields six measures, not factorially based, of a child's abilities: 1) memory; 2) general cognitive; 3) motor; 4) perceptual-performance; 5) quantitative; and 6) verbal.

An experimental test, as yet with little use, is the Kaufman K-ABC Test (Kaufman & Kaufman, 1982). This uses the conception of separate scores on a) simultaneous processing and b) sequential processing of perceptual data. On an inspection basis, it clearly seems to be aiming at a measure of fluid intelligence, g_f, though no factorial evidence has at present been given of its relative saturation in g_f and g_c.

If we turn to tests based on factor analytic structuring in the nursery school range, the most comprehensive study in terms of variety of performances covered is still that developed out of the pioneer work of Cattell and Bristol (1933). The g factor saturations of 18 test types, e.g., form boards, mazes, following directions, immediate memory, and several from Binet, Gesell, Merrill-Palmer, etc. ranged from .24 to .43, and some of those in customary use in the Binet, etc., were among the lowest.

From this research and others eight subtests were chosen to become the *IPAT Culture-Fair Scale 1* for four to eight years. The subtest concept validities finally reached range from .64 to .90 and that of the whole test stands at .95. Although so named because it stands in the Culture-Fair series (Scales 1, 2 and 3), the test actually has a four-subtest, purely culture-fair part and a four-subtest part that is not culture-fair in case one wants to increase its length and to get a contrast of g_f and g_c scores; experiments have indicated that the first part is a measure of g_f, fluid intelligence, and the second of g_c, crystallized intelligence. The question of whether these are still distinguishable in early childhood has received a first answer from a study of three- to six-year-olds by Cattell and Kulhavy, as yet only

published in Cattell (1971a) in a factoring of 12 tests essentially representing primary abilities, as shown in Table 9.9.

Actually, three of these appear to be what have been designated *provincials, p*'s, but the rest may reasonably be interpreted as the familiar 1) *fluid* intelligence most evident in perceiving relations and inductive reasoning, 2) *crystallized* intelligence in verbal facility, following instructions, and even (at this stage of incomplete mastery of the physical world) in spatial relations, and 3) general speed.

It seems very likely that most of the presently available preschool "intelligence tests," with the possible exception of the two parts of the above Culture-Fair Scale 1, which together have a concept validity of 0.95, mix intelligence with other g's and p's, and also with personality factors. This cannot be brought clearly to light at the moment because the nature and measurement of personality factors below the age of eight (except for the tentative Dreger *Pre-School Personality Questionnaire* [Dreger, 1977]) are still obscure. But an alert practitioner working with young children should be prepared to interpret the measures on some tests and "cognitive" developmental scales as involving personality factors.

The question of group and individual administration of tests raised earlier becomes particularly relevant in the testing of younger children. The reader will realize that most of the tests in the older range (e.g., the Lorge Thorndike, the Simplex, Cattell tests) can be either group or individually administered, and in support of this let it be said that, with normal subjects, it is a superstition that the individual administration is in all respects better (granted group proctoring and rejection of spoiled tests). For what is gained in individual testing by certain features is lost by others, notably the bias introduced by the individual testing, in encouragements given and interpretations of borderline responses often at an unconscious level. However, in really young children, ob-

TABLE 9.9

Higher Stratum General Capacities, g's (and certain p's) as found at the 3-6-Year-Old Level

Pre-School Intelligence Structure: Second-Stratum
Factors Among Primary Abilities

Primary Ability Factors	g_f 1	g_c 2	g_s 3	p_m 4	p_v 5	p_k 6
1. Motor Speed		-.2	.7	.5		
2. Memory for Instructions	.3	.3	-.4			.1
3. Verbal Facility	.1	.4			-.2	.1
4. Manipulative Spatial Skill				.3	-.3	.3
5. Perceiving Relationships	.7	.4				
6. Extracting Explicit Spatial Relations	.4	.5	.5			
7. Fast Cube Manipulation		-.2				.4
8. Visual Form Completion	-.2	.2			.6	.3
9. Pyramid Building	.2			.2		.5
10. Inductive, Constructive Reasoning	.7			-.5		-.5
11. Cultural Level in Visual Matters					.3	
12. Visual Perceptual Memory					.5	

Loadings are means, rounded to one decimal place, from 10 researches reanalyzed and integrated by Cattell and Kulhavy (unpublished, 1971).

g_f = fluid intelligence; g_c = crystallized intelligence; g_s = general speed; p_m = "provincial" factor of motor skill; p_v = "provincial" factor of visualization; p_k = possible provincial of kinesthetic awareness

viously, individual testing is vital, and most of the above are individual. The IPAT C.F. Scale 1, however, offers adaptability in designating four subtests as individually administered and four that are designed, if necessary, to be administered to small groups (2 to 10 children) around the psychologist, and in giving complete standardization for both full (22 minutes of testing time) and the abbreviated (approximately 12 minutes) forms. Note this test for four- to eight-year-olds is also applicable for measurement of retarded adults.

SUMMARY

This chapter has looked at the state of the art of the measurement of abilities, and how it has progressed from what may be referred to as the measurement of intuitively-arrived-at constructs to the present measurement of sophisticated, factor analytically obtained constructs.

The main structure of abilities is now well-understood (though outlying areas remain for exploration) through both individual difference and developmental factorings, relation to neurology, etc. Some 20 primary abilities derive directly from test performance and some five or six general factors derive from the primaries. In addition to these two classes of structures—called aids, a's and general capacities, c's—research is beginning to recognize some intermediary provincial, p, structures which have the function of analyzing within each of the special sense domains. This view of g, p, and a structures is known as the triadic theory of intelligence, and guides construction of functional tests.

Intelligence is not the only important upper stratum general capacity. Other general c's are perceptual speed, retrieval capacity or fluency, a second (rote) memory factor, an immediate recall capacity, as well as the provincials, p's, visualization and auditory pattern and pitch discrimination. However, although there are available standardized tests of fluency (Cattell, 1937b), most applied practice seems to have found little use so far for other g's, except in brain injury.

Regarding intelligence itself, the work of Horn, McArdle, Cattell and others has shown conclusively that what was regarded as one factor (Spearman's g) is actually two appreciably correlated ("superimposed") factors, g_f, *fluid intelligence* and g_c, *crystallized intelligence*. These have appreciably different properties, e.g., regarding heritability, age span development, etc., which explain some conflicting results in the past. They need to be measured, respectively, by what can be called *culture-fair* and *traditional* (school knowledge contaminated) tests.

The currently available tests for measuring g_f and g_c are described in sufficient detail, as to psychometric properties, standardization, etc., to guide the practitioner. The IPAT Culture-Fair Scales 1, 2, and 3, the Raven Matrices, and one or two older tests (Lorge-Thorndike) are aimed at g_f measures. The Wechsler Scales (WAIS, WISC) and the Stanford-Binet are the most used in the U.S. for crystallized intelligence (Horn and McArdle have examined their factorial compositeness). The Cattell g_c Scales I, II, and III (published in England) also span the age range, from four years to superior adult level. The Cattell Scale III in this English series and also the IPAT Scale III in the culture-fair have a high ceiling and are used for some graduate selection and by societies like Mensa, evaluating intelligence at highest levels.

The terms "aptitudes" and "abilities" have become used interchangeably, but aptitude has perhaps more frequently been used in the past for what are now defined as *primary abilities*. At the time of Thurstone's pioneer work only about a half dozen were recognized, but these are measured with good psychometric properties by Thurstone's *Primary Abilities Test* (1938). Since then the *Comprehensive Abilities Battery* (CAB), by Hakstian and Cattell, has built upon a demonstration of some 20 primaries. These include verbal, numerical, spatial, perceptual speed, and inductive reasoning, as in the PMA, but also auditory ability, spelling, esthetic judgment, representational drawing, etc. The CAB primaries can be administered separately conveniently taken from a "kit" of tests.

The clinical tests used to assess brain damage and to estimate normal neuro-endocrinal effects from aging have resulted in tests designed a) to assess overall brain damage and b) to determine its locality. The former (overall brain damage) in individuals beyond the school years can be economically assessed by a contrast of g_f (culture-fair) and g_c (crystallized intelligence, in verbal traditional tests) scores. The latter (locality) is approached by such more elaborate tests as the Halstead-Reitan and the Luria batteries. The use of brain waves in the EEG, as by Ertl's method, and by other auxiliary tests (e.g., the Bender), needs to be coordinated with the general (g_f/g_c) ability test approach.

An appreciable number of batteries for testing the intelligence of young children in the two- to eight-year range exists, as well as carefully worked out developmental scales based on general behavior. There is evidence from factorial analysis that the structure in this range still distinguishes fluid from crystallized general intelligence and an initial but still incompletely worked out basis for measuring these in the four- to eight-year range exists in the IPAT Culture-Fair Scale 1. In general, among the seven tests here listed for this range the reliabilities and standardizations are adequate, but the concept validities have not been worked out (except for Culture-Fair Scale 1) to enable one to estimate the almost certain intrusions of other general cognitive factors and even personality factors into test scores in the two- to eight-year range.

CHAPTER 10

Achievement and Proficiency Measures

Daniel D. Blaine and Philip Merrifield

INTRODUCTION

The discussions of instrumentation in the other chapters of this section deal with psychological tests that are used primarily in the prediction or explanation of behavior. In this chapter, the concern is with variables which are more commonly regarded as criterion or outcome variables. The assessment of academic achievement and job proficiency goes back at least to the civil service exams of the Chinese around 1000 B.C. The measurement of educational and job performance has been subjected to the refinement of literally centuries of effort since its beginning.

However, the implication is not necessarily that such assessment has reached a high level of sophisticated application. The application of measurement principles in the assessment of academic achievement and job proficiency continues to be plagued with misunderstandings in selection, administration, and interpretation, to say nothing of the myriad problems encountered in the actual construction

of such tests (see Chapter 22). While it is maintained here that such difficulties are mostly a function of the inappropriate application of tests and measurement principles, the confusion has led many to criticize testing practices beyond reason. Hoffman (1962) exemplifies this rather "antitesting" orientation.

It is interesting to speculate how a teacher or an employer might proceed with the evaluation of students and employees without information on the performance of these persons. It would further seem most reasonable to gather the information relevant to personnel decisions in such a way that the information was most useful. When one studies the principles of testing presented in the earlier chapters of this volume, one discovers that although there are very complex and technical matters involved, the purpose is ultimately to make the information derived from testing as usable as possible against some criterion. This is true whether one is speaking of a teacher concerned with the achievement of individual students in the classroom or a psychologist theorizing about the structure of cognitive abilities. The notion that the information derived from testing should be as usable as possible is in perfect concert with good principles of psychometric theory.

Complaints about testing in the schools or in job situations should not be directed at the tests themselves, but rather to the inappropriate development or to some aspect of the selection, administration, or interpretation phase of the testing application. Those who restrict or eliminate the use of tests would appear, then, to be arguing for the replacement of viable information with that gathered in an informal and haphazard manner. Information collected in such a fashion is not an appropriate foundation upon which to base theories of human behavior, nor is it adequate for personnel decisions.

THE NATURE OF ACHIEVEMENT

When considering the nature of achievement, several related terms come to mind. Such terms as aptitude, ability, and intelligence are examples. The distinction between aptitude and achievement has been dealt with by several authors (e.g., Anastasi, 1980; Fleishman, 1972; Green, 1974; Messick, 1982; Snow, 1980). This distinction has been especially difficult for the lay person to understand because of the high correlation that usually occurs between aptitude and achievement measures and because of the argument against the distinction (Coleman & Cureton, 1954). Although Carver (1974) has argued for a different basis for considering the properties of measures of these constructs, the tests for the two often appear to be very similar. Anastasi (1980) has argued that clarification of the confusion can be found in our willingness to do away with most of the terms as superfluous. Although it is easy to sympathize with the person trying to make sense of the technical jargon that often accompanies discussions dealing with human behavior, it is also necessary to realize that it is a very complex domain with which we are concerned.

This complexity, however, would not seem to argue against an attempt to provide a framework within which achievement and related concepts can be discussed. At the risk of sounding naive, let us start with the idea that our primary concern is human behavior. To be more specific, as scientist-practitioners, we are interested in understanding, predicting, and controlling behavior—that is, we are interested in developing theories of human behavior which specify the patterns and relationships that exist within the variability of human behavior.

The early attempts to conceptualize human behavior in terms of simple S-R notions did not prove very fruitful because persons in the "same" situation did not exhibit the "same" behavior. This forced the expansion of conceptualization to incorporate this added complexity. With the introduction of the concept of latent traits, or the domain "in-between" the input (S) and the output (R), as a way to deal with this apparent lack of isomorphism, the problems associated with representing a concept in a measurement scale presented themselves. If the goal is to develop theories of human behavior so that endeavors such as education can truly become prescriptive, then it is especially important to develop quantitative measures of the aspects of human behavior, since the relationships between these aspects or variables is the "stuff" of psychological theory (see Chapter 3).

Although there is still a long way to go, most social scientists agree that the most productive way to proceed in our study of human behavior is in the examination of the structure of variance/covariance matrices. Before every "experimental" psychologist takes umbrage, it should be rapidly pointed out that analysis of variance can be conceived of as the examination of a matrix structure. It just happens that the independent variables are usually categorical and measured without error (see Chapter 6).

Assuming the advisability of quantitatively measuring the dimensions of human behavior, how then should *achievement* be conceptualized relative to *other domains* of human behavior? Achievement as a domain of behaviors that social scientists attempt to explain can be conceived of as any behavior that can be specified in such a way that the extent to which an individual is capable of its execution can be assessed. The specific behaviors to be focused on depend on the goals of the educational institution or the requirements of job performance. Achievement is distinguished from aptitudes or abilities in that the latter dimensions refer to latent traits which are assumed to be part of the psychological structure of individuals that influence the form of achievement. Abilities are viewed here as developing out of the mastery of. a range of achievement-type behaviors which have superordinate process requirements in common. Such a definition of abilities is similar to that of Ferguson (1954, 1956). For purposes of further discussion the general definitions of Messick (1982) can be used. He refers to achievement as "what an individual *knows* and *can do* in a specified subject area" (p. 1) and to abilities as "stable consistencies *within* individuals (across variations in setting, time, and task) that reliably differentiate *among* individuals" (p. 12).

The dimensionalization of the ability domain has received a good deal of attention in the work of many very capable scholars (e.g., Cattell, 1971a; Ekstrom, French, & Harman, 1976; Guilford, 1967; Thurstone, 1938). The same is true for the domains of personality (Cattell, 1973a; Cattell & Dreger, 1977; Dreger, 1972; Eysenck, 1965; Eysenck & Eysenck, 1969; Guilford, 1975; Thurstone, 1951) and motivation (Cattell, Radcliffe, & Sweney, 1963; Cattell & Warburton, 1967). The specifics of research and theory in these

domains are discussed in the other chapters (Chapter 9) of this volume and will consequently not be dealt with in this context, except in reference to models of achievement. The important consideration at this point is that the domain of achievement probably cannot be characterized by the relatively stable structure that appears to characterize the ability domain. It may in fact be the case that, whereas abilities can be conceptualized as relatively enduring traits residing, in some sense, within the individual, any structure in achievements may actually be a reflection of cultural patterns in the conceptualization of the goals of education.

MODELS FOR THE EXPLANATION OF ACHIEVEMENT

Terms such as achievement and proficiency can be viewed as references to particular types of behavior, patterns of behavior, or situation-related behaviors. Thus, when one discusses "models of achievement," one is really discussing "models of behavior." The nature of the specific achievement or proficiency measures employed will depend on the purpose of testing; that is, what behavior is one interested in understanding and explaining. The purpose of testing is of primary importance and dictates the specific facets of achievement to be assessed. In the discussion of the models which follows, the tests used to assess the variables or dimensions in the respective domains may change as the focus of interest changes, but the general form of the models remains the same.

The most general expression of a model does not necessarily specify the particulars of the interrelations of the variables in that model. Such a model would express achievement as a function of the dimensions of the domains that would theoretically have an effect on achievement. Although there is a wide range of theory and research related to the relevant predictor spaces and their dimensionalization, the majority seem to focus attention on abilities, personality or temperament factors, and aspects of motivation, with a consideration of the importance of situational variables beginning to be integrated. Thus, a general model of achievement could be expressed as:

$$Ach = f(A_i, T_j, M_k, S_n) \qquad (10\text{-}1)$$

where Ach is achievement expressed as a function of i ability dimensions, j temperament dimensions, k motivational dimensions, and n situational dimensions. A consideration of situational factors in the model allows for effects other than those of individual differences. Such a general model does not specify the nature of the functional relationship in terms of how the variables or dimensions of the model contribute to the explanation of achievement nor how they relate to one another.

Bloom (1976) proposed a model for school learning which expressed achievement as a function of *cognitive* entry characteristics, *affective* entry characteristics, and *quality of instruction*. He posited the relations among the predictors as linear, and suggested linear regression as a means of estimating the parameters of the model. This conceptualization of the relationship between achievement and its correlates within the context of the general linear model is probably more common than any other form.

It can readily be seen, however, that such a model is somewhat limited. First, it does not allow for a consideration of the multifaceted nature of achievement nor does it incorporate a consideration of the time dimension. The most global conceptualization of behavior would have the covariance structure of behavioral dimensions moving through time. The covariance structure at any point on the time dimension would describe the *intra*-relationships as well as the *inter*-relationships of the explanatory and response-variable domains. While such a conceptualization

may be more complex than we can functionally manage with current quantitative or statistical models, it does allow us to see where our observations of human behavior (our studies, our experiments) fall in the greater scheme. Although Gordon (1980) has questioned whether such complexity is justified or can be supported by the current school system, ultimately it is difficult to imagine a complete model of achievement behavior which did not incorporate the longitudinal characteristics of the interplay of the dimensions of human behavior.

Cattell (1957c) has proposed (Chapter 23) a model in which the situational aspects are integrated into the model as weights rather than as separate variables in the equation:

$$Y = \overset{a\,=\,x}{\sum b_{ay}A_{ai}} + \overset{t\,=\,y}{\sum b_{ty}T_{ti}} + \overset{d\,=\,z}{\sum b_{dy}D_{di}} \qquad (10\text{-}2)$$

Cattell argues that such a model has the advantages of: 1) keeping the total profile of the individual together in ability, A, general personality temperament, T, and motivation, D, terms; 2) representing the instructional situation (in effect, the school and home situation) by a full profile of determinable factor loadings—the b's; and 3) operating not with an unspecified linear or product relation, but with a tested and predictively effective form used in factor analytic estimations of criterion.

An additional possibility is that the components of achievement are not additive but are more appropriately expressed in a multiplicative relational form, that is, the terms on the right side of equation 10-1 would be multiplied to one another. In such a case a low value on one component is much less likely to be compensated for by a high value on another component, as suggested by the linear model. Such a notion has a certain conceptual appeal in that it is difficult to imagine how any amount of ability could make up for the lack of motivation to achieve. The difficulties of estimating the parameters of the model and the possibly unnecessary complexity of the model, however, lead to the derivation of two linear forms from the product model. To simplify the consideration of the product model, let us reduce it to an expression of achievement as product of the four domains, ignoring, for a moment, the multidimensionality of each, as well as the parameters of the model:

$$\text{Ach} = A * T * M * S \qquad (10\text{-}3)$$

The first model is derived from the product model by merely taking the logarithms of both sides of the equation:

$$\log \text{Ach} = \log A + \log T + \log M + \log S$$
$$(10\text{-}4)$$

The model is in the linear form when the terms are expressed as logarithms. Thus, the model would be linear in a logarithmic transformation of the original scales.

The second derived model is obtained by taking the partial derivatives of the terms of the product model:

$$\delta\text{Ach} = \delta A(T*M*S) + \delta T(A*M*S) + \delta M(A*T*S) + \delta S(A*T*M) \qquad (10\text{-}5)$$

The result is not merely an expression of variation in achievement as a linear function of variation in abilities, temperament, motivation, and situation. Variation in the components is weighted by the product of the other three components. In other words, a change in achievement could be expected from a change in motivation, but the amount of the change would depend upon the location of the individual within the ability and temperament domains, and situational factors. Similarly, changing the situation in order to influence achievement would require explicit consideration of the abilities, temperament, and motivation of the learner—differences in these components would result in differences in achievement of two learners in the same situation. The model in this form makes more explicit the implications for individualization of instruction. Whether or not these latter models hold any potential for the understanding and explanation of achievement behavior is an empirical matter. The immediate difficulty which arises is the relation between the properties of the variables in the models and the mathematical manipulations performed on them. A consideration of such complex models makes the psychometric properties of the variables involved in the models a most critical consideration.

It should be emphasized that the models just discussed are, with the exception of equation 10-2, conceptual representations for purposes of discussion. In the case of equation 10-2, numerous weights for various achievements exist (Cattell & Butcher, 1968). For them to reflect what is probably closer to reality, achievement would have to be considered for its multifaceted character rather than as a single variable as presented in the models. The other noticeable omission is the variable of time which allows for the conceptualization of development; note, however, that the partial differentiation leading to equation 10-5 could well be with respect to time.

As Bock (1976) has pointed out, we may not have a reasonable model of achievement until we can monitor the "continuously moving line of each child's development . . ." (p. 76). Although the structures that are to be dealt with in the ability, personality, and motivational domains have a characteristic stability over time, it must be kept in mind that there is the possibility of a certain degree of variation in the structural relations associated with the achievement and situational domains due to cultural influences.

THE NATURE OF ACHIEVEMENT

Referring back to the definition of Messick (1982), it can easily be seen that there are very few, if any, limitations on the performances that might be measured as achievement. Virtually anything that an individual can learn to know or do can be regarded as achievement. The nature of the achievement behavior to be assessed is then a function of the demands of the circumstances in which the examiner finds him- or herself. Whereas in the domains of ability, personality, and motivation there is an ongoing endeavor to discover the inherent structure and consequently specify the relevant variables for a given model, there is much more occasion for specificity in the structure of achievement variables. Although Bracht and Hopkins (1972) argue that there is a certain stability to achievement structure, there is at least the possibility that, over time, there would be less stability of model parameters related to situational variables than for parameters of the ability, personality, and motivational domains.

Further, any structure that might emerge in the realm of achievement is, at least in part, a function of the cultural circumstances in which it arises. At some point in history, certain cultural goals and values may be reflected in the achievement of students and the tests to which they are subjected. For a time, this provides a structure to achievement which is detectable in the covariance structure of the measured achievement variables. However, as time passes and the emphasis with respect to "desirable" achievement or job requirements changes, the structure as well as the level of achievement can change. As pointed out in Chapters 5 and 20, there are differences among various human groups in the domain of abilities. Given a more dramatic evolution in achievement structure over time, one would expect to find an even greater profusion of variables which would discriminate variously defined groups than would be the case with abilities, for example.

Here, it is maintained that achievement and abilities (or aptitudes) develop out of the same cultural processes. Achievement

refers to the specific behaviors that occur through cultural opportunity. As more and more behaviors with common underlying processes are executed, abilities develop and refer to the general processes underlying these behaviors, which then contribute to a variety of specific tasks or achievements. Thus, because of their commonality with many human behaviors, abilities develop a stability over time that is not displayed by specific achievements. Although there may be changes over time in the structure of abilities, for example, such changes do not mitigate the search for structure as they do in achievement.

THE ASSESSMENT OF ACHIEVEMENT

The above discussion points to the difficulty in determining the particular achievement behaviors to be assessed and in specifying the procedures by which they are to be assessed. This is especially important since the *structure* of achievement is suggested by particular assessment applications. However, with the selection of a set of ability tests, it is more likely a simple matter of particular dimensions being assessed more adequately than others because of the particular tests selected. In dealing with the results of even a rather haphazard measurement of abilities, there is a more established structure from psychological research to aid the interpretation of the structure found in a particular sample of scores. Such structure is not available in the domain of achievement and, it may never reach the specificity of structure to be found with abilities or personality. With a relatively poorly defined structure, it is imperative that a good deal of effort be expended in the efficient assessment of achievement.

This complexity in the conceptualization of achievement is believed to be at the heart of the antitesting movement. Given the lack of definition of the domain and its structure, it is no wonder that detractors have a wealth of data to suggest that achievement testing is inappropriate, especially standardized achievement testing. If one considers the lack of definition in the domain (which really is a symptom of its extensiveness and complexity) and the standardized tests that are available, it is not difficult to imagine that a great deal of testing is, in fact, to some degree inappropriate.

What then is the teacher or the employer to do when confronted with the task of assessing academic achievement or job proficiency? With the painting of such a bleak picture, is there any way that such assessment can be organized so that the needs and purposes of the examiners are satisfied? The answer to the latter question is believed to be resoundingly affirmative. The task is tremendously complex and will take no mean effort on the part of those using tests to measure achievement; but the task is also a very important one involving the assessment of behaviors that are inextricably linked to the goals of society. As Ebel (1962) has pointed out, not only is it important for teachers to be masters of the achievement to be assessed, but they must also master the practice of assessment.

A major consideration of the test user is the particular achievement behavior to be assessed. In the educational domain a great deal of effort has been given to the specification of behavioral objectives (e.g., Bloom, 1956). Such a specification is tantamount to specifying desirable achievement goals. The task then becomes one of determining whether or to what degree the achievement goal has been obtained. How this task of assessment is to be approached depends on the level of specificity of the achievement. Assessing whether or not a student is capable of writing his or her name does not indicate the same assessment problem as determining whether an individual has mastered the concepts of arithmetic sufficiently to move on to algebra.

Unfortunately, it is too often the case that an achievement test is administered because it is "that time of year again," rather than as a logical extension of the perceived value of assessing the state of educational progress. It should be that achievement tests are administered because teacher and other school personnel are interested in making sound educational decisions for individual students in the program. Given that the general goals of education have been specified within the community, then it should be possible to utilize information from achievement tests to determine *what* to focus on in teaching, while assessment of ability, temperament, and motivational and situational variables should provide information relative to *how* instruction should proceed (see Chapter 20).

The reader versed in the relationship between abilities and achievement will respond that the information about "what" and "how" to teach are not limited to achievement and predictor tests respectively. It is well-known that achievement at one point in time is often a very good predictor of subsequent achievement of the same kind. It may well be that the distinction is based more on the language and conceptualizations of the person making use of the results than on characteristics of the respective instruments. A teacher will probably be more interested in how many uses a student can name for a particular object because it is important to subsequent instruction, whereas the psychologist might be interested in the same result, but because it indicates something about the fluency or divergent production ability of the person.

The specificity of the behavior or achievement that is being assessed is a primary consideration. It is important because the level of specificity will determine whether a standardized measure is available or whether the examiner will need to develop his or her own instruments to assess the achievement of interest. In cases where they are available, it is usually advisable to make use of tests for which there are data related to their psychometric properties rather than to devise a new instrument. It is often the case, however, that the examiner will have to resort to the development of a test for a variety of specific purposes, especially in education. The overwhelming majority of the assessment of educational achievement is accomplished with the aid of tests devised by teachers in the classroom. Consequently, it is especially important for teachers to be well-versed in the elements of psychometric theory, especially principles of test construction, since it is rarely the case that such instruments are subjected to the rigorous psychometric evaluation afforded standardized tests.

It is important to understand that the characteristics of a good test, as indicated by the technicalities of psychometric theory, are just as important for a test constructed by a teacher in the classroom as for the standardized test offered by a test publisher. However, since the teacher does not typically have the opportunity to examine the statistical behavior of the test and its items before it is administered, it is especially important that the characteristics of a good test be kept in mind when designing and developing assessment instruments.

If the examiner decides there are no standardized tests appropriate for the particular testing purpose, or there is no already available instrument to provide the information needed to make an educational or personnel decision based on achievement standing, then an instrument must be constructed. Several procedures have been developed which will aid in the construction of an assessment instrument. Since these are principles which lead to the development of the items of the test, they also provide a base from which to evaluate the tests that are available. We now turn to a consideration of these principles and procedures.

Test Content

The most common reason for the lack of availability of suitable tests is that the information sought by the administration of the test is so particular to the individual, classroom, or school that no one could construct an appropriate instrument without familiarity with the specific situation. The developers of standardized tests are typically interested in general measures of achievement which have applicability across a wide range of situations through time; consequently, they may be too general for many situations which require information for decision-making. In such instances, it is very important to have the test reflect the experience that students or employees have actually encountered. (Presumably the activity that occurs in the classroom or on the job is that activity which is judged most relevant to goal performance; otherwise, different activities would occur.) The goal is to have as reasonable a match as possible between what goes on in the referent situation and the performance required on the test.

As a means of aiding the content evaluation of tests, authors of most textbooks dealing with test construction recommend what is commonly referred to as a "table of specifications." Although there are a good many variations presented by different authors, the basic notion is to systematically categorize the activities of a course of instruction or of job performance with the aim of appropriately representing these activities on the test. Immediately, one can ascertain the variety of ways (dimensions in themselves) of classifying such activities. Williams and Haladyna (1982) propose a LOGIQ system which is quite extensive.

A more generic and simplified approach to a table of specifications crosses response modes (recall, evaluation, and application) with levels of content (fact, concept, and principle). Such a crossing yields, in this case, a 3 × 3 table. Each cell represents an activity or process, the importance of which can be assessed to determine the proportion of the test that should be devoted to the assessment of each particular process. (This presumes that some indicator of "importance" is available. The amount of time spent on a particular activity can be used as such an indicator.)

It may be that modifications in the conceptualizations of the dimensions and their respective levels are necessary for the table of specifications to relate appropriately to the achievement to be assessed. The main consideration is that if one has such a special situation where one must construct a test, it is important that there be a match between the nature of the activity and the nature of the test used for assessment. A search of a course text or a job manual for passages from which questions can be easily written may very well not result in a test that is congruent with the activities of a particular course or job. Since a perusal of common texts is often the basis for the development of items for standardized achievement tests, it is wise for the test selector to determine the relationship between the classification of the test items and the table of specifications that is appropriate to the current assessment task.

Tables of specifications need not necessarily be limited to two dimensions. The optimal number of dimensions used to classify activities depends on, among other things, the scope of the achievement being assessed.. The optimal complexity, in terms of dimensions, and the levels on them should provide an adequate conceptual summary of the course activities without fragmenting categories of activities to the point of rendering classifications trivial. Two or three dimensions with three or four levels each are probably as complex as necessary for most purposes. Above all it should be remembered that the goal is not to devise a fancy classification scheme for activities or item types; rather, it is to attempt to ensure the congruence of course content and process with test content and

process, in hopes of increasing the appropriateness of the test for its intended purpose.

Specificity of Assessment

In deciding how to proceed with the task of assessment, the scope of the resulting information must be considered. The relationship between the time of testing and the variety of dimensions assessed has been very well treated in Chapter 4. Assuming a relatively finite testing time, the purposes of testing must govern the relationship between the breadth and depth of assessment. If the purpose of assessment is to determine whether an individual has a level of skill in a narrowly defined area which would enable that individual to attempt to perform a more advanced skill, then the breadth of assessment might be more appropriately sacrificed in order to obtain the more refined assessment. If, on the other hand, the purpose of testing is to screen a variety of areas, it is more appropriate to use an instrument that has relatively few items for each of several different areas and give a more general or "global" description of the individuals tested. As a follow-up assessment, more "tailored" instruments that focus on specific facets of achievement could be administered to different individuals, possibly as a function of potential difficulties in specific areas.

In general, the breadth of the assessment depends upon the purpose of the assessment. One consideration is the degree of generalization that one wishes to make concerning the domain of achievement. If one is interested in how the domains of ability, motivation, temperament, and situations relate to achievement, it is imperative that the complex range of possible achievement behaviors be considered. There is evidence that different levels of achievement can be related to different interactions of abilities, motivation, temperament, and situations (Cattell & Butcher, 1968; Cronbach & Snow, 1977).

It would seem reasonable then to assume that differences in profiles of achievement are affected by these same interactions. Thus, although there are times when the purpose of testing dictates the assessment of a relatively unitary achievement, such an achievement variable exists in the much larger context of achievement variables having varying relations with dimensions of abilities, personality, motivation, and situations (see Chapter 20). Hummel-Rossi (1981) provides an interesting set of longitudinal results that tend to support this conjecture.

Item-Response Form

One of the unfortunate realities of educational measurement is the extent to which practices are adopted and followed for reasons other than sound psychometric or theoretical ones. One theoretical explanation for relatively independent dimensions of achievement behavior is that different cognitive processes are involved and characterize the different dimensions. Yet texts on educational measurement often present discussions of the various item-response forms, without any more consideration of the underlying processes called for than the labeling of items as selected response vs. constructed response. It is not necessarily mentioned that such a distinction could even suggest the possibility of different processes underlying the assessment. It is important to be aware that how the examinee is asked to respond can influence the basis of the achievement assessment process. There may be a change in not only the level of achievement but also the facets of achievement assessed. Although the results are mixed, it has even been suggested that the use of separate answer sheets can have implications for the psychometric properties of a test (Beck, 1974; Muller, Calhoun, & Orling, 1972).

It is especially important for the tester to be cognizant of possible "jangle" effects (Kelley, 1927) in the relationship of tests

and what they are intended to measure. That is, psychological tests that are called by different names do not necessarily measure different things, and tests that are supposed to measure the same thing do not necessarily do so. In this case the researcher has the advantage over the teacher or other practitioner in that an examination of covariance structure will indicate the extent of relationship between variables, and provides the basis for evaluating the psychometric properties of instruments and estimating the structural relations among the concepts they are intended to measure. The teacher, on the other hand, must resort to an informal assessment of the commonality of items and tests which, without the support of objective evidence, can often be misleading. As Ebel (1968) points out, this is further complicated in that "consequences of low reliability in a predictor (imprecise prediction) are mathematically obvious in the low coefficient of predictive validity. The consequences of low reliability in an assessment device (imprecise inferences) are less obvious" (p. 72).

The teacher must also rely on personal judgment in the development of achievement tests. This should not imply, however, that such judgment need necessarily be based on ignorance. Given the variety of item-response formats available to teachers and other constructors of tests (e.g., multiple-choice, true-false, matching, cloze, essay), it should be possible to ascertain at least gross differences in process requirements that might be associated with different items.

It seems not only possible but very reasonable that different item-response formats require different processes. Horn (1966) has even suggested that different "basic abilities" might be required by different item-response formats. If this is the case, then it also seems reasonable that different abilities at least contribute differently to performance on different types of items. Thus, given a mixture of item-response formats, it might be wise to consider separate scores for different formats instead of just a total score. Further, given the strengths and weaknesses in the ability profiles of individuals, there would be differences in achievement as a function of the interaction of abilities and item-response formats. If one is interested in assessing knowledge, for example, one should be aware of the possibility that the level of knowledge demonstrated may be partly a function of the way the individual is required to demonstrate that knowledge.

Norm-referenced vs. Criterion-referenced Testing

With the increased emphasis on concepts of learning for mastery and on criterion-related assessment, which began approximately two decades ago, there arose a good deal of spirited discussion on the relative merits of norm-referencing and criterion-referencing in the interpretation of educational measurement (Berk, 1980; Ebel, 1978; Glaser, 1963; Hambleton, 1978; Livingston, 1972; Mehrens & Ebel, 1979; Popham, 1978; Popham & Husek, 1969; Traub, 1979). The essential distinction between the two approaches as presented by most authors is that norm-referenced scores are related to the distribution of scores of all examinees, whereas criterion-referenced scores are related to some criterion external to actual distribution of scores. While norm-referencing translates an individual score into a standing among other individuals, criterion-referencing relates the score to a standard of performance that has been established (usually independently of any distributional characteristics of the test). Although a variety of other differences can be identified by a thorough examination of the literature, they are for the most part derivable from the basic difference, as mentioned above, in the use of the scores obtained.

The impetus behind the criterion-referencing "movement" was the argument that for many educational purposes information about where an individual stood relative to his or her peers was often not very useful. Knowing that a student scored higher than 60% of the other individuals who had taken the test did not necessarily indicate whether he or she was prepared to receive some *specified* unit of instruction. This difference in the value attached to the informational aspects of test scores led to a division within educational testing. Although at first glance the distinction between the approaches may seem quite important, on closer examination it would seem more apparent than real, and, indeed, statistically inseparable.

Since criterion-referencing was intimately tied to the concept of mastery, there appeared to be no reason to be concerned with the distribution of the resulting scores. Items were to be selected on the basis of their relation to the behavioral objective, with the emphasis on "content validity" coupled with a corresponding deemphasis of the statistical/psychometric properties of the test, since the scores would not necessarily produce a distribution that displayed characteristics appropriate for traditional psychometric examination. One was only interested in whether an individual had attained mastery, which was regarded as the basis for assessment in the first place. This, coupled with the goal of promoting the learning of all students, led to the notion that if instruction were particularly successful all students might obtain very high scores and a normal distribution would not result. Although this may seem like sound reasoning, it can also be viewed as a rather interesting interpretation of the "ceiling effect," which has often been regarded as something to be avoided. When viewed from this latter perspective, it would seem that aspects of the reasoning behind criterion-referenced testing have led to the desirability of ignoring the upper part of a distribution.

It may be that norm-referencing can legitimately be accused of being overly concerned with the generation of a normally distributed set of scores. There are several reasons why a normal distribution of scores is desirable, the most important being that we use the correlation coefficient as the basis of our theoretical inferences about the structure of behavioral processes. Every student in the behavioral sciences has probably encountered the incomprehensible statistics professor raving about the importance of assumptions underlying particular statistical techniques. The importance of such assumptions is extrapolated into the syllabi of comprehensive examinations for graduate students, but unfortunately not far beyond.

The distributional assumptions concerning statistical relationships among variables are important because their violation has implications for the interpretations of the parameter values estimated from the data structure, as well as implications for tests of hypotheses involving those parameters. Distributional considerations are important in avoiding the invalidation of inferences based on statistical values. If we are to base an inference about the relationship between dimensions upon the value of a correlation between measured variables—a correlation that we assume to have a possible range of negative one to positive one—then it is not in our best interests to have the potential values of that correlation artificially restricted nor, in occasional instances, artificially inflated.

In the identification of a possible use of test scores that may not have been properly addressed, a substantial number of people interested in educational measurement seemingly rejected many of the basic principles of sound psychological theory. The fundamentals of criterion-referenced measurement do not seem to contradict the use of norm-referencing in any way, but rather to suggest that scores obtained under the aegis of good psychometric principles have an additional use, the study of which has a great many and valuable

implications for the assessment of achievement. That scores could be used to aid in decisions about whether a student was prepared to go on to a new module of instruction do not appear to be at odds with basic psychometric theory. The issue does not seem to be related to whether scores should be used to estimate an individual's placement in a distribution or standing with respect to some absolute standard of performance. Rather, it seems to be associated with the specification of absolute standards, which is a critical issue, although Glass (1978) has questioned whether it is even possible to talk of an "absolute standard." Regardless of whether the setting of standards is viable, it hardly seems to dictate an alternative to developed psychometric principles. On the other hand, the recommendation that precision at the level of criterion be obtained by asking many questions at that level is an application of the time-honored psychophysical principle of repeated presentation of the same stimulus (in this case, a replicate defined as equivalent within a domain). Hambleton, Mills, and Simon (1983) recommend a minimum of 17-20 items at the same difficulty level in order to assure adequate reliability.

In summary, many of the efforts in the area of criterion-referenced testing appear to be a case of the "tail wagging the dog." In an effort to dichotomize a range of behavior by establishing a criterion of mastery, there has been a flurry of activity associated with the development of alternative assessment procedures whose psychometric properties are evaluated differently (e.g., Linn, 1979a, b; Millman, 1979). The push to "dichotomize" is manifest in the attempt to divide criterion-referencing from norm-referencing. That the purposes of testing could vary from situation to situation does not seem unreasonable. However, that scores which result from the administration of an assessment instrument would be so limited as to require different instruments and underpinning theory for decisions about criterion mastery as opposed to estimating standing in a reference group seems less palatable.

Transformed Scores

Anyone who has ever made use of a standardized test has probably encountered transformed scores. The variety of transformed or standardized scores is almost limitless, and new ones are being devised every day. The transformation of scores is predicated on an attempt to make the scores as informative as possible and/or promoting certain structural relations with variables. Most people have had the experience of receiving some score on a test where the first question that comes to mind is "How did everyone else do?" The basic problem with transformation of scores on educational and psychological instruments is the lack of definition of the "unit" of behavior. The most desirable situation would be to report a score that had inherent meaning. This has been the goal of criterion-referencing, as well as the more recent variation referred to as "domain-referencing." The latter is an attempt to construct tests such that the score on a test is interpretable as the proportion of the "domain" of items that the examinee can answer correctly. The difficulties associated with the specification of the entire "domain" are overwhelming (Bormuth, 1970). Roid and Haladyna (1982) propose that the term "domain" be restricted to the set of all possible items that can be generated from a specified procedure, e.g., an item form.

The norm-referencing approach has, for lack of a better definition of units, accepted the standard deviation as the unit for reporting and interpretation. This, coupled with the assumption of an underlying normal distribution of scores, makes it possible to incorporate a certain "meaning" into reported scores. However, as advocates of criterion-referencing will be quick to point out, there is no absolute criterion against which to evaluate the meaning of a score. Again, this is not the problem of the score or its transformation, but rather the lack of definition of mastery and the inability to establish standards.

The question of norm-referencing of tests is dealt with in several chapters within this volume (see Chapters 5, 6, 18, 22, and 23), but especially in Chapter 23. Elsewhere, Angoff (1971) presents a convenient summary of the basic reasons for transforming the scores that derive from testing: 1) they are convenient for manipulating the data from the testing application; 2) an attempt could be made to rescale the data to achieve an interval level of measurement; 3) transformations may result in an attempt to equate scores from alternate forms of a test; and 4) there is little or no meaning inherent in raw scores.

The user of tests should be very careful when contemplating the transformation of scores that result from tests. Without a consideration of the assumptions underlying a given transformation in a particular situation, there is too great a risk of exchanging one relatively meaningless unit for another.

THE PURPOSES OF ASSESSMENT

In the course of this chapter, several aspects of achievement testing have been considered. There are any number of basic texts which will provide the introductory conceptualizations necessary to begin to tackle measurement problems (Allen & Yen, 1979; Anastasi, 1982; Cattell & Butcher, 1968; Cronbach, 1970; Ebel, 1979; Hopkins & Stanley, 1981; Nunnally, 1972; Thorndike & Hagen, 1977) or pursue them in earnest (Lord & Novick, 1968; Nunnally, 1978). The importance of psychometry in education, psychology, and job performance situations cannot be overemphasized. It is likely that the future will see more psychological measurement rather than less. When one considers this volume together with the literature identified in the attendant references, it is easy to be overwhelmed by the magnitude of the area. It is important, however, that the user of tests respond to the challenge of the developed theory and accumulated technology.

For the test user, the most important consideration in the use of assessment instruments is that of purpose. The vagueness surrounding achievement assessment that can be gleaned from the preceding sections is a function of the inability to be specific about the assessment procedure without being specific about the purposes of testing. The reason for using a test to obtain information is the most important consideration in the development or selection and use of a test and the resulting scores. It determines how the psychometric properties of the test should be evaluated. Whether the goal is to assess a trait, state, or level of mastery determines how one will regard the test and its reported characteristics. It has often been said that the validity of a test is characteristic, not of the test, but of its use. This is true of other aspects of any given test. How a test is to be regarded depends upon the purpose for which it is intended.

It would be very misleading to suggest that the concept of the purpose of a test or the use of the test results is simple and straightforward. This confusion in the use of achievement assessment is indicated by Shutz (1971). At a very gross level, the use of tests can be divided into uses oriented to providing information to be used in decisions about individuals, those with the emphasis on providing information related to programmatic decisions, and those for use in theoretical development. (Cattell, 1937a, surveys this.) Although it is often the case that the same tests are used to provide information relative to all types of decisions, in the development or selection of tests, an emphasis on one or the other of these can have implications for the characteristics of a "better" test. For example, it would generally be more desirable to have a broad, multifaceted measure of achievement when evaluating a program, but a more in-depth assessment when making decisions about an individual student.

With the emphasis on information related to decisions about individuals, measures of achievement and their correlates have been used as follows:

1) as a basis for grades, marks, or other form of informative feedback to students;
2) to make decisions about the selection, placement, or groupings of individual students;
3) as a basis for diagnosis, often in the form of identifying special needs;
4) to motivate students or employees to achieve more proficient levels of performance;
5) to operationalize instructional objectives;
6) as a means of communicating the goals of instruction to the student; and
7) to assess instructional effectiveness.

When the emphasis is more on students or employees as a group, that is, on the program, the outcomes of testing can typically be seen as related to the planning of a program or of the evaluation of that program and its several components. Obviously these are conceptual categories, since the evaluation of one program may be the basis for planning the next. The development of theory related to the variables of interest, while a third emphasis, is also not distinct from the others because research may pertain to interests that fall within any of the uses mentioned above. The orientation that distinguishes theoretical research from the other types of test usage is that the emphasis is on the development of theoretical formulations rather than on the immediate application of the test results in making decisions.

In using test results to determine grades, to make a diagnosis, or to evaluate a program, the primary purpose of the tests is to provide an estimate of the individual's (or group's) "level" of achievement. Such an estimate may be evaluated relative to a norm or a criterion, but in these cases, the concern is with the standing of the individual on the particular construct implied by the test. On the other hand, the remaining uses of achievement tests emphasize not only the standing of individuals on particular tests, but also how scores on tests relate to scores on other tests or assessments. These uses imply a concern with the interrelationship of aspects of achievement with the ability, personality, motivational, and situational domains. Thus, these procedures suggest that the theoretical relationships involved with achievement are being considered in the use of tests to plan a strategy of instruction. Consequently, it may be helpful, if not mandatory, that information on important aspects of related domains be considered in decisions related to planning how to present a unit of instruction or setting up a job performance situation. This presumes that how instruction proceeds or how the job situation is structured will influence the nature of the contributions of the dimensions of the domains relevant to achievement.

SELECTING AN ACHIEVEMENT TEST

In selecting an achievement test, the overriding consideration is the purpose of administering it. Just as the principles of development of a test are applicable or at least have implications for test selection, so, too, principles of selection have implications for development. Although development and selection may be afforded different sections in a presentation of achievement testing, they are both highly interrelated and fall within the general context of good assessment principles. When considering the purpose of assessment in the selection of a test, one should look to the nature of the examinees, the nature of the construct being assessed, and the level of explanation of behavior

to be used when dealing with the results. These considerations must be related to psychometric properties and other characteristics of the test in the selection process.

When selecting a test, it is necessary to consider the relationship between the individuals to whom the instrument will be administered and the procedures by which the psychometric properties of the test were determined. As was pointed out earlier in this volume (see Chapter 4), there are many ways to estimate or consider the consistency of a test. Generally speaking, the consistency of a test indicates the proportion of variance in the test that is due to what is being measured (true scores), as opposed to extraneous influences that have nothing to do with the purpose of the assessment. The various ways of estimating the consistency of a test, however, differ in their appropriateness for different tests and purposes. Whether the reliability of a test for a given purpose is most appropriately assessed through internal consistency or split-half (homogeneity), test-retest (dependability), parallel form (equivalence), or some other procedure depends on the conceptualization of the behavior of the construct variance. For example, it would probably not be reasonable to evaluate a test on the basis of a reliability coefficient estimated from a correlation between two administrations, if the test is to be used to assess the level of a fluctuating state. Or, as Horn (1968) has suggested, a measure of internal consistency (homogeneity) would be a less relevant consideration in a broad-based test of achievement. Another consideration might be whether the test results are to be used to evaluate individuals or groups, since different degrees of reliability might be deemed acceptable (Stanley, 1971). (See also Chapters 4 and 5.)

Validity, which is critical to the appropriate selection and use of tests, is at the base of the whole assessment process. An inappropriate use of a test can very easily render it invalid. A careful consideration of the test in terms of its prescribed use, along with the characteristics of the validation sample, is imperative in good psychometry. It is here that the emphasis on purpose comes to the fore. The validity of a test cannot be regarded as an inherent property of a test. Thus, the validity and use of a test are inextricably linked. Before a test can be evaluated properly, the circumstances of its validation must be carefully examined. For example, do the makeup and size of the validation sample suggest that the test has been validated for the right purpose on enough of the appropriate people? Are the norms that have been developed for this test appropriate for the students or employees with whom it is to be used? The test selector or developer should be very familiar with the concepts dealt with in Chapter 4 before embarking on a testing enterprise.

An aspect of tests which is especially important to the user is the ease with which they can be administered, scored, and interpreted. The questions here are whether the test is appropriate for the testing situation in terms of the time that it takes to administer, the complexity of administration, the number of persons to which the test can reasonably be administered, the difficulty in scoring or obtaining such service, the usefulness of the scores in making the decisions that are necessary, etc.

Finally, probably one of the more important considerations in evaluating a test is in terms of its content. The notion of "content validity" and its significance have been discussed by several authors (Englehart, 1964; Lennon, 1956; Messick, 1975; Willingham, 1980). Most emphasize the importance of the content of the test, especially when the test is to be used for educational measurement and evaluation of achievement. An adequate examination of the test content can only be accomplished by an item-by-item consideration of the test by those who are familiar with the test situation. Whether the test content is appropriate depends on the purpose

for which it is to be used. Cox and Sterrett (1970) have gone so far as to suggest that tests can have increased meaning through the selection of items to make up a subscore that reflects on a particular objective. In such a manner, standardized tests which are typically norm-referenced can yield scores which are more objective-referenced.

One of the characteristics of the field of standardized achievement testing is the large and wide range of instruments available. Thus, it is especially important to be clear of purpose when beginning the task of selecting a test to appropriately assess the relevant achievement. There are not only a number of general achievement batteries available but also an almost overwhelming list of tests for special purposes or tests designed for more detailed assessment of particular achievements in special areas (Buros, 1978). There are tests for all the subject matter areas which may or may not be applicable to assessment in a particular situation. In addition to the presentation of available standardized tests, there are procedures to aid in the construction of instruments for the evaluation of achievement in various academic areas (Bloom, Hastings, & Madaus, 1971).

RECOMMENDED STANDARDIZED TESTS OF ACHIEVEMENT

The tests discussed here were selected in order to present a set of achievement instruments that would be relatively general in their focus on achievement and would also give the practitioner a set of tests to choose from that covered a wide developmental range.

There are many problems associated with the assessment of achievement in young children just as there are in assessing almost anything in the young. That does not, however, suggest that such an endeavor is not a reasonable one. Although the data are still being examined with respect to many of its aspects, CIR-

CUS, a test designed to assess the instructional needs of nursery school, kindergarten, and first-grade children and, monitor and evaluate the educational programs of such children, appears to be one of the potentially better batteries for the assessment of young children. There are two levels: CIRCUS A for nursery school and kindergarten entrants and CIRCUS B for first-grade entrants. CIRCUS A has 14 subtests responded to by the children, two scales which call for teacher ratings of the children, and one scale used by the teacher to evaluate the educational environment. CIRCUS B has essentially the same format with 12 subtests, one scale for teacher ratings of the children, and the environmental rating scale.

The reliabilities reported for CIRCUS (typically alpha coefficients) are quite adequate (averaging in the high seventies), especially given the age to which the tests are oriented. The validities for a test designed for such young children are obviously difficult to establish through correlation with other measures, however, since CIRCUS attempts to convert scores into verbal descriptions as a way to incorporate "meaning" into the test outcomes, the discussion of validity is probably less than adequate at this time. Until more evidence is brought to light on these tests, their use should be based on their relationship to the needs of the testing situation rather than on the basis of the claims of the authors.

The norms for CIRCUS A are based on about 3,000 children from a wide variety of preschool and kindergarten situations, while CIRCUS B norming was based on over 6,000 students in almost 300 classrooms drawn randomly from around the nation. The norms incorporate a consideration of the region of the country, urbanization, and socioeconomic status. Scoring service is available for CIRCUS, but this requires that the answers be transcribed locally to the machine-scored answer sheets. If achievement assessment is oriented to young children, it is worth the time of the test user to consider CIRCUS as a possible battery.*

Once the students have entered the first grade, the Stanford Achievement Test becomes one of the better known, as well as one of the better achievement test batteries available in today's test market.† The battery measures a wide range of achievement appropriate across grades 1.5 to 9.5 in six test levels. Each level spans one year except the Advanced battery, which is appropriate for grades 7.0-9.5. The reliabilities reported (split-half and K-R 20 coefficients) suggest that the tests clearly have adequate reliability. Less than 5% of the coefficients reported are below .80 and these are typically associated with tests designed for the lower grades. The norms are based on very adequate samples of students (approximately 300,000) from a wide variety of situations in terms of community and class size, geographic region, and socioeconomic status. There are, however, no separate norms as a function of these characteristics. Because of the design of the battery, it is possible to derive "objective-referenced" interpretations from the test items. Each item is described in terms of the ability or behavior that it requires, along with the difficulty indices of the items. The items are grouped into clusters of related items and average difficulties reported for the clusters. The manual points out that the reliabilities of these clusters may not be adequate, but this is still a feature with great potential for use by teachers and other personnel making educational/ instructional decisions. A wide variety of machine-scorable answer sheets is available for examinees at grade 4.5 and above, with scoring service available.

Generally it can be said that the Stanford Achievement Test reflects a consci-

---

*Further information on this instrument may be obtained through the publisher, Educational Testing Service, in order to determine its appropriateness for a specified assessment objective.

†It is available, with further information, from the Psychological Corporation.

entious effort on the part of its authors to produce a test battery that is truly of value to the educator in the assessment of pupils and programs.

Two tests that have been commonly used for achievement assessment at about the same levels as the Stanford Achievement Test are the Iowa Tests of Basic Skills (grades 1.7-9), published by Houghton Mifflin Co., and the Metropolitan Achievement Tests (grades k.7-9.5), published by the Psychological Corporation. These tests appear to be quite adequate for the evaluation of groups and programs but are not as well designed in terms of decisions about individuals based on the test results. Unlike the Stanford Achievement Test, these latter tests do not provide the mechanisms for the objective-referenced interpretations of performance. In addition, the California Test Bureau's California Achievement Tests provide an extensive breakdown of objectives suitable for classroom consideration, and state which items in the test correspond to which objectives.*

Although there is a decrease in the use of standardized tests of achievement after the secondary school years, there are situations which call for the assessment of achievement levels of persons in the postsecondary years. In this regard, two tests are worth mention. The Sequential Tests of Educational Progress, developed by Educational Testing Service, is designed to cover grades 4-14 with batteries for levels 10-12 and 13-14 which are beyond the range of the Stanford Achievement Test. The reliabilities for the battery (typically coefficients of internal consistency and correlations between parallel forms) average in the high eighties, with the lower values found for the lower grades as one would expect. This test is worth considering if the assessment of achievement is oriented to older students.†

The second battery of tests that could be of value to the assessment of achievement in older students is the CLEP General Examinations which were designed and administered through the auspices of the Educational Testing Service. These instruments were developed for the assessment of basic achievement areas (English, humanities, mathematics, natural sciences, social sciences, and history) for college level performance. While these tests are most usually administered at specified centers throughout the country primarily as a basis for credit-by-examination, there are "inactive" forms available for local administration and scoring. The reliability coefficients for the battery are all above .90.

The reader should be very careful in the selection of instruments designed to measure achievement. Although general recommendations can be made, characteristics of a specific situation may invalidate those very same recommendations. This applies to achievement measurement much more than the measurement of abilities or personality traits. The importance of the situational variables in the model of achievement cannot be overemphasized and its importance is nowhere more manifest than in the selection of an instrument for achievement assessment.

SUMMARY

In the foregoing presentation on achievement and its measurement, there has been a discussion of the nature of achievement and how it is conceptually distinguishable from abilities. Achievement was presented as a function of abilities, personality traits, motivational factors, time, and characteristics of the ambient situation. The assessment of achievement was discussed from the point of view of development of assessment instruments (content, item-response form, norm- vs. criterion-referencing, transformed scores, purposes) and of the selec-

---

*Inquiries can be directed to McGraw-Hill.

†Additional information may be obtained from the Addison-Wesley Publishing Company.

tion of standardized tests, with recommendations for the use of particular tests to measure a broad spectrum of achievement.

In addition to the specific tests described, there are additional ones available that range from broad spectrum achievement assessment to more narrowly defined tests related to a specific or special purpose. Various considerations associated with the assessment situation influence the appropriateness of these tests. Thus, no procedure of test selection alleviates the consideration of available instruments incumbent upon the test user. Measurement of achievement is a complex arena which necessitates an examination of basic psychometric theory as well as of other domains of psychological inquiry. It is not something that an examiner should undertake lightly. In this regard the *purpose* of the assessment of achievement is given priority.

The overriding reason for almost any testing application is to obtain information related to a decision about an individual or a program. The assumption is that the more informed a decision is, the better that decision will be. Information is typically the goal of all our observations related to inquiry into human behavior and performance. The more systematically observation is conducted, the more appropriate the resulting information will be to the decision that is to be made. Psychometric principles are the basis of systematic observation and assessment.

In the larger scheme, the scientific investigation of human behavior is, in one sense, the search for patterns. These patterns or structure are the basis of our understanding of human behavior. The search for such structure is most evident in the researcher's examination of the variance/covariance matrices which represent the interrelationships of the variables of interest. That the application of sound psychometric principles is important needs no other argument than the avoidance of artifactual relations among the variables with which we are working.

It has been argued that the "dimensions" of a psychological domain are really impositions of structure that derive from psychologists in the first place. We may in fact see only what we choose to see but there is no sound argument against making the dimensions that we "impose" as reasonable an information base for decision-making as possible.

CHAPTER 11

Personality Assessment by Observers in Normal and Psychiatric Data

Ronald C. Johnson

THE LIFE DATA AND THE INTERVIEW SITUATIONS

In most situations where psychologists or psychiatrists evaluate in part by use of ratings, they will also be using help from questionnaires and objective tests, including biographical data. The integration of these is dealt with, for clinicians and industrial psychologists, in Chapters 17, 18, and 19. But in this chapter we shall consider the properties of ratings in and of themselves. By ratings we implicitly and regularly mean *ratings by observers*, for self-rating is fully dealt with under questionnaires in Chapter 12.

The estimation of traits in one person by another has been going on for thousands of years, and probably also in nonhuman mammals, as when a chimpanzee believes his mother has a bad temper or a bulldog decides the dog next door is easily terrified. In the situations a psychol-

ogist meets, we have to distinguish between ratings made over *a lengthy array of known life behavior*, on the one hand, and ratings made in the relatively standardized artificial and brief *interview situation* in a business office or a consulting room. The methods, validities, and reliabilities of these are appreciably different, and we shall consider them separately, beginning with observers looking at life data, i.e., observing subjects in the situations of their everyday life behavior.

RATINGS AND RECORDINGS IN ESTIMATES FROM LIFE DATA

Let us recognize at once two basically different methods of assessment through life data:

1) Behavior and trait *ratings,* as above, in which an unavoidable instrument in

the procedure is the brain of the observer. At once one recognizes that this involves all the virtues and vices of that instrument, the latter occurring in the distortions we encompass in the spectrad model.

2) Behavior *recordings*, e.g., of number of automobile accidents, number of friends met per week, frequency of falling in love, numbers of bottles of whiskey purchased per month, and so on. A particular form of this is the well-known "time sampling" method. This is decidedly less used, and we do not, with a few exceptions (Cattell & Peterson, 1956; Koch, 1942), have correlational studies, as we do with ratings, of how these criterion measures (for so they can be considered) factor into unitary traits estimatable from these behaviors.

The reader is already familiar with the primary division (Chapter 2) into L-, Q-, and T-data. We are now splitting L-data into L(BR)—*behavior rating* from life—and L(R)—*recorded behavior* from life. (Q-data also deals with everyday life material, but is radically different, as the classification in Table 2.1 shows (p. 22), because it is seen uniquely by one person—the subject.) Our examination of L-data in either form involves considering two aspects of its validity:

1) Can it be reliably used to recognize unitary trait and state structures?
2) Can it be dependably used to assign characteristics (traits) to any given individual whence we can predict his or her behavior in further situations?

Obviously, life record (time sampling) L(R) would be the more ideal basis for either task, because it is more concrete and reliable as data. However, research has not yet done more than nibble at the problem of factoring such human data into traits and states. Fortunately, the concept of the *personality sphere*, essential for a comprehensive mapping of personality structure (Chapter 2), *can* be placed on a tolerably satisfactory basis in L(BR) research (though not as well as by measuring what people are doing in each of the 24 hours in a day, as in L(R)). L(BR) gets to this basis by employing the 4,000 or more behavioral words in the dictionary (Allport & Odbert, 1936) as a sampling basis (Cattell, 1946). The latter procedure has been examined by Cattell and Warburton (1967) in the light of the operational basis for extracting ability, temperament, and dynamic modalities from the measurements of the source responses to situations.

THE TWO KINDS OF PROBLEMS IN RATING STRUCTURES

The first problem is that research surveys all too frequently overlook in the analysis and comparison of results that perhaps nine-tenths of published rating studies observe the subject only in a relatively small situational segment of his or her life. For example, a teacher probably can do a good job of rating behaviors in the classroom, but be far off the mark if these ratings were to be used to describe behavior on the playground or in the home. There certainly exists at least *moderate* generality in behavior across situations (we will discuss research showing this to be the case) but, clearly, situational components are also important determinants of behavior.

The factor analytic research on personality structure has shown that unitary personality patterns in L-, Q-, and T-data can be found such that each operates in quite a number of different situations and different responses. There has been confusion about what this means in the writings of psychologists who have not proceeded beyond analysis of variance (ANOVA) to factor analysis and other CORAN methods. For example, some have supposed that a unitary trait means that there should be no variance across situations and that only variance across people is then necessary to account for all observed variance. The factor specification equation, in which loadings express situations, shows that this is a misconception. However, this recognition of *both* sources of variance obviously does not fit such positions as that of Mischel (1968), who argued that behavior is almost solely determined by the stimulus situation. Although this reflexological position was already demonstrated, by hundreds of correlation matrices, to be untenable, this extreme statement perhaps helped to provoke some thinking. If all variance resided with differences of situation, there would be no purpose in obtaining measures of personality through questionnaires or ratings. All that the biographer, the novelist, and the dramatist have taught us about human nature would then logically have to be thrown on the scrap heap.

Nowadays, since the ANOVA analyses of Endler and Magnusson (1976), and the Basic Data Relation Matrix (Cattell, 1966b) (CORAN) analyses by numerous investigators, such opinions as those of some reflexologists and other theorists are not matters for verbal debate. The fractions of variance in behavior from traits, situations, and observer error have been exactly apportioned. There are actually two questions here:

1) The relative *variance* from persons and situation on a particular expression of any one trait.
2) The existence of source trait and state *structures* as demonstrated by R-, dR-, and P-techniques.

The first question is sufficiently answered. The second is fully documented in the research references to Chapter 3, but it may be of interest to glance in history at how far we have come in applying CORAN (correlation analysis) procedures from the early beginnings of application of correlation to the latest factor-analytic procedure.

A very early and classical attempt to recognize trait unity by correlation was made in the personality field by Hartshorne and May (1928), who believed that there were th ee broad domains of dishonesty—lying, stealing, and cheating. They developed a number of behavioral measures of each domain and then tested large numbers of children in these "miniature life situations," i.e., this was somewhat like time sampling in having definite recorded behavior. They concluded that there was basically no correlation cluster of honesty—that one couldn't predict a subject's behavior across situations even within a given domain, such as lying, much less across the domains of lying, cheating, and stealing. This conclusion certainly runs counter to the experience of most of us. However, Burton (1963), in reading Hartshorne and May (1928), recognized that many of the specific measures were unreliable. He selected from the entire battery those measures with a reliability of 0.60 or more, and then factor-analyzed the intercorrelations of scores on these tests. Using this procedure, he found a general factor of honesty to be present. A vast amount of factor-analytic work since has shown that structure abundantly exists in ratings.

Incidentally, there was a very similar sequence in the ability field, where J. McKeen Cattell and Farrand (1896; see also Wissler, 1901) followed up the suggestion of Sir Francis Galton to correlate a diversity of abilities, and were unable to demonstrate a general trait. This cleared up with Spearman's introduction of factor analysis, since correlation clusters and factors can be very different in number and nature. Today, alike in ability, personality, and dynamic modalities, we have firmly established primary, secondary, and other factor patterns demonstrating that some kind of unitary development exists in each of a diversity of traits.

THE BASIC METHODOLOGICAL REQUIREMENTS IN OBTAINING RATING DATA

The data that will be presented below all argue for a moderately high level of consistency in personality as assessed by traits. However, in order to obtain consistency one must obtain reasonably reliable ratings.

First of all, the attribute to be measured must be manifested with some frequency; very rare behaviors are by their very rarity difficult to predict. The attributes to be assessed must be observable—"laughs a lot" really is in a different universe of discourse than, say, "has repressed homosexual tendencies." Secondly, the rater must be really familiar with the individual or individuals to be rated. If the behavioral domain to be assessed is a specific one, e.g., classroom behavior, then the raters should be persons thoroughly familiar with the individual's behavior in that domain, e.g., teachers, classmates. If one is seeking genuinely cross-situational data, then raters should be selected so that, between them, they are rating the individual in a number of important life situations—behavior in the family setting, on the job, during recreation, etc. Thirdly, the raters should be well-motivated and intelligently capable of dealing with a precise definition of a particular kind of behavior. As Cattell noted, "It is not sufficiently realized that in dealing with such abstractions as 'aspects of behavior' distinctly high intelligence is required for effective estimation. The judge need not have the perception of human nature possessed by a Shakespeare or a Freud, but it is a fact that judges of average or low intelligence show a marked falling off of skill, particularly as indicated by validity" (Cattell, 1950, p. 49).

Intelligent and well-informed raters are, in a sense, the equivalent of having intelligent and well-constructed questions in a personality questionnaire. Only a remarkably optimistic constructor of psychometric tests would expect to be able to define a major domain of personality by obtaining individuals' responses to three or four questions. The researcher making use of raters is in an equivalent position. Reliable and valid ratings are much more likely to be obtained as the number of raters increase, up to the point where they become too numerous to know well the persons concerned.

Another problem is that of difference of standards among observers. Some raters are lenient in their ratings of others; other raters—fewer in number—are generally harsh in their judgments. These tendencies must be controlled for as much as possible. If raters are rating any large number of persons (say 25 or more), on one or more traits, one can ascertain the mean and standard deviation for each rater on each attribute being assessed, and convert each rater's assessments to standard scores or T-scores. Another approach to controlling for leniency/harshness is to use a forced-choice technique in which the rater has to choose which of two traits matched in favorability or unfavorability most closely describes the individual being rated. For example, (assuming equal desirability) the rater might have to choose whether to label the person rated as "bully" or "cowardly," or as "reliable" or "persevering." However, as Scott (1963) demonstrated, matching items on desirability across a group of persons rating these traits does not mean that the traits are equally desirable for all individuals. The tedious but conceptually and (with the aid of computers) computationally simple procedure of converting each rater's ratings for each trait to standard scores may be the better approach. If a relatively small number of persons (e.g., 25 or so—which is about the total number of persons we know well anyway) are rated, especially if they are rated on only one trait, then one can have each rater compare each individual on the trait in question in relation to each other individual being rated. This method—paired comparison—would involve, then, persons being compared on a trait (bravery, for example) with each other person; person A with B, A with C, ... A with Z, B with C, B with D, ... etc.—a lot of comparisons, but a thoroughly satisfactory way of controlling for leniency/harshness.

The next difficulty involves the problem of what used to be called halo effects—of the rater allowing overall impressions of the individual to influence his or her ratings of specific traits. Nowadays, in *spectrad theory*, we recognize that it is not that a single dimension or "a favorable impression" (halo) affects scores, but that the whole vector of the rated person's *other* traits affects the rating on one, by what is called the *contextual* effect. (The effect of traits in the rater—the *construing* effect—is also important, but consideration of corrections by both of these more sophisticated concepts of influence is deferred to Chapter 23.) Meanwhile, concise and definitive descriptions of the traits to be rated, anchored in descriptions of overt behavior, can reduce, but not eliminate, such effects. But an equally important corrective is to have all subjects rated or ranked together on *one trait at a time* (see Table 11.1).

As to the first, one is far less likely to obtain reliable and valid measures of an attribute when the characteristic to be rated is a global one, probably confounded as to source trait origins, such as "sociable." Sociable? How? Does the person seek out, as opposed to avoid, large social groups, such as cocktail parties? Does this same person enjoy extended discussions with a few close friends? Is this person shy around the opposite sex, but outgoing with same-sexed friends? That is, what are the observable behaviors that go to make up

"sociable"? Once these are known—and it probably would take a factor analysis to do so—then the person being rated is rated on those behavioral attributes that load heaviest on each of the factors that, in their totality, make up "sociability."

While there are advantages to paired comparisons, a major disadvantage is that the degree to which a given individual manifests an attribute can only be compared with the degree to which others rated in the same paired comparison manifest the same attribute, i.e., the means of different groups are brought to the same value when ranked groups of 20 or so persons are turned to standard scores—and this is not correct. Most investigators desire to compare different groups with one another (e.g., psychiatric patients from different wards who are receiving differing treatments depending on ward assignment) or else to compare a given individual's ratings with population norms. Data obtained through paired comparisons will not serve these purposes, but neither will comparisons of different raters, e.g., in 1955 and 1975, on the same subjects to assess changes in their traits. An example that shows concretely in a practical situation how ratings can be made precise is shown for normals in the lists prepared by Cattell (1946, 1957c) and for clinical cases in the In-patient Multidimensional Psychiatric Scale (IMPS) (Lorr, McNair, Klett, & Lasky, 1962; Lorr, Klett, & McNair, 1963). These latter clinical ratings, however, carry us over from the life setting observation to a psychiatric interview situation, to which we return more fully below. The types of items in the Lorr scales are as follows:

Compared with the normal person to what degree does he or she . . .

1) manifest speech that is slowed, deliberate, or labored?
5) verbally express feelings of hostility, ill will, or dislike of others?
   Cues: Makes hostile comments regard-

ing others such as attendants, other patients, his or her family, or persons in authority; reports conflicts on the ward.

7) express or exhibit feelings and emotions openly, impulsively, or without apparent restraint or control?
   Cues: Shows temper outbursts; weeps or wrings hands in loud complaint; jokes or talks boisterously; gestures excitedly.

19) exhibit a deficit in his memory for events of the last week?
   Cues: Does not know what he or she had for supper last night, what he or she did yesterday, or what treatments he or she received the past week.

How often during the interview did he or she . . .

46) grin or giggle inappropriately (exclude reactions resulting from embarrassment)?

48) exhibit peculiar, inappropriate, or bizarre repetitive gestures and/or manneristic body movements (e.g., rhythmic neck twisting, lip smacking, odd gestures)?

Does he or she know . . .

70) that he or she is in a hospital?
74) the calendar year?

Most of the items in the IMPS, for example, items 1, 5, 7, and 19 above, are rated in terms of the degree to which a behavior is manifested (extremely, markedly, distinctly, quite a bit, moderately, mildly, a little, very slightly, not at all). Other items, such as 46 and 48 above, are scored in terms of frequency—very often, fairly often, a few times, once or twice, not at all. A few items (e.g., 70, 74) are scored yes/no. This scale, discussed further below, is a good example of a well-constructed measuring device measuring clearly defined behaviors.

PROBLEMS AND METHODOLOGICAL CLARIFICATIONS ILLUSTRATED HISTORICALLY IN STRUCTURAL AND DEVELOPMENTAL USE OF RATINGS

Given a sufficient number of trained and seriously motivated raters, as well as thoughtfully constructed rating scales, it is entirely possible, with vigorous methodology, to obtain highly reliable, valid information—provided certain limitations are recognized. The presentation of a selection of the major efforts in personality assessment through ratings will provide evidence illustrating this statement.

The use of observer ratings to measure mean differences between groups or changes in individuals over some time interval has usually too much error to be scientifically very useful—unless it is based on time sampling of literal behaviors. This we shall return to below, but meanwhile let us consider some ordinary rating studies aimed at the two objectives above: a) finding structure by mutually correlating ratings and relating them to other criteria, and b) getting accurate estimates of trait levels in individuals.

Regarding the first, the basic approach to personality structure has been to intercorrelate a number of persons on several attributes. The choice of rated or recorded attributes was initially arbitrary. Galton, a century ago, argued that physical vigor (as might be manifested, in part, by sleep requirements) was an important determinant of eminence.

Gradually some concepts came into use from clinical hunches (extraversion, ego strength) and finally the strategy of starting with a total personality sphere. Alongside the systematically checked, programmatic work on personality rating structure, increasingly refining some 12 to 18 personality factors, as described above, these have come from sporadic studies that are interesting to glance at as illustrating the strengths and limitations of the method.

Kretschmer (1925) believed he had found

psychiatric ratings to correlate substantially with body build (pyknics as cyclothymes). Sheldon, Stevens, and Tucker (1940) took the position that there are essentially three independent aspects of body build/bodily constitution. These are *endomorphy* (the relative proportion of soft roundness throughout various regions of the body), *mesomorphy* (the relative predominance of muscle, bone, and connective tissue; "the mesomorphic physique is normally heavy, hard, and rectangular in outline" (Sheldon et al., 1940, p. 5), and *ectomorphy* (the relative predominance of linearity and fragility). They believed they saw temperament ratings (as surface traits) associated with the three body types: With the endomorphic came *viscerotonia*—sociable, relaxed, love of comfort, slow reaction; with the mesomorphic came *somatotonia*—need for activity and action, assertive, courageous, energetic; and with the ectomorphic came *cerebrotonia* —restrained, inhibited, tense, preferring solitude.

Walker obtained measures of the association between the body build ratings of nursery school children and teacher's ratings of temperament (1962) and of mother's ratings of child behavior (1963). His data are far more convincing than those of Sheldon (1942). He found evidence for associations between body type and personality, but far weaker associations than those previously reported by Sheldon. In general, the significant associations between body type and personality were in the direction predicted by Sheldon, but often were not statistically significant. Sheldon's work has been criticized to the point where some consider it demolished. However, it at least illustrates some of the conveniences that make rating attractive, scientifically perilous, but useful in reconnaissance. The main assertion of the three temperament patterns rested on only 31 cases, rated by only one person and with the usual arbitrariness in surface traits in deciding at what point a variable correlated enough to be in a cluster. Nevertheless, it could perhaps be justified as a pioneer use of ratings that gave sufficient significance to show there is something in the body/temperament relation worthy of more research with improved methods.

In personality structure research, as such, between 1930 and 1970, behavior ratings—L(BR)-data—nevertheless had great strategic value when pursued with the rigorous conditions set out earlier. It had the advantage of providing an operational basis for the total personality sphere, of being suitable for precise factor analytic methods, and of keeping the emerging structural concepts in touch with the world of clinical and other personality theory, which at that time was *also* couched in verbal descriptions of behavior.

As is well-known, the most systematic and comprehensive work in the world on personality structure through ratings was carried out by about 50 psychologists in the U.S. between 1940 and 1970, some working on a consistent methodology with Cattell, who has made technical surveys at regular intervals (1946, 1957a, 1966b, 1979c). A survey has also been made by French (1953), and there have been surveys by Eysenck (1960) in England, Pawlik (1968) in Germany, and Hammond (1977) in Australia. The sufficiently integrated side of this research was achieved with *normal* behavior, but, as mentioned elsewhere in this chapter, Degan (1962), Lorr (1960), Wittenborn (1955), and others used ratings to pioneer in *abnormal* behavior structure (summarized to 1956 in Cattell, 1957c).

This work is too well-known and too widely set out in personality textbooks to call for systematic presentation here. The actual lists of factor source traits most frequently replicated are given above in Chapter 3. At present at least a half dozen precise behavioral variables can be listed (latest list—1979) for rating to give *a summated score for each source trait* (with weights if desired). However, it is not possible to have a stable general standardization for rating scores and each user must get that for his or her own set of raters.

What has methodologically distinguished this work, and helped to give it its clearness of replication, has been attention to the following points, which the reader will find have rarely been fully met in most sporadic factorings of personality ratings, especially those before 1940 or even 1960.

1) Each individual to be rated by six to 10 (or more) raters, the reliability of rating to be taken as the pool of, say, the first four against the second four.
2) The rating to be made preferably by peers rather than persons in a role relation, e.g., not teachers or supervisors.
3) The raters to be in a position to observe behavior for diverse and extensive segments of the day.
4) In the actual rating, one trait to be rated at a time over all subjects to avoid spurious correlations, e.g., halo.
5) The subjects to initially be *ranked*, e.g., by paired comparisons, not rated, and the ranks to be converted to rating *scores*, e.g., stens, by a normal curve.
6) The behavior variable to be rated to be spelled out in concrete instances and incisive definition.
7) The necessary factor analytic checks on number of factors and significance

of simple structure rotation are essential in the subsequent analysis.

These requirements are briefly summarized in Table 11-1. When these conditions are observed, surprisingly high reliabilities are reached. (And, incidentally, Thorndike has shown that at least in rating some objective conditions, e.g., room temperature, the Spearman-Brown formula applies to number of *observers* just as it was known to do for number of *items*.) Thus, when Cattell had ratings made in the above manner in a residential sorority, the reliabilities were as good as for intelligence tests (around 0.8), and they were especially good in soldiers who had seen common service in a tank corps (due to condition 3) above being well met).

When the same rating techniques were carried down to earlier ages, by Coan, Dain, Gruen, Peterson, and others, in the 1950s (see Cattell, 1979c), considerable persistence was found in the form of the source traits, as far as this was carried, namely, to four to six years (Peterson & Cattell, 1959; Koch, 1942). As indicated, the bulk of this experimentally more exact work was carried out in the 1940s and 1950s (see Cattell, 1957c, 1979c), and although rotation was as good then as now (but more laborious, by Rotoplot), the statistical tests for number of factors were not as good as now and the general belief

TABLE 11.1
Some Indispensable Cautions in Reliable Rating

(1) Ratings not based on single words, but on *definitions with concrete behavioral illustrations*, to ensure that terms mean the same for all judges and are anchored in behavioral observations.

(2) Not by persons in special role—e.g., authority, relative—but by peers.

(3) Not by as few as two persons (and certainly not by one only), but by at least eight, and yet not by more than can know the person well. Reliabilities are then to be calculated between averages from two pools of observers, and in such conditions they are usually quite good.

(4) A situational contact with the observed person that is as *broad* as possible, i.e., not restricted to one role segment of his or her daily life, e.g., behavior on the parade ground.

(5) Utilization of a procedure of ranking all persons on one trait at a time, not all traits on one person at a time.

(6) Removal of interrater differences of *means* and, if possible, *standard deviations* by equalizing these across raters or rated subgroups.

From Cattell, Pierson, & Finkbeiner, 1976, pp. 65-66.

(erroneous) was that it was best to under-factor when in doubt. More recent work (Cattell, Pierson, & Finkbeiner, 1976; Cattell, 1985), the latter reanalyzing the most sound data, indicates that the 12 factors there listed were too few. The four extra factors found in questionnaires, and then labeled Q1, Q2, Q3, and Q4, do seem to have rating equivalents. Thus, in the L and Q media, probably because both deal with life behavior *in situ, the number and nature of factors seem to be the same.*

Use of Ratings in Longitudinal and Comparative Personality Research

In the strategic process of personality structure research, beginning with L(BR)-data was absolutely indispensable. It was so because it was the only dependable way to cover a definable personality sphere, and because this rating pattern gave immediate meaning to the source traits, enabling theory to link them up with psychiatric concepts, e.g., those of Kraepelin, Bleuler, Kretschmer, Freud, and Jung.

However, their use in applied psychology and some kinds of research—in spite of the pressure to fall into using them—should be subjected to very careful methodological scrutiny, and there needs to be more caution in accepting results. For example, the comparison of scores on a source trait—say, affectia (A), ego strength (C), or excitability (D)—over a developmental range from, say, 8 to 14 years, has two difficulties. First, though the continuity of such source traits as patterns has been demonstrated, their weighting pattern in behaviors alters somewhat. With care (see isopodic and equipotent scoring, Cattell 1970b), this can be properly handled. Second, as *spectrad theory* (Chapter 23) teaches us, a rating is as much a function of the rater as the ratee. To have two teachers in, say, San Francisco, rate a child who was rated four years earlier, by two different teach-ers in, say, Honolulu, is to deal with a change in score with as much error variance in it from raters and situations as there may be real score change. One may do it for some rough pioneer exploration, but scarcely for a dependable scientific conclusion. The factor *patterns* in, say, 300 children, if based on the mean of about eight raters, are quite likely to be essentially the same, but the *change score* of an individual thereon could be made meaningful only by personality tests on the raters entered into the spectrad model, and various other sophisticated psychometric-statistical correction refinements.

However, it perhaps behooves us to look at some examples, considered as pioneer studies. One of the earliest was that of Huffman who, as chief psychologist to Illinois schools, was able to compare certain ratings on children with observations on those who later, in adult life, needed clinical help. The factoring results are given in Cattell (1957c) and, though Huffman never published the comparative score results, the general evidence in the data was for appreciable constancy of individual level of deviant behavior over this unusually long period of observation. Lowell Kelly (1955) also got a particularly long change period in his study of 300 engaged couples, in 1936-38, whom he reassessed in 1952-53. (World War II prevented his planned follow-up earlier.) His initial interest was in assortiveness of mating and he used a 36-variable rating scale. Most subjects were in their mid-20s at the time of first testing and, with a gap of 16-18 years between measures, were in their early 40s at the time of the follow-up. Two hundred and fifteen of the 300 original males and 231 of the 300 original females were still alive, located, and willing to co-operate. Of these, missing data from the 1936-1938 tests reduced the N's to 176 male and 192 female subjects.

The 10 rated personality attributes were physical energy, intelligence, voice quality, neatness of dress, breadth of interest, conventionality, quietness, kind of temper, modesty, and dependability. Kelly reports on differences in mean scores and on test/retest correlations across this long time span. Changes in mean scores were slight. Test/retest correlations were not too large (about 0.30) but all were statistically significant. Profile similarities were calculated using the 10 scores on each testing occasion; the value obtained was 0.55. The results argue for significant consistency in personality, not only across situations (contrary to Mischel's position), but also across a long span of time.

So long as the examination is kept to correlations dealing with rank order, the artificial difference of *mean* that may arise between the earlier and later raters of the same group of subjects does not matter, but a special difficulty arises in attempting to use ratings in group change research in developmental studies. No really acceptable method exists for comparing the mean of one group of raters with that of quite a different set of raters years later. Some related limitations can be illustrated in the use of ratings in longitudinal research in a study by Digman (1963). In 1959 Digman obtained ratings of 102 first- and second-grade children from four teachers. The children were rated on 38 traits (e.g., nonaggressive, kind, considerate vs. aggressive, tends toward fighting, bullying, teasing, cruelty; unpopular, generally disliked by other children vs. popular, generally liked by other children) previously used by Cattell and Coan (1957), with sex added as a 39th dichotomized variable. Ratings were done as follows:

In the interests of reliability, a scaling procedure was used which was basically a variant of the method of successive categories. The teacher was seated at a table, and a sorting board with nine children were printed on small cards. The trait terms were printed on 5 × 8 in. cards, with arrows indicating the two ends of the continuum under consideration. The traits were then considered by the teacher/judge in order, who was instructed to place the name of the child possessing the characteristic to the

greatest—or least—degree into the extreme cell (1 or 9). Names of the other children were then placed in the remaining cells in such a way as to form an approximation to a normal frequency distribution. (There is no implication that traits are "naturally" distributed thus; depending upon the scale chosen, the normal distribution or something close to it can probably be achieved from any future, more definitive scale by straightforward transformations.) (Digman, 1963, p. 46)

It is unclear as to how many persons rated each child, but one must infer it was close to the minimal number of raters from whom one can hope for reliable results.

In his first report, Digman (1963) derived 11 first-order factors (Superego Strength, Hostility, Surgent Excitement, Autia, General Intelligence, Premsia, Sex, Social Confidence, Neuroticism, an unidentified factor (possibly Shrewdness), and Parental Attitude) and three second-order factors (Successful vs. Unsuccessful Socialization, Introversion vs. Extraversion, and Sex), which fit reasonably well those described in the programmatic researches above.

Digman continued to study this same group of subjects (with the expected attrition of S's) through high school, as well as obtaining data from incoming students not part of the original sample. In more recent studies (Digman & Takemoto-Chock, 1981), the 11 factors were much the same, though they reduced to less than the original 11 factors, and seemed similar to the source trait dimensions found by the programmatic investigations mentioned above (Table 3.2, p. 37). As with Huffman and Kelly, there was tolerably strong evidence for the consistency of behavior across time, both as to patterns and individual levels, as well as for the importance of personality attributes in the prediction of academic performance.

Both Kelly's and Digman's research efforts were conducted under less than optimal circumstances and neither study fulfills all of the necessary conditions for a sound rating study. Even so, these studies shed light on a very important problem—the consistency of personality across time. We scarcely need illustrate here the complementary comparisons to the above—namely, contemporary comparison of two or more different groups. In the majority of the numerous researches published, e.g., of experimental and control groups, the same raters operate and so the gross error of different raters does not apply. A rather serious problem may still arise, however, when the raters know to which group each subject belongs, and often it is not possible to use a "double blind" design. Thus, there are in the applied field many cases where behavioral counting in time sampling would be more satisfactory if it could be achieved.

It was apparent quite early in the factoring of L(BR)- and Q-data—aimed to cover the same total personality sphere —that, as far as *meaning* was concerned, the same source traits could be recognized in both. However, this was not put to the test until comparatively late, by Cattell, Pierson, and Finkbeiner (1976). This study maintained the pure research standards rarely met when people talk of rating in applied situations, as shown in Table 11.1, and the list of rating variables (Table 11.2) was essentially that (Cattell, 1957c, p. 813ff) previously used as a reference set by psychologists seeking a most condensed stratified sample common to important researches. The definitions took the usual form of some spread of behaviors and were intended also as clear hypothet-

TABLE 11.2
List of Bipolar Rating Variables*

Factor for which it is a marker	Number in factor Table 3	
A	1. (28)	*Good-natured, Easy-going.* Does not object when people use his property, time or energy; generous and warm-hearted in his general attitudes; gives people the "benefit of the doubt" when their motives are in question. *vs.* Critical, Exacting. Likes people to be precise and dependable; does not tolerate human failings; is skeptical about people and promises; requires proof of suggestions put to him.
A	2. (13)	*Cool, Reserved.* Tends to be indifferent to personalities and to ignore people; "stand-offish" when personal matters are discussed; cold and aloof toward others; does not mix when in a crowd. *vs.* Interested in Others, Warm. Attentive to people; makes friends easily and quickly; listens to and participates in interests, problems and concerns of others.
B	5. (17 in new list)	*Can Think Abstractly.* *vs.* Has Difficulty with Ideas Concretely Set Out.
B	6. (48 in new list)	6. *Slow to Learn* *vs.* Learns Fast
C	9. (49)	9. *Mature* *vs.* Changeable, Erratic
C	10. (2)	10. *Emotional* *vs.* Stable, Deliberate

TABLE 11.2 *(cont'd)*

E	13. *Assertive* (11)	vs.	Submissive
E	14. *Self-Effacing* (9)	vs.	Egotistical
F	17. *Merry* (26)	vs.	Sober, Solemn
F	18. *Prudent, Careful* (22)	vs.	Happy-Go-Lucky
G	21. *Conscientious* (3)	vs.	Unconscientious
G	22. *Qutting* (7)	vs.	Persevering, Responsible
H	25. *Frank, Friendly* (41)	vs.	Secretive, Shy
H	26. *Nervous, Timid* (20)	vs.	Bold, Adventurous
I	29. *Tender* (8)	vs.	Tough, Hard
I	30. *Ready for Whatever Comes* (18)	vs.	Demanding, Dependent
L	33. *Prone to Jealousy* (5)	vs.	Not Jealous
L	34. *Trusting* (25)	vs.	Suspicious
M	37. *Imaginative, Fanciful* (38)	vs.	Practical
M	38. *Conventional* (4)	vs.	Bohemian
N	41. *Astute, Artful* (51)	vs.	Spontaneous, Natural
N	42. *Naive, Genuine* (32)	vs.	Socially Skillful, Polished
O	45. *Worrying and Depressed* (54)	vs.	Self-Confident
O	46. *Self-Assured, Complacent* (53)	vs.	Guilty and Easily Ashamed
Q_1	49. *Liberal, Experimenting* (55)	vs.	Accepting Tradition
Q_1	50. *Conservative, Accepts* (56) *What Is*	vs.	Radical, Questioning Ideas
Q_2	53. *Resourceful, Takes Initi-* (57) *ative*	vs.	Dependent on Group, Asks What Others Do
Q_2	54. *Socially Dependent* (17)	vs.	Self-Contained, Makes Up His Own Mind
Q_3	57. *Insistently Orderly, Plans* (29) *Ahead*	vs.	Does Not Think of Consequences, Scatterbrained or Disorganized
Q_3	58. *Casual, Careless of Public* (34) *Opinion*	vs.	Mannerly, Shows Regard for His Social Image
Q_4	61. *Tense, High-Strung* (24)	vs.	Relaxed, Seems Under No Pressure
Q_4	62. *Phlegmatic* (58)	vs.	Overwrought, Irritable, Loses Temper Easily

*These 32 variables were given in irregular order to raters, not paired as here. Each member of the pair was rated high in an opposite direction from the other, the italicized being high.

The numbers in parentheses are those given these variables in the standard table of personality sphere variables (Cattell, 1957c, pp. 813-817) to which those of Norman's variables not well represented (a half dozen) have been added in continuation numbers. The letters on the left are, of course, the usual alphabetic primary factor identifications.

The more concrete behaviors for a trait, as given the raters for illustration and definition, are shown here, for economy, only with the two first variables.

ical markers for the factors. Thus, the following variables had to do with factor A, as follows:

Good-natured, Easy-going. Does not object when people use his property, time or energy; generous and warmhearted in his general attitudes; gives people the "benefit of the doubt" when their motives are in question.

Critical, Exacting. Likes people to be precise and dependable; does not tolerate human failings; is skeptical about people and promises; requires proof of suggestions put to him.

The subjects were in groups of nine or 10 for rankable behavior and met for a total of 30 hours in which they discussed their personal problems and personality makeup. Each person rated each other member of the group on each rating variable. Each person also took the 16 P.F. test forms A and B. The internal consistency of the ratings (mean of first five raters against second five) and of the questionnaires (separately for forms A and B) are shown in Table 11.3.

As may be discerned from Table 11.3, the reliabilities of the ratings and of the questionnaire are quite comparable, when ratings are done according to the rules in Table 11.1.

Factor analyses of the rating and of the questionnaire data yielded 23 factors. Of these, 17 were found in both media—that is to say, the markers which had previously been found for factors in ratings, and those previously found for factors in Q-data (forms A and B of the 16 P.F.) now fell on the *same* factors.

The overall consistency of these results shows on the one hand that when ratings are properly carried out they can yield clear-cut, statistically significant, personality factor results, and on the other that the personality factors in L(BR)-data are essentially the same in number and nature as those in Q-data.

The issues in this cross-media area are sometimes discussed in phrases of "multi-method," but, "method" is less appropriate (referring properly to experimental method design concepts) than "instrument," and the model that is more illuminating is one of *instrument factors*. It has been shown that—especially in objective motivation measures—distinct factors can be found running across variables a) with the same psychological meaning, and b) using a common instrumentality, e.g., form of question, media of observation, mode of scoring. There are also, according to spectrad theory, factors in the personality of the observer (outer or inner) that intrude into the correlations in the data actually being examined. However, in L- and Q-data both these instrument intrusions and the everyday behaviors that constitute the substance are evidently so similar that we obtain the result of essentially the same factor appearing in both. In objective tests, T-data, on the other hand, both in general personality and in motivation (dynamic structures), the intrusion of instrument factor variance is greater and is probably one source of the difficulty of matching T and L and Q source traits.

The issue of error from instrument factors is discussed elsewhere in this book (Chapter 23). The general theory (Cattell, 1979) is that there exist *instrument transcending source traits*. However, in estimating scores on them we are bound, in proceeding from concrete test data, to seek to combine scores for the same trait measured in two or more instrumentalities. (This procedure differs from multimethod practice because we first find what the factors are in the methods and weight scores insightfully on that basis.) It would, therefore, be a first approximation to an instrument transcending trait score to combine scores from ratings and from questionnaires. This could be recommended in controlled ratings in research but, as we have seen, the necessary conditions, e.g., the six to eight raters and total day behavior sampling, are rarely reached there. Meanwhile, since the evi-

TABLE 11.3
Internal Consistency of Rating and Questionnaire Variables

(a) Ratings. Homogeneity or "Generalized Reliability"

Factor Marked	No. of Variable		I	II	No. of Variable		I	II
A	1	Good-natured	.58	.59	17	Cool, reserved	.64	.65
B	2	Thinks well abstractly	.78	.78	18	Slow to learn	.74	.74
C	3	Mature	.66	.67	19	Emotional	.66	.67
E	4	Assertive	.88	.89	20	Self-effacing	.67	.68
F	5	Merry	.81	.81	21	Prudent, careful	.66	.67
G	6	Conscientious	.55	.56	22	Quitting	.71	.72
H	7	Frank, friendly	.85	.85	23	Nervous, shy	.80	.80
I	8	Tender	.73	.74	24	Ready and tough	.64	.65
L	9	Prone to jealousy	.62	.63	25	Trusting	.63	.64
M	10	Imaginative, fanciful	.61	.62	26	Conventional	.68	.69
N	11	Astute, artful	.65	.66	27	Naive	.69	.70
O	12	Worrying, depressed	.72	.73	28	Self-assured	.61	.62
Q_1	13	Liberal, experimenting	.73	.74	29	Conservative	.73	.74
Q_2	14	Resourceful	.78	.78	30	Socially dependent	.64	.65
Q_3	15	Insistently ordered	.70	.71	31	Casual	.76	.76
Q_4	16	Tense, high-strung	.54	.55	32	Phlegmatic	.66	.67

As mentioned in the text, column I is Spearman-Brown and Kristof maximum likelihood, while II is the latter converted to an unbiased estimate.

Mean general reliability for ratings = .70

(b) Questionnaire Scales. Reliabilities Calculated as Dependability Coefficients

		Form	
		A	B
A	Affectia	.81	.75
B	Intelligence	.58	.54
C	Ego Strength	.78	.74
E	Dominance	.80	.80
F	Surgency	.79	.81
G	Superego Strength	.81	.77
H	Parmia	.83	.89
I	Premsia	.77	.79
L	Protension	.75	.77
M	Autia	.70	.70
N	Shrewdness	.61	.60
O	Guilt Proneness	.79	.81
Q_1	Radicalism	.73	.70
Q_2	Self-Sufficiency	.73	.75
Q_3	Self-Sentiment	.62	.62
Q_4	Ergic Tension	.81	.87

Mean dependability reliability for questionnaire scales = .74

Most calculations allowing for "error" in the L and Q measures would require the dependability measure, as in 2(b). Since it was not possible to get the same subjects rerated by the same judges it has seemed best here to take in 2(a) the same rated by different judges and consider the error to reside in the difference in people's perception of the same defined variable.

Cairns and Wolf, in Cairns, 1979, p. 215

dence continues that primaries (and secondaries—Cattell, 1957c; Cattell, Pierson, & Finkbeiner, 1976) are closely matched, the applied researcher can use the best questionnaires with tolerable certainty that he is also representing the rating factors.

IPSATIVE RATING: STEPHENSON'S Q-SORT

In ordinary L(BR)-data we rank or point score people relative to one another. In a large group—say 200—ranking all in one series is generally not practicable, because no one rater can know them all well enough. Then we resort to ranking in smaller groups of, say, 16, such that all raters involved can know them all. To combine these we are usually compelled to assume a) that the mean for the groups of 16 is the same, and b) that a normal distribution holds in each. In accordance with the latter, we then assign a point score of 1 to the lowest, 2 to the next 4 in order, 3 to the next 6, 4 to the next 4, and 5 to the highest, i.e., a binomial distribution.

Such procedures must not be confused with what is here discussed, for they are *normative* in standardization, whereas what we are to discuss concerns *ipsative* standardization, to be defined in Q-sort. One should also not confuse Q-technique—a method of factor analysis—with *Q-sort*—a method of scoring—though the former is a superstructure that *can* be built on data from the latter. Q-technique can be studied elsewhere (Burt, 1937, 1940; Cattell, 1978; Stephenson, 1953). It correlates people over tests instead of tests over people, i.e., relatives and referees are reversed, and it yields the same factors as R-technique, with one omissive (Burt, 1937, 1940; Cattell, 1978). It does *not* yield species *types*. Stephenson pointed out its special adaptation to clinical work in which one is sometimes forced to deal with a mere handful of cases—statistically un-

suitable for ordinary R-technique correlation—but may have evidence on 100-200 variables on each, permitting significant correlation of *people*.

It was probably this statistically annoying restriction in clinical research that provoked Stephenson to make a case for factoring by Q-technique, which in turn developed Q-sort, for Q-sort sets up data in the form appropriate for Q-technique, and although few users of Q-sort proceed to Q-technique analysis, they are implicitly bound by the psychometric properties of scores—mainly ipsative standardization—most thoroughly discussed in relation to Q-technique.

Q-sort rests on ranking (and maybe transforming to point scores if one wants) trait behaviors in a given individual *in terms of their relative importance within that individual*. Whereas *normative* scores come from ranks across a set of people, *ipsative scores are relative only to the given individual*. Some clinicians, of whom Rogers was prominent, have felt that *this pattern within the individual* is more important, and thus Stephenson's statistical approach fitted Rogers' clinical approach.

A concrete illustration of this testing procedure would help at this point. A Q deck of statements (e.g., "smiles easily"; "is sarcastic") is prepared. The client or person making the Q-sort puts the cards into stacks ranging from least descriptive to most descriptive. The usual approach is to force a normal distribution. For example, in the Q deck once used by this writer, the cards were distributed as follows:

Number of cards	6	9	13	18	23	18	13	9	6
Pile number	1	2	3	4	5	6	7	8	9
	Least like							Most like	

Q-sorts have been used for a number of different purposes, as follows. Carl Rogers and his associates (see Rogers & Dymond, 1954) were greatly concerned with the degree of discrepancy between real and ideal selves—between persons' descriptions of themselves as they are and as they want to be. Having obtained this information, one then can obtain a mean discrepancy score between real and ideal Q-sorts. Presumably, the lesser the discrepancy, the greater the self-acceptance and the better the adjustment. Presumably, too, psychotherapy, if effective, reduces the discrepancy between real and ideal. Wirt and Briggs (1959) used Q-sorts to describe a group of subjects originally studied by Hathaway and Monachesi (1953). Hathaway and Monachesi reported on the relation between MMPI scores and delinquency for a very large sample of ninth-grade boys. Wirt and Briggs obtained additional data from members of the Hathaway and Monachesi sample with regard to delinquency/criminality about a decade later. All four quadrants were represented: those predicted to be delinquent/criminal on the basis of MMPI scores who, in fact, were so, as opposed to those who were not; those predicted not to be delinquent/criminal who were and who were not so. Among the measures used by Wirt and Briggs was a Q-sort of each subject done by the person who had interviewed that subject. Many significant discrepancies in Q-sort placements were obtained. Clearly, while the MMPI predicted delinquency/criminality at a substantially better than chance rate of success, there were other domains of personality, measured rather poorly, if at all, by the MMPI (in this writer's opinion, chiefly having to do with energy level/stimulation-seeking but also some primary 16 P.F. factors (Cattell & Bolton, 1969). These could also be important predictors of antisocial behavior. MacKinnon and associates (MacKinnon, 1962) used Q-sorts to assess differences in personality between creative and less creative architects, differentially effective army officers, and other groups. Persons under study were observed by trained observers in a variety of circumstances. Q-sorts revealed many differences between such

groups as highly creative vs. other architects. For example, creative, competent persons tend to be 1) very aware of the feelings that others have regarding them, and 2) almost totally uninfluenced by others' feelings toward them—sensitive, yet inner-directed.

A number of other well-known clinical studies have been done using the Q-technique, and despite serious *caveats*, presented below, it seems clear that the Q-sort approach to personality assessment has been a useful one and has the potential of being even more fruitful. Problems involved in using the Q-sort technique are described below, starting with those that are comparatively easy to solve.

1) *The problem of social desirability*. Will Rogers once said, "I never met a man I didn't like." This is a bit Pollyannaish, but if one rephrased the statement to say, "I never met a person who—once I understood the bases of that person's behavior—I did not regard as trying hard to be a decent citizen," most of us would agree, for most, but not all, people whom we know. If one knows a person well enough to rate the person on a number of personality attributes, one also probably will say that most socially desirable attributes are on the most "like" end of the continuum; most socially undesirable ones on the "unlike" end of the rating continuum. Maybe we humans are more good than bad or maybe we, as raters, judge not, lest we be judged. In any case, the social desirability of given attributes does influence their placement on an unlike/like scale. It is clear that social desirability is not a single factor (see Chapter 23). There is no perfect solution to the problem of assessing the influence of social desirability of given statements, as opposed to the actual content of these statements, on their placement in a Q-sort, as contrasted with what can be done (Chapter 23) with ordinary testing by trait view correction. A possible partial solution (Medinnus, 1961) is to have two Q-sort decks, one

dealing with positive attributes, the other with negative attributes. This does not solve the problem of *relative* positiveness or negativeness of attributes; however, this problem seems to be both difficult to deal with (since individual concepts of the desirable vary; Scott, 1963) and trivial in consequence (Rorer, 1965). Positive and negative Q-decks would do much to improve the Q-technique with comparatively little effort.

2) Another problem with the usual Q deck is that of *observability of the behavior in question*. Two kinds of items are found in the middle of the usual Q-deck distribution. One kind deals with behavior that is directly observable, but with regard to which the subject is, in fact, "middling"; e.g., "smiles easily"—not so smiley, not grim either—I'll put that card in the middle. The other kind of item that falls in the middle of the distribution is the kind of item for which the rater is at a loss—e.g., "has an unresolved Oedipus complex." How do I know? I'll put that one in the middle. Q-sort items should be at the same level of observability; otherwise one gets this strange mix of items in the middle of the distribution.

Virtually all of the above uses of Q-sort involve statistical concepts that are open to rather disabling criticism. The first arose in Sir Cyril Burt's criticism (1940) of Stephenson's Q-technique, which does not, however, apply directly to most other Q-sort uses. What *does* apply is: 1) It would be better if the individual were first scored *normatively* on the elements and they were then ranked within him for ipsative scoring. This would be far more objective than asking him to grope to an order on the rather mystical concept of their "importance" to him. 2) To properly estimate resemblance of two profiles, it is necessary to use Cattell's pattern similarity coefficient, r_p, not the correlation coefficient. As both Cronbach (1957) and Cattell (1968) pointed out, a profile has three characteristics: a) a mean level, b)

a shape, and c) a degree of extremity in the shape. r_p takes account of all of these; the correlation coefficient ignores both the first and the third. Thus (see also Guilford, 1959, p. 215), substantial information about the real degree of similarity of, say, actual and ideal similarity is lost in the studies that have used Q-sort and ordinary correlation.

Despite the suggested statistical improvements, the bulk of Q-sort research —and it is a considerable bulk—conducted by mostly nondirective therapists following Rogers, and others cited below, has yielded some interesting psychological indications. One may study further the use of such approaches in Walker (1962, 1963), Wirt and Briggs (1959), and MacKinnon (1962). Each of these made use of ipsative measures obtained from conducting a Q-sort for each of a number of persons. One finds in them various mixtures of ipsative scoring and pattern comparisons based on preliminary normative scores, e.g., on the 16 P.F., as cited above, and simple subjective "importance" ratings where one has no means of telling if the mean of the elements Q-sorted differs or does not differ from person to person. But in none until the last few years was the interpersonal profile similarity measured by r_p rather than r. There may be situations in which the latter is more appropriate, but it certainly involves a loss of information relative to the former and one suspects that what were mere "indications" in 15 years of Q-sort research would, in some cases, become definitive results with the improved method.

RATINGS IN CLINICAL DIAGNOSIS AND PSYCHIATRIC CATEGORIZING

Apart perhaps from some extensive uses of promotional ratings in industry, civil service, and military organizations, quite the most important everyday use of the rating method is in clinical diagnosis and assignment of cases by psychiatrists to categories in the DSM-III (American Psychiatric Association, 1980).

The clinical use covers both L(BR), inasmuch as behavior is observed in home, work, consulting room, etc., and L(R), in which family, court, or other instances of crucial behaviors are recorded. In L(BR) we need to consider both the behavior *in situ* in everyday life, as above, and also behavior in the interview situation, which we have not yet considered, and in which different principles apply.

Let us recognize immediately that in regard to what is being rated considerable confusion continues to prevail in this field. The confusion concerns three structural concepts: the *surface trait*, the *source trait*, and the *species type*. A surface trait is a *correlation cluster* of behavioral variables that have been observed to go together, as in a medical disease syndrome and perhaps in such patterns as Freud's oral

erotic, etc., syndromes. A source trait, as recognized in Chapter 3 and since, is a simple structure factor, a unitary underlying cause of common variation among phenomena.

The first systematic exploration of surface trait and source trait structures in normal traits on the broad basis of the personality sphere concepts revealed (Cattell, 1946), as would be expected, that some correlation clusters were due to a single factor, but that others were due to an overlapping of two factors. (Just as, for example, the features that go together as "luxuriant vegetation" are the overlap of two factors—rainfall and heat.) Thus, as Figure 11.1 shows, the number of factors and the number of clusters are two different things, and commonly the number of surface traits that people think they recognize is greater than the number of factors in that area. (Representation may be

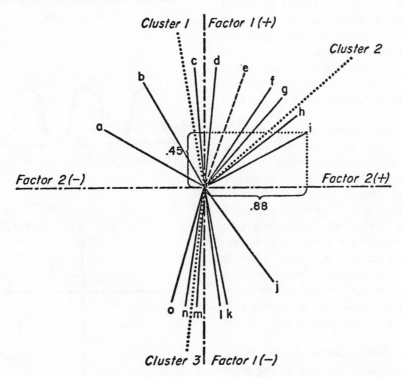

Figure 11.1. Variables resolved into surface traits and source traits*

*Cattell, R. B. (1957). *Personality and Motivation Structure and Measurement*, p. 32.

studied in an introductory way in Cattell, 1957c, pp. 20-48 and with more technical consideration in Cattell, 1978.) Although investigators of structure initially worked by correlation clusters rather than proceed to the more abstract technicalities of factors, the surface trait does not offer clear-cut concepts, due to the arbitrariness of having to decide what degree of correlation justifies entry to a cluster. The problem is precisely that of trying to point to separate sandbanks in an estuary as the tide level changes.

The word "type," as Cattell pointed out in 1946, has possibly over 40 different uses! It is absurd, for example, to say a person belongs to an extravert or introvert type unless we cut the normal distribution by a section down the middle, and in that case (with a one sigma band) more people are unclassifiable than classifiable. All such cases are better handled by scores on a source trait dimension than by talking about types. The type concept is useful when there are distinct species types—cats, dogs, etc. When scores of individuals are plotted on a number of dimensions, it *may* happen that distinct clusters, called segregates (or modes in many dimensions), appear in certain areas, as shown in Figure 11.2.

In psychology, compared, say, to biology, such clearly segregating types are uncommon. They probably exist in occupations, measured on skills, and in ethnic and political groups measured on attitudes. Psychiatrists have long supposed that groups like simple schizophrenics, paranoid schizophrenics, cyclical depressives, and so on, are a complete break away from the normal distribution, due to particular genetic or disease processes, and that it is useful for prognosis and treatment to put each patient into a DSM category.

That these form distinct species types may well be true, but it has never been demonstrated psychometrically. Certainly, the DSM has to admit "schizoid types" as well as schizophrenics, and there

are schizoaffective disorders which seem to be a mixture of affective (manic-depressive) and schizophrenic types. Psychology developed 20 years ago (Cattell, 1957a; Cattell, Coulter, & Tsujioka, 1966) the *Taxonome* method, with its concepts and computer programs permitting an objective sorting of individuals into types on the basis of their profiles (by L(BR), L(R), or testing (Q- and T-data)) on source trait scores. But so far the programmatic experiment necessary to check the real boundaries and numbers of clinical types has not been performed and the DSM rests on the cogitations of committees.

Rating in terms of source traits remains equally unsatisfactory in the abnormal, clinical field. The attempts to provide

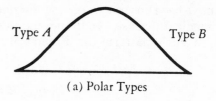

(a) Polar Types

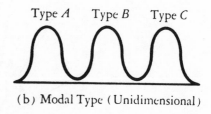

(b) Modal Type (Unidimensional)

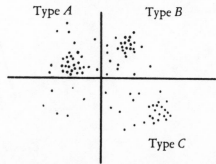

(c) Species Type (Modal Multidimensional)

Figure 11.2. Basic of type

truly factored rating scales for mental hospital work have been rendered uncertain partly by a conceptual confusion of types and factors, and partly by the fact that significance tests for number of factors and completeness of rotation were poorly developed at the time most work was done in this area. (See survey in Cattell, 1957a, 1957c.)

In the questionnaire area things are more satisfactory in the scales of the Clinical Analysis Questionnaire (the CAQ) and the MMPI, the factoring of which has often been checked in recent times. (One should note, however, that the MMPI *began* by seeking items that best assigned individuals to psychiatric *types*, and subsequent factorings find it a hybrid in consequence.) The full technical discussion of handling diagnosis by source traits in a specification equation and, alternatively, by a pattern similarity coefficient, r_p, to see how closely the individual falls into various types, is given in Chapter 23. However, except in questionnaire data, we do not yet have clarity of scales (in rating) or of definition of the psychiatric species types to which individuals can be psychometrically compared, to proceed with demonstrably statistical significance.

One representative psychiatric rating system (Lorr et al., 1962, 1963) was discussed earlier in this chapter. Other widely used instruments include the Schedule for Affective Disorders and Schizophrenia (SADS) (Spitzer & Endicott, 1979). Screening items are presented for each of a number of sets of symptoms—e.g., depression, panic attacks, phobias, delusions, hallucinations, etc. A representative page from the SADS schedule is presented in Table 11.4.

Psychiatric diagnoses based on global ratings have been under attack for decades. As Eysenck put it, after reviewing the literature, "We may then regard it as agreed that psychiatric diagnosis is of doubtful validity and low reliability" (Eysenck, 1952, p. 33). Eysenck has continued to review the diagnosis literature, and has not changed the position quoted above.

Checklists and rating scales (such as those presented herein as examples) have been developed, usually by psychiatrists, as a result of their own questioning of psychiatric diagnoses. They are obviously helpful in the diagnostic process, as will be observed further below. Before such a discussion, let us consider those aspects of the psychiatric interview that work for or against accurate diagnosis and effective treatment.

Pro: The psychiatric interview, whether conducted by a psychiatrist or by some other type of professional such as a psychologist or psychiatric social worker, is conducted by an intelligent and motivated interviewer, trained in interviewing, theoretically sophisticated, and accustomed to presenting and defending diagnoses, based largely on interview ratings, at case conferences. The person to be rated/diagnosed usually manifests behaviors that are sufficiently different from those of the world at large, that they are easily discernible and, therefore, should be reliably observed.

Con: However, the psychiatric interviewer/rater usually has a strong ideological commitment to one as opposed to other theories of causation and of preferred treatment techniques. As a result of the rater's own personality attributes and defense systems, theoretical orientations, or both, psychiatrists vary greatly in the frequency with which they assign different diagnoses.

Even without the problems of theoretical orientations or of own personality/defense systems, the psychiatric rater is at some disadvantage in accurate diagnosis. There are too many attributes to be considered simultaneously, and the rater has no accurate knowledge of how much

TABLE 11.4
Screening Items for Manic Syndrome

The next 5 items are screening items to determine the presence of manic-like behavior. If any of the items are judged present, inquire in a general way to determine how he was behaving at that time with such questions as, *When you were this way, what kinds of things were you doing? How did you spend your time?* Do not include behavior which is clearly explainable by alcohol or drug use.

If the subject has described only dysphoric mood, the following questions regarding the manic syndrome should be introduced with a statement such as: *I know you have been feeling (depressed). However, many people have other feelings mixed in or at different times so it is important that I ask you about those feelings also.*

Elevated or expansive mood and/or optimistic attitude toward the future which lasted at least several hours and was out of proportion to the circumstances.

Have (there been times when) you felt very good or too cheerful or high—not just your normal self?

If unclear: *When you felt on top of the world or as if there was nothing you couldn't do?*

(Have you felt that everything would work out just the way you wanted?)

If people saw you would they think you were just in a good mood or something more than that?

(What about during the past week?)

0 No information

1 Not at all, normal, or depressed

2 Slight, e.g., good spirits, more cheerful than most people in his circumstances, but of only possible clinical significance

3 Mild, e.g., definitely elevated or expansive mood and overly optimistic which is somewhat out of proportion to his circumstances

4 Moderate, e.g., mood and outlook are clearly out of proportion to circumstances

5 Severe, e.g., quality of euphoric mood

6 Extreme, e.g., clearly elated, exalted expression and says "Everything is beautiful, I feel so good"

PAST WEEK 0 1 2 3 4 5 6

Less need for sleep than usual to feel rested (average for several days when needed less sleep).

Have you needed less sleep than usual to feel rested? (How much sleep do you ordinarily need?)
(How much when you were [are] high?)

(What about during the past week?)

0 No information

1 No change or more sleep needed

2 Up to 1 hour less than usual

3 Up to 2 hours less than usual

4 Up to 3 hours less than usual

5 Up to 4 hours less than usual

6 4 or more hours less than usual

PAST WEEK 0 1 2 3 4 5 6

Unusually energetic (which lasted for at least several days), more active than usual without expected fatigue.

Have you had more energy than usual to do things?

(More than just a return to normal or usual level?)

(Did it seem like too much energy?)

(What about during the past week?)

0 No information

1 No different than usual or less energetic

2 Slightly more energetic but of questionable significance

3 Little change in activity level but less fatigued than usual

4 Somewhat more active than usual with little or no fatigue

5 Much more active than usual with little or no fatigue

6 Unusually active all day long with little or no fatigue

PAST WEEK 0 1 2 3 4 5 6

weight to assign to each of them (see Meehl, 1954). Further, there are many attributes of the individual that may be of great importance regarding diagnosis and treatment that the patient is unaware of and, therefore, cannot be expressed in the psychiatric interview or, perhaps, discerned from the case history (see Chapter 18). In addition, patients or clients do change over time. Any mode of assessment that does not take into consideration the fact that many of the observable behaviors vary across situations and across time (even short time intervals) is problematical.

Scales such as those presented above help a bit in sorting out the many variables that must be weighed in any clinical diagnosis. However, surface traits, source traits, and "species types" are totally confounded in the usual psychiatric rating scale. The rating scale and the data derived from it usually are of no help in disentanglement. In the absence of weighing the diagnostic, prescriptive, and prognostic values of each of a number of symptoms, either in the absence of therapy or in the presence of one or another therapy, one can neither diagnose nor prescribe treatment with confidence that one is increasing effectiveness beyond that of base rate ("spontaneous remission"; that is, problems that are solved without intervention, given time). The aid of rating systems such as SADS or checklists such as that used by Lorr et al. in diagnosis does not overcome another problem of the psychiatric rating, that of sheer N. Reliable ratings require a number of raters, familiar with a broad sample of the rated person's behaviors across a substantial segment of time. These conditions are seldom met in psychiatric ratings.

As noted above, Eysenck has been prominent in attacking psychiatric ratings. Another leading psychologist whose name has been closely connected with a general attack on clinical (whether psychiatric or psychological) diagnosis based on global ratings is Paul Meehl. His book,

Clinical vs. Statistical Prediction: A Theoretical Analysis and Review of the Evidence (1954), pointed out the lack of reliability and validity of clinical diagnosis, and demonstrated the general superiority of quantitative data acquired through psychometric measures. Many more papers have been written on clinical vs. statistical (or actuarial) prediction since Meehl's seminal work, and nearly all support the greater value of statistical-actuarial prediction. Meehl has many unkind things to say about the clinical case conference, the data brought to it, and the total inability of the conferees to assign differing levels of confidence in and of diagnostic significance of the various behaviors reported (Meehl, 1973, pp. 225-302). This does not mean, however, that Meehl is opposed to psychiatric diagnosis. He recognizes the problems in such diagnoses, but still feels that they contribute a great deal (see, in particular, Meehl, 1973, pp. vii-xxii, p. 63, pp. 93-94, pp. 132-133).

Diagnostic ratings based on clinical (whether psychiatric or psychological) interview data are nearly always found to be unreliable and low in validity. Further, even with these diagnoses, the preferred mode of treatment frequently is obscure. What Meehl would prescribe appears to be basically what is presented in Chapter 18—a combination of psychometric data and clinical acumen, both brought to bear on developing an effective treatment for a person whose life is not going well. We refer you to Chapter 18.

USE OF EVERYDAY LIFE RECORDED EVENTS: TIME SAMPLING (L(R)-DATA)

Here we get into the area that psychometrists often think of as "criteria" in test prediction. In looking at L(R)-data we shall look as usual at reliability; yet we note that psychometrists frequently correct predictive coefficients for *test* unreliability, but rarely do so for *criterion* unreliability.

As usual there are two aspects of the use of observable variables to consider here: 1) the mode of recording, scaling, standardizing, etc., the variables themselves, and 2) asking what more simplified structure can be found among them to make future use of the domain of variables more economical and more meaningful. In this introduction let us first look ahead to the problems in the second phase.

Theoretically it might seem that the factoring of L(R)-data should lead to the same personality factors as using L(BR)-data. However, although personality expresses itself as systematically in job behavior, recreation, home relations, as in the observer-extracted somewhat more general behaviors in the verbally defined subtrait personality sphere of L(BR)-data, we would expect far more intrusion of local instrument factors in L(R) factoring. These would, indeed, often be what Cattell has discovered as *sems* (sentiments)—see Chapter 3. For example, the individual with a strong sentiment to his mother will modify trait expressions, e.g., of dominance, surgency, in the situation of her presence. Consequently, if we record actual behaviors (intensity or frequency), the correlations to be expected from the *general* personality dominance trait will fall lower in those recorded behaviors in a sample of people varied in strength of maternal attachment. The L(BR) rater intuitively makes allowance for this in ratings that extract the dominance factor, but L(R)-data starkly represent the less smooth terrain.

It is surprising (unless we recognize psychologists to be lazy!) that no one has yet taken a personality sphere of 24-hour everyday life behavior on a sufficient sample of variables and people to conduct a factoring to define the primary personality source traits in quantitatively recorded L(R) behavior. There are a number of studies in the last two decades factoring criteria, but always in limited areas that

cannot easily be fitted together in jigsaw fashion. In some of these, the 16 P.F. or other Q-data personality traits have been correlated in with these samples of criteria, and in virtually every case the correlations have been such that we can conclude that the L(BR) and the L(R) variables have much common factor space, supporting the theory that L(R) factors would be general personality plus instrument factor.

From such criteria factoring studies we may illustrate with classically well done research of Taylor, Smith, and Ghiselin (1963). They obtained 52 measures on 166 scientists, some measures being true L(R), e.g., number of journal articles, number of people supervised, patients per year, and some more like L(BR) assessment. They reached very significant simple structure with 15 factors. Since the number is so close to the 16 often found in ratings, it is tempting to think that these might be personality factors, but inspection suggests that some may be, such as independence as E, but others look like situational instrument factors. Such results and those of Peterson and Cattell below illustrate the inherent complexity of reaching personality structure through L(R)-data and the sophistication of design and factoring that will be needed effectively to reach it. Incidentally, the factoring of criteria by Taylor, Smith and Ghiselin (1963) and several others suggests that much psychometry using a single criterion risks tying the behavioral equation to a composite criterion likely to be unsuitable in composition from one setting to another. A major problem in L(R)-data, both in regard to structuring, above, and to the obtaining and scaling of data, is the sheer number of events occurring in the life of a given individual, the substantial effects of situational components (e.g., behavior in a classroom vs. behavior in the home) and of the specific group with whom the individual is interacting. These add to the difficulty of forming reliable and valid judgments of the attributes of the individual through this sort of general "real life" observation. Generally, too much is happening for one observer to attend closely and record accurately each of several kinds of behavior of a given individual. To get around this we have to resort to a well-stratified sample of variables and limited but standard periods of observation, in what has become known as time sampling.

Time sampling arose as a technique that permitted highly reliable and valid information to be obtained through systematic observation. The first time-sampling study was that of Williard C. Olson (1929), and will serve to illustrate the method. Olson was interested in measuring the nervous habits of children in the social setting. One begins by observing children in a free observational setting and developing a list of well-defined nervous habits—for example, "hirsutal" —pulling or twisting one's hair. Having defined the behaviors to be observed, one then moves to the group of individuals to be observed—e.g., a classroom full of children. Let us say that there are 25 children in a classroom. We would randomly assign numbers from 1 through 25 to each of these children and then observe child 1 during the first one-minute observational interval, child 2 during the second, etc. A different random order would be followed for each successive set of observations of the 25 students. (Clearly, preliminary observations would be needed so that each subject could be instantly recognized.) The observer, stopwatch in one hand, data sheet on clipboard, would record the frequency of each nervous behavior emitted by the child under observation for that one-minute interval. One might expect nervous habits to vary with time of day and with subject matter.

If interested in generalizing across the school day, as theory might require, one might obtain one one-minute observation per hour of the day, or systematically vary the time of observation from day to day in order to obtain a representative sample of nervous behaviors. The observer would keep constant the number of observations of each given child in each behavior context. Thirty minutes observation of each child, taken all at once, will almost certainly give unreliable results. Time of day, type of activity engaged in, daily fluctuations in mood and health, as well as many other variables would almost certainly make any 30-minute segment of behavior unrepresentative of behavior in general. The same 30 minutes, taken from 30 one-minute observations over 30 different days, probably will provide highly accurate information, so long as the behavior or behaviors (e.g., various nervous habits) occur with sufficient frequency. Time sampling is fine for measuring something such as fidgeting.

If the behavior under observation is infrequent or covert, then time sampling is of little or no value as a technique. It has a number of very substantial advantages in assessing those comparatively frequent overt behaviors for which it is appropriate. So long as the behaviors to be counted are clearly defined, even comparatively untrained observers usually will show high interrater reliability in recording their frequency of emission. One needs to provide the observers with a clear, easy-to-follow data recording sheet and to especially impress on observers that once the observational interval is over for a subject, one must then move on to the next one and not yield to the temptation of continuing to observe a subject whose time has ended, even if the subject is doing something interesting or looks as though he or she soon will do so. It's best to take observers through a few dry runs, with each observer, plus the investigator (if someone other than the observers), observing and noting the behavior(s) in question. Unreliability in recording can be discerned and the bases for this unreliability discovered and corrected.

Once the actual experimental observations are obtained, interrater reliabilities and split-half (odd/even) reliabilities are easily obtained and usually are very high. Validities certainly also can be ascertained. For example, in the area of boredom, Sir Francis Galton, that indefatigable measurer of things (including the power of prayer [Galton, 1883]) measured the boringness of papers read at scientific meetings by observing the fidgeting of a set number of persons around him as each paper was read. He had a sharp tack mounted on his thumb and kept his hand in his pocket. He would prick a hole in a piece of cardboard for each fidget observed (new piece, in order, for each paper, in order of presentation). Validation could have been achieved by obtaining boringness ratings of the papers read from the listeners. Given the frankness that characterizes exchanges at English scientific meetings, this would not be a difficult task. Obviously, the boringness of a paper is associated with the degree to which the content is in one's own research domain; even so, boringness per se probably comes through, independent of one's involvement with the topic. This project might be worth doing, even today.

Time sampling got its start in developmental psychology. Arrington (1943) provided a fine review of the early time sampling literature. Barker and Wright (1954) who, with their colleagues observed larger samples of naturally occurring behavior than any other psychologists (e.g., Barker, 1963; Barker & Wright, 1954; Wright & Barker, 1949, 1950) set forth an excellent set of procedures for the use of time sampling techniques (Barker & Wright, 1954).

Cattell and Peterson (1958) and Peterson and Cattell (1959a) attempted to contribute to child development a factoring of a) ratings (L(BR)), and b) time-sampled behavior (L(R)) on the same set of nursery school children, following a pioneer study by Koch (1934). They were unable reliably to relate the rating factors (meaningful in terms of rating factors in older children [Cattell & Coan, 1957]) to the specific ob-

jective behaviors, and concluded that work on a much larger scale would be necessary to separate source traits and instrument traits.

Although the methods of recording, as instanced above, may be considered reasonably established, time sampling analysis has not progressed much. Time sampling measurement of the frequency with which behavior is emitted has, however, become adopted by the behavior modification-reflexological branch of clinical practice, but, being bivariate in concepts, these psychologists neglected research on structure. Others in the tradition of "broad instrument" research, oriented to brief controlled experiment, seem to find time sampling or any other kind of systematic broad life observation too time-consuming, especially since it usually requires at least two observers. Developmental psychologists, perhaps unduly impressed with the respectability of classical experiment, swung away from life observation (L(R) and L(BR)). On the other hand, psychologists from the area of learning theory moved into developmental psychology when they discovered that many of the experiments once conducted using rats could be done with children (and without the expense of maintaining a rat colony!).

Time sampling L(R) is coming back into its own also in terms of change scores, notably in evaluating progress in therapy, where its reliability is better than for ratings (L(BR)). Change can be measured either by clinical use of source trait measures (Cattell 1978; Chapters 17 and 18, this volume) or by a single behavioral symptom. For behavior modification practice one does not worry about intrapsychic structure; one worries about how to change the frequency with which the symptom is manifested. One changes the frequency through reinforcing some behaviors, not reinforcing others. In consequence, behavior modifiers are greatly interested in counting behaviors. They are using techniques pioneered by Olson and by Good-enough with one very important additional element, the control of reinforcement as the "therapy." Two clear examples of this reflexological-behavioral approach will be found in Harris, Wolf, and Baer (1964), one involving the nonreinforcement of a maladaptive behavior, the other the positive reinforcement of a desired behavior. There are hundreds—probably thousands—of such reports in the literature. The clarity and succinctness of the Harris et al. report led to this particular choice of examples. Figure 11.3 is self-explanatory of the relation between a time sampling of frequency of crying of a four-year-old boy (judged excessive in crying) and conditioning by ignoring the crying while giving approving attention to verbal and self-help alternatives.

Developmental psychologists never were shy in rating personality on the basis of data obtained through time sampling. Contemporary behaviorists, on the other hand, have eschewed behavior ratings, almost as John B. Watson, the founder of behaviorism, eschewed the concept of consciousness. Therefore, it comes as a pleasant surprise to find that the use of ratings

has become acceptable in some behavioral circles. Cairns and Green (1979, Table A-1, p. 215) note that most of the potential sources of variance are identical for ratings and for observations. Ratings are more influenced by characteristics of the rater than are observations (see Table 11.5). Other sources of variance characteristics of the child, setting, and type of behavior being observed are identical across types of measures. They conclude, very sensibly, that both ratings and direct behavioral observation have their merits. Each type of measure is superior for attaining certain research goals. If one wishes to measure the processes by which behaviors are evoked and maintained, then observational recording of specific behaviors (L(R)), permitting the recognition of the reinforcements that keep a particular behavior in the individual's repertoire, is the more informative. If, on the other hand, one wishes to measure the personality outcomes of development in terms of demonstrable source trait patterns with consistency and stability over many situations, then (if rating rather than Q- or T-tests are used) L(BR)-data from skilled observers may be superior.

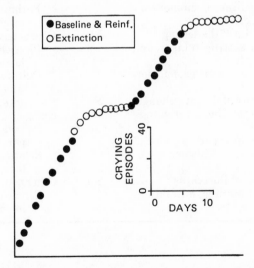

Figure 11.3. Use of time sampling (L(R)) scoring in behavior modification therapy: case of a "cry-baby"

TABLE 11.5

Potential Sources of Variance for Each Assessment Technique

Symbol	Ratings	Symbol	Observations
S^2R	Characteristics of the rater: Idiosyncratic interpretations of the construct or dimension; Idiosyncratic interpretation of the relevant activities; Scaling of individual onto the group distribution; Knowledge of the individual child; Limitations of perception; Personal biases toward subjects (halos); Biases toward groups (stereotyping); Knowledge of reference population; Dispositions of rater (optimistic, etc.); Selective memory factors.	S^2o	Characteristics of the observer: Selective attention factors; Limitations of perception; Personal biases toward subjects (halos); Biases toward groups (stereotyping).
S^2cs	Characteristics of the child —Stable: Enduring dispositions and style of interchange.	S^2cs	Characteristics of the child — Stable: Enduring dispositions and style of interchange.
S^2cr	Characteristics of the child —Temporary: Fatigue, illness, momentary mood, etc.	S^2cr	Characteristics of the child —Temporary: Fatigue, illness, momentary mood, etc.
S^2s	Characteristics of the setting: Physical setting (classroom, home, etc.); Cultural or institutional setting.	S^2s	Characteristics of the setting: Physical setting (classroom, home, etc.); Cultural or institutional setting.
S^2t	Characteristics of the interchange: Behavior of the interchange partner; Relationship of partner to child (age, sex, past history, etc.).	S^2t	Characteristics of the interchange: Behavior of the interchange partner; Relationship of partner to child (age, sex, past history, etc.).
S^2e	Other sources of fluctuation: Errors of recording, mistakes in analysis, etc.	S^2e	Other sources of fluctuation: Errors of recording, mistakes in analysis, etc.

SUMMARY

Everyday life data enter, from a subjective viewpoint however, into questionnaire tests, but are directly observed and evaluated as L-data in two forms: a) L(BR)-data in which observers score subjects on specifically defined behavioral traits, and b) L(R)-data where actual records of frequency or intensity of specific behaviors (sometimes "episodes") are kept.

In principle this division can apply to: a) observation over long periods of everyday life *in situ*, and b) observation in a contrived short situation—the interview —in clinic or business (creating a fourfold table).

L(BR)-data vary greatly in reliability and validity, and in the majority of reports of ratings in applied psychology they are found to reach not very satisfactory levels. However, if some seven conditions set out here are observed (which is more often possible in pure than in applied research), reliabilities reach about 0.8, which is as good, for example, as in some intelligence tests. Thorndike has shown that the reliability follows the Spearman-Brown rule (number of people instead of items over ranges where all have access to what is observable). In comparing rating results and deriving a reliable consensus, it is important to see whether these seven conditions were observed.

The use of ratings requires attention to two objectives: a) the reliability of the single variable ratings, and b) the source trait structure among the variables, whereby numerous variable scores can be converted to a smaller, convenient and psychologically correct number of meaningful source traits. An understanding of the number and nature of source traits in the normal personality sphere was reached in the forties, fifties, and sixties of this century by programmatic factorial research by many multivariate experimenters (see Chapter 3).

It has been shown that the source traits in L-data are essentially the same as those in Q-data, both at the first and second strata (primaries and secondaries), which is not surprising considering they both deal with everyday life behavior. In abnormal behavior, however, the questionnaire factors have been brought to definition, but those in observer ratings are still incomplete.

Ratings have been indispensable in putting personality factoring on a broad personality sphere basis, and in patterns that can be recognized in relation to concepts arising from the clinical phase of psychology, but they suffer from two serious restrictions to their use. First, in developmental psychology, the comparison of subjects after lapse of years suffers from having a different set of familiar raters, and second, comparison of two contemporary groups, known only to two *different* sets of raters, suffers from the same likelihood of differences being due as much to raters as ratees.

The distortions of ratings by different situations begetting different *social desirabilities*, by *halo* effects, by introduction of the rater's personality according to *trait view* and *spectrad theory*, are looked at in some historical instances here, but the systematic treatment of distortion in ratings is deferred to Chapter 23. However, it is recognized that errors of estimation of personality factors arise from the intrusion of *instrument* factors, often peculiar to one medium, so that ideally one would estimate an *instrument-transcending* personality factor from combining L(BR)-data and Q-data source trait scores.

A special use of rating appeared at one time in clinical psychology in the form of Q-sort, in which the individual ranked a series of traits or behaviors in order of declining "importance" in his personality. It is pointed out that this connotes *ipsative* scoring, which is different in some important properties from the more familiar *normative* scoring of tests. If this ranking profile is correlated with another, e.g., actual with ideal, in himself, or in another person, e.g., a central profile for a clinical category, two of the three kinds of information commonly in a profile (level, shape, extremity) are ignored. If values that are first normatized are used in a profile, and r_p rather than r (which loses level and extremity) is used in the comparisons, nothing is lost. (The use of r_p on a subjectively ranked set is, however, too late, since *level* and *extremity* are absent from the beginning.) In spite of these distortions and losses, Q-sort (which, incidentally must not be confused with Q-technique in factor analysis) has yielded indications of interesting psychological generalizations that could be more precisely tested with the use of r_p.

The most widespread current use of what is essentially L-data (as L(BR) *and* L(R)) is in assignment of cases by clinical psychologists into psychiatric categories in the DSM. This involves consideration of both everyday life and interview behavior. Conceptually it also involves a clear distinction of a dimension from a type, which many uses of type have failed to recognize, adding to diagnostic confusion. The taxonome model and computer program enable species types to be objectively discovered and defined, but has not yet been used in clearing up the DSM categories into which clinicians are asked to place cases by ratings. In any case, the ratings themselves, e.g., of anxiety (dimensionally) as made in psychiatric interviews, have been found to have quite a low interpsychiatrist reliability, and the same is true of independent decisions on placing clients in DSM categories. The use of rating methods here is probably susceptible to marked improvement, and so supplementation by source trait tests is strongly indicated (Chapters 11, 12, 16, and 17).

The use of actually recorded behavioral episodes (L(R)-data), which sometimes enters into the scoring of occupational and court criteria, brings higher reliability than observer rating (L(BR)-data). In regard to keeping the personality sphere concept in action, since not all behavior in 24 hours can easily be recorded, *time sampling* has commonly been used. While classical experimenters have employed it negligibly, it has found use in reflexological study of behavior modification therapy of specific symptoms and also in animal learning and ethological studies.

As regards personality structure research, the relation of factoring of L(R) (as in time sampling) to L(BR), where the variables rated are already more abstracted from concrete behavior, remains obscure. That mutual support is not yet reached is unfortunate because there have been accusations (probably unwarranted: see Cattell & Dickman, 1962) that rating on verbal subtraits could give traits unities that are projections of inner stereotypes—which could not happen with recorded episodes. At present some capable factorings of L(R)-data suggest personality source traits mixed in with instrument factors.

CHAPTER 12

Personality Assessment by Questionnaire

Keith Barton

A PERSPECTIVE ON PERSONALITY ASSESSMENT BY QUESTIONNAIRE

It will be obvious from the general principles of Chapter 1 and the specific discussion on structures in Chapter 2 that we shall concern ourselves only with questionnaires which have been thoroughly verified as to the unitary personality structures which they measure, and which contribute to and derive from basic scientific theories of personality structure.

This being the case, we have, first, a series of questionnaires dealing with primary personality patterns at different age levels. These are the 16 Personality Factor Questionnaire for Adults, the High School Personality Questionnaire for the high-school range, the Child Personality Questionnaire for the years of eight to 12 and the Otis School Personality for ages from six to eight. There is now under construction by Dreger the Pre-School Personality Questionnaire, which carries the measures of these same factors down to

the earliest years. The available measures are given in Figure 12.1.

These questionnaires are all roughly one hour in length and, as indicated below, have, with the exception of the Pre-School Personality Questionnaire, which is given on a tape, a standard test form and a standard answer sheet that can be machine-scored. They are also tests that can be given in the individual or the group situation.

It is part of the general usefulness of these tests, and of their integration with general personality theory, that their structures have also been verified in other countries and cultures, such as (as far as the 16 P.F. and HSPQ are concerned) Germany, France, Japan, Italy, Spain, South America, etc. Thus, findings in any one of these countries contribute to a general scientific pool of knowledge about primary personality structure.

In addition to these questionnaires, which span the general normal personality sphere and can be said in their 12 to

16 factors to cover almost any personality dimension one might be interested in, there is a development also into the realm of abnormal behavior, in the Clinical Analysis Questionnaire. The CAQ, which was developed by factorings of the areas previously covered by such measures of abnormal behavior as the MMPI, various depression scales, etc., adds 12 further dimensions to the 16 normal dimensions covered by the 16 P.F. As will be seen in the detailed description, it is divisible into two parts, one of which covers the 16 normal factors in the 16 P.F., and a second which covers the 12 additional abnormal behavior factors for psychiatric purposes. Thus, in fact, one could, if necessary, give the 16 P.F. itself and then just part 2 of the CAQ, but it is more convenient for most people to have in the CAQ shorter measures on the 16 P.F. normal factors which might describe, for example, the prepsychotic personality, and longer, more reliable measures on the 12 clinical abnormal factors. It should be noted, incidentally, that the personality scales for the primary factors in younger children, such as the ESPQ and PSPQ, do not cover quite as many factors as in the adult level. In fact, the HSPQ drops from 16 to 14. This is part of the differentiating that really goes on in personality structure, and it also recognizes that some factors

may be larger and more formed in childhood and others in adult life.

It will be recognized from the psychometric principles discussed in Chapter 3 that omnibus types of tests such as these, which, within an hour or less, cover 12 to 16 personality dimensions, cannot have the validity and reliability levels of, say, an intelligence test that devotes to the measurement of one factor as much time as these do to a dozen factors. However, to meet the needs of the researcher who must reach high validities and can afford more time than a busy practitioner, these tests are constructed with several parallel forms. Thus the 16 P.F. has no fewer than six such parallel forms, namely, A, B, C, D, E, and F, while all the others have at least two parallel equivalent forms. Thus, it can be said that the psychologist can get the validity and reliability level that he or she is prepared to pay for in terms of time of the subject (not necessarily time of his or her own). Researchers have generally given two or three forms, and practitioners have been repeatedly strongly urged to give both forms of the HSPQ and 16 P.F. in cases where it is quite important to be as accurate as possible.

In the case of the 16 P.F., the forms are parallel but are deliberately adapted to somewhat different populations. Thus, the A and B forms are strictly equivalent and

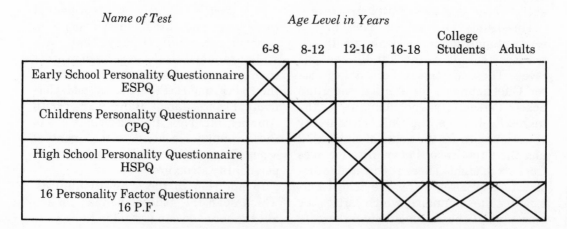

Figure 12.1. Age ranges for personality test series

are applicable to a high-school-educated subject. The C and the D forms have somewhat reduced demand on vocabulary and are also shorter, so that each can be administered in about half an hour or 20 minutes. The E and F forms are called below-literate forms and are brought to the lowest level of reading skill one is likely to meet in our present-day population. It will be noted, incidentally, that all of these questionnaires include an intelligence test of the same length as for the other personality factors. It has been a universal experience that users of the 16 P.F., HSPQ, etc. like to get a first measure of intelligence at the same time, although in various circumstances they will supplement this by an intelligence test as such, described in Chapter 10. These measures on factor *g*, intelligence, move as far as possible in the direction of fluid intelligence without using diagrams, achieving a reduction of the impact of crystallized intelligence, by taking complex relationships among very simple words.

The questionnaires listed in Figure 12.1 are all concerned with the primary normal personality factors. They do not get into motivation and interest as such (see Chapter 14), while the superego and ego structures, as well as the ergic tension factor, Q4, do overlap with the more generalized

motivation. However, essentially they cover what might be called the general personality factors, which change little with incentive and situation.

At certain times psychologists also wish to have measures of second-order personality factors, and here we have 1) the derivation of six or seven second-order personality factors from the 16 P.F., etc., above, 2) the use of the second-order state-trait measures developed by Barton, and 3) the three Eysenck EPI scales. The nature of the second-order factors is set out in Table 12.1 and it is these for which the second-order tables in the 16 P.F. Handbook give weights in scoring. The special scoring services which IPAT supplies automatically calculate these second orders from the primary scores derived from the answer sheet. The alignment of the Eysenck EPI with the main core of second-order factors, exvia, invia and anxiety (or neurosis), is quite good, although the derivation of the former is such that the alignment deteriorates in going to later factors.

The reasons for using second-order factors are not all good. It must be confessed that a principal one has been the desire of the psychologist to score fewer tests and to have a simpler picture than is given by the primary factors. If nature is in fact complex, we pay a big price for oversim-

TABLE 12.1

Second-Order Factors Measured by the 16 P.F. Primaries

Standard Index	Bipolar Title	Chief Primaries Involved
QI	Invia-vs.-*Exvia***	$A+, E+, F+, H+, Q_2-$
QII	Adjustment-vs.-*Anxiety*	$C-, H-, L+, O+, Q_3-, Q_4+$
QIII	Pathemia-vs.-*Cortertia*	$A-, I-, M- (E+, L+)$
QIV	Subduedness-vs.-*Independence*	$E+, L+, M+, Q_1+, Q_2+$
QV	Naturalness-vs.-*Discreetness*	$N+ (A+, M-, O-)$
QVI	Cool Realism-vs.-*Prodigal Subjectivity*	$I+, M+, L-$
QVII	Low Intelligence-vs.-*High Intelligence*	$B+$
QVIII	Low Superego-vs.-*High Superego Strength*	$G+, Q_3+, F-$

plifying it. It is as if a doctor would say he wishes to think of patients as having only lungs and stomachs and to ignore the gall bladder, the pancreas, the large intestine and everything else. It is also a psychometric fact that the prediction of any kind of behavior, clinical or normal, from three to five second-order personality factors is decidedly poorer than the prediction from the full set of primary scores. Truly effective practice is to use primaries and secondaries together in what is called "depth psychometry." As an illustration of this, we may consider that a certain score on the exvia factor can be very differently constituted in different individuals. In some the greatest contribution to the score comes from the primary factors of surgency and effectia. In others it may come from a low score on Q_2 and on H, threctia. This would give us a very different prognosis in the case of, say, a schizophrenic. Depth psychometry, therefore, consists of scoring for a given individual both primary and secondary scores side by side and examining them for telltale differences of this kind.

It perhaps goes without saying that the effective use of these questionnaires requires not only good psychometric calculations following the scores but also a very real insight by the psychologist into the meanings of the different primary factors. It is remarkable how much the psychometric prediction can be improved, in translating into future times and different situations, by psychologists who have a very sure knowledge of these factors at their fingertips. Such knowledge is also very valuable in discussing the results of the tests with a client. Incidentally, age curves are now known for these personality factors, just as for intelligence and other abilities, so that it is possible to project conclusions to some extent into the future. And, of course, it is possible by age corrections to the raw scores, as described in the handbooks.

These questionnaires are very widely applied today in clinical diagnosis, in as-

sessment of causes of school achievement or lack of achievement, and of course in vocational counseling and selection for jobs. It will be argued in Chapter 13 that psychologists should be more frequently using objective tests, i.e., behavioral tests, rather than questionnaires. The arguments for objective tests are that they are not fakable, whereas questionnaires can be faked and can also be sabotaged. Many psychologists have tended to turn a deaf ear to this, even in regard to the use of questionnaires on prison populations, etc., just as people in earthquake areas prefer not to talk about earthquakes. However, while we would argue for objective tests constituting a more shrewd choice in many cases, we would also recognize that recently there have been developments in motivational distortion scales and in trait view theory corrections, which remove a good deal of the risk in using questionnaires. The motivational distortion scales are discussed in Chapter 20, where it is shown that as commonly used (e.g., in the F scales of the MMPI) they are really not adequate in principle. The trait view theory is adequate, but it is more complex and we will leave it to Chapter 20, except to say that the handbooks are now beginning to provide weighting systems that will convert, for any given testing situation, the given raw scores on the factors to more correct underlying scores.

In individual testing with questionnaires it has sometimes been suggested that the questions be read out loud to the subject, especially when there is some question regarding his or her reading ability. This is actually done with the Pre-School Personality Questionnaire.

Personality Questionnaires in Perspective

When teaching a seminar on psychological assessment, I have found it effective to provide students with an initial basic map of the total areas to be covered as a condensed form of the present Chapter 2.

Such a diagram or map puts each area to be treated in overall perspective and facilitates an appreciation of the connectedness of the separate topics. It seems appropriate to begin a chapter such as this with a similar map, and this is shown in Figure 12.2. This, in fact, is to remind the reader of the analysis into L, Q, and T media extensively discussed, in a comparative way, in Chapter 2.

Each of the cubes in the upper part of the figure can be considered to be partitioned into smaller cubes as shown in the lower part of the diagram. Such a model as this not only puts the topic of this chap-

ter into perspective, but also provides a way of defining some of the major issues and problems associated with the measurement of personality by questionnaire. For example, the multitrait-multimethod parameters represented in the lower cube emphasize the need for content validity in assessment by questionnaire, i.e., we need to measure a comprehensive set of traits and view each one in the context of the total profile or configuration.

Of course, in practice, especially when many traits are being measured, the use of many different methods for each trait often becomes infeasible, but even here

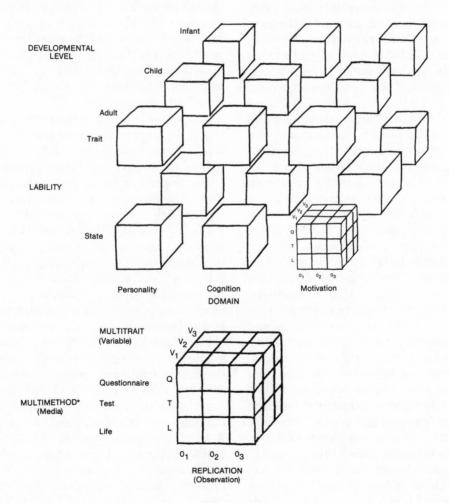

Figure 12.2.

*e.g., traits might be the 16 from the 16 P.F. test

the concept a) underlines the need for a wise choice of method, and b) reminds one of the factor analytic truth that there can exist a media-transcending basic personality factor when pure instrument factors are set aside as such (note one medium— L, Q, or T —may have several instrument factors [see Chapter 2]).

The third dimension of the cube in the lower part of Figure 12.2 is that of replication or the need for multiple measures at different times. This is necessary a) to establish reliability of measurement and b) to provide a check to see whether real changes in traits or states have taken place. This is especially important when the major use of test results is to place people in different educational settings or into different therapy situations. The duty of the test user today is not only to provide a reliable diagnosis but also periodically to check to see if changes have occurred.

Turning to the top portion of Figure 12.2, the "modality" dimension or domain illustrates the need to operationally define personality (and cognition and motivation) and distinguish it from other areas of human behavior. In many ways such distinctions are very artificial (e.g., to what extent is cognitve style a cognitive or personality construct?). But the act of aiming for precise and operational definitions brings in far more benefits than disadvantages. The state-trait distinction illustrated in Figure 12.2 is discussed later in Chapter 16 and in other portions of this book. Suffice it to say here that any comprehensive assessment of personality should not only take into account consistent patterns of behavior over time, i.e., traits, but also labile moods or states that may be induced by specific environmental factors or "ambient situations." The final dimension, that of age in Figure 12.2, has relevance for many aspects of personality measurement by questionnaires. For example, this dimension reminds us a) that since reading levels change with age, different questionnaires will have to be constructed for different age brackets; b)

different sets of behavior will be relevant for the various age groups (e.g., the High School Personality Questionnaire of Cattell et al. has many items related to school behavior which would be inappropriate in the adult level 16 P.F. even though most of the factors tapped by the two tests are identical); and c) there is the possibility that certain personality traits (even though given identical names at different age levels) are qualitatively different and really should be treated as different variables. For example, when we try to assess "anxiety" in a young child, are we really measuring the same kind of dimension that we record at the adult level? One way that is used to check the equivalence of factors across age levels is to give an appropriately aged sample both forms of the questionnaires, say the High School Personality Questionnaire (HSPQ) and the 16 P.F., and factor-analyze the combined data from both instruments.

Of course, the parameters outlined in Figure 12.2 are not the only ones that are relevant to assessment and the measurement of personality in particular. Other important issues include the division of personality questionnaires into those which tap pathological variables or traits (e.g., the MMPI) and those that deal with the "normal" or at least nonpathological sphere of personality, e.g., the 16 P.F. and Central Trait-State Kit (CTS). Yet another important distinction to be made among personality questionnaires is whether or not they have a theoretical background. Eysenck's (EPI) is a good example of a questionnaire with a simple theoretical framework, whereas the more complex MMPI grew out of the clinical experience and intuition of many practitioners, with little if any theory as a guide. A third position is that of the 16 P.F., HSPQ, CAQ, etc. series where the tests were aimed at personality structures definitively located and generating their own theory and where, as Cattell has suggested, the test scales are each a hostage for a personality construct, open to further research checking by psychologists. Related to this is the issue of reasons for the test's construction. The intended use of a test will influence many aspects of its development and the final product. For example, tests intended to be used for group screening will be designed so that they rarely fail to detect the few people who really are in trouble (false positives) although they may falsely identify several people as pathological when, in "reality," they are not that way (false negatives). The rationale here, of course, is that the false negative mistake is the least important since in further and more intensive testing it will be detected and corrected anyway. The false positive mistake amounts to failure to detect a target person and is usually not correctable. However, when the primary use of a test is not merely to diagnose but to identify people as candidates for a radical treatment such as brain surgery, then the priorities are reversed and any test must eliminate the possibility of false negatives, as this would result in people who really did not need a surgical operation getting it anyway.

It is hoped that the brief preceding outline has defined some of the most important issues that must be addressed by any questionnaire that purports to measure personality dimensions. In summary, any such test should attend to the following points:

1) *Multivariate*: The test should tap several of the major personality dimensions to maximize content validity and generalizability.

2) *Multimethod*: The test should be of such a nature as to allow multimethod comparisons with other tests and/or methods. This permits an evaluator to assess relative merits of the various tests under different situations (i.e., evaluation of any method by situation interaction effect).

3) *Replication*: The test should be of such a format to let the user make repeated measurements without the preceding testing interfering with later measures, e.g., equivalent or parallel forms are often useful and sometimes essential.

4) *Age*: Because questionnaires are by their very nature dependent on reading level, forms of the test for different age groups should reflect these reading level discrepancies.

5) *Modality*: In the handbook for the test, "personality" should be operationally defined and distinguished from other areas of human behavior such as cognition and motivation. The relationship between this operational definition of the total personality sphere and the actual variables measured by the test should be specified.

6) *Trait-State*: To do justice to the complexity of personality and in recognition of the fact that situational changes may result in transitory mood (or state) swings, both trait and state measures ideally would be available. (See Chapter 16 for details on measurement of states.)

THE APPROPRIATENESS OF USING QUESTIONNAIRES IN ASSESSING PERSONALITY

Before proceeding to examine in detail specific standards that should be met by personality questionnaires, it is relevant to ask whether it is even appropriate to use such a method of assessment in the realm of personality. An ideal way to answer this question would be to perform a multimedia, multivariable (trait) experiment in which several dimensions of personality were assessed by, say, all three different methods. Assuming that we had some external criterion available, the "best" method of assessment would be the one which produced the score which correlated highest with this criterion. Unfortunately, no such criteria exist (or are agreed on), but some data are available (Cattell & Sweeney, 1964) on a similar design to that mentioned above, in which two different assessment methods (questionnaire vs. objective test) are correlated with each other in two domains: personality and motivation. These researchers found that the correlations between methods were greater in the personality domain and suggest that objective tests are most appropriate in the area of motivation, whereas questionnaires may be satisfactory when we are assessing personality.

The comparative virtues and vices of the three media of personality observation and assessment have been thoroughly examined in Chapter 2. Taking the questionnaire medium as lying within the constraints there analyzed and defined, let us henceforth accept these and put a magnifying glass to the variations and forms that can arise within the Q medium. To begin with, let us consider the effect of varieties of questionnaire form upon the appropriateness of a given questionnaire in measuring personality. The answers to such a question will allow the test user to choose a test and set up such conditions that will maximize the appropriateness of the use of this method. To this end follows a list of some important conditions that should be met to obtain optimizing validity of measurement.

1) Wording of Items

It is often falsely assumed that in order to get a valid picture of a person's personality via a questionnaire, the person being measured must "know" his or her own personality to start with. If the items on the questionnaire refer only to specific and well-defined behaviors (e.g., "how many books have you read during the last year?—a) 0; b) 1 to 10; c) 10 to 20; d) over 20"), then the testee need make no inferences at all about the responses. The wording of items is thus very important and calls for the elimination of vague and ambiguous terms. It is only when items are precisely operationalized that we can con-

sider them as appropriate for personality assessment. As soon as we allow them to include judgments of doubtful validity (e.g., a question like—"Do others consider you very outgoing?"), then the charge that we ask the testee to "know himself" is to a large extent a valid one.

2) Composition of Item Pool

At least in the area of normal or nonpathological personality assessment, the consensus among test designers seems to be to keep to items of a general, noncontroversial nature, avoiding, for example, such areas as religion, sex, and politics. Edwards Personal Preference Scale is an excellent example of this approach, with the author developing his items not only in nonsensitive areas but also making them as neutral as possible in terms of their "social desirability." Another important concern of the pool is that if the test is to be comprehensive of personality factors it shall cover what Cattell has defined as the total "personality sphere," operationally based on all personality descriptive terms in the dictionary.

3) Potential Consequences of Test-taking

If the consequences of taking a personality questionnaire are potentially neutral, then the appropriateness of this method of assessment is probably much higher than when such consequences could be highly negative or positive. When the consequences could be negative, e.g., admission to a mental institution, jail, etc., then there may be a strong motive to fake or otherwise distort responses. Likewise, when the scores on the test could determine some highly desired event, e.g., approval from the therapist, release from jail or institution, etc., then again a strong motive to distort responses could be present. In order to identify and control for these distortions, many tests incorporate lie scales, social desirability estimates, faking good and faking bad scales, scales for detecting random responses and scales that identify several different kinds of response sets, and, on a deeper theoretical basis, the correction by *trait view theory* (Cattell & Krug, 1971). As this last shows, if we simply take out the variance of a "social desirability factor," as Edwards suggests, we also throw away much real information, particularly about the second-order anxiety factor. Trait view corrections (see Chapter 21) show that there is not a *single* "social desirability," but *several* distinct desirabilities according to the test situation. Although it is a little more complicated to use the trait view correction than, say, to try, as Edwards and others have done, to emasculate items of any desirability value, or to correct by an MD (motivational distortion) scale, it is worthwhile to study the process (Chapter 21) if questionnaires are to be brought anywhere near to the objectivity of T-media batteries. However, it is probably better to use a different method of assessment than a questionnaire when one expects in advance that a high degree of distortion may occur due to the nature of the potential consequences for the person taking the test.

Other factors that may influence the degree to which a personality questionnaire is an appropriate instrument in any given situation are a) the *length* of the test (e.g., compare the hundreds of items in the MMPI with the few on Eysenck's EPI); b) the face validity of items (often some items are so annoying, e.g., "this morning my heart was beating" that the whole questionnaire suffers a credibility decrease and a subsequent loss in validity); c) the format of responses, i.e., yes/no forced choice or a *scale* of possible responses ranging from, say, "strongly agree" to "strongly disagree." However, these last three points do not directly deal with the question of when *personality* questionnaires are appropriate instruments to use, but rather concern themselves with the validity of questionnaires in general.

STANDARDS FOR USE OF QUESTIONNAIRES IN PERSONALITY ASSESSMENT

Standards for Factor Analytic Structure

Cattell (1974a) has outlined several general principles that may be used to evaluate the adequacy of modern personality questionnaires. The reader is referred to the original source for details, but it is appropriate here to review these principles (and others), since in the subsequent sections of this chapter we will be examining several specific personality questionnaires and need some guidelines suggesting criteria for evaluation.

Cattell (1974b) noted that the data from Buros's *Mental Measurements Yearbook* showed that in the area of personality assessment by questionnaire, the trend has been towards more instruments based on factor analytical principles (i.e., a structural approach). However, when these factor analyses were examined, the conclusion was made that although quantitative increases had occurred on the number of such instruments, quality (of analyses) had suffered. Cattell identified three issues which need to be taken into account before any evaluation of a specific test can be made. The first issue we have dealt with already: that of appropriateness of the questionnaire in the domain of personality. The second issue he considered was evidence for unitary structure of dimensions, and the third, the vulnerability of the test to distortion and faking.

In order to demonstrate convincingly that a given questionnaire exhibits unitary structure, at least eight conditions must be met in the analysis. By identifying and describing these conditions, Cattell hoped that even a psychologist with relatively little knowledge of multivariate analytical techniques would be in a position to make an evaluation of any personality questionnaire (at least regarding its factor structure). The eight conditions are summarized below:

1) There should be at least three times the number of variables in the analysis as there are number of expected factors.
2) The total number of S's (N) should be at least three times the number of variables and preferably never be less than 200.
3) In order to determine how many factors to extract, some relatively objective test like the Scree test or Kaiser-Guttman unitary rule be applied.
4) Unities should never be used in the diagonal of the correlation matrix; generate communalities instead.
5) Use an oblique, rotational solution and hand rotate after the use of a "canned" program.
6) Use some test for simple structure, e.g., Bargmann.
7) Check structure constancy over several researches, by calculating congruency coefficients for each factor.
8) Examine and report the correlations among the resulting factors.

DeYoung (1972) also realized that adequate standards were necessary to make decisions regarding the quality of any factor analytic structure. He identified three areas in which many questionnaire structure studies show deficits: a) decisions regarding the number of factors to be extracted (like Cattell, DeYoung favors using the Kaiser-Guttman unitary rule and/or the Scree test); b) choice of communality estimates; and c) rotation to simple structure. DeYoung took a study (Howarth & Browne, 1971) which purported to show that the structure of the 16 P.F. was not sound, and illustrated how the above three principles had been violated. In this case, DeYoung considered the result of these violations to be so great as to make the Howarth and Browne conclusion to be totally invalid. Kameoka (in preparation) has also examined, by Bargmann's significance test, the satisfactoriness of simple structure rotation in several prominent questionnaire factorings and found at least 60% to be far from the unique position. The average user and the average reviewer have little time or technical equipment to evaluate the factor completeness and the factor trueness of scales aiming at source traits (see also evidence in Cattell, 1973c), with the result that many conclusions in applied work about the relations of factors to criteria are quite unsound. A mistake as to the number of factors in the domain (as in Eysenck's item pool, which undoubtedly has at least 10 to 12 rather than three factors, and which actually gives, in this case, a coarse approach to second-order factors of extraversion, anxiety, etc.) also leads to erratic conceptions of criterion relations.

Standards for Reliability and Validity

The issues of consistency and validity are so comprehensively dealt with in Chapter 3 that we need here only to summarize in Table 12.2 and then proceed to its bearing on questionnaires. Incidentally, Chapter 2 emphasizes that one should be aware of two systems that do not entirely agree as to concepts and nomenclature—the more analytic and new concepts of researchers (such as Cronbach, Cattell, Gorsuch, Horn, Lord, Nesselroade, and Tatsuoka) on the one hand, and arbitrary, traditional listing of older definitions by APA committees on the other. The present writer believes the newer concepts of Chapter 3 are logically and psychometrically more penetrating and effective in the domain of structurally oriented testing, but will bridge from one to the other where it is called for in explanation.

As to consistency, which includes reliability, several different forms are needed as summarized in the upper part of Table 12.2.

When a proper distinction is drawn, as in the new analysis in Table 12.2, between the dependability and homogeneity forms of consistency, we nevertheless find a dif-

TABLE 12.2
Types of Reliability

Type	Name of Coefficient
1) Test-retest (time interval very small)	Dependability
2) Test-retest (time inverval > 1 month)	Stability
3) Agreement of items with each other in any given scale or subtest	Homogeneity
4) Agreement of one form of a test with another form of same test	Equivalence
5) Consistency when applied to different populations	Transferability

Types of Validity

1) Correlation of the scale with concrete performances	Concrete validity
2) Correlation of scale with the factor	(Direct) Concept validity
3) Correlation of the scale with a sample of psychological variables already known to be highly correlated with the conceptual criteria	Indirect Concept validity (or Circumstantial validity)

ference in conceiving the desirability of the latter. This persists between the "older" tradition which advocates a high degree of correlation among all items within any one scale and the functional testing position which argues that the optimum homogeneity is not the highest possible value. The structuralist argues that high homogeneity could be achieved merely by slightly rewriting the same items many different ways and that even low overall homogeneity may be satisfactory as long as each item correlates well with the factor it is supposed to load on. This point is not a minor issue, since reviewers of tests often naively point to low homogeneity coefficients as evidence of low overall reliability, and the reader who feels unclear on this should study Chapter 3.

Let us now look at some specific personality questionnaires and consider them in the light of the criteria outlined above.

AN OVERVIEW OF MAJOR QUESTIONNAIRES CONCERNED PRIMARILY WITH THE DOMAIN OF THE NORMAL PERSONALITY

A glance at the index or table of contents of any edition of Buros's *Mental Measurements Yearbook* (*the* classic reference text for reviews of psychological tests) shows that by far the greatest coverage is given to questionnaire-type tests of personality. There are now well over 200 such tests published and more available in "experimental" editions. Obviously, in a chapter such as this we cannot think in terms of presenting a comprehensive review, even in a brief format. Instead we will look at the four tests most frequently used in current testing practices. Fortunately, the *Mental Measurements Yearbook* provides us with a clue to the identity of which tests are the most used, since it provides a list of the number of references per test. No direct data on relative magnitude of test usage being available, one might be inclined to assume that the most researched tests are the ones that are most used. This is only a rough and sometimes misleading guide, for there are tests that are coming and tests that are going and the latter are often far more in use by practitioners qualified 10 or 20 years ago, i.e., by most in practice. Accepting this assumption, then the most frequently used tests are 1) the *Minnesota Multiphasic Personality Inventory* (MMPI); 2) the *Edwards Personal Preference Scale* (EPPS); 3) the *California Personality Inventory* (CPI); 4) the *Sixteen Personality Factor Questionnaire* (16 P.F.); and 5) the *Clinical Analysis Questionnaire* (CAQ) and its associated age series (HSPQ, CPQ, ESPQ).

Of these five questionnaires, the CAQ and the MMPI are the only ones that explicitly set out to include pathological personality dimensions. The two, however, are quite different in purpose and design construction from the other three. They are quite different in the principles by which the scale items are selected, the former using factor analysis, the latter a mixed psychometric procedure (not a true discriminant function aimed to separate types).

The Edwards Personal Preference Scale (EPPS) and the Edwards Personality Inventory (EPI)

The EPPS. For an evaluation of the EPPS, the reviews in Buros's *Mental Measurements Yearbook* will be relied on heavily, especially those in the seventh edition (Buros, 1972). The EPPS has by far the most references of any personality questionnaire limited to nonpathological dimensions. Edwards has relatively recently changed the format of the EPPS and constructed a new questionnaire that he calls the Edwards Personality Inven-

tory or the EPI (not to be confused with the Eysenck Personality Inventory!). In fairness to these changes, the EPI will also be briefly considered in this section too.

The EPPS was originally designed to measure 15 "manifest needs," based on the need system theory of Henry Murray. The 15 scales are: achievement, deference, order, exhibition, autonomy, affiliation, intraception, succorance, dominance, abasement, nurturance, change, endurance, heterosexuality, and aggression. The questionnaire was designed for college-age and older adults and takes 40 to 55 minutes to complete. This author argues that the questionnaire medium is unsuitable for validly measuring motivation, compared to *objective tests* (T-data) in the MAT and TAT, and that in any case the clinical-subjective-etymological list of "needs" by Murray has been superseded since the mid-fifties by factor analytically reached ergic patterns, very clear in simple structure. The first part of the argument is relative. In personality most items are intended to describe behavior, whereas in motivation the individual is probably less willing to admit (and frequently does not know) his or her motives. But as the objective test enthusiast will insist, even behavior descriptions are liable to faking. Both Edwards's and Jackson's questionnaires were nevertheless aimed at Murray's need test, though, as stated below, Edwards later dropped this reference to origins.

The first reviewer in Buros (1972, pp. 148-149), Heilbrun, reminds the reader that earlier reviews in 1954 had found the EPPS lacking in validity data and claims that this problem has not been remedied. On the positive side, he compliments the test on the comprehensive set of variables covered and on the satisfactory scale reliabilities, but in conclusion fails to recommend use of the test because of "scanty evidence of validity."

The second reviewer (Buros, 1972, pp. 149-151), McKee, is much more negative and seems to feel that the major worth of the test lies in stimulating discussions in counseling sessions (one of the suggested uses in the test manual). McKee even considers that Edwards's goal of achieving control of "social desirability" (by pairing items of equal social desirability) was not met, since "it has been demonstrated that response to the EPPS can be consciously faked in order to create a particular impression." McKee goes even further in suggesting that even if "social desirability" were controlled, the question of whether or not it is desirable to do so is still not answered. This sentiment seems to be shared by Cattell, who prefers to treat "social desirability" as a useful trait construct rather than "controlling" for it. In conclusion, McKee finds "instruments which have been developed with an emphasis on validity, such as the CPI, more useful in measuring personality characteristics of normally functioning individuals."

From these reviews and earlier ones, it would seem that the EPPS is seen in a positive light with respect to the comprehensiveness and meaning of the scales (content validity) and also in terms of scale reliability, but the consensus is that the test does not offer enough evidence of concrete and construct validity.

The EPI. In constructing the EPI, Edwards no longer used the Murray need system classification and also abandoned the "forced-choice, matched social desirability" format of the EPPS. Instead, items of "neutral" social desirability were chosen and the instructions were changed from the usual self-report format to one in which the person is asked "to predict how people who know you well would mark each statement if they were asked to describe you." A true-false response option is given. The test is designed for 11th graders to adults and consists of 53 scales. The scales are divided among four booklets that each take about 45 minutes to complete. For the sake of space, not all the scales are listed below, but enough from

each booklet to give the reader a sense of the scope of the dimensions involved.

Booklet #1: Plans and organizes things, intellectually oriented, persistent, self-confident, has cultural interests, carefree, conforms, is a leader, kind to others, seeks new experiences, likes to be alone.

Booklet #2: Anxious about performance, avoids facing problems, is a perfectionist, absent-minded, sensitive to criticism, likes a set routine, wants sympathy, avoids arguments, conceals feelings, easily influenced, feels misunderstood.

Booklet #3: Motivated to succeed, impressed by status, desires recognition, cooperative, competitive, articulate, logical, self-centered, makes friends easily.

Booklet #4: Self-critical, critical of others, active, talks about self, becomes angry, helps others, considerate, dependent, shy, virtuous.

Goldberg (1972b) reviewed the EPI in great detail and found little to commend. Specifically, major criticisms centered around a) the standardization sample (size and composition "clearly inadequate"); b) validity ("no section whatever in the manual"); c) test-retest data (none); d) no correlations of scales with other tests. In fact, the only data that Goldberg found satisfactory were the homogeneity coefficients, which for most scales were moderate to high. Goldberg also criticized Edwards for changing the format from the standard self-report method with no empirical evidence that it would improve validity and for ignoring the possibility of response set bias (15 scales have *all* the items keyed for the "true" response). Three other reviewers of the EPI, Norman (1972), Bouchard (1969), and Kleinmuntz (1970), all agree with Goldberg on many points, especially on the lack of validity and test-retest data, but differ from him in taking a more optimistic view of the future of the test when there are more data in concerning norms and validity. All reviewers agree that without such data the test should *only* be considered for research use and the test materials labeled accordingly.

The California Personality Inventory (CPI)

The CPI was designed by Gough for an age level of 13 years through adulthood and provides 18 scale scores taking a total of approximately one hour to administer. A reference list of around 1,000 published reports indicates the extensive usage of this test. The personality dimensions measured are as follows: dominance, capacity for status, sociability, social presence, self-acceptance, sense of well-being, responsibility, socialization, self-control, tolerance, good impression, communality, achievement via conformance, achievement via independence, intellectual efficiency, psychological-mindedness, flexibility and femininity.

In reviewing the CPI in the *Seventh Mental Measurements Yearbook,* Goldberg (1972b, pp. 94-96) starts by reminding the reader that the past three major reviews differed widely in their conclusions (E. Lowell Kelly, very positive; L. J. Cronbach, still waiting for more validity data; R. L. Thorndike, negative). Goldberg proceeded by trying to show why the previous reviewers could not agree. In summary, Goldberg found that the test manual provided excellent validity data and did not agree that it should be faulted for "redundancy" among subtests, since by the nature of the dimensions some scales would be expected to correlate moderately highly with each other (e.g., dominance and sociability). However, Goldberg did identify three weaknesses in the manual. He felt a) that there should be more duplicate items so that reliability checks within scales could be made; b) that there was too much encouragement for the tester to make interpretations of total profiles in spite of the lack of research on the subject; and c) that Gough should provide the user with a detailed description of his test construction procedure.

Walsh (Buros, 1972, pp. 96-97) also reviewed the CPI and concluded that it should not be recommended except for "the most purely empirical purposes." Walsh's major criticism was the criterion-oriented method of test construction which he felt limited considerably the psychological meaningfulness of the scales. He did feel that the normative base was large and varied (over 6,000 men and 7,000 women, spanning many occupations), but finally concluded that "either the 16 P.F. or the EPPS would probably serve as well as the CPI in most prediction situations, and, in addition, the scales of the former inventories possess the advantage of greater generality and clearer psychological meaning." Walsh also raised the issue of the relatively high correlation of about one-third of the CPI scales with the MMPI scales and suggested that this might be due to some kind of common response set influence. However, these high correlations among the scales on the MMPI and CPI should not be surprising since over 200 CPI items were either taken directly from the MMPI pool of items or slightly changed before being incorporated into the final form. Walsh also was not impressed by the magnitude of the test-retest reliabilities for nonincarcerated groups (range from .55 to .75). In the latest review of the CPI (Buros, 1978), Gynther echoed many of the comments of earlier reviewers and found still no evidence to support the clinical interpretations of the CPI profiles and he ended his review with a plea that more multiple regression studies not be undertaken.

The Sixteen Personality Factor Questionnaire (16 P.F.) Considered in Evaluations Over the Past Decade

The 16 P.F. will be considered in two stages: first, here briefly in historical perspective, as with other scales, and second, in the next section in more purely psychological analysis of its traits, in the setting of a whole family of scales (16 P.F., HSPQ, CAQ, etc.) and in terms of setting up flexible combinations of scales for first and second order, state and trait, older and younger versions, etc.

The 16 P.F. was designed for adults and will be so here reviewed. First it has the character of having decidedly more than the number of equivalent forms usually available. Some are in transition. The test takes approximately 50 minutes to complete and covers 16 dimensions of personality. The factors are labeled using two levels of nomenclature, the popular and the professional. In the following list, the professional name is shown in parentheses and just the high scoring end of the scale named:

1) Outgoing (affectothymia);
2) Bright, intelligent (crystallized power measure of intelligence);
3) Emotionally stable (high ego strength);
4) Assertive (dominance);
5) Happy-go-lucky (surgency);
6) Conscientious (superego strength);
7) Venturesome (parmia);
8) Tender-minded (premsia);
9) Suspicious (protention);
10) Imaginative (autia);
11) Astute (shrewdness);
12) Apprehensive (guilt proneness);
13) Experimenting (radicalism);
14) Group independent (self-sufficiency);
15) Controlled (high strength of self-sentiment);
16) Tense (high ergic tension).

Bouchard (1972), who also reviewed the EPI (see above), has examined the 16 P.F. in depth. He disagrees that the factors measured are unique or nonarbitrary "source" traits, as compared to surface traits measured by other tests. He claims that he knows of no arbitrary scales, since all tests are either constructed from a theoretical base or made specifically to tap

relevant variables inherent in the situation in which the test is to be used (e.g., The Strong Vocational Interest Blank). This criticism seems to stem from semantic problems rather than any fundamental theoretical or methodological disagreement. Bouchard praises the 1970 handbook as "an outstanding accomplishment" and suggests that it should serve as a model for other test designers. In particular, Bouchard considers the following to be very positive attributes of the 16 P.F.:

1) the extensive discussion of test construction practices;
2) the large number of statistical aids described for and made accessible to the user;
3) the psychometric properties of the scales;
4) the discussion of the problems and complexities of standardization;
5) the descriptions of the meaning of first- and second-order factors; and
6) the criterion evidence.

This is not to say that Bouchard recommends use of the 16 P.F. without reservation. He does find important deficiencies in the handbook (see below), but these problems are not seen as insurmountable and could relatively easily be incorporated into the next edition of the handbook.

The first negative criticism concerns the fact that, although the *Standards for Educational and Psychological Tests and Manuals* considers it "very desirable" for all test manuals to include a section on the correlations of the test with other tests, the 16 P.F. manual does not contain such data. This would-be valid criticism is actually very ill-informed, since quite systematic tables, with transformation weights from one to the other, have been published for relating the 16 P.F. to the MMPI, Eysenck's EPI, etc. (for example, see Delhees & Cattell, 1970; Cattell & Bolton, 1969).

When considering the topic of validity, Bouchard reminds the reader that there are four forms of the 16 P.F. (A, B, C, and D), as well as old and revised editions. Thus, when examining the validity data, care must be taken to see that it applies to the particular form and edition in question. Again, this criticism has been answered by the acquisition of much more validity data since 1972, the date of the review. In the most recent edition of Buros's *The Eighth Mental Measurements Yearbook* (1978) over 1500 references are given for the 16 P.F., and reviews are mixed. For example, Bloxom, like the authors themselves (Cattell, Eber, & Tatsuoka, 1970), recommends that single forms of the 16 P.F. should not be used, but only either forms A and B together (for shorter use) or C and D together. The scales in any single form (around 10 items) are obviously not long enough (three to four minutes compared to 40 minutes for an intelligence test). Thus the reliabilities will reach .45 to .93 and .67 to .86 respectively. Bolton, on the other hand, although noting that the manual should be revised, concluded that overall for the 16 P.F. "scientific foundation is *at least* as solid as that of its major competitors." Bolton also emphasized the large amount of substantial support for the second-order factors, and the replication in different countries and at different ages of the primary factors.

The fact remains that the 16 P.F. is the only questionnaire 1) factored to meaningful simple structure source traits; 2) permitting scoring also of six second-order factors; 3) demonstrated to have the same factor structure in its translations and standardizations in other cultures: England, Germany, France, Japan, India, Venezuela, and Brazil; 4) linking up developmentally with questionnaires at other ages, e.g., with the same factors in the HSPQ, CPQ, ESPQ, etc.; and 5) with criterion relations on all clinical symptom categories, and on more than 40 occupations. It also has behavioral equations that bring it into the mainstream of personality theory. These clinical interpretations are discussed fully in Chapter 18, while the industrial uses and insights are given by Dr. Noty in Chapter 19.

What conclusions can be drawn on comparisons after reading the reviews of the EPPS, CPI, and 16 P.F.? Leaving aside the details of criticism, it would seem that the major characteristics of any good test fall into two broad categories: internal properties and external properties. By internal properties are meant *definition* characteristics such as origin of items, method of construction, format of items, factor analytic structure, itemetrics or psychometric properties of test, and psychological meaning of scales. External properties have to do with the applied or potential use of the test and include especially concrete validity and the relationships between the test scales and those of other tests. Using this loose dichotomy, when we look at the relative merits and problems of the EPPS, CPI, and 16 P.F., it can be seen that the faults of the EPPS appear to be mainly in the external properties area, since the major criticisms centered around a lack of criterion validity evidence. The CPI, on the other hand, was found to be rich in external validity data but lacking in several internal properties such as psychological meaning of scales, poor test-retest reliabilities, and possible response set bias. The 16 P.F., although by no means judged a perfect instrument, was found to at least be satisfactory in most of the internal *and* external properties. It is on the basis of this more even balance between strengths in internal and external characteristics that this test and its derivative, the Central Trait-State Kit, will be examined in detail in the following section.

FACTORED TESTS FOR FLEXIBLE NORMAL AND ABNORMAL, PRIMARY AND SECONDARY TRAITS, AND YOUNGER AND OLDER SUBJECT USE

In considering the overall utility of a test (see Chapter 3 on the utility coefficient), one asks such questions as:

1) Is it linked to established unitary traits that are meaningful in personality theory and the prediction of everyday life criteria, with age curves, knowledge of degrees of heredity involved, knowledge of origins in the family experience and susceptibility to clinical change, etc.?
2) Is it useful for both normal and pathological insight?
3) Will it yield both primary and secondary traits?

The utility of the 16 P.F. itself, which we shall first discuss in more detail, is that it is actually a *family* of tests: the 16 P.F. for adults, the High School Personality Questionnaire (HSPQ) for ages 12 to 18, the Child Personality Questionnaire (CPQ) for ages eight to 12, the ESPQ for ages six to eight, and (still under research) the orally administered Pre-School Personality Questionnaire (PSPQ) by Dreger. The objective has been to deal (through the whole age range) with the same personality structures, which in most cases have been shown to persist in general form factorially, though with some changing expressions and changes of variance. This family of tests has its value in terms of a) developmental research on personality origins; b) conceptual insights into what the source traits mean; and c) prediction of criteria over spans in time.

The *Clinical Analysis Questionnaire* (the CAQ) is virtually unique as regards 2) and 3), and the 16 P.F. as regards 1) and 2). The ability to get both primary and secondary traits is the basis of *depth psychometry* (Cattell, 1973c; Karoly & Steffens, 1980, p. 163; Chapter 16, this volume), and the coverage simultaneously of normal and abnormal (disease process) dimensions is indispensable to the clinician who needs to know the "prepathological" or prepsychotic personality structure. As described under the CAQ, it covers the 16 normal factors (and sec-

ondaries) of the 16 P.F. (in shorter form), followed by the 12 pathological factors found in a comprehensive pool of MMPI, depression, and other single clinical questionnaires.

Another test construction that has value in terms of adding flexibility to the tool kit is the *Central Trait-State Kit* (CTS). In the early days of Q-data scales, psychologists became accustomed to working with some three to six scales for personality (Eysenck's three, Flanagan's four, Vernon's Boyd scale four, the six Spranger types of the Allport-Vernon, and Bernnenter's six personality factors). The early work was, of course, not very true factor analytically, and often quite subjective in concepts, but the practitioner's handling assessment on three or four factors became entrenched, delaying recognition that the natural complexity of personality really called for some 15 to 20 or more primary scales.

There *is*, however, a way to satisfy both the need for relatively short and simple scales, on the one hand, and the requirements of functional testing on the other. It is to operate with second-order factors—secondaries as they may be called. As many as nine or ten of these are now located and made measurable (Cattell, 1973a), but if we stay with really large variance factors we can cut down to six. It can readily be shown that these secondaries are bound to predict less of any typical real-life criterion than, say, the 16 primaries of the 16 P.F. or the 24 factors in the CAQ; but it is realistic to recognize that there are testing situations so cramped by time demands that accuracy must be sacrificed for brevity. The CTS meets the need for flexibility here by being restricted to six secondaries, which in this case have been thoroughly factorially fixed. Further, as a *kit*, it is, unlike an omnibus test, constructed so that single factors—one, two or more—can be pulled out and used alone, e.g., an exvia-invia or an anxiety scale. Further, it belongs in the category of multi-useful tests in that it measures both *states* and *traits* (see below and Chapter 14). The above three tests will now be considered in the next two sections: the 16 P.F. in the first and the CTS and CAQ in the second.

A FAMILY OF PRIMARY-SECONDARY SCALES ILLUSTRATED BY THE 16 P.F., HSPQ, ETC.

We consider here a set of scales in the normal behavior domain which, as indicated above 1) are shaped to the primary personality factors in Q-data as established over a wide developmental age range; 2) have been replicated across several countries; and 3) first give scores for primaries but have easily applicable weighting systems that give scores on secondaries too (the same as are in the CTS). Because the HSPQ and CPQ deal with the same factors as the 16 P.F., we shall concentrate on the latter and only briefly describe the other members of this "family."

A very complete source for a detailed description of this test (basis, criterion profiles, age changes, etc.) is the handbook for the 16 P.F. (Cattell, Eber, & Tatsuoka, 1970). The test consists of 187 items which load on 16 primary factors (labels mentioned in previous section). These 16 factors or source traits are intercorrelated and, when they are factored, result in six second-order dimensions. These are exvia (extraversion), anxiety, cortertia, independence, superego, and intelligence. Thus, a total of 22 scores is available from the test (actually, eight second-order factors have been extracted but only six of these seem stable enough to warrant anything but experimental use). It is of interest to note that at the second-order level all the dimensions involved have been found to be very useful theoretical and empirical constructs by many psychologists of widely different background. The usefulness of the concepts of anxiety and extraversion, for example, hardly needs to be mentioned, as they are so ubiquitous in psy-

chological research, theory, and practice. "Cortertia," on the other hand (indicating a theory of levels of "cortical alertness"), is newer but has been shown to have powerful predictive power in neurosis (see Chapter 16), in air pilot selection, etc. Data on personality correlates of left and right cerebral hemisphere dominance suggest that such a construct is most useful in categorizing right and left brain associated behavior, and Pawlik and Cattell (1965) have shown significant Q III (Cortertia) relations to brain wave pattern. Thus, left brain activity seems most concerned with logical thinking (i.e., high cortertia or pure cognition), whereas the right side seems to deal with more intuitive processes (i.e., low cortertia or acting from the "heart" or from emotional origins).

Table 12.3 below shows the 16 bipolar primary factors in more detail than discussed previously and Table 12.4 shows how these primary factors combine to form the secondary factors mentioned above. (For even more detailed data on the relative loadings for each of the primaries on the secondaries, the interested reader is referred to page 121 of the 16 P.F. Handbook.)

Scale reliabilities (dependability coefficients), stability coefficients, equivalence coefficients, direct and indirect validities of the full 16 P.F. and some combined forms may all be obtained from the 1970 16 P.F. Handbook. There is also available from the same source a mine of data on regression coefficients to predict a wide variety of criteria such as achievement, accident proneness, leadership, etc.

USE OF THE CTS KIT AND A COMPREHENSIVE QUESTIONNAIRE FOR CLINICAL DIAGNOSIS: THE CAQ

The Central Trait-State Kit: CTS

Until recently, the 16 P.F. user who wished to measure only those dimensions tapped by the second-order factors had no

TABLE 12.3
The 16 Bipolar Primary Factors of the 16 P.F.

Factor	Low Score Description	High Score Description
A	Reserved, detached, aloof	Outgoing, warm-hearted, easy-going
B	Low intelligence, dull	High intelligence, bright
C	Emotionally less stable	Emotionally stable
E	Humble, mild	Assertive, aggressive
F	Sober, serious	Happy-go-lucky, enthusiastic
G	Expedient, disregards rules	Conscientious, moralistic
H	Shy, timid	Venturesome, socially bold
I	Tough-minded, realistic	Tender-minded
L	Trusting	Suspicious
M	Practical	Imaginative
N	Artless, forthright	Shrewd, socially aware
O	Self-assured	Apprehensive
Q_1	Conservative	Experimenting
Q_2	Group dependent	Self-sufficient
Q_3	Undisciplined	Controlled
Q_4	Relaxed	Tense

TABLE 12.4
Second-Order Factors in the 16 P.F.

Factor	Title	Chief Primary Factors Involved
Q I	Exvia	$A+, E+, F+, H+, Q_2-$
Q II	Anxiety	$C-, H-, L+, O+, Q_3-, Q_4+$
Q III	Cortertia	$A-, M-, I-$
Q IV	Independence	$E+, L+, M+, Q_1+, Q_2+$
Q V	Naturalness	$N+$
Q VI	Cool realism	$I+, M+, L+$
Q VII	Intelligence	$B+$
Q VIII	Superego	$G+, Q_3+, F-$

alternative but to give the whole 16 P.F., calculate the primary factor scale scores, and then combine these into second-order scores. Also, since this is an omnibus-type of test (factor items intermixed), this result could be achieved only by giving the whole test of 187 items, whereas the CTS, being in kit form, allows single scales to be lifted out. The Central Trait-State Kit ("central" since it measures only second-order factors) provides the user with five second-order scores on anxiety, extraversion, cortertia, independence, and superego (conscientiousness). Also, it gives both a trait score (founded on an individual difference, R-technique basis) and a trait score (founded on dR-technique—occasion-to-occasion factoring). In addition, two parallel forms are available for each subtest and all forms are printed on a single sheet, which allows the user to be very selective in the choice of variables. For example, if state and trait anxiety is of interest and the experimental design calls for a short-term retest, the researcher or practitioner could use forms A of the state and trait anxiety scale on the first testing and forms B of state and trait anxiety on the second. This option of selectivity not only cuts down on testing time but also increases internal validity of design, since the person tested will be asked to spend only a relatively short time on relevant items.

The "state" scales for the CTS are described in some detail in Chapter 15. It should be mentioned at the outset that the CTS is still in experimental edition form, although the items in the "traits" were taken directly from the 16 P.F. scales. However, initial data on test-retest reliability and factor structure are strong enough to offer the test in an experimental version. Since there are five dimensions covered (it was felt that the "intelligence" factor is adequately dealt with by other tests and probably would show a minimum of state variance), equivalent forms of each test (A or B), and both trait and state versions, the resulting CTS Kit contains no less than *20* subtests. A kit of 20 independently usable subtests provides an enormous variety of combinations and permutations for the test user, but confronts the test designer with many problems in demonstrating overall factor structure, test-retest reliability over time and forms of test, etc., since it is simply not feasible to give all the subtests at any one time. Indeed, with the "state" subtests, even though the testing time is only 50 minutes for all the ten subtests involved, the very fact that they tap "state" variables precludes allowing them to be given together, since they would be expected to interact with each other during the testing session. Consequently, a scheme for the collection of reliability and validity data has been devised, which calls for the administration of several (but not all) subtests at one time and for test-retest data to be acquired separately for each subtest. P-technique and chain P-technique factor analyses have also been planned to examine the structure of the state subtests over time.

What the test measures. The trait scales are identical to the five most stable second-order factors of the 16 P.F., and the state scales (see Chapter 15) are designed to reflect changes in the same factors that may be caused by different environmental or organic situations. Thus, for example,

the trait anxiety scale assesses the usual or average anxiety level of an individual, whereas the state anxiety scale reflects more the mood of the moment, which in turn tends to be influenced by environmental effects (or "ambient" situations using Cattell's terminology). The dimensions are as follows:

1) Extraversion Trait (form A or B)
2) Extraversion State (form A or B)
3) Anxiety Trait (form A or B)
4) Anxiety State (form A or B)
5) Cortertia Trait (form A or B)
6) Cortertia State (form A or B)
7) Independence Trait (form A or B)
8) Independence State (form A or B)
9) Superego Trait (form A or B) (Conscientiousness)
10) Superego State (form A or B) (Conscientiousness)

Each subtest consists of 25 items, is on a single test sheet, and takes about five minutes to administer.

Format of the subtests. The 25 items on each subtest are in the form of self-statements to which the person completing the test must indicate a degree of agreement. A six-point scale of responses is provided ranging from "strongly agree" to "strongly disagree." Items are so written that for half of them a "strongly agree" answer indicates a high score on the factor in question. For the rest of the items a "strongly disagree" response results in a high score. In this way acquiescence response bias is minimized. An example showing the first three items on the trait version of the anxiety subtest (form A) is shown on the following page.

Administrative details, etc. Instructions and other administrative details are given in Chapter 15 but a summary of the major properties and uses of the test are given in Table 12.5.

In summary, the CTS Kit provides the user with a tool to obtain scores on five

FORM A   I.D.# _____
                ASA:1

DIRECTIONS: Please read each item carefully. Then place a check (√) under the column which best reflects
             HOW YOU ARE FEELING RIGHT NOW, IN YOUR PRESENT MOOD.

	Strongly AGREE	Agree	Slightly Agree	Slightly Disagree	Disagree	Strongly DISAGREE
1. In my present mood I feel like doing something shocking just for the fun of it.						
2. I'd describe myself as happy and content today.						
3. All of my usual fears seem even more exaggerated today.						

TABLE 12.5
Summary of Uses and Properties of the CTS Trait Scales

Variables measured:	Anxiety, Extraversion, Cortertia, Independence, Superego (Conscientiousness)
Equivalent forms?	Yes. A-B
Reading level:	General newspaper reading public.
Intended populations:	Adults of "normal" psychological functioning.
Administration time:	Five minutes or less per subtest.
Scoring:	Overlays: one to two minutes to calculate score.
Uses:	Research, Education, Drug Studies, Program Evaluation, Clinical, Vocational Placement, etc.

major personality dimensions recognized to be important by many psychologists. These dimensions have both a strong scientific base and demonstrated predictive power for many criteria. However, the CTS Kit is not a substitute for the 16 P.F.; rather, it is a complement to it and fills a long unmet consumer need.

The Clinical Analysis Questionnaire, CAQ

The difference between the two now most commonly used instruments for clinical diagnosis by questionnaire—the MMPI and the CAQ—is that the former was constructed to separate *types*, such as the DSM recognizes, and the latter to measure underlying source traits, some of them the same in both normals and abnormals. This has considerable "philosophical" importance—it is the antithesis in Aristo- telian versus Galilean taxonomies and analyses—and is also distinct psychometrically. The CAQ can and does permit type classifications, but it does so through first getting profiles on the functionally unitary traits and then classifying by similarities of profiles.

As regards breadth of coverage, the CAQ, which is the later instrument, is more comprehensive. The MMPI 14 scales have repeatedly been factored to show actually five dimensions (Cattell, 1946). The CAQ, taking the MMPI domain and adding other pathological items, factors in its pathologies part to eight. However, it is designed to have a brief test included for the same normal factors as in the 16 P.F., so that it actually has 16 + 8 = 24 dimensions. Incidentally, the overlap in factor space of the MMPI and CAQ is considerable, and so it is possible mutually to translate by tables (Cattell & Bolton, 1969) to an appreciable degree (except for the new space in the CAQ) much as has been done in mutual translation of the 16 P.F. (oblique) and the Guilford-Zimmerman (orthogonal) scale scores. Some differences will also appear through the CAQ being factored on populations stretching from normal through abnormal, whereas the MMPI arose psychometrically by application to pathologies only.

SUMMARY

Questionnaires can only be properly appraised if they are first kept in the perspective of the properties of the three media of assessment—L, Q, and T—as examined in Chapter 2. Thus their measures are subject to distortion of perception, like L and unlike T; belong to a test situation, like T and unlike L; and are couched in real-life behavior, like L and unlike T.

Probably because of the last—common setting—the L and Q personality factors deal with the same source traits, whereas the relation to T-traits is only partially understood—as second-orders in Q tending to match first orders in T. Because of the instrument factors in all three media, but especially L and Q, it is ideally desirable to assess through all, thus hopefully reaching a media-transcending, instrument factor-balanced real personality trait. This has recently become more practicable with the birth of the T-data O-A Battery (Chapter 11).

Among questionnaires themselves many varieties of design exist—multiple choice, forced choice, etc., as well as varieties of administration and scoring. However, on the whole, questionnaires are all susceptible to the same itemetric rules, e.g., of lawful increase of reliability with number of items, effect of private or public review of answers, speed of administration, instruction to guess, number of alternatives, etc.

Perhaps half of the questionnaires in use today linger from an earlier tradition of relatively subjective choice of traits (or of factoring carried out *after* the original layout) and half truly belong to functional testing, being based on prior determination of personality structure. Both are in use and are given description here. In some cases, where they share to an appreciable degree the same space, scales in one can be estimated by multiple regressions from the other, as between the 16 P.F. and the MMPI; and the Guilford-Zimmerman and the 16 P.F. The future almost certainly lies with the structure-related scales for reasons of integration with personality theory.

Unless factor analysis is used in a technically adequate way, e.g., with careful simple structure or cofactor rotation, and with *scientifically* sophisticated strategies, e.g., checks on R- by dR-technique and manipulative experiment, it has no guarantee of real structural meaningfulness. Six conditions for structured questionnaire construction are given. One involves a conflict between an older psychometric view that the homogeneity coefficient should be as high as possible, and the functional view that it should not pass an optimal moderate value, which is calculable.

Differences in construction principles found among presently available tests may be illustrated by these facts: a) the Edwards and the Guilford-Zimmerman scales use orthogonal factoring; the 16 P.F., HSPQ, and Thurstone and Comrey scales have aimed at oblique, natural positions; b) the 16 P.F., HSPQ, and the Guilford-Zimmerman aim at primary source traits, but secondaries can be simultaneously scored (except on the G-Z, the Edwards, etc., since secondaries cannot be recognized with orthogonal primaries); c) equally correct but different principles underlie the MMPI, certain depression scales, etc., on the one hand, which have items maximally separating previously defined types, and, on the other hand, the 16 P.F., G-Z, Edwards, Comrey, etc. which aim at analysis into dimensional traits. Profiles in the latter, however, can be used to assign to clinical types, etc.

Instead of operating with both primary and secondary traits, as in the 16 P.F., HSPQ, CAQ, etc., permitting *depth psychometry*, probably most psychologists use *either* primary *or* secondary trait scores. There are so far around 23 normal primaries discovered and defined, and 12 primaries in pathological behavior, all of which together account for the greater part of variance in most criterion behaviors. There are about eight normal and four pathological secondaries, though only the biggest and most useful five are in the Central Trait-State Kit (CTS).

Although significantly more variance in criterion behavior can, in fact and in principle, be predicted from a full set of primaries than a full set of secondaries, there are a number of situations in practice where one must compromise and be satisfied with use of the smaller number of secondaries (though as few as two in Peterson's factors, three in Eysenck's EPI, and four in Bernnenter, etc., is getting rather threadbare). A test which aims at shorter testing, but with special advantages of flexibility and additional domains of use is the CTS Kit, which a) settles on the five largest and best defined ("central") secondaries; b) switches from omnibus form (in which factor source traits cannot be separately tested) to a *kit*, from which complete single scales can be pulled out one at a time; and c) provides separate measures of the trait and corresponding state, e.g., for anxiety.

There are advantages to having a *family* of tests aimed at the same trait structures across developmental ages, and also checked in structure and standardized in different countries. This is available in three *secondaries* in Eysenck's senior and junior EPI, and for 14 to 16 *primaries* and five *secondaries* in the family of the 16 P.F., the High School Personality Questionnaire (HSPQ), the Child Personality Questionnaire (CPQ), the Early School Personality Questionnaire (ESPQ), etc. These give more opportunity for developmental and cross-cultural studies employing the same constant personality concepts.

In clinical work a broader spectrum of personality traits needs to be examined. A recent test—the Clinical Analysis Questionnaire (CAQ)—combines a relatively condensed set of scores on the 16 P.F. primaries with scales for the 12 pathological primaries from the domain of the MMPI and further pathological, e.g., depression, scales. As far as *questionnaire* approaches are concerned, this offers probably the most comprehensive of clinical tests. However, any questionnaire covering most of the personality sphere, normal or abnormal, cuts down in one form, to so few items per scale that the dependability and equivalence coefficients get low. Consequently, as both reviewers and authors have urged, it is desirable in important situations to use more than one form. The family of tests above and a few others provide equivalent (and standardized) forms—five in the case of 16 P.F.—to use when possible. In these cases there are also adaptations to different literacy levels, and the beginnings of adaptation to ethnic minorities (e.g., the Hawaiian HSPQ).

CHAPTER 13

Personality Assessment by Objective Tests

James M. Schuerger

SYSTEMATIC AND SPORADIC RESEARCH IN THE BACKGROUND OF OBJECTIVE TESTS

It will be recalled, from Chapter 2, that we refer to three media in which human personality is assessed: Q-data, L-data, and T-data. The first two of these have to do with measuring personality through such devices as self-report questionnaires, ratings, behavioral observations, and the like. This chapter is concerned with personality measurement by T-data devices.

We now enter a realm of personality measurements which do not depend either on the person being assessed or on some observer telling us anything directly, self-consciously, about the given personality. More concretely, consider a typical, self-report (Q-data) questionnaire item: "Given a choice, I would live a) in a crowded city, b) not sure, c) far from the center of town where there are fewer people." The assessee's answer to this question, taken in most straightforward manner, indicates his or her liking for persons versus soli-

tude. The assessee is telling us something about him- or herself. On the other hand, an objective test question such as "Most people don't really know what they want a) agree, b) uncertain, c) disagree" might be scored for speed of response time, taken as measuring projection, or measured for GSR response. One might give a test of 20 or so items of this kind and count the number of them that a person would do in a limited time and, discarding any reference to content, get at "speed of social opinion" or some such variable expressing temperament.

The reader familiar with psychological theory generally will by now have begun to suspect the broader implications of this kind of measurement. That is, the most general theoretical framework for this kind of measurement is that personality is well-revealed in everything we *do*. Personality in this sense, as the underpinning for all our behaviors, is consistent with almost any theoretical point of view. The psychoanalytic psychologist will see the behaviors as signs of underlying conflicts or blockages in energy exchange systems; the trait psychologist will see them as quasi-additive indicators of amount of trait; and the reductionist behaviorist will see only the innumerable behaviors and not posit any underlying structure or theoretical explanation. But all will agree that the basis of personality lies in the full range of behaviors. There is an impressive mass of "bitty" research on this kind of personality measurement, most of it highly specific and idiosyncratic.

A scientifically noteworthy exception to those diffuse efforts is the Objective-Analytic Test Kit (Cattell & Schuerger, 1978), an organized collection of miniature situations and response measures based on 25 years of systematic, theoretically advancing programmatic research. The plan followed was, as in Cattell's work in the questionnaire domain, to start free of "prejudices" or popular psychoanalytic and clinical concepts of personality structure, by taking a *personality sphere* of total behavior and factor analytically determining its functional structures.

The reader wishing to find out about the many methodological and theoretical developments which were made in covering nearly a thousand varieties of behavior can best do so in two books: Cattell and Warburton's *Objective Personality and Motivation Tests* (1967) and Cattell, Hundleby, and Pawlik's *Personality Factors in Objective Test Devices* (1965). The first deals with what Cattell calls the toughest part of the enterprise: creating some 500 tests and over 1,000 defined behavior measures to test the gradually emerging hypotheses in the successive factor analytic "distillations." This compendium of defined tests is still a mine from which many personality generalizations can be experimentally extracted. The second is an account of the 20 or more factor analytic studies, overlapping in older and newer (checking) tests which led to the emergence, by cross-matching and special adjunct experiments, of some two dozen factors.

The bulk of this chapter will describe the Objective-Analytic Test Kit as it currently exists, dipping briefly into the research which led up to it. However, a good many other non-questionnaire devices for the measurement of personality exist outside the organized O-A realm, and while for the most part they lack the orderliness and sophistication of the structured approach which the O-A provides, completeness of coverage requires listing and brief description of them. We are referring to the various projective tests—Rorschach, TAT, and so on—and also to a potpourri of others such as the Bender and the various measures of cognitive style, etc. In his chapter on performance measures of personality, Cronbach (1970) lists at least 36 separate measures and points of view from which such measures have been constructed. The reader might properly appreciate the order and comprehensiveness of the O-A Kit by scanning Cronbach's chapter and noting the proliferation of unorganized measures in the T-data medium. For the remainder of this chapter, we will consider, first, the projectives, then a miscellany of other objective measures of personality, then the O-A Kit in some detail. The use of objective measures for dynamic (motivational) traits is detailed in Chapter 14 and will not be covered in this chapter.

THE SO-CALLED PROJECTIVE TESTS

Loosely, by projective tests we mean that class of personality measures which depends on interpretation of the client's responses to a vague but standard stimulus. The term "projection," like many terms in psychology, has in this context lost its precise meaning. As defined in the opening sentence, "projective" tests are a subdivision of objective tests and not all feature true projection (as, for example, in the MAT). As pointed out in Chapter 14, the experimental work on perception by Cattell and Wenig (1952) showed that in addition to *true projection* from the unconscious, as precisely observed and defined by Freud, there is a process of *naive projection*. Here, we are using the loose, more common terminology.

One may conveniently distinguish five main kinds of projectives:

1) Word-association tests, in which the client is asked to respond to stimulus words given by the test administrator. Inferences about personality are made from the quality of the response words. A sample test is the *Kent-Rosanoff* (1910), a standard list of 100 words along with the responses of a norm group of 1000 adults.
   Sample items, with common associations:
   Stimulus—black : *Response*—white
   —cat   :   —dog
   Long response latencies and strange associations are taken as suggestive of emotional disturbance. Unusual associations, in the context of other aspects of the client's life, are taken as signs of unexpressed needs and conflicts.

2) Sentence-completion tests, in which the client is asked to complete short initial stubs of sentences.
   A sample test is the *Rotter Incomplete Sentences Blank*, a standard list of such sentence stubs as:
   My father ....
   My greatest fear ....
   Scoring is possible on the Rotter according to a scheme for rating each response according to its manifest indications of maladjustment. Other scoring procedures involve thematic interpretation of response content.

3) Drawing tests, in which the client is asked to draw something, commonly the human figure.
   Two sample tests are the *Draw-a-Person* (DAP) (Machover, 1971) and the *House-Tree-Person* (HTP) by J. N. Buck (1948). The examinee is instructed to draw the particular figure, and then aspects of the figure (size, position,

characteristics, etc.) are interpreted. For example, a very large drawing is said to be suggestive of impulsivity; heavy, dark lines indicate aggressiveness—and so on.

4) Picture-story tests, in which the client sees a picture and is asked to tell a story or in some way give verbal response to the picture. Sample tests are the *Thematic Apperception Test* (TAT) (Murray et al., 1938), and the *Children's Apperception Test* (CAT) (Bellak, 1975). The TAT is the standard for adults, while the CAT is for children.

5) Inkblot tests, in which the client is shown an inkblot and asked what is seen there or what might be represented by the blot. The classic test of this kind is the *Rorschach* (Rorschach, 1942), which consists of ten cards having on them bilaterally symmetrical inkblots.
   Scoring consists of categorizing the responses for one or more of several categories: location of the area which the client commented on; determinant, or aspect of the blot which influenced the response—form, color, shading, etc.; content of the response—human, animal, anatomical part, etc.

Regardless of particulars, all projectives share the vague stimulus and the relatively unstructured response on the part of the client. Experience has shown that despite the vagueness of stimuli, people tend to give certain responses, or classes of responses, to the stimuli. As experience with the various instruments grew, scoring schemes were developed which took advantage of these similarities and regularities. So, for example, among the picture-story and inkblot tests, both the Rorschach and TAT have elaborate and well-systematized scoring schemes. For the Rorschach there are the systems of Beck (Beck et al., 1961), Klopfer (1954), and others. For the Thematic Apperception Test (TAT), there is, of course, Henry Murray's analytic procedure (Murray et al., 1938), as well as considerable subsequent development by McClelland (1953), Atkinson and Feather (1966), and others.

The TAT is, in fact, one of the more systematic of the projectives and may serve as an example of one of the promising applications. It is considered in more detail in the perspective of motivation measurement in Chapter 14. In this test, the subject views a series of 20 carefully chosen pictures and is asked to tell a story about each in turn. The examiner records the stories just as they are told, and afterwards analyzes them for indication of psychological needs. For example, imagine a picture of a boy with a tool chest. One examinee might begin his story thus:

"John, a young man of 11, is reflecting on his past years of handiwork and is wondering where it is leading him. He has done well for a person his age and for the number of years he has practiced."

A second examinee, to the same stimulus picture, responds:

"The boy in the picture is taking his first look at his new tool chest. He is thinking about the fine things he will be able to make with it. For years he has been working hard. Finally his father has been able to buy him a really fine set of tools."

The first of these might be taken as indication of the client's "need" for introspection, or introception, as Murray calls it, the inward-looking tendency. On the other hand, the second client story is more outward-looking, focused more securely on the future. Also different is the second story's mention of the father, suggestive of affiliative motive on the part of the second client.

The need variables measured by objective (projective) tests are the same variables measured in Q-data medium by the Edwards Personal Preference Schedule (EPPS) or Jackson's Personality Research Form (PRF), which have been shown to be related to personality and motivational

variables (Schuerger, Watterson, & Croom, 1983). Of course, the TAT or any such projective set of pictures can be analyzed with regard to whatever dynamic projections one cares to take as units. The real and serious defect of the TAT is a practical one: that its scoring is open-ended, subjective, and of low interpsychologist reliability. However, in the same year that Murray proposed the TAT to U.S. psychologists, Cattell, in London, published (in *A Guide to Mental Testing*, 1936) a set of projection or misperception tests to cover the clinically most important drives. These were in some ways attractive to psychometry, in that *they were multiple choice* in form and therefore reliable (conspective) in scoring. However, these were never used with the popularity of the TAT, until further developed in the MAT which now replaces them. In Chapter 14 on motivation measurement it is suggested that, despite its lack of conspect reliability, the TAT could well be used with the MAT, to explore the personally *unique* attachments of the common—ergic and semic—quantitatively scored traits on the MAT.

MISCELLANEOUS OBJECTIVE MEASURES OF PERSONALITY

Remembering that we are considering those tests of personality that do not require either self-report by the client or observation/rating by someone else—tests for which the client is not likely to know the personality inferences which are made from the behavior sample—we find a variety of measures outside of projectives and the O-A Kit which a practitioner has available. Under one rubric are found a few tests of perception, notably the Bender and the Embedded Figures Test. The Bender is really only a series of simple line drawings which the examiner presents to the client, asking the client to reproduce them. The figures are generally so simple that most normal adults can reproduce them almost exactly, and any departure from exact reproduction can be interpreted as a strong sign of pathology, often brain dysfunction. A well-known scoring system (Koppitz, 1964) includes expected responses and interpretations of possible pathology, as well as some personological interpretations of certain modifications in design.

The Embedded Figures Test (EFT) has been found by Witkin and followers to correlate substantially (0.3 to 0.6) with more elaborate measures of one variable, field independence. Personological variables fairly consistently found correlating with field independence include curiosity, social autonomy, and healthy body concept (Horn, 1977). It seems, therefore, that the highest scorer on this kind of objective, perceptual task can be expected to share the characteristics reported in the substantial research of Witkin and his associates. As will be noted in more detail later, this variable, field independence, seems quite well subsumed by a variable in the O-A Battery labeled U.I. 19, Independence.

Another kind of objective task for which consistent personological correlates have been found is the configuration of performance measures on some of the rather ordinary measures of ability. We are thinking here of the substantial research on configurational interpretation of the Wechsler tests, for example, and the personological implications of differential verbal-quantitative ability. Among the personality characteristics with various score patterns on the Wechsler, for example, Matarazzo (1972) lists schizophrenia, sociopathy, delinquency, anxiety (both trait and state). In addition, his compilation lists developmental personality correlates of intelligence and Gittinger's Personality Assessment System (Gittinger, 1964), a highly articulated system for deriving personality from the Wechsler tests. Schuerger, Kepner, and Lawler (1979), on a similar but less inclusive tack,

list a number of apparently stable personality correlates of verbal-quantitative differential (the difference between verbal and quantitative score on any standard ability measure). Among such correlates, for example, is the tendency for persons with excess of quantitative ability over verbal to be intolerant of ambiguity. Verbal persons, on the other hand, tend to be interested in art. Men who have excess verbal over quantitative tend to be anxious, and correlatively, women with excess quantitative ability tend to be anxious.

These approaches do not yield valid measures on established unitary personality structures, and thus remain at the same level of description as the available inferences from, say, handwriting or projective tests. On the other hand, and in a more complete conceptual framework, there *are* significant relations unearthed in the last 20 years between ability factors on the one hand and personality factors on the other, as shown by Cattell and Butcher (1968), Cattell and Damarin (1968), and Cattell (1971b). Overall, as Hakstian and Cattell (1978) have shown, all these statistically significant associations, though they throw interesting light (see Cattell, 1971c) on the origins and developmental aids of primary abilities and personality traits, probably do not give large enough multiple correlations from one to the other area to justify any regular practice of inferring personality traits from abilities.

Another approach to objective personality measurement was Freud's *Wit and Its Relation to the Unconscious* (1938) (sometimes translated as *Jokes and the Unconscious*), surely sufficiently clinically convincing to suggest to personality researchers that it be systematically investigated. But actually, in the period since then, only one factored, trait-validated "battery" seems to have been tried. Cattell and Luborsky (1950), Tollefson (1959), and others began by demonstrating that psychiatrists could not divine, with any reliable consensus among them, the underlying dynamic tendency in jokes. But a large collection of jokes given to a large sample *did* evidence consistent correlational groupings and, in fact, from these correlations no fewer than 13 distinct factors could be located. There are difficulties in creating an objective standardized test in this area in that about nine out of ten jokes are local in place and time. But by taking published jokes in the period 1830-1930 that still were applicable (showing no "dating") in the 1960s, these investigators obtained eventually enough to give factor-valid items for a relatively permanent test. In form A, the subject is asked to state which jokes he considers funny (this gives also a personality score, as a by-product, of total funniness — *geniality* in being amused) and in form B, the alternative design is used of asking the subject to state *which of two* he or she considers funnier.

Although this test has been published with keys and standardization since 1963, not enough resourceful application has yet been made by psychoanalysts, clinicians, and educators to give fuller interpretation of these distinct 13 factor traits scorable in humor response. Some, such as that named "hostile derogation," which appears to fit a Freudian concept of repressed aggression, are *dynamic* in nature. But others suggest *general* personality factors such as extraversion (QI), anxiety (QII), premsia, and intelligence, already known in L- and Q-data. For example, the correlation of humor factor 1 with extraversion-introversion measures by QI are quite good; the style of the humor is clearly rather dry and biting in introverts, while extraverts prefer rather "loud" and open slapstick humor, especially with sexual and "friendly aggressive" content. At the present stage of research it has seemed best to give the factors labels that do their best to describe what is common to the given set of jokes, as follows (except for factors 1 and 6, which have been cross-

validated against Q-data), from the Humor Test of Personality:

1) Invia vs. exvia
2) Dry wit vs. good-natured play
3) Compensation vs. tough self-composure
4) Flirtatious playfulness vs. gruesomeness
5) Urbane pleasantness vs. hostile derogation
6) High anxiety vs. low anxiety
7) Theatricalism vs. cold realism
8) Neat wit vs. ponderous humor
9) Damaging retort vs. unexpected "offbeat" humor
10) Cheerful independence vs. mistreatment humor
11) Conscientious concern vs. evasion of responsibility
12) Rebound against feminine aggression vs. scorn of ineffectual male
13) Dullness vs. general intelligence

Obviously, there are some striking theoretical opportunities for research in these descriptive titles, by correlating beyond the rough exploratory 16 P.F. and MAT associations recorded in the handbook. At present one can reasonably hypothesize from initial data that 1 and 6 correspond to secondaries QI and QII, and some to L-Q-data primaries, while others may be primaries (factor 7 is perhaps premsia), and yet others are avenues to assessing the sexual, homosexual, and aggressive dynamic tendencies which Freud described.

From an immediate practical standpoint a much overlooked feature of the Humor Test is its provision of a hidden intelligence test. Whereas the sheer cognitive level of the items is held low, so that variance in appreciation is due to personality differences rather than to g, in the measure which Tollefson constructed for the *g* factor, the emotional types of humor reciprocally are held constant, but appreciation of the jokes now hinges on ability to perceive the wit—the cognitive structure—itself.

Any practitioner knows that there are delicate situations when an ordinary intelligence test is either resented by the subject (as, say, in getting senior executives or bureaucrats to meet a test), or avoided from a sense of insecurity, or faked in the only possible direction (downward) in criminals claiming mental incompetence. This test (located in the B form of the Humor Test of Personality) is apparently the first of its kind to be standardized and validated against intelligence tests. It needs extension in length, but it suffices for many practical needs.

If laughter can tap dynamic and temperamental roots, so also would one expect music to do so. Music had been thought of in the forties, e.g., in research by the Music Research Foundation, more as a means of therapy than of diagnosis: for example, for people's personal experiences (the story of the Sirens), the historical cases of remedying of disturbed moods (David's harping to Saul) gave hope. Unfortunately, though mood changes and degrees of remission can undoubtedly be brought about by such therapy, all available objective research on structural change in pathology from this source has been disappointing. Meanwhile, however, Cattell and Saunders (1954), factor-analyzing preferences for 120 short excerpts (in one case all on piano; in another on diverse instruments), found that consistent and replicable factorial dimensions exist—11 were initially located—and records (33⅓ RPM) were constructed with 100 items, giving scores on 11 dimensions. Cattell and Anderson (1953) showed that these were not dimensions of musical fashions or trained tastes as such, but correlated significantly with personality factors on the 16 P.F. (suggesting second-order lineups, but at present obscurely replicated). Both they and Cattell and McMichael (1960) found numerous significant differences between mental hospital diagnostic groups (schizophrenics, organ-

ics, paranoids, affectives, and alcoholics) and normals, notably on factors 1, 2, 5, 6, 7, 8, 10, and 11. These pioneer data suggest that discriminant function could be used with this test that would be as effective for psychiatric diagnosis as any instruments in use—and especially convenient in that it can be administered to groups, if the patients are capable of reliably recording liking and disliking on an answer sheet.

Neither the Humor nor the Music Preference tests have been researched and developed much beyond basic structure. This lack is attributable to certain misunderstandings: 1) the recordings are not of top musical quality and the jokes are not very funny. This criticism occurs, notably, when the tests are picked up by musicians or connoisseurs of humor, who judge by standards of good music and sophisticated humor and completely miss the purposes in the test design, which are statistically and psychologically to present a broad range of music and humor as judged by the average person; 2) they fall outside the interest of the vast bulk of psychometrists, presently tied to questionnaires or Rorschach, etc.; and 3) many of the personality associations are at present purely empirical. But in these tests, on the credit side, the existence of 10 to 12 distinguishable independent factors has unquestionably been demonstrated, and even at the pioneer stage the relations to known personality structures are statistically significant, even if presently lacking a rationale.

Related to the above is the approach through artistic preference. Here the effect of artistic periods of style is more of an obstacle and, as in both humor and music, the designer has to avoid disturbance of affect through familiarity, by taking items rarely popularly presented. In spite of these difficulties Eysenck found (and Cattell and co-workers independently confirmed) that the second-order exvia-invia factor showed up clearly in a preference by extroverts for bright, clear colors and of introverts for more subtle and somber colorings. Form-vs.-color tests proposed and used by Kretschmer (1925) were tried out in Cattell and Warburton (1967) and found (Cattell, Hundleby, & Pawlik, 1965) to show a weak association (more color) with U.I.34, whereas less academic-abstract aspects of perceptual preference, e.g., for familiar versus unfamiliar art subjects, gave somewhat better associations (U.I. 33(−)). The few checked associations of artistic, color, perceptual emphasis, etc. with general personality factors that reach any significance are described as auxiliaries to the O-A Battery in Cattell and Warburton (1967).

Finally, we turn to somatic and physiological measures that have shown some promise as objective general temperament measures (for their motivation use see Chapter 14). The search for such was most intensive in the first half of this century, and a survey is given by Cattell up to 1946 and again to 1953. Most clear are factors of high general autonomic activity (metabolic rate, systolic pressure) apparently identical with anxiety, and then, separate factors of sympathetic and parasympathetic predominance (Darrow & Heath, 1932). Especially promising is Harrington's finding (1942) of an association of high physiological activity with high psychological and social activity. The possible somatic associations from Kretschmer's and Sheldon's books are well known, are smaller than originally claimed, and need modern factor analytic experiment, so they will not be pursued here.

In the series of published studies on objective personality factors (Cattell, Hundleby, & Pawlik, 1965), there will be found a sprinkling of associations offering some auxiliary individual tests of value in increasing battery validity in the O-A for particular factors, if the psychologists want to get still higher validity. These are generally not put in the main battery because they require individual testing or apparatus, some of which is described later. For example, higher U.I. 20 goes

with lower conditioning rate on the GSR and less pupil dilation on stimulation; U.I. 22 correlates substantially with higher rate of flicker fusion and with reaction time; U.I. 23(−) regression correlates with ataxic sway (as also does U.I. 27) and with lesser GSR response to mental than physical stimuli; high U.I. 24 (Anxiety) individuals show lower handwriting muscular pressure; U.I. 25 substantially relates to two-hand coordination by Thurstone's test; high U.I. 28 persons have a larger area under the pulse wave on the EKG; U.I. 29 (+) goes with higher metabolic rate and with increase of metabolic rate under stimulation, suggesting that the personality correlation with metabolic rate found by Herrington and others describes this factor; U.I. 30 is significantly related to body tempo, and U.I. 32, Exvia, to systolic blood pressure. Pawlik and Cattell (1965) found associations at a predictive level of EEG to personality factors U.I. 16, U.I. 22, and, less consistently, U.I. 32, Exvia.

All in all, therefore, the domain of physiological and somatic measures has promising leads, but not as yet proven predictively high enough to act as more than auxiliaries to T-data and Q-data tests.

THE OBJECTIVE ANALYTIC O-A KIT: ITS HISTORICAL ORIGINS IN PURE RESEARCH AND THEORY

As in all scientific endeavors, one can trace the beginning of objective measurement of functionally unitary personality factors to several sources. Spearman and Thurstone (pure mathematicians aside) developed factor analysis and Burt (1939) and Cattell (1932b, 1933) were the first to apply it systematically to personality, the former to ratings (Burt, 1939, 1940) and the latter to both ratings (Cattell, 1932b) and newly developed objective tests (Cattell, 1933). The break into objective devices also owes much to Eysenck

(1947), though he stopped at three factors whereas Cattell and co-workers eventually replicated close to 20. A historical vista to the present day on objective, behavioristic analysis of personality structure would thus list as main works:

1933	Cattell shifting factor analysis from abilities to personality, working on an array of objective temperament tests
1939-40	Burt's factoring of ratings
1946	Cattell's *Description and Measurement of Personality*, factoring the personality sphere
1947	Eysenck's *Dimensions of Personality*
1948	Burt's factor analysis of temperament traits
	Cattell's factor analysis of objective-analytic measures
1953-56	Cattell, Baggaley, and Schiff, factor-analyzing Air Force O-A data
	Cattell, Dubin, and Saunders —two articles on structure of O-A measures among psychotics
	Cattell's summary article on the principal replicated factors in O-A data
	Cattell and Gruen's article on O-A measures in a young sample
	Baggaley and Cattell's article on O-A devices
1957	Cattell's *Personality and Motivation Structure and Measurement*
	Cattell, Stice, and Kristy write on nature-nurture ratios of personality objective test devices
1958	Scheier and Cattell on relationships among O-A and questionnaire factors
1959	Guilford's *Personality*
	Cattell and Coan's article on O-

A measures in middle childhood

1960	Eysenck's *Structure of Human Personality*
1961	Cattell and Scheier's *Meaning and Measurement of Neuroticism and Anxiety*
1960-65	Knapp's series of reports on O-A measures with U.S. Navy data
1964	Cattell, Horn, Sweney, and Radcliffe publish extension of objective tests into dynamics in the *Motivation Analysis Test*
1965	Hundleby, Pawlik, and Cattell's *Personality Factors in Objective Test Devices*
1967	Cattell and Warburton's *Objective Personality and Motivation Tests*
1973	Cattell, Schmidt, and Pawlik checking structure across three countries
1976	Cattell, Schuerger, Klein, and Finkbeiner's definitive article on structure in O-A devices
1978	Cattell and Schuerger's *Personality Theory in Action*
1980	Cattell's *Personality and Learning Theory*
1982	Cattell's *The Inheritance of Personality and Ability*

Noteworthy in the development over 50 years we see an excellent coordination of theoretical and experimental steps. In the case of anxiety, extraversion, and some few other factors, integration naturally occurred with clinical observation. In other cases the personality concepts were new, and several of the hypotheses for them still invite experimental checks. What at once differentiated this personality theory from most other schools was the precision with which the concepts could be operationalized and measured. With some differences in the methodological development of factor procedures, but with similar results, the theoretical structure in the objective personality measurement research field was advanced by these pioneers. When one considers the amount of labor involved in constructing and administering the devices themselves, and the enormous computational labors of factor analysis before the advent of computerized factor analysis (the algorithm for factor analysis on high-speed computers dates from around 1960, I am told), one is bound to regard this as one of the largest programmatic undertakings in psychology, brought to its present state by a combination of psychological insights and mathematical advances.

In the last half of 1968, this author began work on objective test battery construction as project director in the Laboratory of Personality and Group Analysis, Cattell's lab at the University of Illinois. The position reached by that time in basic research has been sufficiently indicated, especially in the early chapters of this book. Some 30 personality primaries had been checked in Q-data, and some 20 in T-data, and it was beginning to be seen that the answer to the riddle of matching across to those already matching in L-Q media was that primaries in T-data, e.g., exvia, anxiety, intelligence, control, cortertia, were second order among Q-data primaries but first order in T-data. The behavioral equation:

$$a_{ij} = b_{jx}A_{xi} + b_{jy}T_{yi} + b_{jz}D_{zi} \qquad (13\text{-}1)$$

using these new objective test primaries almost at once showed its power to predict life criteria—a_j's. Very soon it was also shown that the factors now known in the three modalities of structures—A, abilities; T, temperament-personality; and D, dynamic motivational—were in "different space."

Hypotheses, rich in means of theoretical testing (in the way Madsen, 1977, defines richness), had been put forward for many

of these source traits. However, after recognition and an acceptable degree of established validity, a great deal remained to be done on plotting the typical life course of these source traits (as had been done for fluid and crystallized intelligence), discovering their relative heritabilities, noting their cross-cultural modifications of pattern, etc. Fortunately, from the clinical studies of Scheier, Tatro, Rickels, Killian and others it was already clear that these common traits had substantial predictive power on life and clinical criteria, recently extended by Schmidt in Germany, Cartwright and Hundleby in the field of delinquency, and Patrick and Campbell in clinical diagnosis.

THE NATURE OF THE PERSONALITY SOURCE TRAITS MEASURABLE IN T-DATA AND CHOSEN FOR THE MAIN O-A BATTERY

The research that I described as beginning in 1968 had three important aspects: 1) improving for practitioners' use the most concept-valid of the measures recorded in Cattell and Warburton's "encyclopedia" (1967); 2) checking once again, in these improved test forms, the factors replicated in the 20 or so studies in Cattell, Hundleby, and Pawlik (1965); 3) proceeding to the convenient instructions, standardization, scoring, and criterion data required in routine use. The details of the last are in the Cattell and Schuerger *Personality Theory in Action* (1978), and the first and second can be traced in the bibliography.

In connection with the first goal, we need pause only long enough to sketch the nature and utility of the indexing system to cover tests, scores, and factors. The response behavior to a given test situation can often be scored for two or three different parameters. For example, scoring of the Rorschach depends almost exclusively on different aspects of the one stimulus. In objective O-A tests there is usually the possibility of focusing on speed, errors, variability, etc. For this reason, two index systems are needed, one to locate a test as such (a T index) and another to find the number for the particular behavior scored (an M.I. or master index). The U.I. (universal index) numbers are, of course, to identify the factors during research required to reach a good interpretive name.

Thus, we have three systems of rubrics: *universal index (U.I.)* numbers for the factors; *test (T)* numbers for the literal test situation and the associated instruction; and *master index (M.I.)* numbers for the variables scored from the tests.

Let us now describe the main factor patterns (of which the best-replicated enter the O-A Battery) and their meanings as presently understood. The U.I. numbers for personality factors actually begin with U.I. 16 (see below) not U.I. 1, because of the first 15 numbers having been reserved for factors of ability, as listed by French (1951) in his survey and matched across researches. The distinction between a test (T) and some behavioral variable derived from the test with an M.I. number may best be illustrated by an example. Under "U.I. 16: Ego Standards" (the battery for which is set out just below), Test 8a is here scored for speed of judgment (M.I. 288). This same test, which consists of questions requiring evaluation of performances (e.g., "How good would you say it is for a six-year-old to be able to tie his or her shoes?"), can also be scored for "criticalness" (M.I. 133) and again for variability of evaluation (M.I. 979). The first of these, M.I. 288, is a simple count of the number done in a given time, while "criticalness" (M.I. 133) is a simple sum of multiple choice response values, where perception of a performance is good = 0, fair = 1, or poor = 2, so the higher score indicates greater criticalness. The various tests and associated variables (M.I.'s), running over 1000, are described for research and other purposes in detail in the compendium by Cattell and Warburton (1967).

So much for the research background

and the extent of the personality dimensions located. From here on we shall cover the 10 factors actually chosen for the O-A Kit, on a basis of best replication, validity and reliability.

U.I. 16: Ego Standards (or Competitiveness)

Many associations suggest this is ego strength in the classical psychoanalytic sense, and also in the sense of factor C$^+$ as ego strength in questionnaires. However, the title hedges on this identification deliberately because U.I. 16 has a stronger emphasis on self-assertion and achievement than is usual in ego strength. "Standards," suggesting a certain competitive assertiveness, is therefore added to avoid risk of premature historical interpretation with the common Freudian ego concept. The subtests show boldness, competitive assertiveness, speed of action, and interests and attitudes. U.I. 16 is lower than normal in psychotics, neurotics, delinquent gangs, in lower social status, in persons of small physique, and in those showing poorer school performance.

Variables that define U.I. 16 in the O-A Kit are:

T	M.I.	
361	244	Quicker social judgment
49a	6d	Higher coding speed
44a	307	Quicker letter-number comparison
8a	288	Quicker judgment, others' performance
20a	282	More seen in unstructured drawings
11a	2409	More logical assumptions done
35a	199	Greater simple numerical performance
43b	2410	Greater fluency on objects (selective)

U.I. 19: Independence vs. Subduedness

This is a factor determining in its subtests independence, criticalness, accuracy, capacity for intensive concentration, and perceptual "field independence," as studied by Witkin (1962) and others. It is a positive predictor of success in school and in some military (submarine) and scientific performances. There is quite a high hereditary component. There are consistent indications of the relation of the factor to the second-order factor of independence in the questionnaire realm, indexed QIV, covering primaries E+, L+, M+, Q_1+, and Q_2+, i.e., the questionnaire dominance, protension, autism (internal values), radicalism, and self-sufficiency. Psychotics and neurotics are significantly lower than normals, and males significantly higher than females.

Variables that define U.I. 19 in the O-A Kit are:

T	M.I.	
35b	120f	Higher accuracy/speed-numerical
37	206	More hidden shapes correctly seen in Gottschaldt figures
6a	167c	Better immediate memory from reading
422	2367	More orderly perceptual series seen
328	1387	More correct in searching task
242a	689	Greater accuracy picture memory
114	51	Higher index of carefulness

U.I. 20: Evasiveness

This quite subtle trait has been the hardest to name, at least in any well-known single term. Descriptively close labels have been offered in "social, emotional evasiveness" (Hundleby, Pawlik, & Cattell, 1965), "dependent instability," and "postering acceptance of social values," which interpretive labels have been given by psychiatrists as "bound anxiety" or "characterological anxiety" and "compensation for insecurity." The individual is superficially culturally conforming, but suggestible also to inconsistent ("delinquent") values. He shows emotional instability (but not of the deep, C-, ego

weakness form) and neurotic lack of objectivity, with some hostility and guilt proneness, but he is sociable and dependent. Adult delinquents score high on the factor, but so, also, do involutional depressives, again suggesting conflicts in the area of guilt and antisocial or reality-evasive behavior. A literary instance might be Mr. Micawber—or even Dickens himself. Pending fuller research interpretations, the only suitable single term for it seems to be evasiveness—suggesting some dubiousness of character, a tendency to posture toward the immediate group style, and some emotional instability.

Variables that define U.I. 20 in the O-A Kit are:

T	M.I.	
10b(1)	34	Greater insecurity of opinion (Area one)
9g(1)	65	Less logical consistency of attitudes
9bj(1)	38	Higher ratio dissonant to consonant
9bj(2)	38	recognition
10b(2)	34	Greater insecurity of opinion (Part of performance 1 above)
38a	211a	More susceptibility to annoyances
16b	100b	More pessimistic insecurity
16b	152b	Greater tendency to agree
16b	67a	Greater extremity of response

As an example of scoring, the scoring instructions for U.I. 20, on the special summary sheet provided in the kit, are presented in Figure 13.1. On this factor, all variables are ratios to remove speed of operation from the variable. Once the variables (derived scores) are scored, they are transferred into partial Z-scores and summed to give an overall Z-score for the factor.

U.I. 21: Exuberance

Because this loads on some tests in the ability field, it has sometimes been confounded with "ideational fluency" or "di-

Performance Score Number	T Number MI Number	Psychologist's Title (Examinee's Title)	Derived Raw-Score Formula	Derived Raw Score	Mean of Derived Raw Scores m	(1) minus (2)	Weight w	(5) Special Subtest Standard Score (3) multiplied by (4) = z'
1	10b(1) 34	Insecurity of Opinion (Opinions I)	$\dfrac{\Sigma(\text{Test }5 - \text{Test }1)}{\text{No. pairs}} =$		1.14		.1	
2	9g 65	Less Logical Consistency of Attitude (Opinions II)	$\dfrac{\Sigma|A_i + B_i - 2C_i|}{\text{No. of complete clusters}} =$		2.67		.2	
3	9bj(1) 38	Not scored as such, but in relation to Test 4, following (Opinions III)	No score here					
	9bj(2) 38	Ratio Consonant/Dissonant Recognition (Memory)	$\dfrac{AY - AN + 15}{DY - DN + 15} =$		.74		.01	
4	10b(2) 34	Not scored as such, but already used in relation to Test 1 (Opinions IV)						
	38a 211a	More Susceptibility to Annoyances (Common Annoyances)	$\dfrac{\Sigma \text{ Item scores}}{\text{No. done}} =$		2.04		.04	
5	16b 100b	More Pessimistic Insecurity (Human Nature I)	$\dfrac{\Sigma \text{ Item scores}}{\text{No. done}} =$		2.8		.8	
6	9g 152b	Tendency to Agree	$\dfrac{\Sigma \text{ MI }152b}{\text{No. done}} =$		3.58		.4	
7	9g 67a	Extremity of Response	$\dfrac{\Sigma \text{ MI }67a}{\text{No. done}} =$		2.20		3.0	

Sum = Factor Score

Figure 13.1. U.I. 20 score summary sheet

From Cattell & Schuerger (1978)

vergent thinking," but it is much broader than a purely cognitive pattern.

All manifestations are clearly those of high spontaneity, fluency, imaginativeness, speed of social and perceptual judgment, fast natural tempo, and sacrifice of accuracy to speed. In the questionnaire domain it shows some relations to surgency $(F+)$, tension (Q_4+), guilt proneness $(O+)$, and imaginativeness $(M+)$, and to ratings of energetic, forceful or dominant, and excitable behavior. It has a high hereditary determination, and some association with broad body build. It has sometimes been called the Winston Churchill factor.

A significantly subnormal score is found on this factor for both neurotic and psychotic patients, and particularly for all depressives. The most promising hypothesis is that it represents a physiological factor determining high metabolic rate in the brain (and perhaps the entire body). The alternative theory, that it represents lack of inhibition, e.g., at the thalamus, should still be entertained.

Variables that define U.I. 21 in the O-A Kit are:

T	M.I.	
411d	335b	Faster marking speed
43a	271	Higher ideational fluency
88a	853	More concrete drawing completion
164a	699	More garbled words guessed
2d	7	Faster speed of closure
3	8	Higher frequency of alternating perspective
51	28b	Greater dynamic momentum: dictation
136a	264	Faster speed of tapping

All tests used for U.I. 21 in the O-A Kit are on expendable (vs. reusable) booklets and require motor performance to one degree or another.

U.I. 23: Capacity to Mobilize vs. Regression

This is also called Mobilization vs. Neu-

rotic Regressive Debility and, by Eysenck, Neuroticism.

The measures are of flexibility, general competence (simulating intelligence at times), emotional balance (especially absence of depression), and endurance of stress. It appears to be about 50/50 hereditary and environmental. At the negative pole it is associated with neuroticism, and at an early stage was called Neuroticism by Eysenck (1961), though it is only one of a half dozen source traits equally or more strongly associated with neuroticism and is better called regression. This negative pole has some qualities of the psychoanalytic concept of regression, in showing a falling-off of interest and vigor along with decline in capacity to organize one's thoughts. The fact that U.I. 23 is low in schizophrenics, depressives, and manics points to its association with disorganization as such. Competence in school, in stressful jobs, etc., is significantly related to the positive pole, as is freedom from "passing out" under stress (as found in the astronaut program). One hypothesis is that U.I. 23 represents an adrenal or other hormone deficiency following prolonged fatigue and impairing the whole dynamic organization.

Variables that define U.I. 23 in the O-A Kit are:

T	M.I.	
38b	242	Higher ratio social/nonsocial annoyances
44c	120b	Higher ratio accuracy/speed letter number
112	609	Higher perceptual coordination
197	401	Less preference for competitive associations
11b	36	Higher ability to state logical assumptions
20b	105	Fewer threatening objects seen
224b	714	Fewer rhyming and alliterative words chosen
1a	2a(1)	Lower perceptual-motor rigidity: backward writing

U.I. 24: Anxiety

This well-defined factor, aligning also well with QII, the second-order anxiety factor in questionnaires (C−, H−, L+, O+, Q_3−, Q_4+), has in some writings been called "emotionality." But it is anxiety, by every criterion—clinical, behavioral, situational, and physiological—that has ever been applied (Cattell & Scheier, 1961; Cattell, Schmidt, & Bjerstedt, 1972; Spielberger, 1966, 1972). It is high in neurotics and highest in anxiety neurotics, but schizophrenics do not differ from normals (hence a diagnostic discriminator). However, high scores are not invariably pathological, since "healthy" anxiety can be high situationally, as has been shown, for example, in measures during school examinations and dangerous military missions.

Variables that define U.I. 24 in the O-A Kit are:

T	M.I.	
430	2404	Preference for outright, rather than inhibited, humor
27b	117b	Less awareness of highbrow tastes
41a	219	More common frailties admitted
36	205	More emotionality of comment
187a	218	More willingness to play practical jokes
163a	1370	Less willing compliance in unpleasant tasks
38c	211b	Higher susceptibility to annoyance involving ego-threats
25	321	Book preferences: more questionable taste preferences

U.I. 25: Realism vs. Tensidia

This is also called Normality vs. Psychoticism by Eysenck and, more descriptively, by Hundleby and Pawlik, Less-Imaginative, Task-Oriented Realism vs. Tense, Inflexible Dissociation from Reality. Tensidia is an acronym for the latter pole.

It loads accuracy, speed, rejection of disturbing, imaginative intrusions, and a realistic orientation to tasks. At the negative pole, which has been rated by some psychiatrists as a form of anxiety and correlates with O+, guilt proneness, and Q_4+, tension, it shows emotional tension and a rigid, subjective, inflexibility of behavior, despite reality demands. Tensidia, as indicated, is an acronym term attempting to capture this tense, inflexible, insensitiveness to reality. It has, by Cattell's results (1982), a moderately strong hereditary determination. At the tensidia pole it correlates significantly with both psychosis and neurosis and is particularly low in depressives. Realism (positive U.I. 25) is higher in normals relative to all pathological syndromes. It is also higher in well-adjusted compared to delinquent adolescents, and (as a mean score) in more cohesive, better functioning groups than less cohesive groups (Cartwright, Tomson, & Schwartz, 1975).

Variables that define U.I. 25 in the O-A Kit are:

T	M.I.	
16b	100b	Less pessimistic insecurity
9bk	2411	Better immediate memory
431	2408	Greater accuracy in digit span
31	144	More agreement with homely wisdom
224a	714	Fewer alliterative and rhyming
118a	249	Better memory proper nouns
49c	120h	Greater accuracy of ideomotor performance

U.I. 28: Asthenia vs. Assurance

This is sometimes called Dependent, Negativistic Asthenia vs. Undisciplined Self-assurance. This is a complex pattern believed to express ambivalence resulting from a conflict between severe, demanding parental upbringing in socialization and the growing individual's own need for self-realization (Cattell, 1964a). There is conformity, but with resentment and a continual asthenia born of unresolved conflict. The questionnaire associations are with toughness (H+), imaginativeness (M+), lack of ambition, lack of agreeableness and cooperativeness, but also with some frustration (Q₄+), jealousy (L+), and depression. It shows as more environmentally determined than hereditary. It has so far shown nothing but zero correlations with clinical data, except in showing paranoid schizophrenics lower (i.e., more self-assured, less asthenic) than nonparanoid, simple schizophrenics. Neurotics are above average, while delinquents, drug addicts, and some kinds of alcoholics are actually below normal, i.e., more self-assured and undisciplined.

Variables that define U.I. 28 in the O-A Kit are:

T	M.I.	
9c(1)	152b	More tendency to agree*
9ek	116	Lower severity and guilt*
9d	125	More institutional values*
16a	100	More cynical pessimism
19	192	Longer estimates of time to do tasks
149	364	Preference for external control (indirect end to story)
96	1160(2)	More grudging skepticism re success
9c(2)	152b	(No score for this on its own. It goes in with Test 1 to give "tendency to agree.")
76	97	Longer estimate of waiting period real time

*These are three performances.

U.I. 32: Exvia vs. Invia

The questionnaire correlations repeatedly found with QI (A+, E+, F+, H+, Q₂−) demonstrate this to be the exvia-invia core of the vaguer, now popular "extraversion-introversion" notion. Schizophrenics, but also manics and depressives, are significantly below normal, i.e., more inviant, as are neurotics. It has no relation, or only a slightly negative relation

(as found also in questionnaire, QI, exvia measures), to school grades. EEG activation measures, when subjects are active (calculating) are greater for exviants than inviants. Contingently, one can assume most proven extraversion-introversion criteria, e.g., in Eysenck (1961), to be related to this factor.

Variables that define U.I. 32 in the O-A Kit are:

T	M.I.	
45	309	Quicker line-length judgment
62b	737	Greater willingness to decide on vague data
142a	356a	More correct attribute-naming responses
97	1169	Less influenced by extenuating circumstances
13a	763a	More fluency concerning people's characteristics
164b	2412	More garbled words heard as family words
121	15	CMS: more circles used
1d	2a(2)	Lower motor rigidity

U.I. 33: Discouragement vs. Sanguineness

This is clearly, from its content and associations, a factor of pessimism and discouragement of a lasting nature. Higher score is associated with lower socioeconomic status, poorer physique, lower self-ratings on confidence, cooperativeness, and calm objectivity. Schizophrenics tend to be above average and delinquents be86w average (both very significantly) on U.I. 33, discouragement.

Variables that define U.I. 33 in the O-A Kit are:

T	M.I.	
22b	108	Less confidence in unfamiliar situations
64b	473	Fewer people who appreciate one as a friend
40c	2413	Less willingness to participate in activities
156b	1245	More depression

39	212	Less belief in attainability to goals
9el	116a	More severe, pessimistic superego
24	112	Greater expectation of unfavorable consequences

ADDITIONAL OBJECTIVE BATTERIES FOR SOURCE TRAIT MEASUREMENTS

Our design of the O-A Battery in the decade 1968-78 recognized that about half an hour would be needed per factor to give acceptable dependability and validity coefficients. Consequently, as a compromise with the aim of covering the whole personality sphere (already reaching to some 20 T-data factors), those 10 were chosen which gave highest concept validity in *group administrable tests*, number of replications, and relevance to criteria dealt with by practitioners. In several factors, however, notably U.I. 22 (Cortertia), excellent validities could be reached if tests requiring individual administration (in this case flicker fusion, ratio of regularly to irregularly warned reaction time, fidgetometer, etc.) could be used. These have been placed in an O-A Extension. Of course, validities of those in the main 10 can be augmented by individual tests if required—and all the main 10 can naturally, though in pencil and paper form, be given as individual tests. In one case, U.I. 17, new results have come in since 1978 that would have placed it in the main 10, namely a) its alignment with the second-order factor of Control in Q-data ($F-$, G, Q_3); b) behavior genetics data showing it to be the most highly learned of factor patterns; and c) evidence of its importance in social reliability.

Any psychologist with normal experimental training can set up batteries for these factors from *Personality Theory in Action* and the descriptions of design in the compendium (Cattell & Warburton, 1967). The researcher will lack norms, but in studies with experimental and control groups these are, of course, unnecessary. The descriptions of these batteries are given below.

U.I. 17: Control: or Inhibition by Good Upbringing

This factor was called general inhibition until it was shown by Wardell and Yeudall (1976) to be apparently identical with QVIII, "restraining upbringing," or *control* in Q-data (second order in 16 P.F.; see Cattell, Eber, & Tatsuoka, 1970). The latter loads high superego, G; high self-sentiment, Q3; and desurgency, $F-$, suggesting exposure to an environment teaching control and inhibition. It correlates with high dependability and carefulness, negatively with military pilot performance, and to some extent with neurosis, as discussed in Chapter 12. The fact that U.I. 17 has a fairly strong genetic determination tells us that the good control is as much due to a receptive, docile, inhibitable temperament as to the family or school/cultural influences.

M.I.

21	Fewer questionable reading preferences
7	Slower speed of closure in gestalt completion
43	Larger G.S.R. deflection in response to threatening stimuli
336	More threatening objects seen in unstructured drawings
117	More responses indicative of "highbrow," educated taste

U.I. 22: Cortertia vs. Pathemia

This has been hypothesized to be high cortical alertness and cognitive activity relative to a predominance of feeling (pathemia) expression, such as might arise from hypothalamic action. It significantly separates (in the pathemic direction) neurotics from non-neurotics, and is potent also in job prediction. It is omitted from the primary O-A only because it demands individual tests.

M.I.

5 Higher ratio of regularly to irregularly warned reaction time

40 More responses to irrelevantly introduced reaction time stimuli

8 High frequency of alternating perspective

83 Higher fidgetometer frequency

9 Better ideomotor performance (cancellation)

A word should finally be said about the nature of some individually administered tests (some for physiological or somatic variables, as above) that can be used to augment the reliability of the O-A Batteries themselves. As stated above, the O-A Kit consists of tests, variables and factors which are conveniently measured without apparatus other than paper, pencil and a tape player. Some examples of how measurement of a particular trait can be improved by the addition of some variables requiring apparatus are:

U.I. 16: Ego Standards

T	M.I.	
138	270	Faster arm-shoulder circling tempo (individual)
304	444	Higher systolic blood pressure (individual)
230	346	Less decrease in muscular endurance over time (leg-rising) (individual)

U.I. 19: Independence

T	M.I.	
122	176	Faster irregularly warned reaction time (individual)
128(a)	80	Less rapid GSR upward drift in skin resistance (individual)
128(b)	469	More rapid GSR conditioning (individual)

U.I. 20: Evasiveness

T	M.I.	
127	42	More body sway suggestibility (individual)
121	78	Less involuntary muscle tension (individual)

An interesting example of the required gadgetry is the fidgetometer (cited above for U.I. 22, Cortertia). It consists of an ordinary-looking chair with loose joints. A person sitting in it will tend to wiggle, and the fidgetometer is rigged with a simple mercury make-break switch or a transducer which picks up the frequency of muscular tension and balance changes while the person is doing some standard task (for example, some other test in the battery).

PSYCHOMETRIC PROPERTIES AND CRITERIA RELATIONS OF THE O-A

Tables 13.1 and 13.2 (after Cattell & Schuerger, 1978) present two chief properties of the O-A Kit: its test consistencies and concept validities. Both are within acceptable bounds compared to questionnaires (cf. Schuerger, Tait, & Tavernelli, 1982; Cattell, Eber, & Tatsuoka, 1970 for comparisons), with U.I. 24 and 32, the two factors most amenable to questionnaire-like measurement, being among the highest in both cases. This finding would be consistent with both theory and experience in this medium, with factors generally being defined by a fairly heterogeneous behavior sample when compared with questionnaires (see Chapter 4 for more extensive discussion of the value of controlled heterogeneity).

It will be recalled again from Chapter 2 that we speak of three media of measurement—Q-data, L-data, and T-data—and that we speak of the *modalities* of *cognitive* ability, *motivation* (dynamic traits), and *personality* (temperamental traits). The O-A Kit is entirely in the T-

TABLE 13.1

Psychometric Consistency: Dependability, Stability, and Trait Constancy Coefficients for Each Source Trait (Calculated for Scoring by Separate Factor Method)

Universal Index No.	Factor Label	Dependability (2-24 hours)	Stability (3-6 weeks)	Trait Constancy
U.I. 16	Ego Standards	.75	.61	.81
U.I. 19	Independence	.75	.73	.97
U.I. 20	Evasiveness	.74	.64	.87
U.I. 21	Exuberance	.93	.78	.85
U.I. 23	Mobilization	.71	.71	1.00
U.I. 24	Anxiety	.90	.85	.94
U.I. 25	Realism	.62	.62	1.00
U.I. 28	Asthenia	.66	.58	.88
U.I. 32	Exvia vs. Invia	.74	.67	.91
U.I. 33	Discouragement vs. Sanguineness	.81	.80	.99

TABLE 13.2

Concept ("Construct") Validities of the 10 Main Battery Factors

Universal Index No.	Factor Label	R
U.I. 16	Ego Standards	.92
U.I. 19	Independence	.79
U.I. 20	Evasiveness	.68
U.I. 21	Exuberance	.80
U.I. 23	Mobilization vs. Regression	.76
U.I. 24	Anxiety	.92
U.I. 25	Realism vs. Tensidia ("Psychosis")	.74
U.I. 28	Asthenia	.64
U.I. 32	Exvia vs. Invia	.71
U.I. 33	Discouragement vs. Sanguineness	.85

(Using only the subtests belonging to the separately administered factor, as one factor battery, with unweighted, i.e., unit weight, subtests)

Note: The values are from a sample of 394 14-16–year-olds (193 boys; 201 girls) in the research of Cattell and Klein (1975).

data realm and in modality is in the region of "general personality," but the principle of media-transcending trait structures (Cattell, 1973a, 1979c) would lead us to expect relationships to general personality as measured by the questionnaire medium (Chapter 12). Although in common usage the modality terms "ability," "motivation," and "personality" seemed clear enough, there had been no clear operational distinction of the concepts until Cattell and Warburton (1967) worked out operational discrimination. However, when the distinction is clearly made, the question remains open whether the particular factor scales and batteries are in fact in the modality in which we imagine them to be. The practical value of knowing the modality correctly resides in a) giving correct expectation of the properties of the trait, and b) not repeating in a prediction certain traits in a way to cause wasteful

TABLE 13.3
Relationship of O-A Variables to 2nd Stratum Q- Variables

	Cattell & Birkett (1980b)	Wardell & Yeudall (1980)	Schuerger et al. (1981)	Cattell (1955b)	Cattell & Scheier (1961)
U.I. 16					
17	QVIII	QVIII	(NA)		
19	QIV (QIII)	(NA)	QIII (?)		
20					
21			QI (?)		
23	QVI (?)				
24	(NA)	QII	QII	QII	
25			QIII		
28					
32	(NA)	(NA)	Neg	QI	QI
33			QI –		

overlap. The latter question is easily answered factor analytically by asking if there is overlap of the ability, personality, and dynamic trait batteries. It has been shown in several studies that in general there is not much overlap in the trait tests described in this book, and that where it does occur it is mainly in broad and complex dynamic traits—such as ego and self-sentiment—appearing also as general personality factors.

Thus, with respect to objective personality tests, there are two questions of broader interest:

1) *Across media.* What are the relationships of the O-A Kit's personality variables (T-data) with personality variables measured in common by questionnaires (Q-data) and rating (L-data)?
2) *Across modalities.* In what places may there be some overlap of the O-A Kit's personality variables with motivational and ability variables also measured by objective devices (see Chapters 8 and 14)—or even by other media?

Addressing the first of these two questions, Cattell (1955a) first opened a vista of alignments of T-data factors with their similarly named Q-data secondaries: U.I. 32 (Exvia) with QI (Exvia); U.I. 24 (Anxiety) with QII (Anxiety), etc. For some time the issue remained tantalizingly moot, until recently three studies have again addressed the problem: those of Cattell and Birkett (1980b), Wardell and Yeudall (1980), and Schuerger, Feo, and Nowak (1981). Results are summarized in Table 13.3. The matches of U.I. 17 with QVIII and U.I. 24 with QII seem well-established. U.I. 32, thought to align with QI, has failed to do so when given the opportunity in recent researches, although Cattell (1982), in a behavior genetics analysis, suggests that this is because U.I. 32 is measuring almost purely the environmentally determined part of exvia-invia while QI (A, F, H, $Q_2(-)$), is largely the genetic part.

On the other hand, in the work with adolescents by Schuerger et al. (1981), QI had partial alignments with U.I. 21 and U.I. 33 (negatively), both of which make psychological sense but are not in simple accord with expectations from Cattell's earlier perspective. Conceivably, the QI alignment is actually with a large second-order factor among the O-A primaries, namely TIII, ardor of temperament, which loads U.I. 21, U.I. 32, and U.I. 33(−) (and also U.I. 16 and some others to a lesser degree). The alignment of U.I. 19 with Q-factors is also problematic. Cattell (1955a) found only the I primary in QIV and QIII significantly loaded. Cattell and Birkett (1980b) found U.I. 19 more clearly lined up with QIV primaries (E, I, L, M), but also with one QIII primary (I), and the latter alignment is also consistent with the finding of Schuerger et al. (1981) that QIII correlates with U.I. 19. Apparently the relationships among O-A and Q variables, although promising and gradually yielding to investigation, are not so straightforward as the first "break-throughs" suggested—except for exvia and anxiety. A new phase of programmatic research, like that which established the primaries, and of high factor analytic precision, is much called for at this juncture, and a sophisticated design could get theoretical guidance from the concepts of instrument factors and the behavior genetic concept of genetic and threptic parts in the eidolon model (Cattell, 1982).

As stated earlier, though ability, personality, and motivation factors behave largely as if in nonoverlapping spaces (Hakstian & Cattell, 1976; Cattell, 1971a, 1979a), there are some significant correlations. In one case—the ego and super-ego—the patterns crop up both as *questionnaire* and the *objective motivation* factors, as was indeed planned and expected, but other relations are more obscure. The main significant relation between ability and general personality factors occurs in T-data but negligibly in Q-data, and is shown in Table 13.4, which summarizes the correlations between certain O-A factors and three measures of mental ability, the 16 P.F. factor B, the Lorge-Thorndike total I.Q., and the WAIS, as found by various researchers. Where no significant correlation coefficient was reported, the *direction* of the relation found is indicated instead. Distinguishing first the pattern of relationships from the magnitude of the correlation coefficients, we

TABLE 13.4

Correlations Between General Ability and O-A Variables

U.I.	Cattell & Birkett 16 P.F. Factor B	Wardell & Yeudall 16 P.F. Factor B	Wardell & Yeudall WAIS Full Scale IQ	King 16 P.F. Factor B	King Lorge-Thorndike IQ
16			+	.21	.48
17	.22				
19		NA	NA	.46	.60
20			−		
21	NA	NA	NA		
23			+	.48	.59
24	NA				− .24
25		+	+	.24	.34
28	NA		−	− .38	− .45
32	NA	NA	NA		
33	NA	NA	NA		

All significant correlations from the studies are entered above. The designation NA indicates that the particular O-A variable was not included in the study. A plus (+) or minus (−) sign instead of a numerical value is used to indicate a significant correlation in the indicated direction where no numerical values were reported.

note that general ability tends to correlate positively with the "fitness" factors (U.I. 16, 19, 23, and 25), and negatively with U.I. 20 and 28. Other correlations are scattered, unsupported by more than one study, or conflicting, and we will not comment on them except to note the lone correlation of the WAIS's fluid-intelligence markers (digit span, digit symbol, etc.; see Chapter 8) with low inhibition, which fits the role of fluency in surgency. This fact of intelligence correlating with some O-A variables is in line with expectations, compared to Cattell and Warburton (1967), who noted that the nature of the objective tests themselves put more demands on intelligence. However, Cattell, in noting the resemblance in age curves, etc. (and probably heritability) between U.I. 1, Intelligence and U.I. 23, Capacity to Mobilize, has suggested a deeper explanation in terms of brain physiology. This hypothesis is that U.I. 1 and U.I. 23, 19, and 25 positively (see above) and U.I. 20 and 28 negatively (see above) form a second-order factor among T primaries because they represent different functional aspects of the same cortical mass. For example, the genetic part of intelligence may well derive from the total cortical nerve cell count, and U.I. 23 from a chemical pacemaker which aids the capacity to mobilize this mass.

With regard to the relationship between personality and motivational (dynamic) variables, very little in the realm of dynamic traits shows correlation with the O-A temperament realm. In Q-data, as indicated above, Cattell and Child (1975) give a matrix of correlations between the Motivational Analysis Test (itself an objective measure—see Chapter 14) and the 16 P.F. (Chapter 8) representing personality in the questionnaire realm. This finding supports the above hypothesis that ego strength and superego strength emerge in both, with some reduction of correlation, however, due to the instrument factors. But though some hypotheses

of O-A and Motivation linkage have been tentatively proposed (Cattell & Warburton, 1967, especially pp. 12-13), no correlations have yet been found. Thus, we can say with tolerable confidence that the O-A and the MAT waste no testing time in mutual overlap, but summate effectively, psychometrically, in the behavioral equation to give maximum prediction of criteria that naturally involve both modalities in the contribution.

Finally, let us turn to the life criterion *relevances* (or validities if one wishes) that clinical, educational, and industrial psychologists are most eager to obtain. Table 13.5 presents research sources for various criterion relevances of the O-A variables to date. Of these, only four—Dielman et al., 1970; Schuerger, Dielman, & Cattell, 1970; King, 1976; Feo, 1980—have used the O-A Kit mostly in its commercial form. The other studies identify the factors by variable matches across research studies (sometimes a problem in itself), which include usually more or fewer factors than the 10 in the O-A Kit. This fact might weaken our conclusions a bit if it were not for the substantial agreement in validities across studies (cf., for illustration, Table 13.6).

Table 13.5 is set up so the interested reader can identify sources at a glance. It includes educational, occupational, and varied clinical applications. The handbook (Cattell & Schuerger, 1978) treats each of these in considerable detail and is still quite up-to-date, so our effort here will be to present validities in outline. We skip presentation of the occupational relevances (see Chapter 19), not because we doubt the potential of the O-A Kit in this area—quite the contrary—but because the data are as yet rather too sketchy to allow confident generalization from Knapp's (1960b, 1962) valuable pioneer studies with military samples and Cattell's (1955a, 1955b) air force studies.

Correlations of O-A variables with academic proficiency are presented in Table

TABLE 13.5
Sources for Criterion Validities of O-A Variables

		Education	Occupation	Delinquency	Neurosis	Psychosis
	Brogden 1940	x				
	Cattell 1955b	x				
	Cattell & Gruen 1955	x				
	Scheier & Cattell 1958	x				
1960	Killian 1960					x
	Knapp & Most 1960		x			
	Knapp 1960a, 1960b	x				
	Cattell & Scheier 1961			x	x	x
	Knapp 1962	x	x			
	Cattell & Rickels 1964				x	
	Knapp 1965			x		
	Cattell, Rickels et al. 1966				x	
	Cattell & Killian 1967			x		
	Tatro 1968					x
1970	Dielman et al. 1970	x				
	Schuerger et al. 1970	x				
	Delhees & Cattell 1971a			x		
	Cattell, Schmidt & Bjerstedt 1972	x			x	x
	Hundleby & Loucks 1974				x	
	Ustrzycki 1974					
	Wardell & Royce 1975				x	
	Cartwright et al. 1975				x	
	King 1976	x				
1980	Wardell & Yeudall 1980	x				
	Feo 1980	x				
	Reuterman, Howard & Cartwright 1980			x	x	
	Patrick, Cattell & Price 1981					x

13.6, adapted from Feo's thesis (1980). Consistent over almost all vagaries of sample and time are positive correlations for U.I. 16, 19, 21, 23, and 25; consistently negative for U.I. 20 and 28. U.I. 24 shows negative correlations in all recent researches, positive in all earlier ones, but for the O-A Kit itself we must endorse the more recent negative correlations. These findings are in line with our understandings of the factors, and bespeak a practical utility as well, adding significantly to the prediction of academic success over that portion attainable from ability alone (King, 1976; see also Cattell & Butcher, 1968).

Clinical relevances are already dem-onstrated to be considerable. Relations of the O-A variables to main clinical syndromes are summarized in Figure 13.2. They are based on the researches listed in Table 13.5, particularly the data from Cattell and Rickels (1964), Tatro (1968), Delhees and Cattell (1971a), and Cattell, Schmidt and Bjerstedt (1972), and can be considered well-founded approximations. Noteworthy are the below-average mean scores for U.I. 16, 19, 21, and 23 over all three types. Neurotics and criminals are also unusually high on U.I. 24, Anxiety. Psychotics have, in addition, a deficit in U.I. 25 and 32 and excess on U.I. 33 (U.I. 25 is Eysenck's "psychoticism," when neg-

TABLE 13.6

Correlations of O-A Variables with Academic Achievement

INVESTIGATOR	UI 16	UI 17	UI 19	UI 20	UI 21	UI 23	UI 24	UI 25	UI 26	UI 28	UI 32	UI 33
Brogden (1940)							.40					
Cattell & Gruen (1955)							.18					
Scheier & Cattell (1958)			.30				.12					
Knapp (1960a, 1960b)				−.13*								
Knapp (1962)											.12*	
Dielman, Schuerger, Cattell (1970)					.31*	.23*	.12	.44**				
Schuerger, Dielman, Cattell (1970)	.23**	.02	.26**	−.13								
King (1976)												
Fresh.	.15		.33**	−.20*	.04	.31**	−.25**	.30**	NA	−.23*	.06	−.07
Soph.	.16	NA	.32**	−.16	.06	.25**	−.20*	.33**		−.22*	.08	−.05
Feo (1980)												
Hist.	.29**	.05*	.33**	−.10**	.13**	.16**	−.26**	.24**	−.14**	−.23**	−.02	.00
Eng.	.27**	.01	.30**	−.08**	.15**	.21**	−.27**	.21**	−.09**	−.20**	−.02	−.05*
Group 1 Math	.27**	.03	.31**	−.13**	.13**	.18**	−.17**	.23**	−.07**	−.16**	.04	−.02
Sci.	.23**	.06**	.26**	−.07**	.11**	.13**	−.21**	.22**	−.10**	−.17**	.03	.01
GPA	.32**	.05*	.36**	−.12**	.16**	.21**	−.28**	.27**	−.12**	−.23**	.01	−.02
Group 2												
Time 1	.12		.38*	.28	.11	.14	−.08	.09	NA	.15	−.14	.25
Time 2	−.11	NA	.23	−.02	−.00	.23	−.10	−.06		.03	−.15	.37*

*Significant at .05
**Significant at .01
After Feo, 1980

ative). In their extensive study with patients on forensic wards, Wardell and Yeudall add some refinements to our knowledge of the relation of O-A variables to criminality, limited however by lack of a group of normal controls within their study. Nevertheless, within their population they found U.I. 17, Control, (not in the main O-A Kit but derivable from it) most promising for separating psychopaths from "overcontrolled" and "violent aggressive" groups. The overcontrolled and psychopathic groups were low on U.I. 17 but also higher, relative to the rest of the patient sample, on U.I. 23 and 25, and lower on a factor tentatively identified as U.I. 20. Cattell, Price, & Patrick (1981)

have recently found a weighting (discriminant function) of factors U.I. 19(−), 23(−), 25(−) and 30(+), which gives a maximum separation of depressives from normals.

In a similar vein, this author and two colleagues, J. Schuler and L. C. Allen, collected follow-up data on the original sample of young men on whom the O-A Kit was tried out. At the time of the first testing, about 12 years ago, they were, on the average, 15 years old. The follow-up data for this phase of the research consisted of a questionnaire sent to their parents, including outcome data in a number of areas. Of relevance here is the area of chemical dependency—of approximately 200 parents responding, 30 reported that

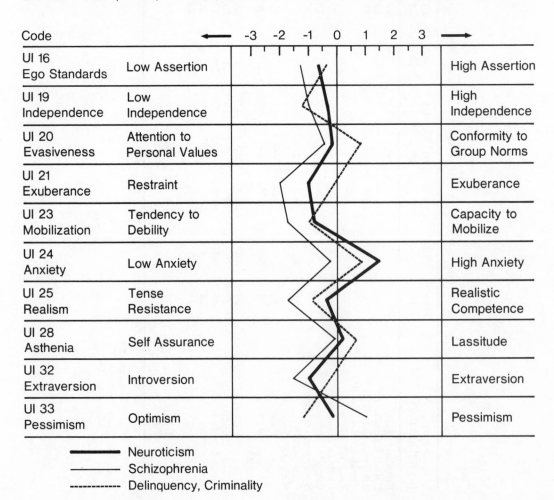

Figure 13.2. Probable pathological personality profiles from the O-A Test Kit

their son(s) had experienced some difficulty with drugs or alcohol. Discriminant function analysis yielded two significant functions which were able to correctly classify over 70% of the young men identified as problem "users," and this from test data 12 years old.

In rough form the weights for the first function included, in order of importance, U.I. 17(−), U.I. 24, U.I. 26(−), and U.I. 33—low inhibition, anxiety, low ego-centeredness, and pessimism. The second function included U.I. 19, U.I. 21(−), and U.I. 23(−) —independence, low exuberance, and regression.

PRACTICAL USE, ADMINISTRATION AND SCORING OF THE O-A BATTERY

Despite its potentially great advantages 1) in dealing with demonstrable unitary traits, around which personality theory in touch with experiment is bound to develop, and 2) in being free of what can sometimes be gross faking in the questionnaire, the O-A Battery has two shortcomings which have unfortunately initially slowed its full use by the practicing psychologist. These are: 1) the greater length of time it requires, and 2) the greater skill required in administration and scoring.

These disadvantages, however, are less real than they appear and, of course, are partly remediable by improved university courses in clinical departments. As to the first, the psychologist has evidence in the handbook (Cattell & Schuerger, 1978) and the literature as to *which* source traits are likely to give the bulk of the needed information and prediction in the case concerned. The construction of the O-A as a *kit*, from which separate factor batteries can be taken out like tools from a chest, enables particular factors or subsets to be used instead of the full battery. For example, the underlying contributions to a depressive response are U.I. 16(−), 19(−), 20(+), 21(−), 23(−), 25(−) and 30(+), and for prediction of school achievement

U.I. 16(+), 23(+) and U.I. 1 (Intelligence). This means that instead of the comprehensive O-A personality testing, which would require a rather threatening five hours, we need in such cases only two to two and a half hours of testing. Only in basic research where a thorough exploration may call for a comprehensive spread of factors are we talking of a five-hour battery, and even then, for convenience or to avoid fatigue, it is likely to be divided into hour or two-hour sessions.

The administration, in demands on skill, is about on a par with the Binet. However, the introduction of *both instruction and timing* on tape is an advance on the latter. The psychologist needs to assemble:

1) one stand-alone reusable test booklet
2) one answer sheet for it
3) a score summary sheet
4) an expendable test booklet for those "open-ended" behaviors that require marking on the test itself and cannot be put in multiple-choice format

One exception to the above is U.I. 21, which has no reusable booklet, and for which *all* subtests are on an expendable booklet.

Any single source trait battery takes about a half hour to administer. Instructions, complete with timing, are available on audiotape and make an otherwise complex job as simple as one could wish. Actually, it is in the scoring, which has to meet the need to give appropriate weight to each subtest, that the user may face some complexity. As will be seen from the carefully designed answer sheet, however, once the *derived raw scores* are obtained, reaching the standardized score is fairly mechanical (see Figure 13.1). To get derived scores one subtracts the relevant mean from each raw score and multiplies by an appropriate weight. One then sums the products to get factor scores. The weights have been precalculated so as to take into account both the raw score standard deviation (population estimate) and the weighted factor estimate value of that variable for the factor.

For some factors, the derived raw scores on which the above calculations are based are often fairly simple—e.g., nothing more than number of items completed, or number correct. In other instances, as with U.I. 20, the raw score derivation is a ratio or difference as may be seen from Figure 13.1. Certain variables also require a "special scoring instruction sheet." Put all together, these complex and simple tasks add up to a sizeable project. In all, it is our experience that to score a complete O-A protocol for one person requires about an hour. However, a computer scoring service to take care of scoring is available by special arrangement with the publisher.

More specific details and instruction on use of the standardization tables (for which age allowances are available) are left to the handbook, which also contains criterion relations organized for particular cases—clinical, educational, etc.—of practice.

SUMMARY

An objective test is defined as one in which the subject reacts to a given situation and instruction without knowing on what aspect of the response the real subjective measurement will be made. Objective tests are thus not as subject as questionnaires to deliberate or unconscious misrepresentation of the self, though, of course, equally subject to sabotage.

An untutored and confusing nomenclature has frequently equated "projective" to "objective." The former are better called *misperception tests*, and only part of the performance therein is due to projection as classically observed and defined in psychoanalysis. Through lack of analysis in terms of demonstrable personality and dynamic structure source traits, the scoring and interpretation of most projective tests have in any case remained at a "rule of thumb" level. Although the conspection reliability of the TAT is unhappily low, if it is used in conjunction with the objective, trait-defined measures of the MAT, it can usefully adumbrate those particular investments of the unitary common dynamic trait structure that are peculiar (unique trait in form) to the individual.

If we use "projective" in so broad a sense that it is almost meaningless, then tests such as the Rorschach, the Bender Word Association, Draw-a-Man, etc., can be considered a projective subclass within the domain of objective tests. By an antlike industry of examining large numbers of possible empirical associations, a number of significant "signs" have been found in these tests relating to psychiatric typologies (the DSM categories), but the reasons in terms of theory and known personality structure remain obscure. They remain thus direct score-to-symptom associations without intermediate personality concept usefulness.

Objective tests of personality factors using a particular instrumentality —humor, art, or music preference—are also available, as are some devices in the somatic-physiological area. Use of the art choice and somatic-physiological devices requires the psychologist to draw on research sources indicated, but the humor and music preference tests are in immediately practicable, standardized form. For psychometrically irrelevant reasons they seem to have had little use, though their span—11 to 12 factors—is almost as comprehensive as others in Q- and T-data.

A considerable literature of attempts to measure personality by some particular objective behavioral device or gadget, often with laboratory apparatus, can be culled between 1920 and 1970. These sporadic attacks have produced some significant relations, but almost invariably the personality differences examined were couched in terms of subjective concepts of personality never subjected to structural examination. The best of these, in terms of having some validity, were later incorporated in the factoring of the whole field of T-data as a basis for the O-A, and are now appropriately organized under its factors.

The construction of the O-A Battery was based on factors found in experiment on a comprehensive basis of over 400 types of subtest and over 2000 specific kinds of behavioral response. In principle the dimensions of its construction rest on the sampling concept in the *personality sphere*, inasmuch as devices were aimed at the factor space concepts already appearing in Q- and L-data. However, although several alignments of T-data primaries with Q-L secondaries are indicated, at present matching is far from complete and one recognizes that there is some space left peculiar to T- and to Q-data measurement areas. However, as far as can be presently seen, the T-data factors in the O-A have at least as much predictive power on everyday life and clinical criteria as questionnaires.

A list is given of the subtests in the battery for each U.I. source trait, along with the concept validities and reliabilities, the theory of the source of the trait, and the criterion relations. Up to a half hour is needed for each battery (akin to an intelligence battery) to get the desired high validities, but if individual tests are added, increases in validity, for special purposes, can be obtained. The standard and standardized 10 factor O-A Kit is called a kit because single-factor batteries or subsets of factors can be chosen according to need. Batteries for source traits beyond these 10—e.g., for personality factors U.I. 17, 20, 22, that are now realized to have significant criterion relations and research importance—are also described here.

Although requiring more time and skill by the psychologist, in group or individual administration, than questionnaires, and more understanding of personality structure reached by multivariate experiment than in the case of the Rorschach, etc., the O-A is a fully practicable, standardized, psychometrically provided (answer sheets, administration tapes, and services) instrument for routine diagnostic and counseling work. Administration and scoring are here discussed.

The dimensions found in objective tests—in the O-A, Humor, projection, etc.—appear in some cases, notably exvia and anxiety, to be identifiable with second-order Q-data factors. In terms of criterion relations, the three or four clinical, industrial, and educational area studies yet done show as high a percentage of "hits" as for other factored L- or Q-data measures. Theory is well-developed around most O-A test factors, and around the humor approach (Freud), but the basis of art and music preference test relations is still a matter for research. Although not suggested as substitutes for the O-A, etc., the humor, music, and art approaches have special values and it is suggested that the intelligence factor in the humor test, especially as augmented by extension items, would be an acceptable approach where ordinary intelligence testing meets resistances.

CHAPTER 14

Evaluating Motivation Structure, Conflict, and Adjustment

Arthur B. Sweney, Michael T. Anton, and Raymond B. Cattell

THE HISTORICAL SITUATION

The assessment of motivation has long been the province of clinical psychology, using such methods as Freud, Adler, Jung, and others employed, e.g., free association, dream analysis, hypnotism. As experimental psychology approached the field, it delivered results largely through animal research, 90% on rats in mazes, though later broadened by quantitative observations in ethology, e.g., by Lorenz, Tinbergen and others. Excellent though this research is, and informative on drives as such, it cannot with scientific confidence be carried over to humans, especially because of the trivial and fragmentary nature of anything that could be called culture in animals, but which is central in the complexities of human motivation.

The most sympathetic survey of *experimental* motivation research in humans as such, between, say, 1930 and 1980, can scarcely evaluate it as a great success. It has been pursued under too many diverse and short-lived concepts, often too ill-defined to contribute to any integrated growth. We shall here first briefly run over some of these concepts in the "historical" literature and then turn to the programmatic dynamic calculus experiments on which modern application is based. However, since our aim is to get to practical tests, we claim nothing more than a brief review of the research and theory.

Among the rather inchoate, but often experimentally well-conducted work we mention as extant, one movement stands out from the rest by the completeness of its theoretical integration, the programmatic march of its research over 30 years, and its operational setting in a mathematical model. This was brought to a clear and comprehensive statement up to 1975 in Cattell and Child's *Motivation and Dynamic Structure*. As the authors have played an active part in this development, we may be accused of overweighting it in this chapter. The reader, however, is left to evaluate its experimental and theoretical superiorities to some other current developments.

Briefly, this line of research began about 1950 by strategically asking, "What is motivation strength?" and took most measurement *devices* then being used by experimenters, plus a creation of many new devices, and intercorrelated all of them. The publications of Baggaley, Barton, Burdsal, Butcher, Cross, DeYoung, Heist, Horn, Kawash, Light, Maxwell, Miller, Radcliffe, Sweney and other coworkers with Cattell between 1945 and 1975 succeeded in clearly focusing a previously unrecognized complexity in motivation strength measurement as such. It was discovered that there were no fewer than seven factorial components in motivation measures, and two main second-order factors, the latter now being familiar as U, unintegrated, and I, integrated, motivation sources. This pattern of χ, β, γ, etc. primaries and two broad second orders was again recently confirmed by Cattell, McGill, Lawlis, and McGraw (1979) using batteries of many devices.

The finding of this totality of factors across the area of motivation manifestations made any new device precisely *concept* validatable by its correlations therewith. With these validated instruments available, this group of researchers and others then set out by similar factorial methods to explore human dynamic structure. This we shall look at more closely later. It led to the first objective determination of the number and nature of mammalian drives in humans (henceforth defined as ergs, to avoid entanglement with the uncertain meaning of "instincts"). The discovery was also made that there are many common structures *culturally acquired*, which emerge as clear factors and are important in the dynamics

of any individual clinically examined. These were called "sentiment structures" at first, and have since been abbreviated to *sems*. The main sems are to home, country, religion, job, spouse, friends, recreation, hobby, and so on.

Before delving more deeply into the nature of ergs and sems, and integrated and unintegrated motivation, it would be beneficial to review some of the experimental concepts generated by earlier research which seem to influence many of existing psychological theories in the area.

OPERATIONS AND CONCEPTS EXTANT IN THE FIELD OF MOTIVATION MEASUREMENT

At least six main concepts are necessary for the clear handling of motivation measurement.

1) A *specific interest* strength in a particular course of action. This, of course, is always in the setting of, and as a response to, a particular situation. We call this, in stimulus-response terms, an attitude, and it has several parts: "In these circumstances I want so much to do this with that." That is to say, it has a life situation, a strength (which may or may not be permitted to act), an object, and a course of action about that object.

2) A drive or *erg* (rhymes with berg), an innate source of energy (hence erg) directed to a particular type of consummatory satisfaction and accompanied by a characteristic emotion. Ergs, which are paralleled by instincts in our mammalian relatives, are the initial sources of human energy and reactivity.

3) A *sentiment* or *"sem."* This is a unitary pattern of interest derived from the investment of ergs in the forms of activity encouraged by institutions in our culture. That is to say, it is an acquired, learned structure, e.g., to home, sport, religion, job, which is unitary in cor-

relational terms and which different people acquire to different degrees according to the degree to which the attitudes in the sem have been conditioned (reinforced, repeated, rewarded).

Any sem has a definite *ergic invest-ment*, i.e., it has come to offer a habitual outlet to the needs of a particular combination of ergs. A sem is thus a source of motivation, as was once perceived in the notion of a "secondary drive," but it is, of course, not a drive in the well-defined sense of an erg, e.g., hunger, fear, or sex, because its unitary structure actually welds several ergic expressions.

4) *Activation* and *arousal*. An erg is *aroused* by a stimulus, but a sem is *activated*. The former involves visceral emotion and conation; the latter is initially the *cognitive* activation of the ideas and connection in a sem, and in turn arouses the ergs channeled in a sem.

5) The distinction of *need strength, drive strength* and directly measured *ergic tension*. Need strength is the constitutional strength of an erg in any given individual. It is partly genetic and partly a result of the kind of experiences which Freud argued affected the fixation and maturation level of an erg. At any given moment, however, an erg is at some phase in a cycle of appetitiveness and of gratification by rewards. If we call need strength, N, and degree and recency of gratification, G, then we define drive strength, D, by

$$D = N - G \qquad (14\text{-}1)$$

But this inner drive strength, fixed by the state of the organism, encounters external stimulation of a strength we will call S. Then what we actually measure, e.g., by a test such as the MAT or the size of a GSR response, is ergic tension level, E, thus

$$E = S \cdot D = S (N - G) \qquad (14\text{-}2)$$

These formulae are dealt with in a somewhat more refined model, and illustrated in Cattell and Child's *Motivation and Dynamic Structure* (1975), and summarized in equation 14-3 below.

6) The distinction of unconscious, U, and integrated conscious motivation, I. This has existed in psychoanalysis but has been given operational and measurable form by the discoveries concerning objective measures of strength of motivation. It has been shown that these devices fall into seven or eight distinct primary factors, indexed as χ, β, γ, etc., and that these fall into second-order factors U and I. The U factor loads such devices as projection, autism, GSR response and other physiological measures, while the I factor loads more cognitive, learned expressions of interest, such as word association, information, etc. Some valuable clinical inferences on conflict, etc. can be drawn from the relations of U and I measures. It should be noted that this is not simply the Freudian conscious and unconscious, but is based on validity-tested objective motivation measures which factor analysis has shown to fall into these two unitary sources.

These basic concepts are encountered in various forms in the general literature of motivation and experimental findings.

$$E_k = (S) [L] = (S_k + Z) [c(C + H + I) + \{(P_k - aG_k) + (N_k - b\tilde{G}_k)\}]$$

Appetitive state strength

Need strength

Resultant ergic tension

$(14\text{-}3)$

For example, *activation* is discussed in Hebb (1949), Duffy (1962), Lindsley (1957). Ergic tension has been studied sometimes simply as muscle tension, but Bindra (1959) and Olds (1956a) conceive it as cited here, namely, as a general onset of motivation which is the initial general state before a specific drive emerges. By factor studies Curran and Cattell (1976) have identified and measured it as a general state, distinct from the specific semic activations in the MAT, but probably connected as Olds indicates.

However, some other concepts in earlier literature fit less well. In Chapter 15 here on *states* it is shown that the *modulation* model for general states is the same as the above $E = S \cdot D$ for ergic tension deriving from a drive, though for activation of a particular sem or arousal of a particular drive its symbolization has been trivially different, namely:

$$\text{Activation} = s_{kx} T_{xi} \qquad (14\text{-}4)$$

where a trait (erg or sem), T_{xi}, is modulated by a value, s_{kx}, specific to the character of T_{xi} and to the life situation k.

When an equilibrium in the process of learning has been reached, s_k will be a function of the reward to trait T_{xi} which people have experienced in the past, e.g., the hunger drive in the course of action motivated by this activation. In discussion of experiments, the reflexological term "reinforcement" is unfortunately ambiguous, sometimes meaning "reward" and sometimes referring to the subsequent *strengthening* of the bond that *may* occur through the experience. Consequently, in structured learning theory, which is closely connected with motivation theory as expressed in measurement practice here, the term *reward* is used. It differs from "reinforcement" even in the latter's "reward" sense because it is not considered general but is always specific to a particular kind of ergic drive and is in fact measured as drive strength reduction (gratification, G, in the above equation). The reason for writing a particular vector of ergic satisfactions for each learning rather than leaving the measure as simply "reinforcement" is based on the evidence that the effect on memory of different ergic rewards may be different. Motivational (interest) analysis by objective tests, as in the MAT below, has made it possible to assign reward indices to specific ergs. Incidentally, no mystery need be construed to the terms "reward," "punishment," and "deprivation." The confusion has arisen from thinking of punishment as pain; but the latter is readily brought into the general conception of punishment as being the deprivation of an ergic goal—as in the case of the goal of the escape erg (fear).

The varieties of terms currently in use being somewhat chaotic, it is necessary in the section that follows to go somewhat further into general motivation and the dynamic calculus.

THE SOURCES OF MOTIVATION AND INTEREST IN HUMAN DYNAMIC STRUCTURES

Speculation into the "whys" of human behavior must be as old as the species itself and may even exist in infrahumans, as many pet owners would testify. The systems developed by McDougall (1900), Freud (1938), Murray et al. (1938) and Maslow (1954) were but a few of the complex systems developed mentalistically to account for internally directed behavior. McDougall's work on instincts and Murray's on "needs" were premature and almost disregarded when the Zeitgeist for behaviorism (reflexology) invaded intellectual circles. Murray was somewhat more careful to include in his explanatory constructs both internal "needs" and external "presses." This, coupled with an operational means for measurement, the TAT, bought him the time needed to develop a productive discipleship. Individual researchers sliced up his pie, with each taking a "need" to study intensely. In this way McClelland (1955) studied the Need for Achievement, Schachter (1959) the need for Affiliation, and Veroff (1957) the need for Power. Meanwhile, clinicians such as Rapaport, Gill, and Schafer (1946, 1968), Bellak (1954, 1975), and many others have advocated and spurred on the clinical use of the TAT as a projective technique for the study of an individual's motivations and personality under many diverse systems.

This very fragmentation may have led to too many "one drive" explanations of motivation and the recognition that these subjective classifications of motives (reaching an ultimate in Maslow) could not be considered part of an experimental science. There followed a radical new beginning characterized by: 1) first finding the validity of objective measures of interest and motivation strength (see lists of devices in χ, β, γ, etc. factors and U and I factors in Cattell and Child, 1975, and 2) factoring a personality sphere of human attitude and interests to discover the dynamic structures (ergs and sems) operating.

(Incidentally, these findings did not prevent such test constructors as Edwards (*Personal Preference Schedule*, 1954) and Jackson (*Personal Research Form Manual*, 1965) from putting considerable itemetric work into constructing questionnaires based on Murray's framework. We shall raise later the issue of whether a questionnaire in any case is suitable for reliable reaching motives, as distinct from temperament traits. Edwards's *Personal Preference Schedule* (1954) strictly does not qualify as a structured instrument, because of the lack of factoring or any other theoretical scheme for relating the catalogue of scales.*)

---

*Although Maslow's notions of what structures exist were totally different from Murray's and from Edwards's and Jackson's concretization of Murray's lists, they were no less devoid of empirical correlational evidence. That system has had a following partly because it fit the cultural swing in the '60s toward "self-realization," and partly because a growing interest in values required a hierarchical emphasis.

In contrast to the trail that petered out from Murray's list, the older theories of Freud are still very much alive in clinical circles. It should be recognized that, although not quantitative and experimental, Freud and Jung, as well as the ethological Lorenz, Tinbergen (and one must add McDougall), were faithful and acute empirical observers. Freud, nevertheless, finished with an almost mystical division into two drives—Eros, as sexual libido, and Thanatos, the death instinct covering aggression and the repetition compulsion. The distortion of Freud's views may have resulted from his observations on a largely prosperous middle class, respectably repressed Viennese sample, free from unsatisfied hunger, thirst, need for security, parental protective expressions, etc. At any rate, in the new experimental phase we shall now briefly explain, the ergs found in man matched none of the above except the instincts observed by ethologists, from Darwin to Lorenz, in primates and other mammals (see Table 14.1).

The experimental inroads into motivation by the necessary multivariate methods, which took place between 1950 and 1980, have already been sketched above as a strategy of a) discovering and introducing valid objective devices for measuring any interest strength, and b) the mapping of dynamic structures by factoring a very broad array of interest-attitudes as defined above. The development may be read in the work of the team Cattell, Heist, Heist, and Stewart (1950), Cattell (1957c), Cattell and Baggaley (1956), Cattell, Blewett, and Beloff (1955), Cattell and Sweney (1964), Cattell, Horn, Sweney, and Radcliffe (1964b), Cattell and Butcher (1968), Sweney and Cattell (1962), Sweney (1969), Cattell and Child (1975), Cattell (1980a), and others. This multivariate programmatic work identified about a dozen primary "instincts" but redefines them as *ergs* to keep initially to the *operational basis* (unlike that of "instincts") on which they actually stand

TABLE 14.1
List of Human Ergs

Goal Title	Emotion	Status of Evidence
Food-seeking	Hunger	Replicated factor; measurement battery exists
Mating	Sex	Replicated factor; measurement battery exists
Gregariousness	Loneliness	Replicated factor; measurement battery exists
Parental	Pity	Replicated factor; measurement battery exists
Exploration	Curiosity	Replicated factor; measurement battery exists
Escape to security	Fear	Replicated factor; measurement battery exists
Self-assertion	Pride	Replicated factor; measurement battery exists
Narcissistic sex	Sensuousness	Replicated factor; measurement battery exists
Pugnacity	Anger	Replicated factor; measurement battery exists
Acquisitiveness	Greed	Replicated factor; measurement battery exists
Appeal	Despair	Factor, once replicated; battery exists
Rest-seeking	Sleepiness	Factor, but of uncertain independence
Constructiveness	Creativity	Factor, but of uncertain independence
Self-abasement	Humility	Factor, but of uncertain independence
Disgust	Disgust	Factor absent for lack of markers
Laughter	Amusement	Factor absent for lack of markers

From Cattell, R. B., *Personality and Learning Theory, Vol. 1: Structure of Personality in Its Environment*, p. 143. Copyright © 1979 by Springer Publishing Company, Inc., New York. Used by permission.

(factoring of objective motivation measures). This nomenclature avoids the trailing assumptions and misunderstandings associated with talk of "instincts" and "drives."* Later the researches of co-workers developed an analysis of *ergs* into *ergic tension* levels, *appetitive components* and an inherent "*need strength*," which

*The use of objective devices to validly measure motivation rather than relying on questionnaire methods is of great significance here for several reasons. Questionnaire methods which depend on self-evaluation are notoriously subject to distortion in the motivational sphere for several important reasons. First of all, the individual responding to the questionnaire may choose to deliberately disguise his motives simply because he does not wish to reveal them. Further, even if he did wish to honestly display all of his most private motives, he is quite unlikely to be able to do so accurately, particularly since a good deal of them are inevitably unconscious or unavailable to him due to his own inner dynamic conflicts. However, object test devices have the distinct advantage of disguising the elements of motivation they are actually measuring. Therefore, they are particularly resistant to the type of distortion which renders questionnaire items largely useless in motivational research. A further limitation of the type of data they produce will be discussed later in relation to the actual components of motivation.

external stimulation brings to an actual ergic tension level at a given moment (Cattell & Child, 1975), as in equation 14-3.

These same multivariate experiments on diverse human behaviors unearthed, however, an important second class of "dynamic factors" which Cattell initially called *sentiments*, after McDougall's concept, and later simply *sems*. These structures are the instrumentalities like money and family which have taken on "secondary drive" value. Cattell and Child (1975) list over 27 of these culturally produced unitary structures based upon their own work and the theoretical positions of others.

Incidentally, the concept of sems has been approached in many nonexperimental writings, such as Allport's (1937a) "functionally autonomous" dimensions, and of course in the popular use of "fixed sentiments." However, as the dynamic lattice in Figure 14.1 shows, the sems are not actually autonomous but eventually subsidiate (to use Murray's term) to ergic goals, as we go from left to right of Figure 14.1.

The actual lists of dynamic structures so far located as common traits in our culture are given in Table 3.6 (ergs) (p. 46) and Table 3.7 (sems)* (p. 47) and should be consulted in what follows.

THE DYNAMIC BEHAVIORAL EQUATION FOR EVALUATING THE ACTION OF STRUCTURES IN SITUATIONS

Since the two steps of a) validating devices for measuring *any* attitude-interest and b) factoring a personality sphere of diverse attitude-interests to define ergs and sems seem often to get confused, a very brief reiteration is probably desirable. In the first, such devices as GSR to stimuli of the attitude, projection of the interest, fluency on the topic, and selective perception have been factored to yield α, β, etc. and finally U and I components. (It should be briefly noted here that questionnaire data tap only the first of these, completely failing to measure six out of these seven independent areas of motivation. Thus, research using solely this type of measuring device must be designated as simply inadequate in a full explanation of this area.) These primary (α, β, etc.) motivation components can be studied elsewhere (Cattell & Child, 1975), but since practice has to economize, the batteries for users, in the MAT, SMAT, and VIM employ only the broad second-

order factors spanning these, namely, the U, unintegrated, and the I, integrated, motivational components. That is to say, correlation shows that a quite distinct U and I score can be given to any attitude or to any aggregate of attitudes measuring an erg or a sem. Both Sweney and Cartwright (1966) have pointed out that these measures may be considered very similar to unconscious and conscious in the Freudian sense (but, as Cattell, 1979c, cautions, these concepts may not be fully identical). Sweney and Vaughan (1976b) have listed a number of possible interpretations, including the Hullian drive strength vs. habit strength (see comment below), and various other possible interpretations can be considered.* The reader will find as complete a discussion as is possible today on this U and I difference in Chapters 17 and 18.

Regarding the second structural research step of factoring a broad span of attitude-interest strengths to reach the *dynamic structure factors*—ergs and sems—it will have been noticed that an attitude is defined differently from the old "for-and-against" polling use. An attitude in this newly defined sense is an *interest in responding with a given course of action to a given situation and object*. When a set of such courses of useful action all operate about a particular object or subgoal, we

---

*As far as sentiment structures are concerned it has turned out that *non*objective measuring devices, such as questionnaires, when factored, discover the same patterns (as far as cross-matching is possible). See references to Guilford, Thurstone, Gundlach & Cerum, Torrs, Ferguson, Humphreys & Strong, Thorndike, Cartar, Pyles & Bretnall, Lurie, Vernon and others in Cattell & Child (1975, p. 46). Recently, Lorr and Brazz (1979) have studied dynamic structure using Holland's (1973) choice of variables through the medium of questionnaire data for which they obtained 10 or 11 factors (11 for boys, 10 for girls). Their work cannot be integrated here due to the lack of identifying markers and other methodological differences.

*Recent interest in the distinctions between intrinsic and extrinsic motivation stimulated by the research of Herzberg (1966), Deci (1975), Kruglanski et al. (1971) and Luyten and Lens (1981) theorize about other possible ways of studying the manifestation facet of motivation. Herzberg's two factors could be considered U and I components if the drive areas themselves were partialed out. Psychology has played with endless terms since Lewin about inner and outer valences, incentives and drives (Hull, 1943), instrumentality (Vroom, 1964; Fowler, 1965), and inner and outer locus of control (Rotter, 1966). It has been a misunderstanding of trait theory (temperamental or dynamic) that it neglects this distinction. In some writings it may, but the basic behavioral equation used throughout this book and Cattell's further development of this in the dynamic calculus, express the inner and outer origins of final behavior both more precisely and more richly than most of these discussions, as will be seen in the next section.

have an acquired sentiment structure—*sem* henceforth—which is psychologically attached to that object, e.g., the mother, a job, a sports team.

Now if we wish to estimate how well a person will perform in a certain course of action, e.g., getting through college, we should use a behavioral equation (equation 2-3, p. 17) incorporating *all three* trait modalities—abilities, temperament traits, and dynamic traits. This reminds us that we should take into account the person's scores on *p*, abilities, *q*, general personality traits, and, *r*, dynamic traits. This

would be written where the summation sign, Σ, says sum over all *p* ability traits, etc.

$$a_{hjk} = \Sigma^{x-p} b_{hjkx} A_{xi} + \Sigma^{y-q} b_{hjky} T_{yi} + \Sigma^{z-r} b_{hjkz} D_{zi} \tag{14-5}$$

That is to say, the total personality will enter into the performance. However, since we want to concentrate on dynamics here, and therefore on an a_{hjk}, which is purely the *strength of interest* in doing what is done (which is often all a clinician or assessor would want to know), we shall

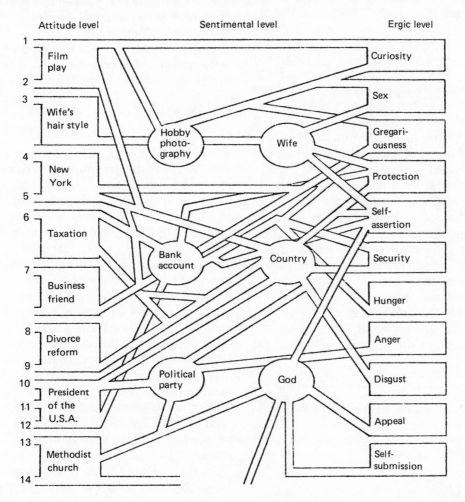

Figure 14.1. Dynamic lattice

From Cattell, R. B., *Personality and Learning Theory, Volume 2: A Systems Theory of Maturation and Structured Learning*, p. 77. Copyright © 1980 by Springer Publishing Company, Inc., New York. Used by permission.

use only the third term. The D's (dynamic traits) in the third term are either E's (ergic drive strengths) or M's (sentiments). An ergic tension level from an aroused erg will be (equation 14-2) in the full symbolization $\bar{E} = s_{ke}E$ and an *activated* sem $\bar{M} = s_{km}M$ and we might expect to write the estimate of strength of an interest, I_j, as

$$I_{hijk} = v_{hjke}s_{ke}E_i + v_{hjkm}s_{km}M_i \qquad (14\text{-}6)$$

(using for the moment only one erg and one sem. The v's are the weights of these two dynamic traits (aroused by s_{ke} and activated by s_{km}) in determining the interest I_{hjk}.

A somewhat more complex formula can be proposed, but for the sake of keeping practical calculations relatively simple here we shall keep to this approximation.*

In the present state of knowledge we conclude that the relative role of the E and the M terms, i.e., their v weights, will depend on what tests we use to measure the interest strength, I_{hjk}. If the battery has a predominance of devices for the U component, then presumably it will register the ergic tension, less conscious E components, while if integrated (I) component devices constitute much of the measurement, the cognitive activation that is in sems will come more into the measurement. However, it has been shown definitely that there is enough cognitive content in the ergs and enough ergic involvement in the sems for both kinds of

---

*The above subtests are suitable for both group and individual administration. The following set of subtests may be added for use in individual administration:

Order of Presentation	5	6
Time	15-20 min.	15-20 min.
Psychologist's Title	GSR to Frustrating Stimulus	Decision Time
Examinee's Title (Client's)	Enforced Moods	Reaction Time

dynamic structure to appear when either U or I measures are factored.

Thus, although in the objective test measurement batteries, such as the MAT and SMAT, we can measure U and I components with some degree of separation, the typical measure of an attitude interest, of an erg or a sem, by such a test is telling us both the ergic tension (drive arousal) and the sem activation contributions to that measure.

Applied psychological research has still to provide us with knowledge of the weights (the v's and s's; or the equivalent b's) for most common human interests. One might speculate, however, from Woliver's (1979) use of the MAT on young married couples, that the interest of one in the other would settle at some such values as the following in the dynamic behavioral equation:

$$I = .5E_1 + .3E_2 + .3E_3 + .2M_1 + .3M_2 \qquad (14\text{-}7)$$

where E_1 is sex erg, E_2 is the need for security, E_3 is the parental protective erg, M_1 is the sem to home and M_2 the self-sentiment. Some checked values are available for various school achievements (Cattell & Butcher, 1968) and Anton is in process of obtaining them for certain sociopolitical attitudes. For the clinician the greatest use lies in the behavioral index values obtained by P-technique, for these give the sources of motivation for some symptom, as Birkett and Cattell (1978) have illustrated in the case of an alcoholic. It is, indeed, quite correct to describe the application of the dynamic calculus to objective ergic and semic measures as "quantitative psychoanalysis." The penetration into clinical understanding and life prediction which the dynamic calculus permits will be developed in the next section. But meanwhile it is important to keep the experimental concepts clear among a mass of semi-experimental, clinical and purely subjective terms. *Need strength* is the constitutionally given value at the time. *Drive strength* is much the same as in the use of Hall, Berlyne, and others, taking account of appetitive additions to need strength. *Ergic tension* is drive strength as finally caused by a situational impact.

In dealing with the learned value of incentives, most writers—Hull (1952), Tolman ("expectancies") (1959), Lewin (1935), Vroom (1964), Porter & Lawler (1968), House & Wahba (1972)—have dealt with a single conditioned piece of behavior, whereas in the dynamic calculus we recognize that factor analysis shows in man the existence of more complex unitary, cognitive networks of acquired response which we call sems. These involve what have sometimes been called "reinforcement values" for a whole set of objects and subgoals. Thereby stimuli have "reward values" which Olds (1956a) operationally defined by the product of the likelihood and the intensity of an elicited response. This is one operationalization of Hull's "habit strength," which is *represented by the M terms in the dynamic behavioral equation.*

However, as just stated, the dynamic calculus model does not stop at habit strength of single responses but recognizes that an M is a common term to several responses, and has other special properties. It is the product of *integration learning* (Cattell, 1979c) which has not often been recognized, although Anderson (1978) does so in the notion of "stimulus integration." This means the combination of separate stimuli into an organized response, and he suggests that a "valuation" exists for the psychological components from various stimuli. This "integration" is represented by the combination of elements within the dynamic lattice (see Chapter 14), and the "valuation" by the weights given in the dynamic equation. Yet another term found in discussions of motivation is "frustration value," originally implied in the "Zeigarnik effect" (1927) and perhaps in Festinger's "cognitive dissonance." It is precisely expressed in the measurement of *ergic*

investment in a sentiment, and of course, the frustration of ergic tension itself. From McDougall's and Lorenz's generalizations of the strength of pugnacity (anger) being proportional to the strength of whatever ergic tension is frustrated (known less richly and accurately as the "frustration aggression" concept), it follows that the "frustration value" (the anger, and contingently, depression) from the loss of a sentiment object, should be proportional to the ergic investment in that sem object. Unfortunately, this hypothesis, now open to experiment with objective motivation measures such as the MAT, has not yet been tested.

Quite the most scholarly and insightful survey of the above field of motivation concepts is available in Madsen's two volumes (1974, 1977). A fully integrated view of the dynamic calculus approach is available in Cattell and Child (1975). A very up-to-date view of the bearing on clinical psychology by experts in the field is available in Chapters 16 and 17 here. However, as a preparation for these latter topics, we shall give in the following section the theoretical background of clinical testing, as a continuation of the foundations already built. This will be followed by a detailed discussion of the actual tests available.

THE MEASUREMENT OF CONFLICT AND ADJUSTMENT

The above basic research advances between 1945 and 1975 have led, as far as testing of structures is concerned, to batteries (such as the MAT, the SMAT, and to some degree the TAT) applying objective devices for a) simply determining the individual's ergic tension levels on his or her main ergs and sems, as a basis for prediction in school achievement, counseling vocationally, and diagnosing in clinics, and b) more complex derivatives in terms of measures of internal conflict, the discovery of particular areas of conflict, and the estimation of total adjustment.

Before turning to actual test use, we need to spend one more section here on research and theory—in this case on the models of conflict and integration. There are three ways in which measurement of conflict has been brought to a rational and objective basis:

1) By discovering the factor loadings for the various ergs and sems for a given course of action or symptom expression. If negative loadings appear we are dealing with conflict—of an *indurated* and possibly unconscious nature. It will be remembered that conflict is either a) overt and unresolved "action conflict" or b) resolved by a compromise leaving a course of action in which some ergs and sems may be dissatisfied. The latter is called "indurated conflict."

2) If there is an excess of the U over the I motivational component, we are dealing with an erg or ergs in which a need for expression exists that has a) never moved out into successful experience and expression, or b) been withdrawn from expression by suppression or repression. This may or may not be conflict: it *could* be merely *deprivation of expression* by circumstances. Let us recognize that all internal conflict begins in conflict with the environment (see the *Adjustment Process Analysis Chart*, Cattell & Child, 1975, p. 68). The (U-I) operational measure therefore needs ancillary data to be sure of an interpretation that we are actually dealing with inner conflict.

3) The recognized clinical signs of conflict—slips of memory, anxiety, muscle tension, fantasy, and other defenses —can be grouped by multivariate research into meaningful dimensions and embodied in a test or rating system (Cattell & Sweney, 1964). This is shown by research analyses, but pragmatic instruments for measuring the conflict dimensions have not yet been made available for general distribution.

Let us expand briefly on each of these three indicators of conflict. As stated above, conflict in a given situation between two courses of action can be fully conscious and sufficiently represented by the dynamic behavioral equation for showing what weights and strengths the various ergs and sems play in it. A simple formula has been suggested for the severity of such overt *action conflict*, namely:

$$C_a = \frac{a_{hixk} + a_{hiyk}}{a_{hixk} - a_{hiyk}} \tag{14-8}$$

where a_{hixk} is the strength of the response course of action x, (the larger)—personality as well as dynamic terms entering—and a_{hiyk} that of the attitude course y. A modification would be to use e_{hixk} and e_{hiyk}—the dynamic part only, as in equation 14-2. What this says is that the amount of conflict and the degree of difficulty in decision are a function positively of the strength of the two impulses and inversely of the difference of magnitude between them.

Such a measure deals only with a particular life situation conflict, and should for greatest accuracy have the loadings determined by P-technique. It does not necessarily tell us anything about the total personality, being situational. However, most set courses of life action have become long settled upon as compromises between satisfaction of one erg and deprivation on another and the dynamic part of the behavioral equation would therefore show what has been called *indurated conflict*, by negative loadings, as illustrated in:

$$e_{hiyk} = .5E_{1i} - .2E_{2i} - .3E_{3i} + .3E_{4i} \tag{14-9}$$

where the outcome of summation is positive, but a total deprivation loading sum of $-.5$ results.

This can be used (multiplied by E

strengths appropriate for individual i) as a clearly conceived measure of indurated conflict in the action a_{hijk}. Summed, say, over the same stratified sample of total life attitudes (giving a score for each of 100 individuals), it should permit comparison of the total conflict in their several adjustments. The inverse of this score, which is essentially *degree of integration*, should theoretically correlate with ego strength and stability measures, which it does (Williams, 1959), and also with the third measure of conflict described earlier, now to be discussed though not yet in test form.

Sweney (1967) found that several of the objective measures of motivation from Cattell, Radcliffe & Sweney (1963), Cattell & Baggaley (1956) and Tapp (1958) were also related to measures of strength of frustration. Taking some two dozen clinically accepted indicators of conflict, as indicated above (muscle tension, defenses, vacillation, slips), Sweney replicated in three independent experiments six basic dimensions of conflict (Cattell & Sweney, 1964). These were meaningful in relation to a number of *loci* (defining the life area, e.g., family, job) and *foci* (defining the dynamic structures involved). This work has been carried further by Krug (1971) with indications of relation between the conflict factors and the motivation components. Unfortunately, as stated above, no psychologist has yet put these objective conflict measurement devices for direct conflict measurement into an easily usable and standardized clinical test, though this should offer no special difficulty.

Before leaving research and theory for actual tests, let us note that suggested ad hoc measurement devices of one kind or another are abundant, but that we have kept here, and in the TAT later, to measures supported by theory and growing from programmatic research. As mentioned above, the reader who wants to get a perspective over the whole field can scarcely do better than see Madsen's *Mod-ern Theories of Motivation: A Comparative Metascientific Study* (1974) covering writing since the clinical phase of Freud, Jung, and Adler. Therein he calculates Hypotheses Quotients, H.Q.s, showing the degree of operational testability of most theories that have been propounded. His tabular summary shows his conclusions. Note that a *low* H.Q. means greater operational definition and a broader testing basis. This is what has been aimed at in Table 14.2.

THE MAT, TAT, SMAT AND OTHER TESTS

In 1936, Murray and Cattell simultaneously and independently, respective in the U.S. and the U.K., published motivation test measures, resting on the theory of *projection*. The *projective* tests, of the style of the Rorschach, the Szondi, the Bender-Gestalt, the Word Association Test, and the Thematic Apperception Test (TAT), must be distinguished from true projection tests, because they depend on unknown collections of misperceptive processes and defenses, whereas the theory of these two pioneer tests was that there would be a true *dynamic projection*, in the sense of Freud's definition, of the motives of the client as he or she interpreted the behavior of perceived others.

The Cattell tests (1936) gave the situation verbally and were multiple choice in scoring, whereas the TAT used pictures and was open-ended in scoring. As research proceeded, Cattell and Wenig (1952) attacked the whole problem of identifying from individuals' interpretive perceptions the main factors that are at work in misperception (defined relative to the norm of the average). Strong factor analytic support was found for projection being only one of several mechanisms, and for the existence of several distinct defense mechanisms, defined by Anna Freud, such as true dynamic projection, autism, ra-

TABLE 14.2
The Hypotheses Quotients

We have made a classification of the theories according to the ratio between the purely *theoretical* (H-H) hypotheses and the partly *empirical* (S-H and H-R) hypotheses. These ratios were calculated according to our formula for the *Hypotheses Quotient*:

$$H.Q. = \frac{\Sigma(H\text{-}H)}{\Sigma[(S\text{-}H) + (H\text{-}R)]}$$

The results of these calculations for both the modern and the earlier theories of motivation are:

Modern Theories:	H.Q.:	Earlier Theories:	H.Q.:
Cattell	0.09	Tinbergen	0.11
Maslow	0.13?	Hebb	0.13
Duffy	0.14	McClelland	0.14
Miller (I)	0.20	Hull	0.36
Pribram	0.29	McDougall	0.43
Bindra	0.30	Lewin	0.50
Atkinson and Birch	0.33	Murray	0.71
Berlyne	0.38	Young	0.82
Brown	0.38	Allport	1.00
Konorski	0.54	Tolman	1.43
Woodworth	0.57		
Miller (II)	0.60		
Festinger	0.84		
Atkinson	0.86		

tionalization, and fantasy. Some primary personality associations were found for these, e.g., factor L on the 16 P.F. with stronger adoption of projection as a defense. A new finding was that the factor of *true* dynamic projection with unconscious processes could be separated from a unitary tendency to *naive projection*, a generalized tendency to interpret events and stimuli in the light of one's own experience.

With this sufficient, but still research-incomplete finding, Cattell abandoned the test design of assuming "mis-interpretation" (personal deviation from the average) to be completely due to projection, and entered on the programmatic research on motivation measurement through use of many defense mechanisms and the whole gamut of physiological and other alleged motivation expressions described above. This culminated in combining the best four to six subtests, as in the MAT, pooling scores actually from true projection, autism, selective memory, word association, fantasy, fluency, etc.

The divergence between designs of Murray's TAT and the modern MAT derived from these 30 years of experimentation is of three kinds:

1) The TAT is interpreted as if the personal (mis)perceptions were due to projection, whereas the MAT is founded on the complete sampling of motivation components.

2) The cards for the TAT were selected to provide responses on Murray's list of rationally defined "needs" (though the psychologist is free to posit his or her

own), whereas the MAT and SMAT cover ten empirically derived factorially checked *dynamic structure* factors—five of the most relevant ergs and five of the strongest sems in most people.

It has been suggested that the TAT can catch not just drive strengths (ergic tensions) but also Jungian archetypes and other more complex situational-involvement patterns such as the tie-up of self-assertion with say, a sibling rivalry pattern, of sex with an oedipal family experience, and so on. If this could be done reliably it would introduce a class of information which the MAT, specifically directed to scores on the ergic tension levels (across the whole area of expression of each) and on the levels of sem development, does *not* claim to supply. Inferences on those more specific dynamic entanglements from the TAT may or may not have validity, but it is psychometrically well-established that the MAT validly and reliably measures the specific ergic tension and sem development levels.

3) The third difference is implicit in the preceding sentence. the MAT is *conspective* (multiple choice) in scoring; the TAT is open-ended, and experience shows that different administrators and scorers show quite poor conspect reliability on the TAT. Where there is poor reliability, there has to be poor final validity. But reliability coefficients are not the main basis for claiming higher ultimate validity for drive level estimates from the MAT and SMAT. The basis, as described in the introductory research above, is that exhaustive multivariate experiment has shown validity of the MAT devices as *concept validity* against the main motivation strength factors, and concrete validity against time and money spent on interests.

What a *thorough* clinical motivation analysis procedure should probably settle down to is a *joint* use of the MAT and TAT:

the MAT to "block in" reliably the main ergic tensions and sem levels and the TAT to explore the unique attachments of these ergs that a common trait study alone does not catch. Because of the nature of the TAT, this second phase will remain an art (see McClelland et al., 1953). It ill-behooves clinicians to think that their artistry can erase the real constraints inherent in the instruments they use and hence they might well depend on the firmer ground of the MAT before turning to what is in part a meretricious crystal ball in the TAT. With this we turn to a brief description of the practical form and use of the tests themselves.

The Thematic Apperception Test

The Thematic Apperception Test (TAT) was introduced by Morgan and Murray in 1935 as a projective technique which would evoke fantasies. The test consisted of a series of pictures meant to represent ambiguous social situations, for which the respondent was to make up stories. It was thought that through this medium the covert and unconscious complexes of the individual would be revealed for scrutiny. The test is based on the assumption that as the individual interprets or "apperceives" (interpreting the stimuli by assimilating it in light of past experience) the pictures, he is actually revealing his own personality by identifying with the material he is describing. This he does by projecting into the characters his own impulses, feelings, and thoughts. As he becomes involved in the task, he becomes less aware of himself and of the examiner, unconsciously becoming less vigilant defensively. In this way, the trained observer may obtain a picture of the person's dynamics, motivations, and most private hopes and fears.

The TAT has been through three revisions since its introduction by Morgan and Murray. In its current form it consists of a series of 31 pictures. The pictures are meant to tap most of the significant relationships with others. About a third are considered appropriate for both sexes, with roughly a third for females and a third for males. The card content varies in stimulus ambiguity from depicting everyday situations to less structured fantasy material. The test has been used with young children through the adult age range. According to Murray (1943), a full test requires two sets of ten cards each, administered in two separate testing sessions. Each session lasts approximately an hour, with about five minutes spent on each card.

As with most aspects of use of the TAT, the procedural details of administration vary among different clinicians. Some have advocated its use as a self-administered instrument where examinees are requested to write stories about each picture. Others have suggested showing the pictures to groups of people by projecting them onto a screen and having each person write his or her own story for the pictures. However, the general mode of administration appears to be to have the person being tested seated in a comfortable chair with his back to the examiner. Two standard sets of instructions have been provided by Murray (1943), with Rapaport et al. (1946) and Bellak (1954) providing similar instructions. A simplified version is used with children and less intelligent adults. The basic instructions are to have the individual make up a story about each picture, including four phases for each. These consist of 1) events leading up to what is happening in the picture; 2) a description of what is happening in the picture at present; 3) an account of what the figures in the picture are thinking and feeling; and 4) the outcome of the story. In the second testing session (separated by at least a day from the first), the individual is encouraged to be more imaginative than in the first, with the cards used being more ambiguous and evocative of fantasy material.

The interpretation of the TAT varies

considerably among its users and seems to follow the theoretical frameworks of Freud (1949) and Murray et al. (1938) from which it arose. Murray advocated analyzing the stories in terms of their content, with each event viewed as a force (need) arising either in the hero (the main character in the story with which the person identifies) or from the environment (press). A list of Murray's 28 needs is then used to classify the individual's motives in terms of needs and presses. Each receives a weighted score, allowing a rank-order system to be calculated. The relationship of the needs to each other is then considered in terms of a hierarchy.

As previously mentioned, various users have utilized the TAT to study different needs and motives (McClelland, 1955; Schacter, 1959; Veroff, 1957). The reader interested in clinical systems of scoring and interpreting of this test may be referred to reviews such as Wyatt (1947) or, more recently, Bellak (1975). We shall now depart from this subjective approach to the study of motivation and take a look at the objective system of the MAT.

The Motivation Analysis Test (MAT)

The ten dynamic structure factors measured by the MAT are listed in Table 14.3.

From the dozens of subtests evaluated in research, the MAT settled on six. Only four are administered in groups; the two only individually administrable are left for description in the handbook. The titles for the subjects, on the test form, are different from the revealing table for the psychologist, as shown in Table 14.4.

As will be seen, half the tests assess predominantly the U component (1, 2, and 5) and half (3, 4, and 6) the I component, though in the usual group (and of course, individual) administrable test without apparatus these will be (1 and 2) and (3 and 4).

Each erg and sem in Table 14.3 is rep-

TABLE 14.3
The Ten Dynamic Structures Measured in MAT

	Order of Appearance* in Final Test Profile	Title	Symbol on the Records	Brief Description
ERGS (Drives)	7	*Mating* Erg	(Ma)	Strength of the normal, heterosexual or mating drive.
	9	*Assertiveness* Erg	(As)	Strength of the drive to self-assertion, mastery, and achievement.
	3	*Fear* (Escape) Erg	(Fr)	Level of alertness to external dangers [This is *not* anxiety; see (34) and p. 22]
	4	*Narcissism-comfort* Erg	(Na)	Level of drive to sensuous self-indulgent satisfactions.
	8	*Pugnacity-sadism* Erg	(Pg)	Strength of destructive, hostile impulses.
SENTIMENTS	6	*Self-concept* Sentiment	(SS)	Level of concern about the self-concept, social repute, and more remote rewards.
	5	*Superego* Sentiment	(SE)	Strength of development of conscience.
	1	*Career* Sentiment	(Ca)	Amount of development of interests in a career.
	10	*Sweetheart-spouse* Sentiment	(Sw)	Strength of attachment to wife (husband) or sweetheart.
	2	*Home-parental* Sentiment	(Ho)	Strength of attitudes attaching to the parental home.

*The order in this table is psychologically clearer than the order necessary in the test answer sheet, which is dictated by convenience of scoring pattern.

TABLE 14.4
Objective Motivation Devices Subtests in the MAT

Order of Presentation		Time	Psychologist's Title	Examinee's Title (Client's)
Group or Individual	1	15-20 min.	Ends for Means (Projection)	Uses
	2	15-20 min.	Autism	Estimates
	3	4-6 min.	Ready Association	Paired Words
	4	15-20 min.	Means end Knowledge	Information
Individual Only	5	15-20 min.	GSR to Frustrating Stimulus	Enforced Moods
	6	15-20 min.	Decision Time	Reaction Time

resented (though hidden in the final structure) by two to eight attitudes, which the record of cumulative research shows to be most highly loaded on the given dynamic trait. Each erg and sem is represented by 2, except the superego by 4 and the self-sentiment by 8, because these are most important. (These variables are set out in the handbook.)

The reliabilities and validities are shown in Table 14.5.

In administration no timing is required, and the test may take from 50 minutes to an hour and longer according to the subject's natural speed. Two answer sheets are used (see Table 14.6).

The scoring can be simple or complex according to the closeness one wishes to come to preferred theoretical bases. There are two reasons why a simple adding of the four subtest scores (after the stencil key or machine scoring of raw scores) cannot be used. First, the sigma of raw scores differs, thus giving subtests unequal weight. Raw must be converted to standard stens on each test before they can be added. Second, one test in U (Uses) and one in I (Word Association) yields an ips-

ative not a normative raw score. This means that in these subtests the sum total of all interests comes out the same for everyone. The informed psychometrist has to heed the special properties of ipsative scores. However, all of the entering of tables which the individual clinician may do on his own can be done—from the answer sheet onwards—by a machine scoring program service available at IPAT, at Psychsystems, and on certain university computers (see Chapter 7).

The School Motivation Analysis Test (SMAT)

This test operates on exactly the same principles as the MAT, merely reducing the items to a cognitive level, and to an experiential domain suitable for children of 12-18 years. Research at the 14-year-old level has shown identical ergic structures as would be theoretically expected, but differences in level and to some extent of pattern in the sems (Sweney & Cattell, 1962). One might expect the dependence on parents to be greater, the focus on a

TABLE 14.5

Reliabilities and Validities for Ten MAT Scales (Attenuation Scoring)

| Dynamic Factor | RELIABILITIES | | | | VALIDITY |
	Dependability Coefficients[1]	Alpha Coefficients[2]	Arbitrary Split-half[3]	Stability Coefficients[4]	Correlation between Factor Estimates[5]
Fear	.70	.58	.54	.48	.60
Mating	.66	.45	.49	.51	.69
Assertiveness	.64	.33	.47	.53	.53
Narcissism	.60	.43	.43	.53	.52
Pugnacity	.51	.39	.33	.41	.72
Career	.53	.42	.37	.39	.66
Sweetheart-spouse	.74	.63	.58	.47	.76
Home-parental	.81	.65	.70	.65	.66
Superego	.67	.44	.50	.46	.61
Self-sentiment	.78	.71	.64	.69	.76

[1]Based on N = 156 Air Force enlisted men.
[2]Based on N = 227 adults in various walks of life (25).
[3]Based on N = 151 college students (51).
[4]Over a five-week period and based on N = 101 college students (51).
[5]Correlation (corrected for overlap) between primary factor scored over all items in the development study and the factor measured by the items actually selected for the test (24, 25).

TABLE 14.6
Title, Order, and Time Required for Subtests

Order of Presentation	Approximate Time	Psychologist's Title	Examinee's Title
1	15-20 min.	Ends-For-Means (Projection)	Uses
2	15-20 min.	Autism	Estimates
3	4-6 min.	Ready Association	Paired Words
4	15-20 min.	Means-End Knowledge	Information

girl- or boyfriend, for boy or girl, to be more inchoate at the 12-15 level, the sem to sport or hobby to be stronger and that to job to be merely forming. The Sweney study actually showed fractionation into more numerous but correlated semic factors. It is surely psychologically very probable that, whereas we know temperament factors to remain steady in number across developmental years (16 P.F., HSPQ, CPQ, etc.), the semic structures (unlike ergs) will in younger children be more fragmentary and transient (except perhaps that to the mother). Consequently, more modification from the MAT and SMAT categories will be needed at the next lower level—the proposed Child Motivation Analysis Test (CMAT)—but for the present the SMAT essentially parallels MAT, with the following 10 dynamic structures.

TABLE 14.7
Dynamic Structures in the SMAT

Ergs	Assertiveness
	Mating
	Fear
	Narcissism
	Pugnacity
	Protectiveness
Sems	Self-sentiment
	Superego
	School
	Home

The practical problems in the measurement of motivation probably call for more alert understanding of basic principles and the impact of situations than in working with the other two modalities—abilities and general personality-temperament dimensions. For these measures—as well as for those given above—we believe our ruling out of the questionnaire medium as too unreliable and invalid in this motivational modality is fully justified. The individual—especially the young person—is far from knowing his various motives. He has developed no skills for comparing his inner interests with those of others. And, as for the adult, the distortions which prevent his being candid were known not only to Freud but to biblical writers, and are the amusement of the man in the street.

However, *every* known form of interest test faces special difficulties, inherent to the psychological realities of cultures, when it comes to preserving validity and standardization across time and place. The investments of ergs in socioenvironmental instrumentalities (the dynamic lattice structure) differ somewhat from culture to culture, and from epoch to epoch in the same culture.* Rectification of items and restandardization of scales need to be done more frequently, making such tests costly in upkeep to publishers and requiring adaptive changes of interpre-

*For instance, one form of transportation (say, the horse) might meet security and self-esteem needs in a more primitive culture or earlier historical period than our own. The automobile would serve the same function in a more industrialized culture or a later period in history. The complexity this type of change brings into assessment can hardly be underestimated.

tations by practitioners. Motivation-interest patterns, even for innate ergs, are inevitably in flux. There is also the problem of ipsative scoring, present in half the MAT subtests, and its possible distorting effect on the correlation among scales, on which our conception of higher strata organization depends. At present the best estimate of correlations among the ergic and semic traits is as in Table 14.8.

These correlations of the oblique factors are quite small (as also are those with the 16 P.F.), perhaps the only noteworthy ones being those of the superego negatively with narcissism and sex, which may well be expected, especially in Christian cultures.

The MAT, TAT, and SMAT apply to *any* area in which motivation, interest, and conflict are to be assessed. Although clinical application has been most focused above, the MAT and SMAT have been well applied in both educational and industrial practice (see Chapters 10, 19, and 20). In-

deed, they have yielded substantial prediction in school achievement beyond what is obtainable from ability and general personality measures, thus illustrating our basic argument on structural testing that intelligent psychological testing must recognize that it is dealing with the same person and the same structure in his job, his education, and his visit to a clinic.

However, we have recognized that in the field of interests, local parameters begin to loom larger. Consequently—and particularly in the industrial job area—there is room for more "special purpose" tests, and we accordingly turn to two of confirmed utility in that field—the Strong Vocational Interest Blank and the Vocational Interest Measure.

The Strong Vocational Interest Blank (SVIB)

The Strong Vocational Interest Blank (SVIB) was first introduced by Strong in

TABLE 14.8

Intercorrelations of Primary Dynamic Structure Factors as Pure Factors and as Scale Estimates on MAT

MAT SCORES	Fear	Mating	Assertiveness	Narcissism	Pugnacity	Career	Sweetheart-spouse	Home-parental	Superego	Self-sentiment
Primary Factor Scores										
Fear		22	01	14	-04	-08	-08	-24	-13	-01
Mating	08		04	13	06	-18	-07	-36	-35	11
Assertiveness	-01	14		12	06	-03	-29	-08	01	-16
Narcissism	-02	12	06		-23	14	-18	-07	-19	34
Pugnacity	02	00	-12	-10		-32	11	-22	-02	-11
Career	-12	-02	00	-09	-02		-13	-12	-02	-18
Sweetheart-spouse	-01	-14	-18	-28	-10	-16		10	-07	09
Home-parental	-13	-31	-06	-32	-16	00	09		-02	-06
Superego	-23	-35	-17	-32	06	06	-06	20		-06
Self-sentiment	-03	18	-23	20	-29	-22	09	-11	-22	

From R.B. Cattell, J. Horn, J. Radcliffe, and A.B. Sweney, *Handbook for the MAT*, Champaign, IL: IPAT, p. 19.

1927. It has since been revised by Campbell (Strong & Campbell, 1974), who has written a rather comprehensive handbook for its use. Previous forms are assumed to be parallel to those currently available, although Williams et al. (1968) have presented some evidence against this assumption. The scale has generated considerable research, with Buros (1972) citing well over a thousand references for it. The test itself is an interest inventory intended for use primarily with late adolescents and young adults. It contains approximately 400 items to which an individual is asked to respond as liking, disliking, or indifferent. The test can be administered in about 40 minutes. The items used have been selected on the basis of their ability to discriminate between criterion groups from different occupations and from people in general. The rationale for the test is that people in different occupations have interests that differentiate them from each other and from people in general. Therefore, people who respond similarly to the interest blank should have similar interests (and differences) in terms of the occupations they will like or dislike.

As stated in Campbell's handbook for the SVIB, the primary function of the test is for use in counseling young people about their career choices. This is done by helping them understand how their preferences are similar or different from those of people in various occupations. This is accomplished by providing individuals with sets of standard scores and profiles for the Basic Interest Scales (which cover areas such as Service, Nature, Law, and Art), Occupational Scales, and Non-Occupational Scales (such as Academic Achievement, Age-Related Interest Scale, and Diversity of Interests Scale). A set of Administrative Indices is used to detect errors in test administration and scoring.

While the Strong test may indeed be useful in the area of vocational counseling, it appears unsuitable for the scientific study of motivational factors. An apparent weakness is that it is a criterion-keyed instrument. In this type of scale construction, artificial correlations arise when the same items are used for more than one scale. Scales sharing items are also somewhat dependent. However, the largest drawback to criterion-keyed scales is that they are not necessarily psychologically meaningful. Grouping individuals on the basis of similarities to a criterion group does not guarantee they will not be dissimilar in a variety of unspecified ways. Further, they do not help to explain underlying influences on behavior, as do factorial scales. A high score on any given scale does not mean a high interest in what the scale claims to measure, for that has not yet been determined empirically. Therefore, we shall leave the Strong test for those who find it useful in the pragmatic domain of vocational counseling.

While the SVIB is what we have defined as a *special-purpose* test, i.e., one that goes directly from test performance to criterion prediction with no intervening use of psychological concepts, the second predictor of job fitness and success on the basis of interest-motivation measurement, VIM, uses measurement of two drives that are found predictive and essentially a set of sems—measured more comprehensively, however, than in the MAT, and with more association with jobs.

The Vocational Interest Measure (VIM)

The Vocational Interest Measure (VIM) (Sweney & Cattell, research form in process of standardization) is an objective test of motivation in the occupational field. It has been developed for use in guidance and personal assessment, and is a complementary instrument to the previously discussed MAT. Both tests measure psychologically meaningful dynamic factors from the motivational domain which have been found through a comprehensive system of factor analytic researches conducted over the past 40 years by Cattell and his colleagues. The MAT utilizes ten of those ergs and sems considered to be most relevant to vocational choice. The factors measured by the VIM are the Protective Erg, Rest-seeking Erg, Career Sentiment, Mechanical Interests, Clerical-Work Interests, Aesthetic-Dramatic Interests, Business-Economic Interests, Scientific Interests, Sports Interests, and Nature-Outdoor Interests. Their relationship to the MAT factors and other known dynamic factors can be seen in Table 14.9 below.

The VIM is an objective test of motivation in the primary sense of using non-questionnaire, behavioral performances and in the secondary sense of being conspective in scoring. The latter means it has an interrater reliability of 1.0, thus eliminating subjectivity on the part of the scorer. In the primary sense it uses four well-tested objective devices (Word Association, Autistic Distortion, Information, and Projection [labeled Uses]). The objective devices are representative of the U and I motivation components, with the usual meaning of that difference, and

cover ten drive areas. Since the respondent is unaware of what the test is actually measuring, it is much less susceptible to distortion or "faking" than the traditional self-report measures. Therefore, through the use of a paper-and-pencil format, adapted as necessary to group administration, the test becomes a set of "standardized stimuli" and the answer sheet a method of gathering "controlled responses." (The interested reader may wish to refer to Cattell and Warburton (1967) for an in-depth discussion of objective test definition and to Cattell and Child (1975) for discussion of the devices.)

Four consecutive subtests make up the VIM, each using one of the objective devices mentioned above. It is not timed and requires approximately 70 minutes for most people to complete. It can be administered either individually or in groups by providing the appropriate number of test booklets and answer sheets. Standardized instructions are read to those taking the test, and questions on instructions are solicited and answered prior to the beginning of the test. Raw scores are obtained

TABLE 14.9

Design for Mutual Supplementation of MAT and VIM

Dynamic Factors Measured in MAT

Ergs	Sentiments
1) Mating (Sexual love)	1) Sentiment to Self
2) Assertiveness (Achievement)	a. Social Reputation
3) Fear (Escape)	b. Control and Understanding
4) Narcissism (Comfort, Sensuality)	2) Superego
5) Pugnacity-sadism ("Aggressiveness" of a specific kind)	3) Career
	4) Sweetheart-spouse
	5) Home-parental

Dynamic Factors Measured in VIM

1) Protectiveness (Altruism)	1) Career
2) Rest-seeking (Lack of energy)	2) Mechanical Interests
	3) Clerical-Work Interests
	4) Scientific Interests
	5) Aesthetic-Dramatic Interests
	6) Business-Economic Interests
	7) Sports Interests
	8) Nature-Outdoor Interests

through the use of four overlay stencils constructed for the instrument. These scores are then converted to "stens" (or ordinary standard scores) through the use of tables provided in the handbook for the test. Stens have a mean of 5.5 and a standard deviation of 2 for the standardization sample, as usual.

Results of the VIM yield several types of information of interest to the employment officer or guidance counselor using the test. Both Integrated and Unintegrated motivation scores are determined for each of the ten dynamic factors in the instrument. Integrated scores have been found to be highly correlated with past experience and training. They seem to be a measure of an individual's motivational history and are likely to reflect intentional goals. Unintegrated scores, as explained with the MAT, appear to be measuring an individual's internal needs, fantasies, and desires with little regard for past experience or external reality. They are considered to be measures of tension, deprivation, and apprehension, but without the goal-directed behaviors necessary to make them functional. Conflict scores are derived from the discrepancy between an individual's Integrated and Unintegrated scores on any given dimension. Conflict is viewed as a measure of current frustration or unsatisfied tension in regard to the external expression of needs. Total Interest scores for the dynamic factors may also be obtained due to the relative independence of the Integrated and Unintegrated scores. These scores are seen as composites of the Integrated and Unintegrated components and are useful as reference points for evaluating the conflict scores.*

---

*Further discussion on interpretation of the dynamic factors measured by the VIM is available in the handbook (Sweney & Cattell, 1980) and will be included in the future with the publication of the manual for the test. Criterion relationships with the factors and useful predictive relationships are in process of calculation by Professor Sweney, to whom requests should be directed at Wichita State University, Wichita, Kansas.

ILLUSTRATIONS OF INFERENCES FROM SCORES ON THE MAT, SMAT, ETC.

In addition to the main profile of 1) *ergic and semic standard scores*, as shown in Figure 14.2 (20 elements, by separate U and I scores and ten total scores), one can derive several further scores of interest in job counseling and clinical work in accordance with the research findings identified elsewhere. These would include:

2) *Conflict* scores for each of the ten dynamic structures, as (U-I) values.
3) A measure of *total conflict* and *total integration*.
4) *Total interest* (from the non-ipsative, subtests 2 and 4 only).
5) *Autism-optimism* as a personality trait, from the total on subtest 2.
6) *General information-intelligence*, from the total on subtest 4.

These by-products in 4, 5, and 6 are not entirely psychometrically clarified or entirely independent, but do contain new information that would otherwise be lost. Since limited general interest is a feature of some clinical conditions (moderately in neurosis and markedly in schizophrenia), scoring the total interest sampled over ten important areas can be useful. It will necessarily overlap, as here calculated, with total information-intelligence in 6. Just what the personality traits are in score No. 5—the total (10 factor) autism score—is still under investigation. On the face of things it is a mixture of optimism about life and some unrealism and so might be expected to be high in manic-hysteric and sociopathic persons. As to the total information, one notes that general information has repeatedly proved, at least in comparable social groups, a reasonably valid measure of crystallized intelligence, g_c. It is certainly practically useful to have available an intelligence measure from the administration of MAT, SMAT, or VIM without further testing time.

Figure 14.2. MAT (Motivation Analysis Test) dynamic structure profile

From R.B. Cattell, J. Horn, & A.B. Sweney, *Motivation Analysis Test*. Copyright © 1961, 1964 by the Institute for Personality and Ability Testing, Inc. Reproduced by permission.

The conflict and integration scores, however, are valuable measures not obtainable elsewhere. They follow the theoretical model discussed earlier, integration being the inverse of the conflict score. It is obtained first diagnostically for each of the 10 areas and finally as a characteristic of the total personality. As already indicated here (and in Cattell & Child, 1975), the U score can be considered ergic drive not successfully invested in real-life expression and, but for there being real individual differences in total interest, they would be inversely correlated. (As directly correlated they are only very slightly negative.) Psychologically the U-I magnitude could arise from two quite different processes: 1) frustration in gaining expression, thus representing conflict; and 2) in the inverse direction (I-U), a highly developed interest system from which the basic ergic motivation had re-

ceded, e.g., to take Allport's example, a retired sailor very knowledgeable about the sea, but now, with a different view, no longer with any vital interest in it. The difference of U and I scores therefore needs ancillary information to ensure meaningful interpretation.

A few examples of concrete criterion relations on the MAT are all that is needed here since other chapters provide several. First, Figures 14.3 and 14.4 show some patterns found for specific groups, first for a group of diagnosed schizophrenics and second for successful businessmen (courtesy of Dr. Charles Noty). The third, Figure 14.5, shows the motivational patterns of a group of the chronically unemployed. An illustrative discussion of their profile shall serve to provide the reader with a glimpse of the descriptive use of the MAT, with clinical examples following in a later chapter.

Sten mean conflict	Sten mean total	Dynamic areas	Standard ten scores (sten) 1 2 3 4 5 6 7 8 9 10	Centile rank conflict	Centile rank total
5.8	8.2	Career sentiment		56.0	91.2
6.5	7.0	Home-parental sentiment		69.2	77.3
5.2	3.5	Fear erg		44.0	15.9
4.2	3.2	Narcism comfort erg		25.8	12.5
6.3	7.5	Superego sentiment		65.5	84.1
7.0	4.4	Self-sentiment		77.3	29.1
7.8	4.6	Mating erg		87.5	32.6
5.6	2.0	Pugnacity-sadism erg		52.0	4.0
6.0	4.7	Assertiveness erg		59.9	34.5
2.5	5.2	Sweetheart-spouse sentiment		6.7	44.0

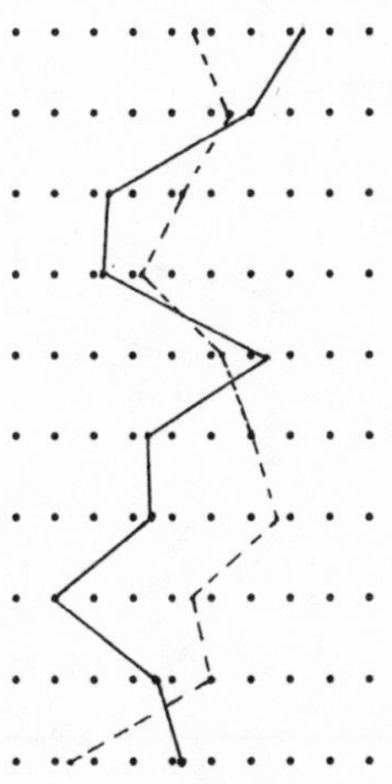

Conflict sten mean -----   Total motivation sten mean _____

Figure 14.3. Diagnostic pattern for the schizophrenic syndrome ($N = 30$)

Lawlis (1968) made a detailed study of 75 chronically unemployed males (had at least six jobs in the last six months and left before completing any assignment) and compared them with the same number of employed males matched for age, I.Q., race, and general educational level. The general profile for U, I, and total scores is given in Figure 14.5. High ergic tension on fear (presumably due to economic insecurity) and low assertiveness (little interest in economic or other competition) mark the chronically unemployed, while, naturally, the integrated

career sentiment is low (but wishful thinking is high). Especially revealing are the MAT conflict scores (excess of U over I scores usually expressed as sten scores). High conflict exists in the sentiments of career, superego, self, and sweetheart-spouse. A high frustration index among the unemployed comes as no surprise and the nonfunctional guilt proneness—a vague intention to be more dependable and conscientious, unimplemented by habits—may explain the high rate of job change typifying this group. The need for affection suggests that conflict occurs be-

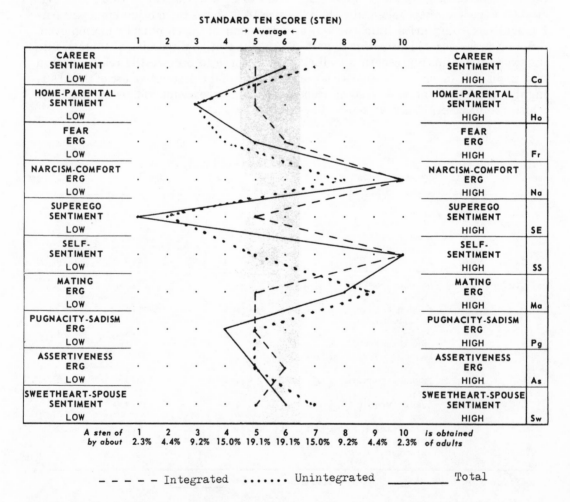

Figure 14.4. MAT profile of executives: Average scores for top executives (20 presidents of insurance and service organizations)

Source: Unpublished work by C. Noty, 1973.

tween man and wife, probably because of the instability created in the home by the frequent unemployment and shortage of money. Finally, the high self-sentiment conflict is very common among those whose self-concept is beset with failures because they are not reaching the goals they have regarded as appropriate for themselves. This conflict is sometimes referred to as the *loser's syndrome* (Sweney, 1969b).

More extensive and intensive interpretive illustrations of profiles of scores on the five ergic and five semic dynamic

traits will be given in clinical examples in Chapters 17 and 18.

SUMMARY

From being the province of clinical psychology and relatively speculative theories, human dynamics has advanced in the last 30 years through experimental psychology, especially in multivariate designs, to measurement-based theory.

The differing views on the human equipment of basic drives supposed by

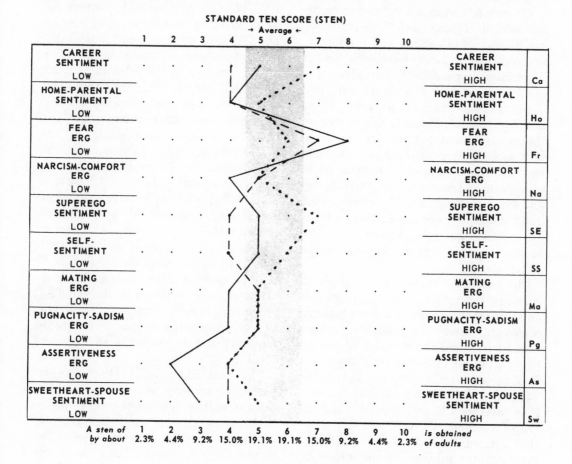

Figure 14.5. Motivational patterns of the chronically unemployed

Source: Lawlis (1968).

Freud, Adler, Jung, Murray, and others have been resolved by objective device measures and factor analysis into about a dozen unitary ergs, which essentially agree in number and nature with the description of mammalian, and especially primate, drives by ethologists.

The same programmatic research has shown that attitudes (courses of action in response to situations) are culturally acquired as instruments to ergic ends in ways that create unitary cognitive-dynamic systems—sems, e.g., to home, job, etc.—which can be measured objectively as to their level of development.

Where motivation and interest strength assessment is concerned, questionnaires are suspect as to validity and reliability, and resorting to more objective devices is imperative for practice. Twenty-five years of experiment with diverse *objective* motivation measurement devices, i.e., those not requiring self-evaluation, have shown that regardless of dynamic area and content, some seven primary (β, γ, δ, etc.) and two secondary (U and I) components of expression and measurement exist for any and every interest. The U, unintegrated, and I, integrated, are uncorrelated, so that for any attitude, interest, sem structure or erg, *two* measures are needed for full information.

The emerging theory of the *dynamic calculus* formulates any ergic tension measure as the result of a constitutional component (*need*), an appetitive component (*drive*), and the strength of the existing stimulus incentive resulting in the final measure (*ergic tension*). This model adequately integrates various concepts that have been in use, such as "tension," "reinforcement value," "deprivation," "habit strength" (Hull, 1943), etc. Though experimental support for the whole dynamic calculus model is only now developing, a large fraction of it can be considered confirmed and capable of predictive action.

Using objective measures of dynamic structures—ergs and sems—the dynamic calculus puts at our disposal a) the hitherto missing dynamic part of the behavioral equation—added to the ability and personality trait part, this can be shown substantially to measure criterion prediction. For example, in school achievement a degree of prediction by the multiple R is reached much in advance of one without weights on ergs and sems; b) a measure of degree of conflict, of general integration, and of the stress levels in decision; and c) dynamic adjustment profiles typical of jobs and clinical symptom groups.

Available tests using objective devices and aimed at ergs and other needs are the TAT, MAT, SMAT, and a few others partially meeting standards of objectivity. The TAT uses one device only— projection —in interpretation, while the MAT and SMAT use four to six validated devices. The MAT, SMAT, VIM, and other structured tests give scores directly on ergic and semic structures, whereas the TAT does not. The TAT is open-ended and has low interpsychologist (conspect) reliability, whereas the MAT and SMAT are completely conspective, i.e., $r = +1.0$ between administrators. They have answer sheets and are computer scorable and standardized in stens.

However, both types of test have a role in clinical examination: the MAT to "block in" the general dynamic adjustment in terms of major *common* traits; the TAT, along with dreams, free association, etc., to expand into the unique trait interest fixations and investments of ergs and sems.

The practical available tests in this personality modality are decidedly fewer than in ability and temperament modalities. As usual there are both structural (analytical) and special-purpose tests. The former are represented in clinical and general work by the MAT and SMAT and in industrial and job counseling by the as yet unstandardized VIM (Sweney, 1980). The area is represented also by Edwards's and Jackson's questionnaires, and by the Strong Vocational Interest Blank, if one accepts the questionnaire as valid in this area and, in the former cases, if one accepts Murray's subjective list of needs.

The special-purpose tests are best represented by the Strong (SVIB), which goes directly from a questionnaire-type preference score to job recommendations, and by the TAT, which relates projection to test-unspecified dynamic needs. It is suggested that the MAT and TAT could advantageously be jointly used, in that order.

Except for the TAT and SVIB, the above tests score on common traits. In the last resort, clinical psychology requires a positive and reliable analysis of unique trait dynamic attachments. This is available in P-technique, as demonstrated in researches by Cross (1951), Shotwell, Hurley, and Cattell (1961), Birkett and Cattell (1978), and Kline and Grindley (1974). It is not discussed here because its technicalities call for special discussion in Chapters 16 and 17. Ideally, P-technique requires that many parallel forms of the MAT be available or that individual motivation device measures like GSR, reaction time, fluency, etc. be used. The highly dependable and penetrating nature of its results suggests that the reduction of testing to suitable clinical convenience will occur in the near future.

In addition to these, there exist at the research stage a series of devices for measuring the magnitude of conflict at various loci and foci, but the requisite development and standardization on the factors remain to be done. Meanwhile, the discrepancy of the U and the I scores on MAT and SMAT has been shown by Sweney and Cattell (1962), Birkett and others, to be, with certain conditions, a good indicator of magnitude of conflict in the area concerned.

An initial example is given of interpretation of the MAT profile (a study of unemployed) but the full discussion of interpretations is in Chapter 16 and, clinically, in Chapter 17.

CHAPTER 15

Measuring Attitudes, Interests, Sentiments, and Values

Richard L. Gorsuch

We can distinguish three distinct areas by our measurement operations, as was noted in Chapter 2. First, we can measure what a person can do, and thus define the area of abilities. Second, we can evaluate what a person usually does, and thus define personality. Third, we can evaluate the direction in which the person—assuming opportunity and ability—is moving, and thus define the area of motivation.

The area of motivation is further subdivided into the basic motivational structure, as detailed in Chapter 13, and the area of sentiments, as detailed in the present chapter. While the differences between these two chapters will become more apparent below, the differences can be summarized briefly: motivation structures (called ergs) are the basic, virtually universal needs we all have, as described in Chapter 13. Basic motivational structures must, however, be expressed by moving towards or away from particular

psychological objects which then take on psychological value in accordance with principles such as those set forth by the dynamic lattice and structured learning theory. Such psychological objects may be actual physical objects, such as people, places, and things, or more abstract entities, such as political parties or moral principles. This chapter is concerned with measurement techniques for this second motivational area.

As the title of this chapter indicates, there are several labels for this area. This results from several models which have been proposed. Our exploration of this area begins with an examination of the classical models used within social psychology and related areas such as vocational counseling.

After the classical models have been discussed, the current bases for a structured model are presented. Common tests and techniques are then reviewed in light of the models available.

THE CLASSICAL MODEL

Typical Definitions

The "classical model" is presented in introductory social psychology texts when attitudes are discussed. Attitudes are generally defined as a predisposition to respond pro or con to an object or idea, a definition long established (Allport, 1935) and essentially the same as the lay use of the term. Much research has used this general definition. This definition still dominates psychology although, as we shall see below, recent advances have led to some redefinitions that enhance understanding and prediction. These advances are sufficiently recent that they have only begun to appear in undergraduate textbooks (e.g., Wrightsman, 1981). Many psychologists are unaware of these advances and are operating by the lay definition of attitudes.

Social psychologists have sometimes defined components of attitudes. Krech and Crutchfield (1948) subdivided attitudes into three components which are often still used: cognitive, affective, and behavioral. The cognitive consists of the beliefs associated with the attitude, the affective consists of the emotional response, and the behavioral is the overt manifestations of the attitude.

Beliefs have been related to this area in one of two ways. First, they have been implicit in the cognitive component of attitudes. A strong attitude, such as a prejudice, could have a belief associated with it, such as believing the outgroup to be "dirty." Second, more recently beliefs have been seen as a broader domain of which attitudes are a part. Rokeach has made this explicit for both attitudes and the closely related area of values. He concludes "an attitude is defined simply as an organization of interrelated beliefs around a common object . . ." (Rokeach, 1968, p. 116).

Definitionally, interests and opinions have much the same history as attitudes. They too have been widely used with lay definitions. They differ from attitudes primarily by the context in which they have been employed.

Interests as a term has been most widely used in vocational counseling. The concern has been with matching a person's interests—generally identified with what he or she personally would enjoy—with those of people in several occupations; the person is encouraged to explore those occupations which contain people with interests like his or hers. Typical scales for this purpose—the Strong-Campbell, Kuder, and VII—are noted later (also see Chapter 18).

Opinions often are concerned with what the individuals feel would be a desirable state of affairs, as when the pollsters ask if a potential voter is in favor of beginning a particular water project in the state. Note that, unlike interests, for which most people would answer from knowledge gained in their personal experiences, "opinion" is a term used when the person responds without the benefit of personal experience. In the water project example, no one has personal experience with it since it would not yet have been built. Opinion is a term which has historically been used by sociologists reporting the views of a group of people. The use of the term "opinion" by social scientists is close to that of nonprofessionals.

In the classical model, actual measurement techniques are the same for attitudes, interests, and opinions. All are measured by Q-type (self-report) data. While the form of presentation and scoring has often differed, those differences are a result of the desired application rather than a difference in definition. Hence, in the classical model, *the terms "attitudes," "interests," and "opinions" are generally interchangeable, and we shall use the term "opinion" to refer to them all.* (Note, however, that many psychologists still use the term "attitude" in the classical model sense; I wish to reserve attitude for a more powerful definition within a structural model.)

Measurement in the Classical Model

The classical measurement techniques began with Bogardus (1925), who needed to evaluate social distances among ethnic groups. He asked each person to indicate whether he or she "would willingly admit members of each race" "to close kinship by marriage," "to my street as neighbors," and so forth. Persons and groups could then be evaluated about whether they wanted to keep a particular group far from them or not.

Thurstone's equal-appearing intervals scales. As Bogardus was developing his social distance measure, Thurstone (1928, 1931) was developing his *equal-appearing intervals* technique. The name of this method comes from Thurstone's concern that a scale should meet the criteria for interval measurement. While it is difficult to prove that any scale is interval (instead of just being ordinal), Thurstone relied on judges to develop a scale that appeared as interval to the judges, and hence its name.

The steps for developing the scale can be summarized as follows:

1) Glean a hundred or so statements regarding the opinion being sampled. Each statement is to contain only one idea or position. All possible positions that could be taken are included. (Note that the opinion being measured should be clear so that everyone can easily agree that the items are relevant.)
2) Have respondents who personally hold a variety of positions judge each *item* as to how positive or negative it is, without regard to their own position about it. (Judges who place unusually large numbers of the items at either the positive or negative end of the scale are dropped.)
3) Calculate the mean and standard deviation (or other measures of central tendency and variability) of the scores assigned to each item. Reject items with high standard deviations as ambiguous (since judges could not agree as to what opinion the item reflected).
4) Give the nonambiguous items to another group of people and have them place a plus in front of items with which they agree and a minus for those with which they disagree. Calculate the percentage agreeing with each item and rank order the items from low to high. Compare the rank order with the rank order from the mean ratings established in 3 above. Any item whose current rank order departs radically from the rank order established by the mean of judge's ratings is not performing as expected, and it is dropped.
5) From the remaining items, select about 20 items that are spaced equally across the possible range of positions.
6) Ask each person who takes the scale to mark the one item that best describes his or her own position. The scale rating of that item, as determined by the judges in 3 above, is the person's score.

The equal-appearing intervals technique is widely applicable. Thurstone and associates applied it to a range of opinion areas, including pacifistic vs. militaristic feelings, views of the Church, and so forth.

Summative (Likert) scales. Likert (1932) generalized from the summative procedures used for ability measures. He asked the respondents to rate a set of items on a scale ranging from 1 for "strongly disagree" to 5 for "strongly agree" with intermediate scores given intermediate meanings. The Likert scale score is the *sum* of the person's ratings across the items. The summative scale is the most widely used technique for obtaining Q-data.

The items are developed by the following procedure:

1) Same as Thurstone's first step. Ideally, half of the items are positively worded and half negatively worded to reduce acquiescence response bias. Negatively worded items are reversed in scoring so that "strongly disagree" is scored as 5 and "strongly agree" is scored as 1. The items are reversed before summing across items.
2) Give the items to a few hundred people. Each rates his or her opinion of each item on the 1 to 5 rating system.
3) Sum across all items for each person for a total score. Correlate each item with the total. Select the 20 or so items that correlate best with the total. (Note that this assumes the total item pool defines exactly what one is interested in measuring; hence, a prior structural analysis is assumed.)

Interest inventories are generally summative scales but substitute a different step 3. The items representing possible differences across occupations are given to people in several occupations. Items are analyzed to identify those that distinguish one occupation from all the rest. The identified items form a scale for that occupation. The items are scored positively if the respondent answers in the same direction as the members of the occupation, and the scores summed across all items.

Guttman scale. Guttman (1944) identified an essential element of a scale: One should be able to reproduce responses to the items from the score the person receives. An example of a scale with this characteristic—and hence called a "Guttman scale"—is height. Implicitly a measure of height is a set of questions such as "Is this person at least 170 cm tall? at least 190? at least 200?" Each "yes" answer receives a score of 1; the person's score is the sum across items. The score of 2 in the example would mean that both

the first two items had been answered "yes" and the last one "no." Hence a scale of height meets the requirements for a Guttman scale.

Construction of a Guttman scale begins with the same step as in Thurstone and summative scales: the generation of items. The items are then administered to many people and the items searched for a subset that produces the desired characteristics. The search can be difficult, and computer programs are available to do it. As in the other scales, it assumes one already knows enough about the structure to adequately select the item pool and that the item pool measures the appropriate opinion.

Self-ratings. The earliest of our ancient ancestors surely turned to a companion and asked, "What do you think of. . . ?" and so was born the self-rating approach to measuring opinions. One is asked his own opinion of his opinion. It is still widely used, particularly by sociologists and pollsters.

In the best uses of self-ratings, several forms of the question are judged to find one item that is least open to misunderstanding. The respondents are asked to rate their opinion for that item on a scale. The rating scale differentiates subtleties of feelings, such as "definitely not," "perhaps not," and so forth. The approach assumes that people know this area of themselves well, and it can be as successful as any other classical technique (e.g., Gorsuch & McFarland, 1972).

Semantic differential technique. The semantic differential approach develops from Osgood, Suci, and Tannenbaum (1957). They were analyzing meanings and found three factors to be generally sufficient to describe the meaning of different words. The factors do not represent the factual meaning—such as object X's being in place Y—but rather more generalized meaning, which includes the area of attitudes as commonly viewed.

The first factor they found differentiating meanings, *evaluation*, is measured by having respondents check the degree to which each of a pair of adjectives describes the action or object being evaluated. A pair of adjectives for this factor is "Like _ _ _ _ Dislike" with the respondent asked to place a check on the line to show the degree to which one or the other term describes that being evaluated. The second factor, *potency*, is measured by adjective pairs such as "Strong _ _ _ _ _ Weak." The third factor, *activity*, is defined by adjectives such as "Active _ _ _ _ Passive." The general conclusion is that the evaluation factor contains the attitudinal component, and so that is often the only one given (e.g., Fishbein & Ajzen, 1974).

A semantic differential is developed by first writing a careful description of that to be measured. This is placed at the top of a page and then appropriate adjective pairs are placed below it. The adjective pairs are selected from the semantic differential research as being appropriate for that attitude. While empirical analysis to evaluate each of the pairs is desirable, it is not necessary if the pairs are carefully selected and checked by others.

Some experience in administering a semantic differential is desirable since communicating the task to the respondents is subtle. People listening to an inexperienced person reading the directions for a semantic differential will have questions, but those listening to an experienced one will immediately understand. This is true even when both read *identical* instructions.

Evaluation of the Classical Approach

Psychometric qualities. The psychometric properties of the classical approach can be excellent. Scale development projects consistently find adequate to excellent reliabilities. Homogeneity coefficients are almost always .7 or higher. Typical coefficients from a half dozen adjective pairs

forming a semantic differential often run .85 to .98. Scales with lower coefficients can usually be revised to increase the reliabilities by, for example, increasing the number of items or dropping the poorer items.

In addition to homogeneity coefficients, stability coefficients are also generally high. As we shall see later, interest tests generally show long-term stability over years. However, stability is not always desired when measuring opinions. People's views do change and their scores should change accordingly. The theory of the content area will suggest whether the opinion should be stable or not.

Another important psychometric feature of the classical measurement techniques is that they correlate very highly together. In studies such as that by Fishbein and Ajzen (1974), the correlations among classical measurement techniques are about the same size as the reliabilities. In fact, if the correlations are corrected for attenuation, they could well approach 1.0. The only conclusion possible is that *the classical techniques measure one factor and hence are psychometrically interchangeable.*

The classical techniques do vary in methods of construction. That variation should be the prime reason for selecting among them. The Thurstone approach, for example, uses judges to provide the information by which the items are selected. Few people from the research population are needed. Hence, it is an excellent approach when the research population is limited, as in research with the mentally retarded. It also has the advantage of giving intrinsically meaningful equal-appearing interval scores.

Self-ratings are highly efficient in many situations. Gorsuch and McFarland (1972) provide a graph by which multiple-item scales and single-item scales can be compared.

The psychometric property of validity is harder to evaluate because of the several types of validity and the multiple studies necessary to evaluate them. In general, content validity is high for the classical measurement techniques. This is almost assured by the method of item development, for each begins with the writing of items for that scale. Psychologists have rarely written items unless they felt that the items did measure that opinion, i.e., had content validity.

Concurrent and predictive validities of classical measurement techniques have been more of a question, in part because of the problems of predictive validity analyzed in Chapter 4. It has long been known, for example, that L-data measures of actual cheating do not correlate well with opinions classically measured. The ground-breaking Hartshorne and May (1928) studies, for example, found very small (e.g., .2) correlations.

In the study noted above, Fishbein and Ajzen (1974) provided further data on this validity question. They measured not only opinions but also reported religious behaviors. When each of the scales was correlated with behaviors, the results were as typically found within the classical model: the modal correlation reported was approximately .16. Fishbein and Ajzen (1974) proposed that this low correlation was a function of correlating a *general* opinion with a *specific* behavior. The general measure implicitly averages across multiple opinions about the multiple behaviors of which, for example, religion consists. Since the general measure is so broad, i.e., a higher order dimension, it cannot be expected to predict a single behavior.

A general opinion measure, Fishbein and Ajzen reasoned, needs a criterion just as general. So they added each of 100 reported religious behaviors as items in a religious behavior scale and correlated that broad behavior scale with each of the classical scales. The results were as expected: the modal reported correlation was .64, a figure almost the same as the scales correlated among themselves. If it were corrected for attenuation, it would

approach 1.0! When the opinion measure is at the same level of generality as its criterion, it is possible for the prediction to be quite high, although correlations of the magnitude reported by Fishbein and Ajzen are still unusual.

Theoretical adequacy. A major characteristic of classical methods for measuring opinions is that they take the person's own evaluations at face value. People are asked their opinion about whether they prefer a particular political candidate, would object to a Mongolian family living on their block, and so forth. It is assumed that people know their own opinions well enough to answer accurately. This approach is functionally close to the lay definition of opinions about one's own attitudes (which is one reason I prefer "opinions" rather than "attitudes" for what the classical model measures).

The Fishbein and Ajzen (1974) results presented above showed the interchangeability of self-ratings—which are the conscious evaluations of one's opinions—with the other measures. This means that *only* the conscious aspect is being measured by the classical techniques. Thus, all these techniques reflect the person's opinion about his attitudes and interests. (And so we have used the word "opinion" to refer to that which social psychology has classically called "attitudes".)

How accurate can we expect conscious evaluations to be? Gorsuch and McFarland (1972) suggested several principles which govern the viability of single-item self-reports—and so conscious measurement. First, it is most accurate when society has clear criteria. Second, the attitudes need to be linked by society with readily identifiable behaviors. Third, the area needs to be widely discussed so that the words take on common meaning and so that a person has practice in making the judgments. Many of the situations investigated with Fishbein and Ajzen's approach seem to fall within these principles. Religious behavior (Fishbein & Ajzen,

1974) certainly does, but so do attitudes towards donating blood, weight loss, buying a particular brand of car, and so forth (see Ajzen & Fishbein, 1980).

But evidence also suggests nonconscious components may be important. First, not everyone has found the Fishbein and Ajzen model to be highly predictive. In particular, Bentler and Speckart (1979) needed an additional element, namely past behavior. If one assumes some consistency in motivational components across time, these findings are not surprising — consistent motivations lead to the same behavior on different occasions and so past behavior predicts current behavior. But since past behavior was needed in the model in addition to the opinion, this finding does suggest that nonconscious areas also need to be measured.

Second, basic research on motivation suggests that elements other than just consciously based ones are needed to evaluate attitudes. On the one hand, Cattell and Baggaley (1956, 1958; see Cattell & Child, 1975 for an overview of this research) included in factor analytic studies almost every procedure devised by psychologists to measure attitudes and motives. The results were presented in Chapter 14. What is conspicuous is that the classical techniques that assume attitudes are conscious were related to only a minority of the motivational factors. Classical attitude measures did load factors alpha and gamma but this still leaves several prominent factors unmeasured. (While it could have been that the conscious attitudes were loading the prominently useful factors, with the others being so small as to be trivial, this is unlikely given the occasional lack of prediction from only the conscious attitudes, as noted above.)

Cattell's conclusions, based on structural analyses of devices to measure attitudes, finds added support in univariate research on people's ability to identify causes of their behavior. Nisbett and Wilson (1977) review this research and find

that people are seldom conscious of the causes of their behavior. Since people are not conscious of the causes of their behavior, it is difficult to argue that a particular cause of behavior, such as attitudes, can be consciously reported with accuracy.

Based on the above data, classical attitude measures are only a person's conscious opinion of his or her attitudes. These opinions are predictive when the person has had ample opportunity to observe behaviors by which he or she can evaluate his or her attitudes. But if that situation does not exist, it seems unlikely that a person's opinions about his or her attitudes are complete descriptions. Prediction in these latter situations will be enhanced by including other motivational components than those measured by the classical methods.

A lack of structured approaches. The classical approaches to attitudes, sentiments, interests, and values have produced few studies on structure. The few studies that have been done (for example, by Ferguson, Eysenck, and Guilford) are seldom cited. The lack of structured approaches is, of course, a major handicap.

Three elements seem to have been important in limiting research on structure. First is the breadth of the area itself. It is difficult for an investigator to have sufficient expertise to effectively sample all areas (and teams of investigators to provide depth across areas are not yet common in psychology). Second is the lack of adequate training in the available tools, such as factor analysis and attitude measurement beyond the classical model.

Third is the narrow behavioral and experimental emphasis of contemporary psychology. This emphasis has placed a demand on social psychologists to be able to predict an overt behavior *now*. Without such prediction, the work does not seem to be widely cited. Unfortunately, the best way to predict an immediate behavior is to gear all the measurement towards that specific behavior without regard for structure. Ajzen and Fishbein (1980) obtain good prediction of a particular behavior by measuring opinions that are just as particular. For example, the behavior might be "contributing blood to the bloodmobile on campus next Tuesday," and then the best predictors naturally refer explicitly to "contributing blood to the bloodmobile on campus next Tuesday." Such work has been excellent for building models of how components of attitudes do relate to behavior but have not encouraged the examination of broader structures, which, as noted previously, will be necessary to understand and predict sets of behaviors.

Unfortunately, the approach taken by the classical model has discouraged a structural approach. Fortunately, as we shall see below, several lines of investigation growing out of the classical model are valuable foundation blocks for developing structural models.

STRUCTURAL MODELS

Toward Structured Measurement

Cattell and Baggaley (1956, 1958; also see review in Cattell & Child, 1975) have presented one structural approach, and their factors have been described in Chapter 14. Except for their MAT, little else exists to provide structured measurement in this area. There is, fortunately, considerable research confirming the importance of at least two factors and to suggest the importance of others.

Factors alpha and gamma: Affect and moral obligation. Developments growing out of the classical approach are reinforcing two factors from structured approaches which are measurable by conscious opinions: alpha and gamma. Alpha is related to preferences and reflects an "I am going to . . ." (Cattell & Child, 1975, p. 11f) feeling, thus primarily reflecting

affect. This appears to be a match for opinions as classically measured. Gamma is also related to preferences but of the "I ought to be interested . . ." type (Cattell & Child, 1975, pp. 12-14); this appears to be a match for moral obligation or values. These factors suggest a clear distinction between affect and moral obligations.

The distinction between affect and moral obligations is supported by research developing out of the classical model. Triandis (1971) separated the classical attitudinal area into several discrete components, in part because of the loose usage of the term "attitude" in classical psychology. One part is the behavioral intention (distinguished from behavior per se, since while the former is determined by psychological factors, the behavior itself is a compromise between the psychological factors and external realities). Others are beliefs about the attitude object and affect (measured by a semantic differential and thus what we have been calling opinion measured by classical "attitude" scales). Finally, Triandis includes values, or moral obligation (often measured by asking if one has a moral obligation in this area).

Are affect and moral obligation, i.e., factors alpha and gamma, both important? Not all psychologists agree that they are. Fishbein (1967) began with both an affective element and moral obligation, but dropped the latter component on finding in his research situations that moral obligations and behavioral intentions seemed interchangeable (Ajzen & Fishbein, 1970).

But Triandis presents evidence in favor of the importance of both factors. In reviewing research on interpersonal attitudes, Triandis (1967) identifies two well-replicated factors. First is "Respect," which involves admiration and thus reflects a moral evaluation (Scott, 1965). Second is "Friendship," which involves liking or affect. Triandis also finds both these elements important for decisions. Davidson, Jaccard, Triandis, Morales, and Diaz-Guerrero (1976) found moral obligations were given more weight in Mexican than in American cultures.

Gorsuch and Ortberg (1983) suggested that the situation determines when affect is more important than moral obligation and vice versa. In analyzing four situations, Gorsuch and Ortberg found that moral obligations were indeed necessary over and above affect. This was particularly so when the situations met criteria suggested by moral philosophy: The choice is nontrivial and the evaluations of the consequences are based on ultimate rather than utilitarian goals. Thus, both affect —factor alpha—and moral obligation— factor gamma—are relevant. Including both is necessary, with situational analyses giving specification equations identifying if and how each relates to specific behaviors.

Still another line of support deriving from the classical model suggests both affect and moral obligation are important yet independent. This work begins with Scott's (1965) investigation of values (Scott used the term values to refer to what was labeled moral obligations above). Defining a "value" as "that which a person holds is ultimately good for all people under all circumstances," he measured values by asking respondents how much they admired a person behaving in a particular manner; a person held the value if he or she almost always admired a person acting to maximize the value.

Generalizing Scott's work to children, values were similarly identified and studied (Gorsuch, 1973). The value constructs were measured by both Scott's admiration approach and a classical measure (a semantic differential). The results also support the usefulness of distinguishing affect (measurable by a semantic differential) and values (measurable by Scott's admiration technique). First, the correlation between the two approaches only averaged approximately .3. Second, the pattern of predictions to teacher ratings of children and children's involvements in critical incidents differed for affect and

values. Third, the relationships of affect and value to the selection and impact of peers differed. This again supports at least two factors in the area classically called attitudes: alpha and gamma.

Thus, Cattell's early work identifying several factors has empirical support from several lines of independent research. Further investigation is needed to better identify the conditions under which factors alpha and gamma are relevant, but each of these must at least be considered.

Other factors. Another line of research from the classical approach has been insufficiently investigated to know how its measurement devices relate to the measurement factors of Chapter 14. The Sherifs (e.g., Sherif & Sherif, 1967), noting that people differed in how they judged items in developing a Thurstone equal-appearing interval scale, thought this to be useful information in its own right. They developed two techniques, based on the Thurstone task of judging items, to measure "ego involvement." In the first, each person sorts 20 or so attitude statements under the directions used in judging items for an equal-appearing interval scale. Ego-involved people place neutral items in the stack opposed to their position ("all those not for us are against us") and use only a few stacks (being more "black and white" in their judgments).

Their second technique is to ask people to mark the one item on an equal-appearing interval scale which best identifies their own position and to cross out all items which are incompatible with their position. The item checked defines their position as classically measured and the number of items they check as incompatible, i.e., the number they reject, measures their ego involvement.

A series of studies has found interesting results with this technique (Sherif & Sherif, 1969). The Sherifs' techniques are recommended, but we do not yet know how they relate to measurement factors.

Classical social psychology has contributed little systematic research on unconscious aspects (or the second-order factor U). Cattell and Baggaley (1956, 1958) identified several factors forming the second-order U factor which need further research. Chapters 17 and 18 suggest this is greatly needed. But measures of unconscious aspects of attitudes can only be effectively used if, first, it is known how they relate to factors alpha and gamma and, second, it is known when they are interchangeable among themselves and when they provide distinctive information. Answers to these questions require structural analysis of the measurement techniques themselves, a task which Cattell and his associates have begun.

Toward Content Structure

Attitudes, sentiments, and higher order sentiments. Fishbein and Ajzen (1974), as shown above, could predict behavioral intentions from classical attitudes but only if the same level of generality held for both the measures of opinion and behavior. Recent research has generally used specific behaviors (e.g., Ajzen & Fishbein, 1980). Specific behaviors—and their prediction from conscious opinions—have, then, become the primary focus of social psychologists rightfully impressed by their work.

Attitudes defined in relationship to specific behaviors are also the basic building block used by Cattell (1957c). He suggests that an attitude be defined by the following paradigm:

"In these circumstances I want so much to do this with that." The first three words define the *stimulus situation*, the fourth defines the *organism* of interest, the fifth to seventh indicate the *intensity*, the eighth to tenth identify the *specific goal, course of action, or response*, and the last two words give the *object identified in the action*. Cattell suggests that we begin at this level and use attitudes as the basic unit for variables to include in the structural

analyses. Thus Cattell also uses "attitudes" to relate to specific behaviors.

Attitudes are defined similarly by Fishbein and Ajzen and Cattell, despite the fact that the former developed their definition because of the classical attitude model's difficulty in predicting behavior and the latter developed his to identify the structure of motivation and related areas such as interests. The primary difference is in the measurement operations. Fishbein and Ajzen measure attitudes by conscious opinion techniques, but Cattell uses techniques to measure unconscious, as well as conscious, attitudes. In keeping with these two approaches, *"attitudes" is used in this chapter to refer to approach/ avoidance tendencies towards specific behaviors.* Since attitudes are specific in nature, they can be expected to relate to equally specific behaviors.

To avoid confusion, a term other than attitude is used to identify approach/ avoidances that are broader than a specific attitude. For example, the attitude might be about taking a social psychology course from Professor X as a part of program Y in year Z. But what of one's general approach/avoidance towards the area of psychology? One term used for broader areas is that of "trait," but that term has now become identified with characteristics that are theoretically stable over time. This chapter follows the practice of some early social psychologists (e.g., McDougall, 1908), of Cattell (1957c), and of psychometricians such as Nunnally (1978): *"Sentiments" are defined as general approach/avoidances (factors) formed by a set of attitudes.* The set might have a common course of action (e.g., achieving) or have a common object (e.g., parents). Following Cattell, the abbreviation "sem" can be used for such factors.

With the term "attitude" reserved for specific approach/avoidances, should we also examine sems? Mischel (1968) argues that specifics are the necessary approach and quotes considerable research in which a classical measure of a sentiment correlated less than .3 with a specific behavior. The answer to Mischel has, in part, already been given in the Fishbein and Ajzen (1974) results, which showed that specific attitudes correlate with corresponding specific behaviors and general sentiments correlate with corresponding general sets of behaviors.

The implication from Fishbein and Ajzen (1974) that sentiments are important to relate to general sets of behavior has been developed further in reviews by Epstein (1979, 1980). He finds that other studies lead to the same conclusions as Fishbein and Ajzen. Sentiment measures relate to behavior provided one develops a generalized measure by aggregating across several relevant behaviors.

Other arguments of Epstein—e.g., that specific behaviors are inherently less reliable and so have attenuated correlations—imply that sentiments may be the best area for relating to behavior, but this conclusion seems of less interest. Surely a science of psychology is incomplete if it fails to explain *both* specific behaviors and aggregated behaviors. Both can be researched by using attitudes to relate to specific behaviors and sentiments to relate to aggregated behavior.

The appropriate structural model to include both attitudes and sentiments—and thus to relate to both specific and aggregated behavior—is a higher order one. At the specific level are attitudes. Through structural analyses these are combined into first strata sentiments. The first strata sentiments aggregate across a limited set of attitudes and so would relate well to limited aggregates of behavior. The first strata sentiments may also be organized into second strata sentiments, which would relate well to broader aggregates of behavior than the first strata sentiments. There might also be still higher order sentiments. At each higher level of sentiments, the prediction to one specific behavior decreases and the prediction to a set of behaviors increases. Such a structural system then allows one to relate to

any level of behavior. If the problem involves a limited set of behaviors, then we would use first strata measurement. If the behavior is broader, such as career planning, then higher strata sentiments are used. A structural model involving both attitudes and sentiments encourages measurement directly related to the task.

For example, a tentative higher order strata can be suggested for American religiousness. Cattell and Child (1975) report a sentiment factor for this sentiment. Gorsuch (1984) finds a broad, higher strata factor of traditional Christianity in the psychology of religion research, and this factor can be subdivided into other factors, such as theistic and ritual-oriented religiousness. The general factor well-represents relationships of variables such as age with religion. The first strata factors add no further predictability when relating to broad phenomena such as age. This does not mean the lower strata factors are unimportant, for they can be important for particular phenomena. In this case lower strata factors of intrinsic religion (religion as an "end") and extrinsic religion (religion as a "means" to other ends) relate differently to several phenomena, particularly prejudice (intrinsics are among the least prejudiced and extrinsics among the most; Gorsuch & Aleshire, 1974) and anxiety (Baker & Gorsuch, 1982).

Developing content structure of sentiments. The areas of attitudes, interests, sentiments, and values include the entire sphere of human activity. Because of its breadth, the identification of structure is slow and only a basic outline of sentiments exists.

The need for building structural models comes from two principles. First is the scientific quest to understand broad ranges of phenomena. This means that we need the prediction of both individual behaviors and sets of behaviors. Second is the need to apply psychology to human problems. Applied psychology often needs to relate to both specific and broad patterns of behavior. Thus, the employer is concerned with the employee's behavior across a given range of situations. The ethicist is concerned with how people treat each other across a range of situations. The clinical psychologist is concerned with how a person copes with several types of stress across several situations. These require a structural approach.

Good structural analysis requires several steps. First is identifying a domain within the area to be the focus of the studies. Without such a focus, initial attempts are likely to collapse under the vastness of the area. Some progress towards structure in the psychology of religion has already been noted, and other areas in which sentiments are prominent likewise need structural analyses of content. The sentiments noted below may each define a specific area worthy of structural analysis.

The second step is to develop a plan for sampling the attitudes. Only with an adequate sample of a well-defined domain can the results include the factors important for psychology.

The third step is to measure each attitude by several measurement devices. It is hoped that sentiments measured by factor alpha will match with, for example, sentiments measured by gamma or unconscious factors.

The fourth step is to expand the attitudes to include any which psychologists have found important but which were not identified by the sampling of the domain. This provides a method of including past insights from classical psychological theory and research.

The fifth step is to refine the measurement procedures for the identified sentiments by, for example, confirmatory factor analyses. The result of this step is twofold. On the one hand, it provides for replication and confirmation of sentiments. On the other hand, it provides scales both for basic research and for applications.

Major sentiments established in factor analytic studies using both conscious and unconscious measurement are summarized by Cattell and Child (1975). These are listed in Table 15.1 with attitudes defining them. Table 15.1 is based on studies of adults, principally air force men. Children's sentiments are similar but more fragmented, as would be expected. Chapter 14 discusses these factors.

The sentiments of Table 15.1 cover a wide area, but undoubtedly more exist. It is not known how these would fit into a

TABLE 15.1
Confirmed Sentiments

Sentiment	Defining Attitudes
Career	
	I want to learn the skills required for this job.
	I want to continue with my present career.
Home-parental	
	I am proud of my parents and want them to be proud of me.
	I want to turn to my parents for affection, comradeship, and guidance.
Mechanical/constructive	
	I enjoy a good car or motorcycle.
	I like to handle mechanical things.
Religious	
	I want to feel that I am in touch with God, or some principle in the universe that gives meaning and help in my struggles.
	I want to see the standards of organized religion maintained or increased.
Self	
	I want to maintain a good reputation and command respect in my community.
	I want never to damage my sense of self-respect.

TABLE 15.1 *(cont'd)*

Sports and games

> I like to watch and talk about athletic events.
>
> I like to take an active part in sports and athletics.

Sweetheart-spouse

> I want to spend time with my sweetheart, enjoying our common interests.
>
> I want to bring gifts to my sweetheart, to share in his or her delight in them.

Superego

> I want to satisfy my sense of duty to others.
>
> I want to be unselfish in my acts.

Adapted from Cattell, Horn, Sweney, & Radcliffe (1964) and Cattell & Child (1975).

higher order strata model; it may be that they are the broader, higher order factors. As noted above, the religious sentiment is known to be a higher order factor which consists of several lower order factors. The same may be true of the other sentiments so far defined. The career sentiment, for example, is also likely to be at a higher order level. Further research is needed within each of the already defined sentiments to identify the lower order factors or to determine that no such factors exist within that area.

The progress towards determining the structure of sentiments is slight. Cattell and his associates have made a beginning but further work is necessary.

CURRENT INSTRUMENTS AND THE STRUCTURES THEY REPRESENT

Vocational Interest Measures

General characteristics of vocational interest measures. The measurement of vocational interests has been for utilitarian

reasons: vocational counseling. It began early, after World War I, and is still very active.

The first approach asked people their interests. However, the respondents seldom had been exposed to the occupation or activity in the question. People's opinions about their interests were therefore not very accurate, and the attempt was abandoned (Anastasi, 1954).

Present procedures generate Q-data by asking each respondent to choose between two or three common activities or interests. Self-ipsatized scales result, a type which is recommended for motivation measurement. Empirical scoring is generally used, which reduces problems from discrepancies between one's opinion of personal interests and one's actual interests.

Scores are computed for structure and empirically keyed scales. The former may be based on a theory of interests and vocations (Campbell & Hansen, 1981), on face validity (Kuder, 1979), or on factor analysis (Lunneborg, 1981). Empirically keyed scales are based on responses from people in particular college majors or occupations, possibly in comparison with a reference sample. The scoring is often through a computer program that provides a general description from structural scales and specific vocational information from empirical scales.

Homogeneity coefficients of these tests are high, with most being at least .8. Stability coefficients exist for the Strong and Kuder scales over as much as 22 years. They generally are .6 or better, provided the first test was given when the person was at least a senior in high school.

Validity coefficients are generally adequate. The odds are good that a person will enter an occupation for which his or her interests match those already in the occupation and enjoy it reasonably well. The inventories discussed in Chapter 19 have generally been revised (or developed) with specific procedures followed to reduce sex bias. Motivation bias is assumed to be trivial in the counseling situations in which they are used.

Possible problems with vocational interest measures. One potential problem lies in their computerized scoring and interpretation. Since the results will be only as good as the program, one could have an invalid interpretation or an excellent interpretation for the same test. It is essential that a manual link the interpretive statements directly to the supporting research. Then a psychologist can determine if a particular interpretation is, for example, based on a sample appropriate to the client (Roid & Gorsuch, 1983). Computer interpretations in no way reduce the professional responsibility to check the reasonableness of interpretations.

The place of interest measures from a structural perspective is unclear. Campbell-Strong, for example, bases its structure on Holland's categories. But Holland (1973) makes explicit that the categories are based on personality rather than motivation, and these scales should add little over a comprehensive personality test with the same research on occupations. Only if occupational scales measure attitudes or sentiments that are distinct from personality per se will they be distinctly useful.

The lack of examined relationships between vocational interest measures and abilities is another problem. Abilities are limiting factors in occupational choices, for example. Vocational interest scale results are, however, validated without that knowledge and the computer interpretations are only beginning to include ability data. While it is beyond the scope of this chapter to discuss use of test batteries for vocational counseling, such systems exist and may be preferable to the traditional vocational interest scales.

Sentiments: Motivation Analysis Test

The Motivation Analysis Test (Cattell, Horn, Sweney, & Radcliffe, 1964) and the companion School Motivation Analysis Test (Sweney, Cattell, & Krug, 1969) are unique in measuring both basic motivation ("ergs") and sentiments ("sems"). The tests and their principles are discussed in Chapter 14 and so this discussion will center on their possibilities for measuring sentiments.

The sems are structurally based in a series of factor analytic studies by Cattell and his associates. The sems measured are Sentiment to Self (Social Reputation, and Control and Understanding), Superego, Career, Sweetheart-spouse, and Home-parental. It is frankly acknowledged that sems are more numerous than the test measures (with the manual listing seven others already established); the ones selected are deemed to be of general clinical importance.

Scores for each sem are calculated for Integrated and Unintegrated motivation components. These are the higher order factors of which alpha and gamma are first-order factors. A total motivation score is also calculated for each sem. While stability coefficients are reported, they are irrelevant because sentiments are not necessarily stable. Homogeneity coefficients are also irrelevant due to the suppressor items and the self-ipsatizing subtests. Split-half reliabilities are problematic, for answering one item may have satiating effects on that motivation, thus decreasing the likelihood of choosing the same motivation on the next item. This may explain the low reliabilities (e.g., .5 for homogeneity and .6 for test-immediate retest), a problem also found among other motivational tests (e.g., McClelland's TAT measure of Need for Achievement).

The scales often measure some other component as part of the measurement vehicle. For example, the Information measures are influenced by general information, in addition to information from sentiment-specific experience. Several techniques are suggested for parceling out general information so only the sentiment-specific information remains. Even so, scales sometimes seem to be measuring general information rather than sentiment-specific information (Gorsuch, 1965).

An experimental variation of the test is also available for vocational counseling.

Value Measures

Allport, Vernon, and Lindzey Study of Values. For many years this was the primary scale for values. The first edition was in 1931 and a third edition of the manual appeared in 1960 (Allport, Vernon, & Lindzey, 1960). Considerable research has been conducted with this scale, although that research has often been theoretically lacking so that little has been integrated into psychology.

The test has six scales: Theoretical, Economic, Aesthetic, Social, Political, and Religious. These originally were to represent Spranger's *Types of Men* but the scales do diverge occasionally from that conceptualization (e.g., Hunt, 1968). The constructs are similar to many of the interest constructs.

The test has 45 self-ipsatized items which are self-scored. Homogeneity coefficients range from .8 to .95, with stability coefficients of .7 to .9. The scale is normed against college students, and it may be inappropriate for noncollege people. Many studies have found the expected group differences.

It has the problems of ipsatized scales. Only relative values are measured and significance tests are difficult due to the experimental dependence among the scales. (This is likewise true of the vocational interest inventories but is less problematic in individual counseling than in basic research.)

Rokeach Value Survey. This scale is currently the one most widely used. Rokeach himself has an active research program which links it with major questions about the nature of values (Rokeach, 1968, 1973, 1979).

In this scale respondents rank 18 instrumental and 18 terminal values for their "importance." The values included were based on Rokeach's views of what people value and whether the values are means to ends, and thus instrumental, or ends in themselves, and thus terminal. Each value is represented by a single word or phrase (e.g., "A COMFORTABLE LIFE") followed by an explanatory phrase (e.g., "a prosperous life"). Stability coefficients over seven weeks are typically .7 or better.

This writer feels the test has several major limitations (Gorsuch, 1969, 1970, 1980). First, since ranks are used, the scale is self-ipsatizing. The implicit assumption is that everyone has values to the same degree; a person cannot have no value commitments on this scale. Neither can a person have several values tied for "first place." Ranking also makes many significance tests questionable since the rankings result in experimentally dependent scores with negative (or suppressed positive) intercorrelations.

Instead of ranking Rokeach's values, people can rate each on a 10-point scale as to how important that value is. The ratings can be changed to ranks if desired, with the resulting ranks correlating .9 or better with the ranks as produced by Rokeach's procedures. The ratings, however, contain additional useful information about whether the person sees anything as important or whether there are ties. The ratings have no statistical problems since rating one value is experimentally independent of all other ratings. In addition, the rating approach has been shown to discriminate better between groups (Aleshire, 1974). There appears to be no reason to use rankings and good reason to use ratings, and ratings are recommended.

The implicit structure of Rokeach's values is problematic. How the values were selected is unclear and no structural analysis was done to guarantee that the area was adequately and efficiently covered. Further, what some people view as an instrumental value others view as terminal.

For example, is Freedom a terminal or instrumental value? What of Forgiving? The work on intrinsic and extrinsic religiousness has demonstrated that whether people see religiousness as instrumental or terminal is *the* question, and so how should rankings of Salvation be viewed?

Rokeach developed his scale before research demonstrated the importance of separating factors such as alpha (affect) and gamma (moral obligation). How evaluations of "importance," as required in this scale, relate to such factors is unknown.

Despite the above-mentioned drawbacks, Rokeach's measure has been used in considerable worthwhile research, as the values sampled cover a broad area. It has the best norms of any values test. Rokeach also argues that the degree of ipsatization is too small to be important and that the ranking procedure reduces social desirability effects.

Scott's Value Surveying and Scales. For Scott (1965), *a value is that which a person holds to be an ultimate for everyone under all circumstances.* He feels that the list of values should come from the people themselves, rather than from the investigator. So Scott analyzes materials people produce to determine the list of values relevant to a group. Then respondents rate behaviors by which the group defines that value on a scale ranging from "never admire" to "always admire." Scott's procedure has produced value scales for college students and for black and white, lower- and middle-class children (Scott, 1965; Gorsuch, 1973).

Value categories are identified by asking each person to think of an individual he or she admires and to list the behaviors that cause him or her to be admired. Content analyses by judges identify the value categories being used. Adequate rater reliabilities are generally found.

Further questions can be asked, as Scott did with college students, to determine if the behaviors are admirable in everyone on every occasion—and thus are valued by that person. Scott himself did not conduct structural analyses with the college students other than that done implicitly by the judges. Scott's college value scales cover the 12 most-mentioned values: Independence, Intellectualism, Creativity, Academic Achievement, Honesty, Religiousness, Self-control, Kindness, Loyalty, Social Skills, Status, and Physical Development. The homogeneity coefficients are all above .8. Norms are available only for the original college sample.

Gorsuch (1973) did structural analyses with fourth- to sixth-grade children, and found only one factor despite obvious differences in content among the items. These results are unusual since parallel analyses were undertaken in four separate samples defined by crossing social class (middle and lower) with race (black and white) to identify any distinctive values in any group—but none were found. The factor was labeled "basic value socialization" and reflected the development of those values necessary to be a part of any group (value enculturation, i.e., developing the values by which people select which group to be a part of, would then occur in adolescence). Items were retained for the final scale if and only if they functioned adequately in each and every one of the eight groups formed by crossing sex with social class with race. The resulting scale is nine items long and reliabilities are generally .7 or better.

The Scott approach is clearly in the value domain in terms of both content and measurement. The former is assured by the sampling procedure and the latter by the measurement procedure. Gorsuch (1973) found values measured by Scott's approach correlated only .3 with a semantic differential approach. This suggests that people can value a value (i.e., feel it is a moral obligation) and/or like a value (i.e., have a particular affect towards it).

Limited norms exist for this approach (as well as Rokeach's), but norms are less critical in measuring values than in other areas. While norms would be useful, knowing that a person or group values X is worthwhile information in its own right.

Measurement of Specifics

Measurement traditionally measures structures of some type. These involve aggregation across a set of objects or behaviors. The classical approach to this area, as well as the structure-based scales discussed above, are generally of this type.

But it is occasionally vital to assess a particular attitude, as the discussion of the Fishbein and Ajzen contributions has shown. One may, for example, assess attitudes toward a program to evaluate it. Or one may assess attitudes toward a particular problem to evaluate success in therapy.

The procedures available for such tasks are implicit in the discussions above, and will be summarized here. For further information on the procedures, the references already mentioned should be consulted.

Affect is readily measured by a variant of the semantic differential. The attitude object, which is often a behavior, is stated and the person rates it on semantic differential scales. Note that it is important to avoid any semantic differential scale which even suggests a moral obligation is involved.

Two methods evaluate the moral obligation or value component. The first is to ask the person if he or she has a moral obligation to engage in an activity or if the object or its existence is morally good in and of itself. A second approach is to have the people rate whether they feel performing that act is always admirable.

Both techniques are simple questions, and they work only if everyone understands the attitude object in the same way. If there is ambiguity in knowing what is being evaluated, the results will be ambiguous.

Obviously, the procedures mentioned here measure only two conscious components (i.e., factors alpha and gamma). Measurement of unconscious components appears, at this time, to require a study to select appropriate items.

SUMMARY

The classical model of social psychology measures pro/con tendencies by using Q-data. Little structural analysis of either measurement devices or of content has occurred. Several procedures exist for developing scales and numerous scales exist for content.

The classical model has scales with excellent reliabilities that correlate highly regardless of the scale development technique used. However, they have questionable validities. This failure is from unquestioned reliance on Q-data, since these measure only a person's conscious opinion of his or her attitude. Further invalidity occurs from failing to recognize that several strata exist and that predicting from a specific stratum to a general one could reduce correlations.

Structural analyses of measurement for attitudes and sentiments suggest several factors are necessary. This is confirmed by postclassical research showing that both factors alpha (concerned with affect) and gamma (concerned with moral obligation) are needed to predict behavior. Factors from structure research are also available for measuring unconscious components of attitudes.

Research on content structure uses attitudes (defined by the paradigm "Under these circumstances I want so much to do this with that") to identify sems or sentiments (i.e., factors consisting of several attitudes). Known sems include Self, Superego, Career, Sweetheart-spouse, Home-parental, Religious, Sports and games, and Mechanical/constructive. These may be higher order sentiments; for example, the evidence suggests that the Religious sentiment is a higher order structure.

Tests are available for measuring vocational interests with excellent reliabilities but with unknown structural relationships. They may be simply another version of personality tests. The Motivation Analysis Test does measure a non-personality area and so adds additional understanding to personality tests. Popular measures for values generally include an arbitrary set of values, but Scott offers a method for sampling the values categories of a specific group, thus providing data for structural analysis of value sentiments.

CHAPTER 16

Measuring Emotional States and Temporary Role Adoptions

Keith Barton

PSYCHOLOGICAL STATES DEFINED

Before we can consider any objective definition of just what psychological states are and how they may be measured operationally, we must first review briefly the context in which the concept evolved. For many researchers this context was that of using trait-like measures as predictors of dependent variables (target behaviors or criteria) generally considered to be important by large segments of our society. Variables of such interest have historically included school achievement level, job success, accident proneness, neuroticism, psychoticism, and the like. Professionals in all fields that involve human performance and interaction need and value any tool that increases their ability to predict important human behaviors, since with the prediction comes control and with control the opportunity to design more efficient systems of education, psychotherapy, medicine, job placement, personnel training, etc. With the advent of such statistical tools as

regression, it became possible to construct prediction equations of increasing complexity. Using trait or trait-like measures as predictor variables in such regression equations led to a substantial increase in successful prediction. Relatively recently, in an attempt to increase predictability still further, the concept of state variables has been introduced. This refinement is discussed below.

The Context of States in the Trait Prediction Model

Much of the work of practicing psychologists today involves the prediction of future behavior and the understanding of past events. This striving for better and better prediction is not a pedantic exercise or an end in itself but is pursued because a knowledge of the laws of prediction brings with it the power to control behavior—or at very least the hope that such control may be attained. Thus, often the clinical psychologist's major task involves assessment of the patient in such a way

334

as to maximize exposing a network of interrelated variables associated with some "target" behavior. Once this network is discovered and defined it offers a) a possible explanation for past behavior, b) a prediction model for future behavior, and c) some clues as to what can be done about controlling such behavior in the future (i.e., what variables should be changed).

Of course, this is an extremely simplified model of what any real-life clinician would do and it leaves much to be desired, but the point here is to underline the fact that in practice the prediction model *has been* very simple. Essentially, the model (formal or informal) involves five basic steps: a) define the "target" behavior (or patient's complaint); b) somehow identify and define variables that seem associated with this target behavior (traits); c) assess the relative importance of the effects of these variables on the target behavior; d) design a program of behavior change (e.g., therapy) for these traits; and e) evaluate the effectiveness of this program in terms of its efficiency in generating changes in the target behavior. Expressed in a more formal manner this strategy may be seen as a way of generating a simple prediction formula (regression equation) in the following form:

$$a_{ij} = b_{ijt1}T_{1i} + b_{ijt2}T_{2i} \ldots . b_{ijtn} T_{ni} \qquad (16\text{-}1)$$

where a_{ij} represents the "target" behavior (response j) of individual i, and b's are beta weights associated with a number of trait scores (T's). Using this formal model, researchers may obtain beta weights by solving the equation when the values for the other two "unknowns" in the equation are available (i.e., T's and a's) for several subjects. At the informal level the T's represent the traits that the clinician purports to be associated with the target behavior and the beta weights the relative importance of those traits among each other.

Using an equation such as the one above to predict behavior, theoretically a high degree of accuracy may be obtained, but in practice this is rare. For example, the prediction of school grades from such cognitive traits as I.Q., etc., results in equations that typically show that half of the variance in grades is shared by the cognitive measures. How could we increase this accuracy? Many researchers try to solve this problem by adding another domain of predictor variables, e.g., personality plus cognitive variables to predict grades. Such approaches typically lead to relatively modest increases in prediction of the target behavior. For example, when personality trait data are included in the prediction equation along with cognitive variables to predict children's school achievement levels, the R^2's obtained average around .7 or so (from .5 when cognitive variables alone are used as predictors) (Cattell, Barton & Dielman, 1972).

A complementary technique to that above involves the inclusion of the concept of psychological "states" and the incorporation of measures of such states into the predictive regression equations.

A Theoretical Model

Given, then, that there is a real need to add state measures to any prediction model, the question arises as to what form the new model will take. Cattell (1971b) has considered this question in detail and it is his model that will be presented here. The reader interested in more detail is referred to the above reference for further clarifications. Essentially, Cattell modifies equation 16-1 to include state measures and this addition results in an equation of the following form:

$$a_{ijk} = b_{jt}{}^1T^1{}_i + \ldots b_{jtg}T_{gi} + b_{js}{}^1S^1{}_{ki} + b_{jsp}S_{pki} \qquad (16\text{-}2)$$

To understand the nature of this equation, it is essential that three new concepts be introduced. These concepts are a) ambient situation, b) modulator index, and c) state liability. The first concept, that of an ambient situation, is perhaps best understood by comparing the lefthand sides of equations 1 and 2. The only difference here is that the predicted ("target") behavior is seen to be influenced not only by an individual's *(i)* responses to an immediate stimulus *(j)*, but also by momentary "ambient situations" *(k)*. These ambient situations are background conditions different from the *focal* stimulus, which is represented in the *j* subscript term.

The concepts of modulator index and state liability are both seen as theoretical components of any *actual* observed state measure *S*. Specifically, Cattell defines any actual *S* value in the form:

$$S_{xki} = s_{kx} L_{xi} \qquad (16\text{-}3)$$

Here the *s* values refer to modulator indices and the *L*'s to state liabilities for any particular state *x*. An individual's actual state value *(S)* is thus seen to be a function of a) a relative permanent proneness (or liability) to experience that particular state (the *L* term in equation 16-3); and b) a modulating influence due to the ambient situation *k* (the *s* in equation 16-3). Or, in reverse calculation, it can be said that any individual's general liability to experience any particular state (say anxiety) is acted on by a modulating influence due to a specific ambient situation *k*, resulting in an observed state value *S*.

One of the major advantages of this theoretical model is that it eliminates the need to obtain state measures *immediately* at the moment of any desired "prediction" (as would be necessary without the concept of the modulator and a knowledge of state proneness). Instead, values of *s*'s and *L*'s can be stored and used along with *b* and *T* values in a "modulated" specification equation of the form:

$$a_{ijk} = \sum_{y=1} b_{jty} T_{yi} + \sum_{x=1} b_{jsx} s_{kx} L_{xi} \qquad (16\text{-}4)$$

Some further explanation of this model is needed not only because it is encountered in several chapters here touching on states, e.g., Chapter 2 on combining with trait measures and Chapter 23 in defining absolute (true zero) scales, but also because the same model applies to roles.

It will be seen that if we plot the relation of the score on a state, *S*, to the strength of the provocation, s_k, from any situation, *k*, assuming a linear relation, we should get a line as shown at L_{11} or L_{12} in Figure 16.1. The first is for a person of lower liability and the second of higher; geometrically, the value of L_{11} is tan α and of L_{12} tan β.

However, the raw scores on the state measurement scale would almost certainly not be such that the 0 thereon would be the absolute zero for the state, and in the present case we have supposed that the true zero of that state, e.g., anxiety, is reached before getting to the bottom of the particular raw score scale. Because we have supposed the best model is that the psychological state disappears when all provocation disappears, i.e., *S* = $s_k L$ becomes zero when s_k becomes zero, it follows that the plots for two people, as in L_{11} and L_{12}, will intersect at the moment when both s_k and the *S* scales reach their true zero.

If the raw score units on the state scale, though not absolute, are essentially equal, it follows that where the two lines come together, as can be seen, without further algebra, from Figure 16.1, the absolute zero in *S* is reached. From this we can begin, as the true zero on situational provocation, to mark off the provocation scores of other situations, such as k_1, k_2, and k_3, from the obtained *S* scores with those s_k values, as shown at three points on Figure 16.1. That is to say, with the absolute zero of *S* determined, we can build up a scale arranging a variety of situations in situational modulation power units, with reference to the given state. This would, of course, be done for many people, to give

s_k values for the average person. In clinical and other practice it would require much less guesswork if we had such s_k figures for, say, anxiety, for a number of important life situations, e.g., sitting for an exam, going to the hospital, making a marriage proposal. Someday we can hope that applied research will have brought such tables into handbooks.

A rider on the Figure 16.1 model is that the standard deviation of a group on a state measure will increase proportionately to its mean. Another derivation is that we can calculate from an individual's S scores his L, (liability to the given emotion) scores for various emotions and dynamic ergic states. It will be noted that,

although we ultimately need absolute scores for this, we can calculate from the S_r (r for raw score) bracketed elevations shown in Figure 16.1. Elsewhere (Cattell & Brennan, 1983) the calculations, given these S_r values, for getting the true zero, the s_k values, and the L values are set out. As defined below, anything in the style of a temporary role gets introduced into action by an ambient situation and, as far as we yet know, the role trait score could behave the same as a state liability.

The Trait-State Distinction and Independence of State Factors

In the above sections we have looked

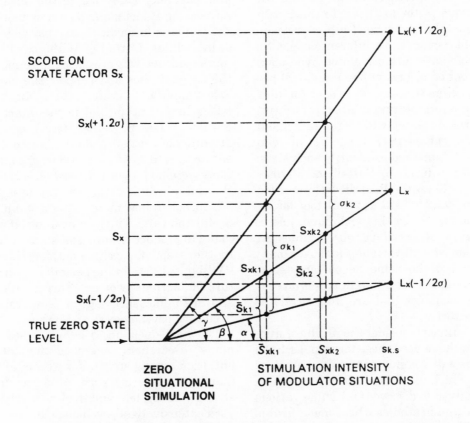

Figure 16.1. Implications of the modulation model for state and role measurement units

briefly at the theoretical distinction between states and traits. Now we will review the evidence that empirically distinguishes the two concepts and that which establishes the independence of various state factors. As was seen in Chapter 12, R-technique factor analysis has played a large role in determining the nature and number of trait factors. In R-technique many variables are intercorrelated with each other over many subjects and the resulting correlation matrix factored. The resulting factors represent traits: patterns or configurations of variables that are characteristic of individuals across time. When defining *states*, two other types of factor analysis are commonly employed: P-technique and dR-technique factor analysis. In the P-technique method, instead of intercorrelating variables over many different people, the variables are intercorrelated over many different occasions for one individual person. Factors resulting from such an intercorrelation matrix reflect changing patterns or states within the individual. As long ago as 1947, Cattell et al. were using this method to identify such states as fatigue (Cattell, Cattell, & Rhymer, 1947). Differential R- or dR-technique factor analysis is also a useful tool for detecting states. In this technique, just as in regular R-technique, observations are made on several variables and over many people but the same people are tested twice and it is the different scores on each of the variables that are intercorrelated and factored.

We will now consider the results of studies that have used these techniques. Such studies fall roughly into two groups: a) those which use P- and dR-technique factor analysis to discover and define various states, and b) studies whose major goal is to differentiate between state and trait factors and to demonstrate the relative orthogonality (i.e., independence) of several state dimensions such as anxiety, stress, and fear. There is insufficient room here for a complete review of the use of

dR- and P-technique factor analysis as applied to state measurement, but an attempt has been made to be as representative as possible of the research literature in the area.

We will first consider some of the evidence that these techniques can be used as tools to discover and precisely define state dimensions. The earliest empirical tests of P-technique were published by Cattell, Cattell, and Rhymer in 1947 and Cattell and Luborsky in 1950. In both studies several psychophysiological factors were identified and tentatively labeled, one study involving an "abnormal" patient and the other a nonpathological subject. Indeed, the results of the Cattell and Luborsky study led to the authors' advocating P-technique as a new tool for the clinician in medicine and psychology. A little later (Cattell & Williams, 1953) more evidence was presented to reinforce the early studies and support the use of P-technique as a useful device "for analyzing functional unities in the intact organism." The new tool attracted the attention of psychologists in many different areas and by the late 1960s the questions were no longer centered on *whether* P-technique could detect and define states but rather in how many areas could it be useful and valid. Thus, for example, it was found to produce meaningful state factors in the area of psychosomatic problems (Williams, 1954), in the personality structure of "normal" women (Curran, 1968), and in the measurement of "depression" in clinical psychology (Van Egeren, 1963).

The next question to be addressed by many researchers concerned the differentiation among states. For example, for many years, terms such as depression, stress, anxiety, fear and the like had been used extensively in psychological practice and theory, but could these concepts be isolated and operationally defined by these relatively new tools of dR- and P-technique factor analysis? Cattell and Scheier (1961) produced the first study in which the major objective was to differentiate between states and they were able to produce several sets of data that suggested that the definitions of stress and anxiety could be best made by looking to factor analytic studies. Following up on this research, further studies showed that by contrasting R- and dR-technique methods, state and trait factors of anxiety, stress, and fear could be uniquely defined (Bartlett, 1968; Cattell & Bartlett, 1971). Later, Cattell, Shrader, and Barton (1974) also produced evidence that showed that anxiety could be differentiated at both the state and trait levels. In one of the few studies that examined both dR- and P-technique simultaneously, Barton, Cattell, and Curran (1973) concluded that examination of factor patterns from both techniques suggested that, although one can make a case for the independence (i.e., orthogonality) of such factors as extraversion, stress, arousal, and fatigue, the data on other state factors are inconclusive. Finally, in a study by Barton and Cattell (1975b) it was demonstrated that state and trait extraversion measures loaded on separate factors, as did state measures of anxiety.

The major conclusions to be made from these kinds of studies are a) that P- and dR-technique factor analysis does indeed enable researchers to identify and operationally define various state factors, and b) that many of the various states so defined can be shown to be independent of each other.

THE USEFULNESS OF STATE MEASURES

In the preceding section several theoretical aspects of states were touched on but now we turn to a more practical question. What are the uses of state measurement? One way to answer such a question is to show a) the wide number of different applications in many different fields, and b) the effectiveness of such applications. Even the briefest of looks at the size of the recent research literature on this subject will convince the reader that a comprehensive review is beyond the scope of this chapter. Instead, a sample of some areas of application will be given and recent studies cited within these areas. This brief sampling will provide the reader with a feel for the enormous scope of state measurement and at the same time effectively lay to rest any questions regarding its usefulness.

Psychotherapy

Changes in affective states both during and after therapy continue to be of great interest to researchers. Measures of states that are reliable, valid, and comprehensive are obviously essential here if we wish to evaluate the effects of various kinds of therapies and to explore affective changes during therapy. For example, Wagoner (1980) used state measures to reveal changes in affect as a function of different therapy types. In a conceptually similar study, Fersching and Kury (1979) investigated changes in psychological states in patients after a four-week treatment period in a mental health center, and Sweney (1975) has endeavored to show relationships among nonverbal behaviors and psychological states. Because mood states are very often the very target phenomenon that therapists try to deal with and change, clinicians will continue to need excellent measures of these states if they are to document the effects of their treatment in any scientific way.

Medicine

Recently, medical research has concerned itself with how and in what ways psychological states are related to specific diseases (especially those thought to be psychosomatic in nature). For example, Ben-Tovim, Marilov, and Crisp (1979) have worked with patients diagnosed as suffering from anorexia nervosa. By administering psychological state measures to these patients, they have been able to show that unique patterns of moods are associated with anorexia nervosa. Agarwal and Sethi (1978) have investigated possible psychogenic factors in bronchial asthma. On such emotional state factors as anxiety, the asthmatic subjects were found to be much higher than siblings free of asthma. Turning to heart disease, Pleszewski (1978) has identified possible state dimensions involved in its etiology and has also examined changes in psychological states brought on by myocardial infarction. Again in this general medical area, Pilowsky (1977) has attempted to identify specific psychological states associated with post-herpetic neuralgia while Houpt, Gould, and Norris (1977) investigated mood states in patients with amyotrophic lateral sclerosis. Achterberg, Lawlis, Simonton, and Mathews-Simonton (1977) have even used psychological state measures as disease outcome predictors in cancer patients. There seems to be an increasing emphasis (in modern medical research) on inclusion of mental or psychological state measures as possible etiological aspects of diseases. Thus, future research in these areas will continue to be dependent on excellent measurement instruments that can detect and reflect changes in psychological states and moods.

Drugs

In this area, researchers continue to use state measures to assess the ways in which different drugs affect mental functioning. One example of the many recent studies is that of Judd (1979), in which the effects of lithium carbonate on several mood states were assessed. Russell and Mehrabian (1977) considered the other side of the issue, asking the question, "In what different mood states do people tend to take different drugs?" The effects of abstinence from such substances as to-

bacco, heroin, and alcohol continue to be an important area of research utilizing psychological state measures. Thus, Williams (1979) used mood state scales to assess the effects of abstinence from tobacco smoking in smokers, and Lorefice, Steer, Fine, and Schut (1976) examined the psychological states of sober alcoholics and former heroin addicts. In another recent and typical study in this area, Mathew, Claghorn, and Largen (1979) compared the psychological mood states of subjects who were experiencing a mild versus severe craving for alcohol. Another area of research interest has centered around the mechanisms involved in the "placebo" effect. Cahill and Belfer (1978), for example, researched the effects of placebos on mood states. Once again, no attempt is made here to try to make the reader aware of the total number of recent studies involving both drug effects and psychological state measures. The few examples mentioned suffice to make the point that state measures in this area are both important and extensively used.

Altered states of consciousness (not drug-induced)

Research on dreaming and sleep is often concerned with psychological state measures. Updegrove (1979), for example, examined emotional states as correlates of dreaming, Cohen (1974) studied the effect of pre-sleep mood state on dream recall and Friedman (1977) researched the effects of gradual sleep reduction on psychological states. There is still much interest in the psychological states associated with extrasensory perception (ESP), as evidenced in studies like that of Schmeidler (1975), in which she related high scores on ESP measures to low anxiety states and high relaxed states. Other lines of research in this general area include the possible effects of differing amounts of stress on psychological states, e.g., Frankignoul and Juchrges (1978), and the results of threatening subjects with pain.

Other areas

There are many recent studies involving psychological state measures. Although these are difficult to categorize, mention of them helps underline the diversity of their usefulness. For example, Kauss (1978) studied the psychological states of athletes and how these states related to their readiness to perform. Again looking at the performance aspect, Barton (1978) noted relationships among psychological state measures and performance on a perceptual motor task. Cruce and Paris-Panzera (1977) noted that film content could affect state score scales. Finally, psychological state scores have been related to such diverse variables as time of day (Barton & Cattell, 1974); physiological variables (Veitch, 1976); obesity (Castelnuovo-Tedesco & Schiebel, 1975); learning (Fuller, 1976); weight reduction programs (Mayo, 1978); delinquency (Lira & Fagan, 1978); and pregnancy (Lebo & Nesselroade, 1978).

When one considers that the above-mentioned studies represent a very small fraction of the total recent research involving psychological state measures, and one notes the importance of the areas involved, the conclusion must be made that there is indeed a very real need for instruments that reliably and validly tap such dimensions. In the next section we will describe some existing state measures and conclude with a specific example of a kit which provides measures of five important dimensions at both the state and trait levels.

HOW MAY WE MEASURE STATES?

Perhaps before we address the question of how states may be measured we should consider how one chooses *which* state dimensions to measure. One major criterion

here is obviously the use to which such state measures will be put. As could be seen in the previous section, the major uses fall into a loosely defined dichotomy which may be labeled pathological vs. nonpathological measures. Thus, when the clinical psychologist and/or psychotherapist uses state measures, because of the nature of the work and interest the tendency is to choose pathological state dimensions such as depression, stress, regression, etc. On the other hand, a researcher with interests in the laws of behavior governing the general population would, when using state measures, tend to study nonpathological variables such as extraversion, general anxiety level, dependence, etc.

Measures of Pathological States

There is no lack of instruments that purport to assess pathological "state-like" behaviors, but unfortunately most suffer from lack of data on validity, reliability, norms, etc., or if such data are available they are of relatively low quality. Lorr (1960), for example, has reviewed a large number of rating scales and behavior inventories that have been consistently used in drug studies. After reviewing this material and the recent literature, the following conclusions are made. The following 15 instruments were considered unsuitable because of the lack of scale reliability, validity and/or norm data: Psychiatric Rating Scale (Wittenborn, 1955—measures nine "cluster" scores and therefore is not concerned with "source" states, only "surface" behaviors); Symptom Rating Scale (Jenkins, Stauffacher, & Hester, 1959—no norms or validity reported); Institute of Living Clinical Rating Scales (Reznikoff & Zeller, 1957—no validity or norms reported); Q-Rating Scale of Ward Behavior (Darbes, 1954—no validity or norms reported); Northampton Activity Rating Scale (Scherer, 1951—no validity, reliability or norm data reported); Elgin Behavior Rating Scale (Wittman, 1948—no reliability, validity or norm data reported); Psychiatric Rating Scale (Malamud & Sands, 1947—no norm data reported, N very low (20) for reliability data); Social Adjustment Scale (Barrabee, Barrabee, & Finestinger, 1955—no reliability, validity or norms reported); Rating Scale for Evaluation of Psychotherapy (Morse, 1953—no reliability or norm data reported); QPSS Rating Sheet (Goodrich, 1953—no reliability, validity or norms given); Clyde Mood Scale (Clyde, 1958—no reliability, validity or norm data reported).

In addition to problems with reliability, validity, norms, etc., most of the above-mentioned scales were designed with a pathological population in mind and are unsuited for a more normal sample, since the items were concerned with behaviors in mental hospital settings, prisons, etc.

Measures of Nonpathological States

When one reviews the scales that attempt to assess nonpathological state measures, the first reaction is surprise at the small number of such instruments available (compared to the more pathological scales). Even when one encounters tests such as Spielberger's State-Trait Anxiety Inventory (STAI), which has reasonable validity, reliability, and norm data, one cannot help wishing for an instrument that taps a comprehensive set of variables and not just one single dimension such as anxiety (Spielberger et al., 1970). In fact, the only test kit that both offers a set of measures, whose choice is based on a functional rationale, and provides scales at both the state and trait levels is the Central Trait-State Kit (CTS) by Barton and Cattell (1981). The dimensions covered in this kit were determined not by fiat, but by second-order factor analytic procedures, and represent normal or nonpathological states. Details regarding this instrument follow in the next section.

A Specific Example of Nonpathological State Measurement: The Central Trait-State Kit (CTS)

History of development of the scales. The history of the development of the CTS parallels that of the development of Cattell's 16 Personality Factor (16 P.F.) test, in that the CTS measures five of the second-order factors found in the 16 P.F. items. Thus, the majority of items in the *trait* scales of the CTS are identical to those of the 16 P.F. and have the same developmental history (for this see the 16 P.F. Handbook, Cattell, Eber, & Tatsuoka, 1970). However, the *state* scales on the CTS are comprised of items, which, although basically tapping the same dimensions as the trait scales, do so with the object of assessing relatively labile moods. For example, the general characterological trait of anxiety is measured by the CTS *trait* scales, whereas shifts in anxiety caused by such factors as situational changes can best be assessed by the CTS *state* scales.

The psychologist in clinical, educational, or industrial and vocational work, who wishes to make a thorough examination of personality by questionnaire, will still find the primary instrument to be the 16 P.F. (with perhaps the 16 P.F. supplement), as together these two questionnaires tap some 23 primary personality traits. If the nature of the investigations requires the assessment of more pathological traits, then an equivalent comprehensiveness in measurement may be obtained with the *Clinical Analysis Questionnaire* (CAQ). However, there are circumstances in which the psychologist may wish:

a) To make observations more quickly (the 16 P.F. takes almost an hour to administer for many people versus five minutes per subtest for the CTS).

b) To measure only one or two factors of interest (compared to the many primary factors in the 16 P.F. and CAQ).

c) To have *both* trait and state measures on the same person at the same time.

d) To make repeated measures on states and/or traits at so short an interval that use of the same instrument would confound the meaning of the results.

When any one or a combination of the above conditions exists, then the CTS would be the appropriate instrument to use. It can thus be seen that the CTS Kit has evolved as a result of unique sets of user needs and is intended to *complement* the CAQ and 16 P.F.

Choice and description of variables. It has been the aim of all test construction at IPAT to orient scales to—and only to—traits and states structures demonstrated by basic research to be functionally unitary entities, and important to general personality theory. Thus, the 23 primary factors in the extended 16 P.F. questionnaire rest on some 40 or more published researches covering behavior ratings, as well as factor analyses of questionnaire and criterion data (see Cattell, 1957a, 1973a; Cattell, Eber & Tatsuoka, 1970).

The present scales are based on the discovery of the *second-order* personality structure by Cattell (1959a), Horn (1963b), Karson and Pool (1958), Karson and Haupt (1968), Krug and Kulhavy (1973), and by the "short-cut" approaches to these factors by immediate item factoring in the work of Sells, Demarce, and Will (1968) and others. A second-order or "secondary" factor is, of course, obtained by factoring primary factor intercorrelations, as in the 16 P.F., and is therefore a central, more general influence which contributes variance to the primaries. That contribution could be small and "secondary" in the sense of importance, too; but actually the contribution is substantial, being more than half the variance if we consider all eight or nine known secondaries.

The best-defined eight second-order factors and their loadings on primaries averaged from 14 different second-order factor experiments are shown in Table 16.1 (taken from Cattell, Eber, & Tatsuoka, 1970).

TABLE 16.1

Mean Loadings of Second Orders on the Normal Primaries A through Q_4*

Source Trait	Females								Males							
	I	II	III	IV	V	VI	VII	VIII	I	II	III	IV	V	VI	VII	VIII
A	85	05	−30	09	34	03	−06	04	62	−07	−59	−04	05	−01	03	−08
B	−02	00	01	02	01	−01	98	02	01	00	00	03	03	01	97	01
C	07	−86	−03	−23	−02	06	02	−03	11	−80	03	−11	−03	05	04	09
E	26	09	29	58	−07	−07	00	01	41	20	02	66	03	−04	−02	00
F	66	−08	13	−08	−04	02	04	−31	84	04	03	−06	−01	−02	04	−19
G	09	−02	−04	−07	−03	06	01	78	07	01	−01	−05	00	06	00	86
H	52	−46	11	01	−06	17	02	−04	78	−18	−05	14	06	05	−08	06
I	−04	−06	−73	05	−05	90	−02	05	03	04	−60	04	−03	67	01	−03
L	01	55	51	37	11	−06	−03	04	05	69	−02	57	07	−29	−02	03
M	−15	−17	−30	54	−16	19	02	−13	−03	−05	−17	50	−02	49	05	−07
N	−01	−06	−01	−05	83	00	04	−01	00	−02	03	−03	90	01	01	01
O	−19	82	−03	−07	−16	−01	00	01	−11	80	−07	−08	−02	08	03	−06
Q_1	05	04	−02	74	07	−16	02	04	02	−01	−12	61	01	05	06	−12
Q_2	−72	11	14	37	−01	−07	−02	04	−01	−78	13	54	02	06	00	11
Q_3	−09	−44	09	−01	07	01	−02	61	−08	−43	01	06	00	−17	01	57
Q_4	08	82	05	09	−04	02	06	12	13	93	03	07	−01	03	06	05

*Key to second-order factor labels

I. Extraversion
II. Anxiety
III. Cortertia
IV. Independence

V. Discreetness
VI. Realism
VII. Intelligence
VIII. Conscientiousness

The CTS Kit, however, concentrates only on the five second-order factors: Anxiety, Extraversion, Independence, Conscientiousness, and Cortertia. Each of these secondaries is broader than any primary factor. Extraversion, for example, contributes to factor A (affectothymia), F (surgency), H (parmia), and $Q_2(-)$ (group dependence). It is this same general influence, stamped into the makeup of all individuals, which increases the endowment in all the "extravert" primaries, A, F, H and $Q_2(-)$. The principal theories suggest a causal interaction or "spiral" effect, whereby a higher level on any one of these factors favors an environmental experience tending to develop the others, e.g., high parmia ("thick-skinnedness") would reduce withdrawal from social problems and thus favor development of more social

skills. Table 16.2 defines these five secondary factors and gives titles, descriptions and sample items for the five secondaries in the kit.

Because there are 20 subtests to the CTS Kit and a need to avoid a verbal title being printed on each test, a simple coding system has been set up which allows the user to easily identify each subtest. The code consists of three components, the first being a letter corresponding to the first letter of each personality factor (A for anxiety, E for extraversion, etc.). The middle code component consists of a T if the subtest measures a trait or an S if the subtest is designed for state assessment. The final code component is an A or B depending which equivalent form of the test is being used. Thus, for example, the code ATA on a subtest means that it measures anxiety

TABLE 16.2

Titles and Sample Items for the Five Secondaries in the CTS Kit*

1)	*Anxiety*: Trait		*Anxiety*: State
Q_1	I tend to take each day as it comes and don't spend a lot of time worrying about the future.	Q_1	In my present mood thinking about my future would really upset me.
Q_2	Even after a hectic day I can easily unwind and relax.	Q_2	I just know that any decisions that I make today will be good ones.
2)	*Extraversion*: Trait		*Extraversion*: State
Q_1	In school I was never one to speak out a lot in class.	Q_1	I'm feeling very talkative and outgoing today.
Q_2	Most people would *not* describe me as the quiet, serious type.	Q_2	In my present mood I'd hate to have to eat dinner alone tonight.
3)	*Independence*: Trait		*Independence*: State
Q_1	On the whole I don't much care what people think of me.	Q_1	In my present mood it would really upset me to know that people think I'm different or odd.
Q_2	I don't think I'm very good at handling things that come up unexpectedly.	Q_2	Having to wait for people to make up their minds would really make me angry.
4)	*Conscientiousness*: Trait		*Conscientiousness*: State
Q_1	My conscience never lets me get away with even small wrongdoings.	Q_1	In my present mood I would tell a lie to get out of something I had said I would do.
Q_2	As long as someone isn't hurting a person or property, I don't think there's anything wrong with breaking rules.	Q_2	The way I am feeling now, I just wouldn't care if I hurt someone's feelings.
5)	*Cortertia*: Trait (cognitive vs. emotional response)		*Cortertia*: State
Q_1	It makes me uncomfortable to see people show their affections in public.	Q_1	I'm feeling very sensitive today and would be easily hurt if someone said the wrong thing.
Q_2	In my opinion there isn't a problem that can't be solved in some practical way.	Q_2	If there was a crisis in my family today, I'd do what my heart, not my head, tells me to do.

*Half of the items for each state and trait dimension are written in positive and negative directions, e.g., half reflect high anxiety and half low anxiety.

at the trait level and is form A of the test. A full explanation of all 20 codes is shown in Table 16.3.

Purpose and uses of the CTS. While Cattell's 16 Personality Factor (16 P.F.) questionnaire has been criticized at the primary-factor level, few researchers would argue that the five major second-order factors do not represent valid and reliable measures of constructs with demonstrable use in psychological theory and practice. These five second-order factors are Anxiety, Extraversion, Independence, Conscientiousness (superego), and Cortertia (cognitive versus emotional response pattern). Until now researchers or clinicians desiring measures on any of these variables have had to administer the whole 16 P.F., obtain scores on all 16 scales and then calculate values for the second-order factors. The CTS Kit allows the researcher or clinician to choose any single factor (or group of factors) of interest and provides a subtest to measure it.

While there has been an increasing amount of attention given to the concept of psychological *states* (compared to traits), except for a few isolated instances (e.g., Spielberger's STAI: State-Trait Anxiety Inventory), there has not been a comprehensive development in the measurement aspect of such variables.

Whether trait or state measures are of interest, the CTS Kit provides equivalent forms of each, i.e., forms A and B for each.

SUMMARY OF USES AND PROPERTIES OF CTS

Variables Measured:	Anxiety, Extraversion, Independence, Conscientiousness, Cortertia.
Trait or State?	Both.
Equivalent Forms?	Yes, A and B for all 5 variables at both trait and state levels.
Intended Population:	Normal adults. Reading level has been kept down to that of the general newspaper-reading public."
Time to Administer:	Five minutes or less per subtest.

TABLE 16.3
Key to Abbreviations of Subtests

Name of Personality	Factor	Trait or State	Form	Abbreviation
Anxiety	(A)	T	A	ATA
"	(A)	T	B	ATB
"	(A)	S	A	ASA
"	(A)	S	B	ASB
Extraversion	(E)	T	A	ETA
"	(E)	T	B	ETB
"	(E)	S	A	ESA
"	(E)	S	B	ESB
Conscientiousness	(Co)	T	A	CoTA
"	(Co)	T	B	CoTB
"	(Co)	S	A	CoSA
"	(Co)	S	B	CoSB
Independence	(I)	T	A	ITA
"	(I)	T	B	ITB
"	(I)	S	A	ISA
"	(I)	S	B	ISB
Cortertia	(C)	T	A	CTA
(Cognitive-Emotional)	(C)	T	B	CTB
"	(C)	S	A	CSA
"	(C)	S	B	CSB

Administrative Details

Materials. Each of the 20 subtests consists of 25 statements arranged over both sides of a single piece of paper. The statements are printed on the left side of each sheet and on the right side is a 6-point scale ranging from "strongly agree" to "strongly disagree."

Instructions. Instructions are printed at the top of each subtest and repeated on the reverse side of the sheet. For the subtest measuring *states*, the instructions are as follows: "DIRECTIONS: Please read each item carefully. Place a check (√) under the column which best reflects HOW YOU ARE FEELING RIGHT NOW, IN YOUR PRESENT MOOD."

For the subtests measuring *traits*, the instructions are as follows: "DIRECTIONS: Please read each item carefully. Then place a check (√) under the column which best reflects HOW YOU USUALLY FEEL."

Timing. The CTS Kit is not a timed test but most people finish any given subtest in five minutes or less.

Scoring. All items to which a "strongly agree" response indicates a high score on the particular variable being tested are scored as follows: strongly agree = 6 points, agree = 5 points, slightly agree = 4 points, slightly disagree = 3 points, disagree = 2 points, and strongly disagree = 1 point. All items to which a "strongly agree" response indicates a low score on that particular state or trait are scored as follows: strongly agree = 1 point, agree = 2 points, slightly agree = 3 points, slightly disagree = 4 points, disagree = 5 points, and strongly disagree = 6 points.

This system has been used to make up transparent overlays for each side of each subtest and is available from the publisher. Each overlay indicates the value to be given to each item depending on

where the user made a check mark on the scale. Using a hand electronic calculator a total score over all items can be obtained in one or two minutes.

Reliability, Validity, and Norm Issues

In order to establish reliability and validity data for the CTS Kit, an ideal theoretical model was first assembled. This model involved a design in which all subtests would be administered to 100 + subjects and then the experiment repeated twice, once to establish short-term reliability and later to estimate long-term reliability (stability, r_s). The model is shown in Table 16.4.

Such an ideal model will allow the assessment of test-retest reliability (both short- and long-term) for all forms and state versions of the five dimensions, forms and state-trait versions, thus permitting an examination of the independence of states and traits and also an estimate of the extent to which the major five dimensions are independent *within* the state and trait concepts.

However, this ideal model unfortunately calls for far more time per participant than is deemed possible to expect without the overall validity suffering, e.g., 20 subtests might take over two hours to finish and certainly might be expected to change the very measures that we are assessing, i.e., states!

As a compromise, data collection is proceeding along the lines defined by the model above but only for the *trait* dimensions. For the *state* subtests, a series of P-techniques have been designed in such a way that independence of the state dimensions, as well as the equivalence of forms of the test, may be assessed. These data are being collected now and, along with test-retest reliability data, will be included in the manual for the CTS Kit. Normative data are also being collected and should be available soon.

TABLE 16.4
Dependability Record

Test Abbreviation*	Original test	Time of Testing Retest same day	Retest at 6 months
ATA ATB ASA ASB	†		
ETA ETB ESA ESB			
CoTA CoTB CoSA CoSB			
ITA ITB ISA ISB			
CTA CTB CSA CSB			

*See Table 16.3 for explanation.   † N = 100 per cell

SUMMARY

This chapter started by defining psychological states by 1) showing the context of states within a trait framework, 2) specifying equations that partition states and traits into separate components of behaviors, and 3) illustrating the independence and unique qualities of specific states. In the course of this definition process, three new concepts were introduced: ambient situations, modulator indices, and state liabilities.

Once states were defined, the usefulness of such measures was illustrated by describing their use in such diverse areas as psychotherapy, medicine, drug studies, etc.

The rest of the chapter was concerned with how states may be measured. The Central Trait-State Kit (CTS) was described in detail as an example of an instrument that allows the measurement of five nonpathological states: anxiety, extraversion, independence, conscientiousness, and cortertia.

PART III

The Art of Testing in Psychological Practice

CHAPTER 17

Clinical Diagnosis and Psychotherapeutic Monitoring

Brian F. Bolton

TRANSITIONS IN MODERN CLINICAL PSYCHOLOGY

Clinical psychology is likely to undergo a greater transition in the '80s than any it has experienced in the previous half-century. Radical improvements are appearing in three directions:

1) A shift from an obsolete armamentarium of rule-of-thumb tests to functional test instruments appearing from basic multivariate research on personality and dynamic structure;
2) Psychotherapy itself shifting from, on the one hand, the wholistic but pre-metric psychoanalytic theories and on the other, from the atomistic, personality-neglecting reflexological ("behavior therapy") to the broader theoretical basis of *structured learning theory*; and
3) A fuller recognition by psychologists of the genetic and physiological aspects of mental disorder, previously more central in psychiatry, but now linking up well with structured personality re-

search on source traits, the dynamic calculus, and the factorially discovered dimensions of state change.

As to the implications for testing, it must be obvious that the whole foundation and spirit of this book calls for recognizing that though such monuments to assiduous "muddling through" as Draw-A-Man, Bender-Gestalt, Rorschach—and even more mystical devices with the attraction of fortune-telling—are still widespread, their reputation is more traditional than scientific. They have repeatedly been shown to have more anecdotal than statistical validity. The exception to this is their hard-won empirical trial-and-error capacity to assign some patients to DSM pigeonholes, but without source trait analysis.

As Chapters 9 through 16 in this book have laid out the evidence, testing can now begin to rest on advances in personality research as such, which have discovered structure in ability, personality, and dynamic traits, on the dimensions of state

348

variation, on indices of conflict and integration, etc. These have now led to a harvest of measuring instruments in questionnaires and a rich variety of nonquestionnaire, objective tests, permitting a far more analytical approach to assessment and diagnosis. Since the instruments themselves already have been presented, their strategic use in diagnosis and psychotherapy can now be discussed.

Clinical assessment via psychological tests is the basis for 1) diagnostic decisions, 2) selection of appropriate therapeutic interventions, and 3) measurement of client progress during the course of the treatment program. It is to be understood that though we are compelled at the present stage of practical aids to handle individuality in terms of scales and batteries for common trait scores, we also recognize theoretically the importance of P-technique with its experimental-statistical structuring of the unique individual. A discussion of the latter appears later in this chapter, but meanwhile we proceed with the review of practicable common trait tests now available.

The factor-analytically located source traits in which we base our procedures are the primary causal influences that account for observed variations in behavior and are measured by such instruments as the 16 P.F., HSPQ, MAT, CAQ, O-A Battery, and others. It is important to explain, however, that we are not suggesting that clinical assessment should be limited to test instruments alone. In fact, a comprehensive evaluation of the client requires that all types of relevant information be ascertained, e.g., family background data, the insights derived from a psychiatric interview, behavioral assessment of maladaptive characteristics, psychosocial and interpersonal skill deficits, as well as traditional psychological testing (see Golden, 1979, for examples of the latter category). Still, consistent with the theme that runs through this entire volume, we believe that source-trait measurement is the foundation of clinical assessment and ac-

cordingly the presentation in this chapter is so restricted.

Clinical assessment with structured tests may take place in a wide range of psychological service settings, e.g., mental health clinics, hospitals, rehabilitation agencies, alcoholism treatment units, child guidance clinics, family counseling services, educational institutions and, especially in the widespread service now offered by individual practitioners. The information produced by source-trait measures is relevant to diagnostic decisions about numerous therapeutic treatments, e.g., individual psychotherapy, group counseling, family counseling, work therapy, various milieu therapies, personal adjustment training, physical fitness training, assertiveness training, and various specific behavioral procedures. While at one time there was a tendency to depend on test instruments specific to the area of practice—e.g., clinical, educational, industrial—the integration of tests in relation to personality structure and theory makes these test collections obsolete. Since it is the same person who enters the job, the clinic, etc., practice is moving toward basic ability, personality, and dynamic measures applicable in all assessment settings and relevant to all diagnostic decisions. And a model rooted in the general behavioral equation and Cattell's (1980b; also see Bolton, 1986) structured learning theory (SLT), provides a comprehensive and quantitative framework for the psychotherapist, ready to handle, with concept and computer, a more refined and analytical approach.

PERSONALITY ASSESSMENT BY QUESTIONNAIRE: THE NORMAL PERSONALITY STRUCTURE BY 16 P.F., HSPQ, ETC.

Factor analytic structuring of personality has found, in a life-broad array of questionnaire items, a now fairly comprehensive taxonomy of factors in normal behavior and abnormal behavior. The former have been caught in the "normal" questionnaire series across most ages—16 P.F., HSPQ, CPQ, ESPQ—and the latter in Part II of the Clinical Analysis Questionnaire (CAQ). These questionnaires and others on a factor structured basis are described in Chapter 12.

In industrial and educational practice the "normal" series commonly suffices. In clinical practice one needs also the 12 pathological behavior dimensions in the CAQ or the MMPI, but it would be a mistake to suppose we do not need the normal dimensions when we measure a client on the "disease process" factors (hence, Part I of the CAQ repeats the 16 P.F.). Much has been written about the concept of disease, and we must recognize at least a difference between disease due to a specific outside agent, as in influenza, and disease as an imbalance or dysfunction in normal processes, as in systemic disorders such as diabetes or cardiac disorder. The most numerous psychopathologies are probably of the latter kind, certainly in neuroses, less definitely so in psychoses. Even in the imbalances it seems from analysis that certain new pathological dimensions may appear that have minimal, unimportant variance in the healthy individual. Thus, the clinician needs, on the one hand, to get a 16 P.F. profile of the normal factors (as when a psychotherapist asks about "the prepsychotic personality") and, on the other hand, to evaluate the pathological processes that have developed, as covered by Part II of the CAQ, the MMPI, etc.

This section concerns 16 P.F. usage, and, by implication, the HSPQ, CPQ, and ESPQ, since these measure the same source traits at other ages. In addition to its extensive use in counseling practice and research, the major reason that the Sixteen Personality Factor Questionnaire (16 P.F.) occupies a prominent place in this chapter is that it is the foundation and cornerstone of source-trait measurement in psychometric personality theory. The primary source-trait structure of hu-

man temperament was originally discovered some 40 years ago (extended in the last 15 to pathological primaries) and has been the focus of continuing research and refinement around the 16 P.F., HSPQ, and CAQ ever since (Cattell, 1946, 1957c, 1965, 1979c). As part of the perspective on that body of research we must recognize the finding of the same factors in several different cultures and countries (U.S., U.K., Brazil, Germany, France, India, Japan, etc.), which supports the fundamental nature of the structures.

During the period from 1971 through 1977, the 16 P.F. was the second most popular test in the published psychological literature, as indicated by the total number of references cited in the *Eighth Mental Measurements Yearbook* (Buros, 1978, p. xxxviii). The relevance of the 16 P.F. to the tasks of clinical assessment is attested to by its inclusion in Golden's (1979) textbook, which reviews ". . . the most widespread and important tests in adult clinical psychology today" (p. ix). Of the ten chapters, only two are devoted to self-report personality inventories, and one of these is the 16 P.F. It is Golden's belief that the clinical application of the 16 P.F. is increasing, as is its use in clinical research. Two recently published manuals that discuss the use of the 16 P.F. in clinical and counseling practice are Karson and O'Dell's (1976) *Guide to the Clinical Use of the 16 P.F.* and Schuerger and Watterson's (1977) *Using Tests and Other Information in Counseling.* The *Handbook for the 16 P.F. Questionnaire* (Cattell, Eber, & Tatsuoka, 1970) is still the basic practical reference, although Krug's (1981b) *Interpreting 16 P.F. Profile Patterns* will also be valuable for practitioners.

The most basic assumption (an axiom of functional testing) in this approach to assessment and diagnosis is that observed behavior is the resultant product of several underlying causal influences—the source traits. This principle of multiple causation of behavior via source-trait structure is embodied in the concept of the specification equation, which states that behavior is determined by a linear combination of temperamental traits, drives, abilities, and mood states. For the individual client, a behavioral prediction or diagnostic estimate can be derived as a weighted sum of the relevant source traits in the individual's unique personality configuration. Alternatively, we can calculate the pattern similarity of the individual's profile with a clinical category (see Chapter 6 for details).

Behavioral specification equations have been developed to estimate marital adjustment, parole success, response to therapeutic intervention, suicide potential, and various diagnostic syndromes. It is important to understand that the specification equation provides a statistical estimate concerning an individual's probable success in a given activity or his or her measured similarity to a specific diagnostic syndrome. The specification equation translates the individual's source-trait profile into the behavioral or diagnostic estimate. A good example of a diagnostic specification equation is that for the general neurotic syndrome (abbreviated from Cattell, Eber, & Tatsuoka, 1970, p. 266):

$$N = 6.3 - 0.3 \, (C) - 0.2 \, (E) - 0.4 \, (F)$$
$$+ \, 0.2 \, (I) + 0.3 \, (O) + 0.4 \, (Q_4) \qquad (17\text{-}1)$$

This equation for neurosis says simply that the diagnosed condition is caused by a combination of six primary source traits: low ego strength $(-C)$, submissiveness $(-E)$, desurgency $(-F)$, emotional sensitivity $(+I)$, apprehension $(+O)$, and excessive ergic tension $(+Q_4)$. As explained below, individual clients typically have unique configurations of neurotic determinants, and these patterns provide especially useful information to the clinician, whose task is to subjectively integrate all relevant data into 1) an in-depth portrait of the client's unique personality structure, and 2) a functional diagnostic statement that will establish the basis for appropriate therapeutic interventions.

Considerable research with the 16 P.F., MAT, CAQ, O-A Battery, and other factored instruments has supported the principle of pathology as, in most cases, a quantitative deviation along a continuum. What this means is that the measured differences between normally adjusted persons and those suffering from various psychiatric disorders are to a great extent a matter of the degree and configuration of the common source traits that span the normal personality sphere. This is especially true for the psychoneurotic, addictive, delinquent, and personality disorder syndromes, which are generally characterized by diminished ego strength, emotional sensitivity, withdrawal, guilt, and excessive tension, though in different profile patterns (see Cattell et al., 1970, for tables of such profiles).

Yet, it is also recognized that there can be bimodal or at least non-normal distributions, and most psychoses (except brain injury cases) seem to be of such a nature, with a fairly distinct break on factor measures. There is an entire class of source-trait dimensions that simply do not emerge as significant factors in studies of normal persons, because by definition normality precludes certain extreme behavioral manifestations, e.g., hallucinations, paranoid delusions, and severe depression. In other words, there is little variation in the normal population on dimensions of psychotic functioning. This, as we have pointed out, puts a limit to use of the 16 P.F. in clinical diagnosis. Hence, as stated, to enable the clinician to diagnose the psychotic conditions objectively via source-trait measurements, the 16 P.F. has been supplemented by 12 psychopathology scales corresponding to the 12 dimensions found in factoring a host of pathological behavior items like those appearing in the MMPI, various depression scales, etc. The resulting instrument is the Clinical Analysis Questionnaire (CAQ), which is discussed in the next section.

Although there is thus an area of personality dysfunction that lies beyond the measuring range of the 16 P.F., it is important to realize that normal and sick can alike be meaningfully described, apart from pathology, in terms of a profile of temperamental variation on the normal source traits. In fact, the extensive evidence reported in Chapter 14 of the *Handbook for the 16 P.F.* documents the substantial diagnostic validity of the 16 P.F. within the psychoneurotic classification, and the somewhat less effective separation of the psychotic syndromes. The explanation for this phenomenon appears to be that there are certain variations among the normal source traits that contribute, along with biochemical factors, to the various forms of psychiatric dysfunction.

It is convenient, while we are still in the domain of the normal personality, to explain *depth psychometry*. The principle of depth psychometry in clinical assessment and diagnosis is based on the important distinction between surface traits and source traits. Surface traits are simply clusters of observed personality characteristics. The psychiatric diagnostic categories (syndromes) are identified by the confluence of a particular set of behavioral manifestations (symptoms). For example, a person who exhibits insecurity, low self-esteem, tension, depression, and quick temper might be diagnosed as suffering from some form of neurotic condition, such as anxiety neurosis or depressive reaction.

In contrast to the more readily observed and measured surface characteristics, psychometric source traits can only be located and operationally defined by careful factor analytic research. Source traits are the *underlying* functional unities—the influences—in human personality that explain the observed variation in surface traits or diagnostic syndromes. For example, we know from the specification equation cited above that the psychiatric disease process known as neurosis results from some combination of the following

source traits: diminished ego strength $(-C)$, submissiveness $(-E)$, desurgency $(-F)$, emotional sensitivity $(+I)$, apprehension $(+O)$, and ergic tension $(+Q_4)$. These, in turn, are generated by environmental trauma, genetic effects, etc.

The basic axiom of depth psychometry states that the same general neurotic syndrome *may* result from *different configurations* of the primary source traits that constitute neurosis. The same degree of neurotic dysfunction can be produced by an overly sensitive $(+I)$, easily upset $(-C)$, overwrought $(+Q_4)$, temperamental inclination in one person and by a submissive, conforming $(-E)$, desurgent $(-F)$, insecure $(+O)$ personality pattern in another person. In other words, an equally severe neurotic condition can have different roots in the unique personality structures of clients and show in different "styles."

The principle of depth psychometry is illustrated in the brief case vignettes presented in this chapter and Chapter 18. The psychologist and psychiatrist typically provide the surface trait descriptions based on traditional test results and the clinical interview, while the 16 P.F., MAT, CAQ, and O-A Battery generate the unique configuration of source traits that guide the clinician in understanding the underlying causal influences in the client's personality structure.

PATHOLOGICAL DEVELOPMENTS ASSESSED BY THE CLINICAL ANALYSIS QUESTIONNAIRE (CAQ)

It has been documented in numerous independently conducted investigations that the major psychoneurotic syndromes—but not the major psychotic syndromes—are characterized by unique source-trait profiles on the normal personality dimensions measured by the 16 P.F. The value of the 16 P.F. in understanding the nature of psychoneurotic dysfunction in the individual case is illustrated by the vignettes presented in this chapter and Chapter 18. As to psychosis, though the light it throws on the general prepsychotic personality is valuable, it was noted by clinical practitioners and psychometric researchers in the 1960s that the 16 P.F. omits pathological loss of reality contact associated with the more severe forms of psychiatric impairment, i.e., the broad category of the psychoses.

In Chapter 12 the structure and the research basis of the CAQ are described by Barton from a series of factor analytic studies by Cattell and his associates (Cattell & Bjerstedt, 1967; Cattell & Bolton, 1969; Delhees & Cattell, 1971b). This programmatic research led to the identification of 12 source traits comprising the *abnormal personality sphere* and produced scales for their measurement. The resulting instrument, the Clinical Analysis Questionnaire (CAQ) (Krug, 1980), consists of 16 scales that measure the source traits of the normal personality sphere as in the 16 P.F. and 12 scales that measure the pathology source traits. Thus, the CAQ encompasses the 16 P.F. and extends the range of questionnaire measurement into the abnormal domain, permitting the psychologist to assess just the latter (by Part II) or all 28 by parts I and II (Part I has much-shortened 16 P.F. scales).

In addition to the 16 dimensions of normal personality functioning that assist the clinician in understanding the prepathological personality, the 12 new scales are:

Hypochondriasis (D_1)
Suicidal Depression (D_2)
Agitation (D_3)
Anxious Depression (D_4)
Low Energy Depression (D_5)
Guilt and Resentment (D_6)
Boredom and Withdrawal (D_7)
Paranoia (Pa)
Psychopathic Deviation (Pp)
Schizophrenia (Sc)
Psychasthenia (As)
Psychological Inadequacy (Ps)

It should be emphasized that, despite the similarity of several of these scale names to those of the MMPI, the CAQ pathology scales measure functionally unitary source traits discovered by factor analysis and are *not* quite the same as the total syndrome categories distinguished by the MMPI, although they do analyze contributors to these.

Since the CAQ in factorial terms subtends most of the "space" of the MMPI, and more besides (especially in conjunction with the normal source-trait scales): 1) a weighting table has been worked out to change scores from one to the other (Cattell & Bolton, 1969; Delhees & Cattell, 1970; Krug, 1980, pp. 44-45), and 2) the CAQ scales are capable of providing fully efficient discrimination of the traditional psychiatric diagnostic categories, e.g., paranoid schizophrenia, anxiety reaction, passive-aggressive personality, psychotic depression, organic brain syndrome, etc.

For illustrative purposes, CAQ profiles for three serious psychiatric disorders are presented in Figure 17.1; the samples consist of 116 male schizophrenics, 230 male alcoholics, and 78 child abusers (from Krug, 1980, Ch. 6). It is immediately apparent that the groups diverge in characteristic directions on the normal source traits, as well as on the pathology scales of the CAQ. Specifically, all three groups exhibit diminished ego strength (C), desurgency (F), shyness (H), shrewdness (N), and guilt proneness (O). However, the schizophrenics differ from the other two groups in that they are within the normal range on suspiciousness (L) and ergic tension (Q_4), while the alcoholics and child abusers score considerably higher. It can be seen that several other normal personality traits discriminate among the three psychiatric groups.

On the 12 abnormal scales of the CAQ the three groups score in the direction of greater pathology (higher) on all scales except Agitation (D_3) and Psychopathic Deviation (Pp), where they are centered

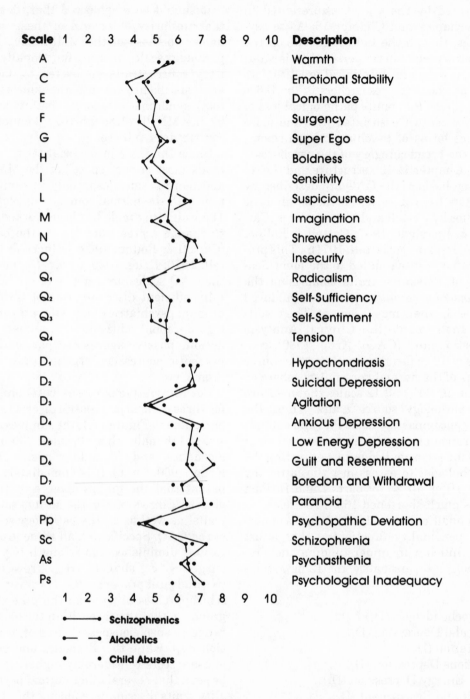

Figure 17.1. CAQ profiles for three groups*

in the normal range. So the first conclusion that can be drawn is that the *individual* CAQ pathology scales discriminate psychiatric groups from normals. It can be logically inferred, then, that the two well-established second-order abnormal factors, General Depression and General Psychosis, because they are additive combinations of the primary scales, produce a highly effective separation of psychiatrically impaired individuals from the normal population. Hence, the broad second-order factors are useful for the preliminary diagnostic identification of all forms of severe pathology.

The second major clinical application of the CAQ pathology scales is in the differential diagnosis of the various types of psychiatric impairment. Careful examination of the three profiles in Figure 17.1 suggests that the abnormal source traits will prove useful in this task. The schizophrenics are uniquely identified by their higher scores on Boredom and Withdrawal (D_7) and Schizophrenia (Sc), scales that deal principally with withdrawal from people, or interpersonal isolation and extreme withdrawal from reality, respectively. These particular source traits correspond closely with the predominant symptomatology associated with the schizophrenic process. The schizophrenics also score higher on Paranoia (Pa), as do the child abusers, and on Psychological Inadequacy (Ps); the alcoholics also score higher on the latter scale, which indicates feelings of self-devaluation.

In contrast to the alcoholics, who score higher on most of the seven depression scales, especially Hypochondriasis (D_1), Anxious Depression (D_4), and Guilt and Resentment (D_6), the child abusers are generally not elevated on the depression source traits, their highest score being just half a standard deviation above the mean on Guilt and Resentment (D_6). The schizophrenics are similar to the alcoholics on the depression scales, in that most scores are well above normal, with Bore-

dom and Withdrawal (D_7) being an especially important characteristic, as was noted previously.

At the intuitive level the reader can sense that these patterns of profile differences on the CAQ scales, both abnormal and normal, establish the psychometric basis for the differential diagnosis of the major psychiatric syndromes via the behavioral specification equation. A good example of such an equation is that for estimating proneness to alcohol addiction (Krug, 1980, p. 39). In simplified form the specification equation is:

$$A = 10 + 0.5 \, (D_6) + 0.3 \, (D_1) - 0.3 \, (Sc) \\ - 0.3 \, (C) - 0.2 \, (D_7) - 0.2 \, (F) \qquad (17\text{-}2)$$

The equation had a validity of 0.63 in the derivation sample consisting of 718 alcoholic and normal cases.

Very briefly, the specification equation for proneness to alcohol addiction indicates that the major psychological determinants of alcoholism include: feelings of guilt, a sense of worthlessness, and an inclination to blame oneself for difficulties (D_6); depression associated with preoccupation with bodily dysfunctions (D_1); extreme sensitivity to reality issues and a hypercritical appraisal of oneself ($-Sc$); emotional instability, easily upset, and subject to fluctuation in mood ($-C$); low tolerance for being alone and strong need to be with other people ($-D_7$); and a serious, introspective attitude toward life ($-F$). This characterization of the alcohol abuser generally confirms clinically based descriptions of this group. However, there are several distinct alcoholic types and although the CAQ specification equation places the analysis within the framework of scientifically developed temperamental source traits, it needs further refinement for special types.

This section concludes with a case vignette that illustrates the interpretation of the CAQ with the individual client. The case of Mr. C demonstrates the value of psychological assessment with a person exhibiting somatic symptoms and illustrates the use of the CAQ in planning a psychotherapeutic program.*

Mr. C is a 30-year-old male who was referred for psychological evaluation by a physician whom the subject had consulted. The presenting symptoms were sleep disturbances, tension, and general feeling of being unwell. The physician requested psychological testing as part of a total health evaluation.

Mr. C's profile (see Figure 17.2) is that of a pathologically withdrawn, threatened, and depressed individual. Two of the most important extraversion primaries, F and H, are at the very bottom of the scale, and Q_2, whose contribution to extraversion is negative, is very nearly at the top of the scale. D_7 (Boredom and Withdrawal) also falls in the high range. Social situations undoubtedly present a real challenge to Mr. C, and he is certainly quite cautious when meeting new people.

Certain elements of his profile, the extreme toughness (factor I), for example, coupled with the elevated anxiety and depression he reports at the present time, suggest that he is an excellent candidate for developing psychosomatic symptoms. D_1 shows there is a very marked focus on and overconcern with health and bodily functions. The particular pattern of sleep disturbances he reported—waking in the middle of the night or early morning, but little difficulty in falling asleep at night—suggests that depression symptoms are of somewhat greater importance than his anxiety. As a consequence, the recommendation was made to the attending physician to consider tricyclic antidepressant therapy.

The clinical scales are revealing. Despite evidence of above-average anxiety

and depression and extreme withdrawal, the possibility of suicide seems relatively remote, since D_3 is at the bottom end of the scale and D_2 (Suicidal Depression) is only minimally elevated. There are many elements of the profile here that underscore the need for counseling and supportive therapy. Although anxiety and depression are prominent features, they have not yet reached extreme levels, and the overall prognosis is fair.

There are several directions therapy might take. First, Mr. C needs to be encouraged to direct his attention out into the world around him and focus less on himself. Next, he needs to define his goals more precisely and more objectively. He does not have huge emotional reserves nor great stress tolerance, so he needs to learn to conserve what he has and channel it more effectively toward attainable goals. Finally, therapy might effectively be directed toward helping him develop avenues for emotional expression.

CLINICAL PERSONALITY ASSESSMENT BY OBJECTIVE TESTS: THE O-A BATTERY

Without doubt the most far-reaching and revolutionary developments in structured testing have occurred in the realm of objective tests. After nearly 30 years of research and refinement, the O-A Battery Test Kit (Cattell & Schuerger, 1978) is available for routine use by clinicians in all human service settings. It can be reasonably predicted that objective personality tests will slowly replace the self-report inventories and professional rating scales that have long been the standard procedures in the measurement of personality and psychopathology for many clinical purposes. The basis for this prediction is the exceptional psychometric characteristics of objective-analytic (O-A) tests: They parallel ability tests in their standardization, their invulnerability to faking, their reliability and validity, and

---

*The vignette is abbreviated from a longer version published in the *Clinical Analysis Questionnaire Manual* (Krug, 1980, pp. 54-55) with the kind permission of Samuel Krug and the Institute for Personality and Ability Testing, Inc., Champaign, IL.

probably in the extent of personality covered.

An *objective* test is one in which the subject performs without knowing which aspect of his or her behavior is being evaluated, while *analytic* refers to the factor analytic derivation of the temperamental source traits, hence the name O-A (objective-analytic) test. The O-A Test Kit consists of 76 objective tests that measure the 10 best-confirmed (by factorial definition) and validated (by criterion relationships) of the 20 or more known temperamental source traits, the basic

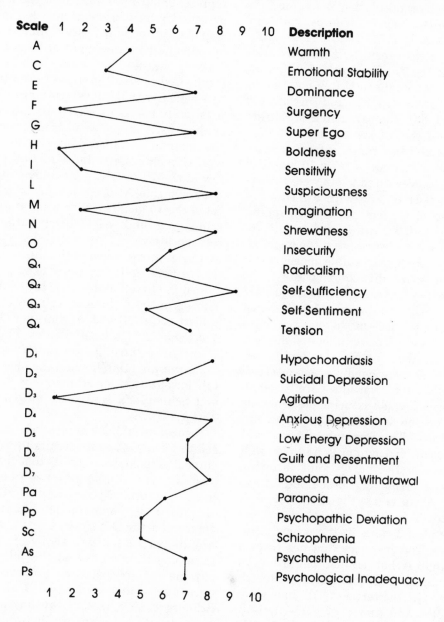

Figure 17.2. Profile for Mr. C*

*From Krug, S.E., *Clinical Analysis Questionnaire Manual.* Copyright 1980 by the Institute for Personality and Ability Testing, Inc. Reproduced by permission of the copyright owners and the author.

and stable dimensions of human nature which have been found across ages and cultures in the T-data (behavioral medium) domain.

A thorough description of the O-A Battery as such and of its research origins has been given by Schuerger in Chapter 13, but a brief recapitulation is appropriate here. The 10 major O-A source traits are Ego Standards (U.I. 16), Independence (U.I. 19), Evasiveness (U.I. 20), Exuberance (U.I. 21), Mobilization (U.I. 23), Anxiety (U.I. 24), Realism (U.I. 25), Asthenia (U.I. 28), Exvia (U.I. 32), and Discouragement (U.I. 33). The psychometric characteristics of the 10 source traits are: a) retest reliabilities ranging from 0.62 to 0.93 with a median of 0.75; b) stability coefficients over three to six weeks ranging from 0.61 to 0.85 with a median of 0.71; and c) concept validities ranging from 0.64 to 0.92 with a median of 0.76. These data demonstrate that the major O-A factors are highly stable measures of replicable personality source traits.

A question that naturally is frequently asked is, "What relation do the O-A source traits bear to those in the questionnaire medium?" Cattell has enunciated the general axiom that the three different media—ratings, questionnaires, and objective tests—when their variables are based on the *personality sphere* principle, must be hitting on the same dimensions "in different dress." This principle of *transcendence of medium* (Chapter 2) has been well borne out in L- and Q- joint factoring (Cattell, Pierson, & Finkbeiner, 1976), but (see Chapter 13) the illumination of the connections of L- and Q- on the one hand, and of T-data on the other, is incomplete. The discovery that has thrown initial light is that second-order factors in L-Q domains are in some cases—exvia, QI; anxiety, QII; cortertia, QIII; independence, QIV; and control, QVIII—first-order—U.I. 32, 24, 22, 19 and 17—in T-data. Research is urgently needed to confirm the U.I. 22 connection and to explore what is happening in the remaining U.I. patterns in the O-A. Meanwhile, however, it is at least clear that the O-A can predict clinical and everyday life criteria that have been tried, just as well as the questionnaires.

Several aspects of the O-A Test Kit merit the attention of clinicians. First, it represents a truly innovative approach to personality measurement and is a major step in the direction of a scientific strategy for personality assessment and research. Second, because the battery can be administered to small groups of examinees by a person with BA-level training or less, it is really not as expensive or time-consuming as it might seem. Furthermore, the instructions for administration are available on cassette tapes and all but a few of the 76 tests use machine-scorable answer sheets. Also, any one factor or subset of the 10 factors can be separately administered since each factor battery is self-contained.

A brief introduction to the theory of objective personality measurement is contained in Cattell and Kline (1977, Ch. 8). The definitive reference volume on the subject is Cattell and Warburton's *Objective Personality and Motivation Tests: A Theoretical Introduction and Practical Compendium* (1967), while the most useful presentation for clinicians is Cattell and Schuerger's *Handbook for the O-A Test Kit* (1978).

A substantial body of research findings relating the O-A source traits to various clinical pathologies suggests that the O-A Test Kit will ultimately prove to be the most diagnostically accurate of all psychometric instruments. The diagnostic potential of the O-A source traits has been quantified in statistical discriminant functions that identified the following psychiatric groups, with proportion of agreements in parentheses (Cattell & Schuerger, 1978, p. 262); involutional depressives (67%), other psychotic depressives (64%), neurotic depressives (45%), schizophrenics (67%), manics (64%), anxiety neurotics (67%), and normal controls

(94%). Thus, in the short time that objective tests have been available, for universal index (U.I.) source traits 16 through 33, an extraordinarily high percentage of significant relations to clinical diagnoses has been found.

Several comments about these data are in order. First, the diagnostic agreement between the O-A Test Kit and psychiatric judgment probably approaches the theoretical limit, given the modest reliability of psychiatric diagnosis. Second, the behavioral and symptomatic distinctions among psychiatric categories are generally small relative to their common symptomatology, making psychometric differentiation all the more difficult. Third, the almost perfect identification of the normal controls (94%) suggests strongly that the O-A Test Kit detects pathological functioning only when it truly exists, producing few false positive diagnoses, as instruments such as the MMPI and Rorschach are prone to do.

While the discriminant functions demonstrate the powerful diagnostic accuracy inherent in the O-A Test Kit, they do not give the practitioner psychological insight unless he or she also has a grasp of the meaning of the particular factors. Although these are given in Schuerger's Chapter 13 on objective tests, and above in diagnostic listings, it is desirable to repeat a brief description here in the context of clinical illustration, as follows:

U.I. 16 Ego Standards. Both paranoid and simple schizophrenics are lower than normals, as are general psychotic and neurotic groups; involutional depressives and neurotic depressives are also lower, but less so than other pathologies.

U.I. 19 Independence. Psychotics and neurotics generally, paranoid and non-paranoid schizophrenics, and hospitalized depressives are all lower than normals, supporting a general psychotic association with schizophrenia and depression, though not necessarily mania.

U.I. 20 Evasiveness. Schizophrenics and neurotics do not differ from normals, but hospitalized depressives are higher; involutional and neurotic depressives are higher than normals while situational and cyclic depressives are lower, establishing a useful diagnostic distinction.

U.I. 21 Exuberance. Neurotics and psychotics generally, paranoid and simple schizophrenics, and all depressives are lower than normals.

U.I. 23 Mobilization. Neurotics are lower than normals and all types of psychotics ranging from schizophrenics to manics are as low as or lower than neurotics; manics are lower than depressives, and paranoid schizophrenics are lower than nonparanoid schizophrenics.

U.I. 24 Anxiety. Depressives, schizophrenics, and most other psychotics do not differ from normals; neurotics are higher than normals while manics are lower than normals.

U.I. 25 Realism. Schizophrenics and psychotics generally, depressives, character disorders, and general neurotics are all lower than normal, supporting the interpretation of this source trait as capacity for self-control and reality contact.

U.I. 28 Asthenia. Depressives, neurotics, and some psychotics are only slightly higher than normals.

U.I. 32 Exvia. Neurotics, schizophrenics, involutional depressives, and manics are lower (more inviant) than normals; nonparanoid schizophrenics are lower than paranoid schizophrenics.

U.I. 33 Discouragement. Neurotics are not different from normals, while schizophrenics and depressives are higher than normals; the pattern of differences is consistent with the interpretation of this source trait as reflecting inhibition and

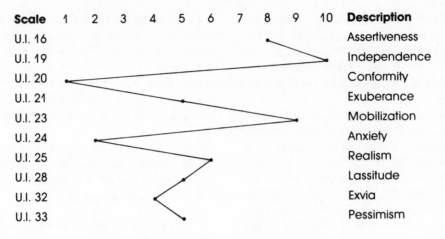

Scale	1	2	3	4	5	6	7	8	9	10	Description
U.I. 16											Assertiveness
U.I. 19											Independence
U.I. 20											Conformity
U.I. 21											Exuberance
U.I. 23											Mobilization
U.I. 24											Anxiety
U.I. 25											Realism
U.I. 28											Lassitude
U.I. 32											Exvia
U.I. 33											Pessimism

Figure 17.3. O-A profile for Mickey*

depression resulting from frustration and deprivation.

Four O-A source traits are common to most of the psychiatric diagnostic syndromes, thus comprising a "pathological core" with the following characteristics: more subdued (U.I. 19 −), greater inhibition (U.I. 21 −), more regressed (U.I. 23 −), and poorer reality contact (U.I. 25 −). In addition to lower scores on U.I. 19, U.I. 21, and U.I. 23, neurotics possess less ego strength (U.I. 16 −) and much higher anxiety (U.I. 24 +). Neurotics also deviate somewhat from normals on evasiveness (U.I. 20 +), realism (U.I. 25 +), and exvia (U.I. 32 −).

The primary diagnostic O-A source traits in differentiating schizophrenics from normals are U.I. 16 −, U.I. 19 −, U.I. 21 −, U.I. 23 −, U.I. 25 −, U.I. 32 −, and U.I. 33 +. While most of these traits are shared with neurotics, there are several critical differences: the U.I. 21 − difference for schizophrenics is less than neurotics, the U.I. 25 − difference is greater for schizophrenics (more disturbed reality contact), U.I. 33 + (discouragement) characterizes schizophrenia but not neurosis, and U.I. 24 + (anxiety) is not a factor in the diagnosis of schizophrenia.

For details regarding the differential diagnosis of the major psychiatric syndromes the reader is referred to the research summary in Cattell and Schuerger (1978, pp. 252-256).

Because the O-A source traits encompass the normal as well as the abnormal personality sphere, the O-A Test Kit can be a useful assessment tool for psychologists working in nonclinical settings with general nonpathological populations. The case vignette which concludes this section illustrates the use of the O-A Test Kit in such a situation.* (See Figure 17.3 for Mickey's O-A profile.)

The second of seven children, Mickey was raised in a secure and loving home where discipline and independent thinking were high priorities. Quiet, slight of build, and congenial, Mickey had the normal childhood diseases, and with the exception of hay fever allergy, has remained throughout his life very healthy; he is capable on occasion, of exhibiting an unusual amount of physical energy. Although his family life was permeated with the spirit and practice of the Roman Catholic tradition, he was not sent to the nearby parochial school, but attended a public elementary school for grades one through

---

*The case was prepared for this chapter by Fr. John Valley of Borromeo College of Wickliffe, Ohio.

six, the local public junior high from grades seven to nine, and he completed a college preparatory course at a very large suburban senior high.

Following high school graduation, Mickey's educational objectives were still uncertain so he decided to test a call he felt to the priesthood. Enrolling in a small liberal arts college designed to aid young men in their choice and preparation for a life of service, he soon realized that the realities of community living were not meeting his more idealistic expectations. But Mickey gave the program a chance and even publicly defended the community style though privately confessing cynical feelings towards it. He finally decided to make God the center of his life. Academically he achieved a steady 2.8 average. No particular course of study was capable of capturing his interest, however, and he once observed that the atmosphere had ". . . the power to allow a person to become lazy and negligent."

By the sophomore year, the inner tension created by his intense vocational reflective process drove Mickey to "playing the stereo and cleaning the room for escape." He was particularly bothered when people were hurt by others and found the actions of some members of the college difficult to reconcile with his concept of fraternal charity. In addition, friends at home were questioning him as to the wisdom of his choice. During the time that Mickey was puzzling over what direction to take, he was loyal to friends and his counselor and extremely capable and conscientious regarding his duties in the college bookstore.

The summer before his junior year Mickey found new life—in working at a camp for the handicapped and retarded, and in working with a special girl who was in charge of the camp. When he returned to school he was looking for new horizons—and he found a way of exploring them in Gestalt psychology. In his evaluation, Mickey showed a new depth which

was characterized by deeper compassion for people's struggles, strong friendships rather than mere alliances, and an integration of the multiple sides of his personality. Mickey was enjoying the new perception and interpretation of the scheme of things of which he was trying to become a part, but at the same time he was still trying to understand "something that just does not fit."

At the end of the first semester of his junior year, he was granted a leave of absence and rated "good" in scholarship ability, "satisfactory" in obedience, "average" in leadership ability, and worthy of recommendation to another school or employment, but only "with caution" to a seminary. His sophomore year had been his best academically, but his energies were subsequently concentrated on a discernment process that eventually resulted in a decision to specialize in psychology at a state university. Mickey worked hard in his senior year there and felt at home in the statistics and science of psychology, bringing better than a 3.0 GPA to graduation. There was no problem finding work at a custodial care mental health hospital and he married the girl who had taught him to care for the handicapped.

Presently, Mickey is awaiting the arrival of his first child, and in order to work more closely with patients, he is pursuing a career as an R.N., with a specialty in psychiatric nursing. He remains a philosopher at heart, but providing for his family and achieving his career have become the most powerful motivating factors in his life. Highly regarded for his work at night in the hospital, and second in a class of 80 at the school of nursing during the day, he still finds time, however, to wonder about the meaning of life and the role he has to play in it.

The O-A Battery was administered during his freshman year and provides a personality profile that in many ways is predictive of Mickey's decisions about the course of his life. His high assertiveness, for example, coupled with an even higher score on independence, and his position in the lowest possible sten on the conformity index are in complete harmony with Mickey's apparent paradoxical posture at the college. He was in academics to be one of the better students, and the best in challenging courses, but his ego standards exhibited themselves as resistance to cliquishness and backbiting, and caused him to question the authenticity of the "more acceptable" lifestyle reinforced by authority figures. Preferring to be more accurate in his judgment than most of his peers, Mickey was primarily an observer. He seldom appeared to be very disturbed, and was generally in the background, easy to live with—perhaps somewhat mysterious and aloof, but always friendly when approached. Although he identified privately with those students who were fighting the system, he devoted more and more time to finding his own way, and to the surprise of many he mobilized very rapidly, chose to leave rather than linger, and made an extraordinarily successful adjustment in a period of a year to a new school, work position, and the responsibility of marriage and a family. He continues to pursue a "better fit" in his career and would like to be a psychologist if he had the necessary time and finances. Until the right opportunity arises, he is realistic enough to know that an R.N. has a better chance in the job market, no matter if he is only one of three males in a nursing program of 80! If pressed, Mickey will characterize himself as cautiously optimistic and still displays the shy, sanguine mannerisms that make most miss the highly achievement-oriented, fiercely independent, and consistently self-sufficient individual dimensions of Mickey. In his case, the O-A profile rivals life experiences as a means of reaching his true personality and, in retrospect, provided a far more valuable aid in understanding him and supporting him in the decisions he has made.

INDIVIDUAL DYNAMICS, CONFLICT, AND INTEGRATION ASSESSED BY THE MAT AND SMAT

Of the three trait modalities—abilities, general personality traits, and dynamic motivational traits—clinicians have always felt that the last are most important to them. Indeed, systems like those of Freud, Jung, Adler, Sullivan, etc., had practically nothing to say on any other. To assess the nature and strength of these dynamic needs and attitudes, conscious and unconscious, clinicians have depended on free association, dream analysis, hypnotism, so-called projection tests like the TAT, Rorschach, etc., and sometimes on questionnaires. These may always have a role, but nowadays, within the framework of objective tests that are conspectively scorable, the TAT and Rorschach suffer from poor interrater reliability and the questionnaire has the inherent weakness that people do not know their unconscious motives and are commonly loath to admit certain motives.

Because the Motivation Analysis Test (MAT) and the School Motivation Analysis Test (SMAT) assess the dynamic trait structures using a series of objective tests of motivational strength which also, unlike the TAT, are conspectively scorable, they constitute an entirely new advance in motivation testing. As in all objective tests, the respondent is not aware of the nature of the trait being measured and thus cannot systematically distort the responses in such a way as to present a desired outcome. Like the 16 P.F., the MAT measures the factorially derived naturally existing structures that account for variation in human behavior. These—the ergs and the sentiments (or "sems")—are described in Chapter 14.

The MAT is the product of a program of scientific research that revealed the principal ergic (drive) structures in humans and led to a model of human motivation known as the dynamic calculus.

The dynamic calculus is an *interaction* model in which behavior is postulated to be the result of 1) stimuli that characterize a particular situation, and 2) unique trait characteristics of the individual. It is further recognized that the individual's existing drive levels (ergic tensions) are the product of situational stimulus levels (acquired from previous learning and physiological predispositions and appetitive levels at the time). It is the entire drive complex of ergs and sentiments that influences and determines what we refer to as motivated behavior.

In brief recapitulation of Chapter 14, we would remind the reader that two kinds of component factors are involved in any specific motivated behavior: 1) motivational components—seven at a primary level and two at a secondary; and 2) ten dynamic structure factors. The two second-order motivational components are the avenues or modes of expression through which any motive may be expressed. The Unintegrated dimension of expression is the unrestrained, spontaneous component that is bound neither by reality considerations nor by the learning implicit in the superego and is evidenced, for example, by appearing in GSR and projection, to be in part unconscious or preconscious. In contrast, the Integrated dimension of expression is the cognitively controlled component that represents the integration achieved through ego function and the impulse control established through cultural values internalized in the superego. In brief, the U component represents the impulsive, undifferentiated aspect of human motivation, while the I component is the reality-oriented, culturally channeled component of goal-directed activity, in which the erg or sentiment has long experienced expression.

The ten dynamic structure factors divide into two main classes of influence that determine the development and course of action of human motives, ergs (basic primate drives), and sentiments (often written "sems" for short). The ergs (or primary drives) represent the basic physiological dispositions, and the sentiments (in reflexology, "secondary drives") are patterns that reflect learned combinations of ergic expressions associated with particular objects and institutions. The MAT measures five ergs (fear, narcissism, mating, pugnacity, assertiveness) and five sentiments (career, home-parental, superego, self-sentiment, and sweetheart-spouse), each in both the Unintegrated and Integrated modes of expression.

Effective use of the MAT in clinical practice is premised on an understanding of the dynamic calculus model of motivation and familiarity with the basic interpretative principles that have emerged from 25 years of research and clinical experience. The primary sources of information about the dynamic calculus model are *Motivation and Dynamic Structure* (Cattell & Child, 1975), *The Scientific Analysis of Personality and Motivation* (Cattell & Kline, 1977), and *Personality and Learning Theory* (Cattell, 1979c). Briefer presentations are available in the chapters by Horn and Sweney (1970) and Dielman and Krug (1977). A very useful source for clinical interpretations of the MAT is the manual by Sweney (1969b).

Through Henry Murray's use of the notion of the *subsidiation chain*, clinicians are always aware that course of action A serves to make possible course of action B, which continues in further links until it reaches a natural ergic goal. The crisscrossing chains meet in certain environmental node objects which constitute the developed sentiment structures and goal-interests involved in the pursuit of particular courses of action. The fundamental principle, then, is that all behavior, represented initially as choices of activities, must ultimately satisfy ergic drives which have their origins in the biological nature of the organism. In other words, the ergs (or instincts) are the energy sources that propel behavior.

Because human behavior is complexly determined and influenced by numerous constitutional and cultural factors, the subsidiation chains for several courses of action are usually interconnected. Rarely does anyone follow a certain course of action for one motive only. Behaviors grow up for the simultaneous attainment of multiple subgoals and the satisfaction of several ergic drives. The *dynamic lattice* is the network that traces the connections among the courses of action and their ergic determinants, thereby outlining the individual's dynamic life patterns. The structures that integrate the subsidiation chains so as to reduce ergic conflict are the sems (sentiments), which are culturally shaped and learned, but derive from the ergs. The function of the sems, then, is to channel ergic energy into socially acceptable behavior while minimizing intrapsychic conflict.

It follows from the intermediate role of sems in the subsidiation process that motivation resulting from the sentiments is typically more stable and dependable than that produced by the ergs. This is so because ergic strength fluctuates from day to day depending on the degree of primitive stimulation and satisfaction occurring, whereas sentiment strength is relatively more constant, reflecting the moderating influence of learning and past experience.

Now it has been factor analytically demonstrated that the ergs and sems constitute factors in "new space" relative to the space of abilities and temperamental personality traits. That is to say, they are independent and add new information not contained in the ability and temperamental traits measured by the 16 P.F., the CAB, the culture-fair tests, etc. At least this is true with the exception of the two largest sentiment structures, the self-sentiment and the superego sentiment, which are alternative objective MAT measures for the same traits measured by questionnaire in the 16 P.F., HSPQ, etc. Inciden-

tally, the main definition of dynamic traits, separating them from general temperament traits is that they are goal-directed, while the temperamental traits are more general orienting or predisposing structures.

Of special relevance to clinicians is the self-sentiment, because of the central organizing role it plays in human personality functioning. The self-sentiment is concerned with the maintenance of self-respect, of social reputation, of self-control, and of personal health and well-being. The self-sentiment not only exercises primary control over the expression of the ergs, but also organizes the less dominant (or subsidiary) sentiments into an integrated personality system, which is the hallmark of the well-adjusted person whose goals and courses of action are consistent and unified.

Assisting the self-sentiment structure in maintaining the regulatory process are the superego sentiment and the ego (factor C of the 16 P.F.). The superego sentiment reflects the ethical values and moral standards that the individual holds and which provide guidelines for the individual's behavior. Ego strength includes the capacity to defer immediate gratification of impulses and to compromise among competing ergic drives, thus reducing psychological conflict and enhancing ultimate drive satisfaction.

The full behavioral equation for any course of action or symptom or performance contains a sum of ability, temperament, and dynamic traits, as shown in Chapter 2. However, many decisions, conflicts, and symptom expressions in clinical psychology hinge largely on dynamic traits—ergs and sems—alone and we can at any rate express the main dynamic calculus calculations without distraction from the other terms. If there are two courses of action open to a client in a given situation, his or her decision will normally be determined by whether his or her motive strength is greater for course of action A or for course of action B. Motive strength for any course of action is the algebraic sum of the relevant ergs and sems.

Common experience suggests that conflict between two courses of action will be more intense the greater the motive strength of the courses of action and the smaller the difference between them. When a person has settled down to a compromise course of action which does not entirely satisfy him but is the best he can do, the result is *indurated* conflict, as opposed to active conflict as defined above, with some ergs positively satisfied and others negatively satisfied. Indurated conflict is a function of the degree of satisfaction of the ergs and sems in the compromise course of action.

These formulations, as well as other developments in the dynamic calculus that may be read in the references above, will not be pursued further here. Unfortunately, it is true that professional psychologists have not yet taken any systematic steps to supply themselves with behavioral index values for the principal predictions with which they have to deal, e.g., the likelihood of schizophrenic breakdown; the chances of recovery, with such and such life situations and therapy, from anxiety neuroses; the likelihood of a depressive suicide, etc. But if psychology is to survive as a profession (vis-à-vis psychiatry), these developments will come.

The first and main purpose of the MAT is to show the strength of ergic and semic investment (Freud's "cathexis") in the cardinal points of the compass of human interests, i.e., the ergic tension levels in sex, assertiveness, pugnacity, security need, etc., and the semic investments in home, mate, church, self, etc. For this purpose the greater reliability of the (U + I) total score indicates its primary use. Many psychiatrists have reported that this has given them the quickest and most objectively reliable insight into the general dynamics of the client; but of course it is necessary after that to fill in the details of the unique life situation attachments of the client. For example, MAT may show that the ergic tension of security need is high, but with this established one has to look at the biographical evidence that it is due, say, to an economic or a health situation. And a high sex erg tension may be explained by any one of several situations that are to be discovered by the usual consulting room procedures starting from the test basis. This aspect of the use of objective motivation measures is best developed in connection with the case that is presented in the next section.

P-TECHNIQUE: INVESTIGATING THE UNIQUE DYNAMICS OF THE INDIVIDUAL

The regard given by functional testing for the *uniqueness* of the individual has already been described as 1) considering the client as a *unique profile*, i.e., a pattern on a sufficiency of measures taken on independent common traits, and 2) approaching uniqueness through P-technique, some rough preliminary notions of which have already been given (Chapters 3 and 14).

In principle, P-technique depends on types of observation which every clinician uses. Ergic tensions rise and fall, and their unitary nature is shown by various investments of a given unitary erg tending to rise and fall *together*. Thus, if we correlate these manifestations over, say, 100 days, on the same person, this unitary influence will be located as a factor. The same establishment of unitary action occurs in the more familiar R-technique, correlating over 100 people instead of 100 occasions, but in P-technique we find what expressions are unique to the given individual. For example, the R-technique loading pattern of the sex erg includes, perhaps surprisingly, love of music, love of travel, and smoking (supporting what Freud had said was an oral erotic substitute for the addiction of masturbation). But in P-technique we might find it loading for a particular person, say, a delight in painting or, as appeared in the mathematician Pascal, a love of geometry. In these specific cases P-technique analysis tells us that for these particular persons, painting and mathematics, respectively, have sexual roots.

No one with scientific perspective can fail to see that P-technique is (at present) the *only* positive, quantitatively reliable method that the psychologist has for exploring unique dynamic connections in the individual. Unfortunately, it is also (at present) a technically difficult and time-consuming form of experiment.

A quite complex development of P-technique has been experimentally pursued by Cattell and his co-workers for the past 30 years and it may be said to constitute a reliable quantitative psychoanalysis (Cattell, 1980b; Cattell & Child, 1975). Only a brief overview of the technique can be given here, and then we shall present a case example. One repeats a strategically chosen (symptom-including) set of dynamic variables daily or half-daily over two to three months. That is to say, the subject is tested on repeatable types of objective motivation instruments that measure relevant dynamic traits, including the known symptom. Factor analysis of the time-correlational data reveals the unique source-trait structure of the client, emphasizing the dynamic causal relationships with the clinical symptom.

Apart from requiring some technical understanding—which any good psychology course can give—the greatest limitation to its use is obviously the time required. However, this is not a problem with clients who are institutionalized or receiving some other form of intensive therapeutic treatment. Readers desiring a thorough review of P-technique research, including a critical analysis of the procedure and a discussion of its possible applications in personality and psycho-

therapy research, are referred to Luborsky and Mintz (1972). Additional useful P-technique experiments are presented by Cattell and Cross (1952), Kline and Grindley (1974), Shotwell, Hurley, and Cattell (1961), and Van Egeren (1977, pp. 663-671).

The case presented here to illustrate the diagnostic potential of P-technique is that of a middle-aged episodic alcoholic. This brief summary focuses on the clinical interpretation of the statistical results; interested readers are referred to the original publication for details (Birkett & Cattell, 1978). The subject of the investigation was a 54-year-old married, professional man. He was on leave of absence from his employment and residing in a residential treatment program for alcoholics. During the five years preceding the study he had been through five different psychotherapeutic treatment programs, all without success. (The diagnoses ranged from mother-fixation to latent homosexuality and lack of father image introjection!)

The investigation was designed to identify the specific dynamic mechanisms that were producing the clinical symptom, i.e., episodic alcoholism. The subject was tested on the same battery of instruments on 100 occasions, typically separated by one-day intervals. The tests included a measure of the strength of the symptom (i.e., the subject's interest in alcohol) and standard objective and self-evaluative measures of the motivational strength of the ten primary ergs and sentiments spanning the domain of dynamic functioning, much as in the MAT. (However, only some of the MAT subtests are repeatable and therefore new devices, including reaction time and GSR, had to be prepared for this use of MAT.) The P-technique analysis statistically examined the simultaneous fluctations over time of the clinical symptom and the strength of the primary motives in order to discover the unique dynamic pattern accounting for the subject's excessive need for alcohol.

The relationships of the dynamic traits to the symptom are summarized as follows: increasing alcohol interest is accompanied by *decreases* in the strength of the narcissistic erg, interest in his wife, and self-sentiment strength, and associated with *increases* in sexual drive, fear, and the demands of the superego. Figure 17.4 contains a graphic portrayal of the empirical relationships comprising the subject's unique dynamic-symptom structure. Considering the pattern of symptom determinants, and the interrelationships among the dynamic traits, as well as biographical, interview, and diary information, the authors were able to specify several clinical hypotheses:

1) As long as the subject's narcissism is satisfied, and his relations with his wife are good, and he receives interpersonal support for his self-sentiment, his need for alcohol remains low.

2) The subject's superego, implanted by a very critical mother, was directed against his narcissism and thus against his self-sentiment and wife sentiment, which later derived sustenance from the primary narcissism.

3) Sex is anarchic in the subject's personality, finding no expression in the main dynamic block in wife, narcissism, and self-sentiment and in fact creating conflict with them, which is the main clue to the alcoholism.

4) The broad causal dynamics in the subject's alcoholism appear to center on a conflict between sex, fear, and superego on the one hand, and narcissism, the domestic sentiment to wife, and the integrity of the self-sentiment on the other.

5) The superego and the self-sentiment are usually positively correlated and the latter subsidiated to the former, but for some reason the subject developed his self-sentiment in a mere social approval context, unrelated to and even opposed by the superego standards which

were implanted early by his extremely critical mother.

These tentative findings considered together with all relevant clinical data led the authors to conclude that in the subject's personality development certain major ergs were not successfully incorporated in sentiments, in particular the sex erg and pugnacity. The anarchic character of the sex erg is seen in its highly negative relationship to the wife sentiment. The key to the subject's episodic crisis seems to the appetitive rise of the sex erg in a sentiment system that cannot accommodate it. The consistent negative relationship with the wife–narcissism–self-sentiment block suggests that when this occurs the stimuli activating the narcissism block are largely shifted from the focus of interest in favor of the sexual cues. From past experience the fear-anxiety and superego forces all contribute to the conflict and the subject resorts to the tension reduction of alcohol.

The therapy in this case was based on the dynamic calculus diagnosis given above and was eventually, with some pharmacological treatment of a concurrent manic-depressive condition, quite successful. It will be realized that with demand for about two hours of testing on each of 100 occasions P-technique must remain, despite its radical advance on most diagnostic methods, an expensive "de luxe" treatment. However, recent work (Cattell & Birkett, 1980a) has shown that the time can be halved, and suggestions have been made for apparatus innovations that would make it far more practical and brief.

MONITORING GAINS AND DIRECTING THERAPEUTIC INTERVENTION

The healing arts, whether they be those of the psychotherapist or the physician, organize their processes into two phases: diagnosis and therapeutic treatment. The

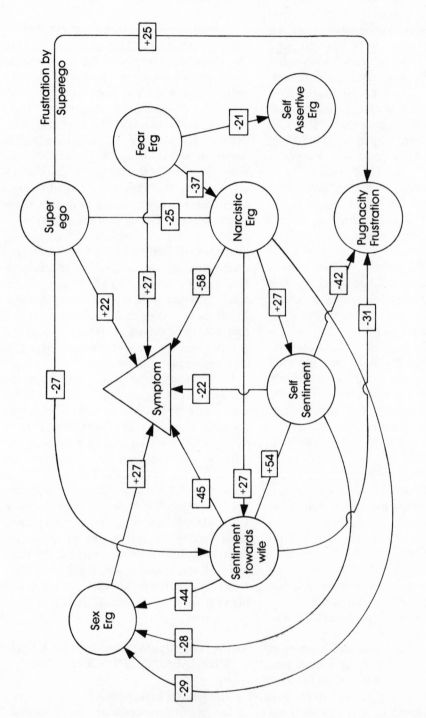

Figure 17.4. Dynamic structure of alcoholism*

*From H. Birkett and R. B. Cattell (1978). Reproduced by permission of the copyright owners.

more their art and understanding improve, however, the more they recognize that the instruments of diagnosis, e.g., a clinical thermometer, need to be continually employed through the treatment period. At the moment this seems better understood by physicians than by many psychologists!

The term "monitoring" is sometimes considered to cover this procedure, but if this is meant to be "seeing if the patient is improving," e.g., by repeated anxiety scale measures, then it recognizes only part of the usefulness of continuing testing. For, as Freud and Jung recognized in the early years of analytical psychology, psychotherapy is a kind of joint voyage by therapist and client, in which tactical changes and new directions must be based on continuously emerging diagnostic insights. If the initial diagnosis is with structurally oriented tests, it follows that the best understanding of change and progress will also be with those tests. Fortunately, most of the tests we have discussed 1) can be given again without any demonstrably significant "practice" effect after about two to four weeks, and 2) if given at shorter intervals have several equivalent forms similarly scorable in stens.

In the first place, the psychotherapist has to convince the public, and some of his own colleagues, that there is any change at all from therapy. During the past 30 years there has been an ongoing debate in the psychological literature concerning the demonstrated value of treatment. Eysenck's (1952) article, which concluded that psychotherapy with neurotics was no more beneficial than no treatment at all, initiated the debate. He claimed that about two-thirds of untreated neurotics showed substantial improvement within two years, which was approximately equal to the success rate for neurotics receiving therapy. While Eysenck's critics have been numerous, attacking almost every aspect of his argument, he has essentially maintained his original line of reasoning and consequently has seen no cause to withdraw his negative conclusion. For the interested reader, the milestone publications in this debate include Bergin (1971), Bergin and Lambert (1978), Eysenck (1966), Meltzoff and Kornreich (1970), Rachman (1971), and Rachman and Wilson (1980).

Only recently has the totality of relevant research on the measured effects of counseling and psychotherapeutic interventions been integrated into a single comprehensive analysis. Glass and his associates (Smith & Glass, 1977; Smith, Glass, & Miller, 1980) examined 830 comparisons between treatment and control groups derived from 375 outcome studies and concluded that the average investigation demonstrated an effect size of two-thirds of a standard deviation on the outcome measure of the treatment over the control group. Stated another way, the typical client receiving therapy was better off than 75% of the untreated control subjects. Unfortunately, the overall conclusion reached by Glass and associates does not specify the psychological or behavioral dimension on which the positive client adjustment occurred. While this meta-analysis was not accepted as valid by everybody (e.g., Eysenck, 1978), it does appear to provide evidence that the various counseling and psychotherapy procedures bring certain kinds of benefit to most clients.

In a subsequent analysis, the investigators grouped outcome measures into ten categories (e.g., anxiety, self-esteem, social behavior, physiological indices, etc.) and calculated average effect sizes for each type of outcome. The largest effects occurred for anxiety reduction and enhanced self-esteem (almost one standard deviation), while considerably less benefit was realized for adjustment indices (about one-half standard deviation) and for educational and vocational improvements (about one-third standard deviation). In an analysis of what is meant by "mental health," Cattell (1973b) suggested that many measures used in this debate on improvement of psychological adjustment do not meet necessary standards.

An important issue that arises in evaluating therapeutic change concerns the relative weight to be given, on the one hand, to test results and, on the other, to changes in everyday life behavior. The latter includes such observations as ability to return to a job, reduction of dissatisfaction reported by a marital partner, cessation of drug or alcohol addiction, improvement of social relations generally, and so on. No psychometrist, as far as one knows, has suggested that this life rating of change is unimportant. A good social worker seeks such evidence and a good psychologist integrates it in an illuminating way with the personality and motivation measures. The view that test monitoring is unimportant has, on the other hand, been crassly expressed by some reflexologists, concentrating on a single, narrow, and admittedly easily observable symptom. The fact is that behaviors of broad importance in life are commonly rated with poor validity and reliability (see Chapter 11). Research under ideal and expensively obtained rating conditions shows that special, highly reliable rating factors *do* correlate as expected with 16 P.F. and other questionnaire factors. Consequently, we can conclude that when good rating is *not* available, the test is actually a better estimate of life behavior than scrappy, biased, and inconsistent reports from one or two raters. If clinics cannot demonstrate high validity and reliability for their outside sources of evidence, they do better to evaluate by source-trait measures.

The above results for different types of outcome measures suggest that psychotherapy has differential effects on various aspects of personality functioning and behavioral criteria, but they do not describe the impact of the treatment on the total personality structure of the individual client, nor do they specify the therapeutic benefits in terms of changes on source-trait dimensions. So, while we may reasonably conclude from the analyses by Glass and his associates that counseling and psychotherapeutic interventions do generally have positive effects on clients, and furthermore that some client characteristics are more amenable than others to therapeutic modification, we cannot identify with scientific precision the nature of the personality changes that occur and, in particular, we don't know how the unitary source traits interact and combine in the individual client to produce therapeutic change.

Raymond Cattell (1966a, 1973b, 1980b) has consistently advocated a comprehensive, psychometrically sound approach to the evaluation of psychotherapeutic treatment. He has suggested that the issue of personality change in psychotherapy be viewed within the broader framework of the measurement of personality change in general. Rather than asking, "Did the client get better?" he has recommended that we ask the more precise question, "On which personality dimensions did the client change?" The latter question requires that we evaluate the benefits of therapeutic treatment in terms of *total personality change*, and not just the alleviation of selected target symptoms. It also recognizes that oftentimes clients change in important personality dimensions not anticipated by the counselor or therapist.

If we accept the argument that client personality change in psychotherapy must be conceived as *multidimensional change* (although it is certainly legitimate to combine particular components into a single index representing "degree of recovery"), then we are faced with the question, "What are the fundamental dimensions on which clients may change and how can such changes be reliably quantified?" The theory of structured personality measurement provides the answer to this question. The major dimensions of client personality change are those functionally unitary source traits that have been precisely identified in 40 years of psychometric research and which are accurately measured by the 16 P.F., MAT, CAQ, O-A Kit, and other structured instruments.

The justification for emphasizing fundamental changes in personality structure in measuring therapeutic benefits is that lasting improvements will occur only when the client's *general adjustive capacity* is enhanced. It simply is not economically feasible for the counselor or therapist to attempt to facilitate the client's adjustment to each and every symptomatic problem that occurs. The nature of the desired changes on the source-trait dimensions can be identified by examining the directions in which pathological groups deviate from the normal population. (The assumption underlying this strategy is that pathological functioning is caused by impaired adjustive capacity.) From the extensive published data on clinical populations we would hypothesize, for example, that greater ego strength (C), enhanced self-sentiment (Q_3), reduced ergic tension (Q_4), higher ego standards (U.I. 16), greater capacity to mobilize resources (U.I. 23), improved reality contact (U.I. 25), and reduced dynamic conflict on the ergs and sentiments will all result in greater general adjustive capacity.

In fact, research suggests that these hypothesized changes in the direction of enhanced adjustive capacity or improved mental health do occur as a result of counseling and psychotherapy. For example, Hunt, Ewing, LaForge, and Gilbert (1959) documented the following changes in neurotic college students after psychotherapy: increased ego strength (C), greater dominance (E), increased surgency (F), less ergic tension (Q_4), decreased anxiety (I), and greater extraversion (II). Cattell, Rickels, Weise, Gray, and Yee (1966) demonstrated that psychoneurotic patients receiving individual psychotherapy from psychiatrists in private practice experience enhanced capacity to mobilize resources (U.I. 23) and reduced anxiety (U.I. 24). Although these and similar investigations are important in specifying the types of source-trait changes that take place as a result of therapeutic treatment, they do not illustrate how the source traits combine and interact in producing psychotherapeutic personality change. For this we must turn to a brief case vignette.

The following case example illustrates how a structured instrument, the Clinical Analysis Questionnaire (CAQ), was able to quantify the source-trait modifications that occurred in one client during psychotherapy.* The reader should note the fairly modest changes in the normal sphere, which is the stable core of human personality, and contrast these to the substantial shifts toward healthy functioning on the pathology source traits. It should be emphasized that this is only one case and illustrates a rather remarkable recovery. Other clients would be expected to exhibit varying patterns of personality change. Clearly there is no substitute for analysis of the individual case to understand the nature of psychotherapeutic personality growth.

Ms. G is a 48-year-old woman who was tested at the beginning of therapy and six months later. (See Figure 17.5 for Ms. G's CAQ profiles.) She was married and had two adult children who were no longer living at home. She had an upper-middle-class background and during the interview reported a very rigid fundamentalist upbringing. There were some suggestions of early childhood sexual abuse by her father. However, this was not confirmed. The primary presenting symptom was depression, which had reached critical levels. At the time she began therapy she was spending all of her time at home, crying most of the day. She had completely withdrawn from all social activity.

---

*The case was prepared by Sherry Skidmore, clinical psychologist in Riverside, California, and is reprinted here with her permission and that of the Institute for Personality and Ability Testing (Krug, 1980, pp. 62-63).

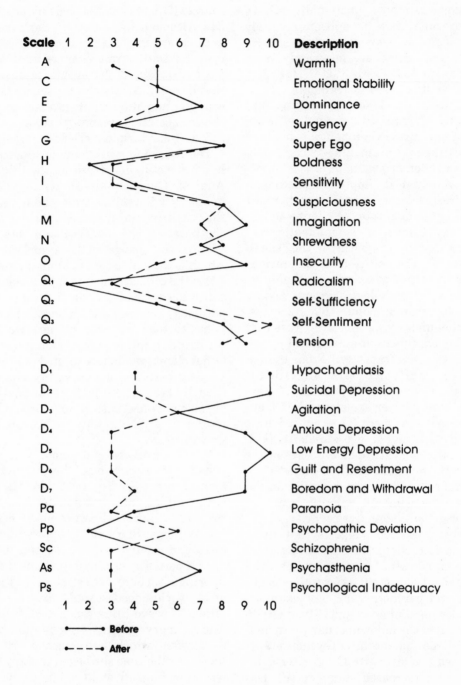

Figure 17.5. CAQ profiles for Ms. G*

With the exception of D_3, all of the depression primaries are in the extreme range. The second-order Depression factor score is 9.4, very near the maximum possible. None of the other clinical primaries is significantly elevated, though there is some hint of rigidity and obsessional forms of behavior in the above-average score on Psychasthenia.

With regard to the normal primaries, more than half fall within the extreme range. She describes herself as extremely conservative and afraid to experiment with new ideas. Most of the important anxiety primaries reach extreme levels. She is quite threat-sensitive (H−), suspicious (L+)—though not to a paranoid extent—guilty and insecure (O+), and tense (Q_4+). Of the remaining anxiety primaries, factor C (emotional stability) falls within the average range, while factor Q_3 (compulsivity) is extreme, but in the nonanxious direction.

Rigidity and obsessiveness are important elements of the profile, with G, Q_3, and L all highly elevated. Despite an immediate impulse to consider this an undesirable feature of the profile, we must entertain the alternate hypothesis that it has some positive value. In the presence of so much pathology it may serve as a useful defense.

This case illustrates the utility of repeated CAQ testing during the course of therapy to monitor the effectiveness of intervention. After six months of psychotherapy, the situation is dramatically and demonstrably different. The most striking changes are evident in the clinical scales: ten have gone down, one (D_5) has stayed the same, and only one (Pp) has gone up. Among the normal primaries there are some shifts but nothing nearly so dramatic as in the clinical scales. Anxiety has dropped slightly, especially the insecurity component represented in the factor O score. Rigidity is, if anything, slightly higher. While G and L have remained at pretherapeutic levels, Q_3 has risen during the six-month period. Despite this increase in obsessional characteristics, the severe depressive and other pathological features of the profile are substantially reduced. From this perspective, the exaggerated compulsivity may not be an immediately undesirable characteristic but a relatively minor problem to be permitted in the presence of so many other more significant problems. The drop on factor M is also a positive indication of better reality contact and less need to dissociate.

As the case of Ms. G dramatically illustrates, a major purpose for monitoring client progress during the course of therapeutic treatment is to provide quantitative estimates of the nature and degree of improvement that is occurring, and thus establish a basis for judgments about the success of the procedure. A second purpose for monitoring client progress is to give the counselor or therapist some indication of difficulties that the client is experiencing, thereby enabling the practitioner to make revisions in the treatment strategy. In addition to the standard source-trait instruments that may be useful for achieving this second goal of therapeutic monitoring, therapists should be familiar with four specialized measures for assessing client personality change. Although space limitations preclude complete descriptions, the four instruments are briefly mentioned here with references cited for further information.

The Anxiety Scale Questionnaire (Krug, Scheier, & Cattell, 1976) is a 40-item measure of the second-order anxiety source trait. The Eight Parallel Form Anxiety Battery (Scheier & Cattell, 1973) consists of eight interchangeable (parallel) measures of anxiety. The battery is especially useful in clinical situations that require repeated testing to monitor client anxiety level. The Depression Scale (Krug & Laughlin, 1976) consists of 40 items that measure the second-order depression factor common to the first seven pathology scales of the CAQ. The Eight State Questionnaire (Curran & Cattell, 1976) measures eight mood states: anxiety, stress, depression, regression, fatigue, guilt, extraversion, and arousal. States refer to the client's emotional condition at the time of testing; states fluctuate considerably over time, in contrast to traits, which are relatively stable characteristics.

SUMMARY

Clinical psychology is moving steadily toward the use of structurally designed source-trait instruments for diagnosis, treatment planning, and monitoring of therapeutic progress. Although current practice with source-trait tests is limited mostly to the use of scales and batteries for common trait dimensions, the emergence of new statistical procedures will bring P-technique strategies for diagnosis of the unique structure of the individual client within reach of the typical practitioner. Structured instruments cover the following domains: primary and general abilities, primary and secondary dimensions of the normal personality sphere, source traits of abnormal behavior, dynamic or motivational traits, i.e., the ergs and sentiments, and the general states, e.g., anxiety, fatigue, arousal, etc. Structured tests are appropriately used with individuals in mental health clinics, hospitals, schools, and industry, i.e., source-trait instruments are general measures of human characteristics independent of the particular setting or application.

The series of structured questionnaires that span the normal personality sphere (16 P.F., HSPQ, CPQ, and ESPQ) provide the foundation of source-trait measurement in psychometric personality theory. These questionnaires, the 16 P.F. in particular, have the most extensive data base of any personality measures, including criterion-relevant profiles and specification equations, thus providing the clinician with a comprehensive view of the client's total personality. Three principles of functional testing via source-trait instruments comprise the basis for clinical practice. The principle of multiple causation of behavior is formalized in the specification equation, which generates behavioral predictions and diagnostic estimates from the relevant source-trait determinants. The principle of pathology as quantitative deviation suggests that most psychiatric disorders can be understood, in part at least, as a unique configuration of normal personality traits, supplemented by appropriate pathology source traits from the CAQ or O-A Battery. The principle of depth psychometry recognizes that a particular diagnostic syndrome may result from various combinations of contributing source traits, thus enabling the clinician to understand the underlying determinants of behavioral dysfunction.

The 16 P.F. and other normal personality questionnaires measure source traits that characterize the psychoneurotic disorders, but do not extend into the realm of pathological loss of reality contact associated with the more severe forms of psychiatric impairment, i.e., the psychoses. Based on a series of factor analytic studies carried out by Cattell and his colleagues in the late 1960s, the pathology source traits comprising the abnormal personality sphere were identified and, scales for their measurement were constructed. The resulting instrument, the Clinical Analysis Questionnaire (CAQ), measures 12 primary pathology source traits (Part II) in addition to the 16 normal primaries (Part I), which were included to assess the "prepsychotic" personality. The value of the CAQ in understanding the nature of psychiatric dysfunction is illustrated with three groups with different etiologies and behavioral manifestations (schizophrenics, alcoholics, and child abusers). A case vignette is presented that demonstrates the role of the CAQ in diagnostic assessment and treatment planning.

Objective tests for clinical diagnosis parallel ability tests in their standardization, reliability, validity, and invulnerability to motivational distortion. Specification equations using the O-A Battery source traits, e.g., Ego Standards, Evasiveness, Mobilization, Anxiety, etc., have been developed for accurate identification of the major psychiatric syndromes, e.g., schizophrenia, anxiety, neurosis, depression, etc. The "pathological core" shared by most forms of psychiatric impairment is: more subdued (U.I. 19 −), greater inhibition (U.I. 21 −), more regressed (U.I. 23 −), and poorer reality contact (U.I. 25 −). Because the O-A Battery seldom diagnoses pathological syndromes falsely, it is equally valuable in personality assessment with relatively normal cases as in clinical situations, as the case vignette presented in the text illustrates.

The assessment of dynamic trait structures using factorial tests of motivational strength is central to the clinician's diagnostic task. The dynamic calculus model of human motivation encompasses situational stimuli and the individual's unique complex of ergs and sentiments, which are expressed through both Unintegrated (unrestrained and spontaneous) and Integrated (impulse control via ego function) modes. The dynamic lattice organizes the interconnections among various courses of action and their ergic determinants. These subsidiation chains are integrated through the sentiments, which function to channel ergic energy into socially acceptable behavior while minimizing intrapsychic conflict. Of special clinical relevance are the self-sentiment, the superego sentiment, and the ego structure, which are central to the achievement of personality integration that characterizes good adjustment. The use of objective motivation tests in the diagnosis of conflict is demonstrated in conjunction with the illustration of P-technique.

The intensive diagnostic procedure known as P-technique enables the clinician to understand the unique dynamic structure of the individual client. P-technique diagnosis requires that the client be assessed daily for two to three months on a battery of carefully selected objective motivation tests that measure the relevant dynamic traits, including the target symptom. The "quantitative psychoanalysis" of the individual client results from factoring the time-correlated data, thus identifying causal connections among the dynamic traits and the clinical symptom. The case of a middle-aged episodic alcoholic illustrates the diagnostic potential of P-technique.

Although it is now known that counseling and psychotherapy do have beneficial effects on most clients, and that treatment may affect different aspects of personality and behavior for different types of clients, the available evidence does not indicate the impact of treatment on the total personality structure of individual clients. Cattell has long advocated that the benefits of psychotherapy and related treatments be evaluated in terms of total (or multidimensional) personality change on replicated source-trait dimensions. The rationale for this strategy is that permanent improvement will occur only when the client's general adjustive capacity is enhanced, in contrast to the narrow symptom-alleviating orientations that characterize some therapeutic strategies. The use of structured instruments in monitoring the progress of a client receiving treatment illustrates how source traits combine and interact in producing positive personality change.

The same instruments and methods are as important for monitoring and tactical direction of treatment as for diagnosis. Most of the tests described have several equivalent forms so that measuring the same traits and states at successive points in treatment is practicable. Considerable theoretical developments for clinical psychology are in progress in the dynamic calculus built on a foundation of measurements by objective tests of motivational strength. They include predictions of decisions on courses of action, evaluating active and indurated conflict levels, estimating an individual's total integration, and tracing the dynamic investments in particular sentiments in the dynamic lattice. An obvious advantage of functional testing based on research-demonstrated structures is that the trained psychologist knows much about those structures—their origins, their normal growth curves, the situations proven to modify them, and their degrees of heritability. It is important for the therapist to be knowledgeable concerning recent evidence on the relative heritability of various source traits, since efforts can be wasted and falsely directed if applied to those of high rather than low heritability.

Because of the developments delineated above, clinical psychologists can anticipate a future of practicing methods radically different from those used in the past. Measurement will become more meaningful, more comprehensive, and more quantitatively precise. If the theoretical developments offered as a foundation, e.g., those of structured learning in personality and the use of systems theory, are carried forward by research, the clinical psychologist will command a specialty beyond present psychiatric and clinical techniques, namely a power in using mathematical models and computer services for thorough diagnosis, evaluation of situation effects, careful monitoring of progress, and direction of therapeutic steps—all on an altogether higher level of insight and reliability than is now customary.

CHAPTER 18

The Art of Clinical Assessment by the 16 P.F., CAQ, and MAT

Heather B. Cattell

INTRODUCTION

Clinical interpretations of the 16 P.F., CAQ, and MAT by Barton, Bolton, Sweney, Cattell, and Anton have been presented in earlier chapters. However, these interpretations served primarily as illustrations, while the present chapter is concerned entirely with interpretation. A secondary purpose of this chapter is to show that, in addition to assigning people to diagnostic categories, the above tests can aid in understanding people as unique human beings. As someone presents himself or herself for psychological services, he or she brings a special history and way of being that requires an integrated understanding on the part of the helping professional, i.e., understanding as a unique constellation of shared human traits. The 16 P.F., CAQ, and MAT can assist the helping professional in obtaining this understanding.

This chapter contains detailed interpretations of the 16 P.F., CAQ, and MAT pro-

files and is divided into three sections accordingly. From among the many ways these tests can be used, only one is discussed in each section. In the first section, the 16 P.F. profiles of a husband and wife are interpreted to reveal the nature of the interaction between the spouses and their different responses to the difficulties facing them. In the second section, the CAQ is interpreted in order to understand the inner experience of a young woman suffering from schizophrenia. Finally, in the third section, two MAT profiles of the same person, a man addicted to alcohol, are interpreted. In this last case the interpreter first identifies problems in order to prescribe an effective treatment plan and, second, assesses the individual's progress in therapy. These accounts are all factual, but changes in the biographical data were made to protect the anonymity of the persons concerned.

Before proceeding we wish to explain our use of certain words. In writing the following text we frequently found ourselves caught between our desire to avoid language which opposes human dignity and our desire to use a clear, succinct literary style. Thus, wherever possible sentences were shaped to eliminate the generic pronoun "he" or "his" when reference was to both sexes. But on those occasions when "he or she" or "his or her" would have been clumsy and monotonous, the male singular pronoun was substituted.

We were also reluctant to classify recipients of clinical services according to the psychological disorders from which they suffer, as this method pigeonholes them according to a "diagnostic" label rather than as whole human beings. Therefore, we have attempted to substitute for terms such as, say, "neurotic" the more encompassing term of "a person suffering from a neurosis." However, in interest of avoiding awkwardness this has not always been possible.

We also chose to refer to the individuals whose test profiles were used in the text as "patients" rather than as "clients," although the latter seems at the moment to be the more popular term among psychologists. Our choice was based on the treatment modality we used, which in these particular cases was along the prescriptive lines of the medical model, i.e., we would make a diagnosis and then a treatment recommendation. Our reasoning was that it is the *role* not *personal characteristics* which are designated. This role is implicit in the type of treatment used and, as Blake and Mouton (1976) have pointed out, there are at least five types. As illustrations: If the treatment had been catalytic—a method of altering perceptions on the basis of acquiring more complete and accurate data—the individuals would have been called clients; if it had been of a didactic theory imparting mode—internalizing more adaptive ways of understanding as a result of new information—then they would have been referred to as students.

INTERPRETATION OF THE 16 P.F. PROFILES OF A MARRIED COUPLE

Interview with Mr. A

Mr. A and his wife are a complex couple, and we selected their profiles for just this reason. Our aim is to show that by uncovering the multiple influences underlying overt behavior the 16 P.F. can go far in explaining why people do as they do.

Mr. A was about to declare bankruptcy and the case promised to create an unusual amount of adverse publicity, as it involved considerable sums of money which Mr. A had borrowed by misrepresenting his financial assets. His lawyer then recommended that he seek psychotherapy because of the resulting situational stresses that he, Mr. A, was experiencing. Mr. A accepted this recommendation but he did so only because he believed that if his creditors understood that he was undergoing psychotherapy they would be inclined to behave more leniently toward him.

After hearing his story, we were surprised that he did not show more distress considering his situation. Mr. A was a 49-year-old retired naval officer with no previous history of litigation. He came from a middle-class family and was presently living with his wife of 25 years; his one child, a daughter, was married and living in another state. The marriage, he claimed, had been a happy one and the only problems between him and his wife arose from their present financial difficulties.

Mr. A gave a childhood history which was uneventful except for an abrasive relationship with his father, whom he described as too strict and against whom he rebelled. He joined the navy after college because of the adventure, security, and active social life. Also attractive to him was the romantic appeal of the military image to women. During his service he had not been disappointed by any of these aspects of naval life but confessed that he nevertheless had seen himself as a "round peg in a square hole." The reason for that was that, contrary to the experience of the majority of his peers, he was frequently bored with the daily routine, disliked following orders, and came into conflict with superior officers whenever taking opportunities to behave autonomously. However, he continued to be promoted on schedule until he reached the age of 45; thereafter, he was passed over several times. After the fifth time, he decided to take an early retirement.

If Mr. A had felt himself to be a round peg in a square hole in the navy, he felt doubly so in civilian life. He had a succession of jobs, usually in sales, where he believed his creative talents were misunderstood and unappreciated by both his employers and co-workers. Meanwhile, he and his wife were spending money far in excess of the income which came from his pension and sporadic earnings as a salesman. The couple made no effort to adjust to their new financial situation, entertaining often and sometimes lavishly, eating out several times a week, spending weekends at neighborhood resorts, and buying expensive clothes. They had borrowed money from various sources to support this lifestyle, and Mr. A, for a time, had kept the creditors at bay by ingeniously circulating a portion of the borrowed money among them. Four months prior to our seeing him, his scheme for keeping the creditors at bay collapsed and he was threatened by foreclosures and lawsuits. He constructed an elaborate but impractical plan to become solvent in six months, which, when showed to his creditors, failed to impress them. We were similarly unimpressed when he later described the plan to us, as it was fraught with blind spots, making it unfeasible.

Although, after carefully listening to him and noting that his reasoning had a certain esoteric quality, we determined that there was no mental disorder. More-

over, he was not overly optimistic about the outcome of his situation, which might have led us to suspect that some manic or hypomanic excesses lay at the root of his financial spending schemes. At the time of our interview and testing, Mr. A was reconciled to the bankruptcy. Also, he realized that the bankruptcy would generate a great deal of adverse publicity. Displaying an almost cavalier attitude toward the entire situation, he at one point mused: "They can't attach my pension so I will have something to live on even if I don't work." Later he commented, "Maybe I will have to find a new lifestyle and a new bunch of friends. That's okay, life is for enjoying yourself and having adventure."

The 16 P.F. was administered three days after the initial interview; the following interpretation is based on the interview and test results. Before continuing the reader may wish to refer back to the description of the 16 P.F. factors in Chapter 12.

Interpretation of Mr. A's 16 P.F. Profile

On the second-order factors, which appear in Table 18.1, Mr. A's scores were high average (6.0) on Extraversion, above average (7.2) on Anxiety, on Tough Poise slightly below average (4.8), and high (8.8) on Independence. Thus, there emerged a portrait of a man whose interests tipped in the direction of the social environment. It also appeared that he was not anxious, acted very independently, and tended to be swayed by feelings rather than rational thought.

TABLE 18.1
Mr. A: Second-Order 16 P.F. Factors

Extraversion	6.0
Anxiety	7.2
Tough Poise	4.8
Independence	8.8

This was the broad picture. Next came the first-order factors, adding depth and subtlety to the portrait. These factors appear in Figure 18.1. What immediately caught our attention was the extreme score of 9 on Ego Strength, C, and Surgency, F. This pair of high scores told us that the examinee was a complex individual who added lively, uninhibited impulsiveness to a basically strong foundation. Ego Strength has recently been demonstrated by Cattell and Cattell (in preparation) to be consistent with the psychoanalytic ego, which controls and directs behavior so that inner needs are gratified or inhibited in accordance with overall long-term satisfactions. Restraint and prudence are the quintessence of Ego Strength. In contrast is Surgency, which resembles the Natural Child in Transactional Analysis (James & Jongeward, 1971).* The Natural Child is the id-gratifying human state that is recognizable in the adult as a carefree, immature, happy-go-lucky, impulsive attitude toward life, which in source traits is low C and high F. Thus, the high Ego Strength† and high Surgency indicated by Mr. A's profile made strange bedfellows.

The high Surgency score was remarkable because the examinee's age was 49 and scores on this factor have been found to steadily decline with age. The examinee's score placed him in the 96th percentile of the general population, but still higher in terms of his age group. We suspected that Mr. A was extremely immature and impulsive. Consequently, his high Ego Strength, which may have been developed to check unruly tendencies, acted as a strong reality orientation.

According to Karson and O'Dell (1976), a high score on Surgency may indicate faulty moral development, as would a low score on Superego, G, and a low or high score on Guilt Proneness, O. Actually, the second-order factor repeatedly (QVIII) has the pattern $F+$, $G-$, and Q_3. This F, G, and O configuration of scores occurred in this profile, with Surgency 9 (high), Superego 4 (below average), and Guilt Proneness 7 (above average). The below-average score on Superego, moreover, showed the examinee was lacking in one of three areas of personal control, namely, concern for maintaining conventional moral values. The other two sources of personal control are Ego Strength and Self-sentiment, Q_3. Self-sentiment is the concern for maintaining self-respect and a good public image. As the Self-sentiment score was only average (5) and the score on Superego below average, it was obvious why Mr. A's decisions would be guided by expediency and pragmatism rather than by moral considerations, self-respect, or the desire to maintain a good public image. This conclusion fits well with Mr. A's rather casual attitude toward the negative personal publicity which lay ahead.

The Guilt Proneness factor is so called because it often measures the intensity of guilt experienced when personal standards are violated. High factor scores indicate insecurity, self-criticism, and a sense of worthlessness, whereas low scores suggest placid self-confidence.* A high

---

*The low end of the Surgency continuum (i.e., with F = 1, 2, 3, & 4) has been recognized by Cattell (1973a) as part of the Good Upbringing factor (Q VIII) and corresponds to a statement of the Adapted Child of Transactional Analysis. In contrast to the Natural Child, the Adapted Child represents the transformation of a child into a socialized being through introjection of society's standards. People who have high scores at this end of the continuum, typically describe their parents as being unusually restrictive and socially conforming. As adults they often are overly conscientious and lack the ability to enjoy life. In the language of psychoanalysis, they experience limited id gratification.

†High C scores have been found in "compensated schizophrenics." Compensated here means that Ego Strength does not issue from an integrated personality but stands apart from the psychopathology.

*Scores at either end of the Guilt Proneness continuum may represent disturbances in superego controls. Above-average scores point to a tendency for excessive self-criticism; below average scores point to a resistance to accepting moral responsibility for wrongdoing. However, deviant scores should be considered in light of their covariance with other factors, especially G, Q_3, and F because they do not always represent superego disturbances.

score on Guilt Proneness may also be interpreted another way. It may arise from the examinee negatively evaluating himself not with a heavy conscience but through self-blame for poor judgment, carelessness, etc., which have landed him into a noxious situation, somewhat like the sinner who is not sorry for his sins but is sorry he is going to hell. Given the examinee's high score on Surgency and low score on Superego, we suspected that this second interpretation of the high Guilt Proneness score was more accurate than the first and that the examinee somewhat regretted the *consequence* of his behavior.

Having examined the most deviant scores on the profile, we next turned to the other scores, which, though less extreme, still fell into the high range, as,

being stens of 8, they placed the examinee into the 89th percentile on the factors involved. These factors were Affectothymia, A, Parmia, H, Premsia, I, Protension, L, and Autia, M. Affectothymia, which is expressed as need for social interaction, and Parmia, as personified by the James Bond, thick-skinned, masculine, swashbuckling image, along with Surgency (discussed above) and Self-sufficiency, Q_2, are regularly the main contributors to the second-order Extraversion Factor pattern. We noted, however, that the level of this Extraversion pattern was within average range. This is primarily because, in contradistinction to the very high scores on other major contributors, Affectothymia, Surgency, and Parmia, the score on Q_2 (Self-sufficiency) fell into the introverted

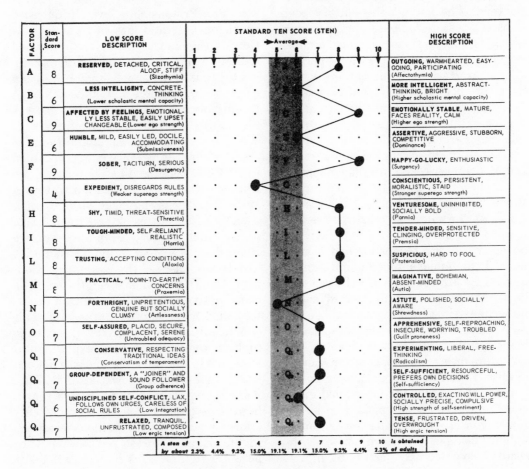

Figure 18.1. Mr. A: 16 P.F. profile of primary factors

direction, giving rise to the mixed social orientation. That is, the examinee was gregarious, exuberant, and socially adventurous, while being something of a "loner" in personal decision-making. Moreover, his score of 8.8 on the second-order Independence factor pattern indicated this tendency would be strongly buttressed by his need to have his own way. These findings went far to aid our understanding of Mr. A's career difficulties, both in the service and civilian life. Mr. A reported that while in the service his dislike of following orders and his disappointment that opportunities for autonomous functioning, though rare, had brought him into conflict with his superior officers. In his civilian life, he felt his creative innovations were misunderstood and unappreciated by his employers and co-workers. If he had sought solitary positions (e.g., as a computer programmer, which is the most satisfactory occupational choice for someone with his personality characteristics), his careers would have run more smoothly. But because of his pull toward social interaction, as indicated by his high scores on Affectothymia and Parmia, he had always sought jobs which involved much personal interaction, teamwork, and interdependence.

On the emotional sensitivity factor, Premsia, I, and on the Imagination factor Autia, M, the scores were both 8. Premsia is what William James had in mind when he described the tender-minded component of the tender-minded/tough-minded dichotomy. Mr. A's score of 8 showed that he had a substantial leaning toward tender-mindedness in that he was soft-hearted and sentimental. This was despite his being intellectually independent and socially brash, as other factors previously discussed indicated. From this we anticipated that he wished to be coddled in his close relationships. Premsia was also a major contributor to the second-order Tough Poise factor pattern, on which he scored below average, portraying him as

an individual with pervasive emotionality.

Autia has been dubbed at the higher pole as the "Absentminded Professor" factor, indicating absorption in one's thoughts rather than alertness to practical needs. While a high score is the strongest indicator of creativity in the 16 P.F., it also often indicates dissociation, a tendency to retreat from and ignore external demands.

This combination of high Autia and Premsia scores is commonly found in artists of all kinds and so we suspected that Mr. A had a very rich inner life. Because of his gregariousness (high Affectothymia), exuberance (high Surgency), and boldness (high Parmia), this inner life was undoubtedly projected out into his environment. We also believed that, given his scores on Protension, L, which indicated suspiciousness and lack of trust, his actions in the environment were performed without prior consultation with others. On this basis, his actions may have been surprising and confusing to others, though intelligible to himself. A case in point was his impractical plan to pay off his bills. While his reasoning was unquestionably creative and imaginative, it contained many flaws because it had not undergone the correction and clarification which results from discussing ideas with others.

Other of his scores outside the average range which have not been discussed are Radicalism, Q_1, and Ergic Tension, Q_4. The first measures the examinee's Conservatism-Radicalism orientation. The conservative pole implies a respect for established ideas and a tolerance of their shortcomings. In comparison, someone high on radicalism has an experimental approach to life and a readiness to discard the old in favor of the new (Cattell, 1973a). Karson and O'Dell (1976) believe that a high score on this scale $(Q_1 +)$ represents a form of sublimated rebelliousness, having its origin in unresolved conflicts with parental figures. This interpretation fits well with Mr. A's childhood history of rebellion toward his father and later conflicts with employers and superior officers. Although Mr. A received only a 7 on this factor, the radicalism reinforced the self-sufficiency and independence that had brought him so much trouble. The score was also important because, when viewed against the low social conformity score (6), it allowed us to predict that following his bankruptcy Mr. A would easily adopt an unconventional lifestyle.

The last factor to be looked at was Ergic Tension, Q_4, which, as a measurement of pent-up feelings and unexpressed needs, is a pattern anticipated in Freud's First Theory of Anxiety. The examinee's score was 7, which was, like the second-order anxiety pattern it entered into, just above average. And, as we have noted earlier, a much higher score would have been expected given the circumstances. That the score was only at the above-average level we attributed to the examinee's high ego strength, which permitted him to remain calm and to avoid the catastrophic thinking that people in his plight often fall into.

Summary

This profile helped us to understand a man who at first puzzled us by defying the usual stereotypes. His career as an officer who functioned in an atmosphere of rigid social conformity did not fit well with his somewhat nonchalant attitude toward his present circumstances. Nor did his difficulty in holding jobs in civilian life fit well with his 23 consecutive years of service. We were also puzzled by his lack of restraint, which had led to his present financial crisis, and by the poor reasoning behind his very elaborate plans for becoming solvent, in light of there being no evidence of thought or mood disorder.

As we interpreted this profile, these issues became clearer and there unfolded a picture of a truly remarkable personality, fraught with many opposing tendencies.

Mr. A appeared gregarious (A, F), yet independent (Q_2), adventurous and bold (H), yet emotionally sensitive and sentimental (I). He was imaginative and probably creative, but reached impracticable ideas because he thought things out in isolation, so that when he implemented his ideas they had not been tempered by the input of other people's opinions. As a result his plans or actions at times contained blind spots or distortions. But above all, he was exuberant, with strong id impulses which could be gratified without concern for midstream moral values and conventionality.

Such a person usually finds himself in trouble, and it was surprising that Mr. A's difficulty had come so late in life. Undoubtedly, the structure of military life contributed to his previous stability, as it placed upon him some of the restraints which are normally superimposed by the internal government of a well-integrated personality. The effect of the military environment could be likened to the external routine and boundaries that set limits for the young child prior to his developing inner controls.

Although his reasons for joining the service revealed a strong Parmic makeup (e.g., "adventure", social life), they also revealed some ego (reality) orientation like the attractiveness of economic security. As we said earlier, in Mr. A's case strange dynamics appear in which a strong ego did not serve its usual role as an integrator of personality. Mr. A's personality was far from being integrated, and so the ego must have presented a strong sense of reality, watching over the warring tendencies and emotions like a faithful guardian but not integrating them. At the time of test administration the strong ego allowed him to face his present crisis without crippling anxiety or depression, as would occur in someone with low or even ego strength. In all, Mr. A came through as a free soul—very independent and motivated by strong id and social needs. He was relatively unfettered by conventional morality and tradition. Therefore, at the very least, we anticipated that given his high ego strength, he would pass through the ordeal ahead relatively unscarred. We wondered what lifestyle Mr. A would eventually adopt, and speculated that it may well be quite unconventional and even artistic.

Mrs. A's 16 P.F. Profile

The following interpretation was made without our having any prior contact with Mrs. A or information other than what was provided about her by her husband. He described her as one who enjoyed good times and liked people, and he claimed that she was "taking everything very well," even better than himself. He said, too, that the only problem between them was her annoyance at not having sufficient money to make her customary purchases. Later, when her annoyance increased and resulted in numerous arguments between the couple, she contacted us with a view towards entering into marriage counseling. After seeing her profile, for reasons which will become clear to the reader, we recommended individual psychotherapy instead of marriage counseling. She did not, however, follow through on this advice.

Mrs. A's profile of second-order factors appears in Table 18.2. What immediately struck us about this profile was the score of 1 on the Anxiety factor. Even for persons in the happiest of circumstances, such low anxiety means that reality contact is amiss, and in view of Mrs. A's situation, the score was so inappropriate that we rechecked our calculations to

TABLE 18.2
Mrs. A: Second-Order 16 P.F. Factors

Extraversion	8.0
Anxiety	1.0
Tough Poise	7.6
Independence	6.6

make sure that we had scored the profile correctly. Having found that our calculations were correct, we turned to an examination of the primaries (see Figure 18.2), which comprised this second-order factor to discern its makeup. The scores indicated that Mrs. A had average ego strength (Ego Strength, $C = 6$), had unruffled self-esteem (Guilt Proneness, $O = 3$), felt relaxed and composed (Ergic Tension, $Q_4 = 3$), was not intimidated by social situations (Parmia, $H = 8$), was not troubled by jealous insecurity (Protensia, $L = 5$), and had a well-developed self-image on which she placed value along with maintaining a good public self (Self-sentiment, $Q_3 = 7$).

The extremities on O, Q_3, and Q_4 pointed to a self-satisfied, confident, self-centered woman who was inordinately tranquil. This meant that she exercised an enormous and effective defense against the anxiety that would have been more appropriate. We wondered which of the various mechanisms she primarily employed. She scored 5 on Ego Strength, so we were reasonably sure that she was adequately processing reality. However, her score on Ergic Tension, Q_4, was only 3, suggesting that she was exercising repression.

According to Anna Freud (1966), there is a correspondence between the magnitude of the defense and the noxiousness of the material against which the defense is employed. The personality characteristics indicated by this profile clearly showed that the trauma of the scandal, which was certain to arise from Mr. A's legal problems, was too much for Mrs. A to bear. She was dependent on others, maybe to the point of being neurotically so (Self-sufficiency, $Q_2 = 1$). Thus, although she was self-satisfied, she was far from being self-sufficient; ostracism from her peers would have been much more painful for her than it would be for the vast majority of people. To complicate matters, we suspected that there was, additionally, a considerable amount of social prestige at stake, as Mrs. A's extremely low score on Self-sufficiency is associated with belonging to organized social groups. And given her high scores of 8 on Dominance, E, and 9 on Shrewdness, N, we guessed that she must have held high positions in these organizations. The Dominance score denoted an enjoyment of authority and command of attention and her score on Shrewdness revealed that she was endowed with enough poise and social astuteness to find her way into positions of leadership.

We also expected that the groups to which Mrs. A. belonged espoused conservative, even reactionary, values and so would be less tolerant of the couple's predicament than would groups with more liberal orientations. This expectation was based on the score of 2 on the Conserva-

tive-Radical Dimension, Q_1, which showed Mrs. A to be extremely traditional and conservative. This bit of insight into Mrs. A's values, moreover, supported the probability of how painful the situation was for her and hence made her need for repression clearer.

The picture thus far showed that Mrs. A faced erosion of values, social disengagement, loss of opportunity to express her power needs, and damage to her concern for preserving her self-image and respectability. Added to these was her great reliance on social channels for personal satisfaction, as denoted by her score of 8 on the second-order Extraversion factor. Unlike her husband, who showed a mixed pattern of both introverted and extraverted qualities, Mrs. A showed an ori-

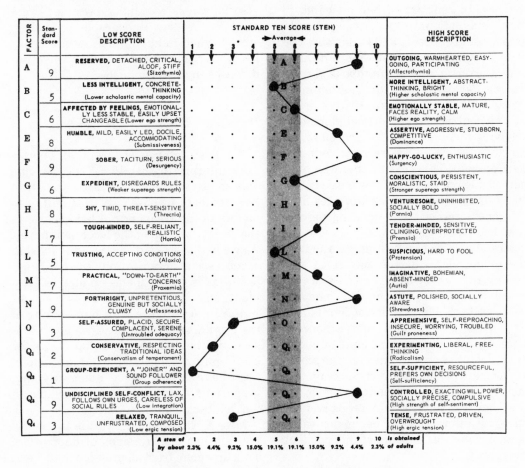

Figure 18.2. Mrs. A: 16 P.F. profile of primary factors

entation wholly in the extraverted direction. The first-order factors which made up this pattern showed her in addition to being a joiner of groups, as already discussed, extremely gregarious (Affectothymia, $A = 9$), exuberant (Surgency, $F = 9$), and socially bold (Parmia, $H = 8$).

It was interesting that Mrs. A shared the same unusually high score of 9 on the Surgency factor as her husband, showing that she too was heavily endowed with the "Natural Child," spontaneous, exuberant, id-gratifying characteristics. We began to see how the couple's financial difficulties must have arisen in a climate of mutual escalation.

The two second-order factors which have not been discussed in this profile are Tough Poise and Independence. Mrs. A scored 7.5 on the Tough Poise factor, showing her, in contrast to her husband, to make unemotional, and possibly harsh, assessments of people and situations. The term Tough Poise is used simultaneously with Cortertia in the *Handbook for the Sixteen Personality Factor Questionnaire* (Cattell, Eber, & Tatsuoka, 1970). Cortertia is a contraction of "cortical alertness" implying mental alertness. Therefore, we concluded that she was responsive to her environment. This gave further weight to our suspicion that her low anxiety resulted from blocking internal forces from awareness rather than in using perceptual defenses.

Mrs. A's score of 6.5 (high average) on the Independence factor may seem surprising in view of her extreme score on group dependence, but the QIV Independence pattern is largely one of dominance, i.e., in the psychological sense, nonreliance on others for emotional support, guidance, or approval. Through the scores on the main primaries which make up this factor, especially Dominance, $E = 8$, we saw that although Mrs. A relies heavily on social interaction for her major satisfactions, she was capable of independent thought.

Most of our conclusions at first centered on the social aspects of Mrs. A's personality. This was because she emerged from the profile as a person for whom the interpersonal field is foremost. However, from her above-average scores on Emotional Sensitivity, $I = 7$, and Imagination, $M = 7$, we realized that she was not lacking in inner emotional life. In particular, her score on Autia suggested that she was not entirely governed by external concerns but that she may have had creative resources. As with her husband, we hoped she would be able to draw on whatever strengths were afforded by these inner qualities.

In concluding the interpretation of this profile, we had none of the optimism that we had for Mr. A, who we believed could weather the coming storm. Almost everything that gave Mrs. A's life meaning —social values, sociability, prestige —were at stake. We saw unbearable anguish in store for her and had the deepest concern for what would happen to her when her defenses finally crumbled.

Interview with Mrs. A

We first interviewed Mrs. A shortly after interpreting her 16 P.F. profile. She was an attractive, well-dressed woman in her late forties whose face was familiar to us due to the frequency of her picture in the society section of the local newspaper. As we had suspected, she was involved in several social organizations and held high positions in two of them—in one, as president, and in the other as vice-president. Again in accordance with our reading of the profile, these organizations had a conservative bent. They were also known for their gala parties and banquets which must have satisfied some of her outgoing, gregarious needs and been enjoyable to her "Natural Child."

Mrs. A was charming in the interview and did not display signs of depression. This freedom from depression had been indicated by her profile. The profile also strongly indicated deep repression, and it became clear in the interview that she denied and rationalized a great deal. Although cognizant of the gravity of her husband's situation, she had little contact with her feelings.·

Her explanation of how their difficulties had arisen was entirely in accord with what we had intuited from the couple's profiles. She said they both "loved people" and "liked to have fun" and had been swept up in a "social whirl." In the navy this lifestyle had been less expensive, because much of it was either provided by the service or was available at a lower cost. Later, in civilian life, when they had become alarmed about their mounting bills, they typically cheered themselves with a night out on the town. She also mentioned that they had often got caught up in each other's enthusiasm.

Also supported by Mrs. A's comments were our suspicions about her husband's thought processes. She saw her husband as a man who did a lot of thinking and rarely consulted others before executing his ideas. She felt that this was one of the main reasons for his continuing problems with co-workers and bosses. She also noted that he behaved similarly in the domestic arena, where he carried out some rather convoluted financial plans without first consulting her. Although she thought some of these plans were "dubious," she did not involve herself in them because she believed her husband's role was to provide for them financially and hers was to care for the home and maintain their active social life.

Unfortunately, Mrs. A did not follow through on our suggestion that she begin psychotherapy. We next heard of her after the bankruptcy proceedings.

Assessment of the Marital Relationship Made From a Comparison of the 16 P.F. Profiles

While the couple's profiles had similarities, especially in the area of extraver-sion, they also had marked differences (see Figure 18.3). These differences were in the areas of values and responsiveness to social opinions, which would be paramount in determining the amount of trauma each was experiencing in the situation at hand.

Mr. A was anticipating the forthcoming bankruptcy and surrounding scandal from a perspective rooted in relative indifference to traditional midstream social values; he also had a low need for group belonging. Conversely, Mrs. A's vantage point was rooted in ultra-conservative values and she had a strong need for belonging and maintaining a respectable public image. Consequently, we believed that their present situation would widen the cleavage between their orientations, making it increasingly difficult for Mr. A to empathize with Mrs. A and understand her distress. This lack of support for her feelings may have been an additional reason for Mrs. A's resorting to such deep repression of her feelings. Concomitantly, because Mrs. A's feelings were repressed and Mr. A's were not intense, it was possible that they did not discuss the situation on an emotional level.

The differences on the Conservative-Radical Dimension made us wonder if the couple moved in separate social circles, as they must have had differing preferences for friends. She must have disliked some of his friends and vice versa. However, Mr. A reported that he found the social life in the navy convivial and so undoubtedly the majority of his peers would have leaned toward conservatism. We concluded, then, that it was also entirely possible that the couple participated in the same social set.

We wondered how this couple's extravagances went unchecked for so long. According to Mr. A, the money had been spent mainly on good times, parties, and dining out, which was compatible with the outgoing, adventurous, and especially the "Natural Child" (Surgent) characteristics appearing in both profiles. It is probable that there was some mutual escalation, with neither party repressing the other's impulsive, id-gratifying styles. We were reminded here of the exploits in the Roaring Twenties of Zelda and Scott Fitzgerald, who undoubtedly must also have had these surgent characteristics. However, Mrs. A, unlike Zelda, did not lack in social poise and concern for respectability. So we were certain that the couple's exuberance was channeled along more dignified lines.

In addition, Mrs. A's traditional orientation suggests that there might be clear role specialization in the marriage along very conventional lines. Moreover, we saw that Mrs. A was dominant yet shrewd and could manipulate, if she desired, expensive purchases.

It was clear that this couple had an ability to enjoy themselves largely because they were not able to exercise mutual restraint. With a free flow of cash their lifestyle before the bankruptcy could have gone on indefinitely; it might have been that the relationship was built around these good times. The question now was what else they had in common. Certainly their values were very different, as indicated by their reactions to their present crisis, and in the long run we could not see enough commonality to keep them bound, as they were now cut off from their shared social life.

Follow-up

Bankruptcy proceedings, the ensuing litigation, and the surrounding publicity occurred as expected, bringing about a

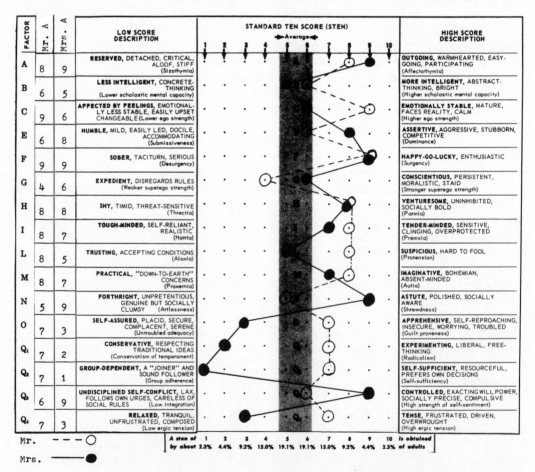

Figure 18.3. Mr. & Mrs. A: 16 P.F. profiles of primary factors

breakdown in Mrs. A's defenses. Subsequently, she went into a deep depression and was hospitalized. Upon recovery she demanded that her husband arrange their move to another state to start their lives anew together. Mr. A refused, and Mrs. A finally left him to live with her married daughter in New England. When we last heard of her she was intensely involved in the rather conservative church in which she had been raised. She held several important positions in it, such as head of the women's auxiliary, and was active in organizing bazaars and church dinners. Her new lifestyle seemed fulfilling and well-suited, as it utilized her extraversion, emotional sensitivity, and imagination (hinted at in her test scores), while offering external structure and control demanded by her high surgency.

Mr. A's lifestyle became more colorful after his wife left. We had noted a proclivity for artistic expression in his 16 P.F. profile. Now his imaginative ideas materialized into art work which brought in a modest income to supplement his pension. It was also favorably noticed by local critics. His interest in art moved him into an unconventional social sphere. Here his surgency no longer brought him trouble as it did in the past, chiefly because he could now enjoy himself without spending great sums of money. However, drug use and alcoholism were prevalent in Mr. A's new social circle, and so we feared that Mr. A's surgency would lead him to substance abuse. He reported to us that, despite experimenting widely, he did not use drugs and alcohol often and then only recreationally. As in the past, we noted the guardianship of his strong ego strength.

INTERPRETATION OF A CAQ PROFILE OF A 32-YEAR-OLD WOMAN WITH A DIAGNOSIS OF SCHIZOPHRENIA

There are several personal accounts of the schizophrenic experience, such as the autobiography of a recovered schizo-phrenic girl by Sechehaye (1951). These accounts are enlightening as they reveal what schizophrenics are unable to reveal about themselves while enmeshed in their symptomatology. Although the CAQ profile discussed here is also essentially a personal account, it differs from these others in that it was obtained under structured conditions; that is, exact measurements were taken on a full sphere of personality traits and clinical dimensions. In the interpretation that follows we make rather extensive use of footnotes (especially when a finding has relevance beyond this particular study) by either providing insight into schizophrenic disorders generally or supporting one or more theories on schizophrenia.

The circumstances under which the CAQ (see Chapter 13) was obtained provides insight into the phenomenological, existential world of a schizophrenic patient. The patient, whom we shall call Ms. X, had been schizophrenic for 15 years prior to taking the CAQ. The CAQ was administered during a brief remission of her schizophrenia. At that time she was completely lucid.* In compliance with our request, her responses to the CAQ did not reflect her behavior or feelings during the test-taking period; instead, they reflected her behavior and feelings of the previous six months. Now, unlike someone in a psychotic state, she was able to make responses based on shared understanding of the CAQ items, i.e., she was free of the intricate private logic which characterizes schizophrenic thinking.† It is noteworthy

---

*Sullivan (1940) was probably the first to draw attention to the discontinuities in psychotic states, in which the characteristic disturbances of thought disappear for varying periods of time.

†As an example of such distortions in schizophrenic thinking, one patient, a paranoid schizophrenic who had puzzled us by obtaining extremely low scores on the L, Suspiciousness, and Pa, Paranoid, scales of the CAQ, later explained that he had interpreted the word "people" to exclude Hungarians, members of his family, persons living in the city in which he resided, and those associated with the United Nations.

that her scores on each factor followed the direction of the group scores for schizophrenics reported in the CAQ handbook, indicating that her profile was representative of that clinical group.

Clinical History

Ms. X's clinical history was quite typical of schizophrenic patients. She was a quiet, shy child who became increasingly withdrawn in adolescence, spending most of her time alone reading religious books. At 17, without the presence of any identifiable psychosocial stressor, she became convinced that her sister's doll was the Christ child and she heard voices commanding her to take care of it. This hallucinatory delusional episode led to her being hospitalized. She was diagnosed as an undifferentiated schizophrenic, because her symptoms could not easily be fitted into a particular subtype. She later experienced several similar episodes, also resulting in hospitalization, and with each succeeding episode her ability to care for her health and safety deteriorated. After some sudden outbursts of apparently unprovoked violence directed toward her parents, she was placed in a Board and Care Home where she had been living for five years prior to the diagnostic testing on the Clinical Analysis Questionnaire. She is now 32 years of age.

Schizophrenia is recognized as involving numerous psychological processes which produce disturbances in affect, interpersonal relations, attachment to the outside world, content and form of thought, identity and subjective experience of control. Even in the residual phase of schizophrenia, the phase on which Ms. X reported, the disorder is still evident. For Ms. X the disorder was apparent in her illogical thinking,* loose associations, pronounced delusions, flat and constricted

---

*The term "illogical thinking" is meant in the psychiatric sense where conclusions arise from contradictory premises as in a thought disorder.

affects, and lack of interest in her surroundings. What was not immediately apparent because it was hidden by the low expressiveness so characteristic of schizophrenia, was her depression, inner turmoil, and emotional sensitivity. However, these came to light after analysis of her CAQ responses. Again, the reader may wish to look at the description of the CAQ factors in Chapter 12 before continuing to the CAQ interpretation that follows.

CAQ Interpretation

Interpretation of Ms. X's CAQ profile involved theoretical knowledge of personality source traits, whatever information was available about the examinee, and an interplay between the test scores and the interpreter's associations.

Scores on the second-order factors in Table 18.3 drew a picture of an extremely introverted (Extraversion = 1.2 on a tenpoint (sten) scale), anxious (Anxiety = 8.3) young woman who was averagely independent (Independence = 5), and controlled by her emotions (Tough Poise = 2.0). Her score on the CAQ General Psychotism factor was 9.8 and on the General Depression factor was 8.14, indicating that she was also depressed and involved in psychotic processes. With respect to her average score on Independence, in view of her score on all other second-order factors, we interpreted it not to reflect competency and self-confidence (as we would if it were embedded in another configuration of second-order factors), but rather disturbances in interpersonal relationships.

TABLE 18.3
Ms. X: Second-Order CAQ Factors

	Sten Score
Extraversion	1.2
Anxiety	8.3
Tough Poise	1.8
Independence	5.1
General Depression	8.1
Psychoticism	9.8

Among the scores in Figure 18.4 for primary factors, the most deviant factor score occurred on the Parmia-Threctia, or H, scale. This score of 1, the lowest possible, indicated that Ms. X was excessively threctic, i.e., susceptible to threat. It is now known that the threctic score is more associated with schizoid tendencies than any other score in the CAQ. Consequently, even if this profile had been "blindly" interpreted, by adding just this one score to the second-order picture, we would have suspected schizophrenia.

Persons achieving threctic rather than parmic scores are described in the 16 P.F. handbook (Cattell, Eber, & Tatsuoka, 1970) as shy, cautious, and restrained.* It is essential to realize, though, that what is described here is not indifference but fear. Indeed, the factor that indicated indifference to social stimuli is A, the Sizothymia-Affectothymia dimension, on which Ms. X scored just below average (4), indicating that her interest in people was far from absent. Such a score is not unusual in schizophrenics, as shown by certain group profiles reported in the CAQ manual. The mean score on Affectothymia in these profiles was 5.4 for males and 4.8 for females. This finding has long puzzled Cattell (Cattell, Eber, & Tatsuoka, 1970).

Looking at Ms. X's A and H scores together, we are forced to conclude that she was not so much cold as afraid and timid. Also, we realized that in past interviews we had confounded these two traits by interpreting the examinee's immobile face,

sparse communication, and lack of enthusiasm as indifference rather than fear.* At that time we would have guessed that her score on Affectothymia would be 1, not 4.

The profile had five other extreme scores just below that of Threctia. These scores were measurements of E, Dominance-Submissiveness (2); F, Surgency-Desurgency (9); D_7, Bored Withdrawal (9); Sc, Schizophrenia (9); and Ps, General Psychosis (9).

The first two mentioned were major contributors to the examinee's second-order introversion pattern, since they indicated social withdrawal and thereby schizoid tendencies. More specifically, the score here on E told us that Ms. X was unusually submissive and could neither protect herself from exploitation nor guide interpersonal situations to meet her needs. According to Karson and O'Dell (1976),

---

*Based partially on research performed by Meeland (1953) which linked the somatic component of Threctia, H−, with dominance of the sympathetic nervous system. Krug (1980) has suggested that threctic individuals are unduly sensitive to external stressors, and they may withdraw to protect themselves from sensory overload. It may be that Threctia has been identified (though not named as such) through investigations performed over the last three decades into the heightened responsiveness to sensory stimulation in schizophrenics. Findings from these investigations have also led to the hypothesis that the withdrawal of schizophrenic patients is an attempt to reduce excessive stimuli, in which case H− would be centrally involved in schizophrenia.

*Extremely low scores on Threctia are consistent with the fear component of the "need-fear dilemma" construct of schizophrenia described by Linn (1980). The dilemma has two complementary components. The first is fear, which forces the schizophrenic person to withdraw. Withdrawal is then followed by intense feelings of loneliness. These in turn generate the second component, delusions and hallucinations, which attempt to compensate for the absence of social stimuli.

The fear-need construct hinges on the hypothesis that the social deprivation resulting from sensitivity to threat is the antecedent variable and the hallucinary experience is the consequence. This hypothesis is intriguing in view of the sensory deprivation experiments performed first by Hebb (1949) and then by Lilly (1972) and others. These experiments have provided compelling evidence that normal subjects will hallucinate in the absence of environmental stimuli.

The practical treatment implication which comes from this line of reasoning is to recognize that withdrawal tendencies will be further reinforced by bleak and inhospitable milieus, such as those of the mental hospital "back wards" of the not too distant past. Under such conditions schizophrenic patients are encouraged, if not forced, to retreat even deeper into their inner worlds of delusions and hallucinations. The key is to create, in both the interpersonal treatment situation between patient and therapist and the broader physical-social environment in which the patient lives, a delicate balance which is at the same time nonthreatening and titillating, much like that which one uses to make contact with a deer or other wild and timid thing.

such persons not only suffer from much frustration, but have difficulty, presumably because of high fear, in expressing hostility toward the source of their frustrations. As a result, angry feelings become directed inward or are vented through sudden and seemingly inexplicable bursts of anger. We wondered if, at least in part, this factor had been involved in the examinee's violent attacks on her parents. The score of 2 on F, Surgency-Desurgency, showed that Ms. X was decidedly desur-

gent. She lacked spontaneity, found life joyless, and interacted little with others. A low score on F does not *in itself* indicate depression as it is also indicative of high inhibitability; however, in this profile there is evidence of strong depressive features.*

*Without elevated scores on the Depression scale, the low Surgency-Desurgency score could have suggested that the examinee was suffering from anhedonia, a complaint of many schizophrenic patients.

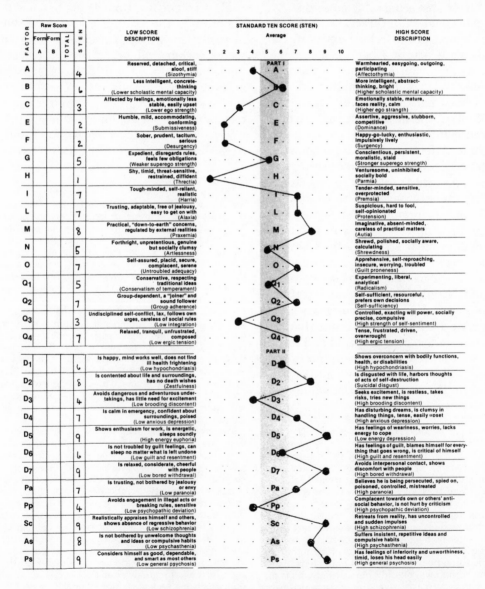

Figure 18.4. Ms. X: CAQ profile

We next looked at the scores of 9 occurring on both the Schizophrenia (Sc) and General Psychosis (Ps) scales. These scales, with Psychasthenia, made up the second-order psychosis pattern on which Ms. X obtained a high score, as already mentioned.

It should be noted—as other clinicians have sometimes found—that we would not have been able to diagnose the patient as schizophrenic based on the Schizophrenic scale score alone. This is because, despite its name, the scale *does not measure symptomatology specific* to schizophrenia. In other words, other clinical groups also tend to score high on this scale and so also do teenagers, whose schizoid behavior is part of adolescence.* What the score of 9 did tell us was that, having endorsed practically every response in the Schizophrenic scale in the direction of symptomatology, Ms. X was describing herself as having difficulty 1) maintaining reality contact, 2) putting her thoughts into words, 3) being controlled by impulses which she didn't understand, 4) dealing with perceptual disturbances, and 5) feeling she was rejected by others.

Just as the score on the Schizophrenic scale does not necessarily indicate a di-

agnosis of schizophrenia, a high score on the General Psychosis scale does not in itself mean an actual psychosis but a condition of personality frequently seen in psychosis.* Actually, the title of the scale may be misleading, as Krug (1980) suggested. Krug has also noticed that what is described on the high end of this scale resembles "learned helplessness,"† since high scorers experience a sense of doom and have little self-worth. Thus, we interpreted Ms. X's score of 9 as meaning that she too felt doomed and unworthy.

The other extreme score in this profile was 9 on D_7, Bored Withdrawal. The highest scorers on this factor tend to be schizophrenic. Ms. X's score told us that Ms. X felt extremely uncomfortable in the presence of others, largely because she saw herself as having nothing to contribute. Also, she was weighed down by what she viewed as the meaninglessness and absurdity of her life.

Not considered extreme scores, but still within the high or low range, were those on C, Ego Strength (3); M, Autism (8); O, Guilt Proneness (8); Q_3, Self-sentiment (8); D_2, Suicide Disgust (8); and As, Psychasthenia (8). The factor scores on Ego Strength, Guilt Proneness, and Self-sentiment were contributors to the second-order anxiety pattern on which Ms. X also scored. This has already been noted.

A low score on Ego Strength, which is typical of all psychotic and neurotic profiles, indicated that Ms. X had difficulty in organizing her behavior to meet her needs. This conclusion was consistent

*A test for schizophrenia, as in any other method of making a differential diagnosis between one kind of disorder and many others, requires that the symptoms involved are 1) *specific* to a clinical group, and 2) occur with *high statistical frequency* within that group. However, as the World Health Organization's (1978) investigation into the classification of schizophrenia revealed, there is an inverse relationship between specificity and frequency variables in schizophrenia, e.g., verbigeration and creation of neologisms, although occurring almost exclusively in schizophrenics, are found in only an estimated 3% of persons diagnosed as schizophrenic. Consequently, scales with high discriminatory power for identifying schizophrenia contain descriptions of symptoms that would identify only a small portion of schizophrenics. In this regard, such scales would have limited utility. Conversely, a scale describing symptoms that are frequently encountered among schizophrenics (e.g., auditory hallucinations as in the Sc scale) are present in other groups and has low discriminatory power. Therefore, the usefulness of this scale is very much dependent on the examinee's scores within the full context of his or her profile.

*High scores on the General Psychosis scale also contribute to the second-order General Depression factor, signifying distortions of self-worth. Although these scores would be elevated in a psychotic depression, they may still be elevated when no psychosis exists at all.

†The construct of "learned helplessness" was experimentally defined by Seligman (1975). It has since been speculated to play a role in the subjective experience of depression, where the depressed person believes he is unable to emit any response that will positively change his situation.

with the ubiquitous observation that schizophrenia involves severe disturbance in ego functions.

Scores on Guilt Proneness and Self-sentiment should be considered together, as both indicate a person's sense of self. In this profile the low Self-sentiment score pointed to severe identity problems, which is a main feature of schizophrenia, while the high score on Guilt Proneness indicates a pervasive sense of self-reproach and unworthiness. Following Karson and O'Dell's (1976) recommendations, we also looked at the two scores in conjunction with the Superego score which, at 5, was within normal range.* Adding to these three scores the average score of 5 on Q_1, the Conservative-Radical dimension, and her below-average score (4) on Pp, Sociopathic dimension (avoidance of illegal acts), we saw that Ms. X had adopted a well-developed, conventional moral code and value system. Thus, we wondered if her high Guilt Proneness may have arisen, at least in part, from her critical self-evaluation against introjected standards of right/wrong and normalcy.

The high score of 8 on M, Autia, was as we would have anticipated in a schizophrenic patient. Autia, the absorption in inner ideas, akin to the "introverted thinking" noticed by Jung, indicates inattentiveness and even dissociation from the physical environment. In the case of Ms. X, we took the score to signify her absorption in inner stimuli and delusional material, as well as in depressive and self-deprecatory thoughts.†

The remaining scores in either the high range or low range are on the clinical

scales, two of which represent depressive factors. Ms. X scored 8 on both D_2, Suicidal Disgust, and D_5, Low Energy Depression. Persons who obtain high scores on the Suicidal Disgust scale are reporting that "they entertain thoughts of death as a viable alternative to their present hopeless situation. In short, they are at the end of their rope" (Krug, 1980). Thus, high scores should always raise concern, especially when they occur in schizophrenics; the suicide rate among such persons is high (Schuettler et al., 1976). We were relieved, therefore, to see that the examinee's score on the agitation factor, D_3, High Brooding Discontent, was below-average; Eber has observed that a high Suicidal Disgust score is not necessarily predictive of suicide if this score is not elevated. Moreover, the score on D_5, Low Energy Depression, was high, suggesting that it would have been difficult for Ms. X to muster the energy to act upon self-destructive impulses. However, should the Suicidal Disgust score have remained high and either the Brooding Discontent score increase or the Low Energy Depression score decrease, we would have been alerted that a possible suicide attempt was imminent and take appropriate measures to protect Ms. X's life.

The last of the high scores on the CAQ clinical scales was on Psychasthenia. This score indicated that Ms. X either felt compelled to perform some repetitive action or believed herself to be the passive object of recurring thoughts.* In schizophrenic patients such a high score is associated with ritualized and stereotyped behavior which has its origin in magical thinking. Nevertheless, the score did not tell us much about Ms. X's thoughts, only that she is obsessive about some of her ideas.

All other deviant scores in the profile were just above or below average, i.e., es-

---

*The average Superego score here is in accord with the schizophrenic group profiles reported in the CAQ handbook. As the onset of adult schizophrenia does not occur before the mid-teens at the earliest, it is not surprising that moral development has occurred.

†As stated in the discussion of Mr. and Mrs. A above, a high score on M, though always indicative of a preoccupation with inner thoughts, often to the exclusion of the external world, can only be interpreted in light of other personality characteristics.

---

*In other clinical groups (for example, in obsessive-compulsive disorders), psychasthenia often takes the form of recording the frequency of some meaningless, trivial event, like counting chairs.

sentially normal. They were on A, Affectothymia vs. Sizothymia (4); I, Premsia vs. Harria (7); L, Protension vs. Alaxia (7); Q_4, Ergic Tension (7); D_3, Brooding Discontent (4); D_4, High Anxious Depression (7); Pa, Paranoia (7); and Pp, Sociopathic Deviation (4). Since the scores on the Affectothymia-Sizothymia, Brooding Discontent, and the Sociopathic Deviation scales had already been considered as part of wider patterns, they needed no further interpretation, so we turned to the scores for Harria-Premsia (I) dimension and then to the remaining scores, which were divisible into a) those which had to do with interpersonal relations and b) those that had to do with anxiety.

The score of 7 on the Harria-Premsia dimension placed Ms. X on the side of emotional sensitivity. This should not have surprised us, as the heightened emotional sensitivity of schizophrenics has long been known to clinicians.* Nevertheless, this score made us realize that we had not been attuned to Ms. X's sensitive feelings during our interviews because of her inexpressiveness.

Other factors which, like Affectothymia vs. Sizothymia (Warmth) and Parmia vs. Threctia (Social Boldness), are indicative of the quality of interpersonal relations are Q_2, Self-sufficiency vs. Group Dependence, L, Alaxia vs. Protension, and Pa, Paranoia, with the last two usually covarying in the same direction. Obtaining a score of 7 on all three of these factors showed that Ms. X did not easily fit into groups, was suspicious and cynical, and felt badly treated by others. As for the Paranoid scale, it is not sufficiently elevated to indicate a classification of paranoid schizophrenia. As we considered this triad of scores, we realized that Ms. X had endured a sense of isolation, but that the scores were what would have been ex-

pected from someone who was as fearful of others as she seemed to be (recall the extreme score on Threctia).

The last two scores to be considered were contributors to the second-order anxiety pattern. They were Ergic Tension, Q_4, and Anxious Depression, D_4. Both scores were 7. The correlation between these scores in the general population is .38, so they each give rise to a fairly similar subjective experience, except, whereas in the former, tension is most prominent, in the latter it is lack of confidence which is foremost.

Summary

We started interpreting this profile by looking at the broad personality dimensions as revealed by the second-order factors. These factors indicated that Ms. X was an extremely introverted, anxious, emotionally sensitive young woman with disturbed interpersonal relationships and marked psychotic, depressive features. We then looked at the primary factors and were able to discern the nuances behind these broad personality dimensions, especially as they related to her social withdrawal, fragile sense of self-worth, and particular depressive style.

Although we conclude the interpretation with an oppressive sense of the tragedy about this individual's life, we had a deeper understanding of her personality organizations and symptomatology.

Follow-up

It has been two years since Ms. X's testing by the CAQ and the interpretation of her problem. Shortly after taking the CAQ, she returned to her previous schizophrenic state. Although her symptoms are not florid, she has become preoccupied with some bizarre religious ideas. In our interviews she often sits silently and appears to have little interest in us or what we are saying.

---

*Lehmann (1980) has documented numerous instances where schizophrenic patients have responded with great hurt to mild rejection and aggression.

Many therapists become discouraged in their work with schizophrenic patients not only because the therapeutic goal is regarded as ameliorative rather than curative, but also because of the tenuousness of the therapeutic relationship. Therapists feel rebuffed and that they have little importance in the lives of their schizophrenic patients. In our contact with Ms. X prior to interpreting the CAQ, we were no exception. However, as a result of the CAQ interpretation, we no longer mistake her fear and shyness for indifference and we have a new awareness of her internal struggles. These discoveries in turn led to the establishment of a much better relationship than there had been previously with Ms. X.*

INTERPRETATION OF TWO MAT PROFILES ON THE SAME INDIVIDUAL: A PRE- AND POSTTREATMENT COMPARISON OF PERSONALITY CHANGE

The Use of the MAT in Clinical Assessment

The Motivational Analysis Test (MAT) which is described in Chapter 13, is a relatively new instrument using objective (not questionnaire) devices for assessing the strength of drives and acquired motivations. Among its many uses, we have found the MAT to be the instrument of choice both for identifying the root difficulties which impel individuals to seek psychological treatment and for assessing the changes that occur in the ensuing intervention. The MAT is useful, regardless

---

*That Ms. X often sat silently in our interviews with seemingly little interest in us may seem to contradict our assertion of an improved relationship. In defense of this position, we refer the reader to the writings of Fromm-Reichmann, an acknowledged expert in the field of schizophrenic treatment. In her book, *Principles of Intensive Psychotherapy* (1950) Fromm-Reichmann describes the reassurance experienced by the schizophrenic patient when the therapist is willing to sit quietly with him.

of what mode of intervention is used, as it addresses the basic intention of all psychotherapies—psychoanalytic, behavioristic, humanistic, and even the more esoteric Eastern remedies—which is to resolve human problems. Here we define "problems" along the lines of Skinner (1953) as ". . . the unavailability of an effective response to a given situation." But we also believe that the effective response must, to some degree, satisfy the responder's need.

Here we must state a theoretical position, but one which we doubt few personality theorists would disagree with, namely, that all human beings are endowed with the same basic psychological needs and differ from one another only in the strength of these needs and how these needs are expressed. Therefore, a problem develops when 1) a need is unmet and the individual finds himself in a state of deprivation; 2) the expression of the need is unsuccessful, as this expression fails to bring the individual the desired amount of satisfaction; or 3) the need or the expression of the need is for some reason troublesome, but the individual persists in the unwanted behavior despite his efforts to stop.

In the first instance an individual seeks treatment to relieve dysphoria resulting from loss or absence. He may complain of a broken attachment, such as the loss of a spouse, or he may complain that he has not been able to find some longed-for object, a job perhaps, or an inner state like peace of mind. He will be angry or depressed, and should the deprivation be experienced as sufficiently intense, he may suffer some personality disorganization and lost insight into what his deprivation actually is; all he knows at this time is that life is unrewarding. In the therapy that follows, it is important for the therapist to gauge the course of the deprived need. If the individual is grieving, or if he has decided to relinquish the need, the therapist will want to know if the internal need pressure is being reduced and what, if any, needs are being substituted.

In the second instance, an individual seeks treatment because he is not behaving in a way that satisfies his need to the extent he wishes. Like Oliver Twist, he wants more—more fulfilling relationships, work experiences, and so on. His deprivation is not absolute but relative. He feels that he is "shortchanged," disappointed. For example, he may say that he wants to find better ways of expressing his anger, being a parent, or talking to his co-workers. With sufficient self-insight, he may see his difficulty as due to the lack of appropriate living techniques and he may present himself at assertiveness training or parenting and communication workshops to acquire these skills. The measurement task, then, is to ascertain the success of these new skills in satisfying the needs they are designed to fill.

Lastly, therapy is sought because an individual sees the way he expresses a need is maladaptive, since this need comes into conflict with others higher on his need hierarchy. He may also find that he is unable to suppress this need. An example here is a sexual impulse disorder such as exhibitionism in an otherwise respectable citizen. Less dramatic, but equally compulsive, are: the woman who wishes to detach herself from a destructive relationship but is unable to; the middle-aged man still bound by his intense desire for his mother's approval, although this approval is irrelevant to his present life situation; and the man driven to succeed beyond reasonable limits, pursuing a goal he himself recognizes as impossible. In these cases the therapeutic task usually becomes one of uncovering the need which is rewarded by this unwanted response, and of assisting the individual towards learning more benign and ego-syntonic ways of meeting the need. Just as the individual is acquiring new skills, it is necessary to judge what the correspondence is between these new responses and the meeting of the need.

The above analysis is summarized in Figure 18.5, the Adjustment Process Analysis Chart (from Cattell, 1982, p. 307).

The MAT has been designed so that it measures the forces in the problems outlined in the preceding paragraphs. Scales for the ten most common needs requiring adaptation in contemporary Western culture have been brought together in the MAT, so that the skilled interpreter can discern which needs are involved in the patient's distress, even though they may be unknown to the patient. The MAT also reflects the conflict between needs, e.g., as seen in the respectable citizen with the sexual impulse disorder, and the degree to which the conflict is being resolved in psychotherapy. It also reflects the level of need strength, as when a need loses potency while an individual works through his grief or relinquishes his longing for the unattainable. And finally, the MAT distinguishes between superficial and actual changes in behavior by revealing real alterations in dynamic expression as represented by new outlets and pathways to satisfaction.

The U and I Components and the Psychological Meaning of Their Various Combinations

The MAT yields for each drive strength or interest a U and an I score. These U and I scores are not figments of conceptual imagination but were discovered by factor analysis of objective motivation measuring devices. The devices and the underlying principles which make up the U (Unintegrated) and the I (Integrated) components have in fact been fully described in Chapter 13. There it is pointed out also that there are five ergs (innate needs) and five sentiments (acquired needs) covered by the MAT, with a U and an I score for each.

Before continuing the MAT interpretation, we need to refresh the reader's memory on the difference and interrelationships between these two components. Within this context we must also introduce what hitherto has not been discussed, the psychological meaning of the combinations of the high, medium, and low U and I scores for any given need. With three for U (high, medium, and low) and three for I, there will be nine combinations to consider.

The U component is that portion of the need or motivation that is unrealized because it has not found its way into awareness or behavioral expression. The fully expressed need is in the I component. Normally, the movement from U to I is in a state of constant flux progressing smoothly from the prepotent, internally generated drive, U, to outer expression, I. However, there are a variety of conditions which

may inhibit expression, causing the need to remain unreleased and pent-up inside the individual.

The U component at the experiential and behavioral level is essentially a desire either renounced or unfulfilled, and so is covert. As it is not directly observable under natural circumstances, it comes to light only by accident such as slips of the tongue, omissions in memory, and other psychological phenomena which have been comprehensively described by Freud. Experimentally this component has been detected and measured by two indirect manifestations of wishful thinking, namely, tests for autism and projection which are included in the MAT.

In contrast to the U component, the I component is that portion of motivation

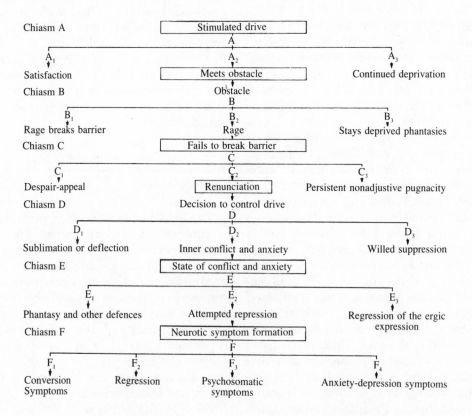

Figure 18.5. The adjustment process analysis chart

Source: Cattell (1965).

which has been realized by awareness and experience. It is overt and as such is subjectively experienced as conscious interest. If the excitation (dynamic investment) which originally molded it has receded, as in the case of an emotionally dead relationship, it is experienced as a well-established habit pattern. The information and word association tests which represent this component in the MAT measure memory of cognitive and motor actions acquired in the service of realizing motivation.

Although ergs and sentiments are alike in possessing U and I components, their internal structures are different. Ergs, as unitary drives, have isomorphic correspondences between components, with the U component being the prepotent need strength and the I the satisfier, e.g., U hunger/I food, U fear/I safety-seeking, and U pugnacity/I pain infliction. Sentiments, on the other hand, although similar on their I components, do not have such isomorphic correspondences. Instead, the U component is the vessel in which ergs and even other sentiments have united in their cathexis to some object, person, idea, or symbolic representation (for a graphic example of sentiment structures, the reader may wish to refer back to the Dynamic Lattice on page 295 in Chapter 14). Undoubtedly, the internal structure of sentiments is somewhat different for each person. Consequently, the U components

of the given sentiments included in the MAT do not tell us anything about their dynamic genealogy, as they represent only end products of dynamic networks.

Psychological Meaning of the Nine MAT U and I Combinations

Any person's score on a dynamic trait (erg or sentiment) may be high, low or middling. Consequently, for any dynamic trait there can be nine possible combinations. These combinations are diagrammed in Table 18.4.

The psychological meaning of the nine U and I combinations has been explored by Cattell and Butcher (1968), Cattell and Child (1975) and Delhees (1968). This research demonstrated the following two basic principles:

1) I scores increase and U scores decrease simultaneously as a motivation is realized in a practical expression.*
2) U scores increase and I scores decrease simultaneously as a motivation is frustrated.

But these two principles, as the reader will quickly see on examining Table 18.4, leave two important points unexplained. First, they account for only six score com-

---

*This is similar to Freud's famous dictum for psychological adjustment: "Where id was, ego will be."

TABLE 18.4
All Possible U & I Combinations

	U High (Stens 7-10)	U Average (Stens 5-6)	U Low (Stens 1-4)
I High (Stens 7-10)	(1) U = I U High/I High	(4) I-U U Average/I High	(7) I-U U Low/I High
I Average (Stens 5-6)	(2) U-I U High/I Average	(5) U = I U Average/I Average	(8) I-U U Low/I Average
I Low (Stens 1-4)	(3) U-I U High/I Low	(6) U-I U Average/I Low	(9) U = I U Low/I Low

binations, those in which one is above average and the other below, i.e., nothing is revealed about the three *equal* strength scores, namely, U High-I High, U Average-I Average, and U Low-I Low. Second, the two principles are purely descriptive and do not immediately give us the psychological reasons for the differences. For example, U-I score (an excess of U over I) indicating that a need is not being expressed may result from any one of the following alternatives: 1) the environment does not allow opportunities for expression; 2) the individual suppresses or represses expression; 3) the individual lacks the capacity to express the need; or 4) the need is so new that it is only now making its way into the individual's awareness and behavior.

Thus, while waiting for further research to expand upon such basic principles, we must make more tentative interpretations of the interplay between a) the *direction* of a score combination (i.e., whether the U score is higher or lower than or equal to the I score; U-I, I-U, or U = I) and b) the *level* (U High-I Low or U Average-I Low) of a score combination as we encounter it.

Table 18.5 lists the alternatives according to the *direction* of the score combination, and Table 18.6 shows which of the alternatives offer the most likely explanation for each of the nine *levels* of score combinations. Table 18.7 is an expansion of Table 18.6, as it provides illustrations, behavioral observations, and examples of verbal clues for each score combination.

TABLE 18.5
Psychological Interpretations of U = I, U-I, & I-U Score Combinations

U = I	*Equal tension.* Dynamic expression does not reduce underlying need state.
U-I, Alternative 1	*Environmental restrictions.* Dynamic expression is limited by the absence of social or physical opportunities, e.g., limited by climate, censorship, and sexual or racial discrimination.
U-I, Alternative 2	*Personal restrictions.* Dynamic expression is limited by personal restrictions, e.g., poor health, shyness, and learning disabilities.
U-I, Alternative 3	*Recency of dynamic development.* Dynamic interest has not had sufficient time or been developed through sufficient experience to find adequate expression, e.g., in the case of a new career or sexual drive in early puberty.
U-I, Alternative 4	*Repression.* Dynamic expression is so anxiety-provoking that the underlying need is kept out of awareness by various defense mechanisms. The need may nevertheless continue to seek indirect expression, e.g., through humor, projection, and slips of the tongue.
U-I, Alternative 5	*Suppression.* Dynamic expression is *consciously* rejected by one of the following three agencies of internal control: 1) the ego, 2) the superego, or 3) the self-sentiment. Rejection by the ego is based on the fear that the expression may be unrealistic and unsafe, e.g., as in a financially risky investment. Rejection by the superego is based on the possibility that the expression is morally reprehensible, e.g., as in the case of stealing. Rejection by the self-sentiment is based on the belief that the expression is damaging to self-respect and/or public image, e.g., as in the situation of public intoxication.
I-U, Alternative 1	*Dynamic realization.* Dynamic expression satisfies by reducing underlying need, e.g., as may happen in obtaining a job in an area of interest.
I-U, Alternative 2	*Dynamic withdrawal.* Interest that initially supported and sustained dynamic expression has withdrawn, leaving a habit formation, e.g., as may happen when a couple continues to perform the daily rituals of married life long after their affection for each other has died.

TABLE 18.6

Most Likely Psychological Interpretation for Each U-I Score Combination

	U HIGH (Sten 7-10)	U AVERAGE (Sten 5-6)	U LOW (Sten 1-4)
I HIGH (Sten 7-10)	#1 U = I U HIGH / I HIGH INTERPRETATION 1) Equal Tension	#4 I-U U AVERAGE / I HIGH INTERPRETATION 1) Dynamic Realization	#7 I-U U LOW / I HIGH INTERPRETATION 1) Dynamic Withdrawal
I AVERAGE (Sten 5-6)	#2 U-I U HIGH / I AVERAGE 1) Environmental Restrictions 2) Personal Restrictions 3) Suppression 4) Recency of Dynamic Development	#5 U = I U AVERAGE / I AVERAGE 1) Equal Tension	#8 I-U U LOW / I AVERAGE 1) Dynamic Realization 2) Dynamic Withdrawal
I LOW (Sten 1-4)	#3 U-I U HIGH / I LOW 1) Repression 2) Environmental Restrictions 3) Recency of Dynamic Develop.nent 4) Personal Restrictions	#6 U-I U AVERAGE / I LOW 1) Repression 2) Suppression 3) Environmental Restrictions 4) Recency of Dynamic Development 5) Personal Restrictions	#9 U = I U LOW / I LOW 1) Equal Tension

TABLE 18.7
Psychological Interpretations of
U = I, U-I, & I-U Combinations of High, Average, & Low Scores

	U HIGH (Stens 7–10)	I U AVERAGE (Stens 5–6)	U LOW (Stens 1–4)
I HIGH (Stens 7-10)	**#1** *U = I (HIGH U = HIGH I)* A) MOST LIKELY PSYCHOLOGICAL INTERPRETATION *Equal tension.* Underlying need remains unsatisfied despite finding outlet for expression. Examples: Religious and political fanatics, "workaholics," addicts. B) BEHAVIORAL OBSERVATIONS Appears driven. Is insatiable, often fixated on one particular interest to exclusion of all others. May have history of extreme deprivation or gratification. C) EXAMPLES OF VERBAL CLUES I can't get enough . . . I can think of nothing else . . . **#2** *U-I (HIGH U = AVERAGE I)* A) MOST LIKELY PSYCHOLOGICAL INTERPRETATION Dynamic expression is average, and not in accordance with its high underlying potential for one of the following reasons: 1. *Environmental restriction.* Lack of opportunities in environment.	**#4** *I-U (HIGH I = AVERAGE U)* A) MOST LIKELY PSYCHOLOGICAL INTERPRETATION *Dynamic realization.* High expressiveness deeply satisfying to underlying need. Example: Persons happily involved in careers or family life. B) BEHAVIORAL OBSERVATIONS Shows high level of sustained interest but without driven, insatiable qualities described in square #1. C) EXAMPLES OF VERBAL CLUES This is very important to me. I am deeply committed. I never get tired of . . . **#5** *U = I (AVERAGE U = AVERAGE I)* A) MOST LIKELY PSYCHOLOGICAL INTERPRETATION *Equal tension.* Average amount of expression does not relieve underlying need state. However, because need state is only of average strength it does not result in uncomfortable excitement as described in square #1.	**#7** *I-U (HIGH I = LOW U)* A) MOST LIKELY PSYCHOLOGICAL INTERPRETATION *Dynamic withdrawal.* High level of motivation has receded leaving strong habit pattern. Example: Bored employee having learned all there is to know about his or her job. B) BEHAVIORAL OBSERVATIONS Makes stereotyped or well-coordinated responses requiring little thought or effort. Goes through the motions. Stores large fund of information but shows little desire to add to it. Always has history of high past involvement. C) EXAMPLES OF VERBAL CLUES I can do it with my eyes closed. It's a habit, nothing more! **#8** *I-U (AVERAGE I = LOW U)* A) MOST LIKELY PSYCHOLOGICAL INTERPRETATION Expression, though average, has little dynamic investment for one of two reasons: 1. *Dynamic realization.* The underlying need is satisfied by the level of expression. Example: Golfer who has achieved score

that is average for his group and does not wish to go above it.

2. *Dynamic withdrawal.* Interest, which probably was not extremely strong originally, has now receded, leaving an adequate habit pattern.
Example: Disinterested parent who continues to provide level of care consistent with cultural standards.

B) BEHAVIORAL OBSERVATIONS
1. *Dynamic realization.* Although information and skills are adequate, does not show ambition for further development. Often has more compelling interests in other areas. Does not express dissatisfaction.

2. *Dynamic withdrawal.* Performs at a purely behavioral mechanical level. Does not stand out from others in group. Review of history shows more interest existed in past. (If the motivational area in question is a sentiment rather than an erg, its main tributary may be:
1) ego (realism), 2) self-sentiment (self-respect), or 3) superego (duty).

I AVERAGE (Stens 5-6)

Example: Pieceworker in garment factory who sustains steady output without need for many breaks.

B) BEHAVIORAL OBSERVATIONS
Shows steady flow of interest but without marked enthusiasm. Does not tire easily. Needs little revitalization.

Example: Person cannot obtain desired advanced training in area in which he has already displayed competence.

2. *Personal restriction.* Lack of opportunity due to limitations within the person.
Example: Young man would like to advance his relationship with a young woman from friendship to romance but is too shy to ask for a date.

3. *Suppression.* Conscious rejection of wish to exercise interest to full potential.
Example: Curtailing expression of anger from physical attack to verbal attack.

4. *Recency of dynamic development.* Interest has not yet had sufficient time to be *fully* expressed, although there is average experience in the area.
Example: Aspiring young musician.

B) BEHAVIORAL OBSERVATIONS
In *Suppression,* will show deliberate effort to modify enthusiasm. In other conditions —*Environmental restriction, Personal restriction,* & *Recency of dynamic development*—seeks out opportunities or makes effort for further expression of interest, while expressing considerable frustration at what is perceived to be the obstruction to satisfaction. However, in *Personal restriction,* may tend to preserve self-sentiment by attributing the obstruction to external causes (e.g., the exam was unfair).

TABLE 18.7 (cont'd)

	U HIGH (Stens 7–10)	I U AVERAGE (Stens 5–6)	U LOW (Stens 1–4)
	C) EXAMPLES OF VERBAL CLUES *Suppression.* "I restrain myself from getting carried away." *Environmental restriction.* "There is no opportunity to advance to a high level, much as I want to." *Recency of development.* "I have as much as the average person, but with time I want to achieve much more." *Personal restriction.* "As much as I try, I can't get more than a 'C' grade."	C) EXAMPLE OF VERBAL CLUES "It's a fairly enjoyable way to pass time."	C) EXAMPLES OF VERBAL CLUES *Dynamic realization.* "I don't want to pursue this any further." *Ergic regression.* "I am less interested now than before but I keep up an acceptable standard."
I LOW (Stens 1-4)	#3 *U-I (HIGH U - LOW I)* A) MOST LIKELY PSYCHOLOGICAL INTERPRETATION There is high internal pressure with little outlet realization for four possible reasons: 1. *Repression.* Although not cognizant of need strength, need may continue to exert considerable psychic pressure and manifest itself in the form of anxiety or somatic symptoms. Example: A case of anxiety neurosis. 2. *Environmental restriction.* Opportunities for realizing the need are almost non-existent rather than moderately available as in square #2. Example: Economically disadvantaged people who are subjected to T.V. advertisements for luxury items. 3. *Recency of dynamic development.* Very early exposure to potentially satisfying experiences or the coming into existence of a	#6 *U-I (AVERAGE U - LOW I)* A) MOST LIKELY PSYCHOLOGICAL INTERPRETATION Expression is minimal although the unintegrated pressure is of average strength. Five possible explanations: 1. *Repression.* Not cognizant of need, and internal pressure is not high. Therefore, there is not the anxiety nor symptoms described in square #1. Example: Unpleasant experience that one has not thought about in years. 2. *Suppression.* Conscious rejection of need does not continue to assert high internal pressure. Example: Comfortably putting aside consideration of a problem till later date. 3. *Environmental restriction.* Expression of need small. But sense of deprivation not intense because dynamic need only of average strength.	#9 *U = I (LOW U = LOW I)* A) MOST LIKELY PSYCHOLOGICAL INTERPRETATION Minimal underlying interest matched by corresponding performance level. Example: Persons conscripted to do tasks against their will, such as slaves.

B) BEHAVIORAL OBSERVATIONS
Does only enough to get by. Apathy. Indifference.

Example: A low-level priority.

4. *Recency of dynamic development.* Very recent exposure to a potentially moderately satisfying experience or coming into existence of latent dynamic.
Example: New worker on job that offers *moderate* rather than *high* potential for satisfaction as in square #3.

5. *Personal restriction.* Despite average interest unable to attain minimally acceptable level of proficiency.
Example: Not being able to perform common task as well as most people.

B) BEHAVIORAL OBSERVATIONS
1. *Repression.* Displays effective defense mechanisms. No symptomatology.

2. *Suppression.* Able to reject unwanted thoughts and behavior. Does not worry. Behavior under conscious control. Avoidance.

3. *Environmental restrictions.* Displays some frustration with perceived environmental barriers, but frustration tolerable. Poor fund of information and skills.

4. *Recency of dynamic development.* Shows willingness but not eagerness to learn. Information and skills very limited.

5. *Personal restriction.* Does not acquire average level of skills despite putting forth average amount of effort.

---

latent dynamic.
Example: Puberty.

4. *Personal restriction.* Despite high motivation, is unable to meet even acceptable standards.
Example: Student with borderline intelligence attempting to pass college entrance exam.

B) BEHAVIORAL OBSERVATIONS
1. *Repression.* Rigid defenses. Anxiety. Somatic symptoms.

2. *Environmental restriction.* Displays frustration toward environment. Anger. Depression.

3. *Recency of dynamic development.* Shows eagerness to learn. Seeks information. Asks questions.

4. *Personal restrictions.* Shows much interest but has little ability to acquire information of skill despite opportunities presented in environment. Often has history of repeated failure. Shows anger. Depression.

TABLE 18.7 (cont'd)

U HIGH (Stens 7–10)	I U AVERAGE (Stens 5–6)	U LOW (Stens 1–4)
C) EXAMPLES OF VERBAL CLUES 1. *Repression.* "I don't remember." 2. *Environmental restriction.* "I want desperately to . . . but can't find a way." 3. *Recency of dynamic development.* "I don't know much now, but one day I will be an expert." 4. *Personal restriction.* "No matter how I try, I can't measure up to normal standards."	C) EXAMPLES OF VERBAL CLUES 1. *Repression.* "I don't remember." 2. *Suppression.* "I don't allow myself to pay attention to that." 3. *Environmental restriction.* "I would like so and so, but it would not upset me too much if it doesn't happen." 4. *Recency of dynamic development.* "I don't want to excel, but I would like to know as much as the next man." 5. *Personal restriction.* "I put out as much effort as others, but I don't seem to be able to learn how to do it."	C) EXAMPLE OF VERBAL CLUES "I couldn't care less."

These tables are self-explanatory, and the reader will find it useful to refer to them as we proceed to discuss an extensive case study in the following section.

Case History

The example we have selected to illustrate what light the MAT can uniquely throw on dynamics is a male alcoholic whom we shall call Mr. Y. Mr. Y's behavior clearly met the WHO (1951) definition of alcoholism, i.e., his drinking was in excess of his cultural norms and created problems in one or more areas of his life. At 41, he was an accountant in a large, prospering firm, and was married with two teenaged children. Though still employed, he was in danger of losing his job, and his family unit was on the verge of breaking up. His life had become unmanageable due to his drinking.

Mr. Y had a typical drinking history. He had started to drink on a regular daily basis eight years ago, after eagerly seeking and winning a job promotion. The promotion, as he later described it, brought him money, prestige, a footing on the climb towards joining the inner circle of the company's elite—and a lot of stress. Initially, two cocktails were enough to help him unwind after a day's work, but gradually, as his alcohol tolerance increased, he required more and more drinks to obtain the desired effect. Noticing that he drank more than others, his wife objected—but to no avail.

Almost insidiously, Mr. Y's drinking began to adversely affect his personal relationships and work performance. About the time he experienced his first blackout (a chemically produced period of amnesia), he became cantankerous and sometimes verbally abusive while drinking. These episodes occurred first in the privacy of his home; later they became more public. After one particularly drunken angry outburst at his country club, his membership there was put in jeopardy.

His wife avoided going out with him and entertaining at home. Friends drifted away.

As time passed, he no longer drank for pleasure but out of need. To use his own words, he "gave up being a workaholic and embarked on a career as an all-out alcoholic." He was preoccupied with finding opportunities to drink and protecting his supply of alcohol. He was soon caught in a complex pattern of excusing, avoiding, denying, and blaming to cover his deteriorating job performance.

When his behavior could no longer be explained away to his supervisor, an ultimatum was declared: Lose his job or stop drinking! He chose the latter alternative. As he was physically addicted to alcohol and knew from several unsuccessful efforts to stop drinking that he could not stop without assistance, he requested a six-week leave of absence from his work. Upon receiving the leave, he presented himself for treatment at a residential treatment program.

Our first meeting with Mr. Y was during his first week of treatment and following five days of medically supervised alcohol withdrawal (detoxification). He appeared anxious, deeply ashamed, and desirous of making restitution to those who had been hurt by his drinking. It was during this time he related the drinking history given above.

He provided some other information at this time which, though not part of his personal drinking history, turned out to be important in our interpretation of the MAT. This information concerned his early home life, particularly his father's alcoholism. Memories of his father's drinking and the difficulties it caused for the family pervaded all of Mr. Y's childhood recollections. His father was given to anger and even physical violence when he drank, and Mr. Y as the oldest child had been the recipient of much of this abuse. Because of the family's resulting financial crises, Mr. Y's mother sometimes held two jobs and so was not home much. When she was home, she was involved in arguments with her husband or rested often in bed. Feeling very much alone and emotionally unnurtured in this home environment, Mr. Y sought his rewards elsewhere. In school he became an excellent student and something of a "teacher's pet." He worked hard and on graduation obtained a scholarship to a college in another state. Thus he escaped his troubled home, visiting it only rarely thereafter.

Until his drinking took its toll on his life, Mr. Y did well on all fronts. He married a woman he genuinely loved, and became the adoring father of two sons. Respected and admired by those who knew him, he had become what he always wanted to be—a "success," one of those people who seemed to have miraculously transcended his ominous beginnings.

Interpretation of the First Administered MAT

In addition to objectively validating what Mr. Y had told us about himself, the first of the sequence of four MATs administered provided information on motivations and conflicts that Mr. Y could not report because they were beyond his awareness. Because this information would be incorporated into a treatment plan, we had two questions in mind in interpreting the first profile.

The initial question was "What needs were met by Mr. Y's drinking?" In the early stages of alcoholism, drinking is used as an effective, albeit ultimately harmful, problem-solving strategy;* it alleviates unpleasant emotions (such as loneliness or anxiety) which signal the underlying need state. In this way it op-

erates by one of three mechanisms: 1) strength reduction of the need state's phenomenological experience;* 2) relaxation of inhibitions that interfered with the expression of needs such as shyness or conscience; or 3) distortion of reality so that needs are satisfied in imagination rather than in actuality.†

It follows that Mr. Y began to drink excessively because he did not have at his disposal, nor was it likely that he had since learned, more appropriate means of satisfying certain of his needs. It was essential that we learn what these needs were, so that we could help him acquire new and better ways of meeting them as part of this treatment. Without this, he probably would eventually return to drinking. Somewhat less likely, but also undesirable, he would persist in a painful self-restraining, "white-knuckled" sobriety, wherein expression of important needs was rigidly controlled.

The second question was "What needs were frustrated by Mr. Y's drinking?" If Mr. Y's drinking had continued to serve the needs for which it was initially intended without interfering with others, then he would be a normal, or social, drinker. But Mr. Y was an alcoholic, which meant that by definition his drinking did interfere with other needs, in that important sources for his life satisfaction had been abandoned or were still unrealized. Without these needs being identified and adaptive ways learned for meeting

---

*The initial impetus for drinking does not become the reason for continuing alcohol abuse. A transition takes place from psychological dependency to tissue dependency, when the need to drink arises out of physical addiction.

*Reduction of the phenomenological experience of the need state is the stress hypothesis motivation for drinking (Sobell & Sobell, 1973). This hypothesis posits that drinking is an operant response that reduces the degree of emotional arousal and number of autonomic signs which accompany a discomforting situation.

†Psychoanalysts have long recognized that needs can at least be partially gratified through wishful thinking. The exaggerations of many people under the influence of alcohol and grandiosity of their ideas are examples of this phenomenon.

them, Mr. Y might find little motivation for staying sober.*

With these two questions in mind our first glance at the MAT profile (which appears in Figure 18.6) was intended to obtain a quick, though rough, idea of which of Mr. Y's needs were being met in the present or had been in the past, and where his major frustrations lay. This required that we look at all three categories of U and I combinations, namely, I-U, U-I, and U = I.

On five factors—Career, Home, Spouse,

_____

*This philosophy is in accord with the growing recognition among clinicians that treatment is most likely to succeed if it is started while there is still a high probability of the person's meeting his needs. The older view, which was to wait until the alcoholic had "hit bottom," when he had lost his health, finances, family, job, etc., is being abandoned. The reason is that an alcoholic at the bottom has irretrievably lost the wherewithal to meet his needs and hence lacks the motivation to stop drinking.

Narcissism, and Assertiveness—the score combinations fell into the I-U category, indicating that there was either dynamic realization or dynamic withdrawal. Three factors—Superego, Self-sentiment, and Pugnacity—had score combinations on the U-I category, indicating frustration. The two remaining factors, Fear and Mating, had score combinations in the U = I category, indicating equal tension but, as will be seen, with quite different meanings for each factor. The high total scores on the former factor pointed to high tension, whereas low scores on the latter pointed to low tension.

Having obtained a bird's-eye view of the profile, we returned to a closer examination of the I-U score combinations, because this category contained the greatest number of scores. There were very different implications for these combinations depending on the level of the scores. Our

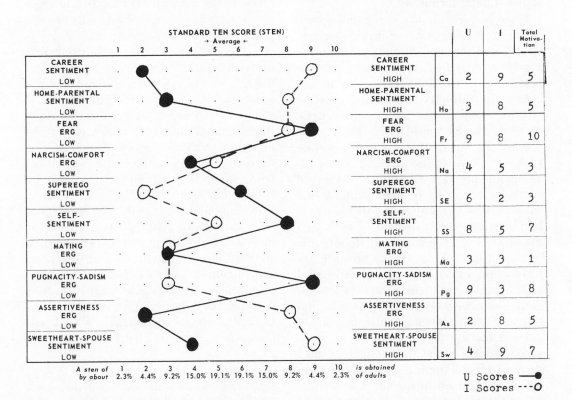

Figure 18.6. Mr. Y: First MAT profile: U, I, and total scores on all ten factors

clinical experience with the MAT suggests that high I scores accompanied by average U scores indicated dynamic realization, High I scores accompanied by low U scores indicated dynamic withdrawal, and average I scores accompanied by low U scores indicated either dynamic realization or dynamic withdrawal.

With the exception of Narcissism, which was the only need in the profile that appeared to be realized at the time, all other I-U score combinations indicated dynamic withdrawal, since all I scores fell into the high range and all U scores into the low range. Thus, a wide chasm existed between present and past interests. The I scores showed that the behavioral patterns associated with need gratification were firmly established, but the high U scores showed that the high drive which had initially molded these behavioral patterns had now receded, leaving empty shells of habit formation.

From Mr. Y's history it seemed appropriate to consider Career and Assertiveness together and Spouse and Home together, as in the first instance they represented his social ambition and in the second his affective concerns. Sweney (1969b) has proposed that Assertiveness, as measured by the MAT, is largely expressed as the motive for social-status-seeking, which is the striving for admiration and prestige through the display of symbols indicative of achievement and success. As with many men, Mr. Y's career had been intimately associated with, and may have been the chief vehicle for, this social-status-seeking. Therefore, we inferred that interest in career and social status must have risen and fallen together, and we were not surprised to find that the two interests shared a similar pattern on the factor scores that measured them. On the Career factor, the I score was 9 and the U score was 2, and on the Assertiveness factor the I score was 8 and the U score was 2, indicating that Mr. Y had been highly motivated in both areas at one time. Although he believed

that they continued to exert strong influences on his life, the total score on each was only average. The main contributor for the total score was habit rather than underlying interest.

High U and low I scores such as these mean dynamic withdrawal, wherein the need state is low and so has lost its emotional potency. As such, it cannot be a motivational influence. Therefore, although Mr. Y had presented keeping his job as the ostensible reason for seeking treatment, we knew we had to look in the U-I and U = I categories for the true reason.

That Mr. Y had withdrawn his interest in career and social status did not mean that this interest could not in the future be restored to its previous strength. However, from a stress standpoint we questioned the wisdom of trying to maintain such unusually strong ambitions, especially in the area of social status, as high scores here often suggest an effort to compensate for low self-esteem. This is especially true of persons who as children grew up with an alcoholic parent, such as Mr. Y's father. These children, because of the emotional turmoil in their families, social conspicuousness of their parent's drinking, frequent financial crises, and other experiences characteristic of such homes, develop a sense of shame and low self-esteem, which they attempt to rise above by heroic efforts to excel. They become what Wegscheider (1981) calls the family heroes, establishing life patterns of overachievement.* Though often highly successful, such individuals find that their self-esteem is largely dependent on other people's admiration and approval. And because they feel continually driven to fend off feelings of inadequacy, they are under much stress. Should they become

---

*Wegscheider's (1981) research, which is based on Satir's (1964) model of the family as a system, has shown that children growing up in homes where one or both parents are dependent on alcohol tend to develop one of four roles: family hero, scapegoat, lost child, or family pet.

alcohol abusers (and many eventually do), they report that they drink to reduce tension.

Mr. Y's account fits this description very closely. He had described himself as a "workaholic" driven to advance in a highly competitive company. His initial impetus for excessive drinking had been to reduce the enormous tension he had experienced after the day's work.

We decided to discuss this "inadequacy compensation" hypothesis with Mr. Y in creating his treatment plan. If, indeed, basic inadequacies were at the root of his overambitiousness, then insight therapy might help Mr. Y develop a more realistic sense of self-worth, and he would no longer need to compensate for his sense of inadequacy. In short, his social status needs would not bring about his former level of stress. However, if the strength of his social status needs was regained, not reduced, therapy might proceed along more direct behavioral lines, specifically, Mr. Y could be trained in relaxation methods such as meditation, jogging, etc.

Just as we grouped the Career and Assertiveness factors together due to their reflection of Mr. Y's status needs, we looked at the Sweetheart-Spouse and Parental-Home factors together as reflections of his major affective needs. While the Parental-Home factor often measures attachment to the examinee's parents and childhood home, in a middle-aged individual it may just as likely measure the quality of his present life with his own family. To distinguish which of the two situations prevails, it is necessary to know something about the examinee's relationship with his parents. When there is a strong affective bond emphasizing mutual pride and this bond has continued from childhood into the present, the Parental-Home factor usually measures attachment to parents and childhood home. But we knew that this was not the case with Mr. Y. He came from an unhappy home and since leaving home at the age of 18 he had little contact with his parents. Given these facts, the high level of interest indicated by the I score could not have referred to the parental home. This we believed was the case, despite the context of dynamic withdrawal, which reflected past rather than present interest. We concluded, therefore, that what was being measured was Mr. Y's present family life.

Having decided that it was his present situation that was being measured, we proceeded to examine the I-U score combination on this factor. Here we saw that the I score was 8 and the U score was 3, which combined came to a total score of 5. These scores indicated that Mr. Y had at one time been strongly involved in his home life but now continued the façade of an active family man. A similar picture of previously high interest coupled with present mechanical role-playing was apparent in Mr. Y's relationship with his wife. On the Sweetheart-Spouse factor the I score was 9 and U score was 4. The total score here was 7, which though high, like all other total scores so far discussed, indicated habit rather than actual interest.

The dynamic withdrawal suggested by both the Parental-Home and Spouse-Sentiment factors was consistent with Mr. Y's own report, which was corroborated by his wife, that prior to his preoccupation with alcohol and despite work pressures, he had made it a point to spend his leisure time with his wife and family. Before the onset of his heavy drinking he had been an unusually devoted husband and father. Even now, when sober, he "ritualistically" played out these roles. His wife described his personality at home as "like a zombie or a sleepwalker."

His wife also complained that the couple's sexual relations had been almost nonexistent. So although the scores on the sexual (Mating) factor did not belong to the I-U score combinations we were considering then, we noted them at that time because of their relevance to the marriage relationship. There was a U = I combination on the sexual factor, but with both U and I having a low score of 3 and a combined total score of 1. These indicated that Mr. Y had lost almost all interest in sex and possibly the ability to perform. This was important information to incorporate into the treatment plan, as sexual impotency in alcoholics often persists after drinking has ceased. At this point sexual therapy is needed.

As previously noted, the only I-U score suggesting dynamic realization on the profile was for Narcissism. This factor measures an enjoyment of basic creature comforts. In college graduates like Mr. Y, the Narcissism erg has been shown to be expressed as a "bon vivant," sensual indulgence, such as concern for good food and physical pleasures. Mr. Y's scores were 4 on U and 5 on I, which came to a total score of 3. These scores showed that, although his narcissistic needs were satisfied, they were low. They were particularly low when compared to others in his reference group, i.e., executives and professional men, who score typically one standard deviation above the population mean (Cattell & Child, 1975). The essence of this factor is rest and relaxation, which are tension-reducing strategies. If Mr. Y had been able to cultivate his narcissistic needs by using other means, for example, sauna or Jacuzzi baths, he might not have resorted to the heavy use of alcohol. Certainly, he should be encouraged to cultivate these narcissistic means of reducing tension as part of his treatment plan.

At this point we had become aware of the intensity of Mr. Y's pre-alcoholic involvements. He had been excessively ambitious, driven to seek status, much concerned with his work, extremely attached to his wife and children, while lacking the ordinary narcissistic outlets for reducing the resulting stress. Therefore, in turning next to the U-I scores, we hoped to be illuminated further on the kinds of conflicts that had caused, and resulted from, this highly pressured lifestyle.

From these U-I combinations it is possible to derive a score of total conflict in the personality (Cattell & Child, 1975; Chapter 13 here) (see Figure 18.7). The term "conflict" has a wider meaning than the intrapsychic ambivalence usually implied when the term is applied to the total personality. Here it means that there is some counter force to the expression of a drive which might arise from internal sources (Repression and Suppression), inexperience (Recency of Dynamic Development), lack of opportunity (Environmental Restrictions), and/or personal inadequacies (Personal Restrictions). Whatever its origin, the result is a surfeit or interest over experience.

There were three U-I (Conflict) scores in Mr. Y's profile. They were on the factors for Superego, Self-sentiment, and Pugnacity. All had maximum Conflict scores. On the Superego factor, which represents an introjection of society's values and at which we looked first, the U score was 6 and the I score was 2, yielding a total score of 3 and the highest possible Conflict score of 10. While we saw from the U score that Mr. Y had an average amount of Superego development, the low I score implied that this development was not translated into behavior. There were five possible explanations. We immediately ruled out Recency of Dynamic Development and Environmental Restriction, as Mr. Y had once displayed an ordinary degree of moral compunctions and did not live in an environment that discouraged the behaviors delineated by the Superego factor. This left a choice between Suppression, Repression, and Personal Restrictions (A. Freud's "restriction of the ego" as described in the Ego and the Mechanisms of Defense, 1966), which meant that he was either attempting to mentally reject his moral standards or was unable to live up to them because of his alcohol dependency. Although we were not able to decide which of these explanations was the most likely, or if all of them were applicable, the ceiling Conflict score indicated that he experienced enormous internal criticism. The subjective experience accompanying this high Conflict score was most likely to be guilt.

The Self-sentiment factor, which we considered next, differs from the Superego factor as it does not represent moral imperatives but rather an interest in maintaining self-respect and an untarnished social reputation. It also differs from what is measured by the Assertiveness factor because it involves a desire for social respectability as distinct from being admired for one's social status. On this factor, Mr. Y's score was 8 on U and 5 on I. His total score was 7 and his Conflict score was 9. These scores indicated that, although he had achieved an average level of self-sentiment expression, it did not satisfy his underlying need, which was unusually high. The result was much frustration and internal pressure. Again, the question was which alternative among five provided the most likely explanation for this score combination. Based again on

what we knew about Mr. Y's situation, we immediately ruled out, as we had on the scores for Superego, inexperience (Recency of Dynamic Development) and an insufficiency of opportunities (Environmental Restrictions). This left two competing hypotheses. The first was that Mr. Y had recognized his excessive self-concern and had attempted to reject it (Suppression). The other was that his strivings to live up to his self- and public image failed because of the sabotaging effect of his drinking (Personal Restriction). But we could not choose between the two hypotheses without discussing them with Mr. Y.

More important than determining which of these two explanations was more plausible was the question of what was meant by his high U score on the Self-sentiment factor. The U score and I score on this factor describe, respectively, the idealized and realized self-constructs, which have

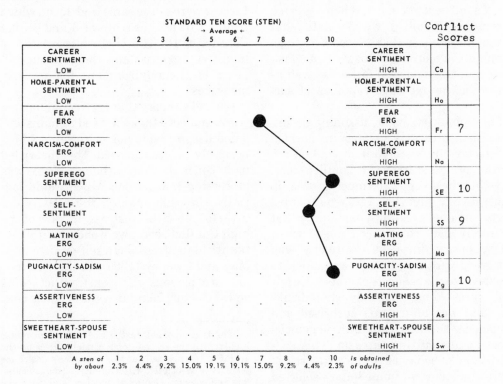

Figure 18.7. Mr. Y: First MAT profile: Conflict scores

been much investigated by Rogers (1951). Rogers demonstrated that substantial outstripping of the realized self by the idealized self leads to lack of personal acceptance. Sweney (1969b) also found that high U scores in the Self-sentiment have implications regarding maladjustment. Therefore, at the very least, this high score showed that Mr. Y's conditions for self-approval were unreasonable, and that he was intensely preoccupied with the need for others to see him as impeccable.

As with Mr. Y's scores on Assertiveness, we surmised that Mr. Y's scores on the Self-sentiment factor reflected an effort to compensate for unrealistic feelings of unworthiness. As with his strong status-seeking aspirations, his need to live up to unrealistic personal standards and public image must have placed him under much stress, from which he eventually sought relief by drinking heavily. Our findings in this area supported our decision to focus on issues of self-esteem in forming the treatment plan. Parenthetically, because Mr. Y's self-sentiment needs had persisted despite his alcoholism, we speculated that it was these needs that caused him to go through the motions of his roles as businessman, husband, and father, as well as maintain the outward trappings of success.

The Pugnacity factor, as its name implies, measures anger at frustration. On this factor Mr. Y scored 9 on U, 3 on I, 8 for the total, and 10 on the Conflict score. Together these suggested much bottled-up anger. In our interview, Mr. Y had denied harboring angry feelings, explaining that he rarely had experienced anger when sober. He saw himself as a "nice guy" who disagreed with no one and was quick to acquiesce to the requests of others. He felt and expressed hostility only when drinking, and was afterwards surprised and ashamed when he recalled his venomous remarks and cutting sarcasm. This self-report told of behavior so characteristic of repression that we immediately selected a repression alternative as the most likely

explanation for the score combination on the pugnacity erg.

It was probable that Mr. Y's drinking alternated between feeding and relieving his anger; i.e., drinking allowed the repressed anger to rise to the surface and be released but it also led to consequences which increased his frustrations, hence his anger. Seen in this light, it seemed clear that, although drinking had a cathartic, problem-solving function, it created new problems by frustrating other needs, especially those in interpersonal relationships. We concluded that learning new and appropriate releases for angry feelings should be incorporated into the treatment plan.

The last score to be interpreted was in the U = I category and was on the Fear factor. This factor is best interpreted as the need for personal security and safety. In contrast to the other U = I score, Mating (discussed earlier in the context of the marriage relationship), this score combination had high equal tension. Both U and I scores were at the same high level, which resulted in a total score of 8 and ceiling Conflict of 10. The U score is related to manifest anxiety* and the I to surveillance of the environment for security measures.

We had a theory that high equal tension scores indicate that the need remains satisfied despite behavior or rewards which normally reduce the need. This theory led us to conclude that, although Mr. Y was processing information which would logically allay his anxiety, the activity did little to relieve his distress. In view of the high Conflict score, we wondered if in actuality his distress was a self-punishment. May and Sweney (1965), in their examination of persons with high Conflict scores on this factor, found in some subjects that

---

*The U component on the Fear factor correlates highly with the second-order Anxiety factor on the 16 P.F. This means that the examinee's desire for security is associated with timidity, suspiciousness, low self-esteem, emotional tension, and poor ego functions.

the denial of reassurance of safety needs came from a belief that personal needs do not deserve to have their needs met. We suspected that Mr. Y's fear resulted from two sources: 1) his appraisal of his predicament and prospects for the future while in a sober state, and 2) lack of tolerance for emotional tension due to having been so accustomed to immediately numbing unpleasant feelings with alcohol. In this sense he had become afraid of fear.

Summary of the First MAT Findings

As stated at the beginning of this section, we viewed this profile to obtain information on the status of Mr. Y's needs, which we divided into two categories: a) those that contributed to or were satisfied by his drinking, and b) those that were abandoned or unrealized as a result of his drinking. After interpreting his scores on all ten factors, we concluded that Mr. Y's drinking was so centrally embedded in his life that all of his major needs were in one way or another involved. Four needs, represented by the Career, Narcissism, Pugnacity, and Self-sentiment factors, fell into the former domain, and five needs, represented by Parental-Home, Fear (security), Superego, Mating (sex), and Sweetheart fell into the latter. With some factors, e.g., Pugnacity, for reasons discussed above, this division implied major contributions to each domain rather than absolute assignments. In virtually every case the insights gained from the MAT scores were confirmed by study of the biographical data and the further revelations in the interview.

Our next step was to discuss these findings with Mr. Y. After Mr. Y had reflected on these findings and given us his associations and insights into them, we were ready to present them, along with other relevant information, in the form of specific psychological problems and incorporate them into the treatment plan.

Documentation of Problems and Formation of Treatment Plan With Reference to MAT Findings

Mr. Y's treatment plan was planned strategically in two steps, both of which involved Mr. Y's active participation. First, problems justifying therapeutic intervention or careful surveillance were identified on the basis of historical information, MAT results, and Mr. Y's further expressed preferences and life goals. These problems were given a descriptive title, assigned a number and listed in the "Problem List," but not put in any priority order.

The second step was to document each of these problems according to the Subjective Data-Objective Data-Assessment Plan (SOAP) format described by Hayes-Roth, Longabaugh, and Ryback (1972), which is widely used in psychiatric facilities and community mental health centers. In this format a problem is presented from the patient's point of view (Subjective Data) and the pertinent clinical findings (Objective Data) stated. An evaluation of the problem follows from a synthesis of these two sets of data (Assessment), and an intervention planned (Plan).

Fragments of Mr. Y's Problem List and Subjective Data-Objective Data-Assessment Plan appear in Tables 18.8 and 18.9. We have not referred to Mr. Y's alcoholism (although we will briefly mention the modalities by which it was treated in the following section) because our purpose here is to focus on those problems directly linked to the MAT results.

Administration of MATS to Monitor Progress Towards Problem-solving

Implementation of the treatment plan delineated above consisted of two phases. The initial phase, which took place in a residential alcoholism treatment facility and lasted six weeks, was designed to 1) assist Mr. Y in obtaining insight into his underlying dynamics; 2) increase his

TABLE 18.8

Mr. Y's Problem List

No.	PROBLEMS	Probable contributor to drinking	Probable consequence of drinking
1.	Apathy. Is apathetic toward major areas of his life, career, spouse, family. If former interest is not substantially restored, may lead to loss of job and dissolution of family.		X
2.	Fear and Anxiety. Responds to present situation with much fear and anxiety, which disrupts general psychological functioning.		X
3.	Deficit of Stress-coping Strategies. Has few strategies for coping with stress. Consequently relies on alcohol for relieving emotional tension.	X	
4.	Guilt. Feels guilt, resulting in self-defeating behavior. Is bent on making overly generous restitution to persons who have been hurt by his drinking. Attempts at restitution may have harmful results for himself.		X
5.	Low Self-esteem. Plagued by low self-esteem originating in childhood. To gain self-esteem, sets himself high standards of achievement, which are unrealistic and overly ambitious. Hence, experiences stress and fails to achieve goals.	X	
6.	Sexual Dysfunction. Has sexual dysfunction which puts further strain on marriage relationship.		X
7.	Anger. Lacks skills for appropriate release of angry feelings. Therefore these feelings are either not expressed or vented in socially undesirable ways.	X	
PROBLEM LIST		NAME: MR. Y	DATE: 6/4/81

TABLE 18.9

Subjective Data-Objective Data Assessment Plan

Problem #1. Apathy
Subjective Data: "All of my energy has been bound up in drinking. The things and people I used to be interested in have faded into the background."
Objective Data: Above statement corroborated by wife. Also, the score combinations on the MAT factors indicate dynamic regression has occurred in areas of career, wife, family, and social status interests.
Assessment: Evidence of typical alcoholic pattern, wherein increasing preoccupation with drinking excludes former interests.
Plan: Former interests in career, wife, family, and perhaps social status may be renewed as interest in drinking recedes. However, marital and family counseling will be instituted for the purposes of mending emotional binds that have ruptured as a consequence of drinking. Vocational counseling will also be implemented to explore career goals, as work-related stress was the original impetus for heavy drinking.

Problem #2. Fear
Subjective Data: "I am overwhelmed with fears. Fear of not being able to stay sober, fear of facing others, fear of not being able to pay my bills, fear of facing reality without a drink. Nothing anyone can say makes me feel better."
Objective Data: Affect is congruent with what is reported. Is not reassured despite efforts of staff. MAT scores suggest strong fear.
Assessment: The patient is very afraid of some specific actualities and possibilities. This apprehension is presently not relieved by reassurance. His fear is exacerbated by the necessity and novelty of dealing with hard facts while in a sober state and by some residual physical withdrawal symptoms.
Plan: With physical detoxification and practice in experiencing his emotions, his fear will grad-

TABLE 18.9 *(cont'd)*

ually be reduced. Nevertheless, he will be counseled to see his fear in perspective and explore what may be the underlying reasons for rejecting reassurance.

Problem #3. Deficit of Stress-coping Strategies
Subjective Data: "Drinking is the only way I know to help me relax."
Objective Data: History reveals drinking was used initially to cope with stress, and the patient is inexperienced with other means of inducing relaxation. The MAT Narcissism scale shows little reliance on physical comforts as relaxation aids.
Assessment: Drinking has been used habitually to cope with stress. The patient will need to use other means to help him rest and relax while maintaining a comfortable sobriety.
Plan: Assist in cultivating effective and harmless strategies for coping with stress.

Problem #4. Guilt
Subjective Data: "I feel extremely guilty. I believe I must do everything in my power to make up for the trouble I caused while drinking, even if I am terribly hurt in the process."
Objective Data: Hangs head and appears genuinely pained when recalls his behavior while drinking. Has talked with other patients about his plans to make amends for his misdeeds. MAT scores also indicate much guilt.
Assessment: Desires to make restitution beyond what is required (i.e., more than the recipients wish and to the extent that it may be harmful to himself). Needs to find more adaptive ways of expiating guilt.
Plan: Counseling to include introduction to the eighth step of Alcoholics Anonymous, which offers practical guidelines for dealing with guilt and making restitution.*

Problem #5. Low Self-esteem
Subjective Data: "Feeling good about myself has always been difficult. I set personal standards I cannot reach. I have worked hard to have other people think I was somebody."
Objective Data: Has insight into his efforts to compensate for low self-esteem. Vestiges of status-seeking still conspicuous, e.g., in designer names prominently displayed on personal items such as wallet. MAT scores point to frustration in area of self-sentiment and to former high social status strivings.
Assessment: Past efforts to gain self-esteem were very stressful and unstable, chiefly because they were overly ambitious and depended on the approval of others.
Plan: Counseling to develop a more realistic self-image and sense of adequacy, and to realize that his low self-esteem is built on childhood perceptions.

Problem #6. Sexual Dysfunction
Subjective Data: "I have lost both interest in sex and the ability to perform adequately."
Objective Data: Patient's self-report is in accord with low MAT scores. Wife has reported that for the past 18 months he has rarely initiated sexual relations, and that when sexual relations have occurred he has not been able to perform adequately.
Assessment: Sexual dysfunction probably results from alcohol abuse.
Plan: Should sobriety not bring a remission of sexual problems, the couple will be referred to a therapist competent in the use of Masters and Johnson's techniques.

Problem #7. Anger
Subjective Data: "My resentments come out only when I drink. On the few occasions that I have had angry feelings when sober, I haven't known who to express them; consequently, I have kept them inside."
Objective Data: Staff's observations of the patient's behavior while in the treatment program suggest that he was not in touch with his anger or that he did not express it when that would have been the most appropriate response. MAT scores indicate that anger was repressed.
Assessment: Repressed angry feelings come to surface and are expressed while drinking. Lacks socially desirable way of expressing anger.
Plan: Teach assertiveness and communication skills to facilitate effective and appropriate expression of angry feelings.

---

*The treatment philosophy of Alcoholics Anonymous is set forth in twelve separate principles called the "Twelve Steps." The eighth step addresses the question of how the recovering alcoholic, without self-punishment, can best redress the difficulties he caused others while drinking.

awareness of alcoholism as a progressive physical and emotional disorder; 3) introduce him to Alcoholics Anonymous as a support system; 4) help him acquire interpersonal and self-management skills; and 5) facilitate healing of the strained relations within his family.

The second phase followed Mr. Y's release from residential treatment and lasted four and a half months, during which he lived at home and resumed his former employment. Here treatment was conducted on an outpatient basis, and consisted of twice-monthly family and marital therapy as well as weekly group therapy sessions which Mr. Y attended with other recovering alcoholics. In addition to these more formal modalities, Mr. Y regularly attended Alcoholics Anonymous meetings, and his wife became actively involved in Alanon. Alanon is a complementary support group to Alcoholics Anonymous, providing peer support for the relatives and friends of recovering or practicing alcoholics. In essence the aim of the second phase was to assist Mr. Y in maintaining a comfortable sobriety, increase mutual understanding and interpersonal skills within the family unit as a whole, as well as help Mr. Y deal with any new problems which might develop.

Several chapters in this book have brought out the importance of using tests not just in a single diagnostic or assessment session but repeated either for reliability or to monitor tactical gains. Cattell's chapter in Karoly and Steffens (1980) on therapeutic change and maintenance describes these procedures. In this case no fewer than four MATs following the initial MAT (discussed above) were administered during a six-month period starting at the conclusion of the first phase and continuing at six-week intervals thereafter. Subsequent MATs were used to monitor Mr. Y's progress in solving the problems that the initial MAT helped identify. *Because it was not possible to discern if the differences among the scores on the profiles reflected maturation*

effects (time and sobriety) or were the result of therapeutic intervention, it can strictly only be said that they indicated changes over the six-month period.

Only the final MAT will be presented here, as space limitations do not permit us to discuss the three that preceded it. This final MAT was administered one week before the conclusion of treatment and just after Mr. Y had celebrated six months of total sobriety.

Interpretation of Final MAT Profile

The purpose of the final MAT interpretation was to assist us in determining how much progress Mr. Y had made towards solving the seven problems enumerated in the Problem List. Our method was to compare each problem in the Problem List with a) its associated MAT scales as they appear in Figure 18.8, and b) clinical assessments which were based on reports provided by Mr. Y and his family, as well as on the observations of the clinical staff. For only one problem, #7, was there a discrepancy between the MAT scales and the clinical assessment; this will be discussed later.

What follows is an analysis of the final status of each problem as it appeared on the Problem List. Each problem is treated separately but with the understanding that the underlying interconnectedness, especially changes in Mr. Y's self-esteem, make this separation more conceptual than real. As before, because we are interested only in what has direct relevance to the MAT scales, Mr. Y's drinking behavior has been excluded from the discussion and documented separately, although in actuality it, along with the sobriety which followed, is central to all changes on the MAT scales.

Problem #1. Apathy. The first MAT alerted us to the fact that, although Mr. Y continued to function in his roles of husband, father, and worker, his interest in these areas (as shown by U scores and to-tal score) had receded with his increasing preoccupation with drinking. At the time he came into treatment, he was in im-minent danger of losing his family and his job. Although it turned out he was some-what ambivalent about the latter, he placed a high priority on restoring his wife and children to their former meaningful places in his life; much of his treatment was directed to this end. His final scores on the Spouse and Parental-Home scales agreed with the opinion of all members of the family that he had reached this goal. As Figure 18.8 shows, both scales had U scores of 7 and I scores of 9, indicating dynamic realization. Also, as we looked at these scores in conjunction with the other scores in the profile, his wife and children emerged as Mr. Y's most important inter-ests.

Mr. Y's interest in his career was more complex, largely because it had been the scapegoat on which he placed much blame

for his stress. Nevertheless, he quite cor-rectly saw that to start over in a different line of work would require a large invest-ment of time and money, which, because of his age and present economic difficul-ties, was impractical. We had suspected from the similarity in score patterns on the Assertiveness and Career scales in the first MAT that Mr. Y's strong social status needs were tied to his career, and that it was such things as jockeying for a better position in the company that created much of the stress he experienced at work. Mr. Y eventually accepted this analysis and was thereby able to separate his en-joyment of the actual tasks involved in his job from the adverse emotional conse-quences of his ambitious strivings. As a consequence, he was able to rethink his career goals, and when he returned to work, it was with the intention of making the most of his technical skills rather than advancing to an executive position in the company. On this last MAT, his score on

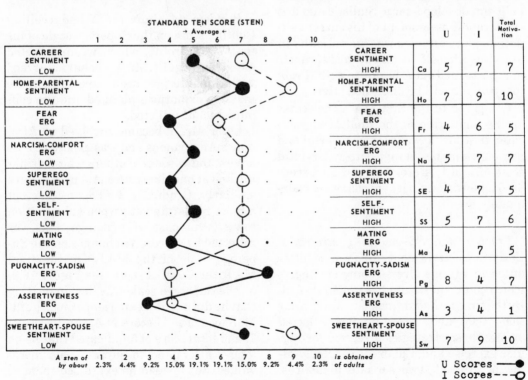

Figure 18.8. Mr. Y: Final MAT profile: U, I, and total scores on all 10 factors

the Career factor was 5 on U and 7 on I, combining for a total score of 7. This total score indicated that his interest in his job had been ignited and was currently realized.

Realizing that Mr. Y was no longer apathetic in his sentiments towards his wife, children, and job, and that all three of these now brought substantial satisfaction to his life, we concluded that this particular problem no longer existed.

Problem #2. Fear and anxiety. The first MAT showed that Mr. Y was experiencing extreme fear and anxiety. We attributed his state to a combination of physiological withdrawal, as he was still in the process of detoxification, and the emotional shock of facing reality without the numbing effects of alcohol. With the passing of time and his increasing sobriety, we expected that Mr. Y's fear would be reduced, and this turned out to be the case. No special intervention was required other than to help him develop a more realistic and less catastrophic assessment of his current situation. More complex was his difficulty in allowing himself to accept reassurance, but this turned out to be due to guilt (Problem #5) and will be discussed later.

Compared to the first MAT, the scores on the Fear scale in the final MAT indicated that Mr. Y was no more fearful and anxious than the average person. His total score of 5, a U score of 4, and an I score of 6 showed security needs were adequately met.

Problem #3. Stress-coping strategies. Early in his treatment, Mr. Y was introduced to various stress-coping strategies which could substitute his use of alcohol. By the time he had returned to work, after some trial and error, he had selected among these strategies a regime for regular exercise and a plan for regularly allowing himself two sensate pleasures: gourmet cooking with his wife on weekends and Jacuzzi baths every night after

work. (Incidentally, we discovered that Mr. Y already possessed Jacuzzi equipment, which—as we could have predicted from the first MAT—had been purchased for the purpose of impressing house guests and therefore had hardly been used at all!)

While none of the MAT scales were designed to pick up the first-mentioned interest, exercise, the Narcissism scale measures the sensuous interests. Mr. Y's scores on this scale on the initial MAT showed that, although his needs in this area were realized, they were low. But for this final MAT, a U score of 5 and an I score of 7 combined to create a high total Narcissism score of 7, indicating high dynamic need and corresponding realization. This finding added weight to our clinical assessment that Mr. Y was finding satisfaction in the tension-reducing strategies that he was currently using. Given the "stress hypothesis of drinking," these satisfactions should go far in replacing his need to drink.

Problem #4. Guilt. Mr. Y had a ceiling Conflict score on the Superego scale of his first MAT profile, which we interpreted as excessive guilt. Mr. Y's behavior agreed with this interpretation, especially in the massive expiations planned and the self-punishment inflicted.

Later Mr. Y became involved in Alcoholics Anonymous and was exposed to the advice and wisdom of others whose drinking had at one time caused them to behave similarly. Gradually, he began to accept a more moderate yet responsible position towards his past wrongdoings. This was reflected by successive changes on the Superego scale of the MAT. On the final MAT, the Conflict score (see Figure 18.9) on the Superego scale was low, indicating that he did not now experience much guilt. Moreover, the U score of 4, the I score of 7, and total score of 5 indicated that he no longer attempted to suppress his moral values, but instead he expressed them so that it was unlikely that his behavior would generate guilt.

Problem #5. Low self-esteem. Mr. Y's low self-esteem was pivotal to much of his difficulties, as his striving for a sense of personal worth created a tension which he relieved through drinking. Drinking, however, only increased his feelings of inadequacy. Much of the therapy, then, focused on raising Mr. Y's self-esteem by increasing his appreciation of personal strength and acceptance of personal limitations. We hoped that this approach would reduce his need to prove his self-worth, ending a vicious cycle.

The scores on two scales on the first MAT alerted us to weaknesses in Mr. Y's self-esteem and to the efforts he made to compensate for these weaknesses. The first was the Self-sentiment scale, which indicated that his strong need to live up to a high personal and public image was frustrated. On the final MAT Self-sentiment scale, however, his U score went down to 5 and his I score went up to 7, indicating dynamic realization of this

need as opposed to frustration. The total score for this scale on the final MAT was reduced to 6, which indicated that he was no longer overly concerned with maintaining an overly high personal and public image. We interpreted these scores as resulting from Mr. Y's greater acceptance of himself and lessened preoccupation with making heavy self-demands in order to impress others with his achievements. Now he could set goals and standards that were more comfortable for himself and were within his reach.

The second scale on the initial MAT that led us to suspect weaknesses in Mr. Y's self-esteem was the Assertiveness scale. On it the score combination pointed to dynamic withdrawals of previously strong social status needs. We reasoned that, as his preoccupation with drinking decreased, these needs might resume their former strengths and again create stress in his life. But our fear was unfounded, as Mr. Y, in forming his treatment plan, said

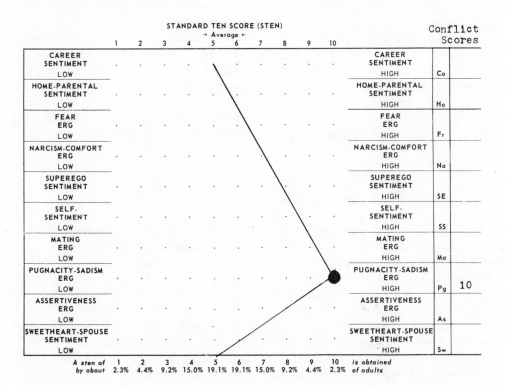

Figure 18.9. Mr. Y: Final MAT profile: Conflict scores

he did not want to strengthen needs that had contributed to his drinking problem. Instead, he wished to revitalize his interest in other areas, such as his family life. The scores on the Assertiveness scale on the final MAT suggested that Mr. Y had been true to his word. The scores were 4 on I, 3 on U, and 1 for the total score. This low, equal-tension score combination and minimum total score suggested that Mr. Y had developed an aversion to status-seeking. Nevertheless, we were concerned about these statistical findings, as they had fallen well below the optimal level required for adequate functioning in the business world. In our final counseling, we suggested to Mr. Y that he return to us at a later date to explore this matter if, indeed, he found himself unable to deal with business concerns.

Problem #6. Sexual dysfunction. Mr. Y's sexual dysfunction seemed to be a result of his alcohol abuse. As with his fearfulness, we supposed that it might disappear as a function of his sobriety, and according to Mr. Y, this is what happened.

Initially, the total score and the score combination on the sexual (Mating) scale were so low as to suggest impairment in sexual functioning. Now, on the final MAT, the total score was within normal range, and the U score of 4 and I score of 5 indicated an average amount of dynamic realization.

Problem #7. Repression and inappropriate release of angry feelings. As noted earlier, although all other scores on the final MAT agreed with our clinical assessments, those on the Pugnacity scale shifted but showed some peculiarities. At the beginning of treatment, repression and the resulting inappropriate release of anger had been identified as a problem; therefore, a treatment goal was set for Mr. Y to learn to acknowledge and appropriately express angry feelings. Later Mr. Y, his family, and the clinical staff all agreed

that this goal had been accomplished, as he was freely using the communication strategies he had been taught in therapy. It was a bit disappointing to find that, less evident than this change in behavior, the final scores on the Pugnacity scale were little less than those on the first MAT. On the first MAT the scores on the Pugnacity scale were 9 on U, 3 on I, 8 on the total score and 10 on the Conflict score, and on this final MAT they were 8 on U, 4 on I, and 7 on the total score. Despite the small changes on the U, I, and total scores, the Conflict score remained at ceiling level. This suggested that strong angry feelings were still being repressed. We thus reasoned that the anger must relate to some unresolved business from the past. We remembered that Mr. Y had been physically and emotionally abused by his father. In such situations, fear prohibits children from expressing angry feelings that arise from the trauma, and the feelings tend to persist into adulthood as frozen resentments. The probability that angry feelings stemming from Mr. Y's childhood still existed had not been addressed in therapy. Consequently, we recommended that Mr. Y attend a special workshop designed to help people who have had these unfortunate childhood experiences. This workshop would enable Mr. Y to come to a greater acceptance of his past and help him to forgive his father.

Summary of MAT findings

Whereas the score combinations on the first MAT indicated dynamic withdrawal for the Career, Home, and Spouse factors and conflict on the Superego and Self-sentiment factors, the final MAT indicated that interest had been restored and conflict resolved. There were two score combinations on the first MAT that suggested equal tension. These were on the Mating and Fear factors, but had different implications because of the different levels of the scores. The scores were low on the former, indicating that Mr. Y's sexual interest was almost extinguished. On the latter, the scores were high, which indicated that he had strong fears which persisted even in the face of reassurance. Now, the scores on the final MAT pointed to a restoration to healthy sexual functioning and an adequate gratification of security needs.

On the first MAT, the only score combination indicative of dynamic realization was on the Narcissism factor. However, the scores had been so low as to suggest that his ability to use creature comforts for stress-reducing purposes was undeveloped, hence a potential alternative to alcohol-induced relaxation was not available. Consequently, on the final MAT we were happy to find that his scores on the Narcissism factor, while still indicating dynamic realization, had increased to average levels.

The difference between the first and final MAT scores on the eight factors mentioned in the two preceding paragraphs suggested that Mr. Y had progressed from a person whose life afforded him barely any pleasures or satisfactions in self or others to someone whose needs on a variety of fronts were adequately met, and who was self-confident and deeply involved in his career and intimate relationships.

There remained on the final MAT two score combinations that caused us concern. The scores in the Assertiveness factor on the first MAT had indicated dynamic withdrawal but now the high I score had fallen into the low range, showing that even the habit formation had collapsed. The result was an equal tension score and total score of just 1. We were concerned that this had fallen well below the optimal level for functioning effectively in the business world. The Pugnacity factor scores which indicated repressed anger remained essentially unchanged. This finding we interpreted as representing some old residual feelings from childhood and

so we suggested appropriate experiences to uncover and resolve them.

Follow-Up

We were concerned by two score combinations on the final MAT. One was on Pugnacity, which we eventually interpreted as anger having to do with past rather than present happenings. We directed Mr. Y to attend a workshop designed specifically to help people resolve feelings of this sort. Later, Mr. Y stopped by our office to tell us about his experience in the workshop, which confirmed our interpretation.

The other score combination was on Assertiveness and indicated that Mr. Y's need for social status was very low. We expected that the attitudes that would accompany such a low score would involve an actual avoidance of competition and disinterest in many of the rewards that normally motivate people in the business world. This turned out to be the case. Fortunately, these attitudes did not matter as they were so peripheral to his new position.

We are happy to report that Mr. Y's total sobriety has continued through the time of the present writing. Moreover, he appears comfortable in his sobriety, as he reports that he has found substitutes for his former use of alcohol as a tension reducer, is less demanding on himself, and has found many new satisfactions antithetical to drinking, such as the peer support of his AA group.

SUMMARY

This chapter concentrates on individual clinical cases. In the last decade tests of unitary source traits have become available spanning all three modalities — personality, temperament, ability and motivation—and much progress is possible when more than one modality is covered. In clinical work personality and motivation factors are most important, and their value in psychotherapy is illustrated here by intensive study of individual cases.

The 16 P.F., which is the test of choice when no real pathology is present, illustrated the nature of the interactions between a husband and a wife. Follow-up information further illustrated the meaning of the measurements.

The Clinical Analysis Questionnaire (CAQ) extends the 16 P.F. by 12 pathological dimensions (factored from items as in the MMPI, various depression scales, etc.). Its use is illustrated in conjunction with the clinical history of a 32-year-old woman suffering from a schizophrenic disorder.

A major increment in the power of clinical analysis has come about through the MAT, measuring the main ergic tensions and unitary sentiment investments. (Unlike the TAT it rests on more than one objective device and is reliably, conspectively scorable.)

The description given elsewhere (Chapter 13) of the difference of I (integrated and U (unintegrated) components in motivation is developed further in the light of clinical cases examined in life situations, and a new tabular schema for interpreting relations between U and I scores is presented.

A documentation of problems as related to MAT scores is presented, and it is shown how the formation of a treatment plan can be guided by such test data. The value of objective motivation measurement in monitoring therapy and understanding readjustments is illustrated by retest on a clinical case.

Although not handled in the above parts of this chapter it is useful to conclude here with a brief perspective on the relevance of the objective measurement of strengths of ergic tensions and of the main sem structures to some current develop-

ments in therapy, such as regression and redecision therapies.

Except by the use of MAT in P-technique (Birkett & Cattell, 1978), no means have been found to make a positive, quantitative assessment of the roots of a particular symptom in the client's dynamic structure. The usual procedure is to enter with the MAT to find the profile of need strengths and the areas of conflict in terms of ergs and sems. After that guidance, the linking of the dynamic problem with particulars in the life situation and biography has to proceed by other methods (free association, TAT, hypnosis, etc.).

An exploration and mobilization of the client's dynamic resources will often bring about the dispersal of a symptom or a powerful and enduring choice of a new course of behavior. The scientific basis for such practice exists in the models of the dynamic calculus (see Chapter 13). Ideally, this calls for P-technique, but the evaluation of choices can also be made with R-technique common-trait formulae. When psychological practice has found the behavioral indices for two courses of action, p and r, the first a "problem," the second a reconsidered desirable alternative, opting in favor of the latter calls for making the terms in r larger in total than those in p.

$$p_i = b_{p1}D_{1i} + b_{p2}D_{2i} + \ldots + b_{pn}D_{ni}$$

$$r_i = b_{r1}D_{1i} + b_{r2}D_{2i} + \ldots b_{rn}D_{ni} \qquad (18\text{-}1)$$

The b values belong in a clinician's handbook, the D values for the n dynamic structures are given by the MAT (n there equals 10) for the individual i. The formula from the dynamic calculus, i.e., the comparison of p and r above for various alternatives provides insight into what dynamic source traits are most advantageously stimulated and what the chances of success are for the given client for a given alternative.

CHAPTER 19

Industrial and Vocational Selection

Charles Noty

A BRIEF HISTORY OF TESTS USED IN INDUSTRIAL/APPLIED SETTINGS

Before reviewing 3000 years of testing history, it will be instructive to define "tests" 1) as they were constructed and used before World War II (and in too many cases after that time) and 2) as used in terms of structure. In the case of the former, we refer to the dictionary definition of "instruments that present a series of questions or problems designed to determine ability, knowledge or intelligence." For a structured test we repeat the definition given in earlier chapters: For our purposes, structural tests to be used in applied/industrial settings are those that have been constructed on a sound theoretical/structural framework. They are theoretical-concept-centered. They are based on an objective analysis of underlying dimensions or traits.

It follows that such a test as used in industry can and should be based on a structural map of human behavior. The requirement of the skill needed by a blueprint drafter to visualize material in three dimensions comes readily to mind. If intelligence is of concern, one could use sep-arate scores for *fluid, g_f* and *crystallized, g_c,* intelligence and know what these scores would predict, e.g., different life courses, susceptibility to brain damage, and achievement in learning different types of tasks. In the case of the drafter, a test based on "three-dimensional ability" can be constructed by the first step of a thorough-going analysis of the job—what the drafter actually does on a daily basis. This can be observed and rated (see description of what is necessary for adequate ratings in Cattell, 1957c, 1971a) before the test items are constructed. Once the job analysis is complete, items can be written or samples of job behaviors constructed that accurately portray the important aspects of the work to be performed.

The selection of personnel has been the province of industrial/organizational psychology since Walter Dill Scott (about 1903) and Hugo Munsterberg (1913) established this specialty. Psychologists and psychometrists did not invent tests; both Gideon and Plato advocated the use of aptitude tests centuries before such "measurement specialists" as Galton and J. McKeen Cattell (1903). Plato was espe-

425

cially concerned with leadership selection in both military and governmental contexts and postulated some of the concepts used in "trait" theory investigated by leadership researchers in the period 1920-1960. In the China of 1000 B.C., mandarins frequently selected civil service personnel by using grading systems that were the forerunner of today's performance appraisal systems and assessment centers. They apparently used a nine-point scale to compare and contrast the personal qualifications of potential government employees. About a decade before J. Cattell (1903) published his research, Wundt (1896) was one of the first to study psychological phenomena and then to develop and classify them into various "mental" tests.

Around 1900, Alfred Binet and Charles Spearman broke ranks with established thought on psychoanalytic and other speculations about personality and intelligence. Each in his own separate but brilliant way was a pioneer in the measurement and specification of underlying dimensions of intelligence. The interested reader is referred to Spearman (1904) for more information on scientific analysis of the concept. As indicated by Cattell (1961a), Spearman's contribution to the field of intelligence testing was his asking of the fundamental question, "Could a person be a genius in mathematics, a perfect fool at expressing himself in writing and mediocre in handling sensitive, social situations?" (For interesting sidelights on these two seminal thinkers and how they came to choose their careers, see Cattell, 1957a).

Binet (Binet & Simon, 1905) had studied pathology and subnormal intelligence as well as microbiology before embarking, at the request of the French government, on the construction of the first intelligence tests. He had been asked by Parisian school authorities to clarify the diagnosis of irremediable forms of backwardness in school children.

Binet started his investigation of the ability exemplified by the current intel-

ligence test by an intensive study of the mental capacities of his own two children. His main purpose was to devise a means of measuring the level of general intelligence possessed by any particular child as by "a metric scale of intelligence." The rationale of his procedure ultimately turned out to be one of sampling a person's ability in all directions by means of ingenious and carefully graded tests of comprehension, memory, judgment, ability to detect absurdities, capacity to resist foolish suggestions, cleverness, and penetration. Although this is the first known systematic realization of standardized tests of intelligence (percentiles and normative tables), the idea of intelligence tests was not new. As indicated previously, Plato and Gideon had advocated the use of tests in the selection of what would today be termed civil service workers.

Interestingly enough, Binet seemed to have both a univariate and multivariate conception of the concept of intelligence. While he looked at various components, he was also an advocate of the view that intelligence is some *one* thing. Binet in one sense was the first individual to use structured psychological tests. Binet introduced his tests to the world in 1904. It was in this same year that Spearman published his paper "General Intelligence, Objectively Determined and Measured." These two sources of scientific endeavor, the practical contribution by Binet and the deeply theoretical and mathematical contribution by Spearman, later fused in a common, harmonious stream of research.

The original Binet test was translated and extensively revised in the early 1900s by Lewis Terman (and his students) of Stanford University. The resulting test, the Stanford-Binet, has now been in use for more than 70 years and has undergone several major revisions and renormings. A complete history of these revisions is found in Terman and Merrill (1960, 1973). The Stanford-Binet and the Wechsler Adult Intelligence Scale (Wechsler, 1958; Matarazzo, 1972) have been used primarily in educational and clinical settings, even though the validity evidence for both still needs further development. Intelligence (or learning ability as one definition) has been used in industrial settings; the first reported large-scale study of intelligence in occupations was that of Cattell (1934) as depicted in Figure 19.1. Cattell (1971a) later updated this study and added other researches, as shown in Table 19.1 below.

If tests could be used to predict learning ability of school children, why not use them to predict the same ability in an industrial setting? The first textbook in the field of industrial psychology attempted to answer this question. Munsterberg (1913) devoted considerable time and attention to the use of tests for selection,

particularly of municipal railway employees, and their later placement on the job. Just ten years later, Freyd (1923) published a three-part article which laid out a thorough procedure for test construction, validation, and implementation. This procedure is as applicable today as it was some 60 years ago. In his extensive, three-installment journal article, he outlined in detail the principles and practices of "measurement and vocational selection." Current-day practitioners would do well to read this three-part article because not a great deal of significance in terms of research design has happened since then. We have, of course, had the advent of the computer and the use of factored and structured tests and the use of multiple-correlational techniques. We have also

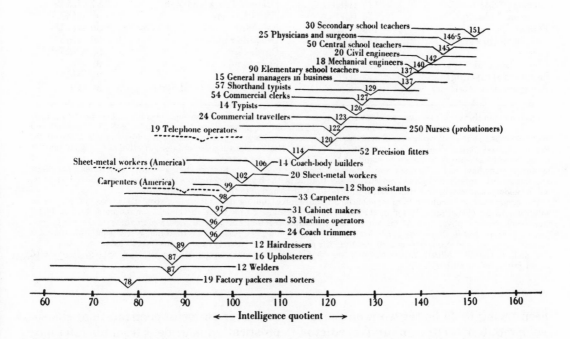

Each line represents the scatter of the middle 50 per cent in that occupation. The position of the median is indicated by a   and a figure above it. For comparison of American results three occupations have been taken at random from Fryer's lists (1922) and represented alongside the same group here by dotted lines. In these the I.Q.s have been calculated from the Army Alpha Scores by the method described in this research. The smaller American scatter (real or apparent) is as evident in each occupation as in the total population distribution.

Figure 19.1. Intelligence levels in various occupations

TABLE 19.1
Distribution of Intelligence in Occupations

Occupation	Mean	Occupation	Mean
Professors and Researchers	134 (C1)	Salesmen	114 (H&H)
Professors and Researchers	131 (C2)	Psychiatric Aides	111 (C&S)
Physicians and Surgeons	128 (C1)	Electricians	109 (H&H)
Lawyers	128 (H&H)	Policemen	108 (C)
Engineers (Civil and Mechanical)	125 (C1)	Fitters (Precision)	108 (C1)
		Fitters	98 (H&W)
School Teachers	123 (C)	Mechanics	106 (H&H)
School Teachers	123 (H&H)	Machine Operators	105 (H&H)
School Teachers	121 (H&W)	Store Managers	103 (C)
General Managers in Business	122 (C)	Shopkeepers	103 (H&W)
Educational Administrators	122 (C)	Upholsterers	103 (H&H)
Pharmacists	120 (H&H)	Butchers	103 (H&H)
Accountants	119 (C)	Welders	102 (H&H)
Accountants	128 (H&H)	Sheet Metal Workers	100 (C)
Nurses	119 (C1)	Sheet Metal Workers	108 (H&H)
Stenographers	118 (C)	Sheet Metal Workers	76 (F)
Stenographers	121 (H&H)	Warehouse Men	98 (H&W)
Efficiency (Time Engineer) Specialists	118 (C)	Carpenters and Cabinet Makers	97 (C)
Senior Clerks	118 (C)	Carpenters, Construction	102 (H&H)
Managers, Production	118 (H&H)	Machine Operators	97 (C)
Managers, Miscellaneous	116 (H&H)	Cooks and Bakers	97 (H&H)
Cashiers	116 (H&H)	Small Farmers	96 (C)
Airmen (USAF)	115 (H&H)	Farmers	93 (H&H)
Foremen (Industry)	114 (C)	Drivers, Truck and Van	97 (H&W)
Foremen	109 (H&H)	Truck Drivers	96 (H&H)
Telephone Operators	112 (C)	Laborers	96 (H&H)
Clerks	112 (C)	Unskilled Laborers	90 (H&W)
Clerks, General	118 (H&H)	Gardeners	95 (H&W)
Salesmen (Traveling)	112 (C)	Farmhands	92 (C)
Salesmen (Door-to-Door)	108 (C)	Miners	91 (H&H)
		Factory Packers and Sorters	85 (C)

The figures in this table are from samples varying in size from some thousands to a couple of dozen, but centering on about 100. They are taken largely from the studies by Fryer (1922), Cattell (1934), Harrell and Harrell (1945), Himmelweit and Whitfield (1949), and some occupational analyses by the present writer, using 16 P.F. Factor B scores, from the Institute for Personality and Ability Testing. The initials C_1, C_2, F, H&H, H&W, indicate these origins. An attempt has been made to bring the various sources to the same standard score I.Q., namely, a sigma of 16 points, and in so doing, a number of approximations have had to be made which makes it pointless to calculate to more than a whole number mean I.Q. These are, thus, results intended to give perspective rather than to be the basis of a definitive occupational list, which, hopefully, will be undertaken soon by institutions with sufficient resources and in terms of culture-fair tests.

The sigmas may be calculated from some of the original sources, but for illustration it is about 12 for accountants, 16 for salesmen, 15 for electricians, 16 for mechanics, 19 for carpenters, 20 for truck drivers, 12 for teachers, 13 and 14 for stenographers, 9 for physicians, 14 for nurses, and practically reaching the general population value (16) for carpenters, factory workers, and laborers. The general tendency is for selection to a lesser value than that of the population (perhaps actually about ⅔), and this is particularly potent in the professions, but scarcely exists in the less skilled occupations.

From R. B. Cattell, *Abilities: Their Structure, Growth & Action*. Boston: Houghton Mifflin, 1971, pp. 481-482. Reproduced by permission of the author.

been trying to do better work on the development of criterion and predictor measures. We have also been fighting battles about the applicability and desirability of looking at and evaluating such constructs as moderator and suppressor variables and differential validity.

Freyd (1923) included a thorough procedure for text construction, validation, and later on for implementation. His sophistication is evident from his reference to such things as cost-effectiveness and deciding upon the department in which selection is to be attempted, job/task analysis as a predecessor both to test and criterion development, and the potential usefulness as predictors of work samples and simulations. Further, he insisted on periodic rechecks of predictive validity —using, for example, the 1920s version of foldback coefficients and multiple discriminant results. Rechecking, he said, should be accomplished at yearly intervals. It is instructive to look at how Freyd thought tests could be used in personnel selection. He had ten steps:

1) Job or task analysis;
2) Developing a criterion measurement;
3) Selecting a sample of individuals for the testing program;
4) Developing a list of the abilities or criteria required for success;
5) Developing or selecting appropriate tests and/or measuring instruments;
6) Administration of tests under carefully controlled conditions;
7) Statistical analysis of test results;
8) Combination of predictors into a battery or other determination of test utility (a precursor of multiple correlation);
9) Development of utility tables, although Freyd would have said, "comparing the predictive accuracy of tests with those of the methods of selection—interviews, etc.—already in use" (modern cost/benefit analysis); and
10) Installation of the new testing program.

A complete explication of these steps and analysis of Freyd's approach is contained in Guion (1976), in Thorndike (1982), in Siegel and Lane (1982) and in standard textbooks on industrial psychology. However, the original article is still a good paradigm.

CURRENT DEVELOPMENTS AND APA AND IAAP POSITION STATEMENTS

In the history of industrial psychological testing 1982 was a significant year. Two events in particular occurred which will have a dramatic impact on the shape of testing programs for the rest of the decade. The first was the appearance of the 5th edition of *Psychological Testing* (Anastasi, 1981). It covers much familiar ground but also new material on ethical/moral considerations. Equal employment opportunity implications clarify some of the debate on "test fairness." The second was a special issue devoted to psychological testing published by the International Association of Applied Psychology. In their journal the IAAP reported on the status of psychological tests in Europe (IAAP, 1982). In this issue McReynolds (1981) was not sanguine about the future of tests in applied situations due to public outcries about test fairness, discrimination, and the "truth in testing movement" advocated by Ralph Nader and others. He advocated a return to "ideographic" methods—the intensive study of autobiographies (DeWaele & Harré, 1979) and perhaps also to an increased application of statistical analysis to single individuals. The former method may be too "clinical" for some practitioners and not much based on norms, guidelines, means, and metrics, and the latter may be inaccessible to the individual practitioner.

However, the advent of distributed data processing (mini-computers) and especially of equipment that provides for interactive psychological testing in the school or industrial office will ameliorate this problem within the next two to five years. The present author has seen mini-computer equipment installations that have cost in the neighborhood of $20,000 to $50,000. However, more recent advances in silicon chip technology will eventually halve this capital equipment figure. This will help the practitioner in administering a great many instruments in a particular situation. At the same time such equipment will provide the clinician or the industrial psychologist with immediate scoring and feedback options. Currently, such questionnaires as the MMPI and similar "clinical" instruments have been adapted for such use. Shortly, it should be possible, for example, to administer a comprehensive battery of ability, personality, interest, and vocational measures to a person applying for a position as a programmer or an individual seeking life/career guidance. An instantaneous comparison and prediction equation can then be made between the individual's test results and the norms for the particular occupation in which there is interest.

It would be advantageous to the practitioner to have the SCII, the 16 P.F., the EAS series, and DAT or PCT and perhaps other measures such as the Watson-Glaser and Allport-Vernon presented to a client in a single testing session. During a counseling interview the client can be presented with suitable feedback from computer printouts which not only provide a qualitative interpretation but also a statistical analysis of the client in terms of a number of reference populations with simultaneous correction of scores for motivational distortion!

A third event is expected to have a significant influence in the 1980s. This is the publication by the American Psychological Association of a special issue (APA, 1981) on psychological testing. In thought provoking articles, it is shown that the future of employment testing and especially the use of "cognitive" measures may not be as clouded as it had been in the 1960s and 1970s (Tenopyr, 1981; Schmidt & Hunter, 1981). Schmidt and Hunter made three telling points: 1) professionally developed cognitive ability tests (the types used in most selection decisions) are valid predictors of performance on the job and for training for jobs; 2) cognitive ability tests are equally valid for minority and majority applicants; 3) the proper use of cognitive ability tests for selection can produce large labor-cost savings ranging from $18 million for a large city police department to $16 billion for a large employer such as the federal government. The interested reader is referred to this special issue as well as to the IAAP issue (1982) for a more complete discussion of the substantive, methodological, and utility issues involved.

The results referred to by Schmidt and Hunter (1981) and those of classical studies reviewed by Ghiselli (1963) may have underestimated the predictive power of cognitive tests in general. These results may have been attenuated not only because of unreliability of predictor problems, but also because the tests used in the 1940-1960 period on which Ghiselli based his research were typically unstructured or not factorially pure. The median validities of about .25 to .40 reported by Ghiselli were not corrected for errors due to criterion and predictor problems. It should be noted that test research projects have typically been done with groups of incumbents in various positions. Some restriction of range is therefore normal. Guilford (1965, pp. 341-345) discusses this problem at length, shows dramatic but real examples of how the coefficient is lowered when variability is restricted (as is the case when working with preselected samples), and presents correction formulas. An average validity coefficient, e.g., of .20, might more nearly have reached .50 if unselected samples had been available for study. The current practice in reporting results of validation studies in industrial situations is to report both obtained and corrected r's as well as complete characteristics of the sample(s) studied in a technical appendix.

Novick (1982) discussed the future of psychological testing with special reference to admissions testing and the role of tests in the evaluation of various types of educational programs. He noted that the area of testing in which there seems to be considerable controversy is that of employment. He indicated that the use of tests in this situation would probably increase in the 1980s as various court jurisdictions tend to emphasize the avoidance of discrimination. He indicated that the more important issues of technical rather than social or political interference need to be resolved if employment testing is to be effective and nondiscriminatory. By this he meant that our current definitions of empirical, content, and construct validation seem out of date with respect to personnel selection. If we refer to Chapters 1, 2, and 3 of the current volume and take a careful look at definitions of a structured psychological test, we will see that major steps in this direction have already been taken by Cattell.

In a similar vein, and in a more general discussion of testing in the educational domain, Linn (1982) reported on recent research in the area of the invalidity of tests for minority group members. He was particularly concerned with the concepts of differential validity and differential prediction. After considering about a dozen studies, he concluded that there were essentially no differences in predictions based on minority and majority group data.

In a cogent study Schmidt and Hunter (1981) presented evidence that cognitive ability tests of the kind generally used in personnel selection are valid predictors of successful performance of all types of jobs in all types of settings. They presented a great deal of evidence countering widely held reservations about suitability of cognitive ability tests for employee selection—selection that was made on the basis of supposed limited applicability, bias, and ultimate contribution to workforce productivity.

Schmidt and Hunter (1981) present a strongly worded argument for greater analysis (more properly, meta-analysis) of published test validity studies over the last few years, rather than for more research in the area. They indicate that more attention should be paid to "making sense" out of many thousands of studies accumulated over the past 50 years. Unfortunately, most of these studies did not use structured tests and it will be necessary to do so before validity generalization procedures can have their full statistical power.

As we shall see later in this chapter, the results of research studies conducted by the present author, as well as by other researchers, indicate that the "state of the art" in current employment and selection testing research does answer some of these research questions. These studies point out the utility of using structured psychological testing—i.e., those tests that measure a particular job domain based on previous research. This could be a test of typing or addition, subtraction, multiplication or division, or general verbal or quantitative skills. As more carefully and completely delineated in Chapters 11 and 12, tests are not (and should not be) the sole criterion for making any kind of selection or evaluation decision. Unfortunately, this has happened in many situations because of the preciseness of test scores and their resultant scientific "look." In the clinical area, for example, interviews, family history, work experience, and other types of data are integrated with clinical test results before making any type of judgment or evaluation. The same holds true in the employment situation. Typically, in most well-organized selection programs the actual use of tests occurs as a fourth or fifth step in any selection process. The procedure, for example, for selection of typists in a large bank involves the following steps:

1) Careful description of duties and responsibilities for the position of typist and comparing and relating it to the standard description in *The Dictionary of Occupational Titles*;
2) Comprehensive recruiting to establish a large pool of candidates for a particular position;
3) Preliminary screening interviews;
4) Additional "depth" and job knowledge interviews;
5) Use of standardized ability tests;
6) Reference checks on previous employment;
7) Physical examination procedures; and
8) Integration of all of the data on each applicant combined into a decision table.

Unfortunately, little is known about the reliability and validity of reference checking, interviewing, and physical examination procedures. An extensive review (Reilly & Chao, 1982) of published and unpublished studies of interview, reference checking, and other selection devices indicated very low validities (correlations of .13-.19). In using tests we have become somewhat more scientific. We can assign appropriate values to the predictive power of our tests.

As we shall see later in the chapter, correlations of .60 to .80 can be achieved using tests as a sole criterion of prediction. This is possible when we have a) excellent predictors of job behavior such as productivity records and b) structured or "factorially pure" measures of cognitive ability or aptitude, intelligence, and personality.

In the same way that personality test instruments are structurally and/or functionally constructed by discovering structural maps of human behavior, aptitude and ability measures used in the industrial and selection situation need also to have a criterion reference. While success as a typist primarily depends upon ability to type, there are additional considerations of motivation, learning, type of supervision received, and organizational dynamics. However, in any case, the test constructed to measure typing ability is rather straightforward. One looks for the typical quantity and quality measures of proficiency in such work and then attempts to develop a set of test items, or job sample, that will measure these proficiencies. The structural map of human behavior in this case is the person's actual ability to produce a page of typewritten copy. While this is not so straightforward in predicting the success of a supervisor, executive, or salesperson, the same principle tends to apply. As has been pointed out in Chapter 1, there are too many *ad hoc* tests which have been constructed without any reference to an underlying theoretical basis. In this chapter we will take a look at a half dozen or so of the

perhaps 30 or 40 most carefully constructed cognitive tests using the definitions of structure and function more fully set out earlier. We will also examine several studies which have used structured personality instruments.

Some 25 years ago Cattell (1957a) made a plea for better training of undergraduate, as well as graduate, students in the psychological disciplines in the areas of multivariate statistical methods. He challenged university psychology departments to incorporate more statistical methodology into the curriculum, particularly those branches dealing with multivariate techniques and methods. While there has been some progress in this direction, there are still many "traditional" teaching faculties who are wedded to the "tried and tested" univariate experimental designs and methods. Is it advisable to ask each undergraduate student in psychology to complete one or two semesters of calculus? This is a current requirement in collegiate schools of business that are accredited by the National Accrediting Association for Business. The level of sophistication that such courses help to produce in terms of logical thinking and analytical ability is most helpful to researchers when they approach the sometimes formidable techniques involved in cluster and factor analysis, multivariate analysis of variance and covariance, multiple correlation, multiple discriminant analysis and similar methods. Should not the student preparing for a career in industrial-organizational psychology be able to use multivariate techniques or at least be familiar enough with these kinds of techniques to be able to interpret computer printouts from various statistical packages such as SPSS, BioMED, and similar programs?

Subsequent to the appeal made by Cattell (1957a) for better trained researchers and graduate students in psychology, the volume *Handbook of Multivariate Experimental Psychology* (Cattell, 1966b) appeared. It is interesting to note the high level technical excellence of this book and in particular the chapter prepared by Sells (1966) on Industrial and Military Personnel Psychology. In a thoughtful review of several hundred studies which attempted to predict success in various types of industrial and military positions, he was quite impressed with the contribution of multivariate technology to the selection and placement decisions made in many large organizations. He was especially impressed by the facts that: 1) factor analysis is now a widely applied technique used in evaluating and describing occupations in various civil and military fields; 2) multivariate concepts and methods have made and are making significant contributions to solving industrial and military problems; 3) evaluating suitability for the job can be conceived either as adjustment, i.e., fitting the profile of the typical person already in the job, or as effectiveness, i.e., scoring high on a criterion of efficiency. The former method proceeds by discriminatory function technique, using perhaps the profile similarity index or pattern analysis, and the latter method proceeds by multiple regression most effectively based on factor measures; and 4) multiple discriminant functions have come into wide use both to define types of individuals and to provide a basis for personnel assignment.

PRACTICAL EXAMPLES OF THE USE OF STRUCTURED TESTS

In Part I of this volume a theoretical presentation was made of the general use of structured psychological tests. Much attention was paid to general matters of reliability and validity—consistency and dependability on the one hand, and predictive possibilities on the other. Other theoretical treatments of the general problems involved in the selection of appropriate psychological tests for selection and placement decisions will be found in Anastasi (1981), Gilmer and Deci (1977),

McCormick and Ilgen (1980), and Kerr (1966). A number of situational factors in the selection process have been covered in detail by Crane (1979). These factors involve the legal and organizational factors involved in sex discrimination, accommodation of religious preferences, affirmative action for the handicapped, and reverse discrimination problems. A comprehensive treatment of practical considerations involved in legal and ethical use of tests is contained in Miner and Miner (1978). The interested reader is referred to these texts and to Dunnette (1976) for a complete discussion of the logic, steps involved, and legal ramifications in the use of occupational testing procedures. As is well known (Ghiselli, 1973), the general use of aptitude tests over the past half century has typically resulted in modest correlations of predictor variables with actual on-the-job performance. A similar case can be made for "intelligence" tests, as documented by Matarazzo (1972). In the realm of personality, the definitive work of Cattell, Eber, and Tatsuoka (1970) and of Guilford and Zimmerman (1949) is well known. We propose to look at the several kinds of test instruments, first as used singly and then in combination, to determine their efficacy. We will examine practical examples of tests used in applied situations with appropriate consideration to the factors of reliability, validity, utility, and cost. We had previously (Table 19.1, Figure 19.1) looked at aptitude measures as predictors. Both published and unpublished studies will be examined.

Document Verifiers

Could aptitude and personality tests predict performance for this group? The general description of the duties involved in this position includes the verification of the filing of documents, the verification of stop payment orders on checks, the completion of reports, the processing of check accounting and stop payment procedures, and debiting and credit verification in check processing areas.

A number of tests were "tried out" in a pilot study and three tests were used in the final analysis. These tests were the Press Test of Baehr, Corsini and Rank, published by the Human Resources Center at the Univerity of Chicago, the Minnesota Clerical Test, published by The Psychological Corporation, and the Short Employment Test (SET), also published by The Psychological Corporation. The tests were administered to a group of one hundred currently employed document verifiers, and criterion data on quality and quantity of work were collected.

As the study progressed and as inspection of the correlation matrices indicated, it was determined that the job performance of document verifiers could be predicted by using a single score—the SET numerical test score. Accordingly, the other predictors originally included in the study were not utilized. The analysis of the SET numerical test predictor yielded a validity coefficient of .397 significant of the .003 level. The criterion was a work output measure.

Sales Representatives

In a study to determine the effectiveness of a measure of "sales aptitudes," the Sales Attitudes Checklist (Gekoski & Schwartz, 1960) was administered to a group of 87 currently employed personnel for a manufacturer and distributor of business forms. The products included carbon interleaved forms typically used in computer printing devices, as well as sales books, sales tags, and letterheads and envelopes used by commercial and institutional organizations. The criterion was the amount of sales in a particular year combined with an index of other profitability. The predictor measurement correlated .41 with the criterion index. This is a moderately positive correlation coefficient, but, given the fact that the test in-

strument takes 15 minutes to administer and about 15 seconds to score, shows the kind of power a relatively short instrument can have in making selection decisions. In a later study using the same group of sales personnel referred to above, one additional instrument was added. This was the Thurstone Test of Mental Alertness (Thurstone, 1960). This test takes approximately 25 minutes to administer and about 30 seconds to score. The test by itself (total score) had a predictor validity of .34 with the criterion indicated above. However, when the two tests were combined into a small battery, the predictive power of the tests jointly was increased to .56.

Krug (1982) developed a model and screening procedure for identifying "high risk" individuals in nuclear plant environments. This study examined the problem of conducting a criterion-related validity study and concluded that this was not feasible. Obviously, incidents such as sabotage and inability to handle nuclear plant problems in emergency cases would be incidents of critical performance. But this could not be a traditional criterion measure, since these incidents cannot normally be allowed to happen. The study concluded that using the 16 P.F. (Cattell & Cattell, 1975), the Motivation Analysis Test (Cattell, 1964c), and the Clinical Analysis Questionnaire (Cattell & Cattell, 1975) would provide components for a security assessment and screening model. The three questionnaires contain 54 scales, 29 of which were represented in the final Screening Index. Various combinations of scoring patterns on the 16 P.F. (personality), CAQ (clinical manifestations of aberrant behavior), and the MAT (motivation and drive) were refined into a predictive index. The final index was validated using construct validity methods. Further evidence of validity was determined by the index's ability to identify "normal" as opposed to "aberrant" individuals.

Several variables other than aptitude are operative in performance, and so it is ordinarily not a reasonable situation to expect a high correlation between any one aptitude test and any valid measure of job success. However, it is possible, where jobs are completely and carefully defined and where the predictor measurements are structured, to have high correlations with indicators of success. In the author's experience the results in Table 19.2 were obtained when installing a test battery for prediction of success for 130 assembly line workers in a vacuum cleaner manufacturing plant.

The correlation coefficients reported in Table 19.2 were for measures from the Flanagan Aptitude Classification Test Battery. When combined into a multiple regression equation, the ensuing R was .90! Interestingly, the predictors in this particular research were not the usual pieces per hour or other quantitative methods of determining performance. In this case the performance criterion was an average of eight ratings of each individual. These ratings were provided by several time study engineers, the immediate

supervisor, the departmental supervisor, the training director, and the director of personnel. All the ratings were converted to standardized scores and then averaged to be used as a criterion measurement. It was felt that this method of developing a criterion measure was reliable and reasonably free from bias, considering the number of ratings used.

The preparation of a utility table indicates the effectiveness of selection procedures when using aptitude tests and where criterion information is precise. As an examination of Table 19.3 indicates, it is possible to achieve perfect selection.

As Table 19.3 indicates, the chances of success for an applicant with a composite score below 159 are nil and no personnel are selected with a score below this level. For scores above 240, selection would be 100% effective, but it would be necessary to interview 16 candidates to select one applicant. In the practical situation this is most often impossible and it is usually necessary to be content with a lower selection ratio.

TABLE 19.2

Correlations of Flanagan* Aptitude Tests with Performance

Predictor	Correlation
FACT—Components	.76
FACT—Assembly	.68
FACT—Spatial Visualization	.70

*FACT, revised, 1960, evaluated in Buros (1978).

TABLE 19.3

Utility of Various Score Levels on FACT* Battery for Selection of Assemblers

Composite Score from FACT Assembly, Components, Spatial Visualization Subtests	Chances of Success	Selection Ratio
0-159	0	0
160-239	5-3	2-5
240-359	8-0	1-15

*FACT, revised, 1960 and evaluated in Buros (1978).

Executives

It is interesting to note how structured tests can be used, not only for theory building but also for actual applied research. In a series of unpublished studies of the present author, cited by Cattell and Child (1975), the Motivation Analysis Test (MAT) was administered to a number of top executives, i.e., presidents of insurance and service organizations. The motivational profile for these top executives is shown in Figure 19.2. Advances in computer technology have now permitted the publishers of the MAT (The Institute for Personality and Ability Testing, Champaign, Illinois) to expand this work considerably. A normative test base of some 1400 top executives has been obtained not only for the MAT but also for the 16 P.F. instruments. The profile of the typical successful businessman shown in Figure 19.2, which in 1970 was based upon less than 100 subjects, has now been expanded to

several thousand and the IPAT Data Base is now representative on a national basis.

Let us see first how structured tests can be used in theory building and later how they can be used in applied settings. Returning to our leadership example, we may ask the question, "What dynamic qualifiers (drives and/or sentiments) and personality factors describe top male executives?"

Several studies, as yet unpublished and confidential to the firms involved regarding the place and detail of the findings, do give a statistically different pattern from the average man, according to the norms. The young, successful executive (Noty, 1975) tends to be the man who has high career drive in the early stages of his climb up the ladder (Figure 19.2). But the well-established executive does not display a similar high career sentiment, possibly because he has already "arrived" and therefore has less need to overtly or covertly express a strong attitude towards

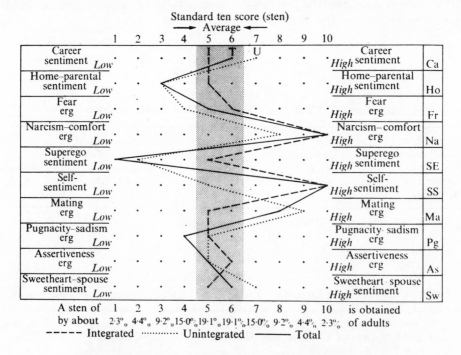

Figure 19.2. Average scores for top executives (20 presidents of insurance and service organizations)

Source: Unpublished work by C. Noty, 1973.

career. The high ambition linked with the bright young man in a career may dampen with success and experience. Interestingly, the college student is typically high on unintegrated career scores, but low on integrated scores. Thus, if we accept the tentative interpretation of U and I scores, one explanation is that a conflict exists at this stage between drives and outlets in reality.

In fact, the work of Sweney, DeYoung, and others suggest that the U component is a relatively unintegrated, unrestrained, and spontaneous component in interest that is susceptible to momentary stimulation and is in part unconscious or preconscious. The integrated component, on the other hand, is relatively firm, reality-oriented, cognitively invested, and experienced—a consciously integrated and controlled interest component. To get a single score for a person's attitude interest strength we could simply add I and U measures, but there is little advantage in doing this if they behave differently with time and circumstances. Thus, adding what a person owns in life insurance to what he owns in real estate might give us a single score of "what he is worth" in worldly wealth, but the two have different reactions to inflation and one is not available to him until he dies! Similarly, U and I components are most meaningfully kept as separate scores on separate kinds of tests.

Sentiment towards home/parents is generally lower than average, possibly reflecting growing independence from parental affiliation and a more satisfactory adjustment. However, even at later ages the men of high achievement show less attachment to the home as such. But, regarding parental home attachment, the high achiever pattern (Sweney, 1969a) appears to be a moderate integrated and low unintegrated score, indicating a low need for parental home dependence. Figure 19.2 shows this very clearly.

Attachment to a wife or sweetheart portrays a need for affection beyond and apart from sexual or gregarious needs. The top executives seem well-balanced in U and I, as well as in total motivation, except that the conflict score (obtained from the difference between U and I) is on the high side and shows a denial on their part of indulging the need for close attachments to, or affection from, a member of the opposite sex. In many high achievers in history, such as Napoleon, the great religious leaders, Newton, and others, there is evidence of cynicism towards romance and domestic affection. It is interesting to see that in lesser ranges of achievement, measurement bears out this pattern, as well as a high rating on conflict (and low on total motivation). It reappears in several professional (or potentially so) groups, such as doctors and college students. The riddle of this connection between professionalism and high conflict with low total spouse sentiment has not been disentangled and is ripe for research. One speculation is that a professional's work makes demands of him similar to those of "affection"—in other words, he becomes attached to his work in a way that depletes the affiliatory energies available for his wife and children.

Not unnaturally, high self-sentiment prevails in executives and leaders, for being good at one's job, maintaining high social standing, and so on, are positive needs of the situation. A carefully planned life in terms of getting a good education, seeking social position, and developing social skills are part and parcel of an executive's bid to fulfill his aspirations. Noty (see Figure 19.3), in a series of studies of businessmen, reports them to be high on integrated self-sentiment and lower on the unintegrated scale—a well-balanced combination (Sweney, 1969a).

Interpretation of the superego scores fits well into popular beliefs about those in positions of responsibility in industry and commerce. Low U scores probably indicate a preoccupation with materialistic and secular affairs. The extremely low score obtained by top executives (Figure

19.2) suggests a misanthropic tendency and reminds us of the findings of Rosenberg (1957) and others that the student of management says he is most frequently "material" (or thing) oriented rather than "person" oriented when asked about those things he values most in his work. On the other hand, at least outside of business, leaders tend to be significantly higher than their followers on superego strength (Cattell & Stice, 1960).

Of the five basic drives, the two most noteworthy for the executives are narcissism and mating. Predictably, the executive has a marked liking for creature comforts. The personal investment of time and effort that goes into any professional training seems very likely to stimulate, exponentially, high self-concern. High scores on both U and I scales, found particularly in affluent societies, is often associated with the "bon vivant" who with insatiable appetite seeks higher and higher levels of comfort. The mating erg appears high on the U score, but average on the

I. This pattern is characteristic of unfulfilled sexual tension—a case of unrequited sexual drive. Have we here a classic example of the Freudian concept of "sublimation," in which sexual energy is being deflected to, and dissipated in, work?

So far we have leaned on the adjustment principle of vocational guidance, which requires as its target the profile of the adjusted job holder. But the present author has also done compilational studies, which yield a specification equation for an efficiency prediction. Here we correlated each dynamic trait level with performance as measured in salesmen by actual sales figures over three years and by compounded company ratings on a merit system. As Tatsuoka and Cattell (1970) have shown, a translation can be worked out between a specification equation and a mean profile, and since so far we have dealt in profiles, the results in Figure 19.2 are similarly expressed. It will be seen that the two approaches (Figures 19.2 and 19.3) give reasonably concordant results.

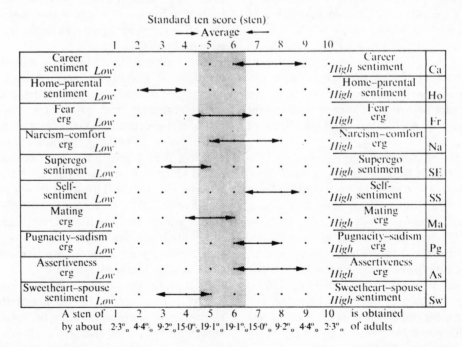

Figure 19.3. Profile of the typical successful businessman (central range shown by arrows)*

Source: Unpublished work by C. Noty, 1973.

STRUCTURED TESTING IN VOCATIONAL GUIDANCE AND SELECTION

Most of the material in this section is excerpted from Cattell (1957a) and Cattell and Butcher (1968). For a detailed examination of the principles and problems involved in matching persons to careers, see Super (1953, 1957) and Super and Bohn (1970). Holland (1973) summarizes findings about vocational preferences of people employed in different occupations. This field has utilized "unstructured" tests since its inception. The two major instruments in the field, the Strong Vocational Interest Blank and the Kuder Preference Record, were not based on factor-analytic or structured methods of construction. However, both the Strong and Kuder measures have come to be widely used, principally because some 50 years of normative development have been employed in refining the tests.

Regardless of whether we deal with vocational guidance, i.e., finding the best fitting job for a given group of individuals in schools, employment agencies, or vocational rehabilitation units, or vocational selection, i.e., picking the best person for a defined necessary job performance, certain general principles apply.

First, the truly comprehensive view requires that we consider society as well as the individual. In society there is a population with certain resources of intelligence, training, emotional stability, etc., partly biological, partly the result of existing training. If one directs more good ability into, say, the fine arts, there may be less in medicine, and if the economic system pays football players more than, say, teachers, the level of intelligence characteristic of teachers may be less than it would otherwise be. All fitness for an occupation is relative to supply.

When we face the choice for one who might do equally well as a lawyer or a painter, we have to consider also how many other people are heading for these occupations and what society needs. Statistical psychologists have worked out some nice mathematical theorems that neatly ensure the maximum utilization of abilities in a system of competing subgroups, each demanding a somewhat different emphasis on abilities for success. But these are beyond an introductory exposition; only the principle can be noted; and, except in an ideally cooperative set of people, it could not be used.

A second general principle concerns the difference between adjustment in a job (largely in terms of satisfaction) and efficiency at a job. For example, in a study by King quoted in Cattell (1970a), several hundred bakery route (door-to-door) salesmen, on equivalent rural types of routes, were measured on intelligence and the 16 P.F. test personality factors. The results of relating scores with the criterion —amount of product regularly sold—were as follows:

$$C + 0.2A + 0.2B + 0.3C + 0.2F + 0.3G + 0.2H - 0.21 - 0.4L - 0.30 - 0.1Q_1 + 0.4Q_3 - 0.2Q_4 \qquad (19\text{-}1)$$

This specification equation says that the effective salesman in this type of situation tends to be of cyclothyme temperament (warm), surgent (talkative), and of sufficient ego strength not to suffer if brushed off—and so on. The combination makes sense in terms of most people's experience of salesmen! The figures could be used as they stand for vocational selection, but for vocational guidance statistical adjustments would have to be made for the salesman already having a different range, in some traits, from that of the general population. Essentially, however, by this method, we should get an "efficiency at the job" estimate through multiplying each candidate's personality source-trait scores by these weights, and adding to a single criterion score estimate.

By contrast, the "adjustment to the job" principle proceeds as follows: One takes a sufficient sample of people who have remained in the job and finds their average profile. Central profiles for each of four different jobs on 16 personality factors and five ability factors (four primaries and general intelligence) are shown in Figure 19.4 and it will be seen that they differ considerably. One could now take the individual profile for a given candidate seeking vocational guidance or selection and set it alongside these (and other occupations similarly analyzed) to decide which it best fits. In a small test installation one might depend on assessing the relative goodness of two people, in the fit of their profiles to the model by eye, but the decision can be made more reliable by working out a pattern similarity coefficient (written r_p to distinguish it from r, the correlation coefficient) between the

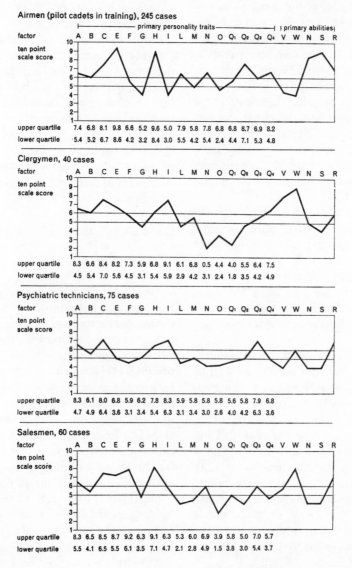

Note: The personality scores on the 16 P.F. are from the number of cases indicated. The Primary Abilities values, however, are based only on demonstration cases and are to be considered only as likely illustration.

Figure 19.4. Four job profiles on personality factors and primary abilities

ideal and actual profiles. One thus sees which of a number of jobs or job families the individual best fits. However, this says how well he is "adjusted" in agreeing with the type of person society has previously called to that job, and who has stayed "successfully" in that job. And there may well be some appreciable discrepancies between the adjustment as thus calculated and the efficiency decisions as found by the estimation from the equation for goodness of performance. For example, Mr. A, who is a business executive, might be more efficient as a janitor than Mr. B, but how long would he stay in the job, and is it good for society to place him there?

Even among those who stay in a job over a long period of time the two indices will rank people somewhat differently. For example, scientific researchers are more premsic (1 + factor) than the general population. That is to say, they are more emotionally sensitive, which is probably due to the fact that more educated persons, especially from homes well-cushioned economically, are in general more premsic, through being relatively protected from harsh demands of reality. But when correlations with a criterion of productivity and effectiveness, such as patents gained, researches published, etc., are made in a group of researchers, it turns out that premsia is negatively weighted. The harric $(I-)$ individual, i.e., the tough and realistic scientist, actually does a better job. Incidentally, since I factor tends to be associated with more indulgent upbringing, the finding of higher art and music interests in premsic individuals fits the statistical finding that scientific leaders, relative to leaders in music and arts, come from less privileged homes.

Formerly (and, alas, in many places today), vocational guidance, however sound the assessment of the individual, was based on comparatively amateur impressions by the counselor of what various jobs demand. A slight advance is made when ideas are derived from some "job analysis"

in terms of what acts the person carries out in the job. But research often shows that a job makes unseen demands, and these confident impressions from job description can be quite wide of the mark. Occupations with apparently very dissimilar activities can demand a very similar personality profile and apparently similar jobs make very different demands. This lack of real knowledge about what a job is really like and what it demands has been a source of criticism of job interest tests, of which the Strong Interest Blank and the Kuder are among the best examples, in which the person literally checks off the occupations and activities he thinks would most interest him. It is true that in these test devices the test constructors have not taken these statements entirely at their face value, but have made statistical analyses showing the choices that people in particular occupations make. However, such vocational guidance does not permit scores to be interpreted and understood through intermediate psychological concepts, such as temperament traits and drive strengths, which would enable one to add psychological to statistical prediction.

The advantage of a vocational guidance system based less on crude empiricism and more on test scores which represent known temperament or dynamic structures is that much can be brought to bear in the latter system from our knowledge of the natural history of the traits and the sociology of the occupation. For example, we know that some source traits, such as cyclothymia, intelligence, and threctic (H-factor), are largely constitutionally given, while others, such as premsia (I factor), superego strength, surgency, etc., are susceptible to substantial environmental change. To know from the scores which of these traits account for the person's fitting the occupational profile or criterion at a given moment is important. Statistically, at the moment of examination, two people might show an equally good fit, but psychologically we would know that one would be doing much better in a year's time, for we know that some factors follow a typical life course, e.g., in the steady decline in surgency after adolescence and the rise of ego strength. Consequently, knowing the natural history of the source trait measured, and the occupational fact that, say, the demands on ego strength do not come until later, one would present different occupational advice, with the help of tests yielding meaningful source-trait scores, from that offered with batteries which merely tie up statistically some inscrutable score on a patent test with some probability of success in a particular occupation.

When well done, vocational guidance is no simple procedure for which a score on an intelligence test and an achievement test will suffice. The number of source-trait scores likely to be needed to reach as good a prediction as is virtually possible may easily reach 30 or 40. Both statistically and psychologically the prediction will gain from going to about 10 abilities, 16 personality traits, and a dozen dynamic traits. Incidentally, in almost any adjustment prediction, one does well to spread the available testing time far more evenly over the three modalities than has hitherto been done—when dynamic traits were neglected and abilities were the focus of concentration.

Incidentally, the above testing principle of spreading one's measurement widely does not apply only to different modalities—ability, personality, motivation. Even in one modality it is better to measure several things, in spite of the reduced reliability found in short tests for each, than to measure only one thing with very high reliability. One great advantage of structured/factored tests of any kind is that one's test measures are guaranteed to be well spread out, each tapping an entirely new aspect of personality, whereas other tests frequently overlap and repeat themselves very wastefully. The time demand, in getting an adequate evaluation of an individual's personality, even with the

most judicious use of tests and scoring methods, is likely to be four hours or more. But, in all conscience, this is not much to take from a person's time for advising him on a life career. Indeed, both industry and the general public have a serious responsibility for remedying two major abuses in personnel selection, affecting the lives of millions. First, there is this absurd discrepancy between the importance to employees and employers of having the right rather than the wrong person in a job, perhaps for years, and the idea that 20 minutes is enough to give to testing. Three or four hours is needed, even with the uncommonly good choice of factored ability and personality tests, to get reasonable coverage. Second, there has been too much dependence on individuals with little qualification in psychological testing and minimum understanding of basic statistics. The almost invariable defense of these types, as they miss the most obvious statistical advantages of procedure, is that they depend on subject insight, experience, and "clinical" feeling.

In large businesses and in organizations such as the civil service, much economy can be brought into the whole testing procedure for promotion and allocation to special jobs by the installation of what has been called the three-file system. As detailed in Chapter 6, these files would consist of: 1) a comprehensive file of tests the psychologist has selected. For example, in selecting executives the file could include the 16 P.F., the Motivation Analysis Test, Thurstone Primary Mental Abilities, Sales Attitudes Checklist, Leadership Opinion Questionnaire, and the Strong or Kuder Inventories; 2) client case records; and 3) types, patterns and behavioral specification equations. In the second file it is desirable to keep records in raw score or other format to permit data collection and research across companies and industrial groupings. In the third file, the specification equations can be obtained from test handbooks or from research. As an example for using the files, the psychologist asks the question, "How do this client's test results compare to those of sales personnel in general and/or to local norms of those successful in a particular organization?"

The three-file system implies a potential matching of every individual's profile from test results of the second file to equations in the third file. The computer is beneficial in the record-keeping and analytic duties required. It could, for example, calculate the congruence of the individual's test scores with those successful in a sales occupation or college setting or with those who are successful in therapy. In the high school guidance situation, the counselor can provide some help to students who are college-bound in terms of likely majors, although, since attitudes and values and motivation are not crystallized at age 17 or 18, guidance here is, at best, tentative.

The advent of distributed data processing (mini-computers) has now made it possible to do a much better job of vocational guidance, in that a client can quickly (and in some testing installations instantaneously) see how a particular pattern of abilities, skills, interests, personality, and motivation coincides with that of individuals who are successful in one or 10 or 100 occupations. What has been a perennial problem is that the guidance counselor frequently is not familiar enough with the actual world of work and the content of many occupations to be able to provide meaningful input on career choices. Here the computer also makes a contribution for the *Dictionary of Occupational Titles,* or some other taxonomic description of the content of jobs can be "computerized." The counselor can then help a client 1) know what a job realistically requires in terms of behaviors and skills; 2) determine how close a particular set of scores is to these requirements; and 3) make decisions based on statistical as well as personal data.

Structured tests now exist for personality and ability. We await the introduction of a structured "interest" measure,

such as suggested by Sweney (1967) and Cattell (1957a). Perhaps the technique used in the 16 P.F. development, which utilized the Allport-Odbert lexicon, can be used here. Meanwhile, the counselor in the guidance clinic and the employment manager in the selection decision area have available to them considerable predictive power in terms of pattern similarity coefficients to make good recommendations or employment decisions. These decisions in the selection case are certainly better when based on structured measurement than when based on interview or other fallible data.

A CALL FOR NEW RESEARCH PROGRAMS AND A RETURN TO "BASICS"

It is now over 25 years since Cattell (1957a) sounded a clarion call for the use of structured tests in industrial and vocational settings. As we have seen in Chapter 3, he has more recently advocated a three-file system to be used in personnel selection. Since the same individual exists in the educational/vocational setting and in the industrial setting, it seems highly logical for a series of measurements to be made over childhood and adult life as the individual progresses from elementary through secondary school, on to college and to his vocational setting. His initial call emphasized personality measures, and in 1967 added cognitive measures to the total picture. This call was reiterated in 1971 when Cattell and Butcher added the dimension of interest to round out the total portrait of the individual who presented himself either for a selection or placement decision.

Even though Cattell, Guilford, and Thurstone pioneered in the development of structured personality and aptitude tests, and even though we have had a half century or more of experience in using such tests in applied situations, many problems still remain. Even though Ghiselli (1963-1973) convincingly demonstrated that a wide variety of tests, when appropriately used, *always* provide significant validity coefficients, the promise of full utilization of such instruments in applied settings has not been realized. It is easy to assess blame for some of the current malaise in testing in applied situations:

1) Should we fault industrial/organizational psychologists? Many are still searching for the best tests, using the best itemetrics, psychometrics, criterion measurements, and statistical procedures. Many are still trying to determine the best way of assembling batteries of tests and to integrate tests into a total selection system.

2) Should test publishers be credited with at least a portion of the other problem? Looking at current catalogs of the major test publishers in the United States, it is interesting to note some rather glaring examples of inappropriate test usage. One large company still lists a "personality" test that was copyrighted in 1945 and has had no significant research done on it since that time. Another large test company lists in its catalog an aptitude test with a preliminary manual dated 1961 and which has not been revised. A number of test publishers have produced rather poorly printed test instruments. Reading Buros's *Eighth Mental Measurements Yearbook* (1978) leads one to the conclusion that very few publishers have statistically adequate technical manuals!

3) It has become popular for some journalists who want to sell books to present "sensational" findings based upon inappropriate interpretation of test validity studies and the use of "straw man" techniques (see *The Brain Watchers* by Gross, 1962).

4) Perhaps the federal and state governments should be ascribed a portion of the blame for fostering a climate of suspicion. It takes a fine legal talent to be able to read and reread the morass of regulations published by various governmental bodies on the use of tests in applied settings.

5) Many individuals who actually use tests in applied settings are also responsible for inappropriate administrative behavior. Tests have been used without rigid adherence to the appropriate standardization measures and testing conditions. Not enough information has been published and not enough attention has been paid to the question of appropriately motivating persons who are taking tests. Many companies have poorly trained test administrators. The problem is similar to physicians' trying to keep up with the advances in medical research and use of drugs and surgical techniques. How many medical practitioners still use instruments the same way they did 10 years ago? How many industrial/organizational psychologists have refined their normative bases, and use a computer in providing actual and standardized scores, as well as linear combinations of these scores? How many industrial/organizational psychologists are aware of the newest theories of the validity of differential validity? How many are still using unfactored, *ad hoc,* or unresearched instruments?

The course of future research seems quite clear. Unfortunately, this course is, in many respects, similar to the one suggested by Freyd (1923) in his classic series of articles. We now have structured personality, aptitude, and cognitive measures that will permit the applied psychologist to do an excellent job of making predictions of performance. It is surprising, in this context, to note that in the Ghiselli volume (1963), levels of validity were still attained when tests that were being reported on were frequently unfactored and unstructured. We now have structured tests typically based on factor-analytic procedure. If the applied psychologist, for example, wants to investigate the phenomenon of leadership or management succession, he must first, of course, determine the underlying structure for leadership success in a particular organization. Having identified this underlying structure he may then use some of the more modern and factorially pure instruments, such as the 16 P.F., the Guilford-Zimmerman Temperament Survey (GZTS), and the FACT and FIT series of Flanagan. Much recent research has been published on the determination of job requirements, as exemplified by the work of McCormick et al. (1972). Stogdill (1974), in his classic treatment of research on leadership for a 50-year period, reported many studies that showed that tests have predictive validity. Unfortunately, many of the tests he reported on were not factorially pure. Coming back again to the question of determining leadership or management succession in prediction, the applied psychologist, for example, can develop a research program as shown in Table 19.4.

But what of the 1980s and beyond? Personnel managers are becoming more sophisticated in the use of quantitative techniques applied to selection decisions. The APA, AERA and NCME are developing even more definitive guidelines for use of tests and we can expect to see these organizations publish a 100+ page set of such instructions in the near future. This will permit governmental organizations such as the Equal Employment Opportunity Commission to base their regulations on more scientific study and eventually to bring some order to case law on the use of tests and other measures in employment decision-making. Tests such as the Primary Mental Abilities (PMA; Thurstone, 1960) and CAB (Cattell, 1971a) mentioned above are continuing to be used (along with other structured intelligence and ability measures) in more and more validation studies. Many firms are organized in cooperative efforts to use tests. We may hope that some 20 years hence procedures will permit a personnel manager to be able to use a set of measures for almost every occupation listed in the government's *Dictionary of Occupational Titles*.

For now, the user of tests in applied settings will need to consider these matters:

1) Are the ability, personality, interest and motivation tests used, structured?
2) What has been their history in generating validity coefficients?
3) Has as much attention been paid to development of "true" criterion measures as to the tests themselves?
4) What is the utility or efficacy of using tests over interviews or other selection devices?

Freyd (1923) had answers to many of these questions. Thurstone, Cattell, Flan-

TABLE 19.4
Model for Test Research Programs

Area Studied	Method
1) Development of basic job dimensions	Position analysis questionnaire of McCormick
2) Development of leadership structure	Factor analysis of leadership research
3) Trial test battery using factored tests	Use 16 P.F., FACT, TAA, GZTS, or similar measures
4) Development of criterion measure	Objective measures of leadership performance such as return on investment
5) Use of multivariate techniques	Factor analysis, multiple regression analysis, discrimination function analysis
6) Utility analysis	Cost/benefit analysis validity generalization

agan and others have answers in terms of instruments to use. Schmidt and Hunter have some additional answers in terms of statistical procedures. For the psychometrist and examiner in applied settings, we need a revision of classics such as Lawshe and Balma (1966) and Dunnette (1966). The present writer confidently predicts that 10 years from now, much of what has been stated here as desirable testing practice will actually take place!

SUMMARY

While testing procedures have been used for as many as 3000 years, only in the last 50 years has much progress been made in terms of structured instruments. The initial research on structured tests centered around mental abilities, but in the 1930s and 1940s research encompassed personality measures. The advent of the computer makes a reality of using many measurements for one person for either a selection or vocational decision.

Major international and national psychological and measurement associations have developed comprehensive sets of guidelines for researchers and practitioners. Psychometric practice will become increasingly scientifically oriented as a result of legislation and demands of organizations for techniques that produce valid, cost-efficient results.

Performance in an occupation depends on personality, abilities, *and* motivation. Achievement can be predicted using factored or structured tests.

A number of structured tests, such as the 16 P.F., Primary Mental Abilities, Motivation Analysis Test, and Clinical Analysis Questionnaire were found to be effective in predicting performance in a wide variety of occupational settings.

Structured testing can be applied to vocational guidance. However, problems are found in counselors who lack an appropriate knowledge of the world of work and of modern psychometric testing practices.

We need to do more consolidation of research studies and to use factored/ structured instruments in replication of research. The "newer" multivariate statistical procedures will produce better research results, and meta-analytic methodology will provide better synthesis across occupational groupings.

CHAPTER 20

Classroom Achievement and Creativity

John S. Gillis

THE NEED FOR FUNCTIONAL TESTS IN EDUCATION

In the preface to their book on *The Prediction of Achievement and Creativity*, Cattell and Butcher (1968) observe that "the standard of living of a country is, in the end, not dependent on the visible natural resources, or on the monetary tricks of the economist, but is a function of the level of attainment and creativity prevailing among its citizens." A similar statement could be made to the effect that the quality of living of individuals within any particular country is to a very large extent associated with their level of educational achievement. Lynn's study (1979), comparing several districts composing the British Isles, shows a substantial unitary trait marked by correlation of mean I.Q., mean educational attainment, percentage of eminent men, low infantile death rate, and average level of real income. For these reasons, both governments and citizens of modern societies invest an enormous amount of time, money, and energy with

the aim of obtaining the highest possible level of classroom achievement, and in time they may also take eugenic measures to raise the mean I.Q. However, at present we are concerned with the level of education and the factors that determine it. In Chapter 10, Merrifield has already concentrated on the validity and reliability of achievement tests as such so we are free to turn to causes and consequences.

As part of this overall quest for knowledge capability within formal academic frameworks and in occupational life (see Chapter 19), psychologists have been asked for many years to develop tests that can be used to assess achievement. As Chapter 10 shows, psychometrists have responded to this request by producing a large number of instruments, which in terms of sheer predictive validity and technical standards of administration, scoring, and norm development can be regarded as some of the finest practical tools that psychology has been able to offer society. Yet, as is amply illustrated in a recent edition of the *American Psychologist* devoted entirely to testing, a considerable number of people have been somewhat less than thankful (Glaser & Bond, 1981) and misunderstandings have run wild. In fact, the present situation has been described as an outright "war upon testing" (Lerner, 1980) waged by unfortunate individuals and some minority groups, who have been taking their battles to court with increasing frequency (Bersoff, 1981). As writers in various fields here have pointed out, there has always been some degree of animosity toward testing (see Haney, 1981), fueled largely by a general feeling of "evaluation apprehension" among those being tested or by a general "revolt against realities." Undoubtedly, the current controversy goes deeper than nominal objections to particular programs and involves many complex motives and situations (e.g., Gordon & Terrell, 1981; Reschly, 1981; Resnick, 1979).

In any case, in this decade we face the social paradox that at the same time as psychologists have developed instruments for predicting achievement with greater and greater precision, the general public has become increasingly uneasy about the use of tests. Some of the blame must go to psychologists in that the public senses—as it does also in courtroom verdicts of psychiatrists—that psychologists are engaging in many blind and out-of-date technical methods, permitting some prediction but no *understanding* of functional testing. When asked what intelligence is, the all-too-frequent reply by psychologists has been the circular statement, "That which is measured by intelligence tests" (see Chapter 8).

One major problem with current testing practices in the classroom, as seen from a functional psychological testing viewpoint, is that psychometrists have become complacent through the aura of success that has surrounded the high levels of reliable discrimination and predictive validity attained in educational measurement. It would seem that there has been a tendency to lose sight of the ultimate goal of

understanding the factors in achievement and making clear distinctions between attainment and the equally important goal for the educated student—creativity. To use what has almost become a scientific cliché, prediction may be a "necessary" condition but is not a "sufficient" condition for understanding a phenomenon such as achievement. Since the time of the ancient astronomers in Egypt and Greece, accurate predictions of the position and movements of the "heavenly bodies" were possible without much understanding of the solar system. Even today astronomical precision alone is a valuable and an indispensable practical contribution to a ship's officer in navigating ships by the stars. Yet this ability to predict without understanding is hardly enough for present-day astronauts, who would not have even gotten into space without the understanding of the solar system produced by Copernicus, Kepler, Newton, and Einstein.

Functional psychological testing has been aimed from its very beginning toward the goal of understanding achievement, with prediction of next year's performance being only a first step. Yet a necessary first step it is. Just as the public can be justifiably wary of those who offer prediction without understanding, fellow psychologists can hardly be expected to listen very carefully to anyone who espouses understanding without the ability to predict.

AMOUNT OF ACHIEVEMENT PREDICTION POSSIBLE WITH FUNCTIONAL TESTS

Cattell and Butcher (1968) recognized the importance of dealing with the question of achievement prediction before addressing the more fundamental topic of understanding achievement. Realizing that any new testing approach would be judged to a great extent on the basis of how well it stacked up in comparison with older techniques, these authors first undertook a survey of previous attempts to predict achievement to see what levels of prediction were typical. Their assessment of past literature led them to the conclusion that traditional ability test correlations with school achievement centered upon a value of about .50 for intelligence and about .60 for a wide array of primary abilities (Cattell & Butcher, 1968, p. 59). A similar conclusion has also been arrived at by Thorndike and Hagen (1969, p. 324), who estimate that correlations of .50 to .60 between intelligence test scores and school marks are fairly representative. In addition, Thorndike and Hagen point out that correlations greater than .70 are typical when standardized achievement tests (see Chapter 10), rather than school marks, are used as the criteria for prediction. This presumably arises from the greater validity and reliability of the criterion built by attainment test experts. Thus, it would appear that correlations of about .60 for teachers' school grades and .70 for achievement test results would be required before many psychologists would be willing to give serious consideration to the merits of more functional tests and personality additives, as proposed here, since .50 to .60 can already be reached by classical ability tests, e.g., WAIS and Binet, alone.

In an attempt to determine the extent to which more analytic functional tests, including personality and dynamic trait measures, could successfully predict academic criteria, Cattell and various coworkers have undertaken a long series of research studies. Portions of the pioneering work carried out between 1958 and 1964 are reported in the book by Cattell and Butcher (1968), but the best overall summary may be found in a research article by Cattell, Sealy and Sweney (1966). In this study, the results of one published work by Butcher, Ainsworth, and Nesbitt (1963) and of four other papers of limited circulation were brought together and made available for a joint analysis. The

findings of most interest regarding the overall degree of prediction of achievement involved the use of multiple regression equations with two separate groups of seventh and eighth grade children. With one group of 278 children a combination of the Culture-Fair Intelligence Test (CFIT), the High School Personality Questionnaire (HSPQ) and the School Motivation Analysis Test (SMAT) resulted in a multiple R of .72 with general school progress as measured by the Stanford Achievement Test. With a second group of 144 children, using the same tests as predictors, the multiple R's were .85 with a standard achievement test and .81 with school grades.

Follow-up research by Cattell, Barton, and Dielman (1972) with 311 children in grades 6 and 7 produced similar results. This study, using the CFIT (Chapter 8), HSPQ, and revised edition of the SMAT resulted in multiple R's of about .71 with social studies and science, .80 with mathematics, and .85 with reading.

Clearly, on the basis of these studies, together involving more than 700 children with an average multiple R of about .80, there is good reason for educational psychologists to take a close look at using the whole behavioral equation. They will need to use it with ability, personality, and dynamic trait modalities, and to have the accompanying knowledge in functional testing of the natural history of those traits. However, it is not the sheer predictive power of the tests that is the most important feature. Rather, as emphasized by Cattell in Chapter 1, it is the manner in which the prediction is obtained that is of most significance. The key element in this type of approach is that, instead of basing prediction upon what might best be called conglomerate (Carroll & Horn, 1981) measures, and what Cattell calls special-purpose tests such as the Bender or the Strong, one rests prediction upon a systematic analysis of achievement into separate source traits of known nature, across the "modalities" of ability, motivation and personality-temperament.

Observant psychologists and educators have long held the opinion that both motivation and personality add to the effect of ability in influencing scholastic achievement. Yet, as Middleton and Guthrie pointed out in 1959, there had, up to that time, been a conspicuous lack of success in empirical demonstration of such a relationship. The problem was that the personality and interest tests used up to that time, constructed in the 1930s and '40s without evidence of personality structure, were of miserable validity. The studies, summarized in Cattell, Sealy, and Sweney (1966) and Cattell, Barton, and Dielman (1972), not only indicate that functional tests can predict at a highly respectable and helpful level, but also demonstrate the magnitude of the separate contributions that come from the modalities of ability, personality, and motivation.

Other researchers have since confirmed that personality and motivation measures add to the prediction of achievement from abilities alone. Cooper, Boss, and Keith (1974) looked at a sample of 582 tenth grade students and found that HSPQ factors C, G, D, Q_2, and Q_3 could discriminate between those having high scholastic performance and those performing less well. Mandryk and Schuerger (1974) studied 469 high school students with the HSPQ and two ability measures, and reported that, as in previous studies, "one-fourth of the variance associated with achievement was accounted for by personality factors." Other research has looked at 164 ninth grade students and affirmed previous findings that "better predictions can be made utilizing both personality and intelligence measures than either alone" (Watterson, Schuerger, & Melnyk, 1976). Hakstian and Gale (1979) have also been able to show with 129 tenth grade students, using composite measures of the HSPQ and SMAT, that the personality and motivational trait domains "add sig-

nificantly to the already-efficient prediction obtained from the ability variables."

The personality and motivation factors associated with achievement are very consistent across these researches and just as an insightful psychologist would expect. We see positive relation especially to the superego, G, the self-sentiment, Q_3, and self-sufficiency, Q_2 (see, for example, Cattell & Butcher, 1968, p. 187), while C, ego strength, comes in somewhat when college years are entered. That intelligence should be implemented by conscientiousness, G, and a well-integrated self-concept, Q_3, is surely not surprising. The psychological action of particular factors, however, is a matter for more detailed discussion below.

These findings, that achievement variance can be accounted for by measures from the separate modalities of ability, motivation, and personality, have important implications for the understanding of many aspects of achievement, both group and individual. For example, in the complicated area of "underachievement" and of stressful, compulsive overachievement, functional tests offer unique possibilities for both the identification and remedy of the problems of individual students. The same is true of the more subtle issues of presence and absence of creativity.

In calling attention to the major increment in prediction of achievement that has come from use of functional tests and the full behavioral equation, we do not intend to forget the situation outside the personality. The child who works in a cold attic and lacks encouragement from his family is unlikely to do as well as a no more gifted but environmentally more fortunate child. In time the psychologist may acquire knowledge of the behavioral indices for a variety of situations, to give them due weight. But in any case a multiple correlation even of 0.8 accounts for only 64% of the achievement variance, and thus it is recognized that at any rate 36% comes from influences outside the personality of the child himself or herself. The work of Cronbach, Gates and others on classroom styles and methods needs to be kept in mind when we concentrate on personality here.

IDENTIFICATION OF UNDERACHIEVERS

Within many highly developed societies there tends to be a group of people who achieve in school at a level that is far below their potential. History brings to mind the more dramatic instances in which early difficulty in school is later overcome by talented individuals. One thinks of the great contributions to the world of Darwin, Edison, Einstein, and Churchill. But these are obviously rare exceptions. History also describes the suicides and frustrated lives of those whose talent neither blooms nor gets recognized by society.

In 1940 an important advance was made toward increasing psychologists' ability to detect underachievement, when an intelligence scale was developed that minimized bias due to culture (Cattell, 1940). The basic theory and practice of culture-fair intelligence tests to measure fluid intelligence is now well worked out, but unfortunately, in spite of a steady accumulation of scientific information indicating the advantages of a culture-fair test of intelligence (see Chapter 9), practitioners have been very slow in adopting the test for widespread use (Cattell, 1979a) and substituting it for the popular idols. One major reason for the lag in practical application of such a test is probably that many psychologists have not recognized that the purpose of testing is analytical and not merely predictive. As mentioned earlier, traditional intelligence tests have been shown to have a correlation of about .60 and occasionally up to .70 with achievement, which means that about 36% to 49% of the achievement variance could be predicted. Some teachers are therefore surprised when the Culture-Fair Intelligence Test (CFIT) typically corre-

lates only about 0.5 with scholastic achievement. What these educational psychologists are perhaps failing to see is that the traditional intelligence test, e.g., WAIS or WISC, *contains an appreciable amount of school achievement as well as intelligence in its score* (see the analysis in Chapter 8 on fluid and crystallized intelligence). It is thus, in part, doing nothing but predicting itself. And indeed, if a high prediction of what a school child will do next semester or even next year is required, quite the best predictor is an achievement test given this semester. Actually, even if prediction alone is wanted, a better estimate than the typical 0.6 of a traditional intelligence test can be reached by adding to the CFIT score the personality spectrum (the HSPQ for example) and a measure of the motivation resources, e.g., the SMAT, since the multiple R, as we have seen, centers on about 0.75. This gives about 56% (0.75^2) of the achievement variance compared to about 36% from the contaminated type of intelligence test, in which, moreover, one does not know how much is intelligence and how much past achievement. If we know the individual's source-trait scores and the behavioral equation weights for achievement, we can see what traits may loom large in the given individual's performance, i.e., it will give an analysis of, say, underachievement, not obtainable by taking into account only a traditional so-called intelligence measurement.

Cultural, situational causes of underachievement can be sheer lack of opportunity due to poverty, a maladjusted family environment, and so on. Low income means fewer books, newspapers, and other educating media being made available to a child. An H. G. Wells may be able to pull himself up by the bootstraps out of economic deprivation, but many others with less determination may falter. For this reason a test for identifying underachievers should be designed to cut through differences in opportunity as effectively as possible. Thus, as far as intelligence is concerned, one necessary characteristic of an I.Q. test is a relatively low relationship to socioeconomic level. Hence, the finding of a correlation of less than .25 by the CFIT with socioeconomic level (McArthur & Elley, 1963), compared to the value of .40 that is more typical of traditional tests (Cattell & Butcher, 1968, p. 50), indicates which instrument is desirable.

Cultural bias in the form of language differences can also make it difficult to predict achievement potential (Olmedo, 1981). Because the CFIT does not involve any linguistic stimulus material (even the instructions may be given in a pantomime form with examples to check if instructions are understood), the impact of language is greatly reduced. One recent application of the CFIT has even shown that it is quite possible for groups with widely differing languages to equal, *or even surpass*, the performance of the language group with whom the CFIT was developed (Buj, 1981).

In addition to socioeconomic level and language differences, sources of cultural bias in tests may arise from reacting differently to items because of membership in a particular ethnic group (Cole, 1981). In this regard it is interesting to note that Smith, Hays and Solway (1977), and Knapp (1960a) found that the CFIT lessened the effect of cultural bias and presented a more accurate picture of the intellectual capacity of Mexican-Americans than did the WISC-R. Similarly, Zoref and Williams (1980) took a careful look at the con tent bias of I.Q. tests and discovered that, of six major ability tests, the CFIT was the only instrument that did not contain any racially or sexually stereotyped content. Other investigators have recently undertaken a careful examination of the culture fairness of the CFIT by comparing item difficulties in American and Nigerian populations (Nenty & Dinero, 1981). These investigators estimated that the six items biased in "favor" of the American group were counterbalanced by five items biased in "favor" of the Nigerian group,

but that the general order of item difficulty was the same for both.

Taken together, the studies of socioeconomic level, language, and ethnicity provide impressive confirmation of the idea that the CFIT substantially reduces cultural bias. There have been, of course, several tests proposed that have avoided cultural material, e.g., form boards, but the evidence is that generally they have also avoided intelligence—at least in any saturated form! A satisfactory test must be both culture-fair and well-loaded with the general intelligence factor, g_f or g_c. Yet all of this would not mean much if the test did not demonstrate "construct" validity in terms of the concept of intelligence. As has been set out in Chapter 9 and given fully and systematically in Cattell (1971a), there is replicated evidence from factor studies in the U.S., Britain, Germany and elsewhere that the CFIT provides a good measure of fluid intelligence, showing substantial concept validity against the pure factor, g_f (sometimes called "construct validity"). Thus, educational psychologists now have at their disposal a test that measures intelligence reliably, and at the same time does not involve the cultural contamination typical of traditional tests of intelligence. Such features make the CFIT, as a good measure of fluid intelligence, the score that is needed to subtract (or "parcel out") from actual achievement results in order to obtain a more accurate evaluation of underachievement (from whatever cause), than has previously been possible.

In considering prediction or analysis of achievement, one should generally apply also a *primary abilities* test, such as Thurstone's or the more recent and extensive CAB (Comprehensive Abilities Battery) —see Chapters 8 and 9. The distinction sometimes attempted between abilities and aptitudes has never reached a firm scientific basis. The implication seems to have been that aptitudes are the innate part of a primary ability (some writers exactly reverse this) and ability is the final capacity. However, the supplementation of a general g_f or g_c test with the CAB scores for verbal, numerical, logical, perceptual, visual, spatial, and other primaries (rather than trying to infer them from the hodgepodge of the WAIS, etc.) provides a firm and clear basis for predictions of achievement in particular areas.

UNDERSTANDING THE ACHIEVEMENT PROCESS

Increased ability to identify underachievers in terms of relation to their ability levels is, of course, a worthwhile accomplishment, but the main task of obtaining a better understanding of the achievement process itself, so that all kinds of problems at educational and child guidance clinics can be better handled, awaits fuller research on the achievement process as seen in the behavioral equation.* However, as the studies aimed at determining the predictive outcome of functional tests are increasingly garnered, a promising beginning has been made at pinpointing important factors in achievement and bringing knowledge gained from research in other areas to bear upon achievement phenomena. In other words, the greater "utility" of functional tests and the linear and typal (interactive) formulations discussed in Chapters 4 and 23 has begun to provide us with some insights about school achievement and, perhaps even more importantly, clues about the most fruitful avenues for research now needed.

In the limited space of a chapter section it is possible to touch only briefly upon some of the main psychological insights on the action of various personality and motivational source traits. We will begin by looking at the area of personality measures, where the most research has been carried out. The results will be first summarized for each individual factor and then certain general findings will be discussed.

Factor A Affectia

There is a consistent tendency for A to be positively related to achievement during the elementary school period, with signs of a reduction later on. The warmth and overall emotional responsiveness of the child higher in A would make for closer relationships with teachers. Later on, in advanced studies, e.g., graduate university performance, the inclination of the low A person better able to cope with extended periods of relative seclusion in a laboratory or library seems to be an asset.

Factor B Intelligence

While this factor, as measured in Q-data in the 16 P.F., HSPQ, etc., was intended largely as a rough estimate of crystallized intelligence, it offers a surprisingly good degree of predictive validity (around 0.4 to 0.5) for such an abbreviated scale. (Careful work should use the B factor score from both A and B forms, or, better, supplement with a half-hour CFIT result.) Research clearly indicates, as far as intelligence weighting is concerned, that in later school years, when more selection on the basis of ability has taken place, achievement is less related to intelligence and more related to personality and motivation. This is noticeable among graduate students selected to proceed to the Ph.D.

Factor C Ego Strength

Although studies with the Children's Personality Questionnaire (CPQ) show that this factor of emotional stability may be positively related to achievement during elementary school, there is surprisingly little (and sometimes even a slight

*For a recent informative discussion of the role of personality assessment in the schools see Krug (1978b).

negative) relation in later years. A similar paradox has been noted by Cattell (1980a) with regard to an expected relationship between C and measures of crystallized intelligence. Why factor C, ego strength, which is the most consistently correlated of any questionnaire factor with freedom from many different forms of emotional problems, is not also connected with scholastic achievement is at first surprising. One must recognize, however, that in the cloistered realm of the classroom or library, little demand is made on real ego strength. One is reminded of Goethe's famous observation "Es entwickelt sich ein Talent in den Stille" ("talent blooms in silence and stillness").

Factor D Excitability

Factor D, the excitability factor, has been found to be sometimes positively and sometimes negatively related to achievement. Perhaps factor D is more importantly associated with situational influences than some of the other factors. It could also be that the effect of factor D is substantially moderated by other factors, such as Q_4, in which case the profile pattern approach recently developed by Krug (1981b) could prove to be particularly valuable in further understanding the role of factor D in achievement.

Factor E Dominance

The role of factor E, dominance, is a very interesting one, showing the need to consider the ambient situation when making prediction of a performance from a measure or a trait. The general relation is a negative one to achievement in the earlier years and even through much of college. At the graduate student level, however, it becomes positive, as the student is thrown back more on his own initiative. In particular, higher dominance

is associated with independent research achievement and productive work in the arts.

The origin of the term "docile," virtually the same as "teachable," suggests that in early years docility and submissiveness (E−) favor imitation and absorption. Possibly, too, the classroom is less competitive in early years. Moreover, the dominant child may expend more energy in social and physical domination of other children (or even the teacher!) and neglect studies. Or, in school adjustment ratings he or she may be seen by authorities as responding inappropriately and as a result will not fare well. On the other hand, children who readily submit to authority and are willing to passively soak up information may attain higher grades. In later school years, particularly at the graduate school level, competition for marks and scholarships is likely to be more intense. At the same time, learning is more inclined to be an active, seeking-out experience, rather than a student-as-sponge process. As a result, the assertive, independent, high E student may encounter more success, explaining why achievement in later school years and particularly in graduate research and later life becomes positively associated with factor E.

Factor F Surgency

At one time it was thought that low factor F was indicative of depression, which would be expected to go along with less achievement. However, more recent work (e.g., Krug & Laughlin, 1977) indicates that factor F is largely independent of depression, and the underlying seriousness of the low F student is one of restraint and is actually correlated with higher achievement. Furthermore, the mercurial life-of-the-party, high F student does not seem as inclined to devote as much attention seriously to the attainment of academic and other proficiencies.

Factor G Superego

Of all the personality factors studied to date, factor G has shown the most consistent pattern of relationship with classroom achievement. In study after study, factor G typically has ranked next to intelligence when it comes to predicting achievement variance. Obviously, factor G deserves careful consideration by anyone trying to understand the complex process of achievement.

Looking at the overall findings about factor G, an interesting picture emerges. The high G person tends to be seen by others as "conscientious," a stickler for rules, and persistent in finishing jobs, while the low G person is described as "expedient," willing to break rules as seems appropriate, and inclined to be casual and even lazy. Clearly, an important ingredient of the factor is a willingness to conform to the rules that are necessary for the functioning of a school. If a student is constantly seeking to circumvent the rules, conflict with teachers seems inevitable. On the other hand, a student who is willing to observe the restrictions upon individual action necessary for group activity will face a less frustrating experience at school. In this sense factor G is a measure of what many educators have described as a student's general "attitude" toward school discipline.

Some writers have even interpreted factor G in a much broader way as an indicator of the extent to which a person has incorporated the ethical values of society within his or her own frame of reference. Cattell has repeatedly pointed to a moralistic, "categorical imperative" or "superego" quality of the high G person's conscientiousness, which he believes calls for an interpretation of factor G that transcends mere group conformity (see Karson & O'Dell, 1976, for a different view). In support of the broader view is the fact that "persistent," "persevering in face of obstacles," and "self-controlled" are among the

highest observer ratings on factor G. Thus, situational conformity to school cannot be the main cause of the achievement association, especially since G correlates with broader achievements outside school, in adult jobs, etc.

Factor H Parmia

Factor H, like factors A and E, has been found empirically to show some change in its relationship with achievement with increasing educational levels. In the early years the bold, adventurous, high H child is more successful at academic work. However, in later years the shyer, more bookish, low H student generally seems to do better than the high H student, who perhaps finds the scholarly life to be rather boring.

Factor I Premsia

Factor I has been found to correlate in some situations positively and in others negatively with school achievement. Unlike factors A, E, and H, which change their relation with achievement as a function of age or the level of educational study involved, the role of factor I seems to depend more upon the nature of the subject being studied. Material emphasizing emotional insights, as in the arts, tends to be more readily learned by those who are high in I. On the other hand, the toughness of low I students appears definitely to favor performance in science and technology.

Factor J Zeppia

Factor J is another factor that has shown statistically significant correlations with achievement but in different directions from one circumstance to another. At the present time we can only speculate about the reasons for these results. Since this factor is believed to be a reflection of how readily a person takes to a group activity, it could be that factor J will either be positively or negatively related to achievement, depending upon whether the entire group of students being studied has adopted a largely positive or negative orientation toward learning. This interesting probability suggests the need for J factor measures to be taken in studying the differences of classroom measures.

Factor L Protension

Factor L has so far been assessed only with adults. Research suggests that the suspicious, hard-to-fool outlook of high factor L is somewhat negatively related to ordinary school achievement, but positively to individualistic learning.

Factor M Autia

Just as with factor L, factor M has not been measured below the adult level. However, the indication from adult studies is that this factor, autia, new to most psychological discussion, plays an important role in achievement in higher education. The rich imagination of those high on M may contribute to impracticality and accident proneness in "real" life, but within the sheltered confines of universities, high M may be an asset in dealing with abstract ideas, especially in developing theory.

Factor N Shrewdness

Research with the 16 P.F. indicates that this factor of a socially shrewd approach to life tends to be moderately associated with achievement. On the basis of the research to date, N is not regarded as a major contributor to general achievement. However, as with some other factors discussed earlier, N could be useful in understanding *particular* types of achievement, e.g., those depending more on social skills. For instance, when marking is not done in an objective manner, high N students might be better able to give "diplomatic" answers that would be less likely to offend sensitive evaluators.

Factor O Guilt Proneness

As would be expected, the excessive apprehensiveness and low self-confidence of the high O person does not seem to be conducive to academic performance. We are not yet sure of the direction of causal action here because scholastic failure could contribute toward making a person more apprehensive and less confident—and school performance is an appreciable part of a child's life. Nevertheless, the "learned helplessness" of O factor, arising from aspects of life other than school, is very likely transferred to produce poor performance in school.

Factor Q_1 Radicalism

Factor Q_1, a measure of radicalness (not just in a political sense but in general attitude to life), has not proven to be a particularly powerful predictor of academic achievement. However, it is the most difficult of the Q factors to measure and may yet show some value in understanding phenomena such as dropping out of school.

Factor Q_2 Self-sufficiency

Factor Q_2 has repeatedly been found to be a potent predictor of achievement. The high level of self-sufficiency associated with this factor seems to be especially helpful in situations where a great deal of individual initiative is expected. Studies carried out in the British school system by Butcher et al. (1963) were among the first to recognize the importance of this dimension in school achievement, which makes good sense in view of the emphasis traditionally placed upon self-motivated study in that country.

Factor Q_3 Self-sentiment

Along with factor G, Q_3 has been the most consistent predictor of high achievement, extending over a variety of studies, and involving quite divergent samples of students. Together with G and to a lesser extent F, Q_3 makes up the broad second stratum *control* factor, which must now be regarded as having a good deal of importance for understanding achievement. The essence of Q_3 seems to be a desire to maintain a high level of self-control and self-respect. It has been termed the "gyroscope" factor by Stice (Cattell, Eber, & Tatsuoka, 1970), representing the action of the self-concept, and seems to play a significant role in guiding long-term planning and promoting the ability to resist impulsive behavior. In this regard, it is worth noting that research by Pierson, Cattell, and Pierce (1966) has shown that, like G, Q_3 shows a substantial increase in subjects exposed to a good course of institutional treatment for delinquency. Such findings reinforce the idea that an overall approach to education which focuses solely upon narrow, cognitive objectives to the exclusion of broad goals such as the development of self-control and self-respect, will fall far short of what is possible.

Factor Q_4 Ergic tension

Factor Q_4 has been found to be significantly related to achievement, but the results have sometimes indicated a positive and other times a negative relationship. Perhaps it will be found eventually that an inverted U relationship will hold between Q_4 and achievement. Such a relation has been postulated frequently by Eysenck (1964), as an instance of the Yerkes-Dodson law for performance and anxiety, of which Q_4 is a component. Being extremely low on Q_4 could result in a state of unproductive lethargy from being too relaxed, while the extreme tenseness of the high Q_4 student could interfere with achievement in an opposite manner. Ratings of "energetic" have shown some positive correlation with Q_4. Again, it will be up to future research to test this curvilinear relation.

Taken altogether, the results of research on achievement with personality measures are summarized in Table 20.1 containing the regression weights for predicting achievement, published in the HSPQ and 16 P.F. handbooks. The results depicted in Table 20.1 make clear that there is definitely not any single personality or ability factor that can be called *the* achievement factor.* As we have seen, factor G comes closest to being the most important factor after intelligence, but in a good prediction the contributions of other factors should be included. Achievement, like the learning process which it encompasses, seems best described as multidimensional change in response to multidimensional stimulation (Cattell, 1980a).

The multidimensionality of the achievement process is emphasized even further by the fact that we have not yet even considered the impact of motivational factors, which previous studies indicate may contribute as much as another 25% of achievement variation.

Research with motivation factors has not gone very far beyond the initial predictive phase, mainly because the functional measuring instruments such as the MAT and SMAT (discussed in Chapter 4) and others are of more recent origin. How-

---

*An excellent new longitudinal study and comparison with previous cross-sectional research on personality factors in academic achievement may be found in Hopkins, Allen, and Schuerger (1983). As in past work, the "control" factors of G, Q_3, and F were found to provide particularly important information above and beyond the intelligence factor, B.

TABLE 20.1
Regression Weights for Predicting Achievement

Factor		HSPQ	16 P.F.
A	Affectia	.08	.08
B	Intelligence	.66	.42
C	Ego strength	.00	−.16
D	Excitability	−.09	
E	Dominance	−.17	.22
F	Surgency	−.06	−.09
G	Superego	.42	.35
H	Parmia	.06	−.17
I	Premsia	−.37	.09
J	Zeppia	.06	
L	Protension		−.08
M	Autia		.35
N	Shrewdness		−.11
O	Guilt proneness	−.26	−.16
Q_1	Radicalism		−.06
Q_2	Self-sufficiency	.34	.34
Q_3	Self-sentiment	.17	.33
Q_4	Ergic tension	.25	−.20

ever, some interesting findings have begun to emerge. For instance, it seems that motives that are manifested in an integrated manner are more predictive of achievement than are the unintegrated motivation components (Cattell, Barton, & Dielman, 1972). According to present theory and experiment, the supergo and self-sentiment factors of the MAT and SMAT are the same factors (in different instrument "dress") as factors G and Q_3 of the questionnaires (Gillis & Lee, 1978). This is supported by their being found to have the same role in determining achievement (Cattell, Barton, & Dielman, 1972; Cattell & Child, 1975; Hakstian & Gale, 1979).

Other dynamic factors also enter in. A comparison of under- and overachievers shows differences, on the total (T = U + I) levels, and the I and U levels as indicated in Figure 20.1.

Other data show both sex (unintegrated) and pugnacity, as well as the unconscious component in attachment to the home (homesickness in college students?), related to poorer performance. The last is not easy to understand, but sex and pug-

nacity have been found before as a second-order factor presumably related to delinquency difficulties in acculturation, such as Freud described in *Civilization and its Discontent*. Much research on meaningful aspects of motivation by functional tests remains to be carried out, but the overall percent of achievement variance predicted increases from 50% by ability and personality, to 65% or more when ergs and sentiments are added.

THE BROADENING TECHNICAL POSSIBILITIES AND THE SOCIAL OBSTACLES THEY FACE

The title of this chapter indicates that it restricts itself to performance in schools. However, this is in many ways an artificial "cutting of the pie," for many other forms of performance are similar. Job performance is dealt with in Chapter 19, and what may be called, in some aspects, social adaptation and marital performance are dealt with in Chapters 17 and 18.

A domain in postschool life which nevertheless comes close to the school situation is that in which formal training is

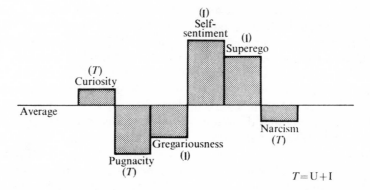

Figure 20.1. Profile showing relationship of dynamic structures to achievement

given to a) recruits for military specialties—a large-scale and vital area for psychologists in time of war; and b) individuals who lack the necessary skills for employment in peace time rehabilitation training. The former made tremendous strides in World War II. The report edited by Flanagan (1948) is a good representative documentation of the varieties of test construction, the criteria, and savings of manpower resulting from all three military programs. The latter was considerable, for example, in reducing crashes and fallout of expensively trained men in later training programs.*

Unfortunately this assault on problems of psychometrics, exceeding in concentration of talent and time anything previously known, occurred before basic research on personality structure and dynamic structure had laid a basis for functional testing. Only in the ability realm had the work of Thurstone and Guilford given clear guidance on test construction. Elsewhere, nine-tenths of the construction was of what we have designated special-purpose (not factored) tests going directly from a test score to a criterion. For example, in personality tests, questionnaires were used and, except for what later became the Guilford-Zimmerman

questionnaire, items, for infantry officer selection, for example, were picked out from a pool of shoveled-in items, by highest correlation with ratings in mock combat training, etc. (Since men already with combat experience were among those being selected, it is not surprising that the computer pushed to the fore as one of the best items an affirmative to "Have you ever been decorated for performance in the field?" for agreement with training rating!) Research producing Cattell's objective test-factored personality battery (a crude precursor of the present O-A Kit, Chapter 12) was brought to administrable form in the Army Adjutant General's Office Personnel Division only in the last three months of the war.

Thus, although this work demonstrated that psychological tests could predict various training and real-life performances well beyond the level of validity and reliability that the general public and the authorities had expected, it did little more theoretically than advance the "itemetric" phase of scale construction—an important step nevertheless. It also showed to the previous generation of educational psychologists, rather unimaginatively confined to ability tests, that personality and motivation were going to be even more important predictors. As we have seen, research has now shown that even in the academic classroom type of performance, personality and motivation tests just about

_____

*See also Psychology in War: The Military Work of German and American Psychologists. Cyril Burt, *Occupational Psychology*, 1942, July, pp. 1-17.

equal in predictive power the ability tests. In the broader types of examination performance and training situations of the military, and also in getting qualified in exams in the civil service, diverse jobs, and scholarship selection for various opportunities in life, it is surely to be expected that the personality and dynamic trait estimations will play a still larger role in relation to abilities.

In these fields (one of which — occupations—is well-illustrated in Chapter 19), the further developments beyond the ordinary classroom technical concepts arise not only by more inclusion of these two modalities, but also with greater knowledge of source-trait psychology. In school we are generally trying to understand the immediate situation or even to predict a year or so ahead. When the question concerns, say, promotion for several years in a civil service niche, or scholarship selection at 18 for, possibly, six or seven years of college work, functional testing becomes vital, for we need to know the typical life curves of various personality traits, and how they are likely to respond to learning situations (Barton & Cattell, 1975; Graffam, 1967).

Although obscured at the moment by a fog of ignorant and politically motivated views, the selection of bright young people to get support for longer and more advanced education is bound to be restored if our society is to survive. We shall glance at those views in a moment, but meanwhile let us consider the psychologist's capability to do a good job on what may briefly be called scholarship selection. The confining of selection to intelligence tests probably persisted partly because it was (rightly, in view of the latest evidence) unlikely to change by more than 5 or 10 points of I.Q. at retesting, whereas personality traits were considered likely to change appreciably during, say, four to six years. It *may* well be that motivation traits change this rapidly—we have as yet no long-term retests on MAT, SMAT and TAT—but, certainly after age 25 or 30

personality source traits do not *on an average* change very much (Kelly, 1955; (Cattell, 1973a). Besides, a few of them have a heritability quotient *virtually* as high as for intelligence. An introduction of personality factors, and even dynamic factors, into scholarship selection—both with due calculation of situations and normal trends—would, therefore, improve assignment of opportunities to those who can make the best use of them.

What has happened to forms of scholarship selection in both Britain and the U.S.A., in the 1950s and '60s, forces us to recognize, however, that classroom testing cannot be considered in this chapter without a brief glance at problems of interpretation to parents, the general public, and legislators. Some thought has already been given in earlier chapters, notably in Chapter 7, to problems of this kind. The "hippie revolt" of the '50s and '60s against examinations of any kind was only the visible expression of a normal constant human evasion of reality-testing, but, happening to coincide with an awareness of poor performance in a minority (of about 10% to 15% in the population), it was sufficiently reinforced to constitute a real setback to the progress of advancement by merit. There was a regression to older practices (judgment by a teacher's impression), which, in fact, have always been less fair, less accurate, and vulnerable to prejudice and personal influence with appointing powers. It is almost incredible that Professor Herrnstein of Harvard should have to write in 1982 (*The Atlantic Monthly*, August, p. 69), "I have now searched the daily and Sunday *New York Times* from 1975 to November of 1981 for all book reviews dealing with I.Q. Of the 15 reviews that I found, every one denigrated I.Q. tests, often vitriolically." It is the misfortune of society in a scientific age that it is served by an excess of literary-trained journalists, whose knowledge of biology, psychology, and genetics is as antiquated as the last generation's writings on progress which they defend with self-styled "righteous" indignation.* Individual differences are the indispensable stuff of evolution, and though no one knows what traits are *absolutely* good, it is everyday common sense that a tone-deaf woman is unlikely to become a good violinist and that a colorblind man should not be entrusted with an airplane control tower. Education being very expensive for society (*too* expensive for half the world's countries), it should be ensured of maximum impact (according to the parable of the talent) by adjustment to the individual differences of school children. And democracy requires similarly that in occupations merit should be assessed as accurately as possible and round pegs in square holes be avoided. Educational and vocational psychologists are presently offering more competent technical assistance than certain ill-informed legislators and public authorities are yet ready to use.

EVALUATING POTENTIAL OF CREATIVITY

Alert educators, at intervals over the last 100 years, have asked themselves whether the methods of education to which they have settled may be smothering creativity rather than fostering it. Examination and associated teaching methods produced in at least one major culture —mandarin China—a rigidity that seemed to reduce creativity below what would be expected from the intelligence manifestly

present in the generations concerned. The rigid diet of Latin grammar and some Greek of English public schools was something that Shakespeare largely escaped, and which creative people like Darwin, Churchill and many others dodged at the cost of being called dunces.

The subject of creativity is a many-faceted one, as the Taylor and Barron (1963) survey shows. Thus, in this section we shall set aside educational methods, which are not the topic of this book, and concentrate on the real advances that have been made in recognizing the talents and personality traits that go with creativity. Although most educators agree that examination-passing capacity is not everything and that multiple-choice test designs, despite reliability, miss this other ingredient, they have had difficulty in deciding just what creativity is. Nevertheless, the cultivation of creativity has become stated as an educational objective. But scientific research has been directed toward the study of creativity only in relatively recent times. Empirical studies of examination-passing date back to the turn of the century, but serious data collection about creativity really began in earnest about the 1950s. A large part of the slowness with which creativity has been studied seems to stem from the difficulty involved in distinguishing creativity from intelligence. In 1962, Getzels and Jackson published a report maintaining that creativity and intelligence were entirely independent phenomena. Within a very short time there was a barrage of criticism directed at Getzels and Jackson's formulation (see Butcher, 1972). More recently, several studies have used tests derived from a functional approach to psychometrics, and have found evidence that serves to clarify the situation.

Rossman and Horn (1972) found that when measures of fluid and crystallized intelligence were factor analyzed along with a variety of creativity measures, dimensions of creativity emerged which were "psychometrically and conceptually

---

*The section of the intelligentsia responsible for blocking progressive new adjustments in journalistic and popular circles is mainly a literary and sociological one. Both seem bogged down in the pre-biological "rationalism" of the French Encyclopedists of the 1750s of which Marxism is an offshoot. Probably the best documented and analyzed treatment of this root in the opposition to individual differences is Zirkle's *Evolution, Marxian Biology and the Social Scene*, 1959. Despite attempting to climb on the bandwagon of Darwin's prestige by asking permission to dedicate *Das Kapital* to Darwin, Marx never perceived the indispensable role of individual and group differences in evolution and, to this day, Russian schools are not allowed to use intelligence tests.

distinct from dimensions of intelligence." Similarly, Crawford and Nirmal (1976) found evidence of a separate creativity dimension when they included measures of fluid and crystallized ability in their factor analysis. In both of these studies, the results indicated that "correlated" but *distinct* factors of intelligence and creativity exist. However, one should bear in mind Spearman's (1930) fundamental position that, cognitively, creativity is relation and fundament eduction and therefore a function of g_f and g_c. Burt has shown, with more statistical sophistication than some of the above, that measures of creativity are highly loaded with intelligence. In the cognitive field, the fluency factor g_r (retrieval) is also important, but, as we shall see, creativity otherwise rests on personality properties which induce an individual to use these cognitive resources in an original fashion.

Believing that the study of only intellectual factors was not sufficient for an understanding of creativity, Cattell and Drevdahl (1955) undertook a research study of eminent researchers, teachers, and administrators in biology, physics, and psychology. Committees were set up from each profession and selections were made from among eminent men listed in

American Men of Science. The personality profile that was found for the research scientists may be seen in Figure 20.2, taken from the 16 P.F. handbook (Cattell, Eber, & Tatsuoka, 1970). Given the difficulty that has traditionally been associated with defining the creativity criterion, the clarity of these results is quite impressive. Even more remarkable is the fact that other researchers, working close to 20 years later with women scientists, have found 16 P.F. profiles that were strongly similar (Bachtold & Werner, 1972).

In another study of personality and creativity, Drevdahl and Cattell (1958) set up committees to select artists from among those people listed in *Who's Who in American Art*, together with writers who had extensive publications of high literary merit. The 16 P.F. was administered to these artists and writers, resulting in the personality profile illustrated in Figure 20.3, taken from the 16 P.F. handbook (Cattell, Eber, & Tatsuoka, 1970). Follow-up research by Cross, Cattell and Butcher (1967), involving a group of British artists showing clear evidence of unusual talent, together with a sample of craft students, produced results that were in "considerable agreement" with the earlier research. Similarly, Csiksz-

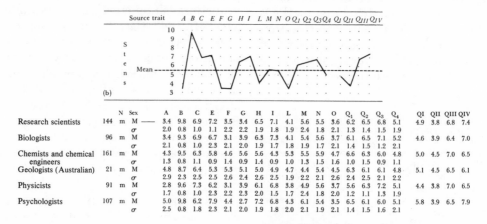

	N	Sex	A	B	C	E	F	G	H	I	L	M	N	O	Q₁	Q₂	Q₃	Q₄	QI	QII	QIII	QIV
Research scientists	144	m M —	3.4	9.8	6.9	7.2	3.5	3.4	6.5	7.1	4.1	5.6	5.5	3.6	6.2	6.5	6.8	5.1	4.9	3.8	6.8	7.4
		σ	2.0	0.8	1.0	1.1	2.2	2.2	1.9	1.8	1.9	2.4	1.8	2.1	1.3	1.4	1.5	1.9				
Biologists	96	m M	3.4	9.3	6.9	6.7	3.1	3.9	6.3	7.3	4.1	5.4	5.6	3.7	6.1	6.5	7.1	5.2	4.6	3.9	6.4	7.0
		σ	2.1	0.8	1.0	2.3	2.1	2.0	1.9	1.7	1.8	1.9	1.7	2.1	1.4	1.5	1.2	2.1				
Chemists and chemical engineers	161	m M	4.3	9.5	6.3	5.8	4.6	5.6	5.6	4.3	5.3	5.5	5.9	4.7	6.6	6.3	6.0	4.8	5.0	4.5	7.0	6.5
		σ	1.3	0.8	1.1	0.9	1.4	0.9	1.4	0.9	1.0	1.3	1.5	1.6	1.0	1.5	0.9	1.1				
Geologists (Australian)	21	m M	4.8	8.7	6.4	5.3	5.3	5.1	5.0	4.9	4.7	4.4	5.4	4.5	6.3	6.1	6.1	4.8	5.1	4.5	6.5	6.1
		σ	2.9	2.3	2.5	2.5	2.6	2.4	2.6	2.5	1.9	2.2	2.1	2.6	2.4	2.5	2.1	2.2				
Physicists	91	m M	2.8	9.6	7.3	6.2	3.1	3.9	6.1	6.8	3.8	4.9	5.6	3.7	5.6	6.3	7.2	5.1	4.4	3.8	7.0	6.5
		σ	1.7	0.8	1.0	2.3	2.2	2.3	2.0	1.5	1.7	2.4	1.8	2.0	1.2	1.1	1.3	1.9				
Psychologists	107	m M	5.0	9.8	6.2	7.9	4.4	2.7	7.2	6.8	4.3	6.1	5.4	3.5	6.5	6.1	6.0	5.1	5.8	3.9	6.5	7.9
		σ	2.5	0.8	1.8	2.3	2.1	2.0	1.9	1.8	2.0	2.1	1.9	2.1	1.4	1.5	1.6	2.1				

Figure 20.2. 16 P.F. profile of eminent scientific researchers*

*From the *Handbook for the 16 Personality Factor Questionnaire*, copyright © 1970, Institute for Personality and Ability Testing, Champaign, IL. Reproduced by permission.

entmihalyi and Getzels (1973) studied the 16 P.F. profiles of students at a well-known art school in the United States, and concluded that the agreement with previous findings was such that an association between certain personality characteristics and a successful artistic vocation "seems firmly established."

(A warning should be issued at this point about confusing the criterion of creativity in a one-hour situation, as in Guilford's studies, which has a large component of the fluency factor, g_r, with the criterion of creativity over the years, as in the studies now being cited. The latter has a far larger personality determination.)

The initially quite unexpected result is that life creativity arises from a remarkably similar personality profile across quite different areas of creation—art, science and literature. Essentially, Cattell and Butcher (1968) define the creativity here being assessed as *the capacity to break through current habits of thought and produce new and more effective ways of attaining desired goals.* One could expand a good deal on the psychological processes associated with the personality profile. It is probable that fluid intelligence, g_f, is more desirable than crystal-lized, g_c, for the latter is rich in current habits and, as the inventor Pickering said, and Edison's life illustrated, "It needs a certain amount of intelligent ignorance to create." The role of dominance, E factor, one can see both in the independence which breaks through custom and in the capacity to bear criticism. Combining the results illustrated in Figure 20.2 and 20.3—along with findings from other research by Chambers (1964), Jones (1964), and Tollefson (1970)—Cattell, Eber, and Tatsuoka (1970) have developed a regression formula for predicting the general criterion of creativity:

Creativity = .99 − .33A + .33 B +
  .17E − .33F + .16H + .33I + .16M −
  .16N + .16Q₁ + .33Q₂   (20-1)

(The first value is a constant to give estimates in stens.) The picture of the "creative personality" that emerges from all of this research with the 16 P.F. is naturally not completely different from that which was summarized earlier in terms of a regression formula for predicting school achievement. For example, the largest positive loading in both is on intelligence, though here an equally high

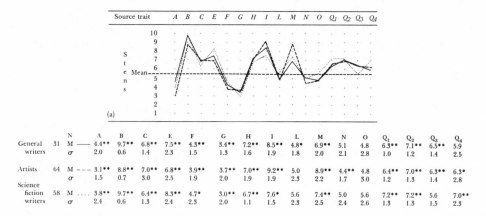

	N	A	B	C	E	F	G	H	I	L	M	N	O	Q₁	Q₂	Q₃	Q₄
General writers	31	M —— 4.4**	9.7**	6.8**	7.5**	4.3**	3.4**	7.2**	8.5**	4.8*	6.9**	5.1	4.8	6.3**	7.1**	6.5**	5.9
		σ 2.0	0.6	1.4	2.3	1.5	1.3	1.6	1.9	1.8	2.0	2.1	2.8	1.0	1.2	1.4	2.5
Artists	64	M --- 3.1**	8.8**	7.0**	6.8**	3.9**	3.7**	7.0**	9.2**	5.0	8.9**	4.4**	4.8	6.4**	7.0**	6.3**	6.3*
		σ 1.5	0.7	3.0	2.5	1.9	2.0	1.9	1.9	2.3	2.2	1.7	3.0	1.2	1.3	1.4	2.8
Science fiction writers	58	M 3.8**	9.7**	6.4**	8.3**	4.7*	3.0**	6.7**	7.6*	5.6	7.4**	5.0	5.6	7.2**	7.2**	5.6	7.0**
		σ 2.4	0.6	1.3	2.4	2.3	2.0	1.1	1.5	2.3	2.5	2.4	2.6	1.3	1.3	1.5	2.3

Asterisks indicate those factors on which differences from the general population are significant at (*) the 5 percent level or (**) the 1 percent level.

Figure 20.3. 16 P.F. profiles for creative artists and writers*

*From the *Handbook for the 16 Personality Factor Questionnaire,* copyright © 1970, Institute for Personality and Ability Testing, Champaign, IL. Reproduced by permission.

loading is found on self-sufficiency. In any case, as usual, it is apparent that many factors are involved rather than a single creativity or achievement factor.

It is likely that even more personality factors will be found to be involved in classroom achievement and creativity, and what we lack at the moment in creativity is research on what further contribution can be gained from dynamic factors assessed by the MAT, TAT, and SMAT. There is also already good reason to believe that the objective-analytic personality factors discussed in Chapter 12 have important connections with achievement and creativity (Cattell & Schuerger, 1978). Nevertheless, it can be said today that substantial progress has been made in using functional tests to understand the complicated processes of achievement and creativity. As elsewhere, the statistics of prediction are likely to proceed further by both the behavioral equation and the use of the pattern similarity coefficient, r_p, which will take account of nonlinear effects.

SUMMARY

The fact that the quality of living of a society—economically and politically—depends on the level of educational achievement has made the measurement of achievement an important and permanent feature of civilized societies. On the one hand, it tests the effectiveness of the schools and on the other, the fitness of individuals for particular jobs.

The question of how efficiently to measure achievement in itself is the subject of Chapter 10. Here we are concerned with factors *determining* achievement, and we concentrate on those in the individual in his life situation, not on those in teaching methods and the classroom environment.

For much of this century the attempts at prediction of achievement, at understanding causes of backwardness, and at selecting for scholarships, etc., have been based almost solely on intelligence tests. The result is typically a correlation of between 0.4 and 0.6 between ability test and achievement currently or in the immediate future.

It has now been shown by enough researches for a dependable conclusion that decidedly more—at least twice as much—of the variance of achievement can be accounted for if we include also measures of general personality factors and motivation. The percentage has typically been raised from 25%-36% to 60%-70% of the variance.

Prediction is not necessarily the main use of school testing. By knowledge of the same equation and its weights we can proceed to understanding the factors in over- and underachievement in the individual. With functional tests aimed at known common trait structures this can be done, but the traditional intelligence test, mixing fluid intelligence with school achievement, and thus giving an immediate higher "prediction" of school achievement, is much less effective for analytical purposes.

The Culture-Fair Intelligence Test (CFIT), the HSPQ 14 factors or 16 P.F. 16 factors in personality, along with the SMAT or MAT measuring dynamic, motivation factors, have been shown to contribute almost equally (and with little overlap) to the prediction of school achievement; about one-fourth of the total variance is accounted for by each in the combined regression equation.

The weights given to the general personality factors in such questionnaire tests as the HSPQ and 16 P.F. can be seen to make good sense psychologically, giving us insight into learning as a process. The self-sentiment, Q_3, and the superego, G, have the most substantive positive relation, but performance is multiply determined and at least eight factors have significant loading in the behavioral equation for achievement behavior.

Dynamic structure factors also show large positive relation to the self-sentiment and superego, while it is found that the integrated interest components are more predictive than the unintegrated. Strong unintegrated sex and pugnacity measures relate negatively to achievement.

Much the same analysis and equation weights are found in training beyond the school classroom level, e.g., in military classification, civil service selection, and occupational rehabilitation work. In these, however, the separate primary abilities have a larger role, and personality profile differences become more important relative to abilities. The greatly expanded use of tests in the emergency of war led to unassailable evidence of the practical gains from testing; however, most of the "itemetric" technical development preceded source trait as intermediate concepts in prediction, to come later in functional testing.

In spite of psychometrics and testing being the most novel and probably the most scientifically well-founded contribution of psychology to society, proper use got caught in a gust of reactionary practice in the 1950s and '60s from which, in some areas, complete recovery is still not evident. Psychologists have a duty to correct the misleading statements popularly made by certain journalists, since both the prosperity of society and the self-realization of the individual are set back by sociolegal obstacles to self-knowledge, good occupational adaptation, and society's best use of the available talent.

Schools have become as concerned about generating creativity as about ordinary examination attainment. In its cognitive processes creativity involves the same capacity to educe relations and correlates as in g_f and g_c, but in "examination room creativity" it also involves g_r, fluency, and in life—a more real criterion—it depends heavily on personality factors. A surprising finding is that, though the primary abilities required in art, science and literature differ appreciably, the test profile defining the creative person seems to require little modification by the area of creativity concerned. The behavioral equation stresses, besides intelligence, relatively introverted qualities in the primaries, namely, sizothymia $(A-)$ and desurgency $(F-)$. It also calls for higher self-sufficiency (Q_2), dominance (E), and premsia (I). The mode of operation of these traits is briefly discussed.

CHAPTER 21

Psychological Characteristics of Groups

John S. Gillis

POPULATION MEASUREMENT AND SYNTALITY MEASUREMENT CONTRASTED

This is the only chapter that addresses itself to the measurement of groups. Because of the needs of social psychology, cultural anthropology, history, sociology, economics, and political science, among academic specialties for quantitative theoretical development, this is becoming an important aspect of psychometry. This is by no means always appreciated by the studies concerned, although in the last 20 years some of them have begun to give considerable attention to quantifiable "social indices." Some of these, especially in economics, are pretty different from what one would think of as psychological measures. Going further afield into, say, agriculture, meteorology, and engineering, one would find variables relevant to groups that are still more remote.

One must recognize that measurement in the physical sciences—the centimeter, gram, second system—developed before

psychometry, and differs largely in not requiring in its foundations statistical reference to groups and norms, which marks the biosocial sciences. Within the biosocial sciences, however, psychology has some claim to having first solved, in psychometry, theorems that run through the biosocial sciences even in their nonpsychological variables. In any case, the life of groups is such that virtually all sociological, economic and political science variables derive from the behavior of people and are thus psychometric in the broadest sense.

Measurements on groups are of three kinds:

1) *Population measures*, which initially deal with the average properties of the individuals, e.g., mean I.Q., mean frequency of mental illness, mean score on an attitude survey, say, of attitude to divorce.
2) *Structural and role measures*, which are measures of relations of individuals within society, e.g., class distribution,

size of family, degree of democracy in political procedures, number of religious subcultures within a nation, and so on.

3) *Syntality measures*, which describe how the group acts when it acts as a unitary group. Syntality, which will be defined more fully below, is analogous in the organized group to personality in the individual. Sports teams, religious bodies, and nations as a whole can be shown to have a certain consistency of conduct over time, which permits us to distinguish them by certain syntality characteristics, e.g., aggressiveness in war, social conservatism, cultural productivity. Syntality characters may be thought of as both "emergents" from the interaction of population characteristics with internal structure and, in turn, as part determiners of population and structure.

Essentially there is nothing new in population measures beyond ordinary psychometry. One must watch sampling and, in comparison, populations of different groups, obtain a common basis for norms from a sample of groups. There is also need for a more sophisticated procedure in factorially defining traits common to all groups (see Cattell, 1970b, on isopodic and equipotent comparisons of factor scores with different patterns). Population measures are made not only for comparisons across groups but also for comparisons of a temporal nature—as in history—within a group. This occurs frequently in opinion polling, where the percentage of the population desiring income tax change, or belonging to a church, or having confidence in the president or prime minister is recorded, say, every month or so to see what change is occurring.

Although one could certainly spend several chapters in detailed discussion of such population measurement techniques as opinion polling methods and surveys of such areas as mental health and family structure, the present chapter will give it quite limited treatment and concentrate on the second and newer aspect of psychometry involved in testing groups *as groups*. (The survey of populations is in any case partly dealt with in the chapters on aptitude testing, intelligence testing, etc.) The justification for substantial discussion on syntality measurement is that human relations, social structure, and the ultimate behavior of Hobbes' "Great Leviathan," which is the group organism, are central to the entire discipline of social psychology, which in turn may be seen as providing the basic psychological foundation for advances of knowledge in other fields of social science, such as sociology, political science, anthropology, social work, and economics.

The kinds of groups that psychologists and other social scientists are called upon to analyze are extremely varied, ranging from basic two-person groups to entire nations. Because of this great variety of groups, the research task confronting psychologists who attempt to understand group behavior is enormously complex. As a result, the need for sophisticated scientific instruments, as have been developed using the functional approach to psychological measurement, is perhaps greater than in any other area of psychology. Yet, nowhere has there been as great an underutilization of functional tests than in the domain of social psychology.

The most important reason for the failure to take advantage of functional testing instruments seems to have been the strong tendency for social psychologists to ignore testing in general. For one thing, until recent years, the prevailing sociological approach has been to look for causes of social behavior almost exclusively in the environment rather than the person. This is partly ideological and partly due to a technical failure of conventional tests to produce consistent findings during the 1930s, 1940s, and early 1950s. For whatever reason, social psychologists turned more and more to an extreme situational point of view. Fortunately, after the situational approach "peaked" (or "valleyed" depending on how one looks at it) in the late 1960s (e.g., Mischel, 1968), a more balanced "interactional" theoretical perspective has become more widely accepted (e.g., Bowers, 1973; Endler & Magnusson, 1976). At the same time, the systematic attention to situational variables by Endler and Hunt (1969), Sells (1963) and others, and the development of an adequate quantitative model in relation to the behavior equation by Cattell (1948a, 1950, 1963a, 1979c, 1980a) rendered "environment-versus-person" an obsolete issue. Henceforth Cattell's method of calculating a taxonomy of environment, of using matrix algebra to catch its multifarious action, and of relating true and subjective perceptions of environment in the spectrad theory (attribution), offered a synthesis that met the needs of a realistic social psychology.

THE SYNTALITY, STRUCTURE, POPULATION MODEL

To deal with the psychology of groups, a group must be defined psychologically. Cattell has suggested "a set of people whose behaviors are so interrelated that most members contribute positively to the satisfaction of other members, who stay in the group because of their satisfaction" (Cattell, 1980a, p. 463). Most definitions of "common purpose," "mutual recognition," etc. follow from this primary dynamic concept that a group is an instrument for the satisfaction of individuals. Viewed in this way groups can be readily distinguished from mere "aggregates" of people temporarily and arbitrarily classified together without regard for psychological forces between members.

According to this view, group behavior is seen as a complex interaction between the psychological disposition of the group and situational factors in the environment. The fundamental formula for group behavior is, therefore:

$$\text{Group Behavior} = (f) \, S \cdot E \qquad (21\text{-}1)$$

where S stands for the "syntality" or personality of the group and E represents the environment. This formula is essentially the same as that set out in Chapter 2 by Raymond Cattell in equation 2-2 (p. 16) as being basic to the understanding of *individual* behavior, thus recognizing a group as having organismic properties.

There is, however, one important difference between the personality of an individual and the syntality of a group. Unlike individuals, whose basic structure has been laid down by nature through the long process of evolution, groups may differ very fundamentally from one another in their overall structure and change their structure more radically than can an individual. As a result, it is necessary to recognize that the syntality of a group needs to be further broken down as follows:

$$\text{Syntality} = (f) \, R \cdot P \qquad (21\text{-}2)$$

where R signifies *group structure* and P means the *population characteristics* of the group. Group structure includes the rules governing such things as:

1) interaction patterns between group members (who reports to whom);
2) how decisions are made by the group;
3) whether the group has any formal officers or leaders;
4) how officers or leaders are chosen; and
5) how funds are raised.

Group structure also encompasses the roles or duties that are prescribed by the group for each member, e.g., who acts as spokesperson for the group, who has responsibility for maintaining records, and other behaviors essential for continued functioning of the group. Population characteristics refer to the personal characteristics of individual members of the group, such as sex, age, religion, ethnicity, social class, and all of the ability, e.g., I.Q., dynamic, and temperament dimensions discussed in previous chapters. In the ultimate systems model (Cattell, 1980a), equation 21-2 is taken only as a simplified aspect of the whole, since there is six-way causal action: population affects structure (and vice versa); structure affects syntality (and vice versa); and syntality (interacting with the environment of the group) affects population character (and vice versa).

As an illustration of Cattell's multivariate, interactionist approach to analyzing group behavior, consider the hypothetical case of a successful large corporation that decided to open up a branch in a foreign country. A group of highly qualified employees were selected and sent to the foreign country with instructions to set up a new branch exactly according to the "tried and true" company policies. Much to the surprise of company executives it was soon apparent that the new venture was failing miserably. What had gone wrong? The syntality (S) of the employees was the same as those back home, since the population characteristics (P) of the group had not been changed, and the group structure (R) had followed a proven formula for success. Clearly, the major difficulty was that the environment (E) was now different.

Faced with such a problem the parent company would basically have the following options:

1) pull out of the new country;
2) try to change E, for example, by taking steps in support of a new government with policies more advantageous to the company;
3) try to change P by bringing in a new group of employees with population characteristics more conducive to personal adjustment in the new culture, or

try to change P by involving employees in a cultural training program; and
4) try to change R by restructuring the rules and roles of the employees.

Which options, or combination of options, selected by a company would depend upon many factors, but one of the most important could well be an analysis made by a psychologist trained in the use of functional tests working within the framework of a multivariate, interactional perspective. Such an analysis would be guided by the research that has already been undertaken with functional tests.

As pointed out earlier, the number of research findings based upon structured psychometrics is not as great in the area of social psychology as in clinical settings or in educational practice. However, many valuable results have been obtained.

In the following sections research will first be considered separately with regard to population characteristics and group structure. Then a brief look will be taken at the complex interaction of population characteristics and group structure involved in the syntality of small and large groups.

THE DIMENSIONS OF POPULATIONS

The demographer of population usually begins with such basic characteristics as size, sex proportions, age proportions, mean real income, urban-rural ratios, birth rates, calories consumed, crime rates, etc. All of these express themselves also in psychological characteristics but until recently, except for opinion polling (see the following section) and the standardizations of intelligence tests, we have had available very little indeed concerning quantitative statements about means and distributions on psychological characteristics such as anxiety score, extraversion level, degree of neuroticism, average ergic tension (Q_4), elation-depression level, ego strength level (C), etc.

For some reason, of all the population characteristics of groups that have been studied by psychologists, the psychological levels associated with difference of sex have been one of the most popular. Because so much has been done in the area of sex differences, one might expect that many basic general findings would have emerged. Unfortunately, as illustrated by the recent controversy that has developed around the notion of psychological "androgyny" (e.g., Bem, 1981), progress in this area has not been as rapid as would be expected. Constantinople (1973), for example, has suggested that masculinity-femininity is one of the "muddiest" concepts in the vocabulary of psychologists.

Fortunately, in recent years the situation has been clarified. After many studies carried out in the 1970s on the topic of androgyny, it finally has been recognized that, just because a single word, such as "androgyny," or two words, such as "masculinity" and "femininity," have been used, this does not necessarily mean that only one or just two dimensions exist. Actually, as may readily be seen in Table 21.1, highly significant sex differences on as many as 11 dimensions have been found consistently in research with the 16

P.F. factors E and I are probably the main components of the "masculine instrumentality" and "feminine expressiveness" dimensions identified by Spence and Helmreich (1980). But this leaves many more personality differences to be taken into consideration.

Had well-replicated findings from functional psychological testing, which have been available since the 1950s and 1960s, been taken into consideration by researchers, the conclusions recently reached by Colwill and Lips (1978), Pleck (1975), and Wesley and Wesley (1977) about the multidimensionality of sex differences in personality could have been arrived at much earlier.

Another population characteristic that has been studied extensively is age. Age constitutes the *sine qua non* variable of developmental psychology, where functional tests have begun to be used to make major advances in knowledge. Because the 16 P.F., HSPQ, CPQ, ESPQ, and PSPQ were designed to measure personality in a comprehensive, interlocking manner, offering continuity in scoring traits over the entire life span, it has been possible to chart the age trends of personality development in a manner that has never

TABLE 21.1

Mean Sex Differences on Primary Personality Factors

(a) Among American Adults (16 PF) [a]

	A	B	C	E	F	G	H	I	L	M	N	O	Q_1	Q_2	Q_3	Q_4
Men																
Mean	18.49	13.44	32.96	24.28	26.18	28.21	28.50	17.83	16.70	22.15	21.93	19.91	20.13	20.49	23.54	22.21
SD	6.84	3.27	6.92	6.28	7.89	5.71	9.82	5.59	5.04	5.89	3.79	6.90	4.60	5.51	4.95	7.93
Women																
Mean	23.14	13.44	33.26	17.30	25.86	28.69	25.43	24.78	14.96	24.17	20.53	23.43	17.61	20.22	22.78	26.78
SD	6.12	3.27	7.87	6.54	7.75	5.01	9.90	4.58	5.67	3.98	7.30	4.32	5.10	4.92	8.30	
Difference [b]	−4.65	0.00	−0.30	6.98	0.32	−0.48	3.07	−6.95	1.74	−2.02	1.40	−3.52	2.52	0.27	0.76	−4.57
t Value	15.50	0.00	0.91	24.93	0.89	2.00	6.67	28.96	7.91	7.21	8.24	11.00	12.60	1.13	3.45	12.35
P	<0.001	NS [c]	NS	<0.001	NS	<0.05	<0.001	<0.001	<0.001	<0.001	<0.001	<0.001	<0.001	NS	<0.001	<0.001

[a] Between men and women corrected to age 35 (raw scores).
[b] Positive if men higher.
[c] NS = not significant.

(b) Among British Adults [a]

	A	B	C	E	F	G	H	I	L	M	N	O	Q_1	Q_2	Q_3	Q_4
Men																
Mean	17.58	14.65	30.80	25.00	26.27	24.63	27.25	17.63	17.72	22.94	20.96	19.69	18.86	20.40	24.86	23.77
SD	5.85	3.47	6.99	7.30	9.23	5.90	10.30	5.76	5.63	4.80	7.79	4.97	5.76	6.00	9.20	
Women																
Mean	21.72	14.16	28.07	19.09	26.42	24.79	23.48	25.01	15.89	21.75	22.34	25.35	16.49	19.68	23.13	28.78
SD	5.02	3.44	6.67	6.69	8.61	5.46	10.36	4.58	4.94	5.92	4.71	7.58	4.71	5.59	5.73	8.16
Difference [b]	−4.14	0.49	2.73	5.91	−0.15	−0.16	3.77	−7.38	1.83	1.19	−1.38	−5.66	2.37	0.72	1.73	−5.01
t Value	17.02	3.18	8.96	18.92	0.38	0.63	8.18	31.78	8.29	4.62	6.50	16.50	10.97	2.84	6.61	12.91
P	<0.001	<0.01	<0.001	<0.001	NS [c]	NS	<0.001	<0.001	<0.001	<0.001	<0.001	<0.001	<0.001	<0.11	<1.112	<2.222

[a] Courtesy of Peter Saville and the National Foundation for Educational Research.
[b] Positive if men higher.
[c] NS = not significant.

been feasible using other approaches to testing. For example, the age trends illustrated in Figure 21.1 are for the well-replicated second-order personality patterns of exvia, anxiety, cortertia, and independence (the primary factor age trends may be found in Cattell, 1973a, from which the present results have been extracted). These age trends may be modified somewhat as new information is obtained using the sophisticated new multivariate designs that have been developed in recent years by Baltes and Nesselroade (1973), Buss (1974), Cattell (1969a, 1970c), and Schaie (1973). However, these initial findings already indicate rich possibilities for the construction of theories about personality development that are based on careful measurement of functional unities rather than guesses about conglomerations of variables or univariate measures.

The ultimate aims of experimental data-gathering on population characteristics are several: data for government; attitudes for politicians; and, for the scientist as such, those comparisons across cultures and across decades that will bring the first steps in the solution of the $S = (f) R \cdot P$ equations, such as is illustrated below in the relation of average population I.Q. to the syntality dimension of enlightened prosperity.

As to population personality parameters, rapid advance has been made in the last decade, inasmuch as the primary source-trait measures in the 16 P.F. have been translated into many different languages and administered to groups of people from different cultures (Cattell, Eber, & Tatsuoka, 1970). Because difficulties in making comparisons between different language and cultural groups still remain (Cattell, 1969a, 1973a), the differences in mean levels of the individual factors so far obtained must still be regarded as being of a tentative nature. However, to illustrate the possibilities of the functional testing approach in the area of national comparisons of personality, a sample of typical results are set forth in Table 21.2, where many interesting differences may be observed.

Further work with different countries has also been undertaken to determine the interrelationships between population characteristics in the form of second-order factors, notably by Lynn (1971, 1979) and associates abroad working with Cattell. Before comparing *levels*, it is important to examine *structure*, in terms of the patterns of primaries that constitute second-stratum factors. The data from these researches are remarkable in their consistency and may be considered to be quite firmly established, in contrast to the conclusions on differences in *levels* of primary factors. As may be seen in Table 21.3, in spite of the immense differences in language and culture among the countries, there is a striking regularity of pattern in the way in which primary factors group together into secondaries.

A variety of other population characteristics, such as social status (Cattell, 1973a, p. 344), religion (Barton & Vaughan, 1976) and geographical region (Krug & Kulhavy, 1973), have been studied using

TABLE 21.2

1. National Culture Differences: National Levels of Primary and Secondary Traits

	Sex	N	A	C	E	F	G	H	I	L	M	N	O	Q_1	Q_2	Q_3	Q_4	I	II	III	IV
Australia	M	694	5.1	5.6	5.2	5.6	5.1	4.5	5.7	6.1	5.3	6.1	5.9	5.6	6.6	5.4	5.5	7.61	6.42	5.28	6.80
Brazil	M	1406	5.6	4.7	4.8	3.7	5.6	5.3	6.4	7.6	7.2	5.0	6.5	6.1	6.1	5.5	6.0	3.06	6.63	5.12	7.23
China	M	425	5.4	3.9	3.9	3.8	5.1	4.8	6.1	7.0	6.5	4.6	5.5	6.0	6.2	6.7	4.8	3.92	9.45	4.61	6.63
Germany	M	1000	5.7	6.1	4.9	5.5	5.5	5.4	3.6	5.7	4.9	6.6	5.7	6.5	5.3	7.1	4.4	4.84	5.04	7.60	6.61
India	M	100	4.6	2.6	3.4	3.5	5.0	4.8	2.4	5.5	5.0	4.2	4.6	5.3	4.7	4.6	3.9	3.96	6.44	4.91	4.63
Japan	M	300	4.2	3.3	5.3	3.2	4.5	3.8	6.0	5.9	7.2	5.7	6.7	7.3	6.8	4.6	6.6	3.05	7.38	6.94	7.92

Note: The above results are in stens on American norms so that comparisons are immediate with the U.S.A. mean (5.5). Thus, for example, all countries but Germany are higher than the U.S.A. on anxiety QII. Details and further examples are available in Cattell, Eber, and Tatsuoka (1970).

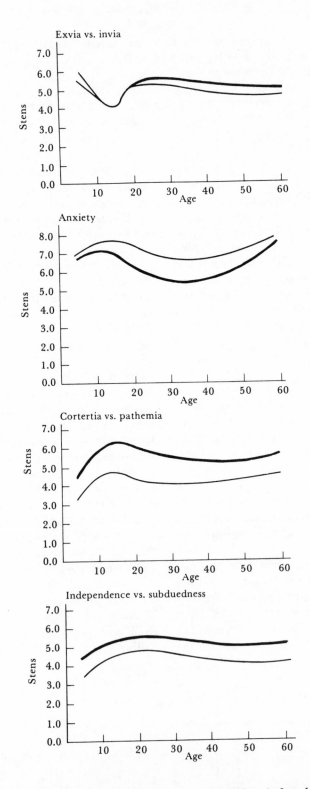

Figure 21.1. Age trends for secondaries I, II, III, and IV (thin line is females; thick line is males)

TABLE 21.3

Agreement of Eight Second-Order Factor Patterns
Across Six or More Diverse Cultures

Adults: First Two Factors

	I: Exvia								II: Anxiety							
	1	2	3	4	5	6	7	8	1	2	3	4	5	6	7	8
A	74	67	61	53	66	37	62	51	01	−08	−02	−04	06	−02	03	−04
B	−01	−10	00	−01	−00	−01	−03	03	00	02	−01	−02	−03	−03	−02	−02
C	09	−22	05	−01	06	16	12	02	−83	−65	−73	−78	−74	−34	−60	−74
E	17	24	05	05	06	04	11	08	15	−09	−00	−01	03	02	−13	06
F	35	54	56	54	53	29	55	57	−02	−00	−03	−08	−08	−01	−00	−16
G	08	−17	01	01	09	08	15	−01	−01	−04	−03	−01	−05	−01	−16	−14
H	65	56	54	56	56	40	47	58	−32	−42	−42	−37	−37	−25	−48	−47
I	01	13	03	07	10	02	13	13	−01	−11	−02	−07	00	−02	02	09
L	03	24	−00	−01	05	−28	03	17	62	66	59	55	56	43	51	79
M	−09	−07	−17	−09	−09	−35	−18	−32	−11	11	10	17	04	06	04	−06
N	−01	−02	00	−01	04	−01	−03	00	−04	12	−01	02	−07	04	−04	04
O	−15	06	−08	−02	−06	04	10	15	82	80	83	81	84	69	68	67
Q_1	04	−32	−01	−01	03	−08	−01	−24	02	−14	−06	−03	−05	−08	−01	−04
Q_2	−75	−33	−61	−69	−70	−54	−62	−88	12	11	−03	−06	−03	00	02	−09
Q_3	−09	11	−10	−03	−08	−07	03	−10	−44	−82	−42	−38	−53	−41	−37	−42
Q_4	11	06	02	03	−01	−06	−05	00	88	83	76	76	86	78	68	87

Note: The boxes pick out the standard primary markers. For exvia and anxiety the samples are in order: American, Japanese, German lower class, German upper class, British, Brazilian, Venezuelan, and New Zealand as specified by Dr. K. E. Nichols (preliminary data in Cattell and Nichols, 1972).

functional tests of basic trait structures.

Although, as will be seen from results on syntality-population relations, we are on the brink of some very important perceptions, the sheer cost of organizing work of this kind and obtaining dependable cooperation abroad, as well as the needed stratified samples, has been a severe obstacle. It remains to be seen whether the next generation of social psychologists and cultural anthropologists will carry on with the necessary persistence and with the reliable strategic choice of population and syntality dimensions to permit integrated advance.

SURVEY MEASUREMENTS IN POPULATIONS

The varieties of social indicators that can be measured on populations, as discussed above, are endless. The developments—except for basic research on population syntality relations—have been largely, in practice, in a) commerce, in terms of market research and advertising; b) government departments and ministries wishing information about mental health, magnitude of drug problems, styles of family living, etc.; and c) political groups wanting to estimate popularities of persons and policies by polling.

In the marketing area such results have turned up as extraverted women wanting brighter varieties of lipstick, and sales of a certain product being increased by giving it the name of a popular stage character. Both psychoanalytic and Skinnerian "experts" have been called on by Madison Avenue to beget theories and test by polling. Fortunately, most of this seduction has used simple polling of attitudes and not availed itself of the dynamic calculus, though one study with the MAT enlightened drug salesmen to the fact that doctors who more freely prescribed a certain tranquilizer were lower on superego scores!

So far the surveying of population qualities has followed essentially simple psychometric procedures scarcely requiring discussion here. There are, first, problems of sampling—obtaining a stratified sample or correcting if one cannot get a satisfactory representation. Second, there are problems of getting the most unambiguous and significant questions, reaching down to low literary levels (as the national census realizes!). Third, there is the question of how to interpret, including how much to allow for temporary influences. The whole development of objective devices for attitude measurement, with recognition of U and I components, in Chapter 13, has shown how superficial, biased and undependable the verbal "for or against checked" attitude measurement is. "For" or "against" can have quite a different ergic vector for different persons. It is not surprising that several instances have occurred in political polling showing that the traditional type of polling measurement (% for) cannot be insightfully corrected for intervening events before the final polling booth count.

In addition to studies of the predominantly biologically based population characteristics of sex, age, and ethnicity, functional testing methods have also been applied to the investigation of more culturally influenced variables, such as socioeconomic status and public opinions.

With regard to socioeconomic status, a variety of indices have been used over the years in the vast amount of research that has been concerned with this topic. Yet, as Stricker (1980, 1982a) has noted, most of these one or two variable measures were never subjected to rigorous psychometric examination. In an effort to redress the situation, Stricker gathered together a comprehensive sample of socioeconomic indices and carried out multifactor oblique factor analyses with samples of blacks and whites in a northern U.S. city. Stricker's results indicate that the whole area of social stratification seems to be much more complicated than many writers had previously assumed. Moreover, the results of this investigation clearly illustrate the advantages of multivariate, concept-based indices of social status over *ad hoc* univariate or bivariate measures. For example, in both the white and black samples there was a well-matched factor of social status in contrast to the more ambiguous results with single measures.

Turning now briefly to the extensive area of public opinion surveys and social attitude assessment, it may be seen that a plethora of special-purpose scales have been developed. Robinson and Shaver (1973) at the Institute for Social Research of the University of Michigan, as well as Shaw and Wright (1967), have done an excellent job of cataloguing all of these specialized instruments. However, the overall end result is similar to that of psychological tests in general. There is a bewildering array of opinion and attitude scales with very little information about whether scales with similar names are actually measuring the same things or whether those with different names may actually be getting at similar phenomena from different angles. In other words, there is a great need for a systematic mapping out of relationships among the variety of opinion surveys and social attitude scales that have been developed by independent researchers. Fortunately, some early research has followed the structured psychometrics approach being advocated in the present volume, and the long-term dividends of building in knowledge of interrelationships between measures through multivariate techniques are beginning to become evident.

Take, for example, the work by Cohen and Streuning (1959, 1962, 1963), in which a factor analysis of opinions of mental illness was carried out. These researchers found evidence of the existence of five factors—1) authoritarianism, 2) benevolence, 3) mental hygiene ideology, 4) social restrictiveness, and 5) interpersonal etiology—underlying the opinions of hospital personnel. A decade later when the Opinions of Mental Illness Scale (OMI) was administered by other researchers to a sample of 138 college students, and the results were analyzed with improved factor analytic techniques, the OMI dimensions proved to be replicable (Dielman, Stiefel, & Cattell, 1973). More recent research also has supported the earlier findings with a sample of community volunteer workers (Wahl, Zastowny, & Briggs, 1980).

Some differences in the loadings of individual items were found, but such minor discrepancies are not surprising in view of the 20-year time period since the OMI construction and the difference in samples involved. The important thing was that the essential pattern of the five dimensions could be demonstrated. Such psychometric sturdiness stands in sharp contrast to the "now you see it—now you don't" quality of the numerous special-purpose opinion scales that have been created with little knowledge of, or regard for, anything other than immediate prediction of specific criteria.

Similar results have also been obtained in the area of political opinion surveys. Using multivariate procedures, Eysenck (1954) developed the Public Opinion Inventory for measuring the dimensions of political ideology which he and other writers have referred to as: 1) radicalism vs. conservatism; and 2) tender-mindedness vs. tough-mindedness.

Although this work contains what may be regarded as technical drawbacks, such as the fact that principal components analysis instead of principal factor analysis was employed (Cattell, 1978), it may be seen in a summary of more than 25 years of research that consistent findings concerning these dimensions of political opinion have tended to emerge (Eysenck & Wilson, 1978). In comparison, other instruments created at about the same time, like the well-known F scale for measuring authoritarian personality (Adorno, Frenkel-Brunswick, Levinson, & Sanford, 1950), seem to have produced a hodgepodge of inconsistent findings paralleling the basic psychometric procedures used in constructing the original scales.

THE MEASUREMENT OF GROUP STRUCTURE

Many novel problems face the psychologist who would go beyond his usual field of personality measurement of popula-tions, on the one hand, and the cultural anthropologist's nonquantitative description of cultural structure, on the other. He needs now to cope with the nature of social status, leadership, numerous role patterns, and interpersonal dealings. Social status has been intensively examined. Factor analysis has been used from the early work of Cattell (1942) to the latest sophisticated analyses of Stricker (1980, 1982a), and a model and method for differentiating role behavior from personality trait behavior have been developed (Cattell, 1980a).

Let us begin with the important topic of interpersonal attraction, so important in friendship, the family, and the army platoon. We shall see later that one of the dimensions of morale in small groups arises from a natural cohesiveness based on interpersonal attraction, or at least interpersonal congeniality and toleration of the others involved. An essential question that has therefore been posed by social scientists has been, "What is the nature of this contribution to psychological forces that serve to hold people together in groups?" At least as far back as Plato, there has been speculation about this question, and in this generation it has particularly focused on the fundamental two-person group of marriage partners.

Let us begin by studying the two-member group. Here several researchers support what has become known as the similarity, likeness or assortive hypothesis of mate selection (see Vandenberg, 1972, for a review). Others have espoused the popular notion about opposites attracting, known as the theory of complementarity (Winch, 1967), though it gets very little support.

Using the 16 P.F., Cattell and Nesselroade (1967) undertook an exploration of the basic ideas of "likeness" and "completeness" in group structure with stably and unstably married couples. These authors found strong evidence that stably married couples were more similar in personality than unstably married couples.

Subsequent studies of the personality structure of married couples have confirmed the likeness finding by showing that the similarity of married couples tends to be general, but is greater on some of the 16 P.F. scales (Barton & Cattell, 1972; DeYoung & Fleischer, 1976) than others. The results of these studies may be seen in Table 21.4.

The DeYoung and Fleischer research and a study by Woliver (1979) with the MAT showed that the law of similarity extends to motivational variables, while the Barton and Cattell (1972) study showed, in addition, that couples "perceive" themselves as being even more similar than is actually the case. The investigation with the 16 P.F. by Sindberg, Roberts and McClain (1970) has provided evidence from a new angle on the importance of personality similarity in marriage partners. They compared the 16 P.F. profiles of 25 couples, who subsequently married after being matched through a computer dating service, with a randomly selected group of clients who did not marry after being matched. This research is of particular importance because the 16 P.F. measurements were taken *prior to the couples ever meeting one another*, thus indicating that the personality resemblance between marriage partners was not simply a result of having lived together.

The hypotheses of Cattell and Nesselroade that a law of supplementation (or complementation) also applied has not been so easy to check upon because of the entanglement of its effect with the similarity principle. This says that the *sum* of the two should reach high levels on adjustive traits for a group among groups, e.g., intelligence, ego strength, and low levels on neurotic traits, e.g., anxiety, O, Q_4. It is at least indicated that marriages breaking up sum more poorly on these.

A second concept beyond personality entering these calculations is, of course, structure ($S = (f) P \cdot R$), in terms of accepted roles. Barton (1976), Barton and Cattell (1973), Barton, Kawash, and Cattell (1972) have measured some aspects of this, and also focused on measuring the intrafamilial attitudes of parents (Barton, Dielman, & Cattell, 1973; Delhees, Cattell, & Sweney, 1970). A theory of effects on children of parental role relations has been checked, with significant relations appearing, by Heather E. P. Cattell (1982).

From the standpoint of a practitioner concerned with marital counseling, the possibilities of insightful diagnosis have improved tremendously through such researches as the above. There is no excuse today for intuitive hit-or-miss methods, since from personality and motivation measures calculations of certain probabilities of sound adjustment can be made,

TABLE 21.4
Husband-Wife Correlations in Personality
Primary 16 P.F. Factors

	A	B	C	E	F	G	H	I	L	M	N	O	Q_1	Q_2	Q_3	Q_4
Cattell and Nesselroade																
(stable group) (N = 102)	16	31	32	13	23	33	23	−1	18	22	18	11	27	15	27	16
Cattell and Barton (N = 171)	30	37	13	35	38	32	12	28	29	33	13	20	26	27	25	16
DeYoung and Fleischer (N = 82)	30	27	01	38	35	29	14	14	19	32	17	11	42	22	23	28

and the traits can be located that need modification for better satisfaction of the similarity and supplementation principles. However, this is only the beginning of a psychometric advance to still more subtle and objective techniques.

Probably the most important structural relations to be investigated (in somewhat larger groups than dyadic ones) are those of leadership (by individual or government) and of social stratification. What happens when you take 1000 men, place them into 100 groups of 10 men each and provide a variety of group tasks to be accomplished? Will the groups structure themselves so that leaders emerge? The answer from research by Cattell and Stice (1960) was that, if the groups faced problems, a desire for leadership tended to develop. Profiles of the personality patterns of elected, effective and technical leaders found by Cattell and Stice (1960) may be seen in Figure 21.2.

In Figure 21.2 it may be seen that regardless of the type of leader selected, whether by elected, effective, or technical criteria, a unique leader personality pattern emerges common to all. When combined with similar findings from other groups, such as military officers, university administrators, and business executives, these results concerning the central personality pattern of leadership have made possible the derivation of a general regression equation (see Table 21.5) for predicting leadership (Cattell, Eber, & Tatsuoka, 1970) mainly based on small group, face-to-face group member interaction. The picture of a leader that emerges from this research makes good psychological sense. According to Table 21.5, leaders may be seen as being somewhat above average in intelligence (B+) and ego strength (C+), emotionally tougher and realistic (I−), with a practical orientation to problems (M−). Above all leaders exhibit an ability to be comfortable in group situations (H+), and seem able to speak up and express opinions (F+), although without being excessively extraverted,

TABLE 21.5
Regression Weights for Predicting Leadership

16 P.F. Factor	Weight
A	.00
B	.12
C	.12
E	.05
F	.24
G	.24
H	.24
I	−.12
L	.00
M	−.12
N	.05
O	−.24
Q_1	.00
Q_2	.00
Q_3	.24
Q_4	−.12
Constant	1.65

since A and Q_2 do not seem to enter into the equation. There is a noticeable inclination away from guilt-proneness (O−), but at the same time a high dependability as to ethical principles (G+) and exacting standards of self-image (Q_3+) are strongly required by the group choice. A problem in the area is that the apparent leader is not always the real leader ("the power behind the throne" role). Certainly the real leader is not always the most popular member of the group, as was often assumed in early research on leadership. The most elegant and useful operational definition of the leader indeed is "that individual whose removal from the group brings the largest (deteriorative) change in group syntality scores" (Cattell & Child, 1975). This brings us, therefore, to the most technical questions in measuring what we have in conceptual terms called "group syntality."

MEASURING THE SYNTALITY OF SMALL GROUPS

We have said that the profile of scores of a group as a group has been called its

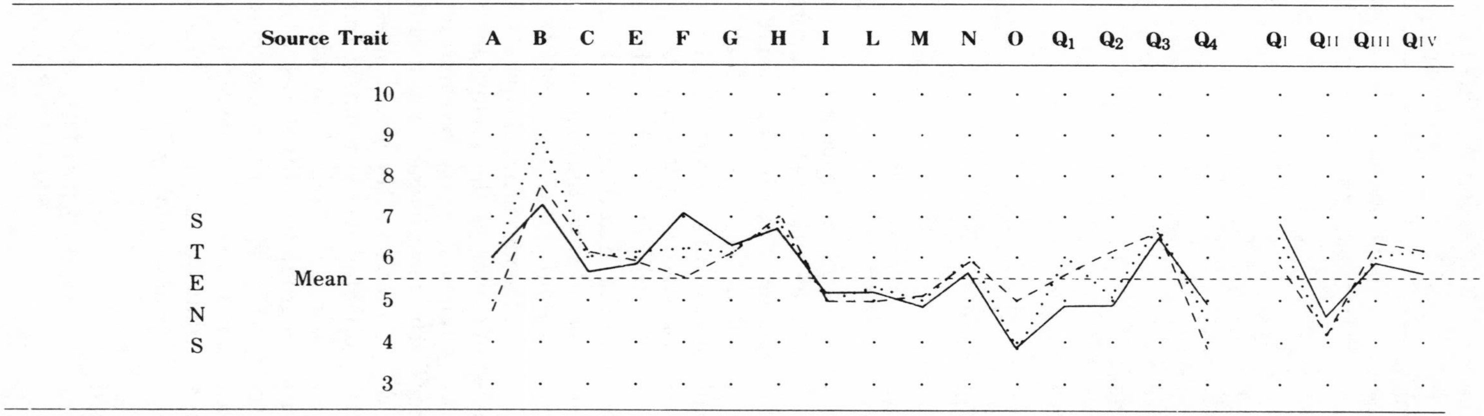

Source Trait	A	B	C	E	F	G	H	I	L	M	N	O	Q_1	Q_2	Q_3	Q_4	Q_I	Q_{II}	Q_{III}	Q_{IV}

Profiles

	N		A	B	C	E	F	G	H	I	L	M	N	O	Q_1	Q_2	Q_3	Q_4	Q_I	Q_{II}	Q_{III}	Q_{IV}
Elected Leaders	92	M ——	6.0	7.3	5.7	5.8	7.1	6.3	6.7	5.2	5.2	4.8	5.7	3.9	4.9	4.9	6.4	4.9	6.8	4.6	5.9	5.6
Effective Leaders	43	M – – –	4.7	7.8	6.2	5.9	5.5	6.1	7.0	5.0	5.0	5.1	5.9	5.0	5.6	6.2	6.5	3.8	5.8	4.2	6.4	6.2
Technical Leaders	90	M ·····	5.8	9.0	6.0	6.1	6.2	6.1	6.9	5.0	5.3	5.0	6.0	3.9	6.0	5.1	6.6	4.5	6.5	4.2	6.0	6.2

Figure 21.2. Sten profiles and specification equation weights for three leader types

syntality as an analogue to *personality* in the individual. But just as in personality, much time was wasted in trying to decide what dimensions to measure by purely subjective guesses. For example, "cohesiveness" was suggested (e.g., Stogdill, 1959) without recognizing what correlates it would empirically involve, and "morale" was defined where later factor analyses showed two distinct dimensions of morale. The same strategic course needed to be followed as with personality, finding the unitary and significant dimensions of syntality by factoring a wide array of performances. Thus one could reach *syntal traits* that are functionally unitary emergents from the group life, analogous to *source traits* in the individual. When they are known and scored for any group, any one of its performances *as a group* can be estimated from the behavioral equation just as for personality, thus:

$$a_{ij} = b_{j1}G_{1i} + b_{j2}G_{2i} + \ldots + b_{jk}G_{ki} \qquad (21\text{-}3)$$

where there are k factored syntal traits, G_1 through G_k.

Although individual humans belong to a variety of social, racial and national populations, each giving some traits peculiar to that population, the number and divergence of personality dimensions are trivial compared to the syntality dimensions required for different kinds of groups: football teams, ships' crews, insurance companies, research teams, etc. The taxonomic task before social psychologists and cultural anthropologists is therefore tremendous. A few sporadic beginnings were accomplished in World War II on submarine crews, bomber crews, etc., and in the Korean War on infantry companies. However, not one of these was on a broad "syntality sphere" of varied group behaviors, in a comprehensive model as will finally be needed. An exception was the study by Cattell and Stice (1960) mentioned earlier, in which 100 groups of air cadets, 10 men in each, were measured on 413 objectively measured and question-naire-reported group performance and motivation variables. Fifteen syntality factors were discovered, most replicated over three examination sessions.

Of these factors the most practicable for general purposes are the three that measure morale, for these account for much of success or failure with small groups. Although "morale" to the military and historical writer is covered by a single word, it proves through this research to have three or four forms, the two largest of which we list here.

Small Group Syntality: Morale of Leadership and Purpose

This is the degree to which the group is motivated by a goal or ideal vitalized by a leader. The tests most distinctively loading it are:

High satisfaction with leader (rating scale)
High influence of leader (rating scale)
High effort on group dynamometer (tug-of-war)
High feeling of freedom to participate
More planning done in a construction task
Low population score on factor A of the 16 P.F.

Small Group Syntality: Morale of Congeniality

High degree of "we-feeling"
High degree of group organization (observer rating)
High degree of interdependence (observer rating)
High degree of leadership activity
High degree of motivation
High dynamometer pull (tug-of-war)
Population low mean on 16 P.F. factor L, Protension
Population high mean on 16 P.F. factor B, Intelligence
Population high mean on 16 P.F. factor C, Ego strength

The strength of this second factor, though having some of the same morale expressions as in the first, e.g., tug-of-war strength, is rooted differently, namely in the cohesiveness through congeniality of the people in the group ("we-feeling"). Military observers and writers, e.g., in *All Quiet on the Western Front*, have noted already this difference in source of morale: the first favors "belief in the cause"; the second, with little thought of the cause, derives from the mutual liking and trust of the people in the group, sometimes called "cohesiveness" (Roby, 1957; Stogdill, 1959). As one would expect, this is aided by population characteristics of higher average intelligence, freedom from protension (L-projecting blame on others), and general freedom from neurotic pathology (C+).

Actual tests and scales for measures of these two factors and others in small groups are given in Cattell and Stice (1960). Just as in measuring factors objectively in personality, here in syntality each is assessed with from six to a dozen variables loaded highly on the factor. Some will be measures of performance, as in "tug-of-war" above, and others in member estimates of group qualities, as in "high degree of interdependence." At present, factoring of groups has very rarely been achieved and most dimensions for defining syntality have been proposed subjectively, as in Bales (1970), Borgatta and Cottrell (1956), Fiedler (1958), Haythorne (1953), Hemphill and Weste (1950), Roby (1957), Stogdill (1959) and others.

For these reasons the psychometrist asked to measure the morale and other dimensions of groups cannot yet call upon ready-made standardized batteries but must go to the research sources indicated, e.g., Cattell and Stice (1960). Furthermore, until he carries out factorings of other species of groups, he will not know to what size business organizations (see Frederiksen, Jensen, & Beaton, 1972), ships' crews, and civil service organizations the above measures for group syntality performance could be carried. However, there seems rough agreement on dimensions applicable to groups of about five to 15.

MEASURING CROSS-CULTURAL SYNTALITY DIMENSIONS OF NATIONS

Psychometrists are often reminded today of the relativity of their measures to culture patterns. Fortunately, as we have seen, the primary personality factors both in Q-data (as in the 16 P.F.) and in objective test T-data, as in the O-A Battery, have been shown (Cattell, Schmidt, & Pawlik, 1973) to preserve their main patterns across cultures. However, the prediction of behavior of the individual still requires regard for the differences of profile levels (means) of cultures, and the measurement of syntality dimensions has importance in its own right in understanding the social psychology of international interactions. In the last 30 years quite extensive research has been done to quantify national and other culture patterns that cultural anthropologists (Benedict, Mead, Malinowski) had left at a descriptive level. In this work, from 50 to 120 countries have been measured (with historical data back to 1830) on both syntality performances (behavior as an organized nation) and on population means, on 200-300 variables (Cattell, 1949a; Cattell, Bruel & Hartman, 1952; Cattell, Graham & Woliver, 1979; Rummel, 1969, 1972, 1975, 1978; Sawyer, 1967) using a wide range of social indicators.

Some 20 distinct syntality dimensions have been covered by these various investigations and probably 8 to 10 of them are today considered sufficiently replicated in factor pattern (Woliver & Cattell, 1981) for reliable measurement. The sorting by taxonome of the syntality profiles into typal groups yields a dozen or more scarcely overlapping culture pattern families or "civilizations" (Toynbee, 1947). In more refined studies one would need to use for measurement the factor patterns *within* these groups; but to cover all countries one needs those extending across all nations, which are: 1) developed technology vs. undeveloped; 2) intelligent affluence; 3) morale—morality; 4) intolerance of cultural pressure; 5) cultural pressure with sublimation; 6) size; 7) conservative, authoritarian, family oriented; plus some 14 other less clear dimensions. The seventh dimension found empirically, factorially, above is probably the same as that which has long been discussed by political scientists on a more direct observation basis as the dimension from an *exchange* society (Boulding, 1964) to an *authoritarian* society.

On each of these dimensions a country can be given a score by adding the standard scores on the variables with high loadings. For example, syntality dimension 1 above, sometimes called Vigorous Adapted Development, takes as markers high ratio of people in tertiary to primary occupations, restriction of birth rate, high degree of industrialization, many calories of food consumed per day per capita. The second dimension has loadings on high per capita real income, high expenditure on

education, high expenditure on travel abroad, low death rate from tuberculosis, greater freedom of the press from censorship. There is some recent evidence (Cattell & Brennan, 1981) that both syntality factors 1 and 2 above are associated (close to $p < .05$) with higher intelligence of the population on culture-fair intelligence tests.

Important new findings have also been reported concerning the relationship between the syntality dimensions of nations and the personality dimensions of their populations (Cattell, Woliver, & Graham, 1980). In this landmark research offering for the first time evidence of relation of population to syntality in the $S = (f) R \cdot P$ formula, correlations were found between several 16 P.F. population factor measures and many of the syntality factors identified in past research. The overall results of the study may be seen in Table 21.6, which gives the syntality factors and notable personality trait relations.

Because these results are based upon a sample of only 18 countries, caution must be exercised in their interpretation. As more national profiles are gathered with the 16 P.F., the results will be brought into sharper focus. Meanwhile it is inter-

TABLE 21.6

Syntality Factors with Notable Population Personality Trait Relations

Syntality Dimension	Population Traits (F~)
1. Vigorous, adapted development	A-, F-, N-
2. Intelligence-Affluence	F-, E-, Q_4-, QI
5. Careless unintegrated society	F, I, QI
6. Intolerance of cultural pressure	F, O-, Q_3-
7. Efficient use of resources-vs-density	
9. Muslim, with ethnic diversity	
10. Political cultural alertness	A, E, G, I, N, QI
13. Nordid-Protestant industriousness	A-, Q_3-, Q_1
14. Oriental self sufficiency	
16. Stable adjustment and restraint	QI, QII-, M-
17. Buddhist East Asian	QII-, C, F
18. Non-conformist religious tendency	L, N, O, Q_1
20. Conservative, authoritarian, family oriented	
21. Insecure, hard-work values	A-, C-, H-, Q_3-, O_2

Of these 14, the personality associations are weaker in 13 and 18, which are nevertheless included because they have been so much discussed, sociologically and historically.

esting to note that factor F, which has recently been found to be among the most substantially inherited of personality characteristics (Cattell, 1982), shows the most consistent tendency to be related to syntality patterns. However, this does not at all imply that the differences in syntality dimensions between nations rest predominantly upon genetic factors. Cattell, Woliver, and Graham (1980) are careful to point out that the best explanation of the relationship between syntality dimensions and personality characteristics seems to be that of a three-way causal action. The authors also stress that any group *behavior* involves not only syntality and personality factors, but also the environmental situation. In other words, the behavior of nations, like any other group, can be analyzed using the multivariate, interactional framework described at the beginning of this chapter.

The furthest developments of this work may be read in Lynn (1971, 1979), who has related national characteristics especially to the (second-order) anxiety factor on the 16 P.F. and to intelligence, and in Rummel (1979) who has made an extensive theoretical development in regard to conflict and the dyadic interactions of nations. These measurement developments have been used rather more by the political scientists and economists, but inasmuch as these are really special branches of social psychology, psychologists will need increasingly to study this branch of psychometry.

A special sector of syntality of which so far little has been said, despite its theoretical importance, is that of the group *synergy*. This has to do with group measurement aspects of all that has been developed in Chapter 14. There it will be recognized that the interest of an individual in maintaining membership in a group can be estimated by a dynamic behavioral equation of weights on his ergic and semic strengths, as in equations 14-5 and 14-6 (pp. 295–296).

Consequently, when individuals belong to a group it calls upon dynamic resources of the nature and extent given by:

$$E_j = \sum_{x=p}^{x=n} \sum_{i=p}^{i=n} b_{jx} T_{xi} \qquad (21\text{-}4)$$

which is the group synergy—the energy it has available for its purposes.

There are a number of useful propositions derivable from this, one concerning the equilibria among group synergies when the same individuals belong to all groups, as frequently happens. No practical experience has yet been gained concerning these formulae; but, as Rummel (1975) points out, the levels of investments of ergs and sentiments in groups is an important aspect of group measurement for predictive purposes.

Fuller treatment of the dynamic calculus as needed for these group derivatives is given in Chapter 13, while Chapter 14 deals with the measurement of attitudes in more conventional ways that cannot be brought into a general calculus.

REGIONAL AND GROUP DIFFERENCES

Popular stereotypes suggest that the modal personalities of persons residing in different parts of the United States vary from one another. Beliefs that East Coast people are cold and tough, westerners conventional and neighborly, Mountain States people independent "loners," and Californians weird, are only some of the existing stereotypes. Krug and Kulhavy (1973) tested out the idea that there are regional differences in personality. They reported on 16 P.F. data from 3,772 male and 2,672 female subjects, aged 16-60. These persons formed a stratified random sample, representative of the population in race and socioeconomic status. The subjects were divided into six groups in terms of area of residence: Northeast, Southeast, Midwest, Western Mountain, Southwest, and West Coast.

The 16 P.F. scores were used in discriminant analyses, separately for each of the six groups, in order to establish regional differences. The first major discriminant function for males was derived from 16 P.F. scores showing high intelligence, imaginativeness, forthrightness, low concern for social acceptance and self-enhancement and low trust and tolerance. The highest scores were obtained by residents of urban, industrialized regions—the West Coast, Northeast, and Midwest. The second discriminant function had a central core of trust, hard work, and tough-mindedness. The Midwest was highest; the West Coast and Southwest lowest. The third major function measured social isolation; it is highest in the Western Mountain and Southwest regions, lowest in the Midwest and West Coast. The fourth function is largely a measure of surgency (happy-go-lucky). Surgency is associated with preference for living in big cities and perhaps for this reason is highest in the Northeast, lowest in the Western Mountain area. The first three discriminant functions for females are very similar to those of males and regional differences are also much the same for the two. The fourth function for females appears to be chiefly a measure of being tense and driven. The West Coast is highest and Southwest lowest in scores.

As Krug and Kulhavy point out, there is no way of ascertaining from these data the degree to which these differences result from differential ethnic migrations into a region or from the characteristics of the region being such as to attract, retain, or nurture a distinctive personality type.

The "differential ethnic migration" referred to above may have influence since, as Krug and Kulhavy pointed out, there are ethnic differences in personality. This is demonstrated in recent research on personality test score differences of persons of European as opposed to Asian ancestry residing in Hawaii (Johnson et al., 1983a, 1983b). Three personality measures were used, seven personality factors derived from the Adjective Check List (ACL), (Gough & Heilbrun, 1965), the 8-factor Comrey Personality Scales (CPS) (Comrey, 1970), and Cattell's 16 P.F. (Cattell, Eber & Tatsuoka, 1970). Caucasians were significantly higher on intraception (rebelliousness) and social attractiveness and Asians were significantly higher on interpersonal abrasiveness and introversion on the ACL factors (Johnson et al., 1983b). Caucasians were more active, stable, extraverted, masculine (basically less squeamish), empathic (CPS), stable, dominant, happy-go-lucky, and venturesome (16 P.F.). Asians were more intelligent, practical, shrewd, and conservative (16 P.F.).

Sex and age differences also were examined in these two reports. Males were significantly higher on interpersonal abrasiveness, ego organization, introversion, and social attractiveness; females were significantly higher on social desirability and internal discomfort (neuroticism) on the ACL factors (Johnson et al., 1983b). Males were significantly more active, masculine (CPS), stable, dominant, tough-minded, and radical (16 P.F.) while females were significantly more trusting, orderly, conforming, empathic (CPS), outgoing, shrewd, apprehensive, and tense (16 P.F.) (Johnson et al., 1983a). Older persons had significantly higher ACL factor scores in social desirability and ego organization, lower scores on social desirability, internal discomfort, and social attractiveness (Johnson et al., 1983b). Older persons had significantly higher ACL factor scores in trust, orderliness, social conformity, emotional stability, and empathy (CPS) and on submissiveness, desurgency (sober, as opposed to happy-go-lucky), trustingness, self-assurance, conservatism and low ergic tension (relaxed) on the 16 P.F. Younger persons were higher in activity and masculinity (CPS), had lower ego strength and superego strength, were more practical, forthright, group dependent and showed higher self-conflict (16 P.F.).

There were very few two-way or three-way interactions between race/ethnicity, sex, and age. Each has a substantial influence on personality scale scores (age most influential, then sex, then race/ethnicity, in terms of amount of association); the absence of interactions suggests that differential (across race/ethnicity; across sexes) cohort effects appear to have had very little influence on personality test scores. (Very large interactions are found in the area of cognitive abilities (see DeFries et al., 1982), suggesting that cognitive abilities are more influenced by cohort effects than is personality.)

SUMMARY

When psychologists are called upon to assist in evaluating business organizations, political science and economic issues, and the interaction of individuals with culture patterns, they face the task of measuring groups. The analogue of personality in the organized individual is *syntality* inferred for an organized group from its behavior as a group.

Syntality dimensions must be distinguished from population dimensions which, of course, are the ordinary ability, personality and attitude dimensions of individuals, averaged. The model considers syntality a product of group structure R, and personality of population P, thus: $S = f(R \cdot P)$.

The unitary dimensions of groups have been subjectively posited in numerous political, historical, and cultural anthropological writings, but only recently has factor analysis, applied to a behavioral sphere of variables, demonstrated that dependable unitary syntality "traits" of groups can be isolated.

Such dimensions have been explored so far for small groups, including married couples, on the one hand, and large historical groups—nations—on the other.

In small groups about a dozen dimensions of syntality have been located and batteries are available for measuring them, though only in the research literature and unstandardized. For example, *morale* (in neonate groups of 10) has been shown to consist of two distinct, almost uncorrelated, dimensions. Dimensions will naturally differ for different species of groups.

Group syntality—as success on various dimensions—has already been shown to relate significantly both to population characteristics and internal structure. Such structural features as type of leadership, status divisions, etc., also relate to syntality. In married couples stability is related to a) a positive assortive relation and probably b) supplementation. Enough sources of measurement and predictive equations therefrom are now available to assist marriage counseling to become a more positive art and science.

The variables for measuring national and other populations are extremely numerous. Demographic variables like age, sex, ethnic group, and earnings can be improved and extended in meaning by better psychological measurement. Conventional polling and survey technique by simple verbal response need to be superseded by objective dynamic attitude measures. The problems in survey work are ordinary ones of sampling and of choosing the fewest measures to give the most information, which requires knowledge of personality and interest structure.

Since individual behavior takes place in the "field" of a national (or other) culture pattern, the psychologist, even when concerned with predicting individual rather than group behavior, must have a psychometry of culture patterns. The last 30 years have seen great progress in factoring variables across some 100 countries, yielding at least seven unitary traits that are well replicated. The behavioral equation applies to predictions from culture patterns as from personality patterns, when weights are experimentally determined. An important sector of syntality is the synergy vector dealing with the dynamic investment which individuals bring to a group.

The measurement discussed in this chapter is especially important to social psychology, which is the central discipline of which political science, cultural anthropology, and economics are special areas. Although still at the research stage, we do have initial factor batteries, with some 8 to 20 scorable variables in each, for measuring small groups and national culture patterns.

CHAPTER 22

Legal Considerations for the Psychologist and Some Practical Suggestions

Paul M. Ganley

Editors' Note: *Ours is a litigious society and any book having to do with psychological testing should consider legal requirements and problems of legal liability. Paul M. Ganley is an attorney-at-law, married to a psychologist (Barbara Dole Porteus, co-author of Chapter 6). He is author or co-author of papers in psychological journals and law journals. He serves on the State of Hawaii Commission on Children and Youth and has devoted considerable time to the development of effective child protective services. He also serves as legal counsel for the Hawaii Psychological Association and its membership and has done work for the American Psychological Association in Washington, DC. As most of us are aware, the use of citations in legal documents makes psychological papers seem almost "precedent free." However, Ganley's experience with the actual needs of protecting psychologists has led him to write a chapter without citations. It was a question of none or a thousand. He chose none. Hence, the different format. He covers very thoughtfully the important legal issues involved in psychological practice and psychological testing.*

THE PSYCHOLOGIST'S EXPOSURE TO LIABILITY

This chapter is intended to give the reader an awareness of those areas in which practitioners come into closest contact with the law as a result of their professional endeavors. Because of the sensitivity of much of the work engaged in by psychologists, whether it is indirect input gained from testing or direct input from a patient or subject's disclosures gained from interviews or therapy, contact with psychologists or psychiatrists can be of the utmost importance even in seemingly unrelated areas. A few examples might be helpful.

A fairly simple employment test attempting to obtain a measure of an individual's intelligence or insight into what personality traits are possessed can have tremendous bearing on an individual's future earnings, the very nature of the employment, or even the amount of dollar damages that may be recovered as a result of some physical injury caused many years later. As a general rule of law, one is not monetarily compensated for preexisting limitations, but only limitations resulting from the physical injuries complained of. The individual injured in an automobile accident who claims some degree, ever so slight, of mental impairment as a result of the accident can be greatly discredited if counsel for the defendant's insurance company has results from previous tests or input from therapy showing a preexisting similar or identical disability or personality defect. Sometimes even inadvertently disclosing the fact that an individual has sought the assistance of a mental health professional is sufficient to cause that individual the loss of a job. Such jobs can and do range from domestic help to that of consideration for the vice-presidency of the United States.

For those working in an area that involves any aspect of psychology, often what is unsaid has almost as much importance as what is said, and clearly exposes the professional to just as much liability. The demands upon the professional are such that the courts, in attempting to reach equitable results in individual cases, often fail to take into consideration the ramifications of the precedent that is being set.

Psychologists and psychiatrists are liable—that is, for damages to the injured party—if they release information and if they don't release information. If, upon request, a professional releases only a scintilla of information, the partial release may be a waiver of confidentiality

as to *all* the information the professional has pertaining to the individual. If the *professional* requested the partial release and, as a result of the partial release, he is ordered by a Court to produce and disclose everything pertaining to the individual, he could be sued. The consent given could be legally viewed as not an "informed consent" because the professional did not advise the individual that release of a limited portion of the confidential information could waive the confidentiality privilege as to all of the information or data under the professional's control. (See informed consent section, pp. 492–493.)

Clearly the exposure to liability runs the gauntlet of potential claims. For example, claims can be made that test results were inaccurate, that test results were improperly used, that test results were improperly released or not released in a timely fashion. Claims also can be based on a failure to respond to a request or subpoena regarding some individual with whom the professional only had limited contact and perhaps little or no contact for years. For the professional it sometimes seems like a no-win situation. There is exposure to liability for keeping too detailed records and for keeping allegedly insufficient records. There is the plight of often having no one to communicate with when a request to release information is made by a client who is only marginally mentally competent and of having individuals confide in the professional not about the past but about intentions for future action that, if carried out, would cause grievous bodily harm or death to other individuals or to an identifiable group of individuals.

It is not enough to have professional guidelines when, more often than not, it seems that professional guidelines of ethical responsibility are in conflict with state or federal statutes. It is even more complicated when the professional is faced with the dilemma of what he must disclose to an individual about the limits of confidentiality. The realm of responsibility is not unlike wandering through an advanced Porteus Maze with seemingly endless alternatives to choose from. As the maze can be conquered with the application of some planning capacity, the following sections of this chapter should provide some guidelines to enable the practitioner to plan ahead so that he can recognize the pitfalls he may have to handle when confronted, directly or indirectly, with the legal aspects arising out of professional endeavors. The guidelines should help regardless of whether the professional is an academician or in government or private practice.

WHO IS THE PSYCHOLOGIST IN THE EYES OF THE LAW?

Under common law, which is the body of law stemming from precedent gained from written decisions handed down on a great many cases, there is little to define the borders of what is a psychologist. The definition has been left almost entirely up to statutory law enacted by the various states. A practitioner should know the definition of a psychologist in the state where he resides. The issue for the professional is really not the definition of a psychologist, but what specifics must be accomplished before an individual can call himself a psychologist. Of course, anyone has the *power* to call himself a psychologist, but whether he has the legal *right* to do so is a different matter. The important point is that, if you call yourself a psychologist even when you have not completed the criteria required in your state, the exposure to liability is tremendous. Furthermore, if you hold yourself out as performing the tasks of a "psychologist" even though you may not refer to yourself as a psychologist, you may have a problem. If you are, in fact, doing those things defined statutorily or by case law as only to be performed by psychologists, then in the eyes of the law you are presenting yourself as a psychologist and accordingly

the standard of conduct and professionalism that you will be required to answer to is that of a properly qualified psychologist in your state. Likewise, the medical doctor who is a general practitioner who also performs general surgery will have his surgical techniques scrutinized and held up to the standards of a surgeon practicing in the community. Suffice it to say that you must be sure you can legally refer to yourself as a psychologist when you practice. You should also be aware that you may be able to refer to yourself as a psychologist in one job but not another. A typical example is that in some states you may be able to do so if working in a university setting, but not in private practice unless certified by the state.

RECORDS

To the psychologist engaged in research, lecturing or clinical work, record-keeping becomes a practical necessity. Whether the data are needed for current or future professional purposes, such as follow-up studies or refreshing the therapist's mind regarding a particular patient, record-keeping, to be *legally sufficient*, must be kept on a regular basis. Records are almost always viewed from a position other than that of the psychologist. To health insurance companies or other third-party payers, the practitioner's records are viewed as the bottom line for information regarding what the practitioner did or did not do for any particular patient or subject on a given date. Accordingly, whenever the practitioner seeks or receives payment from a third party for services rendered or for research performed, records, by necessity, must be kept as a standard practice to show that what the payment was made for was actually performed. To qualify as a business record the entry must reflect that the record was made at the time or shortly after the services were rendered or the research performed and was not reconstructed from memory or notes only when the practitioner was called upon by some agency or government arm seeking to verify that work was performed for the funding received or health benefits paid.

It is the practitioner's obligation to ascertain any local, state, or federal requirements pertaining to the legnth of time that records should be kept for the purposes of third-party payers. Records should be kept for as far back in time as the investigating arm of the payer can sue based on any allegation of fraud for payments made for services or research not performed.

It is also necessary to keep records for a sufficient length of time so that the professional has documentation to protect himself against suits based on a malpractice allegation arising out of professional services previously rendered. A difficulty lies in the fact that the statutory limitations pertaining to when a suit must be brought can be based on either breach of contract or negligence, which usually have different time limitations. Further these statutory time limitations do not usually apply to minors or to those who are deemed mentally incompetent. Accordingly, even if a practitioner specifically researches the applicable statute in his state, the period of his exposure to liability is greatly extended if the potential plaintiff is a minor or incompetent person. It is, however, public policy that an individual or corporate entity should not have a potential lawsuit indefinitely hanging overhead like a black cloud. Consequently, the statutory limits on how long a claim can remain legally valid after the alleged wrong has occurred attempt to give the claimant a fair amount of time to assert his claim in a court of law while not allowing an open-ended period of liability. For instance, in the state of my residence an action based on breach of contract must be commenced within six years from the time of the breach, an action based on negligence within two years after the negligent act has occurred or the injured person

knows or should know that the negligent act has occurred. On the surface, then, it would seem that if a patient, student, or subject accused a psychologist of improperly releasing information or of improper conduct towards him, suit must be commenced within two years if based upon negligence or an intentional wrong or six years if based on a breach of contract. As indicated above, if the complaining patient, student, or subject is under age or is suffering some mental impairment sufficient to make the individual incompetent in the eyes of the law, then the complaining individual would not have to commence an action until two or six years after the date he reached the age of majority or regained his mental competency.

It takes only a moment of thought to realize that in the mental health field where practitioners are working with minors and people with psychological problems, the legal right of a former patient, student, or subject to file suit for alleged wrongdoing may extend for a great many years. The prudent psychologist might place his records on microfilm in a secured storage area for some time, but the resulting costs of keeping all such records could be very high. The only suggestion I have found that psychologists are willing to live with is to ascertain the statutes of limitations in the state of residence for a tortious or contractual claim and keep files for one year longer. By doing so, psychologists are generally keeping records longer than the statute of limitations and will have files on hand for most situations. In addition to keeping files intact for at least a year longer than the statutory requirements by when an action must be filed, in most cases psychologists should have a business policy that dictates that all research subjects and patients are informed that records pertaining to them will not be kept for more than x number of years. Many practitioners also find it beneficial to place on such a form a sentence indicating that no reports or information will be forwarded unless a properly signed consent is executed, the purpose for the records is specifically indicated, and all payments are current. If the patient, student, or subject is a minor or an individual whose competency to sign such a statement could be questioned, then, if at all possible, the individual's guardian should *also* sign the statement.

Unfortunately, the professional ethical codes of many organizations do not limit the time by when a complainant must file a claim against a professional with his professional organization. As a result, a professional may have an extremely stale claim filed against him with his professional organization and be sanctioned because he no longer has the records to refute the claim, even though the complainant would be barred in a court of law for failing to timely file the complaint. Professional organizations should seriously consider extending the protection of limiting liability of its members against stale complaints, at least to the degree that the law does.

In some fields it is becoming common for the professional to keep two sets of records. This ill-conceived practice is due to the mistaken belief that an individual's privacy is best protected by only turning over records containing partial data that would not unduly impose upon the privacy of the individual but would give sufficient information to satisfy government agencies or third-party payers. Such a practice can and does lead to mistrust of the profession and to legal and ethical problems for the individual. The professional seeking to protect the privacy of his patient, subject, or student should follow these guidelines:

- When practical, keep a record of the time, date, tests performed, general impressions, etc., but indicate conclusions that you would otherwise note by labeling (schizophrenic, paranoid, etc.) by a numbering or lettering system known only to you.

- Advise patients, students, or subjects as to the degree of information that any particular insurer, agency or funding source requires, so that they know the limits of confidentiality.
- When, in the view of the professional, the patient, student, or subject, could be construed as mentally incompetent, written consent to proceed with the release of any information or to proceed in any professional capacity whatsoever should *also* be obtained from the natural or legal guardian. In the case of a minor or a mentally incompetent adult, it is not sufficient to obtain the written consent of the natural guardian if a legal guardian has been appointed. If the legal guardian is not an individual, but a department or branch of a municipality or State department of welfare or social services, then the psychologist must be sure that the individual signing for the government has the authority to authorize the consent and to execute the document requested, whether it be a consent for treatment or release of information.
- Whenever the written request or consent is not given by a legally competent individual or his legal or natural guardian, do not release any information without a court order. When using the words "legally competent" in conjunction with the consent to release information, I am referring to an individual who has both reached the age of majority in the state of his or her residence and is mentally competent to authorize the release.

THE LIMITS OF CONFIDENTIALITY

If an issue of privileged communication or confidentiality is perceived then prior to any unauthorized confidence being published, the professional, particularly the psychologist, must keep in mind that the privilege belongs to the patient or client and is not for the protection or use of the professional. Psychologists, not unlike psychiatrists, sometimes attempt to invoke the privilege even when it is a patient, student, or subject who is requesting the release of information. The only situation in which such a position is legally supportable is when the individual requesting the information is legally incompetent, that is, mentally incompetent, or has not reached the age of majority. In all other cases, the professional should not place himself in the position of acting as an omnipotent and omniscient being.

For the most part, the law does not recognize confidentiality dictates contained in professional codes alone, but only recognizes those common law privileges or statutory privileges that address the issue of confidentiality. Historically, the common law only acknowledged the privilege of confidential information as belonging to an individual who intended the information to be confidential and with that intent released the information to his or her attorney, medical doctor, or clergy. Many states have codified and expanded the common law privileges to protect the communications of individuals who confide in certain professionals. In many instances, states have expanded that statutory confidentiality scope to include psychologists. More importantly, the professional code of ethics most psychologists abide by recognizes a duty to protect the confidential disclosures of patients, students, and subjects. In any conceivable situation, however, there are limits to confidentiality and the law is just beginning to deal with the issue of just what a professional must tell a patient, student, or subject about the circumstances under which the confidentiality is limited. Most psychologists feel uncomfortable advising someone that "confidential" information is only partially confidential.

All of the numerous statutory limitations to a privilege of confidentiality are probably nowhere contained in any one jurisdiction. If all of the exceptions to an individual's privilege of confidentiality were contained in a specific jurisdiction, a psychologist looking towards the minimum exposure of liability might be placed in an utterly ridiculous position. He might have to advise his patient, student, or subject as follows:

I want you to realize that all information of a confidential nature that comes to my attention due to your input or because of my association with you will be held in the strictest confidence and will never be disclosed by me, unless of course you indicate that you have . . . battered or sexually abused a minor, neglected a minor psychologically or educationally . . . I would, of course, have to report you to the proper authorities, as required by statute . . . or, if you have abused any elderly individuals under your custody and control, I would have to report you as required by statute . . . or, if you tell me about some future crime you plan to commit that will directly result in bodily injury to others, I must advise the authorities and those individuals if I believe, in my professional capacity, you intend to carry out such acts of violence. Even if I'm not professionally certain that you will actually carry out such acts, I will warn the individuals and authorities so as to protect myself from future liability . . . or, if you attempt to attack me personally by saying in any way that I have committed malpractice or a breach of ethics, then of course everything you have said to me in confidence is no longer in confidence because I have a right to defend myself . . . or, if a spot-check investigation by a third-party payer results in any request for information pertaining to my professional involvement with you, I must release much of the confidential information that I have . . . or if the funding source for my grant requires that I pass certain confidential data on, even though they may identify you as a member of an antisocial group, I must, of course, pass that on in order to honor the terms of the grant, or . . . if your spouse is attempting to gain custody of your children, then in the "best interests of the children" all of the nitty-gritty of the confidential things that you have said must be turned over to the court, since the cloak of confidentiality cannot be used to the detriment of your offspring . . . or, even if you are extremely competent and in touch with reality and can conduct your own affairs, if anyone ever files a court petition claiming that you should have a guardian appointed I must release all confidential information ... or if you have not paid your bill and I must sue you for back fees I must state to the judge what my services were rendered for, which will entail disclosing some general outline of your problems, which will of course reveal many of your confidences, ... or, etc. etc.

If it is any consolation, a psychologist who passes on confidential information pursuant to statutory dictates to do so is generally immune from liability when the statute has made it *mandatory* to report the information, whether it is information of child abuse or neglect, or any other matter alluded to in the contrived statement set out above. Even with statutory protection the fact remains that an individual damaged through the release of confidential information can still sue. Whether the complainant can prevail is another matter, but the defense will take its toll in time, money, and aggravation. Exposure is particularly likely to blossom into problems for the psychologist if the release of "damaging" information was the result of the psychologist's pursuing his own goals, e.g., in publishing case material.

In discussing the limits of confidentiality, the psychologist should focus in on the particular aspects of his involvement with an individual and indicate to that individual the foreseeable areas, if any, where an issue of disclosing confidential information could arise. It is problematic whether psychologists, at least from a legal stance, have to disclose to an individual those statutes that call for the mandatory reporting of certain information by specific categories of involved professionals. (An example in some states would be evidence of child abuse which must be reported by mental health professionals, medical doctors, teachers, and social workers.)

INFORMED CONSENT

Even as late as the early 1970s, informed consent as it involved psychologists and psychiatrists, was not frequently a cause for concern. The term merely meant that, if the individual was a minor, *informed consent* had to be given by the minor's guardian, or, if the individual was not a minor, the professional had to make a determination that the person was sufficiently mentally competent to acknowledge consent to the particulars at hand. By the late 1970s, entire books were being written about informed consent as it applied to particular segments of the public. The important thing to remember in this area is that the days are gone when it was a simple determination of whether the individual was a minor or was sufficiently mentally competent to sign a release of information form. Today, the term informed consent is broad enough so that it encompasses a wide range of research and therapy practices, from what a subject in a psychological study thought he consented to when agreeing to be a subject, to the consent to engage in behavior modification, therapy, or testing.

It is important to realize that any oral statement or any written statement must be in the simplest of language when a consent is being obtained. Many new statutes have sprung up that are commonly referred to as *plain language* statutes. These dictate that releases and consent be plain enough that laypersons can readily understand what it is they are consenting to. If the oral or written statement presented in order to elicit or confirm an individual's consent is not in plain language, it will not be viewed as an informed consent. A plain language form of a consent statement for a release of information or other matters pertaining to a psychologist's practice should be simple enough to be understood by an average sixth or seventh grader. Professionals who plan to use a standard release of information or consent form should have an attorney review or draft the release. An attorney who is familiar with the drafting of such releases and is aware of the plain language bent that hearing officers, courts, and legislators are taking will serve them well.

RELEASE OR DISCLOSURE OF CONFIDENTIAL INFORMATION

Obviously, the release or disclosure of confidential information all ties in with informed consent, the limits of confidentiality, and even record-keeping. The only point in having a separate section on release or disclosure of confidential information is to illustrate the best way to handle the matter of releasing information and add some caveats to earlier recommendations. It is recommended that unless an informed consent is given, psychologists, psychiatrists, and professional organizations release almost no information whatsoever unless specifically ordered to do so by a court of law. However, the psychologist should be aware of the procedures leading up to a jurist or hearing officer ordering the production of records or release of information.

Before describing those procedures, it is appropriate to point out situations where it is not necessary to have a court order before releasing information. The most elementary situation would seem to be where the individual making the request is a patient, student, or subject and who is known to be competent in the sense that he is not a minor and is sufficiently mentally competent to knowledgeably make the request. The second case would be in those situations where a statute requires the professional to report to a Department of Social Services or other specified governmental agency all information pertaining to child abuse, neglect, etc., *and* the particular statute *expressly* states that the individual so reporting is immune from prosecution for so reporting.

Incidentally, failure to report such incidents results in the psychologist's exposing himself to liability should the individual the particular statute is designed to protect be hurt due to the failure to report. Exposure to liability arising out of failure to report when statutorily mandated to do so can and has resulted in monetary or criminal sanctions, even when the failure to report was based upon a defense of ethical considerations and a concern for the confidentiality of the communication.

Some of the situations in which information should not be released without a court order are as follows: The individual who has had contact with the professional is a minor without an adult or guardian to consent to the release of information, a mentally incompetent adult without an appropriate adult or guardian to consent to the release of information, or a competent adult who does not want the information released; the individuals or entities who seek to use the information against the individual who confided in the professional; or it is the professional's view that to state his opinions regarding the individual or to release records would not be in the best interests of the individual.

Once the decision not to release information has been made, the professional should follow these guidelines: Don't disclose any professional contact at all unless authorized. Once so authorized, insist upon a formal, precise, written request stating specifically its purpose. Once received, if you still object, succinctly state the professional and ethical grounds you may have for objecting or for refusing to release the information. Attempt to limit the release of information even when consent is forthcoming. For instance, if the sole purpose is to attempt to find out if any information in the record relates to the person being an unfit parent, and your only involvement was to assist the individual in quitting smoking, those involved with requesting the record might be satisfied by an affidavit that you have no information either in your head or in the file pertaining to anything that could be even remotely relevant to the individual's unfitness as a parent.

For the sake of discussion, let's assume that you cannot extract yourself from the situation by merely giving an affidavit that you have no information pertaining to what is sought, or that for some other reason you feel information should not be disclosed. If subpoenaed to testify, you must appear and respectfully indicate that you refuse to testify on the grounds that the information is privileged and you have not been authorized to release the information by the holder of the privilege (if that is the fact), or that the individual concerned is not legally competent to authorize you to release the information (a minor or mentally incompetent adult without a legal guardian), or from your evaluation of the situation it appears that, although the holder of the privilege has not asked for the protection of the privilege, you feel that release of the information would be detrimental to the holder of the privilege, who may not know the extent of his problems and may not be able to handle the disclosure of the extent of his problems. Whatever your professional reasons, they should be stated to the judge or hearing officer.

If at that point you are ordered by the jurist or hearing officer to disclose some portion of the information, then you should do so, or be prepared to be held in contempt of court, which could involve incarceration until you release the information. You could request that the matter be continued until you retain counsel or ask the judge or hearing officer if he would consider reviewing the material in chambers in order to make a determination if disclosure of the entire file is necessary or disclosure is in the best interest of the involved individual.

The bottom line is that, if all else fails and you are ordered to disclose the information or release the file for inspection and no compromise is acceptable to the court or hearing officer, you may face some unpleasant consequences. Once you have proceeded along the line suggested, you may answer the questions or release the information contained in your records if you are so ordered by the judge or hearing officer.

It may be that you are not subpoenaed to testify in court but only your records are subpoenaed for inspection prior to any court hearing. The procedural steps for you to follow if you are opposing the review of your records is similar to those stated above, with the exception that, instead of proceeding in a timely fashion to the court, you proceed to the place where the record inspection is to be held and state your objections on the record. Because that proceeding is not before a judge, the party seeking the records may then go in to the court or hearing officer with a motion to order you before the court and compel you to release the information. At that time you can state your reasons again and go through the procedure set out above. Be sure, however, that before proceeding to appear at the document production you alert the party requesting the inspection and production of documents (your records) that you feel that you cannot comply unless specifically ordered to do so by the court or otherwise authorized to your satisfaction. If time constraints are involved, it is usually acceptable to send a member of your staff to the document production with your statement, which should be read into the record, as to why you are not producing the records as requested, but you personally must attend the actual hearing. Of course, if you have no objection to producing the documents for inspection, you would notify the requesting party and a member of your staff could take your records to the location of the inspection or you could request that the inspection be made on your premises at a mutually convenient time.

If, for whatever reason, you end up testifying, you are still entitled to be prepared by the counsel of the individual or entity which is calling you as a witness. If counsel who is calling you does not extend to you the courtesy of giving you the time to prepare, or is hostile enough not to do so after you have requested that he meet with you at your office to go over the testimony or questions that he will ask, you should feel perfectly comfortable with answering many questions with words to the effect, "I have told you that I was prepared to meet with you at my office at a mutually convenient time and I could have answered this question quite easily if I had been aware that you were going to ask it because I could have prepared the data or extracted the information from my numerous files, but you did not do so and I cannot answer the question at this time." Of course, such a response should not be given if you have been retained as an expert witness.

SUMMARY

In conclusion, I would like to say that many psychologists and psychiatrists are of the opinion that their actual involvement with anything related to this chapter is extremely remote and that the likelihood of their being called on the carpet through their professional organization, their employer, courts, government agencies, or clients is also remote. Even ten years ago it would have been difficult to disagree with that position, but today most members of society are extremely aware of their rights and what *they* perceive as fairness and due process. However, many of the individuals who professionals may come into contact with have no idea of even the rudimentary aspects of fair play, let alone due process. Being honest and knowledgeable within one's profession is not enough today, even if in addition to honesty and professional competency one is blessed with good common sense. To assume that such attributes will keep professional endeavors from blossoming into anything more than mere exposure to liability is not a practical conclusion.

CHAPTER 23

Dodging the Third Error Source: Psychological Interpretation and Use of Given Scores

Raymond B. Cattell

RELATIVE ROLES OF ERROR SOURCES: SAMPLING ERROR, EXPERIMENTAL ERROR, AND ERROR OF PSYCHOLOGICAL INTERPRETATION OF SCORES

Psychologists are commonly taught that there are two types of error: 1) those of measurement, and 2) those of statistical inference. But there is a third, concerned with inference beyond statistics in the general domain of applying psychological laws to measurement.

The distinct types can best be illustrated by a physical example. A weather specialist, wishing to know the barometric pressure in the state of, say, California, might make a mistake in putting the ruler incorrectly by the mercury column, which would be a measurement error. Next, from only three barometers he might say the pressure is the exact mean of these. That would be a sampling error. With several measures at different levels in plain and mountain, he might not allow for altitude corrections from physical laws, which would be an error of interpretation.

Another way of looking at it is that the first two deal with features of a concrete numerical measure, whereas the last deals with an inference based on a conception of what the measure means. It is true that a sampling, statistical error involves inference, but it is an inference purely in the statistical field, e.g., that the mean I.Q. in New York schools is so and so. The error of psychological interpretation is in a larger domain of laws, as when one infers a student of I.Q. 120 and with such and such a personality profile will average B grades when he goes to college.

Test measurement error is evaluated, within test consistency coefficients (see Chapter 4), by the *dependability* coefficient (retest), and the *administrative reliability* coefficient (across test situations).

(We must not forget that just as these evaluated measurement error in effect on ranks, a reliability *index* also evaluates it in terms of shift of group mean.) We need not return to measurement error here. Sampling error is surely also well understood by the reader. But we may venture to estimate that neither measurement error nor sampling error is as important in psychological practice as the third type of error we are now to discuss.*

The sources of this kind of error in the work of the applied psychologist are very diverse. A miscellaneous sample would include: 1) incorrect understanding of the psychological concept involved in a particular test; 2) failure to consider age corrections; 3) ignorance of the relative role of genetic and threptic influences on a trait; 4) disregard of the vector values for various situations of testing and of life action; 5) wrong assumptions about scaling units; 6) wrong formulae in research on source traits by factor extraction; 7) failure to allow for motivation distortions in ratings and self-ratings; 8) uncertain models for use of difference scores; 9) not allowing for systematic instrument factors; 10) using the *same* source-trait es-

timation weights in different cultures; 11) predicting from only three or four second-order factors where evidence from two to 20 primaries can be gathered in the same testing time, and so on.

The dividing line between the three types of error—measurement, sampling, and interpretation—if we get theoretically casuistic, is not always sharp, in the sense that any given error may involve all three kinds. But, broadly, the third type can be said to arise from insufficient *psychological* understanding of what is necessary to determine—by other than measurement and sampling error in the narrow sense—the interpretation and use of the given numerical score.

The sources of this third, psychological form of error reside in 1) peculiarity of the subject's test reactions, 2) inadequate allowance for the situation in relation to the testing, and 3) defective understanding of laws concerned with the nature of the trait and the situations in future predictions. Let us begin by considering the first: the sources in the subject that affect testing as such and which the psychologist primarily needs to watch. They are: 1) presence of an emotional state, e.g., of fatigue, anxiety, or depression, when one is concerned to measure a trait; 2) in questionnaires, the subject's aiming consciously and unconsciously at giving an approved, more socially desirable impression, frequently called *social desirability* or *spectrad* distortion; and 3) a hostile or noncooperative attitude leading to deliberate sabotage. This last, due to lack of rapport, is so fundamental in its effect that we should consider it first.

ERROR FROM EVALUATIVE SITUATIONS

Sabotage

Enough has been said in numerous test handbooks and throughout this volume about desirable administrative conditions: e.g., the need to develop good mo-

---

*As to the relative importance of these three types of error one might point out that reviewers often give quite excessive concern to the relative reliability of scales. In the first place the coefficients are often on quite small numbers. Secondly, there is a failure to realize that among tests of the same format and type, e.g., three-choice questionnaires, the differences that are reliable are mainly due to length, so that if the Spearman-Brown correction is used they come to essentially the same coefficient for the same test length.

Further, undue regard for sampling error in test standardization results overlooks that the difference of means from a 4,000 and a 50,000 standardization of an intelligence test is only a small fraction of a point of I.Q., whereas in the individual being tested the reliability coefficient tells us there is, say, only a 50/50 chance of being within 4 points of the true I.Q. on account of measurement error. A little considered but very practical point in debates about larger vs. smaller standardizations is that the enormous expense of a 50,000 standardization is likely to deter the publisher from entering soon on that test revision by *progressive rectification* of factor validities, which is so desirable in most tests.

tivation and "rapport" by preliminary discussion and appeal to the motivation system of the particular group; pointing out to them that everyone concerned suffers from any mis-estimate; pointing out in personality tests that there are no "good" and "bad" answers; assuring respect for privacy of results; obtaining sufficient proctors for the size of the group; seeing that all items are answered (except in speeded ability tests); keeping reliable timing on timed tests by a bell rather than a stopwatch which the examiner may fail to catch at the limiting moment, and so on.

In connection with rapport between tester and tested, a fetish has persisted in some texts on testing that individual testing is *always* superior to group administration. But actually, as pointed out in some chapters here, the advantages are by no means all on one side. With young children and disturbed clinical cases, individual testing is undoubtedly required. With normal adult subjects the checking of a questionnaire item is likely to be more dependable in the impersonal situation of a large group than when asked embarrassingly by a stranger. And in individual testing there is often a judgment by the examiner—in, say, an intelligence test—of whether the answer was *barely* or *quite* correct—a judgment likely to be affected by his visual impression of whether the child appears intelligent or attractive. Such individual test atmospheres can accumulate some errors. Coefficients of *administrative dependability*, between different administrators, as advocated (Cattell, 1973a), appear not yet to have been systematically explored to throw light on these effects.

Sabotage may be either a) a noncooperation, aiming at giving a purely random, misleading, uninformative, self-obscuring output, or b) rarely and more mischievously, an attempt to present a definite but totally misleading picture, not necessarily in the sense of social desirability as above, but much as a novelist creates an imaginary character. Short of some fantastically complicated approach, there is no way of *correcting* for either kind of sabotage, and the examiner's aim is simply to recognize its existence and reject the test data.

In perhaps half the cases, the subject adopts a "lazy" way of sabotaging, as can be detected from a mere glance at the answer sheet, when a pattern of all right-hand responses, or alternating right and left, or something equally regular, can be seen.

A more complex examination, probably justified only when sabotage is definitely suspected but not obvious, is to look for internal inconsistency in the factor scores, either between the sum of even and odd items, or between the equivalent A and B forms. With a correlation of, say, 0.8 normally existing in the group between the two parts, the estimated score in the B part from the A part will be .8A (in standard scores, A being the A score). The standard deviation of this estimate will be $\sqrt{1 - .8^2}$, in standard score units. If the difference for a given individual of the actual and the estimated is more than twice this, we can be suspicious that the test has, to say the least, not been carefully answered and probably answered randomly. One would, of course, work this out for all factors in a multifactor test, to give, by the total "deviation," the greatest reliability to the conclusion.

If a subject deliberately set out to give high scores on some factors and low on others, he would, in the first place, show some discrepancy of the kind just discussed, because not even a good psychologist (where factor items are mixed up by cycling) can very reliably pick out which items score on which factors (especially when items with suppressor action are used in construction). Consequently, art would not be as good as nature in producing internal consistency (homogeneity) in the factor item patterns. Secondly, though this is harder to apply, the second order structure implies some similarity in level of certain primary factor scores. For example, exvia requires that a person well above average in A should be significantly above average in F, surgency. A layman unaware of second order structure who faked high and low on various factors would not know this and would produce some improbabilities.

A theoretically less clear, but practically easy examination for sabotage has been suggested, out of their extensive experience, by Karson and O'Dell (1976). This consists simply in noting what proportion of the factor scores lie in extreme ranges. Normally only one factor score in 20 would lie outside a sten score range of from 2 through 9. If, say, in the 16 P.F., there appear three scores of 1 and two of 10 stens, one may be suspicious. Karson & O'Dell (1976) present some empirical results.

Sabotage is possible, in both questionnaire Q-data and objective (T-data) tests, but motivated distortion (to social desirability) is presumably effective only in the former. Except in special circumstances, e.g., with a person with an obsessive prejudice against testing, or with a putative criminal attempting to deceive psychiatrists on an insanity plea, sabotage is, fortunately, quite rare.

Desirability Distortion and Trait View (Spectrad) Corrections

Both questionnaires and observer ratings are liable to motivated distortion. In the past this has been handled by different concepts concocted *ad hoc* for these domains. Discussion has been largely confined to "social desirability" for Q-data and "halo effect" and "projection" for observer rating, L-data. However, it will be shown here that in the end the same broad principles, in *trait view* and *spectrad* theory, can be applied to both, and transcend the limitations of those concepts.

That there are significant shifts in the mean scores, different for different factors, when the same group is asked to do the same test under different conditions is well-known, as shown in Table 23.1.

Edwards (1957) attempted to handle such distortion by the concept of a single "social desirability" factor at work. Cattell, Pierson, and Finkbeiner (1976), however, show that there are *two*, quite distinct social desirabilities at work: 1) in the direction of our culture's accepted morally ideal behavior, as fixed in religion and the establishment; and 2) in the direction of acceptance by the peer group, as a "good fellow" (noticeable particularly in adolescent gangs). But still closer examination indicates additional desirability distortions in as many directions as there are testing purposes and situations. For example, in a situation where testing profiles were exchanged between prospective student dates, the distortion was different again from the above, to what might be called "wooing desirability"!

The ultimate solution in what is called *trait view theory* is to recognize that distortion ("faking") *like any other form of human behavior can be estimated by the behavioral equation*. To use that equation, the behavioral indices, *b*'s, must be empirically found for each situation: e.g., seeking admission to a club; trying to malinger for insurance purposes; being a candidate for the priesthood, and so forth.

Before expressing this in technical form, let us note that, even if there *were* a single pattern of social desirability distortion (as say in one of the profiles in Figure 23.1, p. 509), we should still need to find out how much *any given person* had adopted it. (There would be no point in subtracting the *same* amount—as in any one of the rows in Table 23.1—to finish with the *same* relative positions of the clients as before. Accordingly, the desirability approach invented lie scales and motivated distortion (henceforth MD) scales intended to find out how strongly the given person had set out to fake. They contain items of desirable behavior which it is assumed practically no one could honestly

TABLE 23.1
Differential Distortions Under Different Testing Situations
Mean Score Differences from *Anonymous* Administration to Three Role Situations

Personality Trait	Job-Seeking	Socially Ideal Self	Date-Seeking	General Desirability[a] (Meredith)
Affectothymia	1.2	1.6	1.0	1.4
Intelligence	−0.1	−0.3	0.0	−0.7
Ego Strength	1.0	2.9	1.7	2.3
Dominance	−0.2	−0.6	0.0	−0.3
Surgency	−0.7	−0.1	0.0	0.3
Superego	2.1	2.5	0.6	1.7
Parmia	1.9	2.3	1.7	2.4
Premsia	0.2	−0.2	−0.4	−1.1
Protension	−1.6	−2.1	−1.5	−1.4
Autio	−0.5	−1.1	−0.7	−1.4
Shrewdness	1.1	1.4	0.8	1.5
Guilt Proneness	−2.3	−3.0	−1.9	−2.5
Radicalism	0.9	1.0	0.7	0.6
Self Sufficiency	−0.8	1.3	−0.9	−1.5
Self Sentiment	2.5	2.9	1.4	2.5
Ergic Tension	−2.8	−3.6	−2.2	−3.2

[a]These four patterns of desirability are presented as a difference similarly calculated in the three roles as from Meredith's and DeVoogd's results in Cattell (1973a) with which they should be compared. Virtually all differences, except those for intelligence, surgency, and premsia, are significant at P 0.01 level. In data from Krug and Cattell (1971) positive sign means desirable.

answer positively—as true—such as "Did you never tell a lie?" or "Have you always faithfully returned anything you borrowed?" or "Does everyone admire you?"

Unfortunately, these absurd pretentions have to grade into just conceivably possible real excellencies—so that the scale will not be perceived immediately as a "catch." Consequently, the score on it is actually a composite of some really good traits that some persons might actually possess and several indicators of lying. The possibility therefore exists that if we correlate such an MD scale with each source trait and use the regression to take out the "lie" part from each, we are overdoing it and taking out some true excellence too.

That this is not only a theoretical possibility but an actuality is shown by looking at a majority of the source traits that load when a general factor of social desirability is taken out. Its general nature is sufficiently indicated by Table 23.1, where the personality factors that are common to these distortions, and are lower in the anonymous situation, are, especially, ego strength, C, superego, G, high self-sentiment, Q_3, and low ergic tension, $Q_4(-)$. Higher A, affectia, lower guilt proneness, $O(-)$, and higher surgency, F, are also directions in which some distortion takes place. (The conscious picture of the "ideal self" agrees mainly with these distortions [Table 23.1], but also has some significant new features, by adding higher intelligence, B [not fakable in the last mentioned research], higher dominance, E, higher parmia, H, and lower protension, $L(-)$.)

If one looks around for any known second-order personality factor with decided resemblance to this pattern, the curious discovery is made that the second-order anxiety factor QII (Chapters 12 and 18), loading $C(-)$, $H(-)$, L, O, Q_3 and Q_4, covers the most important "desirability factors" (with the exception of G)—in a negative direction. In short, it is part of the very nature of anxiety that the individual lacks confidence, is self-deprecatory, and gives a low desirability image. Consequently, the proposals to reduce scores by subtracting a general (second-order) factor called "social desirability" would indeed throw away the baby with the bath water, for it would take away most of the variance by which one of the most important clinical factors — anxiety—is recognized and scored.

An understanding of the new trait view and spectrad corrections is better introduced by considering first their role in observer ratings rather than questionnaires. (We need in any case in this chapter to deal with errors in ratings.) As noted above, the first concepts in dealing with rating distortion had to do with the so-called halo effect and the projection of the rater's own less desirable traits. The former supposed that if a rater liked the look of a ratee, or had a friendly role, or was favorably impressed by him on *one* good trait, he would mark him higher toward the favorable pole on other desirable traits. The second concept took over the psychoanalytic notion that a rater battling with some unpleasant trait in his own makeup (strictly, in his unconscious) would project it unduly on others, falsely rating them high thereon. For both of these hypothetical tendencies there is some empirical support, but the first factor analysis of effects of defense mechanisms on perception (Cattell & Wenig, 1952), while a) supporting projection as a real distorter, also b) showed that "projection" actually splits into two distinct kinds: i) *true* (Freudian), and ii) *naive* projection. In the latter the judge simply but honestly judges the other's behavior *on his own limited experience*, i.e., he lacks knowledge that would aid correct empathy. Thus, he explains perceived behavior by motives *he* would have if *he* made the observed reaction. Unlike true projection,

this does not malign; it simply restricts and distorts the accuracy of ratings.

Cattell and Wenig (1952) showed, however, that *other* defense mechanisms than projection alone—in fact, several of those that Anna Freud (1937) had listed—also operate as true unitary tendencies affecting perception of persons. This factoring also showed that the *defense styles had systematic relations to the primary personality factors* in the judges. For example, there are correlations of tendency to true projection with personality factor L, *protension*, and of fantasy with *guilt proneness* (factor O). It is unfortunate that this pioneer study has not been experimentally checked by others; however, at least we may conclude that "misperception" is not just a product of projection only. Indeed, from this and other evidence it surely becomes evident that the degree of misperception derives from *all* the defenses and *all* the traits in the total personality of the perceiver.

This is the position taken in the new development in perception that has been called *trait view* theory (Cattell, 1973a, 1982). It considers two sources that fix the perception of a trait or piece of behavior T_x in a given person by a given judge. First, what is called the *construing* effect arises from the traits of the judge in the given situation in which he is placed, and applies to *any* person he evaluates. It is an ordinary behavioral equation, with the rating of T_x as the behavior, in subject i assessed by observer o, thus:

$$y = m$$
$$T_{xo\bar{i}} = \Sigma b_{xky} T_{yo} \tag{23-1}$$

where T_{yo} is any of the m traits of the observer (judge), o, and k is the situation of the judges. The $\bar{i}$ indicates it is an average effect across *all* observed subjects.

But there is also a *contextual* effect from the *other* traits than T_x in the subject affecting the way T_{xi} is seen, and this will also depend on the *situation* in which the subject is seen by the judges. For example, the intelligence of i, as he is observed in group interaction situations, might be underestimated because he is desurgent $(F-)$ and says little, and this would also be peculiar to the interview situation, k. In a given situation, k, in which the subjects of observation (ratees) stand, c's (*contextual weights*) can be assigned to the way in which every other trait in the individual ratee affects perception of the trait in question, namely, T_{xi}. Holding all judges constant in their situation as observers, and taking the *average* judge's contextual misperception (first setting the equation out more fully for easier understanding), we have:

$$T_{xk'i} = c_{xk'1}T_i + \ldots + c_{xk'n}T_{ni} \qquad (23\text{-}2a)$$

or more briefly,

$$\begin{array}{c} y = m \\ T_{xk'i} = \Sigma c_{xk'y}T_{yi} \end{array} \qquad (23\text{-}2b)$$

Where k' is the situation in which the subjects stand (written with a prime to distinguish from the judges' situation, k). Incidentally, since this is the general, average, contextual effect of subjects' ambient traits on T_x for *all* judges, in the judges' situation k, the score $T_{xk'i}$ should, *in its full regalia, be written* $T_{xk'i\bar{o}k}$, *ō being averaged observer and k their situation.* But equation 23-2a above is an introductory simplification, which is carried further below. It will be noted that the contextual effect in equation 23-2 can be considered a more sophisticated form of the old "halo effect." It does not suppose a *general* halo factor, but weights the distinct effects of various attractive and unattractive, perception-catalytic, and confusable traits upon the perceptual evaluation of trait T_x in the ratee. (The rest of what used to be called "halo" is in the judge, and his situation, as described below.) Incidentally, although we have been talking of "raters," this analysis applies perhaps most vitally to diagnostic assessments by psychiatrists[*] and psychotherapists. Indeed, it presents an essential statement of the end result of the consulting room processes of examination. It follows that if we want to know how trait T_x is being misperceived in a particular individual ratee i by particular individual judge o, the two equations must be put together. Using square brackets, to remind us of the distinct origin of the two constituents, we can write the total effect (assuming no interaction other than addition):

$$T_{xiokk'}{}^{as} = [b_{xk1}T_{1o} + \ldots + b_{xkn}T_{no}] + [c_{xk'1}T_{1i} + \ldots c_{xk'n}T_{ni}] \qquad (23\text{-}3)$$

where $T_{xiokk'}$ is the evaluation of trait T_x in individual i by individual observer (judge) o, the situation of the judges being k and of the subjects k'.

The "situation" of *judges*, k, includes their roles and relations to the ratees. For example, are they teachers rating pupils; magistrates judging the guilt of offenders; psychiatrists assessing sanity; or, say, peers rating peers? The situation of *ratees*, k', is mainly the behavioral settings in which they operate while being observed.

---

[*]Some progress was made 20 years ago in obtaining weights for the contextual terms in psychiatric ratings of anxiety. After the rather alarming discovery that two experienced psychiatrists, selected for reputation as diagnosticians, correlated mutually only .24 in estimates of anxiety level on 86 clients, Cattell and Scheier (1961, p. 100) began to ask what other traits were being mistaken for anxiety, i.e., had high c values. (The psychiatrists, incidentally, both correlated better with the Scheier pure anxiety *factor* scale than with each other.) It was found depressiveness (low U.I. 18, hypomanic optimism) and evasiveness (U.I. 20)—see Chapter 13—were most frequently mistaken for anxiety, i.e., they contextually raised the perception of true anxiety or were confounded with it. Cattell and Scheier also proposed, though without complete available data, that every psychiatrist be helped by being supplied with an index showing what particular traits in the rater and the ratee operated in the overestimation and how one particular psychiatrist's acting concept of anxiety could thus be translated into another's. These aids to objectivity in discussion of a trait concept, and treatment, have unfortunately not been realized in actual tables.

But, if they know they are being observed, it might take on a special character and then the c values would also reflect any "acting up," beyond the formal passive role.

With this description of the separate processes *construing* and *contextual* in the rating of i by o, we are able better to understand what happens in the questionnaire, where the rater and ratee are the same person. The two effects nevertheless continue to exist psychologically, but since *the traits of judge and subject are now identical in score*, the resulting equation becomes simpler, namely a sum of the two expressions in brackets in equation 23-3 (recognizing that now $o = i$ and $k' = k$), thus:

$$T_{xik'} = (b + c)_{xk'1}T_{1i} + \ldots + (b + c)_{xk'n}T_{ni} \quad (23-4)$$

If we reflect on how equations 23-2 and 23-4 are in practice obtained, it will be evident that the values on the left are the distortions from *true* values. But they are, in practice and research, the experimental values with which we have to begin. From these given false values we have to beget the true. Thus in equation 23-3 we, first, in a given situation, allow N_o judges to rate N_i subjects on the trait T_x. From these data we average scores from *all* (N_i) subjects by judge o_1, by judge o_2, and so on, and correlate judges' trait scores (by test) with these values. The resulting correlation matrix, $1 \times N_o$, tells how much the observed trait variance is due to individual differences of judges, and to what factors in judges it is ascribed in various degrees.

Second, one takes reciprocally the same total score matrix (still for trait T_x in situations with vector b_o for judges and b_i for subjects) and averages the scores assigned by *all* (N_o) judges for each subject, i_1, i_2, etc., and correlates the other trait scores (by test) of the subjects with these N_i rated scores on trait T_x. This gives the amount of variance in T_x due to the contextual

effect, and its roots in the b weights assigned to each of the subject's other traits. From this, if we have in a given case in applied practice the rating of a trait T_x for person i by person o, and have the source-trait scores for these rating persons (from tests), we can correct the recorded rating for the construing and contextual effects, since the values calculated as T_{xo} and T_{xi} in equations 23-1 and 23-2 are the needed corrections, positive or negative.

In the case of the correction T_{xic} in the *questionnaire* situation, in equation 23-4, we lack the experimental basis for the true score that is implicit in the averaging of all judges' scores across all subjects in the rating situation, which operationally accepts a mean as the *true* value. If we simply correlate subjects' scores on other traits in the questionnaire with the given T_x score, we should (with oblique factors) be largely including real correlations among the factors, not just perceptual effects. There is thus no way, at least along the above lines, either of separating b and c effects or of evaluating their joint effects in the questionnaire trait scores.

An alternative approach must, therefore, be used as follows. The subjects are asked to evaluate in themselves, in a given questionnaire situation, all of m traits, each represented by at least two subscales. The $2m$ (or, better $3m$) subscales are then factored to yield p factors. By the usual purpose and function of factor analysis these will be the true traits at work, and by the usual factor estimation matrix a weighting of the scale scores can be obtained to estimate the true factor scores, thus:

$$T_{xki} = \sum_{\quad}^{y = 2m} s_{xky}S_{yi} \quad (23-5)$$

where S is a subscale score, and k is attached to T_{xi} to remind us that it is estimated from one situation, k, of questionnaire testing.

It may be wondered whether this same device could be used with judges' data, but in the construing case it would give the true traits of the *judges*, not the subjects. It is of intriguing practical interest, however, that *one thus has a way to score a person's traits from his judgments of others*, though possibly the weights would not be large enough to do so with as much accuracy as is possible by our usual direct testing. In the contextual equation, taking the mean rating of the judges on each individual, but now on two or three slightly different operational definitions of each rated trait, giving $2m$ or $3m$ variables, one could similarly reach true trait estimates as far as the contextual effect is concerned.

Thus we have two methods, which could be cross-checked, for the L-data, rater-subject correction, but only one for the Q-data correction, the construing and contextual effects being taken into account in both L- and Q-data. The results of such analyses for weights would be presented as *correction matrices* (two in the case of ratings) applicable for a given trait in each of several situations. Thus, a handbook for a questionnaire should ideally contain something like Table 23.2 for making all needed distortion corrections.

It should surely be the aim of a well organized applied psychology to pursue research to obtain these weights for each of, say, 15 to 30 traits for each of, say, half a dozen common testing situations.* The computer calculation from a matrix of, say, row 1 across 16 traits and, say, sub-

jects for the day scored on 16 scales would be a matter of seconds, and the correction would be on an altogether higher level of psychological and statistical dependability than by using MD scales, lie scales, gross social desirability corrections, etc.

In the next section the relation of this spectrad model to computer synthesis will be brought out. That other part of trait view distortion that resides in properties of the test itself will appropriately be brought out and discussed in terms of "computer synthesis" correction scores.

Both from the practical standpoint here considered and from the standpoint of discovering laws in social perception, e.g., in attribution theory, this firm model of *trait view theory* should now provide a broad avenue of progress, extending incidentally in *spectrad theory* to the misperception also of situations (Cattell, 1982).

The extent of distortion in a test result is obviously a function not only of the motivational situation of the subject who is taking the test, but also of interaction of the motivational distortion with some intrinsic *degree of vulnerability* of the given test to faking. A well known but not very successful design (by reason of "side effects") for reducing vulnerability in questionnaires was "forced choice" (Nunnally, 1967; Krug, 1985), but others have been tried and probably as much can be done by "artful" wording of items as by forced choice, to make distortion more dif-

---

*We may refer, both in this *situation allowance matrix* and in the (later) *rectification matrix* to a *square* matrix of a kind that would arise as if we had somehow taken the intercorrelations of n scales (say 16 in the 16 P.F.) and derived from them n factors, as in a principal components analysis. Actually, this cannot accurately be done (unless we fall back on principal components), and it is desirable to take two equivalent A and B forms (or more) and factor a $2n \times 2n$ (say 32×32) into n factors. If one wishes to operate only with n scales, one would then cut the factor pattern matrix, V_{fp}, halfway down at an $n \times n$ matrix, and calculate the V_{fe} for estimating the true factors from the scale scores, thus:

$$V_{fe} = R_v{}^{-1}V_{fp}R_f$$

where R_v is the (now) 16×16 correlation of A form

scales, and R_f is the correlation matrix of the (oblique) true factors. Note that this V_{fe} is specific to the *testing situation* in which the questionnaire was filled in and would, in any "third file," have a subscript $k_{(i)a}$, *referent to the given testing situation a*.

To proceed to the true score estimates, on, say, 200 persons, we now use the 200×32 matrix, S_v, of their standard scores on the scale and proceed to the 200×16 matrix, $\hat{S}_f$, of estimated scores on the true factors.

$$S_f = S_v, V_{fe}$$
$$(N \times n)\ (N \times n)\ (n \times n)$$

where N = number of people and n number of factor scores.

The square matrix V_{fe} might well in this usage be referred to as the *test situation allowance* matrix.

ficult. In testing, the ultimate solution to distortion and to test vulnerability is to shift from questionnaires to T-data—objective tests—as in the O-A Kit and the MAT. Meanwhile, among questionnaires and similar tests, though we may have the means in trait view equations to correct for distortion, it would be useful to have for each test an index of *test vulnerability* to distortion. No special term for this en-

TABLE 23.2
Illustration of Use of a Trait View Correction Matrix

a) Hypothetical Trait View Correction Matrix for the 16 P.F. in a Job-Seeking Situation

	A	B	C	E	F	G	H	I	L	M	N	O	Q_1	Q_2	Q_3	Q_4
A	.9		.1													
B	−.1		0													
C	.1		.8													
E	−.2		−.1													
F	−.2		.2													
G	.1		.2													
H	0		−.1													
I	0		−.2													
L	−.1		−.1													
M	0		.1													
N	−.2		−.2													
O	0		−.1													
Q_1	0		−.1													
Q_2	.1		.1													
Q_3	−.2		−.1													
Q_4	0		.1													

Note values here are hypothetical and have not yet been normalized by columns. Only two are illustrated but the whole matrix would normally be full.

b) General Form of Correction Matrix Weight on $T_1 \ldots T_n$ Trait Scores for Estimating Trait T_x

Testing Situation	T_1	T_2		T_n
(a) Job Application	w_{1a}	w_{2a}	$\ldots$	w_{na}
(b) Anonymous Use in Research	w_{1b}	w_{2b}	$\ldots$	w_{nb}
(c) Psychiatric Court Appeal	w_{1c}	w_{2c}	$\ldots$	w_{nc}
(d) "Date" Seeking Matching	w_{1d}	w_{2d}	$\ldots$	w_{nd}

c) Matrix Multiplication Takes the Form:

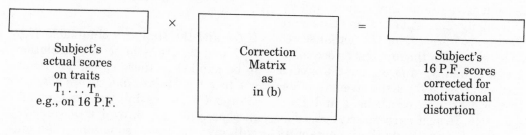

Subject's actual scores on traits $T_1 \ldots T_n$ e.g., on 16 P.F.

×

Correction Matrix as in (b)

=

Subject's 16 P.F. scores corrected for motivational distortion

Trait View Matrix e.g., for Job-Seeking

(cont'd)

TABLE 23.1 *(cont'd)*

d) Illustration of Actual Gain in Validity, as Increase in Obtainable Multiple R with Factor, from Correction by Trait View Theory (a) Personality Traits Alone (b) Personality Traits Plus Role Factor Scores (Cattell & Krug, 1971)

| | | Effect of Correcting for Influence |
Test Situation	Personality Traits	Personality and Role Traits
Job-Seeking	+0.08	+0.10
Date "Seeking"	+0.06	+0.07

Note: Values are multiple R (shrinkage corrected) for trait-view validity minus validity for simple scale scoring. All differences significant at $P < 0.01$ level.

ters into the trait view equation, but, as we shall see, it is implied in the situation vector.

A model for questionnaire distortion should surely ideally include: 1) the individual's intensity of desire to distort on a given trait; 2) the testing situation which modulates that desire; 3) the vulnerability of the test, by its construction, to distortion; and 4) the individual's capacity (cleverness) at distorting such a test (which is different from the strength of his desire to do so).

The design offered for solving for a vulnerability value is to present a) the same test for a given trait T_x under two different situations, one of which stimulates the desire to distort more than the other, and b) two tests, presumably of different degrees of vulnerability, for the same trait, on one and the same situation, i.e., with the same intensity of desire to distort.

To set this out we need no trait subscript since it is the same throughout, and we will simply represent a person's true score therein as T, represent the actual scores as S_{11} and S_{12} for the first test on occasions 1 and 2, and S_{21} and S_{22} for the second test, and D_1 and D_2 as the strength of desire to distort on occasions 1 and 2 respectively. Then, if, as seems most probable, we allow D to multiply the vulnerability U, we have (Model 1):

Test 1
$$(1) \quad S_{11} = T + U_1D_1 \qquad (23\text{-}6a)$$
$$(2) \quad S_{12} = T + U_1D_2 \qquad (23\text{-}6b)$$

Test 2
$$(3) \quad S_{21} = T + U_2D_1 \qquad (23\text{-}6c)$$
$$(4) \quad S_{22} = T + U_2D_2 \qquad (23\text{-}6d)$$

It is assumed all values are in standard scores, so that, although tests 1 and 2 might differ considerably in raw mean and sigma, T will be the same on all four occasions. A moment's algebra shows that we can get from the data on S's the following solutions:

$$\frac{U_1}{U_2} = \frac{S_{12} - S_{11}}{S_{22} - S_{21}} \qquad (23\text{-}7)$$

$$\frac{D_1}{D_2} = \frac{S_{11} - S_{21}}{S_{12} - S_{22}} \, , \qquad (23\text{-}8)$$

$$U_2D_1 = \frac{(S_{21} - S_{11})(S_{22} - S_{21})}{S_{22} - S_{21} - S_{12} + S_{11}} \, . \qquad (23\text{-}9)$$

U_2D_1 (and the similarly obtainable U_2D_2 U_1D_1 and U_1D_2) are the actual correlations to be applied in these cases, but we are out to get U_1 *values and all we obtain is a ratio* U_2. Increasing the experimental measures to, say, 6, by a new value D_3, will give us more equations than unknowns, but the product form of the model is still such that we only get ratios, now overdetermined. Along these lines we can reach a solution if we agree arbitrarily to assign unit vulnerability to a given test and score all other tests relative to it, which is enough for choosing tests. (This also arbitrarily fixes the scale of D's.) This solution could scarcely rest on data from a single individual and one would need to take the mean scores of a whole group under situations provoking a mean change in desire to distort. The results, however, could be applied to an individual, with the assumption that U is a fixed vulnerability of a test and that the situation-tied D has values the same for all people in that situation.

An alternative approach to determining vulnerability values is one that uses factor analysis. Let us suppose we measure N persons on n forms, $a, b, c,$ etc., of measures for trait T, differing presumably in vulnerability, but all in the same testing situation. Although in the same situation, the individuals will differ in desire and capacity to distort. Factored over the n forms, the result will be a factor matrix as follows, when individual factor values are inserted:

Model 2

$$S_{ai} = b_{aT}T_i + U_{aD}D_i + (b_{ea}e_{ai}) \qquad (23\text{-}10a)$$
$$S_{bi} = b_{bT}T_i + U_{bD}D_i + (b_{eb}e_{bi}) \qquad (23\text{-}10b)$$
$$S_{ci} = b_{cT}T_i + U_{cD}D_i + (b_{ec}e_{ci}) \qquad (23\text{-}10c)$$

If the model is correct that the observed score is only true score plus distortion from the subject, plus specific error, the result from such variables should be a two-factor solution. The "loading" U_{aD}, etc., is the vulnerabilities of forms $a, b, c,$ etc., having the usual product relation (as in equation 23-6) to the desire to distort, D, peculiar to the subject.

It will be noted that these values are 1) specific to the given trait, and 2) specific to the situation in which all testing took place (and, of course, to the usual samples, etc.), whereas Model 1 includes the effect of situations in changing the D values. To discover further the effect of either of

these, one would repeat the factoring either with a different trait or with a different testing situation. To assess the effect of a particular style of test, one would average vulnerabilities over such a range of traits and situations.

The aim of getting vulnerability values—U's—is to put a science of comparative test construction on a firm basis. But, when values are known, they of course enable score corrections to be made. With b_{aT} (or U_{aD} if b_{ea} is trivial) fixed, the true score T_i can be derived from S_{ai} on the test form a.

There remains the question of the relation of the *vulnerability* analysis to the *trait view analysis* of distortion. In both we have assumed that the "desire and capacity" to fake (D in the vulnerability model) is a unitary total, though at some later point we might be interested in finding the separate contribution of each trait. It was pointed out that three things enter into the distortion: 1) the drive of the person to fake on a given trait, 2) in a given situation, and 3) in relation to the vulnerability of the test. In the vulnerability model, U, with a situation subscript, gives the two last and D the first. In trait view the D is a set of personality and dynamic traits each weighted by a b. But the vulnerability of the test in the given situation is also contained in these b's, e.g., in a weight on intelligence showing how a more intelligent person can better distort on the given test. Elsewhere, in general personality and perception theory (Cattell, 1980b), it has been shown how b can be broken down into a v and an s, the latter describing how much the situation stimulates the drives, etc., and the former the power of the traits to produce the response behavior. It could be argued that the vulnerability is shown in the weight of the U's, expressing the extent to which people are able to distort for a given strength of the drive to distort.

To apply the trait view approach to assessing vulnerability, one would factor measures for the same trait in the same situation across several different test forms. This would hold the *s* part of the *b*'s constant, whence a comparison of *b*'s for, say, test forms *x* and *y*, showing them larger on *x* than *y*, would describe *x* as more vulnerable than *y*. A ratio of vulnerabilities among tests, equivalent to the *U* value on a scale standing from a test given a unitary *U*, could thus result from trait view as from the initial comparative test vulnerability approach. The difference of the two approaches is that the latter gives a single scalar value for *vulnerability* and for *drive* to distort a particular trait in a particular test situation, whereas trait view gives each as a vector, to be reduced to a scalar by $U = \sqrt{\Sigma U^2}$ and $D = \sqrt{\Sigma s^2}$. Theoretically interesting developments could doubtless be built on the greater information in the vector, but the need for large samples and factor analyses in trait view, compared to a simple fourfold measure (two forms each at two drive-to-distort levels) for results by the comparative vulnerability approach, gives greater appeal to the latter for the practitioner.

As the reader will realize, we are opening up above a new prospect for evaluation of tests, on the important matter of the resistance to different designs to faking, but it enters a domain at present scarcely trodden.

ADULTERATION IN FACTOR SCORES: INSTRUMENT FACTORS, VARIANCE REALLOCATION, AND COMPUTER SYNTHESIS

Pursuing sources of error of interpretation, we come next to misunderstandings about the validity of actual tests and of required allowances for "biased validities." The formal psychometric evaluation of *coefficients of validity*, and their interactions with test *consistency* have already been discussed (Chapter 4). We touch now on two or more diverse test construction models and on calculations on validity not commonly treated.

Much of this can be considered under

perturbation theory (Cattell, 1979a, p. 348). If we begin our study with error in relation to the nature of structure, which must obviously precede considering error on *level of* structures, and look at the structures that emerge from factor analytic research, the outcome is as shown in Figure 23.1. First this sets aside, on the left, "matrix-peculiar," scientifically irrelevant factors that appear through effects in technical procedures. On the right, however, we deal with recurrent *stable* (process-immune) factors not restricted to some coefficient, scoring style, etc. used in calculation. Setting aside first, as "understood," the true substantive factors in organisms, we turn on the extreme right to what concerns us there— *perturbation factors*—which perturb the clear recognition of such substantive factors. Categories (a), (b), and (c) need no explanation, and (c) should be considered an added effect in the domain of trait view concepts that we have just studied. It is category (d), instrument factors, that we now study as having most to do with corrections in psychometric practice.

Of instrument factors there are three main sources—A, B, and C in Figure 23.1. B can be most quickly dealt with. It arises from a biased choice of *situations* in which to observe a given personality trait's manifestations. For example, if a questionnaire deals with dominance behaviors a) in the home and b) in business, it is likely to find two apparent dominance factor patterns each in variables peculiar to one domain. However, they will be much correlated, so that the *general* dominance trait is a second order factor across them (and other situational areas). That is to say, there will be "instrument" factors for each domain, superimposed on a general dominance factor. Some questionnaires that are built on subjective concepts of source traits, rather than reached through factoring of the basic broad personality sphere, e.g., some anxiety scales, are—often unconsciously—restricted to one area or another, and are thus giving a *situation-*

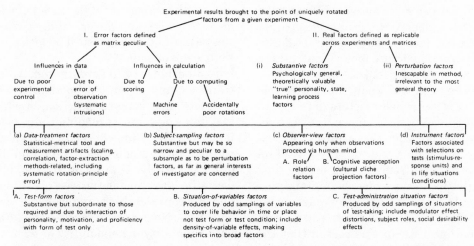

Experimental results brought to the point of uniquely rotated
factors from a given experiment

I. Error factors defined as matrix peculiar

II. Real factors defined as replicable across experiments and matrices

Influences in data

Due to poor experimental control

Due to error of observation (systematic intrusions)

Influences in calculation

Due to scoring

Due to computing

Machine errors

Accidentally poor rotations

(i) *Substantive factors* Psychologically general, theoretically valuable "true" personality, state, learning process factors

(ii) *Perturbation factors* Inescapable in method, irrelevant to the most general theory

(a) *Data-treatment factors* Statistical-metrical tool and measurement artifacts (scaling, correlation, factor-extraction methods-related, including systematic rotation-principle error)

(b) *Subject-sampling factors* Substantive but may be so narrow and peculiar to a subsample as to be perturbation factors, as far as general interests of investigator are concerned

(c) *Observer-view factors* Appearing only when observations proceed via human mind
A. Role relation factors
B. Cognitive apperception (cultural cliche projection factors)

(d) *Instrument factors* Factors associated with selections on tests (stimulus-response units) and in life situations (conditions)

A. *Test-form factors* Substantive but subordinate to those required and due to interaction of personality, motivation, and proficiency with form of test only

B. *Situation-of-variables factors* Produced by odd samplings of variables to cover life behavior in time or place not test form or test condition; include density-of-variable effects, making specifics into broad factors

C. *Test-administration situation factors* Produced by odd samplings of situations of test-taking; include modulator effect distortions, subject roles, social desirability effects

Note that a systematic relation is possible between certain categories here and those of the five dimensions in the data box. Thus, II(ii)(b) deals with sampling on the subject coordinate; II(ii)(c) with the observer coordinate; II(ii)(d)A and B with the stimulus-response coordinates; and II(ii)(d)B and C with selections on the occasions coordinate.

Sources of structural misinterpretation focused on perturbation theory

Figure 23.1. Instrument and other factors that may lead to misinterpretation of source trait and state factors

ally-biased measure of the real general source trait.* Such bias is actually more common in *rating* situations than in questionnaires and is responsible for some debates on number of factors, e.g., suggestions that five rather than 16-20 factors are needed to span the domain (Digman, 1965). For example, a factoring is done only on ratings by teachers made only in school situation, which necessarily omits much home and other behavior.

Instrument factors of type C have al-

ready been sufficiently considered both in test-taking situation effects and in the biasing of the estimation of a trait by too much overlap with a role factor. It is type A, however, that presents the most obvious instances of false factor measurement. If exvia-invia is measured, on the one hand, as a second-order factor in questionnaires (QI; from A, F, H, Q_2^-) and, on the other, by the O-A Battery (U.I. 32), the correlation between the two scores may be relatively low, though both sets of variables, in a factoring common across these media, load only one and the same personality factor. It is reasonable to suppose that each of these two very different media contains one or more instrument factors peculiar to itself. Speculation on what these may be can be read elsewhere (Cattell, 1973a, 1982). The clearest demonstrations have been given in the area of motivation measurement with the objective measures in the MAT and SMAT. Here factor solutions have been reached (Cattell & Digman, 1964; Cattell, 1961a, p. 249), with good simple structure in

---

*Instrument factors have been called by Campbell and Fiske (1959) "methods" in the multitrait-multimethod nomenclature. There are two objections to this: 1) The word method is appropriately used in "scientific methods" and the like as a broad design in research, whereas in tests we are obviously concerned with different kinds of *instrument;* 2) MTMM simply aims at sample measure of one trait across a variety of tests ("methods" or instruments). However, if we go further and find the factors among instruments, the giving of equal weight to instrument factors is very different from multimethod weighting, in which one instrument factor may be represented only twice and another ten times over. The solution is not MTMM but *instrument-transcending* trait measurement.

which the *vehicles* (autism, information projection) clearly stand out as separate instrument factors, beyond the underlying dynamic structure factors, and taking an appreciable slice of the variance.

It is important to know the nature and number of instrument factors in tests, but usually, even though known, they cannot be extirpated from the score by, for example, partialing, and the only way of reducing the bias from any one subtest (just as with specifics in items) is to sum across several, with balance by particular weightings if we know their relative contamination. It is for this reason that the MAT and SMAT are superior (in this respect) to the TAT, for instead of depending on one vehicle only—projection—their source trait scores rest on four: projection, information, autism, and word association. Again, in measuring fluid intelligence, the Raven Matrices use only matrices —in which some training "instrument factor" can be demonstrated —whereas the Culture-Fair Intelligence Scales use four devices, doubtless with some trainable instrument factor or real specific in each, but yielding at least a less biased fluid intelligence measure.

Probably most trait measurements—at least in research where accuracy is important and there is more time to spare—should aim at what have been called *instrument-transcending trait measures*, deliberately using very diverse instruments. For example, exvia-invia would be measured by a) the Q-data secondary, QI; b) the O-A Kit measure U.I. 32; and c) the exvia factor in the Humor Test of Personality. These same distinct approaches could be used in anxiety (using QII and U.I. 24), plus perhaps the purely physiological measures listed by Cattell and Scheier (1961).

A second major form of error in factor source-trait estimation, and one affecting much test interpretation, is *contamination by other common factor scores*. Here we need to keep our concepts clear by refer-

ence to the important difference between *factor trueness* and *factor validity*, which can be most quickly grasped by looking at Figure 4.2 on page 57.

Test designs try to actually remove extraneous, and unwanted, *common* source trait factors by suppressor action, in which two items or subtests loading the wanted factor positively are chosen to load an unwanted factor, one negatively and the other positively. One result of this, incidentally, is to broaden the base of estimate and also considerably to reduce scale homogeneity. (Novices who confuse the latter with reliability-dependability or even validity are apt to write reviews condemning tests of low homogeneity! See Chapter 4.)

Unfortunately, few scales as yet have reached the perfection of adequate suppressor action, so that a factor X scale is likely to have some ingredients of Y, Z, etc. In the last decade some advanced statisticians like Guttman, Kaiser, and Schonemann have issued bloodcurdling warnings on our inability to make true, unique broad factor estimates from sets of variables of the usual moderate loading level. It is easy to see that if one got an estimate on X with positive loadings on Y, Z, etc., and on another set with all negative loadings on these contaminators, these two estimates of X would correlate quite poorly, which is what these statisticians are saying. The fact is that many factor estimates today *are* quite poor, and that construction of source-trait test scales and batteries still awaits a lot of hard work on suppressor action and *progressive rectification* (see below), before the products can be considered truly satisfactory.

Meanwhile, so long as we are working with multifactor "omnibus" tests and batteries, some escape from unwanted factor bias in a scale is possible by what has been called *computer synthesis*, as proposed by Cattell and by Eber. The requirement of an "omnibus" test as a basis, i.e., one in which several factors are scored by a key on subsets of items from a relatively large total set, is inescapable. Usually the correct oblique rotation (by simple structure or confactor) of all items will have left relatively few items (variables) keyed for factor X that also contribute in fact to another factor Y. Then the simplest and usual mode of scoring is for each factor score to be based on the subset formed by its own markers, not overlapping in the items scored with those of any other factor. However, despite a pretty clean factor structure, one may wish to squeeze the last possible bit of validity and dependability from the "omnibus" by scoring X not only on marker items but also on every stray item in any *other* factor's marker set that has *some* loading on X. On a computer this simply calls for multiplying *all* items in the omnibus by the weights in the V_{fe} matrix obtained as in equation 5-7 (p. 98) for the given factor. $S_f = S_t V_{fe}$, where S_f is factor scores of N people on *all* factors and S_t is their test part scores. The only notable drawback of this gleaning is that it tends to produce larger correlations among the estimated primary factor scores than should exist—by the standard of the pure factors. This spuriousness in the primary scores can be a source of error in estimating the secondaries.

An alternative to computer synthesis by items is the shortcut of doing it by factors. Let us remember that primary factor scores even on the restricted base of each factor's own items will be mutually correlated even if the simple structure pure factors themselves are not. Almost invariably simple structure shows that the true factors really are correlated (oblique), and the result of the bias in the item sample is simply that the actual scores are correlated a little differently from the true (simple structure) factors. In the 16 P.F., HSPQ, the CAB, etc., the actual outcome, however, proves to be that the factor scale scores are not correlated much differently from the true factors, and yield essentially the same second-order factors (Cattell, Eber, & Tatsuoka, 1970, pp. 113-123).

Incidentally, this relatively small discrepancy between correlations of true and estimated primaries needs watching really only at two points: 1) as above, in realizing the effect on estimates of the scores on secondaries; and 2) in the behavioral equation estimates of a criterion, when one must keep in mind whether the criterion correlations to be converted into weights came from correlating scales or from factoring the criterion with the items or scale parcels. There are a number of interesting statistical procedures in this area concerning, for example, transforming scale scores to a distinct derived set that correlates mutually just like the true factors (in simple structure). Such tours de force usually have some drawback—in this case reduced validity of the scale score as such, which is discussed elsewhere (Cattell, 1978; Horst, 1962, 1965, 1966; Nesselroade & Cattell, 1985).

The "short" computer synthesis procedure, based on the recognition that the several factor scale scores are mutually correlated, sets up a vector of weights (naturally with highest weight on the scale for the desired factor) over all factors that will multiply *all* the scale scores to get the best estimated factor score for the given factor X. For several factors this collection of vectors becomes a square matrix, e.g., 16 × 16 for the 16 P.F. test. As it happens, this is, formally, algebraically identical with what one does in applying trait view theory, but, whereas trait view takes weights from a particular testing situation, *computer synthesis* is required to *average* the weights over many situations and thus to be dealing with cross-contamination *inherent in the scales*, rather than the effect of a particular situational trait view, invoking weights peculiar to that situation of testing. But it calls similarly for the multiplication of (in the case of the 16 P.F.) a 1 × 16 vector of scale scores by a 16 × 16 matrix of weights to give a new 1 × 16 set of corrected scale scores.

PROGRESSIVE RECTIFICATION; UNIQUE AND LOCAL TRAIT PATTERNS; ISOPODIC COMPARISON

When all is said, one of the largest causes of misinterpretation of test results arises from some psychologists' crude conceptions—one must admit it—of the natures of the source traits being measured. It is true this vagueness does not affect immediate psychometric calculations of, say, criterion estimates—for factor X score is then a number, entered with a recorded weight from a handbook in this or that criterion prediction, or in a diagnostic comparison of psychiatric profiles, regardless of whether the reason is understood. Yet this is not adequate practice, for, as we have insisted from the beginning, psychological practice is an art combining breadth of psychological insight with exact diagnostic and monitoring measurements (see Chapter 18).

Nevertheless, the present writers believe that in the near future many more diagnoses, prognoses, and treatment decisions will be handled by scientific equations than has been done in classical clinical practice. The arguments and the possibilities are set out in the preceding chapter and in such a thorough symposium as that recently put together by Johnson (1981) and in Chapters 7 and 8 in this volume. But to use those equations, with regard to psychological laws, and modify results with a touch of artistic insight, the psychologist will need *to understand the meanings of primary and secondary personality and dynamic source traits* far more thoroughly than most psychologists now do. For example, he will need to have in mind (and in tables) the normal age curves of traits, the heritability coefficients of traits within and between families, the nature and magnitude of the impact on trait levels of various anticipated environments, the usual social reactions of others to the trait, the modification of the trait pattern in subcultures, and so on, as outlined by Heather

Cattell in Chapter 18. There is thus no substitute for the psychologist having as thorough a knowledge of the number and individual characters of source traits and the laws that govern their interaction as, say, that which the medical doctor has of anatomical organs. Chapters 1 through 3 and 9 through 16 are avenues to that knowledge.

The power of such formulae will depend, however, on data precision, i.e., on the degree of source-trait validity in the instrument. The calculation of that validity and its dependence on length, style of test construction, etc., have been dealt with in Chapters 4, 5, and 6. In the preceding section, we have explained further what the psychologist needs to know about "contamination" by instrument factors. We turn now to understanding factor trueness and the need to look at the history of test construction from that standpoint.

Although properly factored tests, of known source-trait content, are well on their way to replacing subjective scales and *ad hoc*, narrow batteries, it is not often that after the first factorial construction the scales for primary source traits have been subjected to what will be defined as *progressive rectification*. A multiple factor space is necessary for the correct *simple structure* definition of any single broad factor, and it is important that at least initially such research on rotation should be based on a deliberately *widely* sampled personality (or ability) sphere of behavior.

It commonly happens that the first sweep through the factor space suffices to indicate the number of factors required in that domain to give a good mutual "fix" by their hyperplanes. But orthogonal to those reasonably reliable hyperplanes, there are often not enough high loaded items to build up an adequate scale. For example, in the first factoring of the Hawaiian (pidgin) version of the HSPQ, factors O and Q_4 had clear hyperplanes but insufficient items at a significant loading for good factor validity. With low loading (say .30) and low homogeneity, such factors look like B in Figure 23.2 (there paired with a well-established factor).

Strategic, programmatic research does not, as a hurried, expediential practitioner might do, abandon such scales, but holds on to their definition by the hyperplane and goes through further experiments with hypothetically promising items to find eventually items standing at higher validities on those hyperplanes.

Now the unique definition of a factorial source trait hinges, in determining simple structure, on having a sufficiency of items high loaded (correlated) on *other* factors than that being fixed. Rectification is a communal effort among factors. Progres-

sive rectification consists of holding on to the broadly discovered factor structure while entering with psychologically better designed items, and factoring again. At each cycle of creation and factorial testing one finds one or two higher loaded items, which a) raise the validity of the scale and b), as better hyperplane material, help to precision the reference vectors (the factor concepts) for all *other* factors. A third outcome is that, with more good items to choose from, one is more likely to find items giving good suppressor action. This action has also been called "buffering" (see next section) by analogy with the chemical concept, for, as Figure 23.2 shows, the balancing of unwanted broad factors

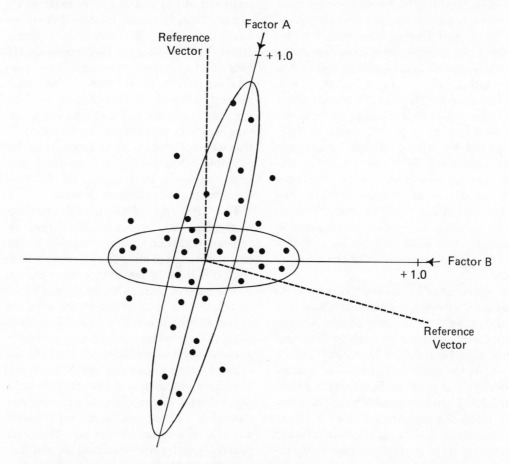

The hyperplane for the large factor A, with items loading up from +.8 to −.8, is actually not as sharply determining as that for factor B, which has no items to measure it above about .4.

Figure 23.2. Goodness of definition possible in a factor of small variance with few markers

helps stabilize the scale at the factor true position.

It seems to be a fact of test history that far too many scales get left at the position of the first research factoring and stay with the initial exploratory items, never undergoing progressive rectification. The costs to the publisher, especially in re-standardization, are high and researchers are apt to leave their scales as orphans. The effect of substitution of a single item y with, say, a $55/45$ "pass-fail," for an older one, x of, say, $62/38$, can be calculated (with approximation), so substitution of a few new items need not entail a complete re-standardization. It may help to glance here at a typical rectification and to bring out the procedures for handling some complexities regarding model and statistics. In functional testing they need to be understood, and few texts have dealt with them. With the usual number of items in an omnibus test, say about 500, there will be a need, in rectification, to try out about 500 new ones. This number may be expected to yield, typically, about 50 truly improved items to substitute for comparative deadwood. With 1000 items the factor operations can easily become forbiddingly large. (Parenthetically, we reject correlating the pool score of items in an existing scale with proposed new items, for this kind of selection perpetuates the factor untrueness of the existing scale.)

It is not only on account of unwieldiness of factor operations in such situations as the above that we contemplate shifting from factoring items as such to factoring what have been called "parcels." In fact, it was on the ground of *instability of properties of items* that we developed (Cattell, 1972, 1974) with Burdsal (Cattell & Burdsal, 1975) the procedures now to be described. Besides suffering from instability (unreliability of a subject's response), single items tend to have so much specific factor in their necessarily particular, narrow behavior that they yield low communality. The low communality means

frustration in the search for precise simple structure, since in the plots the single items are like a globular swarm of bees clinging too close to the origin to show definite hyperplanes.

The method of progressive rectification put forward here differs from past methods in two ways: 1) using *radial parcel* factoring instead of item factoring, and 2) applying a new development on the Dwyer extension (Dwyer, 1940). The first greatly reduces the amount of calculation, and the second avoids what we shall show is a systematic inequitable comparison of items in the Dwyer method. The Dwyer *modification* we may call the *Equity Dwyer*, for reasons below that show it to be apt. Description of the radial parcel method we can safely leave to articles elsewhere (Cattell & Burdsal, 1975; Burdsal & Vaughan, 1974). Briefly, though, the procedure begets relatively factor homogeneous parcels of, say, 4 to 10 items, and, after ascertaining their factor composition, "undoes" them to estimate the factor-belonging of the single constituent items. In this way 800 items can be factored as, for example, 80 parcels of 10 items each covering perhaps 20 factors and defining them with good simple structure.

The "undoing" of the parcels was formerly best carried out by the Dwyer extension equations which require a) the correlations of each of the 80 parcels with the 20 factors (a factor structure matrix in the case of oblique factors), and b) the correlation of each of the items with the parcel to which it belongs. In addition to these 500 items on the test as it presently stands—such as would be constituted, for example, by all items in the A, B, C, and D equivalent forms of the 16 P.F.—the psychologist engaged in progressive rectification will include in his experiment, say, 300 new items, chosen by a thorough psychological understanding of the factors, especially these whose validities suggest they have some deadwood to be replaced. These are also correlated, on the same sample, with the 80 parcels. Thus, instead of operating with an 800×800 item matrix factoring, we have factored an 80×80 and built an 80×800 "extension" matrix, not to be factored, from which, by Dwyer, we can get the correlations of the 800 items with the 20 factors. This extension can be divided into an *old extension* (the existing test items laid out) and a *new extension*, the items hypothetically expected to load the factors better.

Two limitations have always been recognized in the Dwyer method: a) it will not reveal any factors in the new items that were not present in the old. Since the object of progressive rectification is only to improve existing scales this does not matter; and b) it gives the old items some advantage over the new items, in terms of the calculated correlation with the factors. The reason is that the correlation of an old item with its parcel is boosted by its specific factor being included in both, over and above the common factor which alone is of interest, whereas this is not true of the new items. (This might be accepted, however, as a rough "artistic" bias in the right direction, needed because the value for the old item is usually based on several sample factorings, and should have more weight, whereas that of the new is supported only by one sample. But this is too "blind" for good psychometry.) Guilford (1965) provides a formula for reducing the old item correlations to compensate for this spurious gain, but it has to be calculated item by item and makes progressive rectification forbiddingly tedious.

The present writer has introduced a design for old and new extension comparison without bias which may be called the Equity Dwyer or *Equity Rectifying*, ER, calculation. To discuss this let us pass from the numerical illustration above to one of algebraic generality, in which e will stand for the set of *established*, existing items in the scale, and h for the number of hypothesized new items. As usual (Chapter 3, 4, and others above), V_{fs} will stand for

the *factor structure* (correlation) matrix, on the p parcels from the e items. It will be followed by an e subscript ($V_{fs(e)}$) when it derives from factoring the existing, e, parcels, matrix $R_{p(e)}$ and an $(e + h)$ when from factoring parcels from old and new (hypothetical) parcels, from the correlation $R_{p(e+h)}$.

These matrices are shown diagrammatically as well as algebraically in Figure 23.3. The extension matrices are symbolized as E's with subscripts $e(e + h)$ when the r's are of e parcels with $e + h$ items; he when of h parcels with e items; eh when of e parcels with h items, and so on. The corresponding V_{fs}'s will have corresponding subscripts, and the final item weights for getting factor scores will be in V_{fe} (factor estimate) form as usual. The same number of factors, k, holds in all the factor matrices.

The upper part of Figure 23.3 or (a) shows the *usual* Dwyer calculations and needs no comment. The lower part shows that parcels from both the old and new items are put into a common correlation matrix $R_{p(e+h)(e+h)}$ and factored to give $V_{fs(e+h)}$. The items are correlated with all $(e + h)$ parcels to give a common extension matrix $E_{(e+h)(e+h)}$.

The basic innovation is that the factor correlations of the e items are now determined from correlations with the h parcels, giving $V_{fs(h)(e)}$, and conversely those of the h items, by correlation with the e parcels, giving $V_{fs(e)(h)}$ (the first in brackets indicating the parcel origin and the second the free item origin). In this way the contamination (in the ultimate V_{fe} values for election to the scales) of the specific factors in the items is avoided.

Extracting the straight algebraic matrix multiplications from Figure 23.3, we see that the ordinary Dwyer proceeds:

$$E_{(e)(e+h)} \times V_{fe(e)} = V_{fs(e)} \qquad (23\text{-}11)$$
$$(e+h) \times k \qquad p \times k \qquad (e+h) \times k$$

That is to say, the correlations of each and every $(e + h)$ item with each and every

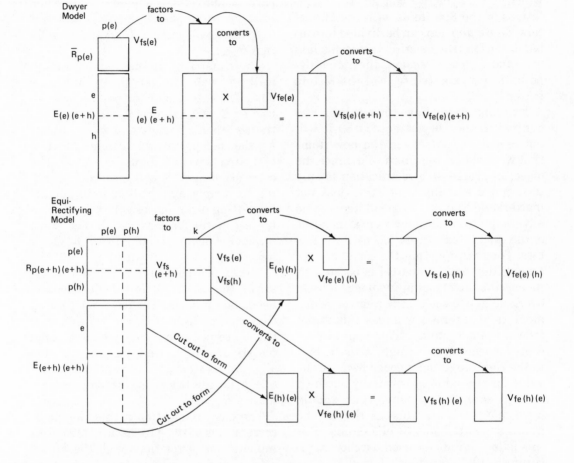

R_p is a *parcel* correlation matrix, whose subscript p(e) refers to parcels among established items and (h) to hypothetically good items.

E is the extension matrix correlating parcels with items. It is either p(e)(e + h) or $(p_{(e)} + p_h)$ (e + h), the first term referring correlations with both sets of parcels.

V_{fsp} is the factor structure among parcels giving k factor by (e) parcels or (k) parcels or both

      $E_{p(e)(k)}$ is factors in $p_{(e)}$ correlated with *k* items

      $E_{p(h)(e)}$ is factors on $p_{(h)}$ correlated with *e* items

$V_{fep(e)(k)}$ is factor estimation weights for k's derived from $p_{(e)}$ set of parcels, for *k* items

$V_{fep(h)(e)}$ is factor estimation weights for k's derived from p(h) set of parcels for *e* items

Figure 23.3. Comparison of matrix processes in the Dwyer and the Equi-Rectification Methods

(*p*) parcel are multiplied by the correlations of those parcels with the *k* factors. The lower part of Figure 23.3 simply repeats this principle with the innovation of taking each item's correlations *only with parcels to which it does not belong*.

Of course, there is a price to pay for this escape from major bias, namely that arising in any failure of the assumption that the same factors are present with approximately equal variance in the *e* and *h* samples of items, so that the factor estimates will remain of about equal accuracy in both. Thus, success depends on a sufficiently clear concept of each factor having emerged at that stage to lead to construction of items at least as good as—and hopefully better than—the old, when entering the next round of progressive rectification. Incidentally, the reader will have noted that it is the V_{fe} and not the V_{rs} matrix of item values on the factor that finally decides the choice of improved items, and this involves some iteration because the former values alter with the set of items already accepted for the factor.

It perhaps hardly needs to be said that, although from a factoring point of view the Dwyer and Equi-rectification methods demand no very large samples—perhaps with 60 parcels (for, say, 16 factors) 200 subjects would suffice—yet to distinguish *reliably between magnitudes of correlation* of different items with a factor (assuming 0.4 about average), one needs a substantial sample—say 400 to 800. And when in doubt between an *old* item and a *new* one, because of close sheer *r* magnitudes and *w* weights, the former should be retained on grounds of having "stood up" in at least one previous analysis.

In conclusion, though progressive rectification is a demanding procedure, it is to be hoped that resources will be made available for its use in the future with the main available factorial source-trait personality tests, for, as we have seen, raising the loadings of markers for a given factor contributes at the same time, through simple structure, to the trueness of rotation of all factors concerned, and therefore the soundness of our theoretical concepts about the nature of the source traits.

A constant interpretation problem that the practitioner needs to watch resides in the fact that the factor estimation weights for items and subtests alter with the sample and population. Actually, most well-known tests pay little attention to this and, even in the intelligence field, tests like the WISC and WAIS simply give the same score to an item regardless of the age or the social status and region of the subject. They also do not, within any given group, weight items differently for *g* saturation, i.e., all items are falsely considered equally good intelligence items.

The Culture-Fair Intelligence Tests deliberately supply scales planned for three different levels, and, as has been shown by cross-national studies, find little or no cultural difference in the validity of the items at each level. Both Horn (1965, 1976; see also Horn & Miller, 1966) and the present writer (1973a) have shown, however, that, within a given group, there is surprisingly little difference in factor score rank between an arithmetically-simply, *equal* weighting and the use of a more refined set of estimation weights. Parenthetically, one should distinguish here between "nominal weights" as actually given to any item or subtest (relative only to the standard deviation of the subtests) and the *true* weights which ultimately ensue due to the existing correlations among subtests (as in beta weights).

However, there are times when what one believes psychologically to be the same factor is measured in such different populations that, despite the identity (or translation equivalence) of items or subtests, the required comparisons cannot safely be made by ordinary procedures, e.g., a t-test on the factor scores using the same weights for the two groups. Indeed, the present writer has reluctantly been compelled to criticize Lynn's conclusions of a 6 I.Q. point superiority of the Japanese, because his results are based on a "translation" of the WAIS rather than on a culture-fair test (which gives about 1 point difference).

For this problem a solution has been worked out by Cattell (1970a) using what are called the *isopodic* and *equipotent* principles. The latter is simpler but less thorough and begins by creating a combined distribution of scores of the two groups on each of the subtests, whence standard scores (if necessary approaching equal interval properties by *pan-normalization*—see the next section) can be given to both. Each group, however, uses its own factor structure weighting matrix, but for each factor the two vectors of weights are brought to equal potency by applying a multiplier to one that will bring the multiple R from its subtests to yield the same sigma of factor score as the other. The isopodic (equal footing) procedure is a little more complex, but begins with the same combining of scores of the same subtest given to the two groups into a single standard score system, and then applies a standardized covariance matrix (mean of the two or more groups) to the raw score deviations of members of all groups in the combined distribution. A more detailed account must be read at the source (Cattell, 1970a), but, despite complexity, whenever cross-cultural or cross-age comparisons of source-trait levels are to be made across groups, these theoretically better founded methods ought ideally to be used.

SOME INFERENCE PROBLEMS RELATING TO EQUAL INTERVAL, ABSOLUTE ZERO, AND DIFFERENCE SCORE SCALE PROPERTIES

Misinterpretation through inattention to scaling units is far more widespread than is commonly recognized. As pointed out earlier (Chapters 5 and 6), we make calculations essentially as in the physical sciences, yet living all the while in a make-believe world that our raw scores are in equal units and even have an absolute zero. Converting to standard scores, of course, does nothing to remedy this.

Yet when psychometry has reduced its shop window to a few thousand tests, as in Buros and in numerous catalogues, and to perhaps three or four highly valid and well designed tests for each personality, ability, dynamic, and state factor, there is hope that it will be able to do the amount of concentrated work on these necessary to make their units more scientifically acceptable. At present we have available four proposed theoretical bases for reaching such units. They are:

1) the *relational simplex*,
2) *pan-normalization*,
3) *inherent properties*, and
4) *state modulation*.

Each involves appreciable attention to assumptions, methods of calculation, and to its relative success in obtaining either a) equal units, or b) true zeros, or both. These issues are most fully addressed in one place in *real base, true zero factor analysis* (Cattell, 1972a).

The Relational Simplex

The relational simplex method of reaching equal unit intervals, already briefly introduced, requires a simultaneous examination of the available scales for several variables, and the determination of their mutual correlations. Since erroneous scaling (departure from equal intervals) behaves in this respect like error of measurement, the correlation between two variables (initially to be considered as attenuated by error) will numerically increase as the raw score units are brought more closely to true values and will reach its natural maximum when equal units are reached. With just two variables, however, the chance would arise that if the raw scores were distorted in just the same way, the same progress to maximum correlation would similarly be reached on this false basis. Consequently, it is necessary to average correlations in a matrix of several variables under several transformations. Since the transformations that produce the best results must be found blindly, by trial and error, and the combinations even with five to 10 variables are very numerous, one might despair. But Lingoes (1966) wrote a computer program that worked quite well, and, incidentally, showed the n-stens on the 16 P.F. to be quite close to equal units. The same process could theoretically reach true *zeros*, since, if a raw score of x on scale A is really zero, correlations with other scales will be impaired when we use raw score numbers below x, and indeed x might be reached by the transformation which collapses all raw scores below x to x.

Pan-normalization

Pan-normalization demands that we lean on an assumption not required in the relational-simplex, namely, that most traits, complexly genetically and culturally determined, and therefore the result of *many* small contributions, will have a normal distribution *when transformed to the right (equal interval) units*. However, it demands that this property exist not just for one group but for overlapping groups spanning different ranges of the new score range. Thus, the best transformation for the raw scores of group A, which overlaps, say, 60% of its cases with group B, may not be the best transformation to give group B itself a Gaussian distribution. The term "pan," therefore, is necessary because *all* overlapping groups giving the data must be acted upon, by one and the same raw score transformation (at least in the overlapping parts) to give the least departure from normality simultaneously for all of them. Brennan has constructed a program which, however, has so far only partly achieved this solution.

Inherent Properties

Inherent properties (Cattell, 1972a, p. 98) defines a class of solutions, each depending on the property taken, and it rests on an almost philosophical assumption that certain properties will be a function of absolute score. Its simplest form can be illustrated concretely by an elastic rubber cord coming through a hole in the ceiling so that we cannot see how far its supporting hook is above the ceiling. If we assume the property that the rubber will extend proportionally to the weight we put on it (Hooke's law), and we compare the length from ceiling to weight with, say, three different weights, we can calculate how far the hook is above the hole in the ceiling. A special case of this was hit upon by Thurstone in his article (1928) on "determining the absolute zero of intelligence," but the principle is widely applicable whenever we can find performances, themselves measurable from zero, that can be considered a product of the absolute amount of the trait.

State True Zeros from Modulation Theory

This is a very practical and promising avenue toward setting up true zeros on state scales, but it does not independently supply equal interval units and, indeed, depends on those being found by other methods. From the sufficient explanation of modulation theory in Chapter 16, it follows that if the model (equation 16-3, p. 336) is correct and the raw score vertical scale (Figure 16.1, p. 337) is equal unit, certain relations will be found to hold. First, the standard deviation of state scores in a group of *any* given standard deviation of liability, (L), scores (and undergoing as a group various levels of environmental arousal) will be simple proportional to the mean score, taken *from the true zero*. Second, the linear plots for three or more groups of different mean state liability scores, taken over several modulating environments, will converge on the same point, which will be the true (absolute) zero of the state scale. An exploratory study showing that the model works, for anxiety and depression states, has been made recently (1985) by Cattell and Brennan.

As far as the authors of this book know, not a single test among the several hundreds recommended in various texts for students and practitioners has yet (with the exception of Lingoes's work on the 16 P.F.) been checked by any one of the above four methods (or others if they exist), nor is the user warned that until equal interval properties are created his further calculations are faulty.

However, psychologists are aware that their complacent assumption of "essentially equal units" is sometimes rudely shaken. Principally this occurs in circumstantial evidence that most scales will tend to show "ceiling" and "floor" effects, i.e., in the ceiling effect, for example, the last few points of raw score at the top of the scale will be gained with disproportionate difficulty, and the true units will be represented cramped at the bottom. Cattell and Brennan (1985), with more direct empirical evidence, supported this "end compression," at least as regards state scales, and gave some indication that in state L scales the true zero tended generally to be *below* the raw score zero. At present, until research in this area is pressed less casually, the psychometrist can only proceed with caution and commonsense hunches about the floor and ceilings of particular scales—plus a seemly blush in the presence of other quantitative scientists!

While ordinary raw scores have been privileged to escape due criticism, difference and ratio scores have been attacked more than they really deserve. Regarding difference scores, the present writer pointed out (1966b, p. 366) that moderate departure from equal interval properties in the original scores is likely to lead to more

severe departures in difference scores. Cronbach and Furby (1970) went further and frightened many from *any* use of difference scores. Nesselroade and Cable (1974), recognizing that a science which could not use difference scores would virtually lose its sight, toned down these criticisms and even added that any difference score could be said to have a true zero —which for some uses is operationally true. A further analysis of the difference score problem is given in Cattell, 1982a. One problem in the discussion of difference scores is that some psychometrists have wanted to tamper with them before using them, and to do so according to various *subjective*, untested models, e.g., to partial out the first score from the second, or the mean of the two from the difference, or from both first and second. This has been done under the impression that statistically there is more error in a difference score than in a single score because one includes the experimental error of measurement at both ends. The variance of a difference score is:

$$\sigma^2_{(a-b)} = \sigma^2_a + \sigma^2_b - 2r_{ab}\sigma_a\sigma_b + \sigma^2_{ea}$$
$$+ \sigma^2_{eb} - 2r_{ea.eb}\sigma_{ea}\sigma_{eb} \qquad (23\text{-}12)$$

where σ^2_a and σ^2_b are the true score variances at occasions a and b, σ^2_{ea} and σ^2_{eb} the error variances. This can be much simplified if we assume, as we commonly must, no correlation of error, and no difference in size of true and error for the parallel occasions. If, also, there is no correlation of the true scores, as if one measured, say, excitement level at 10 A.M. today and 8 P.M. next Friday week, then:

$$\sigma^2_{(a-b)} = 2\sigma^2_{a(\text{or } b)} + 2\sigma^2_{e(a \text{ or } b)} \qquad (23\text{-}13)$$

The ratio of error to true score here is just the same as in a single score ($\sigma^2_a + \sigma^2_e$), i.e., it is σ^2_a/σ^2_e.

What one needs to bear in mind in using

difference scores is that their dependability will vary with a) the dependability of the single occasion scores, b) the correlation between pre- and postinterval scores, c) the pre-post difference of *means*, and d) the difference of pre- and postrelative *standard deviations*. All this generalization has relevance, of course, to the case of the same variables measured twice on the same people, and therefore particularly to the establishment of state and role factor patterns by dR-technique, but also to ordinary repeat measurement in ANOVA designs.

The interaction of the above four conditions requires that we remind the reader of the relations of the *temporal test consistency* coefficients in Chapter 4, called the *test dependability*, r_d, the *stability*, r_s and the *trait constancy*, r_c, coefficients, and apply each appropriately here.

Using more usual test-analytical notation than in the general algebraic statements in 23-8 and 23-9, let us use t for the true score (same on both occasions), e for error and t_f for trait fluctuation, i.e., change in the true trait score from the mean of all occasions to any one occasion. The single occasion dependability coefficient, r_{d1}, is

$$r_{d1} = \frac{\sigma^2_t + \sigma^2_{tf}}{\sigma^2_t + \sigma^2_{tf} + \sigma^2_e} \quad (23\text{-}14)$$

By "single occasion" we mean an immediate retest during an essentially unchanging psychological occasion.

The stability coefficient, over a long enough period for trait fluctuation to have occurred, so that t_f is no longer common, as on equation (23-10), is

$$r_s = \frac{\sigma^2_t}{\sigma^2_t + \sigma^2_{tf} + \sigma^2_e} \quad (23\text{-}15)$$

The problem now is to derive from these the *dependability coefficient for a differ-*ence score, $r_{d(2-1)}$, which, of course, cannot be directly measured but which, on principles of prediction of variance, we know can be written

$$r_{d(2-1)} = \frac{\sigma^2_{tf}}{\sigma^2_{tf} + 2\sigma^2_e} \quad (23\text{-}16)$$

Besides (23-10) and (23-11) we have, as indicated above and in Chapter 4, a third concept in this area, the *trait (or state) constancy coefficient*, r_c, inherent to the psychological structure itself, as follows:

$$r_c = \frac{\sigma^2_t}{\sigma^2_t + \sigma^2_{tf}} \quad (23\text{-}17)$$

From these three one can derive algebraically (Cattell, 1982a) that

$$r_{d(2-1)} = \frac{r_d - r_s}{1 - \dfrac{r_c}{1 - r_c}(r_d - r_s)} \quad (23\text{-}18)$$

And this derivation from r_d, r_s, and r_c coefficients can be reduced to a relation of the two most easily observable coefficients by substituting the relation, stated in Chapter 4, that:

$$r_c = \frac{r_s}{r_d} \quad (23\text{-}19)$$

whereupon

$$r_{d(2-1)} = \frac{r_d - r_s}{1 - r_s} \quad (23\text{-}20)$$

Given this derivation of the dependability of a difference score from the dependability and stability of a single score, it becomes of practical interest to see what dependability exists for a difference score with tests and traits that fall in common ranges of dependability and stability. Schuerger, Tait, and Tavernelli (1982) found stability coefficients over several months for a variety of tests to center on about 0.8 and over four years on about 0.6. Cattell and Scheier (1961), with anxiety measures over a couple of years, found about 0.3 to 0.4. Accepting immediate retest dependability coefficients of .7, .8, and .9 and stability coefficients from − .5 (for they *can* be negative), through 0, .5, .6 and .7, we have set out in Table 23.3 the resulting dependabilities of difference scores.

It will be seen that, with a high trait stability and low test dependability of the original one-occasion scale, little dependence can be placed on difference scores. But the mistake has been to generalize this to all difference scores—see Table 23.3. Thus, in a situation where there is indeed very little real change in rank from one occasion to another, a very high immediate dependability coefficient of the test itself is essential if any conclusion is to be drawn from differences, and in such a case it would be well, for example, to double or treble the length of the test to gain dependability.

We have next to consider the effect of a changing standard deviation between the two occasions. Such a change is precisely what happens according to modulation theory (Figure 23.4), as we pass from one situation to another, so this case is an important one that cannot be neglected. If s_{k1} and s_{k2} are the modulators

at the two occasions and t_1 is the true score on the first occasion, then

$$\sigma^2_{(2-1)} = \sigma^2_{(s_2 - s_1)} + 2\sigma^2_e \qquad (23\text{-}21)$$

Expressing the first term on the right afresh for the condition in which there is a significant pre-post correlation, we have:

$$\sigma^2_{(2-1)} = \sigma^2_{s_2 t_1} + \sigma^2_{s_1 t_1}$$
$$- 2r_{s_2 t_1 s_1 t_1} \sigma_{s_2 t_1} \sigma_{s_1 t_1} + 2\sigma^2_e \qquad (23\text{-}22)$$

But now, according to the modulation model, each person's second score would be an exact multiple of his first, so r would be $+1.0$ and the outcome would be:

$$r_{d(2-1)} = \frac{(\sigma_{s_2 t_1} - \sigma_{s_1 t_1})^2}{(\sigma_{s_2 t_1} - \sigma_{s_1 t_1})^2 + 2\sigma^2_e} \qquad (23\text{-}23)$$

It is thus possible, despite perfect correlations between before and after, as in the state change model, to have a dependable difference score *if the standard deviation changes*. Table 23.4 extends Table 23.3 to show the combined result of change in standard deviation and stability coefficient at a fixed test dependability coefficient, in this case taken at 0.9.

TABLE 23.3

Dependability Coefficients of Difference Scores, $r_{d(2-1)}$, Derived from Values of Single Occasion Scales

		Dependability Coefficient of Single Scale		
		.9	8	.7
Stability	.7	.66	.33	0.0
Coefficient	.6	.75	.5	.25
by	.5	.8	.6	.4
Single	0.0	.9	.8	.7
Scale	− .5	.93	.87	.8

Stability coefficients toward -1.0 would be rare, but it will be seen that with values from -1.0 to 0, difference dependabilities are high. At $+0.5$, which we know is very common, they are still in the .82 to .84 range, with a test of good dependability. Consequently, we may conclude that the "difference score scare" mentioned above was a mistake. One should know their properties, and there are, of course, further aspects to handling difference scores, for several of which the reader is referred to the illuminating article by Nesselroade, Jacobs, and Preshnow (in press).

We would note the importance of insightful use of the above treatment of difference scores to a) state definition and measurement (Chapter 16), b) meaningful therapeutic change measurement, as in Karoly and Steffens (1980), Waskow and Parloff (1975), Parloff, Waskow, and Wolfe (1978), Cattell, Rickels, et al. (1966), and Rickels and Cattell (1965), c) models separating genetic maturation from structured learning (Baltes & Nesselroade, 1973; Cattell, 1982; Goulet, 1968; Schaie,

1973), and d) modulation theory experiments (Cattell & Brennan, 1983). It should be noted that in the last two the parceling out of the initial score from the change score would lose important relational information, e.g., of the relation of maturation level to learning in g_f - g_c studies, though in some covariance analysis designs, where groups are not equal but should be, Lord's (1963, 1965) formulae for this purpose are appropriate.

REVISED COEFFICIENTS OF EQUIVALENCE, HOMOGENEITY, AND OF EXTENDED DEPENDABILITY AND VALIDITY, IN STRUCTURED TESTS

The reader is by now fully alert to radical differences of functional testing from the use of many older, subjective scales, operating as "special applied purpose" tests. Functional testing gives new meaning and possibilities in recognizing age span effects, genetic-environmental interactions, and prognostic and monitoring procedures. However, we felt it desirable,

TABLE 23.4

Difference Score Dependability as a Result of Stability Coefficient and Standard Deviation Relations

Standard Deviations	Stability Coefficient	Formula for 2 (2-1)	Error as % of True Difference	Dependability of Difference Score
$\sigma_{t2} = \sigma_{t1}$	0.0	$2\sigma_{t1} + 2\sigma_e$	11.0	.90
" " "	$+1.0$	$2\sigma_e$	100.0	.00
" " "	-1.0	$4\sigma_{t1} + 2\sigma_e$	5.2	.95
" " "	$+0.5$	$\sigma_{t1} + 2\sigma_e$	22.0	.82
$\sigma_{t2} = 1.5\sigma_{t1}$	0.0	$(1+k^2)\sigma_{t1} + (1+k^2)\sigma_e$	17.0	.90
" "	$+1.0$	$(1+k^2)\sigma_{t1} - 2k\sigma_{t1} + (1+k^2)\sigma_e$	144.4	.41
" "	-1.0	$(1+k^2)\sigma_{t1} + 2k\sigma_{t1} + (1+k^2)\sigma_e$	5.8	.95
" "	$+0.5$	$\sigma_{t1} + 2\sigma_e$	206	.83
$\sigma_{t2} = 2.0\sigma_{t1}$	0.0	k is the ratio of	11.0	.90
" "	$+1.0$	s_2 to s_1 and the gen-	55.5	.64
" "	-1.0	eral formulae here	6.2	.94
" "	$+0.5$	the same. But k is now 2.0	6.2	.84

Note the upper third here deals with the same situation as column one in Table 23.3, i.e., equal standard deviation, $r_d = .9$, but illustrates with more extreme values.

in first introducing psychometric aspects of functional testing, not to pursue the full statistical implications in the opening Chapter 4 and so a few "items of business" in that area remain to be noted here.

Specifically, we plan to show that certain coefficients, notably the equivalence coefficients between different forms of the same test, are differently interpretable from older, itemetric coefficients and that the formulae for the effects of lengthened tests, in particular, are affected. In Figure 23.4 the main possible constructions of equivalent forms are set out. Elsewhere (Cattell & Radcliffe, 1962), we introduced the terms *isometric* and *allometric* to designate equivalent scales that respectively contained a) the *same* factors (besides the common wanted factor) and b) different contaminating common factors. Isometric scales further could contain the same factors in the same variance proportions—i.e., magnitude of loading form—and be called *isomorphous*, or with different weighting emphases and be called *allomorphous*. In the discussion regarding Figure 23.4 we should enter too many complications for a brief introduction if we added various allomorphous proportions, so all will be considered on the isomorphous case.

Figure 23.4 is intended to be largely self-explanatory of four main possibilities in equivalent scales. The first, based on a *simple unitractic* scale (measuring a single pure factor common trait except for item or subscale specifics), is an ideal which one can safely say has never yet been realized. The second is the kind of unitractic scale that is aspired to in the 16 P.F. or in the O-A Kit, in which unwanted common factors (but, of course, not the never-wanted specifics!) are eliminated by suppressor action item choice based on good knowledge of the factor composition of items (to the right of Figure 23.5). Using suppression necessarily reduces the homogeneity coefficient appreciably, but, as we have seen, this low homogeneity brings no reduction in the dependability-reliability r, and is actually

an advantage, psychologically, in spreading the sampling of behavior. However, although if suppression is ideally reached the scale equivalence is as good as in the simple unitractic scale, in practice it never is and we must expect along with the lower internal homogeneity a lower "homogeneity," i.e., equivalence of two parts, between forms. In fact, if the lower homogeneity were random, we might expect proportion of lower equivalence in scales of lower homogeneity. In summary, so long as the forms are allometric, $r_v = \sqrt{r_e}$ holds, but in the more frequent isometric forms this is an upper limit and $r_v < \sqrt{r_e}$.

The term "univectoral" in row 3 is used in the same sense as Guilford's "univocal." If all items have the same mixture of common source trait factors (as in the first and last to the right), a scale may be mistaken as containing a single statistical factor "hence "univocal," but actually "univectoral" in a multiple space of simple structure source-trait factors). This kind of scale, in which both forms share one or two unwanted factors besides the main wanted factor, is a not uncommon compromise end result when one is aiming at the unitractic scale with suppressor action, and, indeed, the *computer synthesis* (variance reallocation) set out above recognizes the existence of this contamination and deals with it. As indicated above, when equivalent forms of non-factor-true scales are used, one cannot estimate validity as the square root of equivalence. But univectorial scale constructions, 3 and 4, will, incidentally, tend to have lower validities than 1 and 2 (Figure 23.4), and are represented today most definitely and frequently in scales based on factor analyses with poor simple structure. Incidentally, the terms α *equivalence* and β *equivalence* coefficients have sometimes been used to distinguish the calculation on the basis of constructions 1 and 2, and of 3 and 4, respectively, the important distinction being that β coefficients give a false idea of the goodness of the equiva-

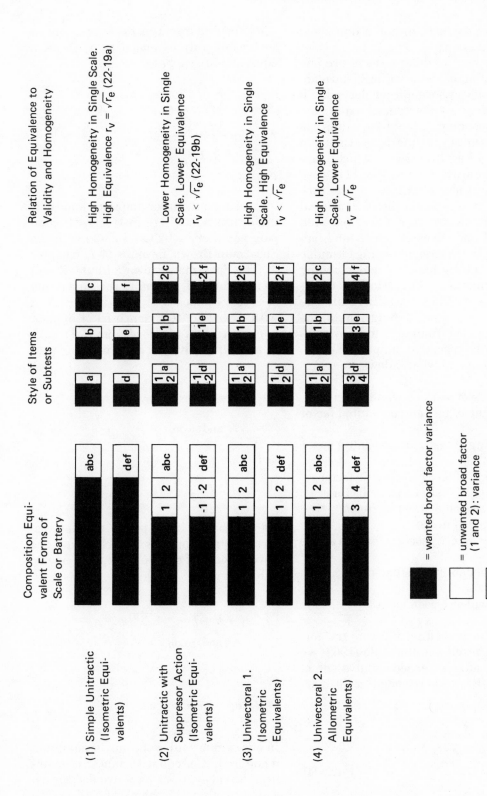

Figure 23.4. Equivalence and homogeneity in different types of scale or battery construction

lence, when one is thinking in functional testing values.

Turning next to differences of use and interpretation of the familiar Spearman-Brown prophecy formula for dependability-reliability (r_d) of extended scales, and the corresponding formula for validity of extended scales, we find a treatment in Cattell and Radcliffe (1962), which is repeated here with the symbols there used in case the reader wishes to connect with the detailed arguments there. Some real differences of meaning arise between structured and itemetric terms and, additionally, the functional testing formulae have the advantages of a) demanding fewer assumptions, b) resting on coefficients somewhat more readily obtainable experimentally, and c) reducing to the older itemetric formulae readily by reintroducing the special assumptions.

The notation in what follows is:

f_j = loading of test j on wanted factor f
u_j = loading of test j on unwanted factor u
y_j = loading of test j on unwanted factor y
s_j = loading of test j on specific factor s
e_j = loading of test j on error factor e
r_{jk} = correlation of any two items
n = number of items
r_{dj} = dependability coefficient for a single item
r_{dn} = dependability coefficient for n-item scale
r_{ef} = equivalence coefficient

From the preceding elementary formulae in Cattell and Radcliffe (1962) we reach, for an n-extended (equivalent of Spearman-Brown n-extended) scale, a dependability

$$r_{dn} = \frac{\sum\limits_{j=1}^{n} r_{dj} + 2\sum\limits_{j<k}^{n} r_{jk}}{n + 2\sum\limits_{j<k} r_{jk}} \quad (23\text{-}24)$$

Proceeding from this to the *equivalence* coefficient duly extended to n (as an α equivalence), we have

$$r_{en} = \frac{\sum\limits_{j=1}^{n} r_{ef} + 2\sum\limits_{j<k}^{n} r_{jk}}{n + 2\sum\limits_{j<k} r_{jk}} \quad (23\text{-}25)$$

To bring out our assumptions and their implications, it will be instructive to compare equations 23-23 and 23-24 with the Spearman-Brown formula (4-7, Chapter 4). The Spearman-Brown formula, it will be remembered, estimates the correlation of a test composed of, say, items j, k, l, with a parallel test composed of items f, q, r, using data obtained from the test of items j, k, l, only, and assuming

(a) $\sigma_j^2 = \sigma_k^2 = \ldots = \sigma_p^2 = \sigma_q^2$

$= \ldots$, and so on. $\quad (23\text{-}26)$

and

(b) $r_{jk} = r_{kl} = \ldots r_{jp} = \ldots = r_{jr} = r_{kl}$
$= \ldots = r_{kp} = \ldots = r_{kr} = \ldots$

As Cronbach (1951) points out, less restrictive assumptions, which allow the development of similar formulae, may be substituted, viz.

(c) $\sigma_{f+k+l+\cdots}^2 = \sigma_{p+q+r}^2$

$+ \cdots$, and, so on. $\quad (23\text{-}27)$

and

(d) $r_{jk}\sigma_j\sigma_k = r_{jl}\sigma_j\sigma_l = r_{jp}\sigma_j\sigma_p = \ldots$
$= r_{jr}\sigma_j\sigma_r = \ldots$

In our own formulae the only assumption made is that of equal variances of members, ((a) above). We have avoided the assumption that the members will *not* be contaminated by unwanted common factors; nor have we assumed equivalence of members in other ways.

In comparing our formula with the Spearman-Brown formula, or such formulae as Cronbach's alpha (1951) and Flanagan's coefficients of extension, the definition of the reliability coefficient involved in each must be kept in mind. Our use of the dependability and x-equivalence reliabilities is adopted on the grounds of their readier availability, their precision of meaning, and their wider utility relative to the alternatives just mentioned. Thus, the Spearman-Brown formula makes no explicit reference to the factorial structure of the items. Its ambiguity arises from the fact that the homogeneity which makes the items correlate equally with one another can arise either from a single wanted common factor or from a combination of common factors. The elements are usually regarded as differing only in specifics (though, as Figure 23.5 on p. 532 shows, the differences are almost always in practice partly psychological specifics and partly unlike common factors), and the "reliability" which the formula measures is, therefore, for most practical purposes, an x-equivalence coefficient. The first two members of x-equivalent scales, between which our correlation is calculated, have the same unwanted common factor and differing specifics (Case 3 in Figure 23.4). But when the x-equivalent scale is extended, each new member may differ in its unwanted common factor, and it *will* invariably differ when the suppressor design is used.

The differences between the assumptions made here and those of other formulae may therefore be summarized as follows: 1) r_{dj} is not r_{ef}; 2) neither r_{dj} nor r_{ej} equals r_{jk}. (Neither the member intercorrelations nor the covariances within or between forms are assumed to be equal. The only assumptions are of equal member variances and equal total variances for the parallel forms.)

If universally equal correlations are assumed (i.e., if $r_{ej} = r_{jk}$), equation 23-22 becomes the Spearman-Brown formula. If equal covariances are assumed equation 23-22 reduces to the formula of Flanagan and others (Cronbach, 1951). If the mean covariance between parallel members is assumed equal to the mean covariance between unpaired members, then equation 23-22 reduces to Cronbach's (1951) alpha formula.

In turning to validity, we retain, of course, the definition as *concept validity*, i.e., correlation with the wanted factor. The validity of a single item is:

$$r_{fj} = \frac{f_{ji}}{f_j + f_{fu}u_j + \ldots + r_{fs}y_f} \qquad (23\text{-}28)$$

On this basis an n-extended scale is as in equation 23-24, which can be simplified to equation 23-25 as follows:

$$r_{fn} = \frac{\sum\limits_{j=1}^{n} fj + r_{fu}\sum\limits_{j=1}^{n} uj + \ldots + r_{fs}\sum\limits_{j=1}^{n} yj}{\sqrt{\dfrac{n}{(n + 2\Sigma r_{jk})}}_{j<k}} \qquad (23\text{-}29)$$

$$r_{fn} = \frac{\sum\limits_{j=1}^{n} r_{fj}}{\sqrt{\dfrac{n}{(n + 2\Sigma r_{jk})}}_{j<k}} \qquad (23\text{-}30)$$

The latter is the more convenient to use in practice. When the factors are orthogonal,

$$\sum\limits_{=1}^{n} r_{fj} = \sum\limits_{j=1}^{n} r_{fi}$$

These equations represent *actual* validity of an ordinary scale of imperfect dependability. *True* validity may be conceived either 1) as that which exists between "true" (i.e., perfectly reliable) scale scores and the factor, or 2) as that which would exist with a test of infinite length. If correction for attenuation is conceived in the first way, the usual formula may be applied; if in the second way, the correction for attenuation cannot be applied with scale dependability or equivalence, because the derivation of the formula rests on the same assumptions as the Spearman-Brown procedure. It could be applied to *item* (or subtest member) *equivalences*, and the corrected values could be included in equation 23-29 to obtain an estimate of *scale* validity, provided that the *item* had perfect equivalence reliability. In practice, this is the most feasible way of estimating the extent to which scale validity could be improved by increasing item reliabilities.

Those who use these formulae should be careful to make the estimates of "reliability" in the sense that is appropriate, namely dependability in equation 23-24 and equivalence in equation 23-25. Equivalence values in equation 23-24 would underestimate extended reliability, and substitution of dependability for equivalence in equation 23-26 would overestimate extended equivalence. Prior factor analyses are necessary to discover overestimate of equivalence so that equivalence coefficients can be calculated. Estimates, however, can be based on assumptions (c) and (d), in equation 23-26, or (e) as in Cronbach's alpha.

So far we have assumed that the n-scale score is simply that which is obtained by giving equal weight to every member. Let us now consider the effect of weighted scoring. One is unlikely to go to that fuss with members that are *items*, but could well do so with subtests, as in the O-A Battery. How are we to determine what particular weights will maximize the multiple correlation with the wanted factor? The solution for the regression weights must be the same as for estimating the factor from any collection of member scores. The only problems therefore are a) to make the solution general, i.e., applicable to oblique as well as to orthogonal

factors, and b) to avoid the practical difficulty of having to compute the inverse of a large matrix of correlations between members. Simplified methods have been suggested by Harman (1967), Dwyer (1940), Guttman (1940, 1944), Creager (1958), and Thomson (1949). These all seek to avoid computing the inverse of the n-member correlation matrix; Harman's appears the easiest to apply. Basing their comparisons on weights obtained by Thomson's formula, Baggaley and Cattell (1956) have shown that the use of the reference vector structure matrix for the matrix of regression weights yields factor scores which are a linear function of those derived from the actual regression weights.

Let f denote the estimated unifactor score from the n-member scale, and w_{fj} (j, k, . . . , n), the regression weight of member j, etc.; then, if

$$r^2_{ff} = R^2_{fjk} \ldots n = \sum_{j=1}^{n} w_{ff} r_{ff} = w^2_{ff} + 2\sum_{j<k} w_{fj} w_{fk} r_{jk}$$

(23-31)

the reliability of this weighted composite will be

$$r_{ff} = \frac{\sum\limits_{j=1}^{n} w^2_{ff} r_{jj} + 2\sum\limits_{j<k}^{n} w_{fj} w_{fk} r_{jk}}{\sum\limits_{j=1}^{n} w^2_{ff} + 2\sum\limits_{j<k}^{n} w_{fj} w_{fk} r_{jk}}$$

(23-32)

which is equivalent to the formula derived by Mosier (1943). In the denominator, r_{jj} may refer to either r_{dj} or r_{ef}, whichever has already been obtained. Except in the final stages of factor scale construction, the gain over unit weighting does not justify the trouble involved in calculating regression weights. An estimate of whether weighted scoring will appreciably increase validity may be obtained from a formula developed by Guttman (1940, 1944) for the orthogonal case and expanded by Creager (1958) to the oblique, namely,

$$R^2_{f \cdot jk \ldots n} = \frac{\Sigma B_{fd} C'_{fl}}{1 + \Sigma B_{fj} C_{fl}} \qquad (23\text{-}33)$$

where $B = V^{-1}_{sp} V_{fs}$; $C' = V'_{fp} V^{-1}_{sp}$; V^{-1}_{sp} = inverse of specific factor pattern matrix; V_{fs} = common factor structure matrix; and V'_{fp} = transpose of common factor pattern matrix. In using this formula we encounter a new question. Is it more important to maximize the correlation of the scale with its unifactor or to maximize it only to a degree consistent with maintaining low correlations with *other* factors? This is a problem which does not arise in calculations with itemetric or homogeneous scales. As we shall see below (suppressor action), the proper principle in constructing scales for meaningful factors is, as far as possible, to keep the factor intercorrelations equal to the population values for the intercorrelations of the true source traits, in the given case; the aim is *not* to reduce them to zero. The correlation of an unwanted factor in a scale with the required unifactor is

$$r_{uf} = \frac{\Sigma w_{fj} r_{uj}}{\sqrt{(\Sigma w^2_{ff} + 2\Sigma w_{fj} w_{fk} r_{jk})}} \qquad (23\text{-}34)$$

Although with weighted scoring r_{ff} may not significantly exceed r_{fn} (with unit scoring), r_{uf} (with weighted scoring) may be considerably less than r_{un} (with unit scoring). In this case the increased purity of the factor measure may more than compensate for the failure of the validity correlation with the wanted factor to increase with weighted scoring. What is happening in these relations can be grasped in visual terms in Figure 23.4.

It remains in this overview of modification of older, itemetric formulae to structured tests to discuss the effect of suppressor variables. If we are right in surmising that behavior in items or subtests which has a large variance from personality factors will generally be factorially complex, then the unwanted common factor variance in scales and batteries will, as a rule, be far less negligible than we would like to think. Hence, in constructing scales, for example, in the 16 Personality Factors omnibus test, the usual practice has been to choose items that will reduce the contribution of unwanted factors by suppression. This method of eliminating variance by internal cancellation may be termed "buffering," for the freeing of a scale from vulnerability to bias due to positive and negative loadings in unwanted factors is a near analogue to a "buffer solution" in chemistry. (Such expressions as a "neutral," "compensated," or "counter-poised" scale might also be considered.) "Buffering" a scale is thus quite distinct from what is sometimes called "purifying" it. The latter would involve throwing out contaminating items or intensifying the scale by replacing such items by others narrower in homogeneity but of a higher wanted factor loading. Actually, the latter is not very likely to be achieved, for few questionnaire items from real life can involve a pure factor (Cattell, 1973a, p. 361), and the items thought to achieve it frequently do so by sharing a narrow specific factor additional to the desired common factor. Meanwhile, it seems that the effects of deliberate adoption of planned suppressor action in test construction have never been examined systematically in terms of effect on reliability and validity; we shall therefore attempt to do so here.

Guilford and Michael (1948), it is true, *have* already examined some suppressor action effects. But their method differs from ours in the following ways: a) It was restricted to abilities only and not extended to the realm of personality; b) the factor scales were limited to *orthogonal* factors; c) consequently, the ideal adopted was to produce zero correlations among scales rather than (as here) to match the true correlation values existing among the pure oblique factors; and d) instead of aiming at complete suppressor action among existing variables, the addition of special variables, having negligible correlation with the required factor, was considered acceptable. Our own aims are sufficiently indicated by saying that we wish to avoid the restrictions stated in a), b), and c), and, in regard to d), to achieve mutual suppressor action entirely through *wanted* items (for validity) instead of by diluting the scale through introducing members for their suppressor action only. Experience suggests that variables can always be found in a large factored pool having the necessary complex factor constitution.

In combining suppressor profiles, our first task is to reduce the algebraic sum of loadings on unwanted factors to zero. As shown below, this will reduce any correlation between the unifactor and the unwanted factor to a minimum. However, beyond the initial goal of reaching minimal values there arises the more sophisticated one of reaching, with the score correlations, the correlations existing among the pure factors when the best simple structure has been obtained. As Chapter 4 points out, "greater validity" has two meanings: a) direct validity, i.e., high correlation with the pure factor, and b) circumstantial validity, i.e., behavior in relation to *other* factors, which shall be as similar as possible to that of the pure factor. The last step above refers to the second of these.

Determining the correlation of the factor scale with unwanted or ulterior factors can be considered first for the scale of n members, and secondly for a weighted scale, oriented as in equation 23-29 above to give the maximum multiple correlation with the pure factor. The correlation with the unwanted factor is given in equation 23-34. And in terms of correlations the relation of the unwanted factor to the scale will be:

$$r_{u(n)} = \frac{\Sigma u_j + r_{fu}\Sigma f_j + \ldots r_{yu}\Sigma y_j}{\sqrt{(n + 2\Sigma r_{jk})}} \qquad (23\text{-}35)$$

Since $\Sigma f_j > 0$, the numerator of equation 23-35 will equal zero only when $\Sigma u_j = r_{fu} = r_{yu} = 0$, or under the unlikely condition when the algebraic signs of the sums and factor correlations are so arranged to produce zero, so that complete orthogonal suppression would normally require perfect suppressor balance and zero factor intercorrelations. If perfect suppressor balance exists, but factors are oblique, r_{un} will approach r_{fu}. Correlations among the scales with n members will approach the true values as suppression and length are increased.*

The calculation of the correlation of the weighted factor estimate, f, with the unwanted (which indicates the degree of lack of success in buffering) will be based on the regression weights discussed in equation 23-24, and is given by equation 23-28. Setting $u_j, \ldots y_f$ equal to zero in equation 23-28, we obtain a condition of nearly maximum suppression; but this will be only an approximation because the inclusion of suppressors will change r_{jk}, increasing it when the suppressors have loadings in the wanted factor, and decreasing it when the suppressors have loadings only on the unwanted factors. Suppressors may reduce the correlation with the wanted factor; and decisions as

---

*Many scales to which these formulae will be applied will be scales associated with others in a whole battery, as in the Guilford-Zimmerman, etc. (4, [3], [6]). The above formulae may then be put into a comprehensive matrix form. However, good battery construction has usually avoided the situation in which all item scores contribute to all scale scores for the following reasons: 1) There are usually more items than can be simultaneously factored; 2) it is easy for common error to produce spurious correlations among items; 3) except with electronic computors scoring becomes quite impracticable if all items have to be taken into account for every scale; 4) many loadings would be almost negligible anyway, except on the wanted factor and one or two others. Consequently, Cattell and Baggaley's postmultiplying matrix [1, eqn. 19] would normally have a predominance of zero entries.

to their use require that the reduction in the unwanted variance be compared with the reduction in the wanted variance.

The practical effectiveness of suppressor patterns in the items of a multidimensional scale is considerable. This is shown by the fact that the scale scores, in the buffered 16 P.F., correlate very similarly to the pure factor scores. This can be seen from the marked degree to which the second order factors obtained by Karson and O'Dell (1976), working on actual scale scores, coincide with those of Cattell (1973c) working on simple-structure-rotated pure factors.

ASSESSING THE VECTORS OF SITUATIONS IN REGARD TO PERCEPTION, MISPERCEPTION (ATTRIBUTION), AND LEARNING EFFECTS

Throughout this book, we have stressed the interaction of the trait and the situation, both in a) *testing* the trait, i.e., in the assessment and diagnosis situation itself, and, b) interpreting, prognosing, and guiding the success of *intervention*. In testing this is evident in Chapters 3, 16, and 18 on including state measurement, in Chapter 8 on social aspects of testing, in Chapter 16 on situational roles, and in Chapters 17 to 20 on psychological practice.

However, up to this point no precise treatment has been given for the quantitative evaluation of situations as such, except in a) pointing out that the *p, e,* and *s* coefficients in the behavioral equation constitute a vector of values defining the situation for the average person, in its cognitive and emotional perception, and b) trait view theory where the situation of the rater and of the subject (or test-taker) are taken into account in correcting for motivational distortion. The behavioral index weights in the ordinary perceptual equation are for everyone in R-technique and for a particular person in P-technique, though the former gives perception values

unique to one person when his particular source-trait scores are inserted.

Psychological testing as previously conceived has *not* included obtaining the psychological vectors for situations. But the general comprehensiveness of the functional testing approach certainly calls for and permits its inclusion, though with a brevity appropriate to the present state of the art. Although concrete results are yet few, there have been no *conceptual* criticisms of the representation of perceptions by the perceptual vector as described above, under *trait view* theory, and some values in formulae exist for understanding misperception of a person. However, the perception by X of what situation a person Y is in, or what Y perceives to be the *situation* in which he acts, has received no precise quantitative formulation prior to what will now be described as *situation view theory*.

Psychologists, who have been interested in evaluating the distortion (faultiness) of attribution of a) *traits* and b) motivating, causal *situations*, have so far done so under the contingent title of "attribution theory." Recently, this area has developed for itself a more adequate framework as a mathematical and experimental model, under the title of *spectrad theory* (Cattell, 1982; Cattell & Raymond, 1982).

Spectrad theory is that branch of the study of perception which is divergent from the substantial but narrower laboratory history of experiment on sensory, cognitive perception. Its aim is to relate perception of all kinds—of personality and of situation—to personality and motivation traits in perceiver and perceived. As Figure 23.5 shows, *Trait View Theory* is a branch of this, while *Situation View Theory*, which we are about to study, is another. To reach measures of distortion of perception of traits, we need four profiles (vectors): 1) the vector of standard scores for the traits of the observer (T_o's); 2) the vector of equation loadings (b's) for the observers' situation; 3) the vector of standard scores for the subjects' observed

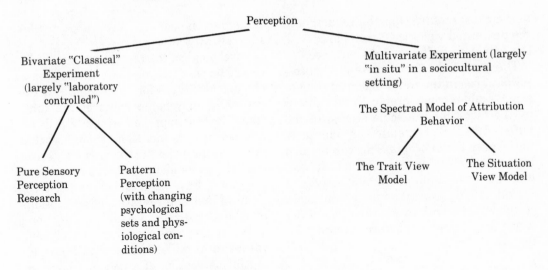

Figure 23.5. The integration of spectrad models of personality and situation perception in the psychology of perception

$(T_i's)$; and 4) the vector of contextual effects (c's) for subjects' traits. The theory thus rests squarely on a *tetrad* of vectors, and since it is concerned with perceptual views (Latin *spectare*, to look at), the whole is aptly named the *spectrad* model—a name reached by condensing these two essentials.

Among the various needs instanced above for quantitatively evaluating situations and their perception, two of the most practically important are a) in social psychology, e.g., in the art of advertising, in commerce, and in the politics of democratic vote getting, and, b) in clinical psychology, e.g., with suspected paranoids and suicidal depressives, in discovering how much reality there is to the patient's perception of a situation. The mode of calculation in defining a situation by a vector has been described in Chapter 3. It remains to develop this a little and to note that, whereas the misperception of traits was analyzed largely in order to proceed from the misperception to separating out the subject's *true* score, the misperception of situations has its more important psychological application, as just cited in clinical work, in the complementary score giving *the estimation of the magnitude of*

the misperception itself. This aspect could alternately be brought to bear in clinical psychology in evaluating paranoia,* or in handling misperceptions of a spouse in marriage counseling, and in social psychology in disputes over the equity of exchanges and services to organizations, in what may broadly be called sociodynamics (Cattell & Child, 1975).

But first let us recognize that ascertaining the formulation of the *true* psychological meaning of a situation is necessary both for correct treatment of trait-situation interaction and also for measuring distortions of perception (false attribution). "Attribution theory" (Cattell & Raymond, 1982) has concerned itself with questions like, "Why did Jones leave his wife, i.e., what in the situation *actually* caused this, and what does *he* think caused it?" and "What traits in Jones were responsible for his action?" As to the lat-

---

*Faced with the precisions of model demanded in spectrad theory, some may express themselves satisfied with judgments of paranoid perception of traits and situations by the clinician's common sense and a few outside witnesses. That common sense can go wrong in judgments of cognitive aberration is amply witnessed by reactions to, say, Pasteur, Galileo, and Copernicus!

ter—the comparison of Jones's observer-perceived traits with his true traits—we have already handled calculations about it in *trait view* theory. In *situation view* theory we attack the comparison of the real situation to which Jones reacted, with that which an observer (or he himself, merely on a conscious level) sees as the cause of his behavior.* The model we have developed as situation view theory within spectrad theory employs four vectors, just as does trait view theory, and applies essentially parallel procedures. Its main aim is a comparison of the true perception and the distorted perception, to obtain a vector of distortion.

First let us consider the true description of a situation itself, with which the false attributions can be compared. By the situation we obviously do not mean the physical demographic and social environment *itself*, e.g., the village of Ipplepen or the factory where a given man works, but *what the situation means psychologically*. The physical basis is a necessary *identifying description*, tagging the situation to which the psychological meaning must be anchored, but the *meaning* of the situation to a given person, or, say, the average person, is the feeling and cognitive associations it evokes, and the action it calls for and permits. The latter, as argued in Chapter 3, is at present most readily susceptible to psychological definition by the vector of loadings, b's, for the main response to be made in the situation. (We shall not repeat here the complication of splitting the b's into components of per-

ceptual p's, or v's, or e's, or modulator s's, and so on as briefly mentioned in Chapter 3.)*

This basic operational concept that the meaning of the perceptions of a situation is given *by the response that people make to it* (or are prepared to make to it), and therefore by the vector of b's, nevertheless requires some further definition. In virtually any "immediate situation" to which just the same kind (but not amount) of response (as in a test) is made by everyone, we recognize the total situation as dividing into a *focal stimulus* and an *ambient situation*, e.g., a door that sticks (focal) when one is in a house on fire (ambient). In the work of the practitioner, however, the educational psychologist thinks of "being at second year in X college," and the clinician of "being a child in a broken family," as the life situation. The main responses could be, respectively, "getting grades" and "entering on gang delinquency." In principle, there is no difficulty in considering these macroscopic situations and responses as summations of a chain of more immediate short "reflex" responses and immediate stimulus situations such as one would deal with in a laboratory. That the macroscopic stim-

---

*In the factor analyses to obtain the prediction of the observer's view of the subject's situation (as derived from the former's situation and his personality), we encounter the problem of having the observer describe his idea of the subject's situation in quantitative terms. That is to say, he is asked to write down (to create the necessary dependent variable) a vector of b's showing what motivates the subject, i.e., what o perceives i's situation to be. This feature of *situation view* experiment requires more technical knowledge—a knowledge of what regression weights mean—than in the rating of a trait, in *trait view* theory. This requirement would be an experimental difficulty with untrained observers.

---

*For the sake of brief communication here we accept the vector of b's as defining the situation, but actually this matter requires much more discussion (see Cattell, 1979b, p. 245). The speed and correctness of a response are defined most by loadings on ability factors, and by the e (execution contribution) part of the b's. The *emotional meaning* of the situation, on the other hand, which motivates the response action (in which the abilities play their part) resides mostly in the s component in b and loads largely the dynamic factors. We assume in the usual equation that we are dealing with *habitual* behavior, in a repeated life situation. Consequently, the *emotional meaning of the situation will then be coincident with the satisfactions that have regularly rewarded the response*. That is to say, the ergs and sentiments aroused by the s modulators, appearing at sight of the situation k, will be those that have habitually been satisfied. In this common case of life action the vector (strictly of s's not the whole b's) represents at once the emotional meaning of the situation and the satisfactions to which it leads. (What may seem the odd case of fear, as in avoiding traffic accidents, is covered by this generalization, because it leads to the satisfaction of the need for security.)

ulus-response is as real and usable a behavioral unit as a "microscopic" laboratory situation and reflex response is shown by the fact (see tables in Chapters 7 and 23) that it is possible to get a definite behavioral equation for the score on the summed response effects that yield the macroscopic response score. In the latter case the score could be the grade at year's end, or the joining or not joining a street gang, or the year's salary. And these total summed outcomes are "responses" to a total life situation which is a pattern of summed, more immediate situations and responses.

The psychological measurement of a situation in terms of its perception (behavioral equation) or degree of misperception (situation view theory) does not constitute the only way in which one might want to evaluate situations. They have also the property of *teaching*, and practicing psychologists would be greatly helped if they had information about what learning (personality change) typically occurs from particular situations, as "life paths" in *path learning analysis* (Catell, 1980a, 1982, 1985; Cattell & Child, 1975).

Applied psychologists have long recognized the need for a development of learning theory that passes beyond the microscopic scale of reflexology to the macroscopic structured learning of everyday life. In *Personality and Learning Theory* (Cattell, 1980a), the pursuit of this development has led among other things to a means of defining and quantifying major life situations in terms of their learning effects. What is set out as path learning analysis (PLA; Cattell & Child, 1975; Cattell, 1980a) shows a means of quantifying the properties of situations in terms of structured *learning* effects, rather than in terms of the perceptual meaning and *immediate* responses as covered in the behavioral equation. We shall not go here into the matrix algebra involved, but shall point out that multivariate design is necessary because, as PLA recognizes, any individual in a total life situation is simultaneously pursuing *several* paths of

experience. One may ask, "How can one situation be several?" and "Does this not contradict the initial statement above that for each physico-social situation there is one corresponding vector of psychological meaning?"

The office of Lombard & Co. is a physico-social situation in which Jack Stevens is simultaneously pursuing the path of advancing himself to a higher business position, and seriously courting Smith's secretary, Joan. We are forced to recognize that our initial statement of the meaning of a situation simply as defined by the *magnitude of the response* to that situation is an introductory simplification. We have fallen into a fixed test response paradigm, when in fact there are several possible responses. For we recognize that the *choice* of a particular response path in a situation alters the vector defining the perception of the situation, and that a *total* meaning of a situation can only be given as a vector sum of *all* goal activity performances the individual (or group) over a period of time is moved to act out in that situation.*

As we have just seen, the life path, in a given situation, has first been recognized and defined in the literature in a *learning* (PLA) context; but we need to return to the initial question of giving a situation a vector corresponding to its *perception*, i.e., the perceptual analogue of the behavior it stimulates. Thus, as far as the meaning of situations is concerned, we have a) a vector of meaning for an immediate situation, e.g., meeting a friend on the street, b) a vector for an integrated chain of behaviors which we call a path, as in PLA, which is one of several being pursued in a given situation, and c) a

---

*The assignment of different vector meanings to different aspects of one and the same socio-physical environment (situation) can be seen from another angle in terms of *determiner potency analysis* (DPA, Cattell, 1980b, p. 304), in which the situation is broken down further into elements which also have vector action on traits. Different aggregates of these elements, along with purposes, could theoretically be equated with the different paths on the same "physical" life situation.

summed vector of meaning for a total environmental situation, in reaction to which the pursuit of *several* response paths is simultaneously going on. Attribution studies might illustrate these respectively by a) "What focal stimulus in the situation caused Jones to get drunk that evening?", b) "What does attending college mean to Jane?", and c) "What does his family mean to the average worker (i.e., what are the diverse satisfactions that its existence provides for him)?"

The rationale and full calculations for the analogue of *trait view* theory in *situation view* theory cannot adequately be pursued in this limited space, and we must let the above sketch show the way to reading elsewhere (Cattell, 1982a). The reader can intuit the general nature of the calculating from the four vectors in trait view theory and grasp the experimental foundations from reading elsewhere (Cattell, 1982; Cattell & Raymond, 1982). The important thing to make clear to the practitioner at this point is mainly that the *psychologically neglected problem of measuring situations as well as people now has a theoretical solution*, which permits, as with people, on the one hand, a *true* vector for various calculations and, on the other, a vector of individually perceived meaning, and hence a derivable measure of perceptual distortion. The spectrad theory which integrates these thus promises, when research gives it actual numerical values for ability, personality, and motivational source traits, and major life situations, the possibility of handling scientifically and precisely what clinicians, counselors, educators, and social psychologists now have to handle by guesswork.

In summary, the aspects of a situation that we may hope eventually to quantify in vector patterns are:

1) The perceptual meaning, cognitive and emotional, of a situation, as bound up in its effect on action.
2) The character of a situation as it enters into the perception of traits in others and oneself.
3) The character of a situation as it influences learning and personality change.
4) The discrepancy between the causal action of a situation (on oneself or others) as it actually exists and as it is consciously perceived (attributed) to exist.

PROBLEMS IN INTERPRETATION AND PRESENTATION OF RECORDS AND DIAGNOSTIC RESULTS

There is available to the psychologist today a much greater diversity in methods of scoring, recording, interpreting, and communicating results than the psychologist commanded a generation ago. The kind of the error that typically arises in these has been discussed as part of previous chapters, e.g., in describing the *conspection* coefficient (degrees of agreement of scorers in relation to open-ended vs. multiple choice tests); the correction for motivational distortions; the use of computer program checks; and the use of screen presentation of tests, etc. But there remain a few special issues to cover in this chapter reviewing sources of interpretational error, e.g., in diagnosis into DSM categories; the use of discriminant functions in diagnosis; the combination of results from different sources.

Among topics that seem to the present writer insufficiently researched and improved upon are the *use* of answer sheets (not just their computer or key scoring), and TV screen test item presentation. If the psychologist handles only a few cases or wants immediate results, he or his secretary scores the sheet forthwith with a key. But if he has a great number, he is likely to send the answer sheets away to a test source to be scored by an optical scanner, as described in Chapter 7. This is done in most E.T.S., IPAT, Psych. Corp., and S.R.A. tests, for example, and it permits the user to buy fewer test booklets than the number of people he proposes to test, and to use them several times over, with the inexpensive answer sheets alone needing to be renewed. The advantages of the answer sheet are mainly three: 1) less expense, as stated, 2) ease of scoring by stencil or machine, and 3) compact storage. The disadvantage is mainly that the answer sheet introduces an extra task for the subject of matching numbers, which may be distracting for children and clinical patients, and this opens the door to a new source of error. This occurs particularly in the "ultimate condensation" practiced in *some* test practices and researches, of having answers made directly on IBM cards. However, an attractive alternative with small children or patients expected to have difficulty is for the psychologist *himself* to record the oral answers in individual test situations, e.g., with the PSPQ. The TV presentation of test items, with immediate pushbutton response, promises to reduce such error.

Originally the machine scoring of answer sheets was available only where a single total was used, as in an intelligence test. Adapted computer programs for multifactor tests are now available, in which several different scores are extracted and recorded (Chapter 7). But it may still often be quicker (avoiding postal delays) and less expensive, to score by clerical help, up to about 40 to 80 cases. On the other hand, a problem of undue delay scarcely arises with organizations like National Computer Systems, Psychsystems, and IPAT Test Scoring Service, which offer return mail service and have machines organized especially to handle tests like the CAQ, MMPI, 16 P.F., WAIS, MAT, Culture-Fair Intelligence Scales, etc.

Regardless of whether scoring be by hand stencil key or computer, one emerges with raw scores to which certain statistical transformations can advantageously be applied in the interests of prediction. The advantage of the computer at this stage is that all kinds of weighted composite scores can easily be built up from the integral raw scores, notably:

1) by giving the very best fractional weights to subtests, e.g., in an intelligence test, instead of equal, of chance, or merely nominal weights, thus improving the validity.

2) by proceeding, in the case of omnibus tests and kits, to *computer synthesis* scoring as described above. This can be done either by items (with very substantial validity increases) or by subtests. On a par with this, in form of computation, is the estimation of second order factors, such as anxiety or extraversion from the primary factors in the HSPQ, etc., as done by the IPAT and NCS programs, to aid *depth psychometry* diagnoses.

3) (a) predictions of particular criteria, by the known behavioral specification equations, or (b) allocations of individuals by their personality patterns to particular groups, e.g., to neurotics, successful technicians, etc., by the multiple discriminant function, can be made directly from the raw scores. These procedures have been more fully discussed in the preceding chapter, in the general psychological context of practice (Chapters 16, 17, etc.), and in the chapters on particular testing areas. Here we need to note that the last stage of test processing includes considering technical matters in obtaining derivative scores of all kinds from the raw scores.

One problem that arises in going from raw scores to standard scores occurs when sophisticated transformation systems are in use. Standardization will normally rest on factor score distributions, in which the factor scores came from item or subtest scores combined in the usual way, simply weighted or unweighted, in the process of addition. If computer synthesis (variance reallocation) is used, with its special weights, such a basic standardization will need to be modified for the synthesis scores. That can be done from a calculation with the older standardization and the synthesis matrix, without a general data restandardization. As noted earlier, the correlations among the primary factor scores will also become somewhat changed under computer synthesis but are not likely to differ from the *true* (simple structure) factor correlations more than do those from the ordinary factor scoring.

Related to this question in the scoring and recording of factor scores is that concerning combined use of primary, secondary, and tertiary factors, as suggested for *depth psychometry* (see Chapters 17, 18, and elsewhere). Several tests, e.g., the 16 P.F. and the CAQ, have scoring facilities which present simultaneously the profile for first-orders (primaries) and secondaries (such as extraversion, anxiety, general psychosis, and the three broad depression factors). This double strata scoring is very desirable from the standpoint of using the principles of depth psychometry, and of course it makes the use of separate questionnaires for the broad secondaries, e.g., anxiety scales, the Eysenck trio and the Briggs-Myers, quite unnecessary. Also, we perceive thereby not only the subject's level on anxiety (QII), for example, but also the components that have most entered into it, such as ego weakness (C−), ergic tension (Q_4), etc., in the given individual.

However, one must face at this point a decision also on the more acceptable theory of personality structure, between, for example, that of a secondary as an *emergent* from primary interactions and as an underlying *broader influence*. If we adopt, as seems most reasonable at this stage, the SUD (stratified unrelated determiners) model (Cattell, 1978, 1979b), we must accept the fact that what we usually call our primary scores, and which should strictly, by the SUD, represent the "stubs," i.e., the primaries in and of themselves, are actually contaminated. For each oblique primary, as usually measured, contains in its score a contribution from the secondary and tertiary trait scores. Conversely, our *estimate* of the secondaries contains error from the inclusion of the

primary stub scores, though the error is rendered relatively unbiased when several primaries are involved. These psychometric issues cannot be expanded upon in this space and the reader is urged to study them elsewhere (Cattell, 1973a, 1978). But in research, and in practice, too, as the real psychological nature of the primary stubs becomes more understood and usable, it would be desirable to get the secondary source trait scores and parcel them out of each initial primary score before considering that one has from the latter the best estimate of the true primary.

In the local drift of language usage some psychotherapists and psychiatrists have in the last decade been using "assessment" for dimensional, profile scoring and "diagnosis" for assignment to a particular "diagnostic category" or type—the latter as in the Diagnostic and Statistical Manual, Third Edition (DSM-III) of the American Psychiatric Association. This usage is a little odd in view of the progressive views that both therapy and statistics have developed in the last 40 years, to the effect that good diagnosis involves much more than pigeonholing the patient in a slot on the shelf. The concept was reached that good diagnosis surely involves more attention to the *dimensional* pattern of the individual, in the Galilean sense of science as dealing with influences rather than in the Aristotelean method of gross categorizing, which marked the dim dawn of science. But, historical perspective aside, the distinction has been clearly discussed in psychometrics between a) measuring (dimensionally) various elements in a profile, and b) assigning to a type. Furthermore, the statistical and mathematical relationships that *systematically exist between types and dimensions* have been worked out, with supporting computer programs, in the last 20 years (Bolz, 1972; Sokal & Sneath, 1963; Cattell, Coulter & Tsujioka, 1966; Cattell & Brennan, 1984a).

Unfortunately, these new taxonomic

methods have not been systematically applied to the psychiatric and psychological illumination of clinical typing. Thus, any study of interpretive error, as in this chapter, has to recognize that the application of the pattern similarity coefficient to known a) central profiles and b) degrees of dispersion in psychiatric categories, first objectively located by taxonome (or the Sokal & Sneath, 1963, numerical taxonomy), has not been developed in psychiatric practice. Incidentally, the reader should not assume we are suggesting the diagnostic profiles should consist only of test performances. The profile matching calculations should cover also elements that are biographical, resting on life data, and the sequences in onset of any disorder.

If we consider as the most used clinical diagnostic system the DSM-III, we find that, though a considerable statistical background exists for the type descriptions, it is in fact not based on the advances in taxonomic methods referred to above but on essentially committee-like decisions. Since one recognizes that a committee of two may suffer from "folie à deux," there is no guarantee that one of a hundred may not suffer from "folie à cent." Consequently, when the clinical psychologist is told that a committee has improved DSM-II and that DSM-III is now authoritative, he must still ask why a purely scientific computer-aided search process by taxonome has not yet been carried out to segregate the naturally existing types, and to provide a numerical vector against which a case could be matched by the pattern similarity coefficient, r_p.

Although prediction from types was historically earlier than from dimensions, it has value as independent evidence, particularly because we use the behavioral equation almost invariably in a linear form, whereas it is certain that some relations of dimensions to criteria are curvilinear. The use of types implicitly recognizes nonlinear and interactive relations among dimensions.

Although the necessary extensive taxonome theory research in pathology has not been done yet to ascertain what truly segregatable ("species") psychological types definitely exist, according to measured profiles, yet a few mean, central profiles have been established, in the domain of pathological diagnosis, e.g., on the 16 P.F. and CAQ factors, and on the MMPI, respectively, in the Handbooks by Cattell, Eber, & Tatsuoka (1970), and Hathaway & Meehl (1952). These test profiles, however, are for types as defined by prior psychiatric inspection. The CAQ is intended for general pathology, and yields distinctive pathological profiles in all fields, whereas it has been shown that the 16 P.F. profiles are really effective only in yielding distinct patterns for various neuroses. Thus Cattell and Scheier (1961) were able to show that the diagnoses by psychiatrists of anxiety neurosis, of obsessional-compulsive forms, of somatic neuroses, etc., corresponded to different, characteristic central source-trait profiles. It was encouraging to find that the psychiatrists from different countries and training backgrounds had concepts of each particular pathological type which resulted in the same central profile in the groups sorted as the same category.

Some further encouragement as to what the mathematical treatment of profiles *could* do is given by the fact that the application of discriminant functions to profiles, in groups separated by psychiatrists, *does* give substantial separation, as shown in Table 23.5. If the typal diagnostic groupings are incompletely reliable (as records of disagreements among psychiatrists indicate, Chapter 11), then one can anticipate that with improvements in the criterion the discriminant function separation would be still more efficient. No systematic treatment has been given in this book to calculation of discriminant functions, which belongs to texts on statistics (Tatsuoka, 1969, 1970, 1971, 1974, 1975); but examples above and in earlier chapters indicate the value of the method

TABLE 23.5
Diagnostic Typal Assignments by Use of Discriminant Functions

(a) Placement of Psychotics and Neurotics by Discriminant Functions Applied to Profiles on the Objective-Analytic O-A Battery

	Psychiatric Diagnoses						
	Involutional Depressives	Other Psychotic Depressives	Neurotic Depressives	Schizophrenics	Manics	(Anxiety Neurotics)	Controls
Involutional Depressives	8(7)	0(1)	0	0	2(1)	0	0
Other Psychotic Depressives	1(1)	7(8)	2(2)	3(2)	0	1(2)	1(1)
Neurotic Depressives	0	2(1)	5(6)	0(2)	0	0	0
Schizophrenics	0(1)	2(1)	2(1)	8(4)	1(2)	1	0
Manics	2(2)	0	1	1(2)	7(6)	1(2)	2(2)
Anxiety Neurotics	1(1)	0	1(1)	0(1)	1(1)	6(5)	0
Controls	0	0	0(1)	0(1)	0(1)	0.	45(45)
Total	12	11	11	12	11	9	48
% valid predictions	67%(58%)	64%(73%)	45%(55%)	67%(33%)	64%(55%)	67%(56%)	94%(94%)

By Tests (row label group)

With the example of the manics we want to explain how to use this table. Following the first classification rule, 7 of the 11 manics (64%) are validly classified; i.e., the *a priori* diagnoses of the psychiatrists and the classification using the individual scores of the discriminant functions are consistent for these *Ss*. Two manics are misclassified as involutional depressives, one as schizophrenic, and one as anxiety neurotic.

If we focus on the rows in the table it shows how *Ss* have been classified according to the prediction. Two involutional depressives are classified as manics as well as one neurotic depressive, one schizophrenic, one anxiety neurotic, and two normals.

The values in parentheses are slightly different, but can be used in the same way. They are based on the classification rule following the highest probability of belonging to either group.

TABLE 23.5 *(cont'd)*

(b) Separation of Depressives from Normal Controls by Source Traits in the O-A Battery

Personality Factors Having Previous Evidence of Separating Depressives From Normals

Source Trait	Magnitude of Association[1]	Direction of Depressive Association[2]	Source[3]
Ego Assertion (UI16)	S	Lower (largely in neurotic and involutional)	2 4
Independence (UI19)	L	Lower (less clearly in involutional)	1234
Evasiveness (UI20)	M	Higher (less in involutional)	123
Exuberance (UI21)	L	Lower (in all depressives)	123
Mobilization (UI23)	L	Lower (in all depressives)	12 4
Anxiety (UI24)	S	Higher (largely neurotics, not in involutionals)	2
Reality Contact (UI25)	M	Lower (scarcely in involutionals)	123
Asthenia (UI28)	S	Higher (in all depressives)	12
Somindence (UI30)	S	Higher (except in involutionals)	3
Discouragement (UI33)	S	Higher (but slight compared to schizophrenics with neurotic depressives	2

In Neurotic Depressives Only

Source Trait	Magnitude of Association[1]	Direction of Depressive Association[2]	Source[3]
Cortertia (UI22)	L	Lower	4
Responsive Will (UI29)	L	Lower (not in psychotic but only in neurotic depressives)	1 4

[1]L = large, M = moderate, and S = slight. The magnitude is assessed both by correlations and amount of replication.

[2]In certain studies—notably Cattell, Schmidt, and Bjerstedt (1972)—these factors have behaved differently for involutional depressives on the one hand and neurotic and general psychotic depressives on the other. This fact is noted when found.

[3]The sources as numbered on the right are as follows:

1 Cattell, Schmidt, and Bjerstedt (1972, p. 59)
2 Cattell and Schuerger (1978, p. 256)
3 Cattell, Price, and Patrick (1981)
4 Cattell and Scheier (1961, p. 67) for neurotic depressives only. Some weight has also been given to Cattell, Eber, and Tatsuoka (1970) and Mahrer (1970).

(c) Separation Achieved by Discriminant Function Based on O-A Battery Source Traits UI19, UI20, UI25, and UI30

As Psychiatrically Classified	Depressives	Normals	Total
Depressives	23(74.19)	8(25.81)	31(100.0)
Normals	5(16.67)	25(83.33)	30(100.0)

Note: Percentages are in parentheses. Percentage of correct classifications is 78.68%.

of diagnostic separation in interpretive use of structured test results.

Discussion has already been given to that source of interpretive error arising from a poor grasp of existing knowledge about personality structure and whatever laws of development of processes we possess. The greatest error of all, of course, is to treat symptoms only, as some behavior therapists do. But there are degrees of blindness to the nature of personality structure, and we would emphasize that the overall view of ability, temperament, and dynamic traits, with a precise understanding of their primary and secondary architecture, as set out in chapters here and elsewhere, is the first requirement in industrial, educational, and clinical psychology. And since research in this field is beginning to move rapidly, it is important to be able to communicate quickly and economically with others in the field. Does the psychologist have such easy command of technical terms, for example, that he has the capacity to communicate, as one medical doctor can communicate to another precisely what organs he finds to be in trouble and with what disease? It is still common today to find communication among psychologists as little better than a layman's level of precision. This is one aspect of the problem, but there is also to be considered the special task of communicating to the client, to the parents in the case of a child, to law courts, and so forth. Here, too, a precision about what needs to be communicated is no disadvantage, even though it has to be translated.

The books and journal articles whereby the testing psychologist can keep up with the latest about theories and findings on the nature of personality, ability and dynamic, motivational factors, their genetics and life courses are surely themselves adequate. That knowledge, in the special field section of this book (Chapters 9 to 16), is brought up to the level of the latest research by eminent workers in the fields concerned. Any further technical discussion here on the avoidance of

errors of interpretation would therefore be superfluous. However, the unevenness of university departments in instruction on ability and personality structure is evident to everyone and there is no harm in professional psychologists suggesting that some college courses could be more up-to-date. What we shall turn to here, therefore, is simply the appropriate use of popular and technical terms in the records and discussions of the professional psychologist.

Obviously, in interpreting for patients, relatives, and even courts, the psychologist has to use everyday terms. However, as set out in Chapter 3 and many other places (Cattell, Eber, & Tatsuoka, 1970; Cattell, 1973a), there are ample translations of technical terms into common language (at least for Q-data; T-data present more problems). These translations, moreover, are skillfully used in the "narrative print-outs" devised for computers, which also cite particular behaviors and accomplishments that the subject would show, thus providing side by side an account intelligible to the layman and a technical record for the psychologist (see Chapter 23).

What psychology has not yet learned to do as well as medicine and psychiatry is to use the *true technical terms* when communicating with other professionals. Medicine has two gains from its Latin-derived technical terms—acute pyelonephritis, hilar lymphadenophy, salmonella infection, etc. First, the usage helps draw a line between the qualified and the amateur quack; second, and more importantly, it permits precise communication among specialists and insightful therapeutic action. Similarly, the psychologist who refers to source traits of affectia, surgency, parmia vs. threctia, premsia, autia, ergic tension, cortertia, capacity to mobilize, etc. (or designates them by their symbols as A, F, H, I, M, Q_4, QIII, and U.I. 23) is saying something precise which conveys far more to another psychologist than the defaced, vague coinage of popular terms. To call A factor "sociability" not only risks the hearer's interpretation as anything from talkative to altruistic, but could in fact mean also surgency, F, or parmia, H, because these also load their own aspects of sociability. To call premsia vs. harria "sensitivity" vs. "toughness" misses the fact that "sensitivity" is understood by a dozen people in a dozen ways. And since the CAQ clearly evidences seven distinct depression factors, which have different origins and probably different responses to chemotherapy, a professional who diagnoses "depression" without quantifying the D_1, D_2, D_3, etc., components is saying little more than could be said by an amateur.

To be realistic, then, at the present stage of common practice, one would have to admit that much of the imprecise language springs from insufficient education in the precise and meaningful grasp of the various source traits, in understanding the different action of primaries and secondaries, in familiarity with the actual source-trait profiles for clinical and other categories, and in utilizing the information on these measures reasonably in behavioral equations. There is even some danger that the psychologist who is vague about the technical meanings will do damage to the client in interpreting to him a source-trait profile, e.g., by talking as if an A(−) score implies a schizophrenic tendency. Admittedly, the psychology of personality, ability, and motivation has still much to learn about structured measurement. The genetic and environmental determiners of source traits are only roughly known, and the predictions and prognoses for normal and pathological behaviors are not as extensively researched as they should be; but there is already a solid fund of scientific knowledge that well educated practitioners can use, and hopefully they will achieve some self-fulfillment by adding thereto by their own experiences and analyses of data.

SUMMARY

Testing can be said to have three sources of error: 1) sampling error, appearing in standardizations, etc.; 2) error of measurement, visible in the departure of the dependability coefficient from +1.0; 3) error of interpretation appearing in faulty inferences through lack of due allowance for test invalidity (in test and testing circumstances) and misunderstanding of what can be predicted from the given traits.

There are formulae for detecting sabotage and motivational distortion toward "desirabilities" peculiar to different testing circumstances. Motivational distortion scales have limited use and *trait view theory* offers the best possibility of corrective formulae. Tests themselves can also be evaluated for their vulnerability to faking, conscious or unconscious.

Faulty inference can arise also from not understanding the role of instrument factors in constructed tests. An "instrument transcending" factor measure is described. *Computer synthesis* (variance reallocation) offers a simple matrix operation to correct for intrusion of instrument factors and unwanted broad-factor intrusions, where multifactor tests are used.

The initial exploration locating and "tying down" primary factors in structured tests by sometimes barely sufficient markers needs to be followed by repetitions of "research and development" experiment in *progressive rectification* of items and subtests. A new *equity* formulae, improving the Dwyer, is described for this purpose.

Although both the primary and secondary source traits, in personality and ability, have been demonstrated to retain recognizable identity across cultures, the best weightings for factor estimation change from culture to culture and have a unique pattern for each. Allowing for this becomes important also in cross-age comparisons. Two methods—the *equipo-*

tent and *isopodic*—have been proposed to make comparisons of trait scores comparable from different populations.

Some "third error" effects arise from psychologists' optimistically assuming better properties than their scales actually possess. To approach equal interval and true zero (ratio scale) properties, four principles of correction have been proposed: 1) the *relational simplex*; 2) *pannormalization*; 3) *inherent properties*; and, 4) for states, the *modulation principle*. Difference scores are especially vulnerable to unequal interval scales, but otherwise need have no disabling properties, granted certain correlations and standard deviation relations of the before and after measures.

The older formulae for dependability, equivalence, and validity of extended test scales need to be given revised forms when dealing with structured tests, i.e., going beyond itemetric principles, and with tests having suppressor action (buffering), while the estimation of first- and second-order factor scores requires attention in terms of the SUD (stratified uncorrelated determiners) theory.

Testing deals with measurement of situations as well as people. A situation has its psychological meaning represented by a vector of behavioral indices by which its perception and misperception (in formulae analogous to those for traits) can be measured. This subsumes "attribution theory" in the broader model of *spectrad theory*. The effect of a situation as a learning experience can also be represented as a vector by path learning analysis.

There is less error of interpretation when *depth psychometry* is used, so that each primary score is considered in the context of the secondaries in which it is involved. The distinction between assessment and diagnosis is presently understood as largely that between assigning a dimensional profile and allocating to a typal category. These have repeatedly been shown to be related by systematic transformations, but, unfortunately, psychiatric types, as in DSM-III, have not yet been shown to be objectively derivable by taxonome from source trait and biographical measures. Meanwhile, however, multiple discriminant functions have been shown to place persons well by source-trait profiles into the psychiatric categories as presently accepted.

The greatest intrusion of error of inference from obtained scores has probably arisen up to the present from inadequate psychological understanding of the full nature of personality, ability, and motivational source traits, primary and secondary. One cause of this is the tendency to linger with popular, unscientific terms. Such a practice is necessary in talking to clients, their relatives, etc., but as between professional psychologists and in relation to precise computer usage there would be less error if technical trait, state, and process terms and symbols were regularly employed. A clear understanding of the technical implications and predictive values of a factorial source trait or state is just as necessary to avoid misleading communication, as to arrest clumsy practice, even though scores have to be interpreted in popular language to the client. However, since understanding of implications of source trait scores through research is still incomplete, there is opportunity for practitioners to contribute to better understanding from their own experience.

References

Achterberg, J., Lawlis, G. F., Simonton, O. C., & Mathews-Simonton, S. Psychological factors and blood chemistries as disease outcome predictors for cancer patients. *Multivariate Experimental Clinical Research*, 1977, *3*(3), 107-122.

Adorno, T. W., Frenkel-Brunswick, E., Levinson, D. J., & Sanford, R. N. *The authoritarian personality*. New York: Harper, 1950.

Agarwal, K., & Sethi, J. P. The personality of the asthmatic. *Journal of Asthma Research*, 1978, *5*(4), 191-198.

Ajzen, I., & Fishbein, M. The prediction of behavior from attitudinal and normative variable. *Journal of Experimental Social Psychology*, 1970, *6*, 466-487.

Ajzen, I., & Fishbein, M. *Understanding attitudes and predicting behavior*. Englewood Cliffs, NJ: Prentice-Hall, 1980.

Aleshire, D. O. *An empirical test of a multivariate model of the values-behavior relationship*. Unpublished doctoral dissertation, George Peabody College, 1974.

Allen, M. J., & Yen, W. M. *Introduction to measurement theory*. Monterey, CA: Brooks/Cole, 1979.

Allport, G. W. Attitudes. In C. Murchison (Ed.), *Handbook of social psychology*. Worcester, MA: Clark University Press, 1935.

Allport, G. W. The functional autonomy of motives. *American Journal of Psychology*, 1937, *50*, 141-156. (a)

Allport, G. W. *Personality: A psychological interpretation*. New York: Holt, 1937. (b)

Allport, G. W., & Odbert, H. S. Trait-names, a psychological study. *Psychological Monographs*, 1936, No. 211, 1-171.

Allport, G., Vernon, P., & Lindzey, G. *Study of values* (3rd ed.). Boston: Houghton Mifflin, 1960.

American Psychiatric Association. *Diagnostic and statistical manual of mental disorders* (3rd ed.), Washington, D.C.: Author, 1980.

American Psychological Association, American Educational Research Association, & National Council for Measurement in Psychology. *Standards for educational and psychological tests*. (rev. ed.). Washington, D.C.: Author, 1974. (Originally published in 1954).

American Psychological Association, Division of Industrial-Organizational Psychology. *Principles for the validation and use of personnel selection procedures* (2nd ed.). Berkeley, CA: Industrial-Organizational Psychologist, 1980.

American Psychological Association. Testing: Concepts, policy, practice and research. *American Psychologist*. Washington, D.C.: Author, 1981, *36*, 997-1189.

Anastasi, A. *Psychological testing* (1st ed.). New York: Macmillan, 1954.

Anastasi, A. *Psychological testing* (4th ed.). New York: Macmillan, 1976.

Anastasi, A. Abilities and the measurement of achievement. In W. B. Schrader (Ed.), *New directions for testing and measurement: Measuring achievement: Progress over a decade*. San Francisco: Jossey-Bass, 1980.

Anastasi, A. *Psychological testing* (5th ed.). New York: Macmillan, 1981.

Anastasi, A. *Psychological testing* (5th ed.). New York: Macmillan, 1982.

Anderson, J. C., & Cattell, R. B. The measurement of personality and behavior disorders by the IPAT musical preference test. *Journal of Applied Psychology*, 1953, *37*, 446-454.

Anderson, N. H. Methods and designs. Measurement of motivation and incentive. *Behavior Research Methods and Instrumentation*, 1978, *10*(3), 360-375.

Anderson, R. C. How to construct achievement tests to assess comprehension. *Review of Educational Research*, 1972, *42*, 145-170.

Angoff, W. H. Scales, norms, and equivalent scores. In R. L. Thorndike (Ed.), *Educational measurement* (2nd ed.). Washington, D.C.: American Council on Education, 1971.

Arrington, R. Time sampling in studies of social behavior. A critical review of techniques and results with research suggestions. *Psychological Bulletin*, 1943, *40*, 81-124.

Atkinson, J. W. Motivation for achievement. In T. Blass (Ed.), *Personality variables in social behavior*. Hillsdale, NJ: Erlbaum, 1977.

Atkinson, J.W., Feather, N. T. (Eds.). *A theory of achievement motivation*. New York: Wiley, 1966.

Bachtold, L. M., & Werner, E. E. Personality characteristics of women scientists. *Psychological Reports*, 1972, *31*, 391-396.

Baggaley, A., & Cattell, R. B. A comparison of exact and approximate linear function estimates of oblique factor scores. *British Journal of Statistical Psychology*, 1956, *9*, 83-86.

Baker, M. & Gorsuch, R. L. Trait anxiety and religiousness. *Journal for the Scientific Study of Religion*, 1982, *21*, 119-122.

Bales, R. F. *Personality and interpersonal behavior*, New York: Holt, 1970.

Baltes, P. B. Longitudinal and cross-sectional sequences in the study of age and generation effects. *Human Development*, 1968, *11*, 145-171.

Baltes, P. B., & Nesselroade, J. R. The developmental analysis of individual differences on multiple measures. In J. R. Nesselroade & H. W. Reese (Eds.), *Life-span developmental psychology: Methodological issues*. New York: Academic Press, 1973.

Barker, R. G. (Ed.). *The stream of behavior*. New York: Appleton-Century-Crofts, 1963.

Barker, R. G., & Wright, H. F. *One boy's day*. New York: Harper, 1951.

Barker, R. G., & Wright, H. F. *Midwest and its children*. Evanston, IL: Row, 1954.

Barrabee, P., Barrabee, E. L., & Finestinger, J. E. A normative social adjustment scale. *American Journal of Psychiatry*, 1955, *112*, 252-259.

Barrett, T. C. Taxonomy of cognitive and affective dimensions of reading comprehension. Cited in G. Wallace & S. C. Larsen, *Educational assessment of learning problems: Testing for teaching*. Boston: Allyn & Bacon, 1979.

Bartlett, H. W. The separation of state and trait anxiety, stress and fear. Unpublished master's thesis, University of Illinois, 1968.

Barton, K. Personality similarity in spouses related to marriage roles. *Multivariate Experimental Clinical Research*, 1976, *2*, 107-111.

Barton, K. Psychological mood states in children related to performance on a perceptual motor task. *Multivariate Experimental Clinical Research*, 1978, *3*(5), 219-231.

Barton, K., & Cattell, R. B. Real and perceived similarities in personality between spouses: Test of "likeness" versus "completeness" theories. *Psychological Reports*, 1972, *31*, 15-18.

Barton, K., & Cattell, R. B. Personality factors of husbands and wives as predictors of own and partners' marital dimensions. *Canadian Journal of Behavioral Science*, 1973, *5*, 83-92.

Barton, K., & Cattell, R. B. Changes in psychological state measures and time of day. *Psychological Reports*, 1974, *35*, 219-222.

Barton, K., & Cattell, R. B. An investigation of the common factor space of some well-known questionnaire scales: The Eysenck EPI, the Comrey Scales, and the IPAT Central Trait-State K + (CST). *Multivariate Experimental Clinical Research*, 1975, *1*, 267-277. (a)

Barton, K., & Cattell, R. B. Changes in personality over a 5-year period. Relationship of change to life events. *JSAS Catalogue of Selected Documents in Psychology*, 1975, *1*, 283-229. (b)

Barton, K. & Cattell, R. B. The Central Trait-State Kit (CTS): Experimental version. Champaign, IL: IPAT, 1981.

Barton, K., Cattell, R. B., & Curran, J. Psychological states: Their definition through P-technique and differential R(dR) technique factor analysis. *Journal of Behavioral Science*, 1973, *1*(5), 273-277.

Barton, K., Cattell, R. B., & Vaughan, G. M. Changes in personality as a function of college attend-ance or work experience. *Journal of Counseling Psychology*, 1973, *20*, 162-165.

Barton, K., Dielman, T. E., & Cattell, R. B. An item factor analysis of intrafamilial attitudes of parents. *The Journal of Social Psychology*, 1973, *90*, 67-72.

Barton, K., Kawash, G., & Cattell, R. B. Personality, motivation and marital role factors as predictors of life data in married couples. *Journal of Marriage and the Family*, 1972, *34*, 474-480.

Barton, K., & Vaughan, G. M. Church membership and personality: A longitudinal study. *Social Behavior and Personality*, 1976, *4*, 11-16.

Beck, M. D. Achievement test reliability as a function of pupil-response procedures. *Journal of Educational Measurement*, 1974, *11*, 109-114.

Beck, S. J., Beck, A. G., Levitt, E. E., & Molish, H. B. *Rorschach's test: I. Basic processes*. New York: Grune & Stratton, 1961.

Bellack, A. A., Kliebard, H. M., Hyman, R. T., & Smith, F. L. *The language of the classroom*. New York: Teachers College Press, 1966.

Bellak, L. *The TAT, CAT, and SAT in clinical use*. New York: Grune & Stratton, 1954, 1975.

Bem, D. J., & Allen, A. A. On predicting some of the people some of the time: The search for cross-situational consistencies in behavior. *Psychological Review*, 1974, *81*, 506-520.

Bem, S. L. Gender schema theory: A cognitive account of sextyping. *Psychological Review*, 1981, *88*, 354-364.

Bender, L. A. *Visual-Motor Gestalt Test and its clinical use*. American Orthopsychiatric Association Research Monograph, No. 3, New York: American Orthopsychiatric Association, 1938.

Bentler, P. M., & Speckart, G. An evaluation of models of attitude-behavior relations. *Psychological Review*, 1979, *86*, 452-464.

Ben-Tovim, D. I., Marilov, V., & Crisp, A. H. Personality and mental state (P.S.E.) within anorexia nervosa. *Journal of Psychosomatic Research*, 1979, *23*(5), 321-325.

Bergin, A. E. The evaluation of therapeutic outcomes. In A. E. Bergin & S. L. Garfield (Eds.), *Handbook of psychotherapy and behavior change*. New York: Wiley, 1971.

Bergin, A. E., & Lambert, M. J. The evaluation of therapeutic outcomes. In S. L. Garfield & A. E. Bergin (Eds.), *Handbook of psychotherapy and behavior change: An empirical analysis* (2nd ed.). New York: Wiley, 1978.

Berk, R. A. (Ed.). *Criterion-referenced measurement*. Baltimore: Johns Hopkins Press, 1980.

Bersoff, D. N. Testing and the law. *American Psychologist*, 1981, *36*, 1047-1056.

Bindra, D. *Motivation: A systematic reinterpretation*. New York: Ronald Press, 1959.

Binet, A., & Henri, V. La psychologie individuelle. *Année Psychologique*, 1895, *2*, 411-463.

Binet, A., & Simon, T. Methodes nouvelles pour le diagnostic du niveau intellectuel des anormaux. *L'Année Psychologique*, 1905, *11*, 191-244.

Birkett, H., & Cattell, R. B. Diagnosis of the dynamic roots of a clinical symptom by P-technique: A case of episodic alcoholism. *Multivariate Experimental Clinical Research*, 1978, *3*, 173-194.

Blake, R. R., & Mouton, J. S. *Consultation.* Reading, MA: Addison-Wesley, Scientific Methods, Inc., 1976.

Blewett, D. B., & Stefanink, W. B. Weyburn Assessment Scale. *Journal of Mental Science*, 1958, *104*, 359-371.

Bloom, B. (Ed.). *Taxonomy of educational objectives.* New York: David McKay, 1956.

Bloom, B. S. *Human characteristics and school learning.* New York: McGraw-Hill, 1976.

Bloom, B. S., Hastings, J. T., & Madaus, G. *Handbook on formative and summative evaluation of student learning.* New York: McGraw-Hill, 1971.

Bloxom, B. M. Review of the 16 P.F. In O. K. Buros (Ed.), *Eighth mental measurements yearbook.* Highland Park, NJ: Gryphon, 1978.

Bock, R. D. Basic issues in the measurement of change. In D. N. M. De Gruijter & L. J. Th. van der Kamp (Eds.), *Advances in psychological and educational measurement.* New York: Wiley, 1976.

Bogardus, E. S. Measuring social distances. *Journal of Applied Sociology*, 1925, *9*, 299-308.

Bolton, B. Review of the 16P.F. In O. K. Buros (Ed.), *Eighth mental measurements yearbook.* Highland Park, NJ: Gryphon, 1978, 1078-1080.

Bolton, B. Multivariate approaches in human learning. In J. R. Nesselroade & R. B. Cattell (Eds.), *Handbook of multivariate experimental psychology* (2nd ed.). New York: Plenum, 1986.

Bolz, C. R. Types of personality. In R. M. Dreger (Ed.), *Multivariate personality research: In honor of Raymond B. Cattell.* Baton Rouge: Claitor, 1972.

Borgatta, E. G., & Cottrell, L. S. On the classification of groups. *Sociometry*, 1956, *18*, 665-678.

Bormuth, J. R. *On the theory of achievement test items.* Chicago, IL: University of Chicago Press, 1970.

Bouchard, J. T. Review of the EPI. *Clinical Psychologist*, 1969, *22*(4), 206-208.

Bouchard, J. T. Review of the 16 P.F. In O. K. Buros (Ed.), *Seventh mental measurements yearbook.* Highland Park, NJ: Gryphon, 1972, 329-332.

Boulding, K. E. *The meaning of the twentieth century: The great transition.* New York: Harper & Row, 1964.

Bowers, K. S. Situationalism in psychology: An analysis and a critique. *Psychological Review*, 1973, *80*, 307-336.

Bracht, G. H., & Hopkins, K. D. Stability of educational achievement. In G. H. Bracht, K. D. Hopkins, & J. C. Stanley (Eds), *Perspectives in educational and psychological measurement.* Englewood Cliffs, NJ: Prentice-Hall, 1972.

Brogden, H. E. A factor analysis of forty character tests. *Psychological Monographs*, 1940, *234*, 35-55.

Broudy, H. S. Impact of minimum competency testing on curriculum. In R. M. Jaeger & C. K. Tittle (Eds.), *Minimum competency testing: Motives, models, measures, and consequences.* Berkeley, CA: McCutchan, 1980.

Buck, J. N. The H-T-P technique: A qualitative and quantitative scoring manual. *Journal of Clinical Psychology*, 1948, *4*, 317-396.

Buj, V. Average IQ values in various European countries. *Personality and Individual Differences*, 1981, *2*, 168-169.

Burdsal, C., & Vaughan, D. A comparison of the personality structure of college students found in the questionnaire medium by items compared to parcels. *Journal of Genetic Psychology*, 1974, *125*, 219-224.

Buros, O. K. (Ed.). *Seventh mental measurements yearbook.* Highland Park, NJ: Gryphon, 1972.

Buros, O. K. (Ed.). *Eighth mental measurements yearbook.* Highland Park, NJ: Gryphon, 1978.

Burt, C. L. *The distributions and relations of educational abilities.* London: King, 1917.

Burt, C. L. Correlations between persons. *British Journal of Psychology*, 1937, *28*, 56-96.

Burt, C. L. The factorial analysis of emotional traits. *Character and Personality*, 1939, *7*, 238-254, 285-299.

Burt, C. L. *Factors of the mind.* London: University of London Press, 1940.

Burt, C. L. Psychology in war: The military work of German and American psychologists. *Occupational Psychology*, 1942, July, 1-17.

Burt, C. L. The factorial study of temperamental traits. *British Journal of Psychology, Statistical Section*, 1948, *1*, 178-203.

Burt, C., & Howard M. The multi-factorial theory of inheritance and its application to intelligence. *British Journal of Statistical Psychology*, 1956, *9*, 95-131.

Burton, R. V. Generality of honesty reconsidered. *Psychological Review*, 1963, *70*, 481-499.

Buss, A. R. A general developmental model for interindividual differences, intraindividual differences, and intraindividual changes. *Developmental Psychology*, 1974, *10*, 70-78.

Buss, A. R. & Poley, W. *Individual differences: Traits and factors.* New York: Gardner Press, 1976.

Butcher, H. J. *Human intelligence: Its nature and assessment.* London: Methuen, 1968.

Butcher, H. J. Creativity. In R. M. Dreger (Ed.), *Multivariate personality research: Contributions to the understanding of personality in honor of Raymond B. Cattell.* Baton Rouge, LA: Claitor's Publishing, 1972.

Butcher, J. N. *Manual for the Minnesota Report.* Minneapolis: Interpretive Scoring Systems, 1982.

Butcher, H. J., Ainsworth, M., & Nesbitt, J. E. Personality factors and school achievement. *British Journal of Educational Psychology*, 1963, *33*, 276-285.

Cahill, M. C., & Belfer, P. L. Word association times, felt effects and personality characteristics of science students given a placebo energizer. *Psychological Reports*, 1978, *42*(1), 231-238.

Cairns, R. B., & Green, J. A. How to assess personality and social patterns: Observation on ratings. In R. B. Cairns, *The analysis of social integration*. Hillsdale, NJ: Erlbaum, 1979.

Caldwell, A. B. *Caldwell Report: An MMPI interpretation*. Santa Monica, CA: Caldwell Report, 1979.

Campbell, D. P. The Minnesota Vocational Interest Inventory. *Personnel and Guidance Journal*, 1966, *44*, 854-858.

Campbell, D. P., & Fiske, D. W. Convergent and discriminant validation by the multitrait-multimethod matrix. *Psychological Bulletin*, 1959, *56*, 91-105.

Campbell, D. P., & Hansen, J. C. *Manual for the SVIB-SCII Strong-Campbell Interest Inventory* (3rd. ed.). Stanford, CA: Stanford University Press, 1981.

Cannon, W. B. *The wisdom of the body*. London: Norton, 1932.

Carpenter, C. R. Field study of the behaviors and social relations of howling monkeys. *Comparative Psychology Monographs*, 1934, *10, 48*.

Carroll, J. B., & Horn, J. L. On the scientific basis of ability testing. *American Psychologist*, 1981, *36*, 1012-1020.

Cartwright, D. S. *Introduction to personality study*. New York: Prentice-Hall, 1974.

Cartwright, D. S. *Theories and models of personality*. Dubuque, IA: Brown, 1979.

Cartwright, D. S., Tomson, B., & Schwartz, H. *Gang delinquency*. Monterey, CA: Brooks/Cole, 1975, pp. 11-12.

Carver, R. P. Two dimensions of tests—Psychometric and edumetric. *American Psychologist*, 1974, *29*, 512-518.

Castelnuovo-Tedesco, P., & Schiebel, D. Studies of superobesity. I. Psychological characteristics of superobese patients. *International Journal of Psychiatry in Medicine*, 1975, *6*(4), 465-480.

Cattell, H. E. P. Sex-roles and dyadic uniqueness in parent-child personality trait relationships. *Multivariate Experimental Clinical Research*, 1982, *6*, 33-46.

Cattell, H., & Cattell, R. B. *Experimental support for the psychoanalytic conflict-free ego*, in preparation.

Cattell, J. McK. A statistical study of eminent men. *Popular Science Monthly*, 1903, *62*, 359-377.

Cattell, J. McK., & Farrand, C. Physical and mental measurements of the students of Columbia University. *Psychological Review*, 1896, *3*, 618-648.

Cattell, R. B. The effects of alcohol and caffeine on intelligent and associative performance. *British Journal of Psychology*, 1929, *19*, 357-386.

Cattell, R. B. Psychologist or medical man. *The Schoolmasters and Woman Teachers Chronicle*, 1932, *8*, 330. (a)

Cattell, R. B. Temperament tests. I. Temperament. *British Journal of Psychology*, 1932, *23*, 308-329. (b)

Cattell, R. B. *Cattell intelligence test, group and individual*. London: Harrap, 1933.

Cattell, R. B. Occupational norms of intelligence and the standardization of an adult intelligence test. *British Journal of Psychology*, 1934, *25*, 1-28.

Cattell, R. B. Objective projection tests. In R. B. Cattell, *A guide to mental testing*. London: University of London Press, 1936, 211-230.

Cattell, R. B. A quoi servent les examens? *Pour L'ère Nouvelle*, 1937, *15*, 13-16. (a)

Cattell, R. B. *The fight for our national intelligence*. London: King, 1937. (b)

Cattell, R. B. A culture-free intelligence test. *Journal of Educational Psychology*, 1940, *31*, 161-179.

Cattell, R. B. The concept of social status. *Journal of Social Psychology*, 1942, *15*, 293-308.

Cattell, R. B. The measurement of adult intelligence. *Psychological Bulletin*, 1943, *40*, 153-193.

Cattell, R. B. *The description and measurement of personality*. New York: Harcourt, Brace, & World, 1946.

Cattell, R. B. The ergic theory of attitude and sentiment measurement. *Education and Psychology Measurement*, 1947, 7, 221-246.

Cattell, R. B. Concepts and methods in the measurement of group syntality. *Psychological Review*, 1948, *55*, 48-63. (a)

Cattell, R. B. The primary personality factors in women compared with those in men. *British Journal of Psychology*, 1948, *1*, 114-130. (b)

Cattell, R. B. The dimensions of culture patterns by factorization of national characters. *Journal of Abnormal and Social Psychology*, 1949, *14*, 443-469. (a)

Cattell, R. B. r_p and other coefficients of pattern similarity. *Psychometrika*, 1949, *14*, 279-298. (b)

Cattell, R. B. *Personality: A systematical theoretical and factual study*. New York: McGraw-Hill, 1950.

Cattell, R. B. *Factor analysis*. New York: Harper, 1952.

Cattell, R. B. *A guide to mental testing* (3rd ed.). Champaign, IL: IPAT, 1953.

Cattell, R. B. The principal replicated factors discovered in objective personality tests. *Journal of Abnormal and Social Psychology*, 1955, *50*, 291-314. (a)

Cattell, R. B. Psychiatric screening of flying personnel: Personality structure in objective tests—a study of 1,000 air force students in basic pilot training. Report No. 9, Project No. 21-0202007. Randolph Field, TX: USAF School of Aviation Medicine, 1955. (b)

Cattell, R. B. A universal index for psychological factors. *Psychologia*, 1957, *1*, 74-85. (a)

Cattell, R. B. Formulae and table for obtaining validities and reliabilities of extended factor scales. *Education and Psychological Measurement*, 1957, *17*, 491-498. (b)

Cattell, R. B. *Personality and motivation structure and measurement*. New York: World Book Co., 1957. (c)

Cattell, R. B. Anxiety, extraversion, and other second-order personality factors in children. *Journal of Personality*, 1959, *27*, 464-476. (a)

Cattell, R. B. The dynamic calculus: Concepts and

crucial experiments. In M. R. Jones (Ed.), *The Nebraska symposium on motivation*. Lincoln: University of Nebraska Press, 1959. (b)

Cattell, R. B. Group theory, personality and role: A model for experimental researches. In F. A. Geldard (Ed.), *Defense psychology*. New York: Pergamon, 1961. (a)

Cattell, R. B. Theory of situational, instrument, second order and refraction factors in personality structure research. *Psychological Bulletin*, 1961, *50*, 160-174. (b)

Cattell, R. B. The relational simplex theory of equal interval and absolute scaling. *Acta Psychologica*, 1962, *20*, 139-158.

Cattell, R. B. Personality, role, mood, and situation-perception: A unifying theory of modulators. *Psychological Review*, 1963, *70*, 1-18. (a)

Cattell, R. B. Theory of fluid and crystallized intelligence: A critical experiment. *Journal of Educational Psychology*, 1963, *54*, 1-22. (b)

Cattell, R. B. Beyond validity and reliability: Some further concepts and coefficients for evaluating tests. *Journal of Experimental Education*, 1964, *33*, 133-143. (a)

Cattell, R. B. The definition(s) of anxiety. *Journal of the American Medical Association*, 1964, *190*, 859. (b)

Cattell, R. B. The parental early repressiveness hypothesis for the "authoritarian" personality factor U.I. 28. *Journal of Genetic Psychology*, 1964, *106*, 333-349. (c)

Cattell, R. B. *The scientific analysis of personality*. Baltimore: Penguin, 1965.

Cattell, R. B. Evaluating therapy as total personality change: Theory and available instruments. *American Journal of Psychotherapy*, 1966, *20*, 69-88. (a)

Cattell, R. B. (Ed.). *Handbook of multivariate experimental psychology*. Chicago: Rand McNally, 1966. (b)

Cattell, R. B. Taxonomic principles in locating and using types. In B. Kleinmuntz (Ed.), *Formal representation on human judgment*. Pittsburgh, PA: Pittsburgh University Press, 1968.

Cattell, R. B. Comparing factor trait and state scores across ages and cultures. *Journal of Gerontology*, 1969, *24*, 348-360. (a)

Cattell, R. B. The diagnosis of schizophrenia by questionnaires and objective personality tests. In D. V. Silva Sankar (Ed.), *Schizophrenia, current concepts and research*. Hicksville, NY: PJD Publications, 1969. (b)

Cattell, R. B. A factor analytic system for clinicians. I. The integration of functional and psychometric requirements in a quantitative and computerized diagnostic system. In A. R. Mahrer (Ed.), *New approaches to personality classification*. New York: Columbia University Press, 1970. (a)

Cattell, R. B. The isopodic and equipotent principles for comparing factor scores across different populations. *British Journal of Mathematical and Statistical Psychology*, 1970, *23*, 23-24. (b)

Cattell, R. B. Separating endogenous, exogenous, ecogenic and epogenic component curves in developmental data. *Developmental Psychology*, 1970, *3*, 157-162. (c)

Cattell, R. B. Estimating modulator indices and state liabilities. *Multivariate Behavioral Research*, 1971, *6*, 7-33. (b)

Cattell, R. B. The structure of intelligence in relation to the nature-nurture controversy. In R. Cancro (Ed.), *Intelligence: Genetic and environmental influences*. New York: Grune & Stratton, 1971. (c)

Cattell, R. B. The 16 P.F. and basic personality structure: A reply to Eysenck. *Journal of Behavioral Science* (Durban, S. A.), 1972, *1*, 169-187.

Cattell, R. B. *A new morality from science: Beyondism*. New York: Pergamon, 1972. (a)

Cattell, R. B. Real base, true zero factor analysis. *Multivariate behavioral research monographs*, Fort Worth, TX: Texas Christian University Press, 1972, 72(1), 1-162. (b)

Cattell, R. B. The nature and genesis of mood states: A theoretical model with experimental measurements concerning anxiety, depression, arousal, and other mood states. In C. B. Spielberger (Ed.), *Current trends in theory and research*, Vol. 1. New York: Academic Press, 1972. (c)

Cattell, R. B. *Personality and mood by questionnaire*. Champaign, IL: IPAT, 1973. (a)

Cattell, R. B. The measurement of the healthy personality and the healthy society. *The Counseling Psychologist*, 1973, *4*, 13-18. (b)

Cattell, R. B. Unravelling motivational and learning developments by the comparative MAVA approach. In J. R. Nesselroade & J. Reese (Eds.), *Life-span developmental psychology*. New York: Academic Press, 1973. (c)

Cattell, R. B. How good is the modern questionnaire? General principles for evaluation. *Journal of Personality Assessment*, 1974, *38*(2), 115-130. (a)

Cattell, R. B. Radial parcel factoring vs. item factoring in defining personality structure in questionnaires: Theory and experimental checks. *Social Biology*, 1974, *21*, 168-177. (b)

Cattell, R. B. *The scientific use of factor analysis in behavioral and life sciences*. New York: Plenum, 1978.

Cattell, R. B. Adolescent-age trends in primary personality factors measured in T-data: A contribution to the use of standardized measures in practice. *Journal of Adolescence*, 1979, *2*, 1-16. (a)

Cattell, R. B. Are culture-fair intelligence tests possible and necessary? *Journal of Research and Development in Education*, 1979, *12*, 3-13. (b)

Cattell, R. B. *Personality and learning theory. I. Structure of personality in its environment*. New York: Springer, 1979. (c)

Cattell, R. B. *Personality and learning theory. II. A systems theory of maturation and structured learning*. New York: Springer, 1980. (a)

Cattell, R. B. The structured learning analysis of therapeutic change and maintenance. In P. Karoly, & J. J. Steffen (Eds.), *Improving the long-term effects of psychotherapy.* New York: Gardner, 1980. (b)

Cattell, R. B. *The inheritance of personality and ability.* New York: Academic Press, 1982. (a)

Cattell, R. B. The development of attribution theory into spectrad theory, using the general perceptual model. *Multivariate Behavioral Research,* 1982, *17,* 169-192. (b)

Cattell, R. B. The voyage of a laboratory, 1928-1984. *Multivariate Behavioral Research,* 1984, *19,* 121-174.

Cattell, R. B. Personality as a scientifically based concept. In J. Kuper & M. Kuper (Eds.), *The social science encyclopedia* (pp. 10-37). London: Routledge & Kegan Paul, 1984.

Cattell, R. B. *Beyondism and current social problems.* New York: Praeger, 1985. (a)

Cattell, R. B. *Motivation and the dynamic calculus.* New York: Praeger, 1985. (b)

Cattell, R. B. *Psychotherapy as structured learning theory.* New York: Springer, 1985. (c)

Cattell, R. B. *Rating revisited: An increase in factor number.* Unpublished manuscript, Honolulu, 1985. (d)

Cattell, R. B. *Abilities: Their structure, growth and action.* Amsterdam: North Holland Press, 1985. (e)

Cattell, R. B. Handling predictions from psychological states and roles. In R. Demaree (Ed.), *Symposium in honor of Saul B. Sells.* Austin: University of Texas Press, in press.

Cattell, R. B., & Anderson, J. C. The measurement of personality and behavior disorders of the I.P.A.T. Music Preference Test. *Journal of Applied Psychology,* 1953, *17,* 446-454.

Cattell, R. B., Anton, M., Child, D., & Cattell, H. *Handbook for the motivation analysis test, Form B (Anglo-American adaptation).* Champaign, IL: IPAT, 1985.

Cattell, R. B., & Baggaley, A. R. The objective measurement of attitude motivation development and evaluation of principles and devices. *Journal of Personality,* 1956, *24,* 401-423.

Cattell, R. B., & Baggaley, A. R. A confirmation of ergic and engram structures in attitudes objectively measured. *Australian Journal of Psychology,* 1958, *10*(1), 287-318.

Cattell, R. B., & Bartlett, H. W. An R-dR technique operational distinction of the states of anxiety, stress, fear, etc. *Australian Journal of Psychology,* 1971, *23*(2), 105-123.

Cattell, R. B., Barton, K., & Dielman, T. E. Prediction of school achievement from motivation, personality, and ability measures. *Psychological Reports,* 1972, *30,* 35-43.

Cattell, R. B., & Birkett, H. Can P-technique diagnosis be practically shortened? Some proposals and a test of a 50-day abridgement. *Multivariate Experimental Clinical Research,* 1980, *5*(1), 1-16. (a)

Cattell, R. B., & Birkett, H. The known personality factors aligned between first-order T-data and second-order Q factors: Inhibitory control, independence, cortertia and exvia. *Personality and Individual Differences,* 1980, *1,* 229-238. (b)

Cattell, R. B., & Bjerstedt, A. The structure of depression by factoring Q-data in relation to general personality source traits. *Scandinavian Journal of Psychology,* 1967, *8,* 17-24.

Cattell, R. B., Blewett, D. B., & Beloff, J. R. The inheritance of personality: A multiple variance analysis determination of approximate nature-nurture ratios for primary personality factors in Q data. *American Journal of Human Genetics,* 1955, 7, 122-146.

Cattell, R. B., & Bolton, L. S. What pathological dimensions lie beyond the normal dimensions of the 16P.F.? A comparison of the MMPI and 16P.F. factor domains. *Journal of Consulting and Clinical Psychology,* 1969, *33*(1), 18-29.

Cattell, R. B., & Brennan, J. Population intelligence and national syntality dimensions. *Mankind Quarterly,* 1981, *22,* 1-17.

Cattell, R. B., & Brennan, J. State measurement: A check on the fit of the modulation model. Unpublished manuscript, 1983.

Cattell, R. B., & Brennan, J. The cultural types of modern nations by two quantitative classification methods. *Social and Sociological Research,* 1984, *68,* 268-295. (a)

Cattell, R. B., & Brennan, J. Fluid and crystallized intelligence structure in the aged: A re-interpretation. *Journal of Applied Developmental Psychology,* 1984. (b).

Cattell, R. B., & Brennan, J. The effect of ipsative scores on the outcome of a factor analysis. Unpublished manuscript, 1984. (c)

Cattell, R. B. & Brennan, J. Methods of deriving equal interval unit scores. *Psychological Bulletin,* 1985.

Cattell, R. B. & Bristol, H. Intelligence tests for mental ages four to eight years. *British Journal of Educational Psychology,* 1933, *3,* 142-169.

Cattell, R. B., Bruel, H., & Hartman, H. P. An attempt at more refined definition of the cultural dimensions of syntality in modern nations. *American Sociological Review,* 1952, *17,* 408-421.

Cattell, R. B., & Burdsal, C. The radial parcelling double factoring design: A solution to the item vs. parcel controversy. *Multivariate Behavioral Research,* 1975, *10,* 165-179.

Cattell, R. B., & Butcher, J. *The prediction of achievement and creativity.* Indianapolis: Bobbs-Merrill, 1968.

Cattell, R. B., Cattell, A. K. S., & Rhymer, R. M. P-technique demonstrated in determining psychophysiological source traits in a normal individual. *Psychometrika,* 1947, *12*(4), 267-288.

Cattell, R. B., & Cattell, M. D. *Handbook for the High School Personality Questionnaire.* Champaign, IL: IPAT, 1969. (a)

Cattell, R. B., & Cattell, M. D. *The High School Personality Questionnaire (HSPQ).* Champaign, IL: IPAT, 1969. (b)

Cattell, R. B., & Cattell, M. D. *The Clinical Analysis Questionnaire.* Champaign, IL: IPAT, 1975.

Cattell, R. B., & Child, D. *Motivation and dynamic structure.* New York: Wiley & Halsted, 1975.

Cattell, R. B., & Coan, R. W. Child personality structure as revealed in teachers' behavior ratings. *Journal of Clinical Psychology*, 1957, *13*, 315-327.

Cattell, R. B., & Coan, R. W. Personality factors in questionnaire responses of six- and seven-year-olds. *British Journal of Educational Psychology*, 1958, *28*, 232-262.

Cattell, R. B., & Coan, R. W. Objective-test assessment of the primary personality dimensions in middle childhood. *British Journal of Psychology*, 1959, *50*, 235-252.

Cattell, R. B., & Coan, R. W. *Handbook for the Early School Personality Questionnaire*. Champaign, IL: IPAT, 1976.

Cattell, R. B., Coulter, M. A., & Tsujioka, B. The taxometric recognition of types and functional emergence. In R. B. Cattell (Ed.), *Handbook of multivariate experimental psychology*. Chicago, IL: Rand-McNally, 1966.

Cattell, R. B., & Cross, P. Comparison of the ergic self-sentiment structures found in dynamic traits by R- and P-techniques. *Journal of Personality*, 1952, *21*, 250-271.

Cattell, R. B., & Damarin, F. L., Jr. Personality factors in early childhood and their relation to intelligence. *Monographs of the Society for Research in Child Development*, 1968, *33*(6, Whole No. 1-2.), 1-95.

Cattell, R. B., DeYoung, G. E., & Horn, J. L. Human motives as dynamic states: A dR analysis of objective motivation measures. *Journal of Multivariate Experimental Personality and Clinical Psychology*, 1974, *1*, 58-78.

Cattell, R. B., & Dickman, K. A dynamic model of physical influences demonstrating the necessity of oblique simple structure. *Psychological Bulletin*, 1962, *59*, 389-400.

Cattell, R. B., & Digman, J. A theory of the structure of perturbations in observer ratings and questionnaire data. *Behavioral Science*, 1964, *9*, 341-358.

Cattell, R. B., & Dreger, R. M. (Eds.). *Handbook of modern personality theory*. New York: Wiley, 1977.

Cattell, R. B., & Drevdahl, J. E. A comparison of the personality profile (16 P.F.) of eminent researchers with that of eminent teachers and administrators, and of the general population. *British Journal of Psychology*, 1955, *46*, 248-261.

Cattell, R. B., Dubin, S. S., & Saunders, D. R. Verification of hypothesized factors in one hundred objective personality test designs. *Psychometrika*, 1954, *3*, 209-230.

Cattell, R. B., Eber, H. W., & Tatsuoka, M. *Handbook for the Sixteen Personality Factor Questionnaire*, Champaign, IL: IPAT, 1970.

Cattell, R. B. & Gibbons, B. D. Personality factors of the combined Guilford and Cattell personality questionnaires. *Journal of Personality & Social Psychology*, 1967, *9*, 107-120.

Cattell, R. B., Graham, R. K., & Woliver, R. E. A reassessment of the factorial cultural dimensions of modern nations. *Journal of Social Psychology*, 1979, *108*, 241-258.

Cattell, R. B. & Green, R. R. Rationale of norms on an adult personality test, the 16 P.F., for American women. *Journal of Educational Research*, 1961, *54*, 285-290.

Cattell, R. B., & Gruen, W. The primary personality factors in 11-year-old children by objective tests. *Journal of Personality*, 1955, *23*, 460-478.

Cattell, R. B., Heist, A. B., Heist, P. A., & Stewart, R. G. The objective measurement of dynamic traits. *Educational and Psychological Measurement*, 1950, *10*, 224-248.

Cattell, R. B., & Horn, J. L. An integrating study of the factor structure of adult attitude-interests. *Genetic Psychology Monographs*, 1963, *67*, 89-149.

Cattell, R. B., Horn, J. L., Radcliffe, J., & Sweney, A. B. The nature and measurement of components of motivation. *Genetic Psychology Monographs*, 1963, *68*, 49-211.

Cattell, R. B., Horn, J. L., Sweney, A. B., & Radcliffe, J. A. *Handbook for the Motivation Analysis Test*. Champaign, IL: IPAT, 1964(a), 1970.

Cattell, R. B., Horn, J. L., Sweney, A. B., & Radcliffe, J. *The Motivation Analysis Test (MAT)*. Champaign, IL: IPAT, 1964. (b)

Cattell, R. B., & Killian, L. R. The pattern of objective test personality factor differences in schizophrenic and the character disorders. *Journal of Clinical Psychology*, 1967, *23*(3), 343-348.

Cattell, R. B., & Klein, T. W. A check on hypothetical personality structures and their theoretical interpretation at 14-16 years in T-data. *British Journal of Psychology*, 1975, *66*, 131-151.

Cattell, R. B. & Kline, P. *The scientific analysis of personality and motivation*. New York: Academic Press, 1977.

Cattell, R. B., Korth, B., & Bolz, C. R. Behavioral types in purebred dogs objectively determined by Taxonome. *Behavioral Genetics*, 1973, *3*, 205-216.

Cattell, R. B. & Krug, S. E. A test of the trait-view theory of distortion in measurement of personality questionnaire. *Educational and Psychological Measurement*, 1971, *31*, 721-734.

Cattell, R. B., & Luborsky, L. B. P-technique demonstrated as a new clinical method for determining personality and symptom structure. *Journal of General Psychology*, 1950, *42*, 3-24.

Cattell, R. B., Maxwell, E. F., Light, B. H., & Unger, M. P. The objective measurement of attitudes. *British Journal of Psychology*, 1949, *40*, 81-90.

Cattell, R. B., Mck., J., & Farrand, L. Physical and mental measurements of the students of Columbia University. *Psychological Review*, 1896, *3*, 618-647.

Cattell, R. B., McGill, J. C., Lawlis, G. F., & McGraw, P. Experimental check on the theory of motivational components, duplicator in two interest areas. *Multivariate Experimental Clinical Research*, 1979, *4*(1 & 2), 33-52.

Cattell, R. B., & McKeen, J. Mental tests and measurements. *Mind*, 1890, *15*, 373-380.

Cattell, R. B., & McMichael, R. E. Clinical diagnosis by the IPAT Music Preference Test. *Journal of Consulting Psychology*, 1960, *24*, 333-341.

Cattell, R. B., & Nesselroade, J. R. Likeness and completeness theories examined by Sixteen Personality Factor measures on stably and unstably married couples. *Journal of Personality and Social Psychology*, 1967, 7, 351-361.

Cattell, R. B., & Nichols, K. E. An improved definition, from 10 researches, of second-order personality factors in Q data (with cross-cultural checks). *Journal of Social Psychology*, 1972, *86*, 187-203.

Cattell, R. B., & Peterson, D. R. Personality structure in 4-5-year-olds, by factoring observed, time-sampled behavior. *Rassegna di Psicologia Generale e Clinica*, 1958, *3*, 3-21.

Cattell, R. B., Pichot, P., Rennes, P. Constance interculturelle des facteurs de personalité mesuré par le teste 16 P.F. II Comparaison franco-americaine. *Revue de Psychologie Applequée*, 1961, *11*, 165-196.

Cattell, R. B., Pierson, G., & Finkbeiner, C. Alignment of personality source traits from questionnaires and observer ratings: The theory of instrument-free patterns. *Multivariate Experimental Clinical Research*, 1976, *2*(2), 63-88.

Cattell, R. B., Price, P. L., & Patrick, S. V. Diagnosis of clinical depression on four source trait dimensions—U.I. 19, U.I. 20, U.I. 25, and U.I. 30—from the O-A Kit. *Journal of Clinical Psychology*, 1981, *37*, 4-11.

Cattell, R. B., & Radcliffe, J. A. Reliabilities and validities of simple and extended weighted and buffered unifactor scales. *British Journal of Statistical Psychology*, 1962, *15*, 113-128.

Cattell, R. B., Radcliffe, J. A., & Sweney, A. B. The nature and measurement of components of motivation. *Psychological Monographs*, 1963, *68*, 49-211.

Cattell, R. B., & Raymond, J. S. The spectrad model for attribution research: An extension of trait view theory. *Interdisciplinaria*, 1982, *3*, 135-154.

Cattell, R. B., & Rickels, K. Diagnostic power of IPAT objective anxiety neuroticism tests. *Archives of General Psychiatry*, 1964, *11*, 459-465.

Cattell, R. B., Rickels, K., Weise, C., Gray, B., & Yee, R. The effects of psychotherapy upon measured anxiety and regression. *American Journal of Psychotherapy*, 1966, *20*, 261-269.

Cattell, R. B., & Saunders, D. R. Beitrage zur Faktoren-Analyse der Personlichkeit. *Zeitschrift für Experimentelle und Angewandte Psychologie*, 1954, *2*, 325-357.

Cattell, R. B., & Scheier, I. H. Personality measurement in applied psychology as illustrated by the 16 Personality Factor Test. *Revista de Psicologia Normal e Patalogica*, 1956, *9*, 42-58.

Cattell, R. B., & Scheier, I. *The meaning and measurement of neuroticism and anxiety.* New York: Ronald, 1961.

Cattell, R. B., Schiff, H., & Baggaley, A. Psychiatric screening of flying personnel: Prediction of training criteria by objective personality factors and development of the seven factor personality test. Report No. 10, Contract No. AF 33(038)-19569, Project No. 21-0202-0007, Randolph Field, TX: USAF School of Aviation Medicine, 1953.

Cattell, R. B., Schmidt, L. R., & Bjerstedt, A. Clinical diagnosis by the objective-analytic personality batteries. *Journal of Clinical Psychology Monograph Supplements*, 1972, *34*, 239-312.

Cattell, R. B., Schmidt, L. R., & Pawlik, K. Cross-cultural comparison (USA, Japan, Austria) of the personality structures of 10- to 14-year-olds in objective tests. *Social Behavior and Personality*, 1973, *1*(2), 182-211.

Cattell, R. B., Schroeder, G., & Wagner, A. Verification of the structure of the 16 P.F. questionnaire in German. *Psychologische Forschung*, 1969, *32*, 369-386.

Cattell, R. B., & Schuerger, J. *The O-A (Objective-Analytic) Personality Battery.* Champaign, IL: IPAT, 1976.

Cattell, R. B., & Schuerger, J. M. *Personality theory in action: Handbook for the Objective-Analytic (O-A) Test Kit.* Champaign, IL: IPAT, 1978.

Cattell, R. B., Schuerger, J. M., Klein, T., & Finkbeiner, C. A definitive large-sample factoring of personality structure in objective measures, as a basis for the high school objective analytic battery. *Journal of Research in Personality*, 1976, *10*, 22-41.

Cattell, R. B., Sealy, A. P., & Sweney, A. B. What can personality and motivation source trait measurements add to the prediction of school achievement? *British Journal of Educational Psychology*, 1966, *36*, 280-295.

Cattell, R. B., Seitz, W. & Rausche, A. Zur konstanz der personlichkeitsfaktoren von Kindern gemessen duren questionnaire Q-datan. *Zeitschrift für Experimentelle und Angewandte Psychologie,* 1971, *18*, 513-524.

Cattell, R. B., & Sells, S. *The Clinical Analysis Questionnaire (CAQ).* Champaign, IL: IPAT, 1974.

Cattell, R. B., Shrader, R. R., & Barton, K. The definition and mesurement of anxiety as a trait and a state in the 12-17 year range. *British Journal of Social and Clinical Psychology*, 1974, *13*, 173-182.

Cattell, R. B., & Stice, C. R. Four formulae for selecting leaders on the basis of personality. *Human Relations*, 1954, *7*, 493-507.

Cattell, R. B., & Stice, G. F. *The behavior of small groups.* Champaign, IL: IPAT, 1960.

Cattell, R. B., & Stice, G. F. *The dimensions of groups and their relations to the behavior of members.* Champaign, IL: IPAT, 1953. Republished Ann Arbor, MI: University of Michigan, Microfilms International, 1976.

Cattell, R. B., Stice, G. F., & Kristy, N. F. A first approximation of nature-nurture ratios for eleven primary personality factors in objective tests. *Journal of Abnormal and Social Psychology*, 1957, *54*, 143-159.

Cattell, R. B., & Sweney, A. B. Components measurable in manifestations of mental conflicts. *Journal of Abnormal and Social Psychology*, 1964, *68*, 479-490.

Cattell, R. B., Sweney, A. B., & Radcliffe, J. A. The objective measurement of motivation structure in children. *Journal of Clinical Psychology*, 1960, *16*, 227-232.

Cattell, R. B. & Tatro, D. F. The personality factors, objectively measured, that distinguish psychotics from normals. *Behavior Research & Therapy*, 1966, *4*, 39-51.

Cattell, R. B., & Tollefson, D. *Humor test of personality*. Champaign, IL: IPAT, 1967.

Cattell, R. B. & Tsujioka, B. The importance of factor trueness and validity, versus homogeneity and orthogonality in test scales. *Educational & Psychological Measurement*, 1964, *24*, 3-30.

Cattell, R. B., & Warburton, F. W. *Objective personality and motivation tests: A theoretical introduction and practical compendium*. Champaign, IL: University of Illinois Press, 1967.

Cattell, R. B., & Wenig, P. Dynamic and cognitive factors controlling misperception. *Journal of Abnormal and Social Psychology*, 1952, *47*, 797, 809.

Cattell, R. B., & Williams, H. F. V. M. P-technique: A new statistical device for analyzing functional unities in the intact organism. *British Journal of Preventative Social Medicine*, 1953, *7*, 141-153.

Cattell, R. B., & Wispe, L. G. The dimensions of syntality in small groups. *Journal of Social Psychology*, 1948, *28*, 57-78.

Cattell, R. B., Woliver, R. E., & Graham, R. K. The relations of syntality dimensions of modern national cultures to the personality dimensions of their populations. *International Journal of Intercultural Relations*, 1980, *4*, 15-41.

Chambers, J. A. Relating personality and biographical factors to scientific creativity. *Psychological Monographs*, 1964, *78*, 584.

Chang, B. H. Selected psychological and somatic variables in asthmatic children. *Dissertation Abstracts International*, 1976, *36*(11-B), 5783-5784.

Chung, K. H. *Motivational theories and practices*. Columbus, OH: Grid, 1977.

Clyde, D. J. *Clyde Mood Scale*. Bethesda, MD: National Institute of Mental Health, 1958.

Cohen, D. B. Effects of personality and presleep mood on dream recall. *Journal of Abnormal Psychology*, 1974, *83*(2), 151-156.

Cohen, J. The factorial structure of the WAIS between early adulthood and old age. *Journal of Consulting Psychology*, 1957, *21*, 283-290.

Cohen, J., & Streuning, E. L. Factors underlying opinions about mental illness in the personnel of two large mental hospitals. *American Psychologist*, 1959, *14*, 339.

Cohen, J., & Streuning, E. L. Opinions about mental illness in the personnel of two large mental hospitals. *Journal of Abnormal and Social Psychology*, 1962, *64*, 349-360.

Cohen, J., & Streuning, E. L. Opinions about mental illness: Mental hospital occupational profiles and profile clusters. *Psychological Reports*, 1963, *12*, 111-124.

Cole, N. S. Bias in testing. *American Psychologist*, 1981, *36*, 1067-1077.

Coleman, W., & Cureton, E. E. Intelligence and achievement: The "jangle fallacy" again. *Educational and Psychological Measurement*, 1954, *14*, 347-351.

Colwill, N. L., & Lips, H. M. Masculinity, femininity, & androgeny: What have you done for us lately. In H. M. Lips & N. L. Colwill (Eds.), *The psychology of sex differences*. Englewood Cliffs, NJ: Prentice-Hall, 1978.

Comrey, A. L. *Manual for Comrey Personality Scales*. San Diego: E.J.Y.S. 1970.

Constantinople, A. Masculinity-femininity: An exception to a famous dictum? *Psychological Bulletin*, 1973, *80*, 389-407.

Cooper, M., Boss, M., & Keith, V. Personality factors as predictors of general and differential performance in high school. *Multivariate Experimental Clinical Research*, 1974, *1*, 46-57.

Coulter, M. A., & Cattell, R. B. Principles of behavioral tendency and the mathematical basis of the Taxonome Computer Program. *British Journal of Mathematical and Statistical Psychology*, 1966, *19*, 237-269.

Cox, R. C., & Sterrett, B. G. A model for increasing the meaning of standardized test scores. *Journal of Educational Measurement*, 1970, *7*, 227-228.

Crane, D. P. *Personnel: The management of human resources* (2nd ed.). Belmont, CA: 1979.

Crawford, C. B., & Nirmal, B. A multivariate study of measures of creativity, achievement, motivation, and intelligence in secondary school students. *Canadian Journal of Behavioural Science*, 1976, *8*, 189-201.

Creager, J. A. General resolution of correlation matrices into components and its utilization in multiple and partial regression. *Psychometrika*, 1958, *23*, 1-8.

Cronbach, L. J. Coefficient alpha and the internal structure of tests. *Psychometrika*, 1951, *16*, 297-334.

Cronbach, L. J. The two disciplines of scientific psychology. *American Psychology*, 1957, *12*, 671-684.

Cronbach, L. J. *Essentials of psychological testing* (2nd ed.). New York: Harper, 1960.

Cronbach, L. J. *Essentials of psychological testing* (3rd ed.). New York: Harper & Brothers, 1970.

Cronbach, L. J. *Designing evaluations for educational and social programs*. San Francisco, CA: Jossey-Bass, 1982.

Cronbach, L. J., & Furby, L. How should we measure "change"—Or should we? *Psychological Bulletin*, 1970, *74*, 60-80.

Cronbach, L., Gleser, G. C., Nanda, H., & Rajaratnam, N. *The dependability of behavioral measurements: Theory of generalizability for scores and profiles*. New York: Wiley, 1972.

Cronbach, L. J., & Snow, R. E. *Aptitudes and instructional methods: A handbook of research on interactions*. New York: Irvington, 1977.

Cronbach, L. J., & Snow, R. E. *Aptitudes and instructional methods* (2nd ed.). New York: Irvington, 1981.

Cross, K. P. Determination of the ergic structure of

common attitudes by P-technique. Unpublished master's thesis, University of Illinois at Urbana, 1951.

Cross, P. G., Cattell, R. B., & Butcher, H. J. The personality pattern of creative artists. *British Journal of Educational Psychology*, 1967, *37*, 292-299.

Cruce, M. A., & Paris-Panzera, E. Psychodynamic effects of a film projection to institutionalized elderly patients. *Archivio di Psicologia, Neurologia e Psichiatria*, 1977, *38*(3), 331-349.

Csikszentmihalyi, M., & Getzels, J. W. The personality of young artists: An empirical and theoretical exploration. *British Journal of Psychology*, 1973, *64*, 91-104.

Cureton, T. K. *Physical fitness appraisal and guidance.* St. Louis: Mosby, 1947.

Curran, J. The dimensions of state change in Q data, and chain P-technique on 20 women. Unpublished master's thesis, University of Illinois, 1968.

Curran, J. P., & Cattell, R. B. *Manual for the Eight State Questionnaire.* Champaign, IL: IPAT, 1976.

Darbes, A. Development of a Q-rating scale of ward behavior of hospitalized psychiatric patients. *American Psychologist*, 1954, *9*, 354.

Darrow, C. W., & Heath, L. L. Reaction tendencies relating to personality. In K. S. Lashley (Ed.), *Studies in the dynamics of behavior.* Chicago: University of Chicago Press, 1932.

Davidson, A. R., Jaccard, J. J., Triandis, H. C., Morales, M. L., & Diaz-Guerrero, R. Cross-cultural model testing: Toward a solution of the etic-emic dilemma. *International Journal of Psychology*, 1976, *11*, 1-13.

Dawes, R. M. The robust beauty of improper linear models in decision-making. *American Psychologist*, 1979, *34*, 571-582.

Deci, E. I. *Intrinsic motivation.* New York: Plenum, 1975.

Dee-Burnett, R., Johns, E. R., & Krug, S. E. *Law Enforcement, Assessment and Development Report (LEADR) Manual.* Champaign, IL: IPAT, 1981.

DeFries, J. C., Corley, R. P., Johnson, R. C., Vandenberg, S. G., & Wilson, J. R. Sex-by-generation and ethnic group-by-generation interactions in the Hawaii Family Study of Cognition. *Behavior Genetics*, 1982, *12*, 223-230.

Degan, J. W. *Dimensions of functional psychosis.* Richmond, VA: Byrd, 1962.

Delhees, K. H. Conflict measured by the dynamic calculus model, and its applicability in clinical practice. *Multivariate Behavioral Research,* 1968, Special Issue, 73-91.

Delhees, K. H. *Motivation und verhalten.* Munchen: Kindler, 1975.

Delhees, K. H., & Cattell, R. B. Obtaining 16P.F. scores from the MMPI and MMPI scores from the 16P.F. *Journal of Projective Techniques and Personality Assessment*, 1970, *34*(3), 251-255.

Delhees, K. H., & Cattell, R. B. Differences of personality factors, by the O-A Battery, in par-

anoid and non-paranoid schizophrenics, manic-depressives, psychoneurotics, and the personality disorders. *Archiv fur Psychologie*, 1971, *123*, 35-48. (a)

Delhees, K. H., & Cattell, R. B. The dimensions of pathology: Proof of their projections beyond the normal 16 P.F. source traits. *Personality*, 1971, *2*, 149-173. (b)

Delhees, K. H., Cattell, R. B., & Sweney, A. B. The structure of parents' intrafamilial attitudes and sentiments measured by objective tests and a vector model. *Journal of Social Psychology*, 1970, *82*, 231-252.

DeWaele, J. P., & Harré, R. Autobiography as a psychological method. In G. P. Ginsburg (Ed.), *Emerging strategies in psychological research.* New York: Wiley, 1979.

DeYoung, G. E. Standards of decision regarding personality factors in questionnaires. *Canadian Journal of Behavioral Science*, 1972, *4*(3), 253-255.

DeYoung, G. E., & Fleischer, B. Motivational and personality trait relationships in mate selection. *Behavior Genetics*, 1976, *6*, 1-6.

Dielman, T. E., & Krug, S. E. Trait description and measurement in motivation and dynamic structure. In R. B. Cattell & R. M. Dreger (Eds.), *Handbook of modern personality theory.* New York: Halstead, 1977.

Dielman, T. E., Schuerger, J. M., & Cattell, R. B. Prediction of junior high school achievement from IQ and the objective-analytic personality factors U.I. 21, U.I. 23, U.I. 24, and U.I. 25. *Personality*, 1970, *1*(2), 145-152.

Dielman, T. E., Stiefel, G., & Cattell, R. B. A check on the factor structure of the opinions of mental illness scale. *Journal of Clinical Psychology*, 1973, *29*, 92-95.

Digman, J. M. Principal dimensions of child personality as inferred from teachers' judgments. *Child Development*, 1963, *34*, 43-60.

Digman, J. M. Child behavior ratings: Further evidence of a multifactor model of child personality. *Child Development*, 1965, *25*, 787-799.

Digman, J. M. The structure of child personality as seen in behavior ratings. In R. M. Dreger (Ed.), *Multivariate personality research.* Baton Rouge, LA: Claitor's Publishing, 1972.

Digman, J. M., & Takemoto-Chock, N. K. Factors in the natural language of personality: Reanalysis, comparison, and interpretation of six major studies. *Multivariate Behavioral Research*, 1981, *16*, 149-170.

Dillon, J. T. Cognitive correspondence between question/statement and response. *American Educational Research Journal*, 1982, *19*, 540-551.

Dixon, L. K., & Johnson, R. C. *The roots of individuality.* Monterey, CA: Brooks/Cole, 1980.

Dollard, J., & Miller, N. E. *Personality and psychotherapy.* New York: McGraw-Hill, 1950.

Dreger, R. M. (Ed.). *Multivariate personality research: Contributions in honor of Raymond B. Cattell.* Baton Rouge: Claitor, 1972.

Dreger, R. M. Development of structural changes in the child's personality. In R. B. Cattell & R. M. Dreger (Eds.), *Handbook of modern per-*

sonality theory. New York: Wiley, 1977.

Drevdahl, J. E., & Cattell, R. B. Personality and creativity in artists and writers. *Journal of Clinical Psychology*, 1958, *14*, 107-111.

Duffy, E. The psychological significance of the concept of "arousal" or "activation." *Psychological Review*, 1957, *64*, 265-275.

Duffy, E. *Activation and behavior.* New York: Wiley, 1962.

Dunlap, J. W. & Kurtz, A. K. *Handbook of statistical nomographs, tables and formulas.* New York: World Book, 1932.

Dunnette, M. D. *Personnel selection and placement.* Belmont, CA: Wadsworth, 1966.

Dunnette, M. D. Abilities, aptitudes, and skills. In M. D. Dunnette (Ed.), *Handbook of industrial and organizational psychology.* Chicago: Rand-McNally, 1976, 473-520.

Dunnette, M. D., & Borman, W. D. Personnel selection and classification systems. *Annual Review of Psychology*, 1967, *3*, 477-525.

Dwyer, P.S. The evaluation of multiple and partial correlation coefficients from the factorial matrix. *Psychometrika*, 1940, *5*, 211-232.

Ebel, R. L. Measurement and the teacher. *Educational Leadership*, 1962, *20*, 20-24.

Ebel, R. L. *Measuring educational achievement.* Englewood Cliffs, NJ: Prentice-Hall, 1965.

Ebel, R. L. The value of internal consistency in classroom examinations. *Journal of Educational Measurement*, 1968, *5*, 71-73.

Ebel, R. L. The case for norm-referenced measurements. *Educational Researcher*, 1978, *7*, 3-5.

Ebel, R. *Essentials of educational measurement* (3rd ed.). Englewood Cliffs, NJ: Prentice-Hall, 1979.

Eber, H. W. Computer interpretation of the 16P.F. test. Paper presented to the American Psychological Association, Los Angeles, 1964.

Eber, H. W. Personality factors in preventive medicine and health maintenance. In S. E. Krug (Ed.), *Psychological assessment in medicine.* Champaign, IL: IPAT, 1977.

Eber, H. W., Cattell, R. B., & Delhees, K. H. Allocation of variance by computer synthesis programs: A strategy for improved use of multifactor scales. *Educational and Psychological Measurements*, 1976.

Edward, A. J. *Individual mental testing. II. Measurement.* New York: Wiley, 1972.

Edwards, A. C. *The Edwards Personal Preference Schedule.* New York: Psychological Corporation, 1954.

Edwards, A. L. *The social desirability variable in personality assessment and research.* New York: Dryden, 1957.

Eggleston, E. *The Hoosier schoolmaster.* New York: Grosset & Dunlap, 1899.

Ekstrom, R. B., French, J. W., & Harman, H. H. *Kit of factor-referenced cognitive tests.* Princeton, NJ: Educational Testing Service, 1976.

Eliot, J., & Smith, J. M. *An international directory of spatial tests.* Atlantic Highlands, NJ: Humanities Press, 1984.

Endler, N. S., & Hunt, J. McV. Sources of behavior variance as measured by the S-R inventory of anxiousness. *Psychological Bulletin*, 1966, *65*, 336-346.

Endler, N. S., & Hunt, J. McV. Generalizability of contributions from sources of variance in S-R inventories of anxiousness. *Journal of Personality*, 1969, *37*, 1-24.

Endler, N. S., & Magnusson, D. Toward an interactional psychology of personality. *Psychological Bulletin*, 1976, *83*, 956-974.

Englehart, M. D. What to look for in a review of an achievement test. *Personnel and Guidance Journal*, 1964, *42*, 616-619.

Epstein, S. The stability of behavior: I. On predicting most of the people much of the time. *Journal of Personality and Social Psychology*, 1979, *37*, 1007-1126.

Epstein, S. The stability of behavior: II. Implications for psychological research. *American Psychologist*, 1980, *35*, 790-806.

Ertl, J. P. Evoked potentials and intelligence. *Revue d'Université d'Ottawa*, 1966, *36*, 599-607.

Eysenck, H. J. An experimental analysis of five tests of appreciation of humor. *Educational and Psychological Measurement*, 1943, *3*, 191-214.

Eysenck, H. J. *The dimensions of personality.* London: Kegan Paul, 1947.

Eysenck, H. J. The effects of psychotherapy: An evaluation. *Journal of Consulting Psychology*, 1952, *16*, 319-324.

Eysenck, H. J. *Uses and abuses of psychology.* Harmondsworth, England: Penguin, 1953.

Eysenck, H. J. *The psychology of politics.* London: Routledge and Kegan Paul, 1954.

Eysenck, H. J. *The structure of human personality.* London: Methuen, 1960.

Eysenck, H. J. *Handbook of abnormal psychology.* New York: Basic Books, 1961.

Eysenck, H. J. *Experiments in motivation.* New York: Macmillan, 1964.

Eysenck, H. J. *The structure of human personality* (2nd ed.). London: Methuen, 1965.

Eysenck, H. J. *The effects of psychotherapy.* New York: International Science Press, 1966.

Eysenck, H. J. *Sense and nonsense in psychology.* Harmondsworth, England: Penguin, 1968.

Eysenck, H. J. *Readings in introversion and extroversion.* London: Staples, 1970.

Eysenck, H. J. An exercise in megasilliness. *American Psychologist*, 1978, *33*, 517.

Eysenck, H. J. Sir Cyril Burt and the inheritance of the I.Q. *New Zealand Psychologist*, 1978, *7*(11), 8-10. (a)

Eysenck, H. J. The general factor in aesthetic judgments. *British Journal of Psychology*, 1980, *31*, 98-102.

Eysenck, H. J. & Eysenck, S. B. G. *Personality structure and measurement.* San Diego: Knapp, 1969.

Eysenck, H. J., & Kamin, L. *The intelligence controversy.* New York: Wiley, 1981.

Eysenck, H. J., & Wilson, G. D. *The psychological basis of ideology.* Lancaster, England: MTP Press, St. Leonard's House, 1978.

Feo, A. Relationship of the Objective-Analytic Test Battery (O-A) with academic success. Unpublished master's thesis, Cleveland State University, 1980.

Ferguson, G. A. On learning and human ability. *Canadian Journal of Psychology*, 1954, *8*, 95-111.

Ferguson, G. A. On transfer and the abilities of man. *Canadian Journal of Psychology*, 1956, *10*, 121-131.

Fersching, A., & Kury, H. Psychological studies of effects of a four-week treatment. *Zeitschrift für Klinische Psychologie*, 1979, *8*(1), 1-16.

Festinger, L. *A theory of cognitive dissonance.* Evanston, IL: Peterson, 1957.

Fiedler, F. *Leader attitudes and group effectiveness.* Urbana: University of Illinois Press, 1958.

Finch, F. H. Enrollment increases and changes in the mental level of the high school population. *Applied Psychology Monographs,* 1946, *10,* 75.

Finch, F. L. A taxonomy for competency testing programs. In R. M. Jaeger & C. K. Tittle (Eds.), *Minimum competency testing: Motives, models, measures, and consequences.* Berkeley, CA: McCutchan, 1980.

Finney, J. C. Programmed interpretation of MMPI and CPI. *Archives of General Psychiatry,* 1966, *15*, 75-81.

Fishbein, M. Attitude and the prediction of behavior. In M. Fishbein (Ed.), *Readings in attitude theory and measurement.* New York: Wiley, 1967.

Fishbein, M., & Ajzen, I. Attitudes towards objects as predictors of single and multiple behavioral criteria. *Psychological Review*, 1974, *81*, 59-74.

Fishbein, M., & Ajzen, I. *Belief, attitude, intention and behavior.* Reading, MA: Addison-Wesley, 1975.

Fiske, D. W. & Maddi, S. R. (Eds.). *Functions of varied experience.* Homewood: Dorsey, 1961.

Flanagan, J. C. *The aviation psychology program in the Army Air Forces.* Washington, D.C.: U.S. Government Printing Office, 1948.

Flaugher, R. C. The many definitions of test bias. *American Psychologist*, 1978, *33*, 671-679.

Fleishman, E. A. On the relation between abilities, learning, and human performance. *American Psychologist*, 1972, *27*, 1017-1032.

Fowler, H. *Curiosity and exploratory behavior.* New York: Macmillan, 1965.

Fowler, R. D. Automated interpretation of personality test data. In J. N. Butcher (Ed.), *MMPI: Research development and clinical applications.* New York: McGraw-Hill, 1969.

Frankignoul, M., & Juchrges, J. Psychophysiological aspects of emotional stress. I. Use of an adjective list for university examinations. *Acta Psychiatrica Belgica*, 1978, *78*(4), 646-657.

Frederiksen, N., Jensen, O., & Beaton, A. E. *Prediction of organizational behavior.* New York: Pergamon, 1972.

French, J. W. The description of aptitude and achievement tests in terms of rotated factors. *Psychological Monographs,* 1951, 5.

French, J. W. *The description of personality measurements in terms of rotated factors.* Princeton, NJ: Educational Testing Service, 1953.

Freud, A. *The ego and methods of defense.* London: Hogarth Press, 1937.

Freud, A. *The writings of Anna Freud, Vol. II* (rev. ed.). New York: International Universities Press, 1966.

Freud, S. The ego and the id. Translated by J. Riviere. *Collected papers.* London: Hogarth Press, 1924.

Freud, S. *Wit and its relation to the unconscious.* New York: Modern Library, 1938.

Freud, S. An outline of psychoanalysis. *Standard edition,* (Vol. 23). London: Hogarth Press, 1940.

Freud, S. Instincts and their vicissitudes. In J. Riviere (Ed. and Trans.), *A collection of papers of Sigmund Freud* (Vol. I). London: Hogarth Press, 1949. (Original work published 1915)

Freud, S. Civilization and its discontents. In *Standard edition* (Vol. 21). London: Hogarth Press, 1961.

Freyd, M. Measurement in vocational selection: An outline of research procedure. *Journal of Personnel Research,* 1923, *2*, 215-249, 268-284, 377-385.

Friedmann, J. Performance and mood during and after gradual sleep reduction. *Psychophysiology*, 1977, *14*(3), 245-250.

Fromm-Reichmann, F. *Principles of intensive psychotherapy.* Chicago: University of Chicago Press, 1950.

Fryer, D. Occupational intelligence levels. *School and Society*, 1922, *16*, 273-277.

Fuller, A. R. A study of the relationship between personality variables, sex, retention interval, arousal, and observational and paired associate learning. *Dissertation Abstracts International*, 1976, *37*(2-B), 1033.

Galton, F. *Inquiries into human faculty.* London: J-M. Dent, 1883.

Ganopole, S. J. Using performance and preference data in setting standards for minimum competency assessment programs. In R. M. Jaeger & C. K. Tittle (Eds.), *Minimum competency testing: Motives, models, measures, and consequences.* Berkeley, CA: McCutchan, 1980.

Gekoski, N., & Schwartz, S. *Manual for the Sales Attitude Checklist.* Chicago: Science Research Associates, 1960.

Getzels, J. W., & Jackson, P. W. *Creativity and intelligence.* New York: Wiley, 1962.

Ghiselli, E. E. Moderating effects and differential reliability and validity. *Journal of Applied Psychology*, 1963, *47*, 81-86.

Ghiselli, E. E. *The validity of occupational aptitude tests.* New York: Wiley, 1966.

Ghiselli, E. E. The validity of aptitude tests in personnel selection. *Personnel Psychology*, 1973, *26*, 461-477.

Gillis, J. S., & Lee, D. C. Second-order relations between different modalities of personality trait organization. *Multivariate Experimental Clinical Research*, 1978, *3*, 241-248.

Gilmer, B. V. H., & Deci, E. L. *Industrial and organizational psychology* (4th ed.). New York: McGraw-Hill, 1977.

Gittinger, J. W. *Personality assessment system* (2 Vols.) Washington, D.C.: Psychological Assessment Associates, 1964.

Glaser, R. Instructional technology and the measurement of learning outcomes: Some questions. *American Psychologist*, 1963, *18*, 519-521.

Glaser, R., & Bond, L. Testing: Concepts, policy, practice, and research. *American Psychologist*, 1981, *36*, 997-1000.

Glass, G. V. Standards and criteria. *Journal of Educational Measurement*, 1978, *15*(4), 237-261.

Goldberg, L. R. Man vs. model of man: A rationale, plus some evidence for a method of improving on clinical inference. *Psychological Bulletin*, 1970, *73*, 422-432.

Goldberg, L. R. Parameters of personality inventory construction and utilization: A comparison of prediction strategies and tactics. *Multivariate Behavioral Research Monographs*, 1972, *72*, 1-59. (a)

Goldberg, L. R. Review of the CPI. In O. K. Buros (Ed.), *Seventh mental measurements yearbook*. Highland Park, NJ: Gryphon, 1972, 94-96, 151-153. (b)

Golden, C. J. *Clinical interpretation of objective psychological tests*. New York: Grune & Stratton, 1979.

Golden, C. J., Hammeke, T. A., & Purisch, A. D. *Luria-Nebraska Neurological Battery: Manual*. Los Angeles: Western Psychological Services, 1980.

Goodrich, B. W. Quantification of the severity of overt psychiatric symptoms. *American Journal of Psychiatry*, 1953, *110*, 334-341.

Gordon, E. W. Three major movements: Relation to educational theory and practice. In W. B. Schrader (Ed.), *New directions for testing and measurement: Measuring achievement: Progress over a decade*. San Francisco: Jossey-Bass, 1980.

Gordon, E. W., & Terrell, M. D. The changed social context of testing. *American Psychologist*, 1981, *36*, 1167-1171.

Gorsuch, R. L. *The clarification of some superego factors*. Unpublished doctoral dissertation, University of Illinois, 1965.

Gorsuch, R. L. Review of *Beliefs, attitudes, and values* by Milton Rokeach. *American Sociological Review*, 1969, *34*, 267-268.

Gorsuch, R. L. Rokeach's approach to value system and social compassion. *Review of Religious Research*, 1970, *11*, 139-143.

Gorsuch, R. L. Value conflict in the school setting. ERIC document files (Ed. 057 410), 1973.

Gorsuch, R. L. *Review of Understanding human values* by Milton Rokeach. *Journal for the Scientific Study of Religion*, 1980, *19*, 316-318.

Gorsuch, R. L. Measurement: The boon and bane of investigating religion. *American Psychologist*, 1984, *39*(3), 228-236.

Gorsuch, R. L., & Aleshire, D. O. Christian faith and ethnic prejudice: A review and interpretation of research. *Journal for the Scientific Study of Religion*, 1974, *13*, 281-307.

Gorsuch, R. L., & McFarland, S. Single versus multiple item scales for measuring religious values. *Journal for the Scientific Study of Religion*, 1972, *11*, 53-64.

Gorsuch, R. L., & Ortberg, J. Moral obligation and attitudes: Their relation to behavioral intentions. *Journal of Personality and Social Psychology*, 1983, *44*(5), 1025-1028.

Gough, H. G., & Heilbrun, A. B., Jr. *The adjective check list manual*. Palo Alto, CA: Consulting Psychologist Press, 1965.

Goulet, L. R. Anxiety and verbal learning. *Psychological Bulletin*, 1968, *69*, 239-247.

Graffam, D. T. Dickinson College changes personality. *The Dickinson Alumnus*, 1967, *44*(1), 2-7.

Graham, F. K., & Kendall, B. S. Memory-For-Designs Test: Revised general manual. *Perceptual and Motor Skills, Monograph Supplement*, No. 2-VIII, 1960, *11(2)*, 147-188.

Green, D. R. (Ed.). *The aptitude-achievement distinction: Proceedings of the Second CTB/McGraw-Hill Conference on Issues in Educational Measurement*. New York: McGraw-Hill, 1974.

Green, S. B., Lissity, R. W., & Mulaik, S. A. Limitations of coefficient alpha as an index of unidimensionality. *Education and Psychological Measurement*, 1977, *37*, 827-889.

Gronlund, N. E. *Measurement and evaluation in teaching* (4th ed.). New York: Macmillan, 1981.

Gross, M. L. *The brain watchers*. New York: The Random House, 1962.

Guertin, W. H., Ladd, C. E., Frank, G. H., Rabin, A. I., & Hiester, D. S. Research with the WAIS: 1960-1965. *Psychological Bulletin*, 1966, *66*, 385-409.

Guetzkow, H. Building models about small groups. In R. Young (Ed.), *Approaches to the study of political science*. Evanston, IL: Northwestern University Press, 1958.

Guilford, J. P. *Manual for the Guilford-Zimmerman Aptitude Survey*. Beverly Hills, CA: Sheridan Supply, 1948.

Guilford, J. P. *Personality*. New York: McGraw-Hill, 1959.

Guilford, J. P. *Fundamental statistics in psychology and education* (4th ed.). New York: McGraw-Hill, 1965.

Guilford, J. P. *Nature of human intelligence*. New York: McGraw-Hill, 1967.

Guilford, J. P. *Nature of human intelligence* (2nd ed.). New York: McGraw-Hill, 1968.

Guilford, J. P. Thurstone's primary mental abilities and structure-of-intellect abilities. *Psychological Bulletin*, 1972, *77*(2), 129-143.

Guilford, J. P. Factors of personality. *Psychological Bulletin*, 1975, *82*, 802-814.

Guilford, J. P., & Hoepfner, R. *The analysis of intelligence*. New York: McGraw-Hill, 1971.

Guilford, J. P., & Michael, W. B. Approaches to univocal factor scores. *Psychometrika*, 1948, *13*, 1-22.

Guilford, J. P., & Zimmerman, W. S. *The Guilford-Zimmerman temperament survey*. Beverly Hills, CA: Sheridan Supply, 1949.

Guion, R. M. Recruiting, selection, and job placement, in M. D. Dunnette (Ed.), *Handbook of industrial and organizational psychology*. Chicago: Rand McNally, 1976.

Gulliksen, H. *Theory of mental tests.* New York: Wiley, 1930.

Gunther, M. D. Review of the EPPS. In O. K. Buros (Ed.), *Eighth mental measurements yearbook.* Highland Park, NJ: Gryphon, 1978.

Guthrie, E. R. *The psychology of learning.* New York: Harper, 1935.

Guttman, L. Multiple rectilinear prediction and the resolution into component, I. *Psychometrika*, 1940, *5*, 75-100.

Guttman, L. General theory and methods for matrix factoring. *Psychometrika*, 1944, *9*, 1-16. (a)

Guttman, L. A basis for scaling qualitative data. *American Sociological Review*, 1944, *44*, 139-150. (b)

Guttman, L. A new approach to factor analysis. In P. F. Lazarsfeld (Ed.), *Mathematical thinking in the social sciences.* New York: Columbia University Press, 1953.

Guttman, L. Some necessary conditions for common factor analysis. *Psychometrika*, 1954, *19*, 149-156.

Guttman, L. Metricizing rank ordered or unordered data for a linear factor analysis. *Sankhya*, 1959, *21*, 257-268.

Guttman, L. Integration of test design and analysis. *Proceedings of the 1969 Invitational Conference on Testing Problems.* Princeton, NJ: Educational Testing Service, 1969.

Haggard, E. A. *Intraclass correlation and the analysis of variance.* New York: Dryden, 1958.

Hakstian, A. R., & Bennet, R. W. Validity studies using the Comprehensive Abilities Battery: Academic achievement criteria. *Educational and Psychological Measurement*, 1977, *37*(2), 425-437.

Hakstian, A. R., & Cattell, R. B. The checking of primary ability structure on a broader basis of performance. *British Journal of Educational Psychology*, 1974, *44*, 140-154.

Hakstian, A. R., & Cattell, R. B. *The comprehensive ability battery: CAB.* Champaign, IL: IPAT, 1976.

Hakstian, A. R., & Cattell, R. B. Higher stratum ability structures on a basis of 20 primary abilities. *Journal of Educational Psychology*, 1978, *70*, 657-660.

Hakstian, A. R., & Gale, C. A. Validity studies using the Comprehensive Ability Battery (CAB): III. Performance in conjunction with personality and motivational traits. *Educational and Psychological Measurement*, 1979, *39*, 389-400.

Hall, J. F., & Kubric, J. L. The relationship between the measures of response strength. *Journal of Comparative Physiological Psychology*, 1952, *45*, 280-282.

Halstead, W. C. *Brain and intelligence.* Chicago: University of Chicago Press, 1947.

Hambleton, R. K. *Validity of criterion-referenced test score interpretations and standard setting methods.* Paper presented at the First Annual Johns Hopkins University National Symposium on Educational Research, Washington, D.C., October, 1978.

Hambleton, R. K., & Eignor, D. R. Competency test development, validation, and standard setting. In R. M. Jaeger & C. K. Tittle (Eds.), *Minimum competency testing: Motives, models, measures, and consequences.* Berkeley, CA: McCutchan, 1980.

Hambleton, R., Mills, C. N., & Simon, R. Determining the lengths for criterion-referenced tests. *Journal of Educational Measurement*, 1983, *20*(1), 27-28.

Hammond, S. B. Personality studied by rating of personality in the life situation. In R. B. Cattell & R. M. Dreger (Eds.), *Handbook of modern personality theory.* Washington, D.C.: Hemisphere, 1977.

Haney, W. Validity, vaudeville, and values: A short history of social concerns over standardized testing. *American Psychologist*, 1981, *36*, 1021-1034.

Harman, H. H. *Modern factor analysis* (2nd ed.). Chicago: University of Chicago Press, 1967.

Harman, H. H. *Modern factor analysis* (3rd ed.). Chicago: University of Chicago Press, 1976.

Harrell, T. W., & Harrell, M. S. Army General classification test scores for civilian occupations. *Educational and Psychological Measurement*, 1945, *5*, 229-240.

Harrington, L. P. The relation of physiological and social indices of activity level. In Q. McNemar & M. A. Merrill (Eds.), *Studies in personality: In honor of Lewis M. Terman.* Stanford, CA: Stanford University Press, 1942.

Harris, F. R., Wolf, M. M., & Baer, D. M. Effects of adult social reinforcement on child behavior. *Young Children*, 1964, *20*(1), 8-17.

Hartshorne, H., & May, M. A. *Studies in the nature of character. I. Studies in deceit.* New York: Macmillan, 1928.

Hathaway, R. R. & McKinley, J. C. *The manual for the Minnesota Multiphasic Personality Inventory.* New York: Psychological Corporation, 1951 (revised 1967).

Hathaway, R. R. & Meehl, P. *An atlas for the clinical use of the MMPI.* Minneapolis: University of Minnesota Press, 1951.

Hathaway, R. R., & Meehl, P. *The MMPI test handbook.* New York: Psychological Corporation, 1952.

Hathaway, R. R., & Monachesi, E. D. *Analyzing and predicting delinquency with the MMPI.* Minneapolis, MN: University of Minnesota Press, 1953.

Hayes-Roth, F., Longabaugh, R., & Ryback, R. The problem-oriented medical record and psychiatry. *British Journal of Psychiatry*, 1972, *27*, 121.

Haythorne, W. The influence of individual members on the characteristics of small groups. *Journal of Abnormal and Social Psychology*, 1953, *48*, 276-284.

Hebb, D. O. *The organization of behavior.* New York: Wiley, 1949.

Heilbrum, A. B. Review of the EPPS. In O. K. Buros (Ed.), *Seventh mental measurements yearbook.* Highland Park, NJ: Gryphon, 1972.

Hemphill, J. K., & Weste, C. M. The measurement of group dimensions. *Journal of Psychology*, 1950, *29*, 325-342.

Herrnstein, R. J. IQ testing and the media. *The Atlantic Monthly*, August 1982, *250*, 68-74.

Herzberg, F. *Work and the nature of man*. London: Staples Press, 1966.

Himmelweit, H. T., & Whitfield, J. W. Mean intelligence test scores on a random sample of occupations. *British Journal of Industrial Psychology*, 1949, *1*, 224-226.

Hine, J. R., Bass, B. M., Dawson, J. G., Wurster, C. R., & Dobbins, D. A. Measures of symptomatic changes in hospitalized psychiatric symptoms. *Diseases of the Nervous System*, 1957, *18*, 3-7.

Hinman, S., & Bolton, B. Motivational dynamics of disadvantaged women. *Psychology of Women Quarterly*, 1980, *5*(2), 255-275.

Hoffman, B. *The tyranny of testing*. New York: Crowell-Collier, 1962.

Holland, J. L. *The psychology of vocational choice*. Waltham, MA: Blaisell, 1966.

Holland, J. L. *Making vocational choices: A theory of careers*. Englewood Cliffs, NJ: Prentice-Hall, 1973.

Holland, J. L. *The self-directed search: Professional manual*. Palo Alto, CA: Consulting Psychologists Press, 1979.

Hopkins, K. D., & Stanley, J. C. *Educational and psychological measurement and evaluation* (6th ed.). Englewood Cliffs, NJ: Prentice-Hall, 1981.

Hopkins, T., Allen, L. C., & Schuerger, J. M. The relationship of Cattellian personality factors to academic achievement, as found in a longitudinal study and across studies. Princeton, NJ: Educational and Psychological Testing, 1983.

Horn, J. L. Equations representing combinations of components in scoring psychological variables. *Acta Psychologica*, 1963, *21*, 184-217. (a)

Horn, J. L. Second-order factors in questionnaire data. *Educational and Psychological Measurement*, 1963, *23*, 117-134. (b)

Horn, J. L. An empirical comparison of methods for estimating factor scores. *Educational and Psychological Measurement*, 1965, *25*, 313-322.

Horn, J. L. Organization of abilities in the development of intelligence. *Psychological Review*, 1968, *75*, 242-259.

Horn, J. L. On the internal consistency reliability of factors. *Multivariate Behavioral Research*, 1969, *4*, 115. (a)

Horn, J. L. The relationship between evoked potential recordings and intelligence test measurements. Paper presented at the International Conference of Society of Multivariate Experimental Psychology, Oxford University, 1969. (b)

Horn, J. L. Organization of data on life span development of human abilities. In L. R. Goulet & P. B. Baltes (Eds.), *Life-span developmental psychology*. New York: Academic Press, 1970.

Horn, J. L. State, trait and change dimensions of intelligence. *British Journal of Educational Psychology*, 1972, *82*, 159-185.

Horn, J. L. Human abilities, a review of research and theory in the early 1970s. *Annual Review of Psychology*, 1976, *27*, 437-485.

Horn, J. L. Personality and ability theory. In R. B. Cattell & R. M. Dreger (Eds.), *Handbook of modern personality theory*. Washington, D.C.: Hemisphere, 1977.

Horn, J. L. Multiple measurement theory and technology for diagnosing intellectual deficiencies of aging adults. In R. Smith (Ed.), *Drugs and Methods in C.V.D.* New York: Pergamon, 1981.

Horn, J. L., & Cattell, R. B. Age differences in primary mental abilities. *Journal of Gerontology*, 1966, *21*, 210-220.

Horn, J. L. & McArdle, J. J. Perspectives on mathematical-statistical model building. In L. W. Poon (Ed.), *Aging in the 1980s*. Washington, D.C.: American Psychological Association, 1980.

Horn, J. L. & Miller, W. C. Evidence on problems in estimating common factor scores. *Educational and Psychological Measurement*, 1966, *26*, 617-627.

Horn, J. L., & Stankow, L. Second order ability factors among auditory and visual primaries. Unpublished manuscript, 1979.

Horn, J. L., & Sweney, A. B. The dynamic calculus model for motivation and its use in understanding the individual case. In A. R. Mahrer (Ed.), *New approaches to personality classification*. New York: Columbia University Press, 1970.

Horst, P. Generalized canonical correlations and their application to experimental data. *Journal of Clinical Psychology*, 1961, Supplement, *14*, 331-347.

Horst, P. Generalized canonical correlations. *Journal of Clinical Psychology*, Monograph Supplement No. 4, 1962.

Horst, P. *Factor analysis of data matrices*. New York: Holt, Rinehart & Winston, 1965.

Horst, P. *Psychological measurement and predictions*. Belmont: Wadsworth, 1966.

Houpt, J. L., Gould, B. S., & Norris, F. H. Psychological characteristics of patients with amyotrophic lateral sclerosis. *Psychosomatic Medicine*, 1977, *39*(5), 299-303.

House, R. L., & Wahba, M. A. Expectancy theory in industrial and organizational psychology: An integrative model and a review of literature. Paper presented at the meetings of the American Psychological Association, Honolulu, Hawaii, 1972.

Howarth, E., & Browne, J. A. An item factor analysis of the 16P.F. Personality Questionnaire. *Personality: An International Journal*, 1971, *2*, 117-139.

Huffman, L. In R. B. Cattell, *Personality and motivation structures and measurement* (Chapter 4). New York: World Book, 1957.

Hughes, D. C., Keeling, B., & Tuck, B. F. Effects of

achievement expectations and handwriting quality on scoring essays. *Journal of Educational Measurement*, 1983, *20*(1), 65-70.

Hull, C. L. *Principles of behavior*. New York: Appleton-Century-Crofts, 1943.

Hull, C. L. *A behavior system*. New Haven: Yale University Press, 1952.

Hummel-Rossi, B. Aptitudes as predictors of achievement moderated by teacher effect. In P. Merrifield (Ed.), *New directions for testing and measurement (No. 12): Measuring human abilities*. San Francisco: Jossey-Bass, 1981.

Hundleby, J. D., Pawlik, K., & Cattell, R. B. *Personality factors in objective test devices*. San Diego: R. R. Knapp, 1965.

Hunt, J. McV., Ewing, T. N., La Forge, R., & Gilbert, W. M. An integrated approach to research on therapeutic counseling with samples of results. *Journal of Counseling Psychology*, 1959, *6*, 46-54.

Hunt, R. A. The interpretation of the religious scale of the Allport-Vernon-Lindzey study of values. *Journal for the Scientific Study of Religion*, 1968, *7*, 65-77.

Hunter, J. E. Maximal decomposition. An alternative to factor analysis. *Multivariate Behavioral Research*, 1972, *7*, 243.

Hunter, J. E. An analysis of validity, differential validity, test fairness, and utility for the Philadelphia Police Officers Selection Examination prepared by the Educational Testing Service. Report to the Philadelphia Federal District Court, *Alvarez vs. City of Philadelphia*, 1979.

Hunter, J. E. *Validity generalization for 12,000 jobs: An application of synthetic validity and validity generalization to the General Aptitude Test Battery (GATB)*. Washington, D.C.: U.S. Employment Service, Dept. of Labor, 1980.

Hunter, J. E., & Schmidt, F. L. Fitting people to jobs: The impact of personnel selection on national productivity. In M. D. Dunnette & E. A. Fleishman (Eds.), *Human performance and productivity: Human capability assessment* (Vol. 1). Hillsdale, NJ: Erlbaum, 1982.

Institute for Personality and Ability Testing, Inc. *Norm Supplement for the 16PF: Forms A and B*. Champaign, IL: IPAT, 1971.

International Association for Applied Psychology. *The status of psychological tests in Western Europe*. Washington, D.C.: Author, 1982.

Izard, C. E. Personality change during college years. *Journal of Counseling Psychology*, 1962, *26*, 482.

Izard, C. E. *Patterns of emotion: A new analysis of anxiety and behavior*. New York: Academic Press, 1972.

Jackson, D. N. *Personality Research Form Manual*. Goshen, NY: Research Psychologist Press, 1965.

Jackson, D. N. *Manual for the Personality Research Form*. Goshen, NY: Research Psychologist Press, 1967.

Jackson, D. N. Comments on evaluation of multimeans factor analysis. *Psychological Bulletin*, 1971, *15*, 421-423.

Jaeger, R. M., & Tittle, C. K. (Eds.). *Minimum competency testing: Motives, models, measures, and consequences*. Berkeley, CA: McCutchan, 1980.

James, M., & Jongeward, D. *Born to win*. Reading, MA: Addison-Wesley, 1971.

Jenkins, R. L., Stauffacher, W., & Hester, R. A system rating sheet for use with psychiatric patients. *Archives of General Psychiatry*, 1959, *1*, 197-204.

Jensen, A. R. *Educability and group differences*. New York: Harper & Row, 1973.

Jensen, A. *Bias in mental testing*. New York: Free Press, 1980.

Jensen, A. R. Test validity: *g* versus the specificity doctrine. Invited address, American Psychological Association Convention, Los Angeles, CA, August 26, 1981.

Jensen, A. R. Test validity: *g* versus the specificity doctrine. *Journal of Social and Biological Structures*, 1984, *7*, 93-118.

Johnson, D. M. Applications of the standard score IQ to social statistics. *Journal of Social Psychology*, 1948, *27*, 217-227.

Johnson, J. H. Computer technology and methodology in clinical psychology, psychiatry and behavioral medicine. *Journal of the Psychonomic Society*, 1981, *13*(4), 1-8.

Johnson, J. H., & Johnson, K. N. Psychological consideration related to the development of computerized testing stations. *Behavior Research Methods and Instrumentation*, 1981, *13*, 421-424.

Johnson, R. C., Ahern, F. M., Nagoshi, C. T., McClearn, G. E., Vandenberg, S. G., & Wilson, J. R. Age and group specific cohort effects as influences on personality test scores. *Journal of Cross Cultural Psychology*, 1985, *16*.

Johnson, R. C., Nagoshi, C. T., Ahern, F. M., Wilson, J. R., McClearn, G. E., Vandenberg, S. G., & DeFries, J. C. Age and cohort effects on personality factor scores across sexes and racial/ethnic groups. *Personality and Individual Differences*, 1983, *4*, 708-713. (b)

Johnson, T. C. Hierarchical clustering scheme. *Psychometrika*, 1967, *32*, 241-254.

Jones, F. E. Predictor variables for creativity in industrial science. *Journal of Applied Psychology*, 1964, *48*, 134-136.

Judd, L. L. Effects of lithium on mood, cognition and personality function in normal subject. *Archives of General Psychiatry*, 1979, *36*(8), 860-865.

Kameoka, V. The nature of the psychological state measures in the Clinical Analysis Questionnaire. Doctoral dissertation, University of Hawaii Library, Honolulu, HI, 1979.

Kameoka, V. An examination of the significance of simple structure by Bargmann's test in 20 published factor analyses. In preparation.

Karoly, P. & Steffens, J. J. *Improving the long-term effects of psychotherapy*. New York: Gardner, 1980.

Karson, S. *Manual for the Karson Clinical Report*.

Champaign, IL: IPAT, 1979.

Karson, S., & Haupt, T. D. Second order personality factors in parents of child guidance clinic patients. In R. B. Cattell (Ed.), *Progress in clinical psychology through multivariate-experimental designs*. Fort Worth, TX: Society of Multivariate Experimental Psychology, 1968.

Karson, S., & O'Dell, J. W. A new automated interpretation system for the 16P.F. *Journal of Personality Assessment*, 1975, *39*, 256-260.

Karson, S., & O'Dell, J. W. *A guide to the clinical use of the 16 P.F.* Champaign, IL: IPAT, 1976.

Karson, S., & Pool, K. B. Second order factors in personality measurement. *Journal of Consulting Psychology*, 1958, *22*, 299-303.

Kaufman, A. S. *Intelligent testing with the WISC-R*. New York: Wiley, 1979.

Kaufman, A. S., & Kaufman, N. L. *Kaufman Assessment Battery for Children (K-ABC)*. American Guidance Service, 1982.

Kauss, D. An investigation of psychological states related to the psychoemotional readying procedures of competitive athletes. *International Journal of Sport Psychology*, 1978, *9*(2), 134-155.

Kelley, H. P. Memory abilities: A factor analysis. *Psychometric Monographs*, 1964, *11*, 1-48.

Kelley, H. P. Are culturally biased tests useful? In S. B. Anderson & L. A. Coburn (Eds.), *Academic testing and the consumer* (New Directions for Testing and Measurement, No. 16). San Francisco, CA: Jossey-Bass, 1982.

Kelley, T. L. *Interpretation of educational measurements*. New York: World Book, 1927.

Kelly, E. L. Consistency of the adult personality. *American Psychologist*, 1955, *10*, 659-681.

Kent, G. H., & Rosanoff, A. J. A study of association in insanity. *American Journal of Insanity*, 1910, *67*, 37-96, 317-390.

Kerr, W. A. *Industrial psychology*. Chicago: William James Press, 1966.

Killian, L. R. The utility of objective test personality factors in diagnosing schizophrenia and the character disorders. Master's thesis, University of Illinois Library, Urbana, 1960.

King, L. D. The correlation of 10 HSOA factor scores to school-related criteria and personality data from HSPQ. Master's thesis, Cleveland State University, 1976.

Kleinmuntz, B. MMPI decision rules for the identification of college maladjustment: A digital computer approach. *Psychological Monographs*, 1963, 77, (Whole No. 477).

Kleinmuntz, B. Review of the EPI. *Journal of Educational Measurement*, 1970, *7*(2), 131-133.

Kleinmuntz, B. *Personality and psychological assessment*. New York: St. Martin's Press, 1982.

Kline, P., & Grindley, J. A 28-day case study with the MAT. *Journal of Multivariate Experimental Personality and Clinical Psychology*. 1974, *1*, 13-22.

Klopfer, B., Ainsworth, M. D., Klopfer, W., & Holt, R. R. *Developments in the Rorschach technique* (Vol. I.). Yonkers, NY: World Book, 1954.

Knapp, R. R. The effects of time limits on the intelligence test performance of Mexican and American subjects. *Journal of Educational Psychology*. 1960, *51*, 14-20. (a)

Knapp, R. R. The nature of primary personality dimensions as shown by relations of Cattell's objective personality test factors to questionnaire scales. Mimeographed report, 1960. (b)

Knapp, R. R. Criterion predictions in the navy from the objective-analytic personality test battery. Paper read at Annual Meeting of the American Psychological Association, New York, September 4, 1961. (a)

Knapp, R. R. Objective personality test and sociometric correlates of frequency of sick bay visits. *Journal of Applied Psychology*, 1961, *45*(2), 104-110. (b)

Knapp, R. R. The validity of the objective-analytic personality test battery in navy settings. *Educational and Psychological Measurement*, 1962, *22*(2), 379-387.

Knapp, R. R. Personality correlates of delinquency rate in a navy sample. *Journal of Applied Psychology*, 1963, *47*, 68-71.

Knapp, R. R. Delinquency and objective personality test factors. *Journal of Applied Psychology*, 1965, *49*, 8-10.

Knapp, R. R., & Most, J. A. Personality correlates of marine corps helicopter pilot performance. *U.S.N. Medical Field Research Laboratory Report*, 1960, No. MR 005.15-1001.1.3.

Koch, A. L. A multi-factor analysis of certain measures of activeness in nursery school children. *Journal of Genetic Psychology*, 1934, *45*, 482-487.

Koch, H. L. Factor analysis of some measures of the behavior of pre-school children. *Journal of Genetic Psychology*, 1942, *27*, 257-287.

Koppitz, E. M. *The Bender Gestalt Test for young children*. New York: Grune & Stratton, 1964.

Kozoll, C. E., & Behrens, C. M. *Timeline: An individualized program for self-growth*. Champaign, IL: IPAT, 1982.

Krech, D., & Crutchfield, R. S. *Theory and problems in social psychology*. New York: McGraw-Hill, 1948.

Kretschmer, F. *Physique and character*. New York: Harcourt Brace, 1925.

Krug, S. An examination of experimentally induced changes in ergic tension levels. Unpublished doctoral thesis, University of Illinois, 1971.

Krug, S. E. *The Marriage Counseling Report: A computerized analysis of paired profiles on the 16P.F.* Champaign, IL: IPAT, 1977. (a)

Krug, S. E. *Psychological assessment in medicine*. Champaign, IL: IPAT, 1977. (b)

Krug, S. E. Further evidence on 16P.F. distortion scales. *Journal of Personality Assessment*, 1978, *42*, 513-518. (a)

Krug, S. E. The role of personality assessment in the schools: A conversation with Dr. Raymond B. Cattell. *School Psychology Digest*, 1978, *7*, 26-35. (b)

Krug, S. E. *Clinical Analysis Questionnaire Manual*. Champaign, IL: IPAT, 1980.

Krug, S. E. Development of a formal measurement model for security screening in the nuclear power plant environment. *Multivariate Experimental Clinical Research*, 1981, *5*, 109-123. (a)

Krug, S. E. *Interpreting 16P.F. profile patterns.* Champaign, IL: IPAT, 1981. (b)

Krug, S. E. *Psychware: A reference guide to computer-based products for behavioral assessment in psychology, education, and business.* Kansas City: Test Corporation of America, 1984.

Krug, S. E. *The adult personality questionnaire* (from the 16 P.F.). Champaign, IL: IPAT, 1985.

Krug, S. E., & Cattell, R. B. A test of the trait-view theory of distortion in measurement of personality by questionnaire. *Educational and Psychological Measurement*, 1971, *31*, 721-734.

Krug, S. E., & Kulhavy, R. W. Personality differences across regions of the United States. *The Journal of Social Psychology*, 1973, *91*, 73-79.

Krug, S. E., & Laughlin, J. E. *Handbook for the IPAT Depression Scale.* Champaign, IL: IPAT, 1976.

Krug, S. E., & Laughlin, J. E. Second-order factors among normal and pathological primary personality traits. *Journal of Consulting and Clinical Psychology*, 1977, *45*, 575-582.

Krug, S. E., Scheier, I. H., & Cattell, R. B. *Handbook for the IPAT Anxiety Scale.* Champaign, IL: IPAT, 1976.

Kruglanski, A. W., Friedman, I., & Zeevi, B. The effects of extrinsic incentive on some qualitative aspects of task performance. *Journal of Personality and Social Psychology*, 1971, *39*, 606-617.

Kuder, G. F. *Manual, Kuder Occupational Interest Survey, 1979 revision.* Chicago: Science Research Associates, 1979.

Kulhavy, R. W., & Krug, S. E. *Individualized stress management.* Champaign, IL: IPAT, 1982.

Labouvie, E. W. Identity versus equivalence of psychological measures and constructs. In L. W. Poon (Ed.), *Aging in the 1950's: Psychological issues.* Washington, D.C.: American Psychological Association, 1980.

Lachar, D. *Automated psychological assessment.* Pontiac, MI: Automated Psychological Assessment, 1976.

Lang, V. R., & Krug, S. E. *Perspectives on the executive personality: A manual for the Executive Profile Survey.* Champaign, IL: IPAT, 1978.

Lawlis, G. F. Motivational aspects of the chronically unemployed. Unpublished doctoral thesis, Texas Technical College, 1968.

Lawlis, G. F. Motivational factors reflecting employment stability. *Journal of Social Psychology*, 1971, *84*, 215-225.

Lawlis, G. F. & Chatfield, D. *Multivariate approaches for the behavioral sciences.* Lubbock, TX: Technological Press, 1974.

Lawshe, C. H., & Balma, M. J. *Principles of personnel testing* (2nd ed.). New York: McGraw-Hill, 1966.

Lebo, M. A., & Nesselroade, J. R. Intraindividual differences in dimensions of mood change dur-

ing pregnancy identified in five P-technique factor analyses. *Journal of Research in Personality*, 1978, *12*(2), 205-241.

Lehmann, H. E. Schizophrenia: History. In H. Kaplan, A. M. Freedman, & B. J. Sadock (Eds.), *Comprehensive textbook of psychiatry, Vol. 2* (pp. 1104-1113). Baltimore: Williams & Wilkins, 1980.

Lennon, R. T. Assumptions underlying the use of content validity. *Educational and Psychological Measurement*, 1956, *16*, 294-301.

Lerner, B. The war on testing: David, Goliath and Gallup. *Public Interest*, 1980, *60*, 119-147.

Lewin, K. *A dynamic theory of personality.* New York: McGraw-Hill, 1935.

Likert, R. A technique for the measurement of attitudes. *Archives of General Psychology*, 1932, *140*, 44-53.

Lilly, J. *The center of the cyclone.* New York: Bantam, 1972.

Lindquist, E. F. *A first course in statistics.* New York: Houghton Mifflin, 1961.

Lindsley, D. B. Psychophysiology and motivation. In M. R. Jones (Ed.), *Nebraska Symposium on Motivation.* Lincoln, NB: University of Nebraska, 1957.

Lindzey, G. & Loehlin, J. *Theories of personality.* New York: Wiley, 1979.

Lingoes, J. C. An IBM-7090 program for Guttman-Lingoes smallest space analysis IV. *Behavioral Science*, 1966, *11*, 407.

Linn, L. Clinical manifestations of psychiatric disorder. In H. Kaplan, A. M. Freedman, & B. J. Sadock (Eds.), *Comprehensive textbook of psychiatry, Vol. 1* (pp. 990-1034). Baltimore: Williams & Wilkins, 1980.

Linn, R. L. Single-group validity, differential validity, and differential prediction. *Journal of Applied Psychology*, 1978, *63*, 507-512.

Linn, R. L. Issues or reliability in measurement for competency-based programs. In M. A. Bunda & J. R. Sanders (Eds.), *Practices and problems in competency-based education.* Washington: National Council for Measurement in Education, 1979a.

Linn, R. L. Issues of validity in measurement for competency-based programs. In M. A. Bunda & J. R. Sanders (Eds.), *Practices and problems in competency-based eduction.* Washington: National Council for Measurement in Education, 1979b.

Linn, R. L. Admissions testing on trial. *American Psychologist*, 1982, *37*, 279-291.

Lira, F. T., & Fagan, T. J. The profile of mood states: Normative data on a delinquent population. *Psychological Reports*, 1978, *42*(2), 640-642.

Livingston, S. A. Criterion-referenced applications of classical test theory. *Journal of Educational Measurement*, 1972, *9*, 13-26.

Loehlin, J. C., & Nichols, R. C. *Heredity, environment and personality.* Austin, TX: University of Texas Press, 1976.

Lord, F. M. Elementary models for measuring change. In C. W. Harris, (Ed.), *Problems on measuring change.* Madison, WI: University of Wisconsin Press, 1963.

Lord, F. M. A strong true score theory. *Psychometrika*, 1965, *30*, 239-270.

Lord, F. M. & Novick, M. R. *Statistical theories of mental test scores*. Reading, MA: Addison-Wesley, 1968.

Lorefice, L., Steer, R. A., Fine, E. W., & Schut, J. Personality traits and moods of alcoholics and heroin addicts. *Journal of Studies on Alcohol*, 1976, *37*(5), 687-689.

Lorenz, K. *Studies in animal and human behavior* (Vol. 2). London: Methuen, 1971.

Lorr, M. Rating scales, behavior inventories and drugs. In L. Urhn & J. G. Miller (Eds.), *Drugs and behavior*. New York: Wiley, 1960.

Lorr, M. *Explorations in typing psychotics*. New York: Pergamon, 1966.

Lorr, M., & Brazz, C. D. Measures of motivation. *Journal of Personality Assessment*, 1979, *43*(1), 64-68.

Lorr, M., Klett, C. J., & McNair, D. M. *Syndromes of psychosis*. Oxford: Pergamon, 1963.

Lorr, M., McNair, D. M., Klett, C. J., & Lasky, J. J. Evidence of ten psychiatric syndromes. *Journal of Consulting Psychology*, 1962, *26*, 185-189.

Luborsky, L. B., & Cattell, R. B. The validation of personality factors on humor. *Journal of Personality*, 1947, *15*, 283-291.

Luborsky, L., & Mintz, J. The contribution of P-technique to personality, psychotherapy, and psychosomatic research. In R. M. Dreger (Ed.), *Multivariate personality research: Contributions to the understanding of personality in honor of Raymond B. Cattell*. Baton Rouge, LA: Claitor's Press, 1972.

Lunneborg, P. W. *Vocational Interest Inventory (VII) Manual*. Los Angeles, CA: Western Psychological Services, 1981.

Luyten, H., & Lens, W. The effect of earlier experience and reward contingencies on intrinsic motivation. *Motivation and Emotion*, 1981, *5*, 25-36.

Lynn, R. *Personality and national character*. Oxford: Pergamon, 1971.

Lynn, R. The intelligence of the Japanese. *Bulletin of the British Psychological Society*, 1977, *30*, 69-72.

Lynn, R. Social ecology on intelligence in the British Isles. *British Journal of Social and Clinical Psychology*, 1979, *18*, 1-12.

Machover, K. *Personality projection in the drawing of the human figure: A method of personality investigation*. Springfield, IL: Charles C Thomas, 1971.

MacKinnon, D. W. The nature and structure of creative talent. *American Psychologist*, 1962, *17*, 484-495.

Madsen, K. B. *Modern theories of motivation: A comparative metascientific study*. New York: Halstead Press, Wiley & Sons, 1974.

Madsen, K. B. The formal properties of Cattellian personality theory and its relationship to other personality theories. In R. B. Cattell & R. M. Dreger (Eds.), *Handbook of modern personality theory*. Washington, D.C.: Hemisphere, 1977.

Magnusson, D. The person and the situation in an interactional model of behavior. *Scandinavian Journal of Psychology*, 1974, *17*, 253-271.

Mahrer, A. H. *New approaches to personality classification*. New York: Columbia University Press, 1970.

Malamud, W., & Sands, S. L. A revision of the Psychiatric Rating Scale. *American Journal of Psychiatry*, 1947, *104*, 231-237.

Mandryk, T. R., & Schuerger, J. M. Cross-validation of the HSPQ as a predictor for high school grades. *Educational and Psychological Measurement*, 1974, *34*, 449-454.

Maslow, A. H. *Motivation and personality*. New York: Harper, 1954.

Maslow, A. H. *Motivation and personality* (2nd ed.). New York: Harper, 1970.

Matarazzo, J. D. *Wechsler's measurement and appraisal of adult intelligence*. Baltimore: Williams & Wilkins, 1972.

Mathew, R. J., Claghorn, J. L., & Largen, J. Craving for alcohol in sober alcoholics. *American Journal of Psychiatry*, 1979, *136*(4-B), 603-606.

May, J. & Sweney, A. B. *Personality and motivational change observed in the treatment of psychotic patients*. Paper presented at Southwestern Psychological Association Meeting, Oklahoma City, 1965.

Mayo, L. G. The correlates of success in a behavioral weight reduction program. *Dissertation Abstracts International*, 1978, *38*(8-B), 3897.

McArthur, R. T., & Elley, W. B. The reduction of socioeconomic bias in intelligence testing. *British Journal of Educational Psychology*, 1963, *33*, 107-119.

McClelland, D. C. The measurement of human motivation: An experimental approach. In *Proceedings, Invitational Conference on Testing Problems, 1952*. Princeton, NJ: Educational Testing Service, 1953.

McClelland, D. C. Measuring motivation in fantasy. In D. C. McClelland (Ed.), *Studies in motivation*. New York: Appleton-Century-Crofts, 1955.

McClelland, D. C., Atkinson, J. W., Russell, A., Clark, R., & Lowell, L. *The achievement motive*. New York: Appleton, 1953.

McCormick, E. J., & Ilgen, D. *Industrial psychology* (7th ed.). Englewood Cliffs, NJ: Prentice-Hall, 1980.

McCormick, E. J., Jeanneret, P. R., & Mecham, R. C. A study of job characteristics and job dimensions based on the Position Analysis Questionnaire (PAQ). *Journal of Applied Psychology*, 1972, *56*, 347-368.

McDonald, R. P. The dimensionality of tests and items. *British Journal of Mathematical and Statistical Psychology*, 1981, *34*, 100-117.

McDougall, W. *An introduction to social psychology*. New York: Scribner, 1900.

McDougall, W. *An introduction to social psychology*. London: Methuen, 1908.

McKee, M. G. Review of the EPPS. In O. K. Buros (Ed.), *Seventh mental measurements yearbook*. Highland Park, NJ: Gryphon, 1972.

McMichael, R. E., & Cattell, R. B. Clinical diagnosis

by the IPAT musical preference test. *Journal of Consulting Psychology*, 1960, *24*, 333-341.

McNemar, Q. *Revision of the Stanford-Binet Scale*. Boston: Houghton Mifflin, 1942.

McReynolds, P. The future of psychological assessment. *International Review of Applied Psychology*, 1981, *31*, 117-138.

Medinnus, G. R. Q sort descriptions of 5-year-old children by their parents. *Child Development*, 1961, *32*, 473-489.

Meehl, P. E. *Clinical versus statistical prediction*. Minneapolis: University of Minnesota Press, 1954.

Meehl, P. E. *Psychodiagnosis: Selected papers*. Minneapolis: University of Minnesota Press, 1973.

Meeland, I. *An investigation of hypotheses for distinguishing personality factors A, F and H*. Doctoral dissertation, University of Illinois, 1953.

Mehrens, W. A., & Ebel, R. L. Some comments on criterion-referenced and norm-referenced achievement tests. *NCME Measurement in Education*, 1979, *10*(1), 1-43.

Meltzoff, J., & Kornreich, M. *Research in psychotherapy*. New York: Atherton, 1970.

Merrifield, P. R. Facilitating vs. differentiating components of creativity. *Journal of Educational Measurement*, 1964, *1*, 103-107.

Merrifield, P. R. An analysis of concepts from the point of view of the structure of intellect. In H. J. Klausmeier & C. W. Harris (Eds.), *Analyses of concept learning*. New York: Academic, 1966.

Merrifield, P. R. A tetrahedral model of intelligence. In P. R. Merrifield (Ed.), *Measuring human abilities* (New Directions in Testing and Measurement, No. 12). San Francisco, CA: Jossey-Bass, 1981.

Messick, S. The standard problem: Meaning and values in measurement and evaluation. *American Psychologist*, 1975, *30*, 955-966.

Messick, S. Abilities and knowledge in educational achievement testing: The assessment of dynamic cognitive structures. Research Report of Educational Testing Service, RR-82-51. Princeton, NJ: December, 1982.

Middleton, G., & Guthrie, G. M. Personality syndromes and academic achievement. *Journal of Educational Psychology*, 1959, *60*, 66-69.

Millman, J. Reliability and validity of criterion-referenced test scores. In R. E. Traub (Ed.), *New directions for testing and measurement* (No. 4): *Methodological developments*. San Francisco: Jossey-Bass, 1979.

Millon, T. *Millon Clinical Multiaxial Inventory*. Minneapolis: Interpretive Scoring Systems, 1982.

Miner, M. G., & Miner, J. B. *Employee selection within the law*. Washington, D.C.: The Bureau of National Affairs, 1978.

Mischel, W. *Personality and assessment*. New York: Wiley, 1968.

Morgan, C. D., & Murray, H. A. A method for investigating fantasies: The Thematic Apperception Test. *Archives of Neurology and Psychiatry*, 1935, *34*, 289-306.

Morse, P. W. Proposed technique for the evaluation of psychotherapy. *American Journal of Orthopsychiatry*, 1953, *23*, 716-731.

Mosier, C. I. On the reliability of weighted composites. *Psychometrika*, 1943, *8*, 161-168.

Muller, D., Calhoun, E., & Orling, R. Test reliability as a function of answer sheet mode. *Journal of Educational Measurement*, 1972, *9*, 321-324.

Munsterberg, H. *Psychology and industrial efficiency*. Boston: Houghton Mifflin, 1913.

Murray, H. A. *Thematic Apperception Test Manual*. Cambridge, MA: Harvard University Press, 1943.

Murray, H. A. et al. *Explorations in personality*. New York: Oxford University Press, 1938.

Nenty, H. J. & Dinero, T. E. A cross-cultural analysis of the fairness of the Cattell Culture-Fair Intelligence Test using the Rasch model. *Applied Psychological Measurement*, 1981, *5*, 355-368.

Nerzberg, F. *Work and the nature of man*. New York: The Mentor Executive Library, 1966.

Nesselroade, J. R. Temporal selection and factor invariance in the study of developmental change. In press.

Nesselroade, J. R., & Bartsch, T. W. Multivariate experimental perspectives on the construct validity of the trait-state distinction. In R. B. Cattell & R. M. Dreger (Eds.), *Handbook of modern personality theory*. Washington, D.C.: Hemisphere-Halstead, 1977.

Nesselroade, J. R. & Cable, D. Sometimes it's OK to factor difference scores. *Multivariate Behavioral Research*, 1974, *9*, 273-282.

Nesselroade, J. R. & Cattell, R. B. (Eds.). *Handbook of multivariate experimental psychology* (2nd ed.). New York: Praeger, 1985.

Nesselroade, J. R., & Jacobs, A. Reliability versus stability in the measurement of psychological states: An illustration with anxiety measures. In press.

Nesselroade, J. R., Jacobs, P. & Preshnow, R. The separation of reliability and stability in short-term change: An example with anxiety. *Psychologische Beitrage*, in press.

Nesselroade, J. R., & Reese, J. (Eds.). *Life-span developmental psychology*. New York: Academic Press, 1973.

Nisbett, R. E., & Wilson, T. DeC. Telling more than we know: Verbal reports on mental processes. *Psychological Review*, 1977, *84*, 231-259.

Norman, W. T. Review of the EPI. In O. K. Buros (Ed.), *Seventh mental measurements yearbook*. Highland Park, NJ: Gryphon, 1972.

Noty, C. *Personality, motivation and attitudinal correlates of persistence in religious vocations*. Unpublished doctoral dissertation, Loyola University, Chicago, 1973.

Novick, M. R. Federal guidelines and professional standards. *American Psychologist*, 1981, *36*, 1035-1046.

Novick, M. R. Educational testing: Inference in relevant subpopulation. *Mid-Western Researcher*, 1982, *3*, 34-35.

Nunnally, J. C. *Psychometric theory*. New York: McGraw-Hill, 1967.

Nunnally, J. C. *Educational measurement and evaluation* (2nd ed.). New York: McGraw-Hill, 1972.

Nunnally, J. C. *Psychometric theory* (2nd ed.). New York: McGraw-Hill, 1978.

Olds, J. *Growth and structure of motives.* Glencoe, IL: Free Press, 1956. (a)

Olds, J. Neuro-physiology of drive. *Psychiatric Research Reports*, 1956, *6*, 15-20. (b)

Olmedo, E., L. Testing linguistic minorities. *American Psychologist*, 1981, *36*, 1078.

Olson, W. C. *The measurement of nervous habits in normal children.* Minneapolis: University of Minnesota Press, 1929.

Osgood, C. E., Suci, G. J., & Tannenbaum, P. H. *The measurement of meaning.* Urbana, IL: University of Illinois, 1957.

Parloff, M. B., Waskow, I. E., & Wolfe, B. E. *Research on therapist-variables in relation to process and outcome.* NIMH, Rockville, MD, 1978.

Patrick, S., Cattell, R. B., Price, P., & Campbell, J. F. The diagnostic power of the O-A Battery in regard to hospitalized depressives. *Journal of Clinical Psychology*, 1981, *37*, 4-11. (a)

Patrick, S. V., Cattell, R. B., Price, P. L., & Campbell, J. F. A discriminant function for diagnosing depressives with selected source trait factor measures from the O-A Kit. *Multivariate Experimental Clinical Research*, 1981, *5*(2), 41-51. (b)

Pawlik, K. *Dimensionen des Verhaltens.* Berne: Huber, 1968.

Pawlik, K., & Cattell, R. B. The relationship between certain personality factors and cortical arousal. *Neuropsychologia*, 1965, *3*, 129-151.

Pearlman, K., Schmidt, F. L., & Hunter, J. E. Validity generalization results for tests used to predict job-proficiency and training success in clerical occupations. *Journal of Applied Psychology*, 1980, *65*, 373-406.

Pervin, L. A. *Personality: Theory, assessment and research.* New York: Wiley, 1975.

Peterson, D. R., & Cattell, R. B. Personality factors in nursery school children as derived from teacher ratings. *Journal of Consulting Psychology*, 1959, *23*, 562-570.

Piaget, J. *Psychology of intelligence.* Paterson, NJ: Littlefield Adams, 1960.

Pierson, G. R., Cattell, R. B., & Pierce, J. A demonstration by the HSPQ of the nature of the personality changes produced by institutionalization of delinquents. *The Journal of Social Psychology*, 1966, *70*, 229-239.

Pilowsky, I. Psychological aspects of post-herpetic neuralgia: Some clinical observations. *British Journal of Medical Psychology*, 1977, *50*(3), 283-288.

Pinneau, S. R. *Changes in intelligence quotient from infancy to maturity.* Boston: Houghton Mifflin, 1961.

Piotrowski, A. Digital computer interpretation of ink-blot test data. *Psychiatric Quarterly*, 1964, *38*, 1-26.

Pleck, J. H. Masculinity-femininity: Current and alternative paradigms. *Sex Roles*, 1975, *1*, 161-178.

Pleszewski, A. Emotional functioning of patients before and after myocardial infarction. *Polish Psychological Bulletin*, 1978, *9*(3), 163-167.

Popham, W. J. *Criterion-referenced measurement.* Englewood Cliffs, NJ: Prentice-Hall, 1978.

Popham, W. J., & Husek, T. R. Implications of criterion-referenced measurement. *Journal of Educational Measurement*, 1969, *6*, 1-9.

Porter, L. W., & Lawler, E. E. *Managerial attitudes and performance.* Homewood, IL: Irwin-Dorsey, 1968.

Porter, R. B., & Cattell, R. B. *Handbook for the Children's Personality Questionnaire.* Champaign, IL: IPAT, 1975.

Rachman, S. *The effects of psychotherapy.* Oxford: Pergamon, 1971.

Rachman, S. J., & Wilson, G. T. *The effects of psychological therapy* (2nd ed.). Oxford: Pergamon, 1980.

Rapaport, D., Schafer, R., & Gill, M. M. *Diagnostic psychological testing, Vols. I & II.* Chicago: Yearbook Publishers, 1946.

Reik, T. *Listening with the third ear.* New York: Farrar, Strauss, 1949.

Reilly, R. R., & Chao, G. T. *Validity and fairness of alternative employee selection procedures.* Unpublished manuscript. American Telephone & Telegraph Co., Morristown, NJ, 1980.

Reilly, R. R., & Chao, G. T. Validity and fairness of some alternative employee selection procedures. *Personnel Psychology*, 1982, *35*, 1-62.

Reschly, D. D. Psychological testing in educational classification and placement. *American Psychologist*, 1981, *26*, 1094-1102.

Resnick, L. B. The future of IQ testing in education. *Intelligence*, 1979, *3*, 241-253.

Reuterman, N. A., Howard, K. I., & Cartwright, D. S. Multivariate analysis of gang delinquency. IV. Personality variables. *Multivariate Behavioral Research,* 1980, *17*.

Reznikoff, M., & Zeller, W. W. A procedure for evaluating the status of schizophrenic patients using combined physical and nurse judgments. *Journal of Clinical and Experimental Psychopathology*, 1957, *18*, 367-371.

Rickels, K. & Cattell, R. B. Diagnostic power of IPAT objective anxiety tests, and coefficients for evaluating tests. *Archives of General Psychiatry*, 1964, *11*, 459-465.

Rickels, K., & Cattell, R. B. The clinical factor validity and trueness of the IPAT verbal and objective batteries of anxiety and regression. *Journal of Clinical Psychology*, 1965, *21*, 257-264.

Rickels, K., Cattell, R., MacAfee, A., & Hesbacher, P. Drug response and important external events in the patient's life. *Diseases of the Nervous System*, 1965, *26*, 782-786.

Rickels, K., Weise, C., Gray, B., Yee, R., Mallin, A., Aaronson, H. G., & Cattell, R. B. Controlled psychopharmacological research in private psychiatric medicine. *Psychopharmacologia*, 1966, *9*, 288-306.

Robinson, J. P., & Shaver, P. R. *Measures of social psychological attitudes.* Ann Arbor, MI: University of Michigan, 1973.

Roby, T. B. On the measurement and description of groups. *Behavioral Science*, 1957, *2*, 119-127.

Rogers, C. R. *Client-centered therapy*. Boston, MA: Houghton Mifflin, 1951.

Rogers, C. R., & Dymond, R. F. *Psychotherapy and personality change*. Chicago: University of Chicago Press, 1954.

Roid, G., & Gorsuch, R. Development and clinical use of test interpretive programs on microcomputers. In M. Schwartz (Ed.), *Microcomputers in private mental health practice*. Boston: Haworth Press, 1983.

Roid, G. H., & Haladyna, T. M. *A technology of test-item writing*. New York: Academic, 1982.

Rokeach, M. *Beliefs, attitudes, and values*. San Francisco: Jossey-Bass, 1968.

Rokeach, M. *The nature of human values*. New York: Free Press, 1973.

Rokeach, M. *Understanding human values*. New York: Free Press, 1979.

Rorer, L. G. The great response style myth. *Psychological Bulletin,* 1965, *63*, 129-156.

Rorschach, H. *Psychodiagnostics: A diagnostic test based on perception*. P. Lemkau & B. Kronenburg, trans. Berne: Huber, 1942. Originally published, 1921.

Rosenberg, M. *Occupations and values*. Glencoe, IL: Free Press, 1957.

Rossman, B. B., & Horn, J. L. Cognitive, motivational and temperamental indicant of creativity and intelligence. *Journal of Educational Measurement*, 1972, 265-284.

Rotter, J. B. Generalized expectancies for internal versus external control of reinforcement. *Psychological Monographs,* 1966, *80* (Whole No. 609.).

Rotter, J. B., & Rafferty, J. E. *Manual: The Rotter Incomplete Sentences Blank*. New York: Psychological Corporation, 1950.

Royce, J. R. *Multivariate analysis and psychological theory*. London: Academic Press, 1973.

Rummel, R. J. Indicators of cross national and international patterns. *American Political Science Review*, 1969, *63*, 1-5.

Rummel, R. J. *The dimensions of nations*. Beverly Hills, CA: Sage, 1972.

Rummel, R. J. *Understanding conflict and war*. New York: Halstead, 1975.

Rummel, R. J. *National attitudes and behavior linkage dimensions*. Beverly Hills, CA: Sage Publications, 1978.

Rummel, R. J. *National attributes and behavior*. Beverly Hills, CA: Sage Publications, 1979.

Russell, J. A., & Mehrabian, A. Environmental effects on drug use. *Environmental Psychology and Non-Verbal Behavior*, 1977, *2*(2), 109-123.

Sahakian, W. S. (Ed.). *Psychology of personality*. Chicago: Rand McNally, 1965.

Sanders, K., Mills, J., Martin, F. I., & Horne, D. J. Emotional attitudes in adult insulin-dependent diabetics. *Journal of Psychosomatic Research*, 1975, *19*(4), 241-246.

Satir, V. *Conjoint family therapy*. Palo Alto, CA: Science & Behavior Books, 1964.

Saunders, D. R. A factor analysis of the information and arithmetic items of the WAIS. *Psychological Reports*, 1960, *6*, 367-383.

Saville, P. *The British standardization of the 16 P.F.* England, Windsor, The National Foundation for Educational Research, 1972.

Sawyer, J. Dimensions of nations: Size, wealth and politics. *American Journal of Sociology*, 1967, *73*, 145-172.

Schachter, S. *The psychology of affiliation: Experimental studies of the sources of gregariousness*. Stanford, CA: Stanford University, 1959.

Schaie, K. W. Methodological problems in descriptive research on adulthood and aging. In J. R. Nesselroade & H. W. Reese (Eds.), *Life-span developmental psychology: Methodological issues*. New York: Academic, 1973.

Schaie, K. W., & Strother, C. R. A cross-sequential study of age changes in cognitive behavior. *Psychological Bulletin*, 1968, *68*, 10-25.

Scheier, I. H., & Cattell, R. B. Confirmation of objective test factors and assessment of their relation to questionnaire factors: A factor analysis of 113 rating, questionnaire and objective test measurements of personality. *Journal of Mental Science*, 1958, *104*, 608-624.

Scheier, I. H., & Cattell, R. B. *Handbook for the IPAT 8-Parallel-Form Anxiety Battery*. Champaign, IL: IPAT, 1973.

Scherer, I. W. *Northampton Activity Rating Scale, Form D*. Springfield, MA: Mee Scientific Apparatus Co., 1951.

Schmeidler, G. R. Personality differences in the effective use of ESP. *Journal of Communication*, 1975, *25*(1), 133-141.

Schmidt, F. L., & Hunter, J. E. Moderator research and the law of small numbers. *Personnel Psychology*, 1978, *31*, 215-232.

Schmidt, F. L., & Hunter, J. E. Employment testing: Old theories and new research findings. *American Psychologist*, 1981, *36*, 1128-1137.

Schmidt, F. L., Hunter, J. E., Pearlman, K., & Shane, G. S. Further tests of the Schmidt-Hunter Bayesian validity generalization procedure. *Personnel Psychology*, 1979, *32*, 257-281.

Schmidt, L. R. *Objective Personlichkeits-messung, in diagnostischer und klinischer Psychologie*. Weinheim U Basel: Beltz, 1975.

Schmidt, L. R. & Häcker, H. O. *Objective test batterie OA TB 75, test hefte*. Weinheim: Beltz, 1975.

Schneewind, K. A. Entwicklung einen deutschra-chigen version des 16 P.F. test von Cattell. *Diagnostica,* 1977, *2*, 188-191.

Schuerger, J. M., Dielman, T. E., & Cattell, R. B. Objective personality factors U.I. 16, 17, 19, and 20 as correlates of school achievement. *Personality*, 1970, *1*, 95-101.

Schuerger, J. M., Feo, A. F., & Nowak, M. J. Personality matches across media in a large high school sample. *Multivariate Behavioral Research*, 1981, *16*, 373-378.

Schuerger, J. M., Kepner, J., & Lawler, B. Verbal-quantitative differential as indicator of temperamental differences. *Multivariate Experimental Clinical Research*, 1979, *4*, 57-66.

Schuerger, J. M., Tait, E., & Tavernelli, M. Temporal stability of personality by questionnaire.

Journal of Personality and Social Psychology, 1982, *43*(1), 176-182.

Schuerger, J. M., & Watterson, D. G. *Using tests and other information in counseling: A decision model for practitioners*. Champaign, IL: IPAT, 1977.

Schuerger, J. M., Watterson, D. C., & Croom, W. C. *An occupational interpretation system for psychological tests and questionnaires*. Unpublished manuscript, Cleveland, OH: University of Cleveland Library, 1983.

Schuettler, R., Huber, G., & Gross, G. Suicid und suicidversuch im verlauf schizophrener erkrankungen. *Psychiatrischer Clinic*, 1976, *9*, 97.

Schumacher, G., & Cattell, R.B. Faktoranalyse des deutschen HSPQ. Unterstuchuengen zur interkulturellen konstanz der primiren personlichkeits faktoren. *Zeitschrift für Experimentelle und Angewandte Psychologie*, 1974, *21*, 1-20.

Scott, W. A. Social desirability and individual concepts of the desirable. *Journal of Abnormal and Social Psychology*, 1963, *67*, 574-585.

Scott, W. A. *Values and organization*. Chicago: Rand McNally, 1965.

Sechehaye, M. *Autobiography of a schizophrenic girl*. New York: Grune, 1951.

Seligman, M.E.P. *Helplessness: On depression, development and death*. San Francisco: W.H. Freeman, 1975.

Sells, S. B. (Ed.). *Stimulus determinants of behavior*. New York: Ronald, 1963.

Sells, S. Industrial and military psychology. In R.B. Cattell (Ed), *Handbook of multivariate experimental psychology*. Chicago: Rand McNally, 1966.

Sells, S. B., Demarce, R. G., & Will, D. P. A taxonomic investigation of personality conjoint factor structure of Guilford and Cattell trait markers. Memo report of project #OEE0072. Washington, D.C.: Office of Education, Department of Health, Education, and Welfare, 1968.

Serow, R. C., & Daview, J. J. Resources and outcomes of minimum competency testing as measures of equality of educational opportunity. *American Educational Research Journal*, 1982, *19*, 529-539.

Shaw, M. E., & Wright, J. M. *Scales of the measurement of attitudes*. New York: McGraw-Hill, 1967.

Sheldon, W. H., Stevens, S.S., & Tucker, W.B. *The varieties of human physique*. New York: Harper, 1940.

Sheldon, W. H., Stevens, S. S., & Tucker, W. B. *The varieties of temperament*. New York: Harper, 1943.

Sherif, M., & Sherif, C. W. The social judgment-involvement approach to attitude. In C.W. Sherif & M. Sherif (Eds.), *Attitude, ego-involvement, and change*. New York: Wiley, 1967.

Sherif, M., & Sherif, C. W. *Social psychology*. New York: Harper & Row, 1969.

Shotwell, A. M., Hurley, J. R., & Cattell, R. B. Motivational structures in a hospitalized mental

defective. *Journal of Abnormal Social Psychology*, 1961, *62*, 422-426.

Shutz, R. E. The role of measurement in education: Servant, soulmate, stoolpigeon, statesman, scapegoat, all of the above, and/or none of the above. *Journal of Educational Measurement*, 1971, *8*, 141-146.

Siegel, L., & Lane, I. M. *Personnel and organizational psychology*. Homewood, IL: Richard D. Irwin, 1982.

Sindberg, R. M., Roberts, A. F., & McClain, D. Mate selection factors in computer matched marriages. *Journal of Marriage and the Family*, 1970, *48*, 132-135.

Skinner, B. F. *Science and human behavior*. New York: Macmillan, 1953.

Smith, A. Neuropsychological testing in neurological disorders. In W. J. Friedlander (Ed.), *Advances in neurology (Vol. 7)*. New York: Raven Press, 1975.

Smith, A., Hays, J., & Solway, K. Comparison of the WISC-R and Culture Fair Intelligence Test in a juvenile delinquent population. *Journal of Psychology*, 1977, *97*, 179-182.

Smith, B. D., & Vetter, H. J. *Theoretical approaches to personality*. Englewood Cliffs, NJ: Prentice-Hall, 1982.

Smith, M. L., & Glass, G. V. Meta-analysis of psychotherapy outcome studies. *American Psychologist*, 1977, *32*, 752-760.

Smith, M. L., Glass, G. V., & Miller, T. I. *The benefits of psychotherapy*. Baltimore: Johns Hopkins University, 1980.

Snow, R. E. Aptitude and achievement. In W. B. Schrader (Ed.), *New directions for testing and measurement: Measuring achievement: Progress over a decade—Proceedings of the 1979 ETS Invitational Conference*. San Francisco: Jossey-Bass, 1980.

Sobell, M.B., & Sobell, L.C. Individualized behavior therapy for alcoholics. *Behavior Therapy*, 1973, *4*, 49-72.

Sokal, R. R. & Sneath, P. H. A. *Principles of numerical taxonomy*. San Francisco: Freeman, 1963.

Spearman, C. E. General intelligence, objectively determined and measured. *American Journal of Psychology*, 1904, *15*, 201-293.

Spearman, C. E. The proof and measurement of association between two things. *American Journal of Psychology*, 1904, *15*, 72-101.

Spearman, C. E. *A measure of intelligence*. London: Methuen, 1929.

Spearman, C. E. *Creative mind*. New York: Cambridge University Press, 1930.

Spence, J. T., & Helmreich, R. L. Masculine instrumentality and feminine expressiveness: Their relationship with sex role attitudes and behaviors. *Psychology of Women Quarterly*, 1980, *5*, 147-163.

Spielberger, C. D. *Anxiety and behavior*. New York: Academic Press, 1966.

Spielberger, C. D. *Anxiety: Current trends in research and theory*. New York: Academic Press, 1972.

Spielberger, C. D., Gorsuch, R. L., & Lushene, R. E.

Manual for the State-Trait Anxiety Inventory. Palo Alto: Consulting Psychologists Press, 1970.

Spitzer, R. L., & Endicott, J. *The psychiatric status schedule.* Unpublished revision, 1979. (Original in *Archives of General Psychiatry,* 1970, *23,* 41-55).

Stanley, J. C. Reliability. In R. L. Thorndike (Ed.), *Educational measurement* (2nd ed.). Washington, D.C.: American Council on Education, 1971.

Stephenson, W. *The study of behavior: Q-technique and its methodology.* Chicago: University of Chicago Press, 1953.

Stogdill, R. M. Leadership, membership and organization. *Psychological Bulletin,* 1950, *47,* 1-14.

Stogdill, R. M. *Individual behavior and group achievement.* New York: Oxford University Press, 1959.

Stogdill, R. M. *Handbook of leadership: A survey of theory and research.* New York: Free Press, 1974.

Stricker, L. J. SES indexes: What do they measure? *Basic and Applied Social Psychology,* 1980, *1*(1), 93-101.

Stricker, L. J. Dimensions of social stratification for whites and blacks. *Multivariate Behavioral Research,* 1982, *17,* 139-167. (a)

Stricker, L. J. Identifying test items that perform differentially in population sub-groups: A partial correlation index. *Applied Psychological Measurement,* 1982, *6,* 261-173. (b)

Stricker, L. J. *Test disclosure and retest performance on the Scholastic Aptitude Test.* Princeton, NJ: College Board Report, No. 82-7, E.T.S., 1982. (c)

Strong, E. K. A vocational interest test. *The Educational Record,* 1927, *8,* 107-121.

Strong, E. K., Jr., & Campbell, D. P. *Strong-Campbell Interest Inventory* (rev. ed.). Stanford, CA: Stanford University Press, 1974.

Sullivan, H. S. *Conceptions of modern psychiatry.* William Alanson White Foundation, Washington, D.C., 1940.

Super, D. E. A theory of vocational development. *American Psychologist,* 1953, *8,* 185-190.

Super, D. E. *The psychology of careers: An introduction to vocational development.* New York: Harper & Row, 1957.

Super, D. E., & Bohn, M. J., Jr. *Occupational psychology.* Belmont, WA: Wadsworth, 1970.

Sweney, A. B. Objective measurement of strength of dynamic structure factors. In R. B. Cattell & F. Warburton (Eds.), *Objective personality and motivation tests: A theoretical introduction and a practical compendium.* Champaign, IL: University of Illinois Press, 1967.

Sweney, A. B. The prediction of adjustment from dynamic source trait measurement. Presented at Midwestern Psychological Association Annual Meeting, Chicago, 1969. (a)

Sweney, A. B. A preliminary descriptive manual for individual assessment by the Motivational Analysis Test. Champaign, IL: IPAT, 1969. (b)

Sweney, A. B. A threshold model for predicting motivational behaviors. Paper presented to Southern Management Association, New Orleans, 1975.

Sweney, A. B. *The Vocational Interest Measure.* Champaign, IL: IPAT, 1980.

Sweney, A. B. The validation of a threshold model for predicting motivated behavior. Presented in abstracts for 20th International Congress of Applied Psychology, Edinburgh, Scotland, 1982.

Sweney, A. B., & Cartwright, D. S. Relations between conscious and unconscious manifestations of motivation in children. *Multivariate Behavioral Research,* 1966, *1,* 447-459.

Sweney, A. B., & Cattell, R. B. *Manual for the Vocational Interest Measure.* Champaign, IL: IPAT, Research edition for limited circulation, 1961, 1970, 1980.

Sweney, A. B., & Cattell, R. B. Relationships between integrated and unintegrated motivation structure examined by objective test. *Journal of Social Psychology,* 1962, *57,* 217-226.

Sweney, A. B., Cattell, R. B., & Krug, S. E. *The School Motivation Analysis Test.* Champaign, IL: IPAT, 1969.

Sweney, A. B., & May, M. J. *Defense mechanisms handbook.* Wichita, KS: Test Systems Inc., 1965, 1970.

Sweney, A. B., & Sweney, V. A. Motivational issues and models influencing organization behavior. In preparation.

Sweney, A. B., & Vaughn, A. Motivation patterns in organizational role pressure and preference. Paper presented to Tenth Annual Personnel Management Conference, London, 1976. (a)

Sweney, A. B., & Vaughn, A. Re-examining motivation: Distinguishing tensions from intentions and action. Paper presented to Tenth Annual Personnel Management Conference, London, 1976. (b)

Sweney, M. A. Non-verbal communication: A study of selected characteristics of an individual in relation to his ability to identify information about human emotional states. *Dissertation Abstracts International,* 1975, *36*(4-A), 2036.

Swenson, W. M. & Pearson, J. S. Automation techniques in personality assessment: A frontier in behavioral science and medicine. *Methods of Information in Medicine,* 1964, *3,* 34-36.

Tapp, J. *An examination of hypotheses governing the motivational components of attitude strength.* Unpublished master's thesis, University of Illinois, 1958.

Tatro, D. F. The utility of source traits measured by the O-A (objective-analytic) Battery in mental hospital diagnosis. *Multivariate Behavioral Research,* 1968, Special Issue, 133-149.

Tatsuoka, M. *Selected topics in advanced statistics.* Champaign, IL: IPAT, 1969, 1970, 1971, 1974, 1975.

Tatsuoka, M. M., & Cattell, R. B. Linear equations for estimating a person's occupational adjustment, based on information on occupational profiles. *British Journal of Educational Psychology,* 1970, *40,* 324-334.

Taylor, C. W., & Barron, F. (Ed.). *The identification of creative scientific talent.* New York: Wiley, 1963.

Taylor, C. W., Smith, W. R., & Ghiselin, B. The creative and other contributions of one sample of research scientists. In C. W. Taylor & F. Barron (Eds.), *Scientific creativity.* New York: Wiley, 1963.

Tenopyr, M. L. The realities of employment testing. *American Psychologist,* 1981, *36,* 1120-1127.

Terman, L. M., & Merrill, M. A. *Stanford-Binet Intelligence Scale: Manual for the third revision, Form L-M.* Boston: Houghton Mifflin, 1960.

Terman, L. M., & Merrill, M. A. *Stanford-Binet Intelligence Scale: 1972 norms edition.* Boston: Houghton Mifflin, 1973.

Thomson, G. H. On estimating oblique factors. *British Journal of Psychology,* 1949, *2,* 1-2.

Thorndike, R. L. *Animal intelligence: Experimental studies.* New York: Macmillan, 1911.

Thorndike, R. L. *Applied psychometric methods.* New York: Academic Press, 1982.

Thorndike, R. L., & Hagen, E. *Measurement and evaluation in psychology and education.* New York: Wiley, 1969.

Thorndike, R. L., & Hagen, E. *Measurement and evaluation in psychology and education.* New York: Wiley, 1977.

Thorndike, R. L. & Woodyard, E. Differences within and between communities in the intelligence of children. *Journal of Educational Psychology,* 1942, *33,* 641-656.

Thurstone, L. L. Attitudes can be measured. *American Journal of Sociology,* 1928, *33,* 529-554. (a)

Thurstone, L. L. The absolute zero in intelligence measurement. *Psychological Review,* 1928, *35,* 175-197. (b)

Thurstone, L. L. The measurement of social attitudes. *Journal of Abnormal and Social Psychology,* 1931, *26,* 249-269.

Thurstone, L. L. A multiple factor study of vocational interest. *Journal of Personality,* 1935, *10,* 198-205.

Thurstone, L. L. *Primary mental abilities.* Chicago: Chicago University Press, 1938.

Thurstone, L. L. The dimensions of temperament. *Psychometrika,* 1951, *16,* 11-20.

Thurstone, L. L. *Manual for the Test of Mental Alertness.* Chicago: Science Research Associations, 1960.

Tiemann, P. W., & Markle, S. M. *Analyzing instructional content: A guide to instruction and evaluation.* Champaign, IL: Stipes, 1978.

Timm, V. Reliabilität und faktorenstruktur von Cattell's 16 P. F. bei einer deutschen stickprobe. *Zeitschrift für Experimentelle und Angewandte Psychologie,* 1968, *15,* 354-373.

Tinbergen, M. *The study of instinct.* Oxford: Clarendon Press, 1951.

Tollefson, D. *Differential responses to humor and their relation to personality and motivation measures.* Unpublished doctoral dissertation, University of Illinois, 1959.

Tollefson, D. Evidence on the selection of researchers for effectiveness, against a criterion, by the Sixteen Personality Factors Test. Unpublished manuscript cited in 16P.F. Handbook, 1970 p. 242.

Tolman, E. C. *Purposive behavior in animals and men.* New York: Appleton, 1958.

Tolman, E. C. Principles of purposive behavior. In S. Koch (Ed.), *Psychology: A study of science* (Vol. II). New York: McGraw-Hill, 1959.

Torgerson, W. S. *Theory and methods of scaling.* New York: Wiley, 1958.

Toynbee, A. J. *A study of history.* New York: Oxford University Press, 1947.

Traub, R. E. (Ed.). *New directions for testing and measurement (No. 4): Methodological developments.* San Francisco: Jossey-Bass, 1979.

Travers, R. W. Rational hypotheses in the structure of tests. *Educational and Psychological Measurement,* 1951, *11,* 128-137.

Triandis, H. C. Toward an analysis of the components of interpersonal attitudes. In C. W. Sherif & M. Sherif (Eds.), *Attitude, ego-involvement, and change.* New York: Wiley, 1967.

Triandis, H. C. *Attitude and attitude change.* New York: Wiley, 1971.

Tsujioka, B., & Cattell, R. B. Constancy and difference in personality structure and mean profile from applying the 16 P.F. test in America and Japan. *British Journal of Social and Clinical Psychology,* 1965, *4,* 287-297.

Tuddenham, R. D. Soldier intelligence in World Wars I & II. *American Psychologist,* 1948, *3,* 54-56.

Updegrove, C. A. Mood and dreaming: Manifestations of personality traits and states in the dream. *Dissertation Abstracts International,* 1979, *39*(12-B), 6148.

Ustrzycki, G. J. *Personality assessment and indices of delinquent behavior.* Master's thesis, University of Guelph, Canada, 1974.

Vandenberg, S. G. Assortative mating, or who marries whom? *Behavioral Genetics,* 1972, *2,* 157-177.

Van Egeren, L. F. *Experimental determination by P-technique of functional unities of depression.* Unpublished master's thesis, University of Illinois, 1963.

Van Egeren, L. F. Multivariate research on the psychoses. In R. B. Cattell & R. M. Dreger (Eds.), *Handbook of modern personality theory.* New York: Halstead, 1977.

Veitch, R. Physiological arousal, affect and interpersonal attraction. *Psychological Reports,* 1976, *38*(1), 43-52.

Vernon, P. E. *Intelligence and cultural environment.* London: Methuen, 1969. (a)

Vernon, P. E. Environmental handicaps and intellectual development. *British Journal of Educational Psychology,* 1969, *35,* 1-22. (b)

Vernon, P. E., & Parry, J. B. *Personnel selection in the British Forces.* London: University of London Press, 1949.

Veroff, J. Development and validation of a projective measure of power motivation. *Journal of Ab-*

normal and Social Psychology, 1957, *54,* 1-8.

Vroom, V. H. *Work and motivation.* New York: Wiley, 1964.

Wagman, M. PLATO DCS: An interactive computer system for personal counseling. *Journal of Counseling Psychology,* 1980, *27,* 16-30.

Wagman, M. Solving dilemmas by computer or counselor. *Psychological Report,* 1982, *50,* 127-135.

Wagoner, J. H. The Emotional Projection Test as an instrument to differentiate affective qualities of personality profiles and as a measure of affective change in four different therapy groups. *Dissertation Abstracts International,* 1980, *40*(12-B), 5835.

Wahba, M. A., & Bridwell, L. B. Maslow reconsidered: A review of research on the need hierarchy theory. *Organization Behavior and Human Performance,* 1976, *15,* 212-240.

Wahl, O. F., Zastowny, T. R., & Briggs, D. A factor analytic reexamination of two popular surveys of mental health attitudes. *Multivariate Experimental Clinical Research,* 1980, *5*(1), 29-39.

Waldrop, J. L., Anderson, T. H., Hively, W., Hastings, C. N., Anderson, R. I., & Muller, K. E. A framework for analyzing the inference structure of educational achievement tests. *Journal of Educational Measurement,* 1982, *19,* 1-18.

Walker, D. A. Answer patterns and score scatter on tests and examinations. *British Journal of Psychology,* 1940, *30,* 248-260.

Walker, R. N. Body build and behavior in young children. I. Body build and nursery school teachers' ratings. *Monographs of the Society for Research in Child Development,* 1962, *27*(3).

Walker, R. N. Body build and behavior in young children. II. Body build and parents' ratings. *Child Development,* 1963, *34,* 1-23.

Walsh, J. A. Review of the 16P.F. In O. K. Buros (Ed.), *Eighth mental measurements yearbook.* Highland Park, NJ: Gryphon, 1978.

Walter, V. W. *Manual for the Personal-Career Development Profile.* Champaign, IL: IPAT, 1978.

Ward, J. H. *An application of linear and curvilinear joint functional regression in psychological prediction.* Research Bulletin 54-86. Lackland AFB, TX: Air Force Personnel Training Center, 1954.

Wardell, D., & Royce, J. R. Relationships between cognitive and temperament traits and the concept of style. *Journal of Multivariate Experimental Personality and Clinical Psychology,* 1975, *1,* 244-266.

Wardell, D., & Yeudall, L. T. A multidimensional approach to criminal disorders. I. The factor analysis of impulsivity. *Journal of Clinical Psychology,* 1976, *32,* 12-21.

Wardell, D., & Yeudall, L. T. A multidimensional approach to criminal disorders: The assessment of impulsivity and its relation to crime. *Advances in Behavior Research and Therapy,* 1980, *2,* 159-177.

Waskow, I. E., & Parloff, M. B. (Eds.). *Psychotherapy change measures: Report of the clinical research outcome measures project.* NIMH, Rockville, MD, 1975.

Watterson, D. G., Schuerger, J. M., & Melnyk, G. I. The addition of personality measures to ability measures for predicting and understanding school achievement. *Multivariate Experimental Clinical Research,* 1976, *2,* 113-122.

Wechsler, D. A. A standardized memory scale for clinical use. *Journal of Psychology,* 1945, *19,* 87-96.

Wechsler, D. *Manual for the Wechsler Adult Intelligence Scale.* New York: The Psychology Corporation, 1955.

Wechsler, D. *The measurement and appraisal of adult intelligence* (4th ed.). Baltimore: Williams & Wilkins, 1958.

Wegscheider, S. *Another chance: Hope and health for the alcoholic family.* Palo Alto, CA: Science & Behavior Books, 1981.

Wenig, P. *The relative roles of naive, autistic, cognitive, and press compatibility misperception and ego defense operation in tests of misperception.* Master's thesis, University of Illinois, 1952.

Wesley, F., & Wesley, C. *Sex-role psychology.* New York: Human Sciences, 1977.

Wessman, A. E. & Ricks, D. F. *Mood and personality.* New York: Holt, Rinehart & Winston, 1966,

Wiggins, J. S. *Personality and prediction: Principles of personality assessment.* Reading, MA: Addison-Wesley, 1973.

Williams, D. G. Different cigarette-smoker classification factors and subjective state in acute abstinence. *Psychopharmacology,* 1979, *64*(2), 231-235.

Williams, H. V. A determination of psychosomatic functional unities by P-technique. *Journal of Social Psychology,* 1954, *39,* 110-142.

Williams, J. R. A test of the validity of the P-techniques in the measurement of internal conflict. *Journal of Personality,* 1959, *27,* 418-437.

Williams, P. A., Kirk, B. A., & Frank, A. C. New men's SVIB: A comparison with the old. *Journal of Counseling Psychology,* 1968, *15,* 187-294.

Williams, R. G., & Haladyna, T. M. Logical operations for generating intended questions (LOGIQ): A typology for higher level test items. In G. H. Roid & T. M. Haladyna (Eds.), *A technology for test-item writing.* New York: Academic Press, 1982.

Willingham, W. W. New methods and directions in achievement measurement. In W. B. Schrader (Ed.), *New directions for testing and measurement: Measuring achievement: Progress over a decade.* San Francisco: Jossey-Bass, 1980.

Winch, R. F. Another look at the theory of complimentary needs in mate selection. *Journal of Marriage and the Family,* 1967, *29,* 756-762.

Winder, P., O'Dell, J. W., & Karson, S. New motivational distortion scales for the 16 P.F. *Journal of Personality Assessment,* 1975, *39,* 532-537.

Wirt, R. D., & Briggs, P. F. Personality and environmental factors in the development of delinquency. *Psychological Monographs*, 1959, *73*, Whole #485.

Wissler, C. The correlation of mental and physical tests. *Psychological Review Monograph Supplement Series,* 1901, *3*(6), Whole #16, 1-62.

Witkin, H. A. *Psychological differentiation: Studies of development.* New York: Wiley, 1962.

Wittenborn, J. R. *Psychiatric rating scales.* New York: Psychological Corporation, 1955.

Wittmann, P. The Elgin checklist of funadmental psychotic behavior reactions. *American Psychologist*, 1948, *3*, 250.

Woliver, R. E. Attraction: An investigation of motivation in mate selection of newlyweds in two cultures, Japanese and American. Unpublished doctoral dissertation, University of Hawaii, 1979.

Woliver, R. E., & Cattell, R. B. Reoccurring national patterns from 30 years of multivariate cross-cultural studies. *International Journal of Psychology*, 1981, *16*, 171-198.

World Health Organization. *Report on the first session of the alcoholism subcommittee.* Expert Committee on Mental Health Technical Report Series, No. 42. Geneva, Switzerland: WHO, 1951.

World Health Organization. *Report of the international pilot study of schizophrenia, Vol. 2.* Geneva, Switzerland: WHO, 1978.

Wright, H. F., & Barker, R. G. Psychological ecology and the problem of psychosocial development. *Child Development,* 1949, *20*, 131-143.

Wright, H. F., & Barker, R. G. *Methods in psychological ecology.* Unpublished manuscript, Lawrence, KS: Dep't of Psychology, University of Kansas, 1950.

Wrightsman, L. *Social psychology for the eighties* (3rd ed.). Monterey, CA: Brooks/Cole, 1981.

Wundt, W. *Grundriss der psychologie.* (C. H. Judd, trans.) Leipzeig: Engelmann, 1896.

Wyatt, F. The scoring and analysis of the Thematic Apperception Test. *Journal of Psychology*, 1947, *24*, 319-330.

Young, P. T. *Motivation and emotions.* New York: Wiley, 1961.

Zeigarnik, B. Uber das Behalten von erledigten und unerledigten Handlungen. *Psychologische Forschung,* 1927, *9*, 1-85.

Zimmerman, I. L., & Woo-Sam, J. M. *Clinical interpretation of the Wechsler Adult Intelligence Scale.* New York: Grune & Stratton, 1973.

Zirkle, C. *Evolution, Marxian biology and the social scene.* Philadelphia: University of Pennsylvania Press, 1959.

Zoref, L., & Williams, P. A look at content bias in IQ tests. *Journal of Educational Measurement,* 1980, *17*(4), 213-322.

Author Index

Achterberg, J., 340
Adler, A., 45, 288, 299, 314
Adorno, T.W., 475
Agarwal, K., 340
Ainsworth, M., 445
Ajzen, I., 320-323, 325, 326, 332
Aleshire, D.O., 326
Allen, L.C., 284
Allen, M.J., 201
Allport, G.W., 143, 209, 253, 311, 330
Anastasi, A., 190, 201, 328, 433
Anderson, J.E., 143, 144, 266, 297
Anton, M., 296, 377
Arrington, R., 232
Atkinson, J.W., 263

Bachtold, L.M., 462
Baer, D.M., 233
Baggaley, A., 268, 289, 292, 299, 322, 323, 325, 528
Baker, M., 326
Bales, R.F., 480
Balma, M.J., 446
Baltes, P.B., 6, 92, 117, 149, 182, 471, 523
Barker, R.G., 232
Barrabee, E.L., 342
Barrabee, P., 342
Barron, F.
Bartlett, H.W. 112
Barton, K., 20, 110, 115, 139, 150, 289, 335, 339, 341, 342, 353, 377, 449, 450, 458, 460, 471, 476
Beaton, A.E., 480
Beck, M.D., 198, 262
Behrens, C.M., 139
Belfer, P.L., 340
Bellak, L., 262, 292, 302
Beloff, J.R., 292
Bem, S.L., 470
Bender, L.A., 184
Bennett, R.W., 180
Bentler, P.M., 322
Ben-Tovim, D.I., 339
Bergin, A.E., 369
Berk, R.A., 199
Bersoff, D.N., 448
Bindra, D., 291
Binet, A., 166, 426
Birkett, H., 124, 279, 280, 296, 315, 366, 367, 424
Bjerstedt, A., 49, 50, 274, 282, 353
Blake, R.R., 378

Bleuler, E., 216
Blewett, D.B., 292
Bloom, B.S., 192, 195, 204
Bloxom, B.M., 252
Bock, R.D., 193
Bogardus, E.S., 318
Bohn, M.J., 439
Bolton, L.S., 112, 232, 251, 252, 349, 353, 377
Bolz, C.R., 24, 537
Bond, L., 448
Borgatta, E.G., 480
Bormuth, J.R., 201
Bouchard, J.T., 249, 251
Boulding, K.E., 481
Bowers, K.S., 468
Bracht, G.H., 194
Brennan, J., 18, 19, 30, 75, 99, 101, 337, 481, 520, 523, 538
Briggs, D., 474
Briggs, P.F., 223, 224
Bristol, H., 186
Browne, J.A., 246
Bruel, H., 480
Buck, J.N., 262
Buj, V., 452
Burdsal, C., 94, 289, 514
Buros, O.K., 3, 15, 58, 67, 89, 105, 132, 159, 204, 245, 247, 248, 250, 307, 350, 444, 518
Burt, C.L., 27, 85, 100, 222, 224, 267, 268, 462
Burton, R.V., 210
Buss, A.R., 123, 471
Butcher, H.J., 7, 12, 112, 122, 138, 139, 167, 173, 193, 197, 201, 264, 282, 289, 292, 296, 399, 439, 443, 447-450, 452, 456, 461-463

Cahill, M.C., 340
Cairns, R.B., 233
Caldwell, A.B., 138
Calhoun, E., 198
Campbell, D.P., 34, 50, 113, 139, 269, 307, 328
Carpenter, C.R., 24
Carroll, J.B., 449
Cartwright, D.S., 33, 123, 269, 274, 294
Carver, R.P., 190
Castelnuovo-Tedesco, P., 341
Catell, A.K.S., 338
Cattell, H.E., 113, 123, 139, 380, 476, 542
Cattell, J.McK., 210, 425, 426
Cattell, M.D., 434

Cattell, R.B., 7, 10, 12, 14, 16, 18, 19, 21, 24, 26, 27, 30-34, 36, 40-43, 48-51, 56, 60, 63, 70, 73, 79, 81, 90, 92, 94-96, 99-103, 105, 110, 112, 113, 115, 116, 122-124, 126-132, 138, 139, 141, 148-152, 159, 167-169, 171-173, 178-180, 186-188, 191-193, 197, 201, 202, 209-212, 214-218, 220, 222-224, 226, 230, 232, 236, 244-246, 249, 251-254, 256, 261, 263, 264, 266-271, 274, 276-282, 284, 285, 289-294, 296-301, 304, 307, 308, 311, 315, 322-326, 327, 329, 335, 337-339, 341-343, 345, 349-351, 353, 356, 358, 360, 363, 366, 367, 370, 374, 375, 377, 380, 382, 391, 397, 399, 412, 418, 424, 425, 427, 430-434, 436, 438, 439, 443, 446-452, 455, 457-460, 462-464, 467-469, 471, 474-477, 479-483, 498, 501, 504, 507-512, 514, 518-524, 528, 529, 531, 532, 534, 537, 538, 541
Chambers, J., 463
Chao, G.T., 432
Chatfield, D., 123
Child, D., 48, 281, 289, 290, 292, 294, 298, 308, 311, 322, 323, 326, 327, 366, 399, 412, 436, 458, 477, 532, 534
Claghorn, J.L., 340
Clyde, D.J., 342
Coan, R.W., 139, 215, 217, 232, 268
Cohen, D.B., 340
Cohen, J., 474
Coleman, W., 190
Cole, N.S., 452
Colwill, N.L., 470
Constantinople, A., 470
Comrey, A.L., 128, 258
Cottrell, L.S., 480
Coulter, M.A., 226, 537
Cox, R.C., 204
Crane, D.P., 433
Crawford, C.B., 462
Creager, J.A., 528
Crisp, A.H., 339
Cronbach, L.J., 60, 74, 92, 94, 104, 197, 201, 224, 246, 250, 261, 451, 520, 527, 528
Croom, W.C., 263
Cross, P., 124, 289, 315, 366, 462

Cruce, M.A., 341
Crutchfield, R.S., 317
Csikszentmihalyi, M., 462
Cureton, T.K., 92, 153, 190
Curran, J.P., 18, 50, 110, 291, 338, 274

Damarin, F.L., 264
Danko, R., 113
Darbes, A., 341
Darrow, C.W., 267
Darwin, C., 292, 451
Davidson, A.R., 323
Dawes, R.M., 137
Deci, E.L., 433
Dee-Burnett, R., 139
DeFries, J.C., 484
Degan, J.W., 214
Delhees, K.H., 123, 128, 251, 282, 353, 399, 476
Demarce, R.G., 343
DeWaele, J.P., 429
DeYoung, G.E., 246, 437, 476
Diaz-Guerrero, R., 323
Dickman, K., 236
Dielman, T.E., 281, 335, 363, 449, 450, 458, 474, 476
Digman, J.M., 34, 217
Dinero, T.E., 452
Dixon, L.K., 148
Dreger, R.M., 14, 26, 46, 111, 123, 186, 191
Drevdahl, J.E., 130, 132, 462
Dubin, S.S., 268
Duffy, E., 291
Dunlap, J.W., 87
Dunnette, M.D., 433, 466
Dwyer, P.S., 514, 515, 517, 528
Dymond, R.F., 222

Ebel, R., 195, 198, 199, 201
Eber, H.W., 26, 29, 73, 75, 90, 128-132, 138, 139, 252, 254, 276, 277, 342, 343, 350, 351, 386, 391, 433, 462, 463, 471, 477, 483, 510, 511, 538, 541
Edwards, A.C., 245, 248, 249, 258, 292, 314, 499
Eggleston, E., 143
Ekstrom, R.B., 191
Eliot, T.S., 15
Elley, W.B., 175, 452
Endicott, J., 227
Endler, N.S., 19, 210, 468
Englehart, M.D., 204
Epstein, S., 326
Ertl, J.P., 112, 188
Eysenck, H.J., 5, 25, 33, 90, 123, 153, 156, 168, 191, 214, 227, 253, 259, 266, 267, 273-275, 282, 322, 369, 457, 475

Fagan, T.J., 341
Farrand, C., 210
Feather, N.T., 263
Feo, A.F., 279, 281, 282

Ferguson, G.A., 104, 191, 322
Fersching, A., 339
Festinger, L., 297
Fiedler, F., 480
Finch, A.L., 89
Fine, E.W., 340
Finestinger, J.E., 342
Finkbeiner, C., 34, 216, 218, 222, 268, 358, 499
Finney, J.C., 138
Fishbein, M., 320-323, 325, 326, 332
Fiske, D.W., 34, 123
Flanagan, J.C., 92, 253, 445, 446, 459, 527
Fleischer, B., 476
Fleishman, E.A., 190
Fowler, R.D., 138
Frankignoul, M., 340
Frederiksen, N., 104, 480
French, J.W., 44, 180, 191, 214
Frenkel-Brunswick, E., 475
Freud, A., 299
Freud, S., 40, 45, 151, 211, 216, 225, 262, 264, 288, 291, 292, 299, 302, 305, 314, 365, 398, 458
Freyd, M., 427-429, 444, 445
Fuller, A.R., 75, 341
Furby, L., 94, 520

Gale, C.A., 450, 458
Galton, F., 210, 213, 232, 425
Gekoski, N., 434
Getzels, J.W., 461, 463
Ghiselli, E.E., 430, 433, 444
Gibbons, B.D., 112
Gill, M.M., 292
Gillis, J.S., 75, 458
Gilmer, B.V., 433
Gittinger, J.W., 264
Glaser, R., 199, 448
Glass, G.V., 200, 369
Gleser, G.C., 60
Goldberg, L.R., 249, 250
Golden, C.J., 177, 184, 185, 350
Goodrich, B.W., 342
Gordon, E.W., 192, 448
Gorsuch, R.L., 50, 65, 246, 319-321, 324, 326, 329, 331
Gough, H.G., 250, 483
Gould, B.S., 340
Goulet, L.R., 523
Graffam, D.T., 150, 460
Graham, F.K., 184, 480-482
Green, J.A., 233
Green, R.R., 116, 190
Gindley, J.A., 315, 366
Gross, M.L., 444
Gruen, W., 215
Guilford, J.P., 5, 61, 104, 112, 123, 167-169, 180, 191, 224, 258, 268, 322, 430, 433, 443, 459, 515, 524, 529
Guion, R.M., 429
Gulliksen, H., 73, 92, 104

Gunther, M.D., 250
Guthrie, G.M., 450
Guttman, L., 67, 92, 96, 246, 319, 501, 528

Hagen, E., 449
Haggard, E.A., 60
Hakstian, A.R., 5, 166-168, 188, 264, 280, 450, 458
Haladnya, T.M., 196, 201
Hall, J.F., 33
Halstead, W.C., 183
Hambleton, R.K., 199, 200
Hammeke, T.A., 184
Hammond, S.B., 214
Haney, W., 448
Hansen, J.C., 139, 328
Harman, H.H., 65, 191, 528
Harré, R., 429
Harrington, L.P., 267
Harris, F.R., 233
Hartman, H.P., 480
Hartshorne, H., 210
Hastings, J.T., 204
Hathaway, R.R., 164, 223, 538
Haupt, T.D., 343
Hays, J., 452
Hayes-Roth, F., 415
Haythorne, W., 480
Heath, L.L., 267
Hebb, D.O., 169, 291
Heilbrun, A.B., 248, 483
Heist, A.B., 289, 292
Heist, P.A., 292
Helmreich, R.L., 470
Hemphill, J.K., 480
Hester, R., 341
Hoffman, B., 189
Holland, J.L., 329, 439
Hopkins, K.D., 194, 201
Horn, J.L., 5, 6, 12, 18, 37, 92, 112, 117, 139, 149, 150, 165, 167-169, 174, 178, 180, 182, 183, 188, 198, 203, 246, 264, 268, 289, 292, 329, 343, 363, 449, 461, 517
Horst, P., 74, 511
Houpt, J.L., 340
House, R.L., 297
Howard, M., 85
Howarth, E., 246
Huffman, L., 216, 217
Hull, C.L., 297, 314
Hummel-Rossi, B., 198
Hundleby, J.D., 5, 24, 41, 123, 261, 267-269, 271, 274
Hunt, J., 19, 150, 330, 468
Hunter, J.E., 73, 144-146, 430, 431, 446
Hurley, J.R., 315, 366
Husek, T.R., 199
Hutt, M., 143

Ilgen, D., 433
Izard, C.E., 150

Jaccard, J.J., 323
Jackson, D.N., 30, 248, 292, 314
Jackson, P.W., 461
Jacobs, P., 523
James, H., 45
James, M., 380
James, W., 44, 45, 382
Jenkins, R.L., 341
Jensen, A.R., 90, 144, 145, 480
Johns, E.R., 139
Johnson, J.H., 140, 512
Johnson, K.N., 140
Johnson, R.C., 148, 483
Jones, F.E., 463
Jongeward, D., 380
Juchrges, J., 340
Judd, L.L., 340
Jung, C., 40, 44, 45, 48, 151, 216,
    288, 292, 299, 314, 394

Kaiser, 67
Kameoka, V., 49, 50, 246
Kamin, L., 144
Karoly, P., 107, 253, 418, 523
Karson, S., 123, 129, 138, 164,
    343, 350, 380, 382, 391, 394,
    455, 499
Kaufman, A.S., 168, 177, 186
Kaufman, N.L., 186
Kauss, D., 341
Kawash, G., 476
Kelley, H.P., 37
Kelley, T.L., 198
Kelly, E.L., 149, 216, 217, 250,
    460
Kendall, B.S., 184
Kepner, J., 264
Kerr, W.A., 433
Killian, L.R., 269
King, L.D., 281, 282, 439
Klein, T., 268
Kleinmuntz, B., 137, 139, 249
Klett, C.J., 212
Kline, P., 151, 315, 358, 363, 366
Klopfer, B., 262
Knapp, R.R., 90, 281, 452
Koch, A.L., 215, 232
Koppitz, E.M., 264
Kornreich, M., 369
Korth, B., 24
Kozoll, C.E., 139
Kraepelin, E., 216
Krech, D., 317
Kretschmer, F., 213, 216, 267
Kristy, N.E., 268
Krug, S., 5, 26, 29, 50, 75, 111,
    119, 128, 129, 138-140, 245,
    299, 329, 343, 350, 353, 363,
    373, 394, 434, 454, 471, 482,
    483, 504
Kuder, G.F., 148, 328
Kulhavy, R.W., 139, 186, 343,
    471, 482, 483
Kurtz, A.K., 87
Kury, H., 339

Lachar, D., 138

Lambert, M.J., 369
Lane, I.M., 429
Lang, V.R., 128, 139
Largen, J., 340
Lasky, J.J., 212
Laughlin, J.E., 373, 454
Lawler, B., 264
Lawler, E.E., 297
Lawlis, G.E., 123, 289, 312, 340
Lashe, C.H., 446
Lebo, M.A., 341
Lee, D.C., 458
Lennon, R.T., 204
Lerner, B., 448
Levinson, D., 475
Lewin, K., 297
Light, B.H., 289
Likert, R., 318
Lindsley, D.B., 291
Lindzey, G., 33, 123, 330
Lindquist, E.F., 92, 104
Lingoes, J.C., 102, 519
Linn, R.L., 431
Lips, H.M., 470
Lira, F.T., 341
Livingston, S.A., 199
Loehlin, J.C., 148
Longabaugh, R., 415
Lord, F.M., 92, 201, 523
Lorefice, L., 340
Lorenz, K., 21, 24, 46, 288, 292,
    297
Lorr, M., 212, 214, 227, 341
Luborsky, L.B., 264, 338, 366
Lunneborg, P.W., 328
Luria, A.R., 184
Lushene, R.E., 50
Lynn, R., 90, 447, 471, 482, 517

Machover, K., 262
MacKinnon, D.W., 223, 224
Madaus, G., 204
Maddi, S.R., 123
Madsen, K.B., 297, 299
Magnussen, D., 19, 210
Malamud, W., 342
Malinowski, A., 480
Mandryk, T.R., 450
Marilov, V., 339
Maslow, A.H., 46, 291
Matarazzo, J.D., 264, 427, 433
Mathew, R.J., 340
Mathew-Simonton, S., 340
Maxwell, E.F., 289
May, R.A., 210
Mayo, L.G., 341
McArdle, J.J., 12, 178, 182, 188
McArthur, R.T., 175, 452
McClain, D., 476
McClelland, D.C., 263, 291, 301,
    329
McCormick, E.J., 433, 445
McDougall, E., 46, 291, 292, 297,
    325
McFarland, S., 319-321
McGill, J.C., 289

McKee, M.G., 248, 249
McKenna, A., 180
McMichael, R.E., 266
McNair, D.M., 212
McNemar, Q., 92, 177
McReynolds, P., 429
Mead, M., 480
Medinnus, G.R., 223
Meehl, P.E., 10, 137, 164, 229,
    538
Mehrabian, A., 340
Mehrens, W.A., 199
Melnyk, G.I., 450
Meltzoff, J., 369
Merrifield, P.R., 447
Merrill, M.A., 426
Messick, S., 92, 190, 191, 193,
    204
Michael, W.B., 529
Miller, T.I., 369
Miller, W.C., 517
Middleton, G., 450
Millman, J., 200
Millon, T., 139
Mills, C.N., 200
Miner, J.B., 433
Miner, M.G., 433
Mintz, J., 366
Mischel, W., 210, 325, 326, 468
Monachesi, E.D., 223
Morales, M.L., 323
Morgan, C.D., 301
Morse, P.W., 342
Mosier, C.I., 528
Mouton, J.S., 378
Muller, D., 198
Munsterberg, H., 425
Murray, H.A., 21, 46, 248, 249,
    262, 263, 291-293, 299-302,
    314, 315, 363

Nader, R., 429
Nanda, H., 60
Nenty, H.J., 452
Nesbitt, J.E., 449
Nesselroade, J.R., 18, 48, 81, 92,
    102, 107, 115, 123, 139, 149,
    182, 246, 341, 471, 475, 476,
    511, 523
Nichols, R.C., 148
Nirmal, B., 462
Nisbett, R.E., 322
Norman, W.T., 249
Norris, F.H., 340
Noty, C., 311, 436, 437
Novick, M.R., 201, 430
Nowack, M.J., 279
Nunnally, J.C., 104, 201, 325

Odbert, H.S., 143, 209
O'Dell, J.W., 123, 129, 138, 164,
    350, 380, 382, 391, 394, 455,
    499
Olds, J., 291, 297
Olson, W.C., 231, 233
Orling, R., 198

Ortberg, J., 324
Osgood, C.E., 319

Page, E., 100
Paris-Panzera, E., 341
Parloff, M.B., 523
Parry, J.B., 160
Patrick, S.V., 50, 269, 284
Pawlick, K., 5, 24, 33, 41, 123, 214, 254, 261, 267-269, 271, 274, 480
Pearlman, K., 145
Pearson, J.S., 138
Pervin, L.A., 33, 123, 151
Peterson, D.R., 215, 232, 259
Piaget, J., 52
Pichot, P., 113
Pierce, J., 457
Pierson, G., 34, 164, 216, 218, 222, 358, 457, 499
Pilowksy, I., 340
Piotrowski, A., 139
Pleck, J.H., 470
Pleszewski, A., 340
Poley, W., 123
Pool, K.B., 343
Popham, W.J., 199
Porter, L.W., 139, 297
Preshnow, R., 523
Price, P.L., 284
Purisch, A.D., 184

Rachman, S.J., 369
Radcliffe, J., 139, 191, 268, 289, 292, 299, 329, 524, 526
Rajaratnam, N., 60
Rapaport, D., 292, 302
Raushe, A., 113
Raymond, J.S., 531, 532, 535
Reese, J., 92, 102, 115, 123, 149
Reik, T., 143
Reilly, R.R., 432
Rennes, P., 113
Reschly, D.D., 448
Resnick, L.B., 448
Reznikoff, M., 341
Rhymer, R.M., 338
Rickels, K., 150, 152, 269, 282, 523
Ricks, D.F., 123
Roberts, A.F., 476
Robinson, J.P., 113, 474
Roby, T.B., 480
Rogers, C., 222, 414
Roid, G.H., 201, 329
Rokeach, M., 317, 330, 331
Rorer, L.G., 224
Rorschach, H., 262
Rosenberg, M., 438
Rossman, B.B., 461
Royce, J.R., 123
Rummel, R.J., 482
Russell, J.A., 340
Ryback, R., 415

Sahakian, W.S., 123

Sands, S.L., 342
Sanford, R.N., 475
Saunders, D.R., 266, 268
Saville, P., 90
Schachter, S., 292, 302
Schafer, R., 292
Schaie, K.W., 92, 149, 182, 471, 523
Scheibel, D., 341
Scheier, I.H., 10, 18, 48, 50, 112, 164, 268, 269, 274, 338, 373, 510, 522, 538
Scherer, I., 341
Schmeidler, G.R., 340
Schmidt, L.R., 50, 75, 123, 144-146, 268, 269, 274, 282, 430, 431, 480
Schneewind, K.A., 123
Schroeder, G., 113
Schuerger, J., 26, 30, 90, 128, 150, 261, 263, 264, 268, 269, 277, 279, 281, 284, 285, 350, 356, 358-360, 450, 464, 521
Schuler, J., 284
Schumacher, G., 113
Schut, J., 340
Schwartz, H., 274
Schwartz, S., 434
Scott, W.A., 211, 224, 323, 324, 331, 333
Scott, W.D., 425
Sealy, A.P., 449
Sechehaye, M., 389
Seitz, W., 112
Sells, S.B., 343, 433, 468
Sethi, J.P., 340
Shane, G.S., 145
Shaver, P.R., 474
Sheldon, W.H., 214, 267
Sherif, C.W., 324
Sherif, M., 324
Shotwell, A.M., 315, 366
Shutz, R.E., 202
Siegel, L., 429
Simon, R., 200
Simon, T., 426
Simonton, O.C., 340
Sindberg, R.M., 476
Skinner, B.F., 396
Smith, A., 185, 452
Smith, B.D., 33
Smith, M.L., 369
Sneath, P.H., 537, 538
Snow, R.E., 190, 197
Sokal, R.R., 537, 538
Solway, K., 452
Spearman, C.E., 5, 28, 92, 110, 166, 167, 173, 178, 267, 426, 462
Speckart, G., 322
Spence, J.T., 470
Spencer, H., 125
Spielberger, C.D., 50, 115, 274, 342, 345
Spitzer, R.L., 227
Stankow, L., 37

Stanley, J.C., 201, 203
Stauffacher, W., 341
Steer, R.A., 340
Steffans, J.J., 107, 253, 418, 523
Stephenson, W., 222, 224
Sterrett, B.G., 204
Stevens, S.S., 214
Stewart, R.G., 292
Stice, C.R., 268, 457
Stice, G.F., 132, 438, 477, 479, 480
Stiefel, G., 474
Stogdill, R.M., 445, 480
Stricker, L.J., 176, 474, 475
Strong, E.K., 148, 307
Strother, C.R., 92, 149
Streuning, E.L., 474
Suci, G.J., 319
Sullivan, H.S., 362
Super, D.E., 439
Sweney, M.A., 5, 139, 164, 191, 268, 289, 292, 294, 298, 299, 304, 307, 313, 314, 329, 339, 363, 377, 410, 414, 437, 443, 449, 450, 476
Swenson, W.M., 138

Tait, E., 277, 521
Takemoto-Chock, N.K., 217
Tapp, J., 299
Tatro, D.F., 116, 269, 282
Tatsuoka, M., 73, 90, 92, 122, 129-132, 246, 252, 254, 276, 277, 342, 343, 350, 351, 386, 391, 433, 438, 457, 462, 463, 471, 477, 483, 511, 538, 541
Tavernelli, M., 277, 521
Taylor, C.W., 461
Tenopyr, M.L., 430
Terman, L., 426
Terrell, M.D., 448
Thomson, G.H., 528
Thorndike, R.L., 28, 90, 201, 235, 250, 429, 449
Thurstone, L.L., 36, 92, 166-168, 180, 181, 188, 191, 267, 318, 319, 434, 443, 446, 452, 459, 519
Timm, V., 75
Tinbergen, M., 288, 292
Tollefson, D., 264, 463
Tolman, E.C., 297
Tomson, B., 274
Torgeson, W.S., 92, 104
Toynbee, A., 480
Traub, R.E., 199
Travers, R.W., 117
Triandis, H.C., 323
Tsujsoka, B., 70, 73, 226, 538
Tucker, W.B., 214
Tuddenham, R.D., 89

Updegrove, C., 340

Vandenberg, S.G., 475
Van Egeren, L.F., 338, 366

Vaughan, G.M., 150, 471, 514
Veitch, R., 341
Vernon, P.E., 89, 114, 160, 253, 330
Veroff, J., 292, 302
Vetter, H.J., 33
Vroom, V.H., 297

Wagman, M., 140
Wagner, A., 113
Wagoner, J.H., 339
Wahba, M., 297
Wahl, O.F., 474
Walker, D.A., 96, 214, 224
Walsh, J.A., 250
Walter, V., 132, 138
Warburton, F.W., 21, 31, 32, 96, 106, 191, 209, 261, 267, 268, 270, 276, 278, 281, 308, 358
Wardell, D., 276, 279, 284
Waskow, I.E., 523

Watson, J.B., 233
Watterson, D.C., 263, 350, 450
Wechsler, D.A., 426
Wells, H.G., 451
Wenig, P., 261, 299, 501
Werner, E.E., 462
Wesley, C., 470
Wesley, F., 470
Wessman, A.E., 123
Weste, C.M., 480
Wiggins, J.S., 33, 130, 151
Will, D.P., 343
Williams, P., 452
Williams, R.G., 196, 299, 307, 338, 340
Willingham, W.W., 204
Wilson, G.D., 475
Wilson, G.T., 369
Wilson, T. DeC., 322
Winch, R.F., 475
Winder, P., 129

Wirt, R.D., 223, 224
Wissler, C., 210
Witkin, H.A., 123, 271
Wittenborn, J.R., 214, 241
Wittman, P., 341
Wolf, M.M., 233
Wolfe, B.E., 523
Woliver, R.E., 21, 296, 476, 480-482
Woodyard, E., 90
Wright, H.F., 232
Wundt, W., 426

Yen, W.M., 201
Yeudall, L.T., 276, 279, 284

Zastowny, T.R., 474
Zeller, W.W., 341
Zimmerman, I.L., 112, 258, 433
Zoref, L., 452

Subject Index

Abilities:
assessment in brain damage, 182-185
assessment in young children, 185-187
classification of, 166-168
cognitive modality, 106
factor analysis of, 167
higher stratum factors, *table* 37
measurement, 166-188
provincial, 169, 186
second order factor, 167, 168, 266
tests for primary, 166-176, 180-182
traits, 36-38
Achievement:
identifying underachievers, 451-453
measuring, 189-207
models for explanation of, 191
nature of, 190, 191, 193, 194
possible prediction with functional tests, 448-451
regression weights for predicting, *table* 458
selecting a test, 203-206
test content, 196-200
Adjective Check List (ACL), 483
Adjustment:
measurement of, 297-315
Adjustment Process Analysis Chart, 51, 298, 397
Affectia (A-factor), 13
Affectothymia:
as second order factor, 344
Sizothymia-Affectothymia factor, 391
A Guide to Mental Testing, 263
Alcoholics Anonymous (Alanon), 418
Alcoholism:
case history, 407-423
Allport-Odbert Lexicon, 443
Allport, Vernon, and Lindzey Study of Values, 330
Allport-Vernon Personality Types, 253, 430
Ambient situation
in behaviorial equation, 16
American Men of Science, 462
American Mensa Society, 180
American Psychological Association, 151, 429, 430, 445, 537
DSM-III, 225

test committee, 161, 162, 246
American Psychologist, 447
Amyotrophic lateral sclerosis, 340
Analysis of Variance (ANOVA), 209, 210, 521
Anorexia nervosa, 339, 340
Anxiety:
as personality factors, 13, 35, 162, 265
as second order factor, 50, *table* 51, 52, 344
as test concept, 67
correlation of states, 48
in L-Q media, 39, 269
measured by CAQ, 390
measured by O-A Battery, 30, 274, 279, 282
measured by 16 P.F., 254
measured by WAIS, 264
ratio of, 83
Anxiety Scale Questionnaire, 373
Apple, 127
Army Adjutant General's Office Personnel Division, 459
Assertiveness
in MAT, 72
Assurance, 274
Asthenia, 274
Atlantic Monthly, 460
A-trait, 13, 46, 216
Attitudes:
classical model, 317, 323
measuring, 316-333
structural measurement:
Alpha and Gamma, 323-325
MAT, 329
values, 330-332
VIM, 328, 329
Attribution theory, 532
Australian Council for Educational Research (ACER), 161
tests, 174
Autia, 382
Autism, 393, 510

Basic Data Relations Matrix (BDRM) (Data Box):
coefficients of evaluations, 56, 62
consistency of test, 77
bases of standardization, 79-83, 103
sources of variation within, *table* 80
factor analysis, 210

Bayley Scales of Infant Development, 165
Behaviorial equation:
behavioral specification equation, 130-132
evaluating action of structures in situations, 294-297
meaning of, 15-18
understanding the achievement process, 453-458
state modulation, 20
teaching of, 6
use of source traits in, 8-10
Behaviorial indices, 17, 18
Behaviorists, 16, 233
Watsonian, 16, 233
Bender-Gestalt test, 3, 143, 184, 188, 299, 349
Bender Word Association Test, 261-263, 286, 299
Benzedrine, 110
Bernnenter Personality Factors, 253, 259
Binet Test, *see* Stanford Binet
Boyle's law, 102
Briggs-Myers Questionnaire, 537
British Mensa Society, 180

California Achievement Tests, 206
California Test Bureau, 14, 206
California Personality Inventory (CPI), 248-250, 252
Campbell-Strong, see Strong-Campbell
Cattell Intelligence Scales, 178, 180, 188, 299
Centiles, 83-88
Central Trait-State Kit (CTS):
flexibility, 253
history of, 342-348
nonpathological measurement with, 242
purpose and use of, 345-347
reliability, validity, 346
secondary traits, 259
state measurement with, 342-345
use of, 254-257
Centre de Psychologie Appliquée, 161
Charles's Law, 102
Child Motivation Analysis Test (CMAT), 305
Children's Aperception Test (CAT), 262

Children's Personality
  Questionnaire (CPQ):
  computer scoring of, 139
  factor loading of, 155
  in clinical assessment, 350
  relationship to achievement,
    453, 454
  relationship to other tests, 252-
    254, 259
  usage of, 248
CIRCUS test battery, 204, 205
Civilization and its discontent,
  458
Clinical Analysis Questionnaire
  (CAQ):
  computer scoring, 29, 139, 141,
    536
  depression factors, 542
  factor analysis of, 227, 253
  in abnormal behavior, 238
  in clinical assessment, 349-
    356, 377-424
  in clinical diagnosis, 257, 259,
    349-356, 377-424
  in pathological diagnosis, 538
  in vocational selection, 439,
    442
  interpretation of CAQ profile
    of schizophrenic women,
    389-396
  measurement of pathology,
    342, 343, 352-356
  measurement of personality
    structures, 242
  monitoring psychotherapy,
    371-374
  occupational reference profiles,
    132
  profile of DSM syndromes, 10
  profiles, figure 354
  scoring secondary factors, 39,
    97
  screening procedure, 434
  similarity coefficient, 122
  usage, 248
Clinical vs. Statistical Prediction:
  A Theoretical Analysis and
  Review of the Evidence, 229
Clyde Mood Scale, 342
Common traits:
  in behavioral equation, 17, 18
  prediction of performance from,
    7
  R-technique factor solutions, 6,
    13
Comprehensive Ability Battery
  (CAB):
  correlation with HSPQ and 16
    P.F., 511
  factor analysis of, 364
  in employment testing, 445
  machine scoring, 29
  measuring primary abilities,
    168, 181-183
  predicting achievement, 452
Computers, 12, 127-141, 269

behavioral equations, 129-132
computer-based test
  interpretation, 137-140,
  163
data bases, 132-136, 141
multivariate experimental
  psychological research,
  contribution to, 127-129
PLATO system, 140
Comrey's Personality Inventory,
  39
  construction principle, 258
  factoring of MMPI scales, 128
  scoring secondary factors, 39
Conflict:
  loser's syndrome, 313
  measurement of, 297-315
Conscientiousness, 344
Control, 276
Correction matrix, 504
  use of a trait view, table 505
Cortertia:
  as mental alertness, 386
  left brain activity, 254
  measured by CTS kit, 344
  second order, 52, 265
  source trait, 45
  vs. Pathemia, 276
Creativity:
  evaluating potential, 461-464
Cronbach's alpha, 4, 59, 527, 528
Culture-Fair Intelligence Test:
  academic bias, 154
  artificial validity, 64
  as classical I.Q. on, figure 85
  assessment of intelligence in
    young children, 185
  correlation with Chinese
    language learning, 172
  cross cultural aspects, 30
  cultural differences, 517, 518
  face validity, 31, 62
  group administration of, 175
  identifying underachievers,
    451
  machine scoring, 536
  nonverbal, 180
  predicting achievement, 449,
    464
  predictive information for, 165
  security of, 163
  standardization of, 90, 188
  test for brain damage, 182
  test sophistication, 114
  test speed, 117, 118
Curran-Cattell Eight State, 49
Curves:
  leptokurtic, 86, 103
  platokurtic, 86, 103

D factor, 216, see also,
  excitability
Data bases:
  growth and management of,
    132, 136

Depression:
  conceptual test for, 63
  diagnosis with CAQ, 356, 371,
    380
  diagnosis with 16 P.F., 386
  DSM categorization, 226
  factors, 49
  state scale, 65
Depression Scale, 373
Description and Measurement of
  Personality, 268
Diagnostic and Statistical
  Manual (DSM):
  clinical diagnosis categories,
    225, 286, 348, 535
  "diagnostic category," 537, 543
  improved DSM-III, 538
  rating clinical types, 226, 236
  24-element profile with CAQ,
    10
  type profiles in, 121
Dictionary of Occupational Titles,
  431, 443, 445
Dimensions of Personality, 268
Discouragement vs.
  sanguineness, 275, 276
Doctorate of Psychology (Psy.D.),
  152
Dominance:
  E factor, 149, 150
  personality factor, 13
dR-techniques:
  common factor analysis, 7, 13
  defining psychological states,
    18, 338
  definition, 6
  dynamic source traits, 48
  exvia-invia trait, 48
  general state dimensions
    discovered by, table 50, 53
  in factor analysis, 5, 77, 258
  occasion-to-occasion factoring,
    255
Draw-a-Man, 27, 62, 100, 286,
  348
  as intelligence test, 100
  conspect reliability, 27
  factor pattern comparison, 62
  obsolescence of, 348
  projective tests, 286
Draw-a-Person (DAP), 262
Dwyer modification, see Equity
  Dwyer
Dynamic trait structures, 45-48
  ergic patterns, as, table 46

E factor, see also ego strength
  dominance factor, 149, 150
Early School Personality
  Questionnaire (ESPQ):
  behavioral equations with 16
    P.F., 132, 252, 253
  computer-based reports for,
    139
  family of tests, 253, 259
  frequency of use, 248

primary factors in, 238
Ectomorphy:
  cerebrotonia, 214
Editest (Bobbs-Merrill), 160
Educational Testing Service, 161,
  162, 206, 535
Edwards Personality Inventory
  (EPI), 251
  construction of, 249
  critique of, 249, 250
Edwards Personal Preference
  Scale (EPPS):
  compared with CPI, 250
  composition of, 244, 292
  critique of, 252
  factoring, 258
  faking, 249
  frequency of use, 248
  need variable measurement,
    263
Ego-strength:
  as ego standards, 270
  as in psychoanalytic ego, 380
  E factor, 149
  increase with therapy, 150
  in personality research, 216
  in schizophrenia, 393, 394
  personality factors, 13
Eight-Factor Comrey Personality
  Scales (CPS), 483
Eight-Parallel Form Anxiety
  Battery, 107, 373
Eight State Questionnaire, 374
Electrocardiogram (EKG), 267
Electroencephalogram (EEG), 30,
  183, 275
Elgin Behavior Rating Scale, 341
Embedded Figures Test (EFT),
  263, 264
Emotional states:
  how to measure, 341-345
  measurement of, 334-347
  usefulness of measures, 339-
    341
Endomorphy:
  viscerotonia, 214
Environmental situation, 18
Equal-appearing intervals
  technique, 318, 319
Equal Employment
  Opportunities Commission
  (EEOC), 445
Equity Dwyer, see also Dwyer
  modification:
  comparison of matrix
    processes, figure 516
  Equity rectifying, 515
  progressive rectification, 514
Ergs:
  drives, 7
  ergic patterns, table 46
  ergic tension, 8, 48, 291, 293,
    297, 314, 382, 383
  in motivation measurement,
    289-294
  in TAT, MAT, SMAT, 314

in VIM, 308
  list of human ergs, table 295
  sex erg, 18, 296, 365
Evaluation:
  clinical psychological, from
    tests, 147
Evasiveness, 271, 277
Excitability, 216
Executive Profile Survey:
  computer based interpretive
    reports, 128, 139, 141
Exhuberance:
  in O-A Kit, 271
  speed measure, 28
Extrasensory perception (ESP),
  340
Exvia:
  conceptual test for, 63
  exvia-invia as
    characterological state, 48
  in 16 P.F., 254
  in T-data, 269, 279
  personality factor, 13
  relation to systolic blood
    pressure, 267
  second order factors, 35, 39, 44,
    52, 266, 390
  temperament traits, 7
  vs. invia, table 43, 275
  Z scores for, 83
Eysenck's Personality Inventory
  (EPI):
  correlation with other tests,
    251
  cross-cultural tests, 30
  depth psychometry, effect of,
    537
  instrument factors, 112
  length of test, 245
  measures of second order
    personality factors, 239,
    259
  personality assessment
    through, 39
  scores on extraversion, 90
  theoretical framework, 242

F factor, see surgency
Factors:
  anxiety, 12
  bipolar rating variables, table
    218
  concepts in psychometry, 60
  homogeneity, 61
  in CAQ, 257, 258
  in CTS kit, 255
  in O-A battery, 50, 65, 269-287
  in I.G.P.F., 68, 72, 76, 239,
    250-252
  instrument transcending
    patterns, 64
  mood change, table 51
  patterns, 7, 46, 48, 62
  personality, 33, 34, 42, 45, 68,
    96, 218
  primary abilities examined,

table 37
  Q-L personality, table 40, 41
  questionnaire variables, table
    221
  second-order, 35, 45, 76, 168
  second-order measurement in
    16 P.F., 256
  16 bipolar primary factors in
    16 P.F., table 255
  structure matrix, 65
  trueness, transferability, 62,
    67
Factor analysis::
  algorithm for, 269
  computerized, 269
  correlation anaylsis (CORAN),
    210
  development of, 267
  in nursery school range, 186
  in projective tests, 299
  of fluid and crystallized
    intelligence, 170, 171, 461
  of 16 P.F., 220
  of WAIS-R and WISC-R, 167
  to define states, 338
Fidgetometer, 276
Flanagan Aptitude Classification
  Test Battery:
  correlation with performance,
    table 435
Flanagan's Coefficients of
  Extension, 527
Flanagan's Personality Scales,
  253
Fluctuations:
  in source traits, 6
  functional, 56
Focal stimulus, 16
Form vs. Color Tests, 267
Formulae and Table for
  Obtaining Validities and
  Reliabilities of Extended
  Factor Scales, 60
Freud's First Theory of Anxiety,
  383

G factor, see superego
General Aptitude Test Battery:
  validity coefficient, 145
General Psychosis Scale, 393
Gesell Development Scales, 185,
  186
Galvanic Skin Response (GSR):
  background of objective tests,
    260
  factor analyzation by
    computer, 140
  measuring interests, 46
  motivation measures, 315
  standardization in relation to
    test scale, 92, 100
  U factor load, 290
  unitegrated expression, 363
  validating devices, 294
  validity factors with O-A Kit,
    267

Gestalt psychology, 361
Gittinger's Personality
    Assessment system *see*
    Personaltiy
    Assessment System
Graduate Record Examination
    (GRE), 176
Graham-Kendall Memory for
    Designs Test, 184
Gross National Product (GNP),
    145
Groups:
    measurement of group
        structure, 475, of nations,
        480-482
    population measures, 466-468
    populations, dimensions of 469-
        473, survey measurements
        in, 473
    psychological characteristics of,
        466-485
    regional and group differences,
        482
    structural and role measures,
        466-468
    syntality measures, 467-469,
        477-480
*Guide to the Clinical Use of the
    16 P.F.*, 350
Guilford-Zimmerman
    Temperament Survey, 258,
    445, 459
    ability testing, 459
    factor analytic value of, 445
    scoring secondary personality
        traits, 39
    weightings for 16 P.F., 112,
        258
Guilt proneness, 380, 381, 393,
    394
Guttman Scale, 319

Hakstian Primary Abilities Test,
    166
Halstead Category Test, 184
Halstead-Reitan
    Neuropsychological Battery
    assessment of brain damage,
        184, 188
    strengths of, 185
*Handbook for the 16 P.F.
    Questionnaire*, 350, 352, 386
*Handbook of Multivariate
    Experimental Psychology*, 81
Harrap, G.G. and Co., 180
High School Personality
    Questionnaire (HSPQ):
    adaptation of minorities, 259
    age level relevance, 242
    age standardization
        allowances, 92
    computer-based reports for,
        139, 141
    construction principles, 258
    cross-cultural verification, 237,
        252

equations for accident
    proneness, etc., 132
factor scale scores, 511
Hawaiian creole, 113
identifying underachievers,
    451
invasion of privacy, 155
personaltiy assessment using,
    349-352, 364
predicting achievement, 449,
    450, 457
predictive information
    availability, 164
relation of primary to second
    order, 48, 254
relation to 16 P.F., 252, 253
reliability level, 238
scoring secondary traits, 39
size of sampling, 163
sten use in, 84
temperament factors, 305
use frequency, 248
Hogkefe and Berne, 161
Homogeneity:
    coefficient, 77
    factor, 61
    test, 61
Houghton Mifflin, 161, 206
House-Tree-Person (HTP), 262
Human Resources Center at the
    University of Chicago, 434
Humor Test of Intelligence, 62,
    110, 265, 266, 510
Hypothesis Quotient (H.Q.), 299

I factor, *see* premsia
Incautia, 45
Independence, 265, 270, 271, 277,
    344, 390
Individualized Stress
    Management Plan, 141
Indifference of indicator:
    principle of, 34
Inherent properties, 519

L (R) data:
    bias, 32
    factoring to L (BR), 236
    homogeneity of, 25
    in clinical diagnosis, 225
    personality assessment, 209,
        216, 242
    subjective evaluation, 27
    time sampling, 229-233
    weakness of, 23
Laboratory of Personaltiy and
    Group Analysis, 269
Lateral Dominance Examination,
    184
Leadership Opinion
    Questionnaire, 442
Liability:
    as L data, 19, 20, 48, 265, 336-
        339
    trait prediction model, 334-337
    trait score, 51

Legal considerations:
    confidentiality, 490-492
    informal consent, 492, 493
    psychologist's liability
        exposure, 486-488
    records, 488-490
    release of confidential
        information, 493-495
Likert Scales, 318, 319
Lithium carbonate, 340
LOGIQ System:
    test evaluation, 196
London School of Economics, 171
Left Hemisphere Scale, 184
Listening With the Third Ear,
    143
Lorge-Thorndike Test, 186, 188,
    280
Luria-Neuropsychological
    Battery, 184, 185, 188

*Manual for the Personaltiy-
    Career Development Profile*,
    135
Marriage Counseling Report, 138,
    141
Mayo Clinic, 138
McCarthy's Scales of Children's
    Abilities, 185
*Meaning and Measurement of
    Neuroticism and Anxiety*,
    268
Media:
    advantages and limitations of
        measurement, 23-25
    objective tests, 21, 22, *table* 23
    observations in life, 21, 22,
        table 23
    of assessment, 15-33
    of measurement, 277-285
    of observation and
        measurement, *table* 22, 23
    questionnaires, 21, 22, *table* 23
Mental Measurement Yearbook,
    58, 105, 132, 159, 245, 247,
    250, 252, 444
Merrill-Palmer Test, 185, 186
Mesomorphy, 214
    somatotomia, 214
Metropolitan Achievement Tests,
    206
Miller Analogies Test, 174, 180
Millon Clinical Multiaxial
    Inventory, 139
Minnesota Clerical Test, 434
Minnesota Multiphasic
    Personality Inventory
    (MMPI):
    abnormal behavior factors, 38,
        238
    atlas to, 164
    computer interpretation of,
        137-139, 141, 429
    Comrey's factoring, 128
    correlation with CPI, 250
    cross-cultural test, 30

factoring of, 4, 27
frequency of use, 248
in clinical assessment, 349-353
standardization, 89
motivated distortion scales,
    with, 240
pathological variables, 242,
    538
pattern similarity coefficient,
    122
predicting personality, 223
relating to 16 P.F., 251
standardization, 89
symbol system, 39
Modality:
cognitive, test, for, 106
dynamic interest, test for, 106
dynamic structure, 53
of behavior, 20-22
of traits, 21, 32, 277
temperment, test for, 106
*Modern Theories of Motivation: A
    Comparative Metascientific
    Study,* 299
Modulation theory, 18, 32, 48, 83
in behavioral equation, 32
in standardization, 83
model for utilizing state
    measures, 18
proneness, 32, 48
Modulator index, 19
Motivated distortion (MD):
correction for distortion, 23,
    240
scales, 245, 499, 500, 504
*Motivation and Dynamic
    Structure,* 289, 290, 363
Motivation structure:
evaluating, 288-297
Motivational Analysis Test
    (Mat):
ability contamination in
    motivation, 99
administering, 109-112
assertiveness in, 72
clinical assessment by, 377-424
clinical motivational analysis
    with, 301, 312
compared with TAT, 300, 301,
    314
computer-based reports, 139,
    141, 165
conspect reliability of, 59
design, 148
ergic tension level, 290, 291,
    296, 314
evaluating creativity, 464
executives' scores, 436
in clinical diagnosis, 363-365,
    367
in occupational testing, 434
in vocational selection, 439,
    442
instrument factors, 510
interpretation of two MAT
    profiles, 396-423

law of similarity, 476
machine scoring, 536
major sentiments covered, 123
measuring motivation, 248,
    329, 330
monitoring psychotherapy, 371
predicting achievement, 457,
    458, 464
prediction of criteria, 281
projective tests, 261-263
second-order factors, 294
source trait test, 124, 286
structured measurement, 323
transformation of scores of, 97
treatment plan based on, 415-
    418
U-I components and their
    meanings, 397-406
vectors for ambient situations,
    20
Multiple regression equation, 9
Music Preference Test, 266
Music Research Foundation, 266
Myers-Briggs Type Indicator, 39
Myograph, 30

National Accrediting Association
    for Business, 432
National Computer Systems,
    163, 536
*National Council for Educational
    Research,* 161
"Natural Child":
in transactional analysis, 380,
    386, 387
Neurotic Regression Battery, 107
New York Times, 460
New Zealand Council for
    Educational Research
    (NZCER), 161
Northampton Activity Rating
    Scale, 341

Objective Analysis Handbook:
in individual testing, 111
objective personality
    measurement theory, 358
vectors for situations, 20
Objective Analysis Personality
    Kit (O-A Kit):
administrations and scoring,
    285, 286
administration of, 107-112, 114
age standardization, 92
clinical assessment by, 377-424
concept validity, 65
conspection correlating, 27
correlation of O-A variables
    with academic
    achievement, *table* 283
"creative response" tests, 116
diagnostic typal assignments,
    table 539, 540
discriminant function, 50
"factor scale," 97
factorial source trait score, 27

group vs. individual dimension
    of, 26
historical origins, 267-269
in clinical diagnosis, 349, 356-
    362, 375
list of source traits, 358
measuring personality
    structure, 261, 264
measuring speed, 28
nature of source traits
    measurable by, 269-277
O-A extension, 276
pathological personality
    profiles, from, *figure* 284
personality factors, life course
    of, 149
physiological aspect, 30, 267
psychometric properties of,
    277, 285
scoring test battery, 128
source trait measurement,
    with, 269-277
*Objective Personality and
    Motivation Tests: A
    Theoretical Introduction and
    Practical Compendium,* 261,
    358
Organization of Petroleum
    Exporting Countries (OPEC),
    146
Organizatione Speciale, 161
Otis School Personality
    Questionnaire, 237

P-technique:
behavioral index values from,
    256
computer analysis of, 141, 164
condensed, 140
diagnostic potential, 366, 375
dynamics of the individual,
    365-367
identifying psychological
    states, 338
in factor analysis, 5
measure of motivation, 298
research by, 18
trait structure of individual, 7,
    13, 50, 53, 124, 315
Pan-normalization:
defining, 519
principle of correction, 543
standardization, 83
Parmia, 344
on 16 P.F. profile, 381, 382
primary order factor, 344, 368
Path Learning Analysis, 126, 534
Pathemia, 276
Pathognomic Scale, 184
Pattern similarity coefficient, 10
Pearson coefficient, 94
Personal Career Development
    Profile, 133, 141
Personality, 268
Personality:
assessment by objective tests.

260-287
by O-A Kit, 269-277
of sexual tendencies, 265
second order factors, 343
theoroy, 5
assessment by questionnaire,
237-259, 349-352
appropriateness, 243-245
standards for use of
questionnaires, 245-247
assessment from psychiatric
data, 208-236
distortion of ratings, 235
methodological requirements
for, 211-222
factor analysis of structures,
50-53, 209
first order factors, 217
ipsative rating, 222-224
main unitary personality
dimensions replicated in
objective (T-data)
measures (with Q-data
matches), *table* 42
profile, 9, 17, 18,
predictive use of, 9
structure, 10
structures in L-Q media, 38-42
structure of primary and
secondary Q-L factors,
table 40, 41, 150
taxonomy, 16
testing, 4, 5, 110
theory, 10-14, 149, 151
trait theory of, 16
Personality and Learning Theory,
151, 268, 363, 534
*Personality and Motivation
Structure and Measurement,*
268
Personality Assessment System,
264
*Personality Factors in Objective
Test Devices,* 268
*Personality Factors in Objective
Test Devices,* 261
Personality Research Form
(PRF), 263, 292
Personality Theory in Action,
268, 269
Peterson's Personality Factors,
259
Phenylketonuria, 119
Philadelphia Police Department,
145
PLATO System, 140
Populations:
dimensions of, 469-473
survey measurements of, 473-
475
Premsia, 7, 8, 150, 265, 381, 382
heritability, 8
Humor Test of Personality,
from, 265
interpretation of 16 P.F.
profile, 381, 382

life effects, 150
primary temperamental traits,
7
Pre-School Personality
Questionnaire (PSPQ):
measurement of personality
factors in young children,
186, 237
primary factors measured by,
238
standard verbal presentation,
26, 111, 240, 253, 536
Press Test, 434
Primary Mental Abilities Test
(PMA):
in executive selection, 442
in vocational selection, 445
intelligence testing, 181, in
young children, 185
predicting achievement, 452
psychometric measurement of,
188
Psyche Cattell Test, 185, 186
Psychiatric Rating Scale, 341,
342
Psychoanalysis:
ego strength, 270
Jungian, 4
state measure in, 359
Psychological Corporation:
Metropolitan Achievement
Test, 434
Minnesota Clerical Test, 434
prosecuting "piracy", 161
scoring by optical scanner, 535
test publishers, 160
Psychological Testing, 429
Psychologist or Medical Man, 151
Psychometric Institute, 161
Psychometrics:
depth psychometry, 40, 52,
240, 352, 537, 543
functional, 10
itemetrics, 4, 10, 27, 28, 77, 92,
95, 96, 104
properties of tests, 54-78, 144,
of O-A, 277-285
public relations of testing, 153-
156
structural, 4, 8, 60, 149, 151
Psychotherapy:
clinical diagnosis, 348-376
by O-A battery, 356-362
by CAQ, 351-356
directing therapeutic
intervention, 368-374
Psychsystems, 536
Public Opinion Inventory, 475

QPSS Rating Sheet, 342
Q-data:
basic personality factors, 242,
258, 265, 269
conspective scoring, 27
correction matrices, 504
correlation between MAT and

16 P.F., 281
cross-cultural patterns, 480
difference from L-data, 209
factor space concepts, 287
factoring L and Q data, 34, 35,
218
firmness of intelligence, 148
in 16 P.F., 230
matching T, L, and Q source
traits, 220
measuring attitudes, 317, 328
media for assessing life
behavior, 21, 32, 216, 260
, 277, advantages, 25,
limitations, 23, 24, 32
need variable measurement,
263
personality structures in L-Q
media, 38-45, 235
physiological measurement,
267
sabotage, 499
second-order Q factors, 49, 276,
287
test construction for, 253
source trait scoring, 226
Q-Rating of Ward Behavior, 341
Q-sort:
decks, 222-224
distribution of traits, 29
ranking of behaviors, 222-224,
235, 236
Q-technique:
factoring by, 222

R-technique:
common trait factors, 13
determining trait factors, 338
factor analysis of, 5-7, 258
in Q-sort, 222
in structural psychometrics, 5
test validity, 77
trait score, 255
Rating Scale for Evolution of
Psychotherapy, 342
Rational simplex theory, 102
Raven Matrices, 174-176, 188,
510
Realism, 274
Reflexologists, 7, 16, 148, 210
Skinnerian, 16, 473
Regression, 273
Reitan-Indiana Aphasia
Examination, 184
Reitan-Klove Sensory-Perceptual
Examination, 184
Relational Simplex:
approach to equal interval
scales, 101, 518, 519, 543
standardization
transformations, 83
*Reliabilities and Validities of
Simple and Extended
Weighted and Buffered
Unifactor Scales,* 60
Rokeach Value Survey, 330, 331

Rorschach test:
  computer interpretation, 139
  conspect reliability, 27, 59
  construction of, 3
  handbook for, 164
  individual to group
    administration, 111
  inkblot test, 262
  interest of psychometrists, 266,
    287
  practice in administering, 109
  prestructural tests, 107, 123
  projective tests, 261, 286, 299,
    362
  scoring of, 269
  use of scores, 4
Rotoplot, 215
Rotter Incomplete Sentences
  Blank, 262

S-factor:
  as observed measure of state,
    336
  as stimulus or situation, 16,
    46, 190
Sales Attitude Checklist, 434,
  442
Sanguineness, 275
Scales:
  centile-sten scoring, 83-88
  meaning of standardized
    scores, 79-104
  population standardization, 88-
    92
  sets in BDRM, 79-83
  simplex and pan-normalization
    principles, 101-104
  standardization
    transformations, 83-88
  test or battery construction,
    92-101
Schedule of Affective Disorders
  and Schizophrenia (SADS),
  227
Schizophrenia:
  CAQ interpretation, 377
  "depth psychometry" of, 240
  diagnostic pattern from MAT,
    figure 311
  diagnosis from CAQ scales,
    353, 389, 396
  difference from normals on 16
    P.F., 266
  DSM categories, 226
  in O-A Kit assessment, 275
  personality questionnaire, 240
  scale, 393
  score pattern on WAIS, 264
School Motivation Analysis Test
  (SMAT):
  computer scorable, 314
  concept validity of, 301
  evaluating creativity, 464
  in clinical diagnosis, 363-365
  instrument factors, 510
  measuring second-order

factors, 294
  objective motivation measures,
    112, 296, 304-306
  predicting achievement, 449,
    450, 457, 458, 464
  source trait tests, 124
  testing of structures, 297
Scores (Scoring):
  adulteration in factor scores,
    computer synthesis, 508-
    511
  computer synthesis, 510, 511,
    536, 542
  dependability index, 59
  ipsative, 29, 81, 82, 99, 222-
    224
  normative, 29, 81
  psychological interpretation of,
    496-543
  reference populations in
    standardization, 88-92,
    115-118
  relative roles of error sources,
    496, 497, administrative
    dependability, 498,
    evaluative situations, 497-
    508
  scales and meaning of, 79-104
  standardization
    transformations, 83-100
Scott's Value Surveying and
  Scales, 331
Scree test, 246
Seashore Rhythm Test, 184
Sems:
  definition, 47
  in MAT, 329
  in motivation measurement,
    289-294, 297, 298, 302,
    364
  in VIM, 307
  main sentiment traits, table 47
Sense and Nonsense in
  Psychology, 156
Sentiments, 47
  developing content structure
    of, 326-328
  main traits obtained by
    questionnaire, table 47
Sequential Tests of Educational
  Progress, 206
Sheppard's correction, 84, 87
Sheridan Company, 160
Short Employment Test, 434
Simplex I.Q. Test, 104, 186
Situation View Theory, 531
Sixteen Personality Factors
  Prediction Questionnaire (16
  P.F.):
  administering, 112, 118
  age standardization, 92, 305
  behavioral equation from, 9
  clinical assessment by, 377-424
  common factor scores, 6
  compared with CTS, 342-345
  comparison with occupational

profiles, 131
computer processing of, 128,
  137, 138, 141
correlation among items, 72,
  table 72
cross-cultural findings, 30, 237
direct to indirect validity, 64
evaluation over past decade,
  250-254
executives' scores, 436-438
factor analyzing with HSPQ,
  242
factor scale scores, 511
frequency of use, 248
in clinical diagnosis, 349-352,
  362, 370
in group structure, 475, 476
in occupational testing, 430,
  434
in pathological diagnosis, 538
in regional and group
  differences, 482-484
intelligence testing with, 148,
  149
internal consistency of rating
  and questionnaire
  variables, table 221
interpetation of P.F. profile of
  married couple, 378-389
machine scoring, 29, 536
monitoring psychotherapy,
  371, 374
number of factor source traits,
  76
personality assessment from,
  237-239, 300
predicting achievement, 457
predicting creativity, 130
sabotage of tests, 499
Sample 16 P.F. Personal-
  Career Development
  Profile, table 133-137
states as related to primary
  factors in, 48, 52
stens in, 84
test length, 68
test time, 74, 118
16 P.F. Handbook and Manual:
  information in, 254
  prediction of achievement, 121,
    122
  reference population in, 89
16 P.F. and MAT correlations,
  265
transformations relating to
  MMPI and EPI, 251
vectors for situations, 20
Social Adjustment Scale, 342
Source traits, 4, 5, 7-10, 33-45,
  76
  developmental study of, 8
  in O-A Battery, 269-277
  in type fitting, 8
  instrument transcending, 220
  personality profile, table 11, 17
  questionnaire scales, 35

stability of coefficients, 8
T-data with Q-data matches, *table* 42, 43
testing for, 54-78, 106, 166-168
use of in the behavioral equation, 8
Spearman-Brown Prophecy Formula:
  dependability-reliability, 526-528
  effects on test reliability, 94, 235
  equivalence homogeneity, 60
  in factor analysis, 210
  in itemtrics, 4
Spectrad theory:
  correcting distortions, 23, 531
  in observer ratings, 501
  integration of spectrad models of personality and situation perception, *figure* 532
  perception of situations, 70
  rating as function of rater, 216, 235
  vector of behavioral indices, 543
Speech-Sounds Category Test, 184
Speed:
  in cognitive performance, 72
  tests, 169
Standards for Educational and Psychological Tests and Manuals, 251
Standford Achievement Test, 205, 206
Stanford Binet Test:
  correlation with Culture-Fair test, 64
  factor analysis of, 186
  in predicting achievement, 449
  intuitive type test, 166, 168
  measuring crystallized intelligence, 176-178, 188
  reliability, *table* 177
  standardization of, 90, 104, 426
  use with young children, 185
Stanford University, 426
State-Trait Anxiety Inventory (STAT):
  comparing psychological states to traits, 345
  measuring nonpathological states, 342
States and situations, 48-53
Statistical prediction, 149-151
Staves, 83
Stens:
  centile-sten scoring, 87, 88, 91
  d-stens, 84, 85, 87, 103
  error estimation, 149
  in MAT, 312, 313
  in 16 P.F., 84, 130
  in VIM, 309
  n-stens, 84, 85, 103

translation from stens to standard scores and centile ranks, *figure,* 85
Stephenson's Q-sort, see Q-sort
Stolpar-somnia, 45
Stratified uncorrelated determiners (SUD), 543
Strong and Kuder scales, see Kuder and Strong
Strong-Campbell Interest Inventory, 139, 307, 329
Strong Vocational Interest Blank (SVIB):
  history and use of, 306, 307
  special-purpose tests, 315
  vs. 16 P.F., 251
Structural psychometrics, 4-8
  advantages of, 149
  dynamic traits, 45-48
  functional testing, 4, 13, 33-53
  natural structures, 5
  source traits, 5, 7-10, 14, 33-45
  systems, 4
  theory for I.Q. tests, 172, 173
  unitary common traits, 5, 7, 13, 14
Structure of Human Personality, 268
Structured Learning Theory (SLT), 349
Subjective Data-Objective Assessment Plan (SOAP), 415
Superego, 48-150, 380
  in 16 P.F., 254
  in MAT, 313
Surgency:
  as trait factor, 4, 7, 13, 72
  life effects of, 150
  on CTS Kit test, 344
  on 16 P.F., 381, 382
  prediction of score, 92
  statistical prediction of, 149
  technical terminology, 45
  test language, 113
Symptoms Rating Scale, 341
Syntality, 21
Szondi Test, 299

T-data:
  as objective test, 27, 32
  as source traits, 9
  as trait scores, 335
  classifying dimensions for test, Q- and T-data, *table,* 26
  cross cultural patterns, 480
  factor analysis of personality structure, 209
  in behavioral equation, 9, 20, 148
  in O-A Kit, 116
  instrument-transcending trait factors, 34
  media of assessment, 21, 258
  matching with L and Q traits, 220

media-transcending personality factor, 242
modulation model, 19
objective tests for personality traits, 269-285
personality structures in, 41-45
profile of source trait scores, 17, 18, 149
ratio of primary Q traits to T-data, 35
reducing test vulnerability, 505
reliability of, 25
sabotage, 499
sorting of individuals by profiles, 226
test performance, 24
test validity, 248
theory of indifference of indicators, 34, 52
Tachistoscopic exposure, 92
Tactual Performance Test, 184
Taxonome program, 14, 538, 543
Tensidia, 274
Telstar, 164
Temperament traits, 7
"Testmanship," 114
Tests, testing:
  administration of, 107-118
  consistency, 56-62
    administrative usage coefficient, 58-59, 112, 496
    conspect coefficient, 58-59, 74, 125
    dependability coefficient, 56-58, 115, 496
    stability coefficient, 59, 115, 159
  cultural bias of I.Q., 452
  definition of, 54-56
  dimensions for classifying, 25-31, *table* 26
  economic value, 144-146
  functional, 7-14, 33-53, 94, 96
  homogeneity, 60-62, 70, 73
    conditions affecting, 66-73
  industrial/applied applications current developments, 429-433
  examples of structured tests, 433-438
  history of, 425-429
  in vocational guidance and selection, 439
  integration from 121-124
  public relations in, 153-156
  qualifications of designers and publishers, 158-162
  revealing results of, 156-158
  scaling, 83 104
  scoring, 29, 30
  selecting, 105-109
  social obstacles, 460, 461
  structural, 4-14, 27, 77, 94, 96, 150, 166-168

taxonomy by internal
    construction, *table* 55
three file system, 18-121
training requirements, 151-153
transferability coefficient, 61,
    62
utility and efficiency of, 73-76,
    141
validities of some well-known,
    table 176
validity per minute, 74
varieties of validity, 62-73
    conditions affecting, 66-73
vulnerability, 76, 77
wider scientific and social
    aspects of, 142-165
*The Absolute Zero in Intelligence
    Measurement,* 102
The Brain Watchers, 444
The Hoosier Schoomaster, 143
*The Inheritance of Personality
    and Ability,* 268
*The Prediction of Achievement
    and Creativity,* 447
*The Scientific Analysis of
    Personality and Motivation,*
    363
Thematic Aperception Test
    (TAT):
    administration, 109, 302
    conspect reliability of, 27, 59,
        124, 286
    determining ergic tension, 297
    dynamic source traits in, 47,
        300-302
    evaluating creativity, 464
    history, 301
    measuring motivation, 248,
        292, 306
    Need for Achievement, 329
    "projective" tests, 123, 261-263,
        299, 314, 362
    test construction, 3
Theory of indifference of
    indicators, 53
Threctia, 240
Three file system, 118-121
Thurstone Test of Mental
    Alertness, 434
Thurstone's Test of Primary
    Mental Abilities (see
    Primary Mental Abilities
    [PMA Test]
Time, 154
Total situation, 16
Tough Poise:
    as corteria, 386
    as second order factor, 390
Trail Making Test, 184

Trait view theory:
    computer scoring, 128
    correcting for distortions, 23,
        245
        with MD scale, 245
    correction by vector of weights,
        52
    corrective formulae, 542
    "faking", 245, 499
    relation to Spectrad theory,
        531
Transferability:
    coefficient of, 61, 77
Triadic theory of ability
    structure
    general capacities, 37, 52
    primary agencies, 37, 52
    provincial powers, 37, 52
    structure, *table* 38
True zeros:
    from modulation theory, 519,
        520
    psychological measurement, 83
Two file system, 164
Types of Men, 330

Uniqueness, 6, 17
University of Illinois, 140
University of London Press, 161
Uses and Abuses in Psychology,
    156
*Using Tests and Other
    Information in Counseling,*
    350

Value measures, 330-332
Vernon's Boyd Personality
    Scales, 253
Veterans' Administration, 14,
    113
Vidal Dominoes, 174
Vocational Interest Measure
    (VIM):
    conspective scoring, 308
    dynamic structure traits, 47
    correlation and conflict, 309
    measuring sentiments, 328,
        329
    multiple test evaluation, 139
    objective test of motivation,
        307

Walker-Guttman Scale, 96
Watson-Glaser test, 430
Wechsler Adult Intelligence
    Scale (WAIS)
    computerization, 139
    concept validity, 34, 97
    correlation with O-A factors,
        280, 281

"creeping norms," 104
crystallized intelligence factor,
    30, 180, 188
    in Halstead-Reitan Battery,
        184
    in predicting achievment, 449
    in vocational testing, 426
    machine scoring, 536
    personality characteristics
        measure, 264
    rank order, 83
    sample and population factors,
        517, 518
    Smith's Survey of WAIS
        predictions, 165
    standardization of, 90
    testing for brain damage, 182
    transferability consistency, 62
Wechsler Adult Intelligence
    Scale-Revised (WAIS-R):
    construction of, 169
    examination for maximum fit
        for difference hypotheses,
        table 179
    factoring of, 167, 168
    measuring crystallized
        intelligence, 176
    multiple factor theory, 178
Wechsler Intelligence Scale for
    Children (WISC):
    assessment of intelligence
        measure, 180, 188
    concept validity
    crystallized intelligence
        measure, 180, 188
    personality characteristic
        measure, 264
    standardization, 90
Wechsler Intelligence Scale for
    Children-Revised (WISC-R):
    factoring of, 167, 168
    measuring crystallized
        intelligence, 176
    multiple factor theory, 178
Wechsler Preschool and Primary
    Scale of Intelligence
    (WPPSI):
    measure of crystallized
        intelligence, 176-177
Wechsler Memory Test, 184
*Wit and its Relation to the
    Unconscious (Jokes and the
    Unconscious),* 264
Who's Who in American Art, 462
World Book, 160
World Health Organization
    (WHO), 407

Zeppia, 455